ESTATE PLANNING

ESTATE PLANNING

William P. Streng, Esq.
Vinson & Elkins Professor of Law
University of Houston Law Center
Houston, Texas
Special Consultant to Tax Management

WILEY Bloomberg BNA

Cover images: Abstract gold background © strizh/iStockphoto;
Business workplace © shironosov/iStockphoto
Cover design: Wiley

Published by John Wiley & Sons, Inc., Hoboken, New Jersey.

This book first appeared in *Portfolio 800-3d Estate Planning* published by Bloomberg BNA.

Published simultaneously in Canada.

Library of Congress Cataloging-in-Publication Data:
Names: Streng, William P., author.
Title: Estate planning / William P. Streng, Esq., Vinson & Elkins Professor of Law, University of Houston Law Center, Houston, Texas, special consultant to Tax Management.
Description: Hoboken, New Jersey : John Wiley & Sons, Inc., 2016. | Includes bibliographical references.
Identifiers: LCCN 2015030346 | ISBN 978-1-119-15712-0 (cloth) | ISBN 978-1-119-19174-2 (ePDF) | ISBN 978-1-119-19175-9 (epub) |
Subjects: LCSH: Estate planning–United States. | Tax planning–United States.
Classification: LCC KF6572 .S757 2016 | DDC 332.024/0160973–dc23 LC record available at http://lccn.loc.gov/2015030346

Printed in the United States of America

FSC
www.fsc.org
MIX
Paper from responsible sources
FSC® C101537

10 9 8 7 6 5 4 3 2 1

Contents

About the Author

William P. Streng
Wartburg College (B.A., 1959); Northwestern University School of Law (J.D., 1962); Law Clerk to Honorable Lester L. Cecil, Chief Judge, U.S. Court of Appeals for the Sixth Circuit, 1963–1964; associated with Taft, Stettinius & Hollister, Cincinnati, Ohio, 1964–1970; Attorney-Advisor, Office of Tax Legislative Counsel (Office of the Assistant Secretary for Tax Policy), U.S. Dept. of the Treasury, Washington, D.C., 1970–1971; Deputy General Counsel, Export-Import Bank of the United States, Washington, D.C., 1971–1973; Of Counsel, Haynes & Boone, Dallas, Texas (1977–1979); Professor of Law, School of Law, Southern Methodist University, Dallas, Texas (1973–1979); Bracewell & Patterson, Houston, Texas (Partner, 1980–1985; Consultant, 1985–2005); Bracewell & Giuliani LLP (Consultant, 2005–2011); Professor of Law, University of Houston Law Center (1985–present); Visiting Professor, The Ohio State University College of Law (1977), New York University School of Law (1990), and The University of Texas School of Law (2002); Lecturer, Rice University (1987–1989); Distinguished Lecturer, University of Hong Kong Law Faculty (1992); Fulbright Professor, University of Stockholm Law Faculty (1993); Visiting Fellow, Victoria University Law Faculty (1996); Visiting Professor, The University of Leiden (International Tax Center), the Netherlands, 1997, 1998, 2000, 2007, and 2009; Visiting Professor, Yokohama National University, Japan (2005); Member: American Law Institute (Tax Advisory Group); the International Fiscal Association (and Council Member, USA Branch); European Association of Tax Law Professors (EATLP); the American Bar Association's Section of Taxation; the BNA Tax Management Advisory Board; and various other professional organizations; Author or co-author of books and Tax Management portfolios, including: 700 T.M., *Choice of Entity* (Bloomberg BNA, 2007); *Tax Planning for Retirement*, with M. Davis (ThomsonReuters/Checkpoint, 2015); "International Business Planning: Law and Taxation—United States," with J. Salacuse (three volumes, 2015, Lexis-Nexis/Matthew Bender); Bittker, Emory, and Streng, "Federal Income Taxation of Corporations and Shareholders—Forms," ThomsonReuters/Checkpoint, 4th ed. (1995, and chapter revisions and supplements to 2015); previously "U.S. International Estate Planning," (RIAG-Warren, Gorham & Lamont, 1996, and updates on ThomsonReuters/Checkpoint).

Introduction

This book is derived from Bloomberg BNA Tax Management Portfolio, *Estate Planning*, No. 800–3rd, which is part of the Bloomberg BNA Tax Management Portfolio Library (for more information, visit www.bna.com/tax). It is designed as an authoritative and practical working tool for attorneys, accountants, and others involved in estate planning practice. The basic estate, gift, and trust planning concepts are presented in a descriptive and conveniently accessible form. The topics treated include: the development by the advisor of an estate planning strategy for the client; fundamentals of the federal transfer tax system and related federal income tax rules; lifetime donative asset transfers; gratuitous property transfers at death; generation-skipping transfers; special property transfer planning considerations (e.g., community property, life insurance, charitable transfers, closely held corporations); and post-mortem planning. Other books in the Tax Management Estates, Gifts, and Trusts series provide detailed coverage of the various specific planning topics surveyed in this book. These books are identified at appropriate locations in the text of this book.

Effective estate planning (particularly, the federal tax planning component) enables a person to make both lifetime and testamentary transfers of assets to that person's beneficiaries of choice and, in the process, conserve wealth for those recipients (often family members). Various methods may be employed to both (1) achieve the estate planning client's objectives regarding the completion of these transfers and the port-mortem management and disposition of the property, and (2) minimize income, gift, and estate tax liabilities on the asset transfers. Effective estate planning, however, requires a working knowledge of both the federal and state tax rules (income, estate, and gift) and the nontax reasons for using traditional wealth-shifting mechanisms such as wills, trusts, gifts, and powers of appointment. Therefore, a familiarity with various state property, trust, probate, and business laws is also essential for the estate planner. This book provides the practitioner with an overview of the estate planning concepts necessary in advising clients concerning these several elements of wealth transfer planning.

The federal transfer tax planning discussed in this book is primarily focused on the period beginning with the year 2013 and thereafter. After a decade of uncertainty, in 2013, Congress finally made permanent many of the estate, gift, and generation-skipping transfer tax changes that were enacted in 2001 and 2010.

CHAPTER 1

Estate Planning Objectives

The primary objectives of estate planning are (1) to secure to the property owner (and his or her family members) during his or her lifetime the maximum economic benefits available from the possession and use of his or her property, and (2) to enable that property owner to transfer the property to the surviving members of his or her family (or other desired beneficiaries, including trusts) with minimal shrinkage from applicable death taxes and other property transfer costs. Estate planning is, therefore, concerned primarily with (1) minimizing federal and state income, estate, gift, and inheritance taxes; (2) reducing probate and associated property transfer costs and similar mechanical burdens; and (3) conserving and enhancing the client's net worth both (i) currently for the benefit of the client and his or her family, and (ii) after the client's death, for the eventual beneficiaries of the primary client's property. Obviously, this estate planning must be consistent with the specific objectives of the client for both (1) the lifetime use of the property by the client, and (2) the testamentary disposition by the client of property to his or her surviving beneficiaries.

In developing a proposed arrangement for both the lifetime and the testamentary disposition of the client's property, the "estate planner" often functions as much more than a legal technician. He or she is both (1) a property/tax planning lawyer and (2) a legal counselor. As a property/tax lawyer he or she must be conversant with the state and federal laws regarding the construction of wills and trusts; property ownership (including community and joint property) rules; asset transfer processes (including for future interests); individual and trust income taxation; inter vivos and death time transfer taxes (both federal and state); probate administration; corporate, partnership, and limited liability company laws and taxation; and rules resolving conflict of laws. As a "counselor," however, he or she must also be skilled in dealing with the human elements of this property/tax planning.[1] He must be able to explain the probate administration processes. Often this must be done on a multigenerational basis where each generation has different perspectives on these questions. Further, he or she must also be able to encourage the client toward appropriate investment strategies for the management and growth of the client's assets during lifetime.

The estate planner must consider the unique objectives of his or her individual clients and attempt to mold a rational wealth accumulation and property transfer plan that is consistent with those clients' specific objectives.[2] In proceeding with this engagement, the attorney/estate planner often will be consulting with the client's other advisors (including, possibly, an accountant, banker, insurance representative, securities broker or investment adviser, and certified financial planner). The estate planner may thereby benefit from a variety of perspectives as to how the estate plan for the individual client may best be formulated and implemented, but the estate planning advisors should be careful to avoid the clients being dominated by one of these other advisors.

Considering these basic objectives of the estate planning process, the function of this book entitled *Estate Planning* is:

- to serve as a fundamental guide for the estate planner to analyze practical and recurring problems confronting clients in the estate planning context (particularly relating to federal tax planning);
- to provide ideas for use in identifying any available options for the resolution of these estate planning issues; and
- to enable the estate planner to formulate specific recommendations and suggestions for implementation by his or her clients.

Increasingly, clients with a reasonable amount of wealth are frustrated by the fluidity of the relevant tax rules in this context, particularly the changes in the estate, gift, and generation-skipping transfer tax rules. This necessitates regular review of the client's estate planning and a continuing response to changing developments. This also suggests structuring substantial flexibility into the client's estate planning documents—about which the client may not be comfortable.

More detailed discussions of many of these matters are included in the various Tax Management portfolios covering estate, gift, and trust income taxation.[3] This book does not deal in depth with such matters as the implementation of (1) a durable power of attorney, (2) anatomical gift documents,[4] (3) a "living will" or "directive to physicians" to evidence an individual's direction to medical caregivers that he or she not be kept alive by life-sustaining procedures in the event of a terminal physical condition,[5] (4) a "durable power of attorney for health care" or a "medical power of attorney,"[6] (5) a declaration of guardianship for oneself,[7] or (6) a burial power of attorney.[8] A "durable power of attorney" is implemented to enable another person to deal with the principal's assets without the requirement of first seeking approval through some type of incompetency or guardianship proceeding in a local court proceeding.[9] Statutes authorizing living wills or advance directives have also been enacted in various states.[10] These statutes generally specify how living will directives are to be implemented and revoked. The objective of legislation permitting a "durable power of attorney for health care" is to enable a person to delegate one's health care decision-making capacity to another person.[11] This document is often used to counteract perceived deficiencies in the use of a living will, including those situations not contemplated by the client when implementing the living will. Because of the occasional reluctance by physicians to recognize these instruments (whether for professional malpractice concerns or for other reasons), the use of both documents might sometimes be useful. In many jurisdictions the use of both documents is the preferred practice.

These matters involving the client's asset management during incompetency and the making of health care determinations are beyond the scope of this book but are discussed in other Tax Management portfolios. These are important questions, however, which the estate planner should carefully examine with his or her clients under appropriate circumstances. In many instances the several types of powers of attorney should be strongly recommended to the estate planning client. The estate planner should be sufficiently organized so that these documents can be produced electronically with limited effort (and, therefore, on a cost-effective basis for both the estate planner and the client).

Much of the discussion in this book is structured to address the situation of the "traditional family." However, demographic trends in the United States suggest that the traditional family is declining in percentage. Increasingly, the estate planner will need to consider a number of variables: (1) a reduction in the number of children and, therefore, a greater necessity to assure that a support network is available for older clients; (2) more second (third, fourth, etc.) marriages, with mixed families including multiple stepchildren[12]; (3) same-sex marriages, domestic partner relationships, and similar arrangements; (4) older heterosexual couples living together without being married and having children from prior marriages; (5) grandparents as heads of households including their grandchildren without the intermediate generation present; (6) more balanced income sources for both spouses contributing to the support of the household; (7) a desire for long-term protection (from various creditors and divorced spouses) for family assets through the use of trusts that continue for extended periods; and (8) children produced using new biological techniques. All these situations can present factual and psychological "wrinkles" in the estate planning that must be carefully addressed in the individualized situation.

Notes

1. The estate planner may determine that the emotional issues, rather than property planning issues, are paramount in the early stages of the estate planning. These might include: (1) determining who should succeed to the property ownership (particularly as to items of tangible personal property), (2) whether this inheritance will change the future behavior

of the beneficiary, and (3) contemplation by the client of his or her death (final arrangements for disposition of one's physical remains). Certain of these issues may be even more psychologically complicated in situations involving second marriages and children of previous marriages.

2. Because of the commoditization of estate planning, the advisor must be able to demonstrate that he/she brings added value to this endeavor. Otherwise, the client may conclude that his estate planning can more easily (and more cost-effectively) be accomplished by using documents available through less expensive websites. *See* Goffe & Haller, *From Zoom to Doom? Risks of Do-It-Yourself Estate Planning*, 38 Est. Plan. 27 (Apr. 2011).
3. Throughout this book reference is made to Tax Management portfolios, where appropriate. For a listing of the portfolios useful in specific estate planning contexts, *see* (1) the Tax Management Estates, Gifts and Trusts Portfolio Classification Guide; and (2) the online BNATAX Management Library (available from Bloomberg BNA Tax Management, telephone 1-800-372-1033 or its website: www.bnatax.com).
4. All states have enacted some form of the Uniform Anatomical Gift Act. This act exists in several versions, being most recently revised in 2006, revising the 1968 and 1987 versions. The 2006 Act indicates how anatomical gift documents can be made, amended, or revoked by an individual. The Act specifies how such gifts can be made by others such as family members. This gift can be accomplished by a testamentary document. The Uniform Act provides that an anatomical gift by last will takes effect upon death of the testator, whether or not the will is probated. If, after death, the will is declared invalid for testamentary purposes, the validity of the anatomical gift is unaffected. Because often a will is not located until after the funeral, many states permit this gift to be evidenced by a separate document designed to be carried by the donor. In some jurisdictions this includes an appropriate designation on a driver's license. This state legislation also often specifies the permissible donees of a person's body or body parts. *See* www.uniformlaws.org for this Act, summaries of this Act, and the status of its adoption in the several states.
5. See *Cruzan v. Dir., Mo. Dep't of Health*, 497 U.S. 261 (1990), where the Supreme Court effectively indicated that quite specific instructions must be provided by an individual to authorize the termination of life support systems.
6. For further discussion of durable powers of attorney for health care and/or medical powers of attorney, see 816 T.M., *Planning for Disability* (Bloomberg BNA).
7. Under state law, an individual may have the capacity to designate a guardian for oneself to manage one's physical care and welfare. This would be different than the designation of a representative to manage one's physical and financial assets. Even though other documents, such as a durable power of attorney and a funded revocable living trust, may be adequate for the management of one's assets, this document may be useful to supplement a health care power of attorney. Further, this document might be used to disqualify an individual who might otherwise have a priority under local law to serve as that person's guardian for physical care and welfare purposes.
8. Under state law, authority may be able to be delegated to a specified agent to control the disposition of the client's physical remains. This may be important where (1) the individual does not want the members of his biological family to control burial arrangements, or (2) prepaid funeral arrangements have not been implemented.
9. See the Uniform Durable Power of Attorney Act, included as Article V of the Uniform Probate Code, for an example of legislation intended to facilitate the implementation of a durable power of attorney. An important objective is to assure that the power granted

to the agent to act on behalf of the principal does not terminate as of the time that the principal becomes disabled or mentally incompetent. This matter of validity of this document is dependent upon state law. State laws as enacted may differ, notwithstanding the Uniform Act. Consequently, if the client has property in several jurisdictions, the estate planner should assure that the durable power of attorney will be effective in each of those jurisdictions to enable the attorney-in-fact designated under that power of attorney to conveniently deal with the property located in each of those jurisdictions. For further information on durable powers of attorney, see 859 T.M., *Durable Powers of Attorney* (Bloomberg BNA), and 816 T.M., *Planning for Disability* (Bloomberg BNA).

10. In some jurisdictions this legislation is identified as a "Natural Death Act." This state legislation specifies such matters as the form of the written directive and the required witnesses.
11. In many jurisdictions a form is prescribed by statute for implementing this authorization. Often an agent under a durable power of attorney for health care may exercise this authority only if the principal's attending physician certifies that the principal lacks the capacity to understand and appreciate the nature and consequences of a health care decision.
12. For example, in this situation the estate planner might need to be concerned about any intended (or unintended) disinheritance of a client's natural children for the benefit of the second spouse.

CHAPTER 2

Inventory of the Client's Assets and Objectives

A. Scope of Factual Analysis

The development of an appropriate estate plan for a client depends on a full and complete understanding of the client's (1) family situation; (2) assets, liabilities, and personal net worth position; and (3) fundamental estate planning objectives. Often the most important, and sometimes the most difficult, element of this process is developing a comprehensive summary of the important and relevant facts applicable to the particular client's situation. If fundamental facts are not made available or are misunderstood by the estate planner, the basic premises for implementing the estate planning may be irrelevant. As a result, in this type of situation the assistance provided by the estate planning professional may be of limited value and, perhaps, counterproductive.

B. Family

The estate planner must initially identify who are the probable beneficiaries of the client's property transfers (i.e., the "objects of the testator's bounty" in probate litigation terminology). A proper inventory of family members (perhaps including an abbreviated family genealogical chart) should be developed for the estate planning professional to show the names, locations, ages, health status, and any mental incompetency issues for the client's spouse, children, parents, and other close relatives.[1]

In addition, the estate planner should attempt to identify the personal family relationships and the net worth situation of each individual who may be an anticipated beneficiary of the client's wealth. This analysis might include each person's present and anticipated financial needs and any special factors that should be considered.[2]

As a part of this process, the estate planner should assure that the client's legal domicile is definitively established. This can (1) avoid multiple state death taxation controversies[3] and (2) facilitate both primary and any ancillary probate proceedings.[4] The assistance by the estate planner might include helping the client (and other family members) to firmly establish domicile in a particular geographic location. This assistance might include filing some designation of domicile with local authorities. This could be in addition to assuring that the important objective criteria for determining residence, such as voting registration, driver's license, and primary bank accounts, evidence a consistent intent concerning the precise location of the client's domicile.[5]

C. Assets and Liabilities

Detailed information should be obtained with respect to the client's assets and liabilities.[6] This will enable an identification of the client's precise net worth position and, therefore, whether an exposure to federal estate tax should be anticipated to exist for the client's estate at the time of death. Various assumptions might be made concerning the date of death, that is, both immediately and at some later date (making alternative assumptions concerning the increase in value of the client's assets, this increase attributable to both inflation and other factors).[7] A client's assets normally may include such items as cash, notes, accounts receivable, mortgages, stocks, bonds, real estate, life insurance policies,[8] employee benefits (e.g., IRA, pension, and profit sharing and "§401(k)" account balances), and business interests (sole proprietorships, partnership interests, limited liability company units, and closely held corporate shares). Other, more unique properties should not, however, be overlooked. These might include oil and gas interests, royalty interests for intangibles such as patents and copyrights, works of art, special collections, and valuable rights (such as a general power of appointment under a trust created by another person).

The precise legal status of these properties should also be established (as determinable under applicable state property laws). For example, are these properties owned outright, held indirectly through a revocable trust, owned with another in a joint tenancy with the right of survivorship, held in a tenancy in common with another person, derived from a contractual right (e.g., a life insurance policy or employee benefits), or wholly or partially characterized as community property? Additionally, both the federal income tax cost (or other) basis and the applicable holding period should be established.[9]

Liabilities must also be identified in determining the client's "net worth."[10] These liabilities may be demand notes, term loans, mortgage obligations, accounts payable, or accrued taxes.[11] These liabilities may be recourse or nonrecourse. Contingent liabilities (including the probability of a liability materializing from personal debt guarantees provided by the client for other family members) should be ascertained and evaluated.

An analysis should be made concerning whether existing casualty insurance and other accident and general liability policies will adequately cover any casualties that occur and liabilities that arise. The client might be advised to consider purchasing an excess risk or "umbrella" insurance policy. Similarly, the estate planner might inquire whether adequate disability income insurance coverage and "long-term care insurance" exists, so that the client's net worth will not disappear during his or her lifetime because of extraordinary living costs incurred during an extended period of physical or mental disability.[12]

D. Cash Flow Analysis

A complete estate planning financial analysis for the client also includes preparing a cash flow schedule identifying (1) present and future sources of cash (not limited to "gross income" for federal income tax purposes) and (2) cash expenditure requirements.[13] Cash inflow items may include earned income (wages, salaries, bonuses, etc.), investment income (interest, including tax-exempt interest income, dividends, and capital gains), other property ownership income (such as rents and royalties), income from trusts, and proceeds from the sale of both liquid and illiquid properties. Future income sources may include items such as Social Security, retirement plan payments, deferred compensation payments and other employee benefits, and investment income.

The cash flow schedule should also identify present and future expenditure needs (e.g., living expenses, income taxes, investment commitments, insurance premiums, and possible health care costs).[14] The cash needs of the client's estate, the surviving spouse, dependent children, and any dependent surviving parents immediately after the client's death should also be identified. If a significant portion of the client's properties are illiquid (e.g., a closely held family business interest or investment real estate), a "liquidity analysis" for the estate planning client may also be appropriate.

E. Present Objectives for Estate Disposition

The client's values, objectives, and priorities concerning property dispositions should be carefully established. These are normally based primarily upon non-tax-motivated factors. For example, questions to be examined might include:

- To whom does the client desire to transfer his or her various properties at death?
- Does the client desire to make lifetime gifts, particularly to take advantage of the federal gift tax annual donee exclusion (and other exclusions)?
- Are the property transfers (whether at death or during lifetime) to be outright and unrestricted?

- Alternatively, does the client desire trust management so the transferred assets are held by a trustee and beneficially managed for his or her spouse or for his or her children and grandchildren and others (whether transferred at death or during lifetime)?
- Should the lifetime management of assets for the principal client (e.g., through a revocable trust or an irrevocable "protective" trust) be recommended?
- To eliminate possible future sources of conflict (which may otherwise generate significant expenses such as legal fees), should the intended beneficiaries of special family heirlooms be specifically identified (whether in the last will or in separate, binding instructions)?
- If no close relatives survive, should a charitable gift program be suggested?

Many such questions, which often evolve from a thorough analysis of the client's individual facts and circumstances, need to be precisely identified and resolved. Without necessarily providing precise recommendations, the estate planner should encourage the client to approach using the property transfer process to create opportunities and incentives to younger-generation members receiving wealth from older-generation members. This might include utilizing a "risk-reward" analysis concerning the distribution of family assets. Some clients will want to use the transfer of wealth to encourage particular behavior on the part of the recipient beneficiaries, but the estate planner should be careful in recommending such arrangements. Certainly, for high-net-worth individuals the advisor should encourage a distribution of wealth that enables all potential beneficiaries to have sufficient funds to enable a minimum level of financial protection, including availability of basic medical care, educational assistance, and long-term care.

In many instances, where adult children are the intended beneficiaries, the estate planner might recommend that the wealth transmission process be discussed among the various family members. This discussion could assure that the client's objectives are consistent with family member expectations and that future intrafamily conflicts are avoided. Sometimes, however, family consultations are contentious or counterproductive, and, consequently, the advisor should carefully analyze how the estate plan basics should be developed.

Notes

1. See the Worksheets for materials designed to assist in this identification process.
2. For example, spouses may be subject to a premarital agreement under which the parties waive spousal rights (or retain certain specific spousal rights). This may not be limited to a second marriage situation but could include a situation in which a wealthy family's younger child is "encouraged" to enter into a premarital agreement prior to a marriage to a young, indebted (e.g., with student loans) prospective spouse. As an incentive to enter into such an agreement, the older-generation member may even specify that trust distributions to the younger-generation member are to be limited until the premarital agreement is in place.

3. This could also involve multiple country conflicts where both the United States and a foreign country assert that domicile exists in their jurisdictions for taxation and testamentary governing law purposes. In this context, a bilateral estate and gift tax treaty may be available to help ascertain the place of residence for transfer taxation purposes through the application of certain "tie-breaker rules."
4. A special mechanism often used to avoid ancillary probate proceedings is a revocable living trust, which is the nominal owner of the out-of-state properties. This does necessitate the actual transfer of ownership of those assets into this trust prior to death. See the discussion of revocable trusts in Chapter 5, B.2.c.
5. In some situations, applicable state law also permits the filing of a statement in local official records that domicile in a particular jurisdiction is being terminated and is being relocated to another jurisdiction. Of course, particularly if state tax revenues are involved, the first state might challenge that the domicile has actually been relocated to another state.
6. See the Worksheets for materials useful in eliciting the various information that should be identified with respect to a client's net worth position. Further, the use of a computer program, such as BNA Software's "Estate Tax Planner," will require a precise identification of these properties, their fair market values, and any associated liabilities. An example of such a spreadsheet analysis in the context of a specific, hypothetical factual situation is contained in the Worksheets.
7. As discussed below, this also necessitates drafting documents to contemplate the changes in the unified credit exclusion amount, which ranged from $1 million for gift tax purposes to $5 million for estate tax purposes in 2010, and $5 million for gift and estate tax purposes after 2010 (with an inflation adjustment after 2011). *See* §2010(c), §2505(a), amended by the 1997 Taxpayer Relief Act, Pub. L. No. 105-34, §501; the Economic Growth and Tax Relief Reconciliation Act of 2001 (EGTRRA), Pub. L. No. 107-16, §521, §531, §901; the Tax Relief, Unemployment Insurance Reauthorization, and Job Creation Act of 2010 (2010 TRA), Pub. L. No. 111-312, §101(a), §301–§304; and the American Taxpayer Relief Act of 2012 (ATRA), Pub. L. No. 112-240, §101(a). For the inflation-adjusted §2010(c) unified credit basic exclusion amount (which is also the inflation-adjusted §2505(a) unified credit basic exclusion amount), see Worksheet 1. All section references herein are to the Internal Revenue Code of 1986, as amended, and the regulations thereunder, unless otherwise stated.
8. Whether life insurance is reflected at its cash surrender value or its date of death value (often quite different amounts) depends upon the purposes for which the net worth statement is being developed. See the discussion in Chapter 9, C., concerning planning techniques to avoid any inclusion of life insurance proceeds in the insured's gross estate for federal estate tax purposes, an objective that should often be pursued.
9. The holding period is often less important when ordinary income and capital gains are subject to tax at the same or an essentially similar tax rate. After the 2003 enactment of a 15% capital gains rate (and a 35% ordinary income tax rate) in the Jobs and Growth Tax Relief Reconciliation Act of 2003 (JGTRRA), Pub. L. No. 108-27, this consideration is more significant. The §1(h) 20% maximum capital gains tax rate and the §1(i) 39.6% maximum income tax rate for most other income types apply to taxable years beginning after 2012. *See* ATRA, Pub. L. No. 112-240, §101(a), §102(b). For tax years beginning before 2013, pre-2013 §1(h) provided for a 15% maximum capital gains tax rate and pre-2013 §1(i) provided for a 35% maximum income tax rate for other income types.

See 2010 TRA, Pub. L. No. 111-312, §101(a), §102 (extending application of sunset provisions in EGTRRA, Pub. L. No. 107-16, §901, and JGTRRA, Pub. L. No. 108-27, §303). Long-term capital gain status is also important in various other contexts including, for example, determining the available amount of an income tax charitable contributions deduction upon a property gift or in categorizing the proceeds received upon a stock redemption. Further, both the tax basis and the holding period of the client's assets will be much more important if the estate of a decedent dying in 2010 elected to apply the §1022 modified carryover basis regime rather than the reinstated estate tax regime as allowed in 2010 TRA, Pub. L. No. 111-312, §301(c), as discussed in more detail in Chapter 4.

10. For materials useful in identifying amounts and types of personal liabilities, see the Worksheets.
11. For some clients the liabilities may be significant. For example, individuals engaged in real estate development may incur significant debt exposure, although this debt might often be collateralized with acquired properties. During periods of economic downturn, the net worth for such highly leveraged individuals may decline dramatically, even though their gross assets remain quite significant.
12. For many families the federal estate tax is not relevant (particularly because of the increasing applicable exclusion amount), but the extensive costs of a last illness constitute the most important factor causing a significant reduction in wealth passing to the next generation. For further discussion of long-term care insurance, see 816 T.M., *Planning for Disability* (Bloomberg BNA).
13. See the Worksheets for materials useful in identifying amounts and types of liabilities that may also be used to identify present income data, present cash flow, and future cash requirements. The examination of the client's previously filed federal income tax returns can materially facilitate this analysis. These income tax returns will not, however, identify particular sources of tax-exempt income and the client's expenditures, particularly for those personal expense items that are not tax deductible but that could be significant.
14. For materials regarding a procedure useful for projecting future cash requirements before death, see the Worksheets. Federal income tax requirements might be projected through the utilization of a personal computer spreadsheet program such as the BNA Software program "Income Tax Planner."

CHAPTER 3

Preliminary Estate Planning Considerations

A. Expanded Responsibilities of the Professional Tax Advisor

The estate planner often functions as more than a lawyer and tax advisor in assisting an estate planning client in the implementation of a program for lifetime and testamentary property dispositions.[1] The planner also often acts as a business and investment mentor, frequently because the client believes (sometimes inappropriately) that the estate planning advisor can provide this assistance. Unless the estate planner has special capacities in this area he or she would not normally provide definitive recommendations on business strategy and investment management questions. He or she should, at a minimum, have developed the capacity to ask important and relevant questions concerning both the client's (1) overall asset investment strategy (if any) and (2) investment returns and continued holding of specific investments.

The estate planner should emphasize to the client the desirability of developing a comprehensive, long-term wealth accumulation and investment strategy to maximize the capital formation for the entire family unit. Income tax planning is an integral part of this process, but certainly not the only component. The structuring (or restructuring) of the ownership of a family business, particularly concerning issues of ownership and management succession, could also be an important element of this family wealth transmission process.

B. Facilitating Lifetime Capital Formation

A detailed inventory and careful analysis of the client's investment positions will reveal not only the financial net worth of the client's estate but also the specific types of property interests held by the client, the client's spouse, and others (e.g., elderly parents). Questions concerning appropriate investment strategy to be raised concerning these property interests should include:

- Is significant cash being held in non-interest- (or very-low-interest-) bearing bank accounts (e.g., checking accounts)? If so, interest-bearing accounts (e.g., cash management or money market accounts) should be established with "sweep" arrangements to assure that the cash is regularly transferred into investment accounts. The identification of appropriate money management options is more difficult to achieve during a period of low market interest rates. This may be particularly frustrating to older clients who have regularly received significant income from investments in certificates of deposits and similar financial instruments and are reluctant to take many market investment risks (preferring to preserve their capital).
- Are checks that should be immediately deposited being held for extended periods, and are similar cash items remaining uncollected? Previously, bonds with coupons attached might have been held with matured, but unredeemed, coupons. In most current situations of debt issuances, that debt is either held in registered or book-entry form.[2] This enables the interest to be paid by check to the registered owner or, perhaps, electronically deposited directly into the owner's bank account. In any event, strategies should be implemented to prevent prolonged and recurring losses of this earning capacity while amounts remain uncollected. In some instances, the bonds may actually have previously matured or have been called for redemption and may no longer be earning interest income. In addition, if depreciated in value, the bonds might be sold to generate currently deductible tax losses. Replacement bonds (particularly if the bonds presently held are U.S. Government Series EE bonds) might produce a higher income return or provide better investment security.
- Are the stocks, bonds, and mutual fund investments held by the client representative of the client's stated investment objectives (i.e., for growth and appreciation or primarily for income)? Has recent or proposed federal tax legislation suggested a redirection of these investment objectives?[3] What is the investment growth potential for particular stocks or mutual funds in the client's investment portfolio? Should losses be realized for federal income tax purposes and should appropriate tax-motivated reinvestments be arranged? Is greater financial asset investment diversity desirable? Should this investment diversity be accomplished through acquiring shares in a mutual fund? If so, will a "no-load" mutual fund accomplish this objective?
- Would other types of less liquid (but reasonably secure) investments provide an enhanced annual rate of investment return? Should these investments be real estate, leased personal property, oil and gas properties, or art and similar collectibles? If investment in real estate is desired, should this be accomplished through an investment in a REIT (real estate investment trust)?

- Is the power and value of compounding (i.e., earning interest on interest) over a longer period recognized by the client? This capacity for increased asset growth (particularly where that compounding growth is untaxed and the deferred tax funds also provide an investment return for the client) should be noted with respect all these alternative types of investments.

These questions are representative of the issues that should be raised with the client (and the investment advisor) to assure maximizing capital formation during the client's lifetime.

C. Fundamental Federal Income Tax Planning

Lifetime income tax planning is an essential part of facilitating capital formation for the estate planning client.[4] Relevant questions in this context might include:

- What is the taxpayer's current marginal income tax rate? Does that rate suggest (from the tax planning perspective) a shift of some investments to tax-exempt municipal bonds, including possibly a tax-exempt bond mutual fund? Alternatively, should the taxpayer shift financial holdings to investments having a lower current yield but a higher appreciation potential (relying on the "total yield" investment concept of combined income and capital appreciation), anticipating an eventual 20% capital gains rate at the time of gain realization? Attitudes concerning investment strategies may change significantly as the relationship between ordinary income rates and capital gains rates change with evolving tax legislation. This is evidenced by the year 2012 legislation enabling a maximum 20% rate for most dividends (including corporate dividends passed through mutual funds).[5]
- Should the taxpayer acquire "tax-advantaged investments"? These tax advantages might be achieved through tax deferral (such as investments in low dividend yield growth stocks), from investments providing "tax write-offs" (e.g., significant tax depreciation deductions) or low-taxed capital gains. The estate planning advisor should caution the client that these arrangements must not only generate the desired federal income tax results, but should also constitute prudent investments (when considered even without the available federal income tax benefits). Relevant questions include whether such an investment should be in improved real estate, leased personal property, farms and agricultural activities, oil and gas properties, research and development (R&D) projects, movies, and other similar arrangements having the potential for generating income tax deductions? In this context, the tax planner must consider the probable applicability of federal income tax accounting provisions such as the "at-risk" rules[6] and the "passive loss" limitation rules,[7] which might limit the current income tax utilization of losses.
- Can current recognition of earned income be deferred where the subsequent federal income tax liability will be sufficiently reduced, thereby offsetting the loss of the current use of those funds (after reduction by the possible federal income tax liability)?

What opportunities exist for deferring that income taxation through tax-deductible contributions to a qualified pension or profit-sharing plan? A self-employed retirement plan (SEP)? A §401(k) plan? An individual retirement account (IRA) or some other variant in the deferred compensation context?
- Will the potential application of the "alternative minimum tax" (or AMT) on items of tax preference income[8] neutralize the economic value of any income tax deferral available under the regular income tax?
- What other planning opportunities exist for reducing current federal or state income tax costs?

When a significant income tax rate differential exists between ordinary income and capital gains, appropriate investment strategy suggests that investments producing capital gains should be emphasized. This is the situation after ATRA when, except for corporate dividends received, the tax rate differential can be at least 19.6% (i.e., 20% for capital gains vs. 39.6% for ordinary income). These maximum 20% and 39.6% rates apply after 2012.[9] Tax code provisions might limit this planning opportunity, however. Further, the client might be concerned about the greater investment risk that might be inherent in growth-potential assets.

D. Managing and Structuring the Closely Held Business Ownership: Family Business Succession Planning

The family business enterprise of which the client is the sole owner or a major participant might be restructured or sold. Important planning questions in this context might include, for example[10]:

- Should the client presently sell the business and retire upon receipt of the sales proceeds, rather than waiting until a later time when a sale of the business might be more difficult to conclude or a key manager for the business is more difficult to identify? Can a key executive be employed who will gradually take over the operations and, possibly, in the future acquire the client's business ownership interest? Can and should recognition of the income to be realized on a sale of the family business enterprise be deferred through an installment sale? Should the parties make use of a "covenant not to compete" or a consulting contract (or a combination of these techniques) to enable the purchaser to secure ordinary deductions for part of the acquisition cost?[11]
- Should sole proprietorship assets or a partnership interest be transferred into a corporation or limited liability company so as to facilitate an after-death transfer of the business interest and its assets? If incorporation (and accompanying property transfers) is decided upon, should S corporation status be elected for this new corporation, if available?[12]
- If the client does not desire to retain his or her business interest after retirement, to be transferred to or for family members after the client's death, should a buy-sell

agreement be arranged with the remaining owners? Should that arrangement be a cross-purchase agreement, an entity stock redemption agreement, or a combination of these two alternatives?[13]

E. Additional Important Preliminary Planning Inquiries

1. Types of Other Property Prompting Estate Planning Analysis

The client often does not hold property directly but through some alternative ownership arrangement, as determined upon applicable local property law concepts. These properties are often governed by contractual arrangements entered into by the client. These properties may have significant economic value and may actually constitute the bulk of a client's net worth. Each of these assets may prompt careful examination concerning estate planning and wealth transfer considerations. Some examples are provided below.

2. Life Insurance

In addition to the personal residence, life insurance is often one of the most important elements of the accumulated wealth for many family units, particularly after the maturity of the policy, at the time of the death of the insured. This insurance can be derived from both personally acquired policies and policies obtained in the employment context. Since the internal build-up of a cash value policy is not included in gross income, life insurance policies are often regarded as the equivalent of tax shelters. There can be, however, a significant start-up cost in establishing a life insurance policy which can reduce the "tax shelter" value. These policies can exist in a variety of forms and, if the appropriate form is not currently held, the possibility exists of engaging in a tax-free exchange to enable tax deferral of accrued gain upon the acquisition of a preferred type of life insurance policy for the policy currently held. Further, because of the structure of the estate tax provisions applicable to the inclusion of life insurance proceeds in the gross estate, prudent planning often suggests that the ownership of these policies be isolated away from the insured (and the insured's spouse).[14] If the policies are held by the insured (and that ownership will be continued), the beneficiary designations should be analyzed by the estate planner since the policy proceeds will be distributed consistent with that contractual designation and beyond the jurisdiction of the probate process for the last will.

3. Joint Tenancy Property

Questions should be raised with the estate planning client concerning whether a joint tenancy property ownership arrangement that provides for survivorship rights should be created to facilitate a death-time transfer of the joint tenancy property to the survivor. This could also enable property transfers without exposure to the complexities of a local probate estate administration. Similar to the life insurance beneficiary designation, the transfer of the interest in joint tenancy with the right of survivorship property will be controlled by the terms of that property ownership arrangement, and not by the client's last will. Some community property jurisdictions even permit joint-tenancy-with-the-right-of-survivorship status for community property when held by spouses. Alternatively, a joint tenancy property ownership including survivorship rights might be severed as part of the estate planning, so as to avoid federal estate and gift tax problems.[15]

4. Conflict-of-Laws Problems

The client may have valuable property interests in several jurisdictions (whether in other states in the United States, in foreign countries, or both). The disposition of these properties (particularly real estate) might be controlled by the testamentary disposition statutes of those nondomiciliary jurisdictions. If this property is owned directly, this could necessitate an ancillary probate administration in each of the relevant nondomiciliary jurisdictions. The estate planner might inquire as to how this potential ancillary probate administration and, particularly, its attendant costs and delays, might be avoided. In some situations, this might be accomplished through the lifetime transfer of the out-of-state properties into an inter vivos revocable trust. The result of this "living trust" arrangement would be that the property would not be owned (in the "local law" property sense) by the decedent at the time of death. Rather, the property would be owned (under local property law rules) by the trust, which would not be treated as dying for purposes of requiring any ancillary probate proceedings.

If it is decided not to avoid ancillary probate administration in the nondomiciliary jurisdiction through the use of a trust, appropriate questions should be asked about the requirements concerning the recognition of wills in those foreign jurisdictions where the various properties are located. Under conflict-of-laws rules, a will is usually recognized if valid where executed, but this status must be carefully documented in each other jurisdiction where this question is relevant. For example, do the rules concerning the formalities of wills or the required testamentary capacity differ from those rules in the client's domiciliary state? Further, notwithstanding the existence of a valid last will, what will be the rights of the surviving spouse and the surviving children with respect to the property in that nondomiciliary jurisdiction, and how are these rights to be preserved or avoided? In addition, the conflict-of-laws rules involving possible state inheritance tax and state succession tax applicability should be carefully examined.

5. Classification of Community Property

A married client may live (or have previously lived) in a community property jurisdiction. This will necessitate an analysis of the actual division of property interests between the spouses and the potential application of ownership tracing rules to situations not clearly defined.

This property classification situation will become more complicated if the client has lived and accumulated property in several jurisdictions. For example, the client residing in a community property jurisdiction previously may have lived in a different community property jurisdiction that applies dissimilar community property law classification concepts from the current residence jurisdiction. These differing rules could affect the community property categorization of the income derived from separate property. Alternatively, the client, although presently living in a common-law property jurisdiction, previously may have lived in a community property jurisdiction. Consequently, the property held in the common-law property jurisdiction may actually be partially owned by the client's spouse because of its community property origin, even though title to the property is only in the name of one of the spouses. Under each of these circumstances, the estate planner will need to assure himself or herself that he or she has properly determined the appropriate allocation of the ownership of properties held by a married couple.[16]

6. Possible Elective Rights of Surviving Spouse and Others

Under applicable state law rules (ordinarily in a separate property jurisdiction), a surviving spouse may have certain elective share rights to property held by the deceased spouse, as specified in the local probate code. Similarly, in a community property jurisdiction, a surviving spouse might be entitled to a life interest, or other rights, in real property such as a homestead. Often, the client has no problem in transferring adequate property to the surviving spouse so that these limitations then become inapplicable. However, in some situations, the client would like to posture his or her planning situation so as to minimize these spousal rights. In these situations the estate planning advisor might suggest that the client change his or her domicile to a jurisdiction where these rules are more hospitable. Often, this will involve physical relocation from a separate property to a community property jurisdiction (where the assumption is that property ownership has already been divided). This necessitates sufficient connection with the replacement jurisdiction so that domicile can adequately withstand jurisdictional challenge. This will also necessitate changing documents, such as a last will, to state the domicile of the client. In some situations, state law may permit the filing of some statement to officially document this change in status. However, the parties must recognize that this transformation in domicile status in another jurisdiction will be prone to attack by the aggrieved party. If the change of domicile is an inadequate planning arrangement, the client might consider a relocation of his or her financial assets into a trust with a trust organization located in a hospitable jurisdiction, with the trust specifying it is subject to the governing laws in that jurisdiction.

7. Disposition of Client's Virtual Assets

With the evolution of the Internet, many individuals have acquired "virtual assets." These are ordinarily identified as one's electronic information stored online on a computer network. This information is often available only through the use of passwords and other security arrangements. This information may also be stored on home computers and other devices not online but where the information is in an electronic format. Access to this information can be difficult when the individual becomes mentally incapacitated or dies. For some persons this electronic "intellectual property" can be quite valuable. In other situations, the unavailability of this information can present serious issues of being able to access important data that is not otherwise available.

For these reasons, the estate planning advisor should advise the client to arrange for the appointment and authorization of some representative to have access to this information in the event of incapacity or death. A durable power of attorney will not ordinarily enable access to this information (during the client's lifetime). Each of the various online accounts will have its own rules for obtaining access to this information by another and, in some situations, preclude access after death. For this reason the advisor might encourage the client to create a "virtual asset instruction letter" or similar document to (1) list all of the individual online accounts and assets, (2) provide web addresses, user names, and passwords, and (3) specify authority to the designated representative to access these accounts. With a durable power of attorney, the delegate is often authorized to act immediately, although in some situations the power of attorney might be structured as a "springing" power, enabling exercise only on the occurrence of some later, specified event. With virtual assets the usual assumption is that this electronic access will be made available only after the occurrence of incompetence or death.

These instructions may be stored in an individual's safe deposit box, accessible by the client's legal representative. Alternatively, they may be stored on a flash memory drive or a CD, enabling prompt access to this information if these items are easily available after the client's death. In some instances, technical assistance should be arranged to facilitate this access.[17]

8. Other Properties and Planning Issues

This list of basic factual inquiries important in the estate planning context is not exhaustive. It does, however, demonstrate the types of questions that should be examined at the preliminary stage of the estate planning process. These inquiries and many similar issues are examined in depth in this book and in the Estates, Gifts and Trusts Series of Tax Management portfolios produced by Bloomberg BNA. The inventory of properties provided by the client should often alert the estate planning advisors to specialized issues arising in this context.

F. Financial Adequacy of the Estate

The estate planner must also determine whether the client's net estate will be financially adequate to satisfy the needs of the client's surviving spouse and dependents. The net estate will consist of the client's properties after the payment of debts and any estate taxes (or other death-related duties). For example, will the client's estate consist of sufficient liquid funds to support the surviving spouse and the children after the death of the primary client? If liquidity is in doubt, should additional life insurance be purchased (assuming the client is insurable)? If so, should this insurance be whole life or term insurance?

An ancillary consideration is whether health insurance, supplemental health insurance, and long-term care insurance should be acquired so that substantial medical bills will not deplete the estate. This mandates an inquiry to assure that appropriate Medicare enrollment has occurred, if the client is eligible. Similarly, should disability income insurance be purchased? Should other casualty and general liability insurance be acquired (e.g., an "umbrella" policy) so that possible catastrophes will not deplete the client's net worth and probable financial estate?[18] For many estates, the significant cost is not estate taxes but depletion of the estate through continuing costs for health care during one's declining years.

G. Hypothetical Probate Administration

The estate planner should analyze what the tax and probate results would be if the client were to die immediately without a last will or with his or her present (perhaps inadequate) will. This analysis would include an estimate of the costs of probate administration and death taxes and the allocation of those costs to the various assets in the anticipated estate.[19] These estimates will be valuable in both (1) determining the liquidity of the estate and (2) in anticipating certain problems as to special assets (such as those mentioned above), which may constitute part of the estate for federal estate tax purposes. This could also include an analysis of who would be the recipients of the estate under either (1) the applicable state laws of descent and distribution, or (2) a will that may be the subject of review and revision. This could identify the net amounts each beneficiary would receive after the allocation of taxes and expenses.[20] This would enable the estate planning client to refine his or her ideas concerning the allocation of his or her assets to be realized by specific beneficiaries after the time of death.

H. Lifetime Asset Management

The estate planner should also anticipate that the client may become mentally incompetent prior to the death.[21] Alternatively, even though not anticipating incompetency, the client may want to delegate the responsibility to another for the handling of his or her investment properties and personal business affairs. A "durable power of attorney,"[22] which is not invalidated as of the time of mental incompetency of the principal, thereby enabling the attorney-in-fact to continue (or begin) to act on behalf of the incompetent, may be used for this purpose.[23]

The usefulness of a durable power of attorney is often underestimated. Most parties relying on a power of attorney will insist on a strict construction as to the authority granted under the power of attorney. Consequently, in drafting the durable power of attorney, an expansive identification of the delegated powers is often useful including, for example, the power to (1) sign tax returns and settle tax disputes, (2) deal with retirement plans and Social Security benefits, (3) access safe deposit boxes (many banks will not let attorneys-in-fact enter a safe deposit box of the principal), (4) deal with life insurance, (5) make property transfers into a previously established revocable or irrevocable trust, and (6) continue or implement a lifetime gift program.[24] An attorney-in-fact under a durable power of attorney will often not be considered authorized to make medical or custodial decisions concerning the incompetent person (although a separate "durable power of attorney for health care" may enable such decisions). Further, many banks, insurance companies, and real estate title companies refuse to recognize the effectiveness of a durable power of attorney unless it is executed on their own special forms previously approved by their own legal counsel. It is recommended that instruments creating powers of attorney be provided to such custodians in advance for review so that a separate form may be prepared if necessary. This will not be possible if the principal has become incompetent, and this possibility of incompetency mandates that the scope of the durable power of attorney, when originally executed, should be carefully examined.

The power of an attorney-in-fact to make gifts on behalf of a principal, or to continue a principal's gifting program, should be set forth clearly in the instrument and should be in conformity with applicable state law. Many states have specific statutes that address this issue. Another area of importance is the power of an attorney-in-fact to transfer property to the principal's revocable trust or to create such a trust. A number of cases have addressed situations where the IRS sought to include in a decedent's taxable estate the property gifted, either into a trust or directly, by an attorney-in-fact. Several decisions approved this gross estate inclusion where the durable power of attorney document was not sufficiently explicit to enable the attorney-in-fact to make gifts of assets of the principal.[25]

Alternatively, a "living trust" (or funded revocable trust) might be used to hold a client's properties.[26] Under this alternative, a trustee (or, often, a replacement, substitute trustee) for the incompetent grantor/original trustee can manage the properties held in the trust. The legal title to those properties, however, must have previously been actually transferred into this trust. Under some circumstances, a durable power of attorney may be sufficiently expansive to enable the transfer of a client's directly owned properties into a previously established revocable inter vivos trust. The durable power of attorney should be drafted to accommodate this possibility, but provisions of applicable state law should be examined carefully to ensure that such property transfers will be recognized.

Notes

1. The estate planner must also be continually aware when assisting his or her client of the professional responsibility obligations applicable in the estate planning context. For further discussion, see Chapter 13.

2. For federal income tax purposes, bonds must be purchased in registered form to enable an interest expense deduction to the obligor. See §163(f) denying a deduction for the interest expense paid on debt obligations not issued in registered form. Similarly, see §149, which specifies that state and local bonds must be registered in order for income to be tax exempt (under §103).
3. For example, the current maximum 20% income tax rate on dividends and the maximum 20% rate on capital gains might encourage some to invest in high-dividend-paying corporate stock or investments to be held for appreciation for longer than a one-year period, rather than financial instruments paying interest income possibly subject to a 39.6% income tax rate. Section 1(h)(11) (treating certain dividends as capital gains) and the general §1(h) 20% maximum capital gains tax rate apply to taxable years beginning after 2012. See the American Taxpayer Relief Act of 2012 (ATRA), Pub. L. No. 112-240, §102(a), §102(b).
4. This income tax planning contemplates the potential application of the federal income tax. State income taxes should also be carefully considered in implementing these planning decisions. Even clients resident in states without income taxes may have properties (e.g., investment real estate) in jurisdictions having state income taxes and for them state income tax exposure also becomes a planning consideration.
5. Section 1(h)(11) provides that "qualified dividend income" is taxed at the capital gain rate (20% for taxpayers in the 39.6% income tax bracket, 0% for taxpayers below the 25% income tax bracket, and 15% for all others). As noted above, §1(h)(11) and the general §1(h) 20% maximum capital gains tax rate apply to taxable years beginning after 2012. *See* ATRA, Pub. L. No. 112-240, §102(a), §102(b).
6. Section 465. Under the "at-risk" rules, the associated deductions cannot exceed actual economic investment (i.e., real financial commitment to the property), rather than the usually larger income tax basis (as defined in §1012 as cost and which, under the decision in *Crane v. Commissioner*, 331 U.S. 1 [1947], includes any nonrecourse indebtedness).
7. Section 469 provides for a limitation on the deductibility of "passive activity losses." Consequently, the income received by a taxpayer from an active trade or business or from securities investments cannot be offset by that taxpayer's losses from "passive activities." Special passive activity loss rules apply to real estate professionals for taxable years beginning after 1993. *See* §469(c)(7).
8. Section 57 identifies the "items of tax preference" for purposes of the alternative minimum tax.
9. The maximum 20% capital gains rate is only applicable to those taxpayers in the §1(i) 39.6% maximum income tax bracket. For most taxpayers, the maximum capital gains rate is 15%.
10. See, generally, 809 T.M., *Estate Planning for Owners of Closely Held Business Interests* (Bloomberg BNA).
11. Note, however, that under §197 the cost for the covenant not to compete would be required to be amortized over a 15-year period (rather than over the specific shorter term for that covenant).
12. Regulations adopting a "check-the-box" approach to entity classification (including the use of limited liability companies) are found at Reg. §301.7701-1 through §301.7701-4 and §301.7701-6, and the rules applicable to electing S corporation status are generally found at §1361–§1362 and the regulations thereunder.
13. See the discussion in Chapter 10, B.3., concerning buy-sell agreements.

14. See further discussion concerning life insurance planning in Chapter 9, C.
15. See further discussion concerning joint tenancy property planning in Chapter 9, A.
16. See 802 T.M., *Community Property: General Considerations* (Bloomberg BNA), and 803 T.M., *Estate Planning for the Mobile Client* (Bloomberg BNA).
17. The client may be advised in appropriate circumstances to consider the use of a commercial service which effectively provides an "online safe deposit box." This arrangement can store the client's virtual assets and provide a procedure through which designated individuals can gain access to the client's virtual assets. The use of any of these online commercial services for the storage of electronic information will need to be carefully investigated since providing access to this information is the equivalent of providing to that designate a power of attorney over one's assets within the particular electronic domain.
18. The enactment of the 1996 Health Insurance Portability and Accountability Act, Pub. L. No. 104-191, made three insurance options more attractive to clients planning for the costs of eventual disability: (1) long-term care insurance; (2) accelerated death benefit riders on life insurance policies; and (3) the sale or assignment of a life insurance policy to a viatical settlement company. For further discussion of these provisions and estate planning for incompetency in general, see 816 T.M., *Planning for Disability* (Bloomberg BNA).
19. See the Appendix for materials regarding projections (such as the BNA Software "Estate Tax Planner") of anticipated and future estate tax costs.
20. This analysis should also consider whether the beneficiary will receive assets with a basis stepped up to fair market value at death or with a carryover basis (e.g., assets consisting of "income in respect of a decedent" or "IRD"). If it has an IRD component, the asset will have an income tax burden that will reduce its net value, unless that income will not be realized for federal income tax purposes until some later date.
21. In addition to granting authority for management of one's assets, the client may also wish to designate someone as guardian of one's person, often a designation authorized by local law.
22. For further discussion of durable powers of attorney, see 816 T.M., *Planning for Disability* (Bloomberg BNA).
23. Local law will ordinarily provide for the possible implementation of a durable power of attorney. The Uniform Durable Power of Attorney Act is included in the Uniform Probate Code at §5-501 through §5-505. Often, a state statute will provide a statutory form of "durable power of attorney" that may be used in this context (but may not be required to be used). The Prefatory Note to this Uniform Act indicates that the purpose of the power of attorney is to assist persons interested in establishing non-court regimes for the management of their affairs in the event of later incompetency or disability. "The purpose was to recognize a form of senility insurance comparable to that available to relatively wealthy persons who use funded, revocable trusts for persons who are unwilling or unable to transfer assets as required to establish a trust." In the 2005 discussion draft revision notes for this Uniform Act, the Prefatory Note indicates that a consensus of opinion exists that a power of attorney should: (1) provide for confirmation that contingent powers are activated; (2) revoke a spouse-agent's authority upon the dissolution or annulment of the marriage to the principal; (3) include a portability provision; (4) require gift-making authority to be expressly stated in the grant of authority; (5) provide a default standard for fiduciary duties; (6) permit the principal to alter the default fiduciary standard; (7) require notice by an agent when the agent is no longer willing or able to act; (8) include safeguards against abuse by the agent; (9) include remedies and sanctions

for abuse by the agent; (10) protect the reliance of other persons on a power of attorney; and (11) include remedies and sanctions for refusal of other persons to honor a power of attorney. The website for the National Conference of Commissioners on Uniform State Laws (www.nccusl.org) will have current drafts of any proposed revisions. The locally enacted version of this legislation may have significant variables that should be identified. Further, if the client has substantial properties in multiple jurisdictions, the client should be assured that the executed durable power of attorney will be recognized in each of those jurisdictions. In many situations involving financial institutions, those organizations will be insistent that their specific form be utilized to enable a transaction involving an attorney-in-fact to be recognized.

24. State law may facilitate a court proceeding to authorize large gifts to be made by the attorney-in-fact, so as to achieve estate tax planning objectives, but a properly prepared power of attorney should be able to avoid the necessity for such a proceeding.
25. For a more detailed discussion of this issue, see 816 T.M., *Planning for Disability* (Bloomberg BNA), and 845 T.M., *Gifts* (Bloomberg BNA).
26. See 860 T.M., *Revocable Inter Vivos Trusts* (Bloomberg BNA).

CHAPTER 4

The Basic Federal Transfer Tax and Income Tax Structure

A. Estate, Gift, and Generation-Skipping Transfer Taxes

1. The Federal Transfer Tax System

a. Disequilibrium in the Transfer Tax System

A necessary prerequisite of any estate planning discussion is a basic understanding of the scope and structure of the federal estate tax, gift tax, and generation-skipping transfer tax system.[1] That tax structure is described below, but it has been and remains subject to significant, continuing revisions. The federal estate and gift taxes have been applicable for a long period, but the transfer tax planning practice during the early twenty-first century has been significantly impacted by year 2001 tax legislative changes.[2] From 2001 until early 2013, there existed much uncertainty in estate planning. Although most tax practitioners believed that Congress would "fix" the potential repeal of the estate tax for years after 2009, Congress failed to act and the result was that estates of decedents dying in 2010 were able to avoid the estate tax altogether.[3] The American Taxpayer Relief Act of 2012 (ATRA)[4] finally brought some stability to the estate tax arena by permanently extending most of the changes made by the Economic Growth and Tax Relief Reconciliation Act (EGTRRA), the Jobs and Growth Tax Relief Reconciliation Act (JGTRRA), and the Tax Reconciliation Act of 2010 (2010 TRA).

As explained below, legislation enacted in early 2013 significantly impacted planning by (1) making permanent many of the EGTRRA provisions; (2) continuing the estate and generation-skipping transfer taxes (as reinstated by the 2010 TRA); (3) providing favorable transfer tax exemption amounts for 2013 and thereafter; and (4) making permanent the spousal portability provision originally provided for in the 2010 TRA.[5]

b. The Estate Planner's Dilemma

Although Congress has provided some certainty as to the post-2012 transfer tax structure with the enactment of ATRA, careful estate planning mandates that tax planners address the uncertainty as to what rules will apply at an estate planning client's death. For example, a client may become mentally incapacitated and may not be able to respond to these changing tax rules with revised estate planning documents. To plan for the situation only when the tax rates and unified credit are higher invites possible catastrophic results if the client dies when the initial assumptions concerning estate tax applicability have become significantly erroneous.[6] Estate planning documents should ordinarily include adjustment clauses to deal with these diverse situations.[7] Planning responses to deal with these variables are noted at various locations below.[8]

c. Summary of the Evolving Transfer Tax Rules

EGTRRA[9] made major revisions in the area of the estate, gift, and generation-skipping transfer taxes.[10] The important details of these legislative changes are summarized here and noted in greater detail in various locations where relevant in the context of specific planning issues. This summary of the EGTRRA changes is followed by a summary of the subsequent changes made by the 2010 TRA and ATRA.[11]

Beginning in 2002 and continuing through 2009, the maximum estate and gift tax rates decreased,[12] and the unified credit effective exemption amount increased.[13]

The generation-skipping transfer tax (GST) exemption amount for 2004–2009 was the same amount as the unified credit exemption amount (as determined under §2010(c)) applicable to decedents' estates in those years.[14]

The estate tax deduction for qualified family-owned business interests for the estates of decedents dying after December 31, 2003, was terminated.[15]

The §2011 credit for state death taxes was phased out and, beginning in 2005, was replaced with the §2058 deduction for death taxes (i.e., estate, inheritance, legacy, or succession taxes) actually paid to any state or the District of Columbia when pertaining to property included in a decedent's gross estate.[16]

Effective for the estates of decedents dying after December 31, 2004, the credit for certain state death taxes allowable against the GST tax was terminated.[17]

The estate tax terminated for decedents dying after December 31, 2009.[18]

The generation-skipping transfer tax terminated for generation-skipping transfers made after December 31, 2009.[19]

The gift tax did not terminate (Congress believing that this gift tax retention would impede the shifting of income-producing assets to other family members, who would probably be in a lower marginal tax bracket for federal income tax purposes).

Along with the termination of the estate tax for the year 2010, the §2056A(b)(1)(B) provision imposing an estate tax on the value of property remaining in a qualified domestic trust at the death of the noncitizen surviving spouse beneficiary was to terminate.[20] However, the §2056A(b)(1)(A) provision imposing an estate tax on lifetime distributions to a surviving spouse from a qualified domestic trust created by a decedent dying before January 1, 2010, is effective through December 31, 2020.[21]

Section 1014, which specifies the rules relating to the tax basis of property acquired from a decedent (to provide for a fair market value basis for such property), was not to apply to decedents dying after December 31, 2009.[22]

Although the estate and generation-skipping transfer taxes were to terminate in 2010, under the "sunset" provision in this legislation, the entire transfer tax system was to be restored, effective January 1, 2011, as it had existed prior to the enactment of EGTRRA.[23]

As indicated above, the 2010 TRA significantly changed the EGTRRA rules for estates of decedents dying, and gifts and generation-skipping transfers made, after 2009 by:

- Reinstating the estate and GST taxes, reinstating the §1014 fair-market-value basis at death provision, and repealing the §1022 modified carryover basis regime after 2009.[24]
- Allowing (in a non-Code provision) executors of estates of decedents dying in 2010 to elect to apply the §1022 modified carryover basis regime rather than the reinstated estate tax regime.[25]
- Increasing the §2010(c) estate tax applicable exclusion amount to $5 million for decedents dying during the period 2010–2012, increasing the §2631(c) GST exemption amount to $5 million for generation-skipping transfers made in 2010–2012, increasing the §2505(a) gift tax applicable exclusion amount to $5 million for gifts made in 2011–2012, and adjusting the $5 million amount for inflation in multiples of $10,000 for 2012.[26]
- Providing for the portability of spouses' unified credits for the estates of decedents dying and gifts made in 2011–2012.[27] Section 2010(c)(2) defines the applicable exclusion amount as (a) the "basic exclusion amount" plus, (b) in the case of a surviving spouse, the "deceased spousal unused exclusion amount" (DSUE amount).[28] Section 2010(c)(3) sets the "basic exclusion amount" at $5 million (as adjusted for inflation in 2012).[29] For surviving spouses of decedents dying in 2011 or 2012, §2010(c)(4) defines the DSUE amount as the lesser of: (1) the basic exclusion amount or (2) the excess of the basic exclusion amount[30] of the last deceased spouse of the surviving spouse over the amount as to which the tentative tax is determined under §2001(b)(1) on the deceased spouse's estate.[31] For a surviving spouse's estate to take into account the DSUE amount, §2010(c)(5)(A) requires the deceased spouse's executor to (a) file an estate tax return computing such amount and (b) make an irrevocable election allowing such amount to be taken into account.[32] If a complete and properly prepared Form 706 is timely filed (taking into account any extensions) in accordance with the Form 706 instructions, the estate will be

considered to have made a portability election if certain conditions are satisfied.[33] The election is not allowed if the deceased spouse's estate tax return is filed after the due date (including extensions).[34] Notwithstanding any §6501 statute of limitations, §2010(c)(5)(B) provides that the IRS may examine the deceased spouse's return to make determinations about the DSUE amount after the expiration of the §6501 period for assessing estate or gift tax relating to the DSUE amount.[35] The portability provisions do not apply to the GST exemption.[36]

- Reducing the maximum estate and gift tax rate to 35% for amounts over $500,000 for taxable estates of decedents dying and gifts made in 2010–2012.[37] The 2010 TRA also extended EGTRRA's repeal of the §2001(c)(2) 5% surtax, which eliminated the unified credit for estates over $10 million, for estates of decedents dying and gifts made in 2010–2012.[38] For generation-skipping transfers made during 2010, the 2010 TRA treats (in a non-Code provision) the applicable rate determined under §2641(a) as being zero.[39] Similarly, for generation-skipping transfers made during 2011–2012, the 35% rate applies for generation-skipping transfer tax purposes.[40]
- Providing special rules to account for the differences in the unified credit resulting from different estate and gift tax rates for estates of decedents dying and gifts made in 2010–2012.[41] Specifically, §2001(b)(2) and §2001(g) state that, in applying §2001(b)(2) to one or more gifts, the tax rates in effect at the decedent's death (rather than the rates in effect at the time of the gifts) are used to calculate the gift tax and the gift tax unified credit allowed. Also, §2505(a) states that, in applying §2505(a)(2) for a calendar year, the gift tax rates for that year (rather than the rates in effect for prior years) are used in determining the gift tax unified credit allowable for preceding years.[42]
- Eliminating §2511(c), which provided a special gift tax rule for certain transfers in trust, effective for gifts made after 2009.[43] Thus, §2511(c) never took effect and, because it was added by EGTRRA, did not return after 2012.
- Extending the due dates for several items. Specifically, for estates of decedents dying after 2009 and before December 17, 2010 (the 2010 TRA's enactment date), a non-Code provision extended, for at least nine months after December 17, 2010, the due dates for: (1) filing an estate tax return under §6018 (including any elections required to be made on such returns) as in effect without the EGTRRA amendments, and without regard to the election to apply the §1022 modified carryover basis rules; (2) making any estate tax payments; and (3) making §2518(b) disclaimers for any property interest passing by reason of the decedent's death.[44] For generation-skipping transfers made after 2009 and before December 17, 2010, a non-Code provision extended, for at least nine months after December 17, 2010, the due date for filing any §2662 GST tax return (including any elections required to be made on such returns).[45]
- Extending EGTRRA's addition of the §2058 state death tax deduction (and delaying the reinstatement of the §2011 state death tax credit) for estates of decedents dying in 2010–2012.[46]

- Extending EGTRRA's repeal of the §2057 qualified family-owned business interest deduction for estates of decedents dying in 2010–2012.[47]
- Extending EGTRRA's modifications to §2031(c)(2) and §2031(c)(8) conservation easement rules (clarifying the value for purposes of the applicable percentage and expanding the definition of land).[48]
- Extending EGTRRA's modifications to the §6166 estate tax installment payment provisions (relating to increasing the number of allowable partners and shareholders in a closely held business, adding qualifying lending and finance businesses, and clarifying the rules on non–readily tradable stock) for estates of decedents dying in 2010–2012.[49]
- Extending EGTRRA's GST tax relief provisions (relating to §2632(c) deemed exemption allocations, §2632(d) retroactive exemption allocations, §2642(a)(3) qualified severances, §2642(b) valuation rules, and §2642(g) relief) for generation-skipping transfers made in 2010–2012.[50]

The EGTRRA and 2010 TRA changes were scheduled to sunset as of December 31, 2012. ATRA generally extended the EGTRRA and 2010 TRA provision with the following modifications:

- Making permanent the increased §2010(c) estate tax applicable exclusion amount of $5 million for decedents dying after 2012, making permanent the increased §2631(c) GST exemption amount of $5 million for generation-skipping transfers made after 2012, making permanent the increased §2505(a) gift tax applicable exclusion amount to $5 million for gifts made after 2012, and making permanent the inflation adjustment in multiples of $10,000 to the $5 million exemption amounts after 2012.[51]
- Making permanent the portability of spouses' unified credits for the estates of decedents dying and gifts made after 2012.[52]
- Increasing the maximum estate and gift tax rate to 40% for amounts over $1 million for decedents dying and gifts made after 2012.[53]
- Making permanent EGTRRA's addition of the §2058 state death tax deduction (and permanently eliminating the §2011 state death tax credit) for estates of decedents dying after 2012.[54]
- Making permanent EGTRRA's repeal of the §2057 qualified family-owned business interest deduction for estates of decedents dying after 2012.[55]
- Making permanent EGTRRA's modifications to §2031(c)(2) and §2031(c)(8) conservation easement rules (clarifying the value for purposes of the applicable percentage and expanding the definition of land) for decedents dying after 2012.[56]
- Making permanent EGTRRA's modifications to the §6166 estate tax installment payment provisions (relating to increasing the number of allowable partners and shareholders in a closely held business, adding qualifying lending and finance businesses, and clarifying the rules on non–readily tradable stock) for estates of decedents dying after 2012.[57]

- Making permanent EGTRRA's GST tax relief provisions (relating to §2632(c) deemed exemption allocations, §2632(d) retroactive exemption allocations, §2642(a)(3) qualified severances, §2642(b) valuation rules, and §2642(g) relief) for generation-skipping transfers made after 2012.[58]

During 2015 an important restriction was enacted to require consistent tax basis reporting between an estate and a person acquiring property from a decedent, as included in the Surface Transportation and Veterans Health Care Choice Improvement Act of 2015, Pub. L. No. 114-41. Section 2004 of that act enacted §1014(f) and §6035. Section 1014(f) provides rules that require that the tax basis of certain property acquired from a decedent, as determined under §2014, may not exceed the value of that property as finally determined for federal estate tax purposes, or, if not finally determined, the value of that property as reported on a statement made under §6035. This provision provides new reporting requirements with regard to the value of property included in a decedent's gross estate for federal estate tax purposes.

Section 6035(a)(1) provides that the executor of any estate required to file a return under §6018(a) must furnish, both to the IRS and to the person acquiring any interest in property included in the decedent's gross estate for federal estate tax purposes, a statement identifying the value of each interest in such property as reported on that return and such other information with respect to the interest as prescribed. Section 6035(a)(2) provides that each person required to file a return under §6018(b) must furnish, both to the IRS and to each other person who holds a legal or beneficial interest in the property to which this return relates, a statement identifying the information described in §6035(a)(1). Section 6018(b) applies when the executor is unable to make a complete estate tax return, but the executor shall then include in his return a description of that part of and the name of each person holding a legal or beneficial interest therein.

Section 6081(a) provides that the Secretary may grant a reasonable extension of time for filing any return, declaration, statement, or other document filed in the estate tax context. Under this authority the IRS has specified that for the statements required under §6035(a)(1) and §6035(a)(2) before February 29, 2016, the due date is delayed until February 29, 2016. As specified in Notice 2015-57, 2015-36 IRB 294, executors and other persons required to furnish a statement under §6035(a)(1) or §6035(a)(2) should not do so until the issuance of forms or further guidance from the IRS addressing the requirements of this provision.

2. The Federal Estate Tax

a. Scope of the Tax: Probate Estate v. Taxable Estate

The federal estate tax is an excise tax imposed on a transfer of property at death.[59] The amount of estate tax liability (imposed at progressive tax rates) depends on the total net value of the property transferred. Applicability of this tax is not limited to property transfers controlled by a last will or by operation of locally applicable laws of descent and distribution (i.e., property that is transferred for local "probate" purposes). Rather, the federal estate tax also extends to other transfers of economic value that are essentially equivalent to testamentary transfers of property but that occur outside the scope of the local probate administration system. At an early stage in the representation of an estate planning client, the advisor should inform the client that his or her taxable estate, as distinct from the probate estate, may include property that the client has given away, as well as property the client has never considered himself or herself as "owning."

b. Determination of a Decedent's Property Rights

Although federal tax law governs in determining the incidence of federal taxation, state law governs in defining the existence of property rights. No distinct property characterization system exists for federal transfer tax purposes. Accordingly, federal transfer tax concepts will be applied to the "property facts" as they are ascertained under pertinent state property laws.

In determining these property interests, the IRS and the federal courts must give "proper regard" to state property definitions (whether derived from state statutes or decisional law).[60] Ascertaining property rights under local law may be difficult because, in a particular situation, the local law may not be well developed. Under these circumstances the federal court (in considering a federal estate tax issue) will need to examine what would be the applicable local law if the state court were to examine the specific property rights at issue.[61]

c. Determination of the Taxable Estate

The computational steps in the process of establishing the taxable estate for federal estate tax purposes are as follows:

- Gross estate (as defined in §2033–§2046 and as valued under §2031–§2032A).
- Less: (1) administration expenses, taxes, losses, indebtedness, etc. (deductible under §2053 and §2054); (2) bequests to the surviving spouse (deductible under §2056)[62]; (3) charitable bequests (deductible under §2055)[63]; and (4) since 2004, the state death tax deduction (§2058).
- Equals: Taxable estate (as defined by §2051).

The net estate tax liability is thereafter computed with the application of available credits.[64]

d. Property Includible in Gross Estate

Section 2033 provides that "[t]he value of [decedent's] gross estate shall include the value of all property to the extent of the interest therein of the decedent at the time of his death."[65] This provision ordinarily contemplates the inclusion in the gross estate of the property subject to probate administration. In addition, various types of property, even though not "owned" (in the local property law sense) at death, are includible in the gross estate for federal estate tax purposes, because economic value is deemed to be gratuitously transferred from the decedent to or for another person at the decedent's death, including:

- the value of property transferred with certain "strings attached" (within the meaning of one of the estate tax "transfer" provisions)[66];
- the value of an annuity (or other payment) receivable by any beneficiary by reason of surviving the decedent and paid under an agreement by which an annuity was payable for the decedent's life (or for any period which does not in fact end before his or her death)[67];
- the value of all property held in joint tenancy (i.e., with a right of survivorship and not as tenants in common), except to the extent that the surviving co-tenant can be shown to have contributed to the acquisition or improvement of the property and except for certain joint interests between spouses[68];
- the value of all property to which the decedent had at the time of his or her death a "general power of appointment"[69];
- the value of life insurance proceeds if[70] (1) receivable by the decedent's executor under any policy on the life of the decedent, or (2) receivable by any other beneficiaries under a policy on the life of the decedent if the decedent possessed at his or her death any "incident of ownership" under the policy;
- if occurring within three years before death, the value of[71] (1) life insurance transferred by the insured, (2) property subject to releases or exercises of general powers of appointment, and (3) property subject to releases of certain powers in property interests retained from previously created inter vivos transfers;
- cash "distributed on account of the death of a beneficiary" from a qualified tuition program, and the portion of the contributions to such account made under the five-year averaging election that are properly allocable to periods after the donor's date of death[72];
- the value of a qualified ABLE account of which the decedent is the designated beneficiary[73]; and
- the value of Coverdell education savings accounts.[74]

e. Deductions from Gross Estate

Deductions from the gross estate allowable in determining the amount of the taxable estate include amounts for[75]:

- certain expenses and indebtedness, such as (1) reasonable funeral expenses, (2) administration expenses,[76] (3) claims against the estate,[77] (4) mortgages and other indebtedness with respect to property included in the gross estate,[78] and (5) certain marital property settlement amounts[79];
- losses[80];

- transfers for public, charitable, and religious uses[81];
- bequests and other transfers to the surviving spouse[82]; and
- state death taxes actually paid in respect of any property included in the gross estate.[83]

Prior to 2004, a deduction was available for a portion of the value of a family-owned business interest.[84] This deduction was limited in amount to $1,300,000. The 2001 Tax Relief Act[85] terminated this deduction for decedents dying after December 31, 2003.[86] Even without legislative termination the increase in the unified credit to enable an exclusion for the year 2004 in the amount of $1,500,000 effectively eliminated this deduction after 2003.

f. Asset Valuation

(1) Valuation Alternatives

The value of a decedent's estate is the value of all property (to the extent of the decedent's interest) as of the time of his or her death.[87] This includes all real or personal property, whether tangible or intangible, wherever situated, owned by the decedent. If the executor elects, the property may be valued on an alternate valuation date, which is usually six months after the decedent's death.[88] If the alternate valuation date is elected, that date controls as to the valuation of all property. The alternate valuation procedure cannot be used by selecting values on an asset-by-asset basis, but must be used on an "all-or-nothing" basis.[89] Additionally, a special valuation procedure is available for certain family farms and other qualified property.[90]

(2) Determining "Fair Market Value": Anticipate Controversies

The property in an estate must be valued at its "fair market value."[91] For this purpose, fair market value is that price at which the property would change hands between a willing buyer and a willing seller, neither being under any compulsion to buy or to sell and both having reasonable knowledge of the relevant facts.[92] Because the application of this standard will obviously be elusive, the estate planner must anticipate controversies concerning the fair market value of assets to be included in the gross estate. Estate tax valuation disputes are the most commonly raised issues during estate tax audits and produce the most estate tax revenues for the IRS since these tax disputes are fact based and are most apt to provide compromises over disputed values.

Valuation problems often occur in the context of business interests held by a decedent.[93] Valuation problems can also occur with respect to real estate held by a decedent and with respect to other property (such as household and personal effects, jewelry, paintings, and stamp collections).[94] The broad subject of valuation is beyond the scope of this book.[95] The estate planner has a responsibility to identify probable estate tax valuation controversies and to attempt to posture the holding of these properties in the best possible environment for a satisfactory valuation when that valuation is required after death in reporting the asset on an estate tax return.

(3) Actuarial Valuations

Valuations of certain assets includible in the gross estate may be required by reference to actuarial and interest rate tables.[96] Current interest rate factors are published regularly.[97] The tables applying these interest rate factors contain actuarial factors to be used in determining the present value of an annuity, an interest for life or for a term of years, or a remainder or reversionary interest.[98]

(4) Alternate Valuation

The alternate valuation method may be elected where a shrinkage in the aggregate value of the gross estate has occurred since death. The alternate valuation date election may be made only if it results in a decrease in both the value of the gross estate and the amount of the federal estate tax liability. If elected, the alternate valuation method must be used for all assets.[99] This precludes the use of the alternate valuation method solely for the purpose of reducing future federal income taxes (i.e., by electing a higher valuation where no federal estate liability exists, thereby establishing a higher tax basis for income tax purposes).[100]

(5) Special Valuation for Farms and Real Property

A special valuation method enables real property that is included in a decedent's gross estate and is devoted to farming or to closely held business use to be valued on the basis of the property's value as a farm or as closely held business property, rather than at its fair market value determined on the basis of that property's highest or best use.[101] This special-use valuation procedure may be used to reduce the total value of the decedent's gross estate.[102]

(6) Minority and Marketability Discounts

In many instances, an assertion may successfully be made that, for federal estate tax purposes, the value of a property interest can be reduced (1) because the property constitutes a minority interest (e.g., in the stock of a corporation) or (2) for lack of marketability, or (3) for both. The IRS has indicated that a minority discount may be available even when ownership interests in a property are divided among family members.[103] Further, the valuation upon the transfer of a minority interest in property (e.g., corporate shares) is not impacted by the transferee's existing ownership of a majority interest in the property.[104] The valuation of minority property interests (including family limited partnership interests) constitutes a recurring federal estate tax audit issue.[105]

(7) Discount to Reflect Asset's Potential Future Income Tax Liability

The asset acquired by a beneficiary may have a built-in potential for a future federal income tax liability. This could include, for example, the stock of a corporation that holds significantly appreciated assets. Those assets, if sold, would reduce the net worth of the corporation because the gain would be taxed to the corporation at the 35% income tax rate. This type of asset with an embedded gain could also include an individual's deferred compensation accounts (which would be includible in the gross income of the successor in interest when receiving the distribution). The IRS was unsuccessful in asserting that the potential corporate level liability should not impact the valuation of stock.[106] The IRS position is that the value of a deferred compensation account (such as an IRA) should not be discounted for estate tax purposes to reflect the income taxes that will be payable by beneficiaries upon the subsequent receipt of distributions from IRAs. The IRS has been successful concerning this position.[107]

3. The Gift Tax—Determining the Taxable Gift

a. Defining Donative Transfers

A federal gift tax is imposed on the transfer of property by gift.[108] For purposes of the federal gift tax, a gift may occur whether the transfer is in trust or otherwise; whether the transfer is direct or indirect; and whether the property transferred is real or personal, tangible or intangible.[109] Donative intent on the part of the transferor is not an essential element in applying the gift tax to the transfer.[110] The tax is applied based on the objective facts of the transfer and the circumstances under which it is made, rather than on the subjective motives of the donor. To constitute a gift for federal gift tax purposes, the property transfer must be complete.[111]

b. Exclusions and Deductions

(1) Annual Donee Exclusion

A gift tax annual exclusion is available to a donor up to a certain amount per donee.[112] When exclusions are combined through gift splitting, which requires filing of a gift tax return, spouses may together transfer double the annual donee exclusion amount (as adjusted for inflation) per donee each year without triggering any gift tax consequence.[113] An annual exclusion is also available for certain gifts made by U.S. citizens or U.S. residents to their non-U.S. citizen spouses, and is provided because no marital deduction is available in this context.[114]

The annual donee exclusion is available only when the gift constitutes a present interest (i.e., an interest or estate in property commencing in possession or enjoyment immediately).[115] Further, this exclusion is not cumulative; that is, the failure to use the annual donee exclusion in one year does not enable a greater exclusion in a subsequent year.[116] Further, many clients believe that annual exclusion gifts may reduce the available unified credit and need reassurance that the annual donee exclusion is in addition to the unified credit.

Example: X has six grandchildren. In 2015 she may transfer $14,000 to each grandchild (an annual total of $84,000), which will be excluded from her tax base for purposes of the federal gift tax but which will not reduce her available unified credit to be applied against gift and estate taxes.

(2) Transfers for Educational or Medical Expenses

In addition to the annual gift tax exclusion, an unlimited gift tax exclusion is allowed for amounts paid on behalf of a donee directly to an educational institution[117] for tuition or to a health care provider for medical services.[118] This exclusion is available without regard to the relationship between the donor and the donee.[119]

(3) Transfers to Section 529 Plans

Contributions to a qualified tuition program[120] are treated as completed gifts to the designated beneficiary of the account and are not treated as a qualified transfer under §2503(e). As a completed gift of a present interest, the contribution to the program qualifies for the §2503(b) annual gift tax exclusion and the exclusion for generation-skipping transfer tax purposes.[121] A distribution from a qualified tuition program is not treated as a taxable gift, except upon a change in the designated beneficiary to a beneficiary in a generation below the generation of the original beneficiary (as determined under §2651).[122]

(4) Marital Deduction

When a gift is made by one spouse to the other spouse, the donor spouse may claim the gift tax marital deduction.[123] Unlimited deductible transfers may be made to the donor's spouse provided the following requirements are satisfied:

- the parties are legally married at the time[124];
- the donee is a U.S. citizen[125]; and
- the gift is not of a "nondeductible terminable interest" (i.e., an interest in property that may terminate upon the passage of time or upon the occurrence or nonoccurrence of some event, with distribution thereafter to another person).

A deduction is allowed, however, for certain qualified terminable interest property transfers.[126]

(5) Gift Splitting

With the spouse's consent, the donor may "split" the gift with the spouse so that the gift transfer is treated as being made one-half by each spouse.[127] This privilege applies to gifts in any amount.[128] The benefit of gift splitting is that it may double the available annual donee exclusion when both spouses are treated as making gifts. Where gifts are taxable (i.e., where the entire unified credit equivalent has been used) the gift tax generally is lower with split gifts by virtue of the use of two graduated gift tax rate structures.[129]

Example: H transfers his separate property securities worth $56,000 to his son, S, and S's wife, X. H's wife, W, consents to the splitting of this gift for federal gift tax purposes. H and W are each considered to have given one-half of the property (or $28,000) each. Since there are two donees (S and X), H and W are each entitled to $28,000 in annual donee exclusions ($14,000 for each donee).[130] Consequently, no gift tax is due on these transfers (and, further, no reduction of the unified credit amount occurs).

To be eligible for gift splitting, the transfer must be made to someone other than the donor's spouse. If the gift-splitting election is made for any gift, all gifts made by either spouse during the calendar year must be treated as being made one-half by each spouse.[131]

4. Determining the Specific Amount of Transfer Tax Liability

a. Outline of the Federal Estate Tax Computation

After determining the taxable estate (i.e., gross estate less available deductions), the determination of the net estate tax liability occurs as follows:

- Gross estate tax (as computed under §2001 prescribing the unified rate schedule, applied to the taxable estate).[132]
- Less the following credits: (1) unified credit (as allowable under §2010)[133]; (2) state death taxes (as allowable under former §2011 but only before 2005)[134]; (3) federal gift taxes (as allowable under §2012)[135]; (4) tax on prior transfers (as allowable under §2013)[136]; and (5) foreign death taxes (as allowable under §2014).[137]
- Equals: Net estate tax liability.

b. Outline of the Federal Gift Tax Computation

The amount of gift tax payable is determined by (1) applying the unified rate schedule to the cumulative lifetime taxable transfers, and (2) subtracting the gift tax payable on lifetime transfers made for prior taxable periods.[138] After determining the tentative gift tax, the available unified credit is applied to determine the net gift tax liability.[139]

c. Unified Rate Schedule

(1) Cumulative Transfer Tax Computation

A single unified tax rate schedule applies for determining estate and gift taxes.[140] The rates are progressive on the basis of both cumulative lifetime transfers and the final transfer at death.[141] This eliminates the preferential rate structure that previously existed for lifetime gift transfers.

For 2001 the rates under the unified rate schedule ranged from 18% for the first $10,000 in taxable transfers to 55% of taxable transfers in excess of $3,000,000.[142] Starting in 2002, the top tax rate was gradually reduced, so that it would be 45% by 2007. Before 2002, the benefit of the graduated rate structure was phased out for taxable cumulative transfers in excess of $10,000,000 but not exceeding $17,184,000.[143] This was accomplished by adding a 5% surtax on taxable transfers in excess of $10,000,000 to the tentative tax computed.[144] The 5% surtax once extended to $21,040,000, which had the effect of also phasing out the unified credit. Amendments made to the former §2001(c)(2) 5% surtax by the Taxpayer Relief Act of 1997 were intended to reflect the increased unified credit beginning in 1998. The conforming amendment, however, was drafted in a manner that had the effect of phasing out the benefit of the graduated rates but not the unified credit. As a result, effective for decedents dying after 1997, the 5% surtax ended at $17,184,000, rather than at $21,040,000. This provision did not otherwise affect the structure of the unified credit. For example, gifts made on or before December 31, 1987, are included in determining the amount of the unified credit subject to this phase-out.[145]

(2) Lifetime Transfers—Gift Tax Computations

The gift tax payable for a calendar year is determined by (1) applying the unified rate schedule to the cumulative lifetime taxable transfers and (2) subtracting the taxes payable at current rates on all taxable gifts made in preceding calendar years and quarters.[146] These taxes payable on lifetime transfers for the prior taxable periods are computed under the unified rate schedule in effect under §2001 for the current taxable period even though the gifts were made before 1977 or under a different unified rate schedule.[147]

(3) Estate Tax—Computation of Liability

The estate tax liability is determined by applying the unified rate schedule to the aggregate of cumulative lifetime transfers and the transfers includable at death. This tentative estate tax amount is offset by the gift taxes payable on lifetime transfers made after December 31, 1976.[148] These taxes are computed under the unified rate schedule in effect as of the date of decedent's death.[149] Thus, if estate tax rates are declining, an amount of gift tax offset may be less than the gift tax actually paid, but the opposite result would occur if estate tax rate increases were implemented.

Special reduced estate tax rates do apply under certain limited circumstances. Section 2201 reduces the federal estate tax rates for the taxable estates of U.S. citizens and residents who are killed in action while serving in combat zones.[150] The §2201 reduced rates also apply to U.S. citizens and residents who die as a result of wounds, disease, or injury suffered while serving in the line of duty in a combat zone by reason of a hazard to which the service member was subjected as an incident to that service.[151] "Combat zone" means an area that the president designates by executive order as an area in which the Armed Forces of the United States are (or have been) engaged in combat.[152] Section 2201 replaces the estate tax rates that otherwise would be imposed by §2001 or §2101 with rates that range from 1% (for taxable estates above $100,000) to 20% (for taxable estates exceeding $10.1 million).[153] Estate tax credits generally available, particularly the §2010 unified credit, may reduce or eliminate the amount of estate tax payable (as determined under this reduced rate structure).

(4) Gift Transfers Included in Gross Estate

Transfers included in the estate tax computational base as lifetime transfers (or "adjusted taxable gifts") do not include those transfers also includible in the decedent's gross estate.[154] Among transfers included in the decedent's gross estate are: (1) interests in property otherwise includible in the gross estate under §2036–§2038 (i.e., the transfer provisions) or §2042 (life insurance), if the power or interest had been retained at death, where the power was relinquished within three years prior to death[155]; (2) gift taxes paid on gift transfers within three years prior to death[156]; and (3) lifetime transfers where the decedent actually retained certain interests, rights, or powers in the property.[157]

(5) Adjustment for Gift Tax Paid by Spouse

The gift tax previously paid by a decedent's spouse is a subtraction, or offset, in computing the estate tax imposed on a decedent's estate where the transfer subject to the tax is included in the decedent's gross estate and was considered a transfer made in part by the surviving spouse under the gift-splitting provisions.[158] The effect of this treatment is to reverse the consequences of treating the surviving spouse as the donor of one-half of a gift made to a third party for gift tax purposes where the property transferred is later includible in the decedent's gross estate.[159]

d. Unified Transfer Tax Credit

A unified credit or "applicable exclusion amount" is available to reduce or eliminate the transfer tax liability.[160] The §2010 unified credit "applicable credit amount," as converted into the "applicable exclusion amount," has provided for the following minimum levels of estate tax exemption: (1) $1 million for estates of decedents dying in 2002–2003; (2) $1.5 million for estates of decedents dying in 2004–2005; (3) $2 million for estates of decedents dying in 2006–2008; and (4) $3.5 million for estates of decedents dying in 2009.[161]

Effective for gifts made after December 31, 2001, §2505 established an effective lifetime exclusion amount for gift tax purposes equal to $1 million.[162] Since the gift tax was not terminated after 2009, this exclusion amount has continued after 2009.[163] In general, any portion of this unified credit used against a gift tax liability applicable to lifetime transfers will reduce the unified credit available to offset the tentative estate tax liability.

As explained in Chapter 4, A.1., the 2010 TRA[164] reunified the estate and gift tax exclusions after 2010 by increasing the §2010(c) estate tax exclusion amount to $5 million for decedents dying in 2011–2012, increasing the §2505(a) gift tax exclusion amount to $5 million for gifts made in 2011–2012 (the amount remains at $1 million for gifts made in 2010), and adjusting the $5 million amount for inflation in multiples of $10,000 in 2012. The 2010 TRA[165] also provides for portability of the exclusion for spouses dying in 2011–2012 (the applicable exclusion amount is the sum of the basic exclusion amount plus, in the case of a surviving spouse, the DSUE amount). ATRA[166] made permanent the 2010 TRA changes with respect to the §2010(c) $5 million estate tax exclusion amount for decedents dying after 2012, the §2505(a) gift tax exclusion amount for gifts made after 2012, and the inflation adjustment for both.[167] ATRA also made permanent the portability of the exclusion for spouses dying after 2012.

5. Filing Requirements

a. Estate Tax Return

The estate tax return must be filed within nine months after the date of the decedent's death.[168] An estate tax return is required only if the decedent's gross estate exceeds the applicable exclusion amount for the year of death and is necessary whether or not any tax will be due in the estate.[169] This gross estate amount filing requirement plateau is reduced by the sum of the adjusted taxable gifts made by the decedent after December 31, 1976, and the amount of the specific gift tax exemption under prior law that was used by the decedent after September 8, 1976.[170]

The executor of a deceased spouse's estate will have the power to file a Form 706 and make the portability election for that estate. This filing of the Form 706 when not otherwise required creates an expense for the estate of that deceased spouse. A conflict of interest can arise concerning who should bear the cost of preparing this return. The executor for the estate of the deceased spouse may seek an agreement on who will fund this cost and, additionally, that executor may seek necessary consents and waivers for this purpose. Although the return is due within nine months, an automatic filing extension of six additional months is available.[171] In certain situations, a further extension for good cause, may be granted by the IRS in the exercise of its discretion.[172]

In addition, the executor or other beneficiary required to file an estate tax return under §6018(a) or §6018(b) is required to file with the Secretary and furnish to each person acquiring an interest in property included in the gross estate a statement setting forth the value of each interest in the property as reported on the return.[173] The statement must be filed no later than the earlier of 30 days after the due date of the estate tax return (including any extensions) or 30 days after the return is actually filed.[174] The Code does not prescribe who is required to file the required statement where the estate is not required to file an estate tax return, but the Secretary has been given authority to prescribe regulations governing that situation.[175] An individual who fails to file the required statement is subject to penalties under §6721 and/or §6722.[176]

b. Gift Tax Return

Gift tax returns are to be filed, and any gift tax is to be paid, on an annual, calendar year basis.[177] In general, the due date for filing the annual gift tax return is April 15 following the close of the calendar year.[178] Any extension of time granted to the donor for filing an income tax return for any taxable year that is a calendar year is deemed to be an extension of time to file a gift tax return for that taxpayer for that year.[179] A special rule exists for the calendar year in which the donor dies. The gift tax return for that year must be filed no later than the due date for filing the deceased donor's estate tax return (including extensions).[180]

A gift tax return is required for any transfer by gift other than a gift transfer (1) excludible under the annual exclusion, (2) excludible under the special exclusion for tuition and health care payments, (3) deductible under the gift tax marital deduction provision, or (4) deductible under the charitable gift tax deduction provision, if certain requirements are met.[181] Where spouses split gifts, a gift tax return is required even though no gift tax will be due.[182]

6. Generation-Skipping Transfer Tax

The assumption of the estate and gift tax structure is that this transfer tax will be imposed at least once each generation. This fundamental objective would be frustrated if this taxation would not occur. Previously, this taxation could be avoided if a transferor created a trust for (1) child for life and (2) remainder to grandchildren. Although a transfer tax (estate or gift tax) would be applicable as of the time of the funding of this trust, no estate tax or gift tax would ordinarily be applicable at the subsequent death of the child (i.e., the intermediate-generation member). This would be the result even though the child enjoyed the lifetime benefit of the property and the property passed to the grandchildren.

The generation-skipping transfer tax was enacted to preclude these arrangements and, thereby, it complements the federal estate and gift taxes.[183] The Code defines a generation-skipping transfer as an event that is either (1) a "direct skip" (i.e., a direct transfer to or for a grandchild), (2) a "taxable distribution" from a trust (or similar arrangement) for the benefit of a grandchild, or (3) a "taxable termination" of a trust (or a similar arrangement) for the benefit of a grandchild.[184]

The applicable requirements relating to the filing of generation-skipping transfer tax returns depend on the type of generation-skipping transfer involved.[185] The variances concern both (1) who is the person liable for this tax and (2) who is required to make the generation-skipping transfer tax return.

B. Related Federal Income Tax Considerations

1. Gifts and Bequests as Gross Income

The receipt by (1) a donee of a gift or (2) an estate beneficiary of a bequest or devise constitutes an accretion to the recipient's economic wealth and, consequently, could be included in his or her gross income under §61 for federal income tax purposes, if Congress so determined. Section 102 provides an exclusion, however, that gross income does not include the value of property acquired by gift, bequest, devise, or inheritance.[186] This exclusion from gross income does not apply, however, to the income from any such property so received.[187] Further, where the gift, bequest, devise, or inheritance is of income from property (rather than the property itself), this gross income exclusion does not apply to the income received.[188]

Although the donee need not treat this gift item as gross income, the donee is required to report to the IRS when the donee receives during a taxable year "aggregate foreign gifts" exceeding $10,000.[189] These are gifts received from a person other than a U.S. person.[190]

2. Income Tax Basis Provisions—Gift Transfers

When property is transferred by gift the transferee takes the transferor's income tax basis for that property if the property when transferred is appreciated.[191] If the property is depreciated as of the time of the gift the donee takes as the tax basis the fair market value of the property as of the time of the gift but only for the purpose of determining any future loss.[192] The donee's basis will be increased by a portion of any gift taxes paid on the gift transfer.[193]

3. Income Tax Basis Provisions—Property Transfers at Death

a. Stepped-Up Tax Basis at Death

In the hands of the recipient, the cost or tax basis of property acquired from or passing from a decedent[194] is its fair market value at the date of death (or at the alternate valuation date, if that date is elected by the decedent's estate for estate tax valuation purposes).[195] Consequently, where the fair market value of the property has increased since the decedent acquired it, the gain that accrued prior to death will disappear from the income tax base at the time of the owner's death and, therefore, never be subject to federal income tax.[196]

Example: Decedent purchased 100 shares of Y Corp. stock on January 1, 2014, for $100x. Decedent died on January 1, 2015, when the fair market value of the stock had increased to $300x. Decedent's estate includes the $300x stock value for federal estate tax purposes. Upon a sale of this stock for more than $300x after decedent's death, whether made by the executor or a beneficiary, the $200x of gain accrued before death will not be recognized for federal income tax purposes because the tax basis will have been stepped up to $300x.

Alternatively, if the property held at death has depreciated in value after the decedent acquired it, when the property is subsequently sold the accrued loss will not be deductible for income tax purposes because (for loss recognition purposes) the income tax basis will have been stepped down to its fair market value at the time of death.[197] The income tax basis of property acquired from or passing from the decedent is often referred to as the "stepped-up basis" (although, if the property is depreciated, the basis will be "stepped down"). For purposes of determining that property which is given a stepped-up basis, the test is generally whether the property is included in the gross estate of the decedent for federal estate tax purposes.[198]

In addition, for income tax basis purposes, the surviving spouse's share of community property also owned by a decedent is treated as if it were acquired from or passed from the decedent and, therefore, that share also acquires a stepped-up (or stepped-down) basis.[199] This occurs even though the surviving spouse's property is not includible in the gross estate of the decedent. For separate property, this same result might be accomplished through the use of a "tax basis revocable trust." This is a trust that is structured to include the separate property of the surviving spouse in the gross estate of the first spouse to die, but without incurring any additional federal estate tax.[200]

During 2015 an important restriction was enacted to require consistent tax basis reporting between an estate and a person acquiring property from a decedent.[201] Section 1014(f) provides rules that require that the tax basis of certain property acquired from a decedent, as determined under §1014, may not exceed that value of that property as finally determined for federal estate tax purposes, or, if not finally determined, the value of that property as reported on a statement made under §6035. This provision provides new reporting requirements with regard to the value of property included in a decedent's gross estate for federal estate tax purposes.

b. Carryover Tax Basis at Death Rules Applicable after 2009

As originally enacted, EGTRRA[202] provided for a new carryover basis regime for the income tax, scheduled to take effect for decedents dying and generation-skipping transfers made after December 31, 2009.[203] EGTRRA further provided that §1014, which provided for tax basis step-up (or step-down) at death, would not have applied to decedents dying after December 31, 2009.[204] Instead, for decedents dying after December 31, 2009, EGTRRA enacted new §1022, which provided that property acquired from a decedent would be treated as if acquired by gift, and recipients of such property would receive a basis equal to the lesser of the decedent's adjusted basis in the property or the fair market value of the property on the date of the decedent's death. As explained in Chapter 4, A.1., the 2010 TRA[205] reinstated the estate tax and the §1014 fair-market-value basis at death provision and repealed the §1022 modified carryover basis regime for decedents dying after 2009. However, a non-Code provision contained within the 2010 TRA allowed the executor of an estate of a decedent dying in 2010 to elect to apply the §1022 modified carryover basis regime; that is, the executor can elect to have the estate tax regime not apply.[206] In May 2015, the IRS released proposed regulations to address the treatment of property with basis determined under §1022 in relation to some three dozen regulatory sections.[207]

For decedents dying in 2010 whose executor elected to have the estate tax not apply, §1022 permitted the decedent's estate to increase the tax basis of assets transferred, as determined on an asset-by-asset basis, by (1) up to a total of $1.3 million and (2) the amount of the decedent's unused capital losses, net operating losses, and certain built-in losses.[208] Section 1022 also allowed an additional $3 million increase to the basis of "outright transfer" property and "qualified terminable interest property" transferred to a surviving spouse.[209] Further, pursuant to this §1022 modified basis regime, nonresidents who are not U.S. citizens may increase the basis of property by up to only $60,000.[210] In no case, however, may the tax basis of an asset be adjusted above its fair market value in the hands of the decedent as of the time of the decedent's death.[211]

As part of EGTRRA, Congress did provide a benefit to those beneficiaries who received the principal residence of someone who died in 2010.[212] Pursuant to §121(d)(11)[213] a beneficiary who received the principal residence of a person dying in 2010 has been allowed to "tack on" the ownership and use of the principal residence by the decedent for purposes of claiming the §121 exclusion.[214] As originally enacted, this provision was meant to apply only to decedents dying in 2010, as EGTRRA §542(f) provided that this provision was applicable only to estates of decedents dying after December 31, 2009, and EGTRRA §901 provided that this provision was not applicable to estates of decedents dying after December 31, 2010.

Although §121(d)(11) was essentially repealed by the 2010 TRA,[215] it remains applicable to decedents dying in 2010 to the extent those decedents' executors elect to have the estate tax regime not apply.[216] Pursuant to §301(c) of the 2010 TRA (i.e., the non-Code provision that allows the executor to elect to have the estate tax not apply), when an executor elects the §1022 modified basis regime, the party who acquires the decedent's principal residence is allowed to use §121(d)(11) to "tack on" the decedent's use and ownership for purposes of the §121 principal residence exclusion.

Neither EGTRRA nor the 2010 TRA provided a date by which the principal residence must be sold. Therefore, the general rules of §121(a) apply.[217] For an estate or trust, presumably, the decedent must have owned and used the property for at least two years out of the five years prior to death, and the trust or estate would be required to sell the property no more than three years after the decedent's death. For individuals who acquire the property from the decedent, that individual can "tack on" any ownership and use by the decedent to satisfy the two-out-of-five-year rule.

Example 1: Dad bought his principal residence on December 31, 2008. Dad died on December 31, 2010, and the principal residence was inherited by Son. The executor of Dad's estate made the election to not have the estate tax apply. Son never lived in the residence and simply maintained it. Since Dad has already met the two-year requirement, Son could sell the house and take advantage of the §121(d)(11) exclusion. However, because there is a five-year look-back, the last date that Son could sell the house was December 31, 2013, as any time past that date would mean that the two-year requirement is no longer met.

Example 2: Dad bought his principal residence on December 30, 2010, and moved in. Dad died suddenly on December 31, 2010, and the principal residence was inherited by Son. Son moved in on Dec. 31, 2010. The executor of Dad's estate made the election to not have the estate tax apply. Son moved out of the property on December 29, 2012. Therefore, in order to meet the two-year requirement under §121(a), Son needs to "tack on" Dad's ownership and use, as he doesn't meet the two-out-of-five-year requirement on his own. Son would, therefore, need to sell the house no later than December 30, 2015 (i.e., this would allow him to meet the two-out-of-five-year requirement of §121(a)), in order to take advantage of §121(d)(11).

c. Gifts to a Decedent Within One Year of Death

The §1014 stepped-up-basis-at-death rules apply regardless of the date at which the decedent acquired the property or the manner of acquisition (unless the estate of a decedent dying in 2010 elects to apply the §1022 modified carryover basis regime in lieu of the estate tax and §1014).[218] Consequently, absent some limiting rule, an heir could transfer appreciated property to a decedent immediately prior to death, anticipating the return of the property at the decedent's death with a higher, stepped-up tax basis resulting at the death of the decedent transferee. The donor-heir might be required to pay gift tax on the fair market value of that gift unless it qualifies for the marital deduction or is within the donor's unified credit or the annual donee exclusion.[219]

Where the donee-decedent bequeaths the property back to the heir, the heir would receive the property with a stepped-up tax basis equal to its fair market value at the decedent's death, absent some limiting rule. The result would be that all of the built-in appreciation in the property will have permanently escaped from the income tax base. The unlimited marital deduction and the unified credit could provide significant incentives for such deathbed transfers because the gift tax can be avoided on the transfers eligible for these benefits.

The stepped-up-basis-at-death rules of §1014 are made inapplicable, however, where (1) appreciated property is acquired by a decedent through a gift transfer within one year of death, and (2) that property passes at death from the decedent to either the original donor or to the donor's spouse.[220]

Example: In 2010, X purchased 1,000 shares of Y Corp. stock for $1,000. X's brother B is terminally ill. X transfers his Y Corp. stock to B on September 1, 2014, when the shares are worth $5,000. B dies on February 1, 2015. B's will leaves the Y Corp. stock to X. On February 1, 2015, the shares had a market value of $7,000. Subsequently X sells the stock for $8,000. X's basis in the stock remains $1,000 and upon the sale he realizes a taxable gain of $7,000.

This denial of a stepped-up tax basis applies where the donor receives the benefit of the appreciated property and regardless of whether the bequest by the decedent to the donor is a specific, general, pecuniary, or residuary bequest.[221] In the situation where appreciated property is sold by the decedent's estate or by a trust to which the decedent was the grantor, and the donor or the donor's spouse is entitled to receive the proceeds of this sale, similar rules apply. The estate does not receive a stepped-up basis in this situation.[222] Consequently, in the above example, if the executor had sold the stock and distributed the proceeds to X, the estate would have realized a taxable gain of $7,000.

The denial of a stepped-up basis applies only to the extent that the donor-heir or his or her spouse is entitled to receive the value of the appreciated property. If the heir or his or her spouse is entitled to only a portion of the property (e.g., because the property must be used to satisfy debts or for administration expenses), this tax basis adjustment limitation rule applies only on a pro-rata basis.

Example: X bought 100 shares of Y Corp. for $1,000. X gives the stock to his terminally ill brother B on September 1, 2014, when the stock is worth $10,000. B dies on February 1, 2015, when the stock is worth $10,000. B leaves the 100 shares to X. B's estate has significant debts, however, and the executor uses 10 shares worth $1,000 to settle debts and administration expenses, as authorized by the will. X is not entitled to the 10 shares and the 10 shares sold receive a stepped-up basis from $100 to $1,000. The remaining 90 shares are distributed to X without receiving a stepped-up basis and retain a basis of $900 in the hands of X (the original tax basis to X as allocated to those shares). X sells the remaining stock for $9,000. The results are: (1) B's estate reports no gain on the sale of the 10 shares for $1,000; and (2) X realizes a taxable gain of $8,100 (90% of $9,000) on the remaining shares.

This basis rule does not apply if the property transfer is made at death by the decedent to someone other than the original donor or the donor's spouse.[223] For example, if (1) the transfer is first from a donor to the donor's parent and (2) the subsequent transfer at the death of the parent is to the original donor's children (the parent/grandparent donee's grandchildren), this basis adjustment limitation rule would not apply.[224] In the planning context, therefore, the objective should be either (1) to make this transfer at a time when the donee is anticipated to live at least one year, thereby avoiding this limitation rule (and arrangements are completed that the property will actually be returned to the donor); or (2) to assure that the property will be transferred to another beneficiary of the first donor's choice.[225]

4. Treatment of "Income in Respect of a Decedent"

a. Purpose of IRD Treatment

As an exception to the §1014 income tax basis adjustment at death rule, §1014(c) specifies inapplicability of §1014 to property that constitutes a right to receive an item of "income in respect of a decedent" under §691.[226] Section 691(a) provides for the treatment of various income items as "income in respect of a decedent" (or IRD).[227] These items are (1) includible in a decedent's estate for federal estate tax purposes[228] and (2) to be treated as generating gross income when subsequently realized. These rules apply, in general, to items of income that have "accrued" (in the economic sense) to a cash basis taxpayer before death, but have not been actually or constructively received by him or her. Accordingly, such items will not have been previously includible in his or her gross income under his or her overall method of accounting for federal income tax purposes. The objective of these IRD rules is to provide equality of income tax treatment between cash basis and accrual basis taxpayers.

The decedent must have been entitled to (or had a right to) a specific item of income for it to be treated as IRD. The recipient of the IRD item is required to include the income in his or her return for that taxable period during which it is received.[229] In addition, the value of this IRD item will be includible in the gross estate of the decedent, causing this item to be subject to both taxes. Because this may produce a high total tax liability, for planning purposes in many circumstances these specific items might be directed (at or after death) to charity (assuming the client desires to make charitable transfers) because both an estate tax deduction will be available and the IRD item will not be included in the gross income of the decedent's estate for federal income tax purposes.[230]

b. Types of Income in Respect of a Decedent

"Income in respect of a decedent" may consist of:

- salary and fringe benefits accrued at death (e.g., salary or wages that a cash basis decedent earned but that were not included in the last payment for compensation received before his or her death)[231];
- fees and commissions based on services performed during life that are indefinite in amount at the time of death or are measured by transactions occurring after death[232];
- an enforceable right to receive amounts under a deferred compensation arrangement[233];
- retirement plan payments[234];
- dividends both declared and payable to a corporate shareholder of record before death, but paid after death;
- interest owed to the decedent at the time of his or her death[235];
- unpaid cash rental payments on an asset owned by a decedent attributable to that portion of the lease term that expired before his or her death;
- the capital gain element of proceeds received after death from a sale essentially completed before death[236];
- certain payments due from business interests (i.e., sole proprietorships and partnerships)[237];
- the income element of installment sales proceeds[238]; and
- alimony.[239]

c. Deductions in Respect of a Decedent

Section 691(b) provides that income tax deductions for business expenses, interest, taxes, and depletion[240] that are not properly allowable on the decedent's last income tax return are allowed, however, on the income tax return of the decedent's estate in the taxable year when paid.[241] This deduction is alternatively allowable to a decedent's successor-in-interest (other than the estate) where the obligation to pay is imposed on that successor-in-interest.[242] This rule affords an opportunity to shift these deductions to that taxpayer where they will produce the greatest income tax benefit.[243]

The general rule that expenses may not be deducted on both the federal estate tax return and the fiduciary income tax return does not apply to deductions in respect of a decedent.[244] If these deductions exceed gross income, payment should be arranged so that they may be taken on the final income tax return of the estate, rather than on an earlier income tax return of the estate. The excess deductions on that final return will then be allocable to the estate beneficiaries on the termination of the estate.[245]

d. Deduction for Estate Tax

Under §691(c), an income tax deduction is available based on the estate tax attributable to the income in respect of a decedent included in the federal estate tax return.[246] This deduction is available to that taxpayer including the IRD item in gross income. The effect of the computation method under §691(c) is to permit a deduction for an amount determined at the highest estate tax rate imposed on the estate.[247] No deduction is available in this context for state estate or inheritance taxes.[248]

5. Gain Recognized on the Satisfaction of Pecuniary Bequests

When an estate or trust distributes property in satisfaction of the right of a beneficiary or a creditor to receive a specified dollar amount, a sale or exchange transaction occurs to the distributing estate or trust. This transaction may result in recognizable gain or loss for federal income tax purposes.[249] This might occur where, under a last will, a child or grandchild is entitled to a cash bequest that, with his or her acquiescence, is actually satisfied with the distribution by the estate of appreciated property. This may also occur when satisfying a marital deduction "pecuniary formula bequest" with property where the surviving spouse (or the qualifying marital trust) is given an "amount" equal to a percentage of the decedent's estate. Thus, in both the estate planning and the estate administration phase, the parties must be aware that gain recognition may be required for federal income tax purposes when the distribution occurs in satisfaction of a pecuniary bequest.[250] This gain recognition will be limited to that gain accrued since the tax basis step-up at death (assuming IRD is not distributed). Further, with the capital gains tax rate being a maximum 20%,[251] this potential income tax cost is limited.

Where property is valued for federal estate tax purposes under the special valuation rules of §2032A for farm and similar property, the income tax basis for that property will be the value as determined under §2032A (and not its fair market value as of the date of death).[252] Where a pecuniary bequest is satisfied with appreciated property eligible for this "special use" estate tax valuation, only the post-death appreciation, as determined without regard to these special use valuation rules, is currently recognized gain.[253] Consequently, if this property, when distributed, has not appreciated from the date of death, no gain recognition will occur on this distribution. A similar gain recognition rule applies to distributions by a trust of property that was specially valued under this provision when that property is distributed from the trust in satisfaction of a right to receive a specific dollar amount.[254] The tax basis of the property in the hands of the distributee is its special use value plus any gain recognized on the distribution.[255]

Notes

1. Information concerning the history of the federal transfer taxes has been summarized in a Congressional Research Service report entitled "A History of Federal Estate, Gift

and Generation-Skipping Taxes," dated January 24, 2011 (Order Code 95-444). *See* www.crs.gov. IRS data available shows that estate tax returns filed with the IRS have declined from about 115,000 in the year 2010 to just over 15,000 in the year 2011. *See* www.irs.gov/pub/irs-soi/10esesttaxsnap.pdf. For the filing year 2010, estates with a gross estate above the tax return filing threshold reported over $130 billion in assets. The combined estate tax obligation was $13 billion. Similarly, see Staff of the J. Comm. on Tax'n, 114th Cong., History, Present Law, and Analysis of the Federal Wealth Transfer Tax System (JCX-52–15) (Mar. 16, 2015), available at www.jct.gov. This report indicates (at Table 2, p. 25) that, for example, for the year 2013 the number of deaths was 2,596,993, but the number of taxable estate tax returns filed was only 4,687 (being 0.18 percent of these deaths). Table 3 (p. 28) in that report specifies that, for the fiscal year 2014, the U.S. government revenue from the estate, gift, and generation-skipping transfer taxes was $19.3 billion, or 0.6 percent of the total federal government receipts.

2. *See* Economic Growth and Tax Relief Reconciliation Act (EGTRRA), Pub. L. No. 107-16.
3. Where a decedent died during the year 2010, the executor of the estate was allowed to elect to apply the Code as if the estate tax and basis step-up rules had not been reinstated. Therefore, the executor could elect to have the EGTRRA law apply, meaning that the estate would not be subject to estate tax and the basis of the assets acquired from the decedent would be determined under the modified carryover basis rules of former §1022. *See* Tax Relief, Unemployment Insurance Reauthorization, and Job Creation Act of 2010 (2010 TRA), Pub. L. No. 111-312, §101(c).
4. Pub. L. No. 112-240.
5. *See* American Taxpayer Relief Act of 2012 (ATRA), Pub. L. No. 112-240, §101.
6. *See, e.g.*, Diane Freida, *Return to 2009 Estate Tax Rates Proposed in President's FY 2014 Budget*, 70 Bloomberg BNA Daily Tax Rep. GG-11 (Apr. 11, 2013).
7. For example, formula clauses based on exemption amounts should be carefully considered. As described below, an important approach (sometimes rejected by the client) may include the use of a disclaimer, for example, leaving the entire estate to the surviving spouse, but providing that any disclaimed assets would be transferred into a nonmarital deduction trust for the spouse and other family members as the trust beneficiaries.
8. The estate planning client may desire a private letter ruling from the IRS concerning the effect of these taxes on a proposed transaction. Rev. Proc. 2015-1, 2015-1 I.R.B. 1, §5.01, specifies that in gift tax matters the IRS generally issues a letter ruling on a proposed transaction and on a completed transaction if the letter ruling request is submitted before the return is filed for the year in which the transaction that is the subject of the request was completed. Rev. Proc. 2015-1, §5.06 specifies that the IRS issues letter rulings on transactions affecting the estate tax on the prospective estate of a living person and affecting the estate tax on the estate of a decedent before the decedent's estate tax return is filed. The IRS will not issue letter rulings for prospective estates on computations of tax, actuarial factors, and factual matters. If the taxpayer is requesting a letter ruling regarding a decedent's estate tax and the estate tax return must be filed before the letter ruling is expected to be issued, the taxpayer should obtain an extension of time for filing the return and should notify the IRS branch considering the letter ruling request that an extension was obtained. In limited circumstances, the IRS will consider a request for an estate tax letter ruling after the estate tax return has been filed but before it has been examined. Rev. Proc. 2015-3, 2015-1 I.R.B. 129, specifies certain areas where private letter ruling letters will not be issued, including in the estate tax, gift tax, and generation-skipping

transfer tax contexts. Rev. Proc. 91-14, 1991-1 C.B. 482, provides a checklist questionnaire containing the information to be included in a request for a ruling relating to estate, gift, and generation-skipping transfer tax issues. This checklist must accompany all such private letter ruling requests.

9. Pub. L. No. 107-16.
10. This discussion deals with federal death transfer taxes. The estate planner should be aware that many states in the United States also have some type of death transfer tax mechanism, whether estate or inheritance taxes. The several state death transfer tax systems are not summarized here because they vary quite substantially and are of significantly less financial importance than the federal transfer tax system. In many instances a state death tax credit (former §2011) was available for federal estate tax purposes but this credit was eliminated for the estates of decedents dying after December 31, 2004. *See* former §2011(f) (struck from the Code by the Tax Increase Prevention Act of 2014 [2014 TIPA]), Pub. L. No. 113-295, Div. A, §221(a)(95)(A). Beginning in 2005, after the elimination of the state death tax credit, a federal estate tax deduction is available for state death taxes paid (§2058). Some state death taxes were effectively made inapplicable by the repeal of the state death tax credit because they were dependent upon the amount of that credit. Some of these states enacted new tax regimes to deal with this automatic repeal. Section 2058 and the repeal of former §2011 were made permanent by ATRA. *See* ATRA, Pub. L. No. 112-240, §101(a) (making permanent the provisions in EGTRRA, Pub. L. No. 107-16).
11. *See* Pub. L. No. 112-240, §101(a) (making permanent the provision in EGTRRA, Pub. L. No. 107-16), §301–§304.
12. §2001(c). See Chapter 4, A.4.c.(1) for further discussion. Because EGTRRA did not change the provision in §2641(a)(1) specifying that the applicable tax rate for generation-skipping transfers is the maximum estate tax rate, the tax rate used for generation-skipping transfers (prior to its termination during 2010) was reduced as the highest estate tax rate declined. After December 31, 2009, §2502, as amended, establishes the highest gift tax rate at 35%. As applicable to gifts made after this date, §2511(c) provides that a transfer in trust is a transfer of property by gift unless the entire trust is treated as a grantor trust for income tax purposes, as to the donor or the donor's spouse and except as provided by regulations. *See* EGTRRA, Pub. L. No. 107-16, §511(e), as amended by the Job Creation and Worker Assistance Act of 2002, Pub. L. No. 107-147, §411(g)(1); Notice 2010-19, 2010-1 C.B. 404 (interim guidance on §2511(c) pending regulations). The 2010 TRA, Pub. L. No. 111-312, §302(e), §302(f), repealed §2511(c), effective for gifts made after 2009 (so that the provision never applied).
13. §2010(c). See Chapter 4, A.4.d., and the Worksheets.
14. *See* §2631(c).
15. *See* EGTRRA, Pub. L. No. 107-16, §521(d), enacting former §2057(j), which provides that former §2057 shall not apply to the estates of decedents dying after December 31, 2003. Former §2057 was struck from the Code as deadwood by the 2014 TIPA, Pub. L. No. 113-295, Div. A, §221(a)(97)(A).
16. *See* EGTRRA, Pub. L. No. 107-16, §531, §532. See Chapter 4, A.4.a.
17. EGTRRA, Pub. L. No. 107-16, §532. *See* former §2604(c) (struck as deadwood by the 2014 TIPA, Pub. L. No. 113-295, Div. A, §221(a)(95)(B)).
18. *See* §2210. *But see* the "sunset" provision of EGTRRA, Pub. L. No. 107-16, §901(a)(2), which provides that the estate, gift, and generation-skipping transfer tax provisions of

the EGTRRA will sunset after December 31, 2010, resulting in reinstatement of the pre-Act federal transfer taxes.

19. *See* §2664. *But see* the "sunset" provision of EGTRRA, Pub. L. No. 107-16, §901(a)(2), which provides that the generation-skipping transfer tax provisions of EGTRRA will sunset after December 31, 2010, resulting in reinstatement of the pre-Act transfer taxes.
20. *See* §2210.
21. *See* EGTRRA, Pub. L. No. 107-16, §501; *see also* §2210(b)(1).
22. *See* EGTRRA, Pub. L. No. 107-16, §541. See the discussion at Chapter 4, B., for further discussion of the revised carryover basis regime.
23. Note also that the Conference Agreement accompanying the Act contains a sunset provision designed to comply with Congressional budget act requirements. The sunset provision specifies that all provisions of and amendments made by the Act, including those applicable to the estate, gift, and generation-skipping transfer taxes, do not apply after December 31, 2010.
24. The 2010 TRA, Pub. L. No. 111-312, §301(a), §301(e), amended each Code provision (§121, §170, §684, §1014, §1022, §1040, §1221, §1246, §1291, §1296, §2210, §2664, §4947, §6018, §6019, §6075, §6716, and §7701) that was amended by Subtitle A or E of Title V of EGTRRA to read as if the EGTRRA amendments had never been enacted. In other words, the EGTRRA amendments to these Code sections are eliminated after 2009 (rather than after 2010 under the sunset provision in EGTRRA, Pub. L. No. 107-16, §901).
25. 2010 TRA, Pub. L. No. 111-312, §301(c). This provision directed the IRS to prescribe the time and manner for making the election, allowed executors to revoke such elections only with IRS consent, and provided that the election did not affect whether any property is considered subject to the estate tax under §2652(a)(1) in determining the transferor for GST tax purposes. *See* Notice 2011-66, 2011-35 I.R.B. 184, specifying that the executor of the estate of a decedent who died in 2010 may make the former §1022 election by filing an IRS Form 8939, *Allocation of Increase in Basis for Property Acquired from a Decedent.* The method for allocating this basis is prescribed in the Notice.
26. 2010 TRA, Pub. L. No. 111-312, §301(b), §301(e), §302(a), §302(b), §302(f).
27. 2010 TRA, Pub. L. No. 111-312, §303. In 2015, the IRS issued final regulations (replacing temporary regulations issued in 2012) providing guidance on the estate and gift tax applicable exclusion amount in general and on portability in particular, including: (1) definitions of certain terms related to portability; (2) an explanation of how to make (or not make) the portability election; (3) details on the portability computation; (4) rules governing the surviving spouse's use of portability; (5) the IRS's authority to examine returns of the deceased spouse; and (6) a description of how portability applies when a qualified domestic trust is involved. *See* §2010(c)(6); Reg. §20.2001-2, §20.2010-0, §20.2010-1, §20.2010-2, §20.2010-3, §25.2505-0, §25.2505-1, §25.2505-2; T.D. 9725, 80 Fed. Reg. 34,279 (June 16, 2015). *See also* T.D. 9593, 77 Fed. Reg. 36,150 (June 18, 2012) (former temporary regulations). The provisions of the final regulations apply generally to estates of decedents dying and gifts made on or after June 12, 2015. Reg. §20.2001-2(b), §20.2010-1(e), §20.2010-2(e), §20.2010-3(f), §25.2505-1(e), §25.2505-2(g). The former temporary regulations apply generally to estates of decedents dying and gifts made on or after January 1, 2011, and before June 12, 2015, however the portions of the former temporary regulations not directly related to portability (former Reg. §20.2010-1T(a), §20.2010-1T(b), §20.2010-1T(c),

§20.2010-1T(d)(1), §25.2505-1T(b), §25.2505-1T(c), §25.2505-1T(d)) apply only to estates of decedents dying and gifts made after June 14, 2012. *See* T.D. 9593. Before issuing the former temporary regulations, the IRS issued two Notices regarding portability - Notice 2012-21, 2012-10 I.R.B. 450 (allowing estates of certain decedents dying between January 1 and June 30, 2011, to obtain six-month extension to file Form 706 for purposes of making portability election) and Notice 2011-82, 2011-42 I.R.B. 516 (guidance on making, or opting out of making, portability election). For a full discussion of the regulations and other guidance, see 844 T.M., *Estate Tax Credits and Computations.*

28. *See also* Reg. §25.2505-1(a), §20.2010-1(d)(2). Section 2505(a)(1) provides that, in determining the amount exempted by the gift tax unified credit, the §2010(c) applicable credit amount is that which would apply if the donor died at the end of the calendar year. *See also* Reg. §25.2505-1(a).
29. Reg. §20.2010-1(d)(3). For the inflation-adjusted amount, see Worksheet 1.
30. *But see* the 2012 temporary regulations, which indicate that the reference here to "basic exclusion amount" is properly interpreted to mean "applicable exclusion amount." Former Reg. §20.2010-2T(c)(1). *See also* ATRA, Pub. L. No. 112-240, §101(c)(2), which made a technical correction replacing "basic exclusion amount" with "applicable exclusion amount."
31. Reg. §20.2010-2(c)(2). *See also* former Reg. §20.2010-2T(c)(2).
32. *See also* Reg. §20.2010-2(a), §20.2010-2(b), §25.2505-1(a). Thus, despite the general rule requiring an estate of a U.S. citizen or resident decedent to file an estate tax return only if the gross estate exceeds the basic exclusion amount (*see* §6018(a)(1)), an estate below the threshold must file to make a portability election. *See* Reg. §20.2010-2(a)(1). In addition, §2010(c)(5)(A) and Reg. §20.2010-2(b) require an estate to include a computation of the DSUE amount to make a portability election.
33. *See* Reg. §20.2010-2(a)(2), §20.2010-2(a)(3), §20.2010-2(a)(7). If the estate of a post-2010 decedent with a surviving spouse does not wish to elect portability, it must make an affirmative statement to that effect on the estate tax return (or an attachment to the return). Reg. §20.2010-2(a)(3)(i). The estate will also be considered to have not made a portability election if the estate fails to file a timely estate tax return. Reg. §20.2010-2(a)(3)(ii). *See also* T.D. 9593 (temporary regulations preamble, §3(d)).
34. §2010(c)(5)(A). *See also* Reg. §20.2010-2(a)(3).
35. *See also* Reg. §20.2001-2(a), §20.2010-2(d), §20.2010-3(d), §25.2505-2(e).
36. The 2010 TRA, Pub. L. No. 111-312, §303(b)(2), §303(c)(2), §304, replaced the §2631(c) reference to the §2010(c) applicable exclusion amount with a reference to the §2010(c) basic exclusion amount.
37. §2001(c), §2502(a), amended by 2010 TRA, Pub. L. No. 111-312 §302(a)(2), §302(b)(2), §302(f), §304.
38. *See* EGTRRA, Pub. L. No. 107-16, §511(b), §901; 2010 TRA, Pub. L. No. 111-312, §101(a), §304.
39. 2010 TRA, Pub. L. No. 111-312, §302(c). In 2011, as referenced in Chapter 8, A., the IRS issued guidance on the GST tax for decedents dying and generation-skipping transfers made in 2010. *See* Notice 2011-76, 2011-40 I.R.B. 479; Notice 2011-66, 2011-35 I.R.B. 184.
40. §2641(a)(1) (referring to maximum federal estate tax rate); 2010 TRA, Pub. L. No. 111-312, §304.

41. §2001(b)(2), §2001(g), §2505(a), amended/added by 2010 TRA, Pub. L. No. 111-312, §302(d), §302(f), §304.
42. *See also* Reg. §25.2505-1(b); former Reg. §25.2505-1T(b).
43. *See* EGTRRA, Pub. L. No. 107-16, §511(e), §901; 2010 TRA, Pub. L. No. 111-312, §302(e), §302(f).
44. 2010 TRA, Pub. L. No. 111-312, §301(d)(1). *See* Notice 2011-66, providing guidance with regard to the time and manner in which the executor of the estate of a decedent that died in 2010 elects (pursuant to 2010 TRA, §301(c)), to have the estate tax not apply and to have the carryover basis rules in former §1022 apply to property transferred as a result of the decedent's death.
45. 2010 TRA, Pub. L. No. 111-312, §301(d)(2). *See* Notice 2011-66, concerning the application of the GST tax to testamentary transfers during 2010.
46. *See* former §2011(f) (struck as deadwood by 2014 TIPA, Pub. L. No. 113-295, Div. A, §221(a)(95)(A)); EGTRRA, Pub. L. No. 107-16, §531, §532, §901; 2010 TRA, Pub. L. No. 111-312, §101(a), §304.
47. *See* former §2057(j) (struck as deadwood by 2014 TIPA, Pub. L. No. 113-295, Div. A, §221(a)(97)(A)); EGTRRA, Pub. L. No. 107-16, §521(d), §901; 2010 TRA, Pub. L. No. 111-312, §101(a).
48. *See* EGTRRA, Pub. L. No. 107-16, §551, §901; 2010 TRA, Pub. L. No. 111-312, §101(a), §304.
49. *See* EGTRRA, Pub. L. No. 107-16, §571-§573, §901; 2010 TRA, Pub. L. No. 111-312, §101(a), §304.
50. *See* EGTRRA, Pub. L. No. 107-16, §561-§564, §901; 2010 TRA, Pub. L. No. 111-312, §101(a), §304.
51. ATRA, Pub. L. No. 112-240, §101(a).
52. ATRA, Pub. L. No. 112-240, §101(a). As noted above, the IRS issued a revised Form 706 in Aug. 2012, which contained a new "Part 6" dealing with the portability election and computation.
53. §2001(c), §2502(a), amended by ATRA, Pub. L. No. 112-240, §101(c).
54. ATRA, Pub. L. No. 112-240, §101(a), removing the sunset provisions found in EGTRRA, Pub. L. No. 107-16, §901, and 2010 TRA, Pub. L . No. 111-312, §304.
55. *See* former §2057(j) (struck as deadwood by 2014 TIPA, Pub. L. No. 113-295, Div. A, §221(a)(97)(A); ATRA, Pub. L. No. 112-240, §101(a), removing the sunset provisions found in EGTRRA, Pub. L. No. 107-16, §901 and 2010 TRA, Pub. L. No. 111-312, §304.
56. ATRA, Pub. L. No. 112-240, §101(a).
57. ATRA, Pub. L. No. 112-240, §101(a)(1).
58. ATRA, Pub. L. No. 112-240, §101(a).
59. The federal estate tax is imposed on the transfer of the taxable estate of every decedent who is a citizen or resident of the United States (and is applied on a worldwide basis). §2001(a). The estate tax will only apply to a nonresident alien on an asset situs basis to those assets treated as U.S. situated. Special rules apply to individuals who are classified as "expatriates" for tax purposes. Effective for an individual whose expatriation date is after June 16, 2008, the Heroes Earnings Assistance and Relief Tax Act of 2008 (HEART Act), Pub. L. No. 110-245, §301(b), §301(g), enacted §2801, which generally taxes certain gifts and bequests a U.S. citizen or resident receives from a "covered expatriate."

See also Prop. Reg. §28.2801-0 through §28.2801-7, REG-112997-10, 80 Fed. Reg. 54,447 (Sept. 10, 2015). An individual whose expatriation date was before June 17, 2008 is subject to special estate tax rules under §2107. The 2004 American Jobs Creation Act, Pub. L. No. 108-357, §804(a), removed the subjective requirement of a "tax avoidance" motive from this provision, effective for an individual who expatriated after June 3, 2004. Section 877 and, consequently, §2107 does not apply to an individual whose expatriation date is after June 16, 2008. *See* §877(h), added by HEART Act, Pub. L. No. 110-245, §301(d). For further discussion of the expatriation provisions, see 837 T.M., *Non-Citizens—Estate, Gift and Generation-Skipping Taxation* (Bloomberg BNA).

60. *Commissioner v. Estate of Bosch*, 387 U.S. 456 (1967). Similarly, *see Scott v. Commissioner*, 226 F.3d 871 (7th Cir. 2000). Note the position of the IRS that it does not acquiesce in the Tax Court's decision in *Estate of Goree v. Commissioner*, T.C. Memo 1994-331, *nonacq.*, AOD 1996-001. In this situation the IRS asserted that the Tax Court should have reviewed the probate court's factual determination de novo in determining whether certain disclaimers were valid for local law purposes.
61. *See* Caron, *Tax Court and Service Stake Out Positions in State Law Debate*, 71 Tax Notes 229 (1996) (and various articles cited in this discussion); Verbit, *State Court Decisions in Federal Transfer Tax Litigation: Bosch Revisited*, 23 Real Prop., Prob. & Tr. J. 407 (1988).
62. See Chapter 5, D. The term "qualified domestic trust" (enabling a marital deduction for a transfer to an alien spouse) is defined in §2056A.
63. See Chapter 9, E.
64. See Chapter 4, A.4., for discussion of the computation of the net estate tax liability (i.e., after the application of available credits).
65. Before October 16, 1962, real property situated outside the United States was excluded from the gross estate (as defined under §2033). This gross estate exclusion was eliminated in the Revenue Act of 1962, Pub. L. No. 87-834, §18, making the U.S. estate tax applicable to a U.S. decedent on a global basis and as to all assets.
66. §2036-§2038. See the discussion at Chapter 6, D.3.e., concerning the application of §2036 (transfers with a retained life estate), §2037 (transfers taking effect at death), and §2038 (transfers with a retained power to alter, amend, revoke or terminate). These tax provisions apply primarily, but not exclusively, in the trust context. *See also* 50 T.M., *Incomplete Lifetime Transfers: Retained Powers Under Sections 2036(a)(2) and 2038* (Bloomberg BNA), and 52 T.M., *Incomplete Lifetime Transfers: Retained Beneficial Interests Under Sections 2036(a)(1) and 2037* (Bloomberg BNA).
67. §2039. See further discussion concerning annuities at Chapter 9, D. *See also* 821 T.M., *Tax Issues of Employee Plan and Commercial Annuities* (Bloomberg BNA).
68. *See* §2040 and the discussion at Chapter 9, A.3.a., concerning the rules regarding "qualified joint interests." *See also* 823 T.M., *Taxation of Jointly Owned Property* (Bloomberg BNA).
69. §2041. A general power of appointment is defined for federal estate tax purposes in §2041(b)(1). The use of general and special powers of appointment in estate planning is discussed at Chapter 5, E. For further discussion, *see* 825 T.M., *Powers of Appointment—Estate, Gift, and Income Tax Considerations* (Bloomberg BNA).
70. §2042. The use of life insurance in estate planning is specifically discussed at Chapter 9, C. For further discussion, *see* 826 T.M., *Life Insurance* (Bloomberg BNA).
71. The value of gifts (other than gifts of life insurance) made by the decedent within three years of death is not includible in the gross estate. Section 2035(a) provides, however,

that interests in property otherwise includible in the gross estate under §2036, §2037, §2038, or §2042, or which would have been included under any of these sections if such interest had been retained by the decedent, are included in the gross estate if transferred within three years of the decedent's death. In addition, the three-year inclusion was retained for the purposes of determining the estate's qualification for special use valuation, deferral of estate taxes, stock redemptions under §303, and for identifying property that is subject to estate tax liens. *See* §2035(c)(1). Under §2035(b) the amount of any federal gift tax paid on gifts made during the three-year period before the decedent's death is also included in the decedent's gross estate. Section 2035(e) permits, however, a gift transfer from a revocable trust without these inclusion rules applying.

72. §529(c)(4), added by the Small Business Job Protection Act of 1996, Pub. L. No. 104-188, §1806, and amended by the Taxpayer Relief Act of 1997, Pub. L. No. 105-34, §211, generally effective on January 1, 1998.
73. §530(d)(3), added by the Taxpayer Relief Act of 1997, Pub. L. No. 105-34, §213, and available beginning in 1998.
74. For further discussion of the estate tax deductions an estate can claim, *see* 840 T.M., *Estate Tax Deductions—Sections 2053, 2054 and 2058* (Bloomberg BNA); 843 T.M., *Estate Tax Marital Deduction* (Bloomberg BNA); 829 T.M., *The Family-Owned Business Deduction—Section 2057* (Bloomberg BNA); and 839 T.M., *Estate and Gift Tax Charitable Deductions* (Bloomberg BNA).
75. Administration expenses may be claimed either as an estate or income tax deduction. *See* §642(g) for the allowance of such expenses as income tax deductions. If no estate tax is payable, §2053 administration expenses should be deducted on the estate's federal income tax return. Otherwise, valuable deductions will be forfeited. Reg. §1.642(g)-1 provides that the waiver of the right to an estate tax deduction cannot be reversed (which would produce detrimental results if, upon estate tax audit, the deduction would be more valuable for estate tax purposes). Note that the IRS may assert that administration expenses, for example, attorney's fees, are not reasonable and that the allowable deduction should be less than the amount actually paid. *See Estate of Calcagno v. Commissioner,* T.C. Memo 1989-677.
76. Section 2053(c)(1)(A) requires that, for a claim against a decedent's estate which is "founded upon a promise or agreement" to be deductible, that claim must be "contracted bona fide and for an adequate consideration in money or money's worth." Intrafamily obligations will be carefully scrutinized under this provision. See *Estate of Shapiro,* 634 F.3d 1055 (9th Cir. 2011), permitting a deduction (under §2053(a)(3)) for a "palimony" claim because it was rooted in a legal obligation. See *Estate of Kosow v. Commissioner,* 45 F.3d 1524 (11th Cir. 1995), where a payment from an estate to children pursuant to a settlement agreement with an ex-wife was deductible as a valid claim against the estate. Similarly, see *Estate of Waters v. Commissioner,* 48 F.3d 838 (4th Cir. 1995), where payments pursuant to a post-divorce settlement were deductible. This "consideration" test applies only to claims against the decedent's probate estate. In *Estate of Harter v. Commissioner,* 3 T.C. 1151 (1944), *acq.*, 1944 C.B. 13, demand notes issued by a trustee to the children of the grantor of a revocable trust were deductible, the Tax Court holding that the "adequate and full consideration" requirement applied only to claims against the estate. *See also Estate of Vose v. Commissioner,* 14 T.C. 113 (1950), *modified,* 20 T.C. 597 (1953), *acq.*, 1953-2 C.B. 6. Considerable controversy exists concerning how to evaluate claims outstanding at the time of death, that is, whether to consider post-death events, such as the

settlement of litigation. In *Estate of Smith v. Commissioner,* 198 F.3d 515 (5th Cir. 1999), *rev'g* 108 T.C. 412 (1997), the U.S. Fifth Circuit Court of Appeals (reversing the Tax Court) held that the amount deductible was the fair market value of the claim on the date of death, rather than the amount paid to settle the claim as argued by the IRS, or the full amount of the claim as argued by the estate. The IRS does not agree with this decision. *See* AOD 2000-04. Similar issues were involved in *Estate of McMorris v. Commissioner,* 243 F.3d 1254 (10th Cir. 2001), and *Estate of O'Neal v. United States,* 258 F.3d 1265 (11th Cir. 2001). See, further, *Estate of Saunders v. Commissioner,* 136 T.C. 406 (2011), *aff'd,* 745 F.3d 953 (9th Cir. 2014), where a deduction was allowed only for the amount paid to settle a legal malpractice lawsuit against the estate of the decedent, and the amount for the original claim for damages was not allowed as a deduction.

77. Section 2053(a)(4) permits a deduction for unpaid mortgages on, or any indebtedness against, property where the value of the decedent's interest therein, undiminished by such mortgage or indebtedness, is included in the gross estate. Note, however, that nonrecourse debt, since not collectible from the estate assets, will reduce the fair market value of property to be included in the gross estate. Reg. §20.2053-7 specifies that, if the decedent's estate is not liable for a mortgage, only the value of the equity of redemption (or the value of the property, less the mortgage or indebtedness) need be returned as part of the gross estate. State law will control whether the debt is recourse or nonrecourse.
78. Under §2043(b)(2), a §2053 estate tax deduction is allowed for transfers pursuant to claims arising under a written agreement in settlement of marital or property rights where the agreement would have qualified those transfers as nontaxable for gift tax purposes under §2516. Under that provision, a transfer of property within a specified three-year period in settlement of marital or property rights or to provide a reasonable allowance for the support of minor children is not treated as a gift.
79. §2054; Reg. §20.2054-1.
80. §2055. See further discussion at Chapter 9, E.
81. §2056. See further discussion at Chapter 5, D., of estate planning techniques with respect to transfers to a surviving spouse.
82. §2058. For a detailed discussion, *see* 840 T.M., *Estate Tax Deductions—Sections 2053, 2054 and 2058* (Bloomberg BNA).
83. Former §2057.
84. EGTRRA, Pub. L. No. 107-16, §521.
85. Former §2057(j).
86. §2031. For further discussion, *see* 830 T.M., *Valuation: General and Real Estate* (Bloomberg BNA).
87. §2032. If the included property is earlier sold or distributed, the date of that sale or distribution constitutes the alternate valuation date for that property. *See* Reg. §20.2032-1(a).
88. Reg. §20.2032-1(a) refers to the valuation of a decedent's gross estate (not portions thereof) at a date other than as of the date of the decedent's death. Similarly, Reg. §20.2032-1(b)(2) indicates that if the election is made, it applies to all the property included in the gross estate, and cannot be applied to only a portion of the property.
89. §2032A. See the discussion at Chapter 10, D., and *see* 833 T.M., *Section 2032A—Special Use Valuation* (Bloomberg BNA).
90. Reg. §20.2031-1(b).

91. *Id.* For an example of the difficulties in applying the willing buyer-willing seller valuation test in the context of mutual fund shares, *see United States v. Cartwright,* 411 U.S. 546 (1973). *See also* Rev. Proc. 84-17, 1984-1 C.B. 432, where the IRS provided guidelines for determining the fair market values of participating interests in bank common trust funds for estate and gift tax purposes if the estate or gift tax valuation date falls between quarterly bank valuation dates. Under these guidelines a weighted average technique is utilized, similar to the method used for valuing stocks and bonds under Reg. §20.2031-2. Often, however, similar to mutual funds, many banks will value their common trust funds on a daily basis. Similarly, see Rev. Proc. 98-34, 1998-1 C.B. 983, setting forth a methodology to value certain compensatory stock options for gift, estate, and generation-skipping transfer tax purposes.
92. Planning for such valuation problems is discussed in greater detail at Chapter 10, B.4. For in-depth analyses of valuation problems, *see* 830 T.M., *Valuation: General and Real Estate* (Bloomberg BNA), and 831 T.M., *Valuation of Corporate Stock* (Bloomberg BNA).
93. See Rev. Proc. 66-49, 1966-2 C.B. 1257, *modified by* Rev. Proc. 96-15, 1996-1 C.B. 627, where the IRS outlined the information to be contained in a competent appraisal report. Rev. Proc. 96-15 informs taxpayers how to request from the IRS a "Statement of Value" that may be used to substantiate the value of art for income, estate, or gift tax purposes. A taxpayer who complies with the provisions of this revenue procedure may rely on the Statement of Value in completing the taxpayer's federal income tax, estate tax, or gift tax return that reports the transfer of art. See also *Estate of Smith v. Commissioner,* 57 T.C. 650 (1972), *acq.,* 1974-2 C.B. 4, where the Tax Court listed various criteria that it applied in valuing for estate tax purposes a large amount of sculpture retained by an artist at his death. Similarly, see the extensive valuation analysis in *Estate of O'Keeffe v. Commissioner,* T.C. Memo 1992-210 (involving the valuation of a large collection of the decedent's self-created art). See further, *Estate of Elkins v. Commissioner*, 767 F.3d 443 (5th Cir. 2014), where a substantial valuation discount was allowed for a partial interest in artwork, suggesting that creating partial interests in artwork can achieve significant valuation reductions.
94. A continuing controversy concerns whether the value of a particular property should be reduced by the income tax cost to be incurred if the property is sold. *See* TAM 200303010, where the National Office advised that, in determining the fair market value of the bonds for estate tax purposes, the estate should not calculate a discount for the income taxes due on the interest that accrued on the bonds from the date of purchase to the date of maturity.
95. See, for example, TAM 9616004 where the National Office advised that a lottery winner's estate must use the §7520 annuity tables to determine the value of lottery payments payable to the estate or a designated survivor. The National Office concluded that certain restrictions on the ability to assign lottery payments did not constitute a restricted beneficial interest, reducing the value of the property interest. Similarly, in *Negron v. United States,* 553 F.3d 1013 (6th Cir. 2009), the Sixth Circuit reversed the district court's decision and held that the IRS annuity tables under §7520 applied in valuing estates' lottery interests, even though the interests were restricted and the tables produced a value higher than the lump-sum payments that the estates received. See, however, *Shackleford v. United States,* 262 F.3d 1028 (9th Cir. 2001), affirming a district court determination that the discount tables did not reasonably approximate the fair market value of lottery payments because California's statutory anti-assignment restriction reduced the

fair market value. Similarly, see *Estate of Gribauskas v. Commissioner,* 342 F.3d 85 (2d Cir. 2003); and *Estate of Cook v. Commissioner*, 349 F.3d 850 (5th Cir. 2003).

96. These interest rates are determined pursuant to §7520. Applicable interest rates are published monthly by the IRS in the Internal Revenue Bulletin.

97. Section 7520(c)(2) (as redesignated by the Tax Increase Prevention Act of 2014, Pub. L. No. 113-295, Div. A, §221(a)(118)) requires the actuarial tables dependent on life expectancy to be updated for the most recent mortality experience not less frequently than once each 10 years. For valuation dates after April 30, 2009, mortality experience from the 2000 census is used. *See* Reg. §20.2031-7T(d)(7) Table S (single life remainder factors for interest rates between 0.2% and 14%) and Life Table 2000CM. The life interest actuarial factor is derived by subtracting the correlative remainder factor in Table S from 1.000000. Reg. §20.2031-7T(d)(2)(iii). For single life remainder factors for a wider range of interest rates, as well as annuity and two life factors, *see* IRS Pub. 1457, *Actuarial Valuations Version 3A.* The actuarial factors used for valuation dates from May 1, 1999, to April 30, 2009, based on mortality information from the 1990 census, appear in Table S and Table 90CM in Reg. §20.2031-7A(f)(4) and IRS Pub. 1457, *Actuarial Values Book Aleph* (7/99). See also Notice 2009-18, 2009-1 I.R.B. 648 (factors for interest rates below 2.2%), responding to the substantial decline in interest rates in the debt market. The actuarial factors used for valuation dates from May 1, 1989, to April 30, 1999, based on mortality information from the 1980 census, appear in Table S and Table 80CNSMT in Reg. §20.2031-7A(e)(4) and IRS Pub. 1457, *Actuarial Values Alpha Volume* (8/89). A fixed interest rate was used for valuation dates before May 1, 1989; see the tables at Reg. §20.2031-7A(a)–(c) and §25.2512-5A(a)–(c). See Reg. §1.7520-3 for various limitations on the use of the §7520 valuation rules and standard actuarial factors.

98. §2032(c).

99. See §1014(a), which specifies that the income tax basis of property acquired from a decedent is its fair market value at death or, in the case of an alternate valuation election, the value so established. Section 1014(f), added by the 2015 Transportation and Veterans Act, Pub. L. No. 114-41, §2004, requires that the basis of certain property acquired from a decedent, as determined under §1014, may not exceed the value of that property as finally determined for estate tax purposes, or, if not finally determined, as reported on a statement required under §6035. This reporting requirement is discussed in Chapter 4, A.1.c. and A.5.a.

100. §2032A. See the more detailed discussion of this valuation procedure at Chapter 10, D.

101. §2032A(a)(2), §2032A(a)(3), added by §501(b) of the Taxpayer Relief Act of 1997, Pub. L. No. 105-34. Initially, a decedent's gross estate could be reduced by up to $750,000, but that figure was adjusted for inflation beginning with decedents dying after 1998. For the §2032A inflation-adjusted amount for recent years, see Worksheet 1. For a detailed discussion of the special use valuation rules under §2032A, *see* 833 T.M., *Section 2032A—Special Use Valuation* (Bloomberg BNA).

102. See Rev. Rul. 93-12, 1993-1 C.B. 202, which specifies that in determining the value of a gift of a minority block of stock in a closely held corporation the block should be valued for gift tax purposes without regard to the family relationship of the donee to other shareholders. Reg. §20.2031-2(f) specifies that a relevant factor in determining the value of shares of unlisted stock is "the degree of control of the business represented by the block of stock to be valued." Note, however, that in *Estate of Adler v. Commissioner,* T.C. Memo 2011-28, the taxpayer transferred realty to five children, each as an undivided

tenant in common, each gift qualifying under Rev. Rul. 93-12 for a fractional interest discount for gift tax valuation purposes. However, the donor retained the exclusive use of the transferred property and this subsequently resulted in §2036(a)(1) inclusion in the gross estate. The Tax Court rejected fractional interest discounts for estate tax valuation purposes because the premise of §2036(a)(1) is that the gifts were never made.

103. See TAM 9432001, where decedent's will provided a bequest of 48.6% of the stock of a closely held corporation to his son who already owned the remaining 51.4% of the shares and the National Office advised that the existing ownership of the son did not impact on the estate tax valuation/minority discount eligibility.

104. See *Estate of Frank v. Commissioner,* T.C. Memo 1995-132, where the court authorized a 20% minority interest discount and a 30% discount for lack of marketability; *Estate of Ford v. Commissioner*, 53 F.3d 924 (8th Cir. 1995), where the court affirmed a 20% minority discount and a 10% lack of marketability discount, the court noting that the "issues of valuation and applicability of marketability and minority interest discounts are factual questions which we review under the clearly erroneous standard." *See also Estate of Hoover v. Commissioner,* 69 F.3d 1044 (10th Cir. 1995), *acq.*, 1998-2 C.B. 1, rejecting the IRS's position that an election to use the special §2032A valuation approach precludes the use of a minority discount factor; *Estate of Bonner v. United States,* 84 F.3d 196 (5th Cir. 1996), rejecting the IRS position that property held in a QTIP trust that is includible in the surviving spouse's gross estate must be aggregated with property otherwise included in the surviving spouse's estate, and allowing a fractional interest discount.

105. See *Estate of Dunn v. Commissioner,* 301 F.3d 339 (5th Cir. 2002), noting that a willing buyer of stock would demand a reduction in price for the built-in gains tax liability. *See also Estate of Jelke,* 507 F.3d 1317 (11th Cir. 2007); *Eisenberg v. Commissioner,* 155 F.3d 50 (2d Cir. 1998); *Estate of Davis,* 110 T.C. 530 (1998). However, in *Estate of Richmond v. Commissioner*, T.C. Memo 2014-26, involving the valuation of a personal holding company whose assets consisted primarily of publicly-traded stock, the Tax Court rejected this dollar-for-dollar discount for unrealized capital gains. The Tax Court, in *Steinberg v. Commissioner*, 145 T.C. No. 7 (Sept. 16, 2015), has also stated that a discount is available in appropriate circumstances where the donee of a gift assumes a contingent tax liability of the donor (such as estate taxes under §2035(b)) as a condition of receiving the gift.

106. TAM 200247001, where the National Office advised that §691 provides a remedy in this context with a deduction for the allocable estate tax paid on this income item when includible in gross income. *See also Estate of Smith v. United States,* 300 F. Supp. 2d 474 (S.D. Tex. 2004), *aff'd*, 391 F.3d 621 (5th Cir. 2004) (rejecting position that value of retirement accounts should reflect eventual federal income tax liability when amounts are received from these accounts); *Estate of Kahn v. Commissioner,* 125 T.C. 227 (2005).

107. §2501(a)(1).

108. Reg. §25.2511-1(a).

109. Reg. §25.2511-1(g)(1).

110. *See* Reg. §25.2511-2(b). Many issues arise concerning whether gifts were actually completed for federal gift tax purposes. See Rev. Rul. 67-396, 1967-2 C.B. 351, describing situations where gifts of notes and checks are treated as complete for gift tax purposes. Rev. Rul. 67-396 was clarified in Rev. Rul. 84-25, 1984-1 C.B. 191 and modified in Rev. Rul. 96-56, 1996-2 C.B. 161, with the result that the delivery of a check will be deemed to be a completed gift for federal gift tax purposes on the earlier of (1) the date on which the donor so parted with dominion and control under local law so that no change in its disposition could be

made or (2) the date on which the donee deposits the check or presents the check for payment, assuming (1) the check was paid when presented for payment; (2) the donor was alive when the check was paid by the drawee bank; (3) the donor intended to make a gift; (4) delivery of the check by the donor was unconditional; and (5) the check was deposited, cashed, or presented in the calendar year in which completed gift treatment is sought. This position is consistent with the decision in *Metzger v. Commissioner,* 38 F.3d 118 (4th Cir. 1994). See also *Muserlian v. Commissioner*, T.C. Memo 1989-493, 493, where checks were issued to children at Christmas and birthdays, but the donees then lent the money back to the donor. No prearranged plan existed that the funds would be re-lent, although relending arrangements were anticipated. The Tax Court held that the frequency of the loans strongly indicated a lack of intent to complete the gifts. Accordingly, noting that the §163 interest expense deduction was dependent upon a bona fide loan, the court determined that the debts were not valid and held the interest expense on the loans to be nondeductible. See also PLR 200308046, where a father's conveyance of a personal residence to his sons with the promise of reconveyance upon the father's request, and the subsequent reconveyance to the father, did not constitute completed gifts (and did not result in income to the father or sons). See, further, Rev. Rul. 98-21, 1998-1 C.B. 975, treating a transfer of a stock option as a completed gift only when the option becomes binding and enforceable.

111. §2503(b), as amended by §501(c) of the Taxpayer Relief Act of 1997, Pub. L. No. 105-34. The §2503(b) exclusion initially was $10,000, but now is adjusted for inflation in $1,000 increments, beginning in 1999. For the §2503(b) inflation-adjusted amount for recent years, see Worksheet 1. From 1942 until the Economic Recovery Tax Act of 1981 an annual exclusion of only $3,000 per year per donee was available.
112. See §2513 for the "gift-splitting" gift tax provision.
113. §2523(i). This exclusion initially was $100,000, but now is adjusted for inflation, beginning in 1999. For the §2523(i) inflation-adjusted amount for recent years, see Worksheet 1. This exclusion is in lieu of a marital deduction because, when the donee spouse is not a U.S. citizen, the unlimited gift tax marital deduction is not allowed. See Reg. §25.2523(i)-1 for the availability of the annual exclusion for gifts to noncitizen spouses.
114. §2503(c); Reg. §25.2503-3. See 845 T.M., *Gifts* (Bloomberg BNA), for a discussion of what constitutes a "future interest." See *Hackl v. Commissioner,* 335 F.3d 664 (7th Cir. 2003), affirming the Tax Court's decision that, because a corporation's operating agreement foreclosed the donees' ability to realize any substantial present economic benefit by restricting the transferability of the shares, the transfers of shares to donees were not gifts of present interests. See also §2503(c), which provides a special, limited exception allowing certain gifts of future interests to individuals under age 21 to qualify for the annual donee exclusion, as discussed at Chapter 6, D.1.b.
115. The use of reciprocal transfers to take advantage of the annual donee exclusion is also not permitted. *See* Rev. Rul. 85-24, 1985-1 C.B. 329 (various partners making reciprocal gifts were not permitted to utilize additional annual donee exclusions). *See also Sather v. Commissioner,* T.C. Memo 1999-309, *aff'd,* 251 F.3d 1168 (8th Cir. 2001) (donors agreed to make gifts to objects of each other's bounty and Tax Court refused to permit each donor to use his annual donee exclusion for gift to other's natural beneficiary); *Estate of Schuler v. Commissioner*, T.C. Memo 2000-392, *aff'd,* 282 F.3d 575 (8th Cir. 2002).

116. The educational institution must be described in §170(b)(1)(A)(ii). See TAM 199941013, indicating that prepaid tuition payments to an educational institution constitute qualified transfers for purposes of the §2503(e) exclusion rule.
117. The medical services must be as defined in §213(e).
118. §2503(e). Consequently, under §2503(e) this support may be provided for both friends and relatives without limitation on the total amount of gifts received for the benefit of a particular beneficiary.
119. A qualified tuition program is a program established to allow individuals to purchase tuition credits or prepay qualified higher education expenses of a designated beneficiary. §529(b)(1), added by the 1996 Small Business Job Protection Act, Pub. L. No. 104-188, §1806. The amendments made by §1806 of the 1996 Act generally apply to taxable years ending after August 20, 1996. Section 402 of EGTRRA, Pub. L. No. 107-16, expanded the definition of qualified tuition programs under §529 to include certain prepaid tuition programs established and maintained by one or more eligible educational institutions (which may be private institutions) that otherwise satisfy the requirements under §529. This provision was effective beginning in 2002 (note that the exclusion from gross income available for certain distributions from a qualified tuition program established and maintained by an entity other than a state (or agency or instrumentality thereof) was effective for taxable years beginning after Dec. 31, 2003). Pursuant to the 2006 Pension Protection Act, Pub. L. No. 109-280, §1304(a), the EGTRRA sunset (Pub. L. No. 107-16, §901) does not apply to the amendments made by EGTRRA, §402 (relating to qualified tuition program modifications).
120. §529(c)(2), added by the 1996 Small Business Job Protection Act, Pub. L. No. 104-188, §1806; amended by the 1997 Taxpayer Relief Act, Pub. L. No. 105-34, §211, and applicable to contributions made after August 5, 1997.
121. §529(c)(5), added by the 1996 Small Business Job Protection Act, Pub. L. No. 104-188, §1806; amended by the Taxpayer Relief Act of 1997, Pub. L. No. 105-34, §211, and applicable to distributions made after August 5, 1997.
122. *See* §2523. For a discussion of the marital deduction in the estate and gift tax context, see 843 T.M., *Estate Tax Marital Deduction* (Bloomberg BNA).
123. No marital deduction is available for a prenuptial gift and, consequently, the donor should make the gift effective immediately after the marriage (perhaps mandated under the requirements of a prenuptial agreement).
124. *See* §2523(i)(1) (precluding marital deduction where spouse was not U.S. citizen at time of gift). This requirement applies to gifts made on or after July 14, 1988. Note Reg. §25.2523(a)-1(a), providing that for gifts prior to July 14, 1988, no marital deduction was allowed for a gift if, at the time of the gift, the donor was classified as a nonresident alien in the United States.
125. See §2523(f), incorporating the "qualified terminable interest property" rules of §2056(b)(7)(B), discussed at Chapter 5, D.3.i.
126. §2513. Because the federal transfer tax has a progressive rate structure applicable to each spouse separately, this enables the spouses to reduce total taxes paid by the family unit on a gift by one of the spouses. Where the required gift-splitting consent is given, the liability for the entire transfer tax of each spouse is joint and several. *See* §2513(d).
127. Note that in the split-gift context the payment of the gift tax liability by one spouse on the gifts by both spouses will not constitute a gift to the other spouse. Reg. §25.2511-1(d).

128. Often, this gift-splitting opportunity will not be important in a community property jurisdiction (where the property has already been divided between two spouses under the locally applicable community property rules) unless one spouse has significantly more separate property which is being given.
129. The annual donee exclusion is $14,000 for 2016. For the §2503(b) inflation-adjusted amount for recent years, see Worksheet 1.
130. §2513(a). Proper gift tax planning should assure that gift splitting will be elected only if the overall federal transfer tax liability will be reduced. If, for example, the husband is in a high transfer tax bracket but the wife is in a low transfer tax bracket, the husband could make gifts during one calendar year, the spouse consenting to gift splitting. The wife could make gifts during the next calendar year without the husband's consent to gift splitting, thereby attempting to equalize the marginal transfer tax rate applicable to each spouse. See 845 T.M., *Gifts* (Bloomberg BNA), for planning opportunities and procedures in using the gift-splitting technique.
131. Under the unified rate schedule, the estate tax is determined as if the transfers at death are the last transfers; that is, any prior gift transfers subject to transfer tax may have absorbed eligibility for the lower tax brackets. Note, however, that although the lifetime gift tax exclusion amount may have been used, an additional exclusion/unified credit amount may be available for estate tax purposes.
132. The §2010 unified credit effective exclusion amounts (the applicable credit amounts) were: (1) $1 million for estates of decedents dying in 2002-2003; (2) $1.5 million for estates of decedents dying in 2004-2005; (3) $2 million for estates of decedents dying in 2006–2008; and (4) $3.5 million for estates of decedents dying in 2009. *See* EGTRRA, Pub. L. No. 107-16, §521. For gifts made after December 31, 2001, §2505 established an effective lifetime exclusion amount for gift tax purposes equal to $1,000,000. As explained in Chapter 4, A.1., the 2010 TRA, Pub. L. No. 111-312, §301(b), §301(e), §302(a), §302(b), §302(f), §303: (1) increased the §2010(c) estate tax exclusion amount to $5 million for decedents dying in 2010-2012, (2) increased the §2505(a) gift tax exclusion amount to $5 million for gifts made in 2011-2012 (the amount remained at $1 million for gifts made in 2010), and (3) adjusted the $5 million amount for inflation in multiples of $10,000 in 2012. The 2010 TRA, Pub. L. No. 111-312, §303, also provides for portability of the exclusion for spouses dying in 2011-2012 (the applicable exclusion amount is the sum of the basic exclusion amount plus, in the case of a surviving spouse, the DSUE amount). The American Taxpayer Relief Act of 2012 (ATRA), Pub. L. No. 112-240, §101(a)(2), made permanent the 2010 TRA changes with respect to the §2010(c) $5 million estate tax exclusion amount for decedents dying after 2012, the §2505(a) gift tax exclusion amount for gifts made after 2012, and the inflation adjustment for both. ATRA also made permanent the portability of the exclusion for spouses dying after 2012. *See* 1997 Taxpayer Relief Act, Pub. L. No. 105-34, §501; EGTRRA, Pub. L. No. 107-16, §901; 2010 TRA, Pub. L. No. 111-312, §101(a), §304; ATRA, Pub. L. No. 112-240, §101(a)(2).
133. The credit for state death taxes was eliminated for decedents dying after 2004 by EGTRRA, Pub. L. No. 107-16, §532(a). See former §2011(f) (before being struck by the 2014 TIPA, Pub. L. No. 113-295, Div. A, §221(a)(95)(A)).
134. This credit is available only for gifts made before 1977. The credit for post-1976 gifts is effectively provided through the estate tax computation mechanism specified in §2001(b). Post-1976 taxable gifts that are not included in the gross estate are added back into the

taxable estate. The amount of gift tax payable on post-1976 gifts is then subtracted from the tentative tax amounts.

135. For a detailed discussion of §2013, see 844 T.M., *Estate Tax Credits and Computations* (Bloomberg BNA).
136. The executor must provide (on IRS Form 706-CE, *Certification of Payment of Foreign Death Tax*) a certificate identifying the actual payment of foreign death taxes. This form is to be certified by the foreign government, but if the foreign government refuses to certify the form, the form should be mailed to the IRS with a copy of the foreign death tax return and an explanation concerning the refusal of the foreign government to provide the certification. If a refund of the foreign tax is subsequently received this will reduce the foreign tax paid credit, and the IRS must be notified of this refund to enable a subsequent adjustment of the U.S. estate tax liability.
137. §2502(a). *See* TAM 9642001 (§2502(a) method used for computing gift tax payable on post-1976 gifts as reduction of tentative tax under §2001(b)). Note that, for gifts made in 2010, the rate structure was provided in §2502(a)(2) rather than in §2001(c). *See* EGTRRA, Pub. L. No. 107-16, §511(d), §901; 2010 TRA, Pub. L. No. 111-312, §101(a), §302(b)(1), §304.
138. §2505. Note that EGTRRA, Pub. L. No. 107-16, §521, amended §2505 to establish an effective lifetime exemption amount for gift tax purposes equal to $1 million for gifts made after December 31, 2001. As a result, the gift tax exemption amount was no longer unified with the estate tax exemption amount after the estate tax exemption amount was increased above $1 million in 2004 and subsequent years. The 2010 TRA, Pub. L. No. 111-312, §301(b), §301(e), §302(a), §302(b), §302(f), §303, reunified the estate and gift tax exclusions after 2010 by increasing the §2010(c) estate tax exclusion amount to $5 million for decedents dying in 2010-2012, increasing the §2505(a) gift tax exclusion amount to $5 million for gifts made in 2011-2012 (the amount remains at $1 million for gifts made in 2010), and adjusting the $5 million amount for inflation in multiples of $10,000 in 2012. For the inflation-adjusted amount for 2012, see Worksheet 1. The 2010 TRA, Pub. L. No. 111-312, §303, also provides for portability of the exclusion for spouses dying in 2011–2012 (the applicable exclusion amount is the sum of the basic exclusion amount plus, in the case of a surviving spouse, the DSUE amount). The American Taxpayer Relief Act of 2012 (ATRA), Pub. L. No. 112-240, §101(a)(2), made permanent the 2010 TRA changes with respect to the §2010(c) $5 million estate tax exclusion amount for decedents dying after 2012, the §2505(a) gift tax exclusion amount for gifts made after 2012, and the inflation adjustment for both. ATRA also made permanent the portability of the exclusion for spouses dying after 2012. *See* 1997 Taxpayer Relief Act, Pub. L. No. 105-34, §501; EGTRRA, Pub. L. No. 107-16, §901; 2010 TRA, Pub. L. No. 111-312, §101(a), §304.
139. The unified tax was enacted in the 1976 Tax Reform Act. See the transfer tax rate schedules in the Appendix. Pre-1976 law was retained for determining (1) when a gift is considered to be completed for gift tax purposes and (2) when property is included in a decedent's estate for estate tax purposes. This is significant in determining whether post–gift transfer appreciation is includible in the gross estate. Before 1977, an estate tax was imposed on transfers at death and a separate gift tax was imposed on transfers during life. Each tax had a separate progressive rate schedule and exemption amount. The gift tax rates were three-fourths of the estate tax rates for the corresponding brackets. The computation of taxable gifts was made on a cumulative lifetime basis. The tax was

based on the fair market value of the gifts, reduced by amounts allowable under the then applicable $3,000 annual donee exclusion, charitable and marital deductions, and any portion of a gift tax lifetime exemption of $30,000 that had not been used for previous gifts. The gift tax base included the value of the property transferred to a donee but did not include the gift tax paid by the donor on that gift transfer. The estate tax base, or taxable estate, was separately determined by deducting from the value of the gross estate the allowable deductions for estate administration and funeral expenses, claims against the estate, casualty and theft losses sustained during the estate administration, the charitable and marital deductions, and the estate tax specific exemption of $60,000. Except for "transfers in contemplation of death" and certain other transfers, the estate tax base was determined solely by reference to transfers at death and without regard to the amount of the decedent's lifetime transfers, or the gift taxes paid on those transfers. Unlike the "tax-exclusive" gift tax base, the estate tax base was the value of the estate without diminution for the amount later used to pay the federal estate tax liability (i.e., determined on a "tax-inclusive" basis).

140. The federal transfer tax burden imposed on transfers of the same amount of wealth is, thereby, the same whether the transfers are made (1) both during life and at death or (2) only upon death. The postponement in completing gratuitous transfers will have delayed, however, the availability of those funds for investment by the donees, rather than by the donor.

141. The 1981 Economic Recovery Tax Act (ERTA), Pub. L. No. 97-34, provided for a reduction of the then top tax rate of 70% to 50% in 5% increments over a four-year period starting in 1982. The 1984 Tax Reform Act, Pub. L. No. 98-368, and the 1987 Revenue Act, Pub. L. No. 100-203, postponed scheduled reductions in the maximum transfer tax rate (applicable to transfers in excess of $2.5 million) by retaining the 55% rate through 1992. The 1993 Revenue Reconciliation Act (1993 RRA), Pub. L. No. 103-66, made the 55% and 53% rates permanent, retroactive to January 1, 1993. The retroactive application of the higher estate tax rates withstood constitutional challenge in *Quarty v. United States,* 170 F.3d 961 (9th Cir. 1999), and *NationsBank of Texas v. United States,* 99-2 USTC ¶60,345 (Fed. Cl. 1999), *aff'd,* 269 F.3d 1332 (Fed. Cir. 2001), *cert. denied,* 537 U.S. 813 (2002). For decedents dying and gifts made in 2002, EGTRRA, Pub. L. No. 107-16, §511, amended §2001(c) to eliminate the two highest rate brackets of 53% and 55% and made the highest rate bracket 50% for transfers over $2.5 million. For subsequent years, §2001(c)(2), as amended, specified that the maximum rates for decedents dying and gifts made were: (1) 49% in 2003; (2) 48% in 2004; (3) 47% in 2005; (4) 46% in 2006; and (5) 45% in 2007-2009. As explained in Chapter 4, A.1., the 2010 TRA, Pub. L. No. 111-312, §302(a)(2), §302(b)(2), §302(f), reduced the maximum estate and gift tax rate to 35% for amounts over $500,000 for estates of decedents dying and gifts made in 2010–2012. ATRA, Pub. L. No. 112-240, §101(c), increased the maximum estate and gift tax rate to 40% for amounts over $1 million for decedents dying and gifts made after 2012, and also imposed a maximum 37% rate for taxable estates between $500,000 and $750,000, and a maximum 39% rate for taxable estates between $750,000 and $1 million. *See* EGTRRA, Pub. L. No. 107-16, §511, §901; 2010 TRA, Pub. L. No. 111-312, §101(a), §304.

142. Former §2001(c)(2). EGTRRA, Pub. L. No. 107-16, §511, amended §2001(c) to eliminate the 5% surtax for decedents dying and gifts made after December 31, 2001. The 2010 TRA, Pub. L. No. 111-312, §101(a), §302(a), §304, extended EGTRRA's repeal

of the §2001(c)(2) 5% surtax for estates of decedents dying and gifts made in 2010-2012. ATRA, Pub. L. No. 112-240, §101(a), §101(c), made the repeal permanent for decedents dying and gifts made after 2012.

143. Former §2001(c)(2). Before the 1993 RRA, Pub. L. No. 103-66, the amount on which the surtax was levied was to be reduced for amounts in excess of $10,000,000 but not exceeding $18,340,000, for decedents dying and gifts made after 1992. Pre-1993 RRA §2001(c)(3). The 1993 RRA, in addition to making the 55% rate permanent, made the higher amounts subject to the surtax permanent. In *National Taxpayers Union v. United States,* 862 F. Supp. 531 (D. D.C. 1994), the court held that no jurisdiction existed to consider plaintiff's action to enjoin enforcement of the 1993 RRA retroactive increase of estate and gift tax rates, the action being barred by (1) the Anti-Injunction Act, 26 U.S.C. §7421(a), which bars any court from enjoining the collection or enforcement of any federal tax, and (2) the Declaratory Judgment Act, 28 U.S.C. §2201(a), which is coterminous with the Anti-Injunction Act.

144. *See* H.R. Rep. No. 100-495, at 994 (1987).

145. §2502(a).

146. Note that, for gifts made in 2010, the rate structure is provided in §2502(a)(2) rather than in §2001(c). *See* EGTRRA, Pub. L. No. 107-16, §511(d), §901; 2010 TRA, Pub. L. No. 111-312, §101(a), §302(b)(1), §304.

147. §2001(b). According to TAM 9642001, the gift tax payable on post-1976 gifts is computed in the same manner as the gift tax on post-1976 gifts under §2502(a). Thus, the gift tax payable is computed based on the cumulative value of all gifts, including pre-1977 gifts. Note that the amount of prior adjusted gifts once could be revalued for purposes of the gift tax subtraction notwithstanding that the limitations period had expired for the gift tax liability. *See Evanson v. United States,* 30 F.3d 960 (8th Cir. 1994); *Estate of Smith v. Commissioner,* 94 T.C. 872 (1990), *acq.,* 1990-2 C.B. 1; *Stalcup v. United States,* 792 F. Supp. 714 (W.D. Okla. 1991). *But see Boatmen's First Nat'l Bank of Kansas City v. United States,* 705 F. Supp. 1407 (W.D. Mo. 1988), for a contrary result. These cases were overruled by the 1997 Taxpayer Relief Act, Pub. L. No. 105-34, §506(a), §506(b), which amended §6501(c) to provide (in §6501(c)(9)) that, if adequate disclosure of gifts has occurred, they cannot be revalued after the gift tax statute of limitations has run. See also §2001(f)(2), providing that, if the statute of limitations expired, those values also cannot be changed for increasing the tax base for estate tax purposes. As a transitional rule under the 1976 Act, the completed lifetime transfers taken into account in determining cumulative transfers at death for purposes of imposing the estate tax include only taxable gifts made after December 31, 1976. *See* §2001(b)(2). Correspondingly, the gift tax paid on gifts made before January 1, 1977, is not included as part of the offset in computing the estate tax. It is, however, available as a credit under §2012(a).

148. For example, if a decedent dying in 2006 made a 1980 gift taxable at the then-highest marginal gift tax rate of 70%, the computation of the gift tax payable for this estate tax computation would be made using the maximum rate in effect as of his or her death in 2006, which would be 46%. In this situation the estate tax would not be reduced by the full amount of gift tax paid on the 1980 gift. However, as explained in Chapter 4, A.1., the 2010 TRA, Pub. L. No. 111-312, §302(d), §302(f) (amending/adding §2001(b)(2), §2001(g), §2505(a)), provides special rules to account for the differences in the unified credit resulting from different estate and gift tax rates for estates of decedents dying and gifts made in 2010-2012. Specifically, §2001(b)(2) and §2001(g) state that, in applying

§2001(b)(2) to one or more gifts, the tax rates in effect at the decedent's death (rather than the rates in effect at the time of the gifts) are used to calculate the gift tax and the gift tax unified credit allowed. Also, §2505(a) states that, in applying §2505(a)(2) for a calendar year, the gift tax rates for that year (rather than the rates in effect for prior years) are used in determining the gift tax unified credit allowable for preceding years.

149. Similarly, the 2001 Victims of Terrorism Tax Relief Act (VTTRA), Pub. L. No. 107-134, §103, amended §2201 by making estates of victims of the September 11, 2001, terrorist attacks, the April 19, 1995, Oklahoma City terrorist attack, and the anthrax attack (who died after September 11, 2001, and before January 1, 2002) eligible for the reduced §2201 estate tax rates. *See* §692(d)(4), added by VTTRA, §101(a). The VTTRA, provided that, if the operation of law prevents an estate, during the one-year period beginning on the date of the enactment of the Act (January 23, 2002), from receiving a refund or credit generated by the amendment to §2201, the refund or credit would nevertheless be allowed if the estate filed a claim for the refund or credit before the end of the one-year period (by January 23, 2003). VTTRA, Pub. L. No. 107-134, §103(d)(2). Further, the 2003 Military Family Tax Relief Act, Pub. L. No. 108-121, §110(c) (adding §2201(b)(3)), made estates of astronauts dying in the line of duty after 2002 eligible for §2201 relief. For purposes of this statute, the term "victim" is limited to someone who was present at the site of one of the specified attacks and dies from wounds or injuries sustained in an attack or in rescue and recovery operations. *See Estate of Kalahasthi v. United States,* 630 F. Supp. 2d 1120 (C.D. Cal. 2008) (term "victim" does not include one who commits suicide, distraught over death of spouse killed in 9/11/01 attack).
150. §2201(b)(1)(B). In Rev. Rul. 2002-86, 2002-2 C.B. 993, the IRS provided sample §2201 estate tax calculations for three situations to show the effects of the former §2011 state death tax credit in 2001 and the §2058 state death tax deduction in 2005.
151. §112(c)(2), §2201(b)(1)(A). In Notice 2003-21, 2003-1 C.B. 817, the IRS identified guidance in a question and answer format on the tax relief provided for U.S. military and support personnel involved in the military operations in "Operation Iraqi Freedom," available as identified in Executive Order No. 12744, 56 Fed. Reg. 2663 (Jan. 23, 1991), applicable to the "Arabian Peninsula Areas" issued during the original Gulf War and not rescinded. In Notice 2002-17, 2002-1 C.B. 567, similar guidance was provided for U.S. military and support personnel involved in the military operations in Afghanistan, this Notice identifying Executive Order 13239, 66 Fed. Reg. 64,901 (Dec. 14, 2001), effective September 19, 2001, designating Afghanistan (including the airspace above) as a combat zone for purposes of the Code.
152. §2201(c). Prior to EGTRRA, Pub. L. No. 107-16, the reduced rates under §2201(c) were determined by reference to the maximum credit that had been available under former §2011(b).
153. §2001(b), flush language.
154. §2035(a).
155. §2035(b).
156. *See* §2036-§2038.
157. §2001(d).
158. See the discussion at Chapter 6, B.1.f.
159. Prior to the Tax Reform Act of 1976 separate specific exemptions were provided for estate and gift taxes. The gift tax specific exemption was $30,000 for each donor. Former §2521. In the case of a married couple, the exemption was $60,000 if the spouse consented

to treat one-half of the gifts made by the donor spouse as being made by him or her. §2513. This specific exemption was in addition to a $3,000 annual donee gift tax exclusion. The estate tax specific exemption was $60,000. Former §2052. The estate tax exemption was not increased for any portion of the gift tax specific exemption that was not used against lifetime gift transfers.

160. Under EGTRRA, Pub. L. No. 107-16, §521. For decedents dying before 1998 this credit provided the equivalent of an exclusion from gift and estate tax of $600,000. Under the 1997 Taxpayer Relief Act, Pub. L. No. 105-34, 501, the unified credit exemption amount was increased to $625,000 in 1998, $650,000 in 1999, and $675,000 in 2000–2001.
161. *See* EGTRRA, Pub. L. No. 107-16, §521.
162. *See* EGTRRA, Pub. L. No. 107-16, §521(b) (enacting §2505(a)(1), as applicable to gifts made after Dec. 31, 2009). Note, however, the applicability of the "sunset provision" enacted in EGTRRA, §901.
163. Pub. L. No. 111-312, §301(b), §301(e), §302(a), §302(b), §302(f), §303.
164. Pub. L. No. 111-312, §303.
165. Pub. L. No. 112-240, §101(a).
166. For the inflation-adjusted amounts, see Worksheet 1.
167. §6075(a). See 822 T.M., *Estate, Gift and Generation-Skipping Tax Returns and Audits* (Bloomberg BNA), for a detailed discussion.
168. §6018(a)(1). *See* §2010(c), amended by the 1997 Taxpayer Relief Act, Pub. L. No. 105-34, §501, and EGTRRA, Pub. L. No. 107-16, §521, identifying the applicable credit amount. The equivalent applicable exclusion amounts are: $600,000 in 1997, $625,000 in 1998, $650,000 in 1999, $675,000 in 2000-2001, $1million in 2002-2003, $1.5 million in 2004-2005, $2 million in 2006-2008, and $3.5 million in 2009. The 2010 TRA, Pub. L. No. 111-312, §301(b), §301(e), §302(a), §302(b), §302(f), §303, increased the §2010(c) estate tax exclusion amount to $5 million for decedents dying in 2010-2012, adjusted the $5 million amount for inflation in multiples of $10,000 in 2012, and provided for portability of the exclusion for spouses dying in 2011-2012 (the applicable exclusion amount is the sum of the basic exclusion amount plus, in the case of a surviving spouse, the DSUE amount). For conformity, the 2010 TRA, Pub. L. No. 111-312, §303(b)(3), amended §6018 to reference the basic exclusion amount rather than the applicable exclusion amount for estates of decedents dying in 2011-2012. ATRA, Pub. L. No. 112-240, §101(a), made permanent the 2010 TRA changes with respect to the §2010(c) $5 million estate tax exclusion amount for decedents dying after 2012, the §2505(a) gift tax exclusion amount for gifts made after 2012, and the inflation adjustment for both. ATRA also made permanent the portability of the exclusion for spouses dying after 2012. *See* 1997 Taxpayer Relief Act, Pub. L. No. 105-34, §501; EGTRRA, Pub. L. No. 107-16, §901; 2010 TRA, Pub. L. No. 111-312, §101(a), §304; ATRA, Pub. L. No. 112-240, §101(a). If the estate of a decedent dying in 2010 elected (under 2010 TRA, Pub. L. No. 111-312, §301(c)) to apply the former §1022 modified carryover basis regime (enacted as part of EGTRRA's repeal of the estate tax for decedents dying in 2010) rather than the 2010 TRA's reinstated estate tax, note that EGTRRA, Pub. L. No. 107-16, §542(b)(1), replaced §6018 with a provision (also known as §6018) requiring a return for large transfers at death, applicable as part of the modified carryover basis regime for estates of decedents dying in 2010 and for whom the election out of the estate tax was made. As explained in Chapter 4, A.1.c., where a

spouse wishes to utilize the portability provisions for a predeceasing spouse, the estate of the predeceasing spouse must file an estate tax return that includes a computation of the DSUE amount. In August 2012, the IRS issued a revised Form 706 that added "Part 6" containing the portability election and the computation provision to determine the DSUE amount. This filing requirement applies to all estates of decedents choosing to elect portability regardless of the size of the estate. The timely filing of Form 706 with a DSUE amount will be deemed a portability election if there is a surviving spouse. Reg. §20.2010-2(a)(2), added by T.D. 9725, 80 Fed. Reg. 34,279 (June 16, 2015) (applicable to estates of decedents dying on or after June 12, 2015). The election is effective as of the decedent's date of death, so the surviving spouse may use the DSUE amount for any transfer occurring after the decedent's death without further action. Reg. §20.2010-3(c), added by T.D. 9725. Once the election for the DSUE amount has been made and the due date for filing the decedent's estate tax return (including extensions) has passed, this portability election becomes irrevocable. Reg. §20.2010-2(a)(4), added by T.D. 9725. Note that the DSUE amount is not indexed for inflation and, therefore, will lose value over time—assuming inflation actually occurs. *See also* T.D. 9593, 77 Fed. Reg. 36,150 (June 18, 2012) (temporary regulations applicable to estates of decedents dying on or after June 15, 2012, and before June 12, 2015).

169. §6018(a)(1). For example, the entire liability may be eliminated by a marital deduction or charitable deduction, or a combination of these deductions. For the estate of a non-resident alien, a U.S. estate tax return must be filed when that part of the decedent's gross estate situated in the United States exceeds $60,000. *See* §6018(a)(2).
170. §6018(a)(3). Now repealed §6018(a)(4) previously specified that an estate tax return was required if the excess retirement accumulation tax was applicable. In the 1997 Taxpayer Relief Act, Pub. L. No. 105-34, §1073, the 15% estate tax on excess retirement accumulations under §4980A was repealed, effective with respect to decedents dying after December 31, 1996.
171. Reg. §20.6081-1(b). Form 4768, *Application for Extension of Time to File a Return and/or Pay U.S. Estate (and Generation-Skipping Transfer) Taxes,* must be filed on or before the due date for the estate tax return to obtain this extension.
172. Reg. §20.6081-1(c).
173. §6035(a)(1), §6035(a)(2), added by the Surface Transportation and Veterans Health Care Choice Improvement Act of 2015 (2015 Transportation and Veterans Act), Pub. L. No. 114-41, §2004(b)(1). The new reporting requirements apply with respect to all estate tac returns filed after July 31, 2015. *See* 2015 Transportation and Veterans Act, Pub. L. No. 114-41, §2004(d).
174. §6035(a)(3)(A), added by the 2015 Transportation and Veterans Act, Pub. L. No. 114-41, §2004(b)(1). The IRS has extended, to February 29, 2016, the deadline to file any statement due before that date in order to allow time to issue guidance implementing the new reporting requirement. Notice 2015-57, 2015-36 I.R.B. 294.
175. *See* §6035(b)(1), added by the 2015 Transportation and Veterans Act, Pub. L. No. 114-41, §2004(b)(1).
176. *See* §6724(d)(1)(D), §6724(d)(2)(II), added by the 2015 Transportation and Veterans Act, Pub. L. No. 114-41, §2004(b)(2). Those filing will be able to raise the reasonable cause defense to such penalties provided under §6724(a).
177. §6019.
178. §6075(b)(1).

179. §6075(b)(2).
180. §6075(b)(3).
181. §6019.
182. *See* §2513, which provides the spousal gift-splitting opportunity.
183. *See* §2601-§2663 and the discussion of generation-skipping transfer tax planning at Chapter 8, E. For a detailed discussion of the generation-skipping transfer tax, see 850 T.M., *Generation-Skipping Transfer Tax.*
184. §2611; Reg. §26.2611-1. The generation-skipping transfer tax regulations explaining these rules were finalized on December 26, 1995 (T.D. 8644, 60 Fed. Reg. 66,898 [Dec. 27, 1995]).
185. See the generation-skipping transfer tax return requirements as prescribed in Reg. §26.2662-1(b).
186. The §102 gross income exclusion applies to settlement proceeds received in lieu of a gift (*Vincent v. Commissioner,* T.C. Memo 1992-21) but does not apply when the payments are actually compensation for services rendered (*Green v. Commissioner*, T.C. Memo 1987-503). See *Roberts v. Commissioner,* T.C. Memo 1995-171, where funds received in settlement of claims against decedent's estate by taxpayer, who cared for decedent for eight years, for breach of contract in failing to provide for her in his will and for services rendered were held not taxable income to taxpayer because the principal claim was based on decedent's failure to provide in his will as promised, rather than for breach of an employment contract; payment was in lieu of a bequest, which is nontaxable under §102(a). See also *Marcus v. Commissioner,* T.C. Memo 1996-190, holding that property sale proceeds were partly excludable from gross income as a settlement of claims against an estate. The Tax Court's holding was partially based upon IRS pleadings admitting that the proceeds received constituted "a substitute for a bequest of property."
187. §102(b)(1). See also *Irwin v. Gavit,* 268 U.S. 161 (1925), decided prior to the enactment of §102(b)(1), differentiating between corpus and income for purposes of this exclusion. The income tax character of a gift or bequest may be an issue in this context. *See Getty v. Commissioner,* 913 F.2d 1486 (9th Cir. 1990), *rev'g* 91 T.C. 160 (1988), where the Ninth Circuit held that an heir's receipt of a lump-sum payment in settlement of litigation against a residuary beneficiary of the estate of the heir's father was equivalent to a nontaxable §102(a) bequest, rather than a taxable payment in lieu of an income interest in a testamentary trust.
188. §102(b)(2). Consequently, when a gift consists of (1) income from specified property to X for life and (2) remainder to Y, the gross income exclusion would be available to Y but not to X.
189. §6039F(a).
190. §6039F(b). Form 3520, *Annual Return to Report Transactions with Foreign Trusts and Receipt of Certain Foreign Gifts,* specifies that this reporting of gifts from a nonresident individual or a foreign estate need only be made when the gifts exceed $100,000, rather than $10,000. However, if the gift is from a foreign corporation or a foreign partnership the lower $10,000 plateau applies, as indexed for inflation. *See* §6039F(d). For the inflation-adjusted §6039F(d) amount for recent years, see Worksheet 1. Section 6039F(c) specifies a penalty for the failure to file this information, subject to a reasonable cause exception.
191. §1015(a). See the more complete discussion of these transferred basis rules at Chapter 6, B.3.b.

192. §1015(a).
193. §1015(d)(6).
194. The date of death of a missing person for federal income tax purposes will be seven years from the time of absence unless state law provides for a different presumption or death can be established earlier. Rev. Rul. 82-189, 1982-2 C.B. 189. *See also* TAM 8526007.
195. §1014(a). Note, however, the §1014(c) exception (discussed below) for "income in respect of a decedent." But see PLR 9436017, where the IRS indicated that when a short sale of securities was closed after death, the basis of the shares will be the fair market value at the time of death and no income in respect of a decedent will be realized. The Taxpayer Relief Act of 1997, Pub. L. No. 105-34, §508(b), added an exception to the step up in tax basis at death rule to the extent that the decedent's executor elected to exclude a percentage of land subject to a qualified conservation easement from the decedent's gross estate under §2031(c). The §2031(c) exclusion applies to estates of decedents dying after 1997. *See* §1014(a)(4). Previously, where a nonresident alien bequeathed shares of a §552 foreign personal holding company to a U.S. citizen, §1014(b)(5) would preclude a stepped-up tax basis. The repeal of the foreign personal holding company provisions made this irrelevant for these shares acquired after January 1, 2005. Note that, until formal guidance is issued, the IRS will not rule on whether the assets in a grantor trust receive a §1014 basis adjustment, for income tax purposes, at the death of the grantor when those assets are not includible in the grantor's gross estate. Rev. Proc. 2015-37, 2015-26 I.R.B. 1196, *amplifying* Rev. Proc. 2015-3, 2015-1 I.R.B. 129, §5.01.
196. See the discussion in Chapter 4, B.3.b., concerning former §1022, the modified carryover basis enacted by EGTRRA, Pub. L. No. 107-16, §542(a), §901, for estates of decedents dying during 2010. As noted in Chapter 4, A.1., the 2010 TRA, Pub. L. No. 111-312, §301(a), repealed former §1022 and reinstated the estate tax for estates of decedents dying after 2009. Note that the 2010 TRA, Pub. L. No. 111-312, §301(c), allows the estate of a decedent who died in 2010 to elect to make inapplicable the estate tax and to apply the modified carryover basis regime instead of the estate tax.
197. This suggests that accrued (but unrealized) losses should be realized for income tax purposes prior to death by selling the property or otherwise disposing of the property in a taxable transaction. If necessary, this disposition transaction might be accomplished by a person's representative acting under a durable power of attorney even when the taxpayer is incapacitated.
198. Property transferred by a decedent at death receives a stepped-up basis for federal income tax purposes even if no federal estate tax is due on the transfer. Thus, if the estate is relying on portability to use the deceased spouse's applicable exclusion amount, the deceased spouse's assets will be transferred to the surviving spouse in a manner that will result in those assets being included in the surviving spouse's gross estate and, therefore, eligible for the §1014 tax basis step-up. This also includes property transferred to a surviving spouse and protected by the estate tax marital deduction. When transfers are exempt for federal estate tax purposes there exists an incentive to overvalue property to enable an increase in its income tax basis.
199. §1014(b)(6). The original purpose of this provision was to enable widows in community property jurisdictions to have the same step-up in basis that often occurred when the working husband in a separate property jurisdiction, accumulated most of the wealth of the marital unit, and was often the first to die. As spouses began to achieve income equality, this provision increased the discrimination against surviving spouses in a separate

property jurisdiction that did not have the benefit of a basis step-up for the property that they acquired during the marriage.

200. *See* TAM 9308002; PLR 200210051, PLR 200101021; Fletcher & Zaritsky, *Tax Basis Revocable Trusts: How They Work After Technical Advice Memorandum 9308002*, 35 Tax Mgmt. Memo. 319 (Oct. 17, 1994); Zaritsky, *Tax Planning for Family Wealth Transfers: Analysis with Forms* (3d ed. 2002). If the estate of a decedent dying in 2010 elected to apply the former §1022 modified carryover basis regime instead of the estate tax (*see* 2010 TRA, Pub. L. No. 111-312, §301), the tax basis trust would not have produced the desired tax result because former §1022(d)(1)(B)(iii) would not allow basis allocations to property that was not owned by a decedent merely because the decedent has a general power of appointment over that property.
201. *See* §1014(f), as enacted by the 2015 Transportation and Veterans Act, Pub. L. No. 114-41. Section 2004 of that act enacted both §1014(f) and §6035. An accuracy-related penalty can be imposed where an inconsistent basis is reported on an income tax return. *See* §6662(b)(8), added by the 2015 Transportation and Veterans Act, Pub. L. No. 114-41, §2004(c). The new consistency requirement does not appear to apply to property passing to a surviving spouse for which the estate claims the estate tax marital deduction. *See* §1014(f)(2). Section 6662(b)(3) imposes, however, an additional penalty on individuals who have an underpayment of income tax attributable to a valuation misstatement regardless of whether §1014(f) applies. *See also* §6662(e).
202. Pub. L. No. 107-16.
203. Former §1022. This is similar to the treatment under the Tax Reform Act of 1976, where the income tax basis of most property acquired from or passing from a decedent who died after 1976 was not to be stepped up (or down) to reflect its fair market value on the date of death. In general, the tax basis of carryover basis property acquired from or passing from a decedent dying after December 31, 1976, was to be the decedent's basis immediately before his or her death, subject to certain adjustments. Former §1023 was enacted to provide rules for determining the basis of such "carryover basis property." In the Revenue Act of 1978, the effective date of §1023 was postponed to make the "carryover basis rules" apply to estates of persons dying after 1979. These carryover basis rules were retroactively repealed in the Crude Oil Windfall Profit Tax Act of 1980, Pub. L. No. 96-223. Under §7401(d) of that Act, however, executors of estates of decedents dying after 1976 and before November 7, 1978, were granted an irrevocable election to have the tax basis of all property of the decedent determined under the carryover basis rules.
204. *See* EGTRRA, Pub. L. No. 107-16, §541.
205. Pub. L. No. 111-312, §301.
206. 2010 TRA, Pub. L. No. 111-312, §301(c). The IRS is to describe the time and manner for making the election, which is revocable only with IRS consent. *Id.* On March 31, 2011, the IRS issued News Release IR-2011-33 stating that the due date for filing Form 8939, *Allocation of Increase in Basis for Property Acquired From a Decedent*, which is the informational return used to establish the income tax basis of property acquired from a 2010 decedent whose estate elected to apply former §1022, was not April 18, 2011 (the due date of the final Form 1040 for 2010 decedents). News Release IR-2011-33 indicated that the IRS planned to issue guidance explaining how to make the former §1022 election, to provide deadlines for making the election and filing Form 8939, and to make Form 8939 available on the IRS website. In late 2011, the IRS issued such

guidance in Notice 2011-66, 2011-35 I.R.B. 184, Rev. Proc. 2011-41, 2011-35 I.R.B. 188, and Notice 2011-76, 2011-40 I.R.B. 479. In Notice 2011-66, the IRS provided guidance to estates of 2010 decedents regarding the time and manner for making the election to apply former §1022 and certain collateral matters relating to the determination of basis if the estate made that election. In Rev. Proc. 2011-41, the IRS provided a safe harbor for estates of 2010 decedents that made the election to apply former §1022 and for recipients of property acquired from such decedents. If the electing estate followed the applicable provisions of Rev. Proc. 2011-41, §4, and took no return position contrary to any provisions of Rev. Proc. 2011-41, §4, the IRS would not challenge the taxpayer's ability to rely on the Rev. Proc. 2011-41, §4, provisions, either on the Form 8939 or on any other tax return. Notice 2011-76 changed the due date to file Form 8939 from November 15, 2011 (as originally specified in Notice 2011-66), to January 17, 2012. Notice 2011-76 stated that the IRS would grant no further extension of time to file Form 8939 (except as provided in Notice 2011-66, §I.D.1 or Notice 2011-66, §I.D.2). *See, e.g.,* PLR 201442019 (granting extension of time to file Form 8939 where original §1022 election was filed late because of accountant's error), PLR 201442015 (denying extension of time to file Form 8939 where estate failed to prove claim that original election was sent via registered mail or was received by IRS), PLR 201343001 (denying extension of time to file Form 8939 where personal representative did not reasonably rely on qualified tax professional), PLR 201246022 (IRS grants extension of time to file Form 8939 pursuant to Notice 2011-66, §§I.D.1, I.D.2). Notice 2011-76 also provided penalty relief to: (1) estates that filed Form 8939 after November 15, 2011, but before January 18, 2012; (2) estates that filed beneficiary statements related to the former §1022 election after December 15, 2011, but before February 18, 2012; and (3) persons who acquired property from 2010 decedents if the basis of the property was determined under former §1022 and the recipient disposed of the property during 2010. In addition, Notice 2011-76 provided guidance on allocating GST exemption when an estate filed Form 8939. *See also* News Release IR-2011-91 (Sept. 13, 2011); PLR 201208005 (estate of decedent dying in 2010 allowed to make §1022 election; maximum federal estate tax for purposes of computing GST tax deemed to be zero).

207. *See* REG-107595-11, 80 Fed. Reg. 26,873 (May 11, 2015) (proposing amendments to Reg. §1.48-12, §1.83-4, §1.179-4, §1.197-2, §1.267(d)-1, §1.273-1, §1.306-3, §1.336-1, §1.355-6, §1.382-9, §1.421-2, §1.423-2, §1.424-1, §1.467-7, §1.617-3, §1.617-4, §1.684-3, §1.691(a)-3, §1.742-1, §1.743-1, §1.755-1, §1.995-4, §1.1001-1, §1.1014-1, §1.1014-4, §1.1014-5, §1.1223-1, §1.1245-2, §1.1245-3, §1.1245-4, §1.1250-4, §1.1254-2, §1.1254-3, §1.1254-4, §1.1254-5, §1.1296-1, §1.1312-7).
208. Former §1022(b)(2)(B), former §1022(b)(2)(C).
209. *See* former §1022(c).
210. *See* former §1022(b)(3).
211. Former §1022(d)(2).
212. EGTRRA, Pub. L. No. 107-16, §542(c).
213. Added as pre-2003 §121(d)(9) by EGTRRA, Pub. L. No. 107-16, §542(c), applicable to the estates of decedents dying after December 31, 2009, subject to the sunset provisions of EGTRRA, Pub. L. No. 107-16, §901 (i.e., effective in 2010 only).
214. The §121(d)(11) exclusion can be utilized by: (1) the estate of a decedent; (2) any individual who acquired such property from the decedent (within the meaning of former §1022); and (3) a trust that, immediately before the death of the decedent, was a qualified revocable trust (as defined in §645(b)(1)) established by the decedent.

215. As originally enacted by EGTRRA, Pub. L. No. 107-16, this provision was contained in §542(c), in subtitle E of title V. Pursuant to §301 of the 2010 TRA, Pub. L. No. 111-312, "[e]ach provision of law amended by subtitle A or E of title V of [EGTRRA] is amended to read as such provision would read if such subtitle had never been enacted."
216. There has been some confusion as to whether the 2010 TRA two-year extension of the EGTRRA sunset provision contained in 2010 TRA, Pub. L. No. 111-312, §101(a) applied to §121(d)(11), thereby allowing the party who inherits a principal residence to use §121(d)(11) for an additional two years. Section §121(d)(11) was only meant to apply to 2010, that is, the year in which there would be no estate tax. *See* CCA 201429022. There is no need for §121(d)(11) when there is an estate tax as §1014 already allows for a step-up in basis and, therefore, essentially eliminates any inherent gain.
217. Pursuant to §121(a), during the five-year period ending on the date of the sale or exchange, such property must have been owned and used by the taxpayer as the taxpayer's principal residence for periods aggregating two years or more.
218. *See* 2010 TRA, Pub. L. No. 111-312, §301; Chapter 4, A.1.; Chapter 4, B.3.b.
219. If gift tax is incurred on this transfer the arrangement would appear ordinarily to be counterproductive because the gift tax rate would probably be greater than the 15% or 20% capital gains rate which would be avoided by any income tax basis step up. The §1(h) 15% maximum capital gains tax rate applies to taxable years beginning before 2013. *See* 2010 TRA, Pub. L. No. 111-312, §101(a), §102 (extending application of sunset provisions in EGTRRA, Pub. L. No. 107-16, §901, and Jobs and Growth Tax Relief Reconciliation Act of 2003 (JGTRRA), Pub. L. No. 108-27, §303). For decedents dying and gifts made after 2012, ATRA, Pub. L. No. 112-240, §101(b)(1), §102(b), increased the maximum §1(h) capital gains tax rate to 20% for taxpayers subject to the §1(i) 39.6% income tax rate.
220. §1014(e). *See* TAM 9308002 (stepped-up basis disallowed where surviving spouse contributed property to joint spousal revocable trust within one year of his spouse's death). Similarly, see PLR 200210051 and PLR 200101021.
221. This might include a situation where the property is transferred into a trust for the donor of the property. In the case of a pecuniary bequest, however, the donor is treated as receiving the benefit of the appreciated property only to the extent that the inclusion of the appreciated property in the estate of the decedent affects the amount that the donor receives under the pecuniary bequest.
222. §1014(e)(2)(B).
223. If that property is to be infused into a "spray or sprinkle" trust for the donor and the donor's children the applicability of this rule seems problematic at best.
224. If the donee parent's estate is subject to federal estate tax, such a transaction might not be advisable, however, depending on the differences between (1) the marginal federal estate tax rate and (2) the marginal income tax rate.
225. In the situation of property to be returned, ethical issues could arise concerning life extending arrangements for the terminally ill individual when the one-year period in §1014(e) is close to being satisfied (particularly when that individual has a living will or other directive).
226. Former §1022(f) likewise provides that former §1022 does not apply to such items. *See also* Prop. Reg. §1.691(a)-3(a), REG-107595-11, 80 Fed. Reg. 26,873 (May 11, 2015).
227. For an analysis of "income in respect of a decedent," see 862 T.M., *Income in Respect of a Decedent* (Bloomberg BNA).

228. See the earlier discussion of TAM 200247001 and *Estate of Smith v. United States,* 300 F. Supp. 2d 474 (S.D. Tex. 2004), *aff'd,* 391 F.3d 621 (5th Cir. 2004), rejecting the position that the estate tax value of IRD items retirement accounts should be reduced to reflect the eventual federal income tax liability when amounts are received from these accounts.
229. This treatment applies whether or not the recipient uses the cash or another method of accounting. Reg. §1.691(a)-1(b)(1), §1.691(a)-2(a)(3). With respect to such income, therefore, accrual basis taxpayers are required to report on the cash method. Assuming earlier accrual for tax purposes, the taxpayer would have an income tax basis for such items later included in income under the IRD rules. Before 1942, all such income was "accrued" at death and included in the decedent's final income tax return. This treatment caused a "bunching" problem that was sought to be alleviated through the subsequent enactment of §691, enabling income recognition postponement until the receipt of cash (or another realization event).
230. The §691(c) income tax deduction for the estate tax attributable to the IRD item might otherwise provide limited relief. See PLR 200234019, describing the tax effects in this type of situation involving a transfer of an IRD item at death. If transferred during lifetime, a charitable deduction would only be allowed to the extent of tax basis that, for ordinary income items, would often be zero. See §170(e), limiting the income tax deduction for charitable transfers of ordinary income and certain capital gain property.
231. *See* Reg. §1.691(a)-1(b)(1). See *Rollert Residuary Trust v. Commissioner,* 752 F.2d 1128 (6th Cir. 1985), where a post-mortem bonus that the decedent, before his death, was "substantially certain" of receiving, was held to constitute IRD.
232. For example, the right of a deceased insurance broker or agent to insurance policy renewal commissions. *See* Reg. §1.691(a)-2(b) *Ex. (2).* See also *Halliday v. United States,* 655 F.2d 68 (5th Cir. 1981), which found that the decedent's right to certain renewal premiums paid after death constituted IRD even though the right to these premiums was not legally enforceable. The insurance company had a long-standing policy of making these payments to the estate of a deceased agent.
233. *See* Reg. §1.691(a)-2(b) *Ex. (1). See also Coleman v. Commissioner,* T.C. Memo 2004-126 (post-death payments received as result of noncompete agreement).
234. See Rev. Rul. 92-47, 1992-1 C.B. 198, holding that proceeds from an individual retirement account (IRA) were IRD items (except for the owner's nondeductible contributions). *See also* PLR 200336020; GCM 39858 (Sept. 9, 1991) (payments received by contingent beneficiary of qualified retirement plan or IRA constitute IRD).
235. For example, the interest element of Series E bonds, to the extent an election was not previously made under §454 to recognize the interest income. *See* Reg. §1.691(a)-2(b) *Ex. (3)*; PLR 9537011.
236. The matter of a sale being "complete" might be determined by applying different tests. See *Trust Co. of Georgia v. Ross,* 392 F.2d 694 (5th Cir. 1967), *cert. denied,* 393 U.S. 830 (1968), adopting a "right to income" test; and *Keck v. Commissioner,* 49 T.C. 313 (1968), *rev'd* 415 F.2d 531 (6th Cir. 1969), adopting an "economic activities" test. In *Estate of Peterson v. Commissioner,* 74 T.C. 630 (1980), *aff'd,* 667 F.2d 675 (8th Cir. 1981), the Tax Court summarized four requirements that have been applied to test whether a decedent has the requisite right to sales proceeds for §691 purposes: (1) the decedent must have entered into a "legally sufficient arrangement," for example, a contract regarding the disposition of the subject matter of the sale; (2) the decedent performed the nonministerial

acts required as preconditions of the sale, that is, the subject matter of the sale was in a deliverable state on the date of decedent's death; (3) no economically material contingencies existed at death that might have prevented the sale; and (4) the decedent would have received the sale proceeds if he or she had lived. See Rev. Rul. 78-32, 1978-1 C.B. 198, where the IRS concluded that obligations remaining to be fulfilled by a decedent at his death were merely "ministerial." Accordingly, the IRS stated that the decedent had substantially fulfilled all of the substantive prerequisites to consummation of the sale and was unconditionally entitled to the proceeds of sale at the time of his death, and therefore the proceeds constituted §691 income. Note, also, PLR 9436017, specifying that the closing of a short sale would not produce IRD.

237. For example, accounts receivable of a professional practice. See *Estate of Cartwright v. Commissioner,* 183 F.3d 1034 (9th Cir. 1999), holding that a portion of proceeds from the disposition of a law practice was attributable to "cases or work in process" and, therefore, was IRD. Note, however, PLR 9549023 (certain copyright agreements did not constitute IRD items). Prior to the Small Business Job Protection Act of 1996, Pub. L. No. 104-188, the tax basis for an inherited partnership interest was reduced to the extent that the value of the interest was attributable to IRD items, but this rule was not applicable to interests in S corporations. Under the 1996 Small Business Act, where a person acquires S corporation stock because of the death of a decedent or by bequest, devise or inheritance, the IRD rules apply to the pro-rata share of any item of income of the S corporation that would have been an IRD item if that item had been acquired directly from the decedent. The fair market value basis of the S corporation stock is reduced by the portion of the value of the stock that is attributable to IRD items of the decedent. *See* §1367(b)(4); Reg. §1.1367-1(j). These provisions became effective for decedents dying after August 20, 1996. Small Business Job Protection Act of 1996, Pub. L. No. 104-188, §1313(a).

238. *See* §691(a)(4).

239. See *Kitch v. Commissioner,* 104 T.C. 1 (1995), *aff'd,* 103 F.3d 104 (10th Cir. 1996), holding that an amount received after death in satisfaction of alimony payment arrearages constituted IRD.

240. Section 691(b) specifically enumerates as eligible for this treatment the deductions "specified in section 162, 163, 164, 212 or 611."

241. For example, assume X owes a bank a principal amount of $5,000, with interest payable semi-annually. If a semi-annual interest payment is due, but unpaid, as of X's death, that amount will be deductible by the estate on its fiduciary income tax return for the tax year in which the interest expense is paid by the estate.

242. §691(b)(1)(B).

243. See 862 T.M., *Income in Respect of a Decedent* (Bloomberg BNA).

244. *See* §642(g) (last sentence).

245. *See* §642(h).

246. *See* Rev. Rul. 92-47, 1992-1 C.B. 198. Rev. Rul. 78-203, 1978-1 C.B. 199, concludes that the §691(c) deduction is allowable as an "itemized deduction" and not as a deduction against gross income in arriving at adjusted gross income.

247. *See* §691(c)(2)(c); PLR 200316008.

248. *See* §691(c)(2)(A).

249. Reg. §1.661(a)-2(f). Note that this treatment also applies if property other than cash and other than the designated property to be transferred as a specific bequest is distributed.

250. *But see* PLRs 200405001–004, PLR 200328032 (distributions occurred without causing gain recognition).
251. For decedents dying and gifts made after 2012, ATRA increased the maximum §1(h) capital gains tax rate to 20% for taxpayers subject to the §1(i) 39.6% income tax rate. ATRA, Pub. L. No. 112-240, §101(b)(1), §102(b). Prior to ATRA, the §1(h) maximum capital gains tax rate was 15% and applied to taxable years beginning before 2013. *See* 2010 TRA, Pub. L. No. 111-312, §101(a), §102 (extending application of sunset provisions in EGTRRA, Pub. L. No. 107-16, §901, and JGTRRA, Pub. L. No. 108-27, §303).
252. §1014(a)(3).
253. §1040(a).
254. §1040(b).
255. §1040(c). See 855 T.M., *Estate and Trust Administration—Tax Planning* (Bloomberg BNA).

CHAPTER 5

Fundamental Testamentary Planning

This section: (1) deals with the most essential matters involved in planning for the gratuitous transfer of property at death, and (2) provides suggestions concerning appropriate property transfer planning alternatives. This planning for testamentary dispositions requires a basic understanding of the local (i.e., state) law requirements concerning the preparation of appropriate testamentary documents, including (1) a last will and testament, (2) testamentary trusts, and (3) revocable inter vivos trusts.[1] Additionally, two important, fundamental estate tax planning mechanisms (i.e., (1) the marital deduction and (2) powers of appointment) are discussed in this segment. The objective in this segment is to blend together an explanation of the fundamental estate planning mechanics, as impacted by the federal transfer tax rules. These fundamental testamentary planning concepts remain generally unchanged despite significant changes to the transfer tax provisions in 2001, 2010, and 2012.[2]

Careful estate planners must confront, however, the possible applicability of any of these alternative situations to clients, including, particularly, to those clients who are mentally incapacitated and cannot alter their estate plans after any future legislative changes do occur. This situation suggests the use of a trust (whether revocable or irrevocable) with sufficient flexibility concerning asset distributions to enable a trustee (other than the grantor) to respond to these possible changes.

Professional advisors are aware that clients often desire simple documents, often too simplistic.[3] The effort must be to balance the desired simplicity and clarity with the necessity of assuring that the documents (1) precisely identify the client's objectives, (2) are comprehensive, and (3) are actually effective under applicable state law and federal transfer tax rules for achieving the desired objectives. Even though, in most instances, the relevant estate planning documents will achieve these objectives, the estate planner should encourage communication between the client and that client's younger generation members (or other intended heirs), including with a letter of wishes or a similar written memorandum, so as to assure both an understanding of the testator's[4] objectives, and an identification of the precise location at the time of death of the will, trust instruments, and properties.[5]

A. Basic Mechanisms for Transferring Property

1. Available Alternatives

The basic instrument for transferring property at death is the "last will and testament," a legal document that permits the testator to direct the distribution of his properties after death. This freedom of property distribution will be contrasted with some foreign jurisdictions which dictate the distribution of a decedent's assets, for example, through a process identified as "universal succession."[6] This last will might also provide for the creation of one or more "testamentary trusts" (i.e., a trust established in this "last will and testament") to be established under instructions in the will and to continue in existence after the termination of the estate probate administration process contemplated by the last will itself. Property held directly and only in the testator's name is subject to the will provisions and to the probate jurisdiction of the local court. Some other properties, for example, a tenancy in common interest in property, would also be subject to probate, but not an interest in a joint tenancy with the right of survivorship (where the property is transferred by the terms of the property ownership instrument). Although the use of a last will may save probate administration costs,[7] federal estate tax savings will not be achieved.[8] If a decedent does not have an effective will, his or her property owned directly and, therefore, subject to probate administration will pass under the laws of descent and distribution prescribed under applicable state law.[9]

Property may also be transferred through arrangements not subject to local probate administration. These property transfers will not be affected by the existence (or nonexistence) of a valid last will. For example, to reduce probate costs or to enable privacy (or both) the client may have placed substantial properties into a revocable inter vivos trust. At the death of the trust grantor, the trust becomes irrevocable. The property held in this trust would be distributed by the trustee (or continue to be maintained in trust) in accordance with the grantor's instructions in the trust agreement, thereby bypassing any probate estate administration. This occurs because the property is not legally owned by the decedent (as ownership is determined under the locally applicable property laws), and it is held by another party (i.e., the trustee) having fiduciary obligations to the beneficiaries under the contractual arrangements creating the trust.

Property held in a joint tenancy with the right of survivorship will also pass directly to the designated survivor outside probate administration by reason of the joint tenancy contractual arrangement. Similarly, pursuant to the contract between the owner of an insurance policy and the insurance company, proceeds receivable under life insurance policies might pass directly to the named beneficiaries, thereby avoiding local probate costs and other local law impediments on these transfers. A comparable transfer regime would be applicable to beneficiary designations under qualified pension and profit sharing plans and individual retirement accounts.

2. Basic Structure of the Last Will

The last will[10] facilitates a variety of functions (both tax and nontax) to enable the transfer of property in the probate estate from the decedent (and the decedent's estate) to the beneficiaries designated under that will.[11] To accomplish these objectives, the will is normally structured with the components described below being included in that instrument (although not necessarily in this order, the sequence often being dependent on local practices).[12]

a. Exordium Clause

This clause functions to:

- identify the testator[13];
- declare his or her domicile (thereby avoiding possible conflicting positions of state taxing authorities concerning the domicile of the decedent at death and the state transfer tax situs of those properties deemed located at the domicile)[14];
- declare the instrument to be his or her "last" will and testament (thereby negating prior executed wills); and
- specifically invalidate all prior testamentary instruments.[15]

b. Payment of Debts Clause

This clause functions to:

- direct the payment by the executor of debts, funeral expenses, and the costs of administration;
- identify the source from which these amounts are to be paid (usually from the residuary estate)[16];
- establish as debts any items that might not otherwise appear to be binding obligations of the testator (e.g., a loan from a child to a deceased parent or an agreement with the testator's business partner)[17]; and
- cover explicitly the method of any payment of secured debts (e.g., whether a mortgage on improved real estate, including the personal residence mortgage, should be paid by the executor of the decedent's estate).[18]

When multiple beneficiaries are designated under the will, the estate planner must carefully advise the client concerning the impact of a provision requiring debts to be satisfied from a particular source, for example, the residuary estate. This could produce significantly different results on a net, after debt allocation basis among the various beneficiaries, than is first anticipated.

c. Payment of Taxes Clause

(1) Purpose of Tax Payment Clause

This clause establishes the source of funds for the payment of all death taxes (including federal estate tax, state death taxes, and, perhaps, foreign death duties). Often, this clause provides that taxes are payable from the residuary estate, rather than being apportioned pro rata to all assets included in the decedent's gross estate, but this approach does not necessarily produce the intended result.[19] The allocation of taxes necessitates careful analysis concerning the impact on the net, after-tax value that will be received by each beneficiary (including trusts), particularly the beneficiaries of the residuary estate. The residuary estate may be inadvertently eliminated by the often-adopted provision in wills allocating all death taxes to the residuary estate. The recipients of large specific bequests and devises might then receive their properties unencumbered by any of these costs. Consequently, in some situations this tax allocation clause may be among the most important provisions in the will when assets (both probate and nonprobate) are distributable to multiple beneficiaries.

Absent a contrary specification in the will, under state law probate and trust codes, death taxes are often apportioned on a pro-rata basis to all property included in the estate for federal estate tax purposes, whether that property passes under the will or outside the will.[20] This property might include specific and general bequests and devises, life insurance proceeds paid directly to designated beneficiaries, jointly owned property with the right of survivorship, inter vivos trust assets, property passing subject to a general power of appointment, and qualifying life income interests described under the qualified terminable interest property (QTIP) marital deduction provisions.[21]

Special care should be taken when a will includes marital deduction provisions[22] or charitable dispositions to ensure that these bequests will not bear a share of the death tax burden.[23] Where this occurs, an interrelated computation is required as the amount of tax (which depends in part on the size of the charitable bequest) will reduce the charitable bequest.

(2) Allocating Tax Payment Burden When Marital Deduction Applies

The burden of the federal estate tax for many estates is eliminated (or diminished) through (1) the unlimited estate tax marital deduction and (2) the unified transfer tax credit. Consequently, where the unlimited marital deduction is used for transfers to the surviving spouse, upon the death of the first spouse to die the tax allocation clause assumes less importance. If, however, not all of the estate transfers qualify for the marital deduction and, further, the estate is not protected by the unified credit, with the result that a federal estate tax liability is incurred, the question of the allocation of the estate tax burden upon the death of the first spouse must be resolved.

The primary focus of the tax payment clause ordinarily is to place the federal and state death tax burden on that part of the estate that does not pass to the surviving spouse in a manner qualifying for the unlimited marital deduction.[24] Thus, any death taxes should usually be paid out of the "credit shelter" or "bypass" trust portion that is funded with the amount of the estate tax exemption equivalent.[25] If no such trust exists (e.g., because properties are transferred outright), or the properties of such a trust are insufficient, with careful drafting the taxes may be charged against any other properties which do contribute to the death tax burden.

(3) Estate Tax Allocation upon Death of Surviving Spouse

If significant assets sourced from the first spouse to die are included in the surviving spouse's estate upon that spouse's subsequent death, any increment in federal estate tax caused by the inclusion of such assets in the gross estate of the surviving spouse should be allocated to the recipient of those assets.[26] The executor of the surviving spouse's estate is allowed to recover from the recipient of such property the incremental estate tax attributable to including this property in the taxable estate of the surviving spouse.[27] The payment of taxes clause should ordinarily affirm the executor's right to recover taxes both under §2207A(a) (pertinent only to federal estate tax) and state law (if applicable), unless applicability of these provisions is explicitly sought to be negated. Language should also be included in the qualified terminable interest trust authorizing the payment of these taxes by the trustee of this trust to the executor of the estate of the surviving spouse. An example of such language is as follows:

> . . . the trustee shall pay from the trust estate, directly or to the personal representative of surviving spouse's estate as the trustee deems advisable, the amount by which the estate and inheritance taxes assessed by reason of surviving spouse's death (including any interest or penalties thereon) is increased because of this trust being includible in surviving spouse's estate for such tax purposes.

Section 2207A(a)(2) requires the surviving spouse's will (or revocable trust) to indicate specifically an intent to waive his or her §2207A recovery right. For example, the surviving spouse might specifically refer to qualified terminable interest property, a QTIP trust, §2044, or §2207A although this provision states that the waiver should be of "any right of recovery under this subchapter with respect to such property." This provision is intended to prevent the inadvertent waiver of the recovery right by a general direction in the surviving spouse's will to pay all taxes from the residuary estate.

(4) Assets Held in Revocable Trust

If a revocable inter vivos trust was created and funded with a substantial portion of a client's assets, the assets of the trust may be subject to a charge for a proportionate amount of the estate taxes accruing at the death of the trust creator.[28] In any event, particularly if the probate estate is anticipated to be illiquid, the trustee of this trust should be authorized to loan necessary funds to the executor to satisfy death tax obligations of the trust grantor.[29] Such a funded trust could enable, in some jurisdictions, avoiding the state inheritance tax on life insurance proceeds and attaining similar state death tax planning benefits.

The tax payment clauses in the will and revocable trust should be coordinated to ensure the desired results, particularly if the estate plan consists of a pour-over will and a revocable trust funded with significant assets.[30] For example, in *Estate of Lewis v. Commissioner,*[31] the tax payment clause in the decedent's will unambiguously directed that the estate taxes were to be paid from the residue of the estate without apportionment. The decedent's revocable trust, however, gave the trustee authority to pay estate taxes, but directed that they be paid only from the credit shelter trust, even if the tax was attributable to marital property. The court concluded that the trust apportionment provisions did not override the clear language of the will.[32]

(5) Summary of Objectives in Structuring Death Tax Payment Provision

The essential objectives in structuring a death tax payment clause in a last will (and, additionally, in another document, such as a revocable trust agreement) are to:

- identify all potential tax liabilities and allocate responsibilities for these taxes;
- identify those bequests and gifts which may need to be specifically exempted from the tax allocation provision (e.g., the marital deduction gift or, in some instances, charitable bequests);
- prepare tax-cost projections to assure, for example, that any unanticipated significant depletion of the residuary assets under the probate estate does not occur by reason of the tax allocation provision; and
- provide immunity from liability to the executor or trustee who exercises any permitted discretion in allocating the responsibility for taxes, because such allocations may be to the benefit of some classes of beneficiaries (e.g., persons holding income interests) and to the detriment of other beneficiaries (e.g., recipients of remainder interests).

Although the applicable tax allocation provision under state law may initially appear sufficient, state law may be changed after the client executes a last will and subsequently becomes incompetent, causing confusion for the original asset disposition structure.[33] Further, carefully structured tax allocation provisions in a specific will can often address these issues on a more precise basis.

d. Disposition of Tangible Personal Property Clause

This clause can provide for the disposition of specific items of tangible personal property (e.g., jewelry, art works, furniture, clothing, automobiles). This clause can also be used to recognize the community property interest of the surviving spouse in such property by indicating that, under community property rules, one-half of the tangible personal property belongs to the spouse. A similar purpose may be achieved with separate property, confirming that the surviving spouse is the sole owner of commonly used furniture, household goods, artwork, or, alternatively, specified designated items.[34] If wills are executed by spouses at approximately the same time, those wills obviously should not both specify that these properties are treated as solely owned by the other spouse (who would be the surviving spouse).

The testator may desire that the identification and the distribution of some specific items (e.g., individual valuable jewelry pieces) not be specifically enumerated in the will. Under such circumstances, a separate document may provide directions to the executor for the disposition of these assets. Whether these separate directions are binding and effective to accomplish this disposition is dependent upon local probate law. Under the laws in most jurisdictions concerning testamentary dispositions, a testator may incorporate in the will a reference to an extrinsic writing, provided that the writing exists at the time the will is executed. In some jurisdictions, a later writing constituting an "act of independent significance" may also be recognized. These writings could be used for the purpose of identifying recipients of specific assets, often tangible personal property.[35] While such a writing in some jurisdictions is not legally binding, beneficiaries usually abide by the wishes expressed.

e. Disposition of Residential Real Estate Clause

This clause may provide specifically for a transfer of either (1) outright ownership or (2) a life estate to the surviving spouse or another beneficiary in the client's residential real estate (including a condominium or a cooperative apartment and, also, second homes). In some situations this may be merely a recognition of a homestead right of the surviving spouse as mandated under local law. This homestead right is ordinarily considered to continue only while the homestead is actually used as the personal residence of the surviving spouse. A primary purpose of this clause is to assure the testator that the family home (and perhaps second residences, such as vacation homes) will be transferred to the appropriate persons and in the form desired (e.g., life estate or outright). This will be particularly important for real properties that have been held by family members for several generations. In addition to the real property to be transferred, the bequest generally should include the benefit of associated items such as any prepaid utilities, casualty insurance policies, homeowners association fees, and local real property taxes. This provision might also indicate whether any mortgage indebtedness on the property is to be paid or is to remain an encumbrance on the property. If the mortgage is on favorable interest rate terms, some funds may also be provided to the real estate transferee, rather than liquidating the mortgage, so as to enable the continued benefit of the preferable interest rate with funds provided to pay this mortgage obligation.

f. Specific Bequests and Devises

In his or her will, the testator may provide for specific bequests and devises of various properties to designated beneficiaries, including to the surviving spouse. This might include gifts of cash, stocks (including privately held companies) and other securities (including partnership and LLC interests), tangible personal property, and real property. These transfers might be made directly to specific, individual beneficiaries, so as to be differentiated from the transfer of the residuary estate (which might be held in trust).

These gifts, if made to someone other than the surviving spouse, will reduce the available unified credit amount. Consequently, to preserve the maximum "credit shelter amount," these properties could be transferred to a surviving spouse (in a form eligible for the marital deduction), coupled with a request (but not an obligation on that spouse) that the surviving spouse thereafter make annual donee exclusion gifts of the transferred properties to various individuals. In many instances, this would enable completion of the desired specific bequests without, however, the reduction of the amount of the surviving spouse's unified credit amount that will be available upon his or her subsequent death. This obviously depends on the size of the subsequent gift transfers. If a binding obligation does exist on the surviving spouse to complete these transfers, the estate tax marital deduction would not be available for these transfers to the surviving spouse, since, in reality, they are not made for the ultimate beneficial use of that spouse.[36]

The format for completing these transfers might be gifts into trust.[37] These could be transfers made for persons other than the beneficiaries of the residuary estate or for the same persons but in a different format. These gifts could include nonresiduary transfers to either (1) a credit shelter trust or (2) a marital deduction trust.

g. Power of Appointment Clause

The client may be the holder of a power of appointment under the will of, or a trust created by, another person. The client may desire to exercise this power of appointment. The document creating that power of appointment will identify how it can be exercised, including possibly through a provision in the power holder's last will. The power of appointment clause in the client/power holder's last will can provide for:

- an identification of both the source and the date of any power of appointment held by the testator, and the specific property subject to that power; and
- the exercise, limited exercise, or nonexercise, or a statement of a prior disclaimer of this power of appointment.[38]

h. Residuary Estate Clause

The clause providing for the disposition of the residuary estate may achieve one or more of the following objectives:

- the outright disposition of all remaining assets not otherwise transferred;
- the transfer of all remaining assets into one or several testamentary trusts (i.e., a trust established under the "last will and testament")[39];

- the transfer of all remaining assets into a previously created inter vivos trust (i.e., a "pour-over" provision), often a trust revocable during the lifetime of the testator/trust creator (which after death subdivides into various trusts for specified beneficiaries);
- the maximum use of the unlimited marital deduction (after considering the available unified credit amount), the optimum amount being determined by application of either a fractional share formula or a pecuniary bequest formula[40];
- disposition of the remaining community property, including using a "widow's election" (whether forced or voluntary), if desired[41]; and
- the implementation of generation-skipping transfer provisions in any testamentary trust.

i. Disposition of Trust Assets Clause

Any property transfers into trust will necessitate prescribing the specific dispositive terms of each trust. This clause should provide the terms for the retention, investment, and disposition of the income and corpus of both marital and nonmarital testamentary trusts.[42] Ordinarily, this will be accomplished with a separate provision for each trust.

(1) Credit Shelter Trust

A "credit shelter trust" or "family trust" (also frequently referred to as a "bypass trust") could be provided to absorb the remaining unified credit amount available to the testator and to retain the property in a form that would not cause estate tax inclusion of this property upon the subsequent death of the surviving spouse.[43] The trust dispositive provisions could include:

- mandatory (or discretionary) payments of income and corpus to the surviving spouse and/or the decedent's children during the lifetime of the surviving spouse;
- if income distributions are delayed, income distributions to the children after the death of the surviving spouse; and
- corpus distributions at the time of death of the surviving spouse or later (e.g., to children or grandchildren when attaining specified ages).

This trust could include an amount of assets greater than the unified credit amount, causing some assets to be subject to estate tax at the first death but not the second. The objective in this situation would be to enable equalization of the several estates of a husband and wife, based on the assumption that their two deaths will occur within a relatively short time frame, thereby benefiting from similar estate tax rate brackets. Of course, if the estates are significant, with both spouses being in the maximum estate tax bracket, the preferable approach would be to postpone the estate tax until the death of the second spouse to die. Portability of the unified credit may also be available for spouses dying after 2010.[44] This type of planning may be of less significance in the current era of high exemption amounts (which makes the estate tax effectively a flat rate tax) and exemption portability.

(2) Marital Deduction Qualified Terminable Interest Trust

This trust (the QTIP trust), for the benefit of the surviving spouse, is structured to qualify for the estate tax marital deduction[45] and should contain the following provisions:

- mandatory payments of all trust income to be made at least annually to the surviving spouse for life, including the "stub period income" (i.e., income earned between the last trust distribution of income and the spouse's later death) to be paid to the estate of the surviving spouse;
- a discretionary power to be held by the trustee (other than the surviving spouse) to invade principal for the benefit of the surviving spouse during his or her life[46]; and
- the specific disposition of the trust corpus upon the termination of the life income interest of the surviving spouse unless the transfer of that property is redirected upon an exercise of any special power of appointment granted to the surviving spouse.[47]

This trust might also include a power to the surviving spouse over the corpus to appoint any part or all of such property among a group of specified persons (perhaps including charities), to be exercisable only at or after the surviving spouse's death. Often, however, the QTIP trust will provide for distribution to specifically designated beneficiaries upon the death of the surviving spouse/trust beneficiary.[48]

This trust is often the preferred form of marital deduction trust because (1) the surviving spouse cannot control the ultimate disposition of these assets after his or her death, and (2) the disposition of these assets at that time is dictated by the terms of the trust as originally structured by the first decedent. This is particularly useful in situations involving a surviving second spouse and the decedent's surviving children of a first marriage.

(3) Marital Deduction Power of Appointment Trust

This clause,[49] creating a marital deduction life estate–power of appointment trust (as an alternative to the QTIP trust provision) would be structured to provide for:

- at least annual payments of all trust income to the surviving spouse, including the "stub period income" (i.e., income earned between the last distribution of income and the spouse's death) to be paid to the estate of the surviving spouse;
- the availability of trust principal for the surviving spouse to satisfy specified needs (e.g., reasonable support and comfort) during the surviving spouse's period of survival;
- a general power of appointment exercisable by the surviving spouse at the time of his or her death, enabling him or her to appoint the property to his or her probate estate (or to the creditors of his or her estate) and, possibly, to others[50]; and
- the specific disposition of the corpus in the event the testamentary general power of appointment is not exercised by the surviving spouse at the time of death (i.e., a gift-in-default clause would be provided).

Various other options are available in structuring some components of this trust, but the ultimate objective is to assure availability of the marital deduction when the first spouse dies (premised upon estate inclusion when the surviving spouse dies). Since enactment of the QTIP alternative, this life estate-power of appointment option is less likely to be used.

(4) Multiple Marital Deduction Trusts to Accommodate Generation-Skipping Tax Planning

Because of the planning requirements relevant to the generation-skipping transfer tax, the creation of more than two marital deduction trusts may be appropriate for larger estates. These trusts might include:

- a credit shelter exemption equivalent trust providing benefits for the surviving spouse and/or children during the survival period and, thereafter, to the children and grandchildren (without estate tax exposure at the death of the surviving spouse);
- a marital deduction trust for which any balance of the generation-skipping transfer tax exclusion is claimed, with the income distributable to the surviving spouse for life and with the trust assets thereafter distributed to or held for the benefit of the grandchildren; and
- a further marital deduction trust for the benefit first of the surviving spouse, thereafter for the decedent's children, and subsequently, if desired, for the decedent's grandchildren. The generation-skipping transfer tax would be applicable in this trust situation upon subsequent transfers to (or for the benefit of) the grandchildren.[51]

j. Appointment of Fiduciaries Clause

The appointment of fiduciaries clause in a last will functions to:

- designate the parties (individual or corporate, or both) who will serve as the executor and, also, as the trustees (and any successors) of any testamentary trusts, assuming eligibility[52];
- waive the posting by the designated fiduciary of a bond or security otherwise required to assure performance by the fiduciary; and
- enable the payment of appropriate compensation to the fiduciaries.

This clause may also identify the circumstances under which (1) the beneficiaries (or others) can replace the current fiduciaries and (2) the fiduciaries can resign and identify their replacements. The "others" who might designate a replacement trustee might include a person identified as a "trust protector."

k. Powers Clause

This clause vests authority in the fiduciary (both the executor and any trustee) to deal with the property held by the decedent at the time of death, including to:

- retain property;
- sell and lease property;

- invest and reinvest estate and trust assets;
- consent to corporate and partnership adjustments (e.g., liquidations and reorganizations);
- manage real estate;
- allocate receipts and disbursements between principal and income;
- lend and borrow funds;
- settle claims;
- exercise employee stock options;
- distribute property in kind;
- make non-pro-rata distributions (from a trust)[53];
- file joint federal and state income tax returns and consent to gift splitting on gift tax returns;
- deal with environmental hazards impacting real property; and
- exercise other powers appropriate to a fiduciary.

The explicit enumeration of these powers will enable the exercise of this authority by the fiduciary without the explicit approval of the probate court. These powers may be in excess of the powers permitted under applicable state trust law (as existing at the time of the execution of the will or at the time of the decedent's death).[54] The enumeration of these powers will often specify that they do incorporate all such powers as enumerated under state law, including as these state laws may subsequently be amended.

In some instances, other persons will be designated to act in an advisory capacity to the fiduciary. For example, if an individual is designated as the trustee, a corporate trustee or an investment advisor may be identified to advise the trustee concerning investment strategies. If a trust company is designated as the trustee, an individual may be designated to advise the trustee on making discretionary income and corpus distributions to the various trust beneficiaries. Sometimes an advisory committee of several individuals might be established to provide this assistance to the corporate trustee. In some instances, an executor or an advisor may be appointed for a limited purpose, that is, to assist in the management of certain assets such as literary properties, intellectual property (e.g., patents and trademarks), or a valuable art collection.

I. Appointment of Guardian

This clause is used to designate the person to act as the guardian of both the person and the property of any minor children (or other incompetent persons) when the decedent dies and the minor children (or other incompetent persons) do not have a surviving parent (or other designated guardian). These designations may be different, one for managing the minor's property and one for protecting the minor's person. Designating a guardian may be (and often is, as permitted by applicable state law) implemented through a separate document, rather than being included as part of a decedent's last will.[55] This enables the identification of the person's capacity as guardian without including such a provision in the last will for this purpose.

m. Common Disaster Provision

A common disaster clause in a will can serve to indicate who is deemed to survive among spouses if they die in a common accident. The ordinary presumption under the locally enacted Uniform Simultaneous Death Act is that, when spouses die in a common accident, each is deemed to survive the other spouse with respect to the transfer of that spouse's assets.[56] The purpose of this provision can be to reverse this presumption. In the absence of such a provision, the applicable simultaneous death act provisions will govern in such situations.[57]

n. Survivorship Provision

To prevent double probate administration and/or taxation if a beneficiary dies soon after the testator, the client's will might specify that a beneficiary must survive for a minimum period (often 30 or 60 days) after the testator's death in order to be treated as having survived the testator for purposes of succeeding to the testator's assets.[58] The estate tax marital deduction is not precluded by such a provision even though the marital deduction gift may not be determinable until the expiration of this survivorship period.[59]

o. Testimonium Clause

The purpose of the testimonium clause is to:

- establish that the testator executed the instrument with full and complete knowledge of the instrument and with a specific intention that the instrument was to be his or her last will and testament;
- establish the date of that document; and
- fix the signature at the end of the document.[60]

p. Attestation Clause

The attestation clause provides assurance of compliance with the requirements of local law as to witnesses and other formalities. If the will is challenged for lack of observance of the formalities of will execution, this clause will at least enable a better litigating position.[61] In some jurisdictions, a "self-proving clause" should be added. The Uniform Probate Code[62] provides for a self-proving acknowledgment, the purpose of which is to eliminate the need after the testator's death for proof of the execution of the last will.[63] Often, the witnesses will need to sign as witnesses and will also be required to separately execute an affidavit verifying their status as witnesses to achieve these benefits.

q. In Terrorem Clause

An "in terrorem" (no contest) clause may be included to provide that, if a beneficiary contests any provision of a will or testamentary trust, the beneficiary's interest in the assets of the estate is reduced or eliminated. In some states or in some situations "in terrorem" clauses are not given effect.[64]

B. Trusts

1. General Purposes of Trusts

Trusts can be created in a variety of contexts (e.g., personal estate planning, business arrangements, sales transactions, and debtor-creditor relationships).[65] The trust "as the term is used in this Restatement [on Trusts] when not qualified by the word 'resulting' or 'constructive,' is a fiduciary relationship with respect to property, arising from a manifestation of intention to create that relationship and subjecting the person who holds title to the property to duties to deal with it for the benefit of charity or for one or more persons, at least one of whom is not the sole trustee."[66] As noted in the commentary to this restatement, in the strict, traditional sense, a trust involves three elements: (1) a trustee, who holds the trust property and is subject to duties to deal with it for the benefit of one or more others; (2) one or more beneficiaries, to whom and for whose benefit the trustee owes the duties with respect to the trust property; and (3) trust property, which is held by the trustee for the beneficiaries.[67]

In the estate planning context, a trust may serve a variety of purposes, including:

- to conserve property for beneficiaries (e.g., to protect them against their own asset mismanagement);
- to enable third-party management of investments;
- to avoid state law guardianship (and related probate court) requirements applicable to property transfers to minors and other persons legally incapacitated;
- to minimize probate costs after death by transferring property prior to death and, therefore, beyond the jurisdiction of the probate court;
- to assure privacy in the transfer of property at death, if the trust is implemented outside the probate system;
- to utilize a legal structure that, when contrasted with a last will, may have greater probabilities of withstanding challenge as to whether (1) the trust grantor had sufficient mental capacity to create the trust and transfer assets into the trust during lifetime and (2) the trust creator was unduly influenced in creating that trust and transferring assets into it; and
- if irrevocable during lifetime (and not otherwise subject to the federal income tax grantor trust rules), to save taxes, including federal income and estate taxes, and state income, inheritance, and estate taxes.[68]

2. Types of Estate Planning Trusts

a. Alternatives

Trusts in the estate planning context can be categorized as:

- inter vivos, that is, created during lifetime by a contract between the grantor and the trustee (including the trust grantor as a possible trustee), or
- testamentary, that is, created under the last will and testament of the trust creator.

The inter vivos trust may be (1) revocable or (2) irrevocable.[69] The testamentary trust (created under the decedent's will) comes into existence and becomes irrevocable at the time of the decedent's death (although it may not actually be funded until the probate process is undertaken). Various specialized types of trusts are examined at various locations later in this book, including (1) a bypass or credit-shelter trust, (2) a QTIP trust, (3) an irrevocable life insurance trust (ILIT), (4) a charitable remainder trust (CRAT or CRUT), (5) a charitable lead trust (CLAT or CLUT), (6) a generation-skipping (or "dynasty") trust, and (7) a special needs trust.

b. Irrevocable Inter Vivos Trusts

An irrevocable trust may be created by a trust grantor during lifetime, ordinarily accomplished mechanically by the grantor entering into a contract with the trustee. Various distinctive irrevocable inter vivos trust arrangements have evolved in response to a variety of federal tax benefits available under specific income and gift tax provisions. For example, §2503(c) identifies a specific type of trust for the benefit of minors. An irrevocable trust may be created and funded with property to reduce the grantor's estate tax liability through the predeath transfer of assets into the trust, perhaps partially protected from gift tax when funded under the annual donee exclusion and the unified credit.[70] Under this arrangement, the trust grantor does not retain a reversionary interest so as to avoid federal estate tax exposure. Where an irrevocable trust is created, the usual purpose is to shift both the property itself and its income from the grantor's gross estate and the grantor's gross income to either the trust (as the taxpayer) or to the trust beneficiaries (or partially to each).[71]

c. Inter Vivos Revocable Trusts

(1) Estate Planning Value

Inter vivos revocable trusts (living trusts) are also of substantial value and commonly used in estate planning. With a revocable trust the grantor retains the power to cause the trust assets to be returned to him or her whenever he or she desires during his or her lifetime. The grantor may specify that the income may be distributed to the beneficiary during lifetime. He or she could specify that this trust would terminate at his or her death, with the trust assets then being distributable as part of the decedent's probate estate. This approach would be inconsistent, however, with the objective of using the inter vivos trust to maintain assets outside of the probate estate. Often, the assets of this trust are specified as (1) being distributable directly to successor trust beneficiaries at the grantor's death or later or (2) to be held by a trustee for the enumerated beneficiaries (receiving benefits after the trust grantor's death).

Such revocable trusts may be created with only a nominal corpus (e.g., $100). The balance of the trust corpus can be added at the time of the grantor's death. This balance may be received by this trust under a will which directs the "pour-over" of the testator's residuary estate into this trust.[72] This addition to the trust assets may also be accomplished by designating the trust as the beneficiary of life insurance proceeds on the trust grantor's life.[73]

Alternatively, during the grantor's lifetime, these trusts may be actually funded with most or a substantial part of the grantor's estate.[74] Under these circumstances, the assets would be transferred into the name of the trustee (1) at the time of the creation of the trust or (2) at some subsequent time before the grantor's death, or (3) at both times.[75]

(2) Federal Tax Applicability

Revocable trusts do not secure any federal income tax advantages for the grantor during his or her life. Income is not shifted to another taxpayer for federal income tax purposes, but belongs directly to the grantor.[76]

Further, for federal estate tax purposes the trust assets are includible in the grantor's estate at the time of his or her death.[77] This results from the applicability of the estate tax provisions requiring inclusion for property subject to a retained interest, the power to control the beneficial enjoyment, or the right to terminate the trust (and retrieve the trust properties).

(3) Nontax Benefits

Nontax reasons provide the primary basis for the creation of inter vivos revocable trusts, particularly if funded during life, including:

- avoidance of the slow and costly process of probate court administration in some states,[78] including any ancillary probate proceedings[79];
- competent asset and investment management through a professional trustee;
- uninterrupted trust administration after the death of the grantor[80];
- avoidance of publicity because the trust assets are not part of the grantor's probate estate at the time of death, and therefore neither the trust agreement (being a contract, not part of the decedent's will) nor the trust property is identified in local probate court records;
- enabling a grantor to choose an out-of-state trustee, thereby authorizing forum shopping in selecting the jurisdiction whose trust laws are to govern the trust (and, if funded, effectively govern the estate plan)[81];
- elimination of lifetime problems encountered because of the mental or physical disability of the trust grantor by enabling asset management to occur through the trust when this type of disability occurs[82];

- possible avoidance of elective share rights of the surviving spouse or children, including illegitimate children[83];
- providing less vulnerability to attack (as being invalid) than a last will because such trusts are not subject to the rules requiring testamentary proof and, additionally, will often have been "seasoned" for some period while being operational before death; and
- avoiding the probate administration restrictions that might be imposed on testamentary trusts (and may continue for an extended period for the administration of this trust).

(4) Specialized Federal Income Tax Considerations

Federal income tax considerations applicable in transferring certain specific assets into the trust might include the following:

- Transfers of unmatured installment notes into a revocable trust will not constitute dispositions that would otherwise accelerate the recognition of the deferred gain embedded in those notes.[84]
- The transfer of S corporation stock to a revocable trust will not result in loss of eligibility for the S corporation election.[85]
- The transfer of §1245 and §1250 property to a revocable trust should not cause recapture of previously deducted depreciation.[86]
- The transfer of investment tax credit property to a revocable trust will not be a disqualifying disposition that triggers recapture of all or part of the investment tax credit.[87]
- The grantor's personal residence may be transferred into trust without the loss of the privilege available under §121[88] for exclusion from gross income of certain of the capital gains derived upon the disposition of the personal residence.[89]
- Interest previously accrued (but not included in gross income) on Series E, EE, and I U.S. savings bonds will not be taxable when the bond owners transfer them into a revocable grantor trust and the bonds are reissued in the name of the trust.[90]
- The trustee of a decedent's "qualified revocable trust" and the decedent's executor (if any) may irrevocably elect (after the death of the trust grantor) to treat the trust as part of the decedent's estate (and not as a separate trust) for federal income tax purposes.[91]

If the trust is a grantor trust, the specific adoption of a calendar year for any federal income tax reporting purposes will not be relevant (because the trust is not categorized as a taxpayer for federal income tax purposes).[92]

(5) Switching to Nongrantor Trust Income Tax Status

The trust grantor may not mind the grantor trust status since, although the grantor is burdened by the income tax liability, the payment of the income tax liability on that income is effectively a "free gift" to the trust beneficiaries (other than the grantor). This results because the assets held in the grantor trust for other beneficiaries do not bear the burden of the associated federal income taxes. However, at some later time the grantor may wish to no longer be burdened with this income tax liability and may transform the trust from grantor to nongrantor status. This change in status will not impact availability of the income tax basis step-up at death for the trust assets, since that result will be determined by whether the trust assets are includible in the grantor's gross estate for federal estate tax purposes. In this situation of terminating grantor trust status, the grantor will be deemed to have transferred to the trust all of the assets in the trust and all of the liabilities of the trust.[93]

d. Testamentary Trusts

A testamentary trust is created under the provisions of a decedent's last will and "testament." Although for local law purposes the trust comes into existence at the time of death, it is usually not activated as a taxable entity for federal income tax purposes until assets are received by this trust. This often occurs upon a distribution from the decedent's probate estate (e.g., from the residuary estate) or from some other source (e.g., a life insurance policy payment where the testamentary trust is the designated beneficiary). A property distribution from an estate into such a trust normally does not occur until the probate administration process is substantially completed.

Similar to inter vivos trusts, the testamentary trust may also function as a receptacle for non-probate assets. For example, (1) insurance proceeds may be made payable to the testamentary trust; (2) inter vivos revocable trusts might be consolidated (or "poured over") into the testamentary trust; and (3) benefits under an employer's qualified pension or profit-sharing plan may be made payable directly to the testamentary trust. All of these properties held in the testamentary trust (including those received from nonprobate sources) will thereafter be subjected to the local probate trust accounting requirements (since the trust is "testamentary"), unless those requirements can be and are waived in the trust provisions.

The continuation of the probate estate as a separate tax entity (for federal income tax purposes) because of significant delays in asset distributions to the testamentary trust may produce some limited income tax benefits.[94] Consequently, the commencement of the existence of the testamentary trust as a separate tax entity may not occur until being funded several years after the testator's death. If the administration of an estate is unreasonably prolonged, the estate may be considered terminated for federal income tax purposes after the expiration of a reasonable period for the performance by the executor of all the duties of estate administration.[95]

e. The "Dynasty Trust" Concept

The "dynasty trust" is a name provided to those trusts that will exist for an extended period, perhaps even on a perpetual basis. These trusts, also sometimes identified as "legacy trusts," are attractive to trust grantors because of numerous benefits. These include:

- after establishment and funding, avoidance of future federal transfer tax provisions, except for possible generation-skipping transfer tax liability;
- the possibility of organizing such a trust in a state (including a jurisdiction not the grantor's domicile) where the rule against perpetuities was repealed, thereby permitting the trust to be perpetual[96];

- the protection of trust assets from the creditors of a particular beneficiary, including liabilities arising from lawsuit judgments and divorce; and
- avoidance of state taxation because the states that offer these trust law benefits also often provide state income and personal property tax immunities.

A negative aspect of these trusts is that the trust "capital" is "locked-in" for a considerable time period. Conservative trustees may be reluctant to undertake investments that might otherwise maximize income from special opportunities available to the trustees and the beneficiaries.

3. Basic Trust Structure

a. Framework of a Trust

A trust, whether (1) created by an agreement during the grantor's lifetime or (2) created as a testamentary trust,[97] will have the following general structure:

Transfer to trust—designates the property constituting the original corpus of the trust and authorizes the trustee to receive additional trust properties.[98]

Designation of trustee—specifies who will function as the trustee. If the trust comes into existence during the grantor's lifetime (i.e., by contractual agreement), the trustee will be a party to the trust agreement.[99]

Dispositive paragraphs—indicate who are the primary and the contingent beneficiaries and the conditions under which they will receive income and corpus distributions from the trust.

Spendthrift clause—provides that a beneficiary's interest under the trust will not be transferable or assignable by the beneficiary, or be subject to the claims of the beneficiary's creditors.[100]

Powers clause—enumerates the administrative powers that may be exercised by the trustee.[101]

Distribution to minors—permits income and property distributions directly to a minor, indirectly to a guardian of the child, application of funds for the benefit of the minor, or the retention of such amounts until the beneficiary reaches majority, thereby avoiding local law impediments such as the necessity to appoint a guardian for the minor's property.[102]

Rule against perpetuities—provides that, notwithstanding any other provisions in the trust document, the trust will terminate not later than 21 years after the death of the last surviving beneficiary living at the time of the trust's creation, thereby saving the trust from termination attributable to an inadvertent violation of the "rule against perpetuities."[103]

Bond—provides that no bond or other security need be provided to assure the performance of the trustee's obligations, thereby saving the annual cost of arranging this security, the assumption being that the trustee will be honest.[104]

Trustee's fee—provides for the payment of reasonable fees to the trustee in an amount commensurate with his or her duties and responsibilities.[105]

Successor trustee—provides for appointment of a successor trustee in the event of the death, resignation, or incapacity of the acting trustee.[106] This provision is particularly necessary where the grantor appointed himself or herself as the initial trustee of an inter vivos, revocable trust: (1) and either he or she becomes mentally incapacitated or dies; and (2) a replacement trustee must be appointed to assure the continued management of the trust.

b. Dispositive Provisions

The trust grantor enjoys many options in providing instructions to the trustee as to how the trust income and corpus should be distributed. The grantor may provide in the trust agreement explicit directions to the trustee as to how and when trust income and corpus are to be distributed. Alternatively, the grantor may provide broad discretion to the trustee as to the time and manner of the distribution (i.e., "spraying" and "sprinkling" of income and corpus among various beneficiaries) before the occurrence of some specified event triggering the termination of the trust (and, thereby, the distribution of the entire remaining corpus and any accumulated income to the designated beneficiaries). As an intermediate position, the trust grantor may provide for (1) mandatory distributions of income and corpus for limited purposes, such as for health, support, education, and maintenance, and (2) the exercise of the trustee's discretion as to the distribution of the remaining corpus and income.[107]

The purpose of this discussion is to outline the basic options available to the grantor in constructing the manner of trust distributions.[108] These are only examples of possible alternatives and the estate planner should mold an arrangement appropriate for his or her client's individual situation.

Income distributions[109]—The trust could provide for (1) the mandatory distribution of current income to a specified beneficiary from the inception of the trust, or (2) mandatory income distributions that commence when the beneficiary reaches a specified age.[110] The trust could require (1) a distribution to a specified beneficiary of income for designated purposes (e.g., subject to an ascertainable standard relating to health, education, support, or maintenance),[111] and discretionary authority to the trustee to distribute income and corpus for other purposes, with all accumulated income distributed to the specified beneficiary upon termination of the trust; or (2) a distribution of income to any of several beneficiaries for specified purposes (e.g., subject to an ascertainable standard relating to health, education, support, or maintenance) and discretionary distributions to be "sprinkled" or "sprayed" by the trustee among a designated group, with the distribution of all remaining, accumulated income on termination of the trust to the several beneficiaries on the basis of a prescribed allocation formula.

Corpus distributions—The trust could provide for the mandatory distribution of (1) corpus at a specified age of a beneficiary (or the distributions of portions of the trust corpus upon attaining various age levels), with interim distributions required for specified purposes (e.g., subject to an ascertainable standard relating to health, education support, or maintenance)[112]; (2) corpus at a specified age of a beneficiary (or the distributions of portions upon attaining various age levels), with interim distributions to this beneficiary solely within the trustee's discretion (i.e., not subject to an ascertainable standard); or (3) an allowable portion of the corpus at a specified age to each of the several beneficiaries, with interim distributions of corpus permitted to be sprinkled among a designated group of beneficiaries within the trustee's discretion (i.e., not subject to an ascertainable standard).

Power of appointment[113]—The "power of appointment" is a valuable estate planning tool that can be incorporated into a trust, usually as a special power of appointment. Through a power of appointment, the "donor" of such a power may confer upon another person the power to alter the donor's dispositive scheme prescribed in the trust agreement and, thereby, to make adjustments for developments that were not (and, often, could not have been) anticipated at the time the original transfer into trust was made. A power of appointment is, in general, a right allowing a person other than the trust grantor to direct the disposition of property that he or she does not own. A power of appointment is created by granting to a person the authority to direct the disposition of such property or, in some instances, the power to remove or replace a trustee. Such a power enables the holder (or donee) of the power to designate future recipients of the benefits of the trust.

To avoid inclusion of the property subject to this power in the power holder's estate for federal estate tax purposes, the "donee" or holder of the power must have only a "special power" (or, other than a "general power of appointment"). The holder, however, may be given the right to invade the property for his or her own benefit without the property subject to that power being included in his or her gross estate if that power is subject to exercise by the power holder only by reference to an ascertainable standard.[114] In addition, any person (not limited to the holder of the nongeneral power of appointment) may be given the annual right (without a qualification such as an ascertainable standard) to withdraw the greater of $5,000 or 5% of the corpus of the trust without the inclusion of the entire trust value in the holder's gross estate.[115]

Generation-skipping—The trust grantor may provide that the principal held by the trust will not be distributed to the grantor's children (or other intermediate level beneficiaries) during their lifetimes. The grantor's children might have substantial enjoyment of the income of the trust property during their lifetimes, and, perhaps, have special powers of appointment concerning the distribution of the trust property among their children. Ultimate, outright ownership of the trust assets would not be made available to the children (i.e., the intermediate generation), however. Although any child will have enjoyed the substantial benefits of economic ownership of the trust property during his or her lifetime and, possibly, at death (through the exercise of the special power of appointment), for federal estate tax purposes the property would not be includible in the child's estate at his or her death. Thus, for the benefit of the next generation, the trust assets will not have been depleted by the amount of federal estate taxes which would otherwise be imposed if the child (i.e., a member of the intermediate generation) had directly transferred the property at death.

A federal "generation-skipping transfer tax" may increase the cost of using such arrangements. Available exemptions and the exclusion under the generation-skipping tax system do make these trusts quite valuable. Careful planning can significantly reduce the impact of the generation-skipping transfer tax.[116]

c. Other Relevant Trust Provisions

Various other issues should be considered in constructing the trust instrument (whether a revocable or an irrevocable trust is involved).

(1) Payment of Taxes, Claims, and Expenses

The extent to which estate and inheritance taxes should be paid from the corpus of a revocable trust, and the extent to which those taxes would be so payable in the absence of specific provisions in the trust agreement or in the grantor's will, should be carefully examined.[117] If the trust contains most of the grantor's property (whether by original transfer or later additions, including insurance proceeds payable to the trust), consideration should be given to providing funds, whether through loans or otherwise, not only for the payment of taxes by the trust but also the payment of debts and funeral and administration expenses.[118] If the trust is irrevocable, the estate tax planning objective often would be to assure that the trust can only loan funds to the grantor's estate on an arm's length basis (or purchase illiquid assets from the estate) to enable the estate to have liquidity to pay taxes and expenses. This would avoid any assertion by the IRS that additional funds, subject to the claims of the executor, should be included in the gross estate of the trust grantor for purposes of the federal estate tax.

(2) Facilitating Estate Liquidity

The trustee may be permitted or encouraged (but not obligated) to either (1) loan funds (on an arm's-length basis) to the executor of the trust grantor's probate estate for purposes other than tax payments, or (2) purchase assets from the grantor's probate estate. This could facilitate the retention of a family business by entities controlled for the benefit of the family and could also enable an asset with high appreciation potential to be transferred (through purchase) to a trust where the federal income tax recognition of the subsequent appreciation of that acquired asset might be postponed for an extended period.

(3) Small Trust Provisions

Where a trust has a small aggregate principal value (e.g., $10,000 or less), the trustee might be authorized, in his or her discretion, to terminate the trust and distribute the trust assets to the trust beneficiaries (or to their guardians).[119]

(4) Merger of Trusts

If the will of a decedent or a member of his or her family contains trust provisions substantially identical (e.g., the same beneficial interests are granted to beneficiaries) to those of an inter vivos trust agreement created by the decedent, and the same trustee is appointed, discretion might be given to the trustee to consolidate and commingle the assets of the trusts, thereafter holding them as one trust.[120] This could enable better coordination of investment strategies and the reduction of trustee's fees.[121]

(5) Facility of Payment Clause

The trustee will not be able to make a distribution directly to a beneficiary if that beneficiary is a minor. The trustee will not want to make a payment to a beneficiary's parent (or other guardian) on behalf of the beneficiary if the trustee knows that the funds will be dissipated by that parent for the benefit of the parent, rather than the trust beneficiary child. Most trust agreements will include a "facility of payment" provision enabling the distribution to occur for the beneficiary, rather than directly to the beneficiary. Often, state law will enable distributions to be made, as determined by the trustee in good faith, to a parent, guardian, other caregiver, or directly to a creditor providing goods or services to the beneficiary.

4. Trust Administration

An executor of an estate is charged with accomplishing various fiduciary responsibilities within a limited time frame, at which point his or her responsibilities as executor will terminate. A trustee may function for a much more extended period, however, sometimes during the life span of two or three generations. Consequently, various important matters of trust administration should be carefully considered when constructing the provisions of a trust instrument.

a. Selection and Responsibilities of Trustees

The designated trustee must have the legal capacity to function as a trustee.[122] The trustee should also be capable of administering the trust in accordance with the grantor's wishes.[123] This will often require (1) the prudent exercise of the discretion accorded to the trustee to sprinkle income and, possibly, corpus to one or more beneficiaries, in accordance with what would be the grantor's probable intentions[124]; (2) prudent investment of the trust principal to assure both sufficient current income distributable to the current income beneficiaries and appropriate capital appreciation to benefit the remainder beneficiaries[125]; and (3) careful record keeping, maintenance of property, and other appropriate custodial and bookkeeping functions.[126] If an individual trustee is appointed, a designation should be made as to a successor trustee. Whatever the choice, the trust grantor should also consider the psychological impact of this trustee designation on the trust beneficiaries.[127]

b. Prudent Investment by the Trustee

The attorney may act as trustee and in these situations may encounter the conflicting interests of income beneficiaries and remaindermen. The interests of these parties must be appropriately balanced (unless the trust instrument specifies otherwise). The "prudent investor rule" will be applicable for the attorney (and others) to apply in reconciling any investment conflicts.[128] Under the prudent investor rule, the trustee must:

- pursue an overall investment strategy;
- consider all the facts and circumstances (e.g., size of the portfolio, duration of the fiduciary relationship, general economic conditions, expected tax consequences, and expected total return);
- invest for total return (maximize total return, having regard to both income generation and capital appreciation, plus preserve purchasing power);
- have adequate investment skills (delegation can be permitted if the trustee exercises care and skill in selecting the delegate and periodically reviewing the activities of that delegate);
- diversify assets (unless the governing instruments dictates retention of certain assets)[129]; and
- consider other matters (e.g., related trusts and the income and resources of the beneficiaries and, perhaps, related parties).

An important element of demonstrating the satisfaction of these requirements by the attorney/trustee will be that person's contemporaneous documentation of the fulfillment of these obligations.[130]

c. Powers of the Trustee

The trustee should be vested with sufficient power to enable him or her to exercise good business judgment concerning the ownership and management of trust property. The trustee is under a duty in administering the trust, to exercise such care and skill as a person of ordinary prudence would exercise in dealing with his or her own property.[131] As indicated above, state law will enumerate the powers that may be exercised by the trustee, but the grantor should consider whether additional powers should be provided to the trustee. In some jurisdictions, those powers enumerated under state trust codes might be quite broad. In other jurisdictions, however, such powers might be restrictive and, therefore, the trust instrument should specifically describe the scope of powers that may be exercised by the trustee.[132] One argument in favor of incorporating statutory powers is that powers legislatively added after the document is executed will be available to the trustee (assuming the document incorporates after-enacted provisions) although liberalized trust powers under locally enacted law may not be applicable to preexisting documents.

d. Controls Over the Trustee

The trust creator will ordinarily appoint an individual (or a trust institution) as the trustee because the trust grantor believes that the designated trustee will manage the trust in accordance with the intentions and desires of the trust grantor. The trust instrument will often provide that the beneficiaries may force the discharge of the current trustee and the appointment of a replacement trustee.[133] This is often a complicated issue because (particularly if an institutional trustee) the trustee will not want its reputation adversely impacted. Sometimes this may be explained by reasons of geographical relocation, but sometimes this is the result of conflict between the trustee and the beneficiaries. Sometimes the grantor may appropriately provide to the trustee a "letter of wishes" to more completely instruct the trustee concerning the grantor's intentions concerning trust administration.

In some situations, the trust grantor may also desire to appoint a "trust protector" or other third-party trust advisor who would be able to terminate the then-current trustee designation and appoint a substitute trustee.[134] This is a mechanism that may be used (particularly by a family member) when a corporate trustee appears to not be responsive to the needs and desires of current trust beneficiaries.[135] Often, the trust protector will want the governing instrument to identify some protection for the protector when exercising (or not exercising) these fiduciary powers.

5. Federal Taxation of Trust Income

a. Basic Income Tax Structure

For federal income tax purposes, a nongrantor trust (like an estate) is a separate taxable entity,[136] much like an individual taxpayer, but with a special deduction for distributions to beneficiaries.[137] The taxable income of trusts is subject to the highest noncorporate federal income tax rate structure.[138] The personal exemption (identified as a "deduction for personal exemption") is $300 for a trust that, under its governing instrument, is required to distribute all of its income currently. All other trusts are allowed a $100 deduction (in lieu of the personal exemption).[139]

The rules for the income taxation of both estates and trusts are set forth in subchapter J of the Code, which has the following subparts:

Subpart A—General Rules for the Taxation of Estates and Trusts (§641–§645);

Subpart B—Simple Trusts (Trusts Which Distribute Current Income Only) (§651 and §652);

Subpart C—Estates and Complex Trusts (Trusts Which May Accumulate Income or Which Distribute Corpus) (§661–§664);

Subpart D—Accumulation Distributions (Treatment of Excess Distributions by Trusts) (§665–§668); and

Subpart E—Grantors and Others Treated as Substantial Owners (§671–§679).

The federal income tax treatment of trusts (and estates) and their beneficiaries is essentially premised upon a modified "conduit principle." As a separate taxable entity, a trust reports its income and computes its tax in a manner similar to individuals. The trust is also allowed, however, a deduction for income distributed (or required to be currently distributed) to the beneficiary.[140] With respect to this distributed income, the trust is thereby a "conduit" through which the income passes onto the beneficiary's income tax return.

The beneficiary must include in his or her gross income the distributions of income actually received from the trust (or estate) and, additionally, that income that must be distributed by the trust (or estate) even if not actually received. The income is taxable to the beneficiary as though he or she had received it directly. Distributions of corpus are not taxable to the beneficiary.[141]

b. Current Distributions

(1) The DNI Concept

The most important element in determining the allocation of the income tax liability between a trust and the trust beneficiaries who receive distributions of current trust income is the "distributable net income" (DNI) concept.[142] The DNI structure basically serves three purposes:

- A limit is imposed on the distributions deduction allowable to the fiduciary.[143]
- A limit is imposed on the amounts of distributed trust income to be included in the gross income of the beneficiaries.[144]
- In determining both the distributions deduction and the income inclusions by the beneficiaries, the tax character of the various items is preserved, thereby separating taxable income from nontaxable income, and long-term capital gains from ordinary income.[145]

(2) DNI Defined

DNI consists of the taxable income of the trust (or estate) (as determined for federal income tax purposes), with certain modifications.[146] In essence, various items of gross income, such as (1) extraordinary dividends and taxable stock dividends, (2) other ordinary taxable income, (3) short-term capital gain, (4) long-term capital gain, and (5) tax-exempt interest, need to be identified and then included or excluded from DNI according to the rules in §643(a).[147] DNI for subchapter J purposes is not necessarily the same as income as defined for local law trust accounting purposes. The distribution of an item that constitutes "principal" for trust accounting purposes might, for example, be classified as an amount to be included for federal income tax purposes in the gross income of the recipient (and deductible by the trust or estate).[148]

(3) Simple vs. Complex Trusts

Two different systems exist for allocating the federal income tax liability between a trust and its beneficiaries, that is, the "simple trust" and "complex trust" regimes. A "simple trust" is a trust for which all income is to be distributed currently and no other amounts (e.g., capital gains) are actually distributed.[149] If the trust is a "simple trust," it is not subject to federal income tax. The trust beneficiaries/distributees are subject to income tax, however. This result occurs even if the income that must be distributed is not actually distributed. This occurs because the trust beneficiary could (through an appropriate local law trust enforcement proceeding) cause the trustee to distribute that income currently.

The taxation of "complex trusts" and their beneficiaries is more complicated. The federal income tax burden is allocated between the trust and its beneficiaries. Different categories (tiers) of distributions to beneficiaries are recognized, with those recipients in the first tier being treated as first receiving income distributions from the trust.[150] A "first-tier" distribution consists of those amounts of income required to be distributed currently to the trust beneficiaries.[151] A "second-tier" distribution is any distribution that does not consist of an amount of income required to be distributed currently.[152] The significance of this income tax categorization of tiered distributions is that the income tax burden will fall first on the recipients of the first tier distributions.[153] Only after DNI is proportionally allocated to all first-tier recipients (and unallocated DNI remains) will an allocation be made of any remaining DNI to the second-tier beneficiaries. To the extent, therefore, that both high and low marginal income tax bracket taxpayers are to be income beneficiaries of a trust, the high-marginal-bracket taxpayers should be the "second tier beneficiaries" (assuming that such an income distribution pattern is consistent with the dispositive intent of the trust grantor). If the trust is to have a long existence, this marginal income tax rate relationship among present and future beneficiaries may be quite difficult to anticipate. Consequently, in this latter situation (from the tax perspective) total discretion to the trustee to "spray and sprinkle" the trust income would often provide the best income tax planning approach for allocating taxable income between the trust and various beneficiaries.

c. Accumulation Trust Rules

(1) Purpose of the "Throwback" Rules

Where a beneficiary's federal income tax bracket is higher than the income tax bracket of the trust, immediate income tax savings can be realized by having trust income taxed to the trust rather than (by reason of the trust income distribution conduit rules) to the beneficiary.[154] Various nontax reasons might also be served by accumulating income at the trust level (e.g., during the minority of a child when a distribution might otherwise necessitate the appointment of a guardian).[155] If, in a later year, the income previously taxed to the trust could be distributed to the high-bracket trust beneficiary taxpayer without further income tax, the income tax savings could be permanently achieved, and the beneficiary could enjoy property (even though after a period of delay) having a more significant value.

To preclude this situation, "throwback rules"[156] were enacted to require, in general, that the recipient of a distribution of accumulated trust income was to be taxed as if he or she had received the income when it had earlier constituted taxable income to the trust. As a result of the tax rate changes in the Revenue Reconciliation Act of 1993, the low individual tax rates (compared to the steeply progressive income tax rates applicable to trusts) make the use of accumulation trusts considerably less valuable for income tax planning purposes. These trusts do remain valuable for other reasons, but the tax costs associated with their usage often mandate making a current distribution to the beneficiaries.[157] For this reason, the "throwback rules" became of less significance and were repealed for distributions from domestic trusts made in taxable years beginning after August 5, 1997.[158]

(2) Accumulation Distribution Tax Computation

To those limited trusts to which the throwback rules apply, the recipient is taxed on the "accumulation distribution" in the year of actual receipt.[159] The presently applicable method of determining the tax on an "accumulation distribution" is summarized as follows:

- Determine the number of preceding taxable years during which the trust had undistributed net income (UNI) not deemed to have been distributed in prior accumulation distributions.[160]
- The beneficiary's base years for determining the additional tax (if any) are to be three of the five preceding taxable years of the beneficiary, determined by eliminating those taxable years with the highest and lowest taxable income.[161]
- The beneficiary must add to his or her taxable income in each of such three preceding taxable years the average of the UNI during the preceding taxable years currently deemed to have been distributed. Taxes paid at the trust level on amounts of UNI currently deemed to have been distributed are also deemed to have been distributed.[162]
- The beneficiary then computes his or her average increase in income tax in those prior three years resulting from the inclusion in his or her taxable income of the amounts deemed distributed from the trust in those taxable years.[163] The average increase in tax is then multiplied by the number of preceding taxable years to determine the additional tax imposed as a result of the current accumulation distribution.[164]
- The beneficiary then credits (except in the case of multiple trusts) against the additional tax liability thereby determined the amount of income taxes paid at the trust level attributed to the UNI retained during such taxable years.[165]

Example: Assume accumulated income distributed during the current year is attributable to 10 prior tax years. One-tenth of the amount distributed would be added to the beneficiary's taxable income in each of the three years chosen from the five years immediately preceding the year of the accumulation distribution. The additional tax is computed for these three years when including that one-tenth amount in the income for each year. The average yearly additional tax for the three-year period is then determined. This amount is multiplied by 10 (the number of years to which the trust income distribution relates). The tax deemed distributed by the trust is applied as an offset in determining the net income tax liability attributable to the accumulation distribution, but no refund is available for any income taxes paid by the trust on an amount in excess of the beneficiary's tax liability.

(3) Accumulation During Minority

The throwback rules (even assuming general applicability) do not apply to any distribution of income accumulated for a beneficiary while he or she was a minor.[166] This encompasses accumulations occurring (1) before the birth of the beneficiary and (2) before the beneficiary attains age 21.[167]

d. Multiple Trusts

(1) Possible Tax Consolidation of Trusts

The use of multiple taxpayer entities has been consistently recognized as a method for reducing the impact of a progressive income tax rate structure and (where applicable) the accumulation trust rules. In the trust context, significant income tax reduction could previously be accomplished by splitting income among several trusts, thereby reducing the marginal income tax bracket applicable to any of such taxable entities.[168]

Multiple trusts have been created in the following situations:

- a different trust for each child (or each grandchild, or both); and
- a new trust for a particular child (or his or her family) in each of several years.

The potential value of these separate trusts might be offset, however, by both the costs of trust administration and the unavailability of a power to sprinkle current income among several trust beneficiaries. Consolidation of multiple trusts for income tax purposes was previously avoided by assuring that the various trusts were meticulously administered as separate entities (including the filing of separate federal income tax returns).[169] A subsequently enacted multiple trust consolidation statutory rule provides, however, that two or more trusts will be treated as one trust if: (1) the trusts have substantially the same grantor or grantors and substantially the same primary beneficiary or beneficiaries; and (2) a principal purpose for the existence of the multiple trusts is the avoidance of federal income tax.[170] For purposes of these rules, a husband and wife are treated as one beneficiary or one grantor.[171] Trusts will not be treated as having different primary beneficiaries merely because the trusts have different contingent beneficiaries. Trusts will not be treated as having different grantors by having different persons making nominal transfers to the trusts.[172]

(2) Accumulation Trust Rules

Under post–August 5, 1997, law, the throwback rules will apply when accumulation distributions are eventually made from domestic trusts created before March 1, 1984, that would be treated as multiple trusts under §643(f) (if §643(f) were applicable to pre–March 1, 1984 trusts).[173] The trustee must consider, of course, the impact of such accumulation distributions on the various beneficiaries, particularly when "sprinkling" distributions are permitted. The primary value of using multiple trust entities is in the income tax deferral (if any) that may be obtained during the period between income recognition and the trust distribution.

A special rule deals with multiple trusts where one beneficiary receives an accumulation distribution from more than two trusts in the same year. Under this rule, in the case of a distribution from a third trust and any additional trusts, the beneficiary recomputes his or her tax under the shortcut method. No credit is given, however, for any taxes previously paid by the trust on this income.[174] The result is double taxation of the accumulated income which is distributed by the third and additional trusts, similar to double taxation of previously taxed corporate income when distributed as dividends to individual shareholders.

Under a "de minimis exception," this special multiple trust rule may not apply. This exception will be applicable where an accumulation distribution from a trust (including all prior accumulation distributions from the trust to the beneficiary for that same year) is less than $1,000.[175]

e. Capital Gains

A maximum 20% tax rate for capital gains eliminated the usefulness of prior tax planning seeking to deflect capital gains recognition from a trust grantor to a trust. This maximum 20% capital gains tax rate applies after 2012.[176] For sales or exchanges on or before August 5, 1997, a special rule covered the possible abuse where (1) the grantor transferred property having unrealized appreciation into a trust and (2) the objective of this transfer was to shift the payment of income tax on that appreciation (when realized) to the trust that was subject to a lower marginal income tax rate.[177] Under that prior rule, where (1) the fair market value of property placed in trust exceeded the price paid (if any) for the property by the trust and (2) the trust sold the property within two years of its transfer into the trust, the total tax on the gain to the trust was equal to (1) the amount of additional tax the transferor would have paid if the gain had been included in the gross income of the transferor for his or her taxable year in which the sale occurred, plus (2) the regular tax imposed on the trust.[178] This treatment was as if the transferor to the trust had realized the gain and subsequently transferred the net after tax proceeds from the sale to the trust as corpus.[179] This treatment could not be avoided through the use of an installment sale, because each installment, when received, was taxed at the grantor's income tax rate, as if the installment sale occurred within the two-year period after the transfer to the trust. Consequently, former §644 applied where a trust elected to report income under the installment sale method as if each installment were a separate sale or exchange of property to which the provision applied, without regard to the two-year rule.[180]

f. Trust Distributions of Appreciated Property

The trustee may often distribute property other than cash to a beneficiary, and the trust provisions ordinarily will (and should) enable the trustee to make such distributions. Distributions of property (other than cash in the form of U.S. dollars) from a trust or estate are treated as carrying out to the beneficiary the distributable net income of the trust only to the extent of the lesser of (1) the property's tax basis or (2) its fair market value at the time of the distribution.[181] The income tax basis of the property in the hands of the recipient beneficiary is the same as the basis for that property to the distributing trust or estate (unless gain is recognized on the distribution, with the basis then being adjusted to reflect that recognized gain).[182] The amount of the deduction to the trust (or estate) upon a distribution of this property is the lesser of that property's tax basis in the hands of the beneficiary or its fair market value.[183]

Alternatively, the trustee or executor may elect to treat the distribution of property as a gain recognition event, resulting in the tax inclusion of all gain (if any) on the distribution as if the property had been sold to the beneficiary at its fair market value.[184] Where properties have depreciated in value, ordinarily the trustee should sell the asset independently and realize the loss for income tax purposes. This could enable possible immediate income tax benefits to the trust. More importantly, where a distribution of loss property is made by a trust to a beneficiary of property having a value less than its basis and the election is made for sale equivalent treatment, a loss deduction is disallowed to the trust because of the relationship between the trust and the beneficiary.[185]

g. Trust Income Tax Planning Ideas

Many planning opportunities do exist to use trusts that might accumulate income, notwithstanding the limitations described above. An important objective in this planning context is to enable flexibility for the trustee concerning the distribution of trust income to those beneficiaries in lower income tax brackets. This may best be accomplished through "spray and sprinkle" powers enabling the trustee to distribute income to multiple beneficiaries, including multiple generations. For example:

- Carefully evaluate the trust's and the beneficiaries' income tax situations after the end of any particular tax year to determine the probable marginal income tax rates for each. Then the trustee can determine whether the greater tax cost will be when the income is taxed to the trust or to the beneficiaries. Within 65 days after the beginning of the tax year, the trustee can make distributions from the trust that are treated as paid as of the last day of the preceding tax year.[186]
- Income tax deferral is possible when the tax bracket of the trust is lower than the ultimate beneficiary's tax bracket. The trust may productively invest the amount that would otherwise have been paid as tax if an immediate distribution to the beneficiary had occurred. Because of the rapid progressivity of the tax brackets applicable to trusts, this opportunity might only be available when the trust beneficiary has quite significant taxable income.

- If the trust is one to which the throwback rules do apply (i.e., it is not a "qualified trust" under §665(c)), the trustee should be vested with discretion to sprinkle trust income. The trustee could sprinkle that income to beneficiaries having an income tax bracket at the time of the income accumulation no higher than the trust's income tax bracket at the time of the accumulation. Included as beneficiaries might be persons not yet born at the time of the accumulation. In such an instance, additional tax would probably not be payable.[187] No income tax refund would be available, however.[188]
- If the throwback rules apply to the trust, upon the ultimate distribution the "short-cut" method of computing the beneficiary's tax may produce a lesser amount of tax than would a current trust income distribution.[189] This situation might arise, for example, where the beneficiary's income has been decreasing, as often occurs after an individual's retirement.

Consequently, for tax planning reasons the trust grantor should not ordinarily mandate the current distribution of all income to a specific beneficiary unless that is his or her specific intent, and this distribution format is compelled by nontax reasons. Significant nontax considerations might dictate that income should be accumulated to achieve the trust grantor's objectives for the trust beneficiaries (e.g., protecting the beneficiary from access to excess resources). In the future, the U.S. Congress may enact a more gradual progressive income tax rate structure applicable to trusts (particularly when contrasted to other taxpayers) than that imposed on trusts as a result of the Revenue Reconciliation Act of 1993 and subsequent law, but conjecture about future tax law changes is always problematic. Of course, the trust may invest so that it does not realize significant income, e.g., accruing but not realizing (for income tax purposes) capital gains from long-term investments. This could avoid the possibility of a significant tax rate differential between the trust and the trust beneficiaries, the capital gains being subject to tax at a maximum 20% rate. This maximum capital gains tax rate applies after 2012.[190] Another investment option (particularly during periods of stock market volatility) may be to invest in bonds producing tax exempt income.[191]

C. Credit Shelter Trust

A specialized trust (known as the credit shelter trust or the "bypass trust") should be considered and implemented by many clients having significant wealth. An exclusion amount (accomplished through the unified credit or "applicable exclusion amount") is available to each estate. This provides immunity for most estates from federal estate tax, with only those estates above the applicable exclusion amount being subject to possible estate tax. The amount of the exclusion was $1 million for estates of decedents dying in 2002–2003, $1.5 million for estates of decedents dying in 2004–2005, $2 million for estates of decedents dying in 2006–2008, and $3.5 million for estates of decedents dying in 2009.[192] The estate tax exclusion amount is $5 million for estates of decedents dying after 2009, and has a portability provision for spouses dying after 2010 (with the basic exclusion amount adjusted for inflation after 2011).[193] An important estate tax planning objective often is to assure the maximum utilization of this exclusion provision, consistent with the objectives of the client.[194] Noting that numerous changes have occurred as to the applicable exclusion amount, and anticipating that further legislative changes might occur as to this amount, the estate planner must implement some type of formula approach to take advantage of whatever this amount might be at the time of death. This does assume the testator's objective is to maximize protection for wealth transfers under this provision whatever the applicable exclusion amount might be.

The applicable credit amount can be employed against direct property transfers (e.g., specific, outright bequests to children) but the remaining portion of this credit is often utilized to eliminate the estate tax on transfers to a trust designated with various names: "credit shelter trust," "bypass trust," or "family trust." The objective of the credit shelter trust arrangement is to assure that (1) an amount of property equal to the decedent's remaining applicable exclusion amount ultimately passes to the next generation (2) without being taxed in the estate of the decedent and, further, (3) without being included subsequently in the gross estate of the surviving spouse upon his or her death.[195] This is achieved by structuring the "credit shelter trust" so that the surviving spouse does not have property and income rights as to the property in this trust that would cause the trust assets to be included in his or her gross estate upon his or her subsequent death. For example, the trust can provide (1) for income and corpus distributions to the surviving spouse (subject to an ascertainable standard), (2) with the remaining income distributable to the children, either subject to an ascertainable standard or in the discretion of the trustee. The trust could provide for discretionary distributions to the surviving spouse, assuming the exercise of that discretion is made by an independent party, that is, not the surviving spouse. Various configurations are available for structuring trust distributions during the period of the spouse's survival. Further, at the time of the surviving spouse's death (or at some later time) the trust (1) might terminate, with the property then being distributed to the children (or, possibly, grandchildren), or (2) be retained in further trust for these beneficiaries.

With careful planning the surviving spouse may be a trustee of the credit shelter trust (for example, by limiting to an "ascertainable standard" the trustee's authority to make distributions to himself or herself). To the extent any additional discretion can be exercised in favor of the surviving spouse, someone other than the spouse (i.e., an independent trustee) must be delegated with this specific authority. This will avoid inclusion of the amounts subject to this discretion in the surviving spouse's (1) income (unless actually distributed to him or her) and (2) gross estate.

Whether the credit shelter trust or, alternatively, the marital deduction trust (if any) should be the recipient of the residuary estate under the will (or upon the reallocation of the assets of a revocable trust that became irrevocable upon the grantor's death) must be determined under the specific factual situation presented. This will involve analyzing (1) the relationship between the potential values of the two trusts, (2) whether gain will be recognized upon the funding with appreciated property of that trust receiving the nonresiduary trust, and (3) other factors, often involving state law.

This careful examination of the relative values of these two trusts will also be essential to assure that the various beneficiaries receive at death the appropriate amounts as initially intended by the client. Many variables may cause complications in this context: (1) the increasing (or decreasing) applicable exclusion amount; (2) significant fluctuations in the net wealth of the client, the spouse, and the client's children and grandchildren, and (3) the timing of the client's death (whether almost immediately after completion of the estate planning or at some later time, including when the client has become mentally incompetent and cannot change his or her last will). For this reason, maximum flexibility is encouraged for structuring the future management and administration of the credit shelter trust.

D. Estate Tax Marital Deduction Transfers

1. Fundamental Elements

A decedent's gross estate can be reduced by a deduction for the value of certain property interests passing from the decedent to the decedent's surviving spouse.[196] Because of its substantial significance, the availability of the marital deduction permeates many areas of estate planning where a decedent might have a surviving spouse. The rules are discussed in detail below.[197] In general, to establish eligibility for the estate tax marital deduction, the executor must demonstrate: (1) that the decedent is survived by a spouse[198]; (2) that the surviving spouse is a U.S. citizen spouse[199]; (3) that the property "passes" from the decedent to his or her spouse[200]; (4) that the property interest transferred is a deductible interest; (5) the value of the property interest; and (6) the value of the decedent's gross estate.

The marital deduction is permitted on the premise that the property interest received by the surviving spouse will be includible in that spouse's estate at that spouse's subsequent death, unless this property is completely consumed during his or her lifetime. This mechanism enables all the marital assets to be used until death by the last surviving member of the marital unit. Under these circumstances, all of the decedent's assets will be exposed to federal estate tax at the decedent's generational level, either at his or her death or at the death of his or her surviving spouse, unless consumed during the survival period. Those assets may not actually be taxed, however, because of the availability of the unified credit.

Historically, because of the progressive estate tax rate structure (as generally in effect for decedents dying before 2006), the total estate tax paid by the two estates would be less where the size of the two estates was equalized and some estate tax was to be paid on the death of each spouse.[201] As noted below, this suggested that the maximum use of the unlimited marital deduction was not always appropriate. Rather, the payment of some tax at the death of the first spouse to die could ultimately be financially beneficial. The benefits of this equalization of the two estates could be offset, however, by the benefits of the current investment use (during an extended period of survival by the spouse) of the funds subsequently to be used for the estate tax.

2. Historical Background and Legislative Purpose of the Estate Tax Marital Deduction

a. Original Enactment

An understanding of the evolution of the estate tax marital deduction, which has a long and tortuous history, is useful to gain perspective on the current marital deduction structure and related planning. From the time of its enactment under the Revenue Act of 1948 until 1977, the sole purpose of the marital deduction was to equalize the estate and gift tax treatment of residents of common law states and residents of community property states.[202] Prior to 1948, each spouse dying in a community property jurisdiction, after accumulating all or most of his or her assets while living in that jurisdiction, would have included in his or her estate only one-half of the total of the community assets. For couples living in community property jurisdictions, this result substantially lessened the impact of the estate tax (because the applicable tax rates were quite progressive), enabling larger net amounts to be passed to younger generations.

At the same time, however, in a common-law state, one spouse generally held in his or her name much of the property accumulated during the marriage, with the result that the entire amount of this property was taxed at a higher estate tax rate than the rate applicable to the two equal portions owned by the marital partnership in a community property state. At the time of the then different workplace environments, these funds were often acquired by the "wage-earner" husband and not the "stay-at-home" wife. To remedy this situation, Congress in 1948 enacted the estate tax marital deduction provision which permitted, but did not require, a division of noncommunity property estates so as to tax a decedent's estate in two equal portions. This was achieved through an estate tax deduction mechanism that allowed the first spouse to die to transfer up to one-half of his or her estate on a tax-deductible basis to his or her surviving spouse.

In community property states, this marital deduction was available only for separate property held by one of the spouses. The recognition of community property ownership had already caused this "split" to occur for transfer tax purposes and, accordingly, community property could not be included in measuring the marital deduction amount. The maximum allowable estate tax marital deduction was roughly one-half of the spouse's separate property.

b. Tax Reform Act of 1976

The estate tax marital deduction provision was liberalized considerably under the Tax Reform Act of 1976, so as to increase the amount of interspousal transfers that could be made without the imposition of a federal transfer tax. Beginning in 1977, the maximum marital deduction for property passing from the decedent to the surviving spouse increased to the greater of $250,000 or one-half of the decedent's adjusted gross estate. Consequently, an estate tax marital deduction up to $250,000 came into existence and these provisions were available for community property estates as well as those containing separate property.

c. Economic Recovery Tax Act of 1981

(1) Quantitative Limits

The Economic Recovery Tax Act of 1981 (ERTA) removed the quantitative limits on the estate tax marital deduction, enabling an unlimited marital deduction (which remains as one of the fundamental principles of the marital deduction). The theory behind this availability of an unlimited marital deduction is to treat the spouses as one economic unit for estate and gift tax purposes (as they can be similarly treated for federal income tax purposes). Accordingly, no federal estate or gift tax is imposed on transfers between a husband and wife. This estate tax immunity is implemented through making available a deduction to the estate of the first spouse to die for the full fair market value of all property transferred to the surviving spouse. The marital deduction is not disallowed for transfers of community property interests between spouses even though the community property system in their state has enabled a 50–50 property ownership split.

The transfer of the entire estate to the surviving spouse, however, may not prevent in all situations the imposition of a federal estate tax when the first spouse dies. Some states impose various types of death taxes on property transferred to the surviving spouse. For federal estate tax purposes the amount of this state tax will be treated as passing to someone other than the surviving spouse. Consequently, this amount does not qualify for the estate tax marital deduction and, accordingly, some federal estate tax could be incurred.[203]

(2) Qualitative Restrictions

The types of property interest transfers that could qualify for the estate tax marital deduction have been gradually expanded over several decades. Property often is, but need not be, transferred outright to the surviving spouse at death. As an alternative property transfer approach, a life estate in property provided for the surviving spouse (which entitles that spouse to all of the income from the property payable at least annually), with a transfer of the remainder interest to other persons upon the death of the surviving spouse, does qualify for the marital deduction on an elective basis.[204] Consequently, the marital deduction remains available if a testator transfers only the current income stream from property to his or her surviving spouse without enabling that spouse to have the power to dispose of that property at his or her death.

Under this option, the transferred property, which is subject to the surviving spouse's income interest, is referred to as "qualified terminable interest property" (QTIP). Upon the death of the surviving spouse, the value of this property is included in that spouse's gross estate and is taxed at the marginal transfer tax bracket applicable to that spouse's estate.[205] If the surviving spouse disposes of all or a portion of the QTIP during his or her lifetime, at that time the spouse will be deemed to make a taxable gift not only of any qualifying income interest which the spouse has in that property but also of the remainder interest in that property.[206] The income tax basis of the QTIP qualifying property will be changed at the surviving spouse's death to the fair market value of the property at that time (because the property is exposed to estate tax inclusion at that time).[207]

(3) Summary of Available Property Transfer Options

The effect of this qualitative change (i.e., the QTIP gift option) in ERTA has provided an additional alternative for marital deduction planning and this option, in most instances, has subsequently become the preferred marital property transfer technique. An important benefit of the QTIP arrangement is that the marital deduction is available even though the surviving spouse is not provided control over the ultimate disposition of the transferred property (e.g., whether by outright ownership or with a general power of appointment). Instead, the first spouse to die may provide for the surviving spouse for life but may also control the ultimate disposition of the QTIP corpus after the death of the survivor spouse. This option is particularly useful in second marriage situations where the decedent (1) wants to benefit the second spouse during the survival period but (2) also has children from the first marriage he or she wants to ultimately share this property after the death of the surviving spouse.

Other available mechanisms for marital deduction eligible transfers include:

- an outright property transfer to the surviving spouse;
- a "life estate/power of appointment trust" (the mechanism often used prior to the QTIP provision enactment);
- a similar arrangement for life insurance proceeds held by the insurer; and
- an "estate trust."

The general requirements imposed by the Code and regulations on these various transfers between spouses for the purpose of qualifying for the marital deduction are discussed below.

d. Qualified Domestic Trust Alternative

Marital deduction transfers to non-U.S. citizen surviving spouses are restricted (under rules included in the Technical and Miscellaneous Revenue Act of 1988 [TAMRA]).[208] For the estates of U.S. citizens and U.S. residents, the estate tax marital deduction is not allowed for property passing to a non-U.S. citizen spouse unless the property is placed in a "qualified domestic trust" (QDT or QDOT).[209] This limitation applies even though the alien spouse is a U.S. resident because the spouse could thereafter relocate to a foreign jurisdiction and, thereby, remove moveable assets from U.S. estate tax jurisdiction. That spouse could also sell the U.S. real property (presumably for little taxable gain if the tax basis has just been stepped-up) and then remove the cash proceeds from the U.S. This limitation on the estate tax marital deduction does not apply if the surviving spouse (1) becomes a U.S. citizen before the date on which the estate tax return is made and (2) was a U.S. resident at all times after the decedent's death and before becoming a U.S. citizen.

3. Transfers Qualifying for Marital Deduction

a. Basic Qualification Requirements

Section 2056 permits an estate tax marital deduction equal to the value of property interests which:

- are included in the decedent's gross estate[210];
- actually "pass"[211];
- pass to a "surviving spouse"[212]; and
- are not terminable interests that are nondeductible.[213]

b. Outright vs. Trust Transfer

Marital deduction gifts may be completed by an outright property transfer directly to the surviving spouse. A marital deduction gift may also be made into a trust (or equivalent) for the benefit of the surviving spouse, but to enable the marital deduction the trust must satisfy the requirements of §2056(b)(5), §2056(b)(6), §2056(b)(7), §2056(b)(8), or §2056A, or be an "estate trust."[214]

c. Factors Affecting the Net Value of a Marital Deduction Bequest

(1) Encumbrances Reduce Available Marital Deduction

In determining the value of any interest in property passing to a spouse, the effect that the federal estate tax and any state and local estate, succession, legacy, or inheritance taxes may have on the net value of the interest passing to the spouse must be considered.[215] Where a property interest is encumbered, that encumbrance will reduce the net value of the property passing to the spouse.[216] Further, an executor may exercise certain tax elections which can affect the value of the property passing to the surviving spouse under a formula provision.[217]

(2) Tax Allocation Clause in First Spouse's Will

Burdening the marital deduction transfer with a liability for either federal estate tax or state estate, succession, or inheritance taxes may usually be avoided by the careful drafting of a tax allocation clause in the will or revocable trust agreement.[218] If no tax allocation provision is included in the will (or the revocable trust agreement), the burden of these taxes may fall on the nonmarital deduction assets by reason of tax allocation provisions included in a state probate code, but such a result should not regularly be anticipated.[219]

Unless charged against specific bequests to other than the surviving spouse, any estate tax burden should generally be specified as chargeable against the unified credit shelter portion of the estate that is exempt from estate tax. If the credit shelter portion is insufficient, the remaining taxes may be charged against properties disclaimed by the surviving spouse. If the will does not so direct and taxes are paid out of property qualifying for the marital deduction (or to the extent the credit shelter and disclaimed properties are insufficient, causing excess taxes to be paid out of such property), a portion of the marital deduction disposition fails to qualify and estate taxes are attributable to that portion. Because these estate taxes must be paid from the marital deduction portion, an additional amount of property fails to qualify for the deduction and more estate taxes must then be paid. The result of this circular phenomenon is sometimes referred to as the "tax-on-tax" problem.[220]

Where substantial property passes outside of the will or in a manner not qualifying for the marital (or charitable) deduction, but is includible in the gross estate, the specific apportionment of taxes may be essential, particularly to those assets not in the probate estate.[221] If those assets do not incur tax obligations and estate obligations are allocated to the marital property, the marital deduction will be reduced.

(3) Use of Administration Expenses as Income Tax Deductions

After the decedent's death (in the "post-mortem estate planning" context) an executor may elect to use administration expenses as deductions for federal income tax purposes rather than as estate tax deductions.[222] For example, where the estate is split between a residuary unlimited marital deduction bequest and a pre-residuary credit shelter gift, no further estate tax deductions are needed. Consequently, all administration expenses should be claimed as income tax deductions rather than as estate tax deductions.

These administration expenses are ordinarily payable out of the residuary estate and, to the extent that they are charged to principal, they would reduce the amount of the marital deduction passing to the surviving spouse (assuming the residuary estate to be for the marital deduction gift).[223] To avoid the resulting increase in the taxable estate, the administration expenses claimed as income tax deductions must be charged against the credit shelter portion.[224] The effect of this is to increase the value of the marital deduction by 100% of the expenses. Accordingly, the surviving spouse's estate is increased because of the larger marital deduction and, in addition, because of the income tax savings produced by the deduction. If the credit shelter can absorb all of these administration expenses, no federal tax will be payable.

The use of administration expenses as an income tax deduction ceases to be advantageous if the credit shelter portion of the estate is exhausted by transfers of property not qualifying for the marital deduction (so that a federal estate tax must then be paid).[225] If the only property available to pay the taxes is marital deduction property, the excess of the expenses over the credit shelter portion reduces the marital deduction disposition and causes a federal estate tax to be paid. The resulting tax itself generates further estate tax and the tax-on-tax problem arises.[226]

Following the uncertainty remaining after the Supreme Court's decision in *Commissioner v. Estate of Hubert*,[227] the IRS issued regulations eliminating the concept of materiality and, instead, established rules providing that only administration expenses of a certain character that are charged to the marital property will reduce the value of the property for estate tax marital and charitable deduction purposes. The regulations define estate transmission expenses and estate management expenses and provide that estate transmission expenses, but not estate management expenses, reduce the value of property for marital and charitable deduction purposes.[228]

(4) Impact of State Death Taxes

If a state does not allow an unlimited deduction or exemption for transfers to a surviving spouse, state death taxes in the estate of a married person using the unlimited marital deduction could have a significant impact. These state death taxes will operate to reduce the federal estate tax marital deduction, resulting in a federal taxable estate. If these taxes exceed the allowable credits (particularly the unified credit), federal estate taxes will be generated, which reduce the federal and state marital deductions further, resulting in the tax-on-tax problem.

d. The Terminable Interest Rule and Its Purpose

Property given outright to a surviving spouse will qualify for the estate tax marital deduction because, unless consumed during lifetime, that property will be included in the surviving spouse's estate at the time of death. Therefore, it will be exposed to estate tax at that time. A property interest passing to a surviving spouse under restrictive conditions that make it a "terminable interest" will not be deductible unless it satisfies one of the specific exceptions to the nondeductible terminable interest rule[229]:

- a limited survivorship requirement[230];
- a life estate-power of appointment trust[231];
- a right to the payment of income derived from life insurance or annuity proceeds held by an insurer, coupled with a general power of appointment in the surviving spouse for the disposition of those proceeds[232];
- a qualified income interest for life in the surviving spouse[233]; and
- a qualified charitable remainder trust where the surviving spouse is the sole noncharitable intermediate beneficiary.[234]

The mere identification of an interest as being "terminable" does not, therefore, cause that interest to be nondeductible for federal estate tax purposes. The fundamental objective of these specific exceptions to the terminable interest rule (except the limited survivorship exception) is to assure that, although not subject to possible estate tax when the first spouse dies, those assets remaining when the surviving spouse dies will be exposed to U.S. estate tax inclusion at that time.

e. Description of a Nondeductible "Terminable Interest"

Two inquiries are applicable in determining the status of a terminable interest as nondeductible: (1) is the interest a "terminable interest," and (2) is the interest a nondeductible terminable interest? A terminable interest in property is an interest that will terminate or fail on the passage of time or on the occurrence, or failure of the occurrence, of some contingency.[235] Examples of terminable interests include certain life estates, terms for years, annuities, patents and copyrights, and, in some instances, a widow's allowance.[236]

An interest that constitutes a terminable interest will be treated as nondeductible for federal estate tax purposes if (1) another interest in the same property passed from the decedent to some person other than the surviving spouse for less than an adequate and full consideration in money or money's worth, and (2) by reason of its passing, the other person or his or her heirs or assigns may possess or enjoy any part of the property after the termination or failure of the surviving spouse's interest.[237] This situation would exist, for example, where the transfer is "to wife for life, remainder to children." A life-income-only interest passing to a surviving spouse will not be treated as a nondeductible terminable interest, however, provided certain conditions are met.[238]

A terminable interest is also nondeductible for estate tax purposes if (1) the decedent directed his or her personal representative to acquire such an interest,[239] or (2) such an interest, which passes to the surviving spouse may be satisfied out of a group of assets that includes a nondeductible terminable interest.[240] Similarly, an interest passing to a surviving spouse under a joint and mutual will, as a terminable interest, does not qualify for the marital deduction.[241]

f. Limited Survivorship Period Exception

(1) Deduction Allowed Under Limited Survivorship Condition

A will may provide that the interest of a surviving spouse will be terminated if that surviving spouse does not survive the decedent for some specified, limited period. A terminable interest will not be disqualified from marital deduction eligibility even though it would be extinguished on the death of the surviving spouse if:

- the death of the surviving spouse will cause a termination of his or her interest only if it occurs (1) within a period not exceeding six months after the decedent's death, or (2) as a result of a common disaster; and
- such termination or failure does not in fact occur.[242]

In this situation the property will then be actually received by (or for) the surviving spouse.

Example: A decedent bequeathed his entire estate to his spouse on condition that she survive him by six months. In the event his wife fails to survive him by six months, his estate is distributable to his surviving descendants, per stirpes. The interest of the surviving spouse will terminate or fail only if she does die within six months following the date of the decedent's death. If she does not die before the expiration of this period, the marital deduction is allowable.[243]

The reason for this exception to the terminable interest rule is the frequently used survivorship clause designed to avoid the multiple administration of estates upon the death of an estate beneficiary occurring shortly after the death of the first decedent. Under such a clause, an heir dying within a short period (e.g., two months) after the testator's death would be considered as having predeceased the testator and, therefore, would not take under the bequest or devise as specified in the will of the first decedent.

In enacting the marital deduction, the continued use of this type of clause, which conditions the spouse's interest upon survival for a limited period, was permitted.[244]

(2) Uniform Simultaneous Death Provisions

The estate planner should give careful consideration to the use of the survivorship provision as specified in the will.[245] The locally enacted Uniform Simultaneous Death Act and a survivorship clause in a will (as described above) may achieve desirable results where the estates of both spouses are approximately the same size. Duplication of administrative costs and increased estate taxes in the estate of the survivor may be avoided. If, however, the decedent has substantial property and the surviving spouse has a nominal amount of property, the passage of a portion of eligible marital deduction property through two estates would probably produce an overall federal estate tax savings. This could occur even though the property would be subject to the expense of two probate administrations. This is, of course, the reason for the inclusion in many wills having marital deduction provisions of a specific presumption that the spouse having fewer assets will be deemed to have survived in a common disaster, notwithstanding the contrary presumption that would otherwise apply under the locally enacted Uniform Simultaneous Death Act.

If significant assets get shifted through this mechanism to the estate of the less wealthy spouse, an imbalance could then occur with this estate then being subject to a larger estate tax. To achieve an equalization of the estates, the simultaneous death presumption should only be partially reversed. This will necessitate the use of some formula causing the value of each estate to be balanced, thereby producing the same amount of estate tax as incurred by each estate.

g. Life Estate—Power of Appointment Trust

(1) Fundamental Requirements

An important exception to the nondeductible terminable interest rule is to permit the use of the life estate power of appointment trust under §2056(b)(5). Under this exception, an interest in property passing from a decedent to his or her surviving spouse qualifies for the estate tax marital deduction if such spouse (1) is entitled for life to all the income from such interest (or all the income from a specific portion of such interest) and (2) holds a general power to appoint the entire interest (or such specific portion).[246]

For such an interest to qualify for the marital deduction the following specific conditions must be satisfied[247]:

- The surviving spouse must be entitled for life to all of the income from the entire interest, or a specific portion of such entire interest, or to a specific portion of all the income from the entire interest.
- The income to which the surviving spouse is entitled must be payable annually or at more frequent intervals.[248]
- The surviving spouse must have the power to appoint the entire interest (or such specific portion) either to himself or herself or to his or her estate.

- The power of the surviving spouse to appoint such property must be exercisable by him or her alone and (whether exercisable by will or during life) in all events.[249]
- The entire interest (or the specific portion) must not be subject to a power in any other person to appoint any part to any person other than the surviving spouse.[250]

With these criteria satisfied, the interest vested in the surviving spouse will, for federal estate tax purposes, be deemed to be the essential equivalent of property ownership to the surviving spouse. With the spouse enjoying the equivalent of ownership of this property, no reason then exists for denying the marital deduction when the first spouse dies. The availability of a testamentary general power of appointment to the surviving spouse will cause the property subject to that power to be included in his or her gross estate at the time of his or her later death, thereby assuring that these assets will be exposed to possible estate tax at the spouses' generational level.[251]

(2) Right to Income

The requirement to provide an income interest to the surviving spouse will be satisfied "if the effect of the trust is to give [the surviving spouse] substantially that degree of beneficial enjoyment of the trust property during her life which the principles of the law of trusts accord to a person who is unqualifiedly designated as the life beneficiary of a trust."[252] Such degree of enjoyment is given only if the decedent's intention was, as manifested by the terms of the trust instrument and the surrounding circumstances, that the trust should produce for the surviving spouse during his or her life such an income, or that the spouse should have such use of the trust property as is consistent with the value of the trust corpus and with its preservation.[253]

The essential issue in this context is whether the overall effect of the trust is to give to the surviving spouse such enforceable rights as will preserve to him or her the requisite degree of current property enjoyment.[254] Consequently, trusts that indirectly accomplish an accumulation of income will not provide the spouse with the required beneficial enjoyment.[255] This might occur where "the corpus of a trust consists substantially of property which is not likely to be income producing during the life of the surviving spouse and . . . the spouse cannot compel the trustee to convert or otherwise deal with the property."[256] If the testator desires to transfer unproductive property into a marital deduction trust, the trust administration rules should require, or at least permit the surviving spouse to require, that the trustee either must make the property productive or convert it to income producing property within a reasonable period.[257] With the acquiescence of the surviving spouse, the nonproductive property could be held by the marital deduction trust without the loss of marital deduction eligibility.[258]

Administrative powers conferred upon the trustee may also have an impact on the estate tax qualification of the marital deduction trust. Provisions granting administrative powers to the trustee should not be treated as having the effect of disqualifying an interest passing in trust unless the grant of those powers evidences the intention to deprive the surviving spouse of the beneficial enjoyment required by the statute.[259]

(3) "Specific Portion"

A marital deduction will be available if a surviving spouse is entitled for life to all the income from (1) the entire interest or (2) a "specific portion" of trust property, payable at least annually, with a power in the surviving spouse to appoint (1) the entire interest or (2) "such specific portion."[260] A partial interest in property will be treated as a "specific portion" of the entire interest only if the portion is determined on a fractional or percentage basis.[261] The surviving spouse's interest or share must reflect the proportionate share of the increment or decline in the whole of the property interest to which the income rights and the power relate.[262] If the spouse's annual income is limited to a specific sum, or if the spouse has a power to appoint only a specific sum out of a larger fund, the interest is not a deductible interest.[263]

This restriction to a fractional or percentage interest on the availability of the marital deduction was initially held invalid by the Supreme Court in *Northeastern Pennsylvania National Bank & Trust Co. v. United States.*[264] The Court held that the spouse's stream of payments (which was stated in a specific dollar amount per month) could be capitalized by the use of assumed interest rates. This capitalized sum would constitute the "specific portion" qualifying for the marital deduction. Consequently, an income interest in property stated in terms of a specific sum (e.g., $300 per month) was determined to qualify for the marital deduction.[265] Regulations were formally amended in 1994 to reflect this decision, but only for arrangements subject to certain transitional rules.[266]

As noted above, in 1992 Congress enacted a rule that defines the term "specific portion" as including only a portion determined on a fractional or percentage basis.[267] The concern was that assets could escape inclusion in either estate because in the surviving spouse's estate the property might not share proportionally in the increase (or decrease) in the value of the entire property. In effect, Congress legislatively overruled both the *Alexander* and *Northeastern Pennsylvania Nat'l Bank & Trust Co.* decisions, effective for decedents dying after October 24, 1992 (the date of enactment).[268]

(4) Power of Appointment

To qualify for the marital deduction under §2056(b)(5), the surviving spouse must be vested with a qualifying power of appointment. To be a qualifying power of appointment, the power must be exercisable[269]:

- in his or her own favor at any time following the decedent's death (as, for example, an unlimited power to invade the trust during lifetime); or
- in favor of his or her estate.

The surviving spouse need not, however, have a general power of appointment exercisable both during his or her lifetime and at death.[270] A power of appointment is often constructed as a testamentary power only so as to preclude the surviving spouse from unadvisedly dissipating the assets during the period of survival (thereby seeking to preserve the assets for next generation survivors). In addition, this limitation on the power of appointment will avoid treatment (under the grantor trust income tax rules) of the spouse as the owner for income tax purposes of the capital gains realized on investments by the trust during the period of survival. If the surviving spouse were vested with an inter vivos general power of appointment, the spouse would be the owner of those capital gains for income tax purposes when realized by the trust.[271]

h. Life Insurance Payments

Another exception to the terminable interest rule is the use of certain life insurance settlement options selected by the decedent-insured.[272] Five requirements must be satisfied to enable eligibility for the marital deduction in this context[273]:

- The proceeds (or a specific portion of the proceeds) must be held by the insurer subject to an agreement either to pay the entire proceeds (or a specific portion thereof) in installments, or to pay interest thereon only to the surviving spouse.[274]
- The installments or interest payable to the surviving spouse must be payable annually, or more frequently, commencing not later than 13 months after the decedent's death.[275]
- The surviving spouse must have the power to appoint all (or a specific portion) of the amounts so held by the insurer to either himself or herself or his or her estate.[276]
- This power in the surviving spouse must be exercisable by him or her alone and (whether exercisable by will or during life) must be exercisable in all events.
- The amounts (or the specific portion of the amounts) payable under such contract must not be subject to a power in any other person to appoint any part thereof to any person other than the surviving spouse.

These five requirements are essentially similar in purpose and in structure to the requirements described above for the life estate–power of appointment exception to the terminable interest rule.[277]

i. Qualified Terminable Interest Property (QTIP)

(1) Basic Requirements

If a client desires a trust to implement a marital deduction transfer, rather than an outright marital deduction transfer to a surviving spouse, the usual practice is to use a QTIP trust, rather than the other alternatives described above. If certain conditions are met, a surviving spouse's income interest in QTIP is treated (although terminable) as a deductible interest for purposes of the estate tax marital deduction. The entire property subject to the income interest is treated as passing to the spouse, and no interest in the property is considered to pass to any person other than the spouse, thereby precluding possible treatment as a nondeductible terminable interest.[278]

QTIP is property that passes from the donor or decedent (1) in which the spouse receives a qualifying income interest for life[279] and (2) for which an irrevocable election is made to treat the property as QTIP property.[280] Therefore, a qualifying income interest must meet the following conditions:

- The property must "pass" from the decedent to the surviving spouse.[281]
- The surviving spouse must be entitled to all of the income from the entire property interest (or a specific portion thereof) payable at least annually for life.[282]
- No power must be held by any person (including the surviving spouse) to appoint any part of the property to any person other than the surviving spouse during that spouse's life.[283]
- The executor must irrevocably elect that the interest be treated as qualified terminable interest property (and, therefore, be deductible, but also, as a result of this election, be includible in the surviving spouse's estate).[284]

(2) Right to Income

For QTIP eligibility, the interest passing from a decedent must entitle the surviving spouse, for a period measured solely by the spouse's life, to all of the income from the entire property,[285] or all of the income from a specific portion thereof, payable at least annually.[286]

A QTIP trust is governed by the same rules and regulations that are applicable in a life estate–power of appointment trust for the required quality of the income interest for the benefit of the spouse.[287] For example, either the trust must contain income-producing property or the surviving spouse must have the power to make the trust property productive.[288] A QTIP trust is not disqualified merely because, upon its termination, "stub period" income is not paid to the estate of the surviving spouse.[289]

Qualifying income interests are not limited to those placed in trust. For example, the right to occupy a residence for life might satisfy this requirement. Whatever the form, the income interest must provide the spouse with a degree of beneficial enjoyment sufficient to satisfy the marital deduction trust rules.[290]

(3) Power to Appoint or Distribute to Spouse Alone

No person can have the power to appoint or distribute property to any person other than the surviving spouse during that spouse's life, including through a limited lifetime power of appointment in the spouse.[291] Further, no invasions of principal may be made by the trustee (or any other person) for anyone other than the spouse.[292] Thus, the surviving spouse cannot make direct lifetime gifts out of the QTIP trust. The spouse may be granted a right of withdrawal from the trusts to enable gifts to be made, but the possibility of the spouse making gifts from this withdrawn property should not be referenced in the instrument. The right would be transformed into a life estate–power of appointment trust and the election opportunity possessed by the executor would be foreclosed. A "five-and-five power" could be provided, but even a limited withdrawal right will foreclose the election option to the extent of that right. The spouse may be granted a special power of appointment over all or a portion of the corpus exercisable only at or after the spouse's death.[293]

(4) Election for QTIP Qualification

The executor must specifically elect on the estate tax return for the QTIP marital deduction to be available.[294] This election, once made, is irrevocable.[295]

Ordinarily, the decedent's will should instruct the executor to make (or not make) the election. Although not required, these instructions can be useful in situations where a substantial conflict would exist among the potential beneficiaries. Making the election is a difficult responsibility for an executor because it involves making choices that may affect both the income received by the surviving spouse and the property ultimately passing to the remainder beneficiaries. The executor should be given explicit guidance in the will and, thereby, be exculpated from liability when making the election.

An absolute limitation should not be placed, however, on the executor concerning this election because the QTIP election permits considerable flexibility in post-mortem planning. If the executor is directed to make the election in a situation where the surviving spouse dies shortly after the first spouse and the equalization of the several estates (rather than estate tax deferral) is then desirable, the executor having the requisite discretion may use the QTIP election to equalize the spouses' estates and to lower the overall estate tax burden on the two estates. In addition, where the advantage of equalization is foreseeable, a will should contain a simultaneous death provision for presumption of survivorship by one spouse to allow the executor discretion to use the election to gain the maximum estate tax benefit.

Previously, a provision in the will directing that (1) if a QTIP election is made, all of the income from the residuary estate must be payable to the surviving spouse, but (2) if an election is not made income may be sprinkled between the spouse and the testator's descendants at the trustee's discretion, could produce a challenge by the IRS concerning the qualification of the entire marital deduction bequest. The assertion was made by the IRS that the income interest in the entire fund did not vest in the surviving spouse as of the date of the decedent's death because of the executor's right to shift income away from the spouse by not exercising the QTIP election. Although this issue now seems resolved,[296] an alternative approach can also be used in this context. The transfer of non-QTIP property to a trust can be solved by enabling the surviving spouse to disclaim a portion of the property, if desirable. The taker in default would be specified as the nonmarital trust.[297] Of course, the surviving spouse may not want to make such a disclaimer and the advisor must be careful about exercising undue influence in encouraging such a disclaimer.

Comment: Great care should be taken to ensure that the QTIP election is made correctly because of both the potential estate tax consequences and the possible liability to the fiduciary for inappropriate advice. The instrument should contain a detailed clause stating that (1) the personal representative is under no liability for making (or forgoing) any QTIP election, and (2) no compensating adjustments or reimbursements shall be made with respect to the economic consequences of any election.

Relief might be obtained for a surviving spouse and his or her estate if the deceased spouse's estate made a QTIP election that was not necessary to reduce the estate tax liability to zero, based on values as finally determined for federal estate tax purposes.[298] According to the IRS, a QTIP election falls into this category (1) if the deceased spouse's taxable estate was less than the §2010(c) applicable credit exclusion amount before application of the marital deduction or (2) if the deceased spouse's estate made a QTIP election for a credit shelter trust.[299] To establish that a QTIP election is within the scope of the procedure, the taxpayer must produce sufficient evidence to that effect, such as a copy of the deceased spouse's estate tax return showing that the QTIP election was not necessary to reduce the estate taxes to zero. The taxpayer should submit this evidence, together with an explanation of why the QTIP election should be treated as void, with the surviving spouse's estate tax return or with a private letter ruling request submitted at any time prior to filing that estate tax return.[300] If the QTIP election is within the scope of the procedure, the IRS will disregard the election and treat it as null and void for purposes of §2044(a), §2056(b)(7), §2519(a), and §2652.

Not all QTIP elections will qualify for relief. For example, a partial QTIP election made for more trust property than was necessary to reduce the estate tax to zero will not qualify.[301] Further, relief is not available for a QTIP election stated in a formula designed to reduce the estate tax to zero.

(5) Qualification of Specific Portion

The QTIP qualification election may be made by the executor for "any property."[302] The term "property" includes an "interest in property."[303] A specific portion of "property" is treated as separate property for this purpose.[304] This treatment will enable a formula approach for determining the precise amount of the marital deduction transfer. The concept of "specific portion" has previously been disputed, as earlier noted.[305] The Code defines a "specific portion" as a fractional or percentile share.[306]

(6) Marital Deduction Amount Contingent on Executor's Election

The will may provide that property is devised to a QTIP trust but may further specify that, if or to the extent that the executor does not make a QTIP election, the property shall be added to another trust not eligible for the marital deduction (e.g., the credit shelter trust). After a change in its position the IRS permits marital deduction eligibility when the executor elects only a portion of the estate for which to claim the marital deduction.[307] This necessitates that the trust that is the receptacle for the non-QTIP property must be carefully structured to assure not only future inclusion in the estate of the surviving spouse but also that appropriate income and corpus disposition provisions are included in this trust.

(7) Disclaimer

As an alternative to a QTIP election by the executor, or as an additional post-death mechanism to adjust the balance between the probable taxable estates of two spouses, a surviving spouse may be given the right to disclaim all or a portion of the trust assets for which the QTIP election would otherwise apply.[308] This disclaimed property could be deflected into a trust which is structured to not otherwise qualify for the estate tax marital deduction and for which the QTIP election is not made (even if eligible). Consequently, the specific structure of that disclaimer trust may be (and often should be) different from the QTIP trust. This disclaimer trust may contain dispositive provisions such as sprinkling powers and remainder beneficiaries who differ from those individuals who take on termination of the QTIP trust. The trust receiving the disclaimed property should not specify that the surviving spouse holds a special power of appointment because the IRS states that such a power in the disclaimant to direct the disposition of disclaimed property is not permissible.[309] Furthermore, the disclaiming spouse should not be sole trustee of a trust into which the disclaimed property passes if the trust has sprinkling provisions.[310]

The surviving spouse holds only a life income interest in the QTIP and uncertainty exists whether, by disclaiming that interest, the spouse may also transfer the corpus relating to the disclaimed income interest. This problem is addressed in several ways: (1) the ultimate beneficiaries of the QTIP and the disclaimer trust should be the same (the remainder beneficiaries are not thereby being divested of any property); and (2) the disclaimer provision in the will may provide that the disclaimer is being made under the will, if state law so allows, and may further provide that the disclaimer of the income interest will include the principal relating to that interest and that such principal will pass to the bypass trust.

Ultimately, this arrangement may fail because the surviving spouse refuses to disclaim her interest even though the disclaimer makes much tax planning sense. The anticipation is that the surviving spouse, with the advice of the deceased's attorney, will make the appropriate disclaimer after death to maximize the marital deduction (and other) planning at that time. However, the surviving spouse may have found replacement counsel that advises retention of the greater property interest permitted through the QTIP provisions. Further, litigation in this context demonstrates that disclaimers can go awry under many circumstances. Consequently, careful structuring (and advice) is essential in this context.

(8) Subsequent Transfer Tax Treatment to Surviving Spouse

(a) Gift Tax on Disposition of the Qualifying Income Interest Ordinarily, the QTIP marital deduction property will be included in the estate of the second spouse to die. The spouse may earlier terminate his or her interest in that property during his or her lifetime. Because it was not subject to a transfer tax (i.e., federal estate tax) at the death of the first spouse to die, the entire value of property subject to a qualified terminable interest election will be subject to transfer tax if, during his or her life, the surviving spouse disposes (either by gift, sale, or otherwise, except consumption) of all or any part of the qualifying income interest.[311] The lifetime disposition of the QTIP interest is treated as a transfer of all the property subject to the QTIP election.[312]

The gift transfer will consist of two elements: (1) the entire value of the remainder interest in the qualified terminable interest property (or a specific portion thereof) and (2) the income interest.[313] The gift of all or any of the income interest would qualify for the gift tax annual donee exclusion.[314] The gift of the remainder interest would qualify for the annual donee exclusion only to the extent that the qualifying income interest is transferred to the remainder beneficiaries (because the remainder interest itself would otherwise be a future interest). Further, even if treated as subject to gift tax, no actual gift tax liability might be incurred if the total gift value is within the unified credit amount.

If, as a result of the donee spouse's lifetime disposition of all or any part of the qualifying income interest, the transfer of the qualified terminable interest property does cause a gift tax liability, the donee spouse does have a right to recover the gift taxes (including penalties or interest paid) from the person or persons receiving the gift property.[315] The gift tax amount paid from the property will reduce the amount of the gift. This right of recovery from the property for the tax amount is only for the federal gift tax attributable to the value of the remainder interest.[316] If the donee spouse waives the right to recover the gift taxes, the amount of these gift taxes will be treated as a further taxable gift transfer.[317] This transfer is deemed final when the right to recovery is no longer enforceable under applicable law and is treated as a gift even if recovery is impossible.[318] A delay in the exercise of the right of this recovery without the payment of sufficient interest for this delay is a below-market loan.[319]

Planners should determine whether lifetime transfers of qualified terminable interest property are appropriate. This would include considering whether a spendthrift clause in the trust instrument should be made applicable to the income interest in the QTIP trust so as to preclude the surviving spouse from completing a lifetime transfer of that interest. Of course, the spouse could continue periodically to receive the regular QTIP trust income distributions and to make gifts of the net proceeds, but the timing of these transfers would be delayed until the receipt of the income.

(b) Transfers at Death of Surviving Spouse If the property subject to the qualifying income interest is not deemed to be transferred (in a gift tax context) prior to the death of the surviving spouse, the value of the QTIP property subject to the qualifying income interest will be included in that spouse's gross estate.[320] Qualified terminable interest property included in the spouse's gross estate is treated as "passing" from the spouse. Thus, for example, this property is to be treated as passing from the spouse for purposes of determining (1) the remainder beneficiary's income tax basis for the property under §1014 (providing for a stepped-up [or stepped-down] tax basis at date of death),[321] (2) the availability of the current use valuation under §2032A, (3) the availability of the charitable deduction under §2055, (4) the availability of the marital deduction under §2056, and (5) eligibility for the installment payment of the estate taxes attributable to interests in closely held businesses available under §6166.[322]

Unless he or she directs otherwise by will,[323] the surviving spouse's estate is granted a right to recover the estate tax paid (including penalties or interest paid) as a result of including the qualified terminable interest property in the spouse's estate.[324] This tax is recoverable from the person or persons receiving such property.[325]

The decedent donor of qualified terminable interest property may direct in his or her will (or the relevant trust agreement) that the taxes (including state death taxes) attributable to the QTIP will be paid from that property before distribution to the remainder beneficiary.[326] This power should not violate the limitation on the availability of a power of appointment[327] because the power is exercisable only at or after the death of the surviving spouse and such a power is permitted.[328]

(9) Summary of QTIP Trust Planning Considerations

(a) Estate Tax Deferral The QTIP trust is useful where the objectives are (1) to provide benefits to the surviving spouse, (2) to enable the first spouse's estate the benefit of the marital deduction, and (3) to limit the surviving spouse's power to subsequently dispose of this property previously transferred by the first, deceased spouse for the benefit of the surviving spouse. This type of trust may also be used to defer the decision to claim the maximum marital deduction. The executor may be authorized (in filing the federal estate tax return) to make (in whole or in part) an election to claim the deduction for QTIP trust property. Thus, if the surviving spouse dies prior to the filing of the federal estate tax return for the first spouse's estate, the executor of the first spouse's estate presumably would not elect to take the maximum marital deduction but would attempt to equalize the two estates by making only a partial election, if financially appropriate.[329]

(b) Mandatory Income Distribution Requirement Similar to the life estate–power of appointment trust, the QTIP trust must hold income-producing property or the surviving spouse must have the power to require that the property be made income producing. All of the trust's income must be paid to the surviving spouse and cannot be sprinkled to other beneficiaries to take advantage of their lower income tax brackets.[330] As income tax marginal tax brackets declined, this concern about income subject to the highest marginal income tax rate might be lessened, and might be further reduced if much of the income received consists of corporate dividends which is subject to a maximum 20% income tax rate.[331] These funds will be accumulated by the surviving spouse (unless consumed or transferred by gift) and subsequently included in his or her estate for federal estate tax purposes.

(c) Limitation on Inter Vivos Gifts The surviving spouse has no ability to make gifts to family members directly from the QTIP trust except by transferring all or a portion of his or her life income interest to those family members.[332] The spouse may receive distributions of principal upon the exercise of discretion by the trustee, and the spouse may then transfer that property to another person. This arrangement will not result in a disqualification of QTIP status unless the surviving spouse is legally bound to transfer the distributed property to another person without full and adequate consideration in money or money's worth.[333]

(d) Possible Impact of Any State Death Tax QTIP property may not qualify for the marital deduction when a state death tax liability arises. For state tax purposes qualified terminable interest property may not qualify for the marital deduction. However, that portion of the testator's estate necessary to qualify for the maximum allowable state death tax marital deduction might be transferred in another form which does qualify for the deduction. If not, a state tax liability would be generated that could reduce the marital gift deductible for federal estate tax purposes (unless under the tax allocation provision in the will this tax liability must be allocated to other property transfers).

j. Charitable Remainder Trusts

(1) The Qualified Charitable Remainder Trust

Another alternative structure for a marital deduction trust is to provide for (1) income to the surviving spouse for life and (2) the remainder to charity as of the death of that surviving spouse. A married couple may prefer to implement this option when they will have no surviving descendants (and have limited interest in providing testamentary transfers to their collateral relatives). Some married couples may wish to use this as an option when they have significant wealth and believe their descendants will be adequately provided for under other transfers made either (1) under the will or (2) from various other sources. The interest transferred to the surviving spouse will be treated as a deductible terminable interest for marital deduction purposes where the surviving spouse is the only noncharitable beneficiary of a qualified charitable remainder trust.[334] For these purposes, the term "qualified charitable remainder trust" means either a charitable remainder annuity trust (CRAT) or a charitable remainder unitrust (CRUT).[335]

The use of this type of trust would enable the property held in trust to be transferred to the ultimate charitable recipient without any federal transfer tax being imposed at any stage. At the time of the death of the first spouse, the marital deduction is available for the income interest transferred to the surviving spouse. The estate tax charitable deduction is available for the gift of the remainder interest because, at the death of the second spouse, the entire property is to be transferred to charity.

(2) Alternative Charitable Transfer Structure

Even though the trust is not structured in the form of a "qualified" charitable remainder annuity trust or a charitable remainder unitrust, federal estate tax may be entirely avoided upon the deaths of both spouses if the fundamental asset disposition structure upon the death of the first spouse is to (1) the surviving spouse for life and (2) remainder to charity. The will could provide for a qualified terminable interest property (QTIP) trust for the benefit of the surviving spouse, with a charitable remainder.[336] In creating this trust, the donor must give the spouse the right to all of the income for the spouse's life. This is unlike the CRAT or CRUT structure where the income interest in the trust must be specified in terms of a percentage. In this alternative QTIP situation the trustee may even be given the power to invade the principal of the trust for the benefit of the spouse (but not for others), consistent with the QTIP trust requirements. On the subsequent death of the surviving spouse, the trust property will pass to the charitable remainder designee as originally identified by the donor spouse. The surviving spouse may be given the right to change the designation of charitable beneficiaries. The power to invade the trust assets for the benefit of the spouse does eliminate the availability of the charitable deduction at the death of the first spouse, but the entire transfer will be protected at that time under the marital deduction (assuming a QTIP election and further assuming eligibility for this election). Although the property would be subsequently included in the estate of the surviving spouse, a charitable deduction would be available at that time equivalent to the value of the assets then transferred to charity pursuant to the directions in the will of the first spouse to die.[337]

k. Estate Trusts

The marital deduction trusts described above require that the current trust income be distributed at least annually to the surviving spouse. The surviving spouse may not need this income. Additionally, the surviving spouse may not have the capability (or the first spouse may so believe) of managing that income and the first spouse's desire may be to avoid forcing this responsibility upon the surviving spouse. Under these circumstances, an "estate trust" might be considered. This type of trust may also be useful where the client wishes to retain unproductive or underproductive property in trust form, but does not wish to include a QTIP required trust provision that the surviving spouse can demand that the property be remarshalled to produce current income.

Pursuant to the "estate trust" arrangement, the income may be accumulated within the trust during the surviving spouse's lifetime.[338] At the death of the surviving spouse the accumulated income and the principal is to be distributed to the spouse's probate estate (as identified for local law purposes). This trust does not violate the nondeductible terminable interest rule because all the trust property will ultimately be included as part of the probate estate of the surviving spouse.[339] Probate costs will be incurred because this property must pass through the spouse's probate estate. The magnitude of those costs will be determined under local law and practice. The ultimate distribution of the property received by the surviving spouse's estate will be governed by the surviving spouse's last will and could, therefore, be transferred to beneficiaries not anticipated by the first spouse to die. Further, the surviving spouse may have accumulated significant debts and these assets would be subject to the claims of the creditors to his or her probate estate.

For federal income tax purposes this distribution will occur without subchapter J throwback income tax consequences.[340] Accumulation at the trust level is often inefficient for income tax purposes, however, because trusts are taxed at the maximum rate of 39.6% at significantly lower levels of income.[341] Consequently, the accumulation at the trust level may produce a much higher federal income tax cost. Considering this situation, the risk exists that the fiduciary might be challenged for incurring excessive income tax costs, unless the trust document precisely specifies that all income should be mandatorily accumulated, or the trustee is otherwise exculpated in the governing instrument. Therefore, under these circumstances, the better option might be to require the current distribution of income but its transfer into a separate account where, although available to the spouse (so as to enable the estate tax marital deduction), the probabilities are substantial that those funds will remain in the receptacle investment account, subject to professional management. Further, the high tax bracket problem could be reduced through a long-term appreciation investment strategy, that is, by trust investments in low-dividend-yield, high-growth potential stocks.

4. Determining the Precise Amount of the Marital Deduction Transfer

a. Objective of Determining the Marital Deduction Amount

An important objective of comprehensive estate tax marital deduction planning is to maximize the total after-tax amount of property ultimately transferred by both the decedent and his or her surviving spouse (upon the spouse's death) to the next generation(s). The question arises, therefore, as to the extent to which the unlimited marital deduction should actually be used by the first spouse to die, particularly after considering the maximum use of the then available unified credit equivalent amounts.

The marital deduction need not be claimed to its available maximum extent when the first spouse dies. A testator has the prerogative to select some specific amount (including property transferred in kind) to be transferred to the surviving spouse, which is less than the total that would qualify for the unlimited marital deduction. The objective, therefore, is to determine that maximum amount to protect with the estate tax marital deduction while achieving the overall testamentary transfer objectives of the two spouses.

b. Basic Marital Deduction Transfer Mechanics

(1) Available Choices

Whether outright or in trust, a marital-deduction-eligible transfer of property to or for the benefit of the surviving spouse may be accomplished through a variety of arrangements. For example, the property conveyance may be accomplished as (1) a gift of specific property, (2) a transfer of money (i.e., a pecuniary amount), or (3) a transfer of a fractional share of a designated fund or specific assets. The amount of the pecuniary gift or the fractional share can be determined with or without a formula approach.

Many marital deduction gifts are identified without any "formula provision." As discussed in this segment, the use of a formula provision has as its objective the identification of a precise marital deduction amount, or credit shelter amount, as of the date of death, therefore accounting for changes in asset values after the time of the original estate planning (and implementation of wills and trusts). Nonformulary approaches might include, for example, the outright transfer of the personal residence, a vacation home, an automobile, and various personal items (without regard to their impact on other transfers to the surviving spouse).

(2) Specific Bequests or Legacy

A marital deduction transfer may be completed by a bequest or devise of specific properties.[342] Examples of such specific bequests and devises are as follows[343]:

> *Example (1):* "I give my 1,000 shares of X Company stock to my wife Y."
> *Example (2):* "I give the 1,000 acres of real estate, which I own in X County, Texas, to the Y Trust Company, as trustee under a trust agreement dated January 1, 2015, for the benefit of my wife, Z."

This type of gift is implemented by the specific identification of the property and without regard to its fair market value at the time of death and without regard to the portion of the total estate represented by this property. The estate planner should ascertain the client's intent concerning these types of gifts if, for example, (1) the property is no longer owned at death, (2) the property was transferred to the designated beneficiary (or to another person) during lifetime, or (3) if the property is changed (e.g., a stock dividend has increased the shares in the example above from 1,000 to 2,000).[344]

(3) Nonformula Pecuniary Bequest

A marital deduction bequest may be made through the transfer of a specific sum of money, that is, a pecuniary bequest.[345]

Example: "I give $500,000 to my wife."

A bequest to a surviving spouse of a specific dollar amount will not ordinarily enable a marital deduction that is precisely equivalent in amount to the marital deduction necessary after the complete use of the unified credit to enable reduction of the estate tax liability to zero. The amount of this bequest may be less than or greater than the amount necessary to maximize the marital deduction amount and will be specified without regard to the availability of the unified credit.

(4) Nonformula Fractional Share Bequest

A transfer to the surviving spouse may be made of a fractional (or percentage) interest in the residuary estate.[346]

Example: "I give three-fifths of my residuary estate, outright, to my wife."

Similar to the provision immediately above, a fractional bequest does not implement a formula approach for the maximum use of the marital deduction. This approach does not take into account (1) the possible availability and amount of the unified credit and (2) the portion of the entire estate represented by this portion of the residuary estate.

c. Formula Clauses for Implementing the Marital Deduction Gift

The estate planner may desire that the estate tax marital deduction, when combined with (1) the unified credit amount (or equivalent applicable exclusion amount) and (2) deductible gifts such as charitable transfers, be used but only in that amount that will reduce to zero the federal estate tax liability for the estate of the first deceased spouse. This may be accomplished through the use of a marital deduction formula clause having this precise objective. The entire estate could be transferred to the surviving spouse (i.e., without the use of a formula to determine the optimum amount) but, in many situations, this will not be estate-tax efficient (as discussed below) because, subsequently, when the surviving spouse dies, gross estate inclusion will occur for those assets although they could have been protected by a credit shelter or "bypass" trust at the death of the first spouse.

Two basic marital deduction formula approaches are available to determine this optimum marital deduction gift amount. The first, a pecuniary formula clause, identifies a marital gift of a precise amount of money, that is, a pecuniary amount to be determined through the applicability of a directive to satisfy this objective. The second, a fractional share formula provision, specifies a marital deduction gift of a portion of the decedent's assets, also as determined under a formula approach. Under this latter alternative, a fractional (or specific percentage) share of the assets in the decedent's residuary estate is bequeathed to the surviving spouse (or to a marital deduction trust). This fraction is stated as having (1) a numerator that is the maximum allowable marital deduction (as reduced by the value of other qualifying marital deduction transfers) and (2) a denominator that is the residuary estate.[347]

d. Maximizing the Marital Deduction Portion

The structure of an arrangement under the will may be to assure the maximum (but no greater than necessary) use of the estate tax marital deduction, thereby deferring the entire estate tax liability until the time of the death of the surviving spouse. Often, this is accomplished by transferring by a nonresiduary bequest (1) an amount equal in value to the maximum marital deduction allowable for federal estate tax purposes that will reduce the estate tax to zero, less (2) the value, for federal estate tax purposes, of all items in the gross estate that qualify for the marital deduction and pass or have passed to the spouse (or into a marital deduction trust) in a form qualifying for the marital deduction otherwise than under this specific transfer provision. Examples of these other transfers would be the outright transfer of the personal residence, household furnishings, and other tangible personal property. The residuary gift then would be made for the credit shelter trust portion.

Alternatively, this type of formula approach could be used to determine the maximum eligible credit shelter transfer amount, rather than the maximum marital deduction amount. The remaining estate would then be distributable to the surviving spouse (or into a marital deduction trust such as a QTIP trust) in a manner qualifying for the estate tax marital deduction.

Income tax considerations often will be important in determining whether the residuary gift should be (1) the marital deduction transfer or (2) the credit shelter transfer. If a pecuniary formula is used for determining that amount to fund the preresiduary gift, gain recognition will occur upon funding that gift.

e. Equalization of the Marital Estates vs. Deferral of Estate Tax

Rather than transferring that amount to the surviving spouse (or a marital deduction trust) that is necessary to "zero out" the tax on the estate of the first to die, the parties may desire that the total estate tax be reduced to the minimum amount applicable in transferring all of the spousal assets to the next generation. In this situation the preferred use of the marital deduction for estate tax purposes may be accomplished when the taxable estates of the two spouses are equalized. This may be accomplished by the transfer to the surviving spouse of only enough marital deduction property to assure that, after taking into account the property already held by the surviving spouse, the taxable estates of both spouses would be essentially equal. This does assume federal estate taxation on both estates at essentially the same time, that is, that both spouses die within a short period.

Both spouses rarely die essentially simultaneously, however.[348] Obviously, precise equilibrium cannot occur because values will change after the first spouse's death. Further, subsequent estate tax legislation may change the exemption amount or the estate tax rate structure. Additionally, taxpayers generally do not prefer to accelerate the payment of taxes, waiting until the liability cannot be avoided. Further, this type of planning has become less prevalent as a result of portability under §2010(c), which enables surviving spouses to utilize the Deceased Spousal Unused Exemption Amount. However, it still will be prudent to analyze the assets of a couple to determine whether any shifting of ownership should occur for the optimal use of each spouse's estate and gift tax credit.

A net financial advantage might be obtained by reason of estate tax deferral through the greater use of the marital deduction in the estate of the first spouse to die. The benefit of any estate tax deferral results from the investment of that amount that would otherwise have been paid in federal estate taxes by the estate of the first spouse to die during the survival period. The offsetting cost would be the increased estate taxes upon the later death of the surviving spouse. This additional cost will be attributable to the stacking of additional assets in that spouse's estate and the higher marginal estate tax rate that might then be applicable. As a general rule, the use of a larger marital deduction upon the death of the first spouse to die will be advantageous unless the surviving spouse is terminally ill. Ultimately, however, a careful analysis must be made with respect to (1) the anticipated survival period for the surviving spouse, (2) the potential appreciation and income stream of the property owned during the estate tax deferral period,[349] (3) whether the surviving spouse might expend his or her assets (held outside a trust) during that period (including through inter vivos gifts), and (4) possible estate tax legislative changes.

This analysis of estate tax legislative changes should include specific consideration of the impact of recent estate tax modifications. For example, the 2010 TRA[350] has included the: (1) elimination of the EGTRRA repeals; (2) reinstatement of the estate tax for estates of decedents dying after 2009 (but allowing estates of decedents dying in 2010 to elect instead to apply the §1022 modified carryover basis regime); and (3) provision of favorable transfer tax rates and exemption amounts for 2010–2012 (including the portability of the exemption amounts for spouses in 2011–2012).[351] In January 2013, ATRA[352] generally made permanent the EGTRRA and 2010 TRA changes, including favorable exemption amounts and portability. When ATRA passed, estate planners believed that after a decade of uncertainty, estate planning had gained some level of certainty. However, before the ink was dry on ATRA, President Obama introduced a budget which would have modified many of the favorable provisions that were made permanent by ATRA.[353] Caution mandates that planning arrangements implemented for the optimum use of the marital deduction must address the uncertainty as to what rules will apply at an estate planning client's death.

If the marital deduction amount is maximized (so as to enable a zero-out of the estate tax liability), the surviving spouse will receive increased income through the investment of assets otherwise used to pay estate taxes on the death of the first spouse. If the deferral period is of sufficient length and the rate of investment return is sufficient, the surviving spouse (or the marital deduction trust) may be able to invest the tax-deferred funds to enable rapid accumulation of funds to more than offset the amount of additional estate taxes to be incurred in the surviving spouse's estate (even further assuming that any increased unified credit applicable exclusion is insufficient). This result could occur during an era of significantly increasing values of the property held by the marital deduction trust (or directly by the spouse). Further, in the situation of illiquid property, through the maximized use of the marital deduction the liquidity problems may be deferred until the death of the surviving spouse because tax funds need not be generated upon the death of the first spouse.

In summary, the estate and gift tax rate structure itself does encourage the use of estate tax deferral opportunities. For example, only a limited estate tax rate differential might exist if the maximum estate tax rate for a decedent dying in 2018 is 45% (after considering the availability of a $3.5 million exemption equivalent).[354] Although only a limited tax rate differential might exist,[355] many couples will be inclined to defer estate taxes. Further, even though the unlimited marital deduction tends to produce the addition of assets to the estate of the surviving spouse, the annual donee gift tax exclusion does afford an opportunity to make subsequent gifts to enable the substantial reduction of the amount subject to federal estate taxation in the surviving spouse's estate. Through the aggressive use of annual donee exclusion transfers, the impact of that stacking may be reduced considerably. Consequently, estate planners must carefully weigh the advantages of achieving the lowest overall estate tax cost against the benefits of the time value of money that is obtained when the maximum marital deduction is used.

f. Dividing Property Between the Credit Shelter and Marital Deduction Dispositions

(1) Alternative Situations

Different marital deduction and credit shelter utilization planning approaches should be considered, dependent upon whether the total assets held by the marital unit are (or are anticipated to be at the death of the surviving spouse):

- less than the amount to be exempted by the estate tax unified credit for the estate of one spouse;
- in excess of the amount exempted by the unified credit for the estate of one spouse but less than the amount of the total unified credits for the estates of both spouses; or
- in excess of the amount exempted by the total unified credits for the estates of both spouses.

The amount exempted by the §2010(c) unified credit may vary depending on the year of the decedent's death, thereby making this type of planning more problematic.[356]

Asset values may significantly change after the death of one spouse and before the death of the surviving spouse. Consequently, the estate planner should anticipate that these planning strategies for the marital unit may need periodic modification.[357] The estate planner should construct documents which contemplate many variables, such as increasing unified credit amounts. These multiple options often cannot adequately contemplate many changes that will actually occur, however. Consequently, the challenge to the estate planner often will be to adequately explain to the client the necessity for (1) this regular reevaluation of the client's estate planning arrangements so as to respond to both changes in asset values and the increasing unified credit amounts, and (2) flexibility in the documents to enable favorable elections and other adjustments after death.

The discussion in the remainder of this section (D.4.f.) and in the next section (D.4.g.) does not reflect the impact of the 2010 TRA's amendment to §2010(c) to provide for the portability of the unified credit amount for spouses dying in or after 2010 (i.e., the availability of the unified credit unused by the estate of the first spouse to die to the estate of the surviving spouse). While ATRA made the portability provision permanent, there are many nontax reasons why spouses may need to consider the relative value of each spouse's estate for planning purposes.

(2) Both Estates Less Than One Spouse's Unified Credit Exemption Equivalent

Where the combined value of the estates of both spouses is less than one estate tax unified credit/exemption equivalent amount, for federal estate tax planning purposes each spouse may leave all of his or her property to the survivor with the assurance that no federal estate tax will result from the ultimate disposition by the survivor of all family assets. In this instance the estate planner will be primarily concerned with nontax property transmission factors, such as the ability of the surviving spouse to handle investments, adequate income and corpus for the spouse during the survival period, and the needs of other beneficiaries.[358]

The first spouse to die may prefer to leave property in trust for the benefit of the survivor spouse so that adequate asset management is assured. Under these circumstances, the trust might be structured without regard to the requirements for qualification for the estate tax marital deduction. The trust might be structured, however, to avoid inclusion in the surviving spouse's estate (using the credit shelter trust techniques, discussed below), taking into account the possibility that the surviving spouse may thereafter realize an increase in his or her net worth. This would limit future estate tax exposure, while adequately providing for the surviving spouse.

This approach often assumes that the first deceased spouse has the primary portion of the marital unit assets, a situation that often occurs in separate property jurisdictions. If the spousal assets are acquired while living in a community property jurisdiction, the ownership of the assets will be more equally divided between the spouses. In the community property situation the same approach will be relevant if the total assets are less than the then applicable unified credit amount, that is, whether the marital deduction is used will not be essential for estate tax planning purposes.

(3) Both Estates Less Than the Spouses' Combined Unified Credit Exemption Equivalents

When the value of the combined estates is in excess of one estate tax unified credit/exemption equivalent amount but less than twice the estate tax unified credit/exemption equivalent, the planning objective ordinarily is to use both unified credit amounts.[359] Under the will of the first spouse to die, the marital deduction bequest should be only for the excess value over the credit shelter/exemption equivalent amount. The nonmarital bequest amount should be placed in the "credit shelter" or "bypass" trust, with the result that these trust-owned assets are not subject to tax (1) on the first spouse's death (because of the available unified credit) or (2) at the death of the surviving spouse (because at his or her death this spouse has no includable interest under the trust). The surviving spouse may be the beneficiary (or one of the beneficiaries) of that credit shelter trust and, thereby, continue to have the economic benefit of those trust assets but would not have any trust power sufficient to cause the inclusion of those assets in his or her gross estate. At the subsequent death of the surviving spouse, another exemption equivalent amount will be available to protect the assets included in that surviving spouse's gross estate (including the current value of any marital deduction assets earlier protected). However, the assets in the previously created credit shelter trust will not be so included.

This planning situation often contemplates that the first spouse to die has a greater amount of assets than the surviving spouse, often a situation arising in separate property jurisdictions, thereby encouraging the wealthier spouse to use the credit shelter trust approach. If these assets are accumulated in a community property jurisdiction while the spouses are married, they would have essentially equivalent asset ownership and presumably also would want to implement credit shelter trusts so that the assets in the credit shelter trust created when the first spouse dies are not includable in the estate of second spouse to die.

If one spouse has a significantly smaller estate than the other (which is less than one exemption equivalent amount), consideration should be given to tax-free lifetime transfers between spouses, made from the more wealthy to the less prosperous spouse. This can accomplish the objective of maximizing the use of each spouse's available unified credit. This approach might be particularly considered where the less wealthy spouse is in precarious physical condition.[360]

(4) Total Marital Assets in Excess of the Spouses' Combined Unified Credit Exemption Equivalents

Where the combined estates exceed two estate tax unified credit exemption equivalents, estate tax savings are often maximized by (1) the use of a credit shelter trust for assets in the estate of each spouse, (2) combined with a maximum eligible marital deduction transfer upon the death of the first spouse.[361] This structure would be arranged in the estate planning documents of each spouse since ordinarily the earlier death of one spouse cannot be predicted with certainty. The tax effect will be the use of two exemption equivalents in transferring the assets to the next generation. If the maximum marital deduction is used at the death of the first spouse, some federal estate tax may be due upon the survivor's death. This assumes that during the period of survival the survivor's estate was not reduced below the exemption equivalent amount by (1) gifts, (2) consumption, (3) a decline in asset values, or (4) an increase in the unified credit exemption equivalent amount.

This planning will be relevant whether the assets of the spousal unit consist of separate or community property or a combination of both. Because of the different property systems, the spouses' estate might vary as to the proportionate interests, but the ultimate objective would be to maximize the marital deduction available above the unified credit amount when the first spouse dies so as to defer the potential future estate tax.

g. Reducing Marital Deduction Utilization

Where the total value of the marital assets is in excess of both spouses' combined estate tax unified credit exemption equivalents, the spouses might be advised that the use of the marital deduction should not be maximized at the death of the first spouse. The choice of this alternative is dependent upon such matters as (1) the anticipated period of survival, (2) the anticipated return on the deferred tax funds, (3) the additional estate tax amount if the estates are not equalized, (4) the possibility of reducing the estate of the surviving spouse, (5) the increasing unified credit amount, and (6) the effect of future estate tax legislation.

The following may be instances where a marital deduction should not be maximized:

- If both spouses are older and the life expectancy of the surviving spouse is quite limited, the deferral period may not be of sufficient length to invest the tax-deferred funds so as to recoup the amount of additional estate tax liability subsequently to be incurred in the estate of the surviving spouse. In addition, in this situation the surviving spouse might not have sufficient time to either consume a portion of the estate or to make significant annual donee exclusion gifts to substantially deplete the estate.
- If (1) the estates of the spouses are approximately equal, (2) the anticipated surviving spouse will have the larger estate, or (3) the assets in the surviving spouse's estate are expected to increase in value substantially after the death of the first spouse, the additional future higher estate tax cost may be unacceptable.
- If the estate of the first spouse to die has great future appreciation potential, the use of a maximum marital deduction may be counterproductive because all of the appreciation after the first spouse's death for the marital deduction assets would be includible in the surviving spouse's estate. In the case of a closely held business interest, real estate being held for appreciation, or mineral properties expected to be productive in the future, a limited first death estate tax might be incurred so that the asset can be shielded from estate tax inclusion at the death of the surviving spouse. The appreciation would thereafter accrue for the benefit of the next generation immune from any estate tax otherwise applicable as of the death of the surviving spouse. Further, for the estate of the first spouse a deferred estate tax payment arrangement may be available if the qualification standards are satisfied.[362]

- The unified credit available against estate tax liability will be an important factor in marital deduction planning. For example, assume the exemption equivalent to be at the $5 million level.[363] The unlimited marital deduction combined with a $5 million exemption equivalent would allow a husband and wife to transfer unlimited amounts between themselves without tax and together to ultimately transfer $10 million to other persons free from transfer tax. If the husband has a net worth of $6 million and the wife has quite limited separate assets of her own, the husband may make a gift of an amount equal to the exemption equivalent ($5 million) to a "bypass" or "credit shelter" trust that provides for the benefit of his spouse for life, with the remainder to the children. The $1 million balance of his estate could be transferred tax free to the spouse in the form of a qualifying marital deduction bequest (when the exemption equivalent is assumed to be $5 million). No estate taxes would be due on the death of the husband. The amount in the exemption equivalent trust (or, credit shelter trust) created by the husband escapes estate tax in the estates of both spouses if the trust is properly structured. In this example, the property constituting the $1 million qualifying marital deduction bequest would be exempt from tax upon the subsequent death of the surviving spouse because of her exemption (assuming during her survival period she has not acquired significant property of her own). To the extent that all her property, including the marital deduction gift property, may have appreciated to an amount greater than her exemption, estate tax exposure will occur to the extent of the excess over that amount.
- Significant nontax considerations may exist to reduce the utilization of the estate tax marital deduction. For example, the surviving spouse may have more than enough assets available for his or her support. Clients may prefer that the children enjoy a portion of their anticipated inheritances at an earlier date. This may be accomplished by leaving some assets to younger generation members upon the death of the first spouse and paying some tax at that time (assuming the transferred value to younger generation members exceeds the estate tax exemption equivalent amount).

Other factors bearing on the use (and the manner of use) of the marital deduction are (1) the degree of confidence in the judgment of the surviving spouse concerning investments, (2) concern about that spouse's possible or probable subsequent remarriage, (3) the probable support needs of the surviving spouse and children, and (4) the possibility of other inheritances for the benefit of the surviving spouse. Some of these issues may be satisfactorily resolved by suspending the assets in a QTIP trust. Consideration should also be given to the survivor's willingness (and mental capability) after the death of the first spouse to make disclaimers and to enter into transactions for the purpose of reducing her estate's potential future estate tax liability (i.e., to make annual exclusion gifts, to enter into estate freeze/property ownership restructurings, or to sell potentially high future appreciation assets to younger family members).

5. Mechanics for Funding the Marital Deduction Formula Amount

a. Fundamental Choices

For estate tax minimization purposes, a formula approach may be used for determining either (1) the maximum marital deduction amount or (2) the maximum credit shelter amount, with the residue being transferred to the other portion. Further, an important question concerns whether the formula to divide the properties between these two portions should be structured on the basis of a "pecuniary formula" or a "fractional share" approach. The fundamental planning questions in this context concern which of various approaches should be used for implementing the formula in a particular situation. Further, the question must be resolved concerning the how to specify instructions to the executor about how the mechanics of funding any of these transfers should be completed.

b. Pre-Residuary or Residuary Marital Deduction Gift?

One important question to be resolved concerns the ordering of (1) the marital deduction bequest and (2) the credit shelter transfer. The division of properties between the credit shelter transfer and the marital deduction transfer presents the following basic options:

- The marital deduction gift may be identified as a gift of a pecuniary amount (determined under a formula) with the credit shelter portion constituting the residuary disposition.
- The credit shelter portion may be determined as a pecuniary amount and the marital deduction gift might constitute the residuary disposition.
- The credit shelter and the marital deduction may each be expressed as fractional shares of the residue with those shares being transferred into trusts for these two purposes.

As described below, when funding a pecuniary gift of either the credit shelter or the marital deduction portion, gains (and losses) accruing during the period of estate administration on those assets used to fund this gift will be realized for federal income tax purposes upon funding and will be required to be recognized for tax purposes. The gain accrued on that property transferred in the residuary disposition will not be treated as realized for federal income tax purposes, thereby being deferred. By contrast, if the residuary estate is divided between the marital deduction portion and the credit shelter portion on a fractional share basis, a proportionate sharing of gains and losses accruing during administration will be allocated to both the credit shelter and the marital deduction dispositions, but this funding event for the residuary components will not cause gain (or loss) realization.

c. Limitation on Funding Pecuniary Bequests—Rev. Proc. 64-19

(1) Pecuniary Formula

A special estate tax planning hazard arises in structuring the funding for a marital deduction bequest (including a marital deduction trust) when the marital deduction amount is to be determined by applying a pecuniary formula provision.[364] The pecuniary formula bequest amount will not change if determined by reference to the values of assets held at the time of death. However, fluctuations in asset values ordinarily will occur after this date if used in computing the allowable marital deduction amount. If this provision is literally applied, if certain assets in the estate have depreciated significantly after the estate tax valuation date, this arrangement would permit the pecuniary formula legacy to be satisfied by the executor with assets having a reduced fair market value on the date of the subsequent, actual estate distribution to the marital deduction distributee (e.g., the individual surviving spouse or a marital deduction trust).

Formula legacy provisions were previously used in conjunction with an authorization in the will allowing the executor to satisfy the pecuniary legacy by distributing assets at their values as determined for federal estate tax purposes (rather than at their fair market values when actually distributed from the estate to the spouse or the marital deduction trust). Consequently, under this earlier approach at the time of funding the marital trust (or other marital deduction bequest), the asset values could be substantially different from the date of death values. The same situation would exist in funding assets into the credit shelter trust.

If not limited, the executor would seek to distribute to the nonmarital trust (e.g., credit shelter trust) the property that might have appreciated since death (i.e., over its tax basis established at date of death) because this property would not be exposed to estate tax on the death of the surviving spouse. The property distributed to the spouse or the marital deduction trust might be that which has depreciated in value from the estate tax valuation date until the date of distribution. This property would be includible in the estate of the surviving spouse upon his or her subsequent death, but the value would be lower unless the value has been recovered since its decline after the death of the first spouse.[365] Thereafter, a lesser amount would quite probably be includible in the gross estate of the surviving spouse upon the subsequent death of that spouse.

(2) Limitations on Available Marital Deduction Bequest Funding Options

To eliminate this opportunity to reduce the value of the marital deduction property when subsequently included in the survivor's gross estate, the IRS published Rev. Proc. 64-19.[366] This revenue procedure specifies important limitations applicable in the structuring of pecuniary formula provisions (particularly as applicable to funding these bequests). The purpose of this revenue procedure is to eliminate the possibility of future estate tax avoidance created by the power to distribute assets at estate tax values in satisfaction of the pecuniary marital deduction gift and without regard to the postdeath appreciation or, particularly, the depreciation of those assets. Rev. Proc. 64-19 indicates that, if the pecuniary bequest can be satisfied at the values as established for estate tax purposes, the value of the property interest passing from the decedent to his or her surviving spouse (or a marital deduction trust) would be treated as not "ascertainable" in amount as of the date of death of the first spouse. Therefore, eligibility for the estate tax marital deduction for that property would not exist. Rev. Proc. 64-19 does offer several alternatives, however, to prevent the disallowance of the marital deduction for pecuniary bequests in conjunction with a power in the executor to satisfy these bequests.

A marital deduction will be allowed where, under (1) applicable state law or (2) the express or implied provisions of the governing instrument, the fiduciary, in funding the marital deduction pecuniary bequest, must distribute assets having an aggregate fair market value at the date(s) of distribution amounting to "no less than" the amount of the pecuniary bequest, as finally determined for federal estate tax purposes.[367] The use of this approach would mean employing a "true worth" or "date of distribution" valuation formula. Assets distributed in kind are to be valued at their date of distribution values.

A marital deduction will also be permitted where, under (1) state law or (2) the express or implied terms of the governing instrument, the fiduciary must distribute, in satisfaction of the marital deduction pecuniary bequest, assets which are "fairly representative of appreciation or depreciation in the value of all property" (since the date of death) available for such distribution.[368] This approach precludes picking depreciated assets to satisfy the marital deduction transfer and appreciated assets to complete the nonmarital transfer.[369]

The "fairly representative" provision in effect converts the marital bequest into the equivalent of a fractional share gift. This approach may be used where the decedent desires that the surviving spouse's portion should share in the postdeath appreciation and depreciation, but does not want a share of each specific asset allocated to the respective funds. A preferable approach, however, might be to use a normal fractional share disposition and give the fiduciary power to make non-pro-rata distributions, as noted below.

Rev. Proc. 64-19 explicitly indicates that its specified limitations do not apply to these situations[370]:

- a bequest (or transfer in trust) of a "fractional share" of the estate under which each beneficiary shares proportionately in the appreciation or depreciation in the value of assets to the date, or dates, of distribution;
- a bequest (or transfer in trust) of specific assets; and
- a pecuniary bequest (or transfer in trust), whether in a stated amount or an amount computed by the use of a formula, if: (1) the fiduciary must satisfy the pecuniary bequest or transfer in trust solely in cash; (2) the fiduciary has no discretion in the selection of the assets to be distributed in kind; or (3) assets selected by the fiduciary to be distributed in kind in satisfaction of the bequest or transfer in trust must be valued at their respective values on the date(s) of their distribution.

In each of these situations the abuse contemplated in Rev. Proc. 64-19 could not be achieved. In many instances, state legislatures have enacted provisions to assure that the standards required by Rev. Proc. 64-19 are not deemed violated by inadvertent will drafting. If local law is not clear, a testator may choose, however, to adopt one of the following alternative formula approaches (as noted above) in the testamentary document:

- a "true pecuniary" marital bequest under which assets equal in value to the marital deduction at the date of distribution must be used to satisfy the bequest;
- the "fairly representative" pecuniary formula approach; or
- a fractional share marital clause.

The discussion below identifies various acceptable approaches in response to these limitations, and the practical implications of implementing any of these approaches.[371]

d. Pecuniary Formula Funding Mechanisms

(1) Types of Pecuniary Formula Provisions

The pecuniary formula marital deduction gift may be implemented on (1) a "pre-residuary" basis or (2) a "residuary" basis.[372] This choice will often be dependent upon whether the marital deduction portion will be smaller or the nonmarital portion (often completely protected by the unified credit) is the lesser amount. If one portion is significantly smaller than the other, that smaller portion will often be designated for the "pre-residuary" transfer. This choice is often made because gain recognition will be required for federal income tax purposes when funding the pecuniary bequest with appreciated property, and the objective would be to limit the gain amount to be recognized. This potential gain amount might be significantly reduced because the tax basis for assets distributed is stepped up to the fair market value at death. Further, the capital gains tax cost might be small due to the enactment of the 20% maximum capital gains tax rate in ATRA. This maximum capital gains tax rate applies after 2012.[373] Various options in this context, combined with provisions to satisfy the Rev. Proc. 64-19 mandates, are described below. The choice among these various approaches is often dependent upon the particular facts and circumstances, rather than that one approach is definitely more preferable than others.

(2) Pre-Residuary or Post-Residuary Approach?

The pre-residuary marital deduction gift approach does enable a possible freezing of the value of that bequest for distribution purposes. This results because all the post-death property value appreciation would be for the benefit of the nonmarital residuary portion (which often will be fully or partially protected by the unified credit). In the event of the depreciation of assets after death, the pre-residuary format would freeze the amount of the marital portion (if a true worth funding approach is used) and the amount of the residuary gift would have declined upon funding.

A residuary (reverse) marital deduction formula may be used if the desire is for the marital gift portion to benefit from postdeath appreciation of property held in the estate. Ordinarily, however, the planning objective is to deflect appreciation away from the marital property transfer, because that property will be subsequently included in the gross estate of the spouse upon his or her death.

A formula may be used, therefore, to identify (in U.S. dollar monetary terms) that maximum amount (but no greater amount) to be transferred as a marital deduction gift on a pre-residuary basis (either to the surviving spouse or a trust for that spouse).

Example (1): Marital deduction formula gift: "I give to (my wife or the trustee of the marital deduction trust) an amount equal in value to the maximum marital deduction allowable to my estate for federal estate tax purposes, less the value for federal estate tax purposes of all items in my gross estate which qualify for the marital deduction and which pass or have passed to (my wife or the trust) in a form qualifying for the marital deduction otherwise than under this gift."

The residuary portion of the estate would then be protected by the unified credit, to the extent available. This formula provision provides a type of computational mechanism to calculate the precise monetary value of the marital deduction gift (with the instrument further providing that the value is to be determined as of the distribution date). The objective is to optimize the marital deduction transfer at an amount that is (1) less than the entire estate and (2) fully deductible under the unlimited marital deduction provision.

Alternatively, a formula may be applied to determine the amount of the maximum value qualifying for the unified credit (rather than the marital deduction), this being the pre-residuary gift, with the remaining portion of the estate being transferred in a form eligible for the marital deduction (i.e., to the spouse or a qualifying marital deduction trust). In this circumstance the marital deduction transfer constitutes the residuary gift.

Example (2): Credit shelter formula gift: "I give to my trustee a sum equal to the largest amount that can pass free of federal estate tax under this gift by reason of the unified credit allowable to my estate but no other credit and after taking account of property disposed of by previous articles in this Will and property passing outside of this Will that is includible in my gross estate and that does not qualify for the marital or charitable deduction and after taking account of charges to principal that are not allowed as deductions in computing my federal estate tax."[374]

This credit shelter pecuniary formula gift is structured so that, when used in conjunction with an unlimited marital deduction residuary gift, it operates to achieve nontaxable status for the estate. Therefore, property that is included in the gross estate, and that passes outside the will or under a preceding article of the will and does not qualify for the marital or charitable deduction, reduces the amount of this credit shelter bequest. The gift is also reduced by principal charges that are not deducted in computing the federal estate tax, for example, administration expenses that are claimed as income tax deductions rather than as estate tax deductions.[375]

(3) Pre-Residuary "True Worth" Funding Approach

Under a "true worth" or "date of distribution" pre-residuary pecuniary bequest funding approach, assets to satisfy the marital deduction bequest (made to the spouse or a marital deduction trust) must be, under the governing instrument, equal in value to the marital deduction amount at the time of the estate distribution. Consequently, any changes in the value of the estate during the probate administration would not have an impact on the amount to be ultimately received in funding this marital deduction bequest. The marital deduction portion would be frozen in amount. No opportunity would exist under this approach to distribute assets having value less than the marital deduction amount and, therefore, exposure to the Rev. Proc. 64-19 risks would be avoided. All asset depreciation would be to the detriment of the residuary estate and not to the marital pre-residuary estate. All asset appreciation would also be for the benefit of the residuary estate and not for the marital bequest. Consequently, if the residuary assets appreciate significantly during the probate process, they would not be transferred to the marital portion. Assuming appropriate structuring of the residuary trust, they would not be taxed at the surviving spouse's death.

(4) Pre-Residuary "Fairly Representative" Funding Approach

The pecuniary marital deduction bequest may be made on a pre-residuary basis, as noted above, with the funding of that bequest being determined using the "fairly representative" approach. Under a "fairly representative" pre-residuary pecuniary bequest funding approach, the assets to satisfy the marital deduction bequest (made to the spouse directly or to a marital deduction trust) must, under the governing instrument, reflect the proportionate change in post death values of all the assets in the estate. This approach precludes choosing (1) depreciated assets (comparing date of death value to distribution date value) to fund the marital portion and (2) appreciated assets (comparing date of death value to distribution date value) to fund the credit shelter portion. Therefore, the mandate of Rev. Proc. 64-19 would be observed.

To assure that this "fairly representative" standard is satisfied, the executor might be permitted to distribute a fraction of each asset to the marital share that represents its pro-rata share. Alternatively, rather than distributing a pro-rata portion of each share, the distribution might be made on the basis of satisfying two tests: (1) the aggregate tax basis of the assets distributed must equal the amount of the marital deduction and (2) the aggregate fair market value at the date of distribution must approximately equal the marital share's pro-rata portion. The language of the instrument should be sufficiently explicit to enable the executor to take either of these approaches when distributing estate assets.

(5) Pre-Residuary "Minimum Worth" Funding Approach

The pecuniary marital deduction bequest could be funded on a pre-residuary basis, using the "minimum worth" approach. Under a "minimum worth" pre-residuary pecuniary bequest funding approach, assets to satisfy the marital deduction bequest (made to the spouse or a marital deduction trust) must, under the governing instrument, reflect the lesser of (1) the tax basis for federal income tax purposes or (2) the fair market value as of the time of distribution.[376] This approach precludes giving the marital share less than it should receive. Therefore, the mandate of Rev. Proc. 64-19 would be observed. This approach could produce overfunding of the marital deduction gift if appreciated assets are distributed, but this could be avoided by the executor selling the asset and then distributing cash proceeds. Of course, under the governing instrument (or applicable state law) the executor must have the authority to do this.

(6) Residuary "True Worth" Funding Approach

A "reverse" "true worth" pecuniary funding formula approach may be used, particularly when (on a comparative basis) the unified credit portion is small and the marital deduction transfer is significantly larger. The unified credit share would be the pre-residuary gift to be funded by using values on the date of distribution. The marital portion would receive the remaining portion, that is, the residuary estate.

This means that the residuary marital deduction gift receives all the post-death appreciation or depreciation.[377] On the assumption that in most situations the post-death investment result is appreciation in value, this additional amount accruing after the first spouse's death must be included in the gross estate of the surviving spouse upon his or her subsequent death (unless these assets are given away or consumed during the spouse's survival period).

(7) Residuary "Fairly Representative" Funding Approach

Alternatively, a "reverse fairly representative" pecuniary funding formula approach may be used when the unified credit portion is small and the marital deduction transfer is large. The unified credit share is the share that must be funded by using values that are fairly representative of the appreciation or depreciation in the estate. The marital portion, that is, the residuary estate, receives the remaining portion. This portion subsequently would be included in the estate of the surviving spouse (unless these assets are given away or consumed during the survival period).

e. Formula Fractional Share Bequests

(1) Structuring the Fractional Share Formula

In making the division between the marital deduction portion and the credit shelter portion, a "fractional share" formula provision may be used as an alternative to the pecuniary funding formula approach.[378] If the formula is to determine the eligible unified credit amount on a fractional share basis, it might possibly be structured, for example, as follows[379]:

> "I give to (the "Credit Shelter Trust" or "Family Trust") that fraction of my residuary estate:
>
> (i) of which the numerator shall be the sum equal to the largest amount that can pass free of federal estate tax under this paragraph by reason of the unified credit and (if available) the state death tax credit (provided the use of this credit does not require an increase in the state death taxes paid) allowable to my estate, but no other credit, and after taking account of property disposed of by previous articles of this Will and property passing outside of this Will, which is includible in my gross estate and does not qualify for the marital or charitable deduction, and after taking account of charges to principal that are not allowed as deductions in computing my federal estate tax; and
>
> (ii) of which fraction the denominator shall be the value of my residuary estate."

Alternatively, this fractional share formula approach might be used to determine the eligible marital deduction amount, with the remaining residue portion then being distributed to the credit shelter or family trust.

(2) Choosing Assets for Completing Fractional Share Transfer

After the pertinent fraction is obtained by means of this formula, that fraction is applied at the date of distribution (i.e., not the estate tax valuation date) to determine those assets receivable by each beneficiary (e.g., the spouse and the credit shelter trust). The beneficiary under a formula fractional share gift is never entitled to a fixed, monetary amount but, rather, is to receive a value that changes with each fluctuation in the value of the property constituting the residuary estate. This will include changes made as a result of an estate tax audit. This fluctuation will occur until the time the credit shelter portion, the surviving spouse's direct share, or the marital trust portion, as applicable, is completely distributed from the estate to the particular recipient. In an environment where estate asset values are appreciating, the fractional share bequest approach means that the amount that will be transferred to the surviving spouse (or marital trust) and subsequently be includible in the spouse's estate will proportionally increase.

In fulfilling this transfer obligation, a fractional interest in each asset is to be transferred to both the credit shelter portion and the marital deduction portion.[380] Alternatively, the language of the governing instrument might be sufficiently expansive to enable the personal representative to pick and choose those assets to distribute to these two beneficiaries, assuming the fraction is proportionately applied to the distributed assets on the dates of distribution.

This type of formula approach may cause administrative difficulties because any non-pro-rata distribution of the marital share and the nonmarital share will mandate a concurrent change in the applicable fraction.[381] If each distribution is fractionalized and made pro rata, this revaluation need not occur but complications may subsequently arise because of the manner in which these fractionalized interests are held. Most state probate laws are not explicit on whether each specific asset available for funding (ordinarily from the residuary estate) must be fractionalized for this purpose.

f. Estate Equalization Formula Clause

A formula clause may be used to equalize the estates of both spouses for federal estate tax purposes rather than to maximize the marital deduction in the estate of the first spouse to die. Consequently, the primary objective in this context would be to not maximize the use of the marital deduction. Rather, the underlying premise in using this type of formula clause is that the balancing of the values of the two estates to avoid a higher estate tax marginal rate upon the death of the surviving spouse is more important than the benefit of any estate tax deferral (which could be achieved through the maximum marital deduction).[382]

Example: "I give to (my wife or marital trust) that percentage interest in my residuary estate that shall, when taken together with all other interests and property that qualify for the marital deduction and that pass or shall have otherwise passed to (my wife or trust), achieve for my estate a marital deduction that would result in the lowest federal estate taxes in my estate and the estate of my wife, on the assumption that my wife died after me, but on the date of my death, and that her estate is valued as of the date on and in the manner in which my estate is valued for federal estate tax purposes."

The reference to a "percentage interest" means that, in this example, this formula utilizes a fractional share approach, rather than a "pecuniary formula" technique. This could be accomplished, alternatively, through the use of a pecuniary formula approach.

This approach does contemplate that the tax rates will remain static. After a decade of uncertainty regarding the unified credit exemption amount and portability, ATRA has provided some level of certainty.[383] However, as mentioned above, caution mandates that planning for the optimum use of the marital deduction address the uncertainty as to what rules will apply at an estate planning client's death. Unless both spouses are in extremely frail condition and both are anticipated to die in the near term, most planners would anticipate that taking the risk to delay any gross estate inclusion until the death of the surviving spouse is most appropriate. An equalization formula might be quite valuable in the event of simultaneous deaths, and the last will might provide for equalizing the estates if this were to occur. Of course, this result might also be accomplished by an executor of one of the estates making a partial marital deduction election (assuming a further provision in the will reversing the usual impact of the state law simultaneous death presumption).

g. Gain Recognition on Funding Marital Deduction and Credit Shelter Bequests

(1) Pecuniary Bequest—Gain Recognition Event to Distributor Estate

If a pecuniary bequest is funded with appreciated property, the transfer of that appreciated property constitutes a gain realization event to the transferor estate. The essence of this transaction is that the estate exchanges appreciated property for a release from an obligation to pay a specified monetary amount to the transferee beneficiary. The estate must recognize gain to the extent that (1) the fair market value of the property on the date of the transfer exceeds (2) the income tax basis for that property.[384] Because the distributed property receives a stepped-up basis at death under §1014, the amount of such recognized gain is ordinarily limited unless substantial post death appreciation has accrued from death and up to the date of funding. This could occur if the probate process is lengthy and appreciation of the property accrues rapidly.

The gain recognized is classified as capital gain if the distributed property is a capital asset.[385] The distributee will receive an income tax basis for that property equal to the fair market value of the property on the date of that distribution, that is, as if the property had been purchased for cash or its equivalent (in this context the release of the obligation to receive a specified monetary amount).[386]

(2) Fractional Share Bequest—No Gain Recognition Event to Distributor Estate

No gain (or loss) is realized by the estate upon transferring appreciated (or depreciated) property to fund a fractional share formula bequest.[387] Generally, because no gain (or loss) is recognized on this distribution, the income tax basis to the recipient of this property is the same as the tax basis of the property in the hands of the distributor estate.[388] If, however, each asset is not split or fractionalized on the basis of the fraction established under the formula clause, gain or loss may be recognized.[389]

(3) Planning Considerations

The selection of the method of partition of the estate pursuant to a formula clause should take into account the income tax consequences when satisfying a pecuniary gift or a fractional share gift with property in kind, whether in the form of a credit shelter bequest or a marital deduction bequest. As noted, upon the funding, in kind, of a pecuniary amount the estate is required to recognize gain. The amount of any gain is equal to the difference between the date of distribution value of the property and its tax basis.[390] If a pecuniary bequest in satisfaction of a marital deduction bequest is large (relative to the residuary disposition), substantial gains may be recognized on funding.[391] Loss should be recognized if the distribution is in satisfaction of a pecuniary bequest.[392] Gain or loss is treated as not realized upon a distribution in kind in satisfaction of a residuary disposition because no property is being distributed in liquidation of a fixed dollar obligation.

When considering these income tax recognition requirements (and assuming that properties tend to appreciate, rather than depreciate in value) a "rule of thumb" often used for determining which gift should be made the specific portion gift is to make the pecuniary amount distribution the smaller gift. Consequently, where the credit shelter amount is large relative to the marital deduction, a marital deduction pecuniary bequest with a credit shelter residuary disposition would seem appropriate. Capital gain realized on funding the marital deduction bequest would be minimized because such gain would be attributable to the smaller portion of the estate. The amount of the marital bequest would be immunized from market fluctuations, with all increases or decreases in value in the period of estate administration being charged to the credit shelter residuary disposition.[393] Conversely, in quite large estates, where the credit shelter is small in relation to the marital deduction, the pecuniary gift might be made to the credit shelter, with the marital deduction constituting the residuary gift. Gain on funding the credit shelter bequest is also minimized. Under this alternative, the credit shelter amount is protected, with the risk of loss (but also the possibility of appreciation) passing to the marital residuary bequest.

The funding of a pecuniary marital deduction gift or credit shelter gift that constitutes a substantial part of the estate can cause problems for the executor. The pecuniary amount resembles an indebtedness of the decedent that has not been satisfied. If the disposition is not funded promptly, decreases in the value of the estate assets may result in a substantial reduction of the residuary gift. Consequently, in the probate administration process the executor ordinarily should seek to fund the pecuniary bequest at an early date.[394]

h. DNI Distributions on Funding the Marital Deduction Bequest

(1) DNI Distribution Effects

Upon the funding of these various bequests a further federal income tax effect might occur, that is, the shifting of gross income from the estate to the recipient. For income tax purposes a distribution made to fund either a pecuniary credit shelter transfer or a marital deduction transfer may constitute distributable net income.[395] This distribution will necessitate inclusion in a recipient's gross income of the distributed amount (even though received in the form of property other than cash).[396] The funding of such a gift is not considered the bequest of a specific sum of money or of property which would enable an exception from the application of the DNI distribution rules.[397]

A distribution in satisfaction of a fractional or percentage share formula bequest similarly constitutes a DNI distribution that does not qualify as a specific bequest.[398] Consequently, this distribution also may carry out the estate's distributable net income to the recipient. This may result whether the transfer is in fulfillment of a marital deduction gift or a credit shelter gift.

The amount of this DNI distribution in the form of any property other than cash (i.e., U.S. dollars) is limited to the lesser of (1) the tax basis of the distributed property in the hands of the distributee beneficiary or (2) the fair market value of the property.[399] The basis of the property received by the beneficiary (e.g., the marital deduction trust) is the basis of that property to the estate, as adjusted for any gain or loss recognized by the estate on the distribution of this property.[400]

(2) Tax Basis Effects to Distributee

On the distribution to fund a fractional share bequest no gain or loss will be recognized by the estate and, therefore, as previously noted, the basis to the distributee (e.g., the marital deduction trust or surviving spouse) of the distributed property will be a carryover basis. The income tax basis of an asset distributed in satisfaction of a pecuniary bequest in the hands of the recipient will be the fair market value of that asset at the date of distribution, to the extent such value is included in the beneficiary's gross income.[401] Because the distribution of appreciated property to satisfy a pecuniary formula bequest constitutes a gain recognition event for income tax purposes, the tax basis to the recipient marital deduction trust (or surviving spouse) for this distributed property will be the fair market value as of the date of distribution.

6. Eligibility of Community Property for Marital Deduction

The original function and purpose of the marital deduction provision, as noted above, was to eliminate the discriminatory effect of the federal estate tax provisions then deemed tilted in favor of persons resident in community property states. Therefore, originally the marital deduction could not be used by the decedent's gross estate for property held by the decedent and his or her surviving spouse as "community property."[402] As presently constructed the marital deduction is unlimited and does not differentiate between separate property and community property. Consequently, all transfers of community property that pass to the surviving spouse in a qualifying form are eligible for the federal gift or estate tax marital deduction.

7. Foreign Recipients or Foreign Decedents

a. QDOT Trust—Alien Spouse as Recipient

An estate tax marital deduction is not allowed where the property transfer is to a surviving spouse who is not a U.S. citizen.[403] Extended residency in the United States by the alien surviving spouse beneficiary is not sufficient to enable marital deduction eligibility for the estate of the deceased transferor spouse. The concern is that the property transferred will entirely escape U.S. estate taxation, (1) upon the first death because of the unlimited marital deduction and, (2) later, upon the death of the alien surviving spouse, because this property may be removed by that spouse from U.S. tax jurisdiction during the period of survival after the death of the first spouse. An exception to this estate tax marital deduction limitation is available where the property passes for the benefit of the surviving spouse in a qualified domestic trust, thereby enabling estate tax postponement.[404]

A "qualified domestic trust" (QDOT) is a trust for the benefit of the surviving spouse.[405] The trust instrument must require that at least one trustee be either an individual citizen of the United States or a domestic corporation and that no distribution, other than of income, be made unless such trustee has the right to withhold the tax imposed by §2056A(b).[406] Trust distributions, except for income and hardship disbursements, made before the death of the surviving spouse will be subject to U.S. estate tax.[407] In addition, the property remaining in the trust at the surviving spouse's death will be subject to estate tax at that time.[408] Unlike a domestic marital deduction trust situation, the spouse need not be entitled to all the trust income at least annually for this trust to qualify for the marital deduction.[409]

Because trusts are not permitted in some countries and some trusts cannot have any U.S. trustees, §2056A(c)(3) grants Treasury regulatory authority to treat certain nontrust arrangements as being trusts for QDOT purposes if they have substantially the same effect as trusts.[410] Further, Treasury has regulatory authority to waive the U.S. trustee requirement.[411] Congress noted that such regulations, if any, would only permit a marital deduction for arrangements under which the United States would retain jurisdiction and adequate security to impose U.S. transfer tax on transfers by the surviving spouse of the property transferred by the decedent.[412]

b. Nonresident Alien Decedent

The estate of a nonresident alien decedent will be subject to U.S. estate tax only for certain property located in the United States at the time of death.[413] A marital deduction is allowed to the estate of the nonresident alien decedent for the transfer of property situated in the United States at the time of the decedent's death if the transferred amount would be deductible under the principles of §2056.[414] These principles include the nondeductible terminable interest rule (and its exceptions) and the requirement that the recipient surviving spouse must be a U.S. citizen.

g. Disclaimers in Marital Deduction Context

a. Disclaimer Planning Options

The disclaimer can be an effective post-mortem estate planning device in the marital deduction context. Dependent upon the circumstances, a disclaimer after the death of the taxpayer might be used either to decrease or to increase the marital deduction amount.

For example, the unlimited use of the marital deduction may lead to significant overfunding of marital transfers in many estates. The disclaimer may be used by the surviving spouse after the death of the first spouse to reduce the amount of the marital deduction transfer. Consequently, the disclaimer is an important addition or alternative to the QTIP election by the executor and to a marital deduction formula provision.

A disclaimer may also be used where another person disclaims an interest receivable under an estate and the disclaimed property is then distributable to the surviving spouse (or a marital deduction trust for that spouse).[415] The objective in this situation would be to cause an increase in the estate tax marital deduction amount. For example, the disclaimer may be implemented by a child to enable the surviving spouse or a marital deduction trust to receive a greater amount of property during the surviving parent's survivorship period (and also to increase the net amount after estate tax eventually to be received by the child). Where a nonmarital family trust is created with contingent or unascertained beneficiaries, difficulties may arise, however, in having all the beneficiaries (such as unborn grandchildren) make effective disclaimers, so as to increase the marital deduction gift.[416]

Whatever the objective in the disclaimer context, the will must contain appropriate provisions concerning the disposition of the assets when the primary beneficiary is deemed not existent for purposes of receiving the testamentary transfer. Ordinarily, a default structure would be included in the governing instrument to assure identification of beneficiaries in default of taking of the property by the primary beneficiary. The parties should ordinarily not rely on the intestate provisions of local law to enable them to achieve this objective.[417]

b. Disclaimers into the Credit Shelter Trust

A disclaimer by the surviving spouse may qualify as a disclaimer even though the spouse holds a continuing interest in the renounced assets. The disclaimed assets could be added to either (1) a credit shelter or bypass trust or (2) a special disclaimer trust.[418]

The provisions of the credit shelter trust must be carefully drafted so as not to jeopardize the validity of the disclaimer. As a result of the refusal to accept the property, the interest must pass without any direction on the part of the person making the disclaimer; that is, a "no direction rule" must be observed.[419] The IRS takes the position that the surviving spouse may not have a special power to appoint among the designated beneficiaries from the trust into which the assets disclaimed by the surviving spouse are transferred.[420] In addition, sprinkling powers held by the surviving spouse as trustee are also prohibited powers (unless limited by an ascertainable standard).[421]

The existence of a special power of appointment in the bypass trust may be neutralized sufficiently to permit a disclaimer by the surviving spouse into the credit shelter trust. The power of appointment may be rendered ineffective for the disclaimed portion being added to the credit shelter trust. Alternatively, the surviving spouse may be able to disclaim the power of appointment, to be followed shortly thereafter by a disclaimer from the marital trust into the credit shelter trust.[422]

The problem of prohibited powers may also be dealt with by creating (e.g., under the decedent's will) an additional trust solely to receive those gifts disclaimed by the surviving spouse. This "disclaimer trust" (often the safest approach) may be structured so as to qualify for the credit for tax on prior transfers in the estate of the surviving spouse if the survivor dies shortly after the first spouse.

9. Marital Trust Postfunding Administration

a. Reduction of Marital Deduction Trust Assets During Survival Period

The marital deduction property received either outright by the surviving spouse or by a marital deduction trust for his or her benefit will be included subsequently in that spouse's gross estate at the time of his or her death.[423] Because the federal estate tax on the surviving spouse's estate is imposed at that later date (rather than at the time of the death of the first spouse to die), if the corpus has been reduced after receipt from the estate of the first spouse to die, but before the death of the surviving spouse, the estate tax liability at the time of the surviving spouse's death can be diminished. The objective, therefore, is to have the marital deduction gift property (whether held outright by the surviving spouse or in trust) reduced in value as of the death of the surviving spouse.[424]

One method of accomplishing this reduction of the subsequently tax-exposed assets is to assure that any principal distributions (in addition to the required income distributions from a QTIP trust) will be made to the spouse from the marital deduction trust before any income or principal distributions are made to the spouse from a nonmarital deduction trust (i.e., from those assets which have already been exposed to estate tax, or were in the credit shelter trust protected from estate tax under the unified credit at the first spouse's death). Another technique to limit the ultimate value of the marital deduction trust assets is to fund that trust with "wasting assets" (i.e., with depreciable and depletable properties that are declining in fair market value). If the executor has a choice in estate asset distributions, he or she may distribute to the marital deduction trust, for example, an apartment building, a patent, or a depleting oil property, while transferring high-appreciation-potential securities to the nonmarital trust. Note, however, that these depreciating properties may not actually be declining in economic value even though they are depreciable or depletable for federal income tax purposes, and these probabilities should be carefully evaluated.

If the nonmarital trust, receiving property distributions from the estate in the amount of the unified credit/exemption equivalent, is structured correctly, the assets in that nonmarital or credit shelter trust (even if significantly appreciated at the death of the surviving spouse) will not be included in the gross estate of that spouse. High-appreciation-potential assets should, therefore, be deflected to this trust, absent other overriding tax and investment planning considerations.

b. Tax Allocation Clause in Surviving Spouse's Will

Consideration must be given to §2207A in drafting a tax allocation clause for inclusion in the will of the surviving spouse. This statutory provision grants the estate of the surviving spouse a right of recovery against the remainder beneficiaries of that qualified terminable interest property which is includible in that surviving spouse's gross estate. The amount of these recoverable taxes under §2207A is the incremental (i.e., not proportionate) estate tax resulting from the inclusion of the qualified terminable interest property in the survivor's gross estate.[425] This means that the tax amount attributable to these includible assets will be determined on the basis of the highest marginal estate tax rate applicable to the estate of the survivor spouse.

Although often the identification of the first spouse to die can be anticipated, this order of deaths may not actually occur. Consequently, the will of each spouse should address the possibility that each spouse will be the surviving spouse. Therefore, each spouse should include an appropriate tax allocation clause in his or her will.

A surviving spouse can direct in his/her will, however, that such taxes are to be paid out of that spouse's own property. That testator must specifically indicate an intent to waive any right of reimbursement for payment of taxes on such property. A waiver of this particular right of reimbursement would be accomplished by a specific reference to the QTIP trust, §2044, or §2207A. A general provision in the survivor's will specifying that all taxes are to be paid by the estate will not be sufficient to waive the right of reimbursement of tax attributable to the QTIP assets.[426]

Where, however, the objects of the surviving spouse's bounty differ from those of the first spouse to die, this waiver clause (assuming compliance with the requirements for the specificity mandated in §2207A(a)(2)) providing for payment of all death taxes from the surviving spouse's residuary estate should probably not be included. Instead, assuming such a provision is appropriate, the surviving spouse's last will might provide for payment from the residuary of only those taxes generated by the property passing under the surviving spouse's will. The tax allocation provision recognizing the principles of §2207A would continue to govern payment of taxes attributable to the qualified terminable interest property that is includible in the survivor's gross estate but passes under the terms of the earlier QTIP transfer.[427]

Ordinarily, to avoid placing the burden on the executor of acting under §2207A, many tax planners prefer to provide in the QTIP governing instrument (usually the will of the first spouse to die) that payments are to be made from the QTIP trust of all taxes attributable to the inclusion of the qualified terminable interest property in the estate of the survivor. This provision must carefully identify that (assuming desired) the incremental tax computational approach is to be applicable in determining the allocable estate tax amount.[428]

E. Powers of Appointment

1. Benefit of the Limited Power of Appointment Technique

The effective tax use of a "special" or "limited" power of appointment can produce quite valuable estate planning results.[429] A limited power of appointment (1) permits the holder of that power to exercise his or her own discretion as to how the property subject to the power should be used or distributed to others (2) without the inclusion of that property in the power holder's gross estate for federal estate tax purposes. Consequently, where the power of appointment is created under a last will, the flexibility permitted under a limited power of appointment allows the testator's dispositive scheme to be altered by the designated holder of the power to account for developments not anticipated at the time of the original disposition by the testator. In effect, the holder (donee) of the power is constituted as a continuing "agent" for the testator/donor in ultimately completing the gift.

2. Applicable Terminology

A "power of appointment" is a power of disposition over property given under a deed of trust or a will.[430] This power is given by the owner of the property to another person who then holds this power.[431] The owner of the property who creates the power of appointment is usually called the "donor." The holder of the power who is delegated the authority to designate who shall take the property or benefit from its enjoyment is called the "donee."[432] The person who receives the property or interest upon the exercise of the power is the "appointee." The person who would take the property upon any default in the exercise of the power is called the "taker in default."

3. Tax Classification of Powers

a. General Power of Appointment

Pursuant to §2041, only property subject to a "general power of appointment" is included at death in a power holder's gross estate for federal estate tax purposes. Consequently, the crucial federal estate tax issue is whether the bundle of rights held by an individual with respect to the treatment and disposition of property constitutes a "general power of appointment" for federal estate tax purposes. The scope of these property rights is defined, however, under applicable state property law.[433]

For federal estate tax purposes a "general power of appointment" is a power under which the holder of the power has the authority to appoint the property subject to the power in favor of anyone, including himself or herself, his or her estate, his or her creditors, or the creditors of his or her estate.[434] A power to appoint in favor of any one or more of these parties is sufficient to satisfy the definition of a general power for federal estate tax purposes.[435] None of the following, however, constitutes (for federal estate tax purposes) a general power of appointment (even though the power is exercisable by the holder of the power in his or her own favor)[436]:

- a power vested in the donee to consume, invade, or appropriate property, even though for his or her own benefit, if such power is limited by ascertainable standards[437] that relate to the holder's health, education, support, or maintenance[438];
- a power exercisable only in conjunction with the creator of the power[439]; or
- a power exercisable only in conjunction with a person holding an adverse interest in the property subject to the power.[440] If the power is exercisable in conjunction with someone other than the creator or a person holding an adverse interest, the value of the assets subject to the power of appointment will be divided equally among those holding the power of appointment.[441]

b. Limited Power of Appointment

A limited (or special) power of appointment is a power permitting appointment of the property only to a special class of takers.[442] For purposes of §2041, any power that is not a general power will be classified as a nongeneral (or limited) power.[443]

c. Scope of Powers of Appointment

The term "power of appointment" for estate tax purposes includes all powers that are in substance and effect powers of appointment, regardless of the nomenclature used in creating the power and regardless of local law terminology.[444] A power in a donee to remove or discharge a trustee and to appoint himself or herself may cause the donee to hold a power of appointment, dependent upon the scope of powers held by the trustee.[445] A power to amend only those administrative provisions of a trust instrument that cannot substantially affect the beneficial enjoyment of the trust property or income will not be classified, however, as constituting a power of appointment.[446]

4. Taxation of Powers of Appointment

a. Estate Tax

(1) Gross Estate Inclusion

Section 2041 requires inclusion in a decedent's estate of all property for which the decedent has, at the time of his or her death, a general power of appointment.[447] The mere existence of the general power is sufficient to cause such inclusion in the power holder's gross estate.[448] A power of appointment is considered to be held on the date of a decedent's death even though the exercise of the power is subject to the precedent giving of notice, or even though the exercise of the power takes effect only on the expiration of a stated period after its exercise, whether or not on or before the decedent's death notice has been given or the power has been exercised.[449] A power exercisable by its terms only upon the occurrence during the decedent's lifetime of an event or a contingency that did not in fact take place or occur during such time is not, however, a power in existence on the date of the decedent's death.[450]

(2) Lifetime Exercise or Release

The holder of the power could possibly exercise the power during lifetime for the holder's direct benefit, in which event the property would be held directly at death and be includible in the holder's gross estate (unless dissipated during lifetime). Further, the prior lifetime exercise of a general power of appointment will cause the property subject to the power to be included at death in a decedent's gross estate for federal estate tax purposes if he or she exercised the power under circumstances such that, if the property subject to the power had actually been owned and transferred by the decedent, the property would be includible in the decedent's gross estate under §2035 (transfers within three years of death), §2036 (transfers with a retained life estate), §2037 (transfers taking effect at death), or §2038 (revocable transfers).[451] For example, the power might have been exercised to put the property subject to the power into a trust where the power holder was entitled to benefits for life. A "release" of a general power of appointment is subject to these same rules, e.g., gross estate inclusion would occur if the power was released and the property was held in a trust under which the (now former) power holder had a life interest.[452]

(3) Disclaimers

A disclaimer or renunciation of a general power of appointment is not considered to be a release of the power.[453] The general disclaimer rules in §2518 apply in the estate tax context under §2041.[454]

(4) Lapses and the "Five-and-Five" Power

A "lapse" of a power consists of the failure to exercise a general power of appointment within a specified time, so that (by its terms) the power expires (i.e., the power holder need take no action and certain changes then occur because of the terms of the trust instrument). A "lapse" is considered to be the equivalent of a "release" and, as noted above, a release may cause gross estate inclusion (because a "release" is treated as the equivalent of a property transfer). A lapse of a general power of appointment during any calendar year is treated as a release, however, only to the extent that the property that could have been appointed by the exercise of the lapsed power exceeds the greater of:

- $5,000; or
- 5% of the aggregate value (at the time of the lapse) of the assets out of which (or the proceeds of which) the exercise of the lapsed power could have been satisfied.[455]

Consequently, the amount protected by a lapsed five-and-five power is not treated as released and, therefore, is not encompassed within the estate tax transfer provisions. When the holder of the power of appointment dies, the property then subject to the five-and-five power will be included in his or her gross estate, however.

Example: X transfers $200,000 worth of securities in trust providing for payment of the trust income to B for life, with remainder to B's issue. B is given a noncumulative right to withdraw 5% ($10,000, based on the $200,000 value) each year from the principal of the trust fund. The failure of B to exercise this right to withdraw will not result in estate tax inclusion with respect to the power to withdraw $10,000 (assuming no property valuation change) which lapses each year before the year of B's death. Absent this five-and-five power lapse exclusion, B would be regarded as having made a transfer to the trust of $10,000 each year (assuming no change in the value of the trust assets) and §2036 would apply at death (because B had a life income interest in the trust) to the extent B would then be treated as a transferor to the trust (by reason of the $10,000 deemed transfers). At B's death the amount that he was then entitled to withdraw at the time his death occurred (e.g., $10,000) will be included in his gross estate, because to that extent, he held a present (rather than a lapsed) power to withdraw.[456]

To the extent of any excess amount over the greater of the $5,000 or 5% withdrawal power, the failure to exercise such a power in any year will be considered a release of the power (and, thereby, a transfer into the trust). This will result in a potential "retained life interest" or similar consequences under the estate tax transfer provisions.[457]

The five-and-five power can be an extremely useful estate planning tool because its availability will not cause the entire trust property to be included in the holder's gross estate. In the year the holder of the power of appointment dies, only that property subject to the five-and-five power is included in the holder's gross estate (to the extent not previously exercised during that year).[458] If the five-and-five power is restricted each year to its exercise during a particular calendar month, and the holder of this power dies in any other calendar month, even the value of the trust corpus subject to the five-and-five power during that year will not be included in the holder's gross estate.[459]

Other mechanisms are available to further limit federal estate tax exposure in this context. If the trust assets are substantial (e.g., $1 million), the trust grantor might limit the five-and-five power to smaller percentages (e.g., the greater of $10,000 or 1% of the trust corpus). Under these circumstances the power will be less than a five-and-five power, further limiting the potential estate tax exposure. If the power is vested in the surviving spouse with respect to assets in a nonmarital deduction trust (which has previously been exposed to estate tax), the trust grantor may wish to require as a condition of the exercise of the power that the marital deduction trust assets be exhausted before authorizing even the availability of a five-and-five power.[460] If the power is vested in a child, the power might be structured to exist only after the child attains a specified age (e.g., age 30) and no gross estate inclusion would then occur if the child dies when under age 30.

Although the primary reason for the existence of the five-and-five power relates to federal estate tax planning, the use of such a power also has federal gift tax implications. For gift tax purposes, a five-and-five power in a trust beneficiary will give that beneficiary a "present interest" in the property subject to the power and serves to make the annual donee exclusion available for gifts to the trust.[461] A power drafted to insure the availability of the annual donee exclusion may be drafted to permit annual withdrawals from the trust on a noncumulative basis of the lesser of (1) the amount of the annual donee exclusion or (2) the fair market value of the property contributed to the trust during the trust year. This is often known as a "*Crummey* power."[462]

A *Crummey* power which takes full advantage of the annual donee exclusion, may exceed the five-and-five power limit unless the trust assets exceed an amount, 5% of which is greater than the gift tax annual exclusion. The amount subject to the *Crummey* power in excess of the five-and-five power limits can result in estate tax inclusion for the holder of the power[463] and can also trigger gift tax liability.[464]

Example: If, in a trust having a $100,000 value, an "annual donee exclusion" power existed to withdraw $14,000 added to a trust in 2015,[465] the lapse of this withdrawal power without exercise would be treated as a "release" as to the $9,000 amount in excess of the first $5,000. As a result, that excess $9,000 would be deemed to be transferred to the trust by the power holder for purposes of applying the estate and gift tax rules concerning powers of appointment and transfer taxation. If the power holder were entitled to receive the trust income or had a special testamentary power of appointment over the trust property and died in 2015 without exercising the power, $9,000 (or a proportionate part of the estate tax value of the assets out of which the power could have been satisfied) would be included in his or her gross estate under §2036(a)(1) or §2038.[466]

Planners should weigh carefully, therefore, the gift tax advantages of securing the full benefit of the annual exclusion against the possible adverse transfer tax consequences resulting from having the excess property subject to the *Crummey* power includible in the gross estate of the holder of the power or, alternatively, treated as a taxable gift by him.[467]

(5) Successive Powers

Although the holding of a limited power of appointment does not ordinarily cause estate tax inclusion, a limited power of appointment exercised to create another power of appointment may be treated as a general power of appointment. Inclusion in the gross estate is required for the value of property for which a decedent[468]:

- by his or her will; or
- in a testamentary manner,[469] exercised a power by creating another power which can be exercised to postpone the vesting of an estate or interest in property.[470]

Example: A decedent has a limited power to appoint by will $100,000 to a group of persons consisting of his children and grandchildren. He exercises the power by making an outright appointment of $75,000 to his children. Further, as permitted by the governing document, he provides one child a power to appoint $25,000. The $25,000 will be includible in the decedent's gross estate.[471]

(6) Certain Imputed Powers

(a) Power to Substitute Trustees The IRS previously took the position that, where an independent corporate trustee has broad discretionary powers over income and principal, the settlor's retention of an unrestricted right to remove that independent corporate trustee without cause and to appoint another corporate trustee would cause the trust corpus to be included in the settlor's gross estate under §2036(a)(2) and §2038(a)(1).[472] The theory behind this rule was that the settlor could remove trustees until a replacement trustee was found who would follow the settlor's instructions and then function, in effect, as the settlor's surrogate. A question then arose as to whether the existence of a "revolving door" trust power might cause the IRS to extend the application of this position to the power of appointment situation.[473] For estate planners, the specific issue under §2041(a)(2) was whether a trust beneficiary holding an apparent non-general power of appointment who was given a similar "revolving door" power concerning trustee replacement would be deemed to possess all of the trustee's powers even though he or she could not be appointed as a successor trustee.[474] This dilemma has been resolved by the Service's withdrawal of its prior position in the §2036 and §2038 context where the IRS asserted gross estate inclusion.[475]

(b) Power to Distribute in Satisfaction of Support Obligation Exposure to federal estate tax inclusion under §2041 may also occur where a decedent has a power to appoint among a class of persons and that power is, or can be, exercised to discharge a legal obligation of the power holder (e.g., an obligation to support the recipient of the appointed trust distribution).[476] For example, the IRS considered the federal estate tax consequences of a settlement option selected by the insured where the proceeds of a life insurance policy were retained by the insurance company during the life of the insured's surviving spouse.[477] The spouse had a life income interest in the funds and could appoint principal to her children for their health, education, support, and maintenance. The IRS determined that the wife/decedent did not hold a general power of appointment over any of the funds because all of the children were adults at the date of the wife's death and the wife had no legal obligation to support them. The power could not be used, therefore, to discharge legal support obligations. The IRS cautioned, however, that if the spouse did have a legal obligation to support the children at her death, she would be regarded as possessing a general power of appointment over the funds to the extent that the funds could have satisfied her obligation to provide support.

This position has important implications when a parent, as a trustee, has the power to distribute trust assets to his or her minor child. Where trust distributions by the parent are deemed desirable, the parent-trustee should be given wide discretion to apply property for the minor's general welfare, not limited for support purposes. As a further precaution, the trust instrument could specifically prohibit the trustee from applying trust assets for the satisfaction of support obligations.[478] As an alternative, a special trustee might be designated for purposes of making these determinations concerning distributions from the trust.[479]

b. Gift Tax

The exercise or release of a general power of appointment will result in a taxable gift under the same circumstances in which a transfer of assets owned outright could result in a taxable gift.[480] The definition of a general power of appointment for gift tax and for estate tax purposes is the same, including the rules concerning (1) ascertainable standards relating to health, education, support, and maintenance; and (2) joint powers. The use of a five-and-five power is also permitted and this exception applies in determining whether a lapse constitutes a taxable release.

The exercise or release of a special power of appointment does not itself constitute a taxable gift. If, however, the effect of such action is to divest a life estate or other beneficial interest belonging to the donee of the power, or to extinguish a general power of appointment, this life estate termination would constitute a transfer of property for gift tax purposes.[481]

c. Income Tax

The holder of a power of appointment will be treated as the owner, for federal income tax purposes, of any portion of a trust from which the holder has a power exercisable solely by himself or herself to vest the corpus or the income therefrom in himself or herself.[482] This rule does not apply if:

- for a power over income, the grantor of the trust is treated as the owner for income tax purposes[483];
- the holder of the power, acting in the capacity of trustee or co-trustee, can apply the trust income to the support or maintenance of a person whom the holder of the power is obligated to support or maintain, except to the extent that such income is actually so applied[484]; or
- the holder renounces or disclaims the power within a reasonable time after first becoming aware of the existence of the power.[485]

For income tax purposes this power must be exercisable "solely" by the holder to cause income taxation to the power's holder.[486]

5. Planning Considerations

a. Creating Powers of Appointment

(1) Reasons for Using Powers of Appointment

The use of the limited (or special) power of appointment permits substantial post-mortem estate planning flexibility in the hands of other parties. This power to postpone decision making on the ultimate disposition of the corpus of a trust enables the established plan of trust distribution to be modified. This can be done on the basis of changes in the family and economic circumstances of the beneficiaries, or other economic and legal changes occurring after the death of the donor of the power. The use of a limited power of appointment may permit a second-generation member to have property benefits almost equivalent to ownership without adverse estate tax consequences at his or her death.[487]

Example: A special power could be made available to permit income or principal to be sprinkled among second generation members as the need arises. Each member of the second generation could be vested with a special power of appointment, with distribution of the trust corpus to be made at his or her death among such of his or her surviving descendants as he or she designates. The use of an appropriate default clause should be implemented to ensure that the property will go to the third generation as a class if the power of appointment is not exercised.[488]

Property over which a beneficiary is given a power of appointment in conjunction with some limited beneficial enjoyment (e.g., income for life) will not normally be subject to claims of dower (by a surviving spouse) or forced heirship at the death of that power holder. Such an arrangement will also normally avoid the claims of creditors of the power holder.

The special power of appointment also may be a valuable estate planning tool in the context of a QTIP marital deduction bequest. As noted above,[489] the marital deduction is permitted where the surviving spouse is vested with a life estate and a general power of appointment (often exclusively a testamentary power). This general testamentary power of appointment will cause the property to be included in the surviving spouse's estate at his or her death, but the property will not have been subjected to estate tax inclusion at the earlier death of the other spouse (by reason of the qualifying marital deduction). This general power of appointment would permit the surviving spouse to transfer that property to anyone. In contrast, where a QTIP trust is used to gain the benefits of the marital deduction, the surviving spouse does not have a general power of appointment. The surviving spouse may be given a special testamentary power of appointment, however. In this context, the spouse would have the capacity to direct the property among a limited number of beneficiaries identified as the class of possible appointees. This would enable the original testator to define the limited scope of the possible recipients for the surviving spouse to consider in possibly readjusting the original property disposition structure.

(2) Drafting Considerations

When including a power of appointment in a trust instrument, the following fundamental planning matters (and their related income, gift, and estate tax consequences) should be carefully analyzed:

- Should the power of appointment be general or limited?
- Who should be included in the group of possible appointees?
- Should any specific persons be excluded from this group?[490]
- Should a special power be "exclusive" or "nonexclusive"?[491]
- Should the power of appointment be exercisable during life, at death, or in both circumstances?
- Should new powers of appointment be permitted to be created by the exercise of the power?

- Should a five-and-five power be made available and, if so, should it be limited either (or both) as to (1) the maximum amount subject to the power or (2) the time of exercise?[492]
- Who should be designated as the takers in default of any exercise of the power of appointment?[493]
- Will the donee of the power be permitted to release such power in whole or in part (and what will be the tax effects of such release)?
- What will be the prescribed specific method for the exercise of the power of appointment?[494]

(3) Rule Against Perpetuities

The common-law rule against perpetuities requires that interests appointed by the donee of a power must vest within lives in being plus 21 years from the date on which the power was created by the donor.[495] In several states, there is a statutory rule against perpetuities; for example, the perpetuities period in Florida is 360 years. A number of states provide a statutory option out of the rule against perpetuities, and others have repealed the rule altogether. Where in effect, the rule against perpetuities does apply to powers of appointment.[496] General powers of appointment presently exercisable are usually treated for these purposes as the equivalent of outright ownership, however, so that the perpetuities period for appointed interests is measured from the date of actual exercise of the power.[497] Special powers and testamentary general powers are often required not only (1) to become exercisable within the perpetuities period but also (2) to be so limited that they must be exercised, if at all, within the time frame dictated by the rule against perpetuities.

b. Exercising the Power of Appointment

The donee of a power of appointment must analyze a variety of considerations pertinent to his or her possible exercise of a power of appointment, including:

- What will be the gift tax consequences?[498]
- What will be the estate tax consequences?[499]
- Are the takers in default those persons the holder of the power wishes to receive the property, and is the proportionate allocation among those persons as desired?
- Is the gift in default of appointment ambiguous and could this ambiguity be resolved by an exercise of the power of appointment?
- If the takers in default receive the property, will their form of ownership (e.g., outright, in trust, other format) be appropriate when considering their particular circumstances?
- Will the exercise of the power of appointment expose (under principles of local law) the appointed property to the claims of creditors of the holder of the power or of the appointees?

- How should a donee of a testamentary power of appointment account for the possibility that the appointee may die before the donee?
- Will the intended appointment violate the rule against perpetuities?

Consequently, both tax and other (e.g., local property law) considerations also must be carefully surveyed in this planning context by the donee of the power.

Notes

1. Another fundamental option, the funded irrevocable inter vivos trust, is ordinarily not a testamentary document, the property transfers into the trust having been completed during lifetime and being immune from the applicability of the federal estate tax at the death of the trust grantor (assuming avoidance of the estate tax "transfer" provisions).
2. See Chapter 4, A.1., regarding the changes made by the 2001 Economic Growth and Tax Relief Reconciliation Act (EGTRRA), Pub. L. No. 107-16, the 2010 Tax Relief, Unemployment Insurance Reauthorization, and Job Creation Act (2010 TRA), Pub. L. No. 111-312, and the American Taxpayer Reform Act of 2012 (ATRA), Pub. L. No. 112-240. Essentially, EGTRRA repealed the estate and generation-skipping transfer (GST) taxes and implemented a modified carryover tax basis regime for estates of decedents dying and generation-skipping transfers made in 2010 and modified the tax rate structure, the tax credit or exclusion amounts, the qualified family-owned business deduction, and the state death tax credit applicable in the years prior to repeal. However, all the changes made by EGTRRA (including the repeal) were scheduled to sunset for decedents dying and transfers made after 2010. EGTRRA, Pub. L. No. 107-16, §901. As explained in more detail in Chapter 4, A.1., the 2010 TRA generally reinstated the estate and GST taxes for estates of decedents dying and generation-skipping transfers made after 2009, repealed the former §1022 modified carryover basis regime that would otherwise have applied in 2010, allowed estates of decedents dying in 2010 to elect to apply former §1022 instead of the estate tax, reduced the rates and increased the exclusion amounts for 2010-2012, and extended various provisions through 2012. Pub. L. No. 111-312, §101(a), §301-§304. ATRA generally made permanent the changes made by EGTRRA and the 2010 TRA, but increased the estate and gift tax rates. ATRA, Pub. L. No. 112-240, §101(a), §101(c).
3. For example, this situation is complicated because of the large availability of widely advertised computer programs that assure that simple documents provided for a limited cost are all that is essential to facilitate a person's estate planning objectives.
4. For simplicity, the term "testator" is used to refer to either a testator or testatrix.
5. This memorandum may often be quite useful in explaining the testator's objectives and expectations in making property transfers and for identifying matters that may be difficult to comprehend without a forensic analysis, or properties that may be difficult to locate, including through the use of computer passwords and other security arrangements. Since this document is probably not implemented with testamentary formalities, it would not be binding for local law purposes, but that is not normally the objective for such a memorandum.

6. If the client has property in foreign jurisdictions, the laws concerning testamentary property transfers must be carefully examined. An appropriate "situs will" may be created for each jurisdiction where property transfers are important to the client. Of course, none of those wills should include a provision which specifies that "I revoke all prior wills" because this provision may then be determined to have worldwide applicability. Alternatively, those foreign-based assets may be inserted into a separate company or trust or other independent mechanism in that jurisdiction.
7. For example, the requirement (and, thereby, the cost) of an executor's bond might be waived in the last will. In some states this cost saving is also accomplished through the appointment of an "independent executor" who is not required by applicable state law to post a bond securing the executor's performance. The assumption of this approach avoiding a third party assurance bond is that this executor will not misappropriate funds from the estate (i.e., that most fiduciaries in this context should be trusted, rather than not trusted).
8. Federal estate tax savings may result, however, through using the will to implement a dispositive scheme taking maximum advantage, for example, of the estate tax marital deduction provision and the "credit shelter trust" mechanism.
9. Each state has laws prescribing how an intestate decedent's probate estate should be distributed. In the event a decedent's properties are located in several jurisdictions, a further determination must be made as to which state's intestate property succession laws control the disposition of those assets (i.e., the laws of the decedent's domicile at death or the laws of the property location).
10. See specimen last wills in the Worksheets and in various estate planning portfolios published by Bloomberg BNA.
11. *See, e.g.,* Tex. Est. Code, §251.051, prescribing the required elements of a will.
12. A question often arising for the estate planning attorney is the method of safeguarding the signed last will after its execution by the client. A variety of alternatives exist: (1) the client keeps the will (whether or not in a "safe-deposit box") but this may sometimes result in the loss of the document or attempted partial and ineffective revocations of the will; (2) the estate planner retains the will, but this may invite ethical challenges because the attorney is attempting to control future legal representation of the deceased client's estate; and (3) the will is deposited in the probate court (consistent with Uniform Probate Code, §2-515, as enacted locally). Few persons know of the latter possibility and it is seldom used. One important condition often imposed on the custodian of such wills is to assure the continued confidential nature of deposited wills.
13. This may be important where a name has been changed (such as upon marriage) or when an individual has always been identified by a "nickname."
14. This may also be important where the will might not be valid under the laws of another jurisdiction where the decedent has significant property and intestate beneficiaries may benefit in this situation.
15. Where a testator wants to implement multiple wills (e.g., a U.S. will and a foreign country will, each governing the disposition of property in separate national jurisdictions) this provision invalidating prior wills must be carefully constructed to assure that these specifications in one last will do not cause the revocation of the other last will dealing with the disposition of property in the other jurisdiction.
16. To assure that the testator understands the impact of this allocation provision when the debts are significant, a tax allocation chart might be prepared to identify the net-after-tax effect of these expenses on each beneficiary's share.

17. These debts must be real, with other documentation evidencing the existence of that debt (based on prior consideration provided), rather than being merely an attempt to transfer property without estate tax exposure.
18. The testator may desire that certain property (e.g., the personal residence) should be transferred subject to the mortgage debt, rather than causing this debt to be liquidated through the use of financial assets held in the decedent's residuary estate. This might particularly be the situation where the long-term mortgage debt is subject to a favorable interest rate at the time of death. Note Uniform Probate Code §2-607 (entitled "Nonexoneration"), specifying that a specific devise passes subject to any mortgage interest existing at the date of death, without right of exoneration, regardless of a general directive in the will to pay debts. This rule is contrary to the common law rule of exoneration for properties subject to a specific devise.
19. Such taxes should ordinarily be defined to include, if desired by the testator, federal estate taxes, state inheritance and estate taxes, foreign death taxes, generation-skipping transfer taxes, federal and state income taxes, and interest and penalties imposed with respect to these taxes. For a more detailed discussion of tax clauses in last wills, see 834 T.M., *Transfer Tax Payment and Apportionment* (Bloomberg BNA).
20. *See* the Uniform Probate Code, Part 9A ("Apportionment of Estate Taxes"), §3-9A-101 through §3-9A-115. Section 3-9A-103(a)(1) specifies that to the extent that a provision of a decedent's will expressly and unambiguously directs the apportionment of an estate tax, the tax must be apportioned accordingly. This provision then provides a series of default rules for the applicability of tax apportionment rules. *See* PLR 200206024 (because decedent's intent on estate tax apportionment was unclear, state apportionment statute was applied to apportion estate taxes generated by residuary bequests among property passing to residuary beneficiaries that did not qualify for marital or charitable deduction).
21. The federal estate tax also has provisions concerning the allocation of federal estate tax liabilities, subject to a contrary indication of intent by the testator. *See* §2206 and §2207 for specific rules in the federal estate tax provisions on proportionately allocating federal estate tax liabilities to life insurance beneficiaries and recipients of property over which the decedent had a power of appointment. Section 2207A provides for the allocation of estate and gift tax liabilities to recipients (surviving spouses) of qualified terminable interest property (see Chapter 5, D.3.d.) when the property benefiting the surviving spouse, and for which a marital deduction was received, is transferred during lifetime or at death. Section 2207A conflicts with many state death tax apportionment statutes because it provides for recovery by the surviving spouse's estate of an incremental amount of federal estate tax, rather than a pro-rata share of this tax, from the person receiving the property. Further, §2207B provides a right of recovery of the federal estate tax liability attributable to the inclusion in the gross estate of property transferred subject to a retained life interest (under §2036), for example, a funded revocable trust. Each of these federal estate tax allocation provisions permits a contrary direction by will, although the manner of complying with this contrary direction will vary. Effective for estates of decedents dying after August 5, 1997, the decedent's will or revocable trust must specifically indicate an intent to waive any right of recovery under §2207A and §2207B in order to waive those rights. §2207A(a)(2), §2207B(a)(2), as amended by the Taxpayer Relief Act of 1997, Pub. L. No. 105-34, §1302. Although a specific intent to waive the §2207B right of recovery must be indicated, a specific reference to §2207B is no longer required.

22. *See* §2056(b)(7)(B)(ii) (describing a qualifying life interest for marital deduction purposes).
23. *See Estate of Bradford v. Commissioner,* T.C. Memo 2002-238 (death taxes were treated as reducing charitable deduction).
24. *See Estate of Lewis v. Commissioner,* T.C. Memo 1995-168, involving a residuary marital gift to a spouse and a tax allocation clause directing that all taxes be paid from the residuary estate. Although the decedent's will showed an intent to maximize the amount of the marital deduction, this intent did not override the clear statement in the will that all estate tax was to be payable from the residue and, consequently, the tax clause in the will superseded the state law (New Hampshire) equitable apportionment statute; and *Leavenworth Nat'l Bank & Trust Co. v. United States,* 1996 U.S. Dist. LEXIS 7046 (D. Kan. 1996). *See also* TAM 199918003 (discretionary authority to pay estate taxes granted to trustee of decedent's revocable trust does not override mandatory direction in will that taxes be paid from residuary estate), TAM 9140005 (where decedent, New York resident, directed in his will that estate taxes be paid as if they were his debts, state apportionment statute was overridden, and, therefore, residue passing to his surviving spouse and estate tax marital deduction was reduced).
25. See TAM 9434004 where, under the will, a portion of the residuary gift was bequeathed to a credit shelter trust, and the remainder passed to a marital trust. The National Office advised that the credit shelter disposition was a pre-residuary bequest (as determined by reference to Florida law) and the entire burden of estate taxes applied to the residuary marital gift. In TAM 199924002, the surviving spouse in effect created a residuary estate from which estate taxes could be paid by disclaiming her interest in specified assets, which then passed as part of the residuary bequest under the dispositive terms of a funded inter vivos trust. The National Office advised that the pre-residuary marital share was not burdened with estate tax because the trust instrument required payment of estate taxes from trust principal but prohibited the use of assets or funds "otherwise excludible in computing federal estate taxes." In *Patterson v. United States,* 181 F.3d 927 (8th Cir. 1999), the court held that death taxes were properly paid from an inter vivos trust, rather than the residuary probate estate, under a will that directed taxes be paid out of the residuary estate but, in the event there was a trust in existence at the decedent's death, authorized the trustee to pay taxes from the trust if it were in the best interests of the beneficiaries. Construing the will and trust together to determine which document governs death tax apportionment, as required by state (Kansas) law, and applying the state law presumption that a decedent intended the estate and surviving spouse to have the full benefit of the marital deduction, the court concluded that payment from the trust was proper because the marital share would not bear the burden of estate taxes if taxes were paid from the trust and the will unambiguously authorized the trustee to make the payment.
26. This gross estate inclusion occurs by reason of §2044 (i.e., qualified terminable interest property is includible even though not "owned" by the surviving spouse at death).
27. §2207A(a)(1).
28. The Uniform Probate Code, §3-9A-104 (incorporating a segment of the Uniform Estate Tax Apportionment Act), contains a provision calling for the apportionment of estate taxes ratably to each person having an interest in the apportionable estate. The apportionable estate consists of the estate (after deductions, including the marital and charitable deductions) as determined for federal estate tax purposes. Thus, this will include an allocation of tax responsibility to that portion of the estate that includes assets held

outside the probate estate in a revocable trust because this provision defines the "estate" as the gross estate as determined for the purpose of the federal estate tax. In TAM 199918003, the National Office advised that §2207B requires a revocable trust to bear the burden of estate taxes generated by the inclusion, under §2036, of the date of death value of the trust property in the decedent's gross estate, because the will did not waive that right of reimbursement. The National Office, however, applied the trust's tax apportionment clause, rather than the will's conflicting clause, to apportion the tax burden attributable to the trust property.

29. A similar loan provision is often included in an irrevocable trust, but the objective in this situation is to assure that the trust assets usable for this purpose are not includible in the trust grantor's estate for federal estate tax purposes.
30. Uniform Probate Code §3-9A-103(a) provides for a hierarchy of priority for estate tax allocation provisions: first, the provisions in the decedent's will; next, the provision of a revocable trust, with the latest revocable trust instrument controlling in the event of conflicting allocation provisions in several revocable trust instruments; and, subsequently, a provision in any other dispositive instrument that expressly and unambiguously directs that any interest in property disposed of by the instrument is or is not to be applied to the payment of the estate tax attributable to the interest disposed of by the instrument.
31. T.C. Memo 1995-168.
32. Similarly, see *Estate of Miller v. Commissioner*, T.C. Memo 1998-416; TAM 199918003. *But see McKeon v. United States*, 151 F.3d 1201 (9th Cir. 1998).
33. Note that, because this allocation may be based on either state or federal law (in the absence of an explicit clause in the governing instrument), the options for sources of this apportionment law may include: (1) common law, including subsequent case law developments; (2) state apportionment statutes, including court decisions interpreting those state apportionment statutes; (3) the apportionment laws of other state jurisdictions where the client might hold real estate interests; and (4) the federal allocation provisions included in the federal estate tax statutes.
34. Note that in such a situation the separate property assets would not receive the income tax basis step-up at death that is available, pursuant to §1014(b)(6), for any interests in community property held by the surviving spouse. This would be important if the assets are significantly appreciated at the time of death. *See* 802 T.M., *Community Property: General Considerations* (Bloomberg BNA).
35. See Uniform Probate Code, §2-513, which specifically permits a testator to implement a separate writing to dispose of tangible personal property (other than money) if the reference is made to that writing in the testator's will. The writing must be signed by the testator and must describe the items and the recipients with reasonable certainty. The commentary to this provision suggests the following clause for inclusion in a will: "I might leave a written statement or list disposing of items of tangible personal property. If I do and if my written statement or list is found and is identified as such by my Personal Representative no later than 30 days after the probate of this will, then my written statement or list is to be given effect to the extent authorized by law and is to take precedence over any contrary devise or devises of the same item or items of property in this will."
36. See §2056(b)(4)(B), which specifies that, where the surviving spouse incurs any obligation imposed by the decedent during the transfer of property to the spouse, that encumbrance or obligation shall be taken into account as if the amount of a gift to the spouse were being determined.

37. Or a similar arrangement, as discussed in the marital deduction trust segment at Chapter 5, D.
38. See the detailed discussion concerning the use of powers of appointment and relevant federal tax planning at Chapter 5, E. See also 825 T.M., *Powers of Appointment—Estate, Gift, and Income Tax Considerations* (Bloomberg BNA). Note the Uniform Probate Code, §2-608, providing that, in the absence of a requirement that a power of appointment be exercised by a reference, or by an express or specific reference, to the power, a general residuary clause in a will, or a will making general disposition of all of the testator's property, expresses an intention to exercise a power of appointment held by the testator only if (1) the power is a general power and the creating instrument does not contain a gift if the power is not exercised or (2) the testator's will manifests an intention to include the property subject to the power. Ordinarily, a gift-in-default clause will be included upon creation of the power of appointment, and the Uniform Probate Code commentary to this article notes the assumption that this clause is ordinarily expected to take effect, stating "it is not merely an after-thought just in case the power is not exercised. The power is not expected to be exercised, and in fact is often conferred mainly to gain a tax benefit . . . inclusion of the property in the gross estate of a younger-generation beneficiary under section 2041 of the Internal Revenue Code, in order to avoid the possibly higher rates imposed by the new federal generation-skipping tax." That contemplated tax rate differential probably is no longer applicable in most situations.
39. See the discussion of testamentary trusts at Chapter 5, B.2.d.
40. See the discussion of the estate tax marital deduction and marital deduction formula clauses at Chapter 5, D. Also see Chapter 4, A.1., regarding the portability of the unified credit amount for spouses dying after 2010. §2010(c), as amended by the 2010 TRA, Pub. L. No. 111-312, §303, §304, and ATRA, Pub. L. No. 112-240, §101(a). This may increase the amount of the unified credit available to the estate of the second spouse to die.
41. See the discussion on estate planning for community property, including the widow's election, at Chapter 9, B. See also 802 T.M., *Community Property: General Considerations* (Bloomberg BNA).
42. See examples of these provisions in the sample wills and trust documents included in the Worksheets.
43. The estate tax exclusion amount may vary: (1) a $5 million amount is available for estates of decedents dying after 2009; (2) a portability provision applies for spouses dying after 2010; and (3) the basic exclusion amount is adjusted for inflation after 2011. Consequently, the amount allocable to the credit shelter trust should ordinarily be determined using a formula approach. See §2010(c), as amended by EGTRRA, Pub. L. No. 107-16, §521, §901; the 2010 TRA, Pub. L. No. 111-312, §101(a), §302-§304; and ATRA, Pub. L. No. 112-240, §101(a); *see also* Chapter 4, A.1. Where an amount less than the applicable credit amount is desired to be transferred into the credit shelter trust a specific amount might be identified in the will, but values of assets includible in the estate may change after execution of the will, causing unanticipated results during asset distributions.
44. See Chapter 4, A.1., regarding the portability of the unified credit amount. *See* §2010(c), as amended by the 2010 TRA, Pub. L. No. 111-312, §303, §304, and ATRA, Pub. L. No. 112-240, §101(a).

45. Under §2056(b)(7). See 843 T.M., *Estate Tax Marital Deduction* (Bloomberg BNA).
46. The exercise of this power might be limited during the period that the surviving spouse has his or her own adequate assets to maintain his or her standard of living, thereby insuring maintenance of the assets in this trust for the eventual benefit of the remainder beneficiaries (and the expenditure of other funds that would otherwise be in the surviving spouse's estate).
47. The qualified terminable interest trust differs from the marital deduction power of appointment trust in that no requirement exists in the QTIP situation that the spouse be given an "all events" general power of appointment (whether exercisable during life, at death, or both). Further, the surviving spouse need not be given a lifetime power of appointment. Otherwise, the trusts require similar administrative provisions.
48. This trust can be particularly useful where the testator wishes to transfer his or her assets (1) for the benefit of his or her second spouse for his or her survival period and (2) then to the children of his or her first marriage.
49. The surviving spouse's right to the annual income and the general power of appointment permits this property transferred into trust to qualify for the estate tax marital deduction under §2056(b)(5). See Chapter 5, D. The general power of appointment held by the surviving spouse will cause estate tax inclusion of the trust assets in the gross estate of the surviving spouse.
50. Alternatively, this power of appointment could be exercisable during lifetime, but this would cause the capital gains realized by the trust during the life of the surviving spouse to be taxable to the surviving spouse (as determined under the grantor trust income tax rules). Even though the maximum capital gains rate is only 20% and it only applies to taxpayers in the maximum §1(i) 39.6% income tax bracket, the surviving spouse would presumably request corpus distributions to enable satisfaction of his or her capital gains liability attributable to these gains. ATRA, Pub. L. No. 112-240, §102(b), increased the maximum capital gains rate to 20% for tax years after 2012. Prior to 2013, the maximum capital gains tax rate under §1(h) was 15%. *See* 2010 TRA, Pub. L. No. 111-312, §101(a), §102 (extending application of sunset provisions in EGTRRA), Pub. L. No. 107-16, §901, and the Jobs and Growth Tax Relief Reconciliation Act of 2003 (JGTRRA), Pub. L. No. 108-27, §303.
51. See Chapter 8 for the discussion of the generation-skipping transfer tax provisions.
52. See, for example, Tex. Est. Code §304.003, indicating that a nonresident of the state may not serve as an executor of an estate unless appointing a resident agent to accept service of process in all actions or proceedings with respect to the estate. This is a common provision in state probate codes to assure availability of service of process on the executor or trustee. The use of an inter vivos trust, implemented by contract, may be accomplished with an out-of-state trustee, eliminating this jurisdictional problem as to an inter vivos trust, but not as to a probate estate.
53. Rev. Rul. 69-486, 1969-2 C.B. 159, specifies that a non-pro-rata distribution from a trust constitutes a gain (or loss) realization event if the trustee is not authorized to make non-pro-rata distributions. The distribution is treated as a pro-rata distribution, followed by an exchange between the beneficiaries, making the distribution a realization event under §1001. This realization event treatment will not be applicable if non-pro-rata distributions are authorized by the governing instrument, because the trustees have the power to act as they deem proper in any partition of trust property (PLR 200328032) or if non-pro-rata distributions are authorized by state law (PLR

200334030). Numerous private letter rulings specify that Rev. Rul. 69-486 is not relevant in those situations because this ruling is distinguishable.

54. See, for example, Uniform Probate Code, §3-711, specifying that, until termination of his or her appointment, a personal representative has the same power over the title to property of the estate that an absolute owner would have, however, in trust for the benefit of the creditors and others interested in the estate. Further, Uniform Probate Code, §3-715, provides an extensive listing of powers exercisable by the personal representative "acting reasonably for the benefit of the interested persons."
55. See, for example, Tex. Est. Code §1104.153, which provides a format for a written "Declaration of Appointment of Guardian for My Children in the Event of My Death or Incapacity."
56. The probable objective in negating such a state law presumption would be to preserve all or part of the marital deduction in deflecting assets to the estate of that spouse treated as surviving. Consequently, the assets are includible in the estate of the "surviving" spouse, even though the survival is only for a very limited period. Even though the property may be required to pass through two probate estates, the allocation of part of the assets to the estate of the (deemed) surviving spouse may enable a significant federal estate tax benefit because of estate tax rate differentials and the equalization of the estates through the (partial) use of a marital deduction provision (though high exemptions and portability make this less likely). In *Estate of Acord v. Commissioner,* 93 T.C. 1 (1989), *aff'd,* 946 F.2d 1473 (9th Cir. 1991), the court held that a state simultaneous death statute requiring survivorship for 120 hours was overridden by a husband's will and inclusion in the wife/decedent's estate of husband's property was required when wife died 38 hours later in a common disaster.
57. The governing provisions may be included in the local probate code, rather than being enacted separately upon adoption of the Uniform Simultaneous Death Act. See Uniform Probate Code §2-104 (applicable in the intestacy context), which specifies that an individual who fails to survive the decedent by 120 hours is deemed to have predeceased the decedent for purposes of homestead allowance, exempt property, and intestate succession, and the decedent's heirs are determined accordingly. Uniform Probate Code §2-702 provides a similar survivorship presumption, but §2-702(d) permits exceptions including where the governing instrument contains language dealing explicitly with simultaneous deaths or deaths in a common disaster and that language is operable under the facts of the case.
58. Additional exposure to estate tax may be avoided in the event of close proximity of the time of deaths because of the "Credit for Tax on Prior Transfers." *See* §2013.
59. See §2056(b)(3), which specifies that the marital deduction is not precluded (because of the terminable interest rule) where (1) the interest of the spouse is conditional on survival for a six-month period after the death of the first spouse to die and (2) the surviving spouse does not actually die within that six-month period. Many states have legislation consistent with this provision. *Cf. Estate of Heim v. Commissioner,* 914 F.2d 1322 (9th Cir. 1990) (provision conditioning spousal transfer on her survival until distribution of estate (indeterminate period not necessarily falling within six-month limitation period of §2056(b)(3)) caused transfer to fail to qualify for marital deduction and state law savings provision did not save deduction because there was insufficient evidence that decedent intended transfer to qualify for marital deduction).
60. See Uniform Probate Code, §2-502(a), which specifies that every will shall be in writing signed by the testator or in the testator's name by some other person in the testator's

conscious presence and by the testator's direction, and shall be signed by at least two persons within a reasonable time after witnessing either the signing or the testator's acknowledgment of the signature or the will. Uniform Probate Code §2-502(b) specifies that a will that does not comply with these requirements is valid as a holographic will, whether or not witnessed, if the signature and material portions of the document are in the testator's handwriting.

61. Uniform Probate Code §2-506, specifies that a written will is valid if executed in compliance with the specifications above or if its execution complies with the law at the time of execution of the place where the will is executed, or of the law of the place where at the time of execution or at the time of death the testator is domiciled, has a place of abode, or is a national. Note that provisions regarding the formalities of will execution vary by state.
62. Uniform Probate Code §2-504.
63. See, for example, Tex. Est. Code §251.102 and §251.103, which indicate that a will or testament may, at the time of its execution or at any subsequent date during the lifetime of the testator and the witnesses, be made self-proved, and the testimony of the witnesses in the probate thereof may be made unnecessary.
64. See Uniform Probate Code §3-905, which specifies that a provision in a will purporting to penalize any interested person for contesting the will or instituting other proceedings relating to the estate is unenforceable if probable cause exists for instituting proceedings. Similarly, Restatement (Third) of Property: Wills and Other Donative Transfers (2003), §8.5 (entitled "No-Contest Clauses"), specifies that a provision in a donative document purporting to rescind a donative transfer to, or a fiduciary appointment of, any person who institutes a proceeding challenging the validity of all or part of the donative document is enforceable unless probable cause existed for instituting the proceeding. *See also* Bekerman, *Is There Terror in In Terrorem Clauses*, 51 Tax Mgmt. Memo. 67 (Mar. 2010).
65. *See* Reg. §301.7701-4(b) (defining "business trusts"); §301.7701-4(c) (defining "investment trusts"); §301.7701-4(d) (defining "liquidating trusts"). See also the regulations adopting a "check-the-box" approach to entity classification at Reg. §301.7701-1 through §301.7701-4 and §301.7701-6. Rev. Rul. 2004-86, 2004-2 C.B. 191, provides a discussion of these rules and identifies an investment trust classified as a trust for federal tax purposes. *But see* Rev. Rul. 2013-14, 2013-26 I.R.B. 1267 (Mexican Land Trust, which allows non-Mexican persons to own residential real property in Mexico is not trust within meaning of Reg. §301.7701-4(a)).
66. Restatement of the Law of Trusts, 3d, §2. *See also* Reg. §301.7701-4(a) (defining trust for income tax purposes).
67. Restatement of Trusts, 3d, §2, ¶ f.
68. Note from the discussion of "defective trusts" at Chapter 6, D.4., a trust may be structured to provide immunity from subsequent estate and gift taxes but not from income tax treatment for the trust grantor.
69. In many states a trust is irrevocable unless a power of revocation is expressly reserved or implied from language in the instrument. Some states reverse this rule, specifying that a trust is revocable unless expressly made irrevocable. *See, e.g.,* Tex. Prop. Code §112.051. Because professional drafters normally identify whether or not a trust is revocable these provisions will have limited applicability. The Uniform Trust Code (UTC), §602(a), specifies that, unless the terms of a trust expressly provide that the trust is irrevocable, the settlor may revoke or amend the trust. UTC §602(b) specifies

that, if a revocable trust is created or funded by more than one settler (1) to the extent the trust consists of community property, the trust may be revoked by either spouse acting alone but may be amended only by joint action of both spouses; and (2) to the extent the trust consists of property other than community property, each settlor may revoke or amend the trust as to the portion of the trust property attributable to that settler's contribution. See, also, Restatement of Trusts, 3d, §63, "Power of Settlor to Revoke or Modify," which provides that: (1) the settlor of an inter vivos trust has power to revoke or modify the trust to the extent the terms of the trust so provide; and (2) if the settlor failed expressly to provide whether the trust is subject to a retained power of revocation or amendment, the question is one of interpretation. Comment c, entitled "Presumptions regarding revocability," specifies that where the settlor failed expressly to provide whether a trust is subject to revocation or amendment, if the settlor retained no interest in the trust (other than by resulting trust), it is rebuttably presumed that the settlor has no power to revoke or amend the trust. If, however, the settlor failed expressly to provide whether the trust is revocable or amendable but retained an interest in the trust (other than by resulting trust), the presumption is that the trust is revocable and amendable by the settlor.

70. Income and estate tax savings can often be accomplished (at the cost of a federal gift tax, except if protected by the annual donee exclusion and the unified credit) by the creation of a funded inter vivos irrevocable trust. See the discussion of irrevocable inter vivos trusts at Chapter 6, D.3.
71. For transfers before March 2, 1986, the "short-term" or "10-year" trust functioned for federal income tax purposes to enable shifting of income to a lower bracket taxpayer within the family group for a limited time period, but the retention of the reversionary interest caused the property to be includible in the grantor's estate for federal estate tax purposes. The Tax Reform Act of 1986 eliminated the opportunity to deflect income through the use of a short-term trust. See §673(a), providing for federal income tax purposes for ownership treatment to the grantor of the trust income when the grantor has more than a 5% reversionary interest in a trust.
72. Most states have adopted the Uniform Testamentary Additions to Trusts Act, presently incorporated into the Uniform Probate Code (as §2-511), as part of their probate codes. *See, e.g.,* Tex. Est. Code §254.001. Pursuant to this Uniform Probate Code provision, under a will a person may validly devise property to the trustee of a trust established or to be established (1) during the testator's lifetime by the testator, by the testator or some other person, or by some other person, or (2) at the testator's death by the testator's devise to the trustee, if the trust is identified in the testator's will and its terms are set forth in a written instrument, other than a will, executed before, concurrently with, or after the execution of the testator's will or in another individual's will if that other individual predeceased the testator, regardless of the existence, size, or character of the corpus of the trust. The devise is not invalid because the trust is amendable or revocable, or because the trust was amended after the execution of the will or the testator's death. The property devised to the trustee is to be administered as a part of the trust and governed by the terms of the agreement, including amendments or modifications made to the trust agreement before or after the death of the testator. Unless the testator's will provides otherwise, a revocation or termination of the trust before the testator's death will cause the devise to lapse.
73. State insurance laws may require special provisions to assure the distribution of policy proceeds into a trust after the insured dies. See the discussion of life insurance trusts at

Chapter 9, C.3.c. *See also* 807 T.M., *Personal Life Insurance Trusts* (Bloomberg BNA); 860 T.M., *Revocable Inter Vivos Trusts* (Bloomberg BNA).

74. If the trustee is a person or entity other than the grantor this arrangement could enable the grantor to test a trustee for investment performance and management during the grantor's lifetime and before the trust becomes irrevocable as of the time of the grantor's death. Of course, this could also be structured with the grantor as trustee (during lifetime) and the investment management responsibilities being delegated to an investment advisor.
75. Careful analysis under state law must occur with respect to the implications of certain asset transfers into the trust, particularly for real estate transfers. Questions arising may include: (1) if the person transfers real property subject to a mortgage with a "due on sale" clause without the lender's consent, will that "due on sale" clause apply to require immediate payment of the loan balance; (2) whether a homestead exemption under local law will be terminated; (3) whether title insurance for the property will be cancelled; and (4) whether certain creditor protections will be voided.
76. Section 676 treats the grantor as the owner of trust income where the grantor retains a power to revoke a trust. Reg. §1.671-3(a) provides that:

> When a grantor or other person is treated under subpart E (section 671 and following) as the owner of any portion of a trust, there are included in computing his tax liability those items of income, deduction, and credit against tax attributable to or included in that portion. For example:
> (1) If a grantor or another person is treated as the owner of an entire trust (corpus as well as ordinary income), he takes into account in computing his income tax liability all items of income, deduction, and credit (including capital gains and losses) to which he would have been entitled had the trust not been in existence during the period he is treated as owner.

Various subpart E, subchapter J, provisions specify grantor trust treatment: §673 for reversionary interests, the value of which exceeds 5% of the value of the trust at creation; §674, the power to control the beneficial enjoyment, subject to eight specific exceptions, such as the power to withhold income from an income beneficiary only temporarily and the power to distribute corpus subject to a reasonably definite standard; §675, certain administrative powers, for example, the power to borrow trust property without adequate interest or adequate security and the power to vote certain voting control stock; §676, the power to revoke a trust and revest title to the asset in the grantor; and §677, where the income can be used either directly or indirectly for the benefit of the grantor or the grantor's spouse.

Additionally, Reg. §1.671-4(a) specifies that:

> . . . items of income, deduction, and credit attributable to any portion of a trust that, under the provisions of subpart E (section 671 and following), part I, subchapter J, chapter 1 of the Internal Revenue Code, is treated as owned by the grantor or another person, are not reported by the trust on Form 1041 . . . , but are shown on a separate statement to be attached to that form.

Reg. §1.671-4(b) specifies, however, that where the trust is all treated as owned by one grantor (or by one other person) other reporting requirements may be applicable.

77. For estate tax purposes the grantor will have retained a life interest causing inclusion in the gross estate under §2036 and also will hold a power to revoke the trust causing inclusion under §2038.

78. In some states, an expeditious, informal probate process is applicable, with general judicial supervision of a testamentary trust not being particularly cumbersome. Consequently, some estate planners suggest that in these contexts a funded revocable trust is not essential but probate will not achieve some of the other objectives such as privacy concerns.
79. Ancillary probate proceedings will be required if a decedent at death owns property in locations other than the residence state, for example, real estate.
80. Pursuant to the terms of the trust agreement, a designated replacement trustee can assume trustee responsibilities immediately after the death (or earlier incompetency) of the trust grantor/original trustee, or another person can be the trustee of the revocable trust from the inception. Requirements of financial institutions to change the account name should ordinarily be able to be accomplished expeditiously after providing a death certificate documenting the death of the original trust grantor.
81. The jurisdiction of choice may have eliminated the rule against perpetuities, may have more flexibility for trustees in the management of assets, and may have other, more convenient trust administration rules than would apply in the trust grantor's jurisdiction.
82. A procedure will need to be specified concerning how that incompetency is to be documented, thereby enabling the successor trustee to assume control and management if the grantor is the original trustee.
83. The Uniform Probate Code, if locally applicable, would include the trust estate of a revocable trust in the deceased grantor's "augmented estate" and would thereby make the revocable trust assets subject to elective share rights. Uniform Probate Code §2-201 through §2-205. Section 2-201 provides that the value of the augmented estate consists of the sum of the values of all property, whether real or personal, movable or immovable, tangible or intangible, wherever situated, that constitute the decedent's net probate estate, the decedent's nonprobate transfers to others, the decedent's nonprobate transfers to the surviving spouse, and the surviving spouse's property and nonprobate transfers to others. The purpose of combining the estates and nonprobate transfers of both spouses is to implement a partnership or marital sharing theory. *See* Uniform Probate Code §2-207, Commentary.
84. Rev. Rul. 74-613, 1974-2 C.B. 153; Rev. Rul. 81-98, 1981-1 C.B. 40.
85. Section 1361(c)(2)(A)(i) provides that an eligible S corporation shareholder includes a trust, all of which is treated (under subpart E of part 1 of subchapter J) as owned by an individual who is a citizen or resident of the United States. See §1361(c)(2) for other trusts that also may be eligible S corporation shareholders. Prior to the Small Business Job Protection Act of 1996, Pub. L. No. 104-188, a grantor trust could continue to be an S corporation shareholder after the grantor's death for a period of only 60 days. As revised for years after 1996, a grantor trust may continue to be an S corporation shareholder for two years from the death of the deemed owner without regard to whether the entire trust corpus is includible in the deemed owner's estate. Further, trusts that receive stock under a will may own S corporation stock during the two-year period beginning on the date the S corporation stock is transferred to them. §1361(c)(2)(A)(iii).
86. *See* §1245(b)(1), §1250(d)(1). Since §1250 recapture is seldom required, this is ordinarily pertinent only in §1245 depreciation recapture situations.
87. Reg. §1.47-3(f)(1)(ii)(b). This provision has limited relevance after the repeal of the regular percentage investment tax credit, but the concept of no disqualifying disposition may be applicable when other types of any subsequently enacted tax credits are claimed.
88. Effective for sales or exchanges after May 6, 1997, the 1997 Taxpayer Relief Act, Pub. L. No. 105-34, §312(a), replaced the over-age-55 exclusion of gain on the sale of the prin-

cipal residence under former §121 with a broader §121 exclusion that does not have an age requirement, allows the exclusion of a higher dollar amount, requires no replacement residence reinvestment, and, in general, may be used every two years.

89. *See* Reg. §1.121-1(c)(3)(i) (during period that taxpayer is treated under §671-§679 as owner of trust or portion of trust that includes taxpayer's principal residence, taxpayer is treated as owning such residence for purposes of satisfying two-year ownership requirement of §121 and trust's sale or exchange of residence is treated as made by taxpayer).
90. *See* Rev. Rul. 64-302, 1964-2 C.B. 1709; PLR 9009053; IRS Info. Letter 2015-0018 (Series I bonds). The IRS has also indicated that continued deferral is also available where the bonds are transferred to an irrevocable grantor trust. *See* IRS Info. Letter 2015-0028 (owner of Series EE bonds may continue to defer reporting of accrued interest where bonds are transferred to irrevocable grantor trust).
91. *See* §645; Reg. §1.645-1. IRS Form 8855, *Election to Treat a Qualified Revocable Trust as Part of an Estate,* is to be used to make the §645 election. This could simplify the process of filing returns but the §645 election would eliminate the opportunity to use lower income tax brackets, which might be available to a separate trust.
92. Rev. Rul. 90-55, 1990-2 C.B. 161. See §644, which states that the taxable year of any trust will be the calendar year.
93. Reg. §1.1001-2(c) *Ex. (5).* If the liabilities deemed transferred to the trust exceed the basis of the assets deemed transferred by the grantor the grantor will recognize gain to the extent of the difference. *See* Regs. §1.1001-2(a)(1). See, further, Rev. Rul. 77-402, 1977-2 C.B. 222, holding that, when a grantor trust owns a partnership interest subject to liability and the grantor renounces all the grantor trust powers, the grantor is treated as having transferred the interest to the trust and will recognize gain or loss on the transfer.
94. The estate would be an additional taxpayer available for the splitting of income. In addition, the estate is not subject to the trust throwback rules on income accumulated during administration, although most domestic trusts are not subject to these rules. §665(c). The advantages of income splitting between the estate beneficiary and the estate are diminished, of course, when marginal income tax rates are lower. With the substantial compression of the lower §1(e) income tax brackets applicable to trusts and estates a significant incentive exists to currently distribute income to beneficiaries who will often be subject to tax on that income in a lower marginal income tax bracket. Section 101 of EGTRRA, Pub. L. No. 107-16, reduced the §1(e) tax rates applicable to trusts and estates beginning after June 30, 2001. The reduced rates (under §1(i)) apply to taxable years beginning before 2013. *See* 2010 TRA, Pub. L. No. 111-312, §101(a) (extending sunset provision in EGTRRA, Pub. L. No. 107-16, §901). ATRA increased the rates (under §1(i)) to a maximum of 39.6% for taxable years beginning after 2012, but kept the estate and trust rates the same. *See* ATRA, Pub. L. No. 112-240, §101(b).
95. See Reg. §1.641(b)-3(a), which further states that "where an executor who is also named as trustee under a will fails to obtain his discharge as executor, the period of administration continues only until the duties of administration are complete and he actually assumes his duties as trustee, whether or not pursuant to a court order." This regulation also specifies that an estate will be considered as terminated when all the assets are distributed, except for a reasonable amount which is set aside in good faith for the payment of unascertained or contingent liabilities and expenses. *See* Rev. Rul. 76-23, 1976-1 C.B. 264 (when sole purpose for retaining stock in S corporation in estate of

deceased shareholder is to facilitate payment of estate tax under §6166, administration of estate will not be considered unreasonably prolonged, and estate will continue to be eligible S corporation shareholder for period during which estate complies with the provisions of §6166); PLR 200226031; PLR 200529006.

96. Such jurisdictions include Alaska (no time limit), Delaware (110-year limit), Florida (360-year limit), South Dakota (no time limit) and Wyoming (1,000-year limit).
97. Restatement of Trusts, 3d, §10, entitled "Methods of Creating a Trust" provides that a trust may be created by:
    (a) a transfer by the will of a property owner to another person as trustee for one or more persons; or
    (b) a transfer inter vivos by a property owner to another person as trustee for one or more persons; or
    (c) a declaration by an owner of property that he or she holds that property as trustee for one or more persons; or
    (d) an exercise of a power of appointment by appointing property to a person as trustee for one or more persons who are objects of the power; or
    (e) a promise or beneficiary designation that creates enforceable rights in a person who immediately or later holds those rights as trustee, or who pursuant to those rights later receives property as trustee, for one or more persons.
98. Often, an inter vivos trust agreement will indicate (on an attachment) that only a nominal amount (e.g., $100) constitutes the original corpus of the trust. This arrangement denies to parties inspecting the trust agreement any access to information about the true value of properties held by the trust. Subsequent additions (not identified in the trust agreement) may be made to the trust, either immediately thereafter or at some later time.
99. Even if the grantor is also the trustee or one of the trustees, as is often the case with a living trust, he or she should provide a written agreement evidencing the trust arrangement. He or she should execute the agreement by signing as both grantor and trustee. Thereafter, any replacement trustee (ordinarily identified in this agreement) will be subject to the provisions of the trust agreement.
100. For a discussion of spendthrift provisions see the Uniform Trust Code (2001), Article 5, and, particularly, §502(b), which specifies that a trust provision stating that the interest of a beneficiary is held subject to a "spendthrift trust," or words of similar import, is sufficient to restrain both voluntary and involuntary transfer of the beneficiary's interest. The Comment to this provision indicates that under this provision a settler has the power to restrain the transfer of a beneficiary's interest, regardless of whether the beneficiary has an interest in income, in principal, or in both. Unless one of the exceptions under this article applies, a creditor of the beneficiary is prohibited from attaching a protected interest and may only attempt to collect directly from the beneficiary after payment is made from the trust. For a spendthrift provision to be effective, it must prohibit both the voluntary and involuntary transfer of the beneficiary's interest, i.e., a settler may not allow a beneficiary to assign while prohibiting a beneficiary's creditors from collecting. Of course, this spendthrift protection exists while the assets are held in trust, and that protection evaporates after the assets are in the hands of the beneficiary. Spendthrift provisions are governed by applicable state law and the potential scope of these provisions varies from state to state. U.S. trust law generally specifies that a person cannot establish a spendthrift trust for his or her benefit and obtain any asset protection benefits. *See* ALI Restatement (Third) Trusts, §58. However, the "full faith and credit" clause of the U.S.

Constitution (Art. 4, §1) seems to enable recognition of a spendthrift clause in a self-settled trust if valid under the governing laws for the trust.

101. Although local trust law normally provides for powers exercisable by a trustee, these laws might be more restrictive than desired, and are subject to change by state legislatures. Such statutory powers also might vary if trust assets are located in multiple jurisdictions. The objective of the powers clause is to assure that any powers specified for the trustee under the trust instrument are in addition to those provided under local trust law. These powers would be similar to the powers vested in the executor under the will. Where a testamentary trust is created (i.e., in a last will), one clause in the last will enumerating fiduciary powers will usually apply to both the executor and the trustee. See the Uniform Trust Code (2001), which provides in §815 for general powers of the trustee, noting that a trustee, without authorization by the court, may exercise (1) all powers conferred by the terms of the trust; or, (2) except as limited by the terms of the trust, (a) all powers over the trust property that an unmarried competent owner has over individually owned property; (b) any other powers appropriate to achieve the proper investment, management, and distribution of the trust property; and (c) any other powers conferred by statute. Further, §816 provides an extensive enumeration of specific powers that a trustee may exercise. The comment to §815 notes that the existence of a power, however created or granted, does not speak to the question of whether it is prudent under the circumstances to exercise the power.

102. The Uniform Trust Code (2001) includes, as one of the "Specific Powers of Trustee," §816(21) which would enable a trustee to "pay an amount distributable to a beneficiary who is under a legal disability or who the trustee reasonably believes is incapacitated, by paying it directly to the beneficiary or applying it for the beneficiary's benefit, or by: (A) paying it to the beneficiary's [conservator] or, if the beneficiary does not have a [conservator], the beneficiary's [guardian]; (B) paying it to the beneficiary's custodian under [the Uniform Transfers to Minors Act] or custodial trustee under [the Uniform Custodial Trust Act], and, for that purpose, creating a custodianship or custodial trust; (C) if the trustee does not know of a [conservator], [guardian], custodian, or custodial trustee, paying it to an adult relative or other person having legal or physical care or custody of the beneficiary, to be expended on the beneficiary's behalf; or (D) managing it as a separate fund on the beneficiary's behalf, subject to the beneficiary's continuing right to withdraw the distribution."

103. *See* Dukeminier, *A Modern Guide to Perpetuities*, 74 Calif. L. Rev. 1867 (1986). Although some jurisdictions have eliminated the rule against perpetuities, best practice suggests inclusion of such a provision, particularly if the trust provisions might be interpreted in multiple jurisdictions, unless the clear intent is to exploit the elimination of the rule against perpetuities, as enacted in a specific jurisdiction. For a further discussion see the Restatement of Trusts, 3d, §29(b), providing that a trust (or provision) is invalid if violating the rule against perpetuities. Comment g to this provision includes an extensive discussion of this limitation, including the fact that some states are limiting the applicability of a rule against perpetuities.

104. The Uniform Trust Code (2001), §702(a), states that a trustee should provide a bond to secure performance of the trustee's duties only if the court finds that a bond is needed to protect the interests of the beneficiaries or is required by the terms of the trust and the court has not dispensed with the requirement. Uniform Trust Code §105(b)(6) does specify that the terms of a trust should prevail over the trust code provisions with certain

exceptions, including the power of a court to require, dispense with, or modify or terminate a bond (and certain other powers as specified in that provision).

105. Uniform Trust Code (2001), §708(a), states that, if the terms of a trust do not specify the trustee's compensation, a trustee is entitled to compensation that is reasonable under the circumstances. Section 708(b) provides that, if the terms of a trust specify the trustee's compensation, the trustee is entitled to be compensated as specified, but the court may allow more or less compensation if: (1) the duties of the trustee are substantially different from those contemplated when the trust was created; or (2) the compensation specified by the terms of the trust are unreasonably low or high. The Comment to this section notes that the relevant factors in determining this compensation include the custom of the community; the trustee's skill, experience, and facilities; the time devoted to trust duties; the amount and character of the trust property; the degree of difficulty, responsibility, and risk assumed in administering the trust, including in making discretionary distributions; the nature and costs of services rendered by others; and the quality of the trustee's performance.
106. Uniform Trust Code (2001), §704(c), provides that a vacancy in a trusteeship of a noncharitable trust must be filled in the following order of priority: (1) by a person designated in the terms of the trust to act as successor trustee; (2) by a person appointed by unanimous agreement of the qualified beneficiaries; or (3) by a person appointed by the court.
107. Note that a "subjective" power as granted to a trustee may enable that trustee to have more influence over the conduct of the beneficiary. If the beneficiary is aware of a mandatory distribution provision (e.g., "beneficiary shall receive all current income") the beneficiary will recognize that the trustee has no control over the beneficiary's behavior. However, where the trustee is obligated to make a judgment concerning distributions, the beneficiary's conduct may be influenced. This might particularly be the situation where the grantor specifies trust distribution provisions having an objective to incentivize the beneficiary towards (or away from) certain conduct. These could include, for example, attaining certain educational goals, achieving specified income goals, or discouraging negative or unproductive behavior.
108. See Gerald R. Jantscher, Trusts and Estate Taxation 2 (1967) at 194, indicating that 61 basic variations are possible. See also Chapter 6, D.3., indicating when adverse estate tax consequences might result by reason of the trust grantor retaining certain powers over the enjoyment of the income or corpus (whether or not acting as trustee) when creating an irrevocable inter vivos trust. If the trust is to qualify for the marital deduction, §2056(b)(5) and §2056(b)(7) require certain dispositive provisions (e.g., mandatory distribution of income to the surviving spouse at least annually and, for power of appointment trusts, a general power of appointment vested in the surviving spouse either during lifetime or at death). See the discussion at Chapter 5, D.
109. Note that for this purpose "income" is defined under the applicable state law (and any specific variances as included in the governing instrument). This includes the concepts included in the Uniform Principal and Income Act, as enacted locally.
110. This determination as to "income" may necessitate application of an adjustment power (if available under state law or the instrument) to recategorize some receipts as income rather than corpus, or vice versa. The adjustment power will not be relevant if, for example, the trust instrument prohibits the trustee from investing assets as a "prudent investor."

111. If a standard such as "support" is included the trustee will be obligated to make a determination as to what amount is necessary to enable that support. This could include an analysis of (1) the beneficiary's standard of living at that time and (2) whether other sources of support exist for this beneficiary. If another person is obligated to support the trust beneficiary the trustee should be able (under local law) to reduce the trustee's distributions by these payments actually being made. Local law may have guideposts as to whether the trustee should "tilt" in favor of an income (rather than remainder) beneficiary in determining the amount of these distributions.
112. Under normal circumstances, these "standards" applicable to distributions should be the same for income and corpus distributions, thereby avoiding confusion as to which standards are applicable to specific types of distributions.
113. See the more detailed discussion of powers of appointment at Chapter 5, E. See also 825 T.M., *Powers of Appointment—Estate, Gift, and Income Tax Considerations* (Bloomberg BNA).
114. §2041(b)(1)(A); Reg. §20.2041-1(c)(2).
115. §2041(b)(2). That property subject to this withdrawal power at the time of death will be includible in the power holder's gross estate.
116. See the discussion of the generation-skipping transfer tax system in Chapter 8. See also 850 T.M., *Generation-Skipping Transfer Tax* (Bloomberg BNA).
117. *See* §2205, §2207B(a); Reg. §20.2205-1. Consideration must be given to the impact (if any) of such a provision on the marital deduction. To avoid any reduction of the marital deduction, the taxes should be payable from the nonmarital portion of the trust when a marital deduction gift is made.
118. If life insurance proceeds or qualified plan distributions excluded from the federal gross estate or exempt from state inheritance tax are received, such amounts can be made available to the grantor's estate through discretionary loans or purchases of assets without negating federal or state estate tax exemptions. The tax allocation provision in the trust (or the "powers" clauses) should negate any possible inference that the trustee has a duty to make these assets available to the grantor's estate.
119. See Uniform Trust Code §414, which suggests that state law provide that, after notice to the qualified beneficiaries, the trustee of a trust consisting of trust property having a total value of less than $50,000 may terminate the trust if the trustee concludes that the value of the trust property is insufficient to justify the cost of administration. In the trust agreement the trust grantor could establish a higher or lower plateau for this purpose.
120. The Uniform Trust Code, §417, suggests a statutory provision that, after notice to qualified beneficiaries, a trustee could combine two or more trusts into a single trust or divide a trust into two or more separate trusts, if the trust does not impact rights of any beneficiary or adversely affect achievement of the purposes of the trust. This provision could be subject to a contrary provision in the terms of the trust.
121. This right would be valuable where one or more such trusts might have only nominal assets. The creation (and continuance) of several trusts, however, might be the result of having sought income tax objectives to split income among several taxpayers, thereby taking advantage of the progressive income tax rate structure applicable to trusts. After the changes made by the Revenue Reconciliation Act of 1993 a trust reached the 39.6% rate bracket at the $7,500 taxable income level (to be annually adjusted for inflation—see Worksheet 1 for recent annual adjustments) and, consequently, the federal income tax planning value of this benefit of splitting income into several trusts was significantly

reduced. *See* §1(e). Section 101 of EGTRRA, Pub. L. No. 107-16, reduced the §1(i) tax rates beginning after June 30, 2001, and JGTRRA, Pub. L. No. 108-27, accelerated the reduction of the top rate to 35%, effective January 1, 2003 (with similar reductions in lower brackets). The reduced rates (under §1(i)) apply to taxable years beginning before 2013. *See* 2010 TRA, Pub. L. No. 111-312, §101(a) (extending sunset provision in EGTRRA, Pub. L. No. 107-16, §901). ATRA, Pub. L. No. 112-240, increased the §1(i) top rate to 39.6% applicable to tax years beginning after 2012. However, the progressivity of the income tax rate applicable to trust income remains much steeper than the progressivity of the rates applicable to individuals.

122. This would include, for example, the legal capacity to take title to property, to continue to hold such property, and to administer the trust. These are questions decided under applicable state property and trust law. See the Uniform Trust Code (2001), Article 8, particularly §801 through §817, for an extensive elaboration of the usual duties and powers of a trustee.
123. The designation of the client's own attorney as the fiduciary will implicate conflict of interest provisions in the model rules of professional conduct when a significant risk exists that the attorney's trustee appointment will materially limit the attorney's independent professional judgment.
124. The trustee would presumably take into account (but not necessarily be controlled by) the federal income tax situation of each beneficiary to assure that the overall income tax liabilities for the trust and the various beneficiaries will be reduced to an extent consistent with the grantor's objectives. The right to exercise such discretion with respect to income and corpus distributions might be vested with a "special trustee" who is familiar with the family situation and who is appointed solely for this purpose. This special trustee, often better than a corporate trustee, might understand the financial needs and spending habits of the various family members. Alternatively, a family member might be designated as the trustee, with the right granted to that family member to delegate other responsibilities (e.g., investment management and custodial activities) to professionals. In this situation the individual trustee would make the determinations concerning the discretionary distributions of income and principal, and often would be in the best position to make those decisions.
125. The grantor may include instructions in the trust instrument for the trustee, in making investment decisions, to emphasize either current income or long-term appreciation. If the corpus is invested so that the principal does not appreciate, the impact of significant inflation could substantially erode the value of the remainder interest. The duties of the trustee in this context may be impacted by the provisions of the locally enacted "Uniform Principal and Income Act (1997)" and the "Uniform Prudent Investor Act (1994)."
126. In choosing the trustee, the trust creator should also consider geographical differences (e.g., to the extent possible should the trustee, beneficiaries, and trust assets be located within reasonable geographic proximity?) and the trustee's particular management expertise (e.g., to deal with farming operations or oil and gas investments).
127. For example, the beneficiaries may perceive a large, corporate trustee to be a faceless, unsympathetic entity. Alternatively, an individual trustee (e.g., an older brother or a stepfather) may generate jealousies and family difficulties, suggesting the possible use of an institutional trustee in this situation, particularly to make decisions concerning discretionary distributions of income and corpus.

128. The Uniform Prudent Management of Institutional Funds Act (UPMIFA) applies the Prudent Investor Rule standard to the management and investment of institutional charitable funds and evidences that standards for managing and investing institutional funds should be the same regardless of whether a charitable organization is organized as a trust, a nonprofit corporation, or some other entity.
129. The trust beneficiaries may request a trustee to maintain a concentrated position in certain investments (despite the trustee's advice to the contrary) and the trustee should then examine whether, under local trust law, some exculpatory agreement is permitted and appropriate to release the trustee from liability and to indemnify the trustee for losses.
130. This may include internal memoranda evidencing a continuing examination of the appropriateness of certain investment holdings, a periodic review of comprehensive investment strategy, and correspondence with various beneficiaries about these decisions.
131. *See* Mark L. Ascher, *Scott and Ascher on Trusts* (5th ed. 2013). Note that many states (e.g., California) have prudent investor laws describing an expansive approach permitted to trustees to emphasize a "total return" approach to implementing an investment strategy. See the "Uniform Prudent Investor Act (1994)" as enacted by various states.
132. See at Chapter 5, A.2., the listing of possible powers authorized to be exercised by an executor under a will. The powers to be exercised by the trustee concerning the management of a trust will be similar. Further, see the elaboration of possible trustee powers in Uniform Trust Code (2001), §815 (General Powers of Trustee) and §816 (Specific Powers of Trustee).
133. This power, if retained by the trust grantor, will not cause gross estate inclusion of the assets, assuming the replacement trustee is not permitted to be the grantor. *See Estate of Helen S. Wall,* 101 T.C. 300 (1993); *Vak v. Commissioner,* 973 F.2d 1409 (8th Cir. 1992), *rev'g* T.C. Memo 1991-503; Rev. Rul. 95-58, 1995-2 C.B. 191.
134. This should not be the trust grantor since adverse estate tax consequences (e.g., §2036–§2038) could arise. If the client is hesitating to identify currently a "trust protector," the client may contemporaneously specify in some type of irrevocable document that one or more beneficiaries, trustees or specified third parties may appoint a trust protector in the future.
135. In some situations, applicable state law may govern the activity of a "trust protector," but in most situations, the activities and responsibilities of that person will be governed exclusively by the terms of the governing instrument (subject, of course, to some general local probate and trust law rules protecting against potential abuse of a trustee's fiduciary responsibility).
136. See 852 T.M., *Income Taxation of Trusts and Estates* (Bloomberg BNA). See also Reg. §301.7701-1(a), which specifies that whether an organization is an entity separate from its owners for federal tax purposes is a matter of federal tax law and does not depend on whether the organization is recognized as an entity under local law. Further, Reg. §301.7701-4(a) specifies that, in general, the term "trust" as used in the Code refers to an arrangement created either by will or by an inter vivos declaration whereby trustees take title to property for the purpose of protecting or conserving it for the beneficiaries under the ordinary rules applied in chancery or probate courts. An arrangement will be treated as a trust under the Code if it can be shown that the purpose of the arrangement is to vest in trustees responsibility for the protection and conservation of property for beneficiaries who cannot share in the discharge of this responsibility and, therefore, are not associates in a joint enterprise for the conduct of business for profit.

137. Section 641(b) provides that the taxable income of a trust "shall be computed in the same manner as in the case of an individual, except as otherwise provided in this part. The tax shall be computed on such taxable income and shall be paid by the fiduciary."
138. Under §1(e) and §1(i)(2), as amended by ATRA, Pub. L. No. 112-240, §101(b)(1), the taxable income over $7,500, as adjusted for inflation, is subject to the highest 39.6% income tax rate. The 39.6% maximum rate applies to tax years beginning after 2012. Note that the 1993 RRA, Pub. L. No. 103-66, §13201–§13202, greatly compressed the income tax brackets for trust income. For 2015, the highest income tax rate begins at $12,301 for trusts compared to $413,201 for single individuals and $464,851 for jointly filing spouses. Rev. Proc. 2014-61, 2014-47 I.R.B. 860, §3.01. For 2016, the top rate beings at $12,401 for trusts compared to $415,050 for single individuals and $466,950 for jointly filing spouses. Rev. Proc. 2015-53, 2015-44 I.R.B. 615, §3.01. Effective for tax years beginning after December 31, 2012, the Health Care and Education Reconciliation Act of 2010, Pub. L. No. 111-152, §1402(a), imposes a new tax on estates and trusts equal to 3.8% of the lesser of the undistributed net investment income for the tax year or the excess (if any) of the taxpayer's adjusted gross income over the dollar amount at which the highest tax bracket begins. *See* §1411(a)(2). For purposes of the additional 3.8% tax, net investment income includes gross income from interest, dividends, annuities, royalties and rents (other than from a trade or business), income from passive activities, or from trading in financial instruments or commodities. *See* §1411(c)(1). For guidance on the application of §1411, see Reg. §1.1411-0 through Reg. §1.1411-10, Reg. §1.469-11(b)(3)(iv); T.D. 9644, 78 Fed. Reg. 72,394 (Dec. 2, 2013). In conjunction with the regulations, the IRS posted on its website, "Questions and Answers on the Net Investment Income Tax" (www.irs.gov/uac/Newsroom/Net-Investment-Income-Tax-FAQs) to provide answers to some basic questions regarding §1411. For a detailed discussion of §1411 as it pertains to trusts and estates, see 852 T.M., *Income Taxation of Trusts and Estates* (Bloomberg BNA).
139. §642(b).
140. §651, §661. Different concepts may apply to the taxation of income distributed to a beneficiary during a tax year after the year for which the income is taxed to the trust. See the discussion of the accumulation trust rules at Chapter 5, B.5.c.
141. For a detailed discussion of the rules governing the income tax characterization of distributions made by trusts or estates, see 852 T.M., *Income Taxation of Trusts and Estates* (Bloomberg BNA).
142. Distributable net income (DNI) is defined in §643(a).
143. A deduction from the trust's gross income for trust distributions made is allowable to the trust under §651 (simple trust) or §661 (complex trust and estate).
144. Such amounts must be included in the beneficiary's income under §652 (simple trust) or §662 (complex trust).
145. *See* Reg. §1.643(a)-0.
146. §643(a). In Reg. §1.643(b)-1, the definition of DNI takes into account certain state statutory provisions identifying income and principal (i.e., to reflect the "total return" concept of investment management). Trust provisions that depart fundamentally from traditional concepts of income and principal (that is, rules allocating ordinary income to income and capital gains to principal) will generally be disregarded. However, amounts allocated between income and principal pursuant to applicable state law will be respected if state law provides for a reasonable apportionment between the income and remainder

beneficiaries of the total return of the trust for the year, taking into account ordinary income, capital gains, and, in some situations, unrealized appreciation. For example, a state law that provides for the income beneficiary to receive annually a unitrust amount of between 3% and 5% of the annual fair market value of the trust assets is a reasonable apportionment of the total return of the trust. Similarly, a state law that permits the trustee to make equitable adjustments between income and principal to fulfill the trustee's duty of impartiality between the income and remainder beneficiaries is a reasonable apportionment of the total return of the trust.

147. Two significant results of the DNI definition are that (1) DNI is reduced by deductible expenses paid from trust principal even though the payments do not necessarily reduce the actual amount of trust income (as defined under the instrument or state law) that beneficiaries receive, and (2) capital gains are normally excluded from DNI (except for the year in which the trust terminates) because that gain is realized on the trust corpus rather than the income of the trust (as determined in the local law trust accounting context). Consequently, the definition of DNI causes capital gains to ordinarily be taxed to the trust (or estate), rather than to the income beneficiaries, because this tax cost pertains to the trust principal (held for the benefit of the trust remainder beneficiaries), rather than to the current trust income (distributable to current income beneficiaries).

148. Assume a distribution is made of 100 shares of Stock X worth $10,000 during a year in which the trust has $25,000 DNI and no other distributions. Even if the stock is deemed "principal" or trust "corpus" for local trust law purposes, this distribution would constitute an income distribution within the scope of subchapter J. The effect would be that, through application of the DNI rules, $10,000 of the trust's $25,000 of income would be shifted from the trust to the distributee because of this in-kind stock distribution.

149. Where all of its income is to be distributed currently, §651 permits a deduction to the trust equal to the amount of such income. Section 652 prescribes that the amount of income required to be distributed currently by the trust will be included in the gross income of the beneficiaries to whom the income is required to be distributed (whether or not actually distributed).

150. An exception to these rules is recognized under §663(a) for a gift or bequest of a specific sum of money or of specific property required by the express terms of a will or trust instrument to be paid or credited in not more than three installments. In this situation the distribution will not be allowed as a federal income tax deduction to an estate or trust under §661, and is not included in the gross income of the recipient beneficiary under §662. Reg. §1.663(a)-1(a). *See* PLR 200210002 (because decedent's pecuniary formula bequest did not qualify as bequest of specific sum under §663(a)(1), amount distributed to satisfy bequest was included in recipient's income pursuant to §662 and estate could deduct that amount under §661).

151. *See* §661(a)(1), §662(a)(1). This provides for income allocation treatment similar to that applicable to "simple trusts."

152. *See* §661(a)(2), §662(a)(2). Section 661(a)(2) specifies that the deduction is available for "any other amounts properly paid or credited or required to be distributed for such taxable year." See also *Buckmaster v. United States,* 984 F.2d 379 (10th Cir. 1993), concerning whether a distribution was "proper" for this purpose because it was made prior to court approval, but court approval was subsequently obtained.

153. Assume that a trust has $7,000 of DNI during a particular tax year and the trustee is required to pay to Beneficiary X $5,000 of income, but may pay to Beneficiary Y $5,000

(from income or principal). A distribution of $5,000 to each of X and Y would cause X to be in receipt of the $5,000 of DNI. Y, the second tier beneficiary (because of the non-mandatory nature of the distribution), would include only $2,000 in her gross income (the remaining undistributed DNI). See Reg. §1.662(a)-3.

154. Note that, by reason of the steep income tax rate progression applicable to trusts under §1(e), only if taxable income amounts for the beneficiaries are minimal will this factual situation exist.
155. The trust agreement should be drafted to preclude this impediment by authorizing trust distributions on behalf of the minor to parents and other representatives of the minor.
156. §665–§667. For an extensive discussion of the throwback rules, see 856 T.M., *Subchapter J—Throwback Rules* (Bloomberg BNA).
157. If the distribution is to a minor child, the trust instrument might permit a distribution into a Uniform Transfers to Minors Act (UTMA) format, avoiding a guardianship. This would partially (but not completely) accommodate the objective to suspend the assets away from the beneficiary. A form of UTMA would need to be enacted under local law to accommodate this result.
158. *See* §665(c), enacted by the 1997 Taxpayer Relief Act, Pub. L. No. 105-34, §507(a)(1). These rules do remain applicable to (1) foreign trusts, (2) domestic trusts that were at any time foreign trusts, and (3) domestic trusts created before March 1, 1984, that would be treated as multiple trusts under §643(f) (if §643(f) applied to pre-March 1, 1984 trusts).
159. Before the 1969 Tax Reform Act, Pub. L. No. 91-172, only income accumulated by a trust in the five-year period before the year of distribution was subject to throwback rules. Further, the rules did not then apply to (1) estates, (2) de minimis ($2,000 or less) distributions of accumulated income, (3) income accumulated before a beneficiary's twenty-first birthday, (4) distributions to meet a beneficiary's "emergency needs," and (5) certain final trust distributions. The Tax Reform Act of 1969 eliminated these exceptions, except for the inapplicability of the throwback rules to estates. Also enacted at that time were capital gain throwback rules, which essentially paralleled the throwback rules pertinent to ordinary income. Before the 1976 Tax Reform Act, Pub. L. No. 94-455, the tax on such amounts could be computed, at the election of the beneficiary, under either of two methods: an "exact method" or a "shortcut method." Under the exact method, the tax was that which would have been payable if the distribution had actually been made in the year the accumulation occurred. The shortcut method, in effect, averaged the tax attributable to the distribution over a number of years, equal to the number in which the income was earned by the trust. In the 1976 Tax Reform Act, the "exact method" was repealed and the "shortcut method" was modified by allocating the average accumulation distribution to three of the five preceding years and excluding those two years with the highest and lowest taxable incomes. §667(b).
160. §667(b)(1)(A).
161. §667(b)(1)(B). Any year in which the beneficiary suffered a loss is treated as a year in which his or her taxable income was zero.
162. §666(b), §666(c).
163. §667(b)(1)(D).
164. §667(b)(1).
165. *Id.*; §666(b), §666(c). Section 666(e) provides, however, that tax payments made by the trust in excess of the income tax liability of the beneficiary will not be refunded to the beneficiary.

166. §665(b). This exception does not apply to foreign trust or certain multiple trust distributions.
167. §665(b). In those states where the age of majority is 18 this "under age 21 exception" is not modified.
168. *See Morris Trusts v. Commissioner,* 51 T.C. 20 (1968), *aff'd,* 427 F.2d 1361 (9th Cir. 1970) (Tax Court held that numerous trusts should not be consolidated, notwithstanding that creation of such trusts was pursuant to tax avoidance purpose; recordkeeping requirements and proper form were strictly observed and court concluded that, under these circumstances, separate identities of each trust would be observed). *Cf. Boyce v. United States,* 190 F. Supp. 950 (W.D. La. 1961), *aff'd per curiam,* 296 F.2d 731 (5th Cir. 1961) (90 trusts were deemed to be sham because they were actually administered as one trust). *See also Judy Trust for David Quinn,* 833 F.2d 563 (5th Cir. 1987) (attempt to create separate trust for each beneficiary of a class trust failed for lack of beneficiary); *Sence v. United States,* 394 F.2d 842 (Ct. Cl. 1968).
169. Reg. §1.641(a)-0(c), which attempted to limit the use of multiple trusts, was held to be invalid in *Stephenson Trust v. Commissioner,* 81 T.C. 283 (1983). The court determined that, by purporting to overrule *Morris Trusts v. Commissioner,* 51 T.C. 20 (1968), *aff'd,* 427 F.2d 1361 (9th Cir. 1970), the regulation exceeded the grant of regulatory authority by the U.S. Congress. Although determined in 1983 to be invalid, this regulation was not withdrawn, perhaps reflecting the subsequently enacted statutory provision concerning trust consolidation.
170. §643(f).
171. *Id.*
172. *See* Staff of the J. Comm. on Tax'n, General Explanation of the Revenue Provisions of the Tax Reform Act of 1984, at 256. This explanation noted that the following trusts, which an individual created with the principal purpose of avoidance of federal income tax, would be treated as one trust for purposes of federal income tax: Trust 1 for the benefit of his sister S1, his brother B1, and his brother B2; Trust 2 for the benefit of his sister S2, his brother B1, and his brother B2; Trust 3 for the benefit of his sister S1, his sister S2, and his brother B1; and Trust 4 for the benefit of his sister S1, his sister S2, and his brother B2. Under each trust instrument, the trustee was given discretion to pay any current or accumulated income to any one or more of the beneficiaries. The explanation also noted, however, that the following multiple trust arrangement was not to be consolidated: X established two irrevocable trusts for the benefit of X's son and daughter. Son is the income beneficiary of the first trust and the independent trustee is required to pay all income currently to son for life. Daughter is the remainder beneficiary. X's daughter is an income beneficiary of the second trust and the trust instrument permits the independent trustee to accumulate or to pay income, in its discretion, to daughter for her education, support, or maintenance. The trustee also may pay the remainder beneficiary, and will receive the trust corpus upon son's death.
173. *See* §665(c)(2)(B). As noted in Chapter 5, B.5.c., the accumulation trust rules also apply to foreign trusts.
174. §667(c)(1). If the beneficiary is trapped by such a rule, he or she can perhaps argue that, pursuant to Reg. §1.641(a)-0(c), several trusts should be consolidated into one trust, thereby preserving the credit for income taxes previously paid by the trust.
175. §667(c)(2).
176. *See* ATRA, Pub. L. No. 112-240, §102(b). This maximum rate applies to those taxpayers in the §1(i) 39.6% maximum income tax bracket. Prior to 2012, the maximum

capital gains rate was 15%. *See* 2010 TRA, Pub. L. No. 111-312, §101(a), §102 (extending application of 15% maximum rate [under §1(h)] to taxable years beginning before 2013 by amending sunset provisions in EGTRRA, Pub. L. No. 107-16, §901, and JGTRRA, Pub. L. No. 108-27, §303).

177. See former §644, repealed by the 1997 Taxpayer Relief Act, Pub. L. No. 105-34, §507(b)(1), effective for sales or exchanges after August 5, 1997. Also note that an unlimited throwback rule for capital gains allocated to the corpus of an accumulation trust was enacted in the 1969 Tax Reform Act, Pub. L. No. 91-172, and repealed by the 1976 Tax Reform Act, Pub. L. No. 94-455.
178. Former §644.
179. Various other exceptions and refinements to these basic rules were prescribed under former §644, for example, a short sale could not be used to circumvent the rules (former §644(d)(1)); interest was chargeable where a delay in tax reporting occurred due to differing tax years (former §644(a)(2)(B)); and the tax character of property included flowed through to the beneficiary (former §644(c)). In addition, various administrative problems sometimes arose, for example, when the trustee did not have sufficient information about the transferor to compute the tax on the includible gain.
180. Former §644(f)(1). This rule did not apply to an installment payment received by the trust after the death of the transferor.
181. *See* §643(e)(2), §661(a)(2).
182. §643(e)(1)(A).
183. §643(e)(2), §661(a)(2).
184. §643(e)(3). This election applies to all distributions made by the estate or trust during a taxable year. Further, this election, once made, may only be revoked with the IRS's consent.
185. *See* §267(a)(1) (providing for disallowance of losses in certain transactions between related taxpayers), §267(b)(6) (specifying that such relationship exists between fiduciary of trust and beneficiary of that trust). Section 267 previously did not apply to deny a tax loss deduction on a distribution by an estate to a beneficiary, but this rule was changed in the Taxpayer Relief Act of 1997, Pub. L. No. 105-34, §1308(a), to deny a loss deduction except in the case of a distribution by an estate in satisfaction of a pecuniary bequest. *See* §267(b)(13).
186. §665(b)(1). Section 665(b)(2) specifies that an election is required to obtain this 65-day treatment.
187. The trust's income tax bracket would probably be higher than that of the beneficiary. In this context, the "kiddie tax" (described below), as specified in §1(g), may be applicable.
188. §666(e).
189. *See* §667(a)(2), §667(b).
190. *See* ATRA, Pub. L. No. 112-240, §102(b). This maximum rate applies to those taxpayers in the §1(i) 39.6% maximum income tax bracket. Prior to 2012, the maximum capital gains rate was 15%. *See* 2010 TRA, Pub. L. No. 111-312, §101(a), §102 (extending application of 15% maximum rate [under §1(h)] to taxable years beginning before 2013 by amending sunset provisions in EGTRRA, Pub. L. No. 107-16, §901, and JGTRRA, Pub. L. No. 108-27, §303).
191. See §103, which provides for exclusion from gross income for income derived from certain state and local government debt obligations.
192. *See* §2010(c), as amended by EGTRRA, Pub. L. No. 107-16, §521. EGTRRA also amended §2505 to establish a lifetime exemption amount for gift tax purposes equal to

$1 million, effective for gifts made after December 31, 2001. See Chapter 4, A., for a discussion of estate planning–related tax changes made by EGTRRA. The §2505(a) gift tax exclusion amount is $1 million for gifts made in 2010, is $5 million for gifts made in after 2010, and has a portability provision for spouses after 2010 (with the basic exclusion amount adjusted for inflation in 2012). See §2010(c), §2505(a), amended by the Taxpayer Relief Act of 1997, Pub. L. No. 105-34, §501, EGTRRA, Pub. L. No. 107-16, §521, §901, 2010 TRA, Pub. L. No. 111-312, §101(a), §301-§304, and ATRA, Pub. L. No. 112-240, §101(a); *see also* Chapter 4, A.1.

193. *See* §2010(c), amended by the 1997 Taxpayer Relief Act, Pub. L. No. 105-34, §501, EGTRRA, Pub. L. No. 107-16, §521, §901, 2010 TRA, Pub. L. No. 111-312, §101(a), §302-§304, and ATRA, Pub. L. No. 112-240, §101(a); *see also* Chapter 4, A.1.

194. Prior to 2004 and after 2010, years when the estate tax applicable exclusion amount is equal to that available for gift tax purposes the entire exclusion amount might be used during a decedent's life and, therefore, would not be available at the time of death in determining the estate tax liability.

195. As discussed at Chapter 5, D.4.f.(2), this planning to protect the applicable exclusion amount upon the death of the first spouse to die is not essential if the total combined value of the estates of the two spouses is less than the applicable exclusion amount, because the applicable credit will protect the entire estate from estate taxation upon the death of the surviving spouse. This assumes that asset appreciation after the death of the first spouse and prior to the death of the second spouse will not cause the value to exceed the applicable exclusion amount available when the second spouse dies. Also see Chapter 4, A.1., regarding the portability of the unified credit amount for spouses dying after 2010. §2010(c), amended by the 2010 TRA, Pub. L. No. 111-312, §303, §304, and ATRA Pub. L. No. 112-240, §101(a).

196. §2056. See Chapter 4, A., and B., for a discussion of estate planning related tax changes made by EGTRRA, Pub. L. No. 107-16. Also see Chapter 4, A.1., regarding the changes made by the 2010 TRA, Pub. L. No. 111-312, §101(a), §302-§304, including the portability of the §2010(c) unified credit amount, and ATRA, Pub. L. No. 112-240, §101(a), which generally made permanent the changes made by EGTRRA and the 2010 TRA.

197. Also, see the extensive discussion of the marital deduction in 843 T.M., *Estate Tax Marital Deduction* (Bloomberg BNA).

198. The question of whether an individual in a "non-traditional" marriage with a decedent constitutes a "surviving spouse" has been addressed by the IRS, the courts, and even (on occasion) by Congress. The question initially arose in the context of common law marriages entered into by opposite-sex couples. *See* Rev. Rul. 58-66, 1958-1 C.B. 60 (ruling that IRS would generally recognize common law marriage as marriage for federal tax purposes where couple entered into such relationship in state recognizing common law marriage); *but see* Rev. Rul. 76-155, 1976-1 C.B. 286 (denying "surviving spouse" status where considerable doubt existed that alleged spouse actually entered into common law marriage with decedent). See also TAM 200132004, where the National Office advised (in the particular situation described) that the marital deduction was not available for an amount paid to an alleged surviving spouse under a settlement agreement because the highest court of the state would conclude that the described decedent and his alleged common law wife did not enter into a common-law marriage. More recently, the question has centered on same-sex marriage and its validity. That question was conclusively resolved when the Supreme Court held that same-sex marriage is a

fundamental right and that all states must license and recognize such marriages. *See Obergefell v. Hodges*, 135 S. Ct. 2584 (2015). As a result, state-recognized marriages of same-sex couples are recognized for the marital deduction (and other federal tax entitlements and responsibilities), the same as for other spouses whose marriages are respected under state law. Prior to 2013, there existed a patchwork among the states regarding recognition of same-sex marriage, but federal recognition of such marriages was prohibited by the 1996 Defense of Marriage Act (DOMA), Pub. L. No. 104-99, §3 (defining "marriage" and "spouse" for purposes of all federal laws and regulations as limited to opposite-sex couples). However, in June 2013, the Supreme Court ruled that §3 of DOMA was unconstitutional. *See United States v. Windsor,* 570 U.S. 12 (2013), *aff'g* 699 F.3d 169 (2d Cir. 2012), *aff'g* 833 F. Supp. 2d 394 (S.D.N.Y. 2012). In response to the ruling, and the Court's refusal to rule on §2 of DOMA (which permitted states to refuse recognition of same-sex marriages performed in sister states), the IRS issued guidance in September of 2013, ruling that the IRS would recognize a marriage of same-sex individuals that was validly entered into in a state (which includes, for federal tax purposes, any domestic or foreign jurisdiction with legal authority to sanction marriages) whose laws authorized the marriage of two individuals of the same sex even if the married couple was domiciled in a state that did not recognize the validity of same-sex marriages. Rev. Rul. 2013-17, 2013-38 I.R.B. 201. Further, the IRS ruled that, where the Code or regulations use the terms "spouse," "husband and wife," "husband," and "wife," such terms would be interpreted to include an individual married to a person of the same sex if the individuals were lawfully married under state law, and the term "marriage" would include such a marriage between individuals of the same sex. *Id.* The ruling applied prospectively from September 16, 2013, but allowed taxpayers to rely on the ruling in filing amended returns or refund claims to the extent the §6511 statute of limitations remained open. Rev. Rul. 2013-17. The IRS has issued proposed regulations that would codify the IRS's definitions of "spouse," "husband," "wife," and "husband and wife" as set out in Rev. Rul. 2013-17. *See* Prop. Reg. §1.7701-18, REG-148998-13, 80 Fed. Reg. 64,378 (Oct. 23, 2015). Note that questions regarding who constitutes a "surviving spouse" can also arise where there are disputes over the validity of a prior divorce or subsequent marriage. *Estate of Goldwater v. Commissioner,* 539 F.2d 878 (2d Cir. 1976) (dealing with validity of second marriage where decedent's first wife challenged validity of divorce decree); *Estate of Spalding v. Commissioner,* 537 F.2d 666 (2d Cir. 1976) (similar); *Estate of Steffke v. Commissioner,* 538 F.2d 730 (7th Cir. 1976), *cert. denied,* 429 U.S. 1022 (1976) (similar). For a detailed discussion of the *Windsor* case and DOMA, see 858 T.M., *Family, Kinship, Descent, and Distribution* (Bloomberg BNA).

199. For estates of decedents dying after November 10, 1988, to qualify for the marital deduction the surviving spouse must be a U.S. citizen, unless the property is placed in a qualified domestic trust or the surviving spouse becomes a U.S. citizen within the specified period after the death of the first spouse. §2056(d). See the discussion of this special "QDOT" trust mechanism at Chapter 5, D.7.a.
200. As described below, property can pass to the surviving spouse in a variety of formats, not limited to either direct transfers or a "marital deduction trust." *See* §2056(c).
201. See the discussion below of the use of an "equalization formula." Except in the case of nonresident noncitizen decedents subject to tax under §2101 with the unified credit defined under §2102(b), the federal estate tax has essentially operated as a flat tax for

estates of decedents dying after 2005 (because of §2001 rate changes and §2010 unified credit increases enacted under EGTRRA, Pub. L. No. 107-16, §511, §521, the 2010 TRA, Pub. L. No. 111-312, §302, §303, and ATRA, Pub. L. No. 112-240, §101(a), §101(c)).

202. See, generally, the discussion of estate planning techniques concerning community property at Chapter 9, B. When the U.S. Congress enacted the marital deduction, it also enacted legislation permitting the splitting of income between husband and wife through the use of the joint federal income tax return to solve a similar problem in the federal income tax context.
203. §2056(b)(4)(A). When the state death tax and other property not qualifying for the marital deduction exceed the amount allocated to the credit shelter disposition (which constitutes the exempt amount), federal estate tax is imposed which reduces the marital deduction and further increases the federal estate tax. The problem previously did not arise if the state death tax was limited to the former §2011 state death tax credit. As noted in Chapter 4, A., former §2011 was repealed for decedents dying after 2004 and replaced with the §2058 state death tax deduction. *See* 2010 TRA, Pub. L. No. 111-312, §101(a) (extending sunset provision in EGTRRA, Pub. L. No. 107-16, §901); ATRA, Pub. L. No. 112-240, §101(a) (generally making permanent changes made by EGTRRA and 2010 TRA, including repeal of state death tax credit).
204. §2056(b)(7). Section 2056(b)(7)(B)(ii) provides that a qualifying income interest for life also exists if the surviving spouse has a usufruct interest for life in the property.
205. Reg. §20.2044-1(a) indicates that, if a decedent has a qualifying income interest for life in any property and a deduction was allowed under §2056(b)(7) or §2523(f), §2044 requires that the trust property is includible in the gross estate of the surviving spouse.
206. Section 2511 provides for gift taxation of the transfer of the income interest (the interest owned by the surviving spouse), and §2519(a) specifies that all other interests are thereby transferred for gift tax purposes.
207. §1014(b)(10).
208. TAMRA, Pub. L. No. 100-647, §5033(a)(1), enacting §2056(d) and §2056A.
209. This trust is described in §2056A. For a further discussion of the qualified domestic trust, see Chapter 5, D.7.a., and 842 T.M., *Transfers to Noncitizen Spouses* (Bloomberg BNA).
210. This would include the myriad of interests subject to the estate tax, for example, real property, securities, cash, insurance, joint property, tangible property, transfers within three years of death, dower rights, and property subject to a general power of appointment. The function of this rule is to assure that a marital deduction will be available only for the property potentially exposed to federal estate tax at the decedent's death.
211. §2056(a). The implication of this statement is that if property otherwise qualifying for the marital deduction is reduced by estate and inheritance tax liabilities, it does not "pass" to the extent used to actually satisfy such liabilities. Section 2056(b)(4) provides that the valuation of a marital deduction transfer will take into account the effect of any taxes or encumbrances on the net value passing to the spouse. Section 2056(c) provides that an interest in property will be considered as "passing" from the decedent to a person only if such interest was (1) bequeathed or devised to such person; (2) inherited by such person; (3) a dower or curtesy interest (or statutory interest in lieu thereof); (4) transferred to such person by the decedent at any time; (5) held in joint ownership with a right of survivorship; (6) received upon the exercise, default, release, or nonexercise of a

power of appointment; or (7) an interest consisting of proceeds of insurance on the life of the decedent. Such property is considered as passing even though received by a surviving spouse exercising his or her right to an elective share or upon disclaimers by children, with the assets thereby being shifted to the surviving spouse. Reg. §20.2056(c)-2(c). See also Rev. Rul. 84-105, 1984-2 C.B. 197, where an estate tax marital deduction was allowable for the entire value of a decedent's pecuniary bequest to a marital trust even though the executor transferred an amount to the marital deduction trust which was less than the full value of the bequest. The spouse could have caused the diversionary transfer to be reversed, did not do so, and was treated as having received the property and then having transferred the property by gift. Similarly, see TAM 200223020.

212. §2056(a). In a common disaster situation, a presumption included in the governing instrument which reverses the usual presumption under the Uniform Simultaneous Death Act will be valuable in establishing that a spouse "survived" the decedent. In such an instance, the marital deduction property must be includible in the gross estate of the spouse treated as the survivor. This property is eligible for the marital deduction at the cost, however, of two probate administrations. *See* Reg. §20.2056(c)-2(e). The reversal of the presumption under the Uniform Simultaneous Death Act should be used with caution where an unlimited marital deduction bequest is made.

213. §2056(b). See Reg. §20.2056(b)-1(b) for a definition of "terminable interests." Reg. §20.2056(b)-1(c) identifies nondeductible terminable interests. Reg. §20.2056(b)-1(d) identifies exceptions to that nondeductible terminable interest rule. Note that not all "terminable interests" are nondeductible for estate tax purposes.

214. See the extended discussion at Chapter 5, D.3.g. and D.3.i., concerning the exceptions to the nondeductible terminable interest rule.

215. §2056(b)(4)(A); Reg. §20.2056(b)-4(c)(1). Reg. §20.2056(b)-4(c)(2) provides an example, indicating that, if the only bequest to the surviving spouse is $100,000, and the spouse is required to pay a state inheritance tax in the amount of $1,500, the actual value for computing the marital deduction is the net amount of $98,500 received by the spouse. *Cf.* Rev. Rul. 88-12, 1988-1 C.B. 330, where under applicable state law the spousal gift was charged with expenses but not taxes.

216. §2056(b)(4)(B). Reg. §20.2056(b)-4(b) *Ex. (1)*, provides that, if a decedent devises a residence valued at $25,000 to his wife with a direction that she pay $5,000 to his sister, the value of the property interest passing to the wife is only $20,000. See PLR 9409018 where the IRS reversed its prior position that any assets passing to a marital trust that could be used to pay off a loan guarantee would not qualify for the marital deduction.

217. *See* §642(g) (election to claim administration expenses as deductions on estate's federal income tax return for years when paid rather than on estate tax return); §2032 (election to value estate assets as of alternative valuation date rather than as of date of death); §213(c) (election to treat expenses for decedent's medical care paid by his or her estate within one year of death as being paid by decedent at time incurred); §454(a) (election to include accrued interest on decedent's final income tax return or any subsequent return for estate in connection with non-interest-bearing obligations issued at discount, usually U.S. Government Series E or EE bonds, on which decedent did not previously accrue interest annually on his or her federal income tax returns).

218. See the general discussion of tax allocation provisions at Chapter 5, A.2.c.

219. Note that under the Uniform Estate Tax Apportionment Act (2003), included as Part 9A (§3-91-101 through §3-9A-115) of the Uniform Probate Code, to the extent that

apportionment of an estate tax is not controlled by a governing instrument, the estate tax is apportioned ratably to each person that has an interest in the "apportionable estate." *See* Uniform Probate Code §3-9A-104. For this purpose the "apportionable estate" is the value of the gross estate reduced by the value of property that qualifies for the marital (or charitable) deduction. *See* Uniform Probate Code §3-9A-102(1).

220. *See* former IRS Pub. 904, *Interrelated Computations for Estate and Gift Taxes,* which demonstrates how to determine the precise tax amount in this context. The IRS no longer publishes IRS Pub. 904 but, in some situations, a request might be made to the IRS to provide the appropriate computation.

221. See the discussion of tax allocation provisions at Chapter 5, A.2.c.

222. See the discussion of this option in 855 T.M., *Estate and Trust Administration—Tax Planning* (Bloomberg BNA).

223. In *Commissioner v. Estate of Hubert,* 520 U.S. 93 (1997), the Supreme Court addressed the conflict among the circuits regarding whether the marital deduction must be reduced by the amount of administration expenses paid from estate income. The Court held that, if administration expenses are chargeable to income, rather than principal, they will not reduce the amount of a residuary marital or charitable bequest as long as the payment of the expenses from income is not a material limitation on the residuary bequest. The decision, however, left many questions unanswered, including when an expense would be considered a "material limitation" on the spouse's right to income. In response, the IRS has taken a regulatory approach to the treatment of administration expenses, discussed below, that would eliminate the concept of materiality.

224. If the decedent's will directs that all administration expenses be paid from income, to the extent that income otherwise allocable to the marital deduction is used, a marital deduction valuation problem exists. *See* Reg. §20.2056(b)-4(a).

225. For example, assume a spouse dies leaving an estate of $1 million to her surviving spouse, but the estate incurs $100,000 in administration expenses. The marital deduction would be limited to $900,000, the amount passing to the surviving spouse, assuming no available unified credit. If the $100,000 in expenses are claimed as income tax deductions and no remaining unified credit is available to absorb the estate tax, federal estate tax will be due. If the estate of the deceased spouse is in a marginal tax bracket of 40% because of her predeath adjusted taxable gifts, $40,000 in estate tax would be payable.

226. In a continuation of the above example, payment of the $40,000 in tax would mean that only $860,000 has passed to the surviving spouse. An $860,000 marital deduction would mean that the taxable estate is not $100,000 but $140,000. This amount, in turn, generates a tax of $56,000 (rather than $40,000). The marital deduction is reduced to $844,000, which means that the taxable estate has increased to $156,000, which, in turn, necessitates further adjustments, each adjustment triggering the necessity for a further adjustment.

227. In *Commissioner v. Estate of Hubert,* 520 U.S. 93 (1997), the Supreme Court held, on the facts presented, that the marital deduction was not to be reduced where three-fourths of the administration expenses had been paid from estate income rather than from the principal of the residuary estate. In affirming the Tax Court, which held for the taxpayer, the Court of Appeals had specified that, where the will permits the allocation of expenses to income, the marital and charitable deductions are not to be reduced by expenses allocated to income. The Supreme Court affirmed, determining that, under Reg. §20.2056(b)-4(a), only material limitations on the right to receive income are to

be taken into account in valuing the interest passing to the surviving spouse. Where the interest is essentially a fee interest (general power of appointment or QTIP trust) the payment of expenses from income is less likely to be material. If the limitation is not material, the expenses paid from income do not reduce the deduction. Whether a limitation is material depends on the facts and the nature of the interest given.

228. Reg. §20.2055-3, effective for estates of decedents dying after December 2, 1999. The regulations specifically address the effect of administration expenses on the valuation of property when all or a portion of the interests in property qualify for the estate tax charitable deduction by adopting Reg. §20.2055-3.
229. Section 2056(b)(1) specifies that no marital deduction is available if the surviving spouse receives only a life estate or other terminable interest, but the subsequent provisions in §2056(b) specify exceptions to this deduction limitation.
230. §2056(b)(3); Reg. §20.2056(b)-3.
231. §2056(b)(5); Reg. §20.2056(b)-5.
232. §2056(b)(6); Reg. §20.2056(b)-6.
233. §2056(b)(7).
234. §2056(b)(8).
235. §2056(b)(1); Reg. §20.2056(b)-1(b).
236. See *Jackson v. United States,* 376 U.S. 503 (1964), where the Supreme Court determined that a widow's allowance was a terminable interest because, under local law, the right to a widow's allowance terminated upon death or remarriage. The Court adopted the view that the character of the widow's allowance must be judged as of the date of death of the decedent. If the interest is not vested until the date of the award of allowance, the interest is nondeductible. The marital deduction status of widow's allowances in numerous state law contexts has been considered by the courts and the IRS because the status of the allowance is dependent upon applicable state law. *See* Rev. Rul. 76-166, 1976-1 C.B. 287. See also *Estate of Snider v. Commissioner,* 84 T.C. 75 (1985), where a deduction was disallowed because, under state law, the allowance was deemed to be contingent and not a vested, unconditional entitlement. *But see Estate of Watson v. Commissioner,* 94 T.C. 262 (1990) (Mississippi widow's allowance was not nondeductible terminable interest because one-year support award to be made would not be reduced or terminated if surviving spouse died or remarried).
237. *See* §2056(b)(1); Reg. §20.2056(b)-1(c)(1). *See also* Rev. Rul. 85-100, 1985-2 C.B. 200, where an employee death benefit annuity was ruled a terminable interest even though another person's contingent interest would be extinguished before the alternate valuation date.
238. Section 2056(b)(7), the QTIP provision, is discussed below.
239. §2056(b)(1)(C).
240. §2056(b)(2). For this reason the will should provide that the marital deduction bequest cannot be satisfied with assets that do not qualify for the marital deduction (e.g., nondeductible terminable interests).
241. *See* TAM 9023004.
242. §2056(b)(3).
243. *See* Reg. §20.2056(b)-3(d) *Ex. 1.*
244. If an event or condition is substituted for a six-month period, this exception to the terminable interest rule will not be available if such event or condition could take more than six months to occur. *See* Reg. §20.2056(b)-3(d) *Ex. 4.* See *Estate of Bond v. Commissioner,* 104

T.C. 652 (1995), where the decedent's will devised his residuary estate to his spouse provided that she "survived distribution of her share of the remainder of my estate." Because the personal property bequeathed to the spouse was contingent upon her surviving until it was actually distributed to her, and because there was no requirement under the will or the law of the State of Washington that personal property be distributed within six months after the decedent's death, her interest in the personal property was terminable and, therefore, the marital deduction was not available. The real property in the residuary estate qualified for the marital deduction, because, under Washington law, the title to real property vested immediately upon the decedent's death. *See also Estate of Robertson v. United States,* 903 F.2d 1034 (5th Cir. 1990); *Estate of Harmon v. Commissioner,* 84 T.C. 329 (1985); *Estate of Shepherd v. Commissioner,* T.C. Memo 1989-610 (marital deduction bequest conditioned on spouse's survival until will's probate did not fall within six-month survivorship exception when will could be probated more than six months after decedent's death). Similarly, see *Estate of Heim v. Commissioner,* 914 F.2d 1322 (9th Cir. 1990), where a provision conditioned the spousal transfer on her survival until distribution of the estate (an indeterminate period not necessarily falling within the six-month limitation period of §2056(b)(3)); TAM 8816001. *Cf. Sowder v. United States,* 407 F. Supp. 2d 1230 (E.D. Wash. 2005), *aff'd by unpub. opin.,* 251 F. App'x 444 (9th Cir. 2007) (decedent's residual gift to spouse in self-drafted will was construed to qualify for marital deduction, despite provision conditioning gift on spouse's survival until distribution of estate, based on Washington law and evidence of decedent's intent).

245. If the spouses die in a common accident, the locally enacted version of the Uniform Simultaneous Death Act (1993) will normally provide that each spouse is deemed to survive the other with respect to the transmission of their separate properties, thereby making the marital deduction unavailable to either estate. Section 3 of this Act provides that, for purposes of a provision of a governing instrument that relates to an individual surviving an event, including the death of another individual, an individual who is not established by clear and convincing evidence to have survived the event by 120 hours is deemed to have predeceased the event. Section 6 of the Act provides that this survival requirement is not applicable if the governing instrument contains language dealing explicitly with simultaneous death or deaths in a common disaster and that language is operable under the facts of the case.

246. §2056(b)(5). Although the QTIP provision is ordinarily the preferred estate tax planning option, many of the concepts that have earlier developed in the life estate–power of appointment context are equally applicable to the QTIP framework. Therefore, this discussion is quite relevant for examining many of the similar concepts applicable in the QTIP context. See the discussion of the §2056(b)(7) QTIP provisions at Chapter 5, D.3.i.

247. *See* Reg. §20.2056(b)-5(a).

248. Reg. §20.2056(b)-5(a)(2). A marital deduction will be allowable for amounts transferred to an otherwise qualifying marital deduction trust that, because of a reasonable delay in the payment of estate administration expenses, was not funded and, consequently, paid no income to the surviving spouse until more than 12 months after the decedent's death. Rev. Rul. 77-346, 1977-2 C.B. 340. The marital deduction will not be available for a testamentary trust where the trustee is required to accumulate the income for the first year after the trust's creation (and such delay is not related to the period of probate administration and distribution of assets). *See* Rev. Rul. 72-283, 1972-1 C.B. 311; Reg. §20.2056(b)-5(f)(9).

249. Reg. §20.2056(b)-5(a)(3). Rev. Rul. 76-446, 1976-2 C.B. 295, indicates that where assets were required to be retained in trust for two years after the death of the surviving spouse, the marital deduction was not allowable because the surviving spouse did not have sole control over the disposition of the assets.
250. Reg. §20.2056(b)-5(a)(5).
251. *See* §2041 (gross estate inclusion for property subject to general power of appointment).
252. Reg. §20.2056(b)-5(f)(1).
253. This income requirement also mandates that accrued but undistributed income at the surviving spouse's death must be paid to the surviving spouse's estate or be subject to a general testamentary power of appointment. Reg. §20.2056(b)-5(f)(8) specifies that this requirement is satisfied for "stub period" income (i.e., income accrued since the last trust income payment date and prior to death) if the spouse had a power of appointment over this income. Reg. §20.2056(b)-7(d)(4) (concerning the QTIP provision, discussed below) provides that income accrued between the last distribution date and the surviving spouse's death need not be paid to the spouse's estate. *But see Estate of Shelfer v. Commissioner,* 103 T.C. 10 (1994), *rev'd,* 86 F.3d 1045 (11th Cir. 1996); *Estate of Howard v. Commissioner,* 91 T.C. 329 (1988), *rev'd,* 910 F.2d 633 (9th Cir. 1990). Note that Reg. §20.2044-1(d)(2) specifies that this amount of undistributed "stub period" income is to be included in the gross estate of the surviving spouse.
254. Reg. §20.2056(b)-5(f)(2). This might be assured through the use of a "savings clause." See Rev. Rul. 75-440, 1975-2 C.B. 372, finding acceptable a clause specifying that any power given to the trustees is void if the power jeopardizes the marital deduction. *See, e.g.,* TAM 200339003. Note, however, the position of the National Office in TAM 200234017, after citing Rev. Rul. 75-440, that a savings clause was not effective and did not operate to create an ambiguity in the instrument. It may only be used as aid in interpreting an instrument where an ambiguity is present in another part of the instrument. See also Rev. Rul. 85-35, 1985-1 C.B. 328, indicating that the "right to income" requirement is not violated where, under state law, a trustee has the power to distribute trust income to a relative or to a court-appointed representative for the benefit of the spouse, or the trustee may spend trust income directly for the benefit of the spouse, if the spouse becomes legally disabled. Similarly, see TAM 9514002.
255. *See* Reg. §20.2056(b)-5(f)(7). Thus, for example, Reg. §20.2056(b)-5(f)(3) provides that the rules to be applied by the trustee in the allocation of receipts and expenses between income and principal must be considered in relation to the nature and expected productivity of the assets passing in trust, the nature and frequency of occurrence of expected receipts, and in the provisions concerning changes in the form of trust investments.
256. Reg. §20.2056(b)-5(f)(5). An example of such a situation might be where raw land is held for appreciation and will eventually benefit the beneficiaries receiving under the exercise of the power of appointment, or the takers in default of the exercise of that power of appointment.
257. Reg. §20.2056(b)-5(f)(4).
258. A personal residence and other personal use property may be held in this trust even though they will not produce income. The rationale is that the personal use of these items by the surviving spouse is comparable to the receipt of income from an investment asset.
259. Reg. §20.2056(b)-5(f)(4). See also Rev. Rul. 69-56, 1969-1 C.B. 224, where the IRS considered the effect on the availability of the marital deduction of various powers

conferred upon a trustee. The IRS noted that directions to, or powers conferred upon, a fiduciary by the governing instrument do not result in the disallowance or diminution of the marital deduction for estate (and gift) tax purposes unless the execution of such directions would, or the exercise of such powers could, cause the spouse to have less than substantially full beneficial enjoyment of the particular interest transferred. The IRS outlined various examples, including where (1) the governing instrument conferred various powers pertaining to the apportionment of receipts and expenditures to or between income and principal, and (2) the income and principal apportionment was governed solely by reference to state law. In all examples the IRS ruled that these powers did not result in a disallowance or diminution of the marital deduction. Under Example 1 of the ruling, the following powers or directions pertaining to the allocation or apportionment of receipts and expenditures to or between income and principal were considered: (1) to apportion or not to apportion, between successive beneficial interests, interest income and expenses, rental income and expenses, real estate taxes, or other items of periodic income and expense; (2) to treat ordinary cash dividends as income when received, regardless of the declaration date or record date; (3) to treat extraordinary cash dividends as principal; (4) to treat stock dividends as principal; (5) to treat capital gains dividends of regulated investment companies as principal; (6) to charge to income or principal executor's or trustee's commissions, legal and accounting fees, custodian fees, and similar administration expenses; (7) to maintain reasonable reserves for depreciation, depletion, amortization, and obsolescence; and (8) to amortize or not to amortize both premium and discount on interest bearing bonds and similar obligations. Example 4 in this ruling described permissible fiduciary powers not pertaining to the allocation or apportionment of receipts and expenditures: (1) to retain cash included in any trust fund without investment thereof for such period of time as the fiduciary deems advisable, whenever he or she determines that it is inadvisable to invest such cash; and (2) to make distributions in cash, or in kind at current values, or partly in cash, allocating specific assets to particular distributees, and for such purposes to make reasonable determinations of current fair market values.

260. §2056(b)(5).
261. §2056(b)(10).
262. Reg. §20.2056(b)-5(c)(2).
263. §2056(b)(10) (to define "specific portion" to only portion determined on fractional or percentage basis).
264. 387 U.S. 213 (1967).
265. This assumes that the other requirements for the marital deduction are satisfied (e.g., at least annual income distributions and a general power of appointment over the specific portion). Just as a right to a fixed dollar amount of income would constitute entitlement to income from a "specific portion" of property so as to satisfy §2056(b)(5), the power to appoint a fixed dollar amount of trust corpus would constitute a power to appoint a "specific portion" of the property so as to satisfy the requirements of that provision. See also *Estate of Alexander v. Commissioner,* 82 T.C. 34 (1984), *aff'd by unpub. opin.,* 760 F.2d 264 (4th Cir. 1985), in which the Tax Court held then Prop. Reg. §20.2056(b)-5(c) invalid, relying on the *Northeastern Pennsylvania Nat'l Bank & Trust Co. v. United States,* 387 U.S. 213 (1967). Reg. §20.2056(b)-5(c) adopted the Prop. Reg. §20.2056(b)-5(c) definition of "specific portion" as a fractional or percentage interest, generally effective for estates of decedents dying after March 1, 1994. The IRS recognized, however, that the *Alexander* decision reflected the law before the Energy Act of 1992, which enacted

the fractional or percentage interest limitation language. Consequently, the final regulations addressing the specific portion rules reflecting changes made by the Energy Act do not apply to estates of decedents dying on or before October 24, 1992. Reg. §20.2056(b)-5(c)(3) provides a transition rule for decedents dying after that date with wills or revocable trusts executed on or before that date and either (1) on that date, the decedent was under a mental disability to change the disposition of the property and did not regain competence to dispose of such property before the date of death, or (2) the decedent died before October 24, 1995.

266. The IRS, by implication, sanctioned the *Northeastern Pennsylvania Nat'l Bank & Trust Co.* approach in Rev. Rul. 79-86, 1979-1 C.B. 311. See Reg. §20.2056(b)-5(c)(3), which formally adopted this rule for estates of decedents dying on or before October 24, 1992, and for certain decedents dying after October 24, 1992, with wills or revocable trusts executed on or before that date.
267. *See* §2056(b)(10), §2523(f)(3); Comprehensive National Energy Policy Act of 1992 (1992 Energy Act), Pub. L. No. 102-486, §1941(a). This definition is applicable for purposes of §2056(b)(5), §2056(b)(6), §2056(b)(7)(B)(iv), §2523(e), and §2523(f).
268. The transitional exception applied for decedents who died within three years thereafter or were incompetent on October 24, 1992, if their estate plans were not executed or amended thereafter in any manner that increased the amount or terms of the marital bequest.
269. §2056(b)(5); Reg. §20.2056(b)-5(g)(1).
270. Note that under §2056(b)(7) (the QTIP provision) no person may have a power to appoint any part of the property to any person other than the surviving spouse.
271. §678.
272. §2056(b)(6). If life insurance proceeds are paid outright in a lump sum to the surviving spouse, no "terminable interest" exists and, therefore, no concern exists about a possible limitation of the marital deduction in this context. Reg. §20.2056(b)-6, §20.2056(c)-2(a)(3), §20.2056(c)-2(a)(3), and §20.2056(c)-2(b)(3)(ii). The result would be the same where the proceeds are payable in a lump sum but the surviving spouse elects to receive them under a deferred payment settlement option. In this situation the surviving spouse is deemed to have received the lump sum payment and, thereafter, to have reinvested it with the insurance company in exchange for a deferred payment contract.
273. Reg. §20.2056(b)-6(a).
274. See 843 T.M., *Estate Tax Marital Deduction* (Bloomberg BNA), for a description of the usual range of settlement options available to the insured in this context.
275. This permissible 13-month delay enables the insurance proceeds to be invested with interest income to be received for the first investment year, rather than requiring an immediate distribution of what would be principal (because income would not yet have accrued).
276. Similar to the §2056(b)(5) life estate/power of appointment option, ordinarily the power of appointment would be structured to be testamentary rather than exercisable during lifetime.
277. Alternatively, the testator could provide (1) that the proceeds are payable in installments to the surviving spouse for life, and after his or her death any remaining installments are payable to his or her estate (Reg. §20.2056(c)-2(b)(3)(iii)), or (2) that interest on the proceeds is payable to the surviving spouse for life, and upon his or her death the principal amount is payable to his or her estate (Reg. §20.2056(c)-2(b)(3)(iv)). This is the insurance equivalent of the "estate trust," discussed below.

278. §2056(b)(7)(A).
279. Section 2056(b)(7)(B)(ii)(I) provides that a qualifying income interest for life exists if the surviving spouse has a usufruct interest for life in the property. Section 2056(b)(7)(C) provides that annuities (1) that are included in the decedent's estate and (2) in which only the surviving spouse has the right to receive payments, qualify for the marital deduction unless the executor elects otherwise. A qualifying income interest could be in the form of the continued usage of property such as a personal residence, but note, however, *Estate of Kyle v. Commissioner,* 94 T.C. 829 (1990), where a surviving spouse's homestead right under Texas law was held to be a terminable interest as not being a "qualifying income interest for life" under §2056(b)(7) because it could have been lost through abandonment by the surviving spouse.
280. For the strictness with which this requirement has been applied, see the IRS's position in TAM 8916002 where a surviving spouse's income interest in a testamentary trust was treated as not constituting QTIP property. The terms of the trust granted the executor the discretion to have a specific portion or all of the trust assets treated as QTIP property. Because the surviving spouse's interest was contingent upon the executor's QTIP election, the interest was not deemed by the IRS as passing from the decedent to the surviving spouse. Substantial controversy previously existed, however, concerning whether the executor could be given the power to determine the amount that passes to the QTIP portion, making an election to accomplish this. The IRS consistently took the position that a property interest could not qualify under the QTIP rules unless it met those tests, whether or not the QTIP election was made. *See* former Reg. §20.2056(b)-7(d)(3), §20.2056-7(h) *Ex. 6.* The Tax Court consistently held that to qualify the interest of the surviving spouse could not be contingent on a valid QTIP election, but that position was rejected on appeal in *Estate of Clayton v. Commissioner,* 976 F.2d 1486 (5th Cir. 1992); *Estate of Robertson v. Commissioner,* 15 F.3d 779 (8th Cir. 1994); and *Estate of Spencer v. Commissioner*, 43 F.3d 226 (6th Cir. 1995). The Tax Court then accepted the position of these courts of appeal in *Estate of Clack v. Commissioner,* 106 T.C. 131 (1996), *acq.*, 1996-2 C.B. 1. Therefore, the QTIP requirements are met if and to the extent that the QTIP election actually has been made. These courts essentially hold that the QTIP election when made during the probate administration phase relates back to the date of the decedent's death so that, once the election is made, the elected property is identified as remaining in the QTIP trust, and nothing in the document dealing with nonelected property affects qualification of the QTIP trust for the deduction. Ultimately, the IRS issued regulations that conformed to *Clayton, Robertson, Spencer* and *Clack* by providing that an interest of a surviving spouse that is contingent on the executor's QTIP election is a qualifying income interest for life. Reg. §20.2056(b)-7(d)(3)(i) provides that a surviving spouse's income interest (or life estate) that is contingent upon the executor's election under §2056(b)(7)(B)(v) will not be precluded, on that basis alone, from being a qualifying income interest for life. Reg. §20.2056(b)-7(h) *Ex. 6*, and §20.2044-1(e) *Exs. 1, 2,* illustrate the amended rule.
281. §2056(b)(7)(B)(i)(I).
282. The governing instrument must clearly identify the right to such income. See, for example, *Estate of Whiting v. Commissioner,* T.C. Memo 2004-68, where the marital deduction trust required the trustee to distribute all of the income from the marital deduction trust to or for the benefit of the surviving spouse, while the disability section permitted the trustee to accumulate the surviving spouse's income received from the marital deduction trust. The court held that the conflicting terms of the marital deduction trust and the

disability section gave way to the decedent's intent to qualify the trust for the marital deduction.

283. §2056(b)(7)(B)(ii)(II).

284. §2056(b)(7)(B)(v).

285. See *Estate of Ellingson v. Commissioner,* 964 F.2d 959 (9th Cir. 1992), where the court concluded that the income distribution requirement was satisfied, notwithstanding conflicting language in the instrument. But see *Estate of Nicholson v. Commissioner,* 94 T.C. 666 (1990), denying the marital deduction where the trustees were required to pay net income to maintain the spouse's customary standard of living. The court ignored a post-mortem modification order of the will. Similarly, see *Estate of Aronson v. Commissioner,* T.C. Memo 2003-189, where the decedent's will gave his surviving spouse only such income from a testamentary trust as she might reasonably need, but not necessarily all the income that she might demand and her interest in the trust did not qualify for the marital deduction.

286. The property that can "pass" for this purpose includes the proceeds from an individual retirement account (IRA). See Rev. Rul. 89-89, 1989-2 C.B. 231, where the IRS ruled that a decedent's estate could elect to treat a distribution from an IRA as qualified terminable interest property because the surviving spouse received a qualifying income interest for life in the IRA, as required by §2056(b)(7). The IRA distribution option required that the date of death balance in the IRA be paid in annual installments to a testamentary QTIP trust along with the income earned on the undistributed balance. Further, provisions of the trust receiving the IRA payments required that the income earned on both the distributed and the undistributed portions of the IRA be paid currently to the surviving spouse. Any remaining balance in the IRA, as well as any portion of the balance previously distributed to the trust, would be includible in the gross estate of the surviving spouse at death. The effect of this arrangement was to enable continued maintenance of the declining balance of the funds in the tax-preferred IRA account form. The IRS obsoleted Rev. Rul. 89-89 in Rev. Rul. 2000-2, 2000-1 C.B. 305, which provided updated guidelines for the funding of a QTIP trust with a decedent's IRA. The IRS still requires a separate QTIP election for both the trust and the IRA and continues to rely on the spouse's power to compel the trustee of the trust to withdraw from the IRA an amount equal to all the income earned that year on the IRA assets, and then to pay that income to the spouse to meet the spousal income requirement. Rev. Rul. 2000-2 clarified that the IRA distributions could be made under the normal distribution rules, rather than in equal amounts annually over the life of the surviving spouse, as implied by Rev. Rul. 89-89. *See* PLR 200241012. In Rev. Rul. 2006-26, 2006-1 C.B. 939, the IRS modified and, as modified, superseded Rev. Rul. 2000-2. Among other things, Rev. Rul. 2006-26 adds scenarios for QTIP treatment of an IRA or other qualified defined contribution retirement plan designating a QTIP trust as beneficiary when income is determined under state law provisions defining income as a unitrust amount or allowing the trustee to make allocations between the income and remainder beneficiaries to fulfill the trustee's duty of impartiality. *See, generally,* T.D. 9102, 69 Fed. Reg. 12 (Jan. 2, 2004) (amending regulations, including marital deduction regulations and Reg. §1.643(b)-1 definition of fiduciary accounting income, to take into account certain developments in state law, effective for taxable years ending after January 2, 2004).

287. *See* Reg. §20.2056(b)-7(d)(2) (cross-referencing Reg. §20.2056(b)-5(f)).

288. Reg. §20.2056(b)-5(f)(5). If the surviving spouse has children by an earlier marriage and wishes to pass his or her own estate to those children, rather than to others who are the

remainder beneficiaries of the qualified terminable interest trust, that spouse will have a strong incentive to assert that the property be income producing. That spouse can, thereby, increase the amount passing to his or her own children and family from funds accumulated after receiving that income.

289. This problem of giving the spouse an unqualified right to all of the income was dealt with in the power of appointment trust by merely making that income subject to a general testamentary power. In the typical QTIP trust, no general power exists. To avoid the creation of an estate where the surviving spouse has no general power, it may be possible to give the surviving spouse a general testamentary power over only the undistributed QTIP income. This issue involves the "stub period" income question and the decision in *Estate of Howard v. Commissioner,* 91 T.C. 329 (1988), *rev'd,* 910 F.2d 633 (9th Cir. 1990). Citing Reg. §20.2056(b)-5(f)(8), the Tax Court in *Howard* held that a trust instrument cannot direct that income accumulated between the last distribution date and the spouse's death pass to the remainder beneficiaries. The court refused to accept former Prop. Reg. §20.2056(b)-7(c)(1), specifying that income accrued between the last distribution date and the spouse's death need not be paid to the spouse's estate. Former Prop. Reg. §20.2056(b)-7(c)(1) was finalized as Reg. §20.2056(b)-7(d)(4), effective for decedents dying after March 1, 1994, and for gifts made after that date. See *Estate of Shelfer v. Commissioner,* 103 T.C. 10 (1994), *rev'd,* 86 F.3d 1045 (11th Cir. 1996), where the Tax Court followed its decision in *Howard* stating that the Ninth Circuit's reasoning that the surviving spouse be entitled to all the income "at the time of its annual . . . distribution" is a limitation that is not imposed by the statute. In *Shelfer,* the 11th Circuit, reversing the Tax Court, held that the failure to pay stub income to the surviving spouse or her estate did not disqualify the trust as QTIP and that the trust property must be included in the surviving spouse's estate under §2044. As noted, the IRS issued regulations to resolve this issue. See Reg. §20.2056(b)-7(d)(4), specifying that an income interest does not fail to constitute a qualifying income interest for life solely because income between the last distribution date and the date of the surviving spouse's death need not be distributed to the surviving spouse or to the estate of the surviving spouse.

290. *See* Reg. §20.2056(b)-7(d)(2) (principles of Reg. §20.2056(b)-5(f) apply in this context). *See also* Reg. §20.2056(b)-7(h) *Ex. 1.* In TAM 9604003, the National Office advised that remainder interests in real property did not qualify for this purpose. In TAM 8948002, the National Office advised that a widower received a §2056(b)(7)(B) qualifying income interest in a bare legal life estate in his wife's residuary estate where both local and common law allowed him to make the property productive. Income interests granted for a term of years, or life estates subject to termination upon remarriage or upon occurrence of a specified event, are not qualifying income interests, however. *See Estate of Peacock v. Commissioner,* 914 F.2d 230 (11th Cir. 1990) (permitting QTIP treatment for right to occupy marital residence "for as long as he desires" because widower was entitled to rental receipts). See also TAM 9229004 denying a deduction where a spouse's lifetime interest in a residence was subject to continued occupancy by the spouse, similar to the decision in *Estate of Kyle v. Commissioner,* 94 T.C. 829 (1990).

291. §2056(b)(7)(B)(ii)(II).

292. *See Estate of Bowling v. Commissioner,* 93 T.C. 286 (1989), indicating that a surviving spouse's life income interest in a trust that could be invaded for the needs of others was not a qualifying interest eligible for the purposes of §2056(b)(7)(B). *See also Estate of Manscill v. Commissioner,* 98 T.C. 413 (1992).

293. §2056(b)(7)(B)(ii), flush language.

294. §2056(b)(7)(B)(v). The election must be clearly evidenced. *See Estate of Higgins v. Commissioner,* 897 F.2d 856 (6th Cir. 1990), holding that the estate did not make a valid QTIP election, where the executor failed both to check the box on the federal estate tax return making the election and to designate the property for which QTIP treatment was elected on the marital deduction schedule.
295. §2056(b)(7)(B)(v). Reg. §20.2056(b)-7(c)(2) provides that a "protective" election also cannot be revoked. See Rev. Proc. 2001-38, 2001-1 C.B. 1335, providing relief for surviving spouses and their estates in situations where a predeceased spouse's estate made an unnecessary qualified terminable interest property (QTIP) election that did not reduce the estate tax liability of the estate. This revenue procedure describes the circumstances in which these QTIP elections will be treated as a nullity for federal estate, gift, and generation-skipping transfer tax purposes, so that the property will not be subject to transfer tax with respect to the surviving spouse. When qualifying under these guidelines the estate may wish to obtain a private letter ruling confirming the QTIP election as a nullity. *See, e.g.,* PLR 201345006, PLR 201131011, PLR 201112001.
296. Reg. §20.2056(b)-7(d)(3)(i).
297. The surviving spouse must not be given rights in the trust, which would prevent the spouse from making a qualified disclaimer. *See* §2518.
298. Rev. Proc. 2001-38, 2001-1 C.B. 1335. The procedure was effective on June 4, 2001, and applies to all QTIP elections within the scope of the procedure, whenever made. If the surviving spouse's estate has already paid gift or estate tax on a transfer subject to the procedure, Rev. Proc. 2001-38 indicates that the taxpayer may file a claim for refund, provided it is within the §6511 limitations period. In various private letter rulings the IRS granted this relief.
299. Rev. Proc. 2001-38 provides several examples of circumstances in which such an election will be treated as a nullity for federal estate, gift, and generation-skipping transfer tax purposes. One example of an unnecessary QTIP election is an election made when the taxable estate (before allowance of the marital deduction) is less than the applicable exclusion amount under §2010(c). The QTIP election is not necessary, because no estate tax would be imposed whether or not the election is made. Another example of an unnecessary QTIP election is one that is made for both a credit shelter trust and a marital trust. The QTIP election for the credit shelter trust is not necessary because no estate tax is imposed on a credit shelter trust funded with an amount that does not exceed the applicable exclusion amount under §2010(c).
300. See PLR 201345006, PLR 201131011, PLR 201112001, PLR 200535026, PLR 200323010, and PLR 200318039 for requests to the IRS to (1) disregard the QTIP election made on a decedent's Form 706 and treat it as null and void in accordance with Rev. Proc. 2001-38, 2001-1 C.B. 1335, and (2) rule that the property for which the election is disregarded under this procedure will not be includible in the gross estate of the spouse under §2044.
301. *See, e.g.,* PLR 200422050.
302. §2056(b)(7)(B)(v).
303. §2056(b)(7)(B)(iii).
304. §2056(b)(7)(B)(iv).
305. See Reg. §20.2056(b)-7(b)(1)(ii), indicating that the term "specific portion of the entire interest" is defined in Reg. §20.2056(b)-5(c). See the discussion involving *Northeastern Pennsylvania Nat'l Bank & Trust Co. v. United States,* 387 U.S. 213 (1967), and *Estate of Alexander v. Commissioner,* 82 T.C. 34 (1984), at Chapter 5, D.3.g.(3).

306. §2056(b)(10)).
307. Reg. §20.2056(b)-7(d)(3). The IRS's position was that, if the income interest provided to the spouse was contingent upon the executor making a QTIP election, the interest did not qualify as QTIP eligible property. This position was consistently rejected by appeals courts, as noted in the discussion above. *See Estate of Clayton v. Commissioner*, 976 F.2d 1486 (5th Cir. 1992); *Estate of Robertson v. Commissioner*, 15 F.3d 779 (8th Cir. 1994), *rev'g* 98 T.C. 678 (1992); *Estate of Spencer v. Commissioner*, 43 F.3d 226 (6th Cir. 1995), *rev'g* T.C. Memo 1992-479. Under this approach, the date of the election is the appropriate date for determining if the property meets the requirements established in §2056(b)(7), rather than some earlier date. The Tax Court subsequently also reversed its position on this question. *See Estate of Clack v. Commissioner*, 106 T.C. 131 (1996), *acq.*, 1996-2 C.B. 1, rejecting the IRS position that a property interest cannot qualify under the QTIP rules unless it meets the tests in the regulations, whether or not the QTIP election is made. *See* Kasner, *Tax Court Concedes Use of Contingent QTIP Election*, 71 Tax Notes 89 (1996).
308. See §2518(b)(4)(A), which indicates that a "qualified disclaimer" includes a refusal by a person to accept an interest in property but only if, in addition to other requirements, the interest (1) passes without any direction on the part of the person making the disclaimer and (2) passes either (a) to the spouse of the decedent or (b) to a person other than the person making the disclaimer.
309. Reg. §25.2518-2(e)(5) *Ex. (5)*.
310. Reg. §25.2518-2(e)(1)(i), §25.2518-2(e)(2), §25.2518-2(e)(5) *Ex. (6)*. The use of an ascertainable standard or the delegation of the sprinkle power to an independent trustee (or other party exercising this power) will change this result.
311. §2511(a) (applicable to life income interest), §2519(a) (applicable to remaining portion). *See* Reg. §25.2519-1(c)(1). See also Reg. §25.2207A-1(b), stating that the waiver of the right to recover gift tax under §2207A(b) due to the disclaimer of a marital share constitutes a gift in the amount of the unrecovered taxes.
312. Section 2519(a) specifies that any disposition of all or part of a qualifying income interest for life in any property where the QTIP deduction was previously allowed will be treated as a transfer of all interests in such property other than the qualifying income interest.
313. The transfer of the income interest is treated as a gift under §2511. The remainder of the transfer is subject to §2519. Note that if a QTIP election was made for only a portion of the property (e.g., for a fractional share), this transfer tax treatment will only apply to that portion to which the election is applicable. Reg. §25.2519-1(c)(2).
314. Section 2503(b), the provision for the annual donee exclusion, requires that the gift be of a "present interest."
315. §2207A(b). The treatment applies because the property transfer actually is sourced to the first spouse to die and those funds should be provided for the tax reimbursement for this transfer.
316. See Reg. §25.2207A-1(c), §25.2207A-1(d), and §25.2207A-1(f) *Ex.*, indicating how the precise amount of gift tax reimbursement must be determined. This amount is determined as if the transfer of the remainder interest is the last gift, subject to the gift tax for each gift transfer being determined on an incremental basis.
317. Reg. §25.2207A-1(b) provides that the surviving spouse makes a gift in the amount of the unrecovered gift tax to the person(s) from whom the spouse could have recovered the gift tax if the spouse fails to exercise the right to recover the gift tax with respect to

a §2519 transfer. Similarly, see *Estate of Morgens v. Commissioner,* 133 T.C. 402 (2009), *aff'd,* 678 F.3d 769 (9th Cir. 2012). Because of the surviving spouse's §2207A right of reimbursement, the §2519 gift is treated as a net gift. Specifically, under Reg. §25.2519-1(c)(4), the amount of a §2519 transfer would be reduced by the amount of the gift tax that the surviving spouse is entitled to recover under §2207A(b) and the amount of the gift tax recoverable and the amount of the remainder interest treated as transferred would be determined according to the same interrelated computation as used for any other transfer in which the transferee agrees to pay the gift tax. The interrelated computation is described in Rev. Rul. 81-223, 1981-2 C.B. 189. *See also* PLR 200530014.

318. The gift is made when the gift tax is no longer recoverable by the surviving spouse.
319. Reg. §25.2207A-1(b)(1); *see also* §7872(b).
320. §2044.
321. §1014(b)(10).
322. Staff of J. Comm. on Tax'n, 97th Cong., General Explanation of the Economic Recovery Tax Act of 1981, at p. 236, n. 4.
323. Considerable litigation has occurred concerning whether this direction actually has been implemented. In *Firstar Trust Co. v. First Nat'l Bank of Kenosha,* 525 N.W. 2d 53 (Wis. Ct. App. 1994), *aff'd in part and rev'd in part,* 541 N.W. 2d 467 (Wis. 1995), the court held that a tax clause in a decedent's will directing her personal representative "to pay expenses of administration of my estate and all valid inheritance and estate taxes payable by reason of my death . . . without seeking reimbursement from or charging any person therefor" did not waive the §2207A right of recovery against a QTIP remainder beneficiary, stating that the tax clause must specifically direct the payment of estate taxes on nonprobate property before that property is exempt from payment. The court also noted (in footnote 4) that, to prevent inadvertent waivers of the §2207A right to recover from the persons receiving the QTIP property, some state legislatures have enacted provisions requiring that any tax direction in the surviving spouse's will must refer specifically to the estate tax attributable to the QTIP trust. *See also Estate of Miller v. Maley,* 595 N.E. 2d 630 (Ill. App. 1992). Precisely to prevent such inadvertent waiver of the right of recovery, §2207A(a)(2) was amended by the Taxpayer Relief Act of 1997, Pub. L. No. 105-34, §1302, to require a specific indication of the intent to waive, for example, reference to the QTIP trust, §2207A, or §2044. *See, e.g., Eisenbach v. Schneider,* 166 P.3d 858 (Wash. Ct. App. 2007) (settlors of trust clearly intended that estate taxes should be allocated pro-rata between QTIP trust and surviving spouse's trust, and effectively waived application of §2207A; pre-1997 waiver of §2207A does not require specific reference to QTIP trust or §2207A).
324. §2207A(a); Reg. §20.2207A-1(a). State death taxes are not so recoverable under federal tax law, but may be recoverable under state law. *See Firstar Trust Co. v. First Nat'l Bank of Kenosha,* 525 N.W. 2d 53 (Wis. Ct. App. 1994), *aff'd in part, rev'd in part,* 541 N.W. 2d 467 (Wis. 1995); *Cleveland v. Compass Bank,* 652 So.2d 1134 (Ala. 1994) (§2207A preempts Alabama apportionment statute for federal estate taxes, but not for state estate taxes, attributable to QTIP property included in surviving spouse's estate). *See also In re Succession of Haydel,* 780 So.2d 1168 (La. Ct. App. 2001) (residual estate, including QTIP property, held liable for state estate taxes). *Cf. Katz, Look & Moison, P.C. v. Shirley (In re Estate of Klarner),* 113 P.3d 150 (Colo. 2005) (QTIP trust had to bear its share of both federal and state estate taxes as apportioned under §2207A formula because, based on Colorado statute coordinating with and paralleling federal law, §2207A preempts Colorado law).

325. Similar to the determination for the gift tax amount, the amount of estate tax recoverable is also calculated on an incremental basis, taking into account the surviving spouse's (or the surviving spouse's estate's) highest marginal rate. *See* §2207A(a)(1). This differs from other estate tax apportionment provisions and most state apportionment statutes, which provide for average or pro-rata allocations of the tax liability.
326. The purpose of such a provision is to avoid cash flow problems in the surviving spouse's estate by forcing the executor to pay the entire estate tax and then proceed with a collection action against the QTIP trust. For example, the direction to pay in the QTIP trust provisions may be made subject to a request by the executor of the surviving spouse's estate to provide funds to pay the amount of incremental tax. The surviving spouse's will should have a compatible tax payment clause and not provide for payment of "all death taxes" from the residue, which would then cause confusion as to whether §2207A reimbursement is to be negated.
327. See §2056(b)(7)(B)(ii)(II), which provides that no person may have a power to appoint any part of the property to any person other than the surviving spouse.
328. *See* §2056(b)(7)(B)(ii), flush language.
329. This assumes that the executor of the first estate has sufficient information concerning the net values of both estates. Even though (under the estate tax apportionment provisions) the entire tax liability attributable to the QTIP marital deduction property is to be sourced from the first estate, a separate executor for the estate of the second spouse may not provide adequate information to the executor of the first estate to enable an informed decision about making the appropriate election to enable equalization of the estates.
330. An income interest does not fail to be a qualifying income interest for this purpose solely because income between the last distribution date and the date of the surviving spouse's death (the "stub period" income) need not be distributed to the surviving spouse or his or her estate. Reg. §20.2056(b)-7(d)(4).
331. The maximum dividend and capital gains rate of 20% was enacted by ATRA, Pub. L. No. 112-240, §102(b), applies to taxpayers in the 39.6% highest marginal income tax bracket under §1(i), and is applicable to years after 2012. Prior to 2013, the highest dividend rate was 15%. The 15% income tax rate for dividends was enacted in the JGTRRA, Pub. L. No. 108-27. *See* §1(h)(11). Section 1(h)(11) and the general §1(h) 15% maximum capital gains tax rate apply to taxable years beginning before 2013. *See* 2010 TRA, Pub. L. No. 111-312, §101(a), §102 (extending sunset provisions in EGTRRA, Pub. L. No. 107-16, §901, and JGTRRA, Pub. L. No. 108-27, §303).
332. §2056(b)(7)(B)(ii)(II). Section 2519 specifies that the disposition of the qualifying income interest for life is treated as a transfer of all interests in that property other than the qualifying income interest. Section 2207A(b) provides that the gift tax attributable to the gift transfer (under §2519) is sourced from the transferred property.
333. Reg. §20.2056(b)-7(d)(6), noting the concern about possible failure to satisfy the requirement of §2056(b)(7)(B)(ii)(II) (possible appointment of property to someone other than surviving spouse).
334. §2056(b)(8).
335. §2056(b)(8)(B)(iii). See §664 and the discussion of these trusts at Chapter 9, E.3.b. If the terms of the will do not satisfy these requirements a local law reformation proceeding may enable this qualification. *See* PLR 200241012, PLR 200232015. *See also Estate of Sansone v. United States,* 2002–2 USTC ¶60,442 (9th Cir. 2002) (unpub. opin.) (trust was not qualified charitable remainder trust because it did not meet requirements of

either CRAT or CRUT; annual payments to the surviving spouse fluctuated based on cost-of-living adjustments).

336. *See* §2056(b)(7). If the surviving spouse is an alien, the additional QDOT requirements must be satisfied. *See* §§2056(d), 2056A.
337. See §2044(c), which specifies that property includible in the gross estate of the decedent under §2044(a) will be treated as property passing from the decedent, thereby enabling the charitable deduction to the estate of the second deceased spouse.
338. This assumes that local law permits this accumulation at the trust level, thereby depriving the surviving spouse of the current income benefits of this property.
339. See Reg. §20.2056(c)-2(b) (particularly the example in Reg. §20.2056(c)-2(b)(1)(iii)), which states that property is treated as passing from the decedent to the surviving spouse where the trust income is to be accumulated for a term of years or for the life of the surviving spouse and the augmented fund is to be paid to the surviving spouse or to his or her estate. *See also* Rev. Rul. 68-554, 1968-2 C.B. 412, Rev. Rul. 72-333, 1972-2 C.B. 530, Rev. Rul. 75-128, 1975-1 C.B. 308; TAM 9109003.
340. Reg. §1.665(a)-0A(d) specifies that the accumulation trust rules do not apply to estates and presumably this rule applies to the estate both as an accumulation vehicle and as a recipient of previously accumulated trust income. Further, §665(c), as enacted in the 1997 Taxpayer Relief Act, Pub. L. No. 105-34, provides for the inapplicability of the throwback rules to most trusts.
341. *See* §1(e), §1(f). The 2015 and 2016 inflation-adjusted income threshold for the maximum rate is $12,301 and $12,401, respectively. *See* Rev. Proc. 2014-61, 2014-47 I.R.B. 860, §3.01; Rev. Proc. 2015-53, 2015-44 I.R.B. 615, §3.01.
342. Section 663(a)(1) permits this bequest to be funded by the estate without being deemed to be a distribution of the DNI of the estate. Further, funding this specific gift with appreciated or depreciated property will not cause the estate to recognize gain or loss for income tax purposes on the distribution. See §643(e)(4) which provides that the §643(e) rules for determining the tax basis of assets distributed by estates and trusts will be inapplicable to distributions described in §663(a).
343. In the case of ambiguity, the determination of the terms of gifts such as specific bequests and devises is a matter of local law.
344. If not sufficiently clear these provisions will need to be interpreted by application of the rules of construction under local wills statutes. See, for example, Uniform Probate Code §2-606, concerning situations involving the nonademption of specific devises (such as where the testator sold the property and received sales proceeds) and §2-609, concerning ademption by satisfaction (i.e., the testator previously transferred the specific property to the designated recipient). This latter provision applies to both specific devises and monetary gifts.
345. If this bequest is actually funded in kind (e.g., by distributing stock or other property having a value of $500,000 but a lower income tax basis), gain will be recognized upon such a funding. *See* Reg. §1.1014-4(a)(3). That gain will ordinarily not be allocated to DNI. The recipient will have an income tax basis for the asset received in an amount equal to the value of the distribution transaction because the gain or loss recognition mandates a §1012 cost basis approach. This provision indicates that, if the distributed property is depreciated, loss must be recognized "to the extent required by the revenue laws." Section 267(a)(1) provides for the disallowance of losses in transactions between certain specified related persons and §267(b)(13) includes as such related persons an executor of an estate and a beneficiary of such estate except "in the case of a sale or exchange in satisfaction of a pecuniary bequest."

346. Because this is not a specific bequest, the exclusion under §663(a) from the applicability of the DNI allocation rules will not apply to the funding of this transfer. Consequently, distributable net income will be carried out of the estate to the beneficiary when the funding of this bequest occurs. The tax basis of the property received by the beneficiary in such a distribution is the adjusted basis of such property to the estate (as adjusted for any gain or loss recognized to the distributor on the distribution). §643(e)(1). That tax basis will have been previously stepped up to a date of death (or alternate valuation date) value, as determined under §1014.
347. The structuring and application of these formulas are discussed at Chapter 5, D.5.
348. In conjunction with making a simultaneous death provision inapplicable, this result could be produced when deaths do occur in a common accident.
349. During periods of low interest rates and limited appreciation in asset values, the better choice often would be estate equalization because the estate tax rate differential might be significantly greater than the investment return on the deferred estate taxes.
350. Pub. L. No. 111-312, §101(a), §301-§304.
351. See Chapter 4, A.1., for more information.
352. Pub. L. No. 112-240, §101(a).
353. Bolen, *Tax Legislation: Obama Says FY 2014 Budget Creates Jobs, Shrinks Deficits, Invests in Economic Growth*, 32 Tax Mgmt. Weekly Rpt. 515 (Apr. 15, 2013) (President's budget proposes estate and gift tax rates of 45%, estate tax exemption of $3.5 million, and gift tax exemption of $1 million in 2018). These proposed changes have continued to be reiterated by the Obama Administration. *See* U.S. Dept. of Treas., General Explanations of the Administration's Fiscal Year 2016 Revenue Proposals (Feb. 2015), at p. 193 (*available at* www.treasury.gov/resource-center/tax-policy).
354. This example assumes some future legislative changes. See, however, §2001(c), §2010(c), as amended by ATRA, Pub. L. No. 112-240, §101(a). As indicated at Chapter 4, A.4.c. and A.4.d., the rates and unified credit exemption equivalent may vary depending on the year of death.
355. Under the amendments made by the 2010 TRA, §301-§304 (made permanent by ATRA, Pub. L. No. 112-240, §101(a)), the difference between the lowest estate tax rate (after applying the exemption equivalent) and the highest estate tax rate disappeared when the estate tax rate was effectively turned into a flat rate tax (after considering the available exemption equivalent).
356. See Chapter 4, A.1., regarding the changes made by the 2010 TRA, Pub. L. No. 111-312, §101(a), §302-§304, and made permanent by ATRA, Pub. L. No. 112-240, §101(a), including the portability of the §2010(c) unified credit amount for spouses dying after 2010. For the inflation-adjusted unified credit amount for the most recent years, see Worksheet 1.
357. The estate planner should also keep in mind the legislative changes in the estate tax, such as those made by EGTRRA, Pub. L. No. 107-16, the 2010 TRA, Pub. L. No. 111-312, and ATRA, Pub. L. No. 112-240, as discussed in Chapter 4, A.1., and possible future legislative changes.
358. The estate planner should be certain that all assets included in the estate for federal estate tax purposes are accurately identified. For example, clients sometimes overlook life insurance policies with proceeds includable in the gross estate, retirement fund balances, the increasing value of a personal residence, and anticipated inheritances.
359. While the portability provision in §2010(c) will typically be utilized in this situation, there are instances where it might not be utilized. Further, as mentioned above, the

possibility of future legislative changes eliminating the portability provision should be considered.

360. Note, however, the possible applicability of §1014(e) concerning the transfer to and the retransfer of property by the decedent if the property initially owned by the decedent is received within one year of death. The income tax basis step up at death is precluded under these circumstances.

361. Whether the assets exceed the spouses' §2010(c) unified credit exemption amounts may be difficult to predict because the §2010(c) amount may vary. See Chapter 4, A.1.

362. See the discussion of the estate tax payment deferral provisions in Chapter 12, E.

363. See Chapter 4, A.1. and A.4.d., for a discussion of the §2010(c) and §2505(a) exclusion amounts after the changes made by the 2010 TRA, Pub. L. No. 111-312, §101(a), §301-§304, and ATRA, Pub. L. No. 112-240, §101(a). Note that this $5 million amount will be indexed for inflation.

364. State law provisions will often resolve problems for inadvertent mistakes in this context but their application can sometimes be problematic and might be challenged by the IRS.

365. This situation would not be possible in the context of a fractional formula share provision because, under the application of this approach, each bequest must share proportionately in the appreciation or depreciation in the value of assets through the date of final distribution of the assets of the estate to the various beneficiaries (including marital and nonmarital trusts).

366. 1964-1 C.B. 682.

367. *See* Rev. Proc. 64-19, §2.02 (permitting "minimum worth distribution"). The effect of this requirement is to put a floor but no ceiling on the bequest. If the objective is to minimize the value of the marital gift, this approach may not, however, produce a better result than the fractional share bequest. If the entire estate depreciates in value, a larger amount of property must then be distributed in satisfaction of this minimum worth bequest than if a fractional share provision were used. This minimum worth provision does add flexibility because the executor is given the choice of minimizing the value of property distributed in satisfaction of the bequest by selling assets and distributing cash or distributing assets in kind, thereby avoiding gain, or combining both approaches.

368. *See* Rev. Proc. 64-19, §2.02 (permitting "fairly representative distribution"). *See also* PLR 9007016 (trusts established for surviving spouse would qualify for marital deduction under §2056(b)(5) and §2056(b)(7), provided that will was amended to insure that property allocated to marital trusts was fairly representative of net appreciation or depreciation; this amendment would enable compliance with requirements of IRS's position in Rev. Proc. 64-19).

369. In Rev. Rul. 90-3, 1990-1 C.B. 174, the IRS concluded that a marital deduction was available (and a nondeductible §2056(b) terminable interest did not exist) where the decedent made a pecuniary bequest to a beneficiary other than the spouse in assets to be valued at the time of distribution and the residuary estate then passed to the surviving spouse. The IRS concluded that, if a pecuniary bequest to a person other than the spouse must be paid with assets valued at the time of payment, the possibility that post-death fluctuations in value might reduce the residuary bequest to the spouse does not cause the residuary bequest to be a nondeductible terminable interest. Of course, the residuary bequest might also increase in this circumstance if the estate assets increase in value after the death of the first spouse to die. TAM 9116003 indicates that the personal representative of the estate need not identify the specific assets that will be used to fund the trust for the marital deduction to be allowed.

370. Rev. Proc. 64-19, §4.01.
371. In this discussion, reference is often made to "date of death value," but this should be understood as being the value for federal estate tax purposes which, alternatively, could be, if elected, the value determined as of the alternate valuation date.
372. The distribution in satisfaction of a pecuniary formula legacy (as distinguished from a specific bequest) will carry out DNI. Reg. §1.663(a)-1(b)(1). Pursuant to Reg. §1.1014-4(a)(3), gain or loss would be recognized by the estate upon a funding in kind with appreciated or depreciated property (subject to a limitation on the loss deduction, as specified in §267). See also Chapter 5, D.5.c., discussing the principles evolving from Rev. Proc. 64-19. This IRS position provides for the possible disqualification of the marital deduction upon the funding of this legacy.
373. *See* ATRA, Pub. L. No. 112-240, §102(b). Prior to 2013, the maximum capital gains tax rate was 15%. *See* 2010 TRA, Pub. L. No. 111-312, §101(a), §102 (extending application of 15% maximum rate [under §1(h)] to taxable years beginning before 2013 by amending sunset provisions in EGTRRA, Pub. L. No. 107-16, §901, and JGTRRA, Pub. L. No. 108-27, §303).
374. Previously, this would also contemplate the state death tax credit, but the elimination of this credit occurred as of the end of 2004. *See* former §2011(f) (struck as deadwood by the Tax Increase Prevention Act of 2014, Pub. L. No. 113-295, Div. A, §221(a)(95)(A)).
375. See, however, the discussion of issues involving the restrictions on the permissible authority for the funding of the pecuniary formula bequest, particularly the applicability of the concepts of Rev. Proc. 64-19 in Chapter 5, D.5.c.
376. Note that fair market value will only be relevant if it is less than the tax basis.
377. Note that Rev. Rul. 90-3, 1990-1 C.B. 174, permits this approach as not violating the mandate of Rev. Proc. 64-19.
378. The limitations specified in Rev. Proc. 64-19, 1964-1 C.B. 682, will not be applicable to the fractional share approach, as indicated in Rev. Proc. 64-19, §4.01(1).
379. The distribution in satisfaction of the formula fractional share bequest will carry out DNI. Reg. §1.663(a)-1(b)(1). Unless an election is made, however, gain or loss will not be recognized to the estate upon the funding distribution made with appreciated or depreciated property. §643(e)(3). This occurs because a fractional portion is being distributed. See §643(e)(1), with respect to the determination of the basis of the distributed assets. Loss recognition on this distribution may also be limited under §267 (relating to the disallowance of losses in transactions between certain related parties).
380. The tax basis for the distributed asset will then be allocated proportionately to the recipients.
381. The issue might also arise whether (for §1001 purposes) an exchange of property is occurring in this context and, if so, whether gain (or loss) is being realized (and must be recognized) for federal income tax purposes. See Rev. Rul. 69-486, 1969-2 C.B. 159, holding that a transaction equivalent to a fractional distribution followed by property exchanges requires gain recognition.
382. See *Estate of Smith v. Commissioner,* 66 T.C. 415 (1976), *aff'd,* 565 F.2d 455 (7th Cir. 1977), *nonacq.,* 1978-2 C.B. 4, *acq.,* 1982-2 C.B. 2; *Laurin v. Commissioner,* T.C. Memo 1979-145, *aff'd,* 645 F.2d 8 (6th Cir. 1981); and *Estate of Meeske v. Commissioner,* 72 T.C. 73 (1979), in which the IRS was unsuccessful in challenging the right of an estate to a marital deduction on the basis that the use of an "equalization clause" transformed the marital transfer into a nondeductible terminable interest. In Rev. Rul. 82-23, 1982-1 C.B. 139, the nonacquiescence in *Estate of Smith v. Commissioner* was

withdrawn. In *Estate of Robertson v. Commissioner,* 98 T.C. 678 (1992), *rev'd,* 43 F.3d 779 (8th Cir. 1994), the Tax Court effectively reiterated its support of this approach, distinguishing the equalization approach from the elective QTIP (a differentiation subsequently abandoned by the Tax Court in *Estate of Clack v. Commissioner,* 106 T.C. 131 [1996], *acq.,* 1996-2 C.B. 1). But see TAM 9010001, where a will provided that the marital trust should be funded in an amount that the personal representative "deems most desirable for reducing the total federal estate tax liability of our respective estates." No marital deduction was allowed because no specific mechanism existed to determine the precise amount intended to pass to the surviving spouse, but the executor had broad discretion in determining the amount of the anticipated marital deduction gift. *See also* TAM 200131001, distinguishing Rev. Rul. 82-23 from the situation in that ruling.

383. *See* §2010(c), as made permanent by ATRA, Pub. L. No. 112-240, §101(a); *see also* Chapter 4, A.1.
384. *See* Reg. §1.1014-4(a)(3).
385. Section 1223(9), eliminates the one-year holding period requirement for long term capital gain qualification when the tax basis is changed by reason of being stepped up (or stepped down) at death under §1014.
386. *See* Reg. §1.1014-4(a)(3).
387. See Reg. §1.1014-4(a)(3), which distinguishes between "an amount" and "a fraction of his residuary estate."
388. Reg. §1.1014-4(a)(1); Prop. Reg. §1.1014-4(a)(1), REG-107595-11, 80 Fed. Reg. 26,873 (May 11, 2015). This basis will be adjusted under §1014 or former §1022, except for items of "income in respect of a decedent." *See* §1014(c); former §1022(f).
389. *See* Reg. §1.661(a)-2(f), §1.1014-4(a)(3); Rev. Rul. 69-486, 1969-2 C.B. 159. If, however, the executor is given authority in the will to make non-pro-rata distributions of estate property, realization of gain should be avoided in these circumstances. See PLR 9422052 involving a revocable trust executed by both spouses and funded with community property. On the death of a spouse the trust was to be divided into three trusts: (1) a survivor's trust (containing the surviving spouse's one-half of the community property), (2) a marital deduction trust, and (3) a credit shelter trust. The IRS ruled that a non-pro-rata division of community property between the three trusts was not a taxable exchange, indicating that this transaction was the same as a partition of jointly held property and the trustee was given the power to make non-pro-rata allocations. See also PLR 9523029, where the shifting of closely held stock between a marital trust and a family trust to abate family disputes did not result in the realization of gain or loss under §1001. In contrast, in PLR 9429012 the IRS ruled that a court-approved non-pro-rata division of a trust into two trusts was a taxable sale or exchange because no authority to make non-pro-rata divisions was granted in the trust instrument or under state law (the situation then being governed by Rev. Rul. 69-486, 1969-2 C.B. 159). However, the IRS has issued numerous private letter rulings citing Rev. Rul. 69-486 and emphasizing that no gain was to be recognized because all the distributions in those situations were pro rata, implying that non-pro-rata distributions might produce a different result.
390. Reg. §1.1014-4(a)(3).
391. If a 20% capital gains rate is applicable, that tax liability might not be significant. *See* §1(h), as amended by ATRA, Pub. L. No. 112-240, §102(b). Prior to 2013, the maximum capital gains rate was 15%. *See* EGTRRA, Pub. L. No. 107-16, §101(c); JGTRRA, Pub. L. No. 108-27, §301. The 15% maximum capital gains tax rate applies to taxable years beginning before 2013. *See* 2010 TRA, Pub. L. No. 111-312, §101(a), §102

(extending sunset provisions in EGTRRA, Pub. L. No. 107-16, §901, and JGTRRA, Pub. L. No. 108-27, §303).

392. Like the trust distribution situation, §267 applies to disallow recognition of a loss realized upon an estate distribution of depreciated property to a beneficiary "except in the case of a sale or exchange in satisfaction of a pecuniary bequest." *See* §267(a)(1), §267(b)(13).
393. An exception exists where the estate decreases in value during the first six months following death and the alternate valuation method available under §2032 is used to value the property. In this instance the marital deduction is charged with all of the losses while the credit shelter remains the same. After passage of the six-month period, the entire risk of loss is on the credit shelter portion, however. A failure to fund the pecuniary bequest promptly continues the risk of substantial reduction of assets passing to the credit shelter residuary.
394. In some very large estates, the pecuniary bequest marital deduction may be used. The result of this arrangement is: (1) if the estate increases in value during the six-month alternate valuation period the accruing market appreciation will pass to the credit shelter disposition (reduced by the capital gains tax incurred on funding the pecuniary bequest); and (2) if the estate decreases in value during the six-month period, the alternate valuation date could be used and the marital bequest would bear the decline in value. The amount passing in the credit shelter is undiminished but only where the marital bequest is funded promptly after the close of the six-month period. Otherwise, a small decrease in value after expiration of the six-month period could result in exhaustion of the credit shelter bequest. For this reason, this technique should be approached with caution.
395. *See* §661(a)(2).
396. *See* §662(a)(2)(B).
397. *See* §663(a)(1). Reg. §1.663(a)-1(b)(1) states that a bequest of money or property, to be selected by the decedent's executor, to the decedent's spouse equal to a fraction of the decedent's "adjusted gross estate" is not a bequest of a specific sum of money because "the identity of the property and the amount of money specified are dependent both on the exercise of the executor's discretion and on the payment of administration expenses and other charges, neither of which are facts existing on the date of decedent's death." The determination of the value of the bequest after the decedent's death but before the bequest is satisfied (so that gain or loss may be realized by the estate in the transfer of property in satisfaction of the bequest) is not material for this purpose. Any distribution in payment of a formula pecuniary bequest also carries with it the estate's DNI because such payment is not in satisfaction of a fixed dollar amount. See PLR 200210002, where a distribution of IRA funds from an estate did not fit within the §663(a)(1) exception.
398. Note that the concept of DNI was impacted by the 2004 regulations revising the definition of DNI under §643(b). T.D. 9102, 69 Fed. Reg. 12 (Jan. 2, 2004).
399. §643(e)(2).
400. §643(e)(1).
401. Reg. §1.661(a)(2)(f) specifies that gain or loss is realized upon an estate distribution of property in kind if the distribution is in satisfaction of a right to receive a pecuniary amount or of specific property other than the property distributed.
402. Residents of community property states could use the marital deduction for the transfer of separate property to the other spouse. This was particularly important for those persons who recently moved from a separate property jurisdiction to a community property jurisdiction or where an individual received a significant bequest (ordinarily categorized

as separate property under applicable state law). Formerly, an adjustment mechanism was provided in §2056 to permit a marital deduction for separate property owned by residents of community property states.

403. §2056(d)(1).
404. §2056(d)(2).
405. Section 2056A(a) enumerates the specific requirements to enable QDOT treatment.
406. §2056A(a)(1). Additional security requirements have been prescribed by regulation to ensure the collection of the §2056A tax. Reg. §20.2056A-2(d). In the 1997 Taxpayer Relief Act, Pub. L. No. 105-34, several amendments were made to the QDOT provisions, including in §1303 of the act, providing a transition rule so that certain trusts created before the enactment of the 1990 Omnibus Budget Reconciliation Act are treated as satisfying the income tax withholding requirement imposed under §2056A(a)(1) if their governing instruments require that all trustees be U.S. citizens or domestic corporations.
407. §2056A(b)(1)(A), §2056A(b)(3)(A), §2056A(b)(3)(B).
408. §2056A(b)(1)(B). For a more detailed discussion of these provisions, see 842 T.M., *Transfers to Noncitizen Spouses* (Bloomberg BNA).
409. An annual income distribution requirement (in former §2056A) was eliminated in the 1989 Revenue Reconciliation Act, Pub. L. No. 101-239, §7815(d)(7)(A)(ii).
410. *See* the 1997 Taxpayer Relief Act, Pub. L. No. 105-34, §1312. See also Reg. §20.2056A-2(b)(3), concerning certain property passing under a nontransferable plan or arrangement and Reg. §20.2056A-4(b).
411. *See* §2056A(a)(1).
412. See H.R. Rep. No. 105-220, at 719 (1997).
413. See §2101-§2107. For more detailed discussions of the rules applicable to nonresident aliens, see 837 T.M., *Non-Citizens—Estate, Gift and Generation-Skipping Taxation* (Bloomberg BNA); 854 T.M., *U.S. Taxation of Foreign Estates, Trusts and Beneficiaries* (Bloomberg BNA).
414. §2106(a)(3). See *Estate of Fung v. Commissioner,* 117 T.C. 247 (2001), *aff'd* 58 F. App'x 328 (9th Cir. 2003), rejecting the assertion of the estate of a nonresident alien that it was entitled to a marital deduction for all of the U.S. property in the residuary estate that passed to the decedent's surviving spouse. The estate maintained that the decedent's interest in the U.S. properties passed to his surviving spouse in recognition of her valid enforceable right under Hong Kong law to an outright distribution of 3/8ths of the residuary estate and thereby qualified for the marital deduction.
415. See PLR 200820023, where disclaimers by children increased the amount distributable to the surviving spouse and eligible for the estate tax marital deduction.
416. See TAM 8926001, where the National Office, disregarding a local court decision holding that the property disclaimed by the children of an intestate decedent passed to the surviving spouse, advised that, as a result of a disclaimer, property passed to the children's children and, consequently, this transfer was not eligible for the marital deduction.
417. If property is located in another jurisdiction, difficulty may even arise in this situation in identifying which intestate law may apply to determine the next taker of a property interest after the disclaimer.
418. An alternative approach could be to seek a ruling that the QTIP election is a nullity because the marital deduction is not necessary to reduce the estate tax liability to zero. See Rev. Proc. 2001-38, 2001-2 C.B. 124, providing relief for surviving spouses and

their estates in situations where a predeceased spouse's estate made an unnecessary QTIP election that did not reduce the estate tax liability of the estate.

419. §2518(b)(4).
420. Reg. §25.2518-2(e)(5) *Ex. 5.*
421. Reg. §25.2518-2(e)(2).
422. Reg. §25.2518-2(e)(5) *Ex. 5.*
423. See TAM 200407018, indicating that a duty of consistency applies to preclude taxpayers from asserting that at the first spouse's death a marital deduction is available under §2056 but that at the second spouse's death no inclusion is required under §2044. Similarly, in *Estate of Letts v. Commissioner,* 109 T.C. 290 (1997), the Tax Court concluded that sufficient privity existed between the two estates to preclude such a position. *See also* TAM 200407018. In *Estate of Posner v. Commissioner,* T.C. Memo 2004-112, the Tax Court refused to apply the duty of consistency to include a trust in the gross estate of the surviving spouse, concluding that the duty of consistency does not apply when the inconsistency arises because of a purely legal issue.
424. As a result of the 2010 TRA, Pub. L. No. 111-312, §101(a), §302-§304, and ATRA Pub. L. No. 112-240, §101(a), the §2010(c) estate tax exclusion amount is $5 million for estates of decedents dying after 2009, and has a portability provision for spouses dying after 2010 (with the basic exclusion amount adjusted for inflation after 2011). See Chapter 4, A.1. These changes may impact the subsequent federal estate tax exposure when the surviving spouse dies even though the marital assets remain the same.
425. See Chapter 5, A.2.c., for a discussion of considerations pertinent in structuring tax allocation clauses.
426. *See* §2207A(a)(2).
427. Local law tax allocation provisions may also be relevant in this context and should be carefully analyzed as to their potential application.
428. The failure of an estate to exercise a right of recovery under §2207A of the allocable estate tax (attributable to the QTIP property) is treated as a gift of the unrecovered amounts from the persons who would benefit from the recovery to the persons from whom the recovery could have been obtained. Reg. §20.2207A-1(a)(2). This transfer is considered made when the right of recovery is no longer enforceable under applicable law. In addition, a delay in the exercise of the right of recovery may be treated as an interest-free loan with appropriate gift tax consequences under §7872, depending on the facts of the particular case. No gift is made, however, if the surviving spouse's will provides that recovery will not be made or to the extent that the beneficiaries cannot otherwise compel recovery. Reg. §20.2207A-1(a)(3). This would also result where the executor has and exercises discretion to waive the right of recovery.
429. This is also known for federal transfer tax purposes as a "non-general" power of appointment because the tax provisions only identify a general power of appointment and, then, exceptions to that categorization. See 825 T.M., *Powers of Appointment—Estate, Gift, and Income Tax Considerations* (Bloomberg BNA). See also an excellent, although dated, analysis of powers of appointment from the American Bar Association. Subcomm. of the Comm. on Est. & Tax Planning, *Use and Drafting of Powers of Appointment,* 1 Real Prop., Prob. & Trust J. 307 (1966).
430. Note that the validity and scope of a power of appointment is a matter of interpretation under state property law, rather than under federal tax law. A power of appointment is ordinarily created under a trust instrument but can be provided in other circumstances,

such as under a contract or a real property deed, although these are cumbersome arrangements and seldom used. See Rev. Rul. 79-154, 1979-1 C.B. 301, where the IRS stated that the principles of §2041 (the estate tax power of appointment provision) apply to the taxation of a life insurance fund subject to powers of appointment in the same manner that the principles are applied to determine the taxability of other forms of property subject to powers of appointment.

431. This power must be distinguished from a power reserved (within the scope of §2036 and §2038) by an owner of property who transfers his or her own property while retaining certain control rights over that property.

432. See Restatement of the Law of Trusts, 3d, Division VI, entitled "Powers of Appointment," and particularly Chapter 17, §17.1, which specifies that "[a] power of appointment is a power that enables the donee of the power, acting in a non-fiduciary capacity, to designate recipients of beneficial ownership interests in the appointive property."

433. Note that the concept of a "power of appointment" is a local law property rule that evolved considerably prior to the enactment of the federal estate tax provisions (including the application of the federal transfer tax provisions in the power of appointment context).

434. §2041(b)(1). Numerous revenue rulings, private letter rulings and cases deal with the question of whether certain powers constitute a general power of appointment. For example, in Rev. Rul. 74-120, 1974-1 C.B. 282, the IRS ruled that a power in a widow to appoint to "such a person or persons as she designates" is, under New York law, a power to appoint to her own estate and is, therefore, a general power of appointment for federal estate tax purposes. State law governs this question, although Reg. §20.2041-1(c)(2) provides specific examples of powers limited by an ascertainable standard that, therefore, would cause the power to be a nongeneral power. This effectively provides a limited federal definition that may be used as a "safe harbor" in this context.

435. Note, however, that the concept of a general power of appointment is not coextensive with the requirements enabling sufficient power over income to enable a QTIP election. *Davis v. Commissioner,* 394 F.3d 1294 (9th Cir. 2005).

436. Because the scope of the power of appointment is determined by reference to applicable local law, the power might be reformed after death in a local court proceeding to assure that the powers held are only coextensive with the scope of a nongeneral power of appointment for federal estate (or income) tax purposes. PLR 200450033.

437. §2041(b)(1)(A). See Rev. Rul. 76-368, 1976-2 C.B. 271, where the IRS ruled that a power of invasion, not limited by an ascertainable standard, that was granted to an independent trustee could not be imputed to the beneficiary of the trust so as to cause the power to be a general power.

438. Reg. §20.2041-1(c)(2) provides that a power is limited by an ascertainable standard if the extent of the holder's duty to exercise and not to exercise the power is reasonably measurable in terms of his or her needs for health, education, and support (or any combination of them). The regulations indicate that the words "support" and "maintenance" are not limited to the bare necessities of life. A power to use property for the "comfort, welfare, or happiness" of the holder of the power is not limited by the requisite standard, however. Numerous cases and rulings address whether an "ascertainable standard" exists for this purpose. *See*, as examples of the process of defining an ascertainable standard, *First Virginia Bank v. United States,* 490 F.2d 532 (4th Cir. 1974); *Estate of Sowell v. Commissioner,* 74 T.C. 1001 (1980), where the court found

that a power to invade corpus for "emergency or illness" was governed by a definite standard but not limited in its exercise to matters relating to the decedent's health, education, support, or maintenance; *Finlay v. United States*, 752 F.2d 246 (6th Cir. 1985), where the court determined that a "right to encroach" given to the decedent's spouse over his residuary trust estate was limited by local law to an ascertainable standard, therefore not constituting a general power of appointment. See Rev. Rul. 78-398, 1978-2 C.B. 237, where the IRS described a situation in which the trustee (who was also the income beneficiary) could apply as much of the trust principal for the benefit of the income beneficiary as the trustee determined to be necessary for the beneficiary's "maintenance and medical care." The IRS concluded that this power was limited by an ascertainable standard and, therefore, the power was not a general power of appointment. *Cf.*, however, Rev. Rul. 77-194, 1977-1 C.B. 283, where a decedent possessed a power to invade corpus for the purpose of "proper comfort and welfare," the power was not limited under the applicable New Jersey law by an ascertainable standard relating to health, education, support, or maintenance, and was held to be a general power of appointment. A general power of appointment also existed where the decedent held a power to invade corpus "to continue the donee's accustomed standard of living" and applicable state law did not restrict or limit the language to support or maintenance. Rev. Rul. 77-60, 1977-1 C.B. 282. This issue ultimately concerns the interpretation of §2041(b)(1)(A) as measured by reference to the rights of the holder of the power as identified under local trust and property law. This type of inquiry is best represented by the discussion in *Estate of Vissering v. Commissioner,* 96 T.C. 749 (1991), *rev'd and rem'd,* 990 F.2d 578 (10th Cir. 1993).

439. §2041(b)(1)(C)(i). This exception is not practically useful in the planning environment because, if the creator holds such a power, the assets will be includible in the gross estate of the creator under the transfer provisions of §2036 and §2038. Such a result would ordinarily be contrary to the estate planning objectives sought by the donor of the power at the time the trust is created.

440. §2041(b)(1)(C)(ii). Such an arrangement invites controversy. The adverse interest must be created in the same instrument that created the power of appointment. *See Witkowski v. United States,* 451 F.2d 1249 (5th Cir. 1971), *cert. denied*, 409 U.S. 891 (1972); Rev. Rul. 79-63, 1979-1 C.B. 302. For examples of situations where this provision was asserted as being applicable see PLR 200150020 and *Estate of Greve v. Commissioner,* T.C. Memo 2004-91.

441. §2041(b)(1)(C)(iii). See Rev. Rul. 77-158, 1977-1 C.B. 285, where the IRS ruled that, where a trust was created by three siblings, each of whom named an adult child as one of the three trustees and the trustees (1) through majority vote had complete discretionary power over the assets of the trust and (2) individually had the right to name a relative as successor, one-third of the value of the trust was includible in a decedent-trustee's estate as property subject to a general power of appointment.

442. Section 2041 only defines a "general power of appointment" and, therefore, what is not a general power of appointment is referred to as a nongeneral power of appointment, although common usage and state law often refers to this latter situation as a "limited" or "special" power of appointment.

443. Obviously, the power cannot be classified as "limited" if the donee is the holder of a power to appoint to his or her estate, his or her creditors, or the creditors of his or her estate.

444. Reg. §20.2041-1(b)(1). For example, if a trust instrument provides that the beneficiary may appropriate or consume the principal of the trust, the power to consume or appropriate is a "power of appointment." Similarly, a power to affect the beneficial enjoyment of trust property or its income by altering, amending, or revoking the trust instrument or terminating the trust is a power of appointment. *See*, for example, *Keeter v. United States,* 461 F.2d 714 (5th Cir. 1972), where the court held that a settlor created a general power of appointment when he elected to place insurance proceeds into a position from which the decedent could withdraw funds for himself. *See also* Rev. Rul. 79-373, 1979-2 C.B. 331.
445. Reg. §20.2041-1(b)(1) indicates that, if under the terms of a trust instrument, the trustee (or his or her successor) had the power to appoint the principal of the trust for the benefit of individuals including himself or herself, and the decedent had the unrestricted power to discharge the trustee at any time and appoint any other person as trustee, including himself or herself, the decedent is considered as having a power of appointment.
446. See Reg. §20.2041-1(b)(1), which indicates that the mere power of management, investment, custody of assets, or the power to allocate receipts and disbursements as between income and principal, exercisable in a fiduciary capacity, whereby the holder has no power to enlarge or shift any of the beneficial interests therein (except as an incidental consequence of the discharge of such fiduciary duties), is not a power of appointment.
447. §2041(a)(2). See, for example, TAM 200014002, where the National Office advised that, where a decedent was a co-trustee and life beneficiary and the trustees could distribute corpus in their discretion, the decedent did not have a general power of appointment because applicable (New York) state law prevented exercise of that power by the decedent for the benefit of the decedent. Ordinarily, this limitation should also be included in the governing trust instrument so that reliance on applicable state law is not essential.
448. For general powers of appointment created on or before October 21, 1942, the property will be included in the donee's gross estate only if the power is actually exercised under the donee's will or by a disposition which is of the nature that, if it were a transfer of property owned by the decedent, such property would be includible in the decedent's gross estate under the transfer provisions of §2035 through §2038. *See* §2041(a)(1). See also *Stewart v. United States,* 512 F.2d 269 (5th Cir. 1975), where the testatrix held a pre-1942 testamentary general power of appointment. Her father's trust, creating the power of appointment, provided it could be exercised merely by her making a will, "any law, custom, or usage to the contrary notwithstanding." The court held that the residuary clause of the testatrix's will constituted an exercise of the power of appointment (although no specific mention was made of the power of appointment), causing the property subject to the power to be included in the testatrix's estate. Although pre-1942 powers of appointment are rare in the twenty-first century, as a precaution an explicit provision should often be included in a last will indicating that no power held by the decedent is exercised under the will unless specific reference is made to a particular power of appointment.
449. §2041(a)(2); Reg. §20.2041-3(b).
450. Reg. §20.2041-3(b). For example, if the power is exercisable only upon reaching a specified age, and as of his or her death the decedent had not reached that age, the power would not exist at the time of death. But see *Estate of Kurz v. Commissioner,* 68 F.3d 1027 (7th Cir. 1995), holding that, in the situation of "stacked" or sequenced trusts, if the

holder of the power exercises control over those contingencies these "contingencies" will be disregarded for this purpose.

451. §2041(a)(2); Reg. §20.2041-3(d)(1). Under these circumstances, the donee need not actually hold a power as of the date of his or her death for the property subject to the power to be included in his or her gross estate.

452. §2041(a)(2); Reg. §20.2041-3(d)(1). The regulations indicate that a release of a power of appointment need not be formal or express in character. See, for example, Rev. Rul. 86-39, 1986-1 C.B. 301, where, in the context of a corporate recapitalization, a shift in economic value occurred, the holder of a general testamentary power of appointment released power over property while retaining an income interest for life in property, and the property was treated as includible under §2041. Reg. §20.2041-3(d)(2) further indicates that §2041(a)(2) does not apply to the complete release of a power of appointment, whether exercisable during life or by will, if the release was not made within the meaning of §2035, and if, after the release, the holder of the power retained no interest or control over the property subject to the power that would cause the property to be included in his or her gross estate under §2036 through §2038 (if the property had been transferred by the holder). Such a release, assuming it were to constitute a gift for federal gift tax purposes, would ordinarily be considered in determining the estate tax liability under the unified tax rate schedule.

453. *See* §2518. Prior to the Tax Reform Act of 1976, a specific disclaimer rule applied to powers of appointment. The Tax Reform Act of 1976 included specific federal tax disclaimer rules in §2518 and deleted the special power of appointment disclaimer rule from §2041(a)(2).

454. *See* H.R. Rep. No. 94-1380, at 67 (1976) (specifically indicating that disclaimer of general power of appointment is not to be treated as "release" of power within meaning of §2041(b)); Reg. §25.2518-3(a)(1)(iii) (specifying that power of appointment for property is treated as separate interest in such property and such power of appointment for all or an undivided portion of such property may be disclaimed independently from any other interests separately created by transferor in property if requirements of §2518(b) are met). *See also* PLR 200003023.

455. §2041(b)(2); Reg. §20.2041-3(d)(3).

456. Regs. §20.2041-3(d)(3).

457. If, in the example, B possessed the right to withdraw $15,000 of the principal annually and the value of the corpus continues to be $200,000, the failure to exercise such power in any year will be considered a taxable release of the power to the extent of the excess of the amount subject to withdrawal over 5% of the trust fund (in this example, the excess being $5,000, or $15,000 less $10,000). Consequently, he would have made a transfer of $5,000 to a trust from which he receives an income distribution, the transfer thereby being equivalent to a §2036 transfer. The purpose of the lapsed power rule is to determine that proportion of the trust property to be includible in a decedent's estate because of the taxable lapse of a general power in a year prior to that in which the decedent died. In the above example, that proportion for the particular year of the lapse is 5,000/200,000 = 1/40. This fraction would increase as nonexempt lapses occur annually thereafter. The value of the taxable proportion must be ascertained as of the decedent's estate tax valuation date, generally by applying the proportion to the estate tax value of the assets from which the lapsed power (greater than the five and five exception) could have been satisfied. The total amount included in the gross estate by reason

of lapses cannot exceed the total value of the trust on the date of death (or, if applicable, the alternate valuation date). Reg. §20.2041-3(d)(4), §20.2041-3(d)(5). *See* Rev. Rul. 85-88, 1985-2 C.B. 201, identifying several *"Crummey"* trust situations where a measurement was made as to the amount of gift transfers in excess of the five-and-five power.

458. See, however, the discussion below as to when property previously subject to a lapsed five-and-five power may be included in the generation-skipping tax base.
459. This exercise period could be even shorter (e.g., a few days at several intervals during the year) if this risk of estate tax inclusion is significant.
460. Note, however, the discussion of *Estate of Kurz v. Commissioner,* 68 F.3d 1027 (7th Cir. 1995), concerning the possible applicability of the power of appointment rules where the power holder has economic power in a "stacked trusts" situation.
461. Under §2503(b), the gift tax annual donee exclusion in only available if the gift consists of a "present interest" in property.
462. See the discussion of the *Crummey* or "demand trust" in Chapter 6, D.3.g.
463. §2041(b)(2).
464. §2514(e).
465. This is the $10,000 annual donee exclusion amount as indexed for inflation for the year 2015.
466. Note, however, that, if the value of the trust is $280,000 (or a greater amount) and the 5% power therefore enables a withdrawal of $14,000 (or a proportionately larger amount), this power will not cause this dilemma.
467. The use of a "hanging power" represents an attempt to avoid this dilemma. A "hanging" power is a power of withdrawal that "hangs" (or continues in effect) until its termination and will not cause a taxable transfer by the power holder. A hanging power is used in conjunction with *Crummey* withdrawal powers in an attempt to utilize the transferor's $14,000 (or $28,000 if the spouse consents to split the gift) annual gift tax exclusion (as adjusted for inflation for both 2015 and 2016; *see* Rev. Proc. 2014-61, 2014-47 I.R.B. 860, §3.35(1); Rev. Proc. 2015-53, 2015-44 I.R.B. 615, §3.35(1)) while retaining the transfer tax benefit provided by the "five and five" power. See TAM 8901004, where the National Office advised that a "hanging" power of withdrawal is invalid and will be ignored for gift tax purposes. Relying on *Procter v. Commissioner,* 142 F.2d 824 (4th Cir. 1944), the IRS concluded that the hanging power mechanism was a condition subsequent and was deemed not valid as tending to discourage enforcement of federal gift tax provisions.
468. §2041(a)(3).
469. Within the meaning of §2035–§2037.
470. §2041(a)(3). Such postponement would occur in a situation where, by reason of state law, the common law "rule against perpetuities" does not apply to prevent the postponement of vesting beyond the lives in being plus 21 years (as determined as of the measurement date).
471. Reg. §20.2041-3(e)(2).
472. In Rev. Rul. 79-353, 1979-2 C.B. 325, the IRS ruled that, where the settlor of a trust retained the power to remove an independent trustee and to appoint another independent trustee at will, this so-called "revolving door" power would cause inclusion of the trust in the settlor's estate. After considerable controversy the IRS's position was reversed in Rev. Rul. 95-58, 1995-2 C.B. 191. In litigation the IRS's position in Rev. Rul. 79-353 was repudiated by *Estate of Wall v. Commissioner*, 101 T.C. 300 (1993) and *Estate of Vak v. Commissioner*, 973 F.2d 1409 (8th Cir. 1992).

473. See PLR 8916032, where a "revolving door" power was treated as creating §2041 exposure.
474. Judicial authority existed to the contrary. See *First Nat'l Bank of Denver v. United States,* 42 AFTR2d 78-6466 (D. Colo. 1978), *aff'd,* 648 F.2d 1286 (10th Cir. 1981), where the issue was whether the beneficiary with powers to remove the trustee could appoint himself trustee. The court construed the trust as requiring the appointment of a bank, thus preventing the decedent from appointing himself, and found that the decedent did not possess a general power of appointment.
475. *See* Rev. Rul. 95-58, 1995-2 C.B. 191; PLR 9607008 (power to replace a corporate trustee is not general power of appointment over income and principal of trust for estate and gift tax purposes). The Service has issued numerous private letter rulings confirming this taxpayer-favorable position. *See, e.g.,* PLRs 200404005-007.
476. Reg. §20.2041-1(c)(1).
477. Rev. Rul. 79-154, 1979-1 C.B. 301.
478. The issue of the existence of a general power of appointment in these circumstances can also be advanced where a parent who is not the donor serves as custodian for his or her child under the applicable state-enacted Uniform Transfers to Minors Act. State property and family law rules should be examined on the issue of §2041(a)(2) includibility of the UTMA account for a non-donor parent acting as custodian. In the majority of jurisdictions, a parent has a legal obligation to support a child without recourse to the child's own funds. Under this view, the obligation of support exists regardless of the child's own funds, and the distribution of those funds should not be regarded as a discharge of the obligation. Consequently, the ability to use the funds should have no §2041(a)(2) consequences. The IRS, however, regards the distribution of a child's funds as a reduction or discharge of the parent's legal obligation. Thus, a parent, acting as a custodian, has the power to utilize the fund in satisfaction of the parent's support obligations and may be deemed to possess a §2041(a)(2) power under a discharge of legal obligation theory. Sections 677(b) and 678(c) (relating to grantor trust income tax treatment) may be regarded as supporting this "discharge of obligation" theory. See Rev. Rul. 56-484, 1956-2 C.B. 23, and Rev. Rul. 59-357, 1959-2 C.B. 212, which reflect the IRS position that distributions made from a UTMA account are regarded, at least for federal income tax purposes, as discharging a parent's legal obligation to support the beneficiary of the account.
479. *See* PLR 9036048 (examining scope of these powers in context of credit shelter trust).
480. §2514(b). In the case of a pre-October 21, 1942, power, taxation is limited to an actual exercise of such a power and does not include a release. §2514(a).
481. §2511(a); Reg. §25.2514-1(b)(2), §25.2514-3(e) *Ex. (3)*; Rev. Rul. 79-327, 1979-2 C.B. 342. *But see Commissioner v. Walston,* 168 F.2d 211 (4th Cir. 1948); *Self v. United States,* 142 F. Supp. 939 (Ct. Cl. 1956). See also PLR 9451049, where the IRS ruled that the exercise by two sisters of special powers of appointment in favor of the other would result in taxable gifts under Reg. §25.2514-1(b)(2), but the IRS did not proceed further to treat these exercises as subject to reciprocal transfer principles.
482. §678(a)(1). If a holder had such a power but modified it or partly released it and retains such controls as would (within the principles of §671–§677) subject a grantor of a trust to treatment as the owner thereof for income tax purposes, the holder will be treated as the owner of the trust for income tax purposes. §678(a)(2). Occasionally this status as "owner" for income tax purposes is important to enable the trust to hold S corporation stock because the person treated as the owner is then an eligible S corporation stockholder. *See* Reg. §1.641(c)-1(k) *Ex. 1.*
483. §678(b); Reg. §1.678(b)-1.

484. §678(c); Reg. §1.678(c)-1.
485. §678(d); Reg. §1.678(d)-1. Unlike the estate and gift tax context, the manner of completing a renunciation or disclaimer for purposes of §678(d) is not specifically defined, but the disclaimer must be within a "reasonable time" after the holder of the power first becomes aware of its existence. *Cf.* §2518, §2046.
486. This is a more restrictive definition than the concept of a taxable power of appointment for estate and gift tax purposes. See, for example, PLR 8926032, where a trustee, who could distribute trust corpus to himself, was not taxable as the trust owner under §678(a) where the distributions required the consent of at least one adverse person. See also PLR 8926066, where a beneficiary was not treated as the owner of a trust because she did not have the power to vest the trust corpus or income in herself, pursuant to §678.
487. See, however, the discussion of the possible application of the generation-skipping transfer tax in Chapter 8.
488. This situation could be subjected to the generation-skipping transfer tax unless the exemption from that tax might be available.
489. See §2056(b)(5) and Chapter 5, D.3.g.
490. For example, the decedent may wish the surviving spouse to not be able to appoint to the spouse from a subsequent marriage.
491. If some of the objects of the power can be completely omitted in making the appointment, the power will be exclusive. If all potential appointees must receive some "substantial" share of the property, the power will be nonexclusive. Whether a power can be exclusive is a matter determinable under applicable state law.
492. For example, to one month per year so as to limit estate tax exposure for the property subject to this power at death.
493. Absent a specific designation of the takers in default in the relevant instrument, state law will determine the heirs at law who will receive this property.
494. This would be to assure that an intent to exercise the power must be clearly manifested by the holder of the power and that a provision such as a residuary clause in a will is not to be deemed to constitute the exercise of the power.
495. *See* Gray, *The Rule Against Perpetuities*, §477 (4th ed. 1942); Simes, *Future Interests,* §121 (2d ed. 1966) (describing the purpose and policy of the rule); Leach, *Perpetuities in a Nutshell*, 51 Harv. L. Rev. 638 (1938); Dukeminier, *A Modern Guide to Perpetuities*, 74 Calif. L. Rev. 691 (1987).
496. For a proposed statutory enactment of a Rule Against Perpetuities *see* Uniform Probate Code, §2-901, which has proposals concerning both the validity of a general power of appointment and the validity of a nongeneral or testamentary power of appointment. Similarly, *see* Restatement of the Law of Trusts, 3d, §29, which specifies that an intended trust or trust provision is invalid if: "(b) It violates rules relating to perpetuities. . . ."
497. *See, generally,* Subcomm. of Comm. on Est. & Tax Planning, Use and Drafting of Powers of Appointment, 1 Real Prop., Prob. & Trust J. 307 (1966). Note that the rule against perpetuities was repealed in several jurisdictions (e.g., Alaska Stat. §34.27.010, effective Jan. 1, 1996) and is under attack in others.
498. Exercise of a general power of appointment is equivalent to a gift transfer (§2514) and the exercise of a special power of appointment may cause a gift to be made (e.g., by the extinguishment of a life estate). *See* Reg. §25.2514-1(b)(2).
499. As described above, §2041(a)(2) requires gross estate inclusion for the property subject to a general power of appointment held by a decedent. A pre-October 21, 1942 general power of appointment generates estate tax inclusion at the power holder's death only if the power is exercised. §2041(a)(1).

CHAPTER 6

Lifetime Asset Transfers

A. Lifetime Gifts—Arguments For and Against

After dealing with the fundamental planning questions concerning gratuitous transfers of property at death, the estate planner should encourage the client to consider the possible use of lifetime gifts to reduce the client's net transfer tax liabilities.[1] A gift program may be motivated, of course, by reasons other than avoiding potential transfer tax liabilities applicable at death.[2] In many situations, however, transfer tax planning is one of the most significant components of implementing a gift program.[3]

Before encouraging implementation of a gift program, the estate planner must be assured that the client's financial position is actually sufficiently secure to enable a gift program. This will necessitate an evaluation of the client's current financial situation, anticipated future income sources, probable cash requirements, and similar matters. If the client's children are involved in this gift program evaluation process, the estate planner must remain vigilant so that his or her commitment to the older generation client's interest in these matters is not compromised by overaggressive children seeking advancements of their anticipated inheritances.

1. Reasons for Making Gifts

A donor may desire to make gift transfers to accomplish one (or more) of the following objectives:

- support his or her elderly parents;
- help a child buy a home;
- help a child start a business or participate in the family business;
- enable a child to learn money management and to initiate an investment program;
- transfer assets anticipated to be difficult to administer by an executor of the donor's probate estate;
- generate federal and state income, estate, and inheritance tax savings; or
- enable a child or other donee to have sufficient liquidity to purchase investment assets that may create an immediate, valuable income tax deduction to the child (such as funding individual retirement accounts and retirement plan contributions).[4]

2. Arguments Against Completion of Gifts

Estate planners are often confronted, however, by their clients making arguments against implementing significant gift programs, such as:

- a loss of control over the property and, particularly, the inability to impact the actions of others (although a trust suspending properties out of the hands of the eventual beneficiaries/trust recipients may solve part of this dilemma);
- an aversion to contemplating one's own death;
- the fear of spoiling others with too much wealth; or
- a dislike for dissipating capital (even though the client's capital is more than adequate to meet reasonable support needs during the client's remaining lifetime).

Whether these arguments against gift programs are rational or otherwise, they often seem to have a significant psychological impact on many individuals. Accordingly, the estate planner should be prepared to respond both rationally and on an emotional level to these arguments.

The estate planner, in considering and recommending a significant gift program, must also take into account the loss of the use of money that may be required to satisfy any resulting gift tax liabilities. This consideration will be particularly pertinent where the gift tax marginal rate is significant and, because the life expectancy of the donor is substantial, any estate tax cost might not accrue until a date substantially in the future, if at all.[5] After the Economic Growth and Tax Relief Reconciliation Act of 2001 (EGTRRA), together with the 2010 TRA, provided estate planners with a decade of uncertainty, ATRA has given estate planners some certainty for the near future. Therefore, a careful financial analysis often suggests that a better long-term overall family net worth position might be realized by currently incurring some limited gift tax cost, with the younger generation transferees then investing the transferred funds into high-appreciation-potential assets with a long-term investment horizon.

In any event, and particularly in light of the certainty provided for by ATRA, these observations emphasize the continued desirability of (1) maximizing the use of annual donee exclusions, (2) making gifts for educational purposes, and (3) gift splitting with a spouse. Over an extended period of time a donor having a substantial life expectancy can achieve a quite significant tax-free transfer of wealth by using only these options.[6] That wealth, when in the hands of the donees (e.g., children and grandchildren, and trusts for those individuals) can then increase in value outside the transfer tax base of the older generation donors

B. Basic Federal Tax Considerations

Depending on the client's situation, and the applicable tax rates and exemption amounts, gift transfers may provide opportunities for significant tax savings.[7] Such savings may be the primary motivation for such transfers but, as noted above, many other factors are also often relevant. Those tax liabilities that may be reduced include federal estate taxes, federal income taxes, and state and local income, estate, and inheritance taxes. The savings of these taxes may, however, be at the immediate cost of a federal (and, sometimes, a state) gift tax.

1. Gift Tax Considerations

a. Tax Rates

For gifts made after 2012, the highest gift tax rate is 40%, which is only 0.4% higher than the 39.6% highest applicable income tax rate.[8] The maximum federal gift tax rate previously was: (1) 48% for gifts made in 2004; (2) 47% for gifts made in 2005; (3) 46% for gifts made in 2006; (4) 45% for gifts made in 2007–2009; and (5) 35% for gifts made in 2010–2012.

b. The Unified Transfer Tax Credit

The amount excluded by the unified credit available for offsetting gift liabilities for gifts made in 2002–2010 was $1 million.[9] Because the estate tax exclusion amount exceeded the gift tax exclusion amount in the period 2004 through 2010, the gift and estate tax credits were not unified in those years.[10] The use of the $1 million exclusion for lifetime gifts could reduce or exhaust the availability of the exclusion when making future gifts and for estate tax purposes at death.[11] When the estate tax credit exceeded the gift tax credit in 2004–2010 the entire credit available during life could be used, although additional credit was available at death. Pursuant to the 2010 TRA and ATRA, the exclusion amount is $5 million for gifts made after 2010 (the same as for estate tax purposes), a portability provision for spouses applies after 2010, and the basic exclusion amount is adjusted for inflation after 2011.[12]

During an estate tax examination, an issue may sometimes arise whether the IRS may revalue prior lifetime gifts by the decedent.[13] The effect of this action could cause the estate tax liability to be increased because the revaluation process moves the estate into a higher estate tax bracket. This previously could occur even though the statute of limitation may have expired for gift tax purposes.[14] The 1997 Act provides that gifts may not be revalued for estate tax purposes after the expiration of the statute of limitations on the gift if adequate disclosure to the IRS occurred at the time of the gift.[15]

c. Annual Donee Exclusion

Other than for gifts of future interests in property, the donor may exclude[16] a certain amount (adjusted for inflation) of gifts that he or she gives to each nonspousal donee,[17] and a certain amount (adjusted for inflation) of gifts to a non-U.S. citizen spouse[18] during each calendar year. This exclusion is available on a donee by donee basis, thereby enabling a significant number of annual donee exclusions, if desired.[19] The annual exclusion, originally $3,000 per donee per year, was intended by Congress to cover wedding and Christmas gifts and occasional gifts of smaller amounts. Because of the substantial increases in price levels, Congress increased the exclusion, effective in 1982, and provided for inflation adjustments, beginning in 1999. To the extent that a gift exceeds the annual exclusion, the unified credit/exemption equivalent must be used to eliminate gift tax liability.[20]

The annual donee exclusion is only available for the gift of a present interest in property.[21] Consequently, careful differentiation between a present interest and a future interest is essential to assure availability of the annual donee exclusion. A right to withdraw property from a trust, even though not exercised, will enable the donor to claim that a present interest exists and, therefore, the annual donee exclusion is available.[22] Such a trust is called a demand trust or a *"Crummey"* trust. As long as the power to exercise a withdrawal right exists, the interest qualifies, even though, as a practical matter, the legal right of a minor to currently exercise the right might require the appointment of a guardian. Notice to an adult beneficiary of the right of withdrawal and a reasonable opportunity to exercise the right is required.[23]

Indirect restrictions may, however, cause what appears to be a present interest to be transformed into a future interest for purposes of this rule.[24] For example, a transfer of restricted corporate shares will be a transfer of a future interest.[25] The transfer of an income interest in a trust, where the trustee has the authority to charge capital losses against income, produces sufficient uncertainty with respect to the payment of income so as to transform an apparent current income interest into a future interest.[26] Past and projected earnings attributable to the interest transferred may determine whether the exclusion is available.[27]

Gifts exempted from gift tax under the annual donee exclusion are not includible in the tax base for purposes of determining federal estate tax. Only "adjusted taxable gifts" are so includible and "adjusted taxable gifts" are limited to taxable gifts (i.e., excluding any annual donee exclusion gifts).[28]

d. Exclusion for Tuition and Medical Payments

Any amounts paid on behalf of any individual (1) as tuition to certain educational organizations for the education or training of such individual or (2) as payment for medical care to any person who provides such medical care for that individual will not be considered transfers subject to gift taxes.[29] This gift tax exclusion for tuition and medical expenses is in addition to the §2503(b) gift tax annual exclusion and is permitted regardless of the relationship between the donor and the donee. Payment under these tuition and medical care exemptions must be made directly to the educational institution or the medical care provider on behalf of the donee and for the qualified purpose.[30] Thus, an intervening trust to pay medical or educational expenses for another person will not satisfy this statutory requirement.

The exclusion is permitted for the educational expenses of both full- and part-time students, but is limited to direct tuition costs.[31] The unlimited exclusion does not apply to amounts paid for books, supplies, and dormitory fees. The unlimited exclusion for medical expenses is not permitted for amounts that are reimbursed by insurance. The exclusion is limited to those medical expenses as defined in §213.[32]

e. Marital Deduction

An unlimited marital deduction is available to a donor for gift transfers to a U.S. citizen spouse.[33] Certain transfers of qualified terminable interest property (QTIP) qualify for the gift tax marital deduction.[34] In general, qualified terminable interest property is property that passes from the donor in which the spouse receives a qualifying income interest for life and for which an irrevocable election is made to treat the property as qualified terminable interest property.[35]

A gift tax marital deduction is available to a donor, regardless of the donor's citizenship or residency, for qualifying gifts to a U.S. citizen spouse.[36] A gift tax marital deduction is not allowed to a donor, however, for gifts to non-U.S. citizen spouses. Instead, the gift tax annual limited exclusion for gifts to a nonresident alien spouse is stated in the Code[37] and adjusted for inflation. To qualify for the indexed exclusion, the transfer must be such that it would have qualified for the marital deduction had the donee spouse been a U.S. citizen.

f. Split Gifts

The donor and his or her spouse may agree to treat one-half of a gift made by one spouse to a third party as made, for gift tax purposes, by the nondonor spouse.[38] The purpose of this gift splitting is to take advantage of two annual donee exclusions, two unified credit amounts, and two progressive transfer tax rate structures.[39]

The gift-splitting privilege does not permit the spouses to allocate proportionate shares of the gift among themselves. Rather, if the gift-splitting option is elected, all gifts made within the particular tax year to third parties must be split on a 50–50 basis. Disproportionate gifts may still be accomplished indirectly, however, by means of interspousal transfers to complete these gifts. These interspousal transfers would be protected from gift tax exposure by the marital deduction.

If subsequent estate tax inclusion is mandated under §2035 (the "transfers within three years of death" inclusionary rule), the total of the donor's split gifts will be within the scope of "adjusted taxable gifts." Accordingly, this total will constitute part of the donor's tax base for estate tax purposes. The gift tax paid by the consenting spouse is to be a subtraction, or offset, in computing the donor's estate tax.[40] When the full amount of the gift is included in the donor spouse's estate, the consenting spouse is placed in a position as if the earlier gift splitting had not occurred. Therefore, these transfers are removed from "adjusted taxable gifts" for purposes of the consenting spouse's subsequent estate tax computation. Further, the gift tax paid by the consenting spouse is not taken into account as a credit against the estate tax of the consenting spouse if it is allowed as a credit to the estate of the donor spouse.[41]

g. Valuation of Gifts

Gifts will often be made of easy-to-value assets, for example, cash and liquid securities. However, concern will arise about a possible valuation challenge by the IRS when the gifted property is illiquid, for example, where it consists of land, oil, or timber interests or closely held stock or family limited partnership interests. The question then arises concerning whether the valuation controversy risks can be limited in this context. Increasingly, "defined value clauses" in making gifts of hard-to-value interests are being accepted by courts.[42] Because of a concern about the validity of such clauses in these cases they have often been structured to provide that, if the property transferred by gift was determined to be in excess of the stated amount, the excess would go to charity (thereby effectively negating the IRS's efforts to collect additional gift tax). However, this approach will probably evolve into a planning situation permitting merely a defined value clause that would permit a gift described as follows: "As donor, I give to my child (or children) the number of shares (or limited partnership interest) in XYZ Company that is equal in value to [specified amount]."[43]

2. Estate Tax Considerations

a. Gifts Made Within Three Years of Death

(1) Inclusion Under Limited Circumstances

Gifts made within a three-year period ending on the date of the decedent's death are not included in the decedent's gross estate.[44] Certain exceptions to this rule are made for transfers of an interest that is included in the gross estate under §2036, §2037, §2038, or §2042,[45] or that would have been included under any of these sections if the interest described in those provisions had been retained by the decedent until death.[46] Because of the cumulative nature of the estate tax computation the impact of this inclusion is to cause the postgift/predeath appreciation to be included in the estate tax base. Property included pursuant to any of those sections will be included whether or not a gift tax return was required for the transfer.

In addition, the three-year inclusion rule is retained for the purposes of determining (1) the estate's eligibility for (a) §303(b) distributions in redemption of stock to pay death taxes, (b) §2032A special use valuation, and (c) §6166 installment payment of estate taxes, and (2) which property is subject to estate tax liens (under subchapter C of Chapter 64).[47] For these purposes, the usual exceptions to §2035 apply so that the gift would not be included where no gift tax return was required (i.e., for marital gifts and small transfers).[48]

(2) Inclusion of Gift Tax Amount

The amount of gift tax paid by the decedent (or the decedent's estate) on any gift made by the decedent (or the decedent's spouse) within three years of death is included in a decedent's gross estate, regardless of whether the gift for which the gift tax was paid is also includible in the gross estate under §2035.[49] This "gross-up" rule eliminates an incentive that would otherwise exist to make deathbed transfers to remove from the transfer tax base an amount equal to the gift tax liability that arises from making these gifts. This inclusionary rule does not extend to a gift tax paid by a spouse on a gift made by the decedent within three years of death that is treated as made one-half by the spouse, because the spouse's payment of this tax would not reduce the decedent's estate at the time of his or her death.[50]

Any deathbed estate tax planning must be done quite carefully. A gift made immediately prior to death may be quite costly because of the loss of the stepped-up income tax basis at death when the gifted asset is not included in the donor's gross estate.[51] This type of planning also generates the danger of lawsuits involving claims of undue influence, incapacity, and similar assertions, even though such gifts might be completed by another person acting for the donor as attorney-in-fact under a valid durable power of attorney.

b. Gifts Made More Than Three Years Before Death

Gifts made more than three years before death are not includible in a decedent's gross estate. To the extent such gifts are "adjusted taxable gifts," they will be includible in determining the estate tax amount under the unified rate schedule.[52] The gift tax paid on these gifts will not, however, be included in the gross estate so as to "gross-up" these gifts.[53]

3. Income Tax Considerations

a. Income Deflection

Substantial income tax may be saved within the family unit by shifting income-producing property from a taxpayer with a high marginal income tax rate to a taxpayer with a lower marginal income tax rate:

Example: In 2015, Father transfers by gift to his daughter, age 24, $100,000 of rental property producing $5,000 in income per annum (capital appreciation is also anticipated). If received and taxed to the father at his 39.6% marginal income tax rate, the $5,000 of rental income would generate approximately a $1,980 income tax liability. If this income is shifted to the daughter, the tax (assuming a 10% marginal income tax rate) on $5,000 taxable income would be $500. Thus, by shifting this asset to the daughter, an additional $1,480 will be retained within the family unit each year after applicable income tax liabilities are satisfied.[54] Additionally, the subsequent accruing appreciation of the transferred asset has been shifted from the father's estate to the child.

Acceleration of the timing of a gift to the earliest part of a calendar year will further facilitate income tax savings for the family unit, particularly if interest rates are relatively high. For example, $20,000 received (under husband/wife annual donee exclusions) on January 1 and immediately invested into tax-free obligations producing a 5% return will produce an additional $1,000 in year 1 for the donee. The effect of compounding this return over a period of years could be substantial.

Income tax provisions that limit these potential income tax savings include:

- The unearned income of minor children under the age of 18 (and certain children under age 24) at the end of the year is taxed (under the "kiddie tax") as if received by the parent.[55]
- The personal exemption is disallowed to an individual to whom a deduction for a personal exemption is allowable to another taxpayer (e.g., such individual's parent).[56]

b. Income Tax Basis for Gift Property

(1) Transferred Basis

When property is transferred by gift, the donee's income tax basis in the property received is a transferred basis. The donee's basis is the donor's basis, possibly increased by a portion of the gift taxes paid.[57] This gift tax portion is the amount of the gift tax attributable to the net appreciation component of the gifted property.[58] This tax basis increase is allocated among gift properties and beneficiaries on the basis of the gift tax paid for each calendar year.[59]

(2) Depreciated Property Exception

The gift transfer of property that has declined in value before the transfer will cause applicability of a loss utilization limitation rule. Upon a subsequent taxable disposition of the gift property, the donee must use as income tax basis, but only for purposes of determining loss, the lower of (1) the donor's basis or (2) the fair market value of the property at the time of the gift.[60]

Example: Property that is transferred to donee by gift has a $100,000 basis to donor and a $90,000 fair market value at the time of transfer. If the property is later sold by the donee for: (a) $95,000—no gain or loss is recognized (basis for gain determination purposes is $100,000 and basis for loss purposes is $90,000); (b) $85,000—a $5,000 loss can be recognized (basis for loss purposes is $90,000); (c) $105,000—$5,000 gain is recognized (basis for gain purposes is $100,000, the cost basis to the donor). Because this property is depreciated in value at the time of the gift, no tax basis adjustment will be pertinent for any gift taxes attributable to the appreciation element of the transferred property.

(3) Special Rules for Spousal Transfers

A special rule applies for transfers of property between spouses. No gain or loss is recognized on a transfer of property from an individual to a spouse (or to a trust for the spouse).[61] As a result, the property is treated as acquired by the transferee by gift and transferred basis rules apply; that is, the basis of the transferee in the property is the adjusted basis of the transferor.[62]

c. Holding Period

The donee's holding period for gift property commences as of the date that property was originally acquired by the donor.[63] This "tacking" of the donor's holding period is relevant for purposes of determining whether, upon the donee's disposition of gift property that is a capital asset, capital gain (or loss) should be categorized as short-term or long-term for federal income tax purposes.[64]

4. Tax Savings Achieved Through Lifetime Gift Program

a. Gift and Estate Tax Considerations

In summary, various gift and estate tax planning incentives to make lifetime gifts are available and should be utilized:

- An annual gift tax exclusion is available for transfers to each donee.[65] The property that is transferred tax free under this exclusion will not be included in the estate tax base.
- The gift tax paid during life is not included in the donor's estate for estate tax purposes, except for gift taxes paid on gifts made within three years of death.
- The growth in value of the gift property from the time of the gift to the date of the donor's death escapes (1) gift tax imposed on the donor and (2) estate tax imposed on the donor's estate (unless the donor retained certain prohibited controls).

b. Income Tax Planning Strategies for Completing Gifts

The summary of applicable income tax rules above indicates that income tax considerations are extremely relevant in determining (1) which of the donor's properties should be transferred by gift and (2) the order of completing those gifts. Basic "rules of thumb" in this area include:

- Make gift transfers of cash or high-basis property, rather than low-basis property (which will be eligible for the stepped-up tax basis at the owner's death), except where high-value–low-basis property will be sold shortly after the gift transfer. In this latter event, the appreciated property might be transferred to a donee who will incur a smaller income tax on the capital gain realized on the property disposition.[66]
- Transfer cash (i.e., U.S. dollars) before other property because, for purposes of determining the amount of gain realized on other property, the income tax basis of the other property will be increased by a portion of the gift tax paid, but not in excess of its fair market value. The tax basis for cash (held as U.S. dollars) cannot be increased above its face value and, therefore, no basis adjustment is

available for cash even if a gift tax liability is incurred upon the transfer of cash to a donee.

- Transfer property producing a high rate of current investment return, particularly if the donee's marginal income tax rate is significantly less than the donor's.
- Transfer property with a high potential for appreciation, so as to permit the post-transfer capital gain to accrue in the donee's hands and, therefore, outside the donor's gross estate.
- Where tax basis exceeds fair market value, sell the property, realize the tax loss, and transfer the sales proceeds to the donee (unless a significant appreciation reasonably may be anticipated after the time of the gift). This assumes that the donor may use the loss in computing his or her income tax liability and, also, that the property need not be retained in the family for sentimental reasons.
- Hold wasting assets (i.e., properties subject to depreciation, amortization, and depletion), assuming the value of these assets (eventually includible in the donor's gross estate) is actually declining in economic value.[67]
- Avoid making any "assignment of income" because the donor could be subject to both income and gift taxes and, further, may have transferred those funds that would otherwise be used to pay the income and gift taxes.[68]
- Avoid unearned income being realized by certain children under the age of 24 (and, thereby, subjected to the "Kiddie Tax"). Rather, in this situation consider investing in delayed income assets, such as Series EE U.S. savings bonds, for the benefit of such children (and other minors). Such bonds could be purchased with maturities occurring when the child is no longer subject to the §1(g) tax, because when the child is no longer subject to the §1(g) tax the income is taxable to the child and subject to the child's income tax rate, rather than the parent's tax rate (i.e., the "Kiddie Tax" is no longer applicable). An alternative investment could be low-income, high-growth-potential stocks where the gain may not be recognized for a considerable period.[69] Even if recognized while the child is subject to the §1(g) tax, the parent's applicable capital gains tax rate would ordinarily be only 20%.

C. Methods of Completing Gifts

1. Concept of Gift Transfers

Any transfer by one person to another is a gift to the extent that the transferor does not receive in return an equal value in money or other property.[70] Donative intent on the part of the transferor is not an essential element for the applicability of the gift tax. The application of the gift tax is based on the objective facts of the transfer and the circumstances under which it is made, rather than on the subjective motives of the donor.[71] Consequently, gifts, although normally made intentionally, may sometimes be unintended. Local law will ordinarily control the determination of the time when a gift is completed.[72]

2. Gift Transfer Variations

Gifts may be made under a variety of circumstances, including[73]:

- direct transfers of (a) cash or promissory notes,[74] (b) securities (e.g., stocks and bonds), (c) real property,[75] and (d) tangible personal property (e.g., paintings, jewelry, and stamp and wine collections);
- the completion of such direct transfers might occur under the Uniform Transfers to Minors Act (as enacted under local law)[76];
- transfers of property to an irrevocable trust[77];
- forgiveness of indebtedness[78];
- assignment of the ownership of a life insurance contract;
- conveying property into (a) a tenancy in common with the donor, (b) a joint tenancy with the right of survivorship with the donor, or (c) a family partnership where the donor is a partner[79];
- the incorporation of a family partnership and the shifting of the pro-rata ownership at the time of the issuance of the stock certificates[80];
- a transfer, for no consideration, to a corporation owned by others[81];
- payment of the liabilities of another[82];
- payment of premiums on life insurance contracts owned by others;
- the use of money (and, possibly, other property) without adequate compensation[83];
- disclaimers and renunciations that are not effective to avoid gift treatment and inadequate waivers of trustee's and executor's commissions[84]; and
- sales, exchanges, and other dispositions where the value of the property transferred exceeds the value of the property received.[85]

This listing is representative of common gift transfers, but certainly is not exhaustive.[86] Note, however, that gifts of uncompensated services, the use of vacation property, and the deflection of investment opportunities do not appear to be gifts for federal gift tax purposes.[87]

3. Gift by Agent on Behalf of Donor

A gift may be completed by another person or entity acting on behalf of the donor. For example, the sole owner of the shares of a corporation may cause the corporation to make a payment or distribution to others (e.g., family members) for inadequate consideration. Such a distribution would ordinarily be reconstructed to be (1) a dividend to the shareholder with (2) a direct gift then being made by the shareholder to the other family member.

Pursuant to a durable power of attorney a gift transfer may be completed by an agent acting on behalf of the principal. The durable power of attorney must be drafted to assure that the power was granted to permit the attorney-in-fact to make gifts (perhaps limited to only the amount of the annual donee exclusion).[88] Significant controversies have arisen whether such authority existed because, if not, the executor will have an obligation to retrieve that property and it will then be includible in the donor's gross estate.[89]

D. Specific Types of Gifts

Several types of common gift transfer techniques are identified in this segment, including (1) gifts to minors, (2) net gifts, (3) irrevocable lifetime trusts, (4) trusts designed to be tax defective, and (5) gift transfers of a personal residence. The primary motivation of each of these transfers is donative; that is, they will be gift transfers for gift tax purposes. In each situation, the income tax and estate tax elements are also examined. Note that, for income tax purposes, the questions may concern such matters as (1) who is the appropriate taxpayer and (2) do any elements of the transaction cause income or gain recognition? In Chapter 7 (Intrafamily Transfer Alternatives to Gifts), additional techniques are examined for transferring wealth to younger-generation members, but those transactions are often structured to avoid a significant gift transfer element. Consequently, many of the transactions described there have a "transfer for consideration" component seeking to avoid gift tax exposure but often causing income recognition for income tax purposes.

1. Gifts to Minors

Many donative transfers made to minimize estate and income taxes consist of gifts from parents to children or from grandparents to grandchildren.[90] If the child is a minor (as determined under locally applicable law), legal and practical problems may arise concerning transfers to those children because they do not have the legal capacity to manage their own financial affairs.[91] Alternatives available to avoid these legal incapacity problems include:

- formal appointment of a guardian of the child's property whereby the management of the minor's property falls under the jurisdiction of the local probate court;
- using the provisions of the Uniform Transfers to Minors Act (as enacted under local law); or
- using a trust (as permitted under §2503(c)) or some other trust structure.

The guardianship alternative is usually not used, if possible, to avoid probate court costs, to escape the formal appointment and accounting requirements, and to assure privacy. If used, the income received by the guardian will be the income of the child for federal income tax reporting purposes, rather than income of a separate taxable entity.[92]

a. Uniform Transfers to Minors Act

(1) Function of the Uniform Transfers to Minors Act (UTMA)

Most states have enacted the Uniform Gifts to Minors Act (UGMA), which was subsequently replaced in most jurisdictions by the Uniform Transfers to Minors Act (UTMA). Under either of these acts[93]:

- A custodian is entrusted with the management of the property (including collecting and investing the income from the property and reinvesting the proceeds); however, the minor has indefeasibly vested equitable title to the property.
- Legal ownership of the property vests in the child at age 21 (or at a younger age where legal capacity is reached earlier, as determined under state law).[94]
- The transfer of securities and other properties into this custodianship status is facilitated.[95]
- Before the minor reaches the age of majority the property may be used for the support, maintenance, education, and benefit of the minor.
- Various mechanical rules are provided covering accounting procedures, the "prudent man rule" for investing assets held in this account, the appointment of a successor custodian, and the right of the minor at age 14 to demand payments for his or her support, maintenance, and education.

(2) Gift Tax Aspects

Under the locally enacted Uniform Transfers to Minors Act a transfer of securities or other eligible property will be made into the name of an individual as custodian for the identified minor child. Dependent upon the type of property, the ownership of such property will be registered in the name of the custodian, often as "Custodian for _______________ [the minor] under the [state] Uniform Transfers to Minors Act." For gift tax purposes, this will constitute a transfer to the child, rather than a transfer to the custodian. The transfer of securities (or other properties) into a UTMA account will constitute a gift of a present interest, eligible for the gift tax annual donee exclusion.[96]

(3) Income Tax Aspects

The income derived from the custodial property during the period of custodianship is gross income to the minor for federal income tax purposes.[97] The income that is actually used for the maintenance and support of a minor is taxable, however, to the parent obligated to provide that support, whether or not that person is the donor or custodian, to the extent of the legal obligation to support (as determined under local law).[98] The UTMA property income should, therefore, either be accumulated for the child during the period of his or her minority or expended for items beyond the scope of the parent's legal support obligation.[99] If the income is distributed during minority for other than support purposes, assuming that this is permitted under the uniform act as locally enacted, the legal guardianship difficulties discussed above may be encountered.

(4) Estate Tax Aspects

Where the donor to the UTMA account is also the custodian for the minor child, the property held in that custodianship will be included in the donor's estate (required under §2038) upon his or her death during the period of custodianship.[100] This gross estate inclusion will occur even if the donor is serving as a successor custodian.[101]

Therefore, in planning transfers of this nature, a donor should make the transfer to his or her spouse as custodian,[102] or to another closely related and interested party, rather than to himself or herself as custodian.[103] Where the property transferred is community property each spouse will be an actual donor of one-half of the property for this purpose, necessitating designation of a third party custodian to assure complete avoidance of the gross estate inclusion risk at the parent/donor level.

A parent who is not a donor may serve as custodian without a §2038 retained interest risk because the parent would not be the transferor for estate tax purposes.[104] A risk of inclusion under the power of appointment provision (§2041) may exist, however, because of a power in the custodian to discharge his or her support obligations by distributions from the custodial fund. Caution dictates, therefore, that a nondonor parent should serve as custodian of large amounts transferred into an UTMA account for a child.[105]

b. Section 2503(c) Trusts

(1) Structure of §2503(c)

Section 2503(b) provides an annual donee exclusion for gifts "other than gifts of future interests in property."[106] If, for example, a transfer is in trust, with the trustee having discretion as to the distribution of trust income, the donee-beneficiary will have received a future interest (rather than a present interest) for purposes of this gift tax exclusion provision. Therefore, the annual donee exclusion will not be available for gift tax purposes in this context. Section 2503(c) provides an exception to this rule, however, making available the annual donee exclusion if the property and income from the transferred property (1) may be expended by, or for the benefit of, the donee before his or her attaining the age of 21 years, and (2) will, to the extent not so expended:

- pass to the donee at the time he or she reaches age 21, and
- be payable to the donee's estate (or as he or she may appoint under a general power of appointment) in the event the donee dies before reaching age 21.[107]

Section 2503(c) is usually used in connection with the creation of a trust, although it is not restricted to such arrangements.[108] If the transfer is to qualify under §2503(c) for the annual donee exclusion, no substantial restrictions under the terms of the trust instrument may be imposed on the current exercise of the trustee's discretion. The trustee must have the discretion to determine (i) the amounts, if any, of the income or property expended for the benefit of the minor, and (ii) the purpose for which the expenditures are made.[109] A mandatory accumulation of income to age 21 would not satisfy this requirement.[110] If a standard for determining distributions is used, the language must be broad.[111] The trust may not provide "sprinkling or spray" powers of distribution among beneficiaries, however, because in this situation the individual beneficiaries are not guaranteed any specific amount.[112]

(2) Definition of "Property"

Section 2503(c) permits an annual donee exclusion "if the property and the income" from the gift are to be expended as prescribed above. Substantial controversy has occurred over the availability of the annual donee exclusion where a trust instrument provides that:

- income can be distributed or accumulated during the beneficiary's minority, at the trustee's discretion;
- all accumulated income is to be paid to the beneficiary at age 21; and
- distribution of the principal to the income beneficiary is to occur at some later age (e.g., 30).

The IRS maintained that such transfers were entirely future interests, but taxpayers argued that, although the rights to income and principal after minority were future interests, the right to receive income distributions during minority was a present interest for purposes of §2503(c). The IRS was not successful in litigating this issue[113] and, thereafter, agreed with the courts (and taxpayers) in ruling that a right to income during minority is to be treated as a present interest, although the rights to income and principal after minority are future interests.[114] Accordingly, the pre-21 income component under a trust transfer will be deemed to be a separate property interest that is a "present interest" where, for example, a trust is created to provide for (1) discretionary distributions of income until age 21, (2) payment of any accumulated income upon reaching that age, (3) mandatory distribution of current income until age 30, and (4) distribution of the principal at age 30.[115] In these circumstances the present income interest (excluding the remainder interest) must be equal to the annual donee exclusion to take full advantage of the annual donee exclusion, and often this will not be the situation (particularly during periods of low interest rates).[116]

(3) Extension of the Trust at Age 21

A present interest for the corpus will be deemed to exist for gift tax purposes only if the property will "pass to the donee on his attaining the age of 21 years."[117] This requirement will be satisfied if the gift property is held under a trust that the minor may extend beyond the time he or she reaches age 21, although the minor may terminate the trust at that time.[118] Alternatively, the trust may be structured to terminate at age 21 but only upon the condition that the minor affirmatively elects to compel distribution.[119] The possibility of a failure to so elect, which would result in continuation of the trust for a specified additional period, will not cause the trust corpus to be treated as a future interest.[120]

(4) Practical Use of the §2503(c) Trust

One of the elements in determining whether to use a §2503(c) trust is that, to gain the full benefit of the annual exclusion, the principal must be made payable at age 21. The instrument may contain provisions for continuation of the trust beyond age 21, but the annual donee gift tax exclusion is available for the full amount transferred into this trust only if the donee has the right to terminate the trust upon reaching age 21. The donor may not wish to allow distribution at age 21 and may want to include further restrictions on distributions in the trust instrument. These restrictions, however, may limit availability of the annual exclusion. If substantial sums are to be transferred in trust, the donor may not be amenable to allowing outright distribution at age 21. Ultimately, in the planning context the possible qualification for the annual donee exclusion should not be allowed to control the terms of a substantial transfer into trust. For example, if $1 million is transferred into trust, the availability (or nonavailability) of an annual donee exclusion should be permitted to have only minimal influence on the determination of the trust structure, for example, whether to use a §2503(c) trust.[121]

If a donor names himself or herself as trustee under a §2503(c) trust, adverse estate tax consequences may occur. The trustee in this situation ordinarily possesses a discretionary power to distribute income and corpus. Therefore, the donor trustee will have retained the power to control the beneficial enjoyment of the property under §2036 and §2038.[122] Where the primary concern of the arrangement is to shift income, the donor might act as trustee, having decided to assume the risk of any estate tax inclusion.

2. Net Gifts

a. Reasons for Net Gifts

A donor may give property to a donee on the express condition that the donee assumes and will pay the federal gift tax liability generated by this gift transfer. The donee agreeing to assume that liability may be an individual gift recipient or an irrevocable trust. A net gift transfer may be constructed because the donor is in a high marginal income tax bracket and the donor does not want to "sell" the property to be transferred by gift. This attitude may prevail even when a 20% capital gains tax rate would be applicable under §1(h). This maximum rate applies after 2012.[123] The property may have substantial potential for future appreciation and the parties may desire that the future appreciation accrue while the property is in the hands of the younger generation. The younger generation may have the funds to pay the gift tax or, if not, could borrow funds to pay the tax, including through using the transferred property as collateral. In some instances, donors will desire to transfer property by gift for estate tax planning purposes, but may feel reluctant to use funds from other sources to pay applicable federal gift tax liabilities. In some situations, the donor merely wants to maintain liquid assets and is prepared to transfer an illiquid asset. The net gift arrangement would circumvent this reluctance by the donor because the donee assumes the associated gift tax liability that arises upon the transfer.

b. Value of the Gift

The value of this "net gift" for gift tax purposes will be measured by (1) the fair market value of the property interest passing from the donor, less (2) the amount of the gift tax liability to be paid by the donee.[124] If the value of the gift is less than the exclusion amount under the gift tax unified credit, no gift tax liability will arise and, accordingly, in these circumstances no "net gift" (as described for gift tax purposes) actually will have been made. Because the amount of the gift and the amount of the gift tax (where arising) are mutually dependent variables, an algebraic formula (or a trial and error computation) is necessary to determine the precise amount of the gift tax.[125] Note that the gift tax actually paid by the donee of a net gift within three years of a decedent's death will be includible in the decedent's gross estate because the tax paid is a statutory liability of the donor/decedent (and remains a statutory liability of the donor notwithstanding a net gift agreement).[126]

c. Income Tax Consequences

(1) Possible Gain Realization

In Rev. Rul. 75-72, concerning the gift tax elements of a net gift situation, the IRS noted that "the donor receives consideration for the transfer in the amount of the gift tax to be paid by the donee," and further observed that "[t]his Revenue Ruling is concerned only with the gift tax consequences of the above transaction and not with the income tax consequences thereof." The IRS's position concerning income tax is that, in a net gift situation, the taxpayer receives an economic benefit that constitutes a taxable accretion to wealth and, therefore, may have the realization of gross income. The IRS has successfully litigated this issue.[127]

Example: If the value of the gift property is $100,000, the tax basis of the property in the donor's hands is $20,000, and the gift tax attributable to the transfer is $30,000, a $10,000 gain is realized by the donor for federal income tax purposes. If, however, the tax basis is $40,000, the gift tax paid (assuming $30,000) would be entirely treated as basis recovery, with no gain being realized. If, therefore, the gift tax liability exceeds the donor's tax basis for the transferred property, for income tax purposes the excess amount constitutes taxable gain to the donor at the time the gift tax liability is paid.[128]

This tax liability assumption is similar to the situation where a donee takes gift property subject to a mortgage. To the extent of the mortgage the transaction will be treated as a "part sale." The transferor will realize gain to the extent that the liability assumed by the transferee exceeds the transferor's tax basis for the transferred property.

(2) Tax Basis to Donee

If no part sale occurred in a net gift transaction, the donee would take as his or her basis for the gift property the donor's basis. This basis might be increased by any gift tax paid attributable to the appreciation element of the property transferred.[129] If a part sale is deemed to have occurred as a result of a net gift situation (because the gift tax exceeds the basis), the tax basis to the donee would be:

- whichever of the following is greater: (a) the transferor's (donor's) basis; or (b) the amount paid by the transferee (donee); and
- the basis adjustment for any gift tax paid on the appreciation element of the property transferred.[130]

The holding periods would be "tacked."[131] This would occur even if the transaction is a part sale.

d. Net Gift Transfer to a Trust

If the net gift transfer is to an inter vivos trust (as the nominal donee), under the grantor trust income tax rules the donor/trust grantor may also be taxed on the income earned by the trust between:

- the date of the net gift creating the tax obligation assumed by the donee trust; and
- the date the donor's gift tax obligation is satisfied.[132]

This potential grantor trust income tax problem may be avoided by having the donee trust borrow money immediately (if necessary, collateralizing the trust property) and use the borrowed funds to pay the donor's gift tax obligation before the trust begins to realize income. The trust income could thereafter be used to liquidate the trust's debt obligation.[133] Alternatively, sufficient trust property could be sold to liquidate the loan. The sale should be structured to occur after the gift tax is paid so that the capital gains are not attributed to the trust grantor.[134]

e. Planning Considerations

"Rules of thumb" to be observed in completing net gifts include:

- To assure that the gift tax value is reduced by the gift tax attributable to the transfer, the donor and donee should agree (preferably in writing) that the donee is assuming the gift tax obligation generated on the gift transfer of the identified property.
- Because the gift tax rates are progressive, if net gifts are completed in years after transfers of other gifts (e.g., cash gifts) have been completed, the gift tax value of the net gifts will be further decreased because the allocable gift tax liability will be greater.
- A donee trust assuming the gift tax liability should satisfy the gift tax liability before income is realized from the transferred property, so as to avoid the applicability of the grantor trust rules to the donor (and the attribution of trust income to that grantor).
- If possible, a donor should be careful to transfer property with a tax basis equal to or slightly more than the applicable gift tax, so that, on the assumption by the donee of the gift tax liability, gain is not treated as realized by the donor for income tax purposes on the gift transfer.
- The donor should consider whether also to specify that any federal and state estate tax liability imposed under §2035(b) must be assumed by the donee if the donor dies within three years of making the gift, that is, the transfer is a "net, net gift."[135] Usually, the actuarial probability of this event occurring is quite small.

3. Irrevocable Lifetime Trusts

a. Function of the Irrevocable Inter Vivos Trust

A funded inter vivos irrevocable trust may be used to shift property value and income to younger-generation beneficiaries. Income may be shifted through the use of an irrevocable trust, for example, to:

- build an educational fund for a child;
- provide current income for an adult child; or
- provide current income for an aged parent (with the principal thereafter distributable to a younger generation member).

The potential income tax savings that are available are evidenced by the following example:

Example: Father, in a 39.6% tax bracket, must earn approximately $1,655 before income tax in order to transfer approximately $1,000 (after approximately $655 in tax) to a child by gift. By deflecting the income stream into a trust, the total income tax liability on this amount could be considerably less than the $655 otherwise payable by the Father. The child could use his personal exemption and a lower tax bracket to enable these substantial tax savings to accrue within the extended family unit, assuming the "Kiddie Tax" is not applicable.[136] As the gross income amounts increase, the benefits may be significant, but will gradually decline proportionately. Current distributions from this trust will ordinarily be appropriate because, for the trust, a 39.6% federal income tax rate will be applicable when taxable income is over $7,500 (with that amount being indexed for inflation).

The value of the transfer will be included in the transfer tax base and be subject to gift tax if (1) annual donee exclusions are not available and (2) the unified credit has been exhausted. If the trust transfer is structured properly, the property transferred into the trust, plus the post-transfer appreciation on that transferred property, should not be included in the transferor's gross estate at death. For an irrevocable trust to achieve this estate tax exclusion objective a person must transfer property by gift to a trust that he or she created to benefit individuals other than himself or herself.[137] He or she must not retain an income interest or a reversionary interest in the income or principal.[138]

Such an inter vivos irrevocable trust might also be a "generation-skipping" trust if the transfers are for the benefit (whether immediately or in the future) of grandchildren. The generation-skipping transfer tax may be applicable, unless protected through the exemption for the grantor and, possibly, an additional exemption for a consenting spouse.[139]

The trust mechanism may enable protection for the trust beneficiaries from their own proclivities to waste these assets. Because an intermediary trustee holds the funds, the trust beneficiary does not have immediate access to the entire funds. The continued receipt of the income from those funds is normally assured through the use of a trust, including the unavailability of those funds to creditors of the beneficiaries (until an actual distribution of those funds is made by the trust to the beneficiary). A spendthrift clause included in the trust agreement, as authorized by applicable state law, prohibiting the beneficiary from anticipating that income will provide assurance concerning the continued protection of those funds in trust. In this situation the beneficiary could not accelerate his access to those benefits through a sale of the beneficiary's trust interest.

b. Possible Income Taxation to Grantor

(1) Basic Structure of Grantor Trust Rules

To effectively shift (for federal income tax purposes) the income from the trust property to either (1) the trust or (2) the trust beneficiaries, the grantor must not have retained any of the "grantor trust" powers (which cause the grantor to be treated as the "owner" of the trust property), such as:

- the power to control the beneficial enjoyment of the trust corpus and income[140];
- certain administrative powers[141]; or
- a power to revoke the transfer.[142]

Additionally, the income must not (1) be able to be held or accumulated for future distribution to the grantor or the grantor's spouse[143] or (2) actually be applied in payment of the grantor's legal obligation of support.[144] These rules are not consistent with (and, in some instances are contrary to) the estate tax transfer provisions requiring inclusion of property in the gross estate.[145]

Section 671–§678 (subpart E) provide specific rules to be observed in formulating trusts to avoid these grantor trust rules which cause attribution of the trust income to the grantor as the owner.[146] Section 671 provides that the grantor is treated as an "owner" of the trust if the trust (or a portion of the trust) does not satisfy the subpart E rules for avoiding this treatment.[147] If the trust grantor is treated as the "owner," the "trust" relationship is, in essence, considered as merely an agency for federal income tax purposes.[148]

(2) Reversionary Interest

The grantor is treated as the owner of any portion of a trust in which he or she has a reversionary interest in either the corpus or the income therefrom, if, as of the inception of that portion of the trust, the value of this reversionary interest exceeds 5% of the value of that portion.[149] The date of measurement of the value of the reversionary interest will be the date the property transfer formalities were actually accomplished.[150] This measurement of value will also be based on an assumption of the maximum exercise of discretion in favor of the grantor.[151] The grantor is not treated as the owner of that portion of a trust solely by reason of a reversionary interest in such portion that would take effect upon the death of a beneficiary before that beneficiary attains age 21 when the beneficiary (1) is a lineal descendant of the grantor and (2) holds all of the present interests in any portion of a trust.[152]

(3) Power to Control Beneficial Enjoyment

The extent of the permissible power of control in the hands of a trustee (or held in some other capacity) will depend upon status, that is, (1) grantor or spouse, (2) related party, or (3) independent trustee. The degree of power to control the beneficial enjoyment that can be retained by the grantor (or accorded to certain related parties) without the grantor being treated as the owner for federal income tax purposes is limited.[153] For example, the grantor will be treated as "owner" of the trust assets if he or she retains the power to sprinkle corpus, unless that power is limited by a reasonably definite standard set forth in the trust instrument.[154] The grantor (as trustee or otherwise) may enjoy the power to distribute income currently or to accumulate such income, however, provided that the income is ultimately payable to the designated beneficiary for a particular portion.[155]

In contrast, a trustee who is other than the grantor or the grantor's spouse, but is not independent, may be vested with the power to distribute, apportion, or accumulate income for specified beneficiaries in accordance with a standard that is reasonably definite.[156] Further, an independent trustee may exercise the right to sprinkle income or corpus (not limited by a standard) without the trust grantor being treated as the owner of the trust corpus and income for federal income tax purposes.[157]

(4) Administrative Powers

The grantor is treated as the owner of a trust if he or she possesses, or has exercised, certain specified administrative powers.[158] These include (1) the power to deal with the trust for less than adequate and full consideration,[159] (2) the power to borrow without adequate interest or security,[160] (3) the actual borrowing of trust funds,[161] and (4) certain general powers of administration exercisable in a non-fiduciary capacity.[162]

(5) Assignment-of-Income Principles

The subpart E regulations indicate that "assignment-of-income" principles may apply to grantor trusts in determining the owner of certain items of income.[163] Therefore, even though the trust grantor is not required to include the trust's gross income in his or her gross income under the statutory subpart E rules, gross income inclusion cannot be avoided where the income was previously economically earned by or otherwise accrued to the trust grantor and is thereafter sought to be deflected to the trust.[164]

c. Trust Income Taxation

Assuming inapplicability of the subpart E rules, a trust will be subject to the income tax rules applicable to nongrantor trusts. These rules categorize such trusts as "simple" or "complex."[165]

The distributable net income of the nongrantor trust will be taxed either (1) to the beneficiaries to whom the income is distributed (or is required to be distributed), or (2) to the trust (treated as a separate taxpayer when the subpart E rules are not applicable). This income tax liability of the trust is based on the amount held by the trust after deductible payments of income made to the beneficiaries (or required to be made to them) are taken as deductions, that is, after application of the subchapter J conduit rules. The income tax treatment of an inter vivos irrevocable nongrantor trust and its beneficiaries is the same as the income tax treatment of a testamentary trust and its beneficiaries.[166]

d. Gift Tax Consequences

A transfer of property into an irrevocable inter vivos trust will result in a completed delivery for gift tax purposes. When no reversionary interest is retained by the grantor, the value of the transfer for gift tax purposes is the fair market value of the entire property when transferred into the trust.[167] If the trust transfer is actually completed within the meaning of the gift completion rules for gift tax purposes,[168] the gift tax will apply even if the transfer is ineffective under the income tax grantor trust rules to shift the income from the grantor's income tax return.[169]

To enable qualification for the annual donee gift tax exclusion, the trust income interest must be a present interest.[170] This will be accomplished by a specification in the trust instrument that trust income be paid currently. When a minor is the beneficiary, the trust could be structured to fit within §2503(c). Alternatively, where a discretionary income distribution structure is desired, a "demand right" provided to the trust beneficiary might be used to achieve eligibility for the gift tax annual donee exclusion.[171]

e. Estate Tax Consequences

(1) Unified Tax Computation

The value of the property shifted to the inter vivos irrevocable trust and treated as a completed gift will be included in the grantor's unified transfer tax base (to the extent in excess of the annual donee exclusion, assuming a present interest transfer).[172] This will impact on the rate of the transfer tax applicable to other transfers made subsequently during life and upon death. The assets previously transferred into trust may also be included in the estate tax base at death, as described below.

(2) Estate Tax Transfer Provisions

In creating an irrevocable trust with the purpose of removing the transferred assets from the gross estate, the grantor must avoid the possible subsequent impact of three important estate tax "transfer provisions."[173]

(a) Section 2036—Retained Life Estate Section 2036 specifies that a decedent's gross estate includes the value of all property to the extent of any interest in the property of which the decedent has at any time made a transfer (except for adequate and full consideration in money or money's worth), by trust or otherwise, under which he or she retained for his or her life:[174]

- the possession or enjoyment of, or the right to the income from, the property[175]; or
- the right, either alone or in conjunction with any person, to designate the persons who shall possess or enjoy the property or the income therefrom.[176]

Such an interest may be treated as retained by applicability of the "reciprocal trust doctrine" where two parties make transfers into trusts for each other and the transactions may reasonably be treated as interrelated.[177] Language in the documents that these arrangements are not being made as consideration for the other party's transfer will not be sufficient to negate reciprocal trust treatment. The planning objective in this context is to assure that dispositive provisions in trusts being implemented contemporaneously do not have substantially similar provisions.[178]

(b) Section 2037—Transfers Taking Effect at Death The trust grantor's gross estate also includes the value of all property to the extent of any interest therein of which the decedent has made a transfer (except for an adequate and full consideration in money or money's worth), by trust or otherwise, if[179]:

- possession or enjoyment of the property may, through ownership of such interest, be obtained only by surviving the decedent; and
- the decedent retained a reversionary interest[180] in the property the value of which, immediately before his or her death, exceeds 5% of the value of the property.[181]

(c) Section 2038—Revocable Transfers The trust grantor's gross estate also includes the value of all property to the extent of any interest therein of which the decedent has at any time made a transfer (except for an adequate and full consideration in money or money's worth), by trust or otherwise, where the enjoyment thereof was subject at the date of the grantor's death to any change through the exercise of a power by the decedent (alone or with another person) to alter, amend, revoke, or terminate the property transfer.[182] This inclusionary rule also applies where any such power is relinquished during the three-year period ending on the date of the decedent's death.[183]

f. Typos of Trust Asset Dispositive Arrangements

A grantor will want to establish the terms upon which trust income and corpus should be distributed by the trustee. The terms of such arrangements will be affected by both tax and nontax considerations. Options for making trust distributions include:

> Income Distribution—(1) mandatory distribution to specifically identified beneficiaries of all trust income or specified portions of the income; (2) absolute discretion delegated to the trustee concerning the timing of income distributions to specified beneficiaries; (3) income distributions to be made subject to a reasonably ascertainable standard (e.g., "health, education, support, or maintenance"); and (4) the right to "spray or sprinkle" income in the discretion of the trustee among a group of designated beneficiaries.
>
> Corpus Distribution—(1) mandatory distribution of the corpus to a specified beneficiary at a specified age (or portions distributed at several specified ages); (2) distribution to a specified beneficiary in the event of certain needs pursuant

to a reasonably ascertainable standard (e.g., "health, education, support, or maintenance"); (3) distribution to a specified beneficiary with the timing of the distribution subject to the exercise of discretion by the trustee; (4) distributions to various beneficiaries subject to the exercise of a "spray or sprinkle" power; (5) distribution upon the exercise of a special power of appointment held by a beneficiary; and (6) retention of the assets in trust at the death of the first generation beneficiaries and the eventual distribution to the second generation beneficiaries (i.e., a "generation-skipping" trust).

This represents merely an outline of basic options available to the grantor in formulating the terms of a trust concerning the distribution of income and corpus. Several of these options might be combined in varying proportions.

g. Demand or "Crummey" Trust

(1) Trust Grantor's Annual Donee Exclusion

A variant in this context is often a trust providing a "demand" withdrawal right (known as a *"Crummey"* trust).[184] The *Crummey* trust's objective is to make the §2503 annual donee gift tax exclusion available[185] while avoiding the mandatory termination of the trust at age 21, as required by §2503(c).[186] The theoretical basis for this treatment is that the annual exclusion should be available where the donee has an unrestricted right to the immediate use, possession, or enjoyment of property.[187] The actual use or possession of such property is not required.[188] Thus, the key element of the *Crummey* trust is the right given to the beneficiary to demand property in the trust.

Early case law allowed the §2503 exclusion where a trust beneficiary possessed an unlimited right to terminate the trust by demanding the trust property even though the other trust provisions did not allow qualification for the annual exclusion.[189] Where the donee was a minor and no guardian had been appointed, the IRS maintained that the interest of the donee was a future interest and not eligible for §2503.[190] The original IRS concession to the *Crummey* trust structure came in Rev. Rul. 73-405.[191] That ruling approved the annual exclusion for a demand power extending to the entire trust property. The IRS concluded that the demand power in a minor beneficiary would create a present interest so long as no impediment existed under the trust or local law to the appointment of a minor's guardian.[192]

The *Crummey* decision extended the demand principle and enabled the annual exclusion even though: (1) the demand power extended only to annual contributions to the trust; (2) the demand right expired at the end of the calendar year during which the transfer into trust was made; (3) the beneficiary–power holder was a minor for whom no guardian had been appointed; and (4) no procedure existed to notify the donee that a transfer was made to the trust. Consequently, the *Crummey* decision allowed the annual exclusion without the necessity of retaining a power to terminate the entire trust. Since recognizing the *Crummey* power concept the IRS has elaborated on its position regarding the availability of the annual exclusion for trust property subject to the power of withdrawal.[193]

Two specific requirements must be met to assure qualification for the annual donee exclusion for property subject to the withdrawal power.[194] The power holder must be given:

- notice of the existence of the withdrawal power; and
- a reasonable time within which to exercise the power.[195]

Even if the demand period extends into a calendar year different from the one in which the transfer was made, the transferor will be entitled to the §2503 annual donee exclusion in the year of the transfer, provided the beneficiaries are given prompt notice of their demand rights and that, for minor beneficiaries, no impediment exists to the appointment of guardians under local law.

(2) Multiple Annual Donee Exclusions

Donors often attempt to include multiple beneficiaries eligible for the withdrawal power, so as to increase the number of available gift tax annual donee exclusions. The IRS regularly challenged such multiple withdrawal powers, however.[196] In the estate planning context, the advice should be to assure that the beneficiaries, for whom an annual donee exclusion is claimed, have real, substantive property interests under the gift transfer. Except for the very wealthiest individuals, the continued, regular use of annual donee exclusion gifts for multiple beneficiaries may achieve significant transfers of wealth over an extended period. This is a better approach than to engage in attempts to create purported annual donee exclusions for numerous beneficiaries when most of the nominal transferees have no real economic interest in the property and understandings were concluded in advance that the withdrawal power will not be exercised.

(3) Multiple Trusts and the "Hanging Power" Issue

A donor may attempt to create several trusts each having withdrawal powers with the objective of enabling multiple annual donee exclusions through multiple withdrawal rights. The IRS has ruled, however, that *Crummey* powers must be aggregated for purposes of the federal gift tax.[197]

Because of the possible difference between (1) the annual donee exclusion *Crummey* withdrawal power[198] and (2) a lesser amount subject to the five-and-five power, some planners attempted to use a "hanging power" to avoid lapses occurring in excess of that power. The concern is that the lapses above the maximum level of the five-and-five power would be transfers for estate tax purposes, that is, a gift from the donee–power holder to the trust beneficiaries.[199]

In this context, the power holder could be given (1) the right to withdraw an amount equal to the annual donee exclusion, but (2) the amount that would lapse each year (for gift and estate tax purposes) would be equal to the five-and-five limitation. The remaining portion would carry over to the following years until being fully absorbed within the five-and-five exception available in subsequent years.[200] If the corpus is appreciating, the 5% amount would also be expanding, thereby increasing the lapsing portion. Eventually, the five-and-five power amount will be exhausted unless the donor continues to make gifts into the trust. Of course, if the donee dies before the hanging power fully lapses, the unlapsed amount would be included in the donee's gross estate as property subject to a general power of appointment.

The IRS has refused to recognize the validity of such a "hanging power" (i.e., a withdrawal power that "hangs" open, closing only at the five-and-five lapse rate).[201] Many practitioners believe, however, that hanging powers continue to be effective where that portion of the withdrawal right which lapses can be calculated without reference to the tax consequences.

(4) Donee's Income Tax Consequences

The use of a *Crummey* trust may generate federal income tax exposure for the donee of the withdrawal right. To the extent that the donee possesses a power to demand property from the trust, the donee is deemed (under the grantor trust rules) to be the owner of that property and is taxed on its income.[202] If the beneficiary's withdrawal power is restricted to annual trust contributions and does not extend to the entire trust property, §678 will have only partial application. Consequently, in these circumstances, for income tax purposes, the beneficiary will be treated as the owner of only a proportionate share of the trust.[203]

(5) Donee's Gift Tax Consequences

A trust with a *Crummey* withdrawal power may generate federal gift tax consequences to the holder of this power.[204] The *Crummey* power is a general power of appointment because it allows the donee to appoint the property to himself or herself, his or her estate, his or her creditors, or the creditors of his or her estate. Section 2514 provides that the exercise or release of a general power is deemed a transfer of property by the power holder. The lapse of a *Crummey* power may cause a taxable gift under §2514, depending on the terms of the trust.[205] Section 2514 may even apply if the trust provides for a remainder over to a secondary donee in the event the primary donee does not survive until termination of the trust.[206]

(6) Donee's Estate Tax Exposure

The *Crummey* power may generate estate tax problems where the primary beneficiary–power holder predeceases the termination of the trust.[207] If any taxable lapses occurred in years prior to death, partial inclusion of the trust property in the donee's gross estate would result.[208] If a taxable lapse occurred in a prior year, a proportionate amount of the value of the trust property at the date of death is included in the gross estate of the power holder.[209] Inclusion as to the amount of property subject to the annual demand right existing at death is mandated even if the donee is a minor not capable of exercising the withdrawal power. As noted above, resolution of this problem through the use of "hanging powers" may be difficult to accomplish.

(7) Life Insurance Trusts

The *Crummey* demand power is often used in conjunction with an unfunded life insurance trust.[210] An irrevocable life insurance trust is often used because the life insurance proceeds can be received by the trustee after death without inclusion of the proceeds in the gross estate of the insured.

If a life insurance policy was transferred to a *Crummey* demand trust, the donor may make annual contributions to the trust in an amount of the annual premium payments and obtain the benefit of the annual donee exclusion for these payments.[211] A question might be raised as to whether the beneficiaries' demand right is illusory (and the annual donee exclusion is, therefore, not available) where (1) the annual contribution to the trust is immediately paid to the insurer,[212] (2) the life insurance in the trust is term insurance (with no cash value),[213] or (3) the trust corpus consists of group term insurance where the employer pays all or most of the insurance premiums directly to the insurance carrier.[214] The IRS ordinarily will not issue a private letter ruling concerning the availability of the annual donee exclusion when (1) the trust corpus consists or will consist substantially of insurance policies on the life of the grantor or the grantor's spouse, (2) the trustee or any other person has a power to apply the trust's income or corpus to the payment of premiums on policies of insurance on the life of the grantor or the grantor's spouse, (3) the trustee or any other person has a power to use the trust's assets to make loans to the grantor's estate or to purchase assets from the grantor's estate, (4) the trust beneficiaries have the power to withdraw, on demand, any additional transfers made to the trust, and (5) there is a right or power in any person that would cause the grantor to be treated as the owner of all or a portion of the trust under §673 through §677.[215]

h. Estate Tax Planning Problems and Opportunities

Both estate and income tax planning problems involving inter vivos irrevocable trusts often arise for the grantor primarily because the grantor (1) wants to function as trustee and (2) in that capacity, wants to exercise various significant powers affecting the beneficial enjoyment of the income and principal. Alternatively, the grantor may decide not to act as trustee but may want to indirectly retain significant control over the enjoyment of the trust income and principal through some other type of power. In either event, the grantor is restricted as to the substantive powers he or she may retain without generating adverse estate tax consequences.

The governing principles in the estate tax area, unlike the income tax context, are substantially based on court decisions. Those principles are highly elusive, and planning in this area is intricate and risky. To avoid these risks, the grantor should designate an independent trustee, retaining for himself or herself (in a non-fiduciary capacity) only those powers clearly permitted under court decisions that enable future avoidance of estate tax.

Those areas involving significant powers or control where substantial estate tax risk is involved, whether such rights are retained by the grantor as a trustee, or otherwise, include:[216]

- Direct powers, such as: (1) the power to defer the enjoyment by the beneficiary of the trust property or its income[217]; (2) the power to accelerate enjoyment by the trust beneficiary by either termination of the trust or invasion of corpus[218]; (3) the power to add or substitute beneficiaries to the trust[219]; and (4) the power to sprinkle or spray to trust beneficiaries the income or principal of the trust, uncontrolled by an external standard.[220]
- Powers of administration, such as broad powers held with respect to: (1) investments; (2) allocation of receipts and disbursements; (3) dealing with trust assets[221]; and (4) voting rights in corporate stock.[222]
- A retained right to designate himself or herself as a replacement trustee.[223] A power by the grantor to remove a corporate trustee and to appoint another corporate trustee ordinarily should not result in inclusion of the trust assets in the gross estate.[224]

A special planning consideration should be noted if the irrevocable trust is to hold S corporation stock. To constitute a "qualified subchapter S trust" only one trust beneficiary is permitted.[225] For taxable years beginning after 1996, an "electing small business trust" may be an S corporation shareholder.[226] Unlike qualified subchapter S trusts, electing small business trusts are permitted to have more than one trust beneficiary.[227]

4. Intentionally Tax Defective Trusts

a. Concept of Intentionally Tax Defective Trusts

Most irrevocable lifetime trusts are structured to avoid in the future both (1) income taxation to the grantor and (2) inclusion of the assets in the grantor's estate for federal estate tax purposes. A trust might intentionally be structured, however, so that it is "tax defective"; that is, it does not satisfy one of these tax avoidance objectives.

The trust might be defective for income tax purposes (so that the trust's ordinary income or capital gains, or both, are treated as directly received by the trust grantor). The trust might be defective for gift tax purposes so that an immediate gift tax liability is not incurred. The trust might be defective for estate tax purposes so that assets are thereafter includible in the grantor's gross estate. This latter situation might be important, for example, where the assets, by being includible in the trust grantor's gross estate, receive a stepped-up tax basis at death. No estate tax may be imposed in this latter situation, however, because of the availability of (1) the unlimited marital deduction, (2) the unified credit, or (3) both. Ordinarily, the tax defective trust is structured to be flawed for income tax purposes but not for estate and gift tax purposes. A revocable inter vivos trust will be defective for income, gift, and estate tax purposes, but may be valuable for non-tax reasons (such as avoiding the applicability of local probate rules), as noted above.

The status as a defective trust for one or more federal tax purposes does not cause the trust to be defective for local trust law purposes. Consequently, the property transfers into trust could be irrevocable for local trust and property law purposes even though federal income tax or transfer tax rules, or both, might treat the trust as incomplete.

b. Income Tax Defective Trust

(1) Fundamental Concept

By avoiding applicability of the grantor trust rules[228] the grantor is not treated as the "owner" of the trust's income. Rather, the income received by a trust is either taxed to the trust or, if distributed (or required to be distributed), taxed to the beneficiaries. Similarly, any capital gain or loss realized by the trust is allocable to the trust (or sometimes, the beneficiaries), but not to the trust grantor.

The trust can be created as not complying with the grantor trust rules, that is, as being "defective." If the trust created by a grantor is defective for income tax purposes, further analysis must be made concerning whether the trust is defective (1) only as to ordinary income, (2) only as to capital gain,[229] or (3) for both purposes. If the trust is defective for ordinary income tax purposes, the ordinary income (or ordinary loss) will be treated as owned by the trust grantor. If the trust is defective for corpus purposes, the capital gain (or capital loss) from those items will be treated as directly received by the trust grantor. If the sales transaction is between the trustee and the grantor trust the transaction will be treated as a nullity for federal income tax purposes.[230] Note that, in this situation, to avoid an unintentional gift being made by the grantor, the sale of assets must be at fair market value. Assuming no estate tax exposure for this trust this transaction will then enable the post transaction appreciation to be removed from the trust grantor's estate for federal estate tax purposes.

(2) Available Income Tax Planning Benefits

A variety of other income tax planning reasons exist for retaining grantor trust status for a trust although the trust is not defective for estate tax planning purposes[231]:

- Interest expense might be paid on funds borrowed by the trust and that interest expense (subject to the limitations of §163) might be beneficial as an income tax deduction to the trust grantor.
- The grantor might obtain the matching of income and deductions, such as capital gains and losses or passive activity income offset by passive activity losses.
- A grantor may have a net operating loss that may be applied against income being received by the trust.
- The steeply progressive income tax rate structure applicable to trusts will not be applicable if the income belongs to the trust grantor.
- A nonresident alien might establish a foreign trust for the benefit of a U.S. beneficiary, thereby enabling the U.S. beneficiary to receive the income on a tax-paid basis.[232]
- A personal residence trust defective as to corpus could, if the property is sold at a gain, enable the availability of the §121 exclusion.[233]
- The transfer of an installment note will not constitute a disposition of that note accelerating gain recognition.
- Stock acquired under an incentive stock option (ISO) plan may be transferred into the trust within two years of the grant of the option or within one year of the exercise of the option without the transfer being treated as a disqualifying disposition.

- Tax-free gifts can be achieved if income taxes that would have been paid by the trust (indirectly for the account of the beneficiary-donee) are paid by the grantor.[234]

(3) Choices for Structuring the Income Tax Defective Trust

For federal income tax purposes a trust will be "defective" to the grantor if only one of the grantor trust provisions is not observed.[235] Often, one of the administrative power provisions is used for this purpose; that is, the grantor of a trust will be deemed the owner of trust property for income tax purposes (both as to ordinary income and as to corpus) if any person may exercise, in a non-fiduciary capacity and without the approval or consent of any one acting in a fiduciary capacity, a power to reacquire trust corpus by substituting other property of an equal value.[236] This non-fiduciary power need not be held by the grantor for §675 to be applicable to effect grantor trust status. Consequently, this power might be given to someone who is not acting as the trustee of the trust. In the process, however, the trust must not be made estate tax defective.

A nonadverse party might be given a power (also exercisable in a non-fiduciary capacity) to vote or direct the voting of stock or other securities of a corporation in which the holdings of the grantor and the trust are significant from the standpoint of voting control.[237] Alternatively, a power might be held by a nonadverse party to control the investment of trust funds, either by directing investments or reinvestments, or by vetoing proposed investments or reinvestments, to the extent that the trust funds consist of stock or securities of corporations in which the holdings of the grantor and the trust are significant from the viewpoint of voting control.[238] In this situation, to enable avoidance of "tax-defectiveness" for estate tax purposes, the power should be held by a person other than the grantor.[239]

Another option for a possible "grantor power" for income tax purposes is to provide to a nonadverse party a power to add beneficiaries. This must be a power other than merely to provide for after-born or after-adopted children.[240] No adverse estate tax consequences should result from the grant of this power.

A nonadverse but independent trustee could have the power to make distributions of income or corpus to the grantor's spouse. The possibility of distributions to the grantor's spouse causes the trust to be income tax defective as to both ordinary income and as to corpus.[241]

(4) Identifying a Nonadverse Party

The existence of the power causing an income tax defective trust is dependent, as noted above, on the power being held by a nonadverse party. This necessitates identification of a nonadverse party. Any "related and subordinate parties" are presumed to be subservient to the grantor for income tax purposes and, therefore, nonadverse.[242] This status should not make the trust defective for federal estate tax purposes, however.

c. Estate Tax Defective Trust

In limited situations, a trust that is defective for estate tax purposes, but not for income tax purposes, may be useful. In this situation, the trust income would be taxed to the actual recipient (trust or beneficiary and not the grantor), but the assets would be included in the estate of the trust grantor for federal estate tax purposes. This would enable an income tax basis step-up at the time of death for the assets held in the trust, because those assets are includible in the gross estate of the trust grantor.[243]

This status as estate tax defective may be achieved through a violation of one of the estate tax transfer provisions (e.g., §2036 or §2038), while not triggering the applicability of any of the grantor trust income tax provisions. This could be accomplished by having the grantor retain a power, in conjunction with an adverse party, to designate the persons who shall possess or enjoy the property or the income from the trust[244] or to revoke the trust.[245] Because the existence of a requirement of the approval or consent of an adverse party makes the income tax grantor trust rules inapplicable,[246] this desired tax defective status could be achieved. This status could also be accomplished through the retention, by the grantor, of a power to accelerate a beneficiary's interest.[247]

The estate planner in this situation must evaluate carefully whether the estate tax exposure negates the income tax benefits being achieved. This estate tax risk might be eliminated or mitigated through the use of the unified credit and the marital deduction. The timing of the event of death, being quite difficult to predict in most situations, may annul the benefits achieved after the trust has been in existence for some reasonable period. In some situations subsequent adjustments to the terms of the trust may enable restructuring to avoid these pitfalls.

5. Transfer of the Family Residence

a. Transfer to Spouse

A gift transfer often used to reduce a donor's gross estate is the transfer of his or her entire interest in the family residence to other family members, for example, the donor's spouse.[248] For example, such a transfer could be from a husband to a wife, based on the assumption that the wife's life expectancy is greater than the husband's. The direction of this transfer might be reversed in the opposite situation. This type of transaction is distinguished from the more complicated arrangement involving a "qualified personal residence trust" where the lead interest is retained by the donor, with only the remainder interest being transferred by gift, thereby reducing the value of the gift transfer.[249] The tax planning objective in the residence transfer gift transaction described here is to entirely and immediately remove the asset from the donor's gross estate. If the residence is transferred to the spouse, gift tax exposure is eliminated, however, because of the availability of the unlimited marital deduction for gift tax purposes.

The IRS previously asserted that the gift of a family residence (or portion thereof) was not effective to remove it from the donor's gross estate for federal estate tax purposes where the donor continued to live in the home for his or her life. The IRS claimed that the donor made a property transfer while reserving the use, possession, or other enjoyment of the property for the remainder of his or her lifetime. The IRS relied on §2036(a)(1) (one of the estate tax "transfer" provisions), which specifies that, if a donor transfers property, but retains a lifetime interest, the property is includible in the donor's gross estate.[250] The IRS lost various cases involving gift transfers between spouses, including the *Gutchess* case,[251] where the Tax Court indicated that the spouses' joint occupancy of a residence after an interspousal transfer of that residence is insufficient in and of itself to indicate the existence of an agreement for retained enjoyment. In such a case there is not such a withholding of use from the transferee as is present where the transferor actually retains income from property he or she transferred. Such post-transfer use is insufficient to indicate any prior agreement or prearrangement for retention of use by the transferor. The IRS later acquiesced in the decision in the *Gutchess* case.[252]

The primary problem for the IRS in contesting these situations was proving that an agreement existed between the spouses that the donor spouse would have continued enjoyment of the transferred property.[253] For planning purposes the spouses obviously should not have an "agreement" or other "understanding" that the donor spouse can live in the residence for the remainder of that spouse's life.[254] Presumably such an understanding might be implied from the marriage relationship itself, but that is not sufficient to constitute an "agreement" for federal estate tax purposes. Certainly the spouse will not transfer the residence to the other spouse if the marriage is undergoing difficulty, recognizing that he or she may lose control of the premises.

The unlimited marital deduction has reduced the significance of this valuable estate planning arrangement in the marital context. The alternate objective might be to retain the residence, obtaining a stepped-up income tax basis, and then transfer the residence to the spouse protected from estate tax by the marital deduction. This would be important if the gain from the sale of the residence would not be entirely excluded from gross income under §121.

A lifetime transfer of the residence to that other spouse may still be appropriate to shift net worth to that spouse for purposes of ultimately using that spouse's unified credit. This would be particularly important if that transferee spouse is anticipated to die first.[255]

b. Transfer to Children

The concepts applicable to residence transfers between spouses may be obsolete in many spousal situations, but this analysis also applies when a gift transfer of a residence is made to children.[256] This is a technique that often is implemented by a parent to transfer a second home or vacation property to younger generation members.

Where a donor transfers the family residence outright to a child, but the donor lives in the residence for the remainder of the donor's life, the probabilities of proof by the IRS are substantially improved that an implicit agreement between the donor and donee existed that the donor could continue to reside in the residence.[257] The donor (e.g., parent) could possibly continue to live in the residence if entering into an enforceable lease agreement with the donee child. However, arm's length criteria must be implemented and continually observed.[258] This should occur even if a transferred vacation property is used only sporadically by the donor. The IRS's position is clear that it will challenge such transfers and, consequently, if estate tax exposure is a potential risk, careful planning is essential to avoid the "retained life interest" risk.[259]

Notes

1. For a more complete discussion of the tax treatment of gifts, see 845 T.M., *Gifts* (Bloomberg BNA).
2. As basic background for this discussion, note that (as explained in Chapter 4, A.1.) the Tax Relief, Unemployment Insurance Reauthorization, and Job Creation Act of 2010 (2010 TRA), Pub. L. No. 111-312, §301(b), §301(e), §302(a), §302(b), §302(f), §303, increased the §2010(c) estate tax exclusion amount to $5 million for decedents dying in 2010–2012, increased the §2505(a) gift tax exclusion amount to $5 million for gifts made in 2011–2012 (the amount remained at $1 million for gifts made in 2010), and adjusted the $5 million amount for inflation in multiples of $10,000 in 2012. The 2010 TRA, Pub. L. No. 111-312, §303, also provides for portability of the exclusion for spouses dying in 2011–2012 (the applicable exclusion amount is the sum of the basic exclusion amount plus, in the case of a surviving spouse, the deceased spousal unused exclusion [DSUE] amount). The American Taxpayer Relief Act of 2012 (ATRA), Pub. L. No. 112-240, §101(a)(2), made permanent all of the aforementioned 2010 TRA changes for decedents dying after 2012. The differential between the gift tax and estate tax exclusion amounts in 2010 may have impeded the completion of large lifetime gifts during that year.
3. See Chapter 4, A.1., for more information about the changes made by ATRA, Pub. L. No. 112-240.
4. *See* §408, §219.
5. The gift tax rate tables are the same as those prescribed for the federal estate tax. *See* §2502(a). However, for gifts made in 2010, the rate structure was provided in §2502(a)(2) rather than in §2001(c). *See* Economic Growth and Tax Relief Reconciliation Act of 2001 (EGTRRA), Pub. L. No. 107-16, §511(d), §901; 2010 TRA, Pub. L. No. 111-312, §101(a), §302(b)(1), §304.
6. Although the transfer tax savings to be achieved can be significant, the effective use of a continuous annual donee exclusion gift program as an estate planning tool is not very widespread.
7. For a more detailed discussion of the gift tax structure, see Chapter 4, A.2. See also 845 T.M., *Gifts* (Bloomberg BNA).
8. *See* §2502(a), §2010(c), as amended by ATRA, Pub. L. No. 112-240, §101(b), §101(c).
9. §2505(a), as amended by EGTRRA, Pub. L. No. 107-16, §521(b), §901, 2010 TRA, Pub. L. No. 111-312, §101(a), §301–§304.
10. The estate tax exclusion amounts were: (1) $1.5 million for estates of decedents dying in 2004–2005; (2) $2,000,000 for estates of decedents dying in 2006–2008; (3) $3.5 million for estates of decedents dying in 2009; and (iv) $5 million for estates of decedents dying after 2009 (with portability for spouses after 2010 and an inflation adjustment after 2011). *See* §2010(c), as amended by EGTRRA, Pub. L. No. 107-16, §521(a), §901; 2010 TRA, Pub. L. No. 111-312, §101(a), §301–§304; ATRA, Pub. L. No. 112-240, §101(a).
11. The use of the unified credit is mandatory. Rev. Rul. 79-398, 1979-2 C.B. 338. This ruling created a problem for pre-August 6, 1997, gifts where the value was not readily ascertainable, such as the stock of a family business. After the statute of limitations for assessing gift tax expired, the fair market value of prior transfers could still be adjusted upward for purposes of computing the gift tax on subsequent transfers, so long as no

gift tax was paid on prior transfers. *See* Reg. §25.2504-2(a). *See also Estate of Smith v. Commissioner*, 94 T.C. 872 (1990); TAM 9250004 (concerning inapplicability of this limitation in estate tax computation context). Where a gift of difficult-to-value property was made before August 6, 1997, the donor often found it advantageous to make the gift large enough to exhaust his or her unified credit so that some tax was paid and the gift tax limitations period began to run.

12. §2010(c), §2505(a), as amended by the 2010 TRA, Pub. L. No. 111-312, §101(a), §301–§304, and made permanent by ATRA, Pub. L. No. 112-240, §101(a). For the inflation-adjusted amounts for recent years, see Worksheet 1.
13. Note that the IRS will not issue a private letter ruling concerning actuarial factors for valuing a prospective or hypothetical gift by a donor. Rev. Proc. 2015-3, 2015-1 I.R.B. 129, §3.01(94).
14. See *Estate of Smith v. Commissioner*, 94 T.C. 872 (1990), *acq.*, 1990-2 C.B. 1, holding that this revaluation during an estate tax examination was possible, although a hypothetical credit needed to be provided for that gift tax liability that would have been incurred at the time of the gift.
15. The Taxpayer Relief Act of 1997, Pub. L. No. 105-34, §506, amended §2001 and §2504(c) to prohibit the IRS from revaluing an adequately disclosed gift made after the date of enactment for which the limitations period has passed for purposes of determining the applicable estate tax bracket and available unified credit. Technical corrections made to §2001(f)(2) in the 1998 Tax Extension Act, Pub. L. No. 105-277, §4003(c), clarify that the value of a prior transfer cannot be redetermined if the transfer was disclosed on a gift tax return or in a statement attached to such a return in a manner to adequately apprise the Treasury Secretary of the nature of the transfer even if no gift tax was imposed on that transfer. This correction was effective as if included in the 1997 Act. Technical corrections made by the IRS Restructuring and Reform Act of 1998, Pub. L. No. 105-206, §6007(e), clarify that in determining the amount of taxable gifts made in preceding calendar periods, the value of prior gifts is the value of such gifts as finally determined, even if no gift tax was assessed or paid on that gift. For this purpose, final determinations include the value reported on the gift tax return (if not challenged by the IRS prior to the expiration of the statute of limitations), the value determined by the IRS (if not challenged in court by the taxpayer), the value determined by the courts, or the value agreed to by the IRS and the taxpayer in a settlement agreement. *See* §2001(f)(2). This correction was effective for gifts made after the date of enactment of the 1997 Act. Section 7477, added by the 1997 Act, Pub. L. No. 105-34, §506, allows a donor to challenge an IRS determination of the value of a gift in an action for declaratory judgment in the Tax Court. The donor must exhaust administrative remedies and must bring the Tax Court action within 90 days of the IRS mailing notice of its determination. Reg. §25.2504-2(b) provides that, for purposes of gift tax finality, the determination as to whether a gift has been adequately disclosed is controlled by Reg. §301.6501(c)-1(f)(1), which provides that a gift tax may be assessed at any time on a gift that is not adequately disclosed on a gift tax return. Reg. §25.2504-2(b) is effective for transfers of property by gift made after August 5, 1997, if the gift tax return for the calendar period in which the transfer is reported is filed after December 3, 1999. Reg. §301.6501(c)-1(f)(1) is effective for gifts made after December 31, 1996, for which the gift tax return for such calendar year is filed after December 3, 1999. In Rev. Proc. 2000-34, 2000-2 C.B. 186, the IRS provided guidance for submitting the information required under §6501(c)(9)

and Reg. §301.6501(c)-1(f) to adequately disclose a gift if a donor filed a Form 709, *United States Gift (and Generation-Skipping Transfer) Tax Return,* for the calendar year in which the donor made a gift, but failed to adequately disclose the gift because (1) the donor did not report the gift on the return or (2) the donor failed to submit with the return the information concerning that gift as required under Reg. §301.6501(c)-1(f)(2). See 845 T.M., *Gifts* (Bloomberg BNA).

16. Under §2503(b).
17. The $10,000 gift tax annual exclusion is indexed for inflation (rounded to the next lowest multiple of $1,000) for gifts made after 1998, using 1997 as the base year. §2503(b), as amended by the Taxpayer Relief Act of 1997, Pub. L. No. 105-34, §501(c). For the inflation-adjusted §2503(b) amounts for the most recent years, see Worksheet 1. Near the end of each calendar year the IRS issues a revenue procedure identifying various inflation adjusted items, including the annual donee exclusion.
18. Under §2523(i), which cross references §2503(b). See Worksheet 1 for the inflation-adjusted §2523(i) amounts for the most recent years.
19. *But see* Rev. Rul. 85-24, 1985-1 C.B. 329, where three partners in a partnership created separate trusts for their respective children and made various reciprocal gifts. Each partner was only entitled to one annual exclusion for the transfer benefiting his child and no exclusions were available for the transfers for the benefit of the other partners' children. *See also Estate of Cristofani v. Commissioner,* 97 T.C. 74 (1991) (permitting annual donee exclusions for transfers in trust to two children and five minor grandchildren). In AOD 1992-09, 1992-1 C.B. 1, the IRS announced its acquiescence "in result" in the *Cristofani* decision but noted its disagreement with the Tax Court's "sweeping interpretation" of the *Crummey* decision. The AOD noted that the IRS will recognize *Crummey* withdrawal powers held by current income beneficiaries and persons with vested remainder interests. In AOD 1996-10, 1996-2 C.B. 1, the IRS subsequently issued a further acquiescence "in result only," noting: "the Service disagrees with the Tax Court's sweeping interpretation of *Crummey.* To extend the benefit of the annual exclusion to illusory gifts of present interests would undermine significantly the unified system of estate and gift taxation and invite flagrant abuse of the benefit that Congress intended in enacting §2503(b). Accordingly, the IRS will continue to litigate cases whose facts indicate that the substance of the transfers was merely to obtain annual exclusions and that no bona fide gift of a present interest was intended." In *Mikel v. Commissioner,* T.C. Memo 2015-64, the IRS claimed an *in terrorem* clause in the trust instrument that, in part, prohibited any beneficiary, on pain of forfeiture of the beneficiary's interest from filing "any action in a court of law," rendered *Crummey* powers held by the beneficiaries illusory. The Tax Court rejected the IRS position, holding that the remainder of the clause and other trust provisions established that the provision was designed only to constrain beneficiaries from challenging distributions made by the trustees (who possessed absolute discretion to make distributions) and did not constrain their ability to enforce their withdrawal rights and, therefore, those withdrawal rights were not illusory so as to render the gifts made to the trust ineligible for per donee annual exclusions. *See Mikel,* T.C. Memo 2015-64, at *18–19.
20. See Rev. Rul. 86-41, 1986-1 C.B. 300, where a gift transfer document indicated (1) that a proportionate interest in real estate was being transferred but (2) that such interest would be reduced if it exceeded a $10,000 value. The IRS indicated that such an adjustment clause would be disregarded for federal tax purposes, the transfer under the

enumerated facts therefore exceeding the then $10,000 exclusion. See similar rejections by the IRS of adjustment clauses in TAM 200337012 and TAM 200245053.

21. §2503(b)(1).
22. *Crummey v. Commissioner*, 397 F.2d 82 (9th Cir. 1968); Rev. Rul. 73-405, 1973-2 C.B. 321; TAM 9141008 (where decedent annually contributed property valued at approximately $350,000 to revocable trust whose primary beneficiaries were her three children). In TAM 9141008, 32 grandchildren and great-grandchildren had contingent remainder interests and all 35 beneficiaries had *Crummey* powers. The National Office advised that the decedent was entitled to annual exclusions only for transfers to the trust for the benefit of the primary beneficiaries, her three children. *See Heyen v. United States,* 945 F.2d 359 (10th Cir. 1991), where gift taxes and fraud penalties were imposed where the donor transferred stock in a family corporation to 29 recipients (each in amounts slightly less than the annual donee exclusion) who then signed the stock certificates in blank so that they could be reissued to members of the donor's family. See the discussion of demand trusts at Chapter 6, D.3.g.
23. See Rev. Rul. 81-7, 1981-1 C.B. 474, and Rev. Rul. 83-108, 1983-2 C.B. 167, where the IRS ruled that a grant to a trust beneficiary of a power to withdraw from trust corpus is a present interest eligible for the §2503(b) annual exclusion in the year of transfer to the trust. This was permitted even though the beneficiary was not informed of the existence of the power until the following calendar year. The trust instrument provided that the trustee must notify the beneficiary of the withdrawal power within a reasonable time of the transfer to the trust and that the power would not lapse for 45 days after notification. *Cf. Estate of Turner v. Commissioner*, T.C. Memo 2011-209 (decedent's direct payments of life insurance premiums on policies held in *Crummey* trust were present interest gifts subject to §2503(b) exclusion, even though beneficiaries did not receive notice of transfers, because beneficiaries had absolute legal right and power to demand withdrawal), *motion for reconsideration denied*, 138 T.C. 306 (2012). The beneficiary's unrestricted right to withdraw principal from a trust will be a power of appointment for gift tax purposes. Reg. §25.2514-1(b)(1).
24. See CCA 201208026, where the IRS concluded that because a threat of severe economic punishment loomed over any beneficiary contemplating action to obtain trust funds the withdrawal rights were illusory. Consequently, no annual donee exclusion was available. *But see Mikel v. Commissioner*, T.C. Memo 2015-64 (clause revoking beneficiary's interest in trust where beneficiary challenged trustees' distribution decisions did not render withdrawal rights illusory because clause did not restrict beneficiary's right to compel trustees to honor withdrawal right).
25. Rev. Rul. 76-360, 1976-2 C.B. 298. Similarly, in *Estate of Stinson v. United States*, 214 F.3d 846 (7th Cir. 2000), the court determined that a gift to corporate shareholders in the form of forgiveness of corporate indebtedness was not eligible for the annual donee exclusion. The court indicated that, when shareholders must liquidate the corporation or declare a dividend to enable enjoyment of the gift, the transfer amounted to an indirect gift to the shareholders of a future interest and, therefore, did not qualify for the exclusion. The court rejected the argument made by taxpayer that the debt forgiveness was an excludable gift of a present interest because it increased the corporation's net worth, as well as the stock value to the shareholders. This same result occurred where a gift was made of an interest in a limited liability company. See *Hackl v. Commissioner,* 118 T.C. 279 (2002), *aff'd*, 335 F.3d 664 (7th Cir. 2003), holding that even though gifts of LLC

units transferred vested ownership interest, gift tax exclusions did not apply since restrictions on withdrawals and distributions, and the lack of present income, precluded substantial present economic benefit being realized to donees. The terms of the company's operating agreement prohibited the donees from withdrawing capital accounts without the company manager's approval and from unilaterally dissolving the company. Further, the company admittedly had no present income to be distributed to the donees and, in any event, the donees' entitlement to income was limited to discretionary distributions. Thus, the economic benefit of the gifts was postponed and did not constitute a present interest as required for the gift tax exclusion. Similarly, see TAM 200212006 where a taxpayer's transfer of publicly traded municipal bonds to a limited partnership constituted indirect gifts of the bonds to children who were limited partners.

26. Rev. Rul. 77-358, 1977-2 C.B. 342.
27. See *Md. Nat'l Bank v. United States*, 609 F.2d 1078 (4th Cir. 1979), where the donor transferred a one-half interest in an unprofitable real estate partnership to a trust for 17 family members. The trust authorized the trustee to hold unproductive property and barred conversion of real estate into stocks, bonds, or other real estate to produce income. The annual exclusion was denied because of the lack of income. *But see Rosen v. Commissioner,* 397 F.2d 245 (4th Cir. 1968), where the gift was of stock in a closely held corporation which had never paid dividends and the exclusion was held to be available. The corporation was a profitable enterprise and was retaining earnings for growth.
28. *See* §2001(b). Note, however, *Estate of Robinson v. Commissioner,* 101 T.C. 499 (1993), where the court determined that the decedent had improperly claimed nine $10,000 annual donee exclusions in a prior year. The court determined that the value of the donor's adjusted taxable gifts was to be adjusted upwards to reflect the improperly claimed gift tax exclusions. The court noted that §2504(c) was inapplicable and, therefore, that the number of annual exclusions to which the decedent was entitled was not a question of valuation.
29. §2503(e). See §529(c)(5), providing for similar treatment for qualified higher education expenses paid under a qualified tuition program (programs sponsored by a state or its agency). Amendments to §529 by the Taxpayer Relief Act of 1997, Pub. L. No. 105-34, §211, changed the treatment of contributions to, and distributions from, qualified tuition programs. Amended §529(c)(2)(A) provides that contributions to such programs do not qualify for §2503(e), but that after August 5, 1997, such contributions are treated as completed gifts of present interests that are eligible for the §2503(b) annual exclusion. Note §529(c)(2), concerning the gift tax treatment of contributions to such a plan, including the right to spread excess contributions over a five-year period for purposes of utilizing the annual donee exclusion. Note that §529(c)(5)(A) specifies that a distribution from a qualified tuition program for qualified higher education expenses will not be treated as a taxable gift. An important (nontax) planning inquiry in this context might concern the cost incurred to the brokerage company or mutual fund manager for creating and maintaining such an account.
30. See Rev. Rul. 82-98, 1982-1 C.B. 141, where the IRS ruled that payments made directly by a donor/father to medical service providers on behalf of his adult son were not subject to the gift tax under §2503(e)(2)(B). If the father had made the payments indirectly by first transferring the funds to the son who then paid the medical service providers, the gift tax would be applicable to the payments. *See* Reg. §25.2503-6(c) *Ex. (4). See also*

Rev. Rul. 82-143, 1982-2 C.B. 220 (tuition payment made directly to foreign educational institution is exempt from gift tax under §2503(e)).

31. Note from TAM 199941013 that this exclusion is available even if the tuition payments are made on a prepaid basis. A condition was that the payments made were not refundable, so the objective could be frustrated if, for example, the student became ineligible to continue at the school. Presumably in those circumstances no charitable deduction would be available for the unutilized tuition amount.
32. *See* §213(d); Staff of J. Comm. on Tax'n, 97th Cong., General Explanation of the Economic Recovery Tax Act of 1981, at 273–274 (1981).
33. §2523(f). Before the Tax Reform Act of 1976, a gift tax marital deduction was allowable to the extent of 50% of the value of property transferred to the spouse. Under the Tax Reform Act of 1976, an unlimited gift tax marital deduction was allowable for the first $100,000 in gifts. No such deduction was available for the next $100,000 of such transfers. For cumulative lifetime transfers in excess of $200,000 to the spouse, a deduction was available to the extent of 50% of the value of the property transferred. The Economic Recovery Tax Act of 1981 (ERTA) removed the quantitative limits on the marital deduction for gift tax purposes and deleted the provisions that imposed restrictions on the use of the marital deduction for gifts of community property.
34. §2523(f)(4) specifies that an election must be made for the gift tax QTIP election. PLR 201025021 indicates that the IRS will not grant extensions to make inter vivos QTIP elections. In this situation the IRS revoked an earlier ruling permitting an extension, noting that the IRS does not have discretion to grant an extension where the time period is expressly dictated by statute.
35. §2523(f)(2). The rules affecting the qualification of a life income interest for both the gift tax marital deduction and estate tax marital deduction are similar and are discussed in Chapter 5, D.3.i.
36. The Revenue Reconciliation Act of 1989, Pub. L. No. 101-239 §7815(d)(2), specifies that this marital deduction provision also applies to nonresident alien donors. This amendment conforms with the Tax and Miscellaneous Revenue Act of 1988 (1988 TAMRA), Pub. L. No. 100-647, provision allowing estates of nonresident aliens an estate tax marital deduction for U.S.-situated property passing to surviving spouses, if such amount would be deductible under §2056. *See* §2106(a)(3). Of course, property situated outside the United States and transferred by a non-resident alien spouse to a U.S. citizen spouse would be beyond the jurisdiction of the U.S. gift tax.
37. §2523(i), added by the 1988 TAMRA, Pub. L No. 100-647, §5033(b). The $100,000 annual exclusion amount for gifts to nonresident alien spouses is adjusted annually for inflation under §2503(b), as cross-referenced. For the inflation-adjusted §2523(i) amounts for the most recent years, see Worksheet 1. Where gifts are made to a spouse who is not a U.S. citizen, the principles of §2515 and §2515A (relating to tenancies by the entirety), as in effect before their repeal by ERTA, apply except for the §2515 election provisions. *See also* Reg. §25.2523(i)-1 through §25.2523(i)-3.
38. §2513.
39. Although the spouses are jointly and severally liable for the gift tax payable on split gifts, one spouse can satisfy the entire gift tax liability without being deemed to make a gift to the other spouse. *See* Reg. §25.2511-1(d). Therefore, the spouse with the larger net worth should consider satisfying the entire gift tax liability (if any) in a split gift situa-

tion. Even if being treated as making a gift to the other spouse, the marital deduction would ordinarily exclude this transfer from the gift tax base.

40. §2001(d).
41. §2001(e). This section applies regardless of the order of death of the spouses. Rev. Rul. 81-85, 1981-1 C.B. 452. Rev. Rul. 82-198, 1982-2 C.B. 206, where, when the non-donor spouse died within three years of the gift, the portion of the gift tax liability was includible in the decedent's gross estate. This was required even though no credit was available against the decedent's estate tax liability because the gift tax liability was considered to be gift tax payable by the donor spouse.
42. *See Estate of Petter v. Commissioner,* 653 F.3d 1012 (9th Cir. 2011); *Estate of Christiansen v. Commissioner,* 586 F.3d 1061 (8th Cir. 2009); *McCord v. Commissioner*, 461 F.3d 614 (5th Cir. 2006); *Wandry v. Commissioner,* T.C. Memo 2012-88, *nonacq.* 2012-46 I.R.B.
43. This specified amount may be, for example, the amount of the donor's available annual donee exclusion(s) plus some part (or all) of the remaining gift tax lifetime exemption amount.
44. §2035(a), as amended by the 1997 Taxpayer Relief Act, Pub. L. No. 105-34, §1310. For a discussion of the prior three-year inclusionary rule and its repeal by ERTA, see 818 T.M., *Section 2035 Transfers* (Bloomberg BNA). Prior to the 1976 Tax Reform Act, gifts made within a three-year period ending on the date of decedent's death were rebuttably presumed to be "in contemplation of death" and were included in a decedent's gross estate to prevent deathbed transfers designed to avoid estate taxes. This law caused considerable litigation concerning the motives of decedents in making gifts within the period shortly before death. As a result, the 1976 Tax Reform Act required the inclusion in a decedent's estate of all gifts made within three years of death without regard to the motives of a decedent. Under the unified transfer tax system adopted in 1976, the inclusion of such gifts in the gross estate had the effect of including in the estate tax base the appreciation of the transferred assets accruing between the time of the gift and the time of death. An exception to these rules existed for transfers of property (other than life insurance) if no gift tax return need be filed concerning the gift.
45. Under ERTA, if the insured transfers by gift the ownership of a life insurance policy within three years of death the proceeds will be includible in the insured's estate under §2035 because the policy would have been includible in the insured's estate under §2042 if the transfer had not been made. This rule does not apply to transfers of a life insurance policy by a noninsured donor within three years of death. If a noninsured decedent owned an insurance policy on the life of another, the policy would be included under §2033, and §2033 is not one of the Code sections mentioned in the statute. The House Committee Report makes a broad statement, however, that "gifts of life insurance" are excepted from the change in §2035. H.R. Rep. No. 97-201, at 187 (1981).
46. §2035(a), as amended by the 1997 Taxpayer Relief Act, Pub. L. No. 105-34, §1310. For example, if the donor made an irrevocable gift to his or her grandchildren and inadvertently retained a §2038 taxable power, he or she could not transfer or release that power within three years of death and avoid estate tax inclusion. See PLR 9509027, where an amendment to a shareholder's agreement did not constitute the retention of a prohibited retained interest for this purpose. Much litigation occurred concerning whether transfers of property from a revocable trust directly to individual donees within three years of the grantor/decedent's death should be includible under §2035(a) and §2038. The IRS refused to characterize the transfers as withdrawals of corpus for the creator's

benefit, followed by direct gifts to third parties. All of these rulings appear to hinge on whether anyone had the power to distribute or direct distribution of the corpus to anyone other than the grantor. *See*, for example, *Estate of Jalkut v. Commissioner*, 96 T.C. 675 (1991), *acq.*, 1991-2 C.B. 1; and *Estate of Frank v. Commissioner*, T.C. Memo 1995-132, where the withdrawal from a revocable trust pursuant to a power of attorney followed by a gift did not trigger the application of §2035. Within three years of the grantor's death his son withdrew funds from a revocable trust under a power of attorney and, subsequently, made gift transfers. The Tax Court treated these arrangements as the grantor's exercise of the power to withdraw assets through his attorney in fact, followed by a gift by the grantor, also through the agency of his attorney in fact. In AOD 1995-006, acquiescing in *Estate of Kisling v. Commissioner*, 32 F.3d 1222 (8th Cir. 1994), *rev'g* T.C. Memo 1993-262, the IRS announced that it would no longer litigate the issue of relinquishment of power to revoke a portion of the trust where the decedent possessed a power to withdraw trust corpus or direct distributions to himself or herself regardless of whether the decedent also had the power to direct distributions to other distributees. In recommending acquiescence in *Kisling*, the Chief Counsel also discussed, without explicitly acquiescing in, the holdings in *Estate of Barton v. Commissioner*, T.C. Memo 1993-583 (where trust instrument permits decedent to invade trust, transfer directly from trust to various beneficiaries is not relinquishment of decedent's retained powers, but rather exercise of decedent's power to invade corpus), and *Estate of McNeely v. United States*, 16 F.3d 303 (8th Cir. 1994) (transfers of marketable securities directly from trust to grantor's descendants is exercise of power to invade and not relinquishment of power to revoke with respect to transferred assets). This problem was solved by the enactment of §2035(e), in the 1997 Taxpayer Relief Act, Pub. L. No. 105-34, §1310(a), which provides that, for purposes of §2035 and §2038, any transfer from any portion of a trust during any period that such portion was treated under §676 as owned by the decedent by reason of a power in the grantor will be treated as a transfer made directly by the decedent. Consequently, an annual donee exclusion gift sourced from the donor's revocable trust would not be included in the gross estate.

47. §2035(c)(1), as amended by the 1997 Taxpayer Relief Act, Pub. L. No. 105-34, §1310. These special rules are discussed elsewhere in this book.
48. §2035(c)(3), as amended by the 1997 Taxpayer Relief Act, Pub. L. No. 105-34, §1310.
49. §2035(b), as amended by the Taxpayer Relief Act of 1997, Pub. L. No. 105-34, §1310.
50. A state gift tax paid on gifts included under the three-year rule is not an asset in the donor's gross estate, however. *Estate of Gamble v. Commissioner*, 69 T.C. 942 (1978), *acq.*, 1981-2 C.B. 1. *Cf.*, Rev. Rul. 75-63, 1975-1 C.B. 294, enunciating the prior position of the IRS to the contrary. That position was revoked in Rev. Rul. 81-302, 1981-2 C.B. 170, when the IRS acquiesced in the *Gamble* decision.
51. This income tax basis step-up treatment is available under §1014. For example, a gift of property with a basis of 10 and a fair market value of 90 on the date of the gift, but worth 100 at the date of death would result in a loss of 90 in tax basis to the donee. The cost of the 90 loss in tax basis step-up would need to be compared to the estate tax incurred on inclusion of the 100 amount. If the asset is a capital asset eligible for a 20% capital gain tax this cost would ordinarily be less than the applicable estate tax (particularly when the property appreciates significantly after the date of any gift). The general §1(h) 20% maximum capital gains tax rate applies to taxable years beginning after 2012. *See* ATRA, Pub. L. No. 112-240, §102(b). Prior to 2013, the maximum capital gains rate was 15%.

See 2010 TRA, Pub. L. No. 111-312, §101(a), §102 (extending application of sunset provisions in EGTRRA, Pub. L. No. 107-16, §901, and JGTRRA, Pub. L. No. 108-27, §303).

52. §2001(b)(1)(B).
53. *Cf.* §2035(b), as amended by the 1997 Taxpayer Relief Act, Pub. L. No. 105-34, §1310.
54. The potential income tax savings from these income deflection arrangements was significantly reduced by income tax rate reductions in the Tax Reform Act of 1986 and subsequent legislation, but income-shifting strategies still remain of importance. Where the income is dividends (subject to a maximum 20% rate under §1(h)(11)), the shifting of such income would not be as beneficial. Section 1(h)(11), the general §1(h) 20% maximum capital gains tax rate, and the §1(i) 39.6% income tax bracket referenced in the Example apply to taxable years beginning after 2012. *See* ATRA, Pub. L. No. 112-240, §101(b), §102(b). Prior to 2013, the maximum capital gains rate under §1(h)(11) was 15%, and the maximum §1(i) income tax rate was 35%. *See* 2010 TRA, Pub. L. No. 111-312, §101(a), §102 (extending application of sunset provisions in EGTRRA, Pub. L. No. 107-16, §901, and JGTRRA, Pub. L. No. 108-27, §303). Previously, the Tax Increase Prevention and Reconciliation Act of 2005 (TIPRA), Pub. L. No. 109-222, §102, had changed the sunset applicable to §1(h)(11) from December 31, 2008, to December 31, 2010.
55. See §1(g) prescribing the "Kiddie Tax." TIPRA, Pub. L. No. 109-222, §510(a), §510(d), increased the §1(g)(2)(A) age threshold from 14 to 18, effective for taxable years beginning after 2005. Under §1(g)(2)(C), as added by TIPRA, Pub. L. No. 109-222, §510(c), the Kiddie Tax does not apply if the child files a joint return for the taxable year. The Small Business and Work Opportunity Tax Act of 2007, Pub. L. No. 110-28, §8241(a), §8241(c), amended §1(g)(2)(A), effective for taxable years beginning after May 25, 2007, to further expand the §1(g) tax to include certain children under the age of 24 (e.g., full-time students). For a complete discussion of the §1(g) tax, see 846 T.M., *Gifts to Minors* (Bloomberg BNA).
56. *See* §151(d)(2).
57. §1015. Also embedded in that donated property is any depreciation recapture potential arising under §1245, §1250, and similar recapture provisions.
58. §1015(d)(6). See Ford & Reed, *The Effect of Gift Taxes on the Basis in Property Received as a Gift*, 71 Tax Notes 527 (1996), noting that the rule for allocating gift tax to the donee's basis is that (1) the numerator of the factor is the appreciation in the gift property and (2) the denominator is the amount of the gift (rather than the fair market value of the property). Consequently, the tax basis adjustment may be understated if the denominator is not reduced by the amount of any annual donee exclusion allowed for the gift.
59. *See* Reg. §1.1015-5. This suggests that a donor should transfer high-tax-basis assets during an earlier year and low-basis assets during a subsequent year. The marginal gift tax rate (and, consequently, the allocation to income tax basis) will be greater in the subsequent year and the appreciation component of these gifts will also be larger.
60. §1015(a); Reg. §1.1015-1(a).
61. §1041(a). Section 1041(e) specifies that this nonrecognition treatment is not applicable where (1) the transfer is into trust and (2) the liabilities attached to the transferred property exceed the total basis for the transferred properties. Section 1041(d) specifies that this nonrecognition rule is not applicable when the transferee spouse is a nonresident alien.

62. §1041(b).
63. §1223(2); Reg. §1.1223-1(b). This holding period tacking is available for loss purposes although a new income tax basis is used for such purposes. See I.T. 3453, 1941-1 C.B. 254, *obsoleted by* Rev. Rul. 69-43, 1969-1 C.B. 310, which held to the contrary.
64. Consequently, upon the transfer of an asset such as inventory (where holding period is irrelevant for income tax purposes) no "tacking" will occur.
65. As earlier noted, this amount may be subsequently adjusted upward by $1,000 increments to reflect inflation adjustments. For the inflation-adjusted amounts for recent years, see Worksheet 1.
66. When the normal capital gains tax rate is 20% this differential may not be significant. The §1(h) 20% maximum capital gains tax rate applies to taxable years beginning after 2012. ATRA, Pub. L. No. 112-240, §102(b). For tax years prior to 2013, the highest §1(h) maximum capital gains rate was 15%. *See* 2010 TRA, Pub. L. No. 111-312, §101(a), §102 (extending sunset provisions in EGTRRA, Pub. L. No. 107-16, §901, and JGTRRA, Pub. L. No. 108-27, §303).
67. In some instances properties such as improved real estate for which tax depreciation is available may actually be increasing in economic value.
68. *See, e.g., Helvering v. Horst*, 311 U.S. 112 (1940).
69. Some mutual fund companies have "tax efficient" funds that seek to achieve the same objective, that is, limitation of currently realized gains for federal income tax purposes.
70. §2511(a), §2512(b); Reg. §25.2511-1(g), §25.2511-1(h), §25.2512-8. *See Stern v. United States*, 436 F.2d 1327 (5th Cir. 1971), where the Fifth Circuit concluded that cash transfers to political campaigns were not gifts because the transfers were "permeated with commercial and economic factors" and motivated by a "desire to promote a slate of candidates that would protect and advance her [the transferor's] personal and property interests." Section 2501(a)(4) specifies that asset transfers to political organizations will not be gifts for gift tax purposes.
71. Reg. §25.2511-1(g)(1). *See Miller v. Commissioner*, T.C. Memo 1996-3, where checks by a mother of $100,000 to each of her sons were treated as constituting gifts, rather than loans, even though each check was identified as being a "loan." The Tax Court concluded that no intent to repay existed from the inception of the transaction.
72. Occasionally, a question arises as to whether the transferor has so parted with dominion and control of the property conveyed so that the ownership change is actually "complete" for federal gift tax purposes. The dominion and control of the property must be irrevocably transferred by delivery to the donee or the donee's agent. See Rev. Rul. 67-396, 1967-2 C.B. 351, addressing the transfer of a check or note, including that a transfer of a promissory note that is unenforceable under state law is not a completed gift; Rev. Rul. 54-135, 1954-2 C.B. 205, and Rev. Rul. 54-555, 1954-2 C.B. 317, with respect to the time of the completion of gift transfers of stock certificates; and Rev. Rul. 76-103, 1976-1 C.B. 293, and Rev. Rul. 77-378, 1977-2 C.B. 347, with respect to completing gifts by transfers into trusts. In Rev. Rul. 96-56, 1996-2 C.B. 161, the IRS stated that, in light of *Estate of Metzger v. Commissioner*, 38 F.3d 118 (4th Cir. 1994), it was modifying Rev. Rul. 67-396. Rev. Rul. 96-56 provides that the delivery of a check to a noncharitable donee will be a completed gift for federal gift tax purposes on the earlier of the date on which the donor parts with dominion and control or the date on which the donee deposits the check. *See also Estate of Rosano v. United States*, 245 F.3d 212 (2d Cir. 2001), and *Estate of Newman v. Commissioner*, 111 T.C. 81 (1998), holding that gifts

by checks not presented and paid before a donor's death were incomplete gifts and were includible in the donor's gross estate. Note that the IRS ruled in PLR 200502014 that a grantor's funding of a trust and the trust distribution committee's transfer of trust property back to the trust grantor would not constitute completed gifts. Only when property was distributed from the trust to other parties would a gift be treated as complete by the trust grantor.

73. *See* 845 T.M., *Gifts* (Bloomberg BNA).
74. *See* Rev. Rul. 84-25, 1984-1 C.B. 191, indicating that a gratuitous transfer of a legally binding promissory note is a gift. *See,* however, *Estate of Dillingham v. Commissioner,* 903 F.2d 760 (10th Cir. 1990), where a gift of checks to donees in year 1 that were cashed in year 2 was completed in the year of cashing and the relation back doctrine was held inapplicable. *But see Metzger v. Commissioner,* 38 F.3d 118 (4th Cir. 1994), where checks were delivered by donor's child, acting under a power of attorney, in December 1985, were deposited by the child in 1985, but were not paid until 1986, the court affirmed the Tax Court position that a "relation back" analysis should be applied. To avoid possible problems in this year-end context the donor (or the donor's agent) should consider the delivery of cash or certified checks prior to year-end.
75. *See* Rev. Rul. 83-180, 1983-2 C.B. 169, where transfers by a donor of specified portions of real property equal in value to the annual gift tax exclusion allowable for the years of the transfers constituted completed gifts each year of the portions transferred. Further, each of the gifts transferred qualified for the annual gift tax exclusion because the donee received the present unrestricted right to immediate use, possession, and enjoyment of an ascertainable proportionate interest in the real property. This ruling distinguished Rev. Rul. 77-299, 1977-2 C.B. 343, where the IRS ruled that the entire property was transferred at the inception of the gift arrangement because no intent existed to enforce a promissory note. The dilemma in transferring only portions of the property is that the property may be appreciating, thereby necessitating future gifts of smaller portions. However, a minority discount valuation argument may be available to reduce the gift amount.
76. *See* the Uniform Transfers to Minors Act, as locally enacted, which has superseded the Uniform Gifts to Minors Act in most jurisdictions.
77. *See* Rev. Rul. 84-105, 1984-2 C.B. 197, where a surviving spouse permitted a marital deduction trust to be underfunded, with certain property intended for that trust, instead, passing to the decedent's son. The property was treated as transferred by a gift made by the surviving spouse to the son.
78. Reg. §25.2511-1(a). See 845 T.M., *Gifts* (Bloomberg BNA).
79. *See Shepherd v. Commissioner,* 115 T.C. 376 (2000), *aff'd,* 283 F.3d 1258 (11th Cir. 2002), where a donor transferred land and bank stock to a general partnership in which the donor held a 50% partnership interest and the donor's two sons each held a 25% partnership interest.
80. See Reg. §1.351-1(b)(1). Similarly, see *Cavallaro v. Commissioner*, T.C. Memo 2014-189, in which parents were held to have made gifts to their sons when the parents and sons merged their separate corporations and the value of the parents' corporation was determined to be grossly undervalued for purposes of distributing shares in the surviving corporation.
81. *See* Rev. Rul. 71-443, 1971-2 C.B. 337, where a donor transferred property to a corporation of which 46% of the stock was owned by his wife and the remaining 54%

of the stock was owned equally by the donor's son and daughter. The IRS, citing Reg. §25.2511-1(h)(1), concluded that the transfers were gifts to the spouse and children to the extent of their proportionate interests, that the gifts were gifts of future interests, and that the transfer benefitting the spouse was not a terminable interest for purposes of determining the availability of the marital deduction. *See also Estate of Stinson v. United States,* 214 F.3d 846 (7th Cir. 2000) (decedent's cancellation of indebtedness owed to decedent by a closely held corporation owned by decedent's five children and two grandchildren constituted a gift of cash to the seven children and grandchildren shareholders of the corporation).

82. *See* Rev. Rul. 78-362, 1978-2 C.B. 248, indicating that a parent made gifts when he made monthly mortgage payments on a mortgage incurred to purchase real estate in a joint and survivorship relationship with his two children. Because any joint tenant could unilaterally sever his or her interest and receive an equal share, two-thirds of the property was owned by the children. Therefore, two-thirds of each mortgage payment constituted a gift.
83. §7872. *See* Prop. Reg. §1.7872-1(a), §1.7872-4(b), §1.7872-8(a). *See also Dickman v. Commissioner,* 465 U.S. 330 (1984). Interest-free loans are taxable gifts to the extent of the value of the use of the money loaned, subject to certain de minimis limitations. *See* §7872(c)(2), §7872(d)(1). See also the discussion in Chapter 7, C.4.
84. See the discussion in Chapter 12, C., on the use of these devices as part of post-death estate planning. The objective, of course, is to avoid any gift tax liabilities by "deflecting" ownership of the disclaimed property to another (often younger generation member).
85. *See* Reg. §25.2512-8; *Ballard v. Commissioner,* 854 F.2d 185 (7th Cir. 1988) (sale of real property to children for less than fair market value constituted bargain sale and gift).
86. Reg. §25.2511-1(c) provides that all transactions whereby property or property rights or interests are gratuitously passed or conferred upon another, regardless of the means or device employed, constitute gifts subject to tax. *See* Rev. Rul. 77-372, 1977-2 C.B. 344, where the IRS ruled that a voluntary cash transfer from one estate beneficiary to another estate beneficiary to equalize the properties received from the estate constituted a gift by the transferor beneficiary.
87. *Hogle v. Commissioner,* 165 F.2d 352 (10th Cir. 1947). *See also Estate of Blass v. Commissioner,* 11 T.C.M. 622 (1952), holding that gift treatment was not applicable to a taxpayer who brought business opportunities to the attention of family trusts and provided services enabling the trusts to purchase property and to sell that property at a profit.
88. This is a matter governed by state law. Many states have adopted some form of the Uniform Statutory Form Power of Attorney Act (1988). This form enumerates many powers included within the capability of the attorney-in-fact, but the making of gifts is not so included. To grant such authority the person appointing the attorney-in-fact must ordinarily provide special instructions to identify that power, unless state law permits such a power.
89. The IRS has asserted that gifts made pursuant to a durable power of attorney are to be treated as revocable transfers for purposes of §2038. *See Estate of Casey v. Commissioner,* 948 F.2d 895 (4th Cir. 1991), *rev'g* T.C. Memo 1989-511 (unrestricted power to make gifts is not found in durable power of attorney that does not expressly grant such power). *Cf. Estate of Ridenour v. Commissioner,* 36 F.3d 332 (4th Cir. 1994), *aff'g* T.C. Memo 1993-41 (gifts made by attorney-in-fact under durable power of attorney not voidable in Virginia pursuant to Va. Code Ann. §11-9.5(A) (Supp. 1992), providing that if a

power of attorney authorizes attorney-in-fact to perform any act that principal might or could do, or evidences principal's intent to give attorney-in-fact full power to handle principal's affairs or deal with principal's property, attorney-in-fact may make gifts in any amount of any of principal's property to any individuals or to organizations described in §170(c) and §2522(a) in accordance with principal's personal history of making or joining in making of lifetime gifts). *See also* TAM 199944005, TAM 9736004, TAM 9731003.

90. See 846 T.M., *Gifts to Minors* (Bloomberg BNA).
91. In some instances children under the age of legal capacity, but sufficiently aware of some financial affairs to understand their import, are permitted to have checking and savings accounts in their own capacity. For example, some states permit bank checking accounts at age 14. Substantial caution is necessary in this area to avoid local law impediments. Further, this arrangement would ordinarily be avoided when larger gifts are planned.
92. This also implies that the Social Security number of the child, not the guardian, must be provided in response to requests from dividend payors and others seeking information concerning payee tax identification.
93. Careful attention must be paid to this Uniform Act as locally enacted because significant variances may have been included when enacted by the state legislature.
94. For example, at age 18 in Texas. *See* Tex. Civ. Prac. & Rem. Code §129.001, §129.002.
95. The Uniform Gifts to Minors Act (UGMA) encompasses gifts of securities, money, life insurance policies, or annuity contracts. In some jurisdictions, UGMA transfers may also be made of other properties such as real property and mineral interests. The Uniform Transfers to Minors Act provides much broader applicability concerning the types of (1) properties and (2) transfers that are within the scope of these rules.
96. §2503(c); Rev. Rul. 56-86, 1956-1 C.B. 449, Rev. Rul. 59-357, 1959-2 C.B. 212. See the discussion in Chapter 6, D.1.b., of §2503(c) and its use in the trust context.
97. This income should be reported on an individual income tax return (Form 1040) filed on behalf of the child, rather than on a fiduciary income tax return. The custodian should not report the income of the custodianship as personally belonging to the custodian. For the custodian to report such income would mean that the income has not been effectively shifted to the minor who, presumably, has a lower marginal income tax rate (absent the application of the "Kiddie Tax" provision under §1(g)).
98. Rev. Rul. 56-484, 1956-2 C.B. 23, provides that custodianship income is taxable to the parent under §61, and Reg. §1.662(a)-4 requires similar treatment of that income if used for support pursuant to will or trust provisions. See Rev. Rul. 59-357, 1959-2 C.B. 212, which indicates, that "[i]ncome derived from property so transferred which is used in the discharge or satisfaction, in whole or in part, of a legal obligation of any person to support or maintain a minor is taxable to such person to the extent so used, but is otherwise taxable to the minor donee."
99. The scope of the support obligation under applicable state law may vary quite considerable from one state to another and, therefore, the estate planner must determine both (1) which state law applies and (2) the scope of the concept of support under the applicable rules.
100. Rev. Rul. 57-366, 1957-2 C.B. 618, Rev. Rul. 59-357, 1959-2 C.B. 212; *Estate of Varian v. Commissioner,* 47 T.C. 34 (1966), *aff'd,* 396 F.2d 753 (9th Cir. 1968); *Estate of Chrysler v. Commissioner,* 44 T.C. 55 (1965), *rev'd on other grounds,* 361 F.2d 508 (2d Cir. 1966). *Cf. Stuit v. Commissioner,* 452 F.2d 190 (7th Cir. 1971).

101. Rev. Rul. 70-348, 1970-2 C.B. 193.
102. Where parents make reciprocal gifts for minor children with each parent naming the other as the custodian of that transferor's donated property, the value of the custodial property held by the decedent spouse at the time of his or her death would be includible in the gross estate under §2036 and §2038. *See Exch. Bank & Trust Co. of Fla. v. United States,* 694 F.2d 1261 (Fed. Cir. 1982), *aff'g* 82-1 USTC ¶13,444 (Ct. Cl. 1981) (applying "reciprocal trust doctrine" in this context).
103. The custodial property would then be includible for estate tax purposes only in the gross estate of the minor donee (i.e., the economic owner of the property). *See* Rev. Rul. 59-357, 1959-2 C.B. 212. An election by the wife under §2513 to treat one-half of a transfer made by her husband as a transfer made by her does not cause any part of the property to be included in the wife-custodian's estate. Rev. Rul. 74-556, 1974-2 C.B. 202.
104. See Rev. Rul. 59-357, 1959-2 C.B. 212, which states that: "In all other circumstances [other than the donor appointing himself custodian and dying in that capacity] custodial property is includible only in the gross estate of the donee."
105. *See* Reg. §20.2041-1(c).
106. The $10,000 exclusion is adjusted for inflation. For the inflation-adjusted §2503(b) amounts for the most recent years, see Worksheet 1. See Chapter 4, A.3.b.(1).
107. In addition to the availability of the annual donee exclusion, the income accumulated for a beneficiary under 21 years (if through a trust) will be exempt from the application of the throwback rules. See §665(b) providing an exception for amounts accumulated before a trust beneficiary reaches age 21. Note that the throwback rules do not apply to distributions from domestic trusts in years beginning after August 5, 1997, making §665(b) essentially irrelevant; the exception in §665(b) for accumulations during minority was not available by its terms to foreign or multiple trusts, which are the only trusts subject to the throwback rules after the enactment of §665(c) by the Taxpayer Relief Act of 1997, Pub. L. No. 105-34, §507(a)(1).
108. Section 2503(c) is also pertinent in permitting transfers under the Uniform Transfers to Minors Act to qualify for the annual donee exclusion.
109. Reg. §25.2503-4(b)(1).
110. Reg. §25.2503-4(b).
111. In Rev. Rul. 67-270, 1967-2 C.B. 349, the IRS ruled that a trustee's discretionary power to use principal and income for a donee's "support, care, education, comfort, and welfare" during his minority satisfied the requirement of §2503(c) that the transferred property be expendable for the benefit of the donee before he attains age 21. The ruling indicated that the trustee's ability to distribute for purposes such as "welfare," "happiness," or "convenience," which would have no objective limitation, would be the equivalent of the term "benefit" as used in §2503(c) in determining that no substantial restriction exists. In Rev. Rul. 69-345, 1969-1 C.B. 226, the discretionary power of the trustee to use property during a beneficiary's minority was subject to the limitation that, in determining whether any need existed, the trustee had to consider other resources available to the beneficiary and other payments made to him or for his benefit. The beneficiary's parents had sources of income more than sufficient to meet their legal obligation of support and the beneficiary held substantial property in his own name. The IRS ruled that the annual donee exclusion was not allowable because the trust instrument (and the surrounding circumstances) evidenced that the trustee realistically would not be authorized to expend

any portion of the trust for the care, support, or education of the minor beneficiary. In *Williams v. United States,* 378 F.2d 693 (Ct. Cl. 1967), the court held a trust provision authorizing distributions only when the trustee finds a necessity for such distributions will still qualify under §2503(c), rejecting the IRS's contention that such a requirement of "necessity" constituted a substantial restriction on the trustee's discretion. In *Duncan v. United States,* 368 F.2d 98 (5th Cir. 1966), the court held that discretion of the trustee to apply "available" funds for the payment of insurance premiums did not foreclose the availability of the annual donee exclusion under §2503(c). The language of a "super support" trust has been held not to create a substantial restriction. This type of trust is drafted with a view toward avoiding application of §677(a), §677(b), and §678(c) by providing that the trust income or principal shall not be distributed so as to discharge a legal obligation of the settlor or a nongrantor trustee. *See Upjohn v. United States,* 72–2 USTC ¶12,888 (W.D. Mich. 1972).

112. Reg. §25.2503-3(c) *Ex. (3).*
113. *See Herr v. Commissioner,* 303 F.2d 780 (3d Cir. 1962); *Weller v. Commissioner,* 38 T.C. 790 (1962), *acq.*, 1968-2 C.B. 3; *Rollman v. United States,* 342 F.2d 62 (Ct. Cl. 1965).
114. Rev. Rul. 68-670, 1968-2 C.B. 413.
115. See *Estate of Levine v. Commissioner,* 63 T.C. 136 (1974), *rev'd and rem'd,* 526 F.2d 717 (2d Cir. 1975), where the pre-age 21 income transfer did not have value equal to the annual donee exclusion amount and the taxpayer was unsuccessful in linking the pre-21 and post-21 income interests for purposes of the annual donee exclusion. If a transfer of property is made in trust with income required to be paid annually to a minor beneficiary and corpus is to be distributed to him or her upon his or her attaining age 25, such transfer is a gift of a present interest of the right to the income, but is a gift of a future interest of the right to corpus. Reg. §25.2503-4(c). Local law problems might arise, however, with respect to any direct distribution to the minor. Such a problem might be solved by transferring the property to the parent as custodian for the minor, if so permitted under local law, including the applicable provisions of the trust instrument.
116. But see *Berzon v. Commissioner,* 534 F.2d 528 (2d Cir. 1976), where annual donee exclusions claimed under §2503(b) were denied because trust income interests could not be valued. Stock in a closely held corporation was transferred to a trust with trust income distributable quarterly to adult beneficiaries. The interests could not be valued because: (1) at the time the gifts were made the closely held corporation was not financially able to pay dividends in the foreseeable future, and (2) restrictions placed on the disposition of stock prevented the trustees from selling the stock and replacing it with income-producing assets. *See also* Rev. Rul. 76-360, 1976-2 C.B. 298.
117. §2503(c)(2)(A).
118. Reg. §25.2503-4(b)(2). See PLR 8521089, where the IRS ruled that transfers to trusts formed for the benefit of minors are gifts of present interests even though the donees may delay the distribution of the trust assets until age 30.
119. In *Heidrich v. Commissioner,* 55 T.C. 746 (1971), *acq.,* 1974-2 C.B. 3, each donee, after attaining the age of 21, had the continuing right to immediate possession of the trust property. At any time after attaining age 21, each donee could make a simple written demand which, upon receipt by the trustee, would require both the termination of the trust and the delivery of the trust property to the donee. The Tax Court held that the §2503(c)(2)(A) requirement was satisfied because the trust funds would pass to the donee at the time the right to make the written demand occurred. The IRS argued that

this situation fit the facts of Rev. Rul. 60-218, 1960-1 C.B. 378, where the IRS ruled that a trust would not satisfy the requirements of §2053(c) if, upon the donee's attaining age 21, the trust agreement provided alternatively that: (1) the donee might compel immediate distribution of the trust; (2) the donee might elect to extend the duration of the trust so that he or she would receive a distribution of one-third of the trust upon attaining 25, one-third upon attaining 29, and the balance upon attaining 33; or (3) if the donee failed to make the election, the trust would continue upon its own terms. The requirement of a "positive act" was deemed fatal to the categorization of the transfer as being of a present interest. Rev. Rul. 60-218 was revoked, however, by Rev. Rul. 74-43, 1974-1 C.B. 285.

120. Rev. Rul. 74-43 states that "a gift to a minor in trust, with the provision that the beneficiary has, upon reaching age 21, either (1) a continuing right to compel immediate distribution of the trust corpus by giving written notice to the trustee, or to permit the trust to continue by its own terms, or (2) a right during a limited period to compel immediate distribution of the trust corpus by given [sic] written notice to the trustee which if not exercised will permit the trust to continue by its own terms, will not be considered to be the gift of a future interest as the gift satisfies the requirements of §2503(c) of the Code. . . ." Similarly, see PLR 8817037.
121. If the income interest is of sufficient value to absorb the annual exclusion, the instrument need not require that the corpus be distributed at age 21. The gift of the corpus, which vests beyond age 21, is a gift of a future interest and, therefore, not eligible for the annual donee exclusion.
122. Section 2041, the power of appointment provision, may also be a problem if the trust was created by another person but the parent is the trustee for the child beneficiary.
123. ATRA, Pub. L. No. 112-240, §102(b). Prior to 2013, the maximum capital gains rate under §1(h) was 15%. *See* 2010 TRA, Pub. L. No. 111-312, §101(a), §102 (extending application of §1(h) 15% capital gains tax rate to taxable years beginning before 2013 by amending sunset provisions in EGTRRA, Pub. L. No. 107-16, §901, and JGTRRA, Pub. L. No. 108-27, §303).
124. See Rev. Rul. 75-72, 1975-1 C.B. 310, indicating that "the gift tax attributable to the transfer of property. . . may be deducted from the value of that property in arriving at the amount of gift where it is shown, expressly or by implication from the circumstances surrounding the transfer, that the donor attached payment by the donee (or out of the transferred property) as a condition of the transfer." In that ruling, the IRS noted Reg. §25.2511-1(e), which provides that, if a donor transfers by gift less than his or her entire interest in property, the gift tax applies to the interest transferred. Rev. Rul. 75-72 superseded Rev. Rul. 71-232, 1971-1 C.B. 275, to the same effect. Before Rev. Rul. 71-232, litigation occasionally occurred over valuation, based on a dispute as to whether the donee had actually assumed a gift tax obligation. In *Harrison v. Commissioner*, 17 T.C. 1350 (1952), *acq.*, 1952-2 C.B. 2, the Tax Court held that, where the donee by agreement obligates himself or herself to pay the gift tax attributable to the transfer, the amount of the gift is reduced by the tax attributable thereto. Similarly, see Rev. Rul. 81-223, 1981-2 C.B. 189, indicating that the gift tax liability assumed by the donee may be deducted from the value of transferred property if the payment of the tax by the donee is a condition of the transfer. The IRS affirmed the applicability of this concept in several situations involving a surviving spouse's transfer of a QTIP interest. *See* PLR 200319002, PLR 200223047. Note PLR 201118007, where IRS ruled that net gift

treatment of a transfer under §2519 is implicit under §2207A(b). Similarly, Rev. Rul. 80-111, 1980-1 C.B. 208, indicated that the value of a gift may be reduced by a state gift tax assumed by the donee. See, however, *Ripley v. Commissioner,* 105 T.C. 358 (1995), *rev'd on other grounds,* 103 F.2d 332 (4th Cir. 1996), rejecting taxpayer's argument that a gift tax lien (under §6324(b)) was a sufficient encumbrance that reduces the value of gifts in donees' hands because the donees were statutorily liable as transferees. Similarly, see *Estate of Armstrong v. United States,* 277 F.3d 490 (4th Cir. 2002).

125. *See* Rev. Rul. 75-72, 1975-1 C.B. 310. See also 845 T.M., *Gifts* (Bloomberg BNA). In making this determination the donor must apply all of his or her previously unused unified credit in determining the amount of tax. *See* Rev. Rul. 79-398, 1979-2 C.B. 338, as explained by Rev. Rul. 84-11, 1984-1 C.B. 201.
126. *Estate of Sachs v. Commissioner,* 856 F.2d 1158 (8th Cir. 1988).
127. The Supreme Court, in *Diedrich v. Commissioner,* 457 U.S. 191 (1982), held that the donor is required to recognize income to the extent that the tax paid by the donee exceeds the donor's basis in the transferred property. The Tax Reform Act of 1984, Pub. L. No. 98-369, §1026, provided that *Diedrich* is not retroactively applicable by specifying that gift tax paid for pre–March 4, 1981, gifts did not result in taxable income to the donor.
128. Note that, unlike in the situation involving a bargain sale to charity (§1011(b)), the tax basis is not proportionately allocated in the net gift situation between (1) the gift portion and (2) the deemed sale portion.
129. §1015(d)(6); Reg. §1.1015-5. The basis increase could be to no more than fair market value of the gift property at the time of the property transfer.
130. Reg. §1.1015-4(a).
131. *See* §1223(2). See *Citizens Nat'l Bank of Waco v. United States,* 417 F.2d 675 (5th Cir. 1969), which found Reg. §1.1015-4 invalid to the extent it may be interpreted to prevent tacking of holding periods in a part sale–part gift to a trust.
132. §677(a)(1); Reg. §1.677(a)-1(d). In *Estate of Sheaffer v. Commissioner,* 37 T.C. 99 (1961), *aff'd,* 313 F.2d 738 (8th Cir. 1963), *cert. denied,* 375 U.S. 818 (1963), the trust income was used to pay directly the gift tax liability and the Tax Court held that income so used was taxable to the settlor because that income discharged his legal obligation. *See also* Rev. Rul. 57-564, 1957-2 C.B. 328; *Krause v. Commissioner,* 57 T.C. 890 (1972), *aff'd,* 497 F.2d 1109 (6th Cir. 1974).
133. See *Estate of Morgan v. Commissioner,* 37 T.C. 981 (1962), *aff'd,* 316 F.2d 238 (6th Cir. 1963), *cert. denied,* 375 U.S. 825 (1963), where the trustee secured a loan to pay the gift tax, paid the gift tax, and used subsequent trust income to repay the loan. The trust income used to repay the loan was not deemed taxable to the donor as a discharge of his legal obligation (because the donor was no longer treated as the grantor of the trust).
134. *See* §677.
135. *See Steinberg v. Commissioner*, 141 T.C. 258 (2013) (noting that determination of this amount requires actuarial calculation and may constitute consideration in money or money's worth in certain circumstances). *See also Steinberg v. Commissioner*, 145 T.C. No. 7 (2015) (holding, after trial on §2035(b) issue, that assumption of liability by donees was sufficient detriment to donees and benefit to donor that willing buyer would require discount in value to account for it).
136. *See* §1(g). The §1(i) 39.6% maximum income tax rate cited in the Example applies to taxable years beginning after 2012. ATRA, Pub. L. No. 112-240, §101(b). Prior

to 2013, the maximum §1(i) income tax rate was 35%. *See* 2010 TRA, Pub. L. No. 111-312, §101(a), §102 (extending application of sunset provisions in EGTRRA, Pub. L. No. 107-16, §901, and JGTRRA, Pub. L. No. 108-27, §303).

137. Trusts created to benefit the grantor (so-called "protective trusts") are not discussed in this book because the objective of such arrangements, although to conserve property, including possibly from the grantor's creditors, is other than "estate planning" (from the estate tax and income tax perspective). Under §2036 the retained income right would cause gross estate inclusion.

138. Cf., however, Rev. Rul. 76-103, 1976-1 C.B. 293, and Rev. Rul. 77-378, 1977-2 C.B. 347, where the grantor provided that the nongrantor trustee had discretion to distribute trust property to the grantor. In the first revenue ruling the transfer was not complete for federal gift tax purposes because, under local law, the grantor's creditors could attach this property. In the second ruling, the creditors did not have this power and the gift was deemed complete for gift tax purposes because any exercise by the trustee to distribute income to the grantor was entirely discretionary.

139. *See* 850 T.M., *Generation-Skipping Transfer Tax* (Bloomberg BNA), concerning the possible applicability of the generation-skipping transfer tax. *See* Chapter 4, A.1., and Chapter 8, regarding the §2631 GST exemption amount. See §2652(a)(2) permitting gift-splitting for generation-skipping tax purposes if gift splitting is elected (under §2513) for gift tax purposes.

140. *See* §674(a). Section 674(b), §674(c), and §674(d), as exceptions to the general rule requiring income inclusion to the trust grantor, permit certain powers to be held by the grantor or others. These exceptions to grantor trust treatment are available on the basis of (1) the type of power retained, and (2) the person who retains this power. The widest discretionary income and corpus distribution powers are permitted to an independent trustee and only the most restricted powers are allowed to the grantor and his or her spouse (*see* §674(b)). *See* 819 T.M., *Grantor Trusts: Income Taxation Under Subpart E* (Bloomberg BNA), for additional discussion concerning the retained powers that will cause a trust to be treated as a grantor trust and those that are permitted under the various exceptions.

141. *See* §675.

142. *See* §676.

143. *See* §677(a)(2).

144. *See* §677(b).

145. *See* §2036(a)(1), §2036(a)(2), §2037, §2038.

146. Under §678, income ownership treatment may also be accorded to a nongrantor of a trust.

147. If the trust is a grantor trust, it is not required (under §644(a)) to adopt a calendar year for any tax reporting purposes because it does not really exist as a taxable entity for federal income tax purposes. Rev. Rul. 90-55, 1990-2 C.B. 161 (prior to the 1997 Taxpayer Relief Act, §644 was designated as §645).

148. Section 672 provides various definitions and rules.

149. §673(a). This 5% exception has little practical significance because only trusts where the reversionary interest is postponed for at least 30 years will qualify under this rule. The precise period will depend on interest rate assumptions as of the time of the creation of the trust, and during periods of low interest rates that period will be even longer. Prior to the Tax Reform Act of 1986, a "short-term trust" was often used to enable the grantor

to shift income to a trust beneficiary while retaining the right to recover the trust corpus at the end of a minimum allowable trust term. *See* former §673. Such a short-term trust (also known as a "Clifford Trust") was most advantageously used to shift investment income subject to a high income tax bracket in the parent's hands to a dependent child having a lower marginal income tax rate. The short-term trust needed to have a trust term of at least 10 years, subject to several exceptions. This 10-year trust opportunity was eliminated by the 1986 Act when the rule allowing only a less than 5% reversionary interest was enacted. See Rev. Rul. 87-127, 1987-2 C.B. 156, where income of a trust established under a pre-need funeral contract that would fulfill a buyer's legal obligation to pay for his funeral was held taxable to the buyer under §673(a), because the buyer had a reversionary interest in the trust. A special rule applicable to a "qualified funeral trust" was subsequently adopted to protect these trusts from the grantor trust rules. *See* §685(b)(6); Notice 98-66, 1998-2 C.B. 810.

150. That is, whether, for grantor trust tax purposes, the value of the reversionary interest is 5% or greater. Under the prior 10-year-term grantor trust provisions, it was particularly important that the transfer of the corpus into trust formally be completed under local property law before the 10-year period began. See *Bibby v. Commissioner*, 44 T.C. 638 (1965), where the completion of transfers of stock to a trust was delayed, with the property actually being held by the trust for less than a 10-year period. This rule is similarly relevant in determining the specific time that transfers into trust are completed for purposes of measuring when the gift tax becomes applicable.
151. §673(c).
152. §673(b).
153. §674(a).
154. §674(b)(5). See *Carson v. Commissioner*, 92 T.C. 1134 (1989), where parents who created a trust for their children were taxable as trust owners under §674(a) because the wife, as a trustee and nonadverse person to the husband, had the power to sprinkle income unequally between the beneficiaries.
155. *See* §674(b)(6). The power to accumulate or pay income amounts to a beneficiary is permitted so long as accumulated income will ultimately be payable (1) to the beneficiary (or his or her estate or appointees) or (2) on termination of the trust to the current income beneficiaries in shares that have been irrevocably specified in the trust instrument. This enables the grantor to indirectly shift income to takers in default of the exercise of a power of appointment although not being treated as the owner of the trust income.
156. §674(d).
157. *See* §674(c)(1), §674(c)(2). If the grantor retained the power to replace the independent trustee with himself or herself, these powers would be imputed to the grantor for purposes of measuring existence of grantor trust status.
158. §675. These are the types of powers some of which are retained when the objective is to assure that the grantor trust is "defective" for federal income tax purposes (i.e., that the trust will be categorized as a grantor trust and not as a true trust for income tax purposes).
159. §675(1). An exception is available where a trustee other than the grantor is authorized under a general lending power to make loans to any person without regard to interest or security.
160. §675(2).

161. §675(3). See Rev. Rul. 86-82, 1986-1 C.B. 253, where the IRS ruled that borrowing from a trust and repaying within the same calendar year caused the grantor to be treated as the owner of the trust under §675(3). This limitation does not apply to a loan providing for adequate interest and adequate security if the loan is made by a trustee other than the grantor and other than a related or subordinate trustee subservient to the grantor. Borrowing by the grantor's spouse is also a prohibited administrative power.
162. §675(4). Powers exercised by a trustee are presumed to be exercisable in a fiduciary capacity. Reg. §1.675-1(b)(4).
163. Reg. §1.671-1(c).
164. *Id.* For example, a person who assigns his or her right to future income under an employment contract to a nongrantor trust will not avoid income tax inclusion of that income. See Rev. Rul. 67-118, 1967-1 C.B. 163, where the IRS indicated that an overriding royalty created out of a 50-year minerals lease (as contrasted with a production payment) was not an assignment of income to a then-permissible short-term irrevocable trust.
165. See the general discussion of the income taxation of trusts in Chapter 5, B.5. Income can be distributed currently or accumulated within the trust for distribution to one or more beneficiaries. Note, however, the discussion above on §674 and powers exercisable by the grantor over the distribution of income (or corpus).
166. Planning aspects in response to such rules are more fully outlined as part of the analysis of testamentary trusts.
167. Note in this context the possible applicability of the special Chapter 14 gift tax valuation rules. The amount of a taxable gift arising from a transfer in trust subject to §2702 is the total value of the transferred property less the value of any interest retained by the transferor.
168. Reg. §25.2511-2.
169. For example, if more than a 5% reversionary interest is retained but a significant trust income interest is transferred, a gift of a property interest will have been completed for gift tax purposes, but the §673(a) non-reversionary interest requirement necessary to shift the income from the grantor for income tax purposes will not have been satisfied.
170. *See* §2503(b).
171. See the discussion of demand or *Crummey* trusts in Chapter 6, D.3.g, and also the discussion of the five-and-five power in Chapter 5, E.4.a.(4).
172. *See* §2001, §2502.
173. These provisions are examined in the planning context in Chapter 6, D.3.h.
174. Alternatively, he or she might have retained such rights (1) for any period not ascertainable without reference to his or her death or (2) for any period that does not in fact end before his or her death. For an in-depth analysis of §2036, see 50 T.M., *Incomplete Lifetime Transfers: Retained Powers Under Sections 2036(a)(2) and 2038* (Bloomberg BNA), and 52 T.M., *Incomplete Lifetime Transfers: Retained Beneficial Interests Under Sections 2036(a)(1) and 2037* (Bloomberg BNA).
175. §2036(a)(1). See, for example, *Estate of Sullivan v. Commissioner*, T.C. Memo 1993-531, holding, consistent with Reg. §20.2036-1(b)(2), that transferred property will be included in a donor's estate if the property is used to discharge the donor's legal obligation.
176. §2036(a)(2). In Notice 2008-63, 2008-2 C.B. 261, the IRS issued a proposed revenue ruling that would provide guidance on the income, estate, gift, and generation-skipping transfer tax consequences when a family creates a private trust company to

serve as trustee of trusts with family members as grantors and/or beneficiaries. In Situation 1 of the Notice, a family formed a private trust company in a state with a private trust company statute. In Situation 2, the family formed the private trust company in a state without such a governing statute (but the family included in the private trust company's governing documents many provisions similar to those in the state statute in Situation 1). In each situation, the private trust company became the successor trustee of various irrevocable trusts for family members. As trustee, the private trust company has discretionary authority to distribute income and/or principal to the trust beneficiaries. The grantor and, after the grantor's death, the primary beneficiary may name a successor trustee other than himself or herself if the current trustee ceases to serve. The proposed revenue ruling would rule that, in Situation 1, neither the appointment of the private trust company nor the service of the company as trustee would alone cause inclusion of the trust assets in a grantor's estate under §2036(a) and §2038(a) because no family member, either alone or with any other person, has a §2036(a) or §2038(a) right or power regarding a trust solely because of the private trust company's service as trustee or the family member's ownership of, or relationship with, the company. The IRS also noted that no family member may insert himself or herself into a position holding such a power. The proposed revenue ruling also would rule favorably on the §2036(a) and §2038(a) consequences in Situation 2 because no family member currently holds a §2036(a) or §2038(a) right or power. The IRS further concluded that a family member will not be able to obtain such a right or power because of the amendment committee and its governing provisions. The IRS will not issue a ruling until guidance is issued on the question of whether §2036 and §2038 apply to the corpus of a trust if the trustee is a private trust company owned, partially or entirely, by members of the grantor's family. Rev. Proc. 2015-3, 2015-1 I.R.B. 129, §5.01(17), §5.01(18).

177. The reciprocal trust doctrine was applied in *United States v. Estate of Grace*, 395 U.S. 316 (1969), to include in the gross estate those transfers by donors that leave the donor in the same economic position before and after the transfer. In *Grace*, the husband transferred property to a trust of which the wife was a life beneficiary and the wife transferred property to a trust of which the husband was a life beneficiary. The trusts had essentially the same dispositive terms except for the life interests. Application of the reciprocal trust doctrine caused the trust to be included in the estate of the donor by reason of §2036.
178. See PLR 200426008, where the IRS, relying on *Estate of Levy v. Commissioner*, T.C. Memo 1983-453, concluded that dispositive provisions were sufficiently different to avoid application of the reciprocal trust doctrine.
179. §2037(a). For an in-depth analysis of §2037, see 52 T.M., *Incomplete Lifetime Transfers: Retained Beneficial Interests Under Sections 2036(a)(1) and 2037* (Bloomberg BNA).
180. Section 2037(b) provides that, for purposes of §2037, the term "reversionary interest" includes a possibility that property transferred by the decedent (1) may return to him or her or his or her estate, or (2) may be subject to a power of disposition by him or her. Such term does not include a possibility that the income alone from such property may return to him or her or become subject to a power of disposition by him or her.
181. Section 2037(b) and Reg. §20.2037-1(c)(3) provide that the value of the decedent's reversionary interest is computed as of the moment immediately before his or her death, without regard to the fact of the decedent's death, and in accordance with recognized valuation principles.

182. See Rev. Rul. 2008-22, 2008-16 I.R.B. 796, ruling that, when the grantor has a power to substitute property held in trust and that power is held in a nonfiduciary capacity, the trust property will not be includible in the grantor's gross estate under §2036 or §2038 if the trustee has a fiduciary obligation to ensure that the grantor complies with the trust terms.
183. For an in-depth analysis of §2038, see 50 T.M., *Incomplete Lifetime Transfers: Retained Powers Under Sections 2036(a)(2) and 2038* (Bloomberg BNA).
184. *See Crummey v. Commissioner*, 397 F.2d 82 (9th Cir. 1968).
185. See Chapter 4, A.3.b.(1).
186. In Rev. Rul. 85-24, 1985-1 C.B. 329, the IRS ruled, in a reciprocal trust situation involving *Crummey* power trusts, that withdrawal powers created under these trusts were complementary and, therefore, based on adequate consideration. Consequently, multiple gift tax exclusions were not available. The §2503(b) annual exclusion was allowed, however, for transfers to trust beneficiaries who, other than for their withdrawal right, have only a contingent interest in the trust. *See Estate of Cristofani v. Commissioner*, 97 T.C. 74 (1991), *acq. in result only*, 1992-1 C.B. 1; AOD 1996-10, 1996-2 C.B. 1.
187. Reg. §25.2503-3(b).
188. *See* Rev. Rul. 73-405, 1973-2 C.B. 321.
189. *See Halsted v. Commissioner*, 28 T.C. 1069 (1957), *acq.*, 1958-2 C.B. 5.
190. Rev. Rul. 59-91, 1959-1 C.B. 207.
191. 1973-2 C.B. 321.
192. *Id.*
193. In Rev. Rul. 80-261, 1980-2 C.B. 279, the IRS indicated that a transfer of a right to demand and receive at least a pro-rata portion of trust corpus conveyed to several donees is a gift of a present interest to the extent of each donee's pro-rata portion and, consequently, the annual donee exclusion is available. Numerous private letter rulings were issued recognizing the existence of *Crummey* powers in specific trust situations.
194. See TAM 200341002, where the National Office advised that substantial impediments caused withdrawal rights not to actually exist.
195. In Rev. Rul. 81-7, 1981-1 C.B. 474, the IRS required that an adult beneficiary of a *Crummey* trust must be informed of the right to a trust distribution and found that three days was not a sufficient period during which such right could be exercised. Although the sufficiency of the withdrawal period was not at issue in *Estate of Cristofani v. Commissioner*, 97 T.C. 74 (1991), *acq. in result only*, 1992-1 C.B. 1, AOD 1996-10, 1996-2 C.B. 1, the IRS tacitly approved a 15-day period by not litigating this issue. See TAM 9628004, where the National Office advised that providing four or fewer days to exercise a withdrawal right in the year the trust was created showed that donor did not intend at creation to make bona fide gifts of present interests and allowance of adequate time to exercise powers in later years did not change that intent; exclusions were denied for all years.
196. *See Estate of Cristofani v. Commissioner*, 97 T.C. 74 (1991), *acq. in result only*, 1992-1 C.B. 1 (where annual donee exclusions were available for two children who were primary trust beneficiaries and five minor grandchildren who were contingent remainder beneficiaries). See also AOD 1992-09 where the Chief Counsel's Office recommended that the gift tax benefit of *Crummey* powers to any beneficiaries with interests more remote than current income or vested remainders would undermine significantly the unified system of estate and gift taxation. In AOD 1996-10, 1996-2 C.B. 1, the Chief

Counsel's Office again recommended acquiescence in result only in *Cristofani*, reiterating that the IRS would continue to litigate cases whose facts indicate that the substance of the transfers was merely to obtain annual exclusions and that no bona fide gift of a present interest was intended. Further, in TAM 9628004, the National Office advised denial of annual exclusions for beneficiaries who had vested remainders and discretionary income interests as well as for beneficiaries who had only naked withdrawal powers. The donor had created three trusts, granting 19 *Crummey* powers to children, grandchildren, great-grandchildren, and various spouses. The National Office advised that the donor did not intend to make bona fide gifts of present interests to any of the beneficiaries, implying that the non-exercise of the withdrawal rights, by itself, indicated that there was a prearranged understanding that the beneficiaries would not exercise the rights.

197. See Rev. Rul. 85-88, 1985-2 C.B. 201, where the IRS ruled that only one five-and-five withdrawal power is available for *Crummey* powers possessed by a beneficiary under identical trusts created by the same grantor.
198. See §2503(b) and Chapter 4, A.3.b.(1).
199. See §2041(b)(2), providing for a lapse above the five-and-five level to be treated as a donative transfer, including being potentially subject to the retained interest estate tax provisions. This problem would not arise if the corpus of the trust subject to the five-and-five power is sufficiently large so that 5% would equal or exceed the annual donee exclusion.
200. *See* §2514(e).
201. See TAM 8901004, noting that such lapses are "conditions subsequent" and, therefore, are invalid as against public policy, citing *Procter v. Commissioner,* 142 F.2d 824 (4th Cir. 1944), *cert. denied,* 323 U.S. 756 (1944). *See also* Rev. Rul. 85-88, 1985-2 C.B. 201.
202. §678.
203. *See* Rev. Rul. 67-241, 1967-2 C.B. 225; Rev. Rul. 81-6, 1981-1 C.B. 385; PLR 9535047 and PLR 9226037 (providing a similar analysis in the S corporation qualification context), PLR 9034004.
204. Note §2514(e) as providing a limited exclusion opportunity in this gift tax context through the use of a lapsing five-and-five power.
205. Reg. §25.2514-3(c)(4).
206. The difficulty with this argument is that, at the time of a lapse, no completed transfer to the secondary donee has occurred. Completion is contingent upon the death of the primary donee before termination of the trust. Consequently, the lapse should not be a taxable lapse. *See* Reg. §25.2511-2.
207. §2041. *See* Rev. Rul. 75-351, 1975-2 C.B. 368. *See also Estate of Rosenblatt v. Commissioner,* 633 F.2d 176 (10th Cir. 1980); *Estate of Gilchrist v. Commissioner*, 630 F.2d 340 (5th Cir. 1980); *Estate of Alperstein v. Commissioner,* 613 F.2d 1213 (2d Cir. 1979), *cert. denied,* 446 U.S. 918 (1980); *Pa. Bank & Trust Co. v. United States,* 597 F.2d 382 (3d Cir. 1979); TAM 9344004.
208. Section 2041 provides that a lapse is taxable only if the lapse is of such a nature that, if it were a transfer of property owned by the decedent, the property would be includible in the gross estate under §2035–§2038. See the discussion of taxable lapses in Chapter 5, E.4.a.(4). Note, further, that if within the ambit of the five-and-five power the lapses in prior years would enable limited protection from estate tax inclusion.
209. *See* Reg. §20.2041-3(d)(4).

210. Where an irrevocable life insurance trust is funded with income producing property, the income of the trust will be taxed to the grantor under §677(a)(3) if the income is used for payment of premiums on policies of life insurance on the life of the grantor or the grantor's spouse. See generally 807 T.M., *Personal Life Insurance Trusts* (Bloomberg BNA). For this reason the trust agreement should specify that trust income cannot be used to pay insurance premiums for insurance on the life of the grantor.
211. *See* §2503(b); Chapter 4, A.3.b.(1).
212. In some situations, the premiums may even be paid directly by the trust grantor to the insurance company to assure that the policy premiums are paid and to enable the trustee not to be required to deal with this funds transfer. This arrangement should be treated constructively as a contribution to the trust and an insurance premium payment by the trustee.
213. *See* PLR 7935091 (IRS ruled favorably on original contribution of term insurance policy and $1 in cash to *Crummey* trust); PLR 8134135 (funding trust with whole life and group term insurance policies).
214. Favorable rulings were issued regarding the §2503(b) exclusion in similar situations. *See* Rev. Rul. 76-490, 1976-2 C.B. 300, Rev. Rul. 79-47, 1979-1 C.B. 312; PLR 8021058, PLR 8006109.
215. *See* Rev. Proc. 2015-3, 2015-1 I.R.B. 129, §4.01(48).
216. See 820 T.M., *Administrative Powers* (Bloomberg BNA).
217. See *Lober v. United States*, 346 U.S. 335 (1953), and *United States v. O'Malley*, 383 U.S. 627 (1966), holding that such authority causes inclusion for estate tax purposes. In contrast §674 provides for a noninclusionary result under the grantor trust income tax rules if the grantor can only postpone enjoyment with respect to a specified beneficiary.
218. Reg. §20.2038-1(a); *Estate of Holmes v. Commissioner*, 326 U.S. 480 (1946). *See also Estate of Skifter v. Commissioner*, 56 T.C. 1190 (1971), *aff'd*, 468 F.2d 699 (2d Cir. 1972), *nonacq.*, 1978-2 C.B. 4 (rejecting IRS's argument concerning applicability of §2042(2) "incidents of ownership" inclusion of life insurance proceeds in this context).
219. Such a power would cause inclusion for estate tax purposes under §2038(a)(1). In Rev. Rul. 80-255, 1980-2 C.B. 272, the IRS ruled that a provision in a trust instrument for the inclusion of the settlor's after-born and after-adopted children as additional trust beneficiaries is not the retention of a power to change the beneficial interests of the trust under §2036(a)(2) and §2038(a)(1). See §674(b)(5), §674(b)(6), §674(b)(7), §674(c), and §674(d), which indicate that the retention of such authority by the grantor causes inclusion of the trust income in the grantor's gross income.
220. In this situation, §2038(a)(1) and either §674(b)(5) or §674(b)(6) require inclusion for both estate and income tax purposes.
221. In *State St. Trust Co. v. United States*, 263 F.2d 635 (1st Cir. 1959), the court held that trust administration powers were so broad that the trustee could shift the economic benefits between a life tenant and a remainder beneficiary. Accordingly, for a trust including such powers, the trust corpus was held includible in the grantor-trustee's estate under §2036(a)(2). Subsequently, courts distinguished the *State St. Trust* decision. *Estate of King v. Commissioner*, 37 T.C. 973 (1962); *Estate of Peters v. Commissioner*, T.C. Memo 1964-167; *Estate of Wurts v. Commissioner*, T.C. Memo 1960-102. The First Circuit, in *Old Colony Trust Co. v. United States*, 423 F.2d 601 (1st Cir. 1970), overruled *State St. Trust*. Consequently, the accepted rule is that a grantor-trustee may retain administrative-type management powers over trust assets, provided that under local law the trustee's activities

will be controlled so that he or she may not arbitrarily favor one beneficiary over another. In several situations, the IRS agreed that managerial and administrative powers are not within §2036(a)(2) and §2038. *See Estate of Budd v. Commissioner,* 49 T.C. 468 (1968), *acq.*, 1973-2 C.B. 1; *Estate of Pardee v. Commissioner,* 49 T.C. 140 (1967), *acq.*, 1973-2 C.B. 3.

222. In *United States v. Byrum,* 408 U.S. 125 (1972), a trust grantor who did not appoint himself as trustee reserved the right (1) to vote shares of unlisted stock; (2) to disapprove the sale or transfer of any trust assets; (3) to approve investments and reinvestments; and (4) to remove the trustee and designate another corporate trustee to serve as successor. The Supreme Court determined that such retained powers did not cause inclusion in the gross estate. The Tax Reform Act of 1976 created §2036(b) to specifically overrule the *Byrum* decision. This provision specifies that the retention of voting rights by a donor is to be treated as the retention of the enjoyment of the stock for estate tax purposes. The capacity in which the decedent exercises the voting rights is immaterial. The voting retention rule is limited to stock of those corporations "controlled" by the decedent and his or her relatives. A corporation is considered controlled for this purpose if, at any time after the transfer and during the three-year period ending on the date of the decedent's death, the decedent or his or her relatives either (1) owned (with attribution of ownership determined under §318) or (2) had the right to vote stock constituting at least 20% of the total combined voting power of all classes of stock of the corporation. Section 2036(b) explicitly applies to indirect transfers, such as the transfer of cash or other property within three years of decedent's death to a trust of which he or she is a trustee, with the trust later using that cash or other property to purchase stock in a controlled corporation from himself or herself. *See generally* Prop. Reg. §20.2036-2. These statutory changes encompass the situation where nonvoting stock is placed in trust and the voting stock is retained by the settlor of the trust. *See* Rev. Rul. 81-15, 1981-1 C.B. 457; PLR 9527025. Such a transfer of nonvoting stock could be accomplished, for example, after an estate planning corporate recapitalization. *See also Estate of Gilman v. Commissioner,* 65 T.C. 296 (1975), *nonacq.*, 1978-2 C.B. 3, *aff'd,* 547 F.2d 32 (2d Cir. 1976) (relying on *Byrum*). See also Rev. Rul. 80-346, 1980-2 C.B. 271, where the IRS ruled that the value of stock transferred to an irrevocable trust was includible in the gross estate under §2036(b) where an oral understanding existed that the trustee would follow the grantor's instructions in voting the stock. The IRS concluded that the decedent indirectly retained the voting rights under an oral agreement with the trustee notwithstanding that the trust instrument made no such provision. In TAM 9515003, the Chief Counsel's Office advised rejection of this "substance over form" approach when the taxpayer, rather than the IRS, sought to use it.

223. The estate of the grantor will include the trust corpus where the grantor has authority to appoint himself or herself as successor trustee and the trustee is vested with discretionary powers. Reg. §20.2036-1(b)(3), §20.2038-1(a). In Rev. Rul. 73-21, 1973-1 C.B. 405, the IRS indicated that if (1) a power was retained by the grantor to appoint himself or herself as successor trustee upon the death, resignation, or inability to serve of the current trustee and (2) the successor trustee (including the grantor) had discretion to distribute trust income, the value of the trust was includible in the decedent's gross estate. If, however, the retained power was limited to the appointment of a successor corporate trustee in the event of the resignation or removal of the original trustee, the trust assets should not be includible under §2036 in the decedent's gross estate. Rev. Rul. 95-58, 1995-2 C.B. 191.

224. In Rev. Rul. 79-353, 1979-2 C.B. 325, *as modified by* Rev. Rul. 81–51, 1981–1 C.B. 458, the IRS ruled that, where a trustee had broad discretionary powers over income and principal, the grantor's retention of an unrestricted right to remove the corporate trustee without cause and to appoint another corporate trustee was a retained life interest, resulting in the application of §2036(a)(2) and §2038(a)(1). The IRS's theory was that the settlor could remove and replace trustees until a trustee was found whose actions would follow the grantor's wishes. This premise ignored the consideration that the trustee, as a fiduciary, is under an obligation to the beneficiaries that transcends any pressures from the grantor. The IRS's position was not supported by strong judicial authority nor by the estate tax regulations, which imply that so long as the power holder could not appoint himself or herself trustee, the power to substitute trustees would not result in estate tax inclusion. *See* Reg. §20.2036-1(b)(3), §20.2038-1(a)(3), §20.2041-1(b)(1). *Cf.* Reg. §1.674(d)-2(a). For a contrary holding, in which the IRS previously acquiesced but which was not cited in Rev. Rul. 79-353, see *Estate of Beckwith v. Commissioner,* 55 T.C. 242 (1970), *acq.*, 1971-2 C.B. 1. The IRS abandoned its position on this issue in Rev. Rul. 95-58, 1995-2 C.B. 191, after the repudiation of Rev. Rul. 79-353 in *Estate of Wall v. Commissioner,* 101 T.C. 300 (1993).
225. §1361(d)(3). See Rev. Rul. 89-45, 1989-1 C.B. 267, noting that a trust, the terms of which provide that a portion of its corpus may be used to fund a new trust for an "after-born" grandchild of the grantor, is not a §1361(d)(3) "qualified sub-chapter S trust." See, further, Rev. Rul. 89-55, 1989-1 C.B. 268, indicating that a trust is not a QSST if its terms permit, in the event the trust no longer holds shares of an S corporation: (1) the trust's termination during the income beneficiary's lifetime; and (2) the distribution of trust corpus to persons other than the current income beneficiary. See also Rev. Rul. 92-20, 1992-1 C.B. 301, concerning income accumulation under such circumstances.
226. §1361(c)(2)(A)(v).
227. An electing small business trust may have multiple current beneficiaries and a charitable remainder beneficiary, may accumulate income and may authorize the trustee to make discretionary distributions of both income and principal. Generally, interests in the trust may only be acquired by gift or bequest and current beneficiaries are limited to individuals and estates. §1361(e); Reg. §1.1361-1(m)(1)(i). Each potential current beneficiary is counted as a shareholder for purposes of the 100 S corporation shareholder limit. §1361(c)(2)(B)(v); Reg. §1.1361-1(m)(4)(vii). A potential negative is that the portion of the trust consisting of S corporation stock is treated as a separate trust for purposes of computing the income tax attributable to the stock held by the trust. This portion is taxable at the highest individual rate, is not included in distributable net income or in the beneficiaries' income, and no deduction is allowed for the amounts distributed to the beneficiaries. §641(c); Reg. §1.641(c)-1.
228. See the discussion of the grantor trust income tax rules Chapter 6, D.3.b.(1).
229. Trusts only defective as to the income from corpus are uncommon because this only results when a permitted reversionary interest is retained. Because of applicable valuation tables this ordinarily necessitates a reversionary interest postponed for more than 30 years (assuming an applicable 10% interest rate). *See* §673; Reg. §1.671-3(b)(2).
230. See *Rothstein v. United States,* 735 F.2d 704 (2d Cir. 1984), where a grantor bought appreciated stock (on an installment basis) from his wife acting as trustee of a trust previously created by the grantor. Even though concluding that, because of §675(3), the trust was a grantor trust, the court permitted an increase in the tax basis to the grantor

purchaser, contrary to the IRS's position. Responding to this decision the IRS issued Rev. Rul. 85-13, 1985-1 C.B. 184, specifying that a transaction cannot be recognized as a sale for federal income tax purposes if the same person is treated as owning the purported consideration both before and after the transaction. *See also* Rev. Rul. 2004-86, 2004-2 C.B. 191.

231. *See* Nicholson, *Sale to a Grantor Controlled Trust: Better Than a GRAT?* 37 Tax Mgmt. Memo. 99 (1996).
232. *See* §672(f)(2)(A) (concerning income attributable through revocable trust).
233. *See* Reg. §1.121–1(c)(3)(i) (during period that taxpayer is treated under §671–§679 as owner of trust or portion of trust that includes taxpayer's principal residence, taxpayer is treated as owning such residence for purposes of satisfying two-year ownership requirement of §121 and trust's sale or exchange of residence is treated as made by taxpayer).
234. This may be particularly valuable if the trust is realizing significant income that might occur, for example, by transferring property equivalent to the full amount of the unified credit by gift to the trust and investing those funds in high-income assets. Concern existed that the IRS would take the position that this payment by the grantor of his or her income tax liability constitutes a gift by the grantor to the trust beneficiary (because, for property law purposes, the obligation is that of the trust, or remainder beneficiaries). But see Rev. Rul. 2004-64, 2004-2 C.B. 7, where the IRS concluded that, when the grantor of a trust, who is treated as the owner of the trust under subpart E, pays the income tax attributable to the inclusion of the trust's income in the grantor's taxable income, the grantor is not treated as making a gift of the amount of the income tax to the trust beneficiaries. Further, if, pursuant to the trust's governing instrument or applicable local law, the grantor must be reimbursed by the trust for the income tax payable by the grantor that is attributable to the trust's income, the full value of the trust's assets is includible in the grantor's gross estate under §2036(a)(1). If, however, the trust's governing instrument or applicable local law gives the trustee the discretion to reimburse the grantor for that portion of the grantor's income tax liability, the existence of that discretion, by itself (whether or not exercised) will not cause the value of the trust's assets to be includible in the trust grantor's gross estate under §2036(a)(1).
235. *See* §671–§678.
236. §675(4).
237. *Id.*
238. *Id.*
239. *See* §2036(b).
240. *See* Reg. §1.674(d)-2(b). *See also Budlong v. Commissioner,* 7 T.C. 756 (1946).
241. §677(a) (income), §676(a), §672(e) (corpus).
242. §672(c).
243. §1014(b)(9). *See* Reg. §1.1014-2(b)(2).
244. §2036(a)(2).
245. §2038(a)(1).
246. *See* §§674(a), §§677(a); Regs. §1.676(a)-1.
247. *Compare* §674(b)(5)(B) (permitting this power for income tax purposes) *with Lober v. United States,* 346 U.S. 335 (1953) (holding that retention of such power does cause estate tax inclusion).
248. Before transferring the family residence by gift, the donor should consider §121 which permits a taxpayer to exclude from gross income a certain amount of gain from the sale

of a principal residence. Certain qualification requirements apply concerning the length of ownership and occupancy of the residence. For a detailed discussion of §121, see 594 T.M., *Tax Implications of Home Ownership* (Bloomberg BNA).

249. The "qualified personal residence trust" is discussed in Chapter 7, J.
250. Reg. §20.2036-1(c)(1)(i) (as redesignated by T.D. 9414, 73 Fed. Reg. 40,173 [July 14, 2008]) states that "[a]n interest or right is treated as having been retained or reserved if at the time of the transfer there was an understanding, express or implied, that the interest or right would be later conferred."
251. *Estate of Gutchess v. Commissioner,* 46 T.C. 554 (1966), *acq.,* 1967-1 C.B. 2. *See also Union Planters Nat'l Bank v. United States,* 361 F.2d 662 (6th Cir. 1966); *Estate of Binkley v. United States,* 358 F.2d 639 (3d Cir. 1966).
252. 1967-1 C.B. 2.
253. *See Estate of Trotter v. Commissioner,* T.C. Memo 2001-250, where the Tax Court concluded that an agreement did exist between spouses.
254. *See, generally,* with respect to problems of applying §2036, 50 T.M., *Incomplete Lifetime Transfers: Retained Powers Under Sections 2036(a)(2) and 2038* (Bloomberg BNA), and 52 T.M., *Incomplete Lifetime Transfers: Retained Beneficial Interests Under Sections 2036(a)(1) and 2037* (Bloomberg BNA).
255. Note in this context the possible applicability of §1014(e) precluding an income tax basis step up where the decedent spouse received the property by gift from the other spouse within one year of death and, at death, the property is transferred back to the donor spouse.
256. *See Estate of Stewart v. Commissioner*, 617 F.3d 148 (2nd Cir. 2010), where, while an adult son was living with his mother in a $2 million residence owned by the mother, she deeded a 49% interest in the residence to the son and filed a gift tax return taking a 20% fractional interest discount. Subsequently rejecting gross estate inclusion in the mother's gross estate under §2036, the following benefits were obtained in this situation: (1) the adjusted taxable gift inclusion was reduced by a fractional interest discount with respect to the donated 49% interest; (2) a 49% portion of the property's appreciation from the time of gift to the time of death was removed from the gross estate; (3) only the value of the 51% interest retained by the mother was included in her gross estate and that interest qualified for a fractional interest discount; and (iv) the mother was able to continue to reside in her home until she died.
257. *See Guynn v. United States*, 437 F.2d 1148 (4th Cir. 1971), holding that the value of a residence purchased by a decedent and deeded to her daughter was includible in the decedent's gross estate where, during the decedent's lifetime, the decedent was the sole resident of the house, paid for all improvements, paid all taxes, and paid no rent. See also Rev. Rul. 70-155, 1970-1 C.B. 189, where the IRS ruled that the value of a residence, possessed and occupied exclusively by the decedent after transferring the property to his children pursuant to an understanding that he would retain use of the property, was includible in his gross estate under §2036(a), and Rev. Rul. 78-409, 1978-2 C.B. 234, where the residence was shared between the donor parent and the donee child (and spouse). *See also Estate of Maxwell v. Commissioner,* 3 F.3d 591 (2d Cir. 1993); *Estate of Rapelje v. Commissioner,* 73 T.C. 82 (1979); *Estate of Cheng Van,* T.C. Memo 2011-22.
258. *Estate of Barlow v. Commissioner,* 55 T.C. 666 (1971), *acq.*, 1972-2 C.B. 1. *See also Estate of Maxwell v. Commissioner,* 3 F.3d 591 (2d Cir. 1993), where rent paid was not adequate

and purchase money notes were not intended to be enforced. The parties entirely disregarded the purported arm's length arrangement that they had initially implemented.

259. In Rev. Rul. 78-409, 1978-2 C.B. 234, the facts indicated that after the decedent's child and the child's spouse moved into decedent-parent's residence, the parent transferred the residence to the child. The decedent continued to occupy the residence until death. The IRS stated that such evidence supported a conclusion that, pursuant to an implied understanding with the child, the decedent retained a right to share possession and enjoyment of the residence for life. See in the spousal transfer context, however, PLR 200240020, where the IRS ruled that the transfer of a long term leasehold interest for a non-U.S. residence to a nonresident alien spouse did not cause retained interest treatment. However, because the transferee spouse was a nonresident alien, no marital deduction was available and, consequently, the transfer was a nondeductible gift. This would permit, however, the shifting of the post-transfer appreciation potential to the nonresident alien donee spouse and that property would not subsequently be includible for U.S. estate tax purposes.

CHAPTER 7

Intrafamily Transfer Alternatives to Gifts

The unified transfer tax system limits the incentives to make lifetime donative transfers to younger generation members. Taxable gifts of substantial value that exceed the unified credit result in a prepayment of estate taxes by the donor.[1] Further, in times of economic uncertainty, whether the expectation is of inflation or deflation, prospective donors recognize the irreversible nature of gifts and that, to achieve the estate tax planning objectives, a severance of all rights to income or principal from the transferred property is required. Gifts are of importance to the estate planner because a gift of significantly appreciating property removes the future accrued gain in the transferred property from the donor's gross estate. The applicability of §2036, §2037, §2038, §2040, and §2042 may result in some or all of the future appreciation being captured in the donor's estate, however.

Techniques other than gifts are available that may enable shifting future appreciation for transferred assets to younger generation family members (and trusts for those persons) while preserving the present value of those assets to the older generation transferor. For example, this retained value may be in the form of an installment sale note or the present value of anticipated payments under a private annuity arrangement among family members. Some of these intrafamily value-shifting arrangements as alternatives to completed gift transfers are possible transactions with family members (or trusts for them) as follows:

- part-gift/part-sale arrangements[2];
- sales (or gifts) and leasebacks;
- installment sales[3];

- low-interest loans by older generation members to younger generation members; credit institution loans made available to junior family members, supported by the use of a senior member's credit rating; and, installment sales at low rates of interest accruing on the deferred payments[4];
- private annuities[5];
- joint or split interest purchases[6];
- sales of remainder interests[7];
- grantor retained annuity trusts[8];
- use of multiple entities or ownership tiers in structuring entities (corporations, partnerships, and irrevocable trusts) to provide senior family members with current income and retirement security while shifting to members of the younger generation much of the potential for realizing the subsequent capital growth of the business[9]; and
- family corporation stock redemptions (and partnership interest purchases).[10]

The recent and prospective legislative changes to the transfer tax provisions should also be considered in evaluating these alternatives to gifts.[11]

A. Intrafamily Sale/Leaseback or Gift/Leaseback

1. Family Sale/Leasebacks

A parent may sell business property to a child (or an irrevocable trust for children) and, thereafter, lease that property back from the purchaser/owner. The underlying premise of such an arrangement is that this transaction will actually be treated as (1) a sale and (2) a leaseback for federal income tax purposes. The objective of such a transaction may be to enable lease income to be realized by the child (or a trust for children), perhaps in a lesser income tax rate bracket than the transferor (unless the Kiddie Tax is applicable). The sale will not permit postponement of tax recognition of any gain on the transferred property unless installment sales reporting treatment is available.[12] The purchaser will have a cost basis for tax depreciation purposes and the depreciation deduction may substantially offset the rental income being received.

One of the major risks in this context is that the IRS will assert that the rent paid by the seller/lessee is not deductible for federal income tax purposes because the rent being paid is not an "ordinary and necessary" business expense.[13] The IRS has litigated numerous cases in this context with mixed results.[14] The determination is often dependent upon whether the particular facts evidence a genuine transaction. The Tax Court established four criteria for determining the deductibility of lease payments in *Mathews v. Commissioner*.[15] These requirements are:

- The donor/trust grantor must not retain substantially the same control over the property that he or she had before he or she made the sale or gift. This requirement is usually met through a transfer to an independent trustee who has the right and opportunity to negotiate regarding the leaseback and who acts for the primary

benefit of the trust beneficiaries, rather than for the trust grantor. This should particularly be the situation where younger participants are involved on the grantee side of the transaction.
- The lease should normally be in writing and must require payment of a reasonable rental.
- The lease (as distinguished from the sale or gift) must have a bona fide business purpose.
- The transferor must not possess a disqualifying interest in the property. A reversionary interest not derived from the lease or the lessor and which would only become possessory after the termination of the trust is not such a disqualifying interest.

This necessitates that the taxpayer carefully construct the arrangements so that the transaction documents clearly identify that a sale and a leaseback occurred, and that the parties continue to conduct the relationship on a business-like basis.

2. Gift/Leaseback

Alternatively, by gift a grantor may transfer assets (e.g., depreciable business properties) to children (or an irrevocable trust for children) and, thereafter, lease those assets back from the owner. If the transaction is properly arranged, the donor/transferor will not be treated as the owner of the transferred property and the new owner/transferee's lease income will be effectively shifted to the children (or a trust for the children) for income tax purposes.

In the gift/leaseback context, the IRS also may assert that the donor/trust grantor (as lessee) is not entitled to a §162 ordinary and necessary business expense deduction for the lease payments being made for renting the business properties from the donee child or donee trust. The disallowance of the deduction for rental expense will cause the arrangement to lose substantial income tax savings value. Assuming the transaction is recognized for tax purposes, for the transferee (child or trust) the rental income will constitute gross income. In the gift context (as contrasted with the sale/leaseback transaction) the donor's tax basis for the transferred asset will carry over to the donee.[16] Accordingly, only limited tax depreciation may be available for the transferee to utilize in offsetting the rental income.

B. Intrafamily Installment Sales

1. Estate Planning Benefits

Intrafamily sales, often arranged on an installment payment basis, may yield numerous family tax planning benefits:

- When appreciated property (which is often the subject of an intrafamily sale) is sold, the seller may spread his or her taxable gain over more than one tax year by arranging an installment sale eligible for installment reporting. The gain may be taxed in multiple years at a lower income tax bracket.[17] After the enactment of the maximum 20% capital gains tax rate (for most properties) the primary benefit may be the value of the deferral of the income tax liability.[18]

- A sale of income-producing property may effectively enable the shifting of the income of that property from a high-bracket seller to a low-bracket family member (or trust), assuming inapplicability of the Kiddie Tax.
- The sale of an asset might remove the future appreciation on that property from the seller's estate for federal estate tax purposes. Simultaneously, without incurring a gift or an estate tax cost (because the transaction is an arm's-length sale), that asset will be placed into the ownership of one or more family members (or trusts for those family members) who would otherwise be beneficiaries of the seller's gross estate.
- The sale may improve the liquidity of the seller's estate by removing illiquid assets and replacing those assets with a negotiable promissory note. This liquidity is improved, however, only if the installment note can actually be paid by the obligor.
- The property sale need not diminish the seller's cash flow because the amount received from the sale will be either in the form of installment payments under a promissory note or cash that may be reinvested to generate replacement income. Further, the seller's actual cash flow might be enhanced, unless the tax amount is sufficiently large that the amount to be reinvested is significantly diluted by this tax. The imposition of the capital gains tax at the rate of 20% will reduce this amount.
- If the seller's income stream is reduced as a result of this sale and other property is required to be consumed by the seller for continued maintenance and support, a reduction in the seller's estate for estate tax purposes might occur.[19]
- A sale may enable the seller's estate to qualify for certain special estate and income tax benefits under those estate and income tax provisions that require that a specific percentage of the gross estate consist of an interest in a closely held business.[20]
- Without incurring significant income tax liability the buyer can resell the property if that property ownership is not consistent with his or her investment objectives. The purchaser's tax basis in the acquired property is the price paid by the purchaser (including the amount of the installment note). This basis, as reduced by any postacquisition tax depreciation deduction available for the acquired property, will constitute the base for measuring gain on this subsequent disposition. The installment sale "related party rules" (discussed below) will determine whether this subsequent sale by the purchaser will accelerate recognition of gain by the initial seller.

2. Income Tax Considerations

Although the intrafamily installment sale may result in substantial estate planning advantages, potentially adverse income tax consequences must be avoided. A seller making an installment sale that fails to comply with the rules of the installment sales tax provision[21] is taxable currently on the entire realized gain. This occurs even though the cash is to be received only on a deferred basis. Thus, the seller might face significant illiquidity if an income tax liability is owed but the receipt of payments is deferred. If the seller does qualify for installment method reporting, he or she is entitled to report the gain on a pro-rata basis as he or she receives payments for the property.[22]

a. Related Party's Purchase and Sale

If a family member makes an installment sale to a "related person," the seller will recognize gain on an accelerated basis if the related purchaser subsequently makes a disposition of the acquired property (i.e., "second disposition") before the first seller receives all installment payments from the first disposition.[23] Recognition of gain will be accelerated to the first seller to the extent that (1) the lesser of (a) the total amount realized from the second disposition of the property or (b) the total contract price for the first disposition exceeds (2) the actual payments made by the related party to the taxpayer on the first sale.[24] Related parties are defined generally for this purpose to include spouses, children, grandchildren, and parents, but to exclude siblings and their descendants.[25]

For sales of property other than marketable securities, this resale rule applies only if the second disposition occurs within a period of two years after the original sale.[26] For installment sales of marketable securities the resale rule specifies no time limit for resales occurring before the installment obligation received by the first seller is satisfied. Note, however, that installment treatment is not available when marketable securities are sold by the first seller and, consequently, this resale rule is not significant in this context.[27] Another exception to this resale rule provides that a transfer after the death of the first seller or the related person will not be a "second disposition."[28]

When an installment sale appears desirable to achieve tax savings but an unrelated purchaser is not available, the use of a related party sale may still be viable. The technique may be used for the installment sale of property other than marketable securities where a resale may be postponed for the two-year period. Even where the resale of the property cannot be postponed for two years, including where the property consists of non-traded securities, an installment sale contemplating a "second disposition" by the purchaser will be available provided that the purchaser is a person not treated as "related" to the seller for purposes of this limitation provision. Consequently, an eligible sale may be made to siblings and their descendants, in-laws, or other similarly-related persons.[29] Where property is difficult to sell outside the family unit, the sale may be made to a related party who may better take the risk of loss pending the property becoming marketable.[30]

b. Sales of Depreciable Property

If installment sales of depreciable property are made between certain closely related parties and the gain is to be treated as ordinary income under §1239, installment sale reporting is not available.[31] All of the gain realized upon this disposition must be recognized in the year of sale.[32] The rule is intended to deter transactions that give the related party purchaser depreciation deductions (calculated on a tax basis that is the recent purchase cost) prior to the time the seller is required to include in income the corresponding gain on the sale. Further, in some limited situations, this treatment of all gain as ordinary income precludes any income tax rate differential that would otherwise occur if (1) the seller could enjoy capital gains treatment while (2) the buyer claimed a depreciation deduction on the purchased property, thereby reducing ordinary income.[33]

c. Gift Cancellation of Installment Obligation

The cancellation of an installment obligation is treated as a disposition of that obligation.[34] This might be done by the holder of the note forgiving all or some portion of the note.[35] At the time of the cancellation the note holder is treated as recognizing gain equal to the difference between the note holder's basis in the note and its fair market value immediately prior to debt cancellation. If the obligor and the note holder are related persons, as defined in the related party installment sale rules, the amount deemed received upon cancellation is at least the face amount of the canceled installment obligation.[36]

d. Bequest of Installment Obligation

A transfer of an installment obligation at death is generally not an event for the estate that triggers recognition of the gain inherent in that obligation.[37] This results whether the installment obligation is transferred though intestacy or under a last will. A tax basis step-up will not occur. The beneficiary who receives the obligation recognizes the gain component of that obligation as portions are subsequently collected. The transfer of an installment obligation to the obligor on the note, whether by bequest, devise, or inheritance, thereby resulting in a cancellation of the debt, will result in the recognition of the previously unreported gain to the decedent's estate. This rule also applies to a cancellation by will of an installment obligation at death or by the executor after death.[38]

3. Estate Tax Considerations

An installment sale would initially appear to remove the value of the transferred property from the seller's gross estate. That value would be replaced, however, by the value of the installment obligation, the down payment received, and any note payments received prior to the date of death. The cash received upon those payments would have been reduced by federal and state income taxes attributable to the installment gain recognized. Further, to the extent the seller, as of the date of death, consumed any cash received under that note, or effectively disposed of the installment obligation, the value of the seller's gross estate is diminished. Any post-transfer appreciation in the property transferred in the installment sale would be excluded from the seller's gross estate because that gain would have accrued in the hands of the purchaser of the property.

The estate tax value of the installment obligation, usually the unpaid principal and accrued interest at death, may be reduced if the fair market value of the obligation is worth less than its face value. This may occur due to such factors as an interest rate lower than the market rate, an unfavorable maturity date, insufficient security, or insolvency of the debtor.[39]

4. Gift Tax Considerations

No gift tax exposure should arise upon an installment sale concluded between family members, assuming that the transaction is a transfer for full and adequate consideration.[40] A taxable gift may occur, however, if the sale price to be received is less than the fair market value of the property transferred.[41] If the property transferred is not readily tradable, an independent appraisal should be obtained to demonstrate that no differential exists between the price and the fair market value.

A differential between the two sides of the transaction may also occur if the installment obligation has a face value equal to the value of the property received, but carries a very low rate of interest to be paid (or no interest specified). This would result in the receipt of a promissory note having a fair market value less than its face amount. This difference between the property transferred and the fair market value of the note would be treated as a taxable gift.[42]

5. Bargain Sale

Although the properly planned installment sale does not normally result in a taxable gift, an intentional "bargain sale" of property (i.e., a sale for less than full consideration) may be made by one family member to another. The purpose of an intentional bargain sale in the intrafamily context may be to permit the seller to transfer an asset to a family member who lacks sufficient resources to purchase the asset for full consideration, or to make a partial gift of property, but at the same time retain for the benefit of the seller some cash from the proceeds received (or to be received under an installment note) from a partial sale of the property.

A bargain sale is in essence two transactions. A gift occurs to the extent that the fair market value of the property transferred exceeds the consideration received by the seller.[43] Gain from a sale occurs to the extent that the value of the consideration received exceeds the seller's adjusted basis.[44] Under gift tax rules, the gift portion of the bargain sale will be protected by the annual donee exclusion and the unified credit or otherwise included in the gift tax base.

No allocation of the seller's income tax basis between (1) the sale portion and (2) the gift portion is required in private bargain sale property transactions.[45] For basis allocation purposes the seller is viewed as selling the entire property for the amount received.[46] The purchaser's basis for the property is the amount paid or the seller's adjusted basis at the time of the transfer, whichever is greater, plus any increase for any federal gift tax paid on the appreciation element of the gift.[47] Thus, an owner of appreciated property who enters into a part-sale–part-gift transaction may minimize his or her gain by offsetting the entire income tax basis of the property against the sales price. This shifts the responsibility for reporting any remaining gain to the transferee (who may be in a lower income tax bracket).[48] The income-splitting potential of this type of transaction is maximized by selling the property for its adjusted basis, thereby shifting to the transferee the entire liability for reporting accrued gain when the property is subsequently sold.[49] Until sold, the benefit of the tax deferral on the postponed gain recognition will continue to accrue.

6. "Self-Canceling" Installment Note (SCIN)

a. Structure of Arrangement Terminating Note Obligation

Under his or her will the holder of an installment obligation may transfer the promissory note to the obligor on that obligation, or the obligation may be explicitly canceled by a provision in the note holder's last will (the executor receiving instructions not to collect on that note). Alternatively, this could be a "self-canceling installment note," or "SCIN," under which, by the terms of the obligation itself, the duty to make installment payments terminates upon the death of the note holder. Under this type of arrangement, the installment sale is made for a sales price that is contingent in amount. The contingency in amount reflects the fact that the note will be terminated if the seller/lender dies prior to the final maturity of the note.

b. Inclusion in Gross Estate

The SCIN terminates by its terms as of the time of death and, accordingly, for federal estate tax purposes, no value is deemed transferred as of that time to a beneficiary of the estate.[50] A termination provision of this character should remove the value of the note from the obligee's gross estate because it has no value as of the moment of death. This assumes, however, that the installment sale was made at arm's length for adequate and full consideration (which would require that at the time of the transaction the contingent note had a value equivalent to the purchased property).[51] If inadequate consideration was received for the property, the IRS might argue that the transfer/retained interest estate tax provisions are applicable, for example, that the transferor retained a life interest in the transferred property.[52] Further, the IRS might assert that the transaction was not bona fide and that a larger amount must be included as "adjusted taxable gifts" when determining the estate tax liability, assuming no expiration of the statute of limitations.[53]

c. Gift Tax Treatment

The effect of the cancellation on death clause on the value of the promissory note must be considered in determining whether the sale actually constitutes a partial gift transaction, particularly where the sale involves related parties. The possible termination of the note prior to its specified term (because of the death of the holder), with less than full payment having occurred, requires that additional consideration must be paid and received for that element of actuarial risk assumed in the sale transaction. This will necessitate examining the life expectancy of the note holder to evaluate the probabilities that the note will be terminated (and when) prior to its specified term upon the death of the note holder. If adequate consideration is not paid for this element (ordinarily as reflected by an increased interest rate paid on the promissory note) a gift transfer will have occurred for gift tax purposes.

d. Income Tax Treatment

The seller is required to report the gain from the contingency note as though all the payments will be received.[54] If the contingency does occur and the selling price will not be received, income (and loss) from the sale is recomputed.[55] If no further payment is received, any excess income previously reported is treated as a loss in the year in which the contingency occurs.[56] To distinguish this arrangement from the gratuitous cancellation of an obligation by the obligee, the contingency of the possible reduction of consideration should be an integral part of the obligation and a bargained-for element of the consideration.[57] When the note is canceled at the death of the obligee under the terms of the note, income is recognized as income in respect of a decedent by the estate of the note holder.[58]

e. Advantages of the Self-Canceling Installment Note

A self-canceling installment note has several advantages over another alternative, the private annuity, which is a somewhat similar arrangement. With a SCIN the purchaser is entitled to an income tax deduction for that portion of each installment payment representing interest expense. Further, the aggregate payments to the seller are finite. In the case of a private annuity transaction the annuitant may outlive his or her life expectancy, with the obligor then being required to continue to make annuity payments for the life of the annuitant. Further, no component of the private annuity payments will be treated for federal income tax purposes as (possibly) deductible interest expense by the payor.

C. Interest-Free Loans of Money

1. Recharacterization of Intrafamily Loans

If an interest-free loan of money (or "below-market" loan) is made in a family context, applicable federal tax rules require the recharacterization of these loans, premised upon an arm's-length transaction having occurred. Before the enactment of §7872 the Supreme Court, in *Dickman v. Commissioner*,[59] resolved the tax treatment of these loans in the gift context, holding that an interest-free loan does result in a gift from the lender to the borrower for federal gift tax purposes. This concept was subsequently incorporated by legislation into §7872, which encompasses both income and gift tax elements concerning interest-free loans.[60]

2. Gift Tax Issues

The gift tax issue arising out of the interest-free loan transaction is whether the lender makes a gift for gift tax purposes by relinquishing the right to receive interest income. In *Crown v. Commissioner*,[61] the court determined that no gift tax liability resulted from the making of interest-free loans to relatives with a demand note being received. This position was challenged for many years until the IRS eventually achieved a successful result in the Supreme Court in *Dickman*.[62]

The IRS previously enunciated its gift timing and valuation position in litigating these gift/interest-free loan cases. In the case of a "demand loan," the amount of the gift was deemed to be the value of the right to the use of the money for such portion of the year as the lender in fact allowed the borrower the interest free use of the money.[63] Under this approach the amount of the gift was calculable as of the last day of each calendar year during which the loan was outstanding.[64] In the context of a "term loan" the amount of the gift transfer was the excess at the time of the loan of (1) the amount of money borrowed over (2) the then–present value of the principal and interest payments to be made under the terms of the loan.[65]

With the enactment of §7872 (described below) the amount of the deemed payment from the lender to the borrower is to be determined solely under this Code provision.[66] This provision is applicable to both income tax and gift tax determinations. Consequently, the amount of the gift is not to be determined under the *Dickman* analysis, even if the applicable federal rate is less than a fair market interest rate.[67]

3. Income Tax Issues

In a commercial loan situation where interest is charged (rather than a discount obligation being issued), on the due date of that loan the borrower must pay to the lender not only the amount of the loan principal but also a specified interest amount for the use of the principal sum. Prior to the Tax Reform Act of 1984, in the case of an interest-free loan, the question arose as to whether a "phantom interest" amount (that would have been charged in a traditional arm's length loan transaction) might be imputed as income to the lender. The federal income tax consequences of these below-market loans was not clear. In the nonfamily below-market demand loan context, the Tax Court had consistently held that the interest free benefit of such loans did not produce taxable income.[68]

4. Section 7872 Below-Market Loan Tax Principles

a. Conceptual Framework

Section 7872 was subsequently enacted, relating to the tax treatment of loans that, in substance, result in a gift, payment of compensation, dividend, capital contribution, or other similar payment from the lender to the borrower. Loans that are subject to this provision and that do not require the payment of any interest, or require interest payments at a rate below the statutory rate (i.e., below the "applicable federal rate"), are recharacterized as an arm's-length transaction in which the lender made a loan to the borrower in exchange for a note requiring the payment of interest at the applicable federal rate. This results in the lender and borrower being treated as if:

- the borrower paid interest to the lender that (for income tax purposes): (1) may be deductible to the borrower and (2) is includible in income by the lender; and
- the lender (at the inception of this transaction): (1) made a gift subject to the gift tax (in the case of a gratuitous transaction, as noted above), or (2) paid a dividend (in the case of a below-market interest loan from the corporation to a shareholder), or (3) made a capital contribution (in the case of a below-market interest loan to a corporation from a shareholder), or (4) paid compensation (in the case of a below-market interest loan by an employer to a person providing services), or (5) because of a below interest loan, made some other payment characterized in accordance with the true, economic substance of the transaction.

b. Gift Tax Rules

In the case of a demand loan, for gift tax purposes the lender is treated as transferring to the borrower and the borrower is treated as receiving from the lender an amount equal to the foregone interest on an annual basis, as of the last day of the calendar year.[69] In the situation of a gift loan,[70] which is a term loan for gift tax purposes the lender is treated as transferring to the borrower and the borrower is treated as receiving from the lender an amount equal to the excess of (1) the amount of the loan over (2) the present value of all principal and interest payments due under the loan.[71] That gift amount is treated as transferred as of the date that the loan is made.

c. Income Tax Rules

For income tax purposes, with a demand loan, (1) the donee/borrower is treated as transferring to the lender and (2) the lender is treated as receiving from the borrower an amount equal to the foregone interest. These events are treated as occurring on an annual basis, as of the last day of the calendar year.[72] Consequently, this foregone interest is (1) included in income by the lender and (2) deductible by the borrower to the same extent as interest actually due on the loan from the borrower.

Example: On January 1, P, a calendar-year taxpayer, loans $200,000 to S, a calendar-year taxpayer, for two years at 5% simple interest payable annually. If the applicable federal rate is 12% compounded semiannually, the amount treated as immediately transferred by the lender to the borrower for gift tax purposes would be $24,760 (i.e., the excess of $200,000 over the present value of all payments due under the loan as discounted at the applicable federal rate [assumed to be 12%]). The amount treated as retransferred by the borrower to the lender on the last day of each of the two calendar years would be $14,720 (i.e., the excess of interest computed at the applicable federal rate, compounded semiannually, over the interest expense actually payable on the loan). This $14,720 interest amount, which would be (i) included in income by the lender and (ii) deductible by the borrower to the extent permitted by the rules governing interest deductions (§163, etc.), would be in addition to the $10,000 interest actually due each year under the terms of the loan.[73]

As noted above, the adequacy of any stated interest and the amount of any deemed payments are determined by reference to an applicable federal rate.[74]

d. Small Gift Loan Exception

No amount is treated as transferred by the lender to the borrower or retransferred by the borrower to the lender for any day during which the aggregate outstanding amount of loans does not exceed $10,000.[75] This small loan rule does not apply, however, if the loan is directly attributable to the purchase or carrying of income producing assets.[76] This exception allows small interest-free loans to children and grandchildren to help them fund short-term cash requirements, medical expenses, educational expenses, and similar costs without incurring income and gift tax consequences.[77]

e. Gift Loan Interest Accrual Limitation

The amount treated as retransferred by the borrower to the lender for any day on which the aggregate amount of loans between the lender and the borrower does not exceed $100,000 is limited to the borrower's net investment income for the year.[78] If the borrower has outstanding two or more gift loans, net investment income is allocated among such loans in proportion to the respective amounts that would be treated as retransferred by the borrower without regard to this limitation.[79] If a borrower has less than $1,000 of net investment income for the year, the borrower's net investment income for the year is deemed to be zero.[80] Accordingly, if the aggregate outstanding amount of loans from the lender to the borrower does not exceed $100,000 on any day during a year and the borrower has less than $1,000 of net investment income for the year, no amount is treated as retransferred by the borrower to the lender for such year.[81] The objective of this provision is to enable greater flexibility to an older generation member in loaning funds without interest to a younger generation member without triggering the application of the §7872 imputed interest rules. For example, this could enable a loan to a child to assist the child in the purchase of a personal residence.

f. Tax Planning Observations

Some tax planning in this context may still be available, notwithstanding the limitations of the below-market interest loans provision, including:

- The client may use the $10,000 and the $100,000 exceptions for loans to children and grandchildren for such purposes as funding their personal expenditures.
- The client may make a gift loan to a child, grandchild, or trust for such individuals when the borrower may receive a significantly larger investment return than

the percentage specified as the applicable federal rate. This could be particularly relevant during periods of low interest rates when the applicable federal rate would also be low.

- The client may use the $100,000 or less exception to provide a loan to facilitate the purchase by the younger generation members of $100,000 of no-yield growth stock, assuming that the stock continues to be held for investment.

The cost of interest-free loans is significantly moderated when interest rates (and the applicable federal rate) are low. Consequently, significant benefits may be realized through exploiting a low interest rate environment.

D. Loans of Property or Credit

1. Loans of Real Property and Tangible Personal Property

Rather than loaning money on an interest-free (or below-market rate) basis, a parent may lend to his or her child certain real property or tangible personal property. For example, a parent could allow a child to live rent free in a personal residence or vacation property owned by the parent. Alternatively, the parent might allow the rent-free use by a child of an automobile, yacht, or airplane. These examples all assume use of such property for personal purposes of the child. Alternatively, the parent might lend some of these types of property to a child for use in the child's business activity.

The utilization of such property on a rent-free basis is often considered to be outside the scope of §7872.[82] Whether gift tax law has sufficiently evolved to require the inclusion of the rent-free use of such property as within the definition of gift transfers is problematic. The concept of the rent-free use of property ultimately is not really economically different than the rent-free use of funds and, accordingly, an appropriate fair rental value should be included in the tax base in this context. In many instances, but certainly not all situations, the amount may be less than an annual donee exclusion. This assumes, of course, that the annual donee exclusion was not otherwise exhausted by cash or direct property gifts made by the donor/lender.

2. Loan of Creditworthiness

The parent might make his or her credit standing available to a child. For example, a parent might guarantee a loan from a bank or other financial institution when the child borrows funds to acquire a personal residence or to start a business. Alternatively, the repayment of a loan obtained from a financial institution by a child might be secured with collateral provided by the parent. This credit assistance might enable securing a reduced interest rate on the loan from the financial institution. This assistance by a family member ordinarily should not be an income or gift tax event.[83]

E. Tax-Free Property Exchanges with Family Members

1. Possible Like-Kind Property Exchange Situations

The client may have appreciated property with substantial potential for future capital growth. The client may not wish to sell this property in a taxable transaction because he or she would then realize substantial gain that must be recognized for federal income tax purposes and would, thereby, incur a significant income tax liability.[84] He or she may wish to transform that asset into another asset, perhaps one that has a higher potential for producing current income but has a reduced capital appreciation potential. In other situations, property may have unique family heritage value and the objective is to assure that this property remains within the family.

Under these alternative circumstances, the client could enter into a tax-free exchange transaction with a younger family member, transferring the highly appreciated property in exchange for a property that is either already held or specially acquired by the exchanging family member for purposes of this tax-free exchange transaction. If property is to be specially acquired for this purpose, the client could possibly identify the replacement property with the desired income and investment potential characteristics. The other, younger family member could then acquire that property for purposes of completing the tax-free exchange transaction with the first family member (i.e., the older generation member). Interim loans could often be obtained to facilitate this purchase.

2. Objective of the Tax-Free Exchange Transaction

The objective of entering into an exchange transaction is to postpone any recognition, for federal income tax purposes, of the gain realized upon the transfer of the property. In the interim, the amount that otherwise would be used for the federal income tax payment remains invested in the property and might be used to generate additional income and appreciation.

If the replacement property received in the exchange is held (presumably by the older-generation member) until death, the potential capital gains tax on the pre- and postexchange appreciation will disappear by reason of the income tax basis step up that occurs at death.[85] In the interim, the client could use the newly acquired replacement property as collateral for a loan to obtain additional funds, if necessary.[86] The interest expense on such a loan might be deductible if that interest is business related or otherwise qualifies under a deduction provision.[87] The value of that interest expense deduction will depend, however, upon the payor's marginal income tax bracket.

3. Income Tax Rules Applicable to the Property Exchange

a. Tax-Free Exchange Treatment

No gain (or loss) is recognized on the exchange of property held for productive use in a trade or business or for investment if such property is exchanged solely for property of like kind, which will be held either for productive use in a trade or business or for investment.[88] Because this provision also applies to exchanges of depreciated property, ordinarily a transferor would seek to avoid its applicability when property has declined in value below its tax basis. This loss recognition may ordinarily be accomplished by a disposition for non-like-kind consideration (therefore not eligible for tax recognition postponement).

Certain property is not eligible for this like-kind tax-free exchange treatment, particularly:

- inventory;
- stocks, bonds, or notes;
- other securities or evidences of indebtedness;
- interests in a partnership;
- certificates of trust or beneficial interests; or
- choses in action.[89]

If an exchange would be a like-kind exchange (as described above), but property received in the exchange consists not only of tax-free exchange eligible property but also of other property or money, gain realized (if any) to the recipient of the non-like-kind property must be recognized. The gain recognized will be in an amount not in excess of the sum of the money and the fair market value of nonqualifying property (i.e., the "boot") received in the transaction.[90]

Example: Client owns raw land having a tax basis of 10x and a fair market value of 25x (thereby having 15x of accrued unrealized gain). He exchanges the land with child (or trust for child) for a replacement parcel ("like-kind" property) having a fair market value of 20x but also receives 5x cash "to boot." The client must recognize the 5x of money received because this is "boot" (or non-like-kind property), rather than like-kind property, and is of an amount that is less than the gain realized in the transaction.

Although this like-kind exchange technique is sometimes suggested for making a transfer of a personal residence, the personal residence transfer will not fit within the like-kind provision because it is not "held either for productive use in a trade or business or for investment." Further, the opportunity under §121 to exclude from gross income $250,000 of gain ($500,000 on a joint return) eliminates the necessity for most taxpayers to even attempt to avoid capital gains realization on the personal residence.

b. Limitation for Like-Kind Exchanges Between Related Persons

A special limitation is imposed on like-kind exchanges with related parties. This provision has similarity to the installment sales provision concerning sales to related parties and a subsequent disposition of the transferred property. If one party exchanges property with a related party[91] and the first party would otherwise be entitled to nonrecognition treatment on the exchange of that property, but within two years of the date of the last transfer that was part of that exchange, either (1) the related party disposes of the property or (2) the taxpayer disposes of the similar or related property received in the exchange from the related party, the original tax-free exchange will not qualify for like-kind exchange treatment (and gain postponement).[92] This gain (or loss) will be recognized[93] as of the date of the subsequent disposition.[94]

A disposition of the transferred property received in the like-kind exchange will not invalidate the nonrecognition treatment of the original exchange if that disposition is due to (1) the death of either party or (2) the involuntary conversion of the property,[95] provided that the original exchange occurred before the threat or imminence of the conversion.[96] A disposition for this purpose does include all transfers of the exchange property, such as tax-free transfers to a corporation[97] or to a partnership,[98] unless it is established "to the satisfaction of the Secretary" that neither the exchange nor the disposition had, as one of its principal purposes, the avoidance of federal income tax.[99] A disposition also includes an indirect transfer of the property, such as by means of conveying of the stock of a corporation or an interest in a partnership that owns the property received in the exchange.[100]

The IRS will not issue a ruling under §1031(f) on whether an exchange described in §1031(f) involving related parties, or a subsequent disposition of property involved in the exchange, has as one of its principal purposes the avoidance of federal income tax, or is part of a transaction (or series of transactions) structured to avoid the purposes of §1031(f), except in the case of (1) a transaction involving an exchange of undivided interests in different properties that results in each taxpayer holding either the entire interest in a single property or a larger undivided interest in any of the properties, or (2) a disposition of property in a nonrecognition transaction.[101]

4. Estate Tax Inclusion of the Exchanged Property

Property transferred in a like-kind exchange for full and adequate consideration should not be includible in a person's estate for federal estate tax purposes.[102] The replacement property will be included in the transferor's gross estate, however. If the exchange transaction is not for equal value, a gift transfer will have been made as of the time of that exchange. Further, if any rights are retained with respect to that transferred property, the IRS might assert that an estate tax transfer provision is applicable as of the time of death.[103]

F. Private Annuities

1. Estate Planning Objectives

a. Planning Environment for Using a Private Annuity

The client, after analyzing his or her net worth and probable future income position, may conclude that there is an asset that he or she may wish to remove from his or her estate (for federal estate tax purposes) because that asset has significant potential to subsequently appreciate. The client may also wish (or may need) to retain, however, the present value of the asset for satisfying his or her personal living costs. Further, because of the unique nature of the asset (for example, a family farm, family residence—including vacation property—or closely held corporate stock), the client may wish this asset to remain within his or her family. Accordingly, he or she may transfer the asset to another family member (often a member of a younger generation) pursuant to a "private annuity" arrangement.[104] This could be an alternative to (1) an installment sale or (2) a like-kind exchange between family members (as discussed above).

As discussed in Chapter 7, F.2.a., the IRS has proposed changes to the income tax treatment of private annuities that could make this planning technique less advantageous.[105]

b. Concept of a Private Annuity

A "private annuity" is created when a person transfers (1) property (usually appreciated in value) to another individual or to a trust or a corporation (other than an insurance company or other organization that regularly issues insurance policies and annuity contracts) in exchange for (2) the transferee's contractual promise to regularly pay the transferor some agreed periodic amount for the duration of the transferor's life.[106]

Example: Annuitant transfers family farm to Child in exchange for Child's promise to pay Annuitant 10x per month for the duration of Annuitant's life. This annuity arrangement is described as a "private annuity" because the payment obligor (i.e., the child) is not in the business of issuing annuity contracts on a commercial basis. Rather, the transaction is entered into on an individualized basis and does not contemplate a spread of any actuarial risks by the obligor undertaking a number of such risks.

c. Federal Tax Planning Objectives

(1) Estate Tax Avoidance Objective

An important tax planning objective of this arrangement is to remove from the individual's estate for federal estate tax purposes the asset being transferred in exchange for the receipt of the annuity promise and annuity payments. The property for which the annuity promise was received by the transferor should be transferred for appropriate consideration contemporaneously with the issuance of that annuity promise. Consequently, the transferred asset should not be includible in the transferor's gross estate because adequate consideration (the annuity contract) has been received for the property.

This property transfer is completed in exchange for a "promise" by the transferee to pay a fixed sum of money at specified periodic intervals over the lifetime of the transferor (or, occasionally, for some specified time certain). Under a lifetime annuity arrangement, the promise made by the transferee expires at the death of the property transferor. Accordingly, having then lapsed, the annuity promise itself no longer has any value for federal estate tax purposes. Under the annuity contract, the transferor/annuitant will receive annuity payments and, if those payments have not been expended as of the annuitant's death, they will remain in the decedent's gross estate.[107]

(2) Gift Tax Avoidance Objective

An important tax planning objective in the private annuity context is to remove the transferred property from the annuitant's estate without triggering a gift tax liability for the annuitant when the annuity promise is acquired. This can occur if the exchange of the property for the annuity promise is completed for full value. The property should be transferred for an annuity promise having equivalent fair market value.[108]

(3) Income Tax Postponement Objective

Additionally, for federal income tax purposes, the timing of the recognition of both property gain and annuity income may be postponed (an annuity transaction income reporting approach is applicable), rather than the exchange of the property for the contract being treated as an immediate gain recognition transaction for all realized gain. Each subsequent annuity payment will include a return of tax basis, a portion of the accrued gain, plus the appropriate interest component. Therefore, the transferor will enjoy the "time value of money" for the taxes payable on the gain derived from the transferred property when the tax payment dates are postponed. The measurement of that value is dependent upon the application of the appropriate actuarial tables, as discussed below. However, as discussed in Chapter 7, F.2.a., the IRS issued proposed regulations in 2006 that would eliminate the gain deferral possibility ordinarily associated with private annuities.[109]

2. Private Annuitant's Income Taxation—Basic Elements

a. Income Tax Components

Prior to the promulgation of the regulation changing the timing rule, the exchange by the transferor of his or her appreciated property (real estate or closely held corporate stock) for an annuity promise would avoid the immediate recognition of all the property value gain (for federal income tax purposes), if the arrangement was structured correctly.[110] Rather, the property gain would be recognized on a periodic basis for federal income tax purposes, that is, as the annuity payments are received. In addition, each periodic payment would include an annuity income (or interest) component. Accordingly, each annuity payment would consist of the following ingredients[111]:

- The recovery of the investor's capital. The investor's income tax basis would be returned without income tax consequences.[112]
- Capital gain. This gain would be attributable to the difference between (1) the adjusted basis of the property transferred and (2) the value of the private annuity promise when received. This value will be measured as of the date that the annuity promise exchange transaction is concluded. This assumes that the value of the annuity promise is equivalent to the value of the transferred property (i.e., that the annuity transaction has no gift element).
- The ordinary income (or interest) element. This represents the return on the investment in the annuity contract (i.e., the payment for the use of the funds).[113]

Where the property, if sold, would cause the realization of recapture of depreciation income (or a similar, special category ordinary income item), that portion must be separately identified (as a split segment of the capital gain portion).[114] Further, where depreciable property is sold to a related person at a gain (including in a private annuity transaction), that gain may be transformed into ordinary income, thereby eliminating the capital gain component noted above.[115]

In 2006, the IRS issued proposed regulations that would eliminate the capital gain deferral possibility associated with private annuities.[116] The proposed regulations would require the immediate recognition of gain on any appreciated property exchanged for an annuity, whether the annuity contract is issued by an insurance company or some other taxpayer and whether the contract is secured or unsecured.[117] Under Prop. Reg. §1.1001-1(j), the amount received for the property would be the fair market value of the annuity contract at the time of the exchange, as determined under §7520. For purposes of calculating the initial "investment in the contract" for the §72(b) exclusion ratio for the annuity payments (which determines the ordinary income component of the payments), the proposed regulations define the "aggregate amount of premiums or other consideration paid for the contract"[118] as the "amount realized attributable to the annuity contract," which the proposed regulations would, in turn, define as the fair market value of the contract at the time of the exchange.[119] The regulations, when final, would generally be effective for exchanges of property for annuity contracts, and annuity contracts received in such exchanges, after October 18, 2006.[120] Although the value of this technique would be reduced for significantly appreciated property, this arrangement may still provide significant benefits in circumstances where the annuitant dies prior to the lapse of the annuitant's normal life expectancy.

b. Significance of Capital Gain Treatment

The differentiation between the capital gain, recapture income, and interest income portions will not be significant when ordinary income and capital gain tax rates are equal or not very dissimilar. When the ordinary income tax rate is 39.6% and the capital gain rate is 20%, this 19.6% differential will often be quite significant.[121] Those differences in tax characterization may not be important, however, for purposes of determining the time at which such income must be recognized for federal income tax purposes.[122]

3. Dividing the "Return of Capital" Portion

a. Dividing Between Basis and Property Gain

To determine the capital return portion of the annuity payment, the annuitant must establish his or her adjusted income tax basis for the transferred property.[123] That occurs by determining the original cost basis and making appropriate adjustments: (1) for additions to basis (often attributable to property improvements) and (2) for reductions to basis attributable to depreciation allowances, etc., and other prior capital recoveries.[124]

The annuitant must then determine the present value of the annuity promise (at the time of the annuity transaction).[125] That value must be divided between: (1) the return of capital portion and (2) the capital gain (including recapture income) portion. These two segments together constitute the amount to be excluded from classification as the ordinary income element that is taxable as regular "annuity income." The amount of each annuity payment to be so excluded as the capital portion is the ratio of the taxpayer's "investment in the contract" to the expected return under the contract.[126]

The "expected return" under the annuity contract is determined by multiplying (1) the annual total payments by (2) the annuitant's life expectancy.[127] This will enable establishing an "exclusion ratio."[128] That exclusion ratio amount (that amount not treated as ordinary annuity income) represents the portion of each payment which, as noted above, constitutes either (1) the nontaxable return of investment or (2) the capital gain portion and any separate recapture income portion. That capital portion is reported, for federal income tax purposes, on the basis of its capital return and gain components.

As discussed in F.2.a. of this chapter, the IRS issued proposed regulations in 2006 that would eliminate the capital gain deferral associated with private annuities.[129] The annuitant's recognition of the entire gain in the transferred property at the time of the transfer would mean that the subsequent annuity payments received would not have a capital gain component.

b. The Capital Gain Portion

The capital gain portion in the annuity transaction is the difference between: (1) the taxpayer's adjusted basis in the transferred property; and (2) the value of the annuity promise when received. Until changed by the proposed regulations, this capital gain may be reported over a period of years measured by the annuitant's life expectancy.[130]

Where depreciable property is transferred in exchange for a private annuity, the depreciation recapture (and similar) provisions may be applicable, as noted above.[131] In an installment sale the depreciation recapture component cannot be postponed.[132] This rule does not appear to be applicable to a private annuity, thereby permitting postponement of recognition of even this depreciation recapture income element (absent applicability of the rule in the proposed regulations).

A private annuity transaction may be concluded with a closely held corporation, rather than with a family member (or a trust for that family member). The annuitant could transfer his or her shares to the corporation for redemption in exchange for the private annuity contract. Capital gain from this "stock sale" might be transformed from capital gain into ordinary income if (1) the property transferred in exchange for a private annuity contract consists of stock in a closely held corporation, (2) the transferee of the stock is the issuing corporation, (3) the transferor does not qualify for "redemption" treatment, and (4) the corporation has "earnings and profits."[133] If dividend treatment (rather than sale or exchange/redemption treatment) is applicable to the transaction, the entire amount received will be gross income until the allocable "earnings and profits" amount of the distributing corporation has been exhausted. Thereafter, the income tax basis attributable to the "redeemed" stock will be treated as recoverable, with any capital gain subsequently being realized after the basis recovery.[134]

c. Annuity Income Portion

The remaining portion of each annuity payment received (other than those items described immediately above) is ordinary income (the equivalent of interest income), similar to the treatment of payments received under a commercial annuity. This treatment will extend for the duration of the annuity payments (until the death of the transferor).

d. Mortality Gain or Loss

An annuitant receiving payments under a private annuity contract usually does not die on the precise date of the lapse of his or her projected life expectancy (as determined on the original date of the private annuity contract). The life expectancy tables are merely an experience average. Accordingly, the annuitant will ordinarily either receive more or less than the amount anticipated under the original life expectancy/expected return computation when the private annuity transaction was concluded. If the annuitant dies before the projected date of death, the entire capital investment will not have been returned through the periodic annuity payments. Because, under the terms of the annuity contract, the annuity payments will terminate as of death, a loss will occur and a loss deduction will be allowed on the annuitant's final income tax return to the extent of the differential between income tax basis and the recovered capital.[135]

If the annuitant lives beyond his or her life expectancy, all of the invested capital will be recovered upon reaching that life expectancy date. The capital gain for the transferred property is fully reportable as of the time the annuitant lives to the length of his or her projected life expectancy (as determined as of the time of the annuity promise). Amounts subsequently received that are attributable to the capital return exclusion portion are not thereafter excludible from gross income. Rather, these amounts are includible in ordinary income, that amount being treated as "mortality gain" (because, from the actuarial perspective, the annuitant has lived too long).[136]

4. Private Annuitant's Gift Taxation

The assumption in the discussion above is that (1) the value of the transferred property and (2) the value of the annuity promise are equivalent as of the date of the exchange transaction. If, however, the value of the annuity promise received by the annuitant is less than the value of the transferred property, the annuitant will have made a gift transfer to the annuity promisor. The gift amount is the difference in values between (1) the property transferred and (2) the property received (the annuity promise).[137] Ordinarily, in this situation, the value of the transferred property might be greater than the value of the annuity promise provided by the younger generation member (or trust for that person). That portion of the transfer that constitutes a gift is eliminated from the required annuity income tax computations described above. If, however, the annuity promise is illusory the entire transfer is treated as a gift.[138]

This gift portion may be excludible from the gift tax base because of the annual donee exclusion. Further, if the transfer has a gift portion and if the annuitant is treated as having a retained income interest in the transferred property, the transferred property eventually will be includible in the annuitant's estate tax base under the estate tax transfer provisions.[139]

The inclusion of a gift tax element will also alter the income tax computation process for determining the taxable and nontaxable elements of each annuity payment. The gift component is excluded from the "return of capital" portion in determining the exclusion ratio under the annuity income tax provision.

5. Transferee's Income Tax Treatment

a. Determining Income Tax Basis for Property Received

In the private annuity transaction the transferee will obtain property in exchange for his or her promise to make periodic annuity payments. Although the value of this promise may be actuarially determined at the time of the private annuity commitment, the transferee will ordinarily pay an amount that is ultimately more or less than the actual value of the annuity promise as of the time of the initial transaction.

The determination of the income tax basis for the property received by the annuity obligor in exchange for the private annuity promise often will not be significant to the obligor for federal income tax purposes until the property is subsequently sold or exchanged by the "purchaser." The income tax basis may be immediately important, however, if depreciation (or other current income tax deductions) may be claimed for the property acquired in the private annuity transaction.

Assuming no gift element in the private annuity transaction, the transferee's tentative income tax basis for the property obtained will equal the value of the annuity promise at the time of the exchange.[140] If a portion of the annuity transaction constitutes a gift, the transferee would make appropriate adjustments to reflect the transferor's income tax basis of that portion.[141]

b. Subsequent Income Tax—Basis Adjustments

To the annuity obligor the value of the annuity promise is the tentative income tax basis of the transferred property as established for federal income tax purposes. That tax basis is used for computing the transferee's depreciation deductions (or any other cost recovery deductions) until the total payments actually made equal the value of the promise.

Each additional payment under the annuity contract would be added to the transferee's current adjusted tax basis and a revised depreciation deduction amount would be determined each year until the transferor dies. At the annuitant's death (when the annuity obligation terminates), the adjusted basis of the asset to the property transferee will be the total of all payments made, less any depreciation deductions previously claimed.

c. Disposition Before Annuitant's Death

If the transferee/annuity obligor disposes of the transferred property before the annuitant's death, the tax basis used in determining the transferor's gain from the property for federal income tax purposes is: (1) the total of the annuity payments actually made under the contract up to that date of disposition, plus (2) the current fair market value of the prospective payments remaining to be made at the date of such disposition. This tax basis would be further (1) increased by any additions to tax basis (such as for improvements to the acquired property) and (2) reduced to reflect depreciation and similar deductions as claimed for federal income tax purposes after the acquisition of the property.[142]

The adjusted basis for determining loss on such a disposition prior to the annuitant's death will be the total of the annuity payments actually made as of the time of disposition (as adjusted for capital improvements, depreciation, etc.). No inclusion of the value of the prospective additional annuity payments will be permitted for purposes of determining any loss from this disposition transaction.

As a result of these differing rules between income tax basis for gain and loss purposes, the selling price may be (1) less than the adjusted basis for gain and (2) greater than the adjusted basis for loss. In this situation, neither gain nor loss would be recognized at the time of the disposition of the property received for the annuity promise. Thereafter, in the gain situation, the continuation of the annuity payments after the sale of the property will not affect the transferee's income tax situation until the total of annuity payments made exceeds the transferee's adjusted basis. After that point, the transferee may deduct the excess loss in the year paid. In the future, in the loss situation, the transferee will incur a loss each time a subsequent annuity payment is made.

d. Interest Paid by Transferor

The property transferor/annuitant will have an ordinary income element in each annuity payment received, as noted above. That annuity income or "interest" segment represents the earnings on the invested funds. The transferee/annuity payor will not be treated as making an interest payment that would be deductible for federal income tax purposes.[143] Rather, all payments made by the property transferee must be capitalized as a cost for the property acquired in exchange for the annuity promise. If interest expense deductions were to be available when the annuity payments were periodically made, presumably those deductions would be in the total amount of the difference between (1) the transferor's expected return and (2) the value of the transferee's annuity commitment as determined at the time of the annuity transaction.

6. Special Precautions for the Transferor

a. Risks

In the private annuity arrangement the transferee of the property ordinarily makes an unsecured and unfunded promise to pay specified amounts to the transferor/annuitant at prescribed intervals for the transferor's lifetime. The transferor may be concerned about the continuation of the annuity payments because of risks that the transferee may be either unable or unwilling to make the payments. However, variations from this unsecured/unfunded promise format may jeopardize certain of the income and estate tax advantages ordinarily available to the transferor in the private annuity transaction. A possible alternative transferee in this context is a trust managed by a competent trustee, but this structure still could present some of the tax issues identified below.

b. Transferred Property Used to Secure Annuity Promise

Prior to the effectiveness of the proposed regulations, the transferor/annuitant in the private annuity arrangement has been permitted to report the realized gain periodically as the annuity payments were being received. If, however, the annuity promise was itself secured by property, the entire gain would be recognized for federal income tax purposes as of the effective date of the annuity transaction.[144] Often, of course, the desire of the annuitant is that the promise should be secured by the transferred property so that the annuitant is more comfortable that the annuity payments will actually be received. Prior to the effectiveness of the proposed revised rule, to avoid gain recognition on the property transfer prior to the time that the cash proceeds for the conveyance of that property were to be periodically received, the annuity promise could not be secured. This obviously mandated that the annuitant/property transferor must feel reasonably satisfied that the annuity promisor would (and would have the financial capacity to) fulfill the annuity promise.

c. Risk of Estate or Gift Tax Inclusion

(1) Gift Transfer Risk

The anticipation in completing a private annuity arrangement is that the transferred property will not be considered a gift for federal gift tax purposes. The premise is that the value of the annuity promise received is fully equal to the property transferred.[145] This gift tax treatment is based on the assumption that (1) although the property received by the annuitant is only a personal commitment by the transferee to make periodic payments, (2) this commitment is based on that promisor's actual ability and real commitment to pay. If the payment of the annuity promise is directly and primarily dependent upon payment from the income stream derived from the transferred property concern might exist concerning the value of the annuity promise.

If the private annuity transaction is arranged so that, in reality, the annuitant actually relies on the income derived from the transferred property to satisfy the annuity payment obligation, rather than the creditworthiness of the obligor, the IRS may successfully assert that a "life interest" in the property was retained by the annuitant. Under these circumstances, the special valuation rules, particularly §2702, would apply and require that the annuity payments be made in a specified form and amount to determine whether a gift transfer was made. If the payments do not comply with this provision, the entire value of the transferred property would be a gift.[146]

Example: "Annuitant" transfers property (an office building having a fair market value of 10x) to Transferee in exchange for an annuity promise also having a fair market value of 10x. The annuity promise is secured by both the rental income from the office building and the equity value in the office building. Under such circumstances, annuitant will probably be treated as having a §2702 "retained interest" in the building for gift tax valuation purposes, with no gift transfer having been made at the time of the annuity promise.

(2) Estate Tax

Even if no gift transfer is treated as occurring, the transferred property could be subject to inclusion in the annuitant's gross estate for federal estate tax purposes. By retaining a life income interest that is tied to the income generated by the property, the annuitant may be considered to have retained a life estate for estate tax inclusion purposes.[147]

d. Illusory Promise/Federal Gift Tax Risk

The assumption in the private annuity transaction context is that the promise of the annuity obligor has genuine value and that, therefore, the value of the annuity promise is equivalent to the value of the property received. As noted above, if value equivalency does not exist, a gift transaction, rather than an arm's-length annuity transaction, would be concluded to the extent of the differential between (1) the value of the transferred property and (2) the value of the annuity promise.

Where the obligor making the annuity promise has no independent financial substance (other than the property received in the annuity transaction), the IRS may assert that the annuity promise itself has no intrinsic value.[148] Under such circumstances, the entire value of the property transferred will be treated as transferred by gift, rather than for valuable consideration.

Example: "Annuitant" transfers a parcel of undeveloped real estate having a fair market value of 100x to a child who has recently reached adult status and, consequently, has the legal capacity to contract. The transfer is in exchange for an annuity promise that purports to have a fair market value of 100x. The undeveloped real estate is producing no income. The child has only a minimal independent personal net worth. Availability of cash flow to the child to enable the annuity promise payments periodically to be made is questionable. The transaction likely will be treated as a gift transfer, rather than as an annuity arrangement, notwithstanding the existence of an enforceable private annuity contract.[149]

e. Illusory Promise/Federal Estate Tax Risk

The IRS also may assert that a private annuity transaction is not genuine for estate tax purposes where the transferor receiving the annuity promise is in the advanced stages of a terminal illness at the time of the annuity transaction.[150] The annuity obligor would be anticipating transferring the property with little consideration actually being paid, but the eventual argument by the taxpayer estate for estate tax purposes would be that the property was transferred for equivalent value. Under these circumstances, the annuity contract would be anticipated to expire shortly after completion of the annuity arrangement.[151] If inadequate consideration is deemed paid, the arrangement could be treated as a retained life interest in the transferred property, causing subsequent inclusion in the gross estate.[152]

f. Use of Irrevocable Trust to Make Annuity Promise

The estate tax inclusion risks described immediately above are particularly applicable if the promisor of the private annuity is an irrevocable trust. Estate tax risks to the private annuitant/property transferor may increase if the annuity promise is made by a trust that is the transferee of the property.[153] For income tax purposes immediate recognition of gain on the exchange by the transferor-annuitant will probably result.[154] If the annuitant is also the grantor of the trust, the grantor trust income tax rules (rather than the annuity income rules) may be applicable, treating the annuitant as the current owner of the trust income.[155] To eliminate or reduce these risks the annuitant/trust grantor should consider the following planning options:

- Fund the trust with additional assets so that the payment of the annuity is not wholly dependent upon the earnings stream from the property transferred in exchange for the annuity promise.
- Use an independent trustee as the trustee of the trust.
- Assure that the annuitant has no retained interest under the trust that would cause inclusion under the estate tax transfer provisions.

G. Joint or Split Purchases

1. Description of Split-Purchase Technique

In a joint or "split purchase," two parties (often a parent and a child) will purchase separate interests in a property being acquired from a third-party seller. They separately purchase "horizontal" interests in a property (an interest in property based on either present or future use), rather than "vertical" interests.[156] For example, in a split-purchase situation involving horizontal interests, the older-generation member may acquire a life interest in the property. The younger-generation member simultaneously may acquire a remainder interest in the purchased property. That remainder interest will vest in the possession of the younger generation member upon the death of the life tenant/older family member. The objective is to have a property ownership arrangement that, due to this joint ownership arrangement, (1) avoids gift tax at the time of the acquisition of the several components of the property, and (2) eliminates gross estate inclusion at the death of the older-generation member for the acquired property.

The allocation of the values and the consideration paid by each family member for the portions of the property acquired will be dependent on the application of actuarial factors (i.e., how much time is anticipated to expire before the remainder interest vests in possession as of the death of the life tenant?).[157]

Example: Mother and Son together buy an apartment building for $100,000. Mother is the life tenant. Her interest in that property is actuarially determined, based on her age at the time of purchase. The remaining portion is attributable to the remainder interest in the property.[158] To constitute an arm's-length arrangement the assumption is that Mother and Son need to pay for their proportionate parts of the purchase price for the apartment building. As the life tenant, Mother receives all of the rental income during her lifetime. At Mother's death, the apartment building is owned outright by Son, without any claim on the ownership of the building by Mother's estate (because her life estate terminates upon her death).

2. Gift Tax Considerations

a. Actuarial Determinations Required

The primary concern in this estate planning context is the possible application of the special valuation rules imposed under §2702 for transfers of various divided ownership interests among family members.[159] Split-interest purchases are governed by the rules under §2702(c)(2). The fundamental purpose of these rules is to ensure that the holder of the life interest does not make a disguised gift to the remainder beneficiary by accepting payments that are other than a fixed annuity or unitrust payment, as determined under §7520, thereby deflecting assets away from the estate of the older generation without appropriate exposure to transfer tax rules. If the payments are in other than the required form, the life interest will be valued at zero, and the remainder interest will be assigned the entire value of the property for gift tax purposes.

If a parent and child make a split purchase of property, with the parent acquiring the life estate and the child the remainder interest, the parent is considered to have made a gift of the entire property to the child, less any consideration furnished by the child.[160] Split purchases are treated (under §2702(c)(2)) as a purchase of the entire property by the party holding the term or life interest, with a subsequent transfer of the remainder interest to the other party.[161] If the person receiving the remainder interest contributes inadequate consideration, as determined by §2702, the individual holding the term or life interest is considered to have made a gift to the remainder beneficiary. Because the portion held by the life interest holder is valued at zero, this causes the entire value to be treated as transferred by gift to the child, except to the extent that the child provided consideration for the purchase.

This rule applies for transactions involving members of the transferor's "family."[162] A family member includes only (1) the transferor's spouse, (2) any ancestor or lineal descendant of such individual or the individual's spouse, (3) any brother or sister of the individual, and (4) any spouse of the individuals identified in (2) and (3).[163] Consequently, these limitations will not apply when the split purchase arrangement is with others (e.g., nieces and nephews). Therefore, in these situations these arrangements might be concluded with these more remote relatives, or trusts for them, without invoking this §2702 zero-value rule.

b. Term Interests in Certain Tangible Property

A special rule does apply to the valuation of a term interest in tangible property if its use does not have a substantial effect upon the valuation of the remainder interest in the property. This exception would be particularly appropriate for joint interests in artwork and similar objects. "Tangible property" for this purpose is tangible property for which no deduction for depreciation or depletion would be allowable if the property were used in a trade or business or held for the production of income and as to which the failure to exercise any rights under the term interest would not increase the value of the property passing at the end of the term interest.[164]

Under this special exception the value of the term interest is to be "the amount which the holder of the term interest establishes as the amount for which such interest could be sold to an unrelated third party."[165] The example in the regulations illustrating this rule identifies a transfer by P of a painting having a fair market value of $2 million to P's child, B, with P retaining the use of the painting for 10 years. The painting does not possess an ascertainable useful life and would not be depreciable if it were used in a trade or business or held for the production of income. Assume the value of the term interest, determined under §7520 (with rates applicable as of the time of the transfer) is $1,220,000 and P establishes that a willing buyer of P's 10-year interest would pay $500,000 for the interest. The amount of the gift would be $1.5 million (the difference between the fair market value of the painting and the value established under the willing buyer/willing seller rule), rather than the gift being for the full value of the property.[166]

This rule appears to be more beneficial than the basic rule permitting an offset only of the amount contributed by the younger generation member. The IRS's premise, however, is that the fair market value of the retained interest will ordinarily be considerably less than the value determined under the §7520 tables. Consequently, the gift tax cost may not be significantly different than if the §7520 tables are applicable, unless a high valuation can be demonstrated for the interim interest. Further, valuations under this special rule will be exceedingly difficult to accomplish.

3. Investment/Income Tax Considerations

a. Investment Return to Life Tenant

During his or her lifetime, the life tenant will receive all the income from the entire property (assuming the property to be investment property rather than tangible property, as noted immediately above).[167] This occurs even though the life tenant has not contributed the entire consideration for the acquisition of the property. Consequently, the life tenant will have "leveraged up" the investment return on his or her investment (at least for the life term).

Example: Mother (M) pays 60x of the purchase price, acquiring a life interest, and Daughter (D) pays 40x of the 100x purchase price for a remainder interest in an apartment building. The building produces net rent approximating a 10% per annum yield. M receives 10x interest per year on her investment of 60x. This constitutes a return of approximately 16% per annum on her invested funds. The excess return received by the life tenant will compensate that life tenant for the continuing economic decline in the value of the life tenant's asset (i.e., the life interest in the property will eventually terminate at death).

The life tenant's interest in the purchased asset will decline in value through the mere passage of time since that interest will terminate at the death of the life tenant and the life tenant is growing older every day. Accordingly, from the investment perspective, if (as determined by reference to the relevant actuarial tables) this premium is insufficient, as of the life tenant's death, to enable recovery of the investment in the life tenancy (plus an appropriate investment return), this investment would have been financially deficient. This would occur when the life tenant actually died prior to the expiration of the life expectancy anticipated under the valuation tables as of the time of the initial completion of the split-purchase arrangement. A greater than anticipated investment return would result, however, if the life tenant lives longer than the life tenant's life expectancy, as determined under the applicable valuation tables as of the time of the split-purchase property acquisition transaction.

b. Life Tenant's Income Taxation

The entire current income from the property is includible in the gross income of the life tenant for federal income tax purposes. This assumes the investment return on the acquired property is taxable income. The acquired asset could be, for example, a state or local government bond and, in that situation, the interest income received from this bond is not includible in the gross income of the life tenant.[168]

The asset the life tenant acquires (a life tenancy) is a "wasting asset" because it expires upon the death of the life tenant. Accordingly, absent any special limitations, for federal income tax purposes, the life tenant should be permitted to amortize (on a straight-line basis) the cost of this interest over the life tenant's anticipated life expectancy.[169] Pursuant to a special limitation, however, no depreciation or amortization deduction is allowed for any term interest in property for any period during which the remainder interest is held (directly or indirectly) by a related person.[170]

The holder of the term interest will be entitled, however, for federal income tax purposes to the depreciation or amortization deduction with respect to the underlying property. Consequently, depreciation would be available for an investment in improved real estate where the rental income is being received by a life tenant.[171]

c. Investment Return to Remainder Beneficiary

During the life tenant's lifetime, the remainder beneficiary receives none of the income from the acquired property.[172] As of the death of the life tenant, the remainder beneficiary will be entitled, however, to the entire, unencumbered interest in the property.[173] Whether, from the investment perspective, this investment is favorable for the remainder beneficiary is also dependent on the duration of the life tenancy.

Example: In the example above, D's investment of 40x results in an asset worth 100x (even assuming no interim fluctuation in the value of the real property) as of the time of M's death. Therefore, the investment of 40x will produce an "income return" of 60x to D as of the time of M's death (because at that time D receives a property worth 100x for the original 40x investment), but this will not constitute a realization event for federal income tax purposes. Whether satisfactory investment results are realized depends on whether the 60x in value accruing for the duration of the life tenancy produces a better return than market rates of return. Where the asset appreciated during the period of the life tenancy, that appreciation will also accrue to the remainder beneficiary at the time possession of the remainder interest commences, thereby enhancing the investment return to the remainder beneficiary.

d. Remainder Beneficiary's Income Tax Considerations

For federal income tax purposes, during the period of the life tenancy the remainder beneficiary will:

- receive no gross income;
- have no amortization deductions for the investment in the remainder interest (it is actually increasing in value as the life tenant gets older); and
- receive no depreciation or depletion deduction for the underlying acquired property (e.g., where a building has been acquired through a split purchase).

When receiving the property at the death of the life tenant, the remainder beneficiary faces no realization event for federal income tax purposes. The income tax basis to the remainder beneficiary for such property is the amount of the remainder beneficiary's original investment, as adjusted.[174] The basis is not "stepped up" (pursuant to §1014) to the fair market value of the property as of the death of the life tenant. This result occurs because no value attributable to this property is included in the gross estate of the life tenant for federal estate tax purposes.

The remainder beneficiary's cost basis will constitute the income tax basis for determining subsequent gain or loss upon the disposition of the property. That basis is adjusted, as noted above, for previously disallowed amortization of the life interest. If the property is depreciable or depletable, this adjustment will impact on the amount of the depreciation or depletion deduction to the remainder beneficiary. If the property is subsequently sold by the remainder beneficiary, the gain will be measured by the difference between: (1) that adjusted basis (as further adjusted by any depreciation or depletion claimed concerning the property) and (2) the sales price.

4. Spousal Joint Purchase Alternative

a. Description of Transaction

A younger generation member can be the purchaser of the remainder interest portion of property acquired in a split purchase transaction (assuming the impact of the

§2702 valuation rules can be satisfactorily resolved), but this is not the only option in arranging such a purchase. When the entire property is acquired from a third party, an alternative may be for one spouse to acquire a life interest in a property while the other spouse simultaneously acquires a remainder interest in that property.[175]

One objective of such an arrangement might be the sole ownership of the property by the remainder beneficiary at the death of the life tenant without a property transfer being subjected to probate court reporting requirements.[176] This assumes, of course, that the life tenant spouse, rather than the spouse holding the remainder interest, dies first. The remainder interest owner should consider providing in his or her last will that (if dying first) the remainder interest should be transferred to children or to a credit shelter trust, rather than being transferred to the life tenant spouse. Another objective might be the possible avoidance of any state inheritance taxes, since a property transfer might not be deemed to occur at death for state tax purposes.

This technique should also avoid the inclusion of the property in the gross estate for federal estate tax purposes upon the death of the life tenant (because nothing will be transferred by the deceased spouse to the surviving spouse). This result might not be important, however, because, if this property is transferred to the spouse, the transfer would be eligible for the unlimited marital deduction for federal estate tax purposes. This result could be detrimental because the property would not receive a date-of-death-value tax basis since it is not included in the decedent's estate (the transfer occurring under circumstances where no estate tax inclusion is required).

b. Gift Tax Applicability

The assumption in this context is that each spouse is actually funding the purchase of his or her interest from his or her own separate funds. In a community property jurisdiction, this will necessitate that each spouse utilize previously segregated separate property funds for the purpose of acquiring his or her particular interest in the property.

The gift tax valuation principles of §2702 would be applicable to this arrangement. The applicability of the gift tax in this situation would not appear to be significant, however, assuming that a gift tax marital deduction will be available for any transfer from one spouse to the other spouse.

c. Federal Income Tax Applicability

Only limited federal income tax benefits are available in this context. If the purchased asset is depreciable or amortizable, a deduction is available to the life tenant for that expense. No deduction is available if the underlying property does not enable qualification for such a current income tax deduction.

As noted earlier, federal income tax benefits could previously be achieved because an annual amortization deduction (attributable to the wasting nature of the interest in the life estate) was available to offset any income being derived by the life tenant. This benefit was available to both spouses through the filing of a joint federal income tax return. Consequently, the net result would be that, by reason of this type of ownership arrangement, the parties could obtain a current income tax deduction to offset all or part of the income being derived from this investment (even though the underlying property was not depreciable). This amortization deduction has been eliminated, but the cost basis for the property when received by the remainder beneficiary will be increased by this disallowed deduction.[177]

5. Split Ownership Estate Tax Planning

The objective of this joint ownership is to have property received by a younger generation member (or spouse) as of the death of an older generation member (or the other spouse) without the property being treated as an asset of the older generation member (or spouse) for federal estate tax purposes. One specific concern is that, for federal estate tax purposes, the life tenant might be treated as having a "retained life estate" in the property, causing inclusion in the gross estate of the life tenant.[178] For example, the junior family member actually must have contributed his or her own funds for the acquisition of the remainder interest to avoid this estate tax inclusion result. If the older family member contributed the entire consideration for the property (even indirectly through a prior but related gift to the younger family member), the IRS may assert that the arrangement is the equivalent of a retained life interest, with the property passing from the life tenant's estate at death.[179]

Each interest owner must have contributed the appropriate portion of the purchase price. This would be accomplished if the gift tax valuation rules are observed when making the allocation. If the actuarial values used are incorrect, resulting in the life tenant paying an excess portion of the purchase price, the IRS could assert that a portion of the consideration was transferred by gift to the remainder beneficiary, with a life interest retained by the life tenant.

6. Implementing the Split-Purchase Transaction

If, notwithstanding the tax impediments noted above, the parties do implement a split-purchase arrangement,[180] the life tenant and the remainder beneficiary should carefully identify their separate rights and responsibilities with respect to the acquired property. Such matters might include:

- Who is entitled to the revenues from the property, particularly when a portion of the cash flow received might be a "return of capital"? For example, this could occur when a bond was purchased at a premium or when oil production proceeds are received.
- Who has the obligation to maintain the property (such as buildings) when both ordinary or extraordinary repairs and improvements are required?
- Who has the responsibility to pay obligations incurred on the split interest property, including property taxes, casualty insurance premiums, and related income tax liabilities?

- How will the proceeds be divided between the two owners in the event of a voluntary (or an involuntary) disposition of the property held in the split-purchase arrangement?
- How will disputes concerning the management of the property be resolved between the life tenant and the remainder beneficiary?

An understanding between the parties concerning the resolution of these items might be appropriately documented in a contract or memorandum, notwithstanding that (or particularly because) this property is held jointly in a family environment.

H. Sale of Remainder Interest in Property

1. Technique Described

The older-generation member may already own a valuable asset that he or she purchased outright and may wish to enjoy during the remainder of his or her lifetime.[181] At some point, he or she may desire to eliminate this asset from his or her gross estate for federal estate tax purposes. In this situation, the older generation member may wish to sell to a younger-generation member of his or her family a remainder interest in this asset.

Example: Father (F) sells a remainder interest in an apartment building to Daughter (D). F is age 70. The value of the property is $1 million. The pertinent actuarial tables indicate that the remainder interest in such property should be sold for a specified percentage of its current fair market value.[182] The price of the remainder interest should be based on that actuarial determination.[183]

The object of this technique would be to eliminate the asset from the seller's gross estate for federal estate tax purposes. This result is sought because at the time of death (1) the life tenant's life estate terminates, leaving no continuing value to be transferred, and (2) the seller is not treated as the owner of the remainder interest in the transferred property. As noted below, however, these objectives are quite difficult to accomplish under current federal tax rules.

2. Estate and Gift Tax Considerations

a. Gift Transfer

This remainder interest sale transaction will often result in a significant taxable gift because of the §2702 gift tax valuation rules. The seller is treated as transferring the entire property in exchange for the consideration paid by the remainder beneficiary unless the retained interest is a "qualified interest."[184] Consequently, upon the sale of a remainder interest in property, the retained term interest or life interest is given a zero value. Therefore, the life tenant is deemed to have made a gift to the remainderman equal to the value of the entire property, less any consideration received from the purchaser.

Example: If Father (F) sells a remainder interest in an apartment building to Daughter (D), F's receipt of the net rental income from the apartment building does not qualify as a "qualified interest" for valuation purposes under §2702, because the income is not a fixed amount.[185] In such a case, F's interest is valued at zero, and he is considered to have made a gift to D of the value of the entire property, less the consideration D provided. Even if F receives fixed payments that qualify under §2702, the gift to D of the remainder is valued by subtracting the value of F's retained interest from the value of the entire property. Thus, if the payments to F are at a rate that is less than the applicable §7520 rate, the remainder has a value that is greater than the value calculated by directly valuing the remainder using the §7520 rate and, consequently, a gift to D may still result.

The purpose of this rule is to prevent the parent from enhancing the value of the remainder interest by accepting less than a market rate of income during his or her life tenancy. However, even if the actuarial value is appropriately determined, the parties may have undervalued the property itself, with the remainder beneficiary paying a value less than fair market value. The excess under these circumstances also constitutes a gift transfer.

The prior rules (not requiring a "qualified interest") do apply, however, to the sale of a remainder interest to a person not within the definition of a member of the transferor's family.[186] For the purpose of this rule, a "family member" includes a spouse, ancestor, lineal descendant, brother or sister, or the spouse of any of them. Not included, however, are nieces, nephews, and cousins. The assumption is that these transactions occur only infrequently, and are less affected with an objective to implement intrafamily transfers. This does suggest, however, that in unique circumstances a remainder interest sale could be arranged without the limiting §2702 valuation rules being applicable.

b. Retained Life Interest/Estate Tax Valuation Provision

Upon a sale of a remainder interest, the seller retains the life interest in the property. This life interest ordinarily is retained by the seller until the time of the seller's death. If the asset is transferred for full and adequate consideration, no estate tax inclusion ordinarily is required.[187]

If the transfer is for consideration that is less than full and adequate consideration in money or money's worth, the transferred asset is included in the transferor's gross estate at its then fair market value (or as of the alternate valuation date), less the actual amount of consideration received. *Gradow v. United States*[188] held that, in a sale of a remainder interest, the existence of full and adequate consideration must be measured against the total value of the property, not just the value of the remainder interest sold. Thus, under the *Gradow* theory, the sale of a remainder interest in property does not remove the property from the owner's estate unless the owner receives consideration equal to the total value of the property. The IRS was initially successful in using the *Gradow* argument in *Estate of D'Ambrosio v. Commissioner,*[189] where the Tax Court held that the entire value of closely held stock was includible in the decedent's estate, even though the decedent sold her remainder interest for an amount equal to its actuarial value, because the decedent had not received consideration in an amount equal to the full value of the stock. In determining the value of the property includible in the decedent's estate, the court subtracted the value of the consideration agreed on for the remainder purchase. The Third Circuit, rejecting the *Gradow* rationale, reversed and held that the adequacy of the consideration is evaluated on the date of the transfer by comparing the value of the remainder transferred to the value of the consideration received by the transferor. The Third Circuit was joined in its conclusion in *D'Ambrosio* by the Fifth and Ninth Circuits. In *Wheeler v. United States,*[190] the Fifth Circuit concluded that the decedent's sale to his sons of the remainder interest in his ranch was a bona fide sale for full and adequate consideration that took the property out of his estate. In *Estate of Magnin v. Commissioner,*[191] the court also held that "adequate and full consideration" is measured against the actuarial value of the remainder interest, rather than the fee-simple value of the property transferred, and remanded the case to the Tax Court for a finding on the value, at the time of the transaction, of the remainder interest and the consideration received in exchange for it. For a decedent outside these circuits, the IRS will probably seek to include in the seller's gross estate the full value of the property less the fair market value of the consideration for the sale of the remainder interest provided by the younger-generation member.[192]

c. Is a Transfer of Wealth Occurring?

Even assuming the gift and estate tax risks noted above are avoided, the question becomes whether this technique will result in an untaxed transfer of wealth from the life tenant to the owner of the remainder interest. Whether this occurs is partially dependent on the relationship between the valuation method used for tax purposes and the actual income productivity and appreciation of the property in which the transferred remainder interest exists.

Wealth is transferred to the remainder beneficiary when the actual income yield of the property is greater than the income yield assumption used for transfer tax valuation. Conversely, if the actual yield of the property is less than the percentage yield assumed for valuation purposes, wealth is transferred by the remainder beneficiary to the life tenant (ordinarily an undesirable result). Consequently, the planner must carefully consider the income potential of the property before determining the income yield to be used for §2702 purposes. Another factor is the current §7520 interest rate, which is revised monthly to follow the market.[193] The parties may wish to conclude this type of transaction when the applicable interest rate is particularly favorable.

3. Income Tax Considerations

a. Sale of Remainder Interest

The sale of the remainder interest will result in the realization of capital gain or loss to the seller. Ordinarily, in determining the amount of gain or loss, the seller's basis for the property must be apportioned between the remainder interest sold and the retained life estate.[194] Only that portion of the basis allocated to the remainder interest is used as the adjusted tax basis for purposes of determining gain or loss on the sale of a remainder interest.[195] Where the sale is between "related persons," any realized loss is to be disallowed as a deduction.[196]

b. Installment Sale/Private Annuity

The timing of the income tax recognition of the gain on the sale of the remainder interest could be postponed by arranging this sale on an installment basis. Alternatively, the remainder interest might be transferred in exchange for a private annuity received by the seller.[197]

Under a private annuity arrangement, the obligation to make additional payments would evaporate at the life tenant's death. In determining the amount of the private annuity payments, the life expectancy factor must be considered. These payments would be larger than the payments required under an installment note to take into account the actuarial element.

In a private annuity situation, the risk is assumed that the seller may "live too long," thereby causing a larger amount to be paid for the remainder interest than would have been paid if the transaction were completed on an installment sale basis. To the extent the payments received by the seller (whether under an installment sale or a private annuity) are not exhausted by the seller/life tenant during lifetime, that net amount is includible in the life tenant's gross estate.

c. Depreciation Deductions

During his or her lifetime, the life tenant (having sold the remainder) is allocated all of the depreciation deductions attributable to the underlying property, if depreciable.[198] As of the life tenant's death, when the remainder beneficiary owns the entire asset, the remainder beneficiary is entitled to the depreciation deductions (if any). The tax basis for these depreciation purposes is the cost to the remainder beneficiary of the property (i.e., the purchase cost for the remainder interest and not a "stepped-up basis").[199]

d. Amortization of Retained Life Interest by Life Tenant

In a remainder purchase situation (as distinguished from a split purchase transaction), the seller retaining the life interest has no income tax deduction for the gradual decline of the value of the retained life interest.[200] Ordinarily, the life tenant may amortize that basis for the life estate over the life tenant's remaining life expectancy. In this context, however, the life tenant is not permitted to amortize the actuarial value of his or her life estate over his or her life expectancy.[201]

e. Recognition Event upon Life Tenant's Death

The IRS may argue that, upon the life tenant's death, the receipt of the property (unencumbered by a life estate) by the remainder beneficiary causes realization of income to the remainder beneficiary (which should be recognized for income tax purposes). What has economically occurred in such a situation is that, upon the termination of the life interest, the remainder interest might be treated as being exchanged for the property itself.

If the property interest obtained upon the termination of the life interest is other than cash or a cash equivalent, the argument might be made that no income realization event occurred. If, however, the remainder interest is transformed into the equivalent of cash at the death of the life tenant, the IRS's position might be that a realization event requiring income recognition has occurred at that time.[202] However, the better argument would seem to be that this is merely equivalent to perfecting title in property, not being a realization event for income tax purposes.

f. Implementing the Sale of Remainder Transaction

Even assuming that the client wishes to enter into a remainder sale transaction, problems may arise in delineating the allocation of property rights (and obligations) between the life tenant and the remainder beneficiary.[203] The types of issues which might arise include:

- Who is entitled to the income, particularly when a portion of the revenue received might be considered to be a return of capital (e.g., when oil royalties or rent from a depreciating commercial building are being received)?
- Who has the obligation to maintain the property? Presumably, ordinary repairs would be the obligation of the life tenant, but extraordinary repairs and improvements would be the obligation of the remainder beneficiary.
- Who has the obligation to assure that the property remains free of encumbrances, including income tax and real estate tax liens?
- Who has the authority to transfer the property? Presumably both parties would need to consent to a property transfer unless an agent for both was appointed for this purpose (or the property is held in trust).
- Who has the right to the proceeds upon a voluntary (or involuntary) disposition of the entire property? Ordinarily, the proceeds would be allocated on an actuarial basis, determined as of the time of the receipt of those proceeds.
- How are disputes concerning fundamental property management decisions to be resolved?

The resolution of these issues might appropriately be identified in a contract or memorandum between the parties.

I. Grantor Retained Annuity Trust and Unitrust

1. GRAT (or GRUT) Technique Described

Pursuant to a "grantor retained annuity trust" arrangement (a GRAT), a grantor transfers assets into an irrevocable trust.[204] The grantor retains a current income interest under the trust for some specified time certain (anticipated to be shorter than the grantor's actual life expectancy). The grantor simultaneously transfers a remainder interest in the trust property to younger-generation beneficiaries.

Under §2702 (the gift tax special valuation provision), the grantor's retained income interest must be in the form of an annuity interest (GRAT) or a unitrust interest (GRUT) to avoid having the entire property transfer treated as a gift for federal gift tax purposes.[205] The annuity must be in the form of a fixed payment, made at least annually, while the unitrust payment is to be an annual payment which is a fixed percentage of the value of the trust property, valued annually. The trust instrument must prohibit the trustee from issuing a note, other debt instrument, option, or other similar financial arrangement in satisfaction of the annuity or unitrust payment obligation.[206] The governing instrument must prohibit the commutation (prepayment) of the interest of the term holder.[207]

The federal tax planning objectives are, upon trust creation: (1) to utilize the favorable aspects of the valuation tables in minimizing the current value of the gift transfer for gift tax purposes and (2) to base the income portion on a time period that the grantor can reasonably be expected to live beyond. If the income interest expires during the grantor's lifetime, the remainder interest vests in the remainder beneficiary at that time without further federal gift tax effect. Additionally, under these circumstances those trust assets will not be includible in the estate of the trust grantor for estate tax purposes, since they are owned outright at that time by the remainder beneficiary, rather than by the trust grantor/prior trust income beneficiary.[208]

2. Gift Tax Considerations

a. Determination of Gift Portion

For gift tax purposes the gift portion of the transfer to a GRAT (or GRUT) will be the entire value of the property transferred to the trust, less the actuarial value of the retained income interest. Consequently, the longer the period for the receipt by the grantor of the trust income (i.e., the "lead" portion of the trust), the lower will be the gift tax value of the remainder portion.

The valuation of the retained interest (and, thereby, the gift component) will be based on tables prescribed by the IRS.[209] The higher the current interest rate assumption, the lower will be the value of the remainder interest since the assumption is that the greater value is in the current interest. Consequently, if the assumed interest rate applicable for current income is lower, the value of the remainder interest (and, accordingly, the value of the gift to the remainder beneficiary) is increased.

Often the gift tax planning objective will be to effectively "zero out" the GRAT, so that the remainder interest has only minimal value (and, therefore, the gift amount is minimal) with most of the value being allocated to the retained lead interest.[210] In addition to a lengthy annuity period, this reduction of the transferred value for gift tax purposes might be achieved with certain retained powers.[211] An alternative approach is to require a quite significant percentage for the annual payout (e.g., 50% of the value of the trust) during a short period so that the remainder interest has minimal value for gift tax purposes. This might be done where the property transferred to the trust is anticipated to appreciate significantly (e.g., closely held shares that will be sold in a public offering at a significantly enhanced value).[212] After the short life of this trust, the residue remaining after realizing the significant appreciation would be transferred to the owners of the remainder interest (with only limited gift tax exposure arising when this arrangement was constructed). A further approach would be to have the lead payment based on multiple life expectancies, subject to earlier termination at the end of a specified period.[213]

b. Time of Gift Completion

An important gift tax planning objective should be to have the gift "completed" (i.e., transferred into the GRAT or GRUT) at a time: (1) when the value of the property is relatively low and, additionally, (2) when that portion of the value of the property which is allocable to the remainder beneficiary is small. This mandates that the gift transfer be completed at the time of the creation of the trust and not at some later date (for example, upon the expiration of some time period or the lapse of some right). This gift completion contemplates that both: (1) the trust instrument is completed and executed and (2) the trust assets to be used to fund this trust are appropriately transferred into the trust. The longer that the completion of the gift transfer is delayed, the greater will be the value of the gift (assuming that the trust property is not economically depreciating and the interest rate is not dramatically increasing).

c. Annual Donee Exclusion

The gift of the GRAT (or GRUT) remainder interest is the gift of a future interest. As such, this transfer will not qualify for the gift tax annual donee exclusion.[214]

d. Trust Termination upon Grantor's Earlier Death

The GRAT (or GRUT) may be structured to provide for the termination of the trust grantor's life interest upon the earlier of: (1) the prescribed term of the income interest, or (2) the death of the grantor. Under normal valuation principles, the addition of a reversionary interest in the grantor's estate if the grantor dies before the expiration of the prescribed term would reduce the value of the remainder since it increases the likelihood that the remainder beneficiary will never receive the property. The Service had taken the position that, under the §2702 valuation principles, the gift tax value of the remainder would not be reduced, since the potential reversion was not a §2702(b) qualified interest. This position was reversed after the Tax Court's decision in *Walton v. Commissioner*.[215] The purpose of providing for such a reversion would be to provide funds with which the estate could pay the estate tax imposed on the decedent's retained interest to the extent that this property is includible under §2036(a).

Under §2207B(a) the estate may also have a right to recover the applicable estate tax from the remainder beneficiary, so it may not be necessary to provide for such a reversion to obtain the tax funds, but the reversion will impact the value of the retained (and transferred) interests. Also, as explained below, if the grantor should die during the term of the retained interest, only the value of the annuity or unitrust interest will be includible in his or her estate, while if the property reverts to the estate on his or her death, its entire value will be includible.

3. Estate Tax Considerations

a. GRAT (or GRUT) Termination Prior to Grantor's Death

When the GRAT (or GRUT) retained income interest terminates, the remainder interest will vest in possession of the remainder beneficiary. For gift tax purposes, however, the transfer of the property to the younger-generation/remainder beneficiaries will have occurred when it was transferred into the trust. Inclusion in the gift tax base will have occurred only with respect to the actuarial value of the remainder interest as of that earlier trust transfer.

The income received by the grantor because of the reserved income interest will, of course, be included in the grantor's gross estate, unless expended. After the expiration of the term interest, the trust property, then entirely vested in the remainder beneficiary without any retained rights being held by the income beneficiary, should not be includible in the grantor's gross estate.[216] This will occur notwithstanding whether a significant increase in the value of the trust assets has occurred while held in trust. The effect of this transfer is that for transfer tax purposes the asset values will have been "frozen" as of the time of the trust creation (and funding), with the only transfer tax event having occurred at the original transfer into the trust. Of course, the grantor should not hold any other retained interest that would cause inclusion in his or her estate.[217]

b. Death Before GRAT (or GRUT) Termination

If the grantor should die at or before the end of the trust term, all or a portion of the trust property will be includible in his or her gross estate.[218] Before the issuance of the 2008 final regulations referenced below, the Service took the position that the trust assets are includible in the trust grantor's gross estate under §2036 and §2039. Section 2039(a) provides that a decedent's gross estate includes the value of an annuity or other payment receivable by any beneficiary by reason of surviving the decedent under any form of contract or agreement if, under the contract or agreement, an annuity or other payment was payable to the decedent. The term "annuity or other payment" is defined broadly to include one or more payments, equal or unequal, conditional or unconditional, or periodic or sporadic.[219] The term "contract or arrangement" is similarly described broadly to include any arrangement, understanding, or plan.[220] Section 2036(a) provides for gross estate inclusion when a retained life interest is held at death.[221]

In 2008, the IRS issued final regulations[222] that amend Reg. §20.2036-1 to provide that, if a decedent transfers property during life to a trust and retains the right to an annuity, unitrust, or other interest for the decedent's life, for a period that does not in fact end before the decedent's death, or for a period not ascertainable without reference to the decedent's death, the decedent has retained the possession or enjoyment of, or right to income from, the property for §2036 purposes.[223] The portion of the trust corpus includible in the decedent's gross estate is that portion of the trust corpus, valued as of the decedent's death necessary to yield the decedent's retained payment or use (without reducing or invading principal) using the §7520 interest rate in effect on the decedent's date of death.[224] Section 2039 does not apply to such trusts if the retained interest or use is described in §2036.[225]

In the planning context, the question becomes how even this potential risk of estate tax inclusion might be lessened.[226] The GRAT (or GRUT) might actually be created so as to have various subtrusts or portions with different terms certain. For example, the trust might be created with terms certain as to separate portions for 5 and for 10 years. If the grantor dies 7 years after the trust is created, that portion subject to the 5-year term certain will not be included since that retained interest will have expired. The property subject to the 10-year term certain would be all (or partially) includible in the grantor's gross estate under the analysis immediately above.

Another possibility would be to sell the retained interest in the trust sufficiently in advance of death so that no gross estate inclusion occurs. A sale by the grantor of his or her retained interest in the trust may be successful in removing the trust from the grantor's estate if that sale occurs more than three years prior to the grantor's death.[227] If the sale occurs more than three years prior to the grantor's death, the GRAT or GRUT should not be includible in the grantor's estate under §2036(a)(1) because the grantor would not have retained for a period not ascertainable without reference to his or her death the possession or enjoyment of, or the right to income from, the trust property. Further, even before the issuance of the 2008 final regulations that apply §2036 rather than §2039 (as referenced above), a GRAT or GRUT should not be includible in the grantor's estate under §2039(a) because no annuity or other payment would be payable to the grantor at the time of his or her death.[228]

4. Income Tax Considerations

a. GRAT (or GRUT) Income Distributions

During the period the retained interest continues the grantor will receive the annuity or unitrust income (as defined in the trust instrument). This income received will be includible in the grantor's gross income for federal income tax purposes under the grantor trust rules, as limited to trust income.[229] For this purpose trust income will ordinarily not include capital gain.

b. Capital Gain and Gain Realization

Capital gain will be taxed to the trust (assuming no retention of a power by the grantor causing the grantor to be treated as the owner of such gain).[230] To avoid capital gain taxation to the trust, the grantor may retain a nonfiduciary power over principal, however.[231] This might be, for example, a power to substitute assets of equal value. In this situation neither the grantor nor the trust would recognize any gain or loss as a result of: (1) the grantor's transfer of assets to fund the trust, (2) the distribution of any appreciated property from the trust to the grantor in payment of the annuity or unitrust amount, or (3) the substitution of assets of the grantor for assets of the trust.[232]

When the retained lead interest terminates but the trust continues, the trust income will thereafter be received by the remainder beneficiary and included in the gross income of the remainder beneficiary for federal income tax purposes. If the trust terminates upon the expiration of the retained lead interest, that income will be received directly by the remainder beneficiary, free of trust restrictions.

Since the objective is to exclude the trust assets from the trust grantor's gross estate, the income tax basis of those assets will not be stepped up to their respective fair market values as of the date of death of the grantor (or as of the alternate valuation date), assuming the estate tax planning objective has been successful.[233] Accordingly, the basis for the assets in the trust will be a carryover basis for those assets contributed to the trust by the grantor and a cost basis for those assets acquired by the trust.[234] If estate tax inclusion of the trust assets does occur, the tax basis for those assets will be stepped up (or stepped down) at the time of death.

5. GRAT (or GRUT) Structuring Strategies

a. Choosing Assets for Trust Funding

The assets in the trust will not be includible in the grantor's gross estate (if actuarially successful), but the income distributed to the grantor will be so included (unless spent). Consequently, the grantor should consider funding the trust with high appreciation potential property and accepting a reasonably low annuity amount. This choice will also be dependent on how much of the trust grantor's unified credit amount might be absorbed by this gift and the interest rate factors at the time of the creation of the GRAT (or GRUT).

b. Limiting Estate Tax Risk of Early Death

If the grantor dies prior to the expiration of the term, all (or at least part) of the trust assets (as noted above) will be included in the gross estate of the grantor. The question then becomes whether such result can be precluded or, at least, moderated. Previously an independent trustee might have been provided with the authority to terminate (or "commute") a trust by distributing the trust assets to the income and remainder beneficiaries in accordance with their actuarial interests in the trust at the time of the trust termination. The regulations preclude this action being taken.[235] The trust grantor might sell his or her interest in the trust for its commuted value. The IRS might challenge this as being the equivalent of the receipt of the value of the remaining term certain interest and, accordingly, may assert that the three-year gross estate inclusionary rule is applicable.[236]

6. Making Assets Available to Grantor After GRAT (or GRUT) Expiration

A problem that can arise in the GRAT (or GRUT) context is that the grantor outlives the term certain but wants to retain use and possession of specific trust property after the expiration of that term certain. This might occur, for example, where the property held under the GRAT (or GRUT) is of special significance to the trust grantor. This might include a personal residence or a vacation home, but these assets would ordinarily be included in a qualified personal residence trust, as discussed below.

In a situation like this, the remainder beneficiaries could arrange to rent the property to the trust grantor for a fair market value rental. If the rental amount is less than fair market value, the IRS might argue, however, that a life interest was indirectly retained for estate tax purposes.[237] The payment of a high rent by the holder of the expired term certain would frustrate this possible estate tax challenge but would also enable additional funds to be transferred to the remainder beneficiaries. This rent would be gross income to the remainder beneficiaries for federal income tax purposes, however. If the property is depreciable, a tax depreciation deduction might be available to partially offset this rental income.

J. Personal Residence Trusts

The §2702 gift tax special valuation rules do not apply if the "transfer involves the transfer of an interest in trust all the property in which consists of a residence to be used as a personal residence by persons holding term interests in such trust."[238] The §2702 regulations permit two types of these personal residence trusts: (1) a personal residence trust (PRT) and (2) a "qualified personal residence trust" (QPRT).[239] Ordinarily, because of its increased flexibility, the QPRT alternative is used. The personal residence trust transaction involves (1) a transfer of a life interest in an owner's personal residence into an irrevocable trust, (2) with the owner retaining a term interest under the trust.[240] The remainder under the trust might be transferred to children or to other younger generation family members who will use the residence property after the expiration of the retained term interest.

1. Primary Use of Property as a Residence

The first requirement to qualify for this special treatment is that the residence transferred into the PRT or the QPRT is actually a "personal residence."[241] A residence is a personal residence only if its primary use is as a residence of the grantor when occupied by the grantor.[242] The trust grantor's principal residence is a personal residence.[243] One other residence can also be a residence of the trust grantor for this purpose.[244] Alternative types of housing arrangements can qualify as a personal residence for this purpose.[245] A personal residence may include appurtenant structures used by the grantor for residential purposes and adjacent land not in excess of that which is reasonably appropriate for residential purposes (taking into account the size of the residence and its location).[246]

The term "personal residence" does not include any household furnishings.[247] Whether an item is a furnishing or a fixture (treated as part of the personal residence) will be determined under locally applicable real estate law.

2. Structuring the "Personal Residence Trust"

If an individual transfers a personal residence into a PRT, the §2702 "qualified interest" valuation rules will not apply.[248] Consequently, the value of the gift transfer can be reduced by the actuarial value of the retained interest and the transfer need not satisfy the "qualified interest" requirements of §2702(b). The PRT must be created by a written instrument. That governing instrument must prohibit the trust from holding, for the original duration of the term interest, any asset other than one residence to be used or held for use as a personal residence of the term holder and "qualified proceeds."[249]

A residence is held for use as a personal residence of the term holder so long as the residence is not occupied by any other person (other than the spouse or a dependent of the term holder) and is available at all times for use by the term holder as a personal residence.[250] The transferor may be required, however, for health reasons to abandon the residence. If the residence remains available at all times for the transferor's use as a residence during the term of the trust, the residence will continue to be held for the transferor's use.[251] Therefore, the trust should not be disqualified even if an elderly transferor cannot currently use the residence.

The residence may be transformed into cash proceeds paid as a result of damage, destruction, or involuntary conversion of the residence. The receipt of these proceeds will not invalidate the trust if the trustee is required to reinvest the proceeds (including any income derived from the investment of those proceeds) in a personal residence within two years from the date on which the proceeds are received.[252]

The PRT arrangement does not enable the trustee to receive proceeds on the sale of the residence, however. Consequently, the residence cannot be voluntarily sold during the term of the trust. Further, the trust will not qualify if the residence may be otherwise transferred by the trust or may be used for a purpose other than as a personal residence of the term holder.[253] Therefore, the governing instrument should include specific prohibitions concerning these requirements.[254]

In addition, the governing instrument must prohibit the trust from selling or transferring the residence, directly or indirectly, to the grantor, the grantor's spouse, or an entity controlled[255] by the grantor or the grantor's spouse, at any time after the original duration of the term interest during which the trust is a grantor trust.[256] For this purpose, a sale or transfer to another grantor trust of the grantor or the grantor's spouse is considered a sale or transfer to the grantor or spouse. However, a distribution (for no consideration) on or after the expiration of the original term to another grantor trust of the grantor or the grantor's spouse pursuant to the express terms of the trust will not be considered a sale to the grantor or the grantor's spouse if the other grantor trust contains the required sale prohibitions.[257]

A grantor who dies before the expiration of the original duration of the term interest may provide for the distribution (for no consideration) of the residence to any person (including the grantor's estate) pursuant to the express terms of the trust or through the exercise of a power retained by the grantor under the trust. Further, the regulations do not prohibit an outright distribution (for no consideration) of the residence to the grantor's spouse after the expiration of the original trust term pursuant to the express terms of the trust.[258]

3. The Alternative "Qualified Personal Residence Trust"

a. Structuring the QPRT Agreement

An alternative to the PRT is the QPRT, the option used in most personal residence trust situations. A QPRT permits considerably greater flexibility than does a PRT. Assets other than merely a personal residence can be held by the trust. No prohibition exists on the residence being voluntarily sold and a replacement residence being subsequently acquired. A specific governing trust instrument is required to be prepared in conformity with the requirements in the applicable gift tax regulations.[259] The governing instrument provisions must by their terms continue in effect during the existence of any term interest in the trust.[260]

The QPRT, enabling more flexibility than the PRT, is permitted to hold certain types of assets in addition to the personal residence.[261] For example, the trust instrument may permit additions of cash to the trust and may permit the trust to hold additions of cash in a separate account under certain circumstances. These can be for the following purposes:

- for the payment of trust expenses (including mortgage payments) already incurred or reasonably expected to be paid by the trust within six months from the date the addition is made to the trust[262];
- for improvements to the residence to be paid by the trust within six months from the date of the addition of cash to the trust[263];
- for the purchase by the trust of the initial residence within three months of the date the trust is created, provided that no addition may be made for this purpose, and the trust may not hold any such addition, unless the transferee has previously entered into a contract to purchase that residence[264]; and
- for the purchase by the trust of a replacement residence within three months of the date the addition is made, provided that no addition may be made for this purpose, and the trust may not hold any such addition, unless the trustee has previously entered into a contract to purchase that residence.[265]

The governing instrument must require, however, that the trustee determine, not less frequently than quarterly, the amounts held by the trust for the payment of expenses in excess of the amounts permitted to be held. The trust instrument must require that those amounts be immediately distributed to the term holder.[266]

If the QPRT has temporary investment assets, it might realize investment income from those assets. The QPRT governing instrument must require that any income of the trust be distributed to the term holder not less frequently than annually.[267]

The governing instrument must prohibit distributions of corpus to any beneficiary other than the grantor prior to the expiration of the primary term.[268] The governing instrument may permit improvements to the residence to be added to the trust. The residence, as improved, must meet the requirements of a personal residence.[269]

The governing instrument may permit the sale of the residence and may permit the trust to hold the sale proceeds. Those proceeds are to be maintained in a separate account.[270] The governing instrument may permit the trust to hold one or more policies of insurance on the residence. Additionally, the governing instrument may permit the trust to hold, in a separate account, proceeds of insurance payable to the trust as a result of damage or destruction to the residence and the proceeds from an involuntary conversion of the residence.[271]

b. Cessation of QPRT Qualification

The governing instrument must specify that the trust ceases to be a QPRT if the residence ceases to be used or held for use as a personal residence of the grantor.[272] A residence is held for personal use of the term holder if the residence is not occupied by any other person (other than the spouse or a dependent of the term holder) and is available at all times for use by the term holder.[273] The governing instrument should further provide that the trustee is permitted to hold the proceeds upon the sale of the residence.[274] If the governing instrument so provides, the trust will thereafter cease to be a QPRT with respect to the proceeds of sale not later than the earlier of:

- two years after the date of sale;
- the termination of the primary term of the trust; or
- the acquisition of a new residence by the QPRT.

The governing instrument must further provide that, within 30 days after the date on which the trust ceases to be a QPRT with respect to certain assets, those assets must be either distributed outright to the grantor or held as a qualified annuity interest for the balance of the primary term.[275] The governing instrument can direct either of these results or can authorize the decision to be made in the discretion of the trustee. Except in extraordinary circumstances, the trustee may elect to convert the QPRT to a qualified annuity interest, rather than to distribute the trust assets outright to the grantor, since the potential is thereby maintained to exclude the assets from the grantor's gross estate for estate tax purposes.

For assets to be converted to and held as a qualified annuity interest, the governing instrument must contain all the provisions required for a qualified annuity interest.[276] The annuity amount must be payable from the "cessation date," which is the date of the sale or destruction or the date the property ceased to be used or held for use as a personal residence.[277]

Upon the termination of the reserved term of the QPRT, the grantor's interest in the residence must terminate. This is necessary to avoid inclusion of the residence in the grantor's gross estate for estate tax purposes.[278]

c. No Commutation of Retained Interest

The governing instrument must prohibit the commutation (or prepayment) of the trust grantor's interest.[279] Commutation is the acceleration of the termination of the grantor's interest by paying the grantor for his or her interest an amount equivalent to its actuarial value as of the date of that payment. Effectively, this requires that the trust be continued until the term expires, thereby maintaining the potential that estate tax inclusion of the residence (and other trust assets) will occur if the grantor dies prior to the expiration of the trust term.[280]

d. Post-Trust Termination Occupancy of Residence

At the expiration of the retained initial trust term the property will be transferred to the holders of the remainder interest.[281] The trust grantor may desire, however, to continue to occupy the residence after the conclusion of the term interest. The grantor may enter into a lease arrangement with the remainder beneficiaries (who then have the sole ownership of the residence). The trust grantor then leasing the property should pay full fair market lease value. If the grantor is paying less than the fair market value for the lease of the residence, the IRS may assert that the trust grantor retained not only (1) a (then expired) term interest but, also, (2) the "possession or enjoyment" of the residence after the expiration of the term interest and, therefore, the residence is to be included in the grantor's gross estate for estate tax purposes.[282]

Rather than entering into a lease arrangement with the remainder beneficiaries, previously the trust grantor could reacquire the residence before the expiration of the primary term. As a result of this transaction, the grantor would retain the residence (in fee simple form) and the remainder beneficiaries would receive cash or other liquid assets. Assuming that the trust was a grantor trust with respect to corpus (i.e., capital gains) for federal income tax purposes, the reacquisition of the residence would have had no income tax consequences.[283] This planning has been foreclosed.

To preclude this opportunity and rejecting this planning possibility, the governing instrument of a QPRT is required to prohibit the direct or indirect sale or transfer of a residence held in the trust to the grantor, the grantor's spouse, or an entity controlled by the grantor or the grantor's spouse during the retained term interest, or at any time after the retained term interest while the trust is a grantor trust.[284] Thus, the regulations prohibit a grantor from placing a personal residence in trust, obtaining all the tax benefits of a QPRT and, thereafter, purchasing the residence from the trust immediately prior to the expiration of the grantor's retained term (or after the expiration of the term if the trust continues as a grantor trust) so that cash or other assets pass to the remainder beneficiaries in lieu of the residence.[285] The residence can be reacquired by the trust grantor after the expiration of the trust from the remainder beneficiaries/owners, but this would constitute a capital gains sales event for them and would necessitate a cash outlay by the trust grantor.[286]

e. Grantor's Death Before Trust Expiration

If the grantor dies before the expiration of the retained term, the regulations do not prohibit the distribution (for no consideration) of the residence to any person (including the grantor's estate) pursuant to the express terms of the trust or through the exercise of a power retained by the grantor under the trust.[287] This enables distribution of the residence under the terms of the trust provisions, rather than through the trust grantor's probate estate. Further, the regulations do not prohibit an outright distribution (for no consideration) of the residence to the grantor's spouse after the expiration of the retained term pursuant to the express terms of the trust.[288]

f. Spousal Joint Interests

Spouses might share (or have previously shared) joint interests in the personal residence and together or separately transfer the residence into a QPRT.[289] This could occur in the following possible situations:

- The property in a common law property jurisdiction was formerly owned directly by both spouses. The interest of one is terminated in anticipation of the transfer of the property into a QPRT.
- Each spouse in a common law property jurisdiction owns an undivided interest in real property and each transfers his or her interest into a QPRT, with the other spouse having a life interest after the termination of the primary term.
- The property could be held as community property, whether under the community property laws of a state in the United States or the community property laws of a foreign jurisdiction.

If spouses contribute their interests in a residence to the same QPRT (or PRT), the governing instrument of that trust must prohibit any person other than one of the spouses from holding a term interest in the trust concurrently with the other spouse.[290] Alternatively, they may each contribute their interest in the residence to a separate QPRT, retaining their interest in the residence for a term.

Each spouse could transfer his or her interest into a QPRT for the life of the other spouse, with the remainder to other beneficiaries. This would immediately remove the residence interest from the trust grantor's gross estate, and the gift to the spouse should be eligible for the marital deduction for gift tax purposes. The reciprocal trust doctrine may be applicable, however, to cause each spouse to be the trust grantor of the trust created by the other spouse (and in this situation a life interest would be treated as having been retained).[291] The spouse could transfer his or her interest in the residence into a trust for a specified term for the other spouse, with the remainder to other beneficiaries. In this event, however, no marital deduction would be available for the transfer for the benefit of the spouse.

4. Gift Tax Consequences

A gift will be completed for federal gift tax purposes upon the transfer of the principal residence to the personal residence trust (a QPRT or PRT). The gift will consist of the remainder interest, since the grantor will have retained the lead or primary interest. The value of that remainder interest will be determined by subtracting the actuarial value of the grantor's retained interest from the entire value of the residence. The transfer to the trust is not valued for gift tax purposes under the special valuation rules of §2702 that mandate that the transferor's retained interest is to be treated as having a value of zero.

These value determinations are made by applying the valuation principles specified in §7520. Because the applicable interest rates change on a monthly basis, the trust grantor should attempt to choose to complete the gift when the interest rates are most favorable for reducing the value of the remainder interest. This would occur when the interest rates are higher since the lead interest under the trust will then have more value.

Additional gift transfers will occur when the grantor makes subsequent transfers of cash into the trust, for example, to be applied to reduce the principal amount of a mortgage obligation or to make improvements to the residence property. The value of each gift is to be actuarially determined as of the date of the additional contribution into the trust. The impact of this valuation process is that, with the lapse of time, the remainder interest will become more valuable (increasing the amount of the then current gift), with the present interest declining in value, since the present interest is closer to termination. These gift transfers must be for the benefit of the remainder beneficiary if they are to be treated as gifts. The payment of current expenses of the residence (e.g., insurance and real estate taxes) would not be attributable to the remainder interest, thereby not constituting a gift. The interest component of any mortgage payments should be similarly treated. If the trust grantor makes these payments directly, rather than first contributing funds into the trust to make these payments, a similar analysis should be applicable.

The gift transfer of the trust's remainder interest is a transfer of a future interest, rather than a present interest. The §2503(b) annual donee gift tax exclusion is only available for gifts of present interests. Consequently, the annual donee exclusion is not available for the gift of the remainder interest upon the creation of a personal residence trust.

5. Estate Tax Consequences

a. Grantor's Death During Trust Term

If the grantor dies during the primary term of the personal residence trust (a QPRT or PRT), the entire value of the trust assets will be included in the grantor's gross estate for estate tax purposes since the grantor has retained the use of the residence for a period that did not end before the grantor's death.[292] This is the estate tax inclusion risk being undertaken in personal residence trust arrangements. The planning should, therefore, balance (i) the desire to limit the gift transfer amount by extending the primary trust term against (ii) the risk that the trust grantor might die before the expiration of that term.[293]

A variety of ancillary estate tax planning considerations should be noted in this context:

- The remainder interest will not ordinarily be transferred to the surviving spouse. If this does occur, however, the estate tax marital deduction should be available if the interest in the residence passes outright to or in a qualifying marital trust for the benefit of the surviving spouse.
- The impact of the mechanism for the computation of transfer tax liability is to assure that the transfer of the interest in the residence will not be subject to both gift tax inclusion and separate estate tax inclusion.
- Allocable estate taxes (if any) can be retrieved from the remainder beneficiaries of the personal residence trust under the provisions of a federal estate tax apportionment provision.[294]

b. Grantor's Death After Trust Term Expires

If the grantor dies after the lapse of the primary term of the trust, the personal residence trust assets ordinarily are not includible in the trust grantor's gross estate. This is the explicit estate tax planning objective of the personal residence trust arrangement. As of the time of the lapse of the primary term, the grantor is to have no further, continuing interest in the trust property and, therefore, has no interest includible for estate tax purposes.

This analysis assumes, of course, that no understandings or other arrangements for the continued use of the property by the trust grantor can be identified or successfully imputed to the parties. As noted above,[295] if the grantor retained some right to remain in the residence without, for example, paying a fair market value rent, some retained life interest might be asserted to exist for estate tax purposes.[296] Since the trust beneficiaries (presumably children or parties in similar status) receiving the remainder interest will be the recipients of rental income if the property is then rented by the grantor, the incentive should exist for the trust grantor to pay excess rent, rather than insufficient rent. This would further deplete the grantor's estate for estate tax purposes. This does assume that the grantor has adequate cash funds available for this purpose.

6. Generation-Skipping Transfer Tax Effects

As of the termination of the primary term of the personal residence trust (a QPRT or PRT), a generation-skipping transfer could occur for purposes of the generation-skipping transfer tax. This could happen, for example, if the residence property is transferred to grandchildren of the grantor, rather than children of the grantor, at the expiration of the term interest.[297]

7. Income Tax Considerations

a. Grantor's Trust Status

The personal residence trust (a QPRT or PRT) will be treated as a "grantor trust" for income tax purposes during the specified term.[298] Consequently, during the period of that term, any income realized by the trust will be treated as income of the grantor directly received.

b. Mortgage Interest Expense and Taxes Deduction

During the continued occupancy by the trust grantor, the grantor will ordinarily continue to make mortgage payments (consisting of both interest and principal or, perhaps, only of interest). The grantor will desire to have a deduction for income tax purposes for the mortgage interest paid (subject to the usual statutory limits).[299]

The inquiry in this context concerns who actually makes the mortgage interest payment. If made by the QPRT, under the grantor trust rules the interest expense deduction flows through the trust to the grantor. If the grantor directly pays the mortgage interest, the interest expense deduction will only be available if the grantor remains personally liable on the mortgage.[300] In the situation of a PRT (rather than a QPRT), as noted above, the grantor must directly pay the mortgage interest. In many instances, the lender will not allow the property transferor/trust grantor to be relieved of the liability for mortgage debt when transferring the residence into a QPRT. Under these circumstances, no difficulty should exist concerning the availability of the interest expense deduction to the trust grantor who resides in the residence.

If the trust is treated as a grantor trust for federal income tax purposes, the payment of real estate taxes by the trustee should also enable deductibility by the trust grantor for income tax purposes. In a QPRT situation, a conservative planning approach would be for the trust instrument to impose on the trust grantor the obligation to pay real estate taxes during the primary term of the trust. If the trust grantor pays these taxes directly, he or she should be entitled to a deduction for any year during which he or she owns a beneficial interest in the residence and pays the real estate taxes to protect that equitable interest.[301]

c. Differentiating Between Income and Corpus

The personal residence trust will ordinarily be a grantor trust for income tax purposes only with respect to the ordinary income portion. It will not be a grantor trust with respect to the corpus portion where the remainder has been previously transferred by the grantor. This will necessitate application of local trust law concepts for differentiating between corpus and income.[302]

If the personal residence is sold by the trust for a capital gain,[303] that gain will be allocable to the trust corpus and not to the grantor. Consequently, the trust (on behalf of the remainder beneficiaries) would be obligated to pay the capital gains tax.[304]

d. Exclusion of Residence Sale Gain

If a QPRT sells the residence to a third party, and the residence is the grantor's principal residence, the question arises as to whether the trust should have the benefit of the §121 election to exclude $250,000 of gain (or $500,000 for married individuals filing jointly)[305] because, from an income tax perspective, the sale would be treated as made directly by the grantor. In several situations, the IRS has recognized the flow through of these benefits in a grantor trust situation.[306] In those situations, however, the grantor held an equitable interest in the remainder (because the grantor could revoke the trust or could otherwise obtain the entire income and corpus).

In the PRT or QPRT situation, the remainder interest is held by persons other than the grantor/occupant of the residence, and the gain is attributable to those holders of the remainder interest. Given that, if the PRT sells the residence, it will be disqualified, and these benefits might be available because this is beyond the authority of the trust. In contrast, if a QPRT sells the residence, the QPRT can continue, with the trust reinvesting the proceeds. The QPRT regulations indicate that the trust is permitted to reinvest in a replacement residence.[307] If the QPRT is a grantor trust with respect to both the income and the corpus portions and it sells the residence to a third party, then the grantor should have the benefit of the §121 exclusion because, from an income tax perspective, the sale is treated as made directly by the grantor.[308]

e. Tax Basis to Remainder Beneficiary

The income tax basis to the trust for the residence transferred into the trust will be the grantor's tax basis in the residence, as increased by any federal gift tax attributable to the appreciation component in the residence included in the gift tax base.[309] If the grantor's income tax basis exceeds the fair market value of the residence at the time of the gift, for purposes of determining any subsequent tax loss, the trust's tax basis for the residence is the fair market value of the residence as of the time of the gift transfer.[310]

When the primary term expires and the remainder beneficiaries obtain the property, the income tax basis for the residence will carry over to those beneficiaries. If the grantor dies prior to the expiration of the initial term and, therefore, the residence is included in the grantor's gross estate for federal estate tax purposes, that basis will be stepped up (or stepped down) to its fair market value as of the date of death (or as of the alternate valuation date).[311] If the property transferred into the trust is classified as community property, the planning objective should be to attempt to retain eligibility for the tax basis step up for the entire property if the grantor dies prior to the expiration of the initial term.[312] The grantor should be able to accomplish this if the community property is transferred into the personal residence trust without having been previously partitioned and local law mandates (or permits) the continued classification of the residence as community property under these circumstances.

K. Transfers of Family Properties Summarized

The discussion in the prior sections of this chapter identifies various strategies that may be implemented concerning family property transfers with the primary objective to achieve tax savings for the family unit. However, with respect to any of these transfers, the advisor must remember that the various family members may have very differing emotions and attitudes concerning the transfers of these properties. These properties may include the family homestead, special vacation properties, multiple parcel properties (such as "family compounds"), and yachts or similar properties. Older generation members may want these properties retained after their deaths, but younger members may want to avoid the burdens of property management. Only some of the younger-generation members may be interested in the retention of these properties after the death of the older-generation members. These divergent perspectives must be examined, with a family property management strategy being developed.

This will necessitate that the estate planner: (1) develop detailed cash requirements and strategies as to how these expenses might be satisfied in the future, (2) construct detailed tax projections for these properties, including variables to contemplate possible tax law changes, and (3) coordinate discussions between various family members concerning the future retention and utilization of these properties. This may necessitate the intervention of a qualified mediator who can help negotiate an acceptable resolution among the various members of the family group, dealing with both the "sentimental" and the "pragmatic" elements of managing this property for the future. This qualified intermediary might be able to independently conduct meetings among the group and arrange individual interviews so that the conflicting perspectives can be accommodated, reducing the potential for future conflicts concerning these properties.

Notes

1. Whether the payment of gift taxes (or prepayment of estate taxes) produces an adverse financial result is problematic. An analysis must include (1) the tax rate differentials between the current gift tax rate and the eventual estate tax rate, (2) the interim loss of the use of funds, including the amount of the anticipated return on those funds, (3) the anticipated tax deferral benefit, (4) the appreciation that could be anticipated to accrue on transferred property between the time of the gift and the date of the donor's death, (5) the relative income tax brackets of the donor and the donee, and (6) various other factors (such as interest rates).
2. See the discussion of net gifts in Chapter 6, D.2.
3. See the discussion of intrafamily installment sales in Chapter 7, B.
4. See the discussion of interest-free and low interest loans in Chapter 7, C., and the discussion of loans of property or credit Chapter 7, D.
5. See the discussion of private annuities in Chapter 7, F.
6. See Chapter 7, G.
7. See Chapter 7, H.
8. See the discussion in this chapter.

9. See Chapter 10 (Special Business Planning Situations). This type of value shifting might include initial multi-class stock capitalizations of corporations, corporate recapitalizations, multi-tiered partnerships, buy-sell agreements, deferred compensation agreements, sales and loans to irrevocable trusts, and corporate splitoffs.
10. See the discussion of corporate and partnership restructuring in Chapter 10.
11. See Chapter 5, A.1., regarding the changes made by the Economic Growth and Tax Relief Reconciliation Act of 2001 (EGTRRA), Pub. L. No. 107-16, the Tax Relief, Unemployment Insurance Reauthorization, and Job Creation Act of 2010 (2010 TRA), Pub. L. No. 111-312, and the American Taxpayer Relief Act of 2012 (ATRA), Pub. L. No. 112-240. Essentially, EGTRRA repealed the estate and generation-skipping transfer (GST) taxes and implemented a modified carryover tax basis regime for estates of decedents dying and generation-skipping transfers made in 2010 and modified the tax rate structure, the tax credit or exclusion amounts, the qualified family-owned business deduction, and the state death tax credit applicable in the years prior to repeal. However, all the changes made by EGTRRA (including the repeal) were scheduled to sunset for decedents dying and transfers made after 2010. EGTRRA, Pub. L. No. 107-16, §901. As explained in more detail in Chapter 4, A.1., the 2010 TRA generally reinstated the estate and GST taxes for estates of decedents dying and generation-skipping transfers made after 2009, repealed the §1022 modified carryover basis regime that would otherwise have applied in 2010, allowed estates of decedents dying in 2010 to elect to apply §1022 instead of the estate tax, improved the rates and exclusion amounts for 2010–2012, and extended various provisions through 2012. 2010 TRA, Pub. L. No. 111-312, §101(a), §301–§304. ATRA generally made permanent the changes made by both EGTRRA and the 2010 TRA, but increased the estate and gift tax rates, personal income tax rates, and the capital gains and dividend tax rates. ATRA, Pub. L. No. 112-240, §101(a), §101(b), §101(c), §102(b).
12. If the property sold is depreciable, recapture of previously deducted depreciation might be required. *See* §1245. Ordinarily, §1239, which treats gain as ordinary income when realized upon the sale of depreciable property between certain related taxpayers, would not be applicable in this context because of the narrow definition of "related persons" in this provision. Consequently, except for the depreciation recapture amount, capital gain could be subject to 20% tax. The §1(h) 20% maximum capital gains tax rate applies to taxable years beginning after 2012. ATRA, Pub. L. No. 112-240, §102(b). Prior to 2013, the §1(h) maximum capital gains tax was 15%. *See* 2010 TRA, Pub. L. No. 111-312, §101(a), §102 (extending sunset provisions in EGTRRA, Pub. L. No. 107-16, §901, and JGTRRA, Pub. L. No. 108-27, §303).
13. §162(a)(3).
14. The courts of appeal are split concerning whether a deduction is available in this context, but ultimately the inquiry seems to be factual. Consequently, careful structuring of these arrangements is essential. Favorable (to the taxpayer) decisions include *Skemp v. Commissioner,* 168 F.2d 598 (7th Cir. 1948); *Brown v. Commissioner,* 180 F.2d 926 (3d Cir. 1950), *cert. denied,* 340 U.S. 814 (1950); and *Quinlivan v. Commissioner,* T.C. Memo 1978-70, *aff'd,* 599 F.2d 269 (8th Cir. 1979), *cert. denied,* 444 U.S. 996 (1979). The Fourth and Fifth Circuits decided against the taxpayer, however. *See Mathews v. Commissioner,* 520 F.2d 323 (5th Cir. 1975), *rev'g* 61 T.C. 12 (1973), *cert. denied,* 424 U.S. 967 (1976); *Perry v. United States,* 520 F.2d 235 (4th Cir. 1975), *cert. denied,* 423 U.S.

1052 (1976). In these circuits a transfer and immediate leaseback is viewed as a single integrated transaction that lacks economic reality and business purpose.

15. 61 T.C. 12 (1973), *rev'd,* 520 F.2d 323 (5th Cir. 1975), *cert. denied,* 424 U.S. 967 (1976).
16. Section 1015 provides for a carryover basis if the transferred property is appreciated above its tax basis when gifted.
17. Note that under §267 loss deductions will be disallowed when incurred in transactions between related persons. The estate planner needs to examine who are related persons for the purpose of this loss disallowance rule. In this context, see PLR 9017008, which indicates that §267 does not disallow a loss deduction on the sale of stock by a father-in-law to a son-in-law, or by a trust grantor to the trustee of the same trust, when the trustee acts in his or her individual capacity and not as a fiduciary.
18. The §1(h) 20% maximum capital gains tax rate applies to taxable years beginning after 2012. *See* ATRA, Pub. L. No. 112-240, §102(b). Prior to 2013, the maximum capital gains tax rate was 15%. *See* 2010 TRA, Pub. L. No. 111-312, §101(a), §102 (extending sunset provisions in EGTRRA, Pub. L. No. 107-16, §901, and JGTRRA, Pub. L. No. 108-27, §303). Note that, as specified in §453A, interest will be charged on the benefit of that deferral when the installment sales tax liability is greater than $5 million.
19. If the property subsequently appreciates after the seller's transfer, the appreciation is still removed from the transferor's estate.
20. *See, e.g.*, §303, §2032A, §6166. In this situation, for example, the asset sold might be property other than the business interest. The sales proceeds might be invested to acquire a greater share of the business (to assure satisfaction of the minimum percentage ownership requirements) or, alternatively, be expended (1) for the seller's living costs or (2) to make annual donee exclusion gifts (thereby indirectly increasing the percentage of the remaining estate assets consisting of the closely held business).
21. §453. For example, installment sales reporting would not be available if the evidence of indebtedness received by the seller is (1) payable on demand or (2) issued by a corporation (or a government or political subdivision thereof) and is readily tradable. *See* §453(f)(4).
22. Pursuant to §453(i) any recapture of depreciation (ordinarily occurring under §1245) must be recognized in the year of asset disposition and only the gain in excess of that recapture income may be reported on the installment method. A detailed discussion of the requirements of §453 in the family tax planning context is beyond the scope of this portfolio. *See* 565 T.M., *Installment Sales* (Bloomberg BNA).
23. §453(e)(1).
24. §453(e)(3). If the second disposition is not a sale or exchange, the fair market value of the property disposed of is treated as the amount realized. §453(e)(4). Subsequent payments actually received by the original seller are recovered tax free until they equal the amount realized from the resale.
25. See §453(f)(1), which defines "related person" as one whose stock would be attributed under §318(a) (other than paragraph (4) thereof) to the seller. "Related person" should not include a spouse of a child or of a grandchild (or other in-laws) because of the prohibition on reattribution in §318(a)(5)(B). Note that, with the recognition of same-sex marriages, this provision could become applicable in situations not previously anticipated. In planning related party sales consider, however, S. Rep. No. 96-1000, at II, F (1980), which states: "It is to be understood that the provisions governing the use of the

installment method to report sales between related parties, and the definition of such relationships, are not intended to preclude the Internal Revenue Service from asserting the proper tax treatment of transactions that are shams."

26. §453(e)(2)(A). The two-year period will be extended for any period during which the original purchaser's risk of loss on the property is substantially diminished by the holding of a put (including a put for similar property), the holding of an option by another person, a short sale, or any other such transaction. §453(e)(2)(B). A typical close corporation shareholders' agreement or an option where the purchase price is to be determined by reference to the fair market value of the property at the time of exercise will not be considered as having the effect of substantially diminishing the risk of loss. S. Rep. No. 96-1000, at II, F (1980).
27. §453(k)(2).
28. §453(e)(6)(C). This exception applies after the death of either spouse when the spouses hold their interests in the installment obligation or the purchased property as community property or as equal undivided joint interests. S. Rep. No. 96-1000, at II, F (1980). See §453(e)(6) for other exceptions.
29. Note that, when the purchaser is an entity such as a trust, a careful analysis of the applicability of the constructive ownership rules to the seller, trust, and the trust's beneficiaries will be necessary.
30. Note, of course, that the loss already accrued at the time of this transaction will not be available as a deduction, as specified in §267.
31. §453(g)(1).
32. Note that §453(g)(2) specifies that this limitation rule shall not apply "if it is established to the satisfaction of the Secretary that the disposition did not have as one of its principal purposes the avoidance of Federal income tax." See *Guenther v. Commissioner,* T.C. Memo 1995-280, where the taxpayer failed to demonstrate the absence of such a tax avoidance purpose.
33. This rule will apply to deferred payment sales between (1) a seller and a partnership or corporation that is 80% owned by the seller and/or the seller's spouse, and (2) partnerships and corporations that are 80% owned by the seller and/or the seller's spouse. *See* §1239(b), §1239(c). Direct transactions between spouses are not between related persons for purposes of this provision.
34. §453B(f)(1), §453(a).
35. The installment note must be received in a genuine transaction to enable its subsequent gift cancellation. See Rev. Rul. 77-299, 1977-2 C.B. 343, where a purported installment transaction was treated from its inception as a completed gift.
36. §453B(f)(2).
37. §453B(c), §691(a)(4).
38. §691(a)(5). See the discussion in Chapter 7, B.6., of "self-canceling installment notes" or "SCINs." This acceleration of gain may be avoided by providing for a bequest of the installment obligation to a trust, for the benefit of the obligor that would continue at least until the taxable year following maturity of the last installment. If the trust provided that only income be distributed currently, the gain realized each year from the installment sales portion would be taxable to the trust (as owner of the corpus) and no further tax would be incurred upon the distribution of the proceeds to the ultimate beneficiary on termination of the trust.
39. Reg. §20.2031-4.

40. §2512(b).
41. Reg. §25.2511-1(g)(1).
42. *See* §7872(c)(1)(A).
43. §2512(b).
44. Reg. §1.1001-1(e)(2) *Ex. (1)*. Consideration received may include the debt on the transferred property whether assumed by the "buyer" or non-recourse debt.
45. Reg. §1.1001-1(e). In a 1933 ruling, the IRS adopted a basis allocation approach for bargain sales, I.T. 2681, XII-1 C.B. 93 (1933), but in 1939 withdrew the ruling as to both transferors and transferees, I.T. 3335, 1939-2 C.B. 193. In contrast, in the situation of a bargain sale to a charity, the adjusted basis for determining gain is allocated between the gift and the sale portions. *See* §1011(b); Reg. §1.1011-2.
46. In 2005, the Joint Committee on Taxation suggested an allocation approach for legislative enactment, but this has not been enacted. *See* Staff of J. Comm. on Tax'n, 109th Cong., Options to Improve Tax Compliance and Reform Tax Expenditures (JCS-02–05), at 59 (J. Comm. Print 2005).
47. §1015(d)(6); Reg. §1.1015-4(a), (b).
48. Prior to 2013, typically both the seller and the buyer would have been in the 15% capital gains tax category, eliminating this as a relevant consideration. The §1(h) 15% maximum capital gains tax rate applied to taxable years beginning before 2013. *See* 2010 TRA, Pub. L. No. 111-312, §101(a), §102 (extending sunset provisions in EGTRRA, Pub. L. No. 107-16, §901, and JGTRRA, Pub. L. No. 108-27, §303). However, after 2012, it is possible that the seller could be in the §1(h) 20% maximum capital gains tax rate, while the buyer would be in the 15% maximum capital gains tax rate, making this relevant once again. See ATRA, Pub. L. No. 112-240, §102(b), increasing the maximum capital gains tax rate to 20%, but only for those taxpayers in the maximum §1(i) 39.6% income tax bracket.
49. *See Fincke v. Commissioner*, 39 B.T.A. 510 (1939), *acq.*, 1939-2 C.B. 12.
50. The amounts previously paid under the note will be includible in the note holder's gross estate, unless expended, including possibly for related income tax on the income component of the note payments.
51. *Estate of Moss v. Commissioner*, 74 T.C. 1239 (1980), *acq.*, 1981-2 C.B. 2; *Cain v. Commissioner*, 37 T.C. 185 (1961), *acq.*, 1962-2 C.B. 4. *But see Buckwalter v. Commissioner*, 46 T.C. 805 (1966).
52. See §2036(a)(1), requiring estate tax inclusion for property transferred when the transferor retained an interest for life.
53. See, for example, *Estate of Costanza v. Commissioner*, 320 F.3d 595 (6th Cir. 2003), *rev'g and rem'g* T.C. Memo 2001-128, where the Sixth Circuit rejected inclusion in the gross estate, based on treatment as a bona fide transaction, indicating that the parties needed to affirmatively show that there existed, at the time of the transaction, a real expectation of repayment and an intent to enforce the collection of the indebtedness to rebut the presumption that a SCIN signed by family members was a gift. The Court of Appeals remanded the case to the Tax Court for the purpose of resolving the IRS's alternative argument that the SCIN constituted a bargain sale that subjected the transfer to gift taxation when the original transaction was concluded. In CCA 201330033 the IRS asserted that a self-cancelling "balloon" installment note transaction resulted in a taxable gift. The IRS concluded there that the §7520 tables should not be used for valuation of the note but that the willing buyer-willing seller standard should be used. The IRS

concluded that because of the decedent's health it was unlikely that the note would be paid and the note actually had a net value significantly less than its stated amount. This CCA was apparently based on the situation involved in *Estate of Davidson v. Commissioner*, as filed in the Tax Court (Dkt. No. 13748-13), where the IRS asserted gift tax, estate tax, and GST liabilities of $2.6 billon. Apparently this case was subsequently settled for a significantly smaller amount, but the heirs of the estate then filed a significant tax malpractice proceeding ($500 million) against the tax advisors who initially advised concerning the structuring of this arrangement.

54. *See* Reg. §15A.453-1(c).
55. See Rev. Rul. 86-72, 1986-1 C.B. 253, which provides that where an installment note is canceled at death, the gain is to be recognized by the estate of the payee.
56. S. Rep. No. 96-1000, at II, J (1980). Related party loss disallowance rules might be applicable, depending on the relationships between the parties. *See* §267.
57. The IRS may take the position that the note that the seller receives is worth less than face value over the term if the actuarial life expectancy of the obligee is less than the term of the note. The result may be treatment as a part-sale/part-gift transaction. This requires that the actuarial possibility of death be taken into account in arriving at the face value of the note.
58. The Tax Court, in *Frane v. Commissioner*, held that the income was includible in the decedent's last income tax return, reasoning that the cancellation was a disposition under §453B(f) and taxable to the individual. *Estate of Frane v. Commissioner*, 98 T.C. 341 (1992), *rev'd in part, aff'd in part*, 998 F.2d 567 (8th Cir. 1993). The Eighth Circuit agreed that income must be recognized when the note is cancelled at death, but held that the income is taxable to the estate, relying on §691(a)(5)(iii), agreeing with the IRS's position in Rev. Rul. 86-72. This provision specifies that a cancellation occurring at the death of the obligee is treated as a transfer by the estate. The court stated that the amount of IRD taxable to the estate is the face amount of the obligation, less its basis in the hands of the decedent.
59. 465 U.S. 330 (1984).
60. Before the Supreme Court's decision in *Dickman*, and the subsequent enactment of §7872, the interest-free loan provided an opportunity for shifting capital for investment within the family unit at little tax cost. If an interest-free loan could be arranged to not trigger income or gift tax results, the following objectives could be achieved: (1) the lender (e.g., the parent) provided the borrower (e.g., a child) with the use of money or property without the lender being treated as making a taxable gift for the value of the use of the funds; (2) the lender did not recognize income in the loan transaction; (3) the lender shifted the income derived from the borrowed funds to the borrower who often was a lower bracket taxpayer for income tax purposes; (4) with the use of a demand note the lender had the right to retrieve the funds immediately from the borrower, rather than waiting for the expiration of some specified term of the loan—when the borrower was a family trust used to achieve the income shifting arrangement (such as, previously, a "*Clifford*" or 10-year trust and, currently, a long term trust) access to those funds could be considerably delayed but the same benefits could be achieved; and (5) the lender could obtain the funds to be loaned in this arrangement by borrowing the funds from a bank and, thereby, secure an interest expense deduction against his or her own income, though this deduction was limited when the opportunities to claim an interest expense deduction were reduced. Using the interest-free loan and the marginal income tax rate

differentials, these transactions could result in significantly greater retention of value within the family unit. *See* Kelley, *Practical Aspects of Intrafamily Loans*, 46 Tax Mgmt. Memo. 539 (Nov. 28, 2005).

61. 67 T.C. 1060 (1977), *aff'd*, 585 F.2d 234 (7th Cir. 1978).
62. In *Dickman*, the Supreme Court did not reach the question of the valuation of the gift. In dicta, however, the Court indicated that "to support a gift tax . . . the Commissioner need not establish that the funds lent did in fact produce a particular amount of revenue; it is sufficient for the Commissioner to establish that a certain yield could readily be secured and that the reasonable value of the use of the funds can be reliably ascertained." *Dickman v. Commissioner*, 465 U.S. 330, n. 14 (1984).
63. Rev. Rul. 73-61, 1973-2 C.B. 408.
64. This was based on the concept that, until the end of the year, the interest amount would not be known because the lender could demand repayment at any time.
65. Rev. Rul. 73-61; Rev. Rul. 81-286, 1981-2 C.B. 176; *Blackburn v. Commissioner*, 20 T.C. 204 (1953); *Mason v. United States*, 365 F. Supp. 670 (N.D. Ill. 1973), *aff'd*, 513 F.2d 25 (7th Cir. 1975); *Dickman v. Commissioner*, 465 U.S. 330 (1984) (all noted in Staff of J. Comm. On Tax'n, 98th Cong., General Explanation of the Revenue Provisions of the Deficit Reduction Act of 1984 [1984 DRA Bluebook], at 525 [1984].
66. *See* 1984 DRA Bluebook, at 535.
67. *See* 1984 DRA Bluebook, at 529. In *Cohen v. Commissioner*, 92 T.C. 1039 (1989), *aff'd*, 910 F.2d 422 (7th Cir. 1990), the Tax Court rejected a donor's argument that Rev. Rul. 73-61, 1973-1 C.B. 408, required the use of the interest rates in the gift tax valuation regulations. The court instead held that interest-free demand loans made before the 1984 Tax Reform Act must be valued for gift tax purposes using the interest rates prescribed in Rev. Proc. 85-46, 1985-2 C.B. 507 (which the IRS issued in response to the Supreme Court's decision in *Dickman v. Commissioner*, 465 U.S. 330 (1984)), rather than the rates used in the valuation tables in former Reg. §25.2512-5(e) and §25.2512-9(e). The court held that the Rev. Proc. 85-46 interest rates, set at the lesser of (1) the statutory interest rate for refunds and deficiencies in §6621, or (2) the annual average rate for three-month Treasury bills, were consistent with the market interest rate standard articulated in *Dickman*. Because the Rev. Proc. 85-46 interest rates mirrored market rates, while the gift tax regulations used significantly below-market interest rates, the court concluded that the donor was not prejudiced by an application of unforeseeable, retroactive interest rates. See also *Estate of Arbury v. Commissioner*, 93 T.C. 136 (1989), in which the Tax Court again upheld the use of Rev. Proc. 85-46 interest rates, even though the prescribed interest rates exceeded the maximum allowable interest rate under state usury laws.
68. In *Dean v. Commissioner*, 35 T.C. 1083 (1961), *nonacq.*, 1973-2 C.B. 4, for example, the controlling shareholders borrowed substantial money interest-free from a corporation. The IRS sought to impute income to the borrowers. The Tax Court held, however, that the transactions did not result in income to the borrowers on the grounds that, if they borrowed the funds in question on interest-bearing notes, their payment of interest would have been fully deductible by them under §163. Additionally, in a pre-§7872 situation, the Claims Court, in *Winter v. United States*, 91-2 USTC ¶50,436 (Cl. Ct. 1991), *aff'd by unpub. opin.*, 972 F.2d 1355 (Fed. Cir. 1992), held that the borrower of an intrafamily interest-free demand loan was not entitled to interest expense deductions.

69. §7872(a). For this purpose, the concept of "demand loan" is any loan that is payable in full at any time on the demand of the lender. *See* §7872(f)(5).
70. The term "gift loan" means any below-market loan where the forgoing of interest is in the nature of a gift. *See* §7872(f)(3).
71. §7872(d)(2).
72. §7872(a)(2).
73. This example is excerpted from the 1984 DRA Bluebook, p. 533. Changes in applicable federal rates could significantly change the amounts in this example.
74. See §7872(e), prescribing the applicability of the "applicable federal rate." As specified in §7872(f)(2), this rate is determined pursuant to §1274(d). Three alternative rates are prescribed for term loans: (1) a short-term rate for loans of three years or less; (2) a mid-term rate for loans over three years but not over nine years; and (3) a long-term rate for loans over nine years. In the case of a demand loan the applicable federal rate will be the federal short term rate applicable for the period for which the amount of forgone interest is being determined, compounded semiannually. *See* §7872(f)(2)(B). These rates are promulgated monthly in a revenue ruling published by the IRS. If the applicable federal rate is low (during periods of low market interest rates) these imputed income amounts will be reduced.
75. §7872(c)(2).
76. §7872(c)(2)(B).
77. Note that this exception is only available where the loan is between natural persons. A loan to a trust for a child will not qualify for this exception. *See* Prop. Reg. §1.7872-8(a)(2).
78. §7872(d)(1). For this purpose, the term "net investment income" has the same meaning as it does for purposes of §163(d)(4). The term generally means the excess of investment income over investment expense. The term "investment income" means: (1) the gross income from interest, dividends, rents and royalties; (2) the net short-term capital gain attributable to the disposition of property held for investment; and (3) any amounts treated as depreciation recapture items.
79. §7872(d)(1)(C).
80. §7872(d)(1)(E)(ii).
81. This exception is inapplicable to any loan whose interest arrangements have as one of their principal purposes the avoidance of federal income tax. *See* §7872(d)(1)(B).
82. In his dissenting opinion in *Dickman v. Commissioner*, 465 U.S. 330 (1984), Justice Powell, noting that the majority did not limit its holding to interest-free loans of money, indicated that "potential tax liability may arise in a wide range of situations involving the unrecompensed use of property."
83. See PLR 9113009, where the IRS (in a marital deduction context) indicated that a guarantee of the indebtedness of a taxpayer's children constituted a taxable gift when the guarantee became binding, without regard to whether the guarantor was actually required to perform on this guarantee. This position was withdrawn, however, in PLR 9409018.
84. This attitude may prevail even though the maximum capital gains rate is only 20%, because the client is aware of the step up in basis at death provision. The §1(h) 20% maximum capital gains tax rate applies only to taxable years beginning after 2012. *See* ATRA, Pub. L. No. 112-240, §102(b). Prior to 2013, the maximum §1(h) capital gains tax rate was 15%. *See* 2010 TRA, Pub. L. No. 111-312, §101(a), §102 (extending sunset

provisions in EGTRRA, Pub. L. No. 107-16, §901, and JGTRRA, Pub. L. No. 108-27, §303).

85. §1014.
86. A "reverse mortgage" may achieve the same objective. Under such an arrangement a person mortgages his or her residence (or other property) and periodically borrows from the lender. The security for that increasing loan balance is the equity value in the residence (or other property). After death, when the income tax basis has been increased to fair market value under §1014, the property may be sold without any gain realization and part of the proceeds may then be used to liquidate the outstanding balance of the property mortgage.
87. See §163(h), which limits the deductibility of personal interest. Interest on a home mortgage remains deductible, however, subject to certain limitations. *See* §163(h)(2)(D), §163(h)(3).
88. §1031(a)(1).
89. §1031(a)(2).
90. §1031(b).
91. For this purpose, the concept of "related party" is defined in §267. *See* §1031(f)(3).
92. §1031(f). This provision has as its objective imposing a limitation on basis shifting and tax-free cashing out of investments. See Rev. Rul. 2002-83, 2002-2 C.B. 927, where the IRS applied this rule to a like-kind exchange transaction accomplished through a qualified intermediary.
93. This treatment would be subject to the loss limitation rules of §267 (restricting loss deductions on transfers of loss properties between related parties).
94. See TAM 200126007 for an extensive discussion of the applicability of §1031(f) in a multiparty exchange where the National Office advised that the limitations of this provision were applicable.
95. §1031(f)(2). An involuntary conversion for this purpose is as defined in §1033.
96. §1031(f)(2)(B).
97. These transfers are accomplished under §351.
98. These transfers are accomplished under §721.
99. §1031(f)(2)(C).
100. See §1031(f)(4), which specifies that like-kind treatment shall not apply to any exchange that is part of a transaction (or series of transactions) structured to avoid the purposes of this two-year rule limiting dispositions.
101. Rev. Proc. 2015-3, 2015-1 I.R.B. 129, §4.01(41).
102. §2036, §2043.
103. *See* §2036, §2038.
104. See 805 T.M., *Private Annuities and Self-Canceling Installment Notes* (Bloomberg BNA).
105. *See* REG-141901-05, 71 Fed. Reg. 61,441 (Oct. 18, 2006). This proposed regulation states that this rule change is effective as of its date of publication. However, nine years later (as of 2015) these regulations have not been finalized.
106. An annuity may exist for a specified term (rather than for one or more lives), but this is ordinarily not the format in the private annuity context.
107. Some of those receipts could have been used for the payment of income tax attributable to the income component of each annuity payment.
108. See Rev. Rul. 84-162, 1984-2 C.B. 200, concerning the determination of the value of an annuity contract. The gift tax and estate tax valuation tables promulgated under §7520 are

used for this purpose. *See* T.D. 8886, 65 Fed. Reg. 36,908 (June 12, 2000), *corrected,* 65 Fed. Reg. 58,222 (Sept. 28, 2000) (providing revised actuarial tables to include longer life expectancies).

109. *See* REG-141901-05, 71 Fed. Reg. 61,441 (Oct. 18, 2006).
110. One potential risk is that the IRS might assert that the receipt of the "promise" from the obligor to pay a monetary amount in exchange for the transfer of property (rather than the subsequent, periodic receipt of the actual funds) is itself sufficient to constitute an amount received (or its equivalent) for having an immediate income tax recognition event for §1001 purposes.
111. This describes the position of the IRS, with respect to the income taxation of private annuities, as evidenced by Rev. Rul. 69-74, 1969-1 C.B. 43. See also PLR 9009064, concerning the application of these concepts when a cost of living (COLI) adjustment factor is included in the private annuity contract. In REG-141901-05, 71 Fed. Reg. 61,441 (Oct. 18, 2006), as discussed below, the IRS proposed to obsolete Rev. Rul. 69-74, effective, with exceptions, for exchanges of property for an annuity contract occurring on or after Oct. 18, 2006.
112. *See* §1001(a).
113. This is the ordinary income component as determined by application of §72, the annuity income taxation provision.
114. See §1245, §1250, concerning potential depreciation recapture.
115. *See* §1239. Note that the concept of "related party" for this purpose is relatively limited.
116. Prop. Regs. §1.72-6(e), §1.1001-1(j), REG-141901-05. The preamble indicates that the IRS issued these proposed regulations in response to perceived abuses of the gain deferral permitted under Rev. Rul. 69-74 and that, as noted above, the IRS plans to obsolete Rev. Rul. 69-74 effective contemporaneously with the effective date of the regulations when they are finalized.
117. REG-141901-05 (preamble); Prop. Reg. §1.1001-1(j).
118. *See* §72(c)(1).
119. REG-141901-05 (preamble); Prop. Reg. §1.72-6(e) (cross-referencing Prop. Reg. §1.1001-1(j)).
120. Prop. Reg. §1.72-6(e)(2)(i), §1.1001-1(j)(2)(i). Therefore, although not finalized, these rules appear to be currently applicable. A transitional rule would delay the effective date until after April 18, 2007, if: (1) the contract issuer was an individual; (2) the contract obligations were unsecured; and (3) the transferee/obligor did not dispose of—including in a transfer to any trust or other entity, even if solely owned by the obligor—property received in exchange for the contract within two years after the exchange. Prop. Reg. §1.72-6(e)(2)(ii), §1.1001-1(j)(2)(ii).
121. The §1(h) 20% maximum capital gains tax rate and the §1(i) 39.6% maximum income tax rate apply to taxable years beginning after 2012. *See* ATRA, Pub. L. No. 112-240, §102(b). Prior to 2013, the §1(h) maximum capital gains tax rate was 15% and the §1(i) maximum income tax rate was 35%. *See* 2010 TRA, Pub. L. No. 111-312, §101(a), §102 (extending application of sunset provisions in EGTRRA, Pub. L. No. 107-16, §901, and JGTRRA, Pub. L. No. 108-27, §303).
122. Under the installment sales provisions, depreciation recapture is not eligible for gain recognition postponement. *See* §453(i). This rule precluding postponement of a depreciation recapture amount is apparently not applicable, however, in the private annuity context (prior to the effectiveness of the proposed regulations).

123. *See* §1011.
124. *See* §1016.
125. Assuming equality of value between the transferred property and the contract, this value will constitute the "investment in the contract" for enabling the required computation of annuity income under §72.
126. §72(b)(1).
127. §72(c)(3)(A).
128. §72(b)(1).
129. REG-141901-05, 71 Fed. Reg. 61,441 (Oct. 18, 2006).
130. This was based on the concept that a modified form of "open transaction" treatment should be permitted in this context. Note, however, that in *Estate of Bell v. Commissioner,* 60 T.C. 469 (1973), the Tax Court held that all capital gain was taxable in the year of the property transfer in a private annuity transaction. In this situation the annuity promise was secured with collateral and, consequently, only limited risk existed that the annuity promise might not be fulfilled. The IRS's position was that no reason for an income tax reporting delay exists in this context, that is, that no "open transaction" reporting position was permissible. As discussed in F.2.a. of this chapter, the IRS issued proposed regulations in 2006 that would eliminate (commencing in 2006) the gain deferral associated with private annuities, whether secured or unsecured. *See* REG-141901-05, 71 Fed. Reg. 61,441 (Oct. 18, 2006). As of mid-2015, these regulations have not been finalized.
131. *See* §1245, §1250. Previously, investment tax credit was to be recaptured (by reason of §47) upon the early disposition of ITC property in exchange for an annuity promise. See §1254 on recapturing certain gain upon the disposition of natural resource properties.
132. *See* §453(i).
133. See the discussion of §302(b)(1), §302(b)(2), §302(b)(3), and §303 corporate stock redemptions in Chapter 12, E.1.
134. If the 20% tax rate on dividends (as enacted in ATRA) remains applicable, this differential will not be important except for the timing of the recovery of the tax basis for the shares redeemed if gain deferral were possible. Section 1(h)(11) and the general §1(h) 20% maximum capital gains tax rate apply to taxable years beginning after 2012. *See* ATRA, Pub. L. No. 112-240, §102(b). Prior to 2013, the §1(h)(11) and the general §1(h) maximum capital gains tax rate was 15%. *See* 2010 TRA, Pub. L. No. 111-312, §101(a), §102 (extending application of sunset provisions in EGTRRA, Pub. L. No. 107-16, §901, and JGTRRA, Pub. L. No. 108-27, §303).
135. §72(b)(3). This will be an ordinary loss and §72(b)(3)(C) specifies that, for net operating loss carry back purposes, this will be treated as a deduction as if attributable to a trade or business of the taxpayer.
136. §72(b)(2).
137. Rev. Rul. 69-74 indicates how the gift element must be determined and eliminated from the income tax computation. In conjunction with the proposed elimination of the capital gain deferral associated with private annuities, REG–141901-05, 71 Fed. Reg. 61,441 (Oct. 18, 2006), as discussed in F.2.a. of this chapter, proposes to obsolete Rev. Rul. 69-74, effective, with exceptions, for exchanges of property for an annuity contract occurring on or after October 18, 2006. *Estate of Bell v. Commissioner*, 60 T.C. 469 (1973), is an example of where the excess of the fair market value of the property transferred over the value of the annuity received was treated as a gift when the transfer was between family members. See also *Fehrs v. United States,* 79-2 USTC ¶13,324 (Ct.

Cl. Trial Div. 1979), *aff'd per curiam,* 620 F.2d 255 (Ct. Cl. 1980), where share transfers by shareholders to a corporation in return for annuities were both redemptions and gifts.

138. See TAM 9513001, where an individual sold real property to his children in return for private annuities but the facts indicated the transferor did not expect payment. The annuity contracts were not recognized, with the adjusted taxable gift amount being increased in the computation of the estate tax applicable to the transferor's estate.
139. §2036(a)(1). See the discussion in F.6.c.(2) of this chapter.
140. See Rev. Rul. 55-119, 1955-1 C.B. 352, for the basis rules applicable to the transferee in this tax basis context.
141. If the annuity transfer has a gift component, the transferee's basis is the greater of (1) the amount paid by the transferee or (2) the transferor's adjusted basis in the property at the time of the transfer. *See* §1015; Reg. §1.1015-4.
142. §1012, §1016.
143. *Rye v. United States*, 92-1 USTC ¶50,186 (Cl. Ct. 1992) and cases cited there. See also §1275(a)(1)(B), which provides, for purposes of the original issue discount rules, that the term "debt instrument" does not include any annuity to which §72 applies and which depends (in whole or substantial part) on the life expectancy of one or more individuals.
144. *See Estate of Bell v. Commissioner,* 60 T.C. 469 (1973); *212 Corp. v. Commissioner*, 70 T.C. 788 (1978). The IRS's position has been that, in this situation, "open transaction" treatment has not been available because payment of the promise is not problematic. The IRS issued proposed regulations in 2006 (but effective immediately) eliminating the gain deferral associated with private annuities, whether secured or unsecured. *See* REG-141901-05, 71 Fed. Reg. 61,441 (Oct. 18, 2006).
145. For an extensive discussion of the valuation of private annuity contracts see *Estate of Gribauskas v. Commissioner,* 116 T.C. 142 (2001), *rev'd and rem'd*, 342 F.3d 85 (2d Cir. 2003), a lottery prize valuation case.
146. See also Rev. Rul. 68-183, 1968-1 C.B. 308 (issued before enactment of §2702), where the grantor of a trust sold stock to a corporation in exchange for an annuity promise. Because the agreement required the income from the transferred property to be utilized to fulfill the annuity promise, the transaction was treated as a contribution to the trust with the retention of a life estate. In Rev. Rul. 79-94, 1979-1 C.B. 296, the obligation to pay under an annuity promise was limited to the income from the transferred property and, similarly, a life interest was deemed to have been retained.
147. §2036(a).
148. See Rev. Rul. 76-491, 1976-2 C.B. 301, where an annuity was to be paid exclusively from the assets of a trust that could be totally liquidated at any time through the exercise by beneficiaries of a power of appointment.
149. §2036(a).
150. See Reg. §1.7520-3(b)(3), §20.7520-3(b)(3), §25.7520-3(b)(3), noting the IRS's position that mortality tables should not be used to predict the survival possibilities of an individual whose time of death is reasonably predictable based on the facts presented. These regulations specify that an individual who is known to have an incurable illness or other deteriorating physical condition is considered terminally ill if at least a 50% probability exists that the individual will die within one year. If, however, the individual survives for eighteen months or longer after the date of the transaction, that individual shall be presumed to have not been terminally ill at the time of the transaction unless the contrary is

established by clear and convincing evidence. This regulation obsoleted Rev. Rul. 80-80, 1980-1 C.B. 194, where the IRS ruled that the actuarial tables in the regulations should be applied unless the individual is known to have been afflicted, at the time of a property transfer, with an incurable physical condition that is in such an advanced stage that death is "clearly imminent."

151. See an estate tax decision, *Estate of McLendon v. Commissioner,* T.C. Memo 1993-459, *rev'd and rem'd,* 77 F.3d 477 (5th Cir. 1995), *on remand,* T.C. Memo 1996-307, *rev'd* 135 F.3d 1017 (5th Cir. 1998), concerning the transfer of partnership interests for the promise of private annuity payments. The Tax Court determined (consistent with Rev. Rul. 80-80) that the use of IRS actuarial tables was not appropriate, but did not expressly find that the decedent's death was clearly imminent. The Fifth Circuit remanded to determine the applicability of Rev. Rul. 80-80. The Fifth Circuit then reversed the Tax Court's decision on remand holding that the Tax Court had incorrectly applied Rev. Rul. 80-80 and that the annuitant was entitled to use the IRS tables. In this situation an adjustment clause was ignored which specified that the amount to be paid to the annuitant was to increase if a determination was made by the IRS or a court that the value of the property transferred was greater than the parties originally specified. Note that Rev. Rul. 80-80 (deemed governing in *McLendon*) was superseded by the §7520 regulations.
152. *See* Reg. §20.7520-3(b)(2)(v) *Exs 1, 2.*
153. The trust property could be includible in the gross estate under §2036(a). *See* Loftis, *When Can a Trust Be Used to Fund a Private Annuity Without Creating a Retained Interest?* 14 Est. Plan. 218 (1987).
154. *See Estate of Bell v. Commissioner,* 60 T.C. 469 (1973); *212 Corp. v. Commissioner,* 70 T.C. 788 (1978). As discussed in F.2.a. of this chapter, the IRS issued proposed regulations in 2006 that eliminate the gain deferral associated with private annuities, whether or not a trust is involved. *See* REG-141901-05, 71 Fed. Reg. 61,441 (Oct. 18, 2006).
155. *See* §677(a)(1); *Estate of Fabric v. Commissioner,* 83 T.C. 932 (1984); *Stern v. Commissioner,* 77 T.C. 614 (1981), *rev'd and rem'd,* 747 F.2d 555 (9th Cir. 1984); *La Fargue v. Commissioner,* 73 T.C. 40 (1979), *aff'd, rev'd, and rem'd in part,* 689 F.2d 845 (9th Cir. 1982). See also *Weigl v. Commissioner,* 84 T.C. 1192 (1985), where the Tax Court held that a grantor of a trust had not entered into a bona fide annuity transaction with the trust and, therefore, the trust grantor was taxable on the trust income pursuant to the grantor trust rules.
156. Vertical interests consist of portions of a tenancy in common or a tenancy with the right of survivorship where each party has both an interest in the current use of the property and the proceeds upon future disposition.
157. Section 7520, enacted in 1988, specifies that the value of a life estate and a remainder interest are to be determined under IRS prescribed tables, using an interest rate equal to 120% of the federal mid-term rate in effect for the month in which the valuation date occurs. For valuation dates after April 30, 2009, see the tables at Reg. §20.2031-7T(d)(7) and IRS Pub. 1457, *Actuarial Valuations Version 3A* (available on the IRS website). For valuation dates after April 30, 1999, and before May 1, 2009, see the tables at Reg. §20.2031-7A(f)(4), IRS Pub. 1457, *Actuarial Values Book Aleph* (7/99), and Notice 2009-18, 2009-10 I.R.B. 648 (factors for interest rates below 2.2%).
158. To determine the actual percentages the advisor will need to examine the valuation tables prescribed under §7520.

159. See 835 T.M., *Transfers of Interests in Family Entities Under Chapter 14: Sections 2702, 2703 and 2704* (Bloomberg BNA); 836 T.M., *Partial Interests—GRATs, GRUTs, QPRTs (Section 2702)* (Bloomberg BNA).
160. Split purchases among family members also previously resulted in estate tax inclusion under former §2036(c). In Example 16 of Notice 89-99, 1989-2 C.B. 422 (interpreting former §2036(c)), the IRS described a split purchase situation, concluding that the parent thereby transferred to the child potential appreciation and that a disproportionate transfer occurred in these situations. Further, as indicated in Example 19 of that Notice, because the income from the property was payable to the parent during the parent's lifetime, the parent was treated as retaining an interest in the income of the enterprise.
161. See Reg. §25.2702-4(d) *Ex. 1*, which provides an illustration of a parent acquiring a term interest and a child acquiring a remainder interest in an apartment building. For gift tax purposes the parent is treated as purchasing the entire property and is effectively treated as transferring the entire interest in the property in exchange only for the amount paid for the remainder interest. The parent's interest is treated as having no value because it is not a "qualified interest."
162. *See* §2702(a)(1).
163. *See* §2702(e), §2704(c)(2). With the recognition of same-sex marriages, the concept of spouse would be expanded for purposes of this rule.
164. Reg. §25.2702-2(c)(2)(i). This special rule could apply to a work of art or undeveloped land being held for appreciation.
165. §2702(c)(4). See Reg. §25.2702-2(c)(1), which states the usual valuation rule as that amount a willing buyer would pay a willing seller for the interest, each having reasonable knowledge of the relevant facts and neither being under any compulsion to buy or sell.
166. Reg. §25.2702-2(d)(2) *Ex. 6.*
167. A detailed discussion of this planning technique is included because (1) in some situations the parties may not be concerned about the special valuation rules and (2) in some situations those rules may not be applicable because the participants are not "members of the family."
168. *See* §103.
169. *See* §167(a)(2); Reg. §1.1014-5(d) *Ex. 1*, as redesignated by T.D. 9729, 80 Fed. Reg. 48,249 (Aug. 12, 2015); *Gist v. United States,* 296 F. Supp. 526 (S.D. Cal. 1968), *aff'd,* 423 F.2d 1118 (9th Cir. 1970); Rev. Rul. 62-132, 1962-1 C.B. 73.
170. See §167(e) (formerly §167(r)), which specifies that: (1) no depreciation or amortization deduction is allowed for a term interest in property for any period during which the remainder interest in such property is held (directly or indirectly) by a related person (for this purpose, a term interest in property means a life interest in property, an interest in property for a term of years, or an income interest in a trust); (2) the taxpayer's basis in the term interest is reduced by the deduction disallowed by this provision; and (3) the remainder beneficiary's basis in the remainder interest is increased by the amount of the disallowed deductions. *See* 1989 Revenue Reconciliation Act, Pub. L. No. 101-239, §7645. *See also Kornfeld v. Commissioner,* 137 F.3d 1231 (10th Cir. 1998), *cert. denied,* 525 U.S. 872 (1998) (owner of bonds may not amortize retained life estate after making gift of remainder interest).
171. Section 167(e)(4)(B) specifies that if, except for the rule above, a depreciation or amortization deduction would be allowable to any person on any term interest in property, the principles of §167(d) shall apply to such term interest. This provision allows a

depreciation deduction for property to a life tenant, rather than partially allocating that deduction to the owner of the remainder interest.

172. Further, because of §167(d), during the existence of the life interest, the holder of the remainder interest receives no part of any depreciation deduction attributable to the wasting asset held by the parties.
173. From the investment perspective, this is the equivalent of purchasing a zero interest deep discount bond, except that (unlike the bond investment) no specified maturity date applies to this interest in property.
174. This adjustment is required by §167(e)(3)(B).
175. See the more detailed discussion of this alternative in Schnepper, Ivers, & Leimberg, *Spousal Purchases of Split Interests: The Sum of the Parts Is Greater Than the Whole*, 36 Tax Notes No. 9, 913 (1987). Note that much of the tax discussion in that article has been superseded by subsequent federal tax legislation.
176. This arrangement is occasionally used by spouses for the purchase of their personal residence.
177. *See* §167(e)(3)(B).
178. §2036(a).
179. A compensating element in this context is that the income tax basis step up (under §1014) would be available, but that would only offset capital gains taxed at the maximum 20% rate, as contrasted to a higher estate tax marginal rate. Prior to 2013, the maximum §1(h) capital gains rate was 15%. *See* 2010 TRA, Pub. L. No. 111-312, §101(a), §102 (extending sunset provisions in EGTRRA, Pub. L. No. 107-16, §901, and JGTRRA, Pub. L. No. 108-27, §303).
180. This might occur where the §2702(c)(2) limitations are not applicable because the parties are not "related."
181. This differs from two family members jointly acquiring a new asset in a split-purchase situation.
182. *See* §7520. Reg. §20.7520-1(a)(1) refers to the valuation tables for remainders in Reg. §20.2031-7(d). *See* Reg. §20.2031-7(d)(7) (providing Table S (single life remainder factors) applicable after April 30, 1999). Note that, if the assumed interest rate declines, the value of the remainder interest will increase. This results because the life interest is assumed to produce a smaller return, making the remainder interest more valuable.
183. Before the enactment of §2702, the remainder could be valued using the applicable actuarial tables and the §7520 interest rate.
184. See §2702(a)(2)(A), specifying that the value of any retained interest that is not a "qualified interest" will be treated as being zero. See also Reg. §25.2702-4(d) *Ex. 2*, noting a situation where a parent holds rental real estate valued at $100,000. Parent sells a remainder interest in the property to child, retaining the right to receive the income from the property for 20 years. Assume that the purchase price paid by the child for the remainder interest is equal to the value of the interest determined under §7520. The parent's retained interest is not a "qualified interest" and is, therefore, valued at zero. Parent made a gift to child in the amount of $100,000, less the consideration received from the child.
185. §2702(a)(2)(B), §2702(b).
186. *See* §2702(a)(1).
187. Section 2036(a) provides that an asset conveyed during life is included in the transferor's gross estate if the transferor retained a life interest in the property transferred. Section

2036(a) further provides for its inapplicability where the property transfer was for full and adequate consideration.

188. 897 F.2d 516 (Fed. Cir. 1990), *aff'g* 11 Cl. Ct. 808 (1987). The significant impact of *Gradow* is that the entire fair market value of the transferred property is includible in the life tenant's gross estate if any excess gift value occurred in the transaction. An offset is available under §2043 to the extent of the consideration received by the life tenant for the remainder interest. The most important aspect in this analysis is that all appreciation subsequent to the remainder interest sale is includible in the gross estate under §2036(a). *See also Parker v. United States,* 894 F. Supp. 445 (N.D. Ga. 1995). The IRS previously took a more lenient position. See TAM 8145012, where the National Office noted that the sale of a remainder interest would not result in the inclusion of any part of the value of the property in the decedent's gross estate by reason of §2036. The IRS could also take the position that §2036 is applicable if the funds for the purchase are provided to the buyer. For example, the parent could give funds to the child and the child could use such funds to purchase the remainder interest. The IRS would assert that adequate and full consideration was not provided by the "purchasing" child. The analysis in this context was that the funds are all sourced from the parent, and the child is not the actual purchaser of the remainder interest.
189. 105 T.C. 252 (1995), *rev'd and rem'd,* 101 F.3d 309 (3d Cir. 1996), *cert. denied,* 520 U.S. 1230 (1997).
190. 116 F.3d 749 (5th Cir. 1997).
191. 184 F.3d 1074 (9th Cir. 1999).
192. *See* Jensen, *Estate and Gift Tax Effects of Selling a Remainder: Have D'Ambrosio, Wheeler, and Magnin Changed the Rules?* 4 Fla. Tax Rev. 537 (1999); Herzog, *Why Gradow Is Still Correct,* 2000 TNT 205-71 (Oct. 23, 2000).
193. Such revisions are required by §7520. During a period of low interest rates the remainder interest would be more valuable, increasing the cost of the remainder interest in this transaction.
194. *See* Reg. §1.1014-5(a)(3). *Cf.* §1001(e), where, on the sale or disposition of a term interest (as contrasted with a remainder interest), the term interest is treated as having no tax basis.
195. *See* §1001(a). Because §2702 only applies to valuation for gift tax purposes, the §2702 value is not necessarily determinative for income tax purposes.
196. §267(a)(1). See §267(b) for determining those relationships that cause the applicability of this loss disallowance provision.
197. See the discussion of the estate planning use of a "private annuity" inChapter 3, F., including the proposed regulations mandating current gain recognition for the transaction.
198. §167(d).
199. This assumes that full and adequate consideration was paid for the property. If this did not occur and the asset is included in the life tenant's estate for federal estate tax purposes (under §2036(a)), the tax basis to the remainder beneficiary is the amount included in the life tenant's gross estate for federal estate tax purposes (§1014).
200. See Reg. §1.1014-5(a)(3) for the determination of tax basis under the uniform basis rules.
201. §167(e)(1).
202. *See Jones v. Commissioner,* 40 T.C. 249 (1963), *vac'd and rem'd,* 330 F.2d 302 (3d Cir. 1964), *on remand,* T.C. Memo 1966-136; *Guthrie v. Commissioner,* 42 B.T.A. 696 (1940).

203. *See* Weinstock, *Sales and Purchases of Remainder Interests and Grantor Income Trusts*, 45th NYU Annual Inst. on Fed. Taxation, Ch. 28 (1993).
204. See 836 T.M., *Partial Interests—GRATs, GRUTs, QPRTs (Section 2702)* (Bloomberg BNA).
205. Reg. §25.2702-3(b)(1)(i) specifies that a GRAT must provide that the interest be an irrevocable right to receive a fixed amount payable to (or for the benefit of) the annuitant for each taxable year of the term of the trust. Reg. §25.2702-3(c)(1) specifies that a qualified unitrust interest is defined as an irrevocable right to receive a payment periodically, but not less frequently than annually, of a fixed percentage of the net fair market value of the trust assets, determined annually. The unitrust amount must be payable to the transferor or the applicable family member retaining such interest for each taxable year.
206. Reg. §25.2702-3(d)(6).
207. Reg. §25.2702-3(d)(5).
208. Note that the IRS periodically issues private letter rulings concerning the various federal tax elements of a GRAT or GRUT and obtaining such a ruling on a unique element of a GRAT or GRUT structure may be valuable.
209. §2702(a)(2)(B); Reg. §25.2702-2(b)(2) (both cross-referencing §7520). Reg. §25.7520-1(a)(1) cross-references the estate tax regulations under §2031 for the valuation of gifts of annuities, unitrust interests for life or a term of years, remainders, and reversions. For valuation dates after April 30, 2009, see the tables at Reg. §20.2031-7T(d) and IRS Pub. 1457, *Actuarial Valuations Version 3A.* For valuation dates after April 30, 1999, and before May 1, 2009, see the tables at Reg. §20.2031-7A(f), IRS Pub. 1457, Actuarial Values Book Aleph (7/99), and Notice 2009-18, 2009-10 I.R.B. 648 (factors for interest rates below 2.2%). These publications are posted on the IRS website at http://www.irs.gov.
210. In Rev. Proc. 2015-3, 2015-1 I.R.B. 129, §4.01(53), the IRS indicated that it generally will not issue rulings as to whether annuity interests are §2702(b) "qualified interests" where either: (1) the amount of the annual annuity is more than 50% of the initial net fair market value of the property transferred to the trust or (2) the present value of the remainder interest is less than 10% of the initial net fair market value.
211. The value of the grantor's power to revoke a qualified annuity or unitrust interest of his or her spouse is treated as the retention of a qualified interest as specified in Reg. §25.2702-2(a)(6). *See* PLR 9451056 (value of retained annuity was enhanced by increasing annuity payments and, also, through retention of revocable contingent annuity for grantor's spouse).
212. *See, e.g.,* TAM 9717008. This appreciation would be anticipated to occur at a greater percentage than the interest rate assumed in valuing the lead interest in the GRAT.
213. In *Schott v. Commissioner,* 319 F.3d 1203 (9th Cir. 2003), each taxpayer's interest in the other taxpayer's annuity, as beneficiary spouses, was contingent on the death of the grantor taxpayer, and the annuity term depended upon the use of two lives, those of the grantor taxpayer and the beneficiary taxpayer. The court determined that the Commissioner's exclusion of the contingency of the spouse being alive at the time her annuity begins was unreasonable and invalid. A two-life annuity, based on the lives of the grantor and spouse with a limit of 15 years, fell "within the class of easily valued rights" that Congress meant to qualify for this purpose.
214. *See* §2503(b).

215. 115 T.C. 589 (2000) (holding former Reg. §25.2702-3(e) *Ex. 5* invalid). In Notice 2003-72, 2003-44 I.R.B. 964, the IRS announced that it would follow the Tax Court's decision in *Walton.* The IRS issued final revised regulations accepting the *Walton* decision, but rejecting (with clarification) the Ninth Circuit's interpretation of the regulations in *Schott v. Commissioner,* 319 F.3d 1203 (9th Cir. 2003), *rev'g and rem'g* T.C. Memo 2001-110. T.D. 9181, 70 Fed. Reg. 9222 (Feb. 25, 2005), effective for trusts created on or after July 26, 2004 (IRS will not challenge any prior application of changes to Reg. §25.2702-3(e) *Exs. 5 and 6*). *See* Reg. §25.2702-7.
216. Any unpaid annuity or unitrust payment would be includible in the annuitant's gross estate under §2033.
217. *See* §2036(a), §2038.
218. To the extent that all or any portion of a GRAT or GRUT is includible in the estate of the grantor because the grantor dies prior to the expiration of the term, the grantor should be entitled to an adjustment in the estate tax determination under §2001(b)(2) for the gift tax payable on the original transfer into the trust. To moderate this potential estate tax cost the trust grantor could possibly fund a life insurance trust to insure against the death of the grantor during the term, thereby providing funds to the estate (e.g., through loans) to facilitate the tax payment.
219. Reg. §20.2039-1(b)(1).
220. *Id.*
221. PLR 9345035 was the first ruling in which the IRS addressed the amount includible in a grantor's gross estate if the grantor retains a qualified interest and does not survive the retained term of the trust. In addition to stating that the trust property would be includible in the grantor's gross estate under §2039, the ruling states that §2036 may require the inclusion of part or all of the corpus of a GRAT in the gross estate of a decedent who was the grantor and annuity beneficiary of the trust, citing Rev. Rul. 82-105, 1982-1 C.B. 133 (addressing charitable remainder annuity trust). The National Office and the Chief Counsel's Office reached the same conclusion in TAM 200210009 and FSA 200036012.
222. T.D. 9414, 73 Fed. Reg. 40,173 (July 14, 2008), finalizing, with modifications, the proposed regulations issued in REG-119097-05, 72 Fed. Reg. 31,487 (June 7, 2007). The regulations incorporate the guidance provided in Rev. Rul. 76-273, 1976-2 C.B. 268, and Rev. Rul. 82-105, 1982-1 C.B. 133, and obsolete both of them as of July 14, 2008. The regulations are effective for estates of decedents dying on or after July 14, 2008. Reg. §20.2036-1(c)(3). *See also* REG-119532-08, 74 Fed. Reg. 19,913 (Apr. 30, 2009) (proposed regulations for determining includible portion of trusts with graduated payments).
223. Reg. §20.2036-1(c)(2)(i). The trusts covered by the regulations include charitable remainder trusts, GRATs, GRUTs, grantor retained income trusts, personal residence trusts, and qualified personal residence trusts, even if those trusts do not qualify under §664(d) or §2702(b), respectively, but do not include trusts constituting employee benefits. *Id.*
224. Reg. §20.2036-1(c)(2)(i) (cross-referencing Reg. §20.2031-7); T.D. 9414 (preamble). The portion of the trust includible in the decedent's estate cannot exceed the fair market value of the trust's corpus on the date of death. Reg. §20.2036-1(c)(2)(i).
225. Reg. §20.2039-1(e), §20.2039-1(f), added by T.D. 9414, effective for estates of decedents dying on or after July 14, 2008.

226. One option would be to create and fund an irrevocable life insurance trust (ILIT) covering the death risk during the remaining term of the GRAT, with the insurance proceeds to be received being an amount equivalent to the estate tax cost.
227. *See United States v. Allen*, 293 F.2d 916 (10th Cir. 1961).
228. See in this context 836 T.M., *Partial Interests—GRATs, GRUTs, QPRTs (Section 2702)* (Bloomberg BNA).
229. §677(a). Grantor trust status for 100% of the trust should allow the trust to qualify as a permissible S corporation shareholder under §1361(c)(2)(A)(i).
230. *See* Reg. §1.677(a)-1(g) *Ex. 2.*
231. This would make the trust "defective" for federal income tax purposes.
232. *See* Rev. Rul. 85-13, 1985-1 C.B. 184. The continuing viability of this ruling was reaffirmed in Rev. Rul. 2004-86, 2004-2 I.R.B. 191, and Rev. Rul. 2007-13, 2007-1 I.R.B. 684.
233. §1014.
234. §1015. Since the infusion of assets into the trust, the basis for those assets may have been reduced by applicable depreciation and depletion deductions.
235. Reg. §25.2702-3(d)(5).
236. *See United States v. Allen,* 293 F.2d 916 (10th Cir. 1961) (three-year rule applicable even though gratuitous transfer had not occurred).
237. Therefore, §2036(a)(1) would cause inclusion of the asset in the trust grantor's gross estate.
238. §2702(a)(3)(A)(ii). As noted above, for gift tax purposes, if a transferor transfers an interest in trust to or for the benefit of a member of the transferor's family and retains an interest in the trust that is other than a "qualified interest," the value of the retained interest is zero (and the entire property is treated as transferred by gift). §2702(a)(1), §2702(a)(2).
239. *See* Reg. §25.2702-5(a).
240. Recognizing that errors in drafting personal residence trusts may be discovered when the gift tax return is prepared, the IRS issued Reg. §25.2702-5(a)(2) to permit trusts to be reformed to comply with the regulatory requirements. The reformation must be commenced within 90 days after the due date (including extensions) for the filing of the gift tax return reporting the transfer of the residence under §6075 and must be completed within a reasonable time after commencement.
241. *See* Reg. §25.2702-5(b)(2)(i), §25.2702-5(c)(2)(i). Note from Reg. §25.2702-5(d) *Ex. 1*, that a residence is a personal residence for this purpose even though the occupant also maintains a principal place of business in one room of the personal residence.
242. Reg. §25.2702-5(b)(2)(iii), §25.2702-5(c)(2)(iii). If the term holder does not actually reside in the residence (e.g., is too ill to reside in the residence), the residence will still qualify so long as it is "available at all times for [the term holder's] use as a residence during the term." Reg. §25.2702-5(d) *Ex. 5.* One impact of this requirement is that the residence cannot be rented. This example notes that the residence would cease to be held for use as a personal residence if the trustee rented the residence to an unrelated party.
243. Reg. §25.2702-5(b)(2)(i)(A), §25.2702-5(c)(2)(i)(A).
244. Reg. §25.2702-5(b)(2)(i)(B), §25.2702-5(c)(2)(i)(B).
245. In PLR 199925027 and PLR 9151046, the IRS indicated that a proprietary lease and the shares in a cooperative housing corporation qualify as a personal residence for this purpose. Similarly, in PLR 9249014, the IRS ruled that the grantor's assignment to a QPRT of the

beneficial title to his shares and the rights under a proprietary lease in a cooperative association, while holding legal title to such shares and leases as a nominee for the trust, was acceptable.

246. Reg. §25.2702-5(b)(2)(ii), §25.2702-5(c)(2)(ii). *See, e.g.,* PLR 200241039 (vacation property with residence, guest house, barn, boathouse, two sheds, and dock, together with adjacent acreage, all of which were subject to conservation easement, qualified as personal residence for this purpose). See 836 T.M., *Partial Interests—GRATs, GRUTs, QPRTs (Section 2702)* (Bloomberg BNA), for a summary of a large number of private letter rulings issued by the IRS responding to the question of whether the particular property constitutes a "residence" for this purpose.
247. Reg. §25.2702-5(b)(2)(ii), §25.2702-5(c)(2)(ii). Reg. §25.2702-5(d) *Ex. 4*, notes that a prohibition on holding tangible personal property is a requirement to be included in the governing instrument of a QPRT.
248. §2702(a)(3)(A)(ii).
249. Reg. §25.2702-5(b)(1).
250. *Id.*
251. *See* Reg. §25.2702-5(d) *Ex. (5).*
252. Reg. §25.2702-5(b)(3). The purchase price for the permitted replacement residence (e.g., when an involuntary conversion has occurred) will not ordinarily be exactly the same amount as the amount received as insurance or involuntary conversion proceeds. The amount to be reinvested is the proceeds, plus any income derived from investing those proceeds.
253. Reg. §25.2702-5(b)(1).
254. The trust could provide for its termination as of the time of the sale of the residence. At that time (as contrasted with the QPRT described below) the interest of the term holder could apparently be commuted with the payment to the term holder of the value of the remaining term interest.
255. See Reg. §25.2701-2(b)(5)(ii) and §25.2701-2(b)(5)(iii) for an explanation of the term "controlled entity."
256. Reg. §25.2702-5(b)(1).
257. Clarified by Reg. §25.2702-5(b)(1).
258. *Id.*
259. Rev. Proc. 2003-42, 2003-23 I.R.B. 993, contains an annotated sample declaration of trust and alternate provisions that satisfy the requirements under §2702(a)(3)(A) and Reg. §25.2702-5(c) for a QPRT with one term holder. Rev. Proc. 2015-3, 2015-1 I.R.B. 129, §4.01(54), specifies that the IRS will not ordinarily rule whether a trust with one term holder satisfies the QPRT requirements of §2702(a)(3)(A) and Reg. §25.2702-5(c).
260. Reg. §25.2702-5(c)(1).
261. Reg. §25.2702-5(c)(5)(ii).
262. Reg. §25.2702-5(c)(5)(ii)(A)(1)(i). PLR 9315010 indicates that an express agreement between the grantor and the trustee that the grantor will pay to the trustee all property taxes, maintenance costs, repair and remodeling costs, homeowner's insurance premiums, and mortgage payments during the primary term of the trust does not disqualify the trust as a QPRT.
263. Reg. §25.2702-5(c)(5)(ii)(A)(1)(ii).
264. Reg. §25.2702-5(c)(5)(ii)(A)(1)(iii).

265. Reg. §25.2702-5(c)(5)(ii)(A)(1)(iv).
266. Reg. §25.2702-5(c)(5)(ii)(A)(2).
267. Reg. §25.2702-5(c)(3).
268. Reg. §25.2702-5(c)(4).
269. Reg. §25.2702-5(c)(5)(ii)(B).
270. Reg. §25.2702-5(c)(5)(ii)(C).
271. Reg. §25.2702-5(c)(5)(ii)(D).
272. Reg. §25.2702-5(c)(7).
273. A residence will not fail to qualify as a personal residence merely because the grantor allows a friend to reside there with him or her (PLR 9249014) or occasionally allows houseguests to use the residence rent free (PLR 9448035). The leasing of a portion of the property to an unrelated third party will not result in disqualification, as long as the property remains the grantor's personal residence (PLR 199916030).
274. Reg. §25.2702-5(c)(7)(ii).
275. Reg. §25.2702-5(c)(8)(i).
276. Reg. §25.2702-5(c)(8)(ii)(A). *See* Reg. §25.2702-3 (prescribing requirements with respect to qualified annuity interests).
277. Reg. §25.2702-5(c)(8)(ii)(B).
278. *See, e.g.,* §2036(a)(1) (retained life interest provision).
279. Reg. §25.2702-5(c)(6).
280. The grantor could possibly sell his annuity interest in the GRAT to the remainder beneficiaries. A transfer for full consideration would be exempt from the three-year transfer rule under §2035(d) for estate tax inclusion of transferred interests, based on this transaction being a sale for full consideration. However, the IRS may assert that this is a prohibited commutation. *See* Rev. Rul. 98-8, 1998-1 C.B. 541.
281. The grantor may desire that at the expiration of the initial term, this property is to be transferred into a trust for the benefit of various remaindermen. This could include various beneficiaries who are children and grandchildren of the trust grantor. In this situation, a separate trust agreement would be required to specify the terms of this trust. Since this separate trust would hold the remainder interest, the terms of this trust might include such matters as: (1) the trustee of this trust maintaining homeowner's insurance coverage on this interest in the residence, and (2) treatment of proceeds upon the disposition of the residence during the initial term or the possible sale of the residence to others.
282. See §2036(a)(1) and Chapter 6, D.3.e.(2)(a). *See also* PLR 9249014 (ruling §2036(a)(1) inapplicable where grantor and remainder beneficiaries agreed at time QPRT was established that grantor had right to continue residing in residence after conclusion of primary term, that grantor would pay fair market value rent as determined by an appraisal, and that grantor would pay all real estate taxes, maintenance, utilities, and repairs).
283. Ordinarily, if the grantor purchased the residence from the trust before the expiration of the primary term of the trust, no gain or loss should have been recognized if the grantor was deemed to be the owner of the trust corpus under the grantor trust rules. *See* §671-§678; PLR 9433016, PLR 9425028 (approving QPRTs that reserved to grantors option to repurchase property). Consequently, the grantor's basis in the residence should have been a carryover basis equal to the trust's income tax basis immediately prior to the purchase, not a purchase price basis. *See* Rev. Rul. 85-13, 1985-1 C.B. 184. For a contrary result, however, see *Rothstein v. United States,* 735 F.2d 704 (2d Cir. 1984).

284. Reg. §25.2702-5(c)(9). This applies to QPRTs created after May 16, 1996. *See* Reg. §25.2702-7.
285. The regulations do specify that distributions (for no consideration) on or after the expiration of the retained term to another grantor trust of the grantor or the grantor's spouse pursuant to the express terms of the trust will not be considered a sale or transfer to the grantor or the grantor's spouse if the other grantor trust contains the required sale prohibitions. Reg. §25.2702-5(c)(9).
286. A possible option in this context is to have the remaindermen establish a new QPRT after the QPRT terminates (identified as a "reverse QPRT"), giving the parent an additional term of occupancy in the house. This arrangement will constitute a taxable gift by the remaindermen. The IRS has ruled that this transaction qualifies under the QPRT rules and is valued without regard to §2702.
287. Reg. §25.2702-5(c)(9).
288. *Id.*
289. *See, e.g.,* PLR 200121015 (approving separate QPRTs husband and wife planned to establish with their respective interests in residence owned as tenants in common).
290. Reg. §25.2702-5(b)(2)(iv), (c)(2)(iv).
291. *See United States v. Estate of Grace*, 395 U.S. 316 (1969) (applying reciprocal trust doctrine when trusts created by spouses for each other are interrelated and trust arrangement, to extent of mutual value, leaves trust settlers in approximately same economic position as they would have been in had they created trusts naming themselves as life beneficiaries).
292. *See* §2036(a)(1).
293. Further planning might contemplate the acquisition of a life insurance policy on the life of the trust grantor for the period of the trust term, enabling the receipt of funds to satisfy the estate tax. The life insurance policy should be owned in a manner to preclude inclusion of the proceeds in the gross estate of the trust grantor.
294. *See* §2207B(a)(1) (when property is includible in decedent's gross estate by reason of §2036, proportionate amount of estate tax can be recovered from person receiving property).
295. See the discussion of §2036(a)(1) and *Estate of Maxwell v. Commissioner,* 3 F.3d 591 (2d Cir. 1993), in Chapter 6, D.5.
296. This might also encompass a retained right, either alone or in conjunction with any other person, to designate the beneficiaries of the trust after the expiration of the period for which the grantor retained the use of the property. *See* §2036(a)(2).
297. However, the predeceased ancestor "move-up" exception of §2651(e), for example, may be applicable. This provides that, if a parent of a descendant of the transferor, or the transferor's spouse or former spouse, is deceased at the time of the transfer, that descendant's own descendants are treated as "moving up" one generation. The exception applies only if the predeceased ancestor was dead at the time that the transfer was first subject to estate or gift tax as to the transferor and, in the case of a transfer to collateral heirs, only if the transferor had no living lineal descendants at the time of the transfer. See the discussion of these generation-skipping transfer tax rules in Chapter 8.
298. *See* §671–§678.
299. *See* §163(h)(4)(D).
300. A further argument might be made that the person holding equitable title to the property (including the term interest holder) is entitled to the mortgage interest expense deduction.

301. *See* §164(a); *Estate of Movius v. Commissioner*, 22 T.C. 391 (1954), *acq.*, 1954-2 C.B. 5; *Horsford v. Commissioner*, 2 T.C. 826 (1943); Rev. Rul. 67-21, 1967-1 C.B. 45.
302. *See* §643; Reg. §1.643(a)-3.
303. If the trust is a PRT (as opposed to a QPRT), the trust would cease to qualify as a PRT after the sale of the residence. Reg. §25.2702-5(b)(1).
304. If the grantor pays this tax, but is not treated as the owner of the corpus, presumably this constitutes a further gift transfer (for federal gift tax purposes) to the remainder beneficiaries.
305. The Taxpayer Relief Act of 1997 (1997 Act), Pub. L. No. 105-34, §312, amended §121 as applicable to sales or exchanges after May 6, 1997. The 1997 Act replaced the over-age-55 exclusion of gain on the sale of the principal residence under former §121 with a broader exclusion that does not have an age requirement, allows the exclusion of a higher dollar amount, and, in general, permits the exclusion to be used every two years. In addition, the 1997 Act repealed former §1034, which provided for a tax-free rollover of gain.
306. *See* Rev. Rul. 66-159, 1966-1 C.B. 162 (gain postponement under former §1034 was available where trust grantor's residence was held by revocable inter vivos trust), Rev. Rul. 85-45, 1985-1 C.B. 183 (benefit of the former §121 exclusion was available where residence was held for beneficiary in grantor trust); PLR 199912026 (owner of revocable grantor trust could use §121 to exclude gain on sale of principal residence held in trust).
307. Reg. §25.2702-5(c)(7)(ii).
308. *See* Reg. §1.121-1(c)(3)(i) (during period that taxpayer is treated under §671–§679 as owner of trust or portion of trust that includes taxpayer's principal residence, taxpayer is treated as owning such residence for purposes of satisfying two-year ownership requirement of §121 and trust's sale or exchange of residence is treated as made by taxpayer).
309. §1015(d)(6).
310. §1015(a).
311. §1014. See Chapter 4, B., for a discussion of §1014.
312. *See* §1014(b)(6) (providing for tax basis step up for entire community property, not merely interest owned by decedent).

CHAPTER 8

Generation-Skipping Transfers

A. Purpose of the Generation-Skipping Transfer Tax

A generation-skipping transfer (GST) tax is imposed on certain gratuitous transfers when the assets transferred may not be subjected to estate or gift tax as applied to the next lower-generation member.[1] Generation-skipping transfers are subject to tax whether accomplished outright, in trust, or in any arrangement similar to a trust, for example, life estates, remainders, estates for years, insurance policies, and annuity contracts.[2] The fundamental premise of this tax is that a federal transfer tax should be imposed on the transfer of wealth at each generational level.[3]

This separate tax is imposed on transfers in which beneficiaries assigned to a generation that is two or more generations below the transferor's generation are benefited.[4] The tax is imposed, therefore, on direct generation-skipping transfers from the transferor to a beneficiary who is assigned to a generation two or more generations below the generation of the transferor when that transfer is a taxable gift or is includible in the estate of the transferor. This tax is also imposed on transfers into trust (and similar transfers) that immediately or thereafter achieve the same objective. In general, to invoke the GST tax: (1) a nonexempt direct skipping transfer must occur; or (2) a nonexempt trust with "skip persons" as potential beneficiaries must make distributions to skip persons or must terminate, making similar distributions, that is, to skip persons.

B. Definitional Provisions

1. Generation-Skipping Transfer

a. Tax Applicability

The taxable event for GST tax purposes is identified as a "generation-skipping transfer."[5] A generation-skipping transfer can occur by reason of[6]:

- a taxable distribution;
- a taxable termination; or
- a direct skip.

A generation-skipping transfer is a transfer of income or principal to or for a beneficiary assigned to a generation at least two generations below the generation of the transferor. Accordingly, only transfers to grandchildren or similar beneficiaries in younger generations are subject to this tax.

Example: An outright transfer by a transferor to a child is not a generation-skipping transfer. However, an outright transfer to the transferor's grandchild would be such a transfer.

b. Exceptions

The term "generation-skipping transfer" does not apply to any direct inter vivos transfer that is eligible for either the §2503(e) exclusion from gift tax for certain transfers for educational and medical expenses,[7] or the §2503(b) annual donee gift tax exclusion.[8] For the gift tax annual donee exclusion transfer to qualify for GST tax purposes, any transfer into trust must be to a trust having only one beneficiary (the skip person) and the trust principal must be included in that beneficiary's estate.[9]

c. Taxable Termination

The termination (by death, lapse of time, release of a power, or otherwise) of a beneficiary's interest in property held in trust is a "taxable termination" unless: (1) immediately after the termination, a "nonskip person" has an interest in the property; or (2) at no time after the termination, may a distribution (including distributions on termination) be made from the trust to a skip person.[10] The taxable termination does not occur until these intervening interests (other than nominal interests of all other nonskip persons) terminate.

Example: A trust is established for Child and Grandchild. At Child's death, a taxable termination occurs if Grandchild is alive and if no other trust beneficiaries exist who have a present interest and are assigned under the GST rules to the same generation as Child or are assigned to an older generation.

The tax planning objective in this context could be to defer the GST tax by having several nonskip beneficiaries of the trust with no trust termination occurring until the death of the last to die of the nonskip beneficiaries. Those interests must be more than nominal to be recognized (and to enable GST tax postponement).

d. Taxable Distribution

Any distribution (other than a taxable termination or a direct skip) from a trust (whether consisting of income or principal) to a skip person is a taxable distribution.[11]

Example: A trust is established for Child and Grandchild. The trustee makes a distribution to Grandchild. That distribution is a taxable distribution.

Often, this type of distribution will occur when a skip person reaches a certain age and that person is then entitled under the trust provisions to a distribution of a significant principal amount or percentage or the trustee is authorized to make a discretionary distribution and does so.

e. Direct Skip

A direct skip is a transfer of an interest in property to a skip person where the transfer is subject to federal estate or gift tax.[12]

Example: Grandparent transfers property outright to Grandchild or to an irrevocable trust solely for the benefit of Grandchild (or for Grandchild and Great-grandchildren). The transfer is a gift for federal gift tax purposes and, also, a direct skip for GST tax purposes.

Note that this transfer might be made directly to a great-grandchild, thereby skipping two intermediate generations, but this is treated as only one direct skip.[13]

2. Definition of Other Terms

a. Skip Person

A generation-skipping transfer will only occur if the transfer is to or for the benefit of a "skip person" (and no intervening interests are held by a nonskip person). A skip person is defined as a person who is assigned to a generation that is two or more generations below the transferor's generation.[14]

Example: A grandchild of the transferor is a skip person since the grandchild is two generations below the transferor.

This term also includes a trust if all the interests in the trust are held by skip persons.[15]

Example: A trust for the benefit of a transferor's grandchild and great-grandchild is a skip person.

The term "skip person" also encompasses a trust if: (1) no person is holding an interest in the trust; and (2) at no time after the transfer may a distribution (including distributions on termination) be made from such trust to a nonskip person.[16]

b. Interest

A person has an "interest" in property held in trust if (at the time the determination is made) the person[17]:

- has a right (other than a future right) to receive income or corpus from the trust;
- is a permissible current recipient of income or corpus from the trust; or
- is described in §2055(a) and the trust is a charitable remainder annuity trust, a charitable remainder unitrust, or a pooled income fund.

Note that an interest that is "used primarily to postpone or avoid any [GST] tax imposed . . . shall be disregarded."[18]

c. Transferor

A transferor for these purposes includes: (i) in the context of the federal estate tax, a decedent[19] and (ii) in the context of the federal gift tax, the donor.[20] If a couple splits a gift (under §2513), the transfer is treated as having been made one-half by each spouse for purposes of the GST tax, that is, each spouse is the transferor of one-half of the transferred amount.[21] For these purposes, a transferor can include a nonresident non-citizen if the property transferred would cause applicability of either the U.S. gift tax or U.S. estate tax.[22]

3. Assignment to a Generation

For purposes of determining the applicability of a GST tax, persons must be assigned to various generations. Ordinarily, this generational assignment is not a problem. All lineal descendants of the grantor's grandparents are assigned to a particular generation on the basis of consanguinity.[23] For example, a child is in the first generation below the grantor, a grandchild is in the second generation below the grantor, a nephew is in the first generation below the grantor, and a first cousin twice removed is in the second generation.

A present or former spouse of a transferor is assigned to that transferor's generation.[24] Spouses of relatives are automatically assigned to the same generation as the relative to whom the spouses are (or at any prior time were) married.[25] For example, a child's spouse is in the first generation below the grantor, even if young enough to be the grantor's grandchild and even if subsequently divorced from the child.

All other beneficiaries (i.e., not lineal descendants) are assigned to a particular generation on the basis of age.[26] The fundamental assumptions are that each generation is 25 years in length and that the grantor is exactly in the middle of his or her generation. Therefore, a person within 12-1/2 years of the grantor is deemed to be in the same generation as the grantor. A person more than 12-1/2 years but not more than 37-1/2 years younger than the grantor is in the first generation below the grantor. A person more than 37-1/2 years but not more than 62-1/2 years younger than the grantor is in the second generation below the grantor.

A special "move-up" rule applies for certain persons who have a deceased parent.[27] This rule recognizes that, when a donor's child is deceased, the primary objects of the bounty of the transferor for the assets that child would have received will probably be the children of that deceased child. Consequently, for purposes of determining whether any transfer is a generation-skipping transfer, if (1) an individual is a descendant of a parent of the transferor (or the transferor's spouse or former spouse) and (2) such individual's parent who is a lineal descendant of the parent of the transferor (or the transferor's spouse or former spouse) is dead at the time the transfer is subject to estate or gift tax imposed on the transferor, that individual is treated as if such individual were a member of the generation that is one generation below the lower of the transferor's generation or the generation assignment of the youngest living ancestor of such individual who is also a descendant of the parent of the transferor (or the transferor's spouse or former spouse).

Example: Donor establishes a trust for Child 1 for life, remainder to the children of Child 2, to be funded by Donor's gift. If Child 2 is deceased at the time the trust is funded, the predeceased ancestor exception applies so the distribution to Child 2's children at the death of Child 1 is not a taxable termination subject to the GST tax. If, however, Child 2 dies after the funding of the trust but before the death of Child 1, the exception does not apply because Child 2 was alive when the transfer was first subject to gift tax (or estate tax for a testamentary trust), and a taxable termination occurs at Child 1's death.

This special rule does not apply with respect to a transfer to any individual who is not a lineal descendant of the transferor (or the transferor's spouse or former spouse) if, at the time of the transfer, the transferor has any living lineal descendants.[28] Consequently, great nephews and great nieces can also be benefited by this move-up rule, but only if they have no living ancestors (and the transferor has no living lineal descendants).

C. Tax Computation

1. Calculating and Paying the Tax

a. Responsibility for the GST Tax

If a GST tax event has occurred, additional issues must then be resolved, including: (1) who has liability for the GST tax, (2) what is the amount subject to tax, (3) what is the amount of the tax, and (4) when must the tax be paid? Unless otherwise directed pursuant to the governing instrument by specific reference to the GST tax, the GST tax on a transfer is charged to the property constituting the transfer.[29] Consequently, the recipient of that property will ultimately bear the burden for the tax.

b. Taxable Distribution Tax Amount

The taxable amount of a taxable distribution is the fair market value of the property when it is received by the transferee, reduced by any expense incurred by the transferee in connection with the determination, collection, or refund of the GST tax with respect to the taxable distribution.[30] If any GST tax on a taxable distribution is paid out of the trust (instead of by the transferee), the amount of that tax paid is treated as a taxable distribution.[31] The transferee is liable for the GST tax.[32] Since the tax must be paid from the amount received, the tax is imposed in this situation on a "tax-inclusive basis" (similar to the estate tax).

c. Taxable Termination Tax Amount

The taxable amount of a taxable termination is the fair market value of all property at the time of termination with respect to which the taxable termination has occurred, reduced by the allocable deductions similar to the deductions allowed under §2053.[33] Thus, the property included in the tax base includes the amount to be used to pay the tax (i.e., an "inclusive" tax base approach is used, similar to the estate tax). The trustee is liable for the GST tax when a taxable termination occurs.[34]

d. Direct Skip Tax Amount

For a lifetime direct skip, the transferor is liable for the tax and required to make the return.[35] For direct skips made from a trust or with respect to property that continues to be held in trust, the trustee is liable for the tax and required to make the return.[36] For a direct skip at death other than from a trust, the person liable for the tax and required to make the return is the executor, subject to special rules for trust arrangements.[37]

The taxable amount of a direct skip is the fair market value of the property received by the transferee.[38] In determining the taxable amount, the GST tax base does not include the amount of any federal estate or gift tax payable with respect to the generation-skipping transfer.

If the direct skip is a taxable gift, the amount of the gift for purposes of the federal gift tax is increased by the amount of any GST tax imposed on the transferor with respect to that gift.[39]

e. Multiple Skips

All taxable distributions are taxed only once, regardless of how many generations are skipped. This results from the definition of a skip person as one who is two "or more" generations below the transferor.[40] There is no distinction among skip persons based on how many levels the beneficiary's generation is below the transferor's.

Example: T creates a trust, the income and principal of which may be paid in the trustee's discretion among T's descendants. The trustee distributes income to T's grandchild, GC, and T's great-grandchild, GGC. Each distribution is a single taxable distribution.

Where a single trust makes transfers to more than one generation of beneficiaries who are assigned to generations below the transferor's generation, a "move-down" rule will apply for purposes of determining whether, subsequently, a generation-skipping transfer has occurred.[41] For example, if a generation-skipping transfer has occurred and, immediately after the transfer, property is held in trust for the benefit of a grandchild and great-grandchild, the trust is treated as if the transferor were assigned to the first generation above that of the highest generation of any person who has an interest in the trust immediately after the transfer.[42]

Example: T creates a trust for T's child, C, for life. On C's death the trust continues for C's child, GC, with distribution on GC's death to GC's then living descendants, per stirpes. On C's death a taxable termination occurs for GST tax purposes. Thereafter the transferor, T, is treated as if assigned to C's generation. Consequently, distributions to GC are not taxable distributions because GC is only one generation younger than C and, thus, is not a skip person. This is the same result that would occur if the trust were included in C's estate on C's death because C would have become the transferor in that situation.

f. Comparisons of GST Tax Costs

The following comparison of transfer tax costs on the different types of GST tax transfers identifies the overall impact of these taxes. These examples show the funds needed to ultimately transfer a net amount of $100,000 to a grandchild. In each case it is assumed that the transferor is in a 50% gift tax and estate tax bracket, all credits and exemptions have been exhausted, and the GST tax rate is 50%.[43] In many instances, of course, these transfers will be protected from tax inclusion by various credits and exemptions.

Example (transfer to grandchild from testamentary trust for child and grandchild [taxable distribution or taxable termination]):

Amount distributed to grandchild	$100,000
GST tax	100,000
Amount in trust before grandchild distribution	200,000
Federal estate tax on original transfer to trust	200,000
Total funds needed for this $100,000 transfer	$400,000

Example (testamentary direct skip transfer to grandchild):

Amount bequeathed to grandchild	$100,000
GST tax on bequest	50,000
Federal estate tax related to bequest	150,000
Funds needed for this $100,000 transfer	$300,000

Example (inter vivos direct skip transfer to grandchild):

Amount given to grandchild	$100,000
GST tax on gift	50,000
Federal gift tax on gift	50,000
Federal gift tax on GST tax	25,000
Funds needed for this $100,000 transfer	$225,000

This comparison evidences that the most tax-efficient approach in this context is a lifetime direct skip transfer to a grandchild (or great-grandchild). This results because (1) the gift tax is a tax exclusive transfer and (2) the estate tax is a tax inclusive transfer and because of the manner of assignment of the liability for the GST tax.

2. Valuation

Property is normally valued at its fair market value at the time of the generation-skipping transfer, reduced by the amount of any consideration furnished by the transferee.[44] Where a direct skip is included in the transferor's gross estate, the value is the value for purposes of the federal estate tax.[45] Where a taxable termination occurs at death, an election may be made to value all the property included in the taxable termination in accordance with the alternate valuation procedure in §2032. This can occur even if the estate does not elect §2032.[46]

3. Applicable Rate

The tax rate applicable to a generation-skipping transfer is the product of[47]:

- the maximum federal estate tax rate[48]; and
- the inclusion ratio with respect to the transfer.

Note that this is a flat rate tax, that is, the rate is imposed at the maximum federal estate tax rate in effect at the time of the transfer.

The "inclusion ratio" is one minus the "applicable fraction."[49] The numerator of the applicable fraction is the GST exemption amount allocated to the property transferred.[50] The denominator of the applicable fraction is the value of the property transferred.[51] The objective of this determination of the inclusion ratio is effectively to divide the property into its GST taxable and nontaxable components. This is mechanically accomplished through a reduction of the applicable transfer tax rate. This allocation is necessary because the property will have appreciated or depreciated in value since the time the transfer was initially completed and before the GST tax event occurs in the trust context. This formulary process enables the division between taxable and nontaxable transfers. This process also means that a proportionate amount of the assets in the generation-skipping trust will be protected from GST tax upon the taxable event occurring, rather than only a specified dollar amount.

Example: Parent (oldest generation) provides for a trust under his will that is funded with $3 million from Parent's estate after the payment of all estate taxes. The trust is for Child for life, remainder to Grandchildren. When Child subsequently dies, the trust has a value of $10 million. Assume that Parent had not used any part of his GST exemption prior to his death in 2005, that his executor allowed the automatic allocation rules to apply, and that this caused $1.5 million of GST exemption to be allocated to the trust.[52] At Child's death, a taxable termination of the trust occurs. Assume (for ease of illustration) that the highest estate tax rate is then 50%. The trustee has an obligation to pay a GST tax from the trust assets. The taxable amount will include that tax. The inclusion ratio will be one less a fraction with: (1) a numerator of $1.5 million (the allocated exemption) and (2) a denominator of $3 million (the value of the property held in the trust as of the time of the transfer into trust). The inclusion ratio is 1/2. Consequently, 1/2 times 50% times $10 million (or $2.5 million) is the GST tax payable upon the taxable termination.

D. Exemptions

1. GST Exemption Amount

Every individual is allowed a GST exemption amount equal to the applicable exclusion amount for estate tax purposes.[53] Since a married couple may "gift split," a married couple is effectively entitled to double the amount of the GST exemption.[54] The amount of the exemption is dependent on the particular year during which the generation-skipping transfer was completed.

2. Allocation of Exemption Amount

The GST exemption may be allocated by the individual (or his or her executor) to any property of which the individual is the transferor.[55] When made, this allocation is irrevocable.[56]

Automatic allocation of the GST exemption will occur under certain statutorily prescribed circumstances. The GST exemption is deemed allocated to a lifetime direct skip to the extent necessary to make the inclusion ratio zero for the direct skip, or to make the inclusion ratio as small as possible if zero is not possible.[57] The transferor can elect out of an automatic allocation on Form 709 by describing the transfer and the extent to which the automatic allocation does not apply.[58] In addition, a timely filed Form 709 with payment of the GST tax as shown on the return with respect to a direct skip is sufficient to elect out.[59]

Further, if a transferor makes an inter vivos transfer into certain trusts, he or she is deemed to have allocated any remaining portion of his or her GST exemption to the transfer unless he or she elects otherwise.[60] Any remaining exemption not allocated on or before the estate tax return due date is deemed allocated to direct skips occurring at death and to all trusts with respect to which a taxable distribution or termination might occur at or after the transferor's death.[61]

In the planning context, the objective is to allocate the GST exemption to that property which will have appreciated most significantly as of the time that the GST tax event occurs. Consequently, a larger amount will be protected from GST tax when that transfer occurs to the next generation.

E. GST Tax Planning Considerations

1. Importance of GST Tax Planning

Many estate planners, concerned about the complexity of the GST tax system, have neglected the structuring of donative transfers to maximize GST tax planning. Rather, they often advise transferring assets to children, thereby also assuring transfer tax exposure when the children transfer assets to their children (except for limited tax relief such as the annual donee exclusion). Significant accumulation of intergenerational family wealth can be achieved on a long-term basis if the planning opportunities under the GST tax system are maximized. To not advise the client having significant wealth to utilize these intergenerational wealth transfer opportunities may generate a challenge of professional malpractice for the advisor. Even though the client may be concerned about access of grandchildren to these funds, trust mechanisms can be used to enable asset protection while still achieving the GST tax planning benefits.

2. GST Exemption

The GST exemption provides significant tax exemption in skipping a generation. An effort to use this exemption should be maximized. In some instances the value of a person's assets may be such that this exemption will sufficiently protect all anticipated generation-skipping transfers from tax.

The GST exemption should be allocated carefully to a trust that can benefit several generations. Allocation is less complicated if the trust transfer or other gift benefits only one generation. The GST exemption can also be leveraged by using it for lifetime gifts and by funding a trust transfer with appreciating property. The total exemption amount can be further enhanced with careful coordination of gift splitting with a spouse for generation skipping transfers.

3. Layering Trusts

Separate trusts (or layering trusts) might be created for nonskip persons and for exempt transfers to skip persons, so as to prevent wasting the GST exemption on nonskip persons.[62] This would enable distributions to be made from the nonskip person trust, protecting the assets in the exempt skip person trust.

4. Exclusions

Opportunities to use exclusions should regularly be carefully examined. This includes gifts protected under the §2503(b) annual donee exclusion. Note, however, that the annual donee exclusion gifts must be direct skips for this exclusion to be available for GST tax purposes.[63] Section 2503(e) transfers for the educational or medical expenses of grandchildren are also excluded from the GST tax base and can enable significant tax protected transfers. Those transfers must be made directly to the educational institution (or medical facility) to enable this exclusion.

5. Reverse QTIP Election

When a qualified terminable interest property (QTIP) election is made to enable a marital deduction (for estate or gift tax purposes), the effect is that all property qualifying for the marital deduction will be subject to estate tax in the estate of the surviving spouse or the donee spouse.[64] The consequence of this treatment is to have the surviving spouse subsequently treated for GST or estate tax purposes as the transferor with respect to the property.[65]

For purposes of the GST tax, the transferor decedent's estate or the donor spouse is permitted, however, to treat the property transfer as if no QTIP election was made. This is accomplished by making a "reverse QTIP election," that is, treating the QTIP election as ineffective for GST tax purposes.[66] Consequently, in this situation, the decedent's estate or the donor spouse will be considered as the transferor for GST tax purposes and can utilize, therefore, his or her GST exemption for the marital deduction trust property.

Example: During 2015, Husband transfers $5.0 million (of his separate assets) to a trust providing that all trust income is to be paid to Spouse for Spouse's lifetime. On Spouse's death the trust principal is payable to Grandchild, a grandchild of Husband and Spouse. Husband elects to treat all of the transfer as a transfer of QTIP assets (thereby enabling a complete marital deduction for gift tax purposes) but he also makes the reverse QTIP election for all of these assets. Because of the reverse QTIP election, Husband continues to be treated as the transferor of the assets after Spouse's death for purposes of the GST tax (including, particularly, the availability of the GST exemption).

A partial reverse QTIP election is not permitted.[67] The reverse QTIP election must be made for the exact portion of the QTIP trust covered by the original QTIP election. This often necessitates a separate trust for achieving this purpose. Once made, a reverse QTIP election is irrevocable.[68]

Often, the reverse QTIP election is not timely made, particularly in the estate tax and estate administration context. In many situations the IRS has permitted an estate to file a late reverse QTIP election after showing good cause in a private letter ruling request.[69] The IRS has provided a simplified alternate method for obtaining relief to make a late reverse QTIP election.[70]

Notes

1. *See* §2601, et seq. The current GST tax was adopted in the Tax Reform Act of 1986 (1986 TRA), Pub. L. No. 99-514. For a more detailed discussion of this tax, see 850 T.M., *Generation-Skipping Transfer Tax* (Bloomberg BNA). The Tax Reform Act of 1976, Pub. L. No. 94-455, contained a prior GST tax structure which was deemed unadministrable. *See* H.R. Rep. No. 94-1380, at 47 (1976). This prior GST tax structure was repealed retroactive to its effective date. *See* 1986 TRA, Pub. L. No. 99-514, §1433(c) (1). As noted in Chapter 4, A., the Economic Growth and Tax Relief Reconciliation Act of 2001 (EGTRRA), Pub. L. No. 107-16, §501, terminated the GST tax for transfers

after December 31, 2009. *See* §2664. However, the Tax Relief, Unemployment Insurance Reauthorization, and Job Creation Act of 2010 (2010 TRA), Pub. L. No. 111-312, §301, §304, reinstated the GST tax (and the estate tax) for generation-skipping transfers (and estates of decedents dying) after 2009. However, for generation-skipping transfers made in 2010, a non-Code provision (2010 TRA, Pub. L. No. 111-312, §302(c)) provided that the applicable rate determined under §2641(a) was zero. *See* PLR 201208005 (estate of decedent dying in 2010 allowed to make §1022 election; maximum federal estate tax rate for purposes of computing GST tax deemed to be zero).

2. The initial GST tax regulations were finalized on December 26, 1995 (T.D. 8644, 60 Fed. Reg. 66,898 [Dec. 27, 1995]). For a summary of these regulations, see 70 Tax Notes No. 1, 41 (1996). *See also* T.D. 8912, 65 Fed. Reg. 79,735 (Dec. 20, 2000) (final regulations relating to application of effective date rules for GST tax).
3. Before the enactment of the GST tax, the transfer tax normally imposed upon transfers of property from one generation to the next could be avoided by placing property in a trust that created a succession of life estates. Only a gift tax or an estate tax was applicable at the creation and funding of the trust. If created in a state that had no rule against perpetuities, these trusts could be created for successive generations and to continue forever. Coupled with flexible powers vested in the trustee, this could constitute (almost) the equivalent of ownership without any transfer tax effects for multiple generations of family members.
4. The 1986 version of the GST tax applies to generation-skipping transfers occurring after the date of enactment. Various exceptions were made, however, for certain post-enactment date transfers, e.g., wills executed before the date of enactment if the decedent died before January 1, 1987 (*see* 1986 TRA, Pub. L. No. 99-514, §1433(b)(2)(B)), or where certain incapacity had previously occurred (*see* 1986 TRA, Pub. L. No. 99-514, §1433(b)(2)(C)). The IRS has issued numerous private letter rulings concerning whether certain proposed actions affecting trusts eliminate "grandfathered" status for this purpose. Reg. §26.2601-1(b), dealing with modifications to grandfathered generation-skipping trusts, was finalized in 2000. T.D. 8912. The regulations also address the effect of the exercise, release, and lapse of general powers of appointment over such trusts. In Rev. Proc. 2015-3, 2015-1 I.R.B. 129, §3.01(96), the IRS indicated that it will not rule on whether a trust that is grandfathered pursuant to Reg. §26.2601-1(b)(1), §26.2601-1(b)(2), or §26.2601-1(b)(3) will retain its exempt status when there is a modification of the trust, a change in the administration of the trust, or a distribution from the trust in a factual scenario similar to a factual scenario set forth in one or more of the Reg. §26.2601-1(b)(4)(i)(E) examples. For examples of situations where litigation was necessary to recognize this grandfathered status, see *Bachler v. United States,* 281 F.3d 1078 (9th Cir. 2002), and *Simpson v. United States,* 183 F.3d 812 (8th Cir. 1999).
5. §2601.
6. §2611(a); Reg. §26.2611-1.
7. §2611(b).
8. *See* §2642(c)(3) (note that this exception applies to "direct skips"); H.R. Rep. No. 99-841, at II-826 (1986); Reg. §26.2642-1(c)(3) (excluding such transfers (if qualifying) from computation of "inclusion ratio").
9. §2642(c)(2); Reg. §26.2642-1(c)(3), §26.2642-1(d) *Ex. 2.*
10. §2612(a)(1). Reg. §26.2612-1(b)(1) provides that no taxable termination occurs if a transfer subject to the federal estate or gift tax occurs with respect to the trust property at

the time of the termination (i.e., a new "transferor" exists with respect to the property). *See* Reg. §26.2612-1(f) *Exs. 8, 9, 10, 11.*

11. §2612(b); Reg. §26.2612-1(c)(1). *See* Reg. §26.2612-1(f) *Ex. 10.*
12. §2612(c); Reg. §26.2612-1(a). *See* Reg. §26.2612-1(f) *Exs. 1, 2.*
13. Reg. §26.2612-1(a). *See* Reg. §26.2612-1(f) *Ex. 2.* This treatment does conflict with the objective of the GST tax, which is to cause assets to be exposed to a transfer tax at each generational level.
14. §2613(a)(1); Reg. §26.2613-1 (making reference to definition of skip person in Reg. §26.2612-1(d)).
15. §2613(a)(2); Reg. §26.2612-1(d) (trust is skip person if all beneficiaries who may currently receive distributions are also skip persons).
16. §2613(a)(2)(B).
17. §2652(c). *See* Reg. §26.2652-1(e) (cross-referencing Reg. §26.2612-1(e)), §26.2612-1(f) *Ex. 14.*
18. §2652(c)(2). Reg. §26.2612-1(e)(2)(ii) specifies that an interest that is used primarily to postpone or avoid the GST tax is disregarded for purposes of Chapter 13. An interest is considered as used primarily to postpone or avoid the GST tax if a significant purpose for the creation of the interest is to postpone or avoid the tax.
19. §2652(a)(1)(A). Reg. §26.2652-1(a)(1) provides that the transferor of property is the individual with respect to whom property was most recently subject to federal estate tax. Reg. §26.2652-1(a)(2) specifies that a transfer is subject to federal estate tax if the value of the property is includible in the decedent's gross estate as determined under §2031 or §2103.
20. §2652(a)(1)(B). Reg. §26.2652-1(a)(1) provides that a person is considered a transferor if he or she makes a gift for purposes of the federal gift tax. Reg. §26.2652-1(a)(2) provides that a transfer is subject to federal gift tax if a gift tax is imposed under §2501(a) (without regard to exemptions, exclusions, deductions, and credits). *See* Reg. §26.2652-1(a)(5) *Ex. 1.*
21. §2652(a)(2). *See* Reg. §26.2652-1(a)(4), §26.2652-1(a)(5) *Ex. 2.*
22. *See* §2663(2); Reg. §26.2663-2; *Estate of Neumann v. Commissioner*, 106 T.C. 216 (1996) (GST tax applies to nonresident alien estate's transfers of U.S. property to grandchildren even though regulations specifically applying to such transfers were not issued until after transfers took place).
23. §2651(b)(1). A relationship by legal adoption is treated as a relationship by blood. §2651(b)(3)(A). A relationship by the half-blood is treated as a relationship of the whole-blood. §2651(b)(3)(B).
24. §2651(c)(1).
25. §2651(c)(2).
26. §2651(d).
27. §2651(e)(1). Note that this "move-up" status can be achieved when the intermediate generation member disclaims his or her interest, with the result that the property transfer (which must be a direct skip) goes directly to the disclaimant's child (or, possibly, grandchild). *See* Reg. §26.2612-1(e)(3) (interest does not exist to extent it is disclaimed pursuant to disclaimer that constitutes qualified disclaimer under §2518).
28. §2651(e)(2).
29. §2603(b).
30. §2621(a).
31. §2621(b).

32. §2603(a)(1).
33. §2622.
34. §2603(a)(2).
35. §2603(a)(3).
36. Reg. §26.2662-1(c)(1)(iv).
37. Reg. §26.2662-1(c)(1)(v).
38. §2623.
39. §2515.
40. §2613(a).
41. §2653(a).
42. §2653(a).
43. For the sake of simplicity of presentation, the maximum transfer tax rates are assumed to be 50%. However, the maximum transfer tax rate is 40% for gifts and generation-skipping transfers made, and estates of decedents dying, after 2012. *See* §2001(c), §2502(a), §2641, as amended by the American Taxpayer Relief Act of 2012 (ATRA), Pub. L. No. 112-240, §101(c). The maximum transfer tax rate was 35% for gifts and generation-skipping transfers made, and estates of decedents dying, in 2010, 2011, and 2012. *See* 2010 TRA, Pub. L. No. 111-312, §101(a) (extending sunset provision in EGTRRA, Pub. L. No. 107-16, §901), §302-§304. A non-Code provision (2010 TRA, Pub. L. No. 111-312, §302(c)) specifies that the §2641(a) applicable rate was zero for generation-skipping transfers made in 2010.
44. §2624(a), §2624(d).
45. §2624(b). This includes the value as determined using the alternate valuation date under §2032 and the special use valuation available under §2032A.
46. §2624(c).
47. §2641(a); Reg. §26.2641-1.
48. *See* §2641(b) ("term 'maximum Federal estate tax rate' means the maximum rate imposed by section 2001 on the estates of decedents dying at the time of the taxable distribution, taxable termination, or direct skip, as the case may be"). As noted in Chapter, A.1., the maximum estate tax rate is 40% for generation-skipping transfers made, and estates of decedents dying, after 2012. *See* §2001(c), §2502(a), §2641, as amended by the American Taxpayer Relief Act of 2012 (ATRA), Pub. L. No. 112-240, §101(c). The maximum estate tax rate was 35% for generation-skipping transfers made, and estates of decedents dying, in 2010, 2011, and 2012. *See* 2010 TRA, Pub. L. No. 111-312, §101(a) (extending sunset provision in EGTRRA, Pub. L. No. 107-16, §901), §302-§304. A non-Code provision (2010 TRA, Pub. L. No. 111-312, §302(c)) specifies that the §2641(a) applicable rate was zero for generation-skipping transfers in 2010. *See* PLR 201208005 (estate of decedent dying in 2010 allowed to make §1022 election; maximum federal estate tax for purposes of computing GST tax deemed to be zero).
49. §2642(a)(1); Reg. §26.2642-1(a).
50. §2642(a)(2)(A).
51. §2642(a)(2)(B).
52. *See* §2632(e)(1).
53. This amount (defined as the "basic exclusion amount" in 2011-2012) is $5 million for generation-skipping transfers made after 2009 (although the §2641(a) applicable rate was zero for 2010) and is adjusted for inflation after 2011. *See* §2010(c), §2631(c), as amended by EGTRRA, Pub. L. No. 107-16, §521 (cross-referencing §2010(c)), the 2010

TRA, Pub. L. No. 111-312, §101(a) (extending sunset provision in EGTRRA, Pub. L. No. 107-16, §901), §302-§304, and ATRA, Pub. L. No. 112-240, §101(a) (generally making permanent changes made by EGTRRA and 2010 TRA).

54. §2652(a)(2).
55. §2631(a), §2632(a).
56. §2631(b). The IRS has provided (in Rev. Proc. 2004-46, 2004-31 I.R.B. 142) a simplified alternate method for obtaining a Reg. §301.9100-3 extension to make an allocation of GST exemption under §2642(b)(1). Effective August 2, 2004, the alternate method may be used in lieu of the normal letter ruling process, provided the requestor satisfies the requirements outlined in Rev. Proc. 2004-46. In 2008, the IRS issued proposed regulations that, when final, would govern requests for extensions of time to allocate GST exemption, to elect under §2632(b)(3) not to have the deemed allocation of GST exemption apply to a direct skip, to elect under §2632(c)(5)(A)(i) not to have the deemed allocation of GST exemption apply to an indirect skip or transfers to a particular trust, and to elect under §2632(c)(5)(A)(ii) to treat a trust as a GST trust for §2632(c) purposes (in lieu of requests under Reg. §301.9100-3). *See* Prop. Reg. §26.2642-7, §301.9100-3(g); REG-147775-06, 73 Fed. Reg. 20,870 (Apr. 17, 2008). The preamble indicates that the proposed regulations would not affect relief available under Rev. Proc. 2004-46 for taxpayers who qualify for relief under that procedure. The 2010 TRA, Pub. L. No. 111-312, §101(a), extended the application of §2632(c) for generation-skipping transfers made in 2010 through 2012 by extending the sunset in EGTRRA, Pub. L. No. 107-16, §901. ATRA, Pub. L. No. 112-240, §101(a), made permanent the application of §2632(c) for generation-skipping transfers.
57. §2632(b)(1).
58. §2632(b)(3).
59. Reg. §26.2632-1(b)(1)(i).
60. §2632(c). The election out of the automatic allocation is described in Reg. §26.2632-1(b)(2). The 2010 TRA, Pub. L. No. 111-312, §101(a), extended the application of §2632(c) for generation-skipping transfers made in 2010-2012 by extending the sunset in EGTRRA, Pub. L. No. 107-16, §901. ATRA, Pub. L. No. 112-240, §101(a), made permanent the application of §2632(c) for generation-skipping transfers.
61. §2632(e)(1).
62. Effective for severances occurring after 2000, §2642(a)(3), as added by EGTRRA, Pub. L. No. 107-16, §562, allows "qualified severances" of existing trusts in certain circumstances.
63. *See* §2642(c). A direct skip for this purpose can include a §2503(c) trust and a custodial gift under the applicable Uniform Transfers (or Gifts) to Minors Act.
64. *See* §2056(b)(7), §2523(f), §2044; *see also* Chapter 5, D.3.i.(4). This assumes that these funds protected by the marital deduction are not exhausted during the lifetime of the surviving (or donee) spouse.
65. §2044(c).
66. *See* §2652(a)(3). Reg. §26.2652-2(b) specifies that this election is made on the return on which the QTIP election is made. If a protective QTIP election is made, a protective reverse QTIP election should also be made.
67. Reg. §26.2652-2(a) specifies that an election under this provision is not effective unless it is made with respect to all of the property in the trust to which the QTIP election applies. This regulation refers, however, to Reg. §26.2654-1(b)(1) (the "separate share rule") which indicates that the severance of a trust that is included in the transferor's gross

estate (or created under the transferor's will) into two or more trust is recognized for GST tax purposes. This severance of the trust must be (1) pursuant to a direction in the governing instrument providing that the trust is to be divided upon the death of the transferor or (2) pursuant to discretionary authority granted under the governing instrument or local law and certain other specified requirements must be satisfied. Reg. §26.2654-1(b)(1). *See also* §2642(a)(3) (allowing qualified severances of existing trusts in certain circumstances).

68. Reg. §26.2652-2(a).
69. See, for example, PLR 201149002 where the IRS approved an extension to make a reverse QTIP election and an election to treat the decedent's marital trust as two separate trusts for GST purposes. The ruling notes that the accountant who had prepared the estate tax return had failed to make either election. Similarly, see PLR 201246020.
70. *See* Rev. Proc. 2004-47, 2004-32 I.R.B. 169. Rev. Proc. 2004-47 provides a simplified alternate method for certain executors of estates and trustees of trusts to request relief to make a late reverse QTIP election. This alternate method may be used in lieu of the normal letter ruling process. No user fee is charged for requests filed under this revenue procedure. The taxpayer must demonstrate, among other things, that the reverse QTIP election was not made on the estate tax return as filed because the taxpayer relied on the advice and counsel of a qualified tax professional and the qualified tax professional failed to advise the taxpayer of the need, advisability, or proper method to make a reverse QTIP election. Rev. Proc. 2004-47 does not apply to inter vivos transfers to or for the benefit of a spouse, or to transfers to or for the benefit of a non-citizen spouse in the form of a qualified domestic trust. Relief under this revenue procedure does not include or grant permission to make a late severance of a trust included in the gross estate or to allocate GST exemption. A letter ruling request will be necessary in these situations.

CHAPTER 9

Special Nonprobate Planning Situations

A. Joint Property

1. Description of Ownership Form

Holding property in joint tenancy with the right of survivorship has traditionally been regarded as a simple method of avoiding probate administration.[1] Under this form of property ownership, joint owners hold concurrent ownership but the survivor of the joint property owners succeeds to the entire property interest at the time of death of the other joint property owner.[2] This situation is contrasted with the tenancy in common, under which each owner possesses a proportionate interest in the property and that proportionate interest may be alienated, devised, or inherited under the local laws of descent and distribution.[3] This property ownership arrangement will also be contrasted with community property (i.e., joint property ownership between spouses) which has often been treated as the equivalent of a tenancy in common. However, certain state laws do permit a survivorship condition to be imposed on community property by agreement between the owners.

This type of property ownership is often arranged between related parties, for example, between a parent and a child.[4] Upon the death of the parent, the child then receives that property without exposure to the estate probate process. This ownership arrangement is not limited to related parties, however, and can be created with another, unrelated person. This might often be in a situation where the survivor would be anticipated to be a recipient of a gratuitous transfer from the deceased joint tenant.

This ownership format is often arranged between spouses. When between spouses, the property ownership under some applicable state laws is described as a "tenancy by the entirety." This causes more severe complexities in terminating the ownership relationship. In the usual joint tenancy, any joint tenant, acting alone, can convey his or her interest to another person and the conveyance of the joint tenant's interest destroys the joint tenancy and, thus, the survivorship feature, as to that joint tenant. The joint tenancy can also be terminated through a partition, whether accomplished by a voluntary arrangement or a state court proceeding. This partitioning (whether voluntary or under court adjudication) can result in: (1) the physical division of the property among the former co-owners, (2) continued ownership of the property as tenants in common, or (3) sale of the property with the proceeds divided among the owners. If, however, the traditional status of a "tenancy by the entirety" exists, both joint tenants ordinarily need to consent to the termination of this joint tenancy relationship.

Since the property interest arises by reason of a survivorship arrangement completed outside the probate administration process, the decedent cannot dispose by will of his or her interest in the joint tenancy with survivorship property. Further, often creditors of the deceased joint tenant cannot reach this property in the hands of the survivor. Rather, during the debtor's lifetime they must force a severance of the joint tenancy so as to reach the interest of the joint tenant that is receivable upon a division of this property during the lifetimes of all the joint tenants. Of course, if the indebted joint tenant is the survivor, holding the entire property outright, his or her creditors could then pursue the property directly in a creditor's proceeding.

Joint tenants may be created through a variety of arrangements: (1) one party may transfer property into the names of that person and another as "joint tenants with the rights of survivorship"; (2) two parties may together acquire property, each contributing 50% of the consideration (or some other portion), and have the property registered in "joint tenancy with the right of survivorship"; and (3) two (or more) parties might receive a bequest from a decedent with the will specifying that the property will be held by those beneficiary parties as joint tenants with the right of survivorship.

A most important consideration in this context is that a client must be cautioned that the implementation of a disposition plan in a last will and trust does not change the designation of the survivor when property is held in joint and survivorship interest. As noted below, some joint accounts (such as bank accounts) can be changed by unilateral action, but other changes in joint accounts necessitate the agreement of both parties. Many surprises occur in this context because significant properties may be held in a joint tenancy (or other probate avoiding arrangements such as life insurance and retirement plans with beneficiary designations) and are not impacted by the provisions of a last will. Consequently, the advisor should counsel clients that these other arrangements must be carefully reviewed to assure the successor designations are as intended by the client.

2. Joint Tenancy Income Tax Considerations

The taxable income and gains with respect to jointly held property and property held as tenants by the entirety are ordinarily allocated among the owners based on the proportion of income to which each co-owner is entitled under local law. This ownership is a matter to be determined under local law, and not under federal income tax rules.[5] Each joint tenant is generally entitled to receive a pro-rata share of the income from the property, although an agreement among the joint tenants to allocate the income on a non-pro-rata basis may be respected for income tax purposes. If the joint tenants are husband and wife and file a joint federal income tax return, the separate ownership of the income will have limited relevance. If, however, both parent and child are joint tenants and are entitled (under local law) to portions of the income, each must report his or her respective portion. Confusion might arise because an income payor will not divide the income on two information statements to be filed with the IRS. In such situations, full disclosure of the relevant facts should be included on the federal income tax return of each joint tenant when reporting his or her correct proportion of the income.

If the joint tenancy property is, for example, a rental real property for which expenses are incurred, a question might arise concerning who is entitled to deduct these expenses for federal income tax purposes. This will also be determined by reference to local law. A co-tenant will be entitled to deduct taxes, interest, and other expenses to the extent paid by the co-tenant, subject to reduction for any right of reimbursement from other co-tenants. A joint tenant will be entitled to deduct all these expenses, to the extent paid, if, under local law, the obligation for these expenses is joint and several.[6]

3. Gift Tax Applicability upon Creation

a. Possible Gift Completion

Gift tax may be applicable upon the creation of a joint tenancy with the right of survivorship. A completed transfer into a joint tenancy arrangement is a prerequisite for imposing the gift tax, but gift completion may not have occurred merely by establishing that relationship. A transfer is not complete if a joint tenant who has furnished all the consideration in creating the joint tenancy is permitted to unilaterally terminate the joint ownership and to retrieve the entire property. Accordingly, no gift is made at the time of the establishment of that type of joint tenancy arrangement. Typically, this situation occurs where a joint bank account is created and, under the deposit arrangement, either party can retrieve the entire deposited amount.[7] Where the transfer into the joint tenancy cannot be completely reversed by the transferor acting alone, a gift transfer will have been made upon the creation of the joint property ownership.[8]

b. Determining the Amount of the Gift

If the creation of a joint tenancy has resulted in a completed transfer for gift tax purposes, the value of the gift will depend on whether, under applicable local law, the right of survivorship may be defeated by either owner acting unilaterally.[9] Often, in this situation, each joint tenant can receive a proportionate share upon a unilateral termination (e.g., each of two joint tenants would receive a one-half interest in the property). If the right of survivorship is severable by any co-tenant acting alone and, at the time of the creation of the joint tenancy one joint tenant furnished consideration in excess of the value of his or her proportionate interest, a gift has been made by that joint tenant in the amount of the excess over that portion which would be received on severance of the joint tenancy.[10]

If the right of survivorship is not severable except by mutual consent, determining the value of the gift requires a calculation that takes into account the ages of both the donor and the other concurrent owner. This calculation is necessary because the younger of the tenants, who has a greater probability of surviving and taking all the property, has a more valuable property interest when determined on the basis of actuarial probabilities.[11] In this situation the amount of any gift transfer would be the difference between the amount contributed to the purchase in excess of the value of the termination right (determined on an actuarial basis), as measured immediately after the creation of the joint tenancy.

c. Joint Tenancies Between Spouses

The establishment of a spousal joint tenancy in real property constitutes a gift to the extent that one spouse provides consideration that exceeds the value of the rights retained by that spouse.[12] If the survivorship rights can be defeated by one spouse acting alone, the retained rights of each are considered equal and a gift of one-half the value of the joint tenancy property is made. Otherwise, actuarial calculations must be made, based on the relative life expectancies of the spouses. No immediate gift tax consequences ordinarily arise, however, because of the unlimited marital deduction for transfers to the other spouse.[13] If, however, the donee spouse is a non-U.S. citizen (whether or not a U.S. resident), gift tax may be incurred because, under these circumstances, the marital deduction is not available.[14]

The same rules result in no gift tax consequences upon the creation of a spousal joint tenancy in personal property[15] because of the unlimited marital deduction.[16] Similarly, a different rule applies when the donee spouse of a joint interest in personal property is a non-U.S. citizen, but the more generous §2523(i)(2) annual donee exclusion is available.

4. Estate Tax Considerations

a. Joint Tenant Spouse

(1) Surviving Joint Tenant Spouse Is U.S. Citizen

Differing estate tax inclusion rules apply to joint tenancy property, depending upon whether the surviving joint tenant is the spouse or another person.[17] One-half of the value of real or personal property held in a tenancy by the entirety or a spousal joint tenancy with the right of survivorship is included in the estate of the first spouse to die.[18] This estate tax result is not conditioned upon whether a gift occurred upon creation of the joint tenancy, that is, the source of the consideration for this acquisition is not relevant.[19] This 50–50 treatment does not apply if a third person is also a joint tenant.[20] The inclusion of only one-half of the value of spousal joint tenancy property in the estate of the first spouse to die results in (1) a tax basis change at death for only one-half the value of the joint tenancy property and (2) a carryover basis for the other one-half of such property.[21]

Example: A personal residence held in joint tenancy has a basis of $100,000 and a fair market value of $350,000 on the date of death of the first spouse to die. The basis of the surviving spouse immediately after the death of the first spouse resulting from inclusion of the one-half interest in the gross estate of the first spouse would be one-half of $350,000 or $175,000. The other one-half attributable to the continuing ownership of the surviving spouse, as to which a carryover basis applies, would be one-half of $100,000 or $50,000. The total basis for the personal residence in the hands of the survivor would be $225,000.

The result evidenced by this example might be counterproductive if the spouse who provided all the consideration for the joint tenancy with right of survivorship property dies first and the tax basis is only stepped up at death for one half of the property.[22] The offsetting elements in this situation are (1) the use of the joint tenancy/survivorship arrangement to avoid probate administration versus (2) the additional cost of the capital gains tax on the appreciation element that did not disappear at death because of the unavailability of the tax basis step up. The estate tax will not be a relevant consideration, assuming a marital deduction is available under either alternative.

If appreciated property is placed in joint tenancy and the donee dies within one year of the gift, this property, although included in the donee's estate to the extent of a one-half interest, will not receive a stepped-up basis.[23] If, however, the property is placed in joint tenancy immediately upon purchase, the basis step up at death should be allowed because the property should not be considered "appreciated property" for purposes of this limitation provision.[24]

(2) Surviving Joint Tenant Spouse Is Not U.S. Citizen

The one-half inclusion rule (discussed above) does not apply to transfers to a non-U.S. citizen spouse unless the property is placed into a qualified domestic trust.[25] Accordingly, in this situation the precise sources of the consideration provided by each joint tenant for the acquisition of the joint tenancy property must be ascertained in determining the amount of such transfers includible in the decedent's estate.[26]

b. Joint Tenancies Between Nonspouses

The opportunity to split the ownership for estate tax purposes between joint tenants is not available when the joint tenants are other than spouses. Joint tenancy property is included in the joint tenant decedent's gross estate, except to the extent consideration has been provided by the surviving joint tenant.[27] Consequently, the burden is on the estate to demonstrate that consideration was originally provided by the surviving joint tenant. Sometimes this can be accomplished by demonstrating that the other party provided "sweat equity" to be credited toward that purchase.[28]

This estate tax inclusion treatment is often most significant with respect to any appreciation in value of the joint tenancy property after the creation of the joint tenancy. The creation of that joint tenancy will be a gift transaction for gift tax purposes, assuming a completed gift. For purposes of the unified tax computation, the joint tenancy property will also be included in the gross estate of the transferor, with (as a result of the §2001(c) tax computation mechanism) an offset effectively being available for the previously paid gift tax. Any appreciation in value after the gift transfer will not previously have been subject to transfer tax, however. Consequently, this appreciation will be fully includible in the gross estate of the joint tenant who provided the consideration for the acquisition (or improvement) of the joint tenancy property.

The income tax basis for the property in the hands of the surviving joint tenant will be dependent on the amount of inclusion in the gross estate of the deceased joint tenant. As noted, if the entire consideration for the property was provided by the deceased joint tenant, the property will be fully includible in the gross estate of that joint tenant. Consequently, a tax-basis step-up will be available for that property in the hands of the surviving joint tenant.[29] No tax-basis step-up will be available for that portion of the property attributable to the consideration provided by the surviving joint tenant.

5. Joint Tenancy Estate Planning

For the smaller estate where exposure to federal estate tax is improbable or minimal,[30] the joint tenancy with a right of survivorship interest is a quite useful transfer mechanism for avoiding the costs of probate administration (since the joint tenancy property transfer to the survivor occurs under the terms of the joint tenancy arrangement and not subject to the provisions of a last will). For this reason, the joint tenancy ownership arrangement is often known as "the poor man's will." Further, estate planning for joint tenancies between spouses is considerably simplified by the unlimited marital deduction. The unlimited marital deduction eliminates any gift liability on creation of a spousal joint tenancy in real or personal property. Further, a greater degree of certainty exists with regard to the estate tax because the property is automatically divided between the spouses.[31] An election to achieve this result is not required.

Particularly if the joint tenancy ownership is between other than spouses the various joint tenants should examine whether they should enter into an agreement for the management and responsibility for expenses for the property. This would enable them to explicitly identify such matters as (1) their respective contributions and contemplated ownership interests, (2) obligations to fund expenses, (3) a possible waiver of a right to partition the property, (4) restrictions on transfers of interests in the property, (5) events requiring the sale of a property interest, (6) terms for any purchases between co-owners, and (7) an agreement to mediate disputes. In appropriate circumstances these considerations would also be relevant, of course, to the owners of property held in a tenancy in common, rather than in joint tenancy.

B. Community Property

1. Community Property Classification Issues

A client may live in a jurisdiction where a community property system is in effect. These jurisdictions are Alaska,[32] Arizona, California, Idaho, Louisiana, Nevada, New Mexico, Texas, Washington, and Wisconsin.[33] Clients may also live in a foreign country where a community property system is in effect.[34] Estate planners must recognize, however, that community property estate planning considerations may be relevant to their clients even if the planner does not practice in one of these community property jurisdictions. The clients may have previously lived in a community property jurisdiction and the property that the clients continue to hold may still be classified as community property.[35]

Under a community property system, any property acquired by a husband or wife during marriage (except property acquired by gift, devise, or descent and in certain other limited circumstances) is usually considered to be community property.[36] The community relationship is considered to be a form of partnership (usually with one spouse as managing partner), both partners having vested, equal, and undivided interests in the community property.[37] Often, this ownership is described as the equivalent of a tenancy in common, arising as of the inception of the property, with additional property management rights accorded to one of the two owners.

On the death of either spouse, the survivor is entitled to one-half of the community property (but not the entire property, unlike joint and survivorship property). This treatment occurs irrespective of any contrary provision in the will of the deceased spouse. The essence of the community property system is that an equal ownership already exists with respect to the property held by the two members of the community and that the surviving spouse already is the "owner" of his or her portion. The survivor's position is often aided in a community property jurisdiction by a presumption that assets owned at death are to be classified as community property unless clearly demonstrated to the contrary.

For spouses whose marital lives have been spent in both community property jurisdictions and noncommunity property jurisdictions (referred to as common law property jurisdictions), the initial process of identifying the property interests of each spouse can become quite complicated. This mixture of community property and noncommunity property assets can be the result of situations similar to the following:

Example (1): Executive X, employed by a large corporation, spent a number of years while married working at divisional headquarters in Houston, Texas (a community property state). For the last 10 years of his career, he was transferred to the Chicago, Illinois, home office and resided in one of the nearby suburbs in Illinois (a common law property state). After retirement he returned to Texas. He and his wife accumulated substantial property sourced from his wages and from earnings on investments made both while residing in Texas and in Illinois.

Example (2): Executive B worked for a number of years for a large company based in New York (a common-law property jurisdiction) and he and his wife lived in suburban Connecticut (also a common-law property jurisdiction). Later, corporate headquarters were moved to Houston, Texas (a community property state), and Executive B was transferred to Houston where he worked for some years before his retirement. Upon retirement, he moved back to a farm in Connecticut that he and his wife had acquired during their earlier residence in Connecticut. They then owned this property completely and unencumbered, having paid the mortgage liability on the farm from wages received primarily while resident in Texas.

Example (3): Mr. C has been a resident of Texas (a community property state) for his entire life. Before his marriage, he accumulated substantial assets from his business activities and, upon the death of his father during his marriage, he acquired substantial additional property by inheritance. A large portion of these assets were used to acquire listed securities. Both before and after marriage the income from these securities, and the proceeds received upon the sale of these securities, have been invested in other listed securities. Mr. C has not kept accurate records reflecting the various sources of funds.

For purposes of making informed estate planning decisions for each of these clients, the estate planner must, in the first instance, identify specifically (1) what property is owned by the "community" and (2) what property is to be classified as separate property.[38] This will include the application of state law presumptions to treat all property as community where the original ownership of separate property cannot be adequately traced.

2. Community Property in the Gross Estate

a. Characterization Rules

(1) Basic Characterization Rules

A decedent's gross estate includes "the value of all property to the extent of the interest therein of the decedent at the time of his death."[39] The ownership of such property is determined by reference to local law. Property can be separate, community, or a combination of both community and separate property.[40] The gross estate of a married decedent will include the value of all of his or her separate property and one-half of the total value of the community property.[41] This necessitates a classification of property as separate or community.

The starting point in this state law property classification process in community property states is the application of the usual presumption that all property owned at the dissolution of the marriage, whether occurring upon the death of one of the spouses or upon divorce, is community property. To negate community property classification, the origin of a particular asset must be "traced" to establish that it was acquired with separate funds.[42]

The community or separate property character of real or personal property acquired by cash purchase during marriage is determined by reference to the separate or community character of the funds used to make that purchase. This involves application of an "inception of title" doctrine. If, for example, the husband's separate funds were used to purchase an asset, that asset is the separate property of the husband. If the asset was purchased in part with community funds and in part with separate funds, the asset is part community and part separate, as determined in proportion to the funds used for the acquisition.

The character of assets purchased on credit or with borrowed funds is usually determined not by the character of the funds ultimately used to discharge the obligation, but, rather, by whether the purchase was made based on community credit or on the separate credit of one of the spouses. The usual presumption is that debt obligations arranged after marriage are based on the credit of the community. When community funds are used to improve or discharge an encumbrance on one spouse's separate property, the other spouse is entitled to reimbursement for that spouse's community share of funds so used. A principle of reimbursement also applies when separate funds are used to improve or discharge an encumbrance on community property.

A division exists among community property jurisdictions as to whether income that is derived from separate property is itself separate property. A similar conflict exists with respect to the categorization of income received from a trust established by a gift or testamentary bequest for the benefit of only one of the spouses.

(2) Life Insurance Characterization

Proceeds from life insurance policies that are community property are treated as belonging one half to each spouse. This categorization will not be important if community property insurance proceeds from a policy on the life of one spouse are payable to the other spouse. If the proceeds are payable to a third party (e.g., children of their marriage or of an earlier marriage of the insured spouse), the surviving noninsured spouse may have a claim to one-half of those proceeds. The validity of this claim would be dependent upon state law and whether the surviving spouse had previously agreed to the beneficiary designation. When the insured spouse does die first, only one-half of the proceeds are includible in the decedent insured's gross estate, regardless of whether those proceeds are payable to the insured spouse's estate, the surviving spouse, or another beneficiary, since the surviving spouse is the owner of one-half of those proceeds.[43]

In categorizing life insurance as being community or separate property two different rules have evolved under applicable state property/insurance ownership laws.[44] Some jurisdictions use an apportionment approach by which the character of life insurance policy proceeds as either separate or community property turns on the proportion of premium payments made from separate or community funds; that is, an apportionment formula is applicable. In other jurisdictions an "inception of title" rule prevails.[45] Under this alternative if, for example, a policy is initiated by the husband before marriage, or after marriage but while the couple is domiciled in a common law property state, the entire policy is treated as the separate property of the husband. If premiums are later paid from community funds, the surviving noninsured spouse would be entitled to be reimbursed for her share of the community funds used to pay premiums on the policy.[46] Under this rule, the surviving spouse would not otherwise share in the policy proceeds (unless designated as beneficiary).

In an alternative situation, the noninsured spouse holding an interest in a community property policy on the life of the insured spouse might be the first to die. The community property interest of the noninsured spouse in the policy is not extinguished in this situation.[47] In the planning context the question becomes whether this first to die spouse should transfer his or her interest in this policy to the insured survivor or should transfer that interest to a third party (e.g., a child). The surviving insured parent may want to control the disposition of the policy and its proceeds in this situation. As noted in the insurance planning discussion,[48] the best approach would be to have the entire insurance policy ownership (and all incidents of policy ownership) held in a form deemed outside the estates of both spouses for federal estate tax purposes.

(3) State Law Property Classification Rules Not Consistent

The local law rules for categorizing property as separate or community are intricate, frequently ill-defined, and not consistent from jurisdiction to jurisdiction.[49] Consequently, the estate planner must carefully identify the property interests under the pertinent local community property laws.[50] Incorrect property classifications could encourage inappropriate estate planning suggestions (which may put the estate planning professional at serious malpractice risk).

b. Choice of Law Rules

For the purpose of classifying marital property, the marital character of property is determined according to the law of the state in which the husband and wife were domiciled at the time the property was acquired.[51] This is normally the rule even if, for example, community funds are used to acquire real estate in a common law property jurisdiction. This occurs because the funds used for the purchase are assumed to be sourced from community assets. Further, the character of that property is not altered from community to separate when the couple relocates to another state.[52]

c. Procedures for Property Identification

(1) Property Identification Process

Where estate planning clients live or previously have lived in a community property jurisdiction, the precise determination of the separate or community property character of assets is often the most essential element of the estate planning process. This identification process can be a highly complicated task, particularly where the various properties have been commingled over an extended period of time.[53] In advising a client, particularly a younger client, the estate planner should suggest that a records maintenance program be implemented to assure that separate property be actually kept segregated from community property. As part of the estate planning process (for example, when insurance policies are to be acquired by an irrevocable insurance trust that will provide benefits for a surviving spouse), the partition of community property into separate property held by each spouse may also be advisable.

Spouses at the time of their marriage and, particularly, when moving into a community property jurisdiction after having lived and acquired property in a common law property state, should identify the separate property interests of each spouse. When this identification process is complete, the spouses might evidence their consensus concerning the ownership of these properties by a memorandum or agreement between them. This might be done with a formal agreement, or merely by a memorandum, the format to be determined by local law considerations. In some states, this agreement might be used to treat property differently than the manner in which it would be characterized under local law.

For example, in Texas corporate dividends received from separate property are categorized as community property. The parties may desire to agree that these dividends should be categorized as the separate property of the holder of the securities. This can often be accomplished by agreement as permitted under local community property law.[54]

(2) Maintaining Separate Property

Having determined which property is actually the separate property of each spouse, a program should be implemented to assure that such status continues. Complete and detailed records should be maintained. This would include separate checking or savings accounts for the husband's separate funds, for the wife's separate funds, and for the community funds. These accounts could then be used to purchase separately other replacement assets. By application of a "tracing" principle, later acquired property will be accurately identified. In those states where the income from separate property is community property (and the parties do not desire to vary this treatment by agreement), the income should be promptly credited to community accounts so that commingling problems will not arise.[55]

Similarly, separate accounts and records should be kept for other properties (e.g., brokerage accounts for securities, real estate, and government bonds). Joint purchases (i.e., the use of both separate and community property funds) should, if possible, not be made, so as to avoid fractionalizing the various interests unless this treatment is fully understood and desired.

d. Partitioning Community Property

(1) Local Law and Gift Taxes

Having determined the community or separate property status of the various properties owned by the spouses, the spouses might determine that, for estate planning purposes, the community property interests should be terminated. This can ordinarily be accomplished under state law through a "partitioning" of the community property. Local law varies as to how this process is to be completed. Most community property jurisdictions permit some form of partition, often achieved through a contractual arrangement between the spouses.[56]

A partition of the community into equal shares of separate property will have no gift tax consequences.[57] When the spouses agree to alter their respective property interests, gift transfers will be considered to have occurred for gift tax purposes.

Example: If a husband and wife agree that what is community property will become the separate property of the wife, the husband will have made a gift of his one-half community interest to his wife.[58] These transfers should ordinarily qualify, however, for the unlimited gift tax marital deduction.[59]

(2) Income Tax Considerations

No gain or loss will result for income tax purposes upon a partition of community property between the spouses.[60] For those assets classified as community property, a stepped-up (or stepped-down) basis at death to fair market value is accorded to the entire property, including the one-half community interest held by the surviving spouse that was not included in the decedent's gross estate.[61] This rule encourages the continuation of community property status for appreciated property held by the marital unit until the death of one spouse, rather than a partitioning of that property into separate property interests. A presumption under local property law that property owned by spouses is classified as community property, rather than separate property, can enhance the benefits of this tax basis step up at the death of the first spouse to die.

3. Lifetime Transfers of Community Property

a. Gift Tax Applicable

In most community property states the sole management power of one spouse over community assets (other than homestead property) is held to include the power to make reasonable gifts. In all community property states some restrictions do exist, however, on one spouse's unilateral power to make gifts of community assets to third parties. This is often a requirement that, under local law, the gift transfer must not be in fraud of the rights of the other spouse.

To avoid the testamentary disposition of community property, a transfer by lifetime gift may be appropriate. The transfer of community property to a third party by gift will constitute a gift by each spouse of his or her interest in the community property.

A transfer by one spouse of his or her community property interest in property to the other spouse, so that the property is held as separate property by only one spouse, will also constitute a completed transfer for gift tax purposes.[62] As noted above, the unlimited marital deduction will ordinarily eliminate any actual gift tax liability, however.[63]

b. Unanticipated Gifts

Gifts of community property can also occur inadvertently, whether to the other spouse or to third parties. This may happen, for example, upon the commingling of separate and community property whereby, under the local law presumption favoring community property status, a gift is made to the other spouse.

In the life insurance context, where (1) property held by a husband and wife as community property is used to purchase insurance upon the husband's life, (2) a third person is designated as beneficiary of the proceeds at death, and (3) the death of the husband makes absolute the transfer of the wife's community property interest, a gift by the wife is deemed made as of the time of the husband's death.[64] The value of such gift, made at the time of death of the insured spouse, is one-half the amount of the proceeds of this insurance.[65]

4. Estate Tax Considerations

Upon a decedent's death, one-half of the value of all community property that the decedent held at death with the surviving spouse will be includible in his or her gross estate (in addition to the full value of his or her separate property).[66] The unlimited marital deduction is available for the transfer of community property interests to the surviving spouse, assuming the nondeductible terminable interest rule does not limit the deduction.[67] This marital deduction qualification eliminates the necessity to differentiate between separate and community property if all property is to be distributed to the surviving spouse. As noted above, an objective would often be to have the entire property (including the interest of the surviving spouse) categorized as community property, so that (as to the appreciated property) the §1014(b)(6) tax-basis step-up at death is available.[68]

5. Widow's Election

a. Concept of the Widow's Election

The will of the first spouse to die may purport to devise the entire interest in the community assets (including that interest of the surviving spouse in the community property that is not actually owned by the deceased spouse). Under local community property law, the decedent is not the owner of the surviving spouse's portion of the community property and, therefore, the decedent does not have the legal power to dispose of that portion.[69] Being the actual owner of that property, under local law the surviving spouse can claim his or her community share of the property outright and free of any apparent restrictions under the decedent's will.

In a "forced widow's election"[70] situation, the will of the deceased spouse may provide, however, for the disposition of the entire community property (i.e., including the portion belonging to the surviving spouse). Of course, the deceased spouse has no legal capacity to dispose of that property. If the surviving spouse elects to separately take his or her community property interest (e.g., outright) against the provisions of the will, the will then often provides that he or she must give up all beneficial interests in the property of the deceased spouse that would otherwise pass to the surviving spouse under the will. If the surviving spouse does decide to take under the deceased spouse's will the surviving spouse would then agree that the disposition of all the community property (or, at least, that property subject to the forced election), including the surviving spouse's interest, would be governed by the terms of the will of the deceased spouse.[71] The usual scheme for asset disposition under this forced widow's election arrangement is to provide (1) a life estate in the entire community property for the surviving spouse with (2) remainder interests for the children in the entire property.[72]

This "forced widow's election" with respect to the disposition of community property must be distinguished from other types of "widow's elections" that might exist in the marital/surviving spouse context:

- The will could provide that community property be entirely placed in a trust providing for (1) the surviving spouse for life, (2) remainder to the children, but that this structure is applicable whether the spouse does or does not agree to this arrangement (i.e., the widow's decision to submit his or her property to this trust structure is not based on a condition).
- In a separate property jurisdiction, when a deceased spouse provides for no (or only limited) benefits under a will to the surviving spouse, that surviving spouse often has the right under applicable state law to elect against the provisions of that will and then receive some minimum portion of the estate of the decedent spouse.

b. Nontax Reasons for Use of Forced Widow's Election

Various factors other than federal tax planning reasons often suggest the possible use of the forced widow's election technique with respect to community property holdings, including:

- to preclude a second spouse of the surviving spouse from managing and using the community property;
- a concern about the surviving spouse's capability to manage the community property;
- a desire for unified management of community property, which might consist of a family business, real estate holdings, or similar property not readily susceptible of divided management; and
- the avoidance of a second probate process at the time of the surviving spouse's death.

The widow's election will (or a revocable trust implementing this same approach) may, therefore, be used as an effective asset dispositive arrangement for the entire property. Significant federal income and estate tax planning issues exist in the forced widow's election context. As noted below, these difficult federal tax issues may ultimately suggest using a voluntary rather than a forced widow's election.

c. Gift Tax Aspects of Widow's Election

Upon the effectiveness of the forced widow's election, the surviving spouse will have transferred a remainder interest in his or her property into trust for the remainder beneficiaries, retaining a life interest. This occurs since the surviving spouse allows the deceased spouse's will to irrevocably govern the disposition of the survivor's share of the community property. This will constitute a completed transfer by the surviving spouse for gift tax purposes.[73]

The amount transferred by the surviving spouse for gift tax purposes will be the value of the remainder interest in the surviving spouse's share of the community property.[74] The value of this remainder interest transferred by the surviving spouse will be offset, however, by the value of the consideration received by the surviving spouse. The consideration received at the time of the gift transfer of the remainder interest by the surviving spouse will be the life income interest in the decedent's share of the community property.[75] If the life interest, as actuarially determined, is anticipated to continue for a significant time period, the value of that interest received may entirely offset the value of the property transferred by the surviving spouse.

This immediate gift tax impact might even be avoided by providing a limited power of appointment to the surviving spouse with respect to the property he or she transfers into this arrangement. If the surviving spouse has the right to distribute that property among a group of possible beneficiaries (not limited to an ascertainable standard), the transfer by the spouse would not be complete for gift tax purposes.[76]

d. Estate Tax Effects to Widow from Widow's Election

The widow's election to accept a life estate in the entire community property will constitute a transfer by the surviving spouse of his or her one-half of the community property with a retained life estate in that transferred property.[77] Consequently, the surviving spouse's portion of the community property would be includible at his or her subsequent death in his or her gross estate by application of §2036.

If a trust property transfer described in §2036[78] is made for a consideration in money or money's worth, but is not a bona fide sale for an adequate and full consideration in money or money's worth, at the time of the death of the surviving spouse only (1) the excess of the fair market value of the property transferred (otherwise to be included on account of such transaction) over (2) the value of the consideration received by the decedent is to be included in the decedent's gross estate.[79] The election by the surviving spouse to take under the will and the acquiescence of the surviving spouse to the transfer of his or her community property interest into the trust will be deemed to be a transfer for consideration for this purpose. The consideration received by the surviving spouse is the right to the income for his or her lifetime from the deceased spouse's share of the community property.

This "consideration offset" under §2043(a) can produce a substantial reduction in the estate tax burden on the assets passing to the remainder beneficiaries at the time of the subsequent death of the surviving spouse.[80] If, however, a general power of appointment over the surviving spouse's assets transferred under the widow's election is made available to the surviving spouse, the "consideration offset" treatment under §2043(a) would probably not be available since, owing to the surviving spouse's control until death, no "transfer for consideration" would have occurred.

The net effect is that often less than 100% of the community estate would be subjected to inclusion in the total gross estates of the two spouses.[81] Any income received by the surviving spouse during the period of survival and not expended at death will also be includible in his or her gross estate. That income would have been sourced from the entire (former) community property held in the trust and not merely the community property interest of the surviving spouse.

e. Income Tax Effects of Widow's Election

(1) Estate as Seller of Life Interest

Income tax concerns could significantly reduce the attractiveness of the forced widow's election technique. The estate may be treated, for example, as the seller of a life interest in the decedent's property transferred into the widow's election trust, receiving in the exchange the remainder interest in the widow's property. The question is whether any gain is realized by the estate on that transaction and, if so, whether that gain is to be recognized for federal income tax purposes.

No gain would be realized if the interest is sold for its tax basis. That basis will have been established (under §1014) at the value as of death. In determining gain or loss from the sale or other disposition of a term interest in property, however, §1001(e) specifies that the portion of the adjusted basis of the interest sold that is determined under §1014 or §1015 is to be disregarded. Whether this provision is applicable to the seller (i.e., the estate) of the life interest in a widow's election situation remains uncertain, but it is probably relevant. If this rule is applicable for the estate, the entire value of the remainder interest received will be treated as an amount received for income tax purposes, an unsatisfactory income tax result. This income recognition result would ordinarily be unsatisfactory even when this transaction is classified as a capital gains event subject to the maximum §1(h) capital gains tax rate.

(2) Capital Gain to Surviving Spouse on the Exchange

The exchange by the surviving spouse of the remainder interest in his or her community property for a life income interest in the deceased spouse's community property is a realization event for capital gains purposes. However, the amount of capital gain would be reduced or eliminated because of the step-up in tax basis allowed at death. This basis step-up also applies (under §1014(b)(6)) to the surviving spouse's share of community property. Accordingly, at the time the surviving spouse exchanges the remainder interest in his or her community property interest for a life interest in the deceased spouse's community property interest, the realization of a significant capital gain will ordinarily be avoided due to the "stepped-up basis" rules. The §1001(e) basis limitation rule (even if applicable in the widow's election context) is only relevant to the disposition of a term interest, not to the transfer of a remainder interest.

The date on which this exchange is deemed to occur will depend on the effective date of the widow's election. If the exchange does not occur until the estate administration has continued for some time (since the surviving spouse must affirmatively elect), and the property subject to the election has appreciated significantly since the death of the other spouse, substantial gain might be realized. This would not result if the exchange is effective as of the death of the spouse. This situation would occur if the surviving spouse has previously executed a document stating that his or her election will be treated as effective as of the moment of the death of the other spouse (i.e., when the will transferring all the community property becomes irrevocable).

(3) Amortization by Purchasing Surviving Spouse

When the widow's election is effective, the surviving spouse will have purchased a life interest in the deceased spouse's community property. That purchased interest is a wasting asset and, ordinarily, for federal income tax purposes the cost for that asset should be recoverable through amortization deductions. A surviving spouse was previously allowed to amortize the income interest that the spouse "purchased" upon electing to take under the will.[82] Consequently, the surviving spouse could shelter a significant portion of the income stream received from the widow's election trust. The income tax basis for amortization purposes would be the fair market value of the life interest in the deceased spouse's community property, determined at the time of the exchange.[83]

No depreciation or amortization income tax deduction is allowed, however, for a term interest in property for any period during which the remainder interest in such property is held (directly or indirectly) by a "related person."[84] In the widow's election context, the remainder interest will often be held by (or for) children (who are related persons for purposes of this deduction disallowance rule).[85] Accordingly, the surviving spouse's purchased life interest will not itself be an amortizable asset for federal income tax purposes.

This deduction limitation provision does not affect a depreciation or amortization deduction that is not allocable to a term of years or a life estate. Consequently, although the owner of a term interest in a building held for rental purposes cannot amortize the term interest, the owner may claim a depreciation deduction with respect to the building itself. The tax basis for that property will have been increased to its fair market value as of the date of death (assuming appreciated property), enabling a larger postdeath depreciation deduction. If the interest of the surviving spouse is held under a trust, the depreciation deduction attributable to the building may be available to offset the taxable income allocable from the trust.[86]

f. Time and Manner of Election by Surviving Spouse

Since the widow's election determines the manner in which the community property assets are held and ultimately distributed, the election must be made before the distribution of the estate of the first spouse to die.[87] The spouses may wish to implement procedures to assure, however, that the widow's (or widower's) election actually will be made. Consequently, an election might be made by each spouse in a separate document. This document could be implemented at the time the other spouse's will is executed or at any later date but before the death of the spouse.

Since a will is revocable until the time of death, this election would also generally be revocable by the surviving spouse at any time during the life of the other spouse. Further, the election would not normally apply to any will subsequently implemented by the other spouse and under which the testamentary scheme is altered. The revocability of this election would also enable the postponement of the surviving spouse's gift tax liability until irrevocability occurs at the time of death (or later if, as noted above, a special power of appointment is implemented).[88] The effectiveness of this election as of the decedent's death will also determine the date of the property exchange transaction, as described above.[89]

6. Structuring Various Trusts Where Community Property Devised

Complications arise in structuring testamentary documents where spouses own both significant community property and substantial separate property.[90] If the first spouse to die desires a trust arrangement for these properties the following trusts might be established:

- a marital deduction trust holding the decedent's separate property;
- a credit shelter trust;
- a trust holding the decedent's share of the community property; and
- a trust funded with the surviving spouse's share of community property with respect to which the surviving spouse retains only a life income interest.

This arrangement can also be accomplished through the participation by the surviving spouse in the creation of an inter vivos revocable trust and funded with these properties during the lifetime of both spouses, using separate trusts for these several types of properties when the trust becomes irrevocable. Whether both a marital deduction trust and a credit shelter trust are essential will be dependent upon the total assets of the marital unit and the unified exemption allowance available as of the time of death.

C. Life Insurance

1. Basic Uses of Life Insurance

a. Estate Planning Objectives

Life insurance can be an extremely valuable component of the estate planning process.[91] Life insurance can be used to create a larger estate for decedents having modest estates, thereby assuring adequate funds for survivors. For a larger estate, life insurance can be used to provide liquidity to pay transfer taxes and probate expenses, thereby enabling the avoidance of a forced sale of valuable illiquid assets. Life insurance may constitute a source of funds for the surviving family members during the interim period of estate administration until more assets are sold to produce greater liquidity. In the business context, life insurance proceeds may be used to fund obligations under agreements with surviving owners to purchase the deceased owner's business interest.[92]

A primary estate tax planning objective with respect to life insurance is to assure that the death proceeds from insurance on the life of an insured are not included in that insured's estate for federal estate tax purposes if the estate would otherwise be exposed to federal estate tax. This estate tax exclusion can be accomplished through the use of an irrevocable trust created to own the policies and to be the beneficiary of those policies, as described more fully in this segment. This can also be accomplished by having younger generation family members own the policy on the life of the older family member, even though the funding of the policy premium costs may come from the older family member.

b. Definition of Life Insurance

(1) Concept of "Risk Shifting"

In determining whether the life insurance estate tax provision (§2042) is applicable a determination must first be made that life insurance exists. The estate tax regulations indicate only that "insurance" refers to life insurance of every description, including death benefits paid by fraternal benefit societies operating under the lodge system.[93] The basic test of whether life insurance exists (as defined for federal estate tax purposes) is whether those amounts are received as a result of a transaction which involves risk shifting and risk distribution.[94] Life insurance for these purposes also includes proceeds from double indemnity clauses and accident insurance policies because these risks with respect to the death of an insured are assumed by the insurer.[95]

Under §7702 a contract will be considered to be "life insurance" only if: (1) it is a contract which is considered under state or foreign law to provide a single, integrated death benefit[96]; and (2) it satisfies one of two alternative tests. Those tests are[97]: (1) a cash value accumulation test[98]; and (2) a combination of a guideline premium requirement and a cash value corridor requirement.[99] When a "life insurance" contract is purchased from a commercial life insurance company the purchaser should be able to reasonably assume that the policy is life insurance for federal tax purposes and, if not, any erroneous representations to this effect will cause liability to the issuer for damages resulting from unanticipated tax expenses. If a contract is not "life insurance" for tax purposes, the income tax and estate tax exclusions described below will be limited when payments are received under the contract. Further, the income tax treatment for credits to the policy will be equivalent to that for interest being received from a bank account.

(2) Policy Types

The types of life insurance policies issued might include:

> Whole life or cash value policies—various types of "permanent" policies that build up cash values during the lifetime of the insured.[100] Ordinarily, the amount of the periodic premium remains constant through the term of this type of policy.[101] The excess contributions in the early years (plus earnings) cover the greater actuarial costs in the later years.

Term insurance—providing only the pure insurance coverage with respect to death occurring within the specified coverage period (e.g., one year or five years).[102] These policies can be issued on an individual basis or on a group basis. No cash value is created and the limited value of the policy expires as of the conclusion of the specified term.

Accidental death—coverage is provided only if death occurs during a specified term as a result of an accident. Flight insurance is a common example of this insurance.

Joint life insurance—this policy insures the lives of two or more persons, often a husband and wife, and the proceeds are ordinarily payable upon the death of the last to die of the two insured individuals. This insurance has become common due to the utilization of the unlimited estate tax marital deduction, which enables complete postponement of estate tax until the death of the survivor.

Universal life—this flexible premium policy is designed to be permanent insurance, similar to whole life. The premiums are not level, however, rather being based on the amount of the insurer's investment and the investment return experience inside the policy.

Variable life—similar to universal life, under this policy the owner selects the type of investments among various choices provided by the insurer to be held within the policy. For example, some insurers may permit the insured to pick one or more mutual funds from a basket of funds for investment of the accumulating premiums.

Many insurers have numerous variations on these alternatives to address various marketing and actuarial concerns.

c. Settlement Options

The life insurance policy is acquired to enable the receipt of cash at some future time, and the question then becomes when that cash will be received after the death of the insured. Proceeds of a life insurance policy are normally paid in full shortly after the insured's death (after the insurance company's formal claim requirements have been satisfied).[103] Insurers often provide various options, however, under which the insurance company will pay out the proceeds over an extended period. These options can either be chosen: (1) by the insured upon the commencement of the policy or (2) by the beneficiary as of the time the policy matures at the death of the insured.

These options normally include:

A life annuity option—under which the insurer provides a sum certain each month for the life of the beneficiary.[104]

A fixed period option—under which a sum certain, including interest, is paid for a specified period, without regard to whether the intended beneficiary predeceases or survives the expiration of the fixed period.[105]

A fixed amount option—under which a sum certain, plus interest (on a declining balance), will be paid in installments to the beneficiaries of the policy, without regard to the length of their respective lives.

An interest only option, with a right of withdrawal—under which only interest will be paid to the beneficiary and, at the beneficiary's death, the principal will be paid to persons as designated by the beneficiary. This option often does give the beneficiary a right of withdrawal.[106]

Many settlement option variations exist. Often a variation can be molded to satisfy the needs and desires of an insured or his or her designated beneficiaries.

2. Fundamental Federal Tax Rules

a. Federal Estate Tax Treatment

(1) Inclusion Under Life Insurance Provision—§2042

A decedent's gross estate includes the value of life insurance proceeds if[107]:

- receivable by the executor—to the extent of the amount receivable by the executor as insurance under policies on the life of the decedent[108]; and
- receivable by other beneficiaries—to the extent of the amount receivable by all other beneficiaries as insurance under policies on the life of the decedent, if the decedent possessed at his or her death any "incidents of ownership," exercisable either alone or in conjunction with any other person with respect to those policies.[109]

No test of direct or indirect payment of premiums as an alternative criterion of gross estate inclusion is applicable.[110] This can enable avoidance of estate tax through an inter vivos transfer to the beneficiary or others (e.g., to an irrevocable trust) of all the incidents of ownership in a life insurance policy.[111]

(2) Proceeds Receivable by the Executor

Proceeds are includible in the gross estate if receivable by the executor.[112] The regulations have given a broad meaning to proceeds "receivable by the executor."[113] Insurance proceeds receivable by a beneficiary who is legally bound to use such proceeds to discharge an estate obligation are included.[114] This would include proceeds under an insurance policy payable in favor of another person (such as a bank) and used as collateral for a loan which is paid with the policy proceeds.[115]

(3) Incidents of Ownership

Insurance proceeds are includible in a decedent's estate if, as the insured under the policy, he or she possessed at his or her death any of the "incidents of ownership" in the insurance policy.[116] An expansive definition is given to the term "incidents of ownership" (as "not limited in its meaning to ownership of the policy in the technical legal sense"),[117] including the power to:

- change the beneficiary[118];
- surrender or cancel the policy[119];
- assign the policy;
- revoke an assignment;
- pledge the policy for a loan; and
- obtain from the insurer a loan against the surrender value of the policy.

The regulations also include as incidents of ownership powers over the choice of settlement option[120] and the retention of a possible reversionary interest by the insured.[121]

"Incidents of ownership" may be held indirectly in other capacities, such as fiduciary powers (e.g., held as executor of a spouse's estate)[122] and administrative powers.[123] Similarly, incidents of ownership can be held indirectly by an insured acting as a trustee of a trust that owns the policy.[124] For this reason, if the insured insists upon being the trustee, the trust agreement should include language precluding the insured/trustee from having any "incidents of ownership" and should specify that decisions concerning any life insurance policies on the trustee's life are to be made by a third party.[125] Similarly, the risk of estate tax inclusion should be avoided (through the use of a third-party trustee) where the spouse is appointed as the trustee of the trust receiving insurance proceeds, but the policy is a "second-to-die" policy (with the proceeds payable upon the death of the surviving spouse/trustee). A decedent does not possess incidents of ownership in an insurance policy on his or her life, however, where the decedent's powers (1) devolved to him or her as a fiduciary and (2) were not exercisable for his or her personal benefit, provided that the decedent did not transfer the policy to the trust and did not furnish consideration for maintaining the policy in force.[126]

Where the insured is a sole or controlling shareholder of a corporation, incidents of ownership possessed by the corporation may be attributed to that shareholder with respect to proceeds payable to a beneficiary other than the corporation.[127] Apparently, attribution-of-stock-ownership rules do not apply in determining whether the decedent was a controlling shareholder for §2042 purposes.[128]

A life insurance policy owned by a partnership, with the proceeds payable other than to, or for the benefit of, the partnership, may be includible in the deceased insured partner's gross estate.[129] If the proceeds are payable to the partnership the proceeds should not be includible in the insured's gross estate under §2042(2), however, if the insured can avoid incidents of ownership in that policy.[130] Ordinarily, this should be able to be accomplished by appropriate provisions in the partnership agreement.

(4) Three-Year Transfer Inclusionary Rule

The proceeds of a policy on the life of the insured may be included in his or her gross estate under estate tax provisions other than §2042.[131] For example, as noted below, §2035 (the three-year transfer rule) requires inclusion of policy proceeds in the gross estate in certain circumstances where, although the policy is owned by another, the insured transferred a §2042 incident of ownership in the policy within three years of his or her death.[132] If the decedent's spouse is, in substance, the purchaser, the decedent should not be deemed, however, to hold "incidents of ownership," even where the designated beneficiary of the policy proceeds is a revocable trust previously created by the decedent.[133]

b. Income Tax Treatment

(1) Income Tax Benefits Available

The primary federal income tax benefits available through investment in life insurance policies are:

- the tax-deferred growth of the cash value accounts inside the policy;
- the tax-free access to the accumulating cash value (through policy borrowings); and
- the income-tax-free receipt of death benefits upon the death of the insured.

(2) Exclusion of Lifetime Increase in Value

During the lifetime of the insured, the internal income element derived from the investment of policy assets will increase the cash surrender value of a policy or will be used to provide additional life insurance coverage.[134] This income component is not included in gross income for federal income tax purposes.[135] However, income will be realized upon the surrender of a policy during lifetime.[136]

(3) Limitation on Interest Expense Deduction

Since the internal buildup of value attributable to income within the policy is not currently included in gross income, restrictions are imposed on the deductibility of interest paid on loans incurred to carry such insurance.[137] Additionally, policy-loan interest will be subject to the general rules that preclude a deduction for consumer interest expense.[138]

(4) Exclusion of Proceeds Received at Death

Amounts received under a life insurance contract (if paid by reason of the death of the insured) are not included in the gross income of the recipient.[139] Accordingly, both (1) the internal interest build-up in the policy and (2) the mortality gain are excluded from gross income when the policy proceeds are received after the death of the insured (assuming the transferee limitation is not applicable). The exclusion of the internal build-up attributable to investment return effectively transforms the policy into a "tax shelter," although a commission to the insurance company (and the salesperson) must be paid to have access to this benefit.

Further, any amounts received under a life insurance contract on the life of individuals who are terminally ill or chronically ill are excluded from gross income as amounts paid as if by reason of the death of the insured.[140] A similar exclusion applies to amounts received for the sale or assignment of any portion of a death benefit under a life insurance contract to a viatical settlement provider if the insured under the life insurance contract is either terminally ill or chronically ill.[141]

(5) Delayed Payment of Proceeds

The insurance proceeds can be paid in full immediately upon death or can be paid on a deferred basis.[142] If a settlement option is elected under which the proceeds are held by the insurer under an agreement to pay interest on those proceeds, the postdeath interest is included in the gross income of the recipient of that interest.[143] If the policy proceeds are payable in installments, the interest element of each installment is includible in gross income.[144]

3. Life Insurance Estate Planning

a. Insurance Tax Planning Issues

In approaching estate planning considerations with respect to life insurance, two questions permeate almost every analysis:

- Should the client transfer presently existing policies under which he or she is the insured and in which he or she holds "incidents of ownership"?
- Should new policies be obtained on the life of the insured and, if so, what types of policies should be acquired and how should they be purchased and owned?[145]

A variety of considerations need to be analyzed in this context including lifetime transfers, the use of insurance trusts (revocable and irrevocable, funded and unfunded), the types of policies and their comparative investment returns, and the availability of the marital deduction upon the payment of death proceeds.[146] In each instance, the estate planner should examine whether, for federal estate tax purposes, the insurance proceeds can properly be placed beyond the gross estate of the insured (and also the gross estates of the spouse and children) through the use of an inter vivos irrevocable trust which acquires and owns the policies.

Where the unlimited marital deduction will be available and liquidity issues at the first spouse's death have become less important (since the estate tax is postponed until the second death), the primary estate planning concerns may become:

- Does a necessity exist to continue policies originally purchased primarily to facilitate liquidity?
- Should complex ownership and premium paying arrangements be continued?
- What need exists for additional insurance in the future (particularly when focusing on non-tax considerations)?
- If acquired, how should the insurance policy ownership be structured?

b. Incentive for Lifetime Policy Ownership Transfers

Estate tax liabilities otherwise accruing at death may be reduced by lifetime donative transfers of life insurance policies.[147] In implementing a gift program, insurance policies are very appropriate for completing gifts. The value of a gift of an insurance policy for gift tax purposes will be the replacement value of the policy at the time of the gift.[148] For estate tax purposes, however, the value will be the face amount, since the policy will have matured at death, except to the extent that value is reduced by any outstanding policy loans existing at the time of death and payable from the policy proceeds.[149]

(1) Advantages/Disadvantages of Policy Transfers

Advantages that arise from using insurance as gift property include:

- The donor does not suffer any current loss of income (since, ordinarily, any investment return is retained within the policy).
- The policy has an income tax basis essentially equivalent to the fair market value of the assets (i.e., the donee does not receive a high-value–low-basis asset with a built-in income tax detriment) unless the policy has been in effect for a considerable period and significant inside build-up has occurred.
- The donor need not be concerned with the donee's investment responsibilities for the transferred property since the investment decision (i.e., the purchase of the insurance policy and the type of policy) has already been made.
- The donee will often be less likely to surrender a life insurance policy to secure cash for nonessential purposes than he or she would be to sell or transfer liquid securities.

If the donee has no independent assets, the donor will need to assure, however, that the donee will have adequate funds to pay any subsequent premiums on the transferred policy. This can be accomplished by subsequent cash gifts to the donee for this purpose, or the donor's direct, periodic payment of the insurance premium amounts.

Gifts of life insurance are not advisable in all instances. A gift of a life insurance policy may remove liquid funds from the estate (which might otherwise be used to satisfy estate obligations and avoid forced sales of illiquid assets).[150] Further, certain transfers of life insurance remain vulnerable to inclusion if transferred within three years of death.[151] The greatest concern may be the required irrevocable nature of the transaction. Future business exigencies (i.e., the need for collateral for loans) or changing family circumstances (such as an illness or a divorce) may create a necessity for the use of the policy benefits by the insured or a change in perspectives about appropriate estate beneficiaries. Further, at that time the donor may not be insurable (e.g., because of adverse health conditions), with replacement insurance not being available.

(2) Choosing Which Policies to Be Transferred

The insured may own several different types of life insurance policies (e.g., term, whole life, and endowment policies). Consideration should then be given to which of these policies should be the subject of any gift transfers and in which order the policies should be transferred. To limit gift tax liabilities, consideration should be given to the transfer first of term insurance policies (having a limited fair market value) and, thereafter, to recently issued ordinary life policies, which will often have a smaller cash surrender value. This will limit the gift tax value of these policy transfers.

(3) Completing the Insurance Policy Transfer

A complete divestiture of all "incidents of ownership" must occur to assure that the desired estate tax planning benefits will actually be realized. This will require: (1) the completion of the insurance company's formal ownership transfer requirements, (2) the delivery of physical possession of the policy to the new owner, and (3) a careful analysis to assure that the donor has not inadvertently retained any incidents of ownership.[152]

(4) Gifts of Policies Within Three Years of Death

Notwithstanding that a decedent has transferred all "incidents of ownership" in a policy insuring his or her life, the proceeds may still be includible in an insured's gross estate if a gift of the ownership of the policy has been made by the insured within three years of his or her death.[153] The statute provides that, if the decedent transfers an interest in or relinquishes a power over a policy within three years of death and the policy would have been includible in the decedent's estate under §2042 if that transfer or relinquishment had not been made, the proceeds are includible in the decedent's estate under §2035.[154] Since §2042 applies only to "incidents of ownership" in a life insurance policy possessed by the insured, the three-year transfer rule should apply only to transfers of policies or incidents of ownership by the insured (and not to transfers of cash to enable the transferee to pay policy premiums).[155]

This three-year transfer rule does not apply to policy transfers by a noninsured donor within three years of death. If a decedent owned an insurance policy at death on the life of another, the policy value would be included in the decedent's gross estate under §2033, not §2042.[156] Further, the three-year rule does not apply to gifts of insurance premiums by a noninsured donor within three years of death, regardless of whether the amount of such premiums is within the annual exclusion.[157]

The basic issue in dealing with §2035 applicability is whether under this three-year inclusionary rule: (1) the policy itself was transferred during the three-year period (under circumstances where an interest in property would have been includible in the estate of the decedent under one of the transfer provisions) or (2) only the premiums were transferred (all rights under the policy having been assigned prior to such period or having originated with another person). Consequently, if the insured has transferred a policy more than three years before his or her death, but continues to pay annual premiums, the policy proceeds should not be subject to §2035 inclusion. This is not the case with accidental death policies or similar situations where each premium creates a new policy.[158]

The application of the three-year rule might be avoided if the noninsured policy owner (including, possibly, an insurance trust) can be treated as directly purchasing the insurance policy from the insurer from its inception, rather than being a transferee of the policy. In this situation, no "transfer" of the policy ever occurs for purposes of the three-year inclusionary rule.[159] If a policy transfer has actually occurred, the donee-owner should pay future premiums from his or her own resources after the transfer of the policy. If this is not feasible, alternatives to assure that cash and not a policy interest is being transferred might include: (1) varying the amounts and dates of cash transfers to a donee to be used to pay premiums, (2) depositing premium payments in advance, and (3) using policy loans to pay premiums.[160] The transfer by the insured of funds to a trust and the trustee's purchase of the policy should not constitute a policy transfer by the insured, but in some situations the trustee could be seen as merely acting as an agent for the insured.[161]

c. Insurance Trusts

(1) Estate Planning Advantages

A trust can be an extremely valuable estate planning tool in holding insurance policies and in receiving the proceeds of various policies at the death of the insured. These trusts can be inter vivos (revocable or irrevocable) or testamentary. If inter vivos, the trust can be funded or unfunded.

Proceeds under a life insurance policy can be paid to a trustee at the time of the insured's death. This arrangement provides substantial flexibility to the trustee to immediately invest the cash proceeds received from the insurer. A trust can also be used to coordinate the collection, investment, and disposition of the proceeds of several policies, as well as the management of other properties such as securities that are part of the corpus of the trust at the death of the insured or that are "poured over" to the trust under the insured's will. This trust can be used for purposes similar to those of any other trust (e.g., sprinkling income and corpus, generation-skipping, marital deduction provisions, if estate tax inclusion is required, and the avoidance of intricate local law problems, such as paying proceeds to minors and dealing with policy ownership when the beneficiary predeceases the insured). This arrangement can be contrasted to the situation where all the proceeds are payable outright to a specified beneficiary who must then invest (or spend) those funds. A trust can also enable avoidance of the expenses and delays of probate administration. The proceeds can escape possible exposure to the creditors of the policy's beneficiary, particularly if the trust was irrevocable prior to the insured's death.

(2) Revocable Insurance Trusts

The grantor may structure the insurance trust so that he or she can revoke, alter, or amend the trust agreement during his or her lifetime, but it will become irrevocable at the death of the grantor. The revocable trust created during the grantor's lifetime may be funded or unfunded. An unfunded revocable life insurance trust exists where the trustee is authorized to collect the life insurance proceeds at the death of the insured and to thereafter administer the trust in accordance with the trust instrument but may have no other responsibilities during the life of the insured. This trust may often be the only designated beneficiary of a policy held by the insured. The trust grantor, however, ordinarily continues to have the obligation to pay the insurance premiums (or at least to provide funds to the trustee to pay the premiums). If the grantor retains the ownership and possession of the insurance policies during his or her lifetime and merely names the trust as the beneficiary under the policies, the trust corpus often will consist only of a nominal amount of cash until the policies become payable at the death of the insured. Alternatively, ownership of the policies, but no other property, might be transferred into this trust.[162]

A funded revocable life insurance trust is created by the grantor transferring cash, securities, or other property to the trust. The trust could then receive sufficient income from these investments to enable the trust to satisfy the premium payment obligations on the insurance policies. The balance of the income, if any, could be paid to the trust grantor or retained in the trust. Since the trust is funded, the trustee will be required to perform the same duties as the trustee of any other active trust. During the grantor's lifetime the grantor might function as the trustee (unless replaced due to mental incompetency). The ownership of the policies will also often be transferred to the trust. Thereafter, the trustee will, for example, receive premium notices and directly pay periodic insurance premium obligations so as to maintain the insurance in force.

No federal tax advantages accrue from using a revocable trust (whether funded or unfunded). The gift is not complete for gift tax purposes and, accordingly, no gift tax liability accrues upon the creation of the trust, the transfer of the policy to the trust, or the periodic payment of insurance premiums.[163] At the grantor's death, the full value of the trust, including the entire proceeds of the life insurance, will be included in the grantor's gross estate.[164] The income of the trust during the grantor's lifetime, including the trust's income applied directly to pay policy premiums, is includible in the gross income of the grantor.[165]

(3) Irrevocable Lifetime Trust

An irrevocable life insurance trust can be created and the ownership of insurance policies can be irrevocably transferred to such a trust. The trust may be otherwise unfunded or may be funded with other financial assets. The unfunded irrevocable trust is ordinarily created by the transfer to an irrevocable trust of only the ownership of the life insurance policies. The trustees will have no funds with which to pay the premiums and those premiums must be paid by another person (e.g., the grantor or a trust beneficiary). The funded irrevocable trust is created upon a transfer of (1) insurance policies on the life of the trust grantor, plus (2) sufficient funds to be used to satisfy (or to generate income to satisfy) the periodic premium payment requirements.[166]

The transfer of the life insurance contracts to an irrevocable trust will be a completed gift for federal gift tax purposes, assuming no retained power by the trust grantor.[167] If the trust is funded with cash or similar assets to enable subsequent premium payments, the fair market value of these other assets transferred to the trust will also be transfers for gift tax purposes. If a trust is unfunded and the grantor pays the premiums on policies owned by the trust, these payments when made will constitute additional gifts.[168] A question can arise concerning the availability of the gift tax annual donee exclusion,[169] particularly if the trust is unfunded and annual transfers are necessary to maintain the policy in effect.[170] In these circumstances the trust should be structured so that the annual donee exclusion is available through the use of a demand (or *Crummey*) power.[171] This will necessitate giving the donee notice of the withdrawal power. Since thereafter this will probably be an annual event (as annual premium payments are made) the estate planner should consider reminding the trustee on a regular basis concerning the necessity of these notices to the trust beneficiaries of the right to withdrawal when premium payments are contributed to the trust.[172]

Since an irrevocable transfer will have been completed during life, no estate tax liabilities should arise upon the death of the grantor. The grantor must be careful not to retain any "incidents of ownership" in the life insurance policies held by the trust and insuring the grantor's life[173] or any beneficial life interest from the trust itself.[174] If the trust instrument directs the trustee to pay debts and taxes of the estate of the decedent from policy proceeds, the funds required for such purposes are includible in the decedent's gross estate.[175] The policy proceeds would also be includible in the gross estate if the policy is transferred to the trust within three years of death.[176]

Since an unfunded trust will not have gross income for income tax purposes, no income tax planning considerations arise in this context.[177] The grantor of a funded trust will be currently taxed on that portion of the income of the trust that is or may be applied to the payment of premiums on policies insuring the life of the grantor or the grantor's spouse.[178]

Another objective of such a trust (in addition to receiving estate tax-free funds) might be to have those funds available for providing liquidity and borrowing opportunities. For example, the insurance proceeds could be used to make loans to the insured's estate to enable the payment of taxes and expenses. Further, the trust could buy certain assets from a decedent's estate (or from a testamentary trust established under the decedent's will). Those assets in the decedent's estate would have an income tax basis stepped up to fair market value at the time of death (or as of the alternate valuation date). The assets might have significant appreciation potential. This subsequent appreciation could thereby be further protected from estate taxation (e.g., at the later death of a surviving spouse) by having the assets acquired by the irrevocable trust (which would not be subject to estate tax at the death of the surviving spouse). This trust might also be used to buy the remainder interest in assets in which the surviving spouse (or a marital deduction trust for his or her benefit) buys a life interest.[179]

(4) Testamentary Trusts

For nontax reasons a decedent/insured may wish to have proceeds of life insurance policies on his or her life paid into a trust created under his or her will, that is, a testamentary trust.[180] The usual dispositive arrangements are available through the use of a testamentary trust funded with life insurance proceeds.[181]

No transfer of the life insurance policy (or proceeds) will have been completed merely by designating the testamentary trustee as beneficiary of the life insurance proceeds. Consequently, no gift tax liability will attach at that time. Further, no estate tax benefits will be achieved by this arrangement. Assuming the insured to be the policy owner, the proceeds of the policies will be includible in the decedent's gross estate for estate tax purposes.[182]

(5) Preparation of the Insurance Trust Agreement

In preparing the trust instrument, the grantor and the trustee must carefully delineate the terms of the life insurance trust arrangement and the responsibilities and obligations of the various parties.[183] These would include:

- Is the trust to be funded or unfunded?
- If unfunded, who has the responsibility for paying periodic insurance premiums?
- If funded, who has the responsibility for paying periodic insurance premiums, particularly if the income generated internally from other trust assets is insufficient for this purpose?
- Is the trustee to be prohibited from using trust income to pay life insurance premiums?
- If trust investment income is in excess of any premium requirements, will that income be accumulated or distributed to trust beneficiaries?
- Will the insurance trust be revocable or irrevocable?
- Will policy proceeds be available after death to alleviate liquidity problems in the grantor's estate, either by a loan, a contribution to the estate (not appropriate for estate tax planning purposes), or a purchase of assets from the estate?
- Can (and should) the trustee use insurance policy settlement options to defer receipt of the proceeds after the death of the insured?
- What administrative powers will be given to the trustee (such as powers to use any corpus to pay insurance premiums and to purchase new policies on the life of the trust grantor or the trust grantor's spouse)?

The usual considerations pertinent to other kinds of trusts should also be analyzed, for example, how the assets are to be distributed and how the assets are to be managed by the fiduciary.

d. Insurance Planning and the Marital Deduction

(1) Use of the Unlimited Marital Deduction

If the trust grantor has a spouse, the insurance trust could be structured to hold assets qualifying for the unlimited marital deduction, assuming the trust assets are includible in the trust grantor's gross estate. This might include the use of one of the exceptions to the terminable interest rule.[184] Ordinarily, however, a better estate tax planning approach would be to cause the proceeds to be outside the gross estates of both spouses, accomplished through the use of an irrevocable life insurance trust, as described above.

(2) Spousal Cross-Ownership

If life insurance policies are owned directly (i.e., outside the trust context), spousal cross-ownership of life insurance policies is unnecessary to obtain estate tax deferral. The same estate tax result can occur where the insured retains the policy and makes the proceeds payable to his or her spouse, qualifying the transfer of the proceeds for the unlimited marital deduction.

Cross-ownership by spouses may still be advantageous in some situations, however. For example, the noninsured spouse can make subsequent policy assignments without the proceeds being subject to inclusion in the estate of the insured should the insured die within three years. For this reason, if the spouses are uncertain about the creation of an irrevocable insurance trust for the benefit of their children, the spouse of the insured should ordinarily make the initial purchase of the policy. This could be the first step toward eventually transferring the policy to an irrevocable insurance trust for the children. If that spouse dies first, the unmatured policy on the life of the surviving spouse could be transferred directly to the children under the will of that spouse without the policy returning to the insured (who cannot assign a policy on the insured's life free of the three-year inclusionary rule).[185]

Various disadvantages of policy cross-ownership can arise in this situation. In the event of divorce or incompetence of the owner-spouse, that owner-spouse (or his or her attorney-in-fact or guardian) is in control of the policy on the life of the other spouse. A prior death of the noninsured spouse creates a risk that the policy will return to the insured unless special planning is implemented.[186] Further, the stacking of assets in the estate of the noninsured spouse may result in greater overall estate taxes.

(3) Joint and Survivor Life Policies

The use of the unlimited marital deduction upon the death of the first spouse to die will shift liquidity needs to the estate of the surviving spouse and to the ultimate beneficiaries of a QTIP trust. An insurance policy providing "joint and survivor life" coverage may solve the liquidity problems that might arise at the death of the second spouse to die. The policy can be issued on the joint lives of the spouses. The proceeds are payable when the surviving spouse dies, that is, when funds are needed to pay estate taxes and related probate transfer costs. Premiums are often structured to be payable only until the first insured dies. The policy can be fully paid up to the face amount, becoming payable at the death of the second insured. If the spouses are in good health and approximately the same ages, the premiums may be significantly less than the premiums on several policies insuring the life of each spouse.

Several disadvantages to these policies do exist. Although such a policy is a whole life policy with significant cash value at the death of the first spouse, no proceeds are available to provide financial support for the surviving family. Borrowing against the cash value may be possible. The disposition of such a policy in the event of divorce may be unclear. Where the policy is owned as the separate property of one spouse, the estate taxation of this type of policy can be summarized as follows:

- If the non-owner-spouse dies first, all of the proceeds when subsequently received will be included in the surviving spouse's estate.
- If the owner-spouse dies first, the value of the policy will be included in that spouse's gross estate. If the policy is then transferred to someone other than the surviving spouse, no proceeds will be included in the surviving spouse's estate upon death. To enhance the possibility that the proceeds will be excluded from the estates of both spouses, the joint lives policy might be owned, therefore, as separate property by the spouse with the shorter life expectancy and at death bequeathed to someone other than the survivor. This ownership by a third party is the most secure method to have all proceeds excluded from the estates of both spouses. If the order of deaths cannot be ordinarily anticipated, the policy should be immediately transferred to children or a trust for children.[187] If the policy premiums are being paid with community

property funds these estate inclusion issues would arise to the extent of one-half to either spouse, suggesting ownership by a third party (including a trust) to remove the policy (and proceeds) from the estate of either spouse.

(4) Using the Irrevocable Life Insurance Trust

In larger estates, an irrevocable life insurance trust is particularly useful to maximize federal estate tax savings. Such a trust may be used to avoid having life insurance proceeds included in either spouse's estate. Further, the insurance proceeds can be available to provide liquidity to the estate of the insured (through loans or asset purchases) without gross estate inclusion.

Even with the deferral of estate taxes available through the use of the unlimited marital deduction, some taxes at the first death may be appropriate to equalize the estates and to moderate the impact of the highest tax bracket at the death of the surviving spouse. The irrevocable life insurance trust could indirectly provide liquidity to pay such taxes if the proceeds are received on the death of the first spouse to die. Even if all estate taxes are deferred at the death of the first spouse, the irrevocable life insurance trust, having received insurance proceeds after the death of the insured, may purchase appreciating assets from (1) the surviving spouse, (2) the deceased spouse's estate, or (3) a marital deduction trust. In this manner, appreciating securities or real estate might be transferred to the life insurance trust where the post-transfer appreciation will be sheltered from estate taxation upon the death of the surviving spouse. Under discretionary income distribution provisions of the trust, the survivor could receive cash that would provide income during life and, if not spent, liquidity to his or her estate at death.

Assuming it is not a marital deduction trust, the life insurance trust can be used to provide income to a lower bracket taxpayer (for income tax purposes) if the trust is drafted with "spray or sprinkle" provisions for the distribution of income. From the investment perspective, the proceeds received in an irrevocable life insurance trust could be invested in assets to grow the trust funds so as to help compensate for the extra estate taxes that might be incurred through the use of the unlimited marital deduction by the first spouse to die and through the stacking of assets into the surviving spouse's estate for federal estate tax purposes.

D. Commercial Annuities

1. Function and Structure of Annuities

An annuity is an arrangement whereby a person, in consideration for the payment of money (or the transfer of other valuable property), receives a contract under which periodic payments are to be received for his or her life or a specified term.[188] Alternatively, those payments might continue for the life or lives of designated survivors.[189]

The arrangement can be in the form of a "commercial annuity," that is, a payment commitment issued by a company regularly engaged in the business of issuing such undertakings, ordinarily a life insurance company. Alternatively, the arrangement can be in the form of a "private annuity," an agreement where an individual transfers cash or, usually, appreciated property, to another individual or to some entity (e.g., a trust or a closely held corporation) not normally engaged in issuing such annuity commitments.[190]

Commercial annuities can be purchased on an individual or a group basis. Often, when issued on a group basis, they are available under an employer-sponsored qualified pension and profit-sharing plan or other deferred compensation plan. Individual commercial annuity purchases are normally made for cash from a life insurance company regularly engaged in the business of issuing annuity contracts and in assuming such risks.

The annuity contract may provide for the periodic payment of a specified amount of dollars throughout a specified period, or it may be a variable annuity. The variable annuity has as its objective the better coverage of inflation risks (i.e., more dollars are expected to be available to be paid out to cover the decline in the annuitant's real purchasing power). The dollar amount of the variable annuity payments would depend upon the appreciation (if any) of the investment securities held by the insurance company to fund the variable annuity commitment in its contract with the annuitant. Of course, when the prices of securities (upon which the value of this annuity is based) are declining, the attractiveness of the variable annuity will also decline.

When the annuity purchase process has been completed, annuity payments will commence, either immediately or later, for example, upon the annuitant reaching some specified age. Annuities can be arranged with a variety of disbursement schedules. These might include (as examples): (1) annuity payments to one annuitant for his or her life; (2) payment of a lifetime annuity to an annuitant, with a similar payment made after his or her death to a designated survivor (e.g., the spouse or another person); or (3) payment of an annuity to one annuitant for his or her life and, at his or her death, a lump-sum payment to a designated beneficiary (the spouse or another person or his or her estate).

Often, the commercial annuity will include a "refund feature." This element assures the minimum return to the annuitant or a successor in interest of the original investment in the contract.[191] A "refund feature" payable at death (because the investment in the annuity has not been fully recovered at the time of death) constitutes a nonannuity element incorporated into the annuity contract. Therefore, as noted below, an amount allocable to the value of this "refund feature" will not constitute an amount paid for the annuity itself. The "investment in the contract" will be reduced by the amount deemed paid for the refund feature (as amount paid for the annuitant's dying too soon).

2. Annuity Income Taxation

The income tax treatment of annuity payments received by a taxpayer is specified in §72. The taxpayer must first determine the amount of "investment in the contract." This is the cost for the annuity contract, reduced by the value of that portion of the total cost attributable to a refund feature, if any.[192] A percentage is then determined that constitutes the portion of each annuity payment attributable to the "investment in the contract."[193] That percentage of each future annuity payment represents a return of capital investment in the annuity contract. The remainder of each payment is treated as annuity income (an interest income equivalent) to be included in the gross income of the annuitant.[194]

The gross income exclusion is limited to the amount of the actual investment in the contract (or tax basis).[195] Accordingly, when the investment has been recovered, additional annuity payments will be fully includible in gross income. The annuitant may die before the time of the recovery of the entire investment in the annuity contract.[196] In this situation an income tax deduction is allowed (to the annuitant on his or her federal income tax return for his or her last taxable year) if the annuity terminates without a complete recovery of investment in the contract.[197]

The annuitant may seek to withdraw funds from the annuity before its specified starting date. The early withdrawal of the investment in an annuity contract will result in immediate gross income to the annuitant to the extent that the cash value of the contract (computed without surrender charges) exceeds the investment in the contract immediately before the distribution.[198] Dividends or similar distributions (to the extent not retained by the insurer as an additional premium), policy loans, and assignments or pledges (agreements to assign or pledge) of the policyholder's interest in the contract are treated as cash withdrawals.[199]

3. Estate Tax

The principal estate tax provision relevant to estate tax inclusion of annuities is §2039,[200] which specifies that the gross estate shall include:

- the value of an annuity or other payment;
- receivable by any beneficiary by reason of surviving the decedent;
- under any form of contract or agreement other than under insurance policies on the life of the decedent; and
- if under such contract an annuity was payable to the decedent or the decedent possessed the right to receive such annuity or payment, either alone or in conjunction with another for his or her life or for any period not ascertainable without reference to his or her death or for any period which does not in fact end before his or her death.[201]

The essence of this provision is that under the annuity contract funded by the decedent, value must pass at death to some successor who thereafter will receive annuity payments.

To be includible in the gross estate, the annuity must have been acquired by the decedent with the decedent's funds. Where a part of an annuity payment payable to the beneficiary is due to contributions made by someone other than the decedent (e.g., a spouse), only that part of the payment attributable to the contributions made by the decedent is includible in the decedent's gross estate. Contributions by an employer made by reason of employment of the annuitant are considered to be made by the employee.[202]

In summary, the following estate tax results occur with respect to annuities:

- A one-life, nonrefundable annuity will not be subject to estate tax on the death of the annuitant since, at the death of the annuitant, the contract terminates and all annuity benefits (and the value of the contract) are extinguished.[203]
- If the contract is to pay an annual sum for a person's life, provided, however, that, if he or she should die before he or she has recovered the full purchase price, the balance would be paid to the annuitant's designated beneficiary, that refundable amount is includible in the annuitant's gross estate.[204]
- If the contract provides for the receipt of periodic payments for an annuitant's life and, thereafter, for the life of a survivor (a survivorship annuity), the value of that survivorship right is includible in the annuitant's gross estate.[205]

E. Charitable Transfers

1. Basic Tax Planning Objectives

a. Tax Planning Issues

Transfers for charitable purposes can generate substantial federal income and estate tax savings.[206] A wide variety of techniques have developed to maximize these tax savings opportunities.[207] The following discussion analyzes: (1) which organizations are eligible recipients of deductible "charitable contributions"; (2) what variations are permissible for differing types of gifts (including, particularly, appreciated property gifts and split-interest transfers); (3) applicable percentage limitations, if any, on this deduction; (4) the private charitable foundation rules; and (5) various planning considerations.[208] This discussion deals with both the income tax planning and the estate tax planning as relevant in the charitable gift context.

b. Income Tax Benefits

The income tax deduction for charitable contributions can effectively function to shelter other gross income, thereby limiting the reduction of the donor's accumulated capital while, simultaneously, currently satisfying the donor's charitable objectives.[209]

Example: In 2015, a donor (in a 39.6% marginal tax bracket)[210] transfers 100 shares of stock of a publicly listed company that he had held for more than one year directly to a public charity. The stock was purchased for $1,000, but the value at the time of the transfer is $10,000. Assuming no percentage limitations apply, the donor will receive an income tax deduction for $10,000, without being required to recognize the $9,000 of capital appreciation as gross income. The net after-tax cost of the transaction to the taxpayer (assuming the stock would otherwise have been sold) can be computed as follows: (1) the value (or cost) of the gift ($10,000) less tax savings attributable to deduction ($3,960) is $6,040; (2) the capital gains tax saved (assuming 20% tax under §1(h) on the $9,000 of untaxed capital gain) is $1,800; and (3) the net after tax cost of the $10,000 charitable contribution ($6,040 less $1,800) is $4,240.[211]

This example demonstrates that the net real cost of a charitable contribution can be significantly moderated, particularly where significant accrued property appreciation need not be included as gross income but the entire fair market value of the contributed property can be claimed as a charitable contributions deduction for federal income tax purposes to offset the highest taxed income.

Even though (as noted below) an estate tax charitable contributions deduction is available, the client with a charitable bequest specified in his or her will should consider making the gift during lifetime, enhancing the overall income tax benefits. That person might specifically authorize in his or her durable power of attorney the right to prepay during lifetime any charitable bequests specified in the last will. A further possibility would be to transfer a specified amount to the surviving spouse with a nonbinding request to the spouse that this amount be contributed to charity. Assuming a nonbinding request (so that the marital deduction is not vitiated) the surviving spouse would then have the benefit of the charitable deduction for federal income tax purposes.

c. Estate Tax Benefits

The estate tax charitable contributions deduction can also be effectively used to achieve substantial tax savings.

Example: Assume that a decedent with a substantial estate dies with a surviving spouse but no children or other close relatives. If he transfers his property to a marital deduction/qualified charitable remainder trust arrangement, no federal estate tax liability will accrue either at his death or the death of the surviving spouse. Further, the decedent can be assured that the property will ultimately be received by charity. Alternatively, for example, using the unlimited marital deduction, the property could be transferred outright to the surviving spouse at the death of the first spouse to die and, thereafter, all property remaining at the surviving spouse's subsequent death could be transferred by that spouse to charity, thereby entirely avoiding estate tax.[212]

Unlike under the income tax, no percentage limitations apply for federal estate tax for contributions made to charity. Therefore, federal estate tax can be completely avoided through the death transfer of assets to charity, including to a private charitable foundation.[213]

2. Eligible Charitable Recipients

A charitable contribution for income tax purposes[214] means a contribution or gift to or for the use of[215]:

- a government entity (e.g., the United States, a state, or political subdivision), if the gift is for exclusively public purposes[216];
- a corporation, trust, or community chest, fund, or foundation[217] if: (1) created or organized in the United States or in any possession thereof, or under the law of the United States, any state, the District of Columbia, or any possession of the United States[218]; (2) organized and operated exclusively for religious, charitable, scientific, literary, or educational purposes, for fostering national or international amateur sports competition, or for the prevention of cruelty to children or animals[219]; (3) no part of its net earnings inures to the benefit of any private shareholder or individual[220]; and (4) it is not disqualified for tax exemption under §501(c)(3) for attempting to influence legislation and it does not intervene or participate in any political campaign on behalf of any candidate for political office[221];
- a post or organization of war veterans, or an auxiliary unit or society of, or trust or foundation for, any such post or organization, if: (1) organized in the United States or any of its possessions, and (2) no part of its net earnings inures to the benefit of any private shareholder or individual[222]; or
- a domestic fraternal society, order, or association operating under the lodge system, but only if the contribution is to be used exclusively for religious, charitable, scientific, literary, or educational purposes, or for the prevention of cruelty to children or animals.[223]

The donor will want to verify that, at the time of the charitable gift, the recipient actually has charitable status as recognized by the IRS. For larger gifts the prospective donor may also want some representation from the charity that charitable tax status remains existent and, perhaps, even a grant agreement specifying that the gift will be returned if the existence (or type) of charitable status was misrepresented.[224]

3. Types of Charitable Transfers

a. Property Transfer Options

Charitable gifts can be completed by a direct and outright gift or by a transfer of a partial interest (perhaps subject to trust restrictions).[225] The transfer can be of cash or property (tangible or intangible).[226] The availability and the amount of the income tax deduction depends on both (1) the type of property being transferred and (2) the type of recipient of this property.

b. Contributions of Property

(1) Benefits from Property Contributions

A donor may contribute a capital asset (eligible for long-term capital gain treatment) that has appreciated substantially in value over its cost basis.[227] Although a sale would produce substantial capital gain, the income inclusion of this gain might be avoided by a charitable transfer, with the present fair market value of the gifted property being allowable as a charitable deduction (without regard to original cost). The gain realized on a later sale by the charitable organization of the contributed property would not be taxable to the recipient charity since the income of that organization is exempt from federal income taxes.[228]

Depreciated property should not be transferred to charity. If the fair market value of the asset is lower than its cost, the asset should be sold by the donor so that the loss can be realized by the owner for income tax purposes. The sales proceeds could then be transferred to charity, permitting a deduction for the amount of cash transferred.

(2) Capital Gain Property

If long-term capital gain property such as appreciated securities or real property (i.e., other than tangible personal property, except in limited circumstances) is transferred to a public charity, the entire value, including the appreciation component, of the gift is deductible for income tax purposes, but the appreciation is not includible in gross income.[229]

Example: X gives to the American Red Cross, a public charity (and not a private charitable foundation), 100 shares of publicly listed company stock that he purchased several years ago for $100 per share and that at the time of this transfer has a value of $250 per share. The amount of the charitable deductible gift would be $25,000 (100 shares times $250 per share), subject to the possible percentage limitation. Further, the $15,000 gain need not be included in the income tax base.

If stock (but not other appreciated property) is transferred to a "private foundation," this charitable contributions deduction for the fair market value is also available, assuming the stock to be "qualified appreciated stock," that is, shares of a publicly listed corporation for which market quotations are available.[230] Any condition that will limit the marketability of this stock can disqualify the stock from the benefit of this rule. Corporate stock can often be subject to special transfer restrictions, such as those under SEC Rule 144.[231] Rule 144 can limit the sale of corporate stock, and the IRS will then take the position that this stock is not readily tradable in the securities markets and, therefore, is not "qualified appreciated stock." Stock that is not publicly tradable but is convertible into stock that is publicly tradable will also not be qualified in this context.[232]

If tangible personal property is contributed for charitable purposes (to a public charity), the amount of the available deduction depends on whether the use by the donee of the contributed property is related to the purpose or function constituting the basis for the recipient organization's exemption.[233] In the "unrelated use" situation, the available charitable contributions deduction amount is reduced by the long-term capital gain component of the gift.[234]

Example: A Picasso painting given to an art museum will be deductible to the extent of its fair market value, but not if the same painting is donated to a church. The museum presumably would retain the painting for its collection, but the church probably would promptly sell that painting to generate funds for church purposes (rather than placing it on display at the church).

This reduction of the charitable contributions deduction is somewhat equivalent to treating the donor as the seller of this property except when the donee is not anticipated to promptly sell this donated property.

(3) Ordinary Income Property

All charitable contributions of ordinary income property, regardless of the identity of the charitable donee, are required to be reduced for income tax deduction purposes by the amount of ordinary income which would have resulted had the contributed property been sold at its fair market value (as determined at the time of contribution).[235] Ordinary income property is defined as "property any portion of the gain on which would not have been long-term capital gain if the property had been sold by the donor at its fair market value at the time of its contribution to the charitable organization."[236] This also includes §306 stock.[237]

Certain corporate charitable contributions of inventory and similar property will be deductible, limited to the extent of the taxpayer's basis in the property and one-half of the unrealized appreciation.[238] This deduction is limited, however, to an amount that is twice the tax basis of the property.

(4) Possible Assignment of Income Risk

Even though property is apparently transferred, in some situations the donor might need to be concerned about the possible applicability of the "assignment of income" doctrine.[239] In this context, the charitable contributions deduction would be available for the amount contributed, but that amount constituting income would also be required to be included in gross income.[240] The risk that then arises is that the charitable contribution deduction may not be fully utilized because of the percentage limitation on charitable contributions and because of other limitations.[241]

(5) Bargain Sales

A "bargain sale" is a sale of property (ordinarily appreciated capital gain property) to charity for a price less than its fair market value. This sale might be arranged where, for example, the seller is prepared to contribute some portion of the value of property to charity but also needs to receive some cash from the transfer (perhaps for living expenses while elderly). In this situation, a charitable deduction will be available for the amount of the charitable transfer, but some of the accrued gain will be required to be recognized on the property transfer.[242]

For federal income tax purposes, in a bargain sale transaction the tax basis of the transferor for this property must be allocated between the "sale" and "gift" portions of the property.[243] Taxable gain is to be recognized on the "sale portion" in the transaction. The transferor, however, is permitted to deduct as a charitable contribution the entire excess of the fair market value of the property over its sales price.[244]

Example: X sold stock worth $1,000 to a charity for the amount of $600. The stock had been originally purchased for $600. X must allocate to the sale component of this transaction that portion of his tax basis that bears the same ratio to his basis as (1) the "sales price" ($600) bears to (2) the fair market value ($1,000) of the property when transferred.

(1) Computation of basis allocation:

$600 total fair market value times 600/1,000 = $360

(i.e., basis for property portion being sold)

(2) Capital gain to be recognized—$240
($600 sales price less $360 allocated basis)
(3) Charitable contributions deduction—$400
($1,000 value transferred less $600 received)

The net effect in this example is that the charitable contribution deduction amount will be in excess of the gain required to be recognized.[245] This results because the appreciation from the $400 contributed portion is not required (under this bargain sale rule) to be included in gross income. Further, a tax rate differential will be realized, since the charitable contributions deduction can be used to offset ordinary income otherwise taxed at ordinary income tax rates while the gain is taxed at the lower capital gains tax rate.

(6) Gifts of Insurance Policies

Because of its unique capability of transferring value at death, the transfer of life insurance benefits is often a convenient method for transferring wealth in the estate planning context.[246] The following are possible options in this context:

- naming the charity as the beneficiary under a policy currently owned by the insured;
- purchasing a new life insurance policy and naming the charity as the owner and beneficiary;
- contributing to charity a paid-up policy already owned by changing the owner and the beneficiary; and
- contributing the ownership of a policy on which the insured is continuing to pay premiums.

An existing policy may be used to complete a current charitable contribution because the policy was intended to protect a spouse or child and that protection is no longer necessary; a policy may have been acquired to support, if necessary, the payment of a home mortgage, and that mortgage may have been paid; a policy may have been acquired to provide adequate retirement income, but other investment sources may have become adequate; or a policy may have been inherited from parents who purchased a policy on the life of the donor and that coverage is no longer necessary. In each of these instances, the policy itself can be given to charity, with the deduction available for the then fair market value of the policy.

c. Partial Interests—Nontrust Transfers

A donor may decide to contribute only a partial interest in property to charity. This partial interest might be of property held either in trust or held directly, that is, not in trust. Examples include: (1) a transfer of a fractional property interest to charity, with the charity and the donor then being tenants in common; (2) the creation of a life estate for the donor's spouse, with the remainder contributed to charity; or (3) the creation of a term interest for charity with the remainder interest to a private beneficiary.

A deduction will be allowed under §170, §2055, or §2522 for a transfer not in trust only if the transferred interest is:

- the taxpayer's entire interest in the property[247];
- an undivided portion of the taxpayer's entire interest in property[248];
- a remainder interest in the taxpayer's personal residence or farm[249]; or
- a qualified conservation contribution.[250]

In the last three situations, the donor would have limited opportunity to manage the property for his or her own benefit after the completion of the partial interest gift, which could frustrate the charitable benefit being transferred.

Special limitations apply to life insurance subject to split ownership arrangements between an individual and a charity. A charitable deduction is disallowed for any split-dollar life insurance arrangement between a charity and the insured (or other private party) where the charity is either paying premiums or where an understanding or expectation exists that such premiums will be paid.[251]

d. Charitable Lead Trusts

(1) Description of Structure

A charitable donor may create a trust with divided beneficial ownership, that is, to charity for a specified term (or for the duration of a measuring life), with the remainder to private beneficiaries (often younger-generation family members). Consequently, in a charitable lead trust situation the charitable interest precedes the remainder interest (which passes to private, noncharitable beneficiaries upon expiration of the precedent interest).[252] This effectively enables a donor to benefit charity while, upon the lapse of the intervening period, retaining the asset in the donor's family.[253] Such a trust may be created by a donor either during lifetime or at death.[254]

(2) Available Income Tax Charitable Deduction

To deduct for federal income tax purposes a charitable gift of an income or "lead" interest (1) that is less than the donor's entire interest in property and (2) that the donor transfers into trust, the income interest for charity must be in the form of (1) an annuity trust interest[255] or (2) a unitrust interest.[256] These trusts are often referred to as "charitable lead trusts." The requirements are similar for estate tax and for gift tax.[257]

To be eligible for a charitable deduction for income tax purposes, the grantor must be the "owner" of the interest under the grantor trust rules and will be taxable on the trust income.[258] As described below, the better approach may be for the charitable lead trust to be a nongrantor trust from its inception. If the donor ceases after inception of the trust to be treated as the "owner" for income tax purposes, he or she will be considered as having received at that time gross income equal to the amount of any income tax deduction previously received for the contribution, as reduced by the discounted value (discounted to the date of contribution) of the income earned by the trust and taxable to him or her before that time.[259] No charitable deduction is allowed, therefore, for a gift of an income interest unless: (1) the interest of the charity is guaranteed by the nature of the transfer, and (2) for income tax purposes, the grantor will be taxable on the income of the trust. Consequently, the trust grantor cannot (1) receive a charitable contributions income tax deduction for the gift of income while (2) not being required to include that income in his or her gross income for income tax purposes.

Notwithstanding these restrictions, some flexibility is available in administering the trust to achieve benefits for the grantor and the remainder beneficiaries. For example, through the investment of the corpus in low-yield, high-growth stocks, the income currently attributable to the trust grantor for federal income tax purposes could be minimized. The objective would be to realize a greater "total return" on the investment than that to be paid to charity in an annuity trust situation. That gain would accrue economically through capital appreciation but remain unrealized and, therefore, would not be taxable to the trust grantor. The net economic gain would eventually accrue for the benefit of the private remainder beneficiaries. The ordinary income received by the trust may be less than the annuity amount, thereby causing "principal cash" to be used to partially fund the annuity payments.

(3) Avoiding the Charitable Lead Trust Requirements

An alternative in this context is to structure the trust not as a grantor trust but, rather, as a nongrantor trust. The grantor will not be entitled to a charitable deduction for federal income tax purposes but will not have derived currently income from the trust. In this situation, the nongrantor trust itself will be entitled to the charitable income tax deduction in an unlimited amount for gross income paid to charity.[260] The more important element, however is that the trust income will not be includible in the income of the grantor, effectively being deflected to the trust, which has the charitable contributions deduction. This means that the trust grantor will have no income but will also have no charitable deduction for income tax purposes. This alternative can be particularly important where, because of charitable deduction percentage limitations, or other restrictions, the charitable contributions deduction would not be available to fully offset the impact of the inclusion of the trust income in the trust grantor's gross income.

(4) Description of Charitable Lead Trust Structuring Options

A charitable lead annuity trust is an arrangement where a fixed dollar amount or fixed percentage of the initial net fair market value of the trust assets is to be paid to one or more charitable organizations for the term of the trust.[261] In contrast, a charitable lead unitrust is a trust where a fixed percentage of the net fair market value of the trust assets, as redetermined annually, is to be paid to one or more charitable organizations for the term of the trust.[262]

(5) Planning Benefits and Valuation

The charitable lead trust is particularly attractive to donors in high estate and gift tax brackets who wish to make a charitable gift of the income or "lead" interest while ultimately passing substantial amounts of property to the noncharitable beneficiaries (usually family members) who receive the remainder interest. The annuity form is usually used to simplify valuation requirements and to pass the appreciation in value to the remainder beneficiaries. The trust may be structured so that no transfer tax is owing upon establishment of the trust.[263]

The use of a charitable lead trust at the time of death, in conjunction with any use of the unified credit, can be quite effective, assuming the children can wait until some future date to receive their inheritances. This occurs because the charitable lead portion is deductible for estate tax purposes. The children in this situation could even be permitted to designate the charitable recipients, thereby enabling them to provide benefits to their favorite charities.

The value of the lead interest will vary depending on the precise valuation date, because §7520 requires transfers to be valued using an interest rate that is 120% of the federal midterm rate (determined under §1274(d)) for the month in which the valuation date falls. If any part of the property transferred qualifies for a charitable contribution deduction, the taxpayer may elect to value the interest using the interest rate in effect for either of the two months preceding the valuation date.[264] Ordinarily, the specified annuity rate will be similar to the §7520 valuation rate, providing for no differential in value. However, if trust assets can be invested at a rate of return in excess of the interest rate used to value the remainder interest, the excess earnings or growth can be accumulated and ultimately (upon the lapse of the intermediate interest) passed on to the donor's heirs at no transfer tax cost.

e. Charitable Remainder Trusts

(1) Types of Charitable Remainder Trusts

Rather than providing a lead interest to charity a donor may wish to provide a remainder interest to charity. Many reasons exist for such an arrangement but this situation often arises where one spouse wishes to provide for the other during that spouse's survival, with the remainder then going to charity, particularly if no children survive. A charitable contribution deduction is immediately allowed for the value of a remainder interest transferred to charity in trust if the trust is[265]:

- a charitable remainder annuity trust[266];
- a charitable remainder unitrust[267]; or
- a pooled income fund.[268]

These charitable remainder trust transfers can be concluded either during lifetime or at death.[269] In the marital transfer context, another alternative is the QTIP trust with a charitable remainder.[270]

If the transfer is made during life, the grantor of a charitable remainder annuity trust or a charitable remainder unitrust is entitled to an income tax charitable deduction and a gift tax charitable deduction based on the present value of the remainder interest which is to ultimately pass to charity. For gift tax purposes, a gift of the income interest might also be made if the income beneficiary is other than the grantor.[271] If no gift tax event occurs but a noncharitable individual beneficiary has an interest at the time of death of the trust grantor, that portion would be exposed to inclusion in the estate tax base.

(2) Income Tax Treatment of Charitable Remainder Trusts

A charitable remainder trust is itself not subject to income tax but (for taxable years beginning after 2006) is subject to a 100% excise tax on any "unrelated business taxable income" the trust has during a taxable year.[272] All or part of its income ordinarily will be distributed currently to the beneficiary of the lead interest in the charitable remainder trust. When distributions are made from the charitable remainder trust to the noncharitable beneficiary, those payments are deemed to be sourced from the trust in the following order: (1) from ordinary income (both current year and accumulated income); (2) from capital gains; (3) from other income (e.g., tax-exempt income); and (4) from trust principal.[273] Consequently, the initial receipt of this income by a charitable, exempt trust will not immunize that income since it is subject to income tax when distributed to the private beneficiary (and distribution is mandated for some or all of that income).

(3) Charitable Remainder Annuity Trusts

A charitable remainder annuity trust is a trust from which a fixed sum (not less than 5% or more than 50%) of the net fair market value of its assets (as valued when originally placed into trust) is to be distributed not less often than annually to the lead, noncharitable beneficiary, with the remainder being distributable to or for the use of a qualified charity.[274] Also, the value of the charitable remainder interest must be at least 10% of the value of the initial net fair market value of all property contributed to the trust.[275]

Example (1): X bequeaths $100,000 to trustees under his will with instructions to pay his surviving spouse $5,000 annually for her life, with the remainder thereafter being distributable to a qualified charity. The $5,000 annuity satisfies the 5% minimum and 50% maximum payout requirements. The trust could fail the 10% minimum remainder requirement, depending on the surviving spouse's age and the applicable §7520 rate on the funding date.

Example (2): X bequeaths the residue of his estate to trustees with instructions to pay annually a sum equal to 5% of the net fair market value of the trust property, as finally determined for federal estate tax purposes, to his surviving spouse for life, with the remainder distributable to a qualified charity. As in the preceding example, this annuity satisfies the payout requirements but the trust will need to be evaluated under the 10% minimum remainder requirement applicable as of the funding.[276]

In either of these situations, the private beneficiary of the lead interest would receive each year a determinable amount without regard to the actual income received by the trust for the year.[277] The annuity payment period must be for the life or lives of the individual beneficiaries (all of whom must be living at the time the trust is created) or for a term of years, not in excess of 20 years.[278] After the initial funding, no additional contributions may be made to a charitable remainder annuity trust (but this limitation is not applicable to a charitable remainder unitrust).[279]

(4) Charitable Remainder Unitrusts

A charitable remainder unitrust specifies that a fixed percentage (not less than 5% or more than 50%) of the fair market value of the trust assets (valued annually) is to be distributed not less often than annually to a noncharitable beneficiary, with the remainder distributable to or for the use of a qualified charity.[280] Also, for each contribution of property to the trust, the value of the charitable remainder interest in such property must be at least 10% of the net fair market value of such property on the date of contribution.[281]

Example: X bequeaths $100,000 to trustees under his will with instructions to pay annually 5% of the net fair market value of the trust property to B for life, with the remainder to a qualified charity. That value is to be determined on December 31 of each year. The 5% unitrust amount satisfies the 5% minimum and 50% maximum payout requirements. However, B's age and the applicable §7520 rate on the date of funding will determine if the trust complies with the 10% minimum remainder requirement.

The payment period must be for the life or lives of the individual beneficiaries (all of whom must be living at the time the trust is created) or for a term of years, not in excess of 20 years.[282]

The unitrust concept permits the beneficiary of the lead interest to receive a specified percentage of the total value of all assets in trust (including accumulated income and unrealized appreciation or depreciation), determined as of a specified date each year and without regard to the actual income of the trust for the year.[283] In this manner, the unitrust, unlike the annuity trust, can function as a hedge against inflation (assuming trust asset values increase at least equal to the rate of inflation).[284]

A unitrust may be a "net income only" unitrust, providing for the payment of the lesser of (1) the fixed percentage or (2) the net income of the trust.[285] This provision can enable more flexibility in investment planning by avoiding the forced sale of assets to obtain funds to satisfy a payout requirement. Consequently, this approach can permit the trust to be initially funded with non-income-producing assets.

This trust may have a "make-up" provision specifying that any amount by which the trust income falls short of the specified percentage (during this "net income only" period) is to be distributed in later years to the extent that the trust's income exceeds the fixed percentage in subsequent years.[286] This make-up provision can enable the investment in growth assets, with the postponement of income distributions, the subsequent sale of those growth assets (without the imposition of income tax on the trust), the reinvestment of those proceeds in financial assets, and the payment of the subsequent investment income received from a much larger base to "make up" earlier shortfalls. This could be convenient, for example, for the supplementation of income during the donor's retirement period (after the donor did not need this income during the pre-retirement phase). The investments for such a unitrust to enable income deferral might include a zero coupon bond in addition to "growth stocks."

In summary, three options are available in the unitrust context: (1) a standard unitrust; (2) a net income unitrust; and (3) a net income unitrust with a make-up provision. If certain requirements are satisfied, a charitable remainder trust can be structured to include a "flip" provision whereby, for example, it commences as a net income unitrust and subsequently changes to a standard unitrust.[287]

(5) Pooled Income Funds

A deduction is also allowed for the value of a charitable remainder interest in property transferred into a "pooled income fund." A pooled income fund is an arrangement by which the donor contributes property to a public charity, retaining for himself or herself (or others) an income interest for life, with an irrevocable remainder interest held by the charity.[288] The property contributed by the donor is commingled by the charitable recipient with property transferred by other donors. The fund must be maintained by the public charity to which the irrevocable remainder interest is contributed.[289] Each income beneficiary is to receive each year an amount of income determined by the rate of return earned by the entire fund for that year.[290] For purposes of computing the amount of the charitable contribution deduction, the present value of the remainder interest contributed to charity is determined by computing the present value of the life income interest at the time of the transfer and subtracting it from the fair market value of the transferred property on the appropriate valuation date.[291]

(6) IRS Procedures Concerning Charitable Remainder Trusts

The requirements for structuring charitable remainder trusts are extremely complicated and drafting errors are not uncommon. To mitigate these risks, the IRS has published several revenue procedures indicating the type of language acceptable in preparing instruments implementing such arrangements.[292] Because the IRS has issued these revenue procedures, the IRS will not ordinarily rule concerning whether a charitable remainder trust that provides for annuity or unitrust payments for one or two measuring lives or for annuity or unitrust payments for a term of years satisfies the statutory requirements.[293] If the charitable remainder trust provisions do not satisfy the statutory standards, under some circumstances a reformation is permitted.[294] In some circumstances the parties may determine to terminate the charitable remainder trust prior to the expiration of the specified lead interest with the division of the trust assets being made between the noncharitable beneficiary and the charitable remainder beneficiary based on the then existing actuarial values of the several interests. However, the IRS will not rule whether this transaction will cause the trust to lose its status as a charitable remainder trust within the meaning of §664.[295]

f. Gift Annuities

Another charitable gift option that is similar to a charitable remainder annuity trust is the charitable gift annuity. Under a gift annuity, the donor transfers a specific amount of money or property to a charitable organization in exchange for a promise from the charity to pay an annuity for life to the donor (or other beneficiaries). The gift annuity is designed to provide a benefit to charity in the amount of value transferred to the charity in excess of the value of the lifetime payments reserved for the beneficiaries.[296] This excess benefit amount enables a current income tax charitable deduction. For the period of the annuity, the annuitant receives payments to use for his or her own purposes.

Although charities are not limited in the interest rate assumptions inherent in the gift annuity rates, many charities base the annuity payout on annuity rates recommended by the American Council on Gift Annuities.[297] The usual assumption is that the charity will have approximately 50% of the original amount contributed for the gift annuity remaining for the charity at the death of the annuity beneficiaries.[298]

A transfer of property to a charity in exchange for a gift annuity is considered to be an immediate gift to a charity under the bargain sale rules.[299] Any gain will be treated as realized under those bargain sale rules. Consequently, if the assets transferred are long-term appreciated securities, real property, or tangible personal property (that the charity uses for its charitable purposes), a portion of the capital gain will not be included in the tax base (i.e., the gain portion attributable to the gift segment). Payments received under a gift annuity are taxable under the regular annuity rules.[300]

An alternative planning option in this context could be to combine a gift to a grandchild with a gift annuity approach. For example, a grandparent may want to remove assets from his or her estate while creating an educational fund for a grandchild. This might be accomplished through the use of a deferred annuity for the grandchild, with the charity as the remainder beneficiary. The annuity for the private beneficiary could be payable during the period that the grandchild is anticipated to be incurring educational expenses. The gift annuity would be a gift for gift tax purposes and a charitable deduction would be available for the value received by the charity in the transaction.

4. Percentage Limitations

a. Income Tax

The income tax provisions include percentage limitations on the amount of the available charitable deduction. These limitations vary, depending on (1) the type of organization to which the contribution is made,[301] (2) the type of property contributed,[302] and (3) the type of taxpayer making the contribution, that is, individual or corporation.[303]

In general, contributions by individuals to charitable organizations may be deducted in an amount up to 50% of a donor's adjusted gross income (computed without regard to any net operating loss carryback for the year).[304] A special 30% limitation applies, however, to capital gain property and contributions "for the use of" any organization.[305] Contributions to certain nonoperating foundations are subject to a 30% limitation for contributions of cash and ordinary income property and to a 20% limitation for contributions of capital gain property.[306] A five-year carryover is allowed for excess contributions.[307]

b. Estate Tax

The estate tax provisions do not contain any percentage limitations on charitable deductions comparable to those applicable to income tax deductions. Consequently, a decedent can transfer his or her entire estate to charity (including, for example, to a private charitable foundation), thereby avoiding any federal estate tax liability for his or her estate.

The amount of the estate tax deduction for any charitable transfer may not exceed the value of the transferred property required to be included in the gross estate.[308] The estate, of course, must have sufficient funds available for full payment of the charitable bequest to obtain the deduction.[309]

Under either the terms of the will, by the law of the jurisdiction under which the estate is administered, or by the law of the jurisdiction imposing the particular tax, the federal estate tax or any other estate, succession, legacy, or inheritance taxes may be payable in whole or in part out of the bequests, legacies, or devises otherwise deductible under §2055. Consequently, the amount deductible is the amount of the bequests, legacies, or devises as reduced by the amount of these taxes.[310] The function of this rule is to assure that the deduction is based on the amount actually available for charitable uses.[311]

The testator should clearly specify in his or her will that a charitable transfer is not liable pro rata for death taxes (assuming this tax immunity result is intended by the testator).[312] Otherwise, an applicable state law tax allocation statute might produce a result contrary to that intended by the testator (i.e., a reduction of the amount of the charitable contribution and, therefore, of the allowable estate tax charitable deduction).

5. Private Foundations

A valuable tool in completing charitable transfers can be the use of a "private foundation."[313] The charitable private foundation (and its investments) can be controlled by the donors, although subject to the limitation that the assets must be maintained for charitable purposes. The private foundation, for example, permits a donor to make an income tax–deductible charitable contribution (to the private foundation), although he or she has not yet definitively determined the ultimate recipient of these funds or how those funds will be otherwise ultimately devoted to charitable purposes.

Substantial limitations are imposed on private foundations to assure that they actually do function for charitable purposes. Practitioners often differ concerning whether these limitations negate the use of a private foundation but, for large transfers, the foundation is often a useful option.[314] These restrictions include the possible imposition of excise taxes on:

- self-dealing[315];
- failure to distribute income[316];
- excess business holdings[317];

- investments that jeopardize charitable purposes[318]; and
- taxable expenditures.[319]

Charitable remainder annuity trusts and charitable remainder unitrusts are subject to certain of these private foundation rules.[320] The specific excise taxes that apply are those on self-dealing, excess business holdings, investments that jeopardize charitable purposes, and taxes on taxable expenditures.[321]

6. Procedural Requirements

A wide variety of procedural and reporting requirements are applicable in the charitable deductions context to assure that the deduction is appropriate:

- No income tax charitable deduction is available for a separate contribution of $250 or more unless the taxpayer has a written receipt or other acknowledgement from the charity of the contribution (including an estimate of the value of any goods or services provided to the taxpayer in exchange for making the gift). A canceled check is not adequate substantiation for this purpose.[322]
- To enable an income tax deduction for a contribution of property valued in excess of $500 the donor must obtain a more detailed receipt from the donee organization.[323]
- If the contributed property has a value in excess of $5,000 ($10,000 for nonpublicly traded stock), the donor must obtain a qualified appraisal of the property for an income tax deduction.[324]
- If the donee charity sells donated property for which an appraisal summary was filed within three years after the gift, the charity must report this sale.[325]
- Each fundraising solicitation on behalf of a charitable organization must identify the portion of a contribution or gift that is not deductible as a charitable contribution.[326]
- A charitable organization must disclose if it receives a quid pro quo contribution in excess of $75.[327]
- An IRS procedure exists for obtaining an IRS Statement of Value fixing the value of a contribution, gift, or bequest of an art work for income, estate, or gift tax purposes.[328]

The regulations require estates to submit certain information to establish the right to an estate tax charitable deduction.[329]

7. Planning Considerations

Each situation involving a potentially large charitable transfer must be carefully analyzed with respect to its income tax and its estate tax impact. The fundamental inquiry often is whether (1) the gift should be completed during lifetime (enabling present income tax savings), (2) the gift should be made at the time of death, or (3) property should be transferred to survivors (with those survivors making charitable gifts with stepped-up basis property and obtaining income tax deductions for themselves rather than for the estate). For example:

- If the donor is elderly and intends to transfer substantial assets to his or her spouse, the income tax savings from the proposed charitable gift might be postponed, with the spouse receiving all assets by reason of an unlimited marital deduction and, thereafter, making a charitable contribution.
- If the donor is elderly and has a charitable contributions deduction carryover, any carryover will expire at his or her death. In this situation, income realization might be accelerated, with such income to be absorbed by this carryover.
- Where the donor has a substantial life expectancy and, even if the estate tax savings and income tax savings would be approximately equal, the value of the present use of an income tax deduction will often produce better net after-tax results.

F. Foreign Trusts

1. The Foreign Trust Planning Context

The use of a foreign trust presents an arcane estate planning option, but this is risky and may invite careful IRS scrutiny. A foreign trust has allure to many U.S. taxpayers who believe (in many instances, quite inappropriately) that the use of this device will enable them to avoid U.S. income tax and U.S. transfer taxes. Unfortunately, some taxpayers are prepared to take bad advice to this effect. The challenge to the estate planner is to identify those limited situations where the possible use of a foreign trust may be appropriate. This could include when the client is interested in maximizing protection from the claims of creditors through the use of an offshore creditor protection trust. In this situation, the obligation of the estate planner is to clearly inform the U.S. client implementing such an arrangement of the continuation of U.S. tax obligations for the income from and transfer of the funds located offshore. A foreign trust may also be appropriate and useful where the client is resident outside the United States, has foreign-based assets, or has foreign resident family members.

Numerous federal income tax restrictions apply to assure that income derived through the use of foreign trusts does not disappear from the U.S. tax base.[330] These include (1) required gain recognition on the transfer of assets to a foreign trust, (2) special grantor trust rules, and (3) special rules to capture the benefit of any U.S. tax deferral. If the trust is located in a foreign jurisdiction where foreign country income tax is incurred on that income, a foreign tax credit will ordinarily be available to offset, reduce, or eliminate the impact of U.S. income tax on that same income. However, many foreign trusts are organized in jurisdictions where little or no income tax is imposed.

2. Identifying a Foreign Trust

If a trust is a U.S. trust (i.e., a U.S. resident for U.S. income tax purposes), the U.S. tax system applies to that trust on a global basis.[331] The worldwide income of the trust is included in U.S. gross income of the trust. A foreign trust,[332] however, is taxed only on its U.S. income.[333] For U.S. individuals, a foreign trust is of limited use in the estate planning context.[334]

3. Foreign Trust Formation and Funding

Except as provided in regulations, gain is required to be recognized on the transfer of appreciated property by a U.S. person to a foreign trust or estate as if the property were sold for fair market value at that time.[335] Before August 5, 1997, an excise tax was imposed on the transfer by the U.S. person of appreciated property to a foreign trust.[336] The excise tax rate was imposed at the rate of 35% of the appreciation portion of the transferred property.[337] The payment of this excise tax liability did not result in an increase in the tax basis of the transferred assets for income tax purposes (since no gain realization event had occurred for income tax purposes), the excise tax being a transactions tax. Accordingly, the appreciation would again be subject to income tax upon disposition of the asset if then subject to U.S. income tax.

This gain recognition treatment under §684 does not apply to a transfer to a foreign trust by a U.S. person to the extent that any person is treated as the owner of the trust under the grantor trust rules.[338] This gain recognition treatment also does not apply to any transfer of property by reason of the death of the U.S. transferor if the basis of the property in the hands of the foreign trust is determined under §1014(a).[339]

4. U.S. Income Taxation of Foreign Trust

Assuming not treated as a "grantor trust"[340] for U.S. income tax purposes, the foreign trust has the status of a nonresident alien individual and is taxed as such in the United States on its U.S. income.[341] If the foreign trust is not engaged in business in the United States:

- its non-U.S. source income is not subject to tax;
- its U.S. source income, such as interest (other than exempt "portfolio interest" and bank interest),[342] dividends, and royalties, is subject to a withholding tax imposed at source at the rate of 30%[343] (or at any lesser rate, to the extent reduced by an applicable U.S. income tax treaty); and
- its capital gains on the sale of U.S. securities are not subject to tax.[344]

If the foreign trust is "engaged in trade or business within the United States" during the taxable year[345]:

- its income "effectively connected" with the conduct of a trade or business within the United States is subject to the graduated rate structure applicable to domestic trust taxpayers[346];
- its U.S. source income such as interest (other than portfolio and bank interest), dividends, and royalties is subject to tax at the rate of 30%[347] (or any lesser rate to the extent reduced by an applicable U.S. income tax treaty); and
- its capital gains on the sale of securities (assuming not effectively connected with the conduct of a U.S. trade or business) are not subject to U.S. income tax.[348]

5. U.S. Taxation of Trust Grantor

Special grantor trust rules are applicable to an irrevocable foreign trust created by a U.S. person.[349] In general, any U.S. person transferring property to a foreign trust having a U.S. beneficiary is treated under a special grantor trust rule as the owner of that portion of the trust attributable to the property transferred by the U.S. person.[350] If a U.S. person directly or indirectly transfers property to a foreign trust, the IRS may treat the trust as having a U.S. beneficiary for purposes of §679 unless the U.S. person submits information as required by the IRS and demonstrates to the satisfaction of the Secretary that (1) under the terms of the trust, no part of the income or corpus of the trust may be paid or accumulated during the taxable year to or for the benefit of a U.S. person, and (2) if the trust were terminated during the taxable year, no part of the income or corpus of the trust could be paid to or for the benefit of a U.S. person.[351] If any person has the discretion (by authority given in the trust agreement, by power of appointment, or otherwise) to make a distribution from the trust to, or for the benefit of, any person, the trust is treated as having a U.S. beneficiary unless (1) the terms of the trust specifically identify the class of persons to whom such distributions may be made, and (2) none of those persons is a U.S. person during the taxable year.[352]

Any U.S. person treated under this provision as the owner of a portion of a trust is taxed on the income of that portion of the trust in the same manner as an owner of a trust is taxed under the domestic grantor trust rules.[353] These grantor trust rules also apply to: (1) nonresident alien individuals who directly or indirectly transfer property to foreign trusts and then become U.S. residents within five years of the transfer; and (2) U.S. persons who transferred property to a domestic trust if the trust later becomes a foreign trust while the transferor is still alive.[354] As noted above, a specific rule precludes a foreign grantor from being treated as the owner of the foreign trust income when the trust has a U.S. beneficiary.[355] An exception to this rule applies to a revocable trust or a trust where the trustee can only distribute income or principal to the grantor or the grantor's spouse.[356] Further, if a U.S. trust beneficiary provides funds to a foreign trust grantor who then creates a trust for the U.S. beneficiary, that U.S. beneficiary will be treated as the trust grantor; that is, the foreign trust grantor will be treated as only an intermediary.[357]

Transfers by U.S. persons to a foreign trust having a U.S. beneficiary that take place by reason of the death of the U.S. person are not subject to the §679(a)(1) grantor trust rule.[358] Consequently, the income of a foreign testamentary trust created by a U.S. person is not taxed to the estate of the U.S. person. Further, transfers in exchange for fair market value consideration are excepted from this grantor trust treatment.[359]

The impact of these rules in the planning context is that the U.S. grantor cannot place assets in a foreign trust for the benefit of current U.S. beneficiaries and achieve avoidance of current U.S. income tax. The U.S. grantor can transfer assets into a foreign trust for the benefit of foreign beneficiaries and avoid the application of these rules. The trust grantor then might possibly need to be concerned about the beneficiary becoming a U.S. person and causing grantor trust status to then be applicable.

If the foreign beneficiary becomes a U.S. person within five years of the transfer to the trust, the grantor trust rules will then apply to the trust grantor. This will not be the result if the non-U.S. beneficiary becomes a U.S. person more than five years after the transfer.[360]

6. U.S. Income Taxation of Trust Beneficiaries

a. Inbound Trust Distributions

U.S. citizens and residents are taxed on their worldwide income. This includes the income received as beneficiaries from foreign trusts (assuming that income has not been taxed to the grantor under §679). Under §643(h), if an amount is paid to a U.S. person directly or indirectly from a foreign trust, and the payor of the amount is not the grantor of the trust, the payment is treated as a direct transfer from the foreign trust to the U.S. person in the year of payment. A transfer of property, including cash, to a U.S. person from a foreign intermediary who received the property from a foreign trust, is treated as a direct payment to the U.S. person, if the intermediary received the property pursuant to a plan that had a principal purpose of avoiding U.S. taxes.[361]

The characterization of the components of the distributable net income of a foreign trust is made at the trust level, even though, as the equivalent of a nonresident alien, a foreign trust is not taxable and is not required to file a U.S. income tax return (which would otherwise identify those income components).[362] If the foreign trust makes a distribution to a U.S. beneficiary of the trust's accumulated income, the beneficiary will be subjected to the trust income throwback rules.[363] In addition, the multiple trust rules apply equally to distributions from foreign trusts as to the distributions from domestic trusts.[364] A beneficiary receiving distributions attributable to the same taxable year from three or more trusts is not permitted to gross-up his or her distributions by the amount of trust tax paid, or to receive a tax credit for distributions from any trust beyond the first two.[365]

Further, where the income of a foreign trust is not taxed to the grantor under the grantor trust rules, §668 imposes an interest charge on trust distributions, based on the length of time during which the U.S. income tax was deferred because of the trust's income accumulation. This charge is in addition to any tax incurred by beneficiaries upon the receipt of the distribution.[366] This interest cost is not deductible.[367] Since January 1, 1996, this interest has been compounded and based on the federal tax underpayment rate.[368] It is imposed on tax amounts determined under the accumulation distribution rules, including the total simple interest for pre-1996 periods, if any. For purposes of computing the interest charge, the accumulation distribution is allocated proportionately to prior trust years in which the trust had undistributed net income (and the beneficiary receiving the distribution was a U.S. citizen or resident), rather than to the earliest of such years.[369] An accumulation distribution is treated as reducing proportionately the undistributed net income from prior years.[370]

The effect of these rules is to assure that all the tax benefits to U.S. beneficiaries upon distributions from a foreign trust have been curtailed. Particularly, this includes enabling the U.S. Treasury Department to recover the benefit of the deferral through the imposition of an interest charge, often making the distribution quite tax expensive to the beneficiary.

b. Outbound Trust Distributions

Trust distributions may be made by either a U.S. or a foreign trust to a foreign beneficiary. If U.S. sourced income is realized by a foreign trust, the foreign trust itself will be treated as a foreign person for U.S. income taxation purposes. Through applicability of the trust distribution conduit rules, the U.S income tax liability may be transferred from the foreign trust to the foreign beneficiary if a current trust income distribution is made to the foreign beneficiary.

If U.S. income is realized by a U.S. trust, the completion of a current income distribution to a foreign beneficiary may be quite important. If no current distribution is made, the income tax will be imposed at the trust level on a U.S. taxpayer, that is, the U.S. trust. If, however, a current distribution is made, the distributed income will retain its character for the foreign beneficiary. This may enable income tax exemption of certain types of gross income, for example, where the distributed income would be tax-exempt portfolio interest.[371]

7. Foreign Trust Tax Planning

The usefulness of foreign trusts by or for U.S. persons is significantly limited by §668 (providing for an interest charge on accumulation distributions from foreign trusts) and §679 (providing a special grantor trust ownership rule). A foreign trust may have value where the beneficiaries are nonresident aliens, or will be at the time of the trust income distribution. This can insulate the foreign beneficiaries from any U.S. income tax upon receiving trust distributions.

Further planning considerations in this context might include:

- If significant investment returns are anticipated the compounding of reinvested foreign trust income may produce greater accumulated wealth than would have been the situation had the foreign trust not been used, notwithstanding the interest charge to U.S. beneficiaries on eventual distributions.[372]
- Discretionary distributions to the U.S. beneficiary of a foreign trust might be coordinated with the beneficiary's low tax bracket income years (including when a net operating loss may be available).
- The foreign trust might make interim loans to U.S. beneficiaries and family members. This arrangement might be subject, however, to the applicability of conduit rules and "substance over form" rules.[373]

Reporting requirements require the reporting of the creation of a foreign trust by a U.S. person, a transfer of property to a foreign trust by a U.S. person, or the death of a U.S. person if any portion of a foreign trust is included in the decedent's gross estate or was taxable to the decedent under the grantor trust rules.[374] Unfortunately, many taxpayers (notwithstanding contrary advice from estate planning advisors) have utilized foreign based trusts to achieve self-help tax planning. Many of these arrangements have severe limitations, as noted from the various Code provisions described above. Depending on the effectiveness of future compliance initiatives by the IRS, many estate planners may be assisting their clients in unwinding these arrangements, rather than formulating them.

Notes

1. See 823 T.M., *Taxation of Jointly Owned Property* (Bloomberg BNA). Joint tenancy property should be differentiated from that property where another party is designated as an owner solely for the sake of convenience, thereby only having an interest in the property as a nominee, and being subject to a "trust" obligation to deliver that property to another in accordance with the understanding between the principal and the nominee. Under state law this ownership status may be specified for certain bank account arrangements in specific legislation.
2. The common law developed the doctrine of the four "unities" of time, title, interest, and possession as the test for the existence of a joint tenancy. Under this doctrine, in order for a joint tenancy to exist, all of the co-owners must have (1) acquired their interests at the same time, (2) acquired these interests by the same instrument, (3) identical interests in terms of quality, and (4) the same rights of possession.
3. Previously, most applicable state law presumed that common ownership contemplated a survivorship condition, but state law in most instances now includes a contrary presumption, that is, that no survivorship condition was contemplated unless explicitly specified in property conveyancing documents.
4. Often the joint tenancy is between two persons, but more than two individuals can hold property in joint tenancy. This latter situation might occur, for example, when property is held by spouses and a child, with the child anticipated to be the surviving owner.
5. Note, however, Rev. Rul. 54-143, 1954-1 C.B. 12, where the IRS indicated (applying an assignment of income analysis) that the interest income derived from a U.S. Treasury obligation is entirely attributable to the person providing the consideration for the purchase of the debt instrument. If that obligation is a Series E U.S. savings bond permitting (under §454) deferral of the accruing interest income, this reporting obligation will be postponed until the bond is liquidated, even if the bond is passed through an estate if the purchaser dies before collecting the income.
6. Rev. Rul. 71-268, 1971-1 C.B. 58. Similarly, see CCA 201451027.
7. *See* Reg. §25.2511-1(h)(4). This provision notes that if one person creates a joint bank account for himself or herself and another person (or a similar type of ownership by which the first person can retrieve the entire property without the consent of the other), a gift will (only) occur when the second person draws upon the account for his or her own benefit. Similar treatment is to occur with respect to the purchase of a U.S. savings bond.
8. Reg. §25.2511-1(h)(5) notes that if one person with his or her own funds purchases property and has the title conveyed to himself or herself and another as joint owners and the purchaser then only has the right to unilaterally retrieve one-half of the property, a

gift has resulted to the extent of one-half of the property. Existence of the authority to completely retrieve the entire property (or only a portion) will be determinable under applicable state law, not federal tax rules.

9. *See, generally,* Reg. §25.2515-2(b); H.R. Rep. No. 94-1380, at 18 (1976).
10. Reg. §25.2511-1(h)(5).
11. Only in unique situations (as determined under local property law) is the consent of both tenants who are not spouses required to terminate a joint tenancy with survivorship rights.
12. Former §2515, which provided that the creation of a tenancy by the entirety in real property was not treated as a gift unless the donor elected gift treatment, was repealed by the Economic Recovery Tax Act of 1981 (ERTA), Pub. L. No. 97-34, §403. If the donor made the election, former §2515(c)(3) eliminated the need for actuarial calculations where the right of survivorship was not unilaterally severable. For tax purposes, a "tenancy by the entirety" is the essential equivalent of a joint tenancy with the right of survivorship between spouses. Minor variations exist under local property laws. Former §2515 also applied to the creation of a spousal joint tenancy in real estate with rights of survivorship. Former §2515(d). In either type of tenancy, if the donor did not make the former §2515(c) election, a taxable gift was not considered to have been made until the termination of the tenancy (assuming the termination occurred otherwise than by death of a spouse). Former §2515(b). Thus, taxability was automatically postponed.
13. §2523(a).
14. §2523(i)(1). In the case of a noncitizen spouse, some relief is available because of the provision in §2523(i)(2) permitting a §2503(b) $100,000 annual gift tax exclusion for gifts to a non-citizen spouse. This $100,000 exclusion is limited to gifts that would be eligible for the marital deduction, but for the general rule disallowing the deduction for gifts to noncitizen spouses. For example, a gift of a nondeductible terminable interest will not qualify for this $100,000 exclusion. The annual exclusion amount for gifts to noncitizen spouses is adjusted annually for inflation. §2523(i), §2503(b). For the inflation-adjusted §2523(i) amounts for the most years, see Worksheet 1.
15. Reg. §25.2511-1(h)(5).
16. §2523(a).
17. Estate tax inclusion is governed by §2040 entitled "Joint Interests." Section 2033 provides that a decedent's gross estate "shall include the value of all property to the extent of the interest therein of the decedent at the time of his death." Although the language of §2033 could be construed to cover all concurrent interests in property, including joint tenancies, only §2040 applies to interests that pass by the right of survivorship.
18. §2040(b). Before the Tax Reform Act of 1976 (1976 TRA), Pub. L. No. 94-455, §2040 provided that, on the death of a joint tenant (regardless of whether the tenants were spouses), the entire value of the property owned in joint tenancy with the right of survivorship was included in a decedent's gross estate, except for the portion of the property attributable to the consideration furnished by the survivor. Thus, if the decedent furnished the entire purchase price of the jointly owned property, the value of the entire property was included in his or her gross estate. The surviving joint tenant (e.g., a spouse mostly working in the home) could sometimes argue successfully in a family business context that he or she had also contributed to the acquisition cost of the joint tenancy property. *See, e.g., United States v. Neel,* 235 F.2d 395 (10th Cir. 1956); *Estate of Otte v. Commissioner,* T.C. Memo 1972-76. *See also* Rev. Rul. 78-418, 1978-2 C.B. 236

(where jointly held property was purchased with proceeds from sale of community property, one-half of consideration for jointly held property was furnished by each spouse). Before the enactment of §2040(b) in the 1976 TRA, unnecessary estate taxation often occurred. If the first spouse to die contributed the entire consideration, the entire value of the joint tenancy was included in his or her gross estate, subject to any available exclusion under the marital deduction (which was then limited). Upon the death of the first joint tenant, the surviving joint tenant would hold a fee simple in the property, and the property would be again included in that survivor's gross estate. For an example of how this taxation might occur upon the simultaneous deaths of the joint tenants, see Rev. Rul. 76-303, 1976-2 C.B. 266. Under state property law, the use of the joint tenancy ordinarily precluded giving the survivor a life estate with the remainder to another and, thereby, avoiding taxation at the survivor's death. The 1976 TRA introduced the "qualified joint interest" for spousal joint tenancies created by either or both spouses under §2040(b). One half of the value of a "qualified joint interest" was includible in the gross estate of the decedent at the date of the decedent's death (or alternate valuation date), regardless of which joint tenant furnished the consideration. As originally enacted, an interest was a "qualified joint interest" only if the following requirements were satisfied: (1) the interest was created by the decedent or his or her spouse or both; (2) in the case of personal property, the creation of the joint interest must have been a completed gift for purposes of the gift tax provisions; (3) in the case of real property, the donor must have elected to treat the creation of the joint tenancy as a taxable event at that time; and (4) the joint tenancy could not be between persons other than the decedent and his or her spouse. Former §2040(b)(2), as enacted by 1976 TRA, before amendment by ERTA, P.L. 97-34, §403(c)(1). Thus, if a donor created a joint interest with his or her spouse in personal property or in real property and made the former §2515 election to have the creation of the real property joint tenancy treated as a taxable gift, upon the death of one spouse only one-half of the value of the property was includible in the gross estate of the decedent. In addition, under pre-1976 TRA law, the services performed by the surviving spouse in connection with a family-owned business were to be taken into account as consideration furnished for the purchase of jointly owned property used in the trade or business if a partnership were used to conduct business. *See* Staff of J. Comm. on Tax'n, 94th Cong., General Explanation of the Tax Reform Act of 1976, at 534 (J. Comm. Print 1976) (1976 Bluebook) (citing *Otte*). This rule applied even though the applicable local law would treat the income and, therefore, the "consideration furnished" with respect to a jointly operated family business that was not conducted under the partnership form of business, as belonging to the husband during the marriage. *See id.;* H.R. Rep. No. 94-1380, at 19 (1976). The 1976 TRA amended former §2515(c) to provide that, if the election for immediate gift treatment was made, the retained interest of each spouse was treated as one-half of the value of the joint interest. This treatment applied even if the joint tenancy, under local law, could be terminated only with mutual consent. According to the legislative history, the effect of the 1976 TRA's amendments to §2040 and former §2515 was to implicitly recognize a spouse's services towards accumulating joint property even if the services could not be valued easily. 1976 Bluebook, at 535-536. Also, if the joint tenancy could not be unilaterally severed, the actuarial computations normally necessary to determine value were not required. The donor was to make the former §2515(c) election by including the transfer in the gift tax return for the calendar quarter in which the joint tenancy was created. If the donor did not elect, in the case of real property, to treat the transfer as a gift at the time of creation of the interest then, upon the death of a spouse, the joint property was subject to inclusion in the gross estate under §2040(a) at the full value of the property less the value attributable to any contribution that could be traced to the survivor. The Revenue Act of 1978 (1978 RA), Pub. L. No. 95-600, §511, added former §2040(c), which permitted excluding a portion of the value of jointly owned real or tangible personal property used in a farm or other business. The exclusion was based on the number of years the surviving joint tenant spouse materially participated in the operation or management of the business. The purpose of this provision was to provide estate tax recognition to services performed by the surviving spouse without regard to whether the creation of the joint interest was a gift for gift tax purposes and to avoid differences in treatment in cases that were substantially identical except for the form of the arrangement (partnership or other type). *See* Staff of J. Comm. on Tax'n, 95th Cong., General Explanation of the Revenue Act of 1978, at 286–287 (1979). The aggregate decrease in the value of the decedent's gross estate under this provision was not to exceed $500,000. With the enactment of the unlimited marital deduction, former §2515 (dealing with tenancies by the entirety in real property and the gift election in connection therewith), former §2515A (dealing with tenancies by the entirety in personal property and eliminating the need for actuarial computation, as enacted by the 1978 RA, Pub. L. No. 95-600, §702), former §2040(c) (material participation test), and former §2040(d) (providing for qualified joint interest treatment for pre-1977 tenancies, as enacted by 1978 RA, Pub. L. No. 95-600, §702) were repealed by ERTA, Pub. L. No. 97-34, §403(c)(3)(A), §403(c)(3)(B).

19. *See* §2040(b).
20. §2040(b)(2)(B).
21. Section 1014 specifies that property must be acquired from the decedent to enable the tax basis adjustment as of death. A possible exception to this rule may be community property held in joint tenancy. Under §1014(b)(6), the surviving spouse's one-half share of such property is considered as having been acquired from or as having passed from the decedent and receives a tax basis change. *But cf. Stanley v. Commissioner,* 40 T.C. 851, *aff'd,* 338 F.2d 434 (9th Cir. 1964) (if step up in basis would have been denied to interest had it not been community property, such as where it was "income in respect of a decedent" [IRD], step up would also be denied where interest consisted of surviving spouse's community property interest in IRD item).
22. For this reason, if the joint tenancy property is also community property, the retention of community property status (as determined under applicable local law) is essential to enable the tax basis step up at death for the entire property. *See* §1014(b)(6).
23. §1014(e)(1).
24. *See* §1014(e)(2)(A) ("The term 'appreciated property' means any property if the fair market value of such property on the day it was transferred to the decedent by gift exceeds its adjusted basis").
25. Section §2056(d)(1)(B) specifies that if the surviving spouse of the decedent is not a U.S. citizen, §2040(b) (providing for a 50-50 allocation) does not apply. See, further, PLR 200910019 applying this rule. The qualified domestic trust, described in §2056A, could possibly be used to enable a marital deduction in this context.
26. Section 2056(d)(1)(B) applies to estates of decedents dying after November 10, 1988. The Revenue Reconciliation Act of 1989, Pub. L. No. 101-239, §7815(d)(16), provides,

however, a special rule in applying §2040(a) with respect to jointly held interests to which §2040(b) does not apply solely by reason of §2056(d)(1)(B).

27. §2040(a).
28. *See, e.g., Estate of Anderson v. Commissioner,* T.C. Memo 1989-643 (joint tenant's management services were treated as adequate §2040 consideration to support exclusion of one-half of joint tenancy property). The party providing the services then has a dilemma since ordinarily the property interest received for these services will constitute gross income for federal income tax purposes. *See* §61.
29. §1014. The Economic Growth and Tax Relief Reconciliation Act of 2001 (EGTRRA), Pub. L. No. 107-16, §541, §542, repealed §1014 and implemented a carryover basis regime under former §1022, effective for decedents dying after 2009. Although, as noted in Chapter 4, A.1., the Tax Relief, Unemployment Insurance Reauthorization, and Job Creation Act of 2010 (2010 TRA), Pub. L. No. 111-312, §301(a), repealed former §1022 and reinstated §1014 and the estate tax for estates of decedents dying after 2009, that Act (in §301(c)) allowed the estate of a decedent dying in 2010 to elect to apply the modified carryover basis regime instead of the estate tax. Former §1022(b) permitted a decedent's estate to increase the basis of assets transferred, as determined on an asset-by-asset basis, by up to a total of $1.3 million and to further increase the basis of assets by the amount of the decedent's unused capital losses, net operating losses, and certain built-in losses. Former §1022(c) allowed an additional $3 million increase to the basis of property transferred outright to a surviving spouse and for qualified terminable interest property (QTIP) transferred to a surviving spouse. Former §1022(b) and §1022(c) applied, however, only to property "owned by the decedent at the time of his death." For purposes of determining the decedent's ownership of jointly held property, the statute applied rules similar to present (but then-repealed) §2040(a) and §2040(b). *See* former §1022(d)(1)(B).
30. This potential exposure is less when the estate tax exclusion amount is $5 million, as it is for estates of decedents dying after 2009 (with portability for spouses after 2010 and an inflation adjustment after 2011). *See* §2010(c), as amended by the 2010 TRA, Pub. L. No. 111-312, §101(a) (extending sunset provision in EGTRRA, Pub. L. No. 107-16, §901), §301-§304; American Taxpayer Relief Act of 2012 (ATRA), Pub. L. No. 112-240, §101(a) (generally making permanent the EGTRRA and 2010 TRA changes); Taxpayer Relief Act of 1997, Pub. L. No. 105-34, §501; *see also* Chapter 4, A.1.
31. As noted above, an income tax–basis step-up will not result for the portion deemed owned by the surviving spouse rather than by the deceased joint tenant spouse.
32. Effective May 23, 1998, Alaska adopted the Alaska Community Property Act, an elective community property system. 1998 SLA CH. 42; Alaska Stat. §§34.77.010, et seq. Alaska residents must opt into the community property regime. Alaska also allows nonresidents to establish trusts with an Alaska trustee that are governed by community property law under some circumstances. Note from IRS Pub. 555, *Community Property,* that the IRS may not recognize the elective community property system in Alaska as a community property regime for federal tax purposes. *See also* Blattmachr, Zaritsky & Ascher, *Tax Planning with Consensual Community Property: Alaska's New Community Property Law,* 33 Real Prop. Prob. & Tr. J. 615 (Winter 1999).
33. Wisconsin has adopted the Uniform Marital Property Act (1983), which implements community property law principles. *See* Wis. Stat. §§766.001, et seq. The rights of the

spouses are community property rights for purposes of federal income taxation. *See* Rev. Rul. 87-13, 1987-1 C.B. 20.

34. These provisions could have applicability to U.S. individuals either resident in a foreign jurisdiction or owning real property in a foreign jurisdiction.
35. See 803 T.M., *Estate Planning for the Mobile Client* (Bloomberg BNA); Reinecke, Community Property Issues for Noncommunity Property Practitioners, in "Estate Planning in Depth," ALI-ABA Course of Study Materials, Vol. II, at 969 (2001); Moore & Moore, The Importance of Community Property in an Age of Increased Migration, 10th Annual Estate Planning Symposium, Vol. 2, §U (1999).
36. Note that, as evidenced by the discussion below, this is a local law matter and state laws can vary in the process of defining what property is categorized as community property. For example, Tex. Fam. Code Ann. §3.001 provides: "A spouse's separate property consists of: (1) the property owned or claimed by the spouse before marriage; (2) the property acquired by the spouse during marriage by gift, devise, or descent; and (3) the recovery for personal injuries sustained by the spouse during marriage, except any recovery for loss of earning capacity during marriage." Tex. Fam. Code Ann. §3.002 provides: "Community property consists of the property, other than separate property, acquired by either spouse during marriage."
37. Differences might arise concerning applicability of community property rules in "same-sex marriages" and similar arrangements. For example, California has extended the community property system to registered domestic partners. In PLR 201021048, the IRS ruled that a division of income under this statute does not constitute a gift to the nonemployed "spouse." The IRS did note that these domestic partners must file separate income tax returns, however, each reporting one-half of their community income. Similarly, see CCA 201021050. Note that after the decision in *United States v. Windsor*, 570 U.S. 12 (2013), concerning the recognition of same sex marriages, the IRS in Rev Rul. 2013-17, 2013-2 CB 201, specified that, for federal tax purposes, the term "marriage" does not include registered domestic partnerships, civil unions, or other similar formal relationships recognized under state law that are not denominated as a marriage under that state law, and the terms "spouse," "husband and wife," "husband," and "wife" do not include individuals who have entered into such a formal relationship. This conclusion applies regardless of whether individuals who have entered into such relationships are of the opposite sex or the same sex.
38. For a detailed analysis of community property and related estate planning problems, see 802 T.M., *Community Property: General Considerations* (Bloomberg BNA). See also 803 T.M., *Estate Planning for the Mobile Client* (Bloomberg BNA).
39. §2033.
40. This latter situation can occur, for example, where improvements made to separate property are paid for with funds belonging to the community, or, alternatively, improvements made to community property are paid for with separate property funds. These properties would have a mixed separate and community property character. The method of identifying those several portions may vary, depending on local law.
41. This will be the property subject to the decedent's power of testamentary disposition (or other power, such as a designation of beneficiary with respect to life insurance proceeds).
42. In most states, the recording of the property title in the name of one spouse alone will not conclusively resolve this separate versus community property ownership issue. Rather, in most community property jurisdictions, community property can be recorded in the name

of only one member of the community, with that party being the "manager" for the community.

43. Reg. §20.2042-1(b)(2). Proceeds not receivable by or for the benefit of the estate are includible in a decedent's gross estate only if the decedent had incidents of ownership in the policy. §2042.
44. *See* TAM 8928003 (estate included only one-half of certain life insurance proceeds where: (1) decedent appeared to be owner of policies; (2) premiums were paid from community funds; and (3) beneficiaries were surviving spouse and children). *But cf.* Rev. Rul. 2003-40, 2003-17 I.R.B. 813 (if Louisiana decedent purchases life insurance policy on decedent's life during marriage, names decedent as owner of policy, and does not transfer ownership of policy, policy is presumed to be community property under Louisiana law and, consequently, one-half of proceeds is includible in decedent's gross estate under §2042); Rev. Rul. 94-69, 1994-2 C.B. 241 (in Louisiana, presumption that property in possession of either spouse during marriage is community property does not apply to life insurance policy transferred by or between spouses; thus, where decedent had transferred ownership of policy on his life and retained no incidents of ownership, surviving spouse became sole owner of policy, with no proceeds of policy being includible in insured's gross estate even though policy had been purchased with community funds).
45. *See, e.g.*, Rev. Rul. 80-242, 1980-2 C.B. 276 (recognizing Texas "inception of title" doctrine).
46. If the surviving spouse receives at least his or her community share as policy beneficiary at the insured's death, no gift will ordinarily be deemed to have been made of the amounts payable to third persons. *Kaufman v. United States,* 462 F.2d 439 (5th Cir. 1972). If, however, community property is used to purchase life insurance upon the life of a spouse, a third person is designated as revocable beneficiary, and under state law the death of the spouse is considered to make absolute the transfer by the surviving spouse, a gift is made by the surviving spouse at the other spouse's death of one-half of the life insurance proceeds. Reg. §25.2511-1(h)(9); *Commissioner v. Chase Manhattan Bank,* 259 F.2d 231 (5th Cir. 1958).
47. *See Estate of Cavenaugh v. Commissioner,* 51 F.3d 597 (5th Cir. 1995), *rev'g* 100 T.C. 407 (1993) (involving Texas community property law and reversing Tax Court which had essentially rejected concept that any property interest in term insurance policy on life of spouse was held by noninsured spouse). *See also Estate of Cervin v. Commissioner,* T.C. Memo 1994-550, *rev'd,* 111 F.3d 1252 (5th Cir. 1997) (Tax Court did not recognize rights of predeceased spouse in insurance policies on life of surviving spouse); TAM 8951003 (wife who predeceased insured husband did not have community property interest in proceeds of policy on life of her husband, who subsequently died, and 100% of proceeds were includible in husband's estate under §2042; husband died after previously deceased wife's estate had been settled for tax purposes without claim to proportionate interest in insurance covering husband's life).
48. See Chapter 9, C.
49. Note that the IRS also permits alternative treatment for a conduit entity owned by two spouses as community property. In Rev. Proc. 2002-69, 2002-45 I.R.B. 831, the IRS indicated that, at their option, a conduit entity owned as community property by two spouses can be treated as either (1) disregarded or (2) a partnership.

50. As indicated above, 802 T.M., *Community Property: General Considerations* (Bloomberg BNA), analyzes in depth the rules for identifying community property and estate planning techniques with respect to such property.
51. Restatement (Second) of Conflicts of Laws, §529, provides that where a husband and wife move from a community property state to a common law state, the property they acquired with community funds, and property traceable to those community funds, continues to be community property even though the couple subsequently lives in a common law jurisdiction. This Restatement §529, Comment (b), specifies that considerations of fairness and convenience require that the spouses' marital property interests in a chattel or right embodied in a document should not be affected by the mere removal of the chattel or document to another state. Likewise, these interests are not affected by a change of domicile to another state by one or both of the parties.
52. *See* Uniform Disposition of Community Property Rights at Death Act (which has been enacted in several states). This uniform act has as its objective the recognition of community property rights previously established in property. However, in *Estate of Richman v. Commissioner*, T.C. Memo 1994-421, the spouses, resident in a community property jurisdiction (Texas), used community funds to purchase shares in a Massachusetts business trust, taking title as tenants with the right of survivorship. The trust agreement provided that the rights of all parties to the agreement were governed by Massachusetts law. The Tax Court rejected the position of the IRS that, in determining the ownership of personal property between spouses, Texas would apply the law of marital domicile. The Tax Court concluded that (1) the spouses made a valid choice of law, and (2) no fundamental policy of the community property jurisdiction was contravened by implementing this choice of law.
53. This is particularly complicated in some states where income from separate property will be treated as community property and, therefore, commingling will occur upon each receipt of income.
54. If property interests of the spouses are altered under this agreement from those prescribed under local law, transfers might be treated as occurring for gift tax purposes, but the marital deduction ordinarily should be available to protect these transfers from gift tax.
55. This assumes that the rule categorizing such income as community property cannot be varied by an agreement between the spouses.
56. If the property and the couple's residence are in different jurisdictions, conflict of laws principles also need to be examined to determine how the partitioning process should be implemented to satisfy these requirements in each jurisdiction.
57. *Commissioner v. Mills*, 183 F.2d 32 (9th Cir. 1950); Rev. Rul. 55-709, 1955-2 C.B. 609. *But cf.* Rev. Rul. 70-401, 1970-2 C.B. 197 (concerning this situation in New Mexico).
58. This assumes the arrangement is not offset by a separation of property of similar value in favor of the husband. *See Fleming v. Commissioner*, 3 T.C. 974 (1944), *aff'd*, 155 F.2d 204 (5th Cir. 1946).
59. §2523(a).
60. §1041. *See* PLR 8929046 (no gain or loss is recognized when spouses transmute their community property interests into the separate property of the other spouse because gifts are gifts between spouses for purposes of §1041). Section 1041 specifies that no gain or loss is to be recognized for income tax purposes on transfers between spouses or to a former spouse if incident to a divorce. Note, however, Rev. Rul. 87-112, 1987-2 C.B.

207, indicating that §1041 does not supersede the assignment of income doctrine. In Rev. Rul. 87-112, the assignment of Series E U.S. Government bonds triggered the required recognition of accrued interest. Rev. Rul. 2002-22, 2002-1 I.R.B. 849, clarified Rev. Rul. 87-112 by eliminating references to assignment of income principles and reaffirmed Rev. Rul. 87-112 with respect to the application of §454 and the regulations thereunder to the transfer and determination of the transferee's basis. Rev. Rul. 2002-22 dealt with the assignment of nonstatutory stock options and nonqualified deferred compensation in a divorce property division context where §1041 was applicable. Similarly, see PLR 201016031.

61. §1014(b)(6). *See, e.g.*, Rev. Rul. 92-37, 1992-1 C.B. 195 (surviving spouse's basis for calculating cost depletion on property that represents surviving spouse's one-half share of community property for taxable year of other spouse's death is surviving spouse's adjusted basis in property as of end of surviving spouse's taxable year); PLR 9326043 (with respect to copyright licenses held as community property at death).
62. Of course, a transfer of community property to one of the spouses with only the nominal ownership but not the community property status changed may not be a transfer for gift tax purposes if no real transfer of economic interests has occurred.
63. For estate tax purposes a "retained life interest" problem formerly arose in this context under §2036 where local law treats income from separate property as being community property. *See* Rev. Rul. 81-221, 1981-2 C.B. 178, *revoking* Rev. Rul. 75-504, 1975-2 C.B. 363 (abandoning position that §2036 inclusion was required). *See also Estate of Wyly v. Commissioner*, 610 F.2d 1282 (5th Cir. 1980).
64. This assumes that, under local law, the community property interest in the policy can be realized upon during life and that this right disintegrates as of the time of death, when the policy proceeds become irrevocably payable to the designated beneficiary.
65. Reg. §25.2511-1(h)(9).
66. §2031, §2033.
67. §2056.
68. *See* Rev. Rul. 68-80, 1968-1 C.B. 348 (proceeds of community property sale used to purchase property in separate property jurisdiction as equal tenants in common lost its community character and §1014(b)(6) tax basis step-up for nondecedent's portion was not available).
69. The surviving spouse's interest in the community property will not be included in the decedent's gross estate since the decedent does not own that property. *See* Rev. Rul. 67-383, 1967-2 C.B. 325 (only deceased spouse's community property interest was includible even though surviving spouse elected that entire community property would be governed by provisions of decedent's will). *See also* Rev. Rul. 72-443, 1972-2 C.B. 531.
70. For simplicity, the election is referred to as a "widow's election" but the concept applies equally to widowers.
71. *Cf. United States v. Stapf*, 375 U.S. 118 (1963) (illustrating use of widow's election where separate property was held at death, and impact on then-available marital deduction). *See also* Reg. §20.2056(b)-4(b) *Ex. 3* (evidencing an arrangement forcing widow to make election concerning disposition of her community property interest, and noting: "[a] decedent bequeathed certain securities to his wife in lieu of her interest in property held by them as community property under the law of the state of their residence. The wife elected to relinquish her community property interest and to take the bequest. For the

purpose of the [estate tax] marital deduction, the value of the bequest is to be reduced by the value of the community property interest relinquished by the wife").

72. Mechanically, this arrangement implementing a forced widow's election could also be used with a revocable inter vivos trust that prior to death has been funded with community property and imposed these described conditions.
73. See 802 T.M., *Community Property: General Considerations* (Bloomberg BNA).
74. This will be distinguished from the value of the surviving spouse's transfer for estate tax purposes, being his or her entire share of the community property, as noted in the discussion below.
75. §2512; *Commissioner v. Siegel,* 250 F.2d 339 (9th Cir. 1957); *Estate of Sparling v. Commissioner,* 60 T.C. 330 (1973); *Turman v. Commissioner,* 35 T.C. 1123 (1961), *acq.,* 1964-2 C.B. 7.
76. *See* Reg. §25.2511-2(c).
77. §2036(a)(1); *Estate of Vardell v. Commissioner,* 307 F.2d 688 (5th Cir. 1962); *Estate of Sparling v. Commissioner,* 60 T.C. 330 (1973); *Estate of Bomash v. Commissioner*, 50 T.C. 667 (1968), *rev'd on other grounds*, 432 F.2d 308 (9th Cir. 1970); *Estate of Gregory v. Commissioner,* 39 T.C. 1012 (1963).
78. Alternatively, the trust might be described in §2037, §2038, or §2041.
79. §2043. *See also* Reg. §20.2043-1(a).
80. The value of the surviving spouse's one-half share of the former community assets is reduced by the actuarial value of the surviving spouse's life estate in the decedent's share of those assets, as determined at the time of decedent's death. Section 7520, the valuation table provision, requires the applicable interest rate to be redetermined monthly, based on 120% of the federal midterm rate under §1274(d). Consequently, the relative values of the life estate and remainder interests will vary, depending on the valuation date.
81. *But see* PLR 8929046 (in measuring adequacy of any consideration received, value of interest transferred by widow would be full value of property transferred, notwithstanding that widow effectively retained life estate in those assets and transferred only remainder interest). In PLR 8929046, the IRS relied on the Court of Claims' decision in *Gradow v. United States,* 11 Cl. Ct. 808 (1987), *aff'd,* 897 F.2d 516 (Fed. Cir. 1990). In *Gradow,* the estate had argued that the widow's election fell within the full and adequate consideration exception of §2036(a)(1), causing the value of the property the surviving spouse transferred to the trust to be excluded from her gross estate. The court disagreed, upholding the IRS view that if the surviving spouse makes the widow's election, the full date of death value of the entire property (less the value of consideration received) will be includible in the surviving spouse's estate unless the consideration equaled the fair market value of the fee simple interest in the property transferred to the trust (and not just the actuarial value of the remainder) at the time of the transfer. Therefore, in evaluating whether a widow's election constituted full and adequate consideration for §2036(a) purposes, the consideration flowing from the surviving spouse consists of the property which would otherwise have been included in his or her gross estate by virtue of his or her retention of a life estate, that is, his or her half of the community property. Stating that the *Gradow* analysis would make the statutorily contemplated sale of a remainder virtually impossible, the Third Circuit (in a case not involving a widow's election) rejected *Gradow*'s reasoning in *Estate of D'Ambrosio v. Commissioner,* 101 F.3d 309 (3d Cir. 1996), *rev'g* 105 T.C. 252 (1995), *cert. denied*, 520 U.S. 1230 (1997), and held that the sale of a remainder interest in property for an amount equal to its then

actuarial fair market value succeeded in excluding the property from the decedent's gross estate. The Fifth Circuit also analyzed *Gradow* in detail in *Wheeler v. United States,* 116 F.3d 749 (5th Cir. 1997), because the IRS's position concerning adequate consideration for the sale of a remainder interest rested principally on an analogy to the widow's election mechanism. The court concluded, however, that the widow's election cases present factually distinct circumstances that preclude the wholesale importation of the *Gradow* rationale into cases involving sales of remainder interests. The Fifth Circuit held that the sale of a remainder interest for its actuarial value was a sale for adequate consideration. Adopting the above view of the Third and Fifth Circuits, the Ninth Circuit in *Estate of Magnin v. Commissioner,* 184 F.3d 1074 (9th Cir. 1999), *rev'g and rem'g* T.C. Memo 1996–25, also held that "adequate and full consideration" was measured against the actuarial value of the remainder interest rather than the fee-simple value of the property transferred to the trust by the decedent.

82. Several cases held a life estate to be amortizable even though the income being received was tax exempt (e.g., from §103 bonds). *Gist v. United States,* 423 F.2d 1118 (9th Cir. 1970); *Estate of Christ v. Commissioner,* 54 T.C. 493 (1970), *aff'd,* 480 F.2d 171 (9th Cir. 1973); *Manufacturers Hanover Trust Co. v. Commissioner,* T.C. Memo 1969–132, *aff'd,* 431 F.2d 664 (2d Cir. 1970).
83. This discussion assumes no gift element in the transfer.
84. §167(e)(1).
85. *See* §167(e)(5)(B), §267(b)(1).
86. *See* §167(d) (regarding allocations of the depreciation deduction in a trust context).
87. If the surviving spouse dies during probate, a question might arise as to whether, under local law, the personal representative has an affirmative duty as a fiduciary to elect against the predeceased spouse's will, thereby maximizing the estate of the surviving spouse. This difficulty could be avoided by an appropriate provision in the will of the surviving spouse, permitting the fiduciary to exercise discretion concerning this choice.
88. The surviving spouse might otherwise be considered to have irrevocably gifted a remainder interest in that spouse's half of the community property to the remainder beneficiaries under the other spouse's will, as offset by the life estate in that other spouse's one-half of the community.
89. Since conflicts of interest can easily arise in this context, the estate planner advising both parties must be careful to assure that both parties understand the complexities of this arrangement and that, if appropriate, they can obtain independent advice on this matter from other counsel.
90. *See, generally,* Johanson, *Revocable Trusts, Widow's Election Wills and Community Property: The Tax Problems*, 47 Tex. L. Rev. 1247 (1969) (for drafting ideas). Note, however, that significant tax law changes have occurred since the date of this article.
91. See, generally, 826 T.M., *Life Insurance* (Bloomberg BNA); 827 T.M., *Life Insurance—A Practical Guide for Evaluating Policies* (Bloomberg BNA).
92. In the business context, for a discussion of split-dollar insurance, see Chapter 11, E.2.
93. Reg. §20.2042-1(a)(1). If includible in the gross estate, whether an asset is life insurance (as distinguished from other property) is not of substantial estate tax significance since, if a death benefit to be paid is not life insurance, its value might be taxed under §2033 (probate estate assets) or §2039 (annuities). Early in the history of the estate tax a $40,000 exemption was available for life insurance proceeds, which made this classification process of greater significance.

94. *See Helvering v. Le Gierse,* 312 U.S. 531 (1941) (noting that historically and commonly insurance involves risk-shifting and risk-distributing). *See also* §7702(a) (providing definition of "life insurance contract" for federal tax purposes [discussed below]); *Commissioner v. Treganowan,* 183 F.2d 288 (2d Cir. 1950) (proceeds received from New York Stock Exchange Gratuity Fund constituted life insurance since risk of loss from premature death was effectively shifted from individual to group of other members of Exchange); Rev. Rul. 86-80, 1986-1 C.B. 79 (noting that payments to beneficiary from Board of Trade Gratuity Fund constituted life insurance and premiums paid were not deductible for income tax purposes); PLR 200002030 (providing extensive definition of what constitutes life insurance for purposes of §101 gross income exclusion).
95. The fact that ordinary life insurance is payable upon an inevitable event (death) whereas accident policies are payable only upon an evitable event (accidental death) is not relevant in determining whether "insurance" exists. *See, e.g., Commissioner v. Estate of Noel,* 380 U.S. 678 (1965). The concept of insurance also includes death benefits paid under a policy issued pursuant to a local law no-fault insurance statute when the payment of death benefits is not a substitute for a wrongful death suit. *See* Rev. Rul. 83-44, 1983-1 C.B. 228.
96. *See* Staff of J. Comm. on Tax'n, 98th Cong., General Explanation of the Revenue Provisions of the Deficit Reduction Act of 1984, at 646-647 (J. Comm. Print 1984). For example, the portion of any contract that provides annuity benefits (other than as a settlement option) will not be considered life insurance. *Id.* Further, in an arrangement that is considered to be a combination of term insurance and an investment fund, only the term insurance portion will be treated as life insurance proceeds upon the insured's death. *Id.*
97. *See* §7702(a)(1). Further, a variable life insurance contract must meet a diversification requirement to qualify as a life insurance contract. *See* §817(h).
98. This test is generally used to qualify the traditional whole life policy as life insurance. This test requires that, by the terms of the contract, the cash surrender value may not at any time exceed the net single premium that would have to be paid at such time to fund future benefits, assuming a maturity date of no earlier than the insured's age 95 or later than the insured's age 100. §7702(b), §7702(e).
99. *See* §7702(c), §7702(d). This test is generally used to qualify "universal life" and adjustable life policies. *See, e.g.,* PLR 9517042 (describing certain flexible premium universal life insurance contracts).
100. Policy dividends can be paid to the insured but are often used to acquire additional paid-up insurance.
101. A policy can be a single-premium policy only; that is, only one payment ever need be made to have fully paid-up insurance coverage under the particular policy.
102. A term policy can be a level term policy, enabling the payment of the same premium amount during the period of the policy. A term policy may be in a decreasing coverage amount, recognizing that the increasing age of the insured means a higher actuarial risk, with the coverage being reduced, rather than the premium being increased.
103. Note that pursuant to §2206 the recipient of the proceeds will be responsible for a proportionate share of the federal estate taxes attributable to the policy proceeds (if includible in the gross estate), unless the decedent provides otherwise in his or her will, thereby reducing the net amount of life insurance proceeds received.

104. If the proceeds are includable in the insured's gross estate, this option is selected by the insured, and the surviving spouse is the sole beneficiary of the annuity payments, the transfer of value under the policy will qualify for the estate tax marital deduction because no payments can be made to anyone other than the spouse (or his or her estate). Like many annuities, this annuity may have a refund feature enabling the full return of the investment were the annuitant to die before that occurs.
105. If the proceeds are includible in the gross estate and if selected by the insured, this option will not qualify for the marital deduction (if the payments are to be made to the surviving spouse) since the surviving spouse beneficiary might not receive all the payments under the settlement arrangement.
106. Where this option is chosen by the insured, if a right of withdrawal is provided and if any restrictions on the right of withdrawal are merely formal, the proceeds should qualify for the marital deduction (assuming inclusion of the proceeds in the insured's gross estate). *See Estate of Cornwell v. Commissioner,* 37 T.C. 688 (1962), *acq.*, 1964-1 C.B. 4; *Estate of Jennings v. Commissioner,* 39 T.C. 417 (1962), *acq.*, 1964-2 C.B. 6. If no right of withdrawal is provided, naming the surviving spouse as the beneficiary under the policy will not qualify the proceeds for the marital deduction unless qualification can occur under the QTIP rule in §2056(b)(7).
107. Section 2042 deals only with inclusion of life insurance proceeds in the estate of the insured. The value of a life insurance policy may also be taxed in the estate of someone other than the insured. For example, where the wife owns a policy on the life of her husband and predeceases him, the value of the unmatured policy is includible in her estate under §2033 as property owned at her death. The estate tax value of such property will normally be the interpolated terminal reserve value (rather than the cash surrender value), assuming valuation through the sale of comparable contracts is not readily ascertainable. *See* Reg. §20.2031-8(a). *See, e.g.,* Rev. Rul. 78-137, 1978-1 C.B. 280 (single-premium life insurance policy owned by decedent for many years on life of another person may not be valued, under Reg. §20.2031-8(a), by comparing cost, at time of decedent's death, of similar policy of same face amount with lesser cash surrender value). Use of the interpolated terminal reserve may also be appropriate when the insured and the owner-beneficiary die in a common disaster. *See, e.g., Estate of Wien v. Commissioner,* 441 F.2d 32 (5th Cir. 1971); *Estate of Chown v. Commissioner,* 428 F.2d 1395 (9th Cir. 1970).
108. §2042(1).
109. §2042(2). If the insurance contract does not satisfy the requirements of §7702(a)(1), only the excess of the amount of death benefits paid over the net cash surrender value of the contract will be treated as "life insurance" for tax purposes upon receipt at the death of the insured. §7702(g)(2).
110. The "payment of premiums" test was dropped in enacting the 1954 Code "to place life insurance policies in an analogous position to other property." *See* S. Rep. No. 83-1622, at 124 (1954). The Committee Report indicated that "no other property is subject to the estate tax where the decedent initially purchased it and then long before his death gave away all rights to the property." The House Minority Report however indicated (with respect to the elimination of the premium payment test) that: "[i]t is sought to justify the change as merely putting life insurance on a par with other property which may be given away free from estate tax if the gift is not made in contemplation of death. But life insurance is not like other property. It is inherently testamentary in nature. It is designed,

in effect, to serve as a will, regardless of its investment features. Where the insured has paid the premiums on the life insurance for adding to what he leaves behind at his death for his beneficiaries, the insurance proceeds should certainly be included in his taxable estate." *See* H.R. Rep. No. 83-1337, at B-14 (1954).

111. This assumes no transfer of the policy within three years of death or that is otherwise subject to the transfer provisions, §2036–§2038. *See* §2035(a).
112. §2042(1). Often, except when required under a creditor life policy, this beneficiary designation is to be avoided since policy proceeds are ordinarily exempt from the claims of creditors unless the estate is designated as the beneficiary. Similarly, in some common-law property jurisdictions the insurance proceeds payable to other than the estate cannot be reached by the surviving spouse in the exercise of his or her statutory right of election to receive a specified portion of the deceased spouse's assets. Ordinarily, if the proceeds are receivable by the executor, the incidents of ownership will be vested in the decedent and the proceeds will, therefore, also be includible in the gross estate under §2042(2).
113. Proceeds of insurance on a decedent's life are included in the gross estate if receivable by the executor or administrator or payable to the decedent's estate. Reg. §20.2042-1(b)(1).
114. Reg. §20.2042-1(b)(1). For example, where a policy is owned by an irrevocable trust, an obligation on the trustee to use proceeds to pay estate expenses of the insured would cause these proceeds to be includible in the insured's gross estate.
115. For example, this would be applicable to creditor life insurance proceeds. Such proceeds are included in the gross estate under §2042(1) even though not "receivable by the executor." The amount of the loan outstanding at the date of the decedent's death (which is eliminated by these insurance proceeds) will be deductible in determining the taxable estate. *See* Reg. §20.2053-4, §20.2042-1(b)(1). The net effect is that the insurance proceeds eliminate the debt as a deductible item, and the creditor no longer is concerned about pursuing the estate for payment of the loan balance.
116. Ordinarily, the insured will apply for a policy on the insured's life and will retain the ownership of the policy until death, causing inclusion under §2042(2). This provision does not require, however, as a prerequisite of gross estate inclusion of the proceeds, that the insured have applied for the policy or have been the original owner of the policy.
117. *See* Reg. §20.2042-1(c)(2) (also indicating that "the term has reference to the right of the insured or his estate to the economic benefits of the policy").
118. *See* Rev. Rul. 75-70, 1975-1 C.B. 301 (right retained by transferor of insurance policy to veto owner's choice of beneficiary was "incident of ownership"). Where a divorce decree required the decedent to maintain his minor children as beneficiaries of his group accident and health insurance, he had no incidents of ownership, regardless of contrary terms of the contract. *Estate of Beauregard v. Commissioner*, 74 T.C. 603 (1980), *acq.*, 1981-1 C.B. 1. *See also* TAM 8819001 (power to terminate spouse's interest in policy by obtaining divorce is not incident of ownership).
119. See the discussion Chapter 11, E.1.b., concerning the assignment of incidents of ownership in a group term life policy. In Rev. Rul. 79-46, 1979-1 C.B. 303, the IRS ruled that a decedent's right to prevent cancellation for nonpayment of premiums on an insurance policy owned by the employer on the decedent's life by purchasing the policy for its cash surrender value caused the insurance proceeds, less the cash surrender value, to be included in the gross estate. The Tax Court held, however, that the right of an

employee to acquire a policy in order to prevent cancellation did not require inclusion, at least where the employee had no significant stock ownership interest in the employer policy owner. *Estate of Smith v. Commissioner,* 73 T.C. 307 (1979), *acq. in result only,* 1981-1 C.B. 2. The court did note that the beneficiary designation in Rev. Rul. 79-46 (the employee's spouse) was different from that in the case (the corporation). *See also* Rev. Rul. 69-54, 1969-1 C.B. 221 (power of employee to convert group policy into individual policy was incident of ownership although exercisable only when insured terminates his employment). The Tax Court rebuffed the IRS on this issue. *See Estate of Smead v. Commissioner,* 78 T.C. 43 (1982) (stating that conversion right is too remote or contingent to be considered incident of ownership). The IRS subsequently modified its position on this issue, ruling that a conversion privilege exercisable only in the event of the termination of employment is not an incident of ownership for these purposes. Rev. Rul. 84-130, 1984-2 C.B. 194.

120. Reg. §20.2042-1(c)(4); *Estate of Lumpkin v. Commissioner,* 474 F.2d 1092 (5th Cir. 1973). *But see Estate of Connelly v. United States,* 551 F.2d 545 (3d Cir. 1977). In Rev. Rul. 81-128, 1981-1 C.B. 469, the IRS announced it will follow *Lumpkin* in all cases other than those identical to *Connelly* in the Third Circuit. *See also* AOD 1983-032.
121. Reg. §20.2042-1(c)(3). Accordingly, having the insured's estate as a contingent beneficiary creates a risk that the reversionary right will be large enough to cause inclusion in the gross estate. *See* Rev. Rul. 79-117, 1979-1 C.B. 305.
122. Reg. §20.2042-1(c)(4) specifies that incidents of ownership can be held "as trustee or otherwise." Certain circuit courts of appeal hold that policies are includible only if the insured can exercise fiduciary powers for his or her own personal benefit. *Estate of Skifter v. Commissioner,* 468 F.2d 699 (2d Cir. 1972); *Estate of Fruehauf v. Commissioner,* 427 F.2d 80 (6th Cir. 1970). *See also Hunter v. United States,* 474 F. Supp. 763 (W.D. Mo. 1979), *aff'd,* 624 F.2d 833 (8th Cir. 1980). *Cf. Gesner v. United States,* 600 F.2d 1349 (Ct. Cl. 1979). The Fifth Circuit has held that incidents of ownership held in a fiduciary capacity do require inclusion in the insured's estate. *Rose v. United States,* 511 F.2d 259 (5th Cir. 1975); *Terriberry v. United States,* 517 F.2d 286 (5th Cir. 1975), *cert. denied,* 424 U.S. 977 (1976).
123. See Rev. Rul. 2011-28, 2011-49 I.R.B. 830, holding that a grantor's retention of the power, exercisable in a nonfiduciary capacity, to acquire an insurance policy held in trust by substituting other assets of equivalent value will not, by itself, cause the value of the insurance policy to be includible in the grantor's gross estate under §2042, provided the trustee has a fiduciary obligation (under local law or the trust instrument) to ensure the grantor's compliance with the terms of this power by satisfying itself that the properties acquired and substituted by the grantor are in fact of equivalent value, and further provided that the substitution power cannot be exercised in a manner that can shift benefits among the trust beneficiaries.
124. *See Estate of Skifter v. Commissioner,* 468 F.2d 699 (2d Cir. 1972), *aff'g* 56 T.C. 1190 (1971), *nonacq.*, 1978-1 C.B. 3.
125. See, for example, PLR 200947006, PLR 200948001, and PLR 200949004 where a partner in a partnership released all powers over a policy on his life and was treated as not having incidents of ownership.
126. *See* Rev. Rul. 76-261, 1976-2 C.B. 276 (adopting Fifth Circuit position in *Rose* and *Terriberry*). However, in Rev. Rul. 84-179, 1984-2 C.B. 195, the IRS revoked Rev. Rul. 76-261 and ruled to this effect for purposes of §2042(2). For a further discussion of Rev.

Rul. 84-179, see PLR 200404013, where the IRS ruled that an irrevocable trust arrangement did not result in the existence of "incidents of ownership."

127. Reg. §20.2042-1(c)(6). In *Estate of Levy v. Commissioner,* 70 T.C. 873 (1978), proceeds from insurance policies owned of record by a corporation, insuring the life of a controlling shareholder and payable to his widow, were included in the gross estate of the controlling shareholder. The Tax Court rejected a challenge to the validity of Reg. §20.2042-1(c)(6), which provides that if any part of the proceeds of a policy on the life of a decedent who is a sole or controlling shareholder of a corporation are not paid to or for the benefit of the corporation, the incidents of ownership will be attributed to the decedent with respect to such part. Note that, if policy proceeds are payable to or for the benefit of the corporation, and are thus not includible in the insured's estate as insurance, the proceeds would, nevertheless, be reflected in the increased value of the corporation's stock as included in the gross estate for estate tax purposes. Reg. §20.2042-1(c)(6) (cross-referencing Reg. §20.2031-2(f)). *See also* Rev. Rul. 90-21, 1990-1 C.B. 172 (gratuitous assignment of life insurance policy by corporation within three years of death of corporation's controlling shareholder is transfer of incidents of ownership in policy by controlling shareholder).
128. Constructive ownership rules are provided, for example, in §318 (applicable in the corporate taxation context).
129. *See* Rev. Rul. 83-147, 1983-2 C.B. 158 (proceeds of life insurance policy owned by partnership, but payable other than to or for benefit of partnership, are includible in deceased insured partner's gross estate because incidents of ownership were held in conjunction with other partners).
130. See PLR 200214028 (no estate tax inclusion results under §2042 when proceeds of insurance policy owned by partnership were payable to partnership). See PLR 200947006, PLR 200948001, and PLR 200949004, where by contract only the other partners could exercise authority concerning the life insurance policy on the life of the deceased partner.
131. See Reg. §20.2042-1(a)(2).
132. §2035(a). *See* Rev. Rul. 90-21, 1990-1 C.B. 172 (concerning applicability of §2035 in controlling shareholder/corporation context).
133. *Estate of Margrave v. Commissioner*, 71 T.C. 13 (1978), *aff'd*, 618 F.2d 34 (8th Cir. 1980). The IRS approved this decision in Rev. Rul. 81-166, 1981-1 C.B. 477 (upon insured's death, completed transfer by policy owner occurs, with life estate being retained (within meaning of §2036(a)) by policyholder).
134. The traditional life insurance policy is separated into three independent elements: i.e., the protection, investment, and expense components. Each gross premium is credited to the policy's investment account against which is charged the insurance protection for the period, as well as expenses. The essential question is whether this investment fund is an integral part of the risk-shifting process (which occurs upon the payment of premiums on life insurance), so as to come within the safe harbor of the gross income exclusionary provision, §101(a)(1). After much controversy concerning universal life policies (flexible premium policies), §7702 was enacted in the Deficit Reduction Act of 1984 (DEFRA), Pub. L. No. 98-369, §221. Flexible premium contracts continue to come within the §101(a)(1) gross income exclusion, provided the contracts satisfy one of two alternative tests: (1) a cash value accumulations test or (2) a test consisting of a "guideline premium requirement" and a "cash value corridor requirement." *See* §7702(a). Any contract not satisfying either of the two tests will be treated as providing a combination of a term life

insurance policy and an annuity. §7702(g). For income tax purposes, if a contract does not satisfy the requirements for any taxable year, the policyholder will be treated as having received or accrued ordinary income during that year. §7702(g)(1)(A). Income will be based on the sum of the increase in net cash surrender value during a taxable year, plus the cost of life insurance protection during that year, less the amount of premiums paid. §7702(g)(1)(B). All income on a contract for all prior taxable years will be treated as received or accrued during the taxable year in which the contract fails to satisfy the definition of a life insurance contract. §7702(g)(1)(C).

135. Section 72(e) addresses the income tax treatment for amounts received from a life insurance policy. Growth of cash value is not included as gross income within §72(e) triggers and the inference is that the mere buildup of cash values inside a life insurance policy prior to accessing those values is not a taxable event.
136. Rev. Rul. 2009-13, 2009-1 I.R.B. 1029, specifies that the surrender of a policy for its cash value (or amounts received upon the lapse of a policy) will result in ordinary income (rather than capital gain) for the amount received in excess of tax basis.
137. *See* §264(a). This limitation applies to a single premium life insurance contract (which includes a contract where substantially all the premiums are paid within the first four years). §264(a)(2), §264(c)(1). This limitation does not apply if no part of four of the first seven annual premiums is paid through borrowings. *See* §264(d)(1). For additional exceptions to the interest deduction disallowance, see §264(d)(2)–§264(d)(4) and §264(e). The IRS will not rule (under §264(c)) whether "substantially all" the premiums of a contract of insurance are paid within a period of four years from the date on which the contract is purchased or on whether §264(d)(1) applies. Rev. Proc. 2015-3, 2015-1 I.R.B. 129, §3.01(34), (35).
138. §163(h)(1).
139. §101(a)(1). Section 101(a)(2) provides, however, that no exclusion for insurance policy gain is permitted where the policy is transferred for consideration, unless the transfer is by gift (see §101(a)(2)(A)) or among members of a limited group of business associates (as defined in §101(a)(2)(B)). Not included in this limited group are transfers between corporate shareholders (although a transfer of the policy to a corporation is within this exception). Various private letter rulings have been issued by the IRS where shareholders were permitted to create parallel partnerships for effectively circumventing this policy transfer limitation. For tax treatment guidance for buyers and sellers of life insurance contracts, see Rev. Rul. 2009-13, 2009-21 I.R.B. 1029 (for policyholders who surrender or sell their life insurance contracts) and Rev. Rul. 2009-14, 2009-21 I.R.B. 1031 (for investors who buy life insurance contracts). Rev Rul. 2009-14 describes the rule that death proceeds received by an unrelated purchaser of a life insurance policy will produce ordinary income.
140. §101(g)(1), as added by the Health Insurance Portability and Accountability Act of 1996, Pub. L. No. 104-191, §331, applicable to amounts received after December 31, 1996. Section 101(g)(4)(A) specifies that the "term 'terminally ill individual' means an individual who has been certified by a physician as having an illness or physical condition which can reasonably be expected to result in death in 24 months or less after the date of the certification."
141. §101(g)(2).
142. Often some delay will be encountered in seeking immediate payment on a life insurance policy while processing requirements are satisfied. The life insurance company may pay

some small amount of interest for its use of funds during that period. That interest will be included in gross income.

143. §101(c). Formerly, if the recipient was a surviving spouse, the first $1,000 of interest paid each year on deferred insurance proceeds was exempt (pursuant to former §101(d)(1)(B)), but this gross income exclusion was eliminated.
144. §101(d)(1). For example, if the insurance proceeds are $100,000, an option might be elected to receive $10,000 per year for 15 years (or a total of $150,000). One-third of each year's payment would constitute interest income for these purposes. This computational formula does effectively allow income tax postponement since, economically, a greater principal amount held during the early payout years produces larger interest income amounts. Therefore, the gross income inclusion for these interest payments being received is not on a constant yield basis.
145. Additionally, the estate planner will want to consider: (i) the estate tax impact of any policies held by the client as a beneficiary and insuring the lives of other persons, and (ii) whether those policies should be transferred by gift to assure that any unexpended proceeds received in the event the client survives the insured will not be includible in the client's gross estate.
146. See 827 T.M., *Life Insurance—A Practical Guide for Evaluating Policies* (Bloomberg BNA).
147. See the general discussion of gifts in Chapter 6, A.
148. Reg. §25.2512-6(a). The replacement value is usually not the cash surrender value. Rather, the replacement value is ascertained by adding to the interpolated terminal reserve of the policy at the date of the gift the proportionate part of the gross premium last paid before the date of the gift which covers the period extending beyond that date. *Id.* Upon request, this valuation will ordinarily be provided by the life insurance company.
149. Reg. §20.2042-1(a)(3) (including in gross estate "the full amount receivable under the policy").
150. The recipient of that policy could possibly loan those proceeds to the estate to eliminate these liquidity problems. See the discussion of irrevocable insurance trusts in C.3.c.(3) of this chapter. A right to demand access to these funds cannot be retained by the policy transferor, however, without causing inclusion of those proceeds in the insured's gross estate.
151. *See* §2035(a).
152. The retention by the donor of physical possession (e.g., in his or her safe deposit box) might cause him or her to have "incidents of ownership" where the policy itself would need to be surrendered to change the designated beneficiary. This risk should normally not exist if the policy ownership is by a trust and the possession of the policy held by the insured for the trustee is merely as a matter of convenience.
153. §2035(a), as amended by the 1997 Act, Pub. L. No. 105-34, §1310 (pre-1997 Act §2035(d)(2)). The 1997 Act revised §2035 to improve its clarity as to the ERTA, Pub. L. No. 97-34, §403, amendments.
154. This treatment applies even if the policy transfer occurs only indirectly. *See* Rev. Rul. 90-21, 1990-1 C.B. 172 (if shareholder disposes of his or her controlling share interest in corporation within three years of death, and corporation holds nonbusiness insurance policy on shareholder's life, policy proceeds are includible in the shareholder's gross estate under §2035).

155. *See* Rev. Rul. 82-141, 1982-2 C.B. 209 (involving transfer by corporation controlled by insured; policy proceeds includible under §2035), *amplified by,* Rev. Rul. 90-21, 1990-1 C.B. 172 (controlled corporation's gratuitous transfer of ownership of policy insuring life of controlling shareholder within three years of controlling shareholder's death will be attributed to controlling shareholder for purposes of §2035 even if after transfer of policy controlling shareholder disposes of control of corporation); GCM 39815 (Apr. 23, 1990). *See also Knisley v. United States,* 901 F.2d 793 (9th Cir. 1990) (one-half of proceeds of life insurance policy owned and payable to decedent's wife were includible in decedent's gross estate where community funds were used to acquire policy and to pay premiums within three years of death).
156. Caution should be exercised in this area because the legislative history on the ERTA amendments to §2035 broadly states that "gifts of life insurance" are excepted from the general rule of §2035 (providing for no gross estate inclusion for transfers within three years of death). *See* H.R. Rep. No. 97-201, at 187 (1981).
157. As noted above, §2035(a) applies only to life insurance policies the proceeds of which would have been includible under §2042 had the relevant rights or powers over the policies been retained by the decedent.
158. *Bel v. United States,* 452 F.2d 683 (5th Cir. 1971), *cert. denied,* 406 U.S. 919 (1972). Rev. Rul. 82-13, 1982-1 C.B. 132, expressly distinguishes a group term policy from the accidental death policy in *Bel,* pointing out that the payment of the premium on the group policy at the time for the policy's renewal did not create new rights but merely effectuated the continuation of the existing agreement. In *Bel,* the payment of each annual premium after the creation of the policy was considered a purchase of a new policy.
159. *See* TAM 9323002 (describing this issue in significant detail). *See also Estate of Perry v. Commissioner,* 927 F.2d 209 (5th Cir. 1991), *aff'g* T.C. Memo 1990-123; *Estate of Headrick v. Commissioner,* 918 F.2d 1263 (6th Cir. 1990), *aff'g* 93 T.C. 171 (1989), *acq. recommended,* AOD 1991-012; *Estate of Leder v. Commissioner,* 893 F.2d 237 (10th Cir. 1989), *aff'g* 89 T.C. 235 (1987) (where trustee initially applied for insurance policy, decedent must actually have possessed incidents of ownership and must have transferred those incidents of ownership to third party within three years of insured decedent's death for §2035 to apply); *Estate of Richens v. Commissioner,* T.C. Memo 1991-23; *Estate of Ard v. Commissioner,* T.C. Memo 1990-294; *Estate of Chapman v. Commissioner,* T.C. Memo 1989-105.
160. See 826 T.M., *Life Insurance* (Bloomberg BNA); 807 T.M., *Personal Life Insurance Trusts* (Bloomberg BNA).
161. The IRS has successfully argued that the trustee is merely acting for the insured in buying the policy so that, in reality, the insured purchases and then transfers the policy into the trust. *See Detroit Bank & Trust Co. v. United States,* 467 F.2d 964 (6th Cir. 1972), *cert. denied,* 410 U.S. 929 (1973); *Hope v. United States,* 81-2 USTC ¶13,434 (N.D. Tex. 1981). The IRS has lost most of the post–ERTA §2035 cases involving policy transfers, but caution in this context remains advisable.
162. Retention of ownership of the policies would enable the grantor to deal with insurance policies without involving the trustee and without the expense of an active trust administration. If an insured who retained the ownership of policies but later became mentally incompetent and needed the cash surrender value of his or her life insurance policies for living expenses, the exercise of the privilege of surrendering life insurance

policies for their cash value could be a complicated, expensive problem involving the appointment of a guardian, unless a durable power of attorney is available to enable this. If, however, the ownership of the policies is vested in the trust, the appointment of a guardian could be avoided since, if necessary and appropriate, the trustee could exercise the privilege of surrender of the policy, or borrow against the policy, and use the proceeds for the insured's benefit. As a revocable trust, the insurance proceeds (and any other trust assets held at death) would be includible in the trust grantor's gross estate.

163. The retention of the power to alter, amend, or revoke the trust causes the gift to be incomplete. *See* Reg. §25.2511-2(b). Similarly, payments of premiums by the trust grantor or the trustee will not constitute gifts since the trust assets can be retrieved by the trust grantor.

164. Section 2038 requires inclusion where a decedent has made a trust transfer but has retained a power to alter, amend, revoke, or terminate. Section 2036 requires inclusion where the decedent has retained during his or her lifetime the right to designate the person(s) who will enjoy the transferred property or its income. Reg. §20.2042-1(c)(4) provides that a decedent is considered to have an "incident of ownership" in an insurance policy on his or her life held in trust if, under the terms of the policy, the decedent has the power (as trustee or otherwise) to change the beneficial ownership in the policy or its proceeds. The trust may be used, of course, to shelter all or a portion of the insurance proceeds from federal estate tax by way of the estate tax marital deduction, assuming the marital trust provisions in the trust agreement are appropriately constructed to satisfy the requirements of §2056(b)(5) or §2056(b)(7).

165. The income of the trust will be taxable to the grantor by reason of the retained power to revoke the trust. §676(a).

166. Any excess income could be either accumulated or distributed to the beneficiaries in accordance with the dispositive provisions of the trust instrument.

167. Reg. §25.2511-2(b). Reg. §25.2512-6(a) specifies rules for the valuation of life insurance contracts transferred by gift.

168. Later payments of premiums made from the income of an irrevocable funded trust would not constitute additional gifts, since sourced from funds previously subjected to gift tax.

169. Note, in this context, Rev. Proc. 2015-3, 2015-1 I.R.B. 129, §4.01(48), indicating that the IRS will not ordinarily rule whether the transfer of property to a trust will be a gift of a present interest in property when: (1) the trust corpus consists or will consist substantially of insurance policies on the life of the grantor or the grantor's spouse; (2) the trustee or any other person has a power to apply the trust's income or corpus to the payment of premiums on policies of insurance on the life of the grantor or the grantor's spouse; (3) the trustee or any other person has a power to use the trust's assets to make loans to the grantor's estate or to purchase assets from the grantor's estate; (4) the trust beneficiaries have the power to withdraw, on demand, any additional transfers made to the trust; and (5) there is a right or power in any person that would cause the grantor to be treated as the owner of all or a portion of the trust under §673 through §677.

170. If the trust is unfunded, the gift will probably be a gift of a future interest unless the beneficiary of the trust can compel the conversion of the insurance policy to income-producing assets or can withdraw some portion of the trust (including forcing a borrowing against the policy). If the trust is funded, only the value of the right to receive

the income after deducting the amount of income necessary to pay the premium on the policies might seem to qualify as a gift of a present interest.

171. See the discussion of the demand (or *Crummey*) trust in Chapter 6, D.3.g. If each beneficiary of the trust can withdraw principal in an amount equal to annual additions to the trust (up to $14,000 per annum, as indexed for inflation from $10,000, for the years 2015 and 2016, or $28,000 in the case of split gifts between spouses), gifts of policies or future premium payments should qualify for the §2503(b) annual donee exclusion. This *Crummey* withdrawal right is often drafted to permit annual withdrawal from the trust on a noncumulative basis of the lesser of the amount of the annual exclusion or the fair market value of the property transferred into trust. To avoid estate and gift tax problems associated with a §2514(e) lapse of a power, the withdrawal right is frequently limited to $5,000, however, unless the trust corpus is greater than $280,000 (in which event the 5% would enable a $14,000 withdrawal for 2015 or 2016 gifts). See the discussion of the estate and gift tax ramifications of five-and-five powers in Chapter 5, E.4.a.(4), and Chapter 6, D.3.g. For persons creating new life insurance trusts where annual premium payments are substantial, the planning choice is whether to shelter the premium payments from gift taxes through the use of the full annual exclusion or to protect the beneficiary from subsequent adverse estate and gift tax consequences. If the beneficiary is a lifetime beneficiary of the trust (e.g., a spouse) the $5,000 limit should probably be retained unless the trust is a large trust. If the beneficiary is likely to survive the grantor and to receive the trust property outright at a future date, the trust proceeds will be taxed in the beneficiary's estate in any event if death occurs in the natural order. The only risk of estate tax due to the unrestricted *Crummey* power then occurs in the event of the beneficiary's death prior to the termination of the trust. In many cases, a donor faced with annual gifts for premium payments in excess of $5,000 will prefer to ignore the $5,000 (or 5%) limit, rather than use the unified credit amount or pay a gift tax currently.

172. Note TAM 9532001, where the IRS denied the annual donee exclusion where the *Crummey* powerholder waived notice of any future annual additions to the trust. The IRS indicated that a present interest cannot exist over assets that the beneficiary has no opportunity to enjoy.

173. Within the meaning of §2042(2). This would preclude the grantor from acting as the trustee of the trust unless those powers over the policies that would be "incidents of ownership" are explicitly delegated to another person, therefore beyond the control of the grantor-trustee. *See* Reg. §20.2042-1(c)(4).

174. Reg. §20.2036-1(b)(2) provides that the decedent will be regarded as having retained the right to income from property where the income was to be applied "for his pecuniary benefit." The IRS has unsuccessfully argued that, where the income from the trust is used to maintain the grantor's life insurance, the grantor has retained the income throughout his or her life and the value of the noninsurance assets held by an irrevocable trust should also be included in his or her gross estate. *See First Nat'l Bank of Birmingham v. Commissioner,* 36 B.T.A. 651 (1937), *acq.*, 1937-2 C.B. 24; *Bennett v. United States,* 185 F. Supp. 577 (N.D. Ill. 1960), *aff'd*, 293 F.2d 323 (9th Cir. 1961).

175. Reg. §20.2042-1(b)(1). This planning problem can be circumvented by providing in the irrevocable trust instrument that the trustee may make loans to the executor for this purpose or, on behalf of the trust, may purchase assets from the grantor's probate estate. *See also* Rev. Rul. 81-164, 1981-1 CB 458 (with respect to trust grantor's power to borrow from insurance trust during his lifetime).

176. §2035(a). This rule should not be applied, however, if the policy is acquired directly by the trust from the insurance company. *See, e.g., Estate of Headrick v. Commissioner,* 93 T.C. 171 (1989), *aff'd,* 918 F.2d 1263 (6th Cir. 1990) (proceeds of life insurance policy purchased by irrevocable trust within three years of insured's death were not includible in his gross estate under §2035).
177. If policy dividends are received, they will not normally constitute gross income. Such dividends represent a return of premiums and are not taxable. *See* §72(e)(1)(B). Further, as noted above, the internal buildup in the policy does not constitute current gross income.
178. *See* §677(a)(3) (requiring that grantor be treated as owner of any portion of trust whose income, without approval or consent of any adverse party or in discretion of grantor or nonadverse party, is or may be applied to the payment of premiums on policies of insurance on the life of the grantor or the grantor's spouse). Section 672(a) defines "adverse party" as "any person having a substantial beneficial interest in the trust which would be adversely affected by the exercise or nonexercise of the power which he possesses respecting the trust." In PLR 8839008, a trust had income producing assets and an insurance policy insuring grantor's life, but the terms of the trust prohibited trust accounting income from being used to pay premiums on insurance insuring the life of the grantor or his spouse. The IRS ruled that §677(a)(3) was applicable for income tax purposes since the source of the premium payments for trust accounting purposes was not relevant. Many practitioners do insert in their irrevocable insurance trust documents a provision stating that trust income cannot be used to pay premiums on the life of the grantor, assuming this is sufficient to negate the applicability of §677(a)(3). Various decisions have adopted exceptions to the broad rule, applying §677(a)(3) only if an insurance policy whose premiums can be paid with trust income is in existence during the taxable year. *See Corning v. Commissioner,* 104 F.2d 329 (6th Cir. 1939); *Weil v. Commissioner,* 3 T.C. 579 (1944). In some instances, taxpayers rely on §677(a)(3) to assert that a trust is intentionally defective and should be treated as a grantor trust for income tax purposes.
179. Note, however, the discussion of split-interest purchases and the probable gift tax impediments under §2701 in Chapter 7, G.
180. Before designating the testamentary trustee as a beneficiary under the policy, the estate planner should carefully analyze pertinent local law considerations, including: (1) whether policy proceeds can be paid directly to a testamentary trustee (alternatively, the proceeds could be paid to the estate for distribution to the testamentary trustee); (2) whether, if desired, the insurance policy proceeds paid to the testamentary trust will be safeguarded from the claims of creditors; (3) whether these assets will be includible in determining the base for computing probate administration costs (if computed on a value, rather than time, basis); (4) whether beneficiary designations and similar insurance documents must be completed with testamentary formalities; and (5) whether periodic probate accountings with the local probate court will be required for the testamentary trust even though specifically waived in the trust instrument.
181. For example, sprinkling of income and corpus, discretionary distributions, a special power of appointment, avoidance of local probate restrictions on asset transfers to minors, and limited generation skipping.
182. Since the trust will not come into existence until the decedent's death, the trust will not realize income for income tax purposes at any prior time. Therefore, no grantor trust

income tax problem will arise in the testamentary trust context since §677(a)(3) will not apply.

183. For an example of an irrevocable funded trust agreement, see 807 T.M., *Personal Life Insurance Trusts* (Bloomberg BNA).
184. *See* §2056(b)(5), §2056(b)(7); Chapter 5, D.3.d., concerning the QTIP trust.
185. Practitioners often include a specific clause in a will that any insurance on the life of the surviving spouse will be transferred to children (or a trust for children) rather than to that spouse.
186. For example, if the surviving spouse is the executor of the estate of the spouse who owned a policy on the life of the executor/surviving spouse, that executor could be treated as holding "incidents of ownership" until the probate process is completed.
187. A lifetime gift of a joint and survivor policy followed by the death of one of the two insured parties within three years does not appear to be subject to the three-year transfer rule. Section 2035 applies only if §2042 would have been operative had there been no transfer. Section 2042 applies only to life insurance "proceeds" payable at death. In this situation, if the joint and survivor policy had been retained, no "proceeds" payable upon the death of the first to die would have been received. Section 2035 would be applicable, however, when the policy is transferred after the death of the first insured and the surviving spouse dies within three years of that transfer.
188. Reg. §1.72-1(b) specifies that "amounts received as an annuity" are amounts that are "payable at regular intervals over a period of more than one full year from the date on which they are deemed to begin, provided the total of the amounts so payable or the period for which they are to be paid can be determined as of that date."
189. See 821 T.M., *Tax Issues of Employee Plan and Commercial Annuities* (Bloomberg BNA), for a complete discussion of the federal estate and gift tax rules relevant to annuities. An annuity can be payable on a joint and survivor basis, thereby based on several lives. Although unusual, a person could receive annuity payments based on another person's life.
190. See the discussion of private annuities in Chapter 7, F., and in 805 T.M., *Private Annuities and Self-Canceling Installment Notes* (Bloomberg BNA).
191. This element is often mandated by applicable state insurance laws. Note that the refund amount is based on a return of cash equivalent to the amount of the original investment, rather than the return of the annuitant's tax basis (while excluding gross income from this computation).
192. §72(c)(1), §72(c)(2).
193. §72(b)(1). This computation is made by applying the following fraction against each annuity payment received: Investment in the contract ÷ Expected return
194. §72(a), §72(b). Compare this to the special rule for the treatment of payments received under a private annuity, as discussed in Chapter 7, F. Previously, in the case of certain employee annuities, where only part of the consideration paid for the annuity contract was contributed by the employee and, during the three-year period beginning on the date on which an amount was first received under the contract as an annuity, the aggregate amount receivable by the employee was equal to or greater than the consideration for the contract contributed by the employee, all amounts received as an annuity under the contract could be excluded from gross income until the employee had recovered his or her investment in the contract. This provision (former §72(d)) was repealed by the Tax Reform Act of 1986 (1986 TRA), Pub. L. No. 99-514, §1122(c) (effective generally for

individuals whose annuity starting date was after July 1, 1986). Post-1986 TRA §72(d) was amended by the Small Business Job Protection Act of 1996 (SBJPA), Pub. L. No. 104-188, §1403, effective with respect to annuity starting dates beginning 90 days after August 20, 1996, to provide that basis recovery on annuity payments from qualified plans generally is determined under a method similar to a simplified alternative method then provided by the IRS. This provision was further amended in the 1997 Act, Pub. L. No. 105-34, §1075(a), to provide a simplified method when payments are to be made for more than one life. The portion of each annuity payment that represents a return of basis equals the employee's total basis as of the annuity starting date, divided by the number of anticipated payments under the following table from §72(d)(1)(B)(iii) and §72(d)(1)(B)(iv):

If the age of the annuitant on the annuity starting date is:	The number of anticipated payments is:
Not more than 55	360
More than 55 but not more than 60	310
More than 60 but not more than 65	260
More than 65 but not more than 70	210
More than 70	160

If the annuity is payable over the lives of more than one individual, the number of anticipated payments is determined as follows:

If the combined ages of the annuitants are:	The number of anticipated payments is:
More than 110	410
More than 110 but not more than 120	360
More than 120 but not more than 130	310
More than 130 but not more than 140	260
More than 140	210

A refund feature in the annuity contract will not impact the application of this simplified method. §72(d)(1)(C).

195. *See* §72(b)(2).
196. *See* §72(b)(4) (definition of "unrecovered investment"). For this purpose the taxpayer's investment in the contract as of the annuity starting date is determined without regard to the value of the refund feature. §72(b)(4)(A). This will enable the entire investment in the contract to be recovered tax-free.
197. *See* §72(b)(3).
198. §72(e)(2)(B).
199. §72(e)(4). Note that this income inclusion treatment compares unfavorably to a borrowing against the cash surrender value of a life insurance policy, which does not constitute the receipt of gross income.
200. Section 2039 is not the only provision affecting the estate tax status of annuity payments. If, under a contract purchased by a decedent, payments that accrued before his or her death have become payable to his or her estate, the value of those anticipated payments

will be includible under §2033. A reservation of a power to surrender an annuity contract for cash or to change the person named to succeed him or her as annuitant will result in inclusion of the value of the contract as a revocable transfer under §2038 (even though not held in trust).

201. Examples of contracts to which §2039(a) was intended to apply include: (1) a contract under which the decedent immediately before his or her death was receiving (or was entitled to receive) for the duration of his or her life an annuity, with payments thereunder to continue after his or her death to a designated beneficiary if surviving the decedent (i.e., a "self and survivor" annuity); (2) a contract under which the decedent immediately before his or her death was receiving (or was entitled to receive), together with another person, an annuity payable to the decedent and that other person for their joint lives, with payments to continue to the survivor following the death of either (i.e., a joint and survivor annuity); (3) a contract entered into by the decedent and his or her employer under which the decedent immediately before his or her death and following retirement was receiving (or was entitled to receive) an annuity (or other stipulated payment) payable to the decedent for the duration of his or her life and, thereafter, to a designated beneficiary, if surviving the decedent (whether the payments after the decedent's death are fixed by the contract or are subject to an option or election exercised or exercisable by the decedent); and (4) a contract under which the decedent immediately before his or her death was receiving (or was entitled to receive) an annuity for a stated period of time, with the annuity to continue to a designated beneficiary upon the decedent's death before the expiration of that period, if that beneficiary survived the decedent.
202. §2039(b). Before DEFRA, Pub. L. No. 98-369, §525, repealed former §2039(c)-§2039(g), $100,000 of the value of certain annuities paid from a qualified retirement plan was excludible from the gross estate. Elimination of that exclusion in DEFRA mandates that qualified plan benefits are fully includible in the annuitant's gross estate for federal estate tax purposes.
203. This would accord with the treatment of a life estate which expires at death (i.e., since no property interest survives the decedent, no value is transferred for estate tax purposes).
204. If the "refund" is paid to the estate, that amount would be includible in the gross estate under §2033. Otherwise (i.e., if paid to other than the probate estate), since an amount is payable by reason of the annuitant's death, from property with respect to which decedent had retained a life interest, that amount would be includible in the gross estate under §2036.
205. This assumes that the annuitant (or his or her employer), and not the survivor, provided the consideration for the annuity. *See* §2039(b).
206. *See* Staff of J. Comm. on Tax'n, 112th Cong., Present Law and Background Relating to the Federal Tax Treatment of Charitable Contributions (JCX 55-11) (Oct. 14, 2011). This document can be found at www.jct.gov.
207. The value of the charitable deduction for federal income tax purposes will be dependent in many instances, as noted below, both on the donor's marginal income tax rate and the amount of appreciation inherent in the contributed property (if not to be included as recognized gain).
208. Tax Management has published a number of portfolios analyzing various aspects of these issues, including: 839 T.M., *Estate and Gift Tax Charitable Deductions* (Bloomberg BNA); 863 T.M., *Charitable Contributions: Income Tax Aspects* (Bloomberg BNA); 865 T.M., *Charitable Remainder Trusts and Pooled Income Funds* (Bloomberg BNA); 866

T.M., *Charitable Lead Trusts* (Bloomberg BNA); 456 T.M., *Private Foundations and Public Charities—Definition and Classification* (Bloomberg BNA); 877 T.M., *Private Foundations and Public Charities—Termination (§507) and Special Rules (§508)* (Bloomberg BNA); 468 T.M., *Private Foundations—Section 4940 and Section 4944* (Bloomberg BNA); 470 T.M., *Private Foundations—Self-Dealing (Section 4941)* (Bloomberg BNA); 472 T.M., *Private Foundations—Distributions (Section 4942)* (Bloomberg BNA); 473 T.M., *Private Foundations—Excess Business Holdings* (Bloomberg BNA); and 474 T.M., *Private Foundations—Taxable Expenditures (Sec. 4945)* (Bloomberg BNA).

209. Before the Tax Reform Act of 1969, Pub. L. No. 91-172, taxpayers could actually produce net gain from a charitable transfer, particularly where the transfer consisted of ordinary income property. See the example in S. Rep. No. 91-522, at 80 (1969). Since 2013, with a maximum 20% federal income tax rate on corporate dividends received (pursuant to §1(h)(11)), considerable benefit can be obtained through receiving corporate dividends (including from one's closely held corporation) subject to the 20% tax rate, and then contributing the entire dividend amount to charity (including to a private charitable foundation) and receiving a deduction to offset ordinary income otherwise taxed at a maximum rate of 39.6% under §1(a)-§1(e) and §1(i) (therefore producing a positive 19.6% differential). Note, however, the possible applicability of the charitable contributions percentage limitation on deductions for federal income tax purposes. *See* §170(b). Section 1(h)(11), the general §1(h) 20% maximum capital gains tax rate, and the §1(i) 39.6% maximum income tax rate apply to taxable years beginning after 2012. *See* ATRA, Pub. L. No. 112-240, §101(b), §102(b). Prior to 2013, the §1(h) maximum capital gains tax rate was 15% and the §1(a)–§1(e) and §1(i) maximum income tax rate was 35%, producing a 20% difference. *See* 2010 TRA, Pub. L. No. 111-312, §101(a), §102 (extending sunset provisions in EGTRRA, Pub. L. No. 107-16, §901, and JGTRRA, Pub. L. No. 108-27, §303).

210. *See* §1(a)-§1(d), §1(i).

211. Before 1993, the appreciation element of contributed property was treated as a tax preference item for purposes of the alternative minimum tax. *See* former §57(a)(6), before amendment by the Revenue Reconciliation Act of 1993, Pub. L. No. 103-66, §13171(a). This tax cost could have reduced the benefit of the charitable transfer.

212. This assumes that in this situation the surviving spouse will implement that subsequent charitable gift, rather than diverting it to some newly found individual beneficiary.

213. *See* Reg. §20.2055-1(a).

214. For income tax purposes, the term "charitable contribution" is defined in §170(c). Section 2055(a)(1), the estate tax provision permitting a charitable contributions deduction, is similar. A prerequisite is that the transfer must be for a charitable purpose. *See Hernandez v. Commissioner,* 490 U.S. 680 (1989) (payments to Church of Scientology in exchange for "auditing" sessions were held to be not deductible as §170 charitable contributions, since donors were treated as expecting and receiving something of value for their payments). *But see* (partially in response to *Hernandez*) §170(f)(8), §6115 (receipt of "intangible religious benefit" does not constitute receipt of consideration in charitable contributions context). See, further, *Sklar v. Commissioner,* 549 F.3d 1252 (9th Cir. 2008), where the taxpayer was not permitted a charitable deduction for tuition paid to a religious school for religious education for taxpayer's children.

215. *See Davis v. United States,* 495 U.S. 472 (1990) (taxpayers were not entitled to charitable contribution deduction for payments made to their children serving as Mormon missionaries since payments were not "for the use of" qualifying charitable organization).
216. §170(c)(1). *See also* §2055(a)(1) (estate tax), §2522(a)(1) (gift tax).
217. §170(c)(2). *See* §508(a) (specifying procedural requirements necessary for such organization to be treated as tax exempt within meaning of §501(c)(3)). The "private foundation" (which can qualify as a charitable organization under §501(c)(3)) functions as a convenient receptacle for charitable contributions, although subject to various restrictions. *See also* Rev. Proc. 2015-9, 2015-2 I.R.B. 249 (prescribing procedures for organizations when seeking recognition of tax-exempt status under §501).
218. §170(c)(2). *See also* §2522(a)(2). The estate tax deduction provision specifies that the contribution must be "to or for the use of" a corporation or must be "to" a trustee and does not refer to community chests, funds, and foundations. §2055(a)(2). The estate tax regulations use the phrase "corporation or association." Reg. §20.2055-1(a)(2). Unlike the income tax deduction provision, the estate and gift tax deductions are not limited to charitable transfers to domestic corporations. Foreign corporations are, accordingly, permissible recipients for estate and gift tax deduction purposes. *See* Reg. §§20.2055-1(a), §25,2522(a)-1(a). Difficulties may sometimes arise in demonstrating that the foreign charity is organized exclusively for charitable purposes.
219. The estate tax provision for contributions to or for the use of corporations and the gift tax provision also specifically include transfers for "the encouragement of art." §2055(a)(2), §2522(a)(2). The estate tax provision refers to amateur sports competitions only in the context of contributions to or for the use of corporations. §2055(a)(2).
220. Section 2055(a)(2) and §2522(a)(2) are similar to this income tax provision.
221. *See also* §2055(a)(2), §2055(a)(3), §2522(a)(2) (similar estate and gift tax rules).
222. §170(c)(3). *Cf.* §2055(a)(4), §2522(a)(4).
223. §170(c)(4). *Cf.* §2055(a)(3), §2522(a)(3).
224. This status can ordinarily be verified by consulting the IRS's *Exempt Organizations Select Check* system, available at www.irs.gov/Charities-&-Non-Profits/Exempt-Organizations-Select-Check. See, also, the database at www.guidestar.org, which provides essential information on each charity's mission, programs, leadership, and finances. A copy of each organization's IRS Form 990 is available for examination.
225. To qualify for an estate tax charitable deduction, an effective transfer of property must occur. The validity of a charitable bequest is to be determined under local law. If the bequest is void under local law, for whatever reason, no estate tax deduction is allowable, notwithstanding that no objection to the void bequest is raised by other legatees or heirs.
226. Certain capital gain property that has appreciated in value is particularly appropriate for lifetime gifts, due to the resulting income tax benefits, as discussed below.
227. For income tax purposes, §170(a)(1) provides that a charitable contribution is deductible only if verified in the manner prescribed by Treasury regulations. *See also* §170(f)(11). Substantiation rules are prescribed in Reg. §1.170A-13(a), §1.170A-13(b), and §1.170A-13(c). Additional information must be attached to the donor's income tax return using Form 8283 in the case of a donation of property for which a deduction exceeding $500 is claimed. Appraisals are required with respect to contributed property with a claimed value of more than $5,000 except as to securities for which market quotations are readily available. *See* Reg. §1.170A-13(c). Rules are prescribed for obtaining an appraisal from a qualified appraiser and for attaching an appraisal summary signed by

the appraiser to the return on which a deduction is first claimed for such contribution. Further, §6050L provides that if a donee charity sells, exchanges, transfers, or otherwise disposes of any "charitable deduction property" within three years of the date of receipt of such property, the donee must furnish an information return to the IRS setting forth the donor's name, address, and tax identification number and certain other information. Effective for returns filed after September 1, 2006, the Pension Protection Act of 2006, Pub. L. No. 109-280, §1215(b), §1215(d)(2), increased the two-year reporting period in §6050L(a)(1) to three years and added to the information the donee must report. Form 8282 is prescribed for providing this information.

228. If the recipient is a private charitable foundation, a nominal tax would be incurred by the charity. *See* §4940(a).

229. *See* §170(e)(1) (which does not limit amount of this gift). In some instances of gifts of appreciated property, the amount of the charitable gift is reduced to tax basis. *Id. See also* §170(b)(1)(C)(i) (imposing requirement that deductions for appreciated property charitable gifts may not exceed 30% of taxpayer's contribution base for such year).

230. Section 170(e)(1)(B)(ii) reduces to tax basis the deduction for gifts of appreciated long-term capital gain property to a private foundation, that is, the gift is reduced by the long-term capital gain amount which would have been recognized if a sale of these shares had been made. However, §170(e)(5) provides that this limitation for private foundation gifts is not applicable for the contributions to private foundations of certain stock for which market quotations are readily available.

231. *See* 17 C.F.R. 230.144.

232. *See* PLR 199915053.

233. §170(e)(1)(B)(i). The IRS may rule that tangible personal property gifted to a charity may be related to the purpose or function constituting the basis for the charity's exemption. *See* PLR 200223013.

234. §170(e)(1)(B)(i). Effective for contributions made after Septemeber 1, 2006, §170(e)(1)(B)(i)(II), as added by the Pension Protection Act of 2006, Pub. L. No. 109-280, §1215(a)(1), §1215(d)(1), contains a long-term capital gain reduction rule for certain contributions of related-use tangible personal property if the donee disposes of the property before the end of the year in which the contribution was made and does not provide a §170(e)(7)(D) certification. Long-term capital gain reduction rules also apply for certain contributions of intellectual property (as noted in E.3.c. of this chapter) and taxidermy property (under §170(e)(1)(B)(iv), as added by the Pension Protection Act of 2006, Pub. L. No. 109-280, §1214, effective for contributions made after July 25, 2006).

235. §170(e)(1)(A).

236. *See* Reg. §1.170A-4(b)(1). Examples of ordinary income property include inventory, art works created by the donor, a manuscript prepared by the donor, letters and memoranda prepared by or for the donor, and a capital asset held by the donor for less than the applicable long-term capital gain holding period.

237. In *Pescosolido v. Commissioner*, 883 F.2d 187 (1st Cir. 1989), the court held that a taxpayer's deductions for the charitable contribution of §306 stock was limited to the income tax basis in the stock. The court noted that §306(c)(1)(A) specifies that the amount realized from the sale of §306 stock is ordinary income and that §170(e)(1)(A) requires that the amount of the deduction for the donation of appreciated property must be reduced in this situation by the amount of any ordinary gain inherent in the property. The court

concluded that the taxpayers did not qualify for the §306(b)(4) exception to ordinary income treatment, since they had failed to satisfy their burden of proof by showing that the disposition of the stock was not part of a plan having as one of its principal purposes the avoidance of federal income tax. *See also* TAM 8930001 (indicating that deduction is not available for contribution of §306 stock since full fair market value of stock would have been treated as ordinary income if stock had been sold). Note, however, the possible impact in this context of §306(a)(1)(D) (enacted in the Jobs and Growth Tax Relief Reconciliation Act of 2003 (JGTRRA), Pub. L. No. 108-27, §302(e)(3)) which specifies that for "purposes of §1(h)(11) and such other provisions as the Secretary may specify" any ordinary income amount is treated as a dividend. Under §1(h)(11), the corporate dividend is treated as capital gain (subject to a maximum 20% rate). Certainly an argument can be appropriately made that under §306(a)(1)(D), the §306 gain has been transformed into capital gain and, therefore, this limitation on the charitable deduction amount has been eliminated.

238. §170(e)(3). *See* §170(e)(4) (rules concerning contributions of research property).

239. *See Caruth Corp. v. United States,* 865 F.2d 644 (5th Cir. 1989) (where dividends were declared on nonvoting preferred stock, but were not paid before charitable contribution of stock, court held that dividends were not includible in shareholder-donor's income, noting that neither "assignment of income" nor "sham transaction" doctrines were applicable). *Cf. Ferguson v. Commissioner,* 174 F.3d 997 (9th Cir. 1999) (anticipatory assignment of income doctrine was applicable to transfer of appreciated stock).

240. In *Greene v. United States,* 13 F.3d 577 (2d Cir. 1994), the donors were determined not to make an "assignment of income" by making gifts of commodity future contracts to a private foundation. The donors donated only the long-term capital gains portion of these contracts, and not the short-term capital gains portion. The donors relinquished control over the accounts. The court determined that no "assignment of income" had occurred. Subsequently, however, in *Greene v. United States,* 79 F.3d 1348 (2d Cir. 1996), the court determined that the charitable donation of futures contracts constituted a "termination" under §1256(c) and, therefore, the mark-to-market rules required income inclusion for the contributed amount.

241. *See* Rev. Rul. 2004-27, 2004-12 I.R.B. 625 (in "frivolous tax shelter" context, IRS enunciated position that services income will not be successfully shifted to charity/religious entity formed to avoid individual gross income inclusion). *See also* IRS News Release IR-2004-81 (June 22, 2004).

242. This assumes that no limitation otherwise exists on the charitable contribution of appreciated property, for example, because of the type of property or type of intended charitable recipient. *See* §170(e)(1).

243. §1011(b). Effectively, this is treated as two transactions, a sale and a gift, with the tax basis proportionately allocated to each transaction (based on the relative fair market values of each portion).

244. A surprise to some tax planners is that, for purposes of this provision, a gift of mortgaged property is a bargain sale to the extent of the transferred debt, since the charitable recipient provides consideration in the form of the assumption of debt. The amount of indebtedness must be included in the sales price even if the debt is nonrecourse (and, therefore, is not "assumed"). Reg. §1.1011-2(a)(3); *Guest v. Commissioner,* 77 T.C. 9 (1981), *acq.*, 1982-1 C.B. 1. *See* Rev. Rul. 75-194, 1975-1 C.B. 80 (gift of limited partnership interest); PLR 9533014.

245. This technique is occasionally used for the sale of a personal residence to charity where the first $250,000 of gain ($500,000 for a joint return) is excluded from gross income under §121.
246. See, however, the discussion below of §170(f)(10) and the deduction limitations when only a partial interest in a life insurance policy is contributed.
247. Reg. §1.170A-7(a)(2). *See also* §170(f)(3), §2055(e)(2), §2522(c)(2). For example, D may be given an interest in Property X for life, with the remainder in that property to B. If B gives her remainder interest to charity, this will be a deductible gift. In response to concerns in this context where intellectual property is contributed to charity, the American Jobs Creation Act of 2004, Pub. L. No. 108-357, §882, added §170(e)(1)(B)(iii) and §170(m), effective for contributions made after June 3, 2004. Section 170(e)(1)(B)(iii) generally limits the donor's income tax deduction for contributions of patents and other intellectual property to the lesser of fair market value or basis. Section 170(m), however, may allow additional income tax charitable deductions for certain amounts the charity receives or accrues on such property. *See also* Notice 2004-7, 2004-1 I.R.B. 310; Rev. Rul. 2003-28, 2003-1 I.R.B. 594.
248. §170(f)(3)(B)(ii), §2055(e)(2), §2522(c)(2); Reg. §1.170A-7(b)(1), §1.170A-5(a)(2), §20.2055-2(e), §25.2522(c)-3. For example, this could include the contribution of a 50% interest in land owned by the taxpayer or the transfer of a one-half undivided interest in a painting to a donor's wife and the transfer of the other one-half interest to an art museum. Note, in this context, the IRS acquiescence at 1989-1 C.B. 1, to the Tax Court's decision in *Winokur v. Commissioner*, 90 T.C. 733 (1988), permitting a charitable contribution for the donation of an undivided interest in an art collection, where the donee was given the immediate right to possession of the property for a portion of every year equal to its proportionate interest, but did not take actual possession within one year of delivery of the deed of gift. *See also* PLRs 200223013–014, PLR 9303007. Effective for contributions made after August 17, 2006, §170(o), as added by the Pension Protection Act of 2006, Pub. L. No. 109-280, §1218(a), §1218(d), generally: (1) disallows a §170 deduction for a contribution of an undivided portion of the donor's entire interest in tangible personal property unless the donor (or the donor and the donee) held all interests in such property immediately before the contribution; (2) applies special rules for valuing subsequent gifts in such property; and (3) imposes recapture rules and penalties if the donor does not contribute the remainder of such property or if the donee does not satisfy certain possession and related-use requirements within a specified time period. Section 2522(e), as added by the Pension Protection Act of 2006, Pub. L. No. 109-280, §1218(c), §1218(d), applies similar rules for gift tax purposes (except for the special rules for valuing subsequent gifts), effective for gifts made after August 17, 2006. Former §2522(e)(2) and former §5022(g), originally added by the Pension Protection Act of 2006, Pub. L. No. 109-280, §1218(b)-§1218(d), effective for gifts and bequests made after August 17, 2006, had provided that the fair market value of a subsequent contribution of the property for gift or estate tax purposes would be determined by using the lesser of the property's fair market value at the time of the initial contribution or at the time of the additional contribution. These special valuation provisions were repealed retroactively by the Tax Technical Corrections Act of 2007, Pub. L. No. 110-172, §3(d), §3(j). The legislative history to the Pension Protection Act of 2006 mentions a fractional interest contribution in artwork as an example to which §170(o) and §2522(e) might apply. Staff of J. Comm. on Tax'n, 109th Cong., Technical Explanation of H.R. 4, the

'Pension Protection Act of 2006,' at 307–308 (J. Comm. Print 2006). The application of §170(o) is described in detail in 863 T.M., *Charitable Contributions: Income Tax Aspects* (Bloomberg BNA).

249. §170(f)(3)(B)(i), §2055(e)(2), §2522(c)(2); Reg. §1.170A-7(b)(3), §1.170A-7(b)(4), §20.2055-2(e)(2)(ii), §20.2055-2(e)(2)(iii), §25.2522(c)-3(c)(2)(ii), §25.2522(c)-3(c)(2)(iii). In valuing the remainder for determining the available income tax charitable contributions deduction, depreciation and depletion should be taken into account. §170(f)(4). This charitable gift strategy is especially attractive when interest rates are low. An income tax deduction is available for the actuarial value of the remainder, and the lower the §7520 rate at the time of the gift the greater is the amount of the income tax deduction for the gift of the remainder.
250. §170(f)(3)(B)(iii), §170(h), §2055(e)(2), §2522(c)(2); Reg. §1.170A-7(b)(5), §1.170A-7(b)(14), §20.2055-2(e)(2)(iv), §25.2522(c)-3(c)(2)(iv).
251. §170(f)(10) (cross-referencing deductions under §2055 and §2522). Such a deduction for similar arrangements concluded prior to the 1999 enactment of §170(f)(10) has been rejected in several court decisions. *Addis v. Commissioner*, 374 F.3d 881 (9th Cir. 2004); *Weiner v. Commissioner*, 94 AFTR2d 2004-5202 (9th Cir. 2004), *cert. den.* 543. 1151 (2005).
252. See 866 T.M., *Charitable Lead Trusts* (Bloomberg BNA).
253. The charitable lead annuity trust functions similarly to the grantor retained annuity trust, that is, if the trust assets produce a total return in excess of the §7520 rate applicable when the trust was created the gift to the remainder beneficiaries will be undervalued for gift tax purposes.
254. The IRS has provided sample forms for testamentary charitable lead annuity trusts and unitrusts with one or more noncharitable remainder beneficiaries. *See* Rev. Proc. 2008-46, 2008-30 I.R.B. 238 (unitrusts); Rev. Proc. 2007-46, 2007-29 I.R.B. 141 (annuity trusts). In addition, the IRS has provided sample forms for inter vivos grantor and nongrantor charitable lead annuity trusts and unitrusts with one or more noncharitable remainder beneficiaries. *See* Rev. Proc. 2008-45, 2008–30 I.R.B. 224 (unitrusts); Rev. Proc. 2007–45, 2007–29 I.R.B. 89 (annuity trusts).
255. §170(f)(2)(B).
256. *Id.*
257. §2055(e)(2)(B), §2522(c)(2)(B).
258. §170(f)(2)(B). For example, a grantor transfers $100,000 into a trust specifying the payment of $5,000 per year to X University for nine years, with the property then reverting to the grantor. The immediate income tax deduction is the present fair market value of the $45,000 transfer. Thereafter, the grantor is taxed on $5,000 each year for nine years (with no offsetting charitable deduction). The present value of the $45,000 amount is determined using actuarial tables promulgated under §7520.
259. §170(f)(2)(B).
260. *See* §642(c).
261. An income interest is an "annuity trust interest" only if it consists of an irrevocable right under the governing instrument to receive a guaranteed annuity. Reg. §1.170A-6(c)(2)(i)(A), §25.2522(c)-3(c)(2)(vi). *See also* Reg. §20.2055-2(e)(2)(vi).
262. An income interest is a "unitrust interest" only if it is an irrevocable right under the governing instrument to receive payment, not less often than annually, of a fixed percentage of the net fair market value of the trust assets, determined annually. Reg. §1.170A-6(c)(2)(ii)(A), §25.2522(c)-3(c)(2)(vii). *See also* Reg. §20.2055-2(e)(2)(vii).

263. Because the trust is to terminate in favor of a noncharitable beneficiary other than the donor, an immediate taxable gift of the remainder interest will occur when the charitable lead trust transaction is completed. The value of that gift to private beneficiaries is determined by subtracting the value of the charitable lead interest from the entire value of the gift property. If the annuity is sufficiently large and continues for a sufficient period of time, the value of the annuity may essentially equal the value of the gift property. In this situation, no taxable gift to private beneficiaries results. The gift to the remaindermen may be protected for gift tax purposes by the unified credit amount. However, this remainder interest will be larger when interest rates are low. The same rules apply with regard to valuation of a charitable lead trust established at the death of the creator of such a trust.
264. Reg. §1.7520-2(a)(2), §20.7520-2(a)(2), §25.7520-2(a)(2). Note, however, that the IRS will not allow the §7520 tables to be applied when the donor's physical condition at the time of the property transfer evidences that death is imminent. For example, in TAM 9504004 the National Office advised that the term interest tables could not be used in valuing a charitable lead trust.
265. §170(f)(2)(A), §2055(e)(2)(A), §2522(c)(2)(A). See 865 T.M., *Charitable Remainder Trusts and Pooled Income Funds* (Bloomberg BNA). These limitations effectively prevent the trustee from deflecting excess trust assets to the private beneficiaries since the amount distributable: (i) is either determined pursuant to a precise formula or (ii) for the "pooled income fund," is under the control of other than the donor.
266. As described in §664(d)(1).
267. As described in §664(d)(2).
268. As described in §642(c)(5).
269. If created during lifetime, the charitable remainder trust can enable the donor to diversify his or her assets, increasing the donor's income without a capital gains cost being incurred. Stocks can be contributed to a charitable remainder trust, sold without a capital gains cost, and the proceeds invested by the charitable remainder trust into higher yielding assets.
270. *See* §2056(b)(7); Chapter 5, D.3.i. Unlike the charitable remainder trust, in the QTIP charitable remainder context, the trustee may be given the power to invade the principal for the benefit of the spouse. The surviving spouse may be given the right to change the designation of the charitable beneficiaries. Since the remainder interest in the QTIP trust is a partial interest and the QTIP trust is not a qualified annuity trust, unitrust or pooled income fund, no income tax deduction is available for the gift of the remainder interest in the QTIP trust when the transfer is made during lifetime. *See* §170(f)(2). The treatment is not significant in the gift and estate tax context, however, because a full marital deduction will be available in that situation and, further, at the death of the surviving spouse, the transfer to charity as specified in the QTIP provisions will enable a complete charitable deduction for estate tax purposes for the estate of the deceased surviving spouse. One disadvantage of the QTIP approach is that any capital gains will be subject to income tax during the continued lifetime of the surviving spouse.
271. The donor might reserve the right to revoke or terminate the interest of any noncharitable beneficiary (exercisable only by will). Reg. §1.664-2(a)(4), §1.664-3(a)(4). Since the life interest is revocable, no gift occurs as of the time of the creation of the trust.
272. *See* §664(c)(2) (unrelated business taxable income is defined in §512, determined as if part III of subchapter F of Code applied to trust), as amended by the Tax Relief and

Health Care Act of 2006, Pub. L. No. 109-432, §424. This amendment replaced the former §664(c) rule that taxed a charitable remainder trust on all its income for any year in which the trust had unrelated business taxable income.

273. §664(b). In 2005, the IRS issued final regulations to recognize tax rate changes, including the treatment of capital gains in 1997, 1998, and 2003 tax legislation. T.D. 9190, 70 Fed. Reg. 12,793 (Mar. 16, 2005) (amending ordering rules under Reg. §1.664-1(d)(1)). The thrust of these rules is to assure that the income subject to the highest tax rate is deemed first distributed by the trust.
274. §664(d)(1)(A), (C). The 50% maximum was added by the 1997 Act, Pub. L. No. 105-34, §1089, generally effective for transfers after June 18, 1997.
275. §664(d)(1)(D). This 10% minimum was added by the Act 1997, Pub. L. No. 105-34, §1089, effective for transfers after July 28, 1997. Whether a trust satisfies this requirement depends on the applicable §7520 rate on the date assets are transferred to the trust, as well as the noncharitable beneficiary's age, if the trust is for the beneficiary's life, or the trust's term, if the trust is for a specified term of years. Because of the uncertainty this creates for testamentary trusts, the 1997 Act also added §2055(e)(3)(J)(ii), which allows a trust that fails the 10% requirement to be reformed or voided if certain requirements are satisfied.
276. Using a percentage rather than a specific amount to define the annuity might avoid valuation miscalculations. Under both examples, the transfer to the surviving spouse would qualify for the unlimited marital deduction. *See* §2056(b)(8).
277. As an additional option, the right to sprinkle the annuity amount among several beneficiaries might be provided. Reg. §1.664-2(a)(3)(i). However, Reg. §1.664-2(a)(3)(ii) indicates that the governing instrument may not grant the trustee the power to allocate the annuity among members of a class unless such power falls within one of the exceptions to §674(a). Such a power, if retained by the grantor upon an inter vivos transfer (rather than at death), will cause estate tax inclusion under §2036 and §2038. At that time, a charitable deduction will be available for the remainder interest gift.
278. §664(d)(1)(A). In some cases, the annuity amount may be paid after the end of the year in which payment is due if the payment is made within a reasonable time period. *See* Reg. §1.664-2(a)(1)(i)(a).
279. Reg. §1.664-2(b).
280. §664(d)(2)(A), §664(d)(2)(C). The 50% maximum was added by the 1997 Act, Pub. L. No. 105-34, §1089, generally effective for transfers after June 18, 1997.
281. §664(d)(2)(D). This 10% minimum was added by the 1997 Act, Pub. L. No. 105-34, §1089, effective for transfers after July 28, 1997. Whether a trust satisfies this requirement depends on the applicable §7520 rate at the time assets are transferred to the trust and the noncharitable beneficiary's age at that time, if the trust is for the beneficiary's life, or the trust's term, if the trust is for a specified term of years. Because of the uncertainty this creates for testamentary trusts and additional contributions, the 1997 Act also added §2055(e)(3)(J), which allows a trust that fails the 10% requirement to be reformed or voided if certain requirements are satisfied, and §664(d)(4), which allows the severance of an additional contribution that would otherwise cause the trust to fail the 10% requirement.
282. §664(d)(2)(A). In some cases, the unitrust amount may be paid after the end of the year in which payment is due if the payment is made within a reasonable time period. *See* Reg. §1.664-3(a)(1)(i)(g).

283. In the "standard" charitable remainder unitrust, the payout is made from net income and, to the extent the net income is insufficient, from principal. *See* §664(d)(2). Note that in Notice 94-78, 1994-2 C.B. 555, the IRS announced that it would challenge the validity of charitable remainder trusts with short terms and high percentage unitrust payouts. The concern of the IRS was that in this situation the charitable remainder unitrust could be used to convert appreciated assets into cash while avoiding a substantial portion of the tax on the gain. To negate the intended treatment, the IRS stated that it would assert both a "substance over form" approach and the "assignment of income" doctrine. Subsequent changes to the charitable remainder trust provisions under the 1997 Act, Pub. L. No. 105-34, and under regulations were also part of the effort to combat the abusive trust described in the Notice.
284. The right to sprinkle the unitrust annual payment among several private beneficiaries might be provided. *See* Reg. §1.664-3(a)(3)(i), §1.664-3(a)(3)(ii) (governing instrument may not grant trustee power to allocate fixed percentage among members of class unless such power falls within exception to §674(a)).
285. *See* §664(d)(3)(A). The IRS will not ordinarily rule whether a trust that will calculate the unitrust amount under §664(d)(3) qualifies under §664 when a grantor, a trustee, a beneficiary, or a person related or subordinate to a grantor, a trustee, or a beneficiary can control the timing of the trust's receipt of trust income from a partnership or a deferred annuity contract to take advantage of the difference between trust income under §643(b) and income for federal income tax purposes for the benefit of the unitrust recipient. Rev. Proc. 2015-3, 2015-1 I.R.B. 129, §4.01(36).
286. *See* §664(d)(3)(B).
287. *See* Reg. §1.664-3(a)(1)(i)(c), effective for trusts created on or after December 10, 1998. The "flip" must be triggered "on a specific date or by a single event whose occurrence is not discretionary with, or within the control of, the trustees or any other persons." Examples of such events (which must be specified in the trust agreement) include the sale of unmarketable assets, as well as marriage, divorce, death, or the birth of a child. The conversion date must be the beginning of the taxable year immediately following the year containing the date of the triggering event. Any "make-up" amount is forfeited upon the conversion.
288. *See* §642(c)(5) (providing detailed requirements). *See, e.g.*, PLR 9542011, PLR 9503018 (usual process is for taxpayer to follow model provisions for pooled income funds in Rev. Proc. 88-53, 1988-2 C.B. 712, in lieu of seeking advance approval of fund as qualified under §642(c)(5)). *See also* Rev. Proc. 2015-3, 2015-1 I.R.B. 129, §4.01(34) (IRS will not ordinarily rule whether pooled income fund satisfies requirements described in §642(c)(5)). In some situations, however, the IRS will issue rulings on the qualification of pooled income funds if the provisions of Rev. Proc. 88-53 are not completely applicable. *See, e.g.*, PLRs 200608002, PLR 200329035, PLR 200329031.
289. The fund is not permitted to invest in tax-exempt securities. §642(c)(5)(C).
290. This mandates the estate planning advisor to ascertain the rate of return from investments for the pooled income fund contemplated to be the donee. Since this fund essentially functions as a mutual fund, similar investment returns should be anticipated when comparing its investment approach to mutual funds having a similar investment strategy.
291. Reg. §1.642(c)-5(a)(4), §1.642(c)-6.
292. The IRS issued revised sample annuity trust forms in 2003. *See* Rev. Proc. 2003-53, 2003-31 I.R.B. 230 (inter vivos annuity trust for one measuring life); Rev. Proc.

2003-54, 2003-31 I.R.B. 236 (inter vivos annuity trust for term of years); Rev. Proc. 2003-55, 2003-31 I.R.B. 242 (inter vivos annuity trust for two consecutive measuring lives); Rev. Proc. 2003-56, 2003-31 I.R.B. 249 (inter vivos annuity trust for two concurrent and consecutive measuring lives). *See also* Rev. Proc. 2003-57, 2003-31 I.R.B. 257; Rev. Proc. 2003-58, 2003-31 I.R.B. 262; Rev. Proc. 2003-59, 2003-31 I.R.B. 268; Rev. Proc. 2003-60, 2003-31 I.R.B. 274 (testamentary annuity trusts for same four types of distribution plans). The IRS issued revised sample unitrust forms in 2005. *See* Rev. Proc. 2005-52, 2005-34 I.R.B. 326 (inter vivos unitrust for one life); Rev. Proc. 2005-53, 2005-34 I.R.B. 339 (inter vivos unitrust for term of years); Rev. Proc. 2005-54, 2005-34 I.R.B. 353 (inter vivos unitrust for two consecutive lives); Rev. Proc. 2005-55, 2005-34 I.R.B. 367 (inter vivos unitrust for two concurrent and consecutive lives). *See also* Rev. Proc. 2005-56, 2005-34 I.R.B. 383; Rev. Proc. 2005-57, 2005-34 I.R.B. 392; Rev. Proc. 2005-58, 2005-34 I.R.B. 402; Rev. Proc. 2005-59, 2005-34 I.R.B. 412 (testamentary unitrusts for same four types of distribution plans). The IRS will recognize a trust as satisfying all the charitable remainder trust requirements if the trust document: (1) creates a valid trust under local law; (2) makes reference to the appropriate Revenue Procedure; and (3) is substantially similar to the sample instrument. *See also* Rev. Rul. 82-38, 1982-1 C.B. 96 (with respect to declarations of trust and instruments of transfer that may be used to satisfy pooled income fund requirements of §642(c)(5)), *amplified by*, Rev. Rul. 85-57, 1985-1 C.B. 182; Rev. Rul. 90-103, 1990-2 C.B. 159.

293. Rev. Proc. 2015-3, 2015-1 I.R.B. 129, §4.01(16), (35), (46), (51).

294. §2055(e)(3). Numerous private letter rulings and a few cases concern whether reformations were acceptable. *See, e.g., Estate of Johnson v. United States*, 941 F.2d 1318 (5th Cir. 1991); *Estate of Hall v. Commissioner*, 93 T.C. 745 (1989), *aff'd*, 941 F.2d 1209 (6th Cir. 1991) (Tax Court held no "qualified reformation" had occurred since amendment proceeding was not initiated on timely basis); PLR 201125007. Another option may exist in this context, that is, the immediate payment to a qualifying charity of an agreed amount, if in settlement of a bona fide will contest where a split-interest charitable remainder gift does not otherwise qualify for charitable deduction purposes. *See* Rev. Rul. 89-31, 1989-1 C.B. 277 (in situations involving settlements of will contests IRS would no longer challenge direct payments to charities solely on basis that they were made in lieu of nondeductible split-interest remainder, however, will contest settlements will continue to be scrutinized in order to assure that settlement reached is not attempt to circumvent law by means of collusion).

295. Rev. Proc. 2015-3, 2015-1 I.R.B. 129, §3.01(68).

296. The charity is limited to providing gift annuities only for the life of one or two beneficiaries and not for a specific term. *See* §514(c)(5) (specifying that "acquisition indebtedness," which causes unrelated debt-financed income to be realized by charity, does not include obligation to pay annuity that: (1) is sole consideration issued in exchange for property if, at time of exchange, value of annuity is less than 90% of value of property received in exchange; (2) is payable over life of one individual in being at time annuity is issued or over lives of two individuals in being at that time; and (3) does not (a) guarantee minimum amount of payments or specify maximum amount of payments and (b) provide for any adjustment of amount of annuity payments by reference to income received from transferred property or any other property). Note that the charity issuing the gift annuity must comply with applicable state insurance law and regulations.

297. These rates are available at www.acga-web.org. *See Ozee v. American Council on Gift Annuities,* 110 F.3d 1082 (5th Cir. 1997) (extended discussion concerning charitable gift annuities in antitrust challenge to charitable annuities interest rates). See PLR 200742010 noting were an annuity was based on these rates.
298. The value of the annuity must be less than 90% of the value of the property exchanged for the annuity. When gift annuities are arranged by young individuals and simultaneously the market interest rates are extremely low this test may not be satisfied.
299. *See* Reg. §1.170A-1(d)(3).
300. *See* PLR 200230018 (where taxpayer contemplated transferring his IRA balance to charity at death in exchange for charitable gift annuity payable to another, annuity amounts would constitute ordinary income because they were attributable to IRA account and did not receive basis step up at death).
301. *See* §170(b)(1)(A) (differentiating between public and private charities).
302. *See* §170(b)(1)(D). Different classifications made on the basis of the type of property include (1) cash, (2) long-term capital gain property, (3) ordinary income property, and (4) contributions "for the use of" a charitable organization.
303. Section 170(b)(2) provides that a corporation's charitable deductions cannot exceed 10% of its taxable income. In the situation of a closely held corporation subject to a 35% rate of tax under §11(b), a contribution by the corporation "in honor of the sole shareholder" may be more tax efficient. If the corporation is in a lower tax bracket, the corporation could distribute its earnings as dividends (subject to a 20% tax rate under §1(h)(11)) with the shareholder then contributing those funds, enabling a charitable deduction against his or her (possibly) 39.6% taxable income under §1(a)–§1(d), §1(i). Section 1(h)(11), the general §1(h) 20% maximum capital gains tax rate, and the §1(i) 39.6% maximum income tax rate apply to taxable years beginning after 2012. *See* ATRA, Pub. L. No. 112-240, §101(b), §102(b). Prior to 2013, the §1(h) maximum capital gains tax rate was 15%, and the §1(i) maximum income tax rate was 35%. *See* 2010 TRA, Pub. L. No. 111-312, §101(a), §102 (extending sunset provisions in EGTRRA, Pub. L. No. 107-16, §901, and JGTRRA, Pub. L. No. 108-27, §303). Effective for contributions made in tax years beginning after 2005 and before 2015, more favorable percentage limitation rules (and carryover provisions) apply to certain §170(h) qualified conservation contributions by some corporate farmers and ranchers under §170(b)(2)(B), as added by the Pension Protection Act of 2006, Pub. L. No. 109-280, §1206(a)(2), §1206(c). *See* §170(b)(2)(B)(iii).
304. §170(b)(1)(A), §170(b)(1)(G).
305. §170(b)(1)(B), §170(b)(1)(C). These rules, which are quite complicated as to how they relate to each other and to available charitable contribution deduction carryovers, are analyzed in detail in 863 T.M., *Charitable Contributions: Income Tax Aspects* (Bloomberg BNA).
306. *See* §170(b)(1)(C), §170(b)(1)(D).
307. *See* §170(d)(1) (gifts of money), §170(b)(1)(C)(ii) (gifts of securities and real estate held short term), §170(b)(1)(D)(ii) (gifts of capital gain property to private foundations). Effective for contributions made in tax years beginning after 2005 and before 2015, more favorable percentage limitation rules and carryover provisions apply to certain §170(h) qualified conservation contributions made by individuals under §170(b)(1)(E), as added by the Pension Protection Act of 2006, Pub. L. No. 109-280, §1206(a)(1), §1206(c). *See* §170(b)(1)(E)(vi).

308. §2055(d). Consequently, property transferred or to be transferred to charity must have first been included in the decedent's gross estate. Reg. §20.2055-1(a).
309. If the estate holds insufficient funds, the deduction will be denied. *See Estate of Dorsey v. Commissioner,* 19 T.C. 493 (1952). This result will occur even though the charity receives some payment because of the application of estate income to debts and taxes (thereby relieving the charitable residue of those burdens). *See Alston v. United States,* 349 F.2d 87 (5th Cir. 1965); *Republic Nat'l Bank of Dallas v. Commissioner,* 334 F.2d 348 (5th Cir. 1964); *Estate of Luehrmann v. Commissioner*, 287 F.2d 10 (8th Cir. 1961); *Rogan v. Taylor,* 136 F.2d 598 (9th Cir. 1943); *Waldrop v. United States,* 137 F. Supp. 753 (Ct. Cl. 1956).
310. §2055(c); Reg. §20.2055-3(a).
311. *See* Reg. §20.2055-3(a) (providing example that if $50,000 is bequeathed for charitable purpose and is subjected to state inheritance tax of $5,000 payable out of $50,000 bequest, amount deductible is $45,000). Reg. §20.2055-3(b) notes that, in such a situation, a circular computation is involved (i.e., if the federal estate tax is payable out of a charitable transfer so that the amount of the transfer otherwise passing to charity is reduced by the amount of the tax, the resultant decrease in the amount passing to charity will further reduce the allowable deduction).
312. Often, a tax allocation provision will specify that the tax liabilities are to be allocated only to the taxable transfers.
313. As defined in §509. A charitable foundation is ordinarily organized under a state law not-for-profit corporation statute, but it can be organized as a charitable trust.
314. An option in this context is a "donor-advised fund." Large mutual fund companies (and others) facilitate these arrangements by enabling charitable contributions to charitable investment pools that these companies manage. The donor can recommend grants to public charities to be made by the mutual fund manager from funds in the account. Individual account records are ordinarily private and donor gifts to charity may be made anonymously, if desired. The private foundation excise tax provisions are not applicable. However, the Pension Protection Act of 2006, Pub. L. No. 109-280, §1231-§1235, enacted a number of provisions, including excise taxes in §4966 and §4967, designed to improve the accountability of donor advised funds and their sponsoring organizations. These provisions (and their specific effective dates) are discussed in detail in 450 T.M., *Tax-Exempt Organizations: Organizational Requirements* (Bloomberg BNA).
315. §4941. See, more specifically, 470 T.M., *Private Foundations—Self Dealing (Section 4941)* (Bloomberg BNA).
316. §4942. See, more specifically, 472 T.M., *Private Foundations—Distributions (Section 4942)* (Bloomberg BNA).
317. §4943. See, more specifically, 473 T.M., *Private Foundations—Excess Business Holdings* (Bloomberg BNA).
318. §4944. See, more specifically, 468 T.M., *Private Foundations—Section 4940 and Section 4944* (Bloomberg BNA).
319. §4945. See, more specifically, 474 T.M., *Private Foundations—Taxable Expenditures (Sec. 4945)* (Bloomberg BNA).
320. §4947(a)(2).
321. *Id.*
322. §170(f)(8)(A). Reg. §1.170A-13(f)(13) indicates that the §170(f)(8) substantiation requirements do not apply to transfers to charitable remainder or charitable lead trusts.

Effective for a cash, check, or other monetary contribution made in taxable years beginning after August 17, 2006, §170(f)(17), as added by the Pension Protection Act of 2006, Pub. L. No. 109-280, §1217, provides that no §170 deduction is allowed unless the taxpayer retains as evidence a bank record or a written communication from the donee showing the donee's name and the contribution's date and amount.

323. §170(f)(11); Reg. §1.170A-13(b)(3). Form 8283 is required in this context.
324. §170(f)(11); Reg. §1.170A-13(c). *See* Form 8283. The IRS is periodically successful in challenging the validity of a taxpayer's appraisal. *See, e.g.*, *Schrimsher v. Commissioner*, T.C. Memo 2011-71.
325. §6050L, as amended by the Pension Protection Act of 2006, Pub. L. No. 109-280, §1215(b), §1215(d)(2), effective for returns filed after September 1, 2006 (increasing two-year reporting period to three years and adding to information donee must report). This report must be provided on Form 8282. Section 6050L also requires the charity to report certain information on qualified intellectual property contributions.
326. §6113(a).
327. §6115(a). Section 6115(b) specifies that "the term 'quid pro quo contribution' means a payment made partly as a contribution and partly in consideration for goods or services provided to the payor by the donee organization."
328. *See* Rev. Proc. 96-15, 1996-1 C.B. 627 (prescribing procedures enabling taxpayer to request that IRS issue "Statement of Value" for item of art transferred as charitable contribution within meaning of §170(c)). This procedure prescribes a number of requirements, including that the request for the Statement of Value include a copy of an appraisal (consistent with a prescribed format).
329. *See* Reg. §20.2055-1(c). *See also* Reg. §25.2522(a)-1(c) (regarding proof for gift tax charitable deduction).
330. *See, generally,* 854 T.M., *U.S. Taxation of Foreign Estates, Trusts and Beneficiaries* (Bloomberg BNA). Prompted by concerns about foreign trust abuses, the SBJPA, Pub. L. No. 104-188, added compliance provisions and expanded the scope of U.S. taxation of foreign trusts.
331. *See* §61.
332. Formerly, §7701(a)(31) had stated that a foreign trust meant a trust the income of which, from sources without the United States that was not effectively connected with the conduct of a trade or business within the United States, was not includible in gross income. However, amendments to §7701(a)(30) and §7701(a)(31) by the SBJPA, Pub. L. No. 104-188, §1907, established a two-part objective test for determining, for tax purposes, whether a trust is foreign or domestic. If both parts of the test are satisfied, the trust would be treated as domestic. Under the first part of the test, in order for a trust to be treated as domestic, a U.S. court (i.e., federal, state, or local) must be able to exercise primary supervision over the administration of the trust. §7701(a)(30)(E)(i). This test would ordinarily be satisfied by any trust instrument that specifies that it is to be governed by the laws of any state in the United States. Under the second part of the test, in order for a trust to be treated as domestic one or more U.S. fiduciaries must have the authority to control all substantial decisions of the trust. §7701(a)(30)(E)(ii). This test would ordinarily be satisfied in any case where fiduciaries that are U.S. persons hold a majority of the fiduciary power (whether by vote or otherwise), and where no foreign fiduciary, such as a "trust protector" or other trust advisor, has the power to veto important decisions of the U.S. fiduciaries. In applying this test, a reasonable period of

time would be allowed for a trust to replace a U.S. fiduciary who resigns or dies before the trust would be treated as foreign. A foreign trust would be defined as a trust other than a trust that is determined to be domestic under both the court-supervision test and the U.S. fiduciary test. §7701(a)(31)(B). As amended, §7701(a)(30) and §7701(a)(31) apply to taxable years beginning after December 31, 1996, or at the irrevocable election of the trustee, to taxable years ending after August 20, 1996. In 1999, the IRS issued final regulations that provide guidance for determining whether a trust is domestic or foreign. Reg. §301.7701-7, T.D. 8813, 64 Fed. Reg. 4967 (Feb. 2, 1999), generally applicable to taxable years ending after February 2, 1999. The final regulations provide a safe harbor for the court test in §7701(a)(30)(E) but not for the control test. The final regulations also provide guidance regarding the election by certain trusts to remain domestic trusts for taxable years beginning after 1996, incorporating the guidance contained in Notice 98-25, 1998-1 I.R.B. 979. For further discussion of the regulations, see 854 T.M., *U.S. Taxation of Foreign Estates, Trusts and Beneficiaries* (Bloomberg BNA).

333. Section 871 prescribes the applicable U.S. income tax rates for foreign individuals, differentiating between (1) income not connected with a U.S. business (§871(a)) and (2) income connected with a U.S. business (§871(b)). Further, special rules apply for taxation of investment gains by a foreign party in U.S. real property. *See* §897.
334. Foreign trusts are occasionally used, as noted, however, in the "asset protection trust" context to transfer assets into an irrevocable trust in a foreign jurisdiction so as to enable frustrating the claims of creditors of the trust grantor.
335. §684, enacted by the 1997 Act, Pub. L. No. 105-34, §1131, which also repealed former §1491-§1494, effective on August 5, 1997. The IRS issued final §684 regulations on July 20, 2001. T.D. 8956, 66 Fed. Reg. 37,897. The regulations apply to transfers of property to foreign trusts and estates after August 7, 2000. Reg. §1.684-5. In the preamble to the proposed regulations (REG-108522-00, 65 Fed. Reg. 48,198 [Aug. 7, 2000]), the IRS stated that an immediate effective date was necessary to inform taxpayers of the exceptions to §684 in the regulations (and presumably to prevent taxpayers from taking advantage of a later effective date).
336. Former §1491, repealed by the 1997 Act, Pub. L. No. 105-34, §1131. *But see* Rev. Rul. 87-61, 1987-2 C.B. 219 (excise tax not applicable when appreciated property transferred to foreign grantor trust but would be imposed at time grantor trust status terminated during grantor's lifetime).
337. Former §1491. This excise tax did not apply, however, if: (a) the transfer was one to which §367 applied; (b) the transfer was not described in §367, but the taxpayer elected the application of principles similar to the principles of §367; or (c) an election was made under former §1057 with respect to the transfer. Former §1492, repealed by the 1997 Act, Pub. L. No. 105-34, §1131. Under former §1057, which was repealed by the 1997 Act, Pub. L. No. 105-34, §1131, a taxpayer could elect to treat a transaction subject to former §1491 as a sale or exchange of the property transferred and to recognize as gain on such transfer the excess of the fair market value of the property transferred over the adjusted basis (for determining gain) of the property in the hands of the transferor. Thus, to the extent that gain was recognized under this election, the transfer was not subject to the former §1491 excise tax and normal rules would have applied to increase the transferee's income tax basis for the transferred assets by the amount of gain recognized. Former §1492(3). In this situation, the election to apply §367 principles would often be made since not all transfers were immediately subject to gain recognition. *See*

§367(a) (providing various exceptions to required gain recognition, such as upon transfer of assets of trade or business and for securities anticipated to be held for extended period).

338. *See* §684(b); Reg. §1.684-3(a). Reg. §1.684-2(e) specifies that if the grantor trust rules become inapplicable, a deemed transfer is then treated as occurring, causing gain recognition then to be required.
339. Reg. §1.684-3(c). However, the gain recognition treatment would apply where the foreign trust's basis is determined under former §1022. *See* Prop. Reg. §1.684-3(c)(2), REG-107595-11, 80 Fed. Reg. 26,873 (May 11, 2015).
340. See the discussion immediately below.
341. *See* §641(b). Income taxation is imposed by §871 and §872 .
342. The 30% tax does not apply with respect to "portfolio interest" received from U.S. sources by a nonresident alien. *See* §871(h). The 30% tax is also not applicable to interest received from banks and other financial institutions. *See* §871(i)(2)(A), §871(i)(3).
343. §871(a)(1), §1441(a).
344. *See* §871(a)(2); Rev. Rul. 62-154, 1962-2 C.B. 148. Under §897 (enacted in the Foreign Investment in Real Property Tax Act of 1980, Pub. L. No. 96-499), tax will be applicable, however, if the shares being sold by the foreign trust have been issued by a U.S. real property holding company.
345. Note that under the U.S. tax entity classification rules a trust engaged in business activities will not be treated as a trust for U.S. tax purposes but will be classified as either a partnership or a corporation under the business entity rules. *See* Reg. §301.7701-2, §301.7701-4. To maintain trust status, the arrangement must function as protecting and conserving property for beneficiaries and not be engaged in a profit-making business.
346. §871(b). Gain from the disposition of U.S. real property interests will be treated as effectively connected with a U.S. trade or business. §897(a)(1).
347. §871(a)(1). If that income is "effectively connected" with the U.S. trade or business (see §864(c)(2)), it will be subject to progressive rates. *See* §871(b)(2).
348. §864(c)(2), §871(a)(2).
349. *See* §679. Before the 1976 TRA, Pub. L. No. 94-455, the grantor trust rules under §671 through §678 (which tax the income of a trust to the grantor under certain conditions) applied equally to domestic and foreign trusts. If these grantor trust rules were satisfied, the income of the trust, while being accumulated offshore, could be immunized from U.S. income taxation. In addition, these trusts were generally situated in countries that did not tax interest and dividends paid to foreign investors and, therefore, these trusts would pay no income tax. This enabled a foreign-based tax-free accumulation of income, pending ultimate distributions to beneficiaries resident in jurisdictions where tax would be imposed on these receipts.
350. A year-to-year determination is to be made of whether or not a trust has a U.S. beneficiary. If a foreign beneficiary becomes a U.S. person (and thus, becomes a U.S. beneficiary), the grantor trust treatment applies to the transferor beginning with the transferor's first taxable year in which the foreign person becomes a U.S. beneficiary. However, §679(c)(3), added by the SBJPA, Pub. L. No. 104-188, §1903(d), provides that a beneficiary is not treated as a U.S. person with respect to any transfer of property to a foreign trust if the beneficiary first becomes a U.S. person more than five years after the transfer, effective for transfers after February 6, 1995. Under a special conduit rule, §672(f), as added by the Revenue Reconciliation Act of 1990, Pub. L. No. 101-508, §11343, a U.S. beneficiary

of a foreign trust is taxed as the grantor to the extent he or she has transferred any property to the foreign grantor. §672(f)(5). Amendments to §672(f) by the SBJPA, Pub. L. No. 104-188, §1904, apply with respect to a foreign trust created by a foreign person. A foreign person is prevented from being treated as the trust owner by applying the grantor trust rules only to the extent their application results in amounts being included in the income computations of a U.S. citizen, resident, or corporation, effective August 20, 1996 (subject to transitional rules for certain grantor trusts in existence on September 19, 1995). §672(f)(1). Limited exceptions were maintained to allow grantor trust status for certain revocable trusts that can only distribute to the grantor or the grantor's spouse and for trust distributions that are taxable as compensation. This income would be treated as received and, therefore, "marked to market" for tax purposes. *See* §672(f)(2)(A). Also, §957 foreign controlled corporations are treated as domestic corporations for this purpose. §672(f)(3)(A). In 2001, the IRS issued final regulations under §679 that provide definitions and operating rules for determining when a U.S. transferor is taxable on the income of a foreign trust with U.S. beneficiaries. T.D. 8955, 66 Fed. Reg. 37,886 (July 20, 2001). Generally, these regulations are effective for transfers made after August 7, 2000. Reg. §1.679-7. Reg. §1.679-1 makes it clear that §679 applies to any transferor to a foreign trust that satisfies the statutory definition, even if the transferor does not have any powers over the trust under §673-§678 that would make it a grantor trust under subchapter J. Reg. §1.679-5 applies to any nonresident alien who becomes a U.S. person within five years after making a transfer to a foreign trust with a U.S. beneficiary. The regulation treats the person as making a transfer to the trust on the date on which he or she becomes a U.S. resident. The amount transferred is the portion of the trust attributable to the property originally transferred, increased by the trust's undistributed net income (as defined in §665) from property deemed transferred. Reg. §1.679-4(a)(1)-§1.679-4(a)(3) (exceptions to general rule) provides that §679 does not apply to any transfer to a foreign trust by reason of the transferor's death (per §679(a)(2)(A)), to a foreign trust that qualifies under U.S. law as a retirement trust, or to any trust described in §501(c)(3) without regard to the notice requirements of §508(a). Reg. §1.679-2(b) reiterates the rules of §679(c)(2) to describe how a trust may be subject to §679 by having indirect beneficiaries. A foreign trust will be deemed to have U.S. beneficiaries if any amount is paid to or accumulated for a controlled foreign corporation under §957(a), a foreign partnership of which a U.S. person is a partner, or a foreign trust or estate that has a U.S. beneficiary. The rules for indirect U.S. beneficiaries also apply when an agent or intermediary is used to transfer the benefits of the trust to a U.S. person. For further discussion of these regulations, see 854 T.M., *U.S. Taxation of Foreign Estates, Trusts and Beneficiaries* (Bloomberg BNA).

351. §679(d), as enacted in the Hiring Incentives to Restore Employment Act (HIRE Act), Pub. L. No. 111-147, §532(a).
352. §679(c)(4), as enacted in the HIRE Act, Pub. L. No. 111-147, §531(b). The Joint Committee on Taxation's, General Explanation of Tax Legislation Enacted in the 111th Congress (JCS-2-11) (March 2011), specifies (at p. 239) that this provision is meant to be consistent with existing regulations under §679.
353. *See* §671, §679(a). Form 3520, *Annual Return To Report Transactions With Foreign Trusts and Receipt of Certain Foreign Gifts*, must be filed for the taxable year of the creation of a foreign trust. In addition, an annual return on Form 3520-A, *Annual Information Return*

of Foreign Trust With a U.S. Owner, must be filed for any foreign trust that has a U.S. owner under the grantor trust rules.

354. §679(a)(4), §679(a)(5), added by the SBJPA, Pub. L. No. 104-188, §1903, applicable to transfers after February 6, 1995.
355. §672(f)(1). The IRS adopted final regulations implementing the SBJPA amendments to §672(f) in 1999. T.D. 8831, 64 Fed. Reg. 43,267 (Aug. 10, 1999), generally effective for transfers after August 10, 1999. The regulations explain the rule under §672(f)(1) that prevents a foreign grantor from being treated as the owner of the trust and discuss the exceptions in §672(f)(2) for compensatory trusts and for trusts that can only make distributions to the grantor.
356. §672(f)(2).
357. Section 672(f)(5) provides that, if a trust has a foreign grantor and a U.S. beneficiary, the U.S. beneficiary is treated as the grantor of the trust to the extent that the U.S. beneficiary has transferred property, directly or indirectly, to the foreign person. The IRS issued regulations that define a grantor as any person who creates a trust or who makes a gratuitous transfer of property, that is, a transfer for less than fair market value, to the trust. Reg. §1.671-2(e), T.D. 8890, 65 Fed. Reg. 41,332 (July 5, 2000), effective for transfers on or after August 10, 1999. Reg. §1.671-2(e)(7). For further discussion of these regulations, see 854 T.M., *U.S. Taxation of Foreign Estates, Trusts and Beneficiaries* (Bloomberg BNA).
358. *See* §679(a)(2)(A); Reg. §1.679-4(a)(1).
359. §679(a)(2)(B); Reg. §1.679-4(a)(4). As originally enacted, §679(a)(2)(B) applied to a sale or exchange for fair market value if the transferor recognized all of his or her gain on the transfer, either at the time of the transfer or as provided under the §453 installment sales election. No exception was available, however, for transfers to a foreign trust in exchange for a private annuity. *See* 1976 Bluebook, at 222. The SBJPA, Pub. L. No. 104-188, §1903(a), amended §679(a)(2)(B) to eliminate the gain recognition requirement and added restrictive rules (in §679(a)(3)) for when obligations issued (or to the extent provided by regulations, guaranteed) by the trust, any grantor or beneficiary of the trust, or any related person (as defined in §643(i)(2)(B)) are treated as having value for purposes of qualifying for the §679(a)(2)(B) fair market value exception, effective for transfers after February 6, 1995. *See* Reg. §1.679-4(c), §1.679-4(d) (regarding obligations that are taken into account for §679(a)(2)(B) purposes).
360. §679(c)(3); Reg. §1.679-2(a)(3).
361. Reg. §1.643(h)-1, T.D. 8831, 64 Fed. Reg. 43,267 (Aug 10, 1999). For further discussion of these regulations, see 854 T.M., *U.S. Taxation of Foreign Estates, Trusts and Beneficiaries* (Bloomberg BNA).
362. Under §643(a)(6)(C), the capital gain of foreign trusts is to be allocated to income rather than to corpus, without the availability of any capital gains deduction. Accordingly, capital gain is treated in a manner similar to ordinary income when distributed by a foreign trust. Section 667(d) provides for a flow-through of the foreign tax credit to the beneficiary.
363. §665-§668. See the discussion of the "throwback rules" in Chapter 5, B.5.c. Although the 1997 Act, Pub. L. No. 105-34, §507(a)(1), repealed the throwback rules for most domestic trusts (by enacting §665(e)), the throwback rules remain applicable to distributions received from foreign trusts.
364. §643(f).

365. §667(c).
366. *See* §667(a), §668.
367. §668(c).
368. §668(a)(1), as amended by the SBJPA, Pub. L. No. 104-188, §1906(a). The interest charge for pre-1996 years was 6% per year on the amount of tax imposed on the beneficiary, after reduction for any foreign tax credits attributable to the distribution and for any U.S. taxes paid by the trust.
369. §668(a)(2)–§668(a)(4).
370. §668(a)(5).
371. *See* Rev. Rul. 81-244, 1981-2 C.B. 151 (applicability of conduit rule to distributions of U.S. bank interest through simple trust to nonresident alien beneficiaries). *See also* Rev. Rul. 86-76, 1986-1 C.B. 284 (amplifying Rev. Rul. 81-244, and distinguishing between current distribution [producing conduit treatment to foreign beneficiary] and current accumulation with delayed distribution [producing taxation to the trust or estate]); TAM 9413005.
372. *See* §668.
373. *See* §7701(l) (conduit rules).
374. §6048(a), as amended by the SBJPA, Pub. L. No. 104-188, §1901(a). The reporting requirements added by the SBJPA are described in Notice 97-34, 1997-1 C.B. 422.

CHAPTER 10

Special Business Planning Situations

A. Family Business Planning Options

An essential part of a comprehensive estate planning structure for a family is achieving the effective transfer to younger family members of interests in a closely held family business. This shifting of ownership can cause both (1) the management control of a family business and (2) the potential for future capital appreciation of the business interest to be vested in younger-generation members. At the same time, however, the older-generation members can retain a significant income stream for life from a retained interest in the business without having their transitions to senior ownership positions in the business enterprise constitute income recognition events for U.S. income tax purposes. This situation frequently occurs where a parent wants to shift effective control of a family business to one or several of his or her children, sometimes to the exclusion of the other children. In this situation, the existence of another child who will not participate in the business introduces additional complexities, but the parent may want that child to benefit equally from the family wealth that is represented substantially by the family business. Often, the most significant challenges in this context involve not the tax planning but the transfer of ownership in complicated family situations and the risk that the successor generations will not adequately manage the enterprise.[1] This will necessitate the involvement of accountants, insurance advisors, financial advisors, appraisers, and others in the process of facilitating this business ownership shifting.

Income, gift, and estate tax planning in this context is quite important and complicated. The valuation rules of §2701 through §2704 are of particular importance in this context.[2] These rules are controlling for determining the amount of value shifted to others (ordinarily younger-generation members) in a lifetime restructuring of the ownership of a closely held family business.

A variety of ownership formats and structural options occur and should be considered in this context when engaging in business ownership rearrangements motivated for estate planning purposes[3]:

- corporate form, whether a regular "C" corporation or a tax-option "S" corporation;
- a general partnership or limited partnership (LP), including a "family limited partnership" (or "FLP"); and
- a limited liability company ("LLC").

In addition, a variety of other arrangements between family members and enterprises might be used in the business context to shift value to younger-generation members, including (1) leases of property, (2) employment and independent contractor arrangements, (3) joint venture contracts, and (4) licensing arrangements.

B. Closely Held Family Corporations

1. Shifting Ownership by Incorporating an Operating Business

a. Planning Alternatives

A family business may already be functioning in partnership form. Alternatively, the business may be operating as a sole proprietorship, but the parent may feel that the time is appropriate to include his/her child (or multiple children) in the ownership of the business. To accomplish this objective the parent and child may consider restructuring the family enterprise, whether (1) in partnership form, (2) in limited liability company form (treated as a partnership for U.S. tax purposes), or (3) by incorporating the business in a tax-free incorporation under §351. That corporation can be either a regular ("C corporation") or a tax-option ("S corporation") corporation. This latter format permits the conduit treatment of tax items as if received directly by the shareholders (and eliminating the corporate level income tax).

Such an incorporation will create business interests (i.e., corporate shares) which may be more easily transferable than partnership interests or sole proprietorship assets. An incorporation will also permit the receipt by the older generation of shares limited as to voting rights and, particularly, as to their potential for post-incorporation appreciation.[4] These would ordinarily be designated as "preferred" shares for corporate law purposes.

b. Gain Recognition on Incorporating Transfer of Assets

If the corporate format is desired, a tax planning objective would be to assure that no gain recognition occurs upon the transfer of appreciated property from the proprietorship or partnership into the corporation in exchange for the stock of that corporation. Neither gain nor loss will be recognized if property is transferred to a corporation[5]:

- by one or more persons;
- solely in exchange for stock in such corporation[6]; and
- immediately after the exchange, such person or persons are in "control" of such corporation.[7]

In the family business planning context, this structure can enable the issuance of corporate shares in multiple classes, for example, as follows:

Situation 1—	
Parent—	100% nonvoting preferred stock
Child—	100% voting common stock
Situation 2—	
Parent—	80% nonvoting preferred stock 20% voting common stock[8]
Child—	20% nonvoting preferred stock
	80% voting common stock

Note, however, that S corporation classification will not be available when the corporation has multiple classes of stock.[9]

After this transaction the parent might (under either situation) use the nonvoting preferred stock for gifts to another child (particularly a child not subsequently participating in the business). The parent could also use either nonvoting preferred or common stock for gifts to the child participating in the business enterprise. Thus, under Situation 2 (above), voting common stock could be available for gifts to the participating child at the same time that gifts of nonvoting preferred stock are made, for example, to a child not participating in the family business.

c. Gift Tax Risk on Incorporation

(1) Possible Transfer of Value

The shares issued on incorporation to the parent and the child (or children) should represent the relative fair market values of the properties transferred into the corporation by each of these shareholders. Otherwise, a gift will be deemed to have been made to the extent that a disproportionate stock issuance occurs.[10] This occurs because greater value is held by the younger generation after the transaction than before the transaction.

(2) Special Valuation Rules when Divided Equity Structure

Of particular importance in this context in measuring the amount of the transfer is the applicability of the special Chapter 14 valuation rules relevant in the gift context. The special valuation regime specified in §2701 may apply in measuring (1) whether a gift of a corporate (or partnership) interest is made to certain family members (spouses, lineal descendants, and spouses of lineal descendants) and (2) the amount of any gift transfer. These special valuation rules can apply in the context of the restructuring of the family business upon incorporation. They can also apply when a partnership is restructured and when a corporation is recapitalized. The essence of §2701 (applicable for measuring gift transfer amounts) is that all property (e.g., the entirety of the equity of a corporation) is treated as being transferred to the younger-generation member(s) except the portion that can be specifically quantified under prescribed rules as being retained by the older-generation members.[11]

2. Corporate Recapitalizations

a. Objectives

Ownership interests of family members may be shifted within an already existing corporate structure, thereby accomplishing estate planning objectives through the use of a "recapitalization" of the corporation.[12] In the recapitalization, several classes of shares can be issued in exchange for one preexisting class of shares. The benefits to be achieved through a recapitalization stock redistribution can include (1) enabling incentives to new managers (including younger family members), (2) easing the ultimate separation of the older managers, (3) maintaining existing capital (although rearranging the corporate structure), (4) protecting the interests of senior management through the use of preferred stock, (5) precluding an increase in estate tax liability (by eliminating the potential for subsequent appreciation of stock held by the older generation), and (6) making available a stock interest appropriate for future gift transfers to younger-generation members.

The tax traps in this area are numerous, however.[13] A number of tax pitfalls must be avoided in this context including:

- classifying the exchange as other than a tax-free corporate reorganization[14];
- avoiding ordinary dividend treatment on the exchange;
- if possible, avoiding preferred stock bailout treatment of preferred stock received in the exchange;
- complying with the special gift tax valuation rules; and
- possible other valuation questions.

b. Tax-Free Reorganization Treatment

A "recapitalization" is a type of tax-free corporate reorganization engaged in by only one corporation.[15] A recapitalization may occur whenever a stockholder transfers his or her stock to the issuing corporation in exchange for a different kind or class of stock in that corporation.[16] Unlike most other corporate reorganizations, the recapitalization is a reshuffling of capital interests within the corporate structure of one entity, rather than a combination of two or more existing corporations or a division of one corporation into several corporate entities.

For the exchanging interest holder, a corporate recapitalization can be either "upstream" (an exchange of common stock with preferred stock received) or "downstream" (an exchange of preferred stock for common stock received). In the estate planning corporate recapitalization context, the "upstream" recapitalization is ordinarily used, with the older-generation members upgrading their equity position from common stock to preferred stock.[17]

A recapitalization is a tax-free corporate reorganization for both the stockholders and the corporation,[18] assuming it has a valid business purpose.[19] If a shareholder, therefore, exchanges his or her common stock in the corporation for preferred stock or for a different class of common stock, he or she normally would recognize no gain (or loss) as a result of this share exchange. If he or she receives both stock and cash (or some form of property other than stock of the exchanging corporation), gain will be recognized. That gain will be recognized, however, only to the extent of the cash or the fair market value of the other property.[20]

c. Possible Dividend Treatment of Recapitalization Exchange

Ordinary dividend treatment may arise immediately from the corporate recapitalization, notwithstanding that the exchange is treated as a tax-free corporate reorganization. The general rule is that gross income does not include the amount of any distribution of the stock of a corporation made by such corporation to its shareholders with respect to its stock.[21] A number of important exceptions to this general rule exist, however.[22] The purpose of these exceptions is to tax immediately those shareholders who elect (or can elect) to receive stock of the corporation in lieu of periodic cash dividends or other property interests that differ substantially from a corporation's voting stock. These taxable transactions include, for example:

- A distribution, at the election of the shareholders, payable either in (a) stock of the distributing corporation or (b) property.[23]
- Disproportionate distributions, that is, those distributions that result in the receipt of property by some shareholders and in an increase for other shareholders in their proportionate interests in the earnings and profits of the distributing corporation.[24] To fit within this rule, two classes of distributions must occur before a disproportionate distribution results.[25]
- The distribution of common stock to some common shareholders and preferred stock to other common shareholders.[26]
- Any distribution on preferred stock (except antidilution adjustments of convertible preferred).[27]
- Certain distributions of convertible preferred stock even if pro rata.[28]

Quite importantly, these rules imposing income taxation are inapplicable to a single and isolated exchange that occurs in the estate planning context.[29]

d. Possible Preferred Stock Bailout Treatment

Section 306 (the provision restricting the potential tax-free bailout of dividends) also may be applicable to the preferred stock received in an estate planning recapitalization transaction. This provision was enacted to restrict the conversion of potential dividend income into a return of capital and capital gains. This provision applies even where no dilution of a shareholder's underlying equity investment and comparable dilution of control of the corporation occurs. Section 306 stock (ordinarily preferred stock), when issued, obtains a "taint" and its later disposition generates "ordinary income" (rather than capital gain) treatment. Even if for some taxpayers no income tax rate differential exists between capital gain and ordinary income, §306 remains significant because the stock value serves as the measure of the amount of income possibly to be treated as received when the stock is subsequently sold to a third party. Note that amounts treated as "ordinary income" on the disposition of §306 stock are treated as "dividends" for purposes of applying the reduced rates (ordinarily 20%) applicable to dividends under §1(h)(11).[30]

Section 306 stock consists of any stock distributed (other than common on common) to a shareholder if any part of the distribution is not included in the gross income of the distributee under §305(a).[31] This stock can include preferred stock received in connection with a reorganization under §368, provided the effect of the transaction is substantially the same as the receipt of a stock dividend.[32] Attribution of ownership rules apply in this context for measuring this effect of the distribution.[33]

At the time of a later disposition of the §306 stock, the amount realized (in other than a redemption of this stock) is treated as ordinary income (which, under §306(a)(1)(D), is a dividend). This treatment is limited, however, to the ratable share of earnings and profits at the time of the distribution of the §306 stock.[34] If the §306 stock is subsequently redeemed (i.e., acquired by the issuing corporation), the entire amount realized is treated as a dividend to the extent of the corporation's earnings and profits at the time of this subsequent redemption, rather than at the time of issuance of this stock.[35] Certain exceptions are applicable to the §306(a) ordinary income recognition: (1) the termination of a shareholder's entire interest in the corporation,[36] (2) a complete termination of the shareholder's interest in a redemption transaction,[37] (3) the redemption of the shares in a partial liquidation,[38] (4) a redemption pursuant to a complete liquidation,[39] or (5) where the taxpayer establishes that the transaction "was not in pursuance of a plan having as one of its principal purposes the avoidance of Federal income tax."[40]

If the owner of §306 stock holds this stock until death, the §306 taint will likely disappear.[41] If cash is needed for consumption purposes during lifetime, funds could possibly be borrowed, with the §306 stock pledged as security to the lending institution. Depending upon the stockholder's life expectancy, this would ordinarily produce a better net financial result than selling part of the §306 stock with the objective of using the after-tax proceeds for consumption purposes.[42]

Any disposition of §306 stock by lifetime gift is not a satisfactory tax planning alternative. If this stock is given to a private donee, this stock continues with the §306 "taint" in the hands of the donee.[43] If §306 stock is donated to a charitable organization, the income tax charitable contributions deduction will be limited to the shareholder's tax basis in the §306 stock.[44]

e. Gift Tax Valuation Issues

(1) Elements of the §2701 Valuation Rules

Various other tax planning issues arise from the possible value shifting to younger-generation members as a result of an estate planning recapitalization.[45] That shift of value could constitute a taxable gift for federal gift tax purposes (even when, as noted above, a bifurcated capital structure is not created).[46] An unanticipated transfer tax liability may be incurred when ownership of the common stock is provided to the younger generation. The amount of the gift to these common shareholders will ordinarily be the difference between the value of the preferred stock received by the older-generation shareholder and the common stock exchanged for it, subject to the further application of the §2701 valuation rules.

The §2701 valuation provision is triggered only when a transfer occurs of a junior equity nonmarketable interest in a corporation (or partnership) for the benefit of a family member. If only one class of stock (or one class of partnership interest) is involved, these special valuation rules are not applicable.[47] If market quotations are readily available for the retained or the transferred interest, the transaction is outside the scope of these special valuation rules.[48] A further exception is applicable for those retained interests that are proportionally the same as those interests which are transferred. Consequently, differences in voting power with respect to corporate stock (and differences in management and liability limitations with respect to partnership interests) are disregarded in determining the applicability of these valuation rules.[49]

(2) Subtraction Valuation Approach

Under §2701, the evaluation of the transferred interests is done on a "subtraction method." The entire entity is first valued. The value of the interests retained by the transferor is then subtracted from the total entity value.[50] The resulting amount is the value of the interest transferred for gift tax purposes. Applicable valuation criteria require that certain rights connected with the retained interest be prescribed a zero value.[51] These might include noncumulative dividends, puts, calls, and certain liquidation rights.

The effect of this valuation approach is to ascribe a nominal value for the interest retained by the transferor. Consequently, for gift tax purposes, the value of the transferred interest can be at or near the entire value of the entity.[52] This could generate a high gift tax exposure at the time of the business restructuring transaction, rather than at the later death of the senior family member.

(3) Defining Family Member

Section 2701 applies when the transfer of ownership interests in a business entity is to a member of the transferor's family. For this purpose a "member of the family" includes the transferor's spouse, lineal descendants of the transferor or the transferor's spouse, and the spouse of any descendent.[53] This term does not include, however, transfers to collaterals such as uncles, aunts, or cousins or transfers to an ancestor of the transferor or the transferor's spouse.

(4) "Qualified Payments"

The gift tax impact of an entity ownership restructuring transaction can be reduced if the senior equity interest incorporates a right to receive a "qualified payment." For this purpose, a "qualified payment" is a dividend that is payable on a periodic basis and at a fixed rate or at a variable rate with a fixed relationship to a market interest rate.[54]

Even where value is placed on a retained interest based on a "qualified payment" right appearing to be equivalent to the entire value of the enterprise, the junior equity interest of the entity is to be assigned a value of at least 10% of the total value of the corporation (or partnership), as noted above.[55] For making this measurement the total value of the enterprise consists of all of the entity's equity interests plus the total debt owed by the entity to the transferor or to an "applicable family member."[56]

(5) Failure to Make Qualified Payments

Section 2701 assumes that receipt of the preferred payments (e.g., cumulative preferred dividends) actually occurs as scheduled. If payment delays extend beyond the statutorily permitted four-year grace period, additional gift tax must be paid upon a subsequent lifetime transfer of the retained interest in the entity (or the termination of the interest).[57] Alternatively, an additional estate tax is to be paid at the death of the transferor.[58]

Any accumulated qualified payments are deemed to increase the value of the retained interest by a compounded amount computed as if the dividend was paid when due and then invested at an annually compounding rate.[59] The increase in value under this unpaid dividend rule cannot exceed the increase in the value of all the junior equity interests accruing after the transfer at issue.

(6) Elections

Several elections are provided with respect to the applicability (or nonapplicability) of §2701. One election would waive the qualified payment treatment to preclude application of the compounding rules if dividend payments are not made as scheduled.[60] A further election is to treat an otherwise nonqualifying distribution right as a qualified payment, so as to assign value to the retained interest for gift tax purposes.[61]

(7) Planning Considerations

These special gift tax valuation rules applicable to family corporate (and partnership) ownership restructurings suggest consideration of a variety of planning options, including: (1) implementing these ownership reshufflings when values are low (e.g., at the bottom of an economic cycle); (2) considering divided ownership (perhaps with reserved voting rights) when the family enterprise is being organized; and,

(3) implementing ownership changes when the gift transfer value can be substantially absorbed by the lifetime gift tax exemption amount, including, perhaps, with gift splitting with the spouse to enabling the doubling of that possible exclusion amount.

3. Stock Purchase Agreements

A stock purchase agreement (often referred to as a "buy-sell agreement") will often be entered into by the shareholders of a corporation with the important objective being to impose restrictions on the transferability of stock held by each of the parties to the contract.[62] The use of a binding stock purchase agreement by the shareholders as an estate planning tool will assure:

- convertibility of a shareholder's stock in the closely held business into liquid assets (upon that shareholder's death or earlier retirement);
- diversification of the assets to be received by the shareholder's estate beneficiaries;
- avoiding the risk of oppressive tactics by the surviving shareholders[63]; and
- establishment of the value of the stock for estate tax purposes (to avoid extensive negotiations concerning valuation with the IRS estate tax representative).[64]

The purposes of the corporation are also served by a binding stock purchase agreement since an effective buy-sell agreement can:

- prevent shareholder deadlock or harassment by the deceased shareholder's beneficiaries who may be minority shareholders (causing distraction from the corporation's implementing its operating objectives);
- permit the corporation to retain profits for corporate expansion (rather than being pressured to distribute dividends to the deceased shareholder's nonemployee surviving spouse and children);
- eliminate possible S corporation disqualification because of shares being transferred to a nonqualifying trust or into the hands of a shareholder who may not be contractually restricted from terminating the S corporation election; and
- in family situations, control those family members who will participate in future ownership, including if desired, precluding participation by spouses of family members and, possibly, other business partners.

a. Potential Purchasers

(1) Alternative Plans

As specified in the buy-sell agreement, the possible purchasers of the deceased shareholder's shares can be:

- the corporation (through the use of an "entity purchase" or "stock redemption" plan); or
- the surviving shareholder(s) (through the use of a "cross-purchase" arrangement).

Occasionally, these two options are combined to achieve the desired objective. The stock redemption plan will usually impose a smaller after-tax combined cost on the corporation and the surviving shareholders than will a cross-purchase agreement. This occurs since the shareholder funds necessary to be accumulated to satisfy obligations under a cross-purchase agreement will often have been taxed to both the corporation and shareholders (assuming that the corporation does not have S corporation status). The funds used by the corporation to satisfy its obligations under a stock redemption agreement will have been taxed, however, only to the corporation (again, assuming no S corporation status). A reduced shareholder cost might arise in a cross-purchase agreement context where: (1) the individual purchaser has a lower effective income tax rate than the corporation[65] and (2) the funds used by that purchaser have been received through compensation income deductible by the corporation when paid to the employee. Of course, if an S corporation election has been made, only one level of income tax will occur in any event.

(2) Stock Redemption Plan

Under a stock redemption plan, the corporation must have sufficient assets to redeem the shareholder's stock when required under the stock purchase agreement. This may be accomplished through the retention by the corporation of liquid assets. For example, the corporation might invest a portion of each year's earnings in liquid assets to establish a reserve fund to satisfy this potential obligation under the stock redemption agreement. The corporation may have insufficient funds, however, if the shareholder dies before the corporation has had adequate time to accumulate sufficient funds to satisfy its stock redemption obligation, or if the value of the business enterprise appreciates significantly so that previously accumulated funds are inadequate to cover the required redemption amount. Alternatively, if sufficient time has elapsed and sufficient funds have been accumulated, the corporation may be subject to the accumulated earnings tax for its failure to distribute the accumulated funds as dividends to the shareholders.[66]

Often, life insurance funding is used for the purpose of assuring sufficient funds, the corporation being the owner of a policy on the life of each of the shareholders. The proceeds of the policy would be made payable to the corporation as the beneficiary upon the death of the shareholder. The corporation would not be entitled to a deduction upon the payment of the insurance premiums.[67] The corporation's payment of annual insurance policy premiums will not be included in the income of the shareholders who are parties to the buy-sell agreement.[68]

The proceeds of life insurance received upon the death of a shareholder will ordinarily be excluded from the gross income of the corporation.[69] These proceeds representing gain from the policy will, however, be included in determining the corporation's "earnings and profits" account. This is important for purposes of measuring the amount of dividends distributed by the corporation.[70] These proceeds will often be used to satisfy the requirement to redeem the shares held by the decedent.[71] No dividend will be deemed paid to the remaining shareholders by reason of the redemption of the shares of the deceased shareholder, although the percentage interests of the remaining shareholders in the corporation are increased by this redemption.[72]

The sale of the shares by the estate of the deceased shareholder to the corporation may cause the redemption of these shares to be treated as a distribution of corporate earnings and profits (i.e., a dividend). Redemption proceeds will be treated as a dividend distribution under §302(d) unless it may, within the meaning of §302(b), be treated as an "exchange." A redemption can be treated as an "exchange" if it is[73]:

- "not essentially equivalent to a dividend"[74];
- a "substantially disproportionate" redemption of stock[75];
- a "complete termination" of the shareholder's interest[76]; or
- a partial liquidation distribution.[77]

The redemption may also qualify for exchange treatment under §303.[78] The complete stock redemption alternative is ordinarily the safest method for achieving sale or exchange treatment and avoiding dividend distribution categorization, assuming the attribution of ownership rules can be avoided.[79] If sale or exchange treatment is applicable, the sale often will not produce any realized capital gain (or loss). This occurs because the income tax basis for the shares being redeemed will have been "stepped up" to fair market value at death.[80] This analysis concerning the tax basis assumes, however, that the buy-sell agreement is binding for estate tax valuation purposes. Even though the tax on dividends received by individuals is 20% under §1(h)(11), where the proceeds are received as dividends (rather than stock redemption proceeds) that tax will apply, rather than the proceeds merely constituting a recovery of tax basis (as stepped up at death). This maximum rate applies after 2012.[81]

If the redemption does not constitute an exchange and is of the stock of an S corporation, the income tax effects of the distribution will be determined under the S corporation provisions.[82] The redeeming shareholder will not recognize gain so long as the redemption payments do not exceed the corporation's "accumulated adjustments account" plus the shareholder's aggregate basis in the S corporation stock.[83]

(3) Cross-Purchase Plan

The cross-purchase plan is a share ownership arrangement solely between the shareholders; that is, the corporation that issued the shares subject to the agreement is not involved. The funding of the obligation under this type of agreement must occur at the purchaser shareholder level. To fund this obligation, often the individual shareholders will own, pay premiums on, and be the beneficiaries of insurance policies on the lives of the other shareholders. If more than several shareholders are involved, a number of policies will be required (each shareholder often being required to own a policy on the life of each other shareholder), making the process of multiple policy ownership quite cumbersome.[84] Further, the life insurance premium cost may be substantial for younger shareholders needing to acquire insurance on the lives of older shareholders. Relief might be obtained by increasing deductible salary payments to the shareholders needing to make these premium payments (with the corporation thereby bearing a part of the cost indirectly), assuming unreasonable compensation/deduction limitation problems can be avoided.[85] An alternative approach might be a split-dollar life insurance plan.[86]

No income tax deduction for the insurance premium payments made by the shareholders will be available.[87] Insurance proceeds when received will be excluded from the gross income of the surviving shareholder/beneficiary.[88] Since the purchase arrangement is between two shareholders, and no funds are received from the corporation in the completion of this arrangement, no exposure to possible dividend distribution treatment exists.[89] The sale under the cross-purchase arrangement that occurs shortly after death will not produce realized gain or loss to the selling shareholder estate, again assuming the stock price in the agreement is binding for estate tax valuation purposes, since the income tax basis for the shares is "stepped up" to the fair market value at the death of the decedent/owner.[90] The tax basis to the surviving owner for the newly purchased business interest will be equal to the amount paid for the stock, that is, a cost basis.[91]

(4) Simultaneous Redemption and Cross-Purchase

Because of inadequate capital surplus or other restrictions imposed under local law, a corporation may be unable to redeem all the stock owned by the shareholder whose interest is required to be acquired under an entity purchase agreement. An arrangement might be concluded to have the remaining shareholders purchase the stock not to be acquired by the corporation. Under these circumstances, the cross-purchase between the shareholders should ordinarily occur before the stock redemption by the corporation, so that the redemption by the corporation will effect a complete termination of the shareholder's interest, eligible for sale or exchange treatment (i.e., avoiding dividend treatment).[92]

b. Fixing the Price to Be Paid

(1) Estate Tax Valuation Limitations

A variety of mechanisms can be used in a stock purchase agreement to establish the price to be paid for each share.[93] An important objective in the intrafamily context will be to assure that the valuation as determined under the buy-sell agreement will also be binding for purposes of establishing the value for federal estate tax purposes.[94] The price set in a buy-sell agreement will represent the estate tax value of the property restricted by the agreement only if the decedent's estate is obligated to offer the stock (or, e.g., partnership interest) for sale at that price. The assumption is that, if the agreement price is less than the fair market value of the property, any offer of sale will be accepted and, accordingly, the estate will not be able to realize more than the price established in the agreement.

Little weight will be accorded a price contained in an option or contract, however, under which the decedent was free to dispose of the underlying securities (or other property) at any price he or she chose during his or her lifetime.[95] Consequently, the objective of a lifetime restriction must be to preclude a shareholder (or partner) from realizing a higher price on a lifetime transfer than the amount that would be realized on a sale by the shareholder's (or partner's) estate. This lifetime restriction is often imposed through the implementation of a "right of first refusal." Under this approach a shareholder (or partner) cannot accept an outside purchase offer without first offering that business interest to the other parties at the agreement price (i.e., the price at which it must be offered for purchase after death).[96]

Under the special valuation rules of Chapter 14, any restrictive agreement or purchase options in a buy-sell agreement may be disregarded for valuation purposes, however.[97] An exception to this limitation is provided if the taxpayer can establish that the restriction or option under such an agreement is[98]:

- a bona fide business arrangement[99];
- "comparable to similar arrangements entered into by persons in an arms' length transaction"[100]; and
- not a device to transfer property to the natural objects of the transferor's bounty for less than full and adequate consideration.[101]

The terms of the option or agreement must be comparable to similar agreements entered into among unrelated persons.

(2) Mutually Agreed Specific Dollar Amount

In setting the price in a buy-sell agreement, the parties may simply agree on a specified price per share. This method assumes that the parties themselves are the best judges of the value of their business interests. Further, although they can evaluate the relative actuarial risks, they cannot be assured whether their estate will be the seller or they will be the survivor and, therefore, the buyer. Since values change (sometimes quite substantially), this type of agreement should include a provision requiring the review of the agreed amount at specified periodic intervals. If a revised amount per share (if necessary) is not established within that time frame, an alternative valuation method might be specified as thereafter being applicable.[102]

(3) Book Value

The net book value of the enterprise might be used to establish the price per share for purposes of the buy-sell agreement. Often, net book value is not reflective of the actual value of an ongoing business.[103] The parties might agree, however, that some multiple of the net book value will accurately reflect the current total value of the business assets (including goodwill). Alternatively, the net worth statement might be restated, with certain assets (e.g., listed securities) required to be valued at fair market value and book value (or a multiple thereof) being used for the remaining operating assets.

Adjustments might be specified if the corporation is a cash basis taxpayer, rather than an accrual method taxpayer.[104] These adjustments can reflect items such as accounts receivable, accounts payable, and tax liabilities on current earnings that may not be currently reflected in determining the net worth of a cash basis taxpayer, but which are clearly relevant in determining the net value of the enterprise. Additional adjustments might be made with respect to partially completed work reported on the completed contract method, outstanding installment payments, and last-in, first-out (LIFO) inventories. If the corporate business has subsidiaries, the book value (to which a multiple might be applied) should be determined on a consolidated financial statement basis. If a subsidiary has essentially liquid assets the fair market value, rather than book value, might be used in restating the value of that subsidiary.

(4) Appraised Value

The shareholders may agree that, for purposes of establishing value for purposes of the buy-sell agreement, the business assets are to be appraised as of the date of death. The shareholders (or their successors) may together designate an appraiser to act impartially for this purpose, or they (or their successors) may each desire to appoint his/her own appraiser, with appropriate conflict resolution procedures. When adopting this approach some references in the buy-sell agreement should often be made to the specific appraisal techniques to be applied (e.g., market value, replacement value, inclusion of goodwill, etc.).

(5) Capitalization of Earnings

The earnings of the enterprise, as determined over a specified number of years, might be capitalized to establish the value per share.[105] Matters to be considered in capitalizing earnings for this purpose include:

- defining the representative period over which earnings should be computed (particularly in a cyclical business);
- defining the appropriate capitalization rate; and
- defining what are the "earnings," for example, earnings as determined for financial accounting purposes or, alternatively, for tax accounting purposes, and what adjustments need to be made to assure the appropriate measurement of these earnings.

Further, the parties may desire to give more weight to the most recent earnings experience and less weight to financial results in more remote years.[106]

(6) Impact of Life Insurance Proceeds

Where the obligation under a stock redemption agreement is to be satisfied with life insurance proceeds, a special problem exists in determining whether, for purposes of the buy-sell agreement, those insurance proceeds are to be included or excluded in determining the fair market value of the stock to be sold pursuant to the agreement. Before the death of the insured, the insurance policies will be carried on the books of the corporation at their cash surrender values (unless subject to policy loans that reduce the net value). Immediately after death, the value of the corporation itself will have been increased by the excess of the face values over the cash surrender value of the policies on the life of the deceased shareholder.[107] The corporation will have a liability, however, to satisfy its obligation under the buy-sell agreement.

The issue to be resolved is whether the estate of the deceased shareholder (then still being a shareholder) should share in the insurance policy gain accruing to the corporation at the death of that shareholder. This is ordinarily a matter to be negotiated between the shareholders but is an important matter that should not be overlooked.

This insurance inclusion issue is not a consideration where the insurance policies are acquired by the individual business owners for funding their obligations to other shareholders under a cross-purchase agreement. Each owner will individually hold policies insuring the lives of the other business owners. Concern might exist in this situation about whether each owner will perform his or her obligations under the cross-purchase agreement as of the death of the other owner. As noted above, a trust might be arranged, with an independent trustee, to hold these policies and to perform the obligations under the cross-purchase agreement.[108]

c. Methods of Payment

The stock purchase agreement can also specify the method for the payment of the price established under the agreement. These options might include (1) a lump-sum amount payable by a specified date after death, (2) installment payments to be made over a specified period after death, or (3) some other arrangement. An installment payment arrangement will often be necessary where insurance proceeds are insufficient (or unavailable) to fund the entire purchase price and a lump-sum payment would seriously deplete the liquid assets of the corporation.[109] Ordinarily, installment sales treatment available under §453 will be unimportant to defer income tax on the sale (although appropriate interest must be paid). This occurs since the income tax basis for the shares being sold will have been stepped up to their fair market value at death, thereby eliminating any capital gain potential.

In any deferred payment arrangement, the fiduciary for the selling shareholder's estate should, of course, insist upon an adequate arrangement to assure the delayed payments actually will be made. This might include, for example, having the shares held in escrow pending the actual receipt of all payments. Potential future income tax problems exist with the use of the redeemed or purchased stock as collateral.[110] The selling shareholder should not receive any interest in the corporation other than that of a creditor. Otherwise, the waiver of the §318(a) family attribution rules pursuant to §302(c)(2) may be negated.[111]

4. Retaining the Closely Held Stock

a. Potential Valuation Controversy

Stock in a closely held corporation may not be subject to a buy-sell agreement because the probable beneficiaries of the older shareholder want to receive those shares and participate (or continue to participate) in the family business. Since no binding buy-sell agreement exists to possibly establish the fair market value of those shares for federal estate tax purposes, an estate tax controversy might arise as to their value.[112] This controversy concerning value does not impact the remaining shareholders, since the estate of the deceased shareholder will continue to hold the stock interest (and subsequently distribute the stock interest to the beneficiaries of the estate). Consequently, the estate planner should often design a strategy to deal with these tax valuation problems after the death of the client and, also, to possibly posture the business before death to enable a favorable estate tax valuation for these shares.

b. Relative Tax Considerations

In approaching any valuation problem, the estate planner must analyze both the potential overall estate tax impact and the related income tax implications. A higher value for estate tax purposes could generate an increased federal estate tax liability. A higher estate tax value may enable, however, an estate to satisfy the percentage qualification tests for §303 stock redemption treatment and the deferred estate tax payment options.[113]

A higher estate tax value would cause a higher income tax basis for the property, since the property passing through an estate will have a tax basis equal to the fair market value of that property as of the date of death (or as of the alternate valuation date).[114] The increase in income tax basis would correspondingly decrease any capital gain on a later sale of that property.[115] A higher estate tax value may be preferable, consequently, where the unified credit will eliminate any estate tax liability. If the unlimited marital deduction is also used so that estate taxes on all asset transfers are deferred, incentives will exist to establish the highest value which can be reasonably supported. The approach of asserting a higher value would only be useful when the total net asset value is protected from estate tax, since a subsequent capital gains tax (at the rates specified in §1(h)) will be less than any estate tax assessed at a higher rate.

c. Value Defined

The value of property for estate tax purposes is its fair market value at death (or as of the alternate valuation date).[116] Fair market value is defined as "the price at which the property would change hands between a willing buyer and a willing seller, neither being under any compulsion to buy or to sell and both having reasonable knowledge of relevant facts."[117]

Where selling prices or bid and ask prices are not available, relevant stock valuation factors include[118]:

- the company's net worth;
- the prospective earning power; and
- the dividend-paying capacity of the corporation.

This information will be developed by analyzing:

- the business's goodwill;
- the economic outlook for the particular industry;
- the company's position in the industry;
- the company's management;
- the degree of control represented by the block of stock to be valued; and
- the value of securities of companies engaged in the same or similar lines of business that are listed on a stock exchange.

The position of the IRS concerning fundamental business valuation approaches is enumerated in the long outstanding Rev. Rul. 59-60.[119] That ruling indicates that a variety of valuation techniques might be used, such as:

- book value;
- capitalization of net earnings;
- market value of underlying assets;
- recent sales of the stock being valued; and
- the comparable value of stocks traded regularly, including reference to the price-earnings ratios, the book value per share, and the dividends per share for those other regularly traded stocks.

The use of any one factor (or combination of such factors), depends, of course, on the individual circumstances. Of particular relevance during a substantial inflationary cycle is, for example, that:

- inventory value may be substantially understated[120]; but
- depreciation and depreciation reserves may also be substantially understated (in light of very significant increased costs for any replacement of currently existing capital equipment).[121]

These are merely examples of situations where significant variance might exist between book value and fair market value. In such event, corporate earnings may be significantly understated or overstated and should be restated for business valuation purposes. Reference to cost replacement and inflation accounting rules developed by the Financial Accounting Standards Board will be of value in this context. In each individual situation, a careful analysis will be essential.

d. Availability of Discounts and Premiums

The determination of the fair market value of a block of stock will depend, as noted above, on factors that include "the degree of control of the business represented by the block of stock."[122] Several important discounts may be available in this context, including (1) a discount for lack of marketability and (2) a discount because the position held is a minority interest and, therefore, no control exists over corporate policy.

A discount for lack of marketability may be available because no regular market exists for the sale either (1) of the particular corporate shares or (2) for the number of shares that are held. This will necessitate demonstrating the difference in value resulting because special negotiations or an extended time interval will be necessary to complete a sale. The discount for a minority or fractional interest would be available because of the lack of immediate control and the problems associated with dealing with co-owners of the property. Owners of closely held businesses ordinarily do not have the unilateral right to realize their pro rata share of the business (or its assets) through causing the dissolution of the business.

Alternatively, the IRS may assert that various blocks of stock should be aggregated for purposes of determining whether control, and, therefore, a control premium, exists.[123]

The IRS has recognized in this context that family ownership attribution rules are not to be applied when valuing minority interests in closely held companies for estate and gift tax purposes.[124]

e. Posturing for an Estate Tax Valuation Controversy

The estate planner has an obligation to structure the estate and the dispositive instruments so that any valuation controversy will be resolved expeditiously and favorably to the client's estate.[125] This can be accomplished by anticipating estate tax valuation problems and creating an environment in which these problems might be resolved in favor of the estate.[126]

The client might be encouraged to make sales and purchases of the stock that will later be valued in his or her estate.[127] Other shareholders might also make sales under favorable conditions. The IRS would analyze these transactions carefully, particularly if related persons are involved, but the transactions should have some effect on the ultimate valuation. Additionally, the presentation of the profit and loss statement and the balance sheet might be improved by the following[128]:

- realize accumulated economic capital losses, thereby depressing the income statement[129];
- use accelerated depreciation to decrease income (for federal income tax purposes);
- when in an inflationary environment, use the LIFO inventory method (to decrease income for federal income tax purposes);
- create significant reserves for potential liabilities (available for financial accounting purposes but not for federal income tax purposes); and
- implement changes in facilities to incur start-up costs (as well as generating increased depreciation expense).

The parties should remember that in this valuation process the financial statements prepared for reporting to shareholders and creditors will normally be more relevant than tax basis balance sheets. The corporation might also be encouraged to conduct an analysis showing future cash demands for replacing capital equipment and an analysis showing future prospects (particularly if declining) for the industry, including projections for increased research and development costs necessary to maintain a competitive position in the particular business sector. The persuasiveness of such surveys would be enhanced to the extent they are developed by competent, independent consultants.

C. Closely Held Partnerships and Limited Liability Companies

1. Estate Planning Options for Partnership Structures

A partnership (including a limited liability company categorized for federal tax purposes as a partnership) may be an appropriate alternative to a closely held corporation for purposes of: (1) conducting a family business or investment enterprise and (2) enabling the allocation of income and value to younger-generation members. A "family partnership" has often been the vehicle used to shift income and economic value from older-generation members to younger family members.

A family partnership organized as a limited partnership, that is, a "family limited partnership" (or "FLP") has been regularly used in the estate and gift tax planning context. The family limited partnership is a mechanism used especially to divide family assets among family members for transfer tax purposes, while taking advantage of rules permitting a reduced valuation of the amount being transferred. The particular benefits of the family limited partnership are: (1) by reason of the ownership format, for senior-generation members the values can be significantly reduced for transfer tax purposes, (2) the senior family member may be able to continue to control the partnership (assuming §2036 can be made inapplicable), and (3) the partnership interests transferred to younger family members should not be includible in the estate of the older transferor at the death of that transferor (even though subject to management control by reason of being the managing partners of the partnership, again, assuming §2036 does not apply).

The traditional choices of the partnership form in this planning context have been: (1) a limited partnership (where the liability of the limited partners is confined to the amount of their partnership contribution obligation, but a general partner has unlimited liability) and (2) a limited liability company treated as a partnership for federal tax purposes. A limited liability company can be categorized as a corporation for U.S. tax purposes, but ordinarily is a partnership for these purposes.[130] Under applicable state business association laws, all of the owners of interests in the limited liability company have limited liability for the debts of the entity (i.e., limited to their respective capital commitments). Local business organization laws should be verified concerning this treatment.

2. Family Partnerships Enabling Income and Transfer Tax Benefits

a. Purpose of Family Partnerships

The family business may be held as a sole proprietorship (i.e., in unincorporated form) by an older family member and that family member may wish to include younger family members as owners in the enterprise. Alternatively, a partnership including family members may already exist and the expansion of partnership equity participation to other family members may be desired.[131] For federal income tax planning purposes the retention of partnership status, including through the use of a limited liability company rather than a corporation, may be preferred.[132]

In this situation, a business owner may wish to utilize the tax planning opportunities available with a "family partnership" or "family limited partnership."[133] This is merely the name used for a partnership when created in a closely knit family environment, particularly when the objective is to deflect income to younger-generation members. In a manner similar to that permitted through the use of an irrevocable trust for shifting passive investment income, with the family partnership the income of the family business can be deflected from the highly taxed parent to children having lower marginal income tax rates.[134] The donor-parent can still retain limited controls in the functioning and management of the partnership. The Code and the regulations recognize the family partnership as a valid mechanism to enable the deflection of certain income to other, younger family members, including trusts for those younger persons.[135]

For federal income tax purposes, in allocating partnership income among the various partners substantial flexibility exists to establish: (1) the compensation portion (i.e., the earned income to the parent who manages the partnership) at the lowest reasonable level, and (2) the economic return from the capital investment (i.e., the unearned income being split between the parent(s) and the children as partners) at the highest reasonable level. Outside the narrow tax planning context the partnership can serve a useful family psychological purpose; that is, the transfer of an ownership interest in the family business to a child can be used to instill in that child a respect for the process through which the family unit obtains its economic sustenance.

b. Creation of the Family Partnership

A person will be recognized as a partner in a partnership if he or she owns a capital interest in a partnership in which capital is a "material income-producing factor."[136] This partner status is to be recognized whether the partnership interest was derived by purchase or gift from another person.[137] Accordingly, a donee's distributive share of partnership income will be includible in the donee's gross income (and not the donor's gross income).[138] Before determining the distributive share for the donee partner(s), an allowance of reasonable compensation must be made for services rendered to the partnership by the donor partner.[139] In addition, for a donee of a partnership interest to be recognized as a partner, the donee must be the substantive owner; that is, a complete and bona fide transfer of a partnership ownership interest to the donee must be made (as determined under applicable state property law principles).[140]

c. Partnership Interest Ownership Tests

Not only must the donor comply with requirements with respect to creating a family partnership, but the partnership must also regularly function as a genuine partnership to achieve and maintain this status for federal tax purposes.[141] Consequently, to avoid being treated as the owner of the transferred property interest, the donor/partner must not have:

- retained control over the distribution of amounts of partnership income, except to the extent he or she is the managing partner and is authorized to retain amounts for the reasonable needs of the business[142];
- limited the discretionary right of the donee partner to liquidate or sell his or her interest in the partnership without financial detriment[143];

- retained control of assets essential to the business[144]; or
- retained extraordinary management powers.[145]

These powers are acceptable if the donee partner at his or her discretion can liquidate his or her interest without financial detriment.[146] Those controls deemed inconsistent with ownership by other partners would be unacceptable whether retained directly or indirectly.[147]

Substantial participation by the donee in the control and management of the partnership's business would be strong evidence of a donee-partner's exercise of dominion and control over his or her interest.[148] Actual distributions to a donee-partner of his or her share of the business income for the sole benefit and use of the donee would also be substantial evidence of the economic realities of the donee's ownership interest.[149] Further, the business itself must be conducted so as to evidence its partnership characteristics to the general public.[150]

Special ownership tests will be applied where either trustees or minor children are to be treated as partners.[151] A trust holding a partnership interest will be recognized as a partner if: (1) the trustee is independent, or (2) the grantor (or a subordinate party) as trustee actively represents and protects the interests of the beneficiaries in accordance with the obligations of a fiduciary.[152] A minor child generally will not be recognized as a partner unless: (1) he or she is shown to be competent to manage his or her own property and participate in partnership activities, or (2) control of the property is exercised by another person as fiduciary for the sole benefit of the child and judicial supervision of the conduct of the fiduciary occurs as required by law.[153]

d. Allocation of Family Partnership Income

When the existence of a partnership interest created by gift is recognized for income tax purposes, the distributive share of partnership income of the donee is includible in his or her gross income. As noted above, an allowance of reasonable compensation must be made, however, for services rendered to the partnership by the donor to assure that income attributable to that personal effort (rather than income from capital investment) is not shifted to an individual having a lower tax bracket (and not providing services to the partnership).[154] Income allocations to the donor and donee must be proportionate to their respective interests in the partnership capital.[155]

Example: X is in the business of selling specialized equipment at wholesale. X owns a warehouse which includes office space. The warehouse, fixtures, inventory, and goodwill are worth $2 million. Net income from the business is $500,000 annually. X creates a partnership in which he gives his child a one-half interest in the capital of the partnership. Assuming that the net income of the business allocable to these capital investment assets is $250,000 (12-1/2% return on $2,000,000 invested capital), the $500,000 income of this partnership would be allocated as follows[156]:

Father:	
(1) allocable to personal services	$250,000
(2) 1/2 of income attributable to capital	125,000
Total	$375,000
Child: 1/2 of income allocable to capital	125,000
Total	$500,000

e. Income Tax Advantages

For federal income tax purposes, the family partnership enables possible income shifting where other arrangements (such as leases) would not be available.[157] The partnership permits income shifting and a reduction of the overall income tax cost within the family unit. This income shifting can also reduce the accumulation of assets by the parent which otherwise would, upon his or her death, be includible in his or her gross estate for federal estate tax purposes.

f. Transfer Tax Advantages

At the time of the creation and funding of the limited partnership, significant gift tax advantages can be achieved through the applicability of discounting in the valuation of the transferred assets. The fundamental premise is that a minority discount must be applied to the partnership interest received by the donee because the donee–limited partner has only a minority position in the partnership, cannot participate in the management of the enterprise, and is restricted from selling the interest. Wealthy individuals could see significant gift tax savings by implementing transfers of limited partnership interests to children and grandchildren when, for example, the gift tax exclusion (as indexed for inflation) is $5.43 million (as in the year 2015, rising to $5.45 million in 2016). If gifts are made by two spouses and, for example, a 30% minority discount could be available, each spouse could transfer value of $7 million (discounted to $5 million) without gift tax effect (assuming no prior usage of the unified credit equivalent amount).

Care must be taken to assure that the minority (or lack of control) discount will be available; that is, the transfer is treated as being a transfer of a minority interest in a funded limited partnership, rather than being a transfer of a proportionate interest in the underlying partnership assets. Further, the taxpayers may successfully assert the applicability of a discount for lack of marketability. IRS has unsuccessfully asserted on several occasions that no discounts should be available because gifts of property were made directly to donees, rather than in the form of interests in a limited partnership holding those properties. For the estate planner this necessitates careful attention to structuring the form and timing of the transaction in these situations so that the gift transfer being made is of a partnership interest itself.[158]

3. Family Limited Partnerships

The family partnership is also being used to achieve estate tax savings.[159] This can be accomplished through the use of a partnership normally designated as a "family limited partnership" (FLP).[160] The fundamental FLP estate planning objective is to create a partnership to hold certain family assets and to then transfer those partnership interests to other family members: (1) at a limited gift tax cost and (2) without subsequent inclusion in the estate of the donor for federal estate tax purposes of the transferred partnership interests then held by others.

The partnership interests being transferred ordinarily would be limited partnership interests, enabling the senior family member to continue to control the partnership assets as the general partner. Alternatively, a corporation might be formed to act as the general partner, and the various family members might be shareholders in this corporation. Various other ancillary benefits might be achieved through the use of a family limited partnership including: (1) putting these assets into a form which would be protected from the transferor's creditors (except for the transferor's own partnership interest) and (2) encouraging other family members to be interested in the management of these family assets.

The federal gift tax objective would be to significantly limit for federal gift tax purposes the value of the partnership interests being transferred by gift to (or for) younger family members. This could result because the transfer consists of illiquid, minority partnership interests. This would enable valuation discounts to be applied because of both the holding of minority interests and the lack of marketability of transferred property.[161] In some situations, these discounts have been successfully asserted even where the partnership whose interests are transferred has assets consisting exclusively or predominantly of readily tradable securities.[162]

One primary objective for estate tax purposes (in addition to achieving significant discounts) would be to assure that the transferred partnership interests are not includible in the estate of the transferor.[163] To confirm this result, the partnership agreement might specify (the obvious) that the general partner, in managing and operating the partnership, is bound by fiduciary obligations to the other partners.

The IRS has had only partial success in resisting the use of family limited partnerships to create valuation discounts: (1) for gift tax purposes, especially if the partnership was created shortly before the death of the senior family member in order to create discounts in his or her estate; and (2) for estate tax purposes.

4. Estate Exclusion and Freeze Arrangements for Family Limited Partnership Interests

a. The Family Limited Partnership Estate Planning Objective

Similar to a corporate estate planning freeze (e.g., the estate planning recapitalization), the structure of an existing partnership can be rearranged to achieve the objective of shifting future appreciation potential to younger-generation members for many of the family held assets, both liquid and illiquid. This could be achieved through the use of a family limited partnership but, as noted, that arrangement might generate undesirable gift tax exposure.

A partnership capital freeze can involve the formation of a new partnership or the restructuring of an old partnership to include several classes of partnership interests. A "frozen" partnership interest would be the senior interest and would have a preference as to partnership income and distributions and priority as to liquidation proceeds. A regular or "non-frozen" partnership interest would be the typical partnership interest, which is secondary to the frozen interest as to the distribution of both partnership income and liquidation proceeds.

In many respects, the "frozen partnership interest" is comparable to the senior position of preferred stock issued by a corporation and the regular partnership interest is similar to common stock. Both the corporate estate planning recapitalization and the partnership freeze transaction are subject to the gift tax valuation rules prescribed in Chapter 14 of the Code.

b. Estate Tax Planning Purpose

The purposes and functions of the multitiered partnership are analogous to those of the corporate recapitalization in the intrafamily context. The primary purposes are: (1) to freeze the asset value owned by the senior family members and (2) to cause much of the future appreciation in those assets to accrue for the benefit of younger family members. This freeze can also assist in establishing a value for the business interest, so as to reduce the valuation uncertainties that arise when an interest in a closely held business is included in a decedent's gross estate. A frozen partnership interest held by a senior family member can assure a more constant cash flow and offers that family member the financial security derived from such income certainty.

The multitiered partnership freeze technique can be used outside the family context. For example, when a retiring owner wishes to transfer ownership to new, unrelated younger owners, the transfer might be accomplished through the use of a preferred partnership interest. This could enable postponing a tax on disposition of the partnership interest until the tax basis is stepped up at the time of death. Since no transfer to a family member occurs in this context, the Chapter 14 valuation rules will not apply to possibly expand gift tax exposure.

c. Partnership Restructurings vs. Corporate Recapitalizations

The formation of both partnerships and corporations are nontaxable events.[164] No control requirements are present with respect to the organization of partnerships, while the corporate tax rules impose specific control tests that must be satisfied on the formation of a corporation to result in a nontaxable organizational transaction.[165] Control may be retained by the frozen partner in a manner unrelated to the percentage equity ownership of the business enterprise. Consequently, through the drafting of the partnership agreement, equity ownership can be disassociated from legal rights with regard to the entity. In addition, no corporate-type dividend distribution concerns[166] exist when using the partnership form.

The partnership offers a flow-through of earnings and avoids the double taxation involved through use of the regular corporate entity.[167] Likewise, the tax character of such items as percentage depletion deductions, accelerated cost recovery deductions, and capital gains or losses pass through to the partners. Further, the partnership vehicle avoids the potential corporate tax liabilities associated with: (1) personal holding company status and (2) the possible penalty tax imposed upon the unreasonable accumulation of corporate earnings. Property distributions by partnerships are usually not events causing gain recognition to the distributor.[168] Consequently, a partnership can "downsize" or terminate without significant federal income tax cost. The opportunities to achieve the same results in a corporate form are more limited.

d. Description of the Frozen Partnership Interest

The frozen partnership interest may be in the form of a cumulative preference as to partnership profits that is required to be paid by the partnership at specified intervals and irrespective of whether sufficient funds exist to fund this commitment.[169] In lieu of a cumulative commitment, payment of income to the frozen partnership interest may be guaranteed only to the extent funds are available from the current year's partnership profits.[170]

If a frozen partner has an interest consisting only of a guaranteed payment, he or she may not be treated for income tax purposes as a partner in the partnership.[171] The source of the concern in this context is that the frozen partner who receives only a guaranteed payment determined without regard to the income of the partnership may not be determined to be sharing partnership profits.[172] Consequently, the frozen partner should have at least some interest in residual partnership profits, in addition to the guaranteed payment.[173] The frozen partner may continue to participate in management without resulting income tax problems but, should he or she retain control, income tax issues[174] and estate tax issues will arise.[175]

e. Regular Partnership Interest

The regular partnership interest (as contrasted with the frozen, senior partnership interest) is simply the standard partnership interest permitting the distribution of profits and requiring an allocated responsibility for losses. The regular partners are subject to the normal partnership risks (unlike the frozen interest, if transformed into limited partnership interests). Any subsequent capital appreciation is allocated to the regular partners. Income generated in excess of the amount required to satisfy the preferred profits interests is allocated to the regular partnership interests. To achieve effective estate planning in this context, the regular partnership interests are generally held by the junior family members. To achieve limitation of liability for these junior family members, these portions can be structured as limited partnership interests.

f. Income Tax Considerations

The regular partners may acquire their partnership interests by several methods. The controlling partner contemplating diffusion of ownership through a FLP can make direct gifts of the partnership interests to family members, but the income allocation strictures of the family partnership rules will apply.[176] The preferable approach would be to have the junior members of the family who are to be partners make direct contributions of their original capital amounts. This can eliminate the application of the family partnership rules. Those partners may not have the financial capability, however, to make such contributions in formation and capitalization of the partnership.

The formation of a new partnership or the restructuring of an old partnership to have divided ownership interests is normally a tax-free transaction.[177] The potential for generating gain realization in the restructuring of an existing partnership does exist if a limited partnership interest is created as a result of restructuring a general partnership.

For the creation of a frozen partnership interest to be tax free, the interest received from the partnership must be for capital and not for debt. Otherwise, the transaction will be treated as a sale or exchange under §707, rather than a tax-free contribution under §721.[178] The explicit subordination of the partnership interest to the claims of creditors may be appropriate to evidence that the interest is economically a capital interest in the partnership.[179]

g. Gift Tax Considerations

If the partner in a partnership freeze arrangement receives a partnership interest with a value less than that of the assets he or she contributed, a taxable gift to the other partners may result.[180] In the FLP context, this inquiry is particularly impacted by the Chapter 14 special gift tax valuation rules enacted in the 1990 RRA.[181] These rules are applicable for measuring the value being gratuitously transferred to younger-generation members through the partnership structuring or restructuring.[182]

Generally, similar to the corporate restructuring arrangement, the process in the partnership context is to treat the entire amount of the interest received by the younger-generation members as being a gift transfer, except as reduced by the value of any "qualified payment" retained by the older-generation partner.[183] In the partnership context, a "qualified payment" is a payment comparable to a dividend payable on a periodic basis under any cumulative preferred stock, if determined at a fixed rate.[184] For this purpose, a payment will be treated as fixed as to rate (even though varying) if the payment is determined at a rate that bears a fixed relationship to a specified market interest rate.[185] The junior interest being shifted to younger-generation members will be treated, however, as being not less than 10% of the value of the enterprise (including debt to the transferor).[186]

Therefore, if, because of the family control relationship, these rules are applicable, the partnership interests held by the senior family members need to be carefully constructed to assure that the retained distribution right constitutes a "qualified payment." In this context, the amount of the gift transfer will be reduced, but the transfer tax premise is that the qualified payment will produce the receipt of value to be subsequently includible in the transferor's gross estate in an amount equivalent to the prior interest held and not subject to gift tax treatment.

h. Estate Tax Considerations

If all or a portion of a regular partnership interest is transferred by gift from a "frozen partner," an additional inquiry will be whether estate tax inclusion under §2036 and §2038 will result to the estate of the donor. For example, §2036(a)(2) may be applicable if the frozen partner wants to retain exclusive control over partnership profit distributions.[187] A frozen partner's power to liquidate the partnership should not be considered a power to alter, amend, or terminate the contributed interest under §2038 because such a power would apply only to that partner's capital interest. The IRS has ruled in the family limited partnership context that specific facts did not cause the applicability of these estate tax transfer rules. The arrangements in any frozen partnership situation mandates, however, that careful analysis be made concerning the possible applicability of the estate tax transfer provisions to the estate of the senior family members who transferred partnership interests to younger-generation members.[188] This is an area particularly prone to challenge in an IRS estate tax audit.[189]

5. Partnership/Limited Liability Company/Corporation Choice

Ultimately, in advising concerning estate planning in the family business enterprise context, the estate planner should reexamine the appropriate form of investment entity to be utilized. In determining the choice of business entity in the context of estate planning, the decision is often in the direction of the partnership form, unless the S corporation option can be used.[190] The S corporation option is not available, for example, where several classes of stock are desired.[191] In considering the partnership form, an increasingly popular option is the limited liability company, created with a format to satisfy the criteria enabling classification as a partnership for federal tax purposes.[192]

The use of a regular corporation will generally result in a greater income tax burden on the corporation and its shareholders than if a pass-through entity (such as a partnership, limited liability company, or S corporation) is used. Moreover, distributions of appreciated property by a corporation (including an S corporation) to shareholders will result in corporate-level gain recognition,[193] as well as taxation at the shareholder level. These rules, among others, significantly encourage the utilization of a "flow-through" entity.

The S corporation form and the limited liability company form are often desirable to limit liability at the owner level. Benefits of the limited liability company (treated as a partnership) over the S corporation include: (1) more flexibility over the form of ownership, (2) possible tax basis step up of the entity's assets under §754, (3) no gain recognition upon the contribution of appreciated assets by members to the capital of the entity, (4) deductibility by the partners of losses of the entity (to the extent of the owner's tax basis), and (5) no gain recognition to the entity upon distribution of appreciated assets to owners (as owners).

Alternatively, the limited partnership vehicle may be appropriate, although this often involves additional organizational costs that the owners may not wish to incur and does require at least one general partner. To solve the "liability exposure" issue in the partnership context, adequate insurance coverage can sometimes be obtained for this purpose.

6. Terminating the Partnership Interest of a Deceased Partner

After the death of a partner, a partnership may make payments or distributions of cash or property to the estate of a partner in liquidation of the deceased partner's interest.[194] The income tax basis for that partnership interest will be its date of death value, plus the allocable share of liabilities, less the value of the items of "income in respect of a decedent" (IRD).[195] No basis step-up at death will be available for the IRD items.[196]

The estate of the deceased partner will have gross income to the extent of its distributive share of the partnership income when attributed to the estate. The estate can shift income and deductions to the beneficiaries, however, by making current distributions that carry out distributable net income (DNI) to the beneficiaries. This would be important to accomplish if the estate's marginal income tax rate is in excess of the marginal tax rate of the recipient beneficiaries.

During estate administration, the estate may distribute the partnership interest itself, rather than (or in addition to) the income received from the partnership. The distribution of a partnership interest from a residuary estate can itself carry out DNI from the estate. Gain or loss realized on the distributed assets is ordinarily not recognized to the estate on this distribution. A distribution of a partnership interest in satisfaction of a pecuniary bequest will cause gain recognition to the estate on this distribution, however. This transfer of a partnership interest may then close the partnership's year with respect to the estate.[197]

D. Special Valuation for Family Farms and Real Property

1. Usual "Highest and Best Use" Valuation Standard

Property included in the gross estate of a decedent is ordinarily reported at its "fair market value" as of the date of the decedent's death, or as of the alternate valuation date (if elected).[198] "Fair market value" is that price at which the property would change hands between a willing buyer and a willing seller, neither being under any compulsion to buy or to sell, and both having reasonable knowledge of the relevant facts.[199] One of the most important factors applied in this valuation process is the "highest and best use" for which the property can be used.

2. Special Valuation Procedure Available

If specified conditions are satisfied,[200] the executor may elect to value certain property under a method that will produce a lower value for federal estate tax purposes.[201] Real property included in the decedent's estate that is devoted to farming or to closely held business use may be valued on the basis of the property's value as a farm or as used in the closely held business, rather than at its fair market value determined on the basis of "highest and best use."[202] This special use valuation cannot be used, however, to reduce the decedent's gross estate by more than $750,000, as adjusted for inflation after 1998.[203] This special valuation procedure is available for community property.[204]

3. Qualification Requirements for Special Valuation

a. Qualification by the Estate

Various tests must be satisfied before the decedent's estate can qualify for the §2032A special valuation procedure[205]:

- the decedent must have been a U.S. citizen or resident at death[206];
- the property in the estate must have passed from the decedent to a qualified heir[207];
- 50% or more[208] of the adjusted value of the decedent's gross estate must consist of the adjusted value of real or personal property that: (1) on the date of the decedent's death was being used for a qualified use by the decedent or a member of the decedent's family, and (2) was acquired from or passed from the decedent to a qualified heir of the decedent[209];
- at least 25% of the adjusted value of the gross estate must consist of the qualified farm or closely held business real property that: (1) was acquired from or passed from the decedent to a qualified heir, and (2) satisfies the following two requirements[210];
  - such real property must have been owned by the decedent or a member of his or her family and used or held for "qualified use" for five of the last eight years immediately before the decedent's death[211]; and
  - the decedent or a member of his or her family must have materially participated in the operation of the farm or closely held business in five out of the eight years immediately preceding the earlier of the date of decedent's death, the date the decedent became disabled, or the date the decedent began receiving Social Security benefits.[212]

For purposes of the 25% and 50% tests, the value of the property sought to be qualified for the special valuation procedure is to be determined without regard to its special use value.[213] This will necessitate: (1) a valuation at the "highest and best use" (to determine eligibility for §2032A) and (2) another valuation under the methods established under §2032A (to determine the amount to actually be included in the gross estate).

b. Qualifying Real Property

(1) Qualified Use Requirement

Real property must have had a "qualified use," to be eligible for §2032A special use valuation. The property must be located in the United States,[214] and be devoted to either[215]:

- use as a farm for farming purposes; or
- use in a trade or business other than the trade or business of farming.

Therefore, to be specially valued: (1) real property must be used in the trade or business,[216] and (2) the material participation in that trade or business must be that of the decedent or a member of his or her family.[217] Consequently, a cash rent lease to a family member during the pre-death period will satisfy the qualified use test so long as the family member bears the associated financial risk.[218] The rental of property to a nonfamily member for qualified use under a lease where the rental is not substantially dependent upon production will not satisfy the qualified use requirement.[219]

(2) Farm Defined

A "farm" for §2032A purposes includes stock, dairy, poultry, fruit, furbearing animals, and truck farms, plantations, ranches, nurseries, ranges, greenhouses, or other similar structures used primarily for the raising of agricultural or horticultural commodities.[220] Farms also include orchards and woodlands.[221] In determining whether real property is used as a farm for farming purposes, the activities actually conducted on the real property are to be determinative.[222]

In addition to cultivation of the soil and raising or harvesting of agricultural or horticultural commodities, and preparing such commodities for market, the term "farming purposes" as used in these provisions includes:

- handling, drying, packing, grading, or storing on a farm any agriculture or horticultural commodity in its unmanufactured state (but only if the owner, tenant, or operator of the farm regularly produces more than one-half of the commodity so treated); and
- the planting, cultivating, caring for or cutting of trees, and the preparation (other than milling) of trees for market.[223]

(3) Adjacent Farm Property and Buildings

In the case of qualifying real property where the material participation requirement is satisfied, the real property that qualifies for special use valuation includes the farmhouse or other residential buildings and related improvements located on qualifying real property, if these buildings are occupied on a regular basis by the owner or lessee of the real property (or by employees of the owner or lessee) for the purpose of operating or maintaining the real property or the business conducted on the property.[224] Qualified real property also includes roads, buildings, and related improvements that are functionally related to the qualified use. Those elements of value not related to the farm or business use are not eligible for the special use valuation.

Example (1): If an oil lease has been entered into to exploit oil under the farm, the full market value of the mineral rights will be taken into account for estate tax valuation purposes.[225]

Example (2): Buildings or other improvements on or contiguous with the farm and the farm buildings may be neither functionally related to the farm nor qualify as a farmhouse and "related improvements."[226] Such buildings and other improvements are not to be treated as qualified farm real property.

(4) Nonfarm Real Property

Although primarily directed toward farming property, the §2032A special use valuation rule also provides that real property used in a trade or business other than farming may qualify for special use valuation. The property must have been used in a trade or business in which the decedent or a member of his or her family materially participated before the decedent's death.[227] This rule may have substantial application where land having significant value is used for a purpose other than its highest and best use (e.g., use as a car dealership facility, rather than use for an apartment or office building).

(5) Qualifying Real Property Held by Entities

Real property otherwise qualifying for the special valuation procedure may be held in a partnership, corporate, or trust form that, with respect to the decedent, is an interest in a closely held business. A decedent's estate is generally able to use the benefits of special use valuation where the decedent held the qualifying real property indirectly through an interest in a partnership, corporation, or trust. This treatment is available, however, only if the business in which the property is used constitutes a closely held business and the related property would qualify for the special use valuation if it were held directly by the decedent.[228]

c. Material Participation Test

A "material participation" requirement functions to exclude inactive investors from eligibility for §2032A special use valuation.[229] The deceased owner or member of the owner's family must have materially participated in the operation of the farm or of the business. Reg. §20.2032A-3(a) states, "[w]hether the required material participation occurs is a factual determination, and the types of activities and financial risks which will support such a finding will vary with the mode of ownership of the property itself and of any business in which it is used." This regulation also indicates that "[p]assively collecting rents, salaries, partnership distributions, dividends, or other income from the farm or other business is not sufficient for material participation." Neither is "merely advancing capital and reviewing a crop plan or other business proposal and financial reports each season or business year" sufficient for material participation.[230]

The required material participation must last: (1) for periods totaling five years or more during the eight years immediately preceding the date of the decedent's death and (2) for periods totaling three years or more during any eight-year period ending after the date of decedent's death (up to a maximum of 10 years when the recapture provisions cease to apply).[231] The pre-death material participation requirement is relaxed for landowners who are disabled or are retired and receiving Social Security benefits.[232]

A special rule is applicable to enable a surviving spouse to satisfy the pre-death material participation requirements where the deceased spouse held qualified real property.[233] The surviving spouse is treated as having materially participated in the operation of the farm or business during periods when the surviving spouse engaged in the "active management" of the farm or other business.[234] "Active management" means the making of management decisions of a business other than daily operating decisions.[235] The surviving spouse must be personally involved in active management for five or more of the last eight years before retirement, disability, or death.[236]

An alternative to the post-death material participation requirement is provided to certain qualified heirs. The material participation requirement is considered satisfied through "active management" by an eligible qualified heir or by a fiduciary if the qualified heir is a person under age 21 or a disabled individual.[237]

"Material participation" is to be determined in a manner similar to the way the term is used for purposes of imposition of social security tax on net earnings from self-employment.[238] Physical work and participation in management decisions are the principal factors to be considered in determining the presence of material participation.[239]

With regard to indirectly owned property, (i.e., ownership through a corporation, partnership, or trust), even for full-time involvement, an arrangement must exist necessitating material participation in the business by the decedent owner or a family member and specifying the services to be performed.[240] The same participation standards apply where property is owned by a qualified closely held business as where the property is directly owned.[241]

d. Present Interest Test

The legislative history to the Tax Reform Act of 1976[242] stated that "[t]rust property shall be deemed to have passed from the decedent to a qualified heir to the extent that the qualified heir has a present interest in the trust property."[243] Questions previously arose concerning compliance with the present interest test for trusts in which the trustees had discretionary spray powers or the discretionary right to invade principal to benefit individuals in addition to those holding the income interest. The discretionary payment of trust income or principal does not make land ineligible for special use valuation if all the beneficiaries of the trust are qualified heirs.[244]

4. Income Tax Considerations

The income tax basis for §2032A special valuation property is the value as determined for special valuation purposes.[245] This tax basis will be adjusted (as discussed below) if a disqualifying disposition of the property occurs.

Upon a distribution of special use valuation property in satisfaction of a pecuniary bequest, or upon a sale to a qualified heir, gain will be realized by the distributing estate to the extent of the differential between (1) the tax basis and (2) the asset's fair market value. The estate must recognize only a portion of the appreciation in the property. This appreciation amount to be recognized is equal to the difference between: (1) the property's fair market value on the date of that distribution or sale and (2) its estate tax value as determined without regard to the special valuation provision.[246]

If the special use valuation property is purchased (or otherwise acquired) by a qualified heir from the estate, the qualified heir's income tax basis is the special use value increased by the amount of gain recognized to the estate.[247] These rules create a trap for the unwary purchaser because the purchaser does not obtain a cost basis. QTIP assets included in the surviving spouse's estate pursuant to §2044 are treated as passing from that spouse for purposes of determining the availability of the special use valuation and, therefore, are subject to these same tax-basis rules.[248]

5. Special Use Valuation Methods

There are two approved methods for valuing special use property: the farm method and the multiple factor method.[249] Each is discussed below.[250]

a. Farm Method

If a farm qualifies for special use valuation, its value is generally to be determined by dividing[251]:

- the excess of: (1) the average annual gross cash rental (or average annual net share rental) for comparable land used for farming purposes located in the locality of such farm,[252] over (2) the average annual state and local real estate taxes for such comparable land, by
- the average annual effective interest rate for all new Federal Land Bank loans.[253]

Each average annual computation is to be made on the basis of the five most recent calendar years ending before the date of the decedent's death.[254]

The purpose of this special farm valuation method is to permit the executor to achieve substantial certainty in arriving at use valuation for farmland, as well as to eliminate nonfarm factors in valuing farmland. This special farm valuation method does not apply where[255]:

- no comparable land exists from which the average annual gross cash rental (or average annual net share rental) may be determined, or
- the executor elects to have the value of the farm determined by applying the "multiple factor method."

b. Multiple Factor Method

Under the alternative "multiple factor method," the valuation of real property is to be determined by applying the following five factors[256]:

- the capitalization of income that the property can be expected to yield for farming or closely held business purposes over a reasonable period of time under prudent management using traditional cropping patterns for the area, taking into account the soil capacity, terrain configuration, and similar factors;
- the capitalization of the fair rental value of the land for farming or closely held business purposes;
- assessed land value in a state that provides a differential or use value assessment law for farmland or land used in closely held businesses;

- comparable sales of other farm or closely held business land in the same geographical area far enough removed from a metropolitan or resort area so that nonagricultural use is not a significant factor in the sale price; and
- any other factor that fairly values the farm or closely held business value of the property.

Because of the subjective nature of the criteria and the lack of guidance as to how these criteria are to be applied, the five-factor method is used infrequently in practice when the capitalization of rents method is available.[257]

c. Special Rule for Standing Timber

The executor may elect to treat standing timber as part of the qualified real property on which the timber is located instead of valuing it as other growing crops based on fair market value.[258] Standing timber is valued by reference to similar timber located on comparable land where both land and timber are rented for timber growing purposes under a cash or share rental lease.[259] If no comparable timber and land are so rented in the locality, the timber and land are to be specially valued using the multiple factor method.[260]

6. Recapture of Additional Estate Tax Amounts

a. Basic Recapture Requirements

If, within 10 years after the death of the decedent (but before the death of the qualified heir), the special use valuation property is transferred to nonfamily members[261] or ceases to be used for farming or other closely held business purposes, all or a portion of the estate tax benefits obtained by virtue of the originally reduced estate tax valuation is to be recaptured.[262] This is to be accomplished through the imposition of an additional estate tax.[263]

The amount of the tax benefit potentially subject to recapture is the excess of: (1) the estate tax liability which would have been incurred had the special use valuation procedure not been used over (2) the actual estate tax liability based on the special use valuation provisions. This amount is called the "adjusted tax difference."[264] In general, if a recapture event occurs within 10 years of the decedent's death, the amount of the additional or recapture tax imposed is equal to the lesser of: (1) the adjusted tax difference attributable to the interest, or (2) the excess of the amount realized with respect to the interest over the value of the interest determined under the special use valuation.[265]

b. Cessation of Qualified Use

As noted above, where a cessation of qualifying use or a sale or exchange to someone other than a family member has occurred, the amount of the additional tax imposed would be the lesser of the adjusted tax difference or the excess of the fair market value of the interest over the special use valuation.[266] A cessation of qualified use that constitutes a disposition occurs if[267]

- the qualified property ceases to be used in the manner in which it qualified for special valuation[268]; or
- during any period of eight years ending after the date of the decedent's death and before the date of the qualified heir's death, no material participation by the qualified heir or a member of his or her family occurs in the operation of the farm or other business during an aggregate three-year period.[269]

A special two-year grace period immediately following the date of the decedent's death exists during which failure by the qualified heir to commence the qualified use of the property will not result in the imposition of a recapture tax.[270]

c. Several Recapture Events

If two recapture events occur with respect to one property interest, a recapture would be imposed on the first "recapture event." No recapture tax would be imposed on the second "recapture event."[271]

Example: Two recapture events would occur when the qualified heir first changes the use of the property and, thereafter, that same person sells that property.

d. Several Qualified Heirs

Where more than one qualified heir receives qualified real property with respect to which special use valuation has been elected, or receives an interest in such property, the "adjusted tax difference" is to be allocated among the property interests in proportion to their respective reductions in estate tax value when the estate tax return was initially filed (or as later revised as a result of audit or litigation).[272]

Comment: If one qualified heir sells or otherwise disposes of his or her interest, note that the disposition must be to a "family member" of that qualified heir, rather than to another "qualified heir" who is not a family member of the disposing qualified heir, to avoid recapture.[273]

e. Lapse of Recapture Requirement

If the qualified heir dies without having disposed of the property or converted it to a nonqualified use, or a period of 10 years from the decedent's death has lapsed, the potential liability for recapture will cease.[274] If the decedent leaves qualified property for which special use valuation has been elected to two of his or her children as tenants in common, the death of one of the children would free that child's interest in the property from any further potential liability for the recapture tax, but not the interest of the remaining tenant in common.[275] If, however, the special use valuation was elected and two or more qualified heirs have successive interests in the property, potential liability for the recapture tax is not diminished and none of the property is to be released from potential liability for the recapture tax until the death of the last of the qualified heirs.[276]

f. Adjustment to Tax Basis

A special income tax basis provision applies for property on which a recapture tax has been paid. A qualified heir may make an irrevocable election to have the income tax basis of the formerly qualified real property increased to the fair market value of the property as of the date of the decedent's death (or the alternate valuation date, if selected by the estate).[277] This increase in basis is effective as of the date immediately before disposition or cessation of qualified use.[278] Therefore, no retroactive changes in depreciation or other deductions or credits may be made. If the heir elects this basis adjustment, the heir must pay interest on the amount of recapture tax from the date nine months after the decedent's death until the due date of the recapture tax.[279] If the qualified heir does not make this election and pay the interest, no adjustment is made to the basis of the property.[280]

g. Liability for Recapture Tax

A qualified heir is expressly made personally liable for the recapture tax imposed with respect to his or her interest in qualified property.[281] In addition, a special lien is imposed on all qualified farm or closely held business real property with respect to which an election to use the special use valuation provision has been made.[282] This lien continues until the tax benefit is recaptured or until the potential liability for recapture ceases.[283] The IRS is authorized to establish procedures under which other security could be substituted for the special use real property.[284] A three-year period of limitations on assessment of the tax on disposition or cessation of use is applicable, starting with a notification to the IRS of a disposition or cessation of use.[285]

7. Election to Use Special Valuation

The election to use §2032A special valuation is made on the decedent's estate tax return.[286] The election can be made even if that return is not timely filed.[287] Accompanying such an election must be a written agreement signed by each person who has any interest in the property with respect to which the use valuation is elected. This agreement must evidence the consent of each of these parties to the application of the recapture tax provisions to the property interest.[288]

The executor may have a reasonable time (not to exceed 90 days after the estate is notified that a defect in the election exists) in which to cure certain technical defects in a §2032A election.[289] To qualify for this treatment, the original election must have been timely made.[290] Technical defects for this purpose include failures to provide all the information required in the election notice or to include the signatures of all persons having an interest in the property.

8. Using the Special Valuation Method

If property held by the client is of the type that will qualify for the special use valuation method, the asset composition in the estate should be structured to assure that the qualifying percentage tests specified under §2032A are satisfied. If the possibility exists that the percentage requirements might not be satisfied (e.g., if 50% or more of the adjusted gross estate does not consist of qualified use real or personal property), the client might be advised to give away nonspecial use property (thereby increasing the percentage of qualified property held). This should particularly be the situation if that non–special use property has high appreciation potential in the hands of the donee. Alternatively, or in addition, the client could transform certain of his or her nonqualifying property into qualifying property. One detrimental aspect of such a planning approach, however, is quite probably a loss of liquidity in the estate.

E. Qualified Family-Owned Business Interests

1. Small Business Relief Deduction Provision

This segment examines the former §2057 special estate tax relief for "family-owned business interests."[291] This relief has terminated for estates of decedents dying after December 31, 2003.[292] Because this provision could reappear, and because litigation concerning the applicability of this provision and the 10-year recapture period provisions will continue for a considerable period, the following discussion examines this special relief provision. Former §2057 was struck from the Code as deadwood by the Tax Increase Prevention Act of 2014.[293]

As one of the small business relief initiatives in the 1997 Act,[294] Congress enacted former §2033A with the purpose of protecting and preserving family farms and other family-owned enterprises and preventing the liquidation of such enterprises in order to pay estate tax. As enacted, former §2033A allowed the executor of an estate of a U.S. citizen or resident decedent dying after 1997 to elect special estate tax treatment for "qualified family-owned business interests" (QFOBIs). In general, §2033A was to operate with the unified credit to allow the exclusion of $1.3 million from the decedent's gross estate. Since this $1.3 million amount was not scheduled to increase as the unified credit increased, for years after 1998 the benefit of the former §2033A family-owned business exclusion would have been reduced with each increase in the unified credit. Because of the interaction between former §2033A and the increases in the unified credit (referred to below as the applicable exclusion amount) through 2006 (as in effect under the 1997 Act), the estate tax on estates with family-owned businesses were to increase over time.[295]

In addition to the problems inherent in the interaction of former §2033A and the unified credit, the statute was generally believed to be too complex and confusing.[296] In response to these concerns, the IRS Restructuring and Reform Act of 1998[297] converted the QFOBI exclusion into a deduction and redesignated former §2033A as §2057.[298] Many of the requirements for qualification for the deduction for QFOBIs remained the same as the requirements for qualification under former §2033A. The §2057 deduction was not available for GST tax purposes.

2. Description of Section 2057 Deduction

Section 2057 retained many of former §2033A's similarities to the §2032A special use valuation provision, another statutory benefit important to small businesses and family farms, including many of the definitions applicable for §2032A purposes and the concepts of material participation, qualified use, and recapture. The following discussion gives an outline of the §2057 deduction and describes the coordination of the §2057 benefit with the unified credit.

If the executor elected to use §2057, the estate tax liability was calculated as if the estate were allowed a maximum QFOBI deduction of $675,000 and an applicable exclusion amount of $625,000, regardless of the year in which the decedent died. If the estate included less than $675,000 of QFOBIs, the applicable exclusion amount was increased on a dollar-for-dollar basis, but only up to the applicable exclusion amount generally available for the year of death.[299]

Example: D died in 2002, when the applicable exclusion amount was $1,000,000, with an estate that included QFOBIs valued at $675,000 or more. The estate tax liability was calculated as if the estate were allowed a deduction of $675,000, and the applicable exclusion amount was limited to $625,000. If, instead, D's estate included QFOBIs of $300,000, all of the QFOBIs would have been deductible from the estate and the applicable exclusion amount would have been $1,000,000. If D's estate included QFOBIs valued between $300,000 and $675,000, all of the QFOBIs would have been deductible and the applicable exclusion amount would have been calculated as the excess of $1.3 million over the amount of the QFOBIs. Thus, if D's QFOBIs were valued at $600,000, the applicable exclusion amount would have been $700,000.

The estate was required to satisfy four requirements to qualify for the §2057(a) deduction: (1) the decedent must have been a U.S. citizen or resident at death; (2) the executor must have elected application of this section and have filed a recapture agreement; (3) the adjusted value of the QFOBIs must have exceeded 50% of the decedent's adjusted gross estate; and (4) the decedent or members of the decedent's family must have materially participated[300] in the operation of the business in an aggregate of at least five years of the eight-year period ending on the decedent's death.[301]

For purposes of determining whether the 50% test was satisfied, the adjusted value of the QFOBIs included those interests included in the decedent's gross estate and those that were acquired by or passed to a qualified heir from the decedent, along with those interests the decedent transferred by gift (either a taxable gift or a gift that qualified for the §2503(b) annual exclusion).[302] To be included, the gifted interests must have been continuously held by members of the decedent's family (other than the decedent's spouse) between the date of gift and the date of the decedent's death.

3. Identifying a QFOBI

A QFOBI could include a sole proprietorship interest as well as an interest in an entity carrying on a trade or business.[303] An interest in an entity was a QFOBI if the decedent and his or her family members owned: (1) at least 50% of the entity; or (2) at least 30% of the entity if the members of two families owned at least 70% of the entity or the members of three families owned at least 90% of the entity.[304] A decedent was treated as engaged in a trade or business for this purpose if any member of the decedent's family was engaged in the business.[305] For corporations, the family must have owned the required percentage of the total combined voting power of all classes of stock entitled to vote and the required percentage of the total value of shares of all classes.[306] For partnerships, ownership was determined by the percentage of the capital interest held.[307] If there were tiered entities, each was to be tested separately.[308] With respect to individual ownership of entities, the entity was proportionately owned by its shareholders, partners, or beneficiaries having a "present interest."[309]

Section 2057 specified that an interest in property would not be disqualified as a QFOBI where the decedent leased that interest on a net cash basis to a member of the decedent's family who used the leased property in an active business.[310] The rental income derived by the decedent from the net cash lease in those circumstances was not treated as personal holding company income for §2057 purposes.[311]

The following interests could not be QFOBIs: (1) interests in a trade or business whose principal place of business was outside the United States[312]; (2) interests in an entity if the stock or debt of the entity (or a controlled group in which the entity was a member) was readily tradable on an established securities market or secondary market within three years of the decedent's death[313]; (3) any interest in a trade or business if more than 35% of the adjusted ordinary gross income of the business for the year of the decedent's death would have been personal holding company income if the trade or business had been a corporation[314]; and (4) the portion of an interest in a trade or business that was attributable to cash and/or marketable securities in excess of the reasonably expected day-to-day working capital needs of the business and to certain passive assets.[315]

4. Possible Recapture of Deduction

As noted above, the recapture provisions of §2057 continue to apply to the estates of pre-2004 decedents that elected to use the QFOBI deduction. Specifically, the estate tax benefit of the deduction is to be recaptured if within 10 years after the decedent's death and before the qualified heir's death[316]: (1) material participation requirements are not satisfied with respect to interests acquired from the decedent; (2) the qualified heir disposes of a portion of the QFOBI, other than to a member of the qualified heir's family or through a qualified conservation contribution under §170(h); (3) the qualified heir loses U.S. citizenship or no longer is a U.S. resident and does not satisfy certain additional security requirements; or (4) the principal place of business ceases to be located in the United States.[317] A qualified heir is not treated as disposing of a QFOBI by ceasing to be engaged in a trade or business so long as the property to which such interest relates is used in a trade or business by any member of the individual's family.[318]

The entire estate tax benefit is recaptured if the recapture event occurs within six years following the decedent's death; the percentage recaptured thereafter is reduced in 20% increments, until only 20% is recaptured in the 10th year.[319] If a recapture event occurs with respect to any QFOBI, the total amount of estate taxes potentially subject to recapture is calculated as the difference between (1) the actual amount of estate tax liability for the estate, and (2) the amount of estate taxes that would have been owed had the QFOBI election not been made.[320] The estate is also liable for interest on the recaptured amount at the §6621 underpayment rate.[321]

Section 2057 takes a more expansive view than §2032A of a decedent's qualified heirs, including in addition to the family members considered qualified heirs under §2032A(e)(1) any active employee who has been employed in the business for at least 10 years at the decedent's death.[322]

If a qualified heir was not a U.S. citizen, the QFOBI had to pass to, be acquired by, or be held in a qualified trust for the interest to be a QFOBI.[323] Like a §2056A qualified domestic trust used to qualify property passing to a non-U.S. citizen surviving spouse for the marital deduction, the qualified trust had to be organized under and governed by the laws of the United States or a state and, except as otherwise provided in regulations, had to require that at least one trustee be an individual U.S. citizen or a domestic corporation.[324]

5. Future for Family Owned Business Interest Deduction

Although this provision does not apply to estates of decedents dying after December 31, 2003,[325] it has continuing application concerning (1) estate tax audit examinations which may not be concluded (particularly if litigation is pursued) and (2) possible recapture of the benefit of the deduction.

Notes

1. In many instances the failure of the business in the hands of successor family members/generations is attributable either to (1) the failure of those members to adequately interact between themselves as the new owners, or (2) their not being prepared to manage the enterprise.
2. *See* Chapter 14 (§2701–§2704), as enacted in the Revenue Reconciliation Act of 1990 (1990 RRA), Pub. L. No. 101-508. Technical corrections, effective as if enacted originally as part of Chapter 14, were made by the Small Business Job Protection Act of 1996, Pub. L. No. 104-188, §1702(f). See Chapter 4, A. and B., for a discussion of estate-planning related tax changes made by the Economic Growth and Tax Relief Reconciliation Act of 2001 (EGTRRA), Pub. L. No. 107-16, the Tax Relief, Unemployment Insurance Reauthorization, and Job Creation Act of 2010 (2010 TRA), Pub. L. No. 111-312, and the American Taxpayer Relief Act of 2012 (ATRA), Pub. L. No. 112-240.

3. See, generally, 700 T.M., *Choice of Entity* (Bloomberg BNA) (by the author of this book). *See also* Reg. §301.7701-1 through §301.7701-4, §301.7701-6, §301.7701-7 (regulations for "check the box" entity classification, effective January 1, 1997).
4. See, generally, 758 T.M., *Transfers to Controlled Corporations: In General* (Bloomberg BNA); 759 T.M., *Transfers to Controlled Corporations: Related Problems* (Bloomberg BNA).
5. §351.
6. Note that §351(b) permits the receipt of "boot" in a tax-free incorporation transaction, but gain (limited to the amount of the boot) would be required to be recognized to the extent of the gain realized. This provision might be applicable when the corporation issues both stock and promissory notes in the incorporation transaction. The use of debt would enable an interest expense deduction to the corporation, thereby potentially increasing earnings per share. The issuance of debt would enable, under the installment sales provision, the postponement of the recognition of the boot gain until the subsequent receipt of payments on the note.
7. Section 368(c) defines "control" to be the ownership of stock possessing 80% of the voting control and 80% of the total shares of all other classes of stock of the corporation.
8. In Situation 2, the ownership of 20% of the common stock will cause the parent to benefit from 20% of the equity growth of the corporation, but the objective may be to eliminate all growth potential from the estate of the older-generation member.
9. Section 1361(b)(1)(D) specifies that an S corporation cannot have more than one class of stock, but §1361(c)(4) specifies that a corporation will not be treated as having more than one class of stock solely because there are differences in voting rights among the shares of common stock. Therefore, the S corporation can issue both voting and nonvoting common stock but cannot issue both common and preferred stock.
10. *See* Reg. §1.351-1(b)(1). Reg. §1.351-1(b)(2) *Ex. (1)*, indicates that where a father transfers property worth $8,000 in exchange for 20 shares of stock and a son transfers property worth $2,000 in exchange for 80 shares of the same type of stock, the transfer of value from father to son through the incorporation transaction would be a gift. *See also Estate of Trenchard v. Commissioner*, T.C. Memo 1995-121, *reh'g denied*, T.C. Memo 1995-232 (transfers of property to closely held corporation in exchange for debentures and preferred stock resulted in taxable gifts to holders of common stock because value of property transferred to corporation exceeded aggregate value of stock and debt received in transaction). For a further discussion of the applicability of this concept, see *Caracci v. Commissioner*, 118 T.C. 379 (2002), *rev'd*, 456 F.3d 444 (5th Cir. 2006).
11. See the discussion of the §2701 provisions B.2.e. of this chapter.
12. *See* Rev. Proc. 81-60, 1981-2 C.B. 680 (setting forth checklist questionnaire to be used in private letter ruling requests with respect to recapitalizations); 774 T.M., *Single Entity Reorganizations: Recapitalizations and F Reorganizations* (Bloomberg BNA). However, Rev. Proc. 2015-3, 2015-1 I.R.B. 129, §3.01(48), specifies that the IRS generally will not rule concerning the status of an "E" recapitalization as a tax-free reorganization. *See also* Chapter 14 (§2701–§2704).
13. In addition to the various tax considerations described below, see Rev. Rul. 86-39, 1986-1 C.B. 301, where, in a corporate recapitalization, certain value was transferred from a trust, and the IRS ruled that, thereby, a power of appointment of the trust would be treated as having been released for purposes of §2041 (the power of appointment provision).

14. As noted above, the IRS will not issue a ruling for a closely held corporation as to whether a transaction constitutes a corporate recapitalization within the meaning of §368(a)(1)(E), except when the reorganization status request involves a "significant issue," as determined by the IRS. *See* Rev. Proc. 2015-3, 2015-1 I.R.B. 129, §3.01(48).
15. §368(a)(1)(E). Other acquisitive and divisive reorganizations are also described in §368(a)(1).
16. *See, e.g.*, Reg. §1.368-2(e)(3) (recapitalization occurs where corporation issues preferred stock for outstanding common stock).
17. See the several examples of recapitalizations in Reg. §1.368-2(e).
18. §354, §361.
19. Reg. §1.368-1(b). A change in the voting control of a corporation is a sufficient business purpose. Rev. Rul. 74-269, 1974-1 C.B. 87. For transactions on or after February 25, 2005, Reg. §1.368-1(b), as amended by T.D. 9182, 70 Fed. Reg. 9219 (Feb. 25, 2005), no longer requires a transaction to satisfy the continuity of business enterprise test or the continuity of interest test to qualify as a recapitalization under §368(a)(1)(E).
20. §356. Such "other property" would include "securities" from the corporation. §356(d).
21. §305(a).
22. §305(b).
23. §305(b)(1).
24. §305(b)(2) (as amplified in §305(c)).
25. If a corporation is organized with a class of common stock upon which stock dividends are paid and a class of preferred stock upon which cash dividends are paid, a disproportionate distribution will not result (since the ownership relationships are not changed in this transaction). Further, if nonconvertible preferred stock is distributed pro rata to shareholders of the only class of common stock, a disproportionate distribution will not result. Such a distribution fits, however, within the classic §306 preferred stock bailout pattern, as described below.
26. §305(b)(3).
27. §305(b)(4). This could encompass a redemption premium. *See* Rev. Rul. 83-119, 1983-2 C.B. 57, *obsoleted by* Rev. Rul. 2003-99, 2003-34 I.R.B. 388.
28. §305(b)(5). A "likelihood of conversion" test will be applied to determine whether a substantial objective of the distribution is to accomplish a shifting of proportionate ownership interests in the corporation.
29. Before the amendment of §305(b) by the Tax Reform Act of 1969, Pub. L. No. 91-172, tax advisors planning recapitalizations could rely on the principles evolving from *Dean v. Commissioner,* 10 T.C. 19 (1948), *acq.*, 1949-1 C.B. 1, and *Hartzel v. Commissioner,* 40 B.T.A. 492 (1939), *acq.,* 1939-2 C.B. 16, in structuring an "estate planning recapitalization" involving the distribution of preferred stock to senior family members. In both of these situations, corporate capital restructurings enabled older shareholders to upgrade their equity positions on a tax-free basis. The *Dean-Hartzel* type recapitalizations appear, however, to fit precisely within the technical description of a §305(b) distribution that would trigger immediate taxation. For example, §305(b)(2) contains broad language generally designed to treat as taxable those stock dividends that increase the proportionate equity interests of some shareholders while permitting other shareholders to receive "property." A recapitalization in which some common shareholders receive common stock and other stockholders receive preferred stock paying fixed dividends and perhaps redeemable at a specified price is also within the general intent of this provision. Section 305(b)(3), dealing with the distribution of common stock to some shareholders and

preferred stock to others, would also appear to be pertinent. Reg. §1.305-3(e) *Ex. 12,* indicates, however, that §305 dividend treatment does not apply to a "single and isolated" transaction where a restructuring of corporate ownership occurs. The regulations describe a situation where a corporation had 2,000 shares of Class A stock outstanding, with five shareholders owning 300 shares each and five other shareholders owning 100 shares each. In preparation for the retirement of the five major shareholders, the corporation in a "single and isolated transaction" had a recapitalization in which each share of Class A stock could be exchanged either for: (1) five shares of new Class B nonconvertible preferred stock, plus 0.4 shares of new Class C common stock, or (2) two shares of new Class C common stock. As a result of the various exchanges, each of the five major shareholders received a total of 1,500 shares of Class B nonconvertible preferred stock and 120 shares of Class C common stock. Each of the five remaining shareholders received 200 shares of Class C common stock. The older group thereby received 600 shares of the new common stock, while the younger group attained majority control with the 1,000 shares. The regulations indicate that this exchange is not within the purview of the exceptions specified in §305(b) (which would cause income recognition). Accordingly, at least for purposes of avoiding §305 dividend classification, the estate freezing recapitalization remains as an effective estate planning tool, assuming the ownership restructuring arrangement is consummated in a "single and isolated transaction" within the meaning of these regulations.

30. §306(a)(1)(D), as amended by the Jobs and Growth Tax Relief Reconciliation Act of 2003 (JGTRRA), Pub. L. No. 108-27, §302(e)(3), §302(f). Section 1(h)(11), as amended by JGTRRA, Pub. L. No. 108-27, §302(a), §302(f), treats qualified dividend income as net capital gains, generally effective for taxable years beginning after 2002. After several extensions as to the sunset of this provision, ATRA, Pub. L. No. 112-240, §102(a), permanently extended the taxation of qualified dividend income as net capital gain by removing the sunset provision from JGTRRA.
31. §306(c)(1)(A).
32. §306(c)(1)(B).
33. §306(c)(4).
34. §306(a)(1).
35. §306(a)(2), §301.
36. §306(b)(1)(A).
37. §306(b)(1)(B).
38. *Id.*
39. §306(b)(2).
40. §306(b)(4). The IRS will not ordinarily issue a ruling as to "[w]hether the distribution or disposition or redemption of 'section 306 stock' in a closely held corporation is in pursuance of a plan having as one of its principal purposes the avoidance of federal income taxes within the meaning of §306(b)(4)." Rev. Proc. 2015-3, 2015-1 I.R.B. 129, §4.01(23). In Rev. Rul. 89-63, 1989-1 C.B. 90, the IRS indicated that the fact that §306 stock is issued by a corporation whose stock is widely held is not sufficient grounds for the application of §306(b)(4). Therefore, the §306(b)(4) exception does not automatically apply even when a widely held corporation issues §306 stock.
41. Under Reg. §1.306-3(e), where the basis of §306 stock is determined under §1014, the stock ceases to be classified as §306 stock. However, Prop. Reg. §1.306-3(e), REG-107595-11, 80 Fed. Reg. 26,873 (May 11, 2015), would continue to apply the taint where the stock's basis is determined under former §1022.

42. The applicability of a 20% tax rate to the "dividend" amount (under §1(h)(11)) will moderate this impact. Section 1(h)(11) and the general §1(h) 20% maximum capital gains tax rate apply to taxable years beginning after 2012. *See* ATRA, Pub. L. No. 112-240, §102(b). Prior to 2013, the §1(h) maximum capital gains rate was 15%. *See* 2010 TRA, Pub. L. No. 111-312, §101(a), §102 (extending sunset provisions in EGTRRA, Pub. L. No. 107-16, §901, and JGTRRA, Pub. L. No. 108-27, §303). Whether the interest expense paid on the borrowed funds is deductible (under §163) will depend on the application of those borrowed funds.
43. Reg. §1.306-3(e).
44. *See* §170(e)(1)(A).
45. Because of its importance in the corporate recapitalization context, the discussion of the §2701 valuation rules (included in Chapter 14) is included here. These rules also have important application in other contexts, for example, in the family limited partnership ownership restructuring context.
46. Before the enactment of §2701, Rev. Rul. 89-3, 1989-1 C.B. 278, identified a recapitalization of a corporation controlled by a parent where value was shifted (for gift tax purposes) from the parent to a trust created by the parent for descendants. Alternatively, when the younger shareholders are unrelated to the older owner involved in the recapitalization, taxable compensation could be treated as received by those younger shareholders as a result of the restructuring. Reg. §1.83-6(d) specifies, for example, that such a transaction may be viewed as a transfer by the shareholder of capital to the corporation followed by the corporation's paying such amount immediately to the employee/recipient in the form of compensation. *See also* Reg. §1.162-7; Rev. Rul. 74-269, 1974-1 C.B. 87. A deduction cannot be claimed by the shareholder because the transaction was not incurred in connection with his or her trade or business, but rather was incurred in connection with the corporation's trade or business.
47. §2701(a)(2)(B); Reg. §25.2701-1(c)(3). A class is the same class as the transferred interest if the rights are identical to the rights of the transferred interest, except for nonlapsing differences in voting rights. Reg. §25.2701-1(c)(3).
48. §2701(a)(1), §2701(a)(2)(A); Reg. §25.2701-1(c)(1), §25.2701-1(c)(2).
49. §2701(a)(2)(C).
50. Reg. §25.2701-1(a)(2). In valuing gifted junior interests, generally any "applicable retained interests" in the entity are valued at zero, unless an available exception applies. §2701(a)(3)(A); Reg. §25.2701-1(a).
51. §2701(c)(1)(B).
52. Even if an attempt is made to "zero out" the gift transfer amount, a minimum 10% of the equity will be treated as transferred to the holders of the junior equity. §2701(a)(4).
53. §2701(e)(1); Reg. §25.2701-1(d)(1).
54. §2701(c)(3). Periodic payments must be made at least annually. Reg. §25.2701-2(b)(6)(i)(A), §25.2701-2(b)(6)(i)(B).
55. §2701(a)(4).
56. §2701(a)(4)(A). For this purpose, indebtedness does not include: (1) short-term indebtedness incurred with respect to the current conduct of the entity's trade or business; (2) indebtedness owed to a third party solely because it is guaranteed by the transferor or an applicable family member; or (3) amounts permanently set aside in a qualified deferred compensation arrangement, to the extent the amounts are unavailable for use by the entity. Reg. §25.2701-3(c)(3)(i). "A lease of property is not indebtedness, without regard

to the length of the lease term, if the lease payments represent full and adequate consideration for use of the property." Reg. §25.2701-3(c)(3)(ii).

57. §2701(d).
58. §2701(d)(1)(A).
59. §2701(d)(2).
60. §2701(c)(3)(C)(i).
61. §2701(c)(3)(C)(ii).
62. For a more detailed analysis of this topic, see 809 T.M., *Estate Planning for Owners of Closely Held Business Interests* (Bloomberg BNA). In addition to the considerations below, an appropriate legend ordinarily should be placed on the stock certificates to indicate, in accordance with local law stock transfer rules, that contractual restrictions apply to the transfer of this stock.
63. This might occur, for example, by accomplishing a "starve-out" of the survivors of the deceased shareholder through inappropriately increasing salaries of remaining corporate employees or by reducing (or eliminating) dividends, or by implementing both strategies, thereby adversely affecting the nonemployee shareholders' value in the enterprise.
64. Under Reg. §20.2031-2(h), the basic requirements for this agreement to fix the estate tax value are that: (1) the decedent's estate must be obligated to sell, (2) the agreement must prohibit the shareholder during life from disposing of the stock without first offering it to the prospective purchaser at the contract price (i.e., a right of first refusal), and (3) the purchase price at death must have been established through an arm's-length business bargain (and not as a device to pass the decedent's shares to the natural objects of his or her bounty for less than an adequate and full consideration in money or money's worth). These requirements were strengthened with the enactment of §2703 in the 1990 RRA, Pub. L. No. 101-508, §11602(a), effective for agreements entered into, or substantially modified, after October 8, 1990. Section 2703 provides that values under a buy-sell agreement will be determinative for estate, gift and generation-skipping transfer (GST) tax purposes only if the agreement: (1) is a bona fide business arrangement; (2) is not a device for transferring property to members of the transferor's family for less than full and adequate consideration; and (3) has terms that are comparable to similar arrangements entered into by persons in an arms' length transaction. *See* §2703(b); Reg. §25.2703-1(a), §25.2703-1(b). These requirements are deemed satisfied if more than 50% by value of the property subject to the right or restriction is owned directly or indirectly by individuals who are not members of the transferor's family. Reg. §25.2703-1(b)(3). Note that the effective date provision enables, if possible, the retention of a buy-sell agreement implemented prior to that effective date. The IRS has issued various private letter rulings indicating that in specific situations the "grandfathered" status of a pre-existing buy-sell agreement was maintained, notwithstanding certain changes, because the right or restriction was not "substantially modified." Reg. §25.2703-1(c)(1), §25.2703-2. Reg. §25.2703-1(c)(2) indicates that a substantial modification does not include: (1) a modification required by the terms of a right or restriction; (2) a discretionary modification of an agreement conferring a right or restriction if the modification does not change the right or restriction; (3) a modification of a capitalization rate used with respect to a right or restriction if the rate is modified in a manner that bears a fixed relationship to a specified market interest rate; and (4) a modification that results in an option price that more closely approximates fair market value. Occasionally, a proposed change does constitute a substantial modification. *See, e.g.*, *Estate of Blount*

v. Commissioner, T.C. Memo 2004-116 (concluding that change to buy-sell agreement did constitute substantial modification for this purpose), *aff'd*, 428 F.3d 1338 (11th Cir. 2005).

65. For tax years after 2012, the maximum individual income tax rate (39.6%) is higher than the maximum corporate income tax rate (35%). §1(a), §1(d)(i), §11. The cost to the shareholder may be reduced when dividends are paid, subject to a maximum 20% rate. *See* §1(h)(11). Section 1(h)(11), the general §1(h) 20% maximum capital gains tax rate, and the §1(i) 39.6% maximum individual income tax rate apply to taxable years beginning after 2012. *See* ATRA, Pub. L. No. 112-240, §101(b), §102(b). Prior to 2013, the maximum §1(h) capital gains rate was 15% and the maximum §1(i) income tax rate was 35%. *See* 2010 TRA, Pub. L. No. 111-312, §101(a), §102 (extending sunset provisions in EGTRRA, Pub. L. No. 107-16, §901, and JGTRRA, Pub. L. No. 108-27, §303).
66. *See* §531. An accumulation of liquid assets to redeem stock when the accumulation occurs before the shareholder's death is not a "reasonable need of the business" (since serving a shareholder rather than a corporate need). *See* §537(b)(1) (allowing post-death accumulations for §303 redemptions). *Compare Mountain State Steel Foundries, Inc. v. Commissioner*, 284 F.2d 737 (4th Cir. 1960), *with Pelton Steel Casting Co. v. Commissioner*, 28 T.C. 153 (1957), *aff'd*, 251 F.2d 278 (7th Cir. 1958). *See also John B. Lambert & Assoc. v. United States*, 212 Ct. Cl. 71 (1976); *Otto Candies, LLC v. United States*, 288 F. Supp.2d 730 (E.D. La. 2003) (redemption of stock of minority shareholder was valid business purpose and funds retained for such purpose were retained for reasonable needs of corporation's business); GCM 36605 (Mar. 3, 1976). Funds may be reserved to satisfy future redemption obligations long in advance of the actual circumstances triggering the redemption where a company is bound to make future redemptions pursuant to a stock purchase agreement. The use of the S corporation option (if available) should eliminate the accumulated earnings tax risk.
67. Section 264(a)(1) provides that no deduction is allowed for premiums paid on any life insurance policy covering the life of any officer or employee, or of any person financially interested in any trade or business carried on by the taxpayer, when the taxpayer is directly or indirectly a beneficiary under the policy.
68. *See* Rev. Rul. 59-184, 1959-1 C.B. 65. In this ruling, the IRS indicated that whenever a corporation purchases life insurance on the lives of its stockholders, the proceeds of which are to be used in payment for the stock of any stockholder, the premiums on such insurance do not constitute income to any stockholder, even though the stockholder has the right to designate a beneficiary, if such right of the beneficiary to receive the proceeds is conditioned upon the transfer of corporate stock to the corporation. The payment of premiums by the corporation is merely an independent act by the corporation by which it converts one asset, cash, into another asset, an insurance policy, and such action has no relationship whatsoever to the receipt of income by the stockholders. *See also Prunier v. Commissioner*, 248 F.2d 818 (1st Cir. 1957); *Sanders v. Fox*, 253 F.2d 855 (10th Cir. 1958). If, however, the insurance is payable to a beneficiary other than the corporation/policy owner, the shareholder benefiting from these payments by the corporation will receive gross income from the periodic premium payments.
69. §101(a)(1). The exclusion does not apply if a transfer of the policy for value has occurred. *See* §101(a)(2).
70. *See* §312; Rev. Rul. 54-230, 1954-1 C.B. 114.

71. To assure this stock redemption result, the parties may agree to a trust or escrow arrangement to receive the insurance proceeds to be applied for this purpose by the trustee or escrow agent.
72. Rev. Rul. 58-614, 1958-2 C.B. 920.
73. The IRS will not rule on whether §302(b) applies when: (1) the consideration given in a redemption by a corporation consists entirely or partly of its notes payable and the stock is held in escrow or as security, with the possibility that the stock will be returned to the shareholder on the happening of certain defaults by the corporation (Rev. Proc. 2015-3, 2015-1 I.R.B. 129, §3.01(39)); (2) the consideration consists entirely or partly of its promise to pay an amount based on, or contingent on, future corporate earnings, when the promise is contingent on working capital being maintained at a certain level, or "any other similar contingency" (*Id.* at §3.01(40)); or (3) after the redemption, the distributing corporation uses property owned by the redeeming shareholder and the corporation's payments for the use of the property are dependent on its future earnings (unless the payments are based on a fixed percentage of receipts or sales) or are subordinate to the claims of the corporation's general creditors (*Id.* at §3.01(41)).
74. §302(b)(1). This dividend equivalence test requires a "meaningful reduction" in the shareholder's proportionate interest after applying the attribution of ownership rules. *United States v. Davis,* 397 U.S. 301 (1970). A reduction in majority shareholder status to exactly 50% is a "meaningful reduction" since, at that point, the shareholder's voting situation declines from control to a possible deadlock position. Rev. Rul. 75-502, 1975-2 C.B. 111. *See also* Rev. Rul. 85-106, 1985-2 C.B. 116; Rev. Rul. 76-364, 1976-2 C.B. 91; Rev. Rul. 75-512, 1975-2 C.B. 112.
75. §302(b)(2). The §318 attribution of ownership rules will apply in determining whether the redemption is "substantially disproportionate." §302(c).
76. §302(b)(3). A problem in achieving the protection of §302(b) is that each of the three tests for exchange treatment depends upon the shareholder's pre-redemption and post-redemption stock interest, which includes the stock the shareholder owns both (1) directly and (2) through attribution from related parties under the rules of §318. Fiduciaries attempting redemptions in complete termination under §302(b)(3) have commonly encountered problems with the family attribution rules of §318(a)(1) and the beneficiary attribution rules of §318(a)(3). One escape from the burden of these rules is found in §302(c)(2), which specifies that the family attribution rules may be waived under specific conditions. If the redemption occurs after death, uncertainty has existed as to whether the estate (or a testamentary trust) could waive the attribution rules to gain sale or exchange income tax treatment. The problem arises because: (1) the beneficiary attribution rules become applicable upon the creation of the estate or testamentary trust; (2) §302(c)(2)(A) has allowed waiver of only the family attribution rules; and (3) the IRS had maintained that only natural persons have the privilege of waiving family attribution rules. Rev. Rul. 68-388, 1968-2 C.B. 122 (no waiver allowed to estates), *obsoleted by,* Rev. Rul. 2003-99, 2003-34 I.R.B. 388; Rev. Rul. 59-233, 1959-2 C.B. 106 (no waiver allowed to trusts),, Rev. Rul 2003-99. *But see* Rev. Rul. 77-93, 1977-1 C.B. 80 (estate can file waiver where stockholder redeemed prior to death). The Tax Court has previously held that the term "distributee" in §302(c)(2) is applicable to trusts and estates and that those entities can waive the family attribution rules. *Johnson Trust v. Commissioner,* 71 T.C. 941 (1979); *Crawford v. Commissioner,* 59 T.C. 830 (1973), *nonacq.,* 1974-2 C.B. 5. *See Rickey v. United States,* 592 F.2d 1251 (5th Cir. 1979) (approving waiver by trust of entity/beneficiary attribution rules). The Tax Court rejected the *Rickey* holding as to

waiver of entity attribution in *Metzger Trust v. Commissioner,* 76 T.C. 42 (1981), *aff'd,* 693 F.2d 459 (5th Cir. 1982), *cert. denied,* 463 U.S. 1207 (1983). *Metzger* supported the IRS position that the attribution of ownership rules apply without regard to the existence of hostility among family members. Pursuant to subsequently enacted §302(c)(2)(C), an entity is permitted to waive the family attribution rules if those through whom stock ownership is attributed to the entity join in this waiver. Only family attribution rules may be waived by an entity and its beneficiaries. The waiver rules have not been extended to waivers of attribution to and from entities and their beneficiaries. This legislative change was expressly intended to overrule *Rickey.* This change presumably also caused the IRS to obsolete the rulings noted above. *See also* §302(c)(2)(B) (certain acquisitions and dispositions of stock with related persons). The IRS will not rule on whether, for purposes of §302(c)(2)(B), such an acquisition or disposition of stock has, or did not have, as one of its principal purposes the avoidance of federal income taxes within the meaning of that provision, unless the facts and circumstances are materially identical to the facts identified in certain specified revenue rulings. Rev. Proc. 2015-3, 2015-1 I.R.B. 129, §3.01(42). Further, an interest in the corporation will be treated as retained by the redeeming shareholder (i.e., no "complete termination" will occur) if that person thereafter serves as a salaried employee or as a consultant to the corporation (or an affiliated company). *See Lynch v. Commissioner,* 801 F.2d 1176 (9th Cir. 1986); *Seda v. Commissioner,* 82 T.C. 484 (1984).

77. §302(b)(4). Only distributions to noncorporate shareholders can qualify under this provision. A distribution qualifies under this provision if it: (1) is not essentially equivalent to a dividend (with reference to the effect on the corporation and not on the shareholders), (2) is made pursuant to a plan of liquidation, and (3) occurs within the taxable year the plan is adopted or the succeeding year. §302(e)(1).
78. See the discussion of §303 in Chapter 12, E.1.
79. Various private letter rulings have been issued to taxpayers to assure this result in their individualized facts and circumstances, including where the redeeming taxpayer files the agreement described in §302(c)(2)(A)(iii). *See, e.g.*, PLR 200939011 (§302(b)(3) applied to complete termination of interest in closely held corporation even taxpayer gave shares in corporation; redemption was in exchange for 15-year notes equal to purchase price, and treatment was dependent upon filing agreement specified in Reg. §1.302-4).
80. *See* §1014(a).
81. *See* ATRA, Pub. L. No. 112-240, §102(b). Prior to 2013, the maximum tax on dividends for individuals was 15% under §1(h)(11). *See* 2010 TRA, Pub. L. No. 111-312, §101(a), §102 (extending application of §1(h)(11) and general §1(h) 15% capital gains tax rate to taxable years beginning before 2013 by amending sunset provisions in EGTRRA, Pub. L. No.107-16, §901, and JGTRRA, Pub. L. No. 108-27, §303).
82. *See* §1368.
83. Rev. Rul. 95-14, 1995-1 C.B. 169; PLR 201207002, PLR 200402019, PLR 200402009, PLR 200401009.
84. Consideration might be given to the use of a trustee to purchase and maintain the policies in force. Such an arrangement assures all parties that the agreement will be carried out (assuming the policies remain in force through regular premium payments) and can offer possible protection from creditors of the individual shareholders.
85. See §162(a)(1) providing the payor a deduction for a "reasonable" allowance for salaries paid.
86. See Chapter 11, E.2., for a discussion of split-dollar life insurance plans and the potential issues involved.

87. §264(a)(1).
88. §101(a)(1). This assumes the transfer for consideration rule of §101(a)(2) is not applicable to limit the amount excludible from gross income.
89. If the buy-sell agreement imposes an unconditional purchase obligation on the individual shareholders and that obligation is subsequently discharged by the corporation, the amounts distributed in redemption may be treated as dividend income to the surviving shareholders. *See* Rev. Rul. 69-608, 1969-2 C.B. 42; *Sullivan v. United States,* 363 F.2d 724 (8th Cir. 1966), *cert. denied,* 387 U.S. 905 (1967); *Wall v. United States,* 164 F.2d 462 (4th Cir. 1947); *Smith v. Commissioner,* 70 T.C. 651 (1978); *Stephens v. Commissioner,* 60 T.C. 1004 (1973). Consequently, dividend treatment will result to the remaining shareholder if the corporation effectively assumes an obligation under a cross-purchase agreement binding on that shareholder. *See Holsey v. Commissioner,* 258 F.2d 865 (3d Cir. 1958). If the surviving shareholders simply have an option to purchase the stock and do not exercise their option but, alternatively, cause the corporation to purchase the stock the redemption should not be treated as a dividend distribution to those shareholders. Further, if the corporation immediately redeems the stock from the buying shareholder, and the court treats the buying shareholder as a mere agent or conduit for the corporation, the original seller may be treated as if his or her stock had been redeemed directly from that seller. *See Fox v. Harrison,* 145 F.2d 521 (7th Cir. 1944); *Bennett v. Commissioner,* 58 T.C. 381 (1972), *acq.*, 1972-2 C.B. 1*; Bunton v. Commissioner,* T.C. Memo 1968-3.
90. §1014(a).
91. §1012.
92. This redemption will qualify under §302(b)(3) as a complete termination of the shareholder's interest in the redeeming corporation. *See, e.g., Zenz v. Quinlivan,* 213 F.2d 914 (6th Cir. 1954) (discussing integrated treatment of this transaction). *See also* Rev. Rul. 77-226, 1977-2 C.B. 90 (if redemption by corporate shareholder occurred before sale and did not constitute sale or exchange, this sequence would not be relevant for purposes of availability of dividends received deduction to corporate shareholder recipient, where both transactions were undertaken as part of integrated plan).
93. For a detailed discussion of this subject, see 809 T.M., *Estate Planning for Owners of Closely Held Business Interests* (Bloomberg BNA).
94. Estate tax values will be determined with respect to "an option or a contract to purchase securities owned by a decedent at the time of his death." Reg. §20.2031-2(h).
95. *See* Reg. §20.2031-2(h); *Estate of Blount v. Commissioner,* T.C. Memo 2004-116 (where decedent has unilateral ability to change buy-sell agreement while alive, agreement will not be considered binding during lifetime and, therefore, cannot control value for federal estate tax purposes), *aff'd on this issue,* 428 F.3d 1338 (11th Cir. 2005).
96. This is an acceptable approach for creating a lifetime restriction, since it limits the amount that can be realized from the sale. *May v. McGowan,* 194 F.2d 396 (2d Cir. 1952).
97. §2703, effective for agreements entered into, or substantially modified, after October 8, 1990. Reg. §25.2703-1(c)(1) specifies that, for purposes of this "grandfathering" rule, a substantial modification is one that results in more than a de minimis change to the quality, value or timing of the parties' rights or restrictions. Reg. §25.2703-1(c)(2) indicates that a modification is not considered a substantial modification if it is required by the terms of the agreement, if it does not change the right or the restriction, or if it modifies a capitalization rate in a manner tied to a specified market interest rate. An

exception is also provided for a modification that results in an option price that more closely approximates fair market value. *See* Reg. §25.2703-1(c)(2)(iv).

98. §2703(b). Reg. §25.2703-1(b)(2) indicates that each of these three requirements must be independently satisfied for a right or restriction to satisfy this exception. For example, the mere showing that a right or restriction is a bona fide business arrangement is not sufficient to establish the absence of a device to transfer property for less than full and adequate consideration.
99. Reg. §25.2703-1(b)(3) indicates that a right or restriction will be treated as having satisfied the bona fide business requirement, the device test, and the similar arrangements test, if more than 50% of the value of the restricted property is owned directly or indirectly by individuals who are not members of the transferor's family.
100. Reg. §25.2703-1(b)(4).
101. Reg. §25.2703-1(b) uses the term "natural objects of the transferor's bounty" rather than "members of the decedent's family" as specified in §2703(b)(2).
102. The problem of failure to review values when using the fixed price approach might be partially solved by specifying that the agreed price per share will be increased or decreased by the corporation's per share fluctuation in retained earnings during some specified measurement period.
103. This might occur, for example, because the enterprise has significant goodwill that is not reflected as an asset on the financial books.
104. Often a corporation will be required to be an accrual basis taxpayer unless engaged in a service business. *See* §448.
105. For example, assume Y and B each own 50% of the shares of Corporation X. They could agree that the value of the corporation will be determined by capitalizing at a 10% rate the average earnings for the five-year period before the year in which the sale is to occur. Assume the average earnings over the five-year period are $300,000. The net worth of the corporation would be determined to be $3 million (based on the multiple of 10 times earnings), and the value of each shareholder's interest would be $1.5 million.
106. *See* Reg. §20.2031-3(b) (endorsing use of corporation's "demonstrated earning capacity" as relevant factor for valuation purposes).
107. The gain on that policy will not be included in gross income of the policy owner, unless the policy has been transferred for consideration. *See* §101(a)(1), §101(a)(2). Note, however, that the corporate alternative minimum tax includes, as an adjustment item, the death proceeds in excess of cash value. §56(g)(4)(B)(ii).
108. In PLR 9511009, for example, life insurance policies were transferred to business owners who assigned these policies to a trust named as the beneficiary of the policies. The owners were to make payments into the trust to pay the premiums necessary to maintain the policies in force. The IRS ruled that neither owner would hold incidents of ownership (for estate tax purposes) while the independent trustee held the policies. *See also* PLR 9622036 (where shareholders created irrevocable trust and transferred policies to trust, naming trust as beneficiary, policy proceeds were not includible in insured's gross estate under §2042(2)).
109. This contemplates a closed transaction with an exchange of all the stock for promissory notes, rather than periodic stock sales or periodic stock redemptions (which could cause dividend treatment because the periodic transactions do not qualify for sale or exchange treatment under §302(b)).
110. In an entity purchase situation, the IRS will not rule regarding the applicability of §302(b) if the notes are secured by a pledge of the stock that has been repurchased or

redeemed. Rev. Proc. 2015-3, 2015-1 I.R.B. 129, §3.01(39). Further, the regulations imply that the acquisition of this stock upon default by the obligor may constitute acquisition of an "interest" in the corporation, negating any waiver of the family attribution rules under §302(c)(2). Reg. §1.302-4(e).

111. The regulations indicate that the notes received by the selling shareholders should not be subordinate to claims of general creditors. Interest and principal payments on the notes should be fixed and not contingent on corporate earnings. *See* Reg. §1.302-4(d). Likewise, the notes should be structured so as to not be regarded as an equity interest in the corporation (i.e., the notes should not be another class of stock under the §385 rules differentiating debt from corporate equity).
112. Even if the stock is substantially disbursed among several primary shareholder groups and their family members, the stock might not be listed on a stock exchange, or otherwise be regularly traded, and, consequently, this share valuation problem would arise. See 831 T.M., *Valuation of Corporate Stock* (Bloomberg BNA). *See also* §2703 (restricting relevance of buy-sell agreements for valuation purposes).
113. See Chapter 12, E.1. and E.2.
114. §1014(a). Section 2032(c) provides that the alternate valuation date election may be made only if the election will decrease both the value of the gross estate and the amount of the tax. Before the amendments to §2032 made by the Deficit Reduction Act of 1984, Pub. L. No. 98-369, §1023, and the Tax Reform Act of 1986 (1986 TRA), Pub. L. No. 99-514, §1432, the alternative valuation date might have been elected (if, as of the date of death, the value of the gross estate exceeded a specified minimum amount), so as to achieve a higher income tax basis. *See also* §6662 (accuracy-related penalty provisions).
115. See, however, §1014(f), enacted in 2015, which provides rules concerning the consistency in basis values for income tax and estate tax. These rules require that the tax basis of certain property acquired from a decedent, as determined under §2014, may not exceed the value of that property as finally determined for federal estate tax purposes, or, if not finally determined, the value of that property as reported on a statement made under §6035. This provision provides new reporting requirements with regard to the value of property included in a decedent's gross estate for federal estate tax purposes. See §1014(f), as added by the Surface Transportation and Veterans Health Care Choice Improvement Act of 2015, Pub. L. No. 114-41, §2004.
116. Reg. §20.2031-1(b).
117. *Id.* If the corporation holds significant real estate, the estate may be able to use the special valuation procedure available under §2032A. *See* Reg. §20.2032A-3(b)(1).
118. Reg. §20.2031-2(f).
119. 1959-1 C.B. 237. Rev. Rul. 59-60 has been amplified by Rev. Rul. 77-287, 1977-2 C.B. 319, which provides the IRS's perspective on how to value unregistered securities issued by a company whose stock is actively traded on one or more securities markets. The problem addressed is how to determine the difference in fair market value between registered shares that are actively traded and unregistered shares. In *Estate of McClatchy v. Commissioner,* 106 T.C. 206 (1996), *rev'd,* 147 F.3d 1089 (9th Cir. 1998), the Tax Court determined that a decedent's shares of stock in a family business should be valued without regard to securities law restrictions that applied to the stock during the decedent's life (i.e., SEC Rule 144) but expired at the time of death. However, the Ninth Circuit held that restrictions on stock owned by affiliates, which applied to the decedent but not to his estate, were to be considered in valuing stock for estate tax purposes where the nonaffiliate status of decedent's estate, rather than decedent's death, caused the restrictions to be removed.

120. For example, Widget Co. makes a $1.50 widget from $1 worth of parts. When the price of the parts increases from $1 to $2, Widget must raise its prices to an amount such as $2.50. If Widget has an inventory of parts that it bought for $1 per unit, it will have an embedded profit of at least $1.50 per unit, rather than $.50 per unit, until that inventory is exhausted.
121. For example, in its operations, Widget Co. uses a machine purchased for $50,000, claiming depreciation over five years (at $10,000 per year). When this machine must be replaced at the end of the five-year cycle, the new machine might cost $75,000, substantially more than the $50,000 accumulated depreciation on the old machine (and the possible depreciation reserve).
122. Reg. §20.2031-2(f). Note that any transfers of interests in corporations and partnerships must involve consideration of the potential gift and estate tax valuation impact of §2704, regarding when the lapse of voting or liquidation rights is treated as a transfer.
123. *See* TAM 9403002 (two blocks of stock, one includible under §2033 and other includible under §2038, should be aggregated for purposes of applying control premium). Note that in *Estate of Mellinger v. Commissioner,* 112 T.C. 26 (1999), *acq.,* 1999-2 I.R.B. 763, the court rejected an aggregation argument, but in *Estate of Fontana v. Commissioner,* 118 T.C. 318 (2002), the Tax Court ruled that, for estate tax valuation, stock owned by decedent was correctly aggregated with stock over which he possessed a testamentary general power of appointment because, at the moment of death, he had control and power of disposition over the property.
124. Rev. Rul. 93-12, 1993-1 C.B. 202. *See also Estate of Bright v. United States,* 658 F.2d 999 (5th Cir. 1981) (rejecting family attribution in estate tax valuation context).
125. For an example of taxpayer's success in a large valuation case, see *Estate of Newhouse v. Commissioner,* 94 T.C. 193 (1990), *nonacq.,* 1991-2 C.B. 1, where the Tax Court rejected the Commissioner's alleged deficiency and fraud penalty of over $900 million on the valuation of closely held stock. See, further, the extended dispute concerning valuation in *Morrissey v. Commissioner,* 243 F.3d 1145 (9th Cir. 2001), *rev'g Estate of Kaufman v. Commissioner,* T.C. Memo 1999-119. The Ninth Circuit rejected the Tax Court's analysis concerning valuation.
126. *See, e.g., Estate of Hall v. Commissioner,* 92 T.C. 312 (1989) (value of Hallmark stock was determined to be "adjusted book value" because of transfer restrictions and buy-sell agreements).
127. *See Estate of Jung v. Commissioner,* T.C. Memo 1990-5 (information relating to sale of assets of business 27 months after decedent's death was relevant to value determination).
128. This assumes no substantial, countervailing desire to report a more favorable earnings position to shareholders (and other interested parties, such as creditors).
129. This will, however, increase the corporation's after tax net worth, and its dividend-paying capacity, to the extent these losses are currently used to offset otherwise taxable income.
130. Under Reg. §301.7701-3(a), a business entity not classified as a corporation (organized as such under applicable state incorporation laws) will be an "eligible entity" that can elect its classification for federal tax purposes. Under default rules, this entity (i.e., not a "corporation") will be categorized for federal tax purposes as a partnership if it has two or more members, although it can elect to be treated as a corporation. Reg. §301.7701-3(b).
131. For a discussion of the income tax treatment of family partnerships, see 812 T.M., *Family Limited Partnerships and Limited Liability Companies* (Bloomberg BNA), and 710 T.M., *Partnerships—Conceptual Overview* (Bloomberg BNA).

132. Noncorporate form can enable the application of personal income tax rates under §1, which can be lower than the corporate income tax rates under §11 (except when individual income is subject to tax in the highest bracket). Additionally, this form will avoid such corporate income tax issues as: (1) constructive dividends; (2) unreasonable accumulation of corporate earnings; (3) personal holding company status; (4) payments of unreasonable compensation; (5) earnings and profits computations; and (6) tax-free merger or other tax-free reorganization qualification. Some of these corporate tax issues will not be relevant if the corporation makes a subchapter S (or tax option) election (assuming eligibility). Section 1 provides that the maximum individual income tax rate will be 39.6% and §11 provides for a maximum corporate income tax rate of 35%, but a second tax (at a maximum 20% rate) will be applicable under §1(h)(11) to dividend distributions received by shareholders, unless the corporation has S corporation status. Section 1(h)(11), the general §1(h) 20% maximum capital gains tax rate, and the §1(i) 39.6% maximum individual income tax rate apply to taxable years beginning after 2012. *See* ATRA, Pub. L. No. 112-240, §101(b), §102(b).
133. This can function as an alternative to shifting family business income through the incorporation of the business and the gift transfer of stock to children (and, e.g., trusts for children and grandchildren).
134. This assumes inapplicability of the "Kiddie Tax" (see §1(g)), which mandates that the unearned income of certain children under age 24 is taxed at the marginal income tax rate of the parent.
135. *See* §704(e), §702. If a partnership exists for income tax purposes, the partners include in their own individual income tax returns their pro rata shares of the partnership gains, losses, deductions, and other items. Although a partnership tax return is required, this return is for informational purposes only and no income tax liability is imposed at the partnership level. *See* §701, §702.
136. §704(e)(1). Capital is a "material income-producing factor" if a substantial portion of the business's gross income "is attributable to the employment of capital in the business conducted by the partnership." Reg. §1.704-1(e)(1)(iv). Capital is not a material income-producing factor where the business's income "consists principally of fees, commissions, or other compensation for personal services performed by members or employees of the partnership." *Id.* Capital is ordinarily a material income-producing factor if the business's operation "requires substantial inventories or a substantial investment in plant, machinery, or other equipment." *Id. Carriage Square, Inc. v. Commissioner,* 69 T.C. 119 (1977), confuses the meaning of capital as a material income-producing factor. The Tax Court there held that outside construction financing and permanent financing does not constitute "capital" within the meaning of §704(e)(1). The IRS will not rule with respect to matters relating to the validity of a family partnership when capital is not a material income-producing factor. Rev. Proc. 2015-3, 2015-1 I.R.B. 129, §3.01(79). The IRS apparently will rule, however, whether capital is a material income-producing factor. *See* PLR 9808010.
137. §704(e)(1). *See also* Reg. §1.704-1(e)(1)(ii).
138. This shift of income through the use of a family partnership is also subject to possible applicability of the "assignment of income" doctrine. Consequently, where the sole partnership asset following the sale of its office building was a claim for unpaid rent and the partnership was in the process of liquidation, the assignment of a partnership interest was ineffective to shift the taxability of the assignor's distributive share. *Seyburn*

v. Commissioner, 51 T.C. 578 (1969). *See also Haggard v. Wood,* 298 F.2d 24 (9th Cir. 1961) (reaching similar result where sole partnership asset was cotton crop).

139. §704(e)(2); Reg. §1.704-1(e)(1)(ii), (3)).
140. Reg. §1.704-1(e)(1)(iii). This requirement would contemplate the execution and delivery of appropriate transfer documents (deeds, etc.), the satisfaction of local property law requirements concerning the completion of gifts, and an effective partnership agreement (as determined under local partnership law).
141. Reg. §1.704-1(e)(2)(i).
142. Reg. §1.704-1(e)(2)(ii)(a).
143. Reg. §1.704-1(e)(2)(ii)(b).
144. Reg. §1.704-1(e)(2)(ii)(c). This might occur, for example, through the retention of assets leased by the donor to the partnership.
145. Reg. §1.704-1(e)(2)(ii)(d).
146. *Id.*
147. Reg. §1.704-1(e)(2)(iii).
148. Reg. §1.704-1(e)(2)(iv). Under applicable state law, however, the participation by a limited partner in the management could cause the loss of the liability limitation.
149. Reg. §1.704-1(e)(2)(v).
150. Reg. §1.704-1(e)(2)(vi). This is evidenced in relations with customers and creditors, compliance with local partnership laws, recognition of the donee's rights in distributions of partnership property and profits, in written agreements, records, or memoranda, and by the filing of partnership income tax returns showing income allocations. *Id.*
151. For an example of the use of a family partnership arrangement, see *Sharon v. Commissioner,* T.C. Memo 1989-478. There, a father had transferred a general partnership interest to his two children by assignment to himself as their natural guardian. He deposited the income from the partnership in segregated bank accounts in his own name, but his records did indicate that the funds belonged to his children. He subsequently purchased investment property using income from the partnership in his own name using some of his own funds and some of the income from the partnership. He deposited a proportionate amount of income from the investment property in segregated bank accounts. The money in the bank account was used to pay for private high school and college tuition, camps, foreign travel, and similar items. The money was not used to satisfy parental support obligations. Based on these facts and circumstances, the court held that the partnership interests and bank accounts in reality belonged to the children. This suggests that careful segregation of separate accounts is essential.
152. Reg. §1.704-1(e)(2)(vii).
153. Reg. §1.704-1(e)(2)(viii).
154. Reg. §1.704-1(e)(3)(i)(a).
155. Reg. §1.704-1(e)(3)(i)(a), (b).
156. Allocation methods are not clearly defined. For example, is a reasonable allowance for personal services first debited against total partnership income, with the remainder attributable to capital allocated proportionately, or is the income reasonably attributable to each element determined and the total partnership income then divided proportionately?
157. The family partnership can be used where a sale-leaseback transaction is not possible (e.g., where the capital requirements of the business are for funding accounts receivable, inventory, and other assets not normally appropriate to be leased). *See, e.g., Skemp v. Commissioner,* 168 F.2d 598 (7th Cir. 1948); *Oakes v. Commissioner,* 44 T.C. 524

(1965), *nonacq.*, 1967-1 C.B. 3. *But cf. Van Zandt v. Commissioner*, 341 F.2d 440 (5th Cir. 1965), *cert. denied*, 382 U.S. 814 (1965) (concerning sale-leaseback transactions).

158. See, for example, *Pierre v. Commissioner*, 133 T.C. 24 (2009) (*Pierre I*) where the Tax Court held that petitioner's single-member LLC was not to be disregarded for gift tax valuation purposes under the "check-the-box" regulations of Reg. §301.7701-1–§301.7701-3. Accordingly, a transfer by petitioner of an interest in her single-member LLC was treated as such and subject to discounts for lack of control and marketability, rather than as the transfer of a proportionate share of the underlying assets owned by the LLC. Subsequently, in *Pierre v. Commissioner*, T.C. Memo 2010-106, the Tax Court decided that the step transaction doctrine applied, that an 8% lack of control discount applied, and that a 30% lack of marketability discount applied. Further, see *Linton v. United States*, 630 F.3d 1211 (9th Cir. 2011) where the Court of Appeals reversed a decision of the District Court that held that (1) funding of a single member LLC and the transfer of LLC assets to the trusts for children were indirect gifts of the underlying LLC assets to the children's trusts and (2) the step transaction would collapse the funding of the LLC and the gift of LLC interests to the children's trust in to a single gift of the underlying assets contributed to the LLC.

159. See 812 T.M., *Family Limited Partnerships and Limited Liability Companies* (Bloomberg BNA).

160. See Halperin, *Dr. Jekyll and Mr. Hyde: The IRS States that Final Anti-Abuse Regulation Does Not Apply to Family Limited Partnerships, But What Is Next?* 36 Tax Mgmt. Memo. 115 (Apr. 17, 1995).

161. See Rev. Rul. 93-12, 1993-1 C.B. 202 (permitting minority discounts in determining valuation for gift tax purposes of block of stock of closely held corporation even though other stock was held by family members).

162. See *IRS Issues Settlement Guidelines on Discounts for Family Limited Partnerships*, "Providing Appeals Settlement Guidelines—Family Limited Partnerships and Family Limited Liability Corporations," at 2007 TNT 20–21, Jan. 29, 2007. This extensive IRS release describes various litigated family limited partnership cases and the results concerning various discounts which were authorized.

163. The IRS has issued various rulings confirming that an individual, as a general partner, may retain significant control over assets contributed to a family limited partnership without causing the applicability of the transfer provisions (i.e., §2036(a)(2) and §2038) at the death of the transferor. *See, e.g.*, PLR 9415007, PLR 9332006, PLR 9310039; TAM 9131006. Subsequently, however, as noted in the estate freeze discussion in Chapter 10, C.4.h., the IRS has often asserted that §2036(a)(1) applies to cause assets transferred to a FLP to be included in the transferor's estate. This argument has been successful if the court can find that: (1) the transferor had an implied agreement to retain possession or enjoyment of, or the right to the income from, the transferred assets; and (2) the transfer did not satisfy the exception for bona fide sales for full and adequate consideration.

164. §721; *cf.* §351 (which has certain requirements applicable to corporate formations, as specified in Chapter 10, B.1.b.).

165. §351, §368(c).

166. These include the possible applicability in the corporate context of §305 (stock distribution dividend treatment) or §306 (preferred stock bailout delayed dividend income treatment).

167. §701. If eligible, multiple levels of income taxation can be avoided in the corporate context through the use of an S corporation election.

168. §731. In the corporate context, §311(b) requires gain recognition when a corporation distributes appreciated property to a shareholder.
169. To the extent any insufficiency exists, the preference amount is payable by the partners. This type of income interest is treated as a "guaranteed payment" under §707(c). It is ordinary income to the frozen partner but is not treated as a return of capital for tax or accounting purposes. The payment does not reduce, therefore, the frozen partner's capital account. As described below, this cumulative preference is also required under §2701 if the retained interest is to have value for gift tax purposes, that is, for reducing the amount treated as transferred by gift.
170. If the payment to the frozen partner is payable only to the extent available from the current year's partnership profits, it is not a guaranteed payment for income tax purposes but is instead treated as a distributive share of partnership profits. The significant income tax difference in the two distribution methods results from the operation of the flow-through characteristic of a partnership. Under the distributive share rules, the tax attributes of particular items flow through to the qualifying partner. Where a true guaranteed payment exists, the source of the payment and the tax attributes are not relevant. Note from the Chapter 14 discussion below, however, that if the payment is not guaranteed, the payment commitment does not have value for purposes of the §2701 valuation rules, resulting in no offset for a retained interests in determining the value of a gift transfer for gift tax purposes.
171. The nonrecognition principles of §721 will then not apply and the assignment of income principles will prevent the allocation of profits in proportions differing from capital ownership.
172. *See Luna v. Commissioner,* 42 T.C. 1067 (1964) (citing other cases); *Haas v. Commissioner,* 12 T.C.M. 1117 (1953).
173. Generally, subject to §704(e)(2), partners do not have to share profits in proportion to capital interests. Therefore, a frozen partner can be given only a limited interest in residual profits.
174. Reg. §1.704-1(e)(1), (2).
175. §2036, §2038.
176. See the discussion in Chapter 10, C.2.d. Further, the special valuation rules in Chapter 14 may apply.
177. Section 721 specifies that no gain or loss will "be recognized to a partnership or any of its partners in the case of a contribution of property to the partnership in exchange for an interest in the partnership." Contrast Reg. §1.1031(a)-1(a)(1), which specifies that §1031(a)(1) (permitting tax-free like-kind exchanges) "does not apply to any exchange of interests in a partnership regardless of whether the interests exchanged are general or limited partnership interests or are interests in the same partnership or in different partnerships."
178. Reg. §1.721-1(a).
179. *Hartman v. Commissioner,* T.C. Memo 1958-206; Rev. Rul. 72-350, 1972-2 C.B. 394. Note, also, that a frozen partnership interest that is contingent upon actual earnings and not guaranteed at a certain rate or amount more clearly resembles a joint venture profits interest than a debt with an interest preference.
180. §2512(b).
181. Pub. L. No. 101-508, §11602.
182. See CCA 201442053, where the recapitalization of a limited liability company resulted in a gift to children as a result of §2701. The IRS here noted that a gift can occur through

a recapitalization. The IRS described the process for applying the rules of §2701 in this situation for determining the gift amount.

183. §2701(a), §2701(b).
184. §2701(c)(3)(A). *See* PLR 200138028 ("Guaranteed Preferred Return" [as described in ruling] was distribution right that was qualified payment right because it was right to receive distribution that was: (1) payable on periodic basis [at least annually]; (2) with respect to partner's partnership interest; and (3) determined as fixed amount to extent of "Guaranteed Preferred Return").
185. §2701(c)(3)(B).
186. §2701(a)(4)(A). *See* Reg. §25.2701-3(c)(1).
187. The Supreme Court's analysis in *United States v. Byrum,* 408 U.S. 125 (1972) (dealing with retained controls over corporate dividend policy and rejecting estate tax inclusion on this basis), may be available to negate such an argument.
188. *See, e.g., Kimbell v. United States,* 371 F.3d 257 (5th Cir. 2004) (decedent's transfer to partnership was bona fide sale for full and adequate consideration that was not entitled to recapture into estate under §2036(a); transfer that actually occurred was not disguised gift but was entered into for substantial business reasons); *Estate of Strangi v. Commissioner,* T.C. Memo 2003-145, *aff'd,* 417 F.3d 468 (5th Cir. 2005) (99% of net asset value of family limited partnership was includible in decedent's gross estate; governing documents contained no restrictions precluding decedent from being designated as recipient of income of partnership). In *Turner v. Commissioner,* 382 F.3d 367 (3d Cir. 2004), the decedent transferred assets, primarily securities, to family partnerships and the estate applied a discount to the value of decedent's partnership interests for lack of control and marketability in the decedent's estate tax return. The appellate court held, however, that the full value of the transferred assets was includible in the decedent's gross estate under §2036. The decedent retained lifetime control and enjoyment of the transferred assets, and the transfer was not a bona fide sale for adequate and full consideration. The decedent lacked de jure control over the transferred property. However, the fact that decedent did not retain sufficient assets to support himself and family members and that he sought financial advice assuring that he could withdraw assets as necessary indicated an implied understanding that decedent would continue to be the principal economic beneficiary of the contributed property. Note, further, *Estate of Turner v. Commissioner,* T.C. Memo. 2011-209, *recon. den.,* 138 T.C. 306 (2012), where the court held (1) inclusion under §2036(a)(1) (implied retention of economic benefits) and (2) inclusion under §2036(a)(2) (power to control the beneficial enjoyment), based on the decedent being the sole general partner and having sole and absolute discretion to make pro rata distributions of partnership income.
189. *See* IRS "Appeals Settlement Guidelines—Family Limited Partnerships and Family Limited Liability Corporations," 2007 TNT 20-21, Jan. 29, 2007, for an extensive discussion by IRS of litigated FLP cases and probable settlement guidelines.
190. See 700 T.M., *Choice of Entity* (Bloomberg BNA).
191. Section 1361(b)(1) prohibits an S corporation from having more than one class of stock (except, pursuant to Reg. §1.1361-1(l)(1), voting and nonvoting stock of the same class). This generally limits the use of an S corporation for estate tax freezing purposes.
192. See 725 T.M., *Limited Liability Companies* (Bloomberg BNA). *See also* Reg. §301.7701-1 through §301.7701-4, §301.7701-6. Before the adoption of these check-the-box regulations, unincorporated business entities could be taxed as partnerships only if they lacked at least two of the following four characteristics of corporations: (1)

limited liability; (2) continuity of life; (3) free transferability of interests; and (4) centralization of management. The check-the-box regulations make it less difficult for owners to structure an unincorporated business entity that will satisfy both tax and nontax goals.

193. *See* §311(a), §311(b).
194. For a discussion of estate planning with respect to partnership successions and terminations, see, e.g., 718 T.M., *Partnerships—Disposition of Partnership Interests or Partnership Business; Partnership Termination* (Bloomberg BNA).
195. §1014; Reg. §1.742-1. However, an interest acquired from a 2010 decedent where the estate elected application of former §1022 would have a basis determined under that section and not under §1014. *See* Prop. Reg. §1.742-1(a), REG-107595-11, 80 Fed. Reg. 26,873 (May 11, 2015).
196. *See* §1014(c).
197. *See* §706(c).
198. §2031, §2032.
199. Reg. §20.2031-1(b), §25.2512-1. See 830 T.M., *Valuation: General and Real Estate* (Bloomberg BNA).
200. For a discussion of §2032A, see 833 T.M., *Section 2032A—Special Use Valuation* (Bloomberg BNA). In addition to this special valuation procedure, deferral of the estate tax payment may be available under §6166. See the discussion in Chapter 12, E.2.
201. §2032A. This concept has no application to federal gift tax calculations. Consequently, for example, the value of a gift of property subject to a special use valuation recapture agreement (described below) is the fair market value of the property at the time of the gift as unreduced by the amount of any potential §2032A recapture tax. Rev. Rul. 81-230, 1981-2 C.B. 186. Special use valuation is available with regard to the GST tax, limited, however, to direct skips of that property included in a decedent's gross estate. *See* §2624(b).
202. §2032A(b)(2), §2032A(b)(3). In implementing these provisions, the Congressional tax writing committees concluded that the valuation of land on the basis of its potential "highest and best use" was not appropriate when such farming and small business uses were involved, especially since the encouragement of the continued use of property for these purposes is desirable. The concern was that, under such circumstances, the heirs might be forced to sell the land for land development purposes, thereby terminating the family farm operation. *See* H.R. Rep. No. 94-1380, at 21-22 (1976).
203. §2032A(a)(2). For the inflation-adjusted amounts, see Chapter 4, A.2.f.(5).
204. §2032A(e)(10). The interest of the surviving spouse in the community property is to be taken into account under §2032A to the extent necessary to provide a result under §2032A with respect to the property that is consistent with the result obtained if such property had not been community property. *See id.;* Rev. Rul. 83-96, 1983-2 C.B. 156 (holding that, where executor elects §2032A special use valuation, full limitation imposed by §2032A(a)(2) applies to decedent's qualified community property interest if decedent was noncontributory spouse towards acquisition of property; this result is same regardless of extent to which decedent contributed towards purchase of property).
205. Even though qualified real property may be valued under §2032A, the full amount of the mortgage on such property may be deductible for estate tax purposes. In Rev. Rul. 83-81, 1983-1 C.B. 230, for example, a mortgage was fully deductible although the value of the property as included in the estate was less than the value of the mortgage. The decedent was personally liable for the mortgage and the mortgage was enforceable

as a claim against the estate. *See also* TAM 8528008 (estate was not personally liable on mortgage).

206. §2032A(a)(1)(A).

207. §2032A(b)(1). The circumstances in which property is considered to be acquired from the decedent include property purchased from a decedent's estate by a qualified heir. §2032A(e)(9). Further, §2044(c) specifies that qualified terminable interest property (QTIP) includible in the estate of a surviving spouse is treated as passing from the spouse (including, therefore, for purposes of the special use valuation provision). *See* Reg. §20.2044-1(b).

208. §2032A(b)(1)(A), §2032A(b)(3). For a ruling identifying application of these percentage requirements, see Rev. Rul. 85-168, 1985-2 C.B. 197, where an estate was allowed to combine the adjusted values of personal property used in farming, farm property, and a building used in a business other than farming to qualify for special use valuation. If the deceased spouse holds such interest as community property, the entire property, including the surviving spouse's community interest, will be considered in determining whether this percentage test is satisfied. §2032A(e)(10). Rev. Rul. 87-122, 1987-2 C.B. 221, specifies that for meeting these percentage requirements the decedent's estate takes into account the qualified real property transferred by the decedent within three years of death. *See* §2035(c)(1)(B).

209. §2032A(b)(1)(A)(ii). The term "qualified heir" means a "member of the family" of the decedent. §2032A(e)(1). The definition of "member of family" excludes uncles and aunts and first cousins. §2032A(e)(2). "Member of the family" includes the ancestors of the decedent, his or her spouse and his or her lineal descendants, the lineal descendants of his or her parents (e.g., brothers and sisters), and the spouse of any lineal descendant. *Id.* The spouse of a lineal descendant remains a family member even when the descendant dies. Rev. Rul. 81-236, 1981-2 C.B. 172. *See also* Rev. Rul. 89-22, 1989-1 C.B. 276 (recapture tax was imposed when specially valued farm property was transferred by qualified heir to heir's cousin within 10 years of decedent's death). The term "member of family" is utilized in the special use valuation context to determine: (1) who can be a "qualified heir" (§2032A(e)(1)); (2) who can provide material participation before death (§2032A(b)(1)(C)(ii)); (3) who can satisfy the ownership and qualified use tests before death (§2032A(b)(1)(C)(i)); (4) who can provide material participation to avoid recapture after death (§2032A(c)(6)(B)(i))); and (5) who can acquire qualified real property after death from a qualified heir without triggering recapture (§2032A(c)(1)(A)).

210. §2032A(b)(1)(B). For purposes of §2032A(b)(1)(A) and §2032A(b)(1)(B), the "adjusted value" of the gross estate means the value of the gross estate reduced by mortgage and similar liabilities deductible under §2053(a)(4). *See* §2032A(b)(3)(A). A special use value election need not include all eligible real property in an estate but sufficient realty must be covered by the election to equal or exceed 25% of the adjusted value of the gross estate. Reg. §20.2032A-8(a)(2).

211. §2032A(b)(1)(C)(i). The "tacking" of the ownership, qualified use, and material participation requirements is permitted in the case of replacement property acquired in conjunction with a tax-free exchange under §1031 or an involuntary conversion under §1033. §2032A(e)(14). Tacking is permitted only to the extent that the fair market value of the qualified replacement property does not exceed the fair market value of the replaced property. §2032A(e)(14)(B). The replacement property must be for the same use as the replaced property. §2032A(e)(14)(C)(i).

212. §2032A(b)(1)(C)(ii), §2032A(b)(4)(A).

213. *See* §2032A(b)(3)(B).
214. §2032A(b)(1).
215. §2032A(b)(2).
216. *Id.*
217. §2032A(b)(1)(C)(i). The predeath qualified use test may be satisfied if either the decedent or a member of his or her family is using the property for the qualified use. *See* Reg. §20.2032A-3(b)(1).
218. §2032A(b)(1)(C)(i); Reg. §20.2032A-3. No provision was originally made for the post-death period. Therefore, except for the two-year grace period of §2032A(c)(7), cash rental of land in the period after death would trigger recapture unless the rental was by the surviving spouse to a member of the family. Former §2032A(b)(5), §2032A(c)(6). The Taxpayer Relief Act of 1997 (1997 Act), Pub. L. No. 105-34, §504, added §2032A(c)(7)(E) and amended §2032A(b)(5)(A) to provide that the cash lease of specially valued real property (effective for leases after 1976) by a lineal descendant or the spouse of the decedent to a member of the lineal descendant's or spouse's family, who continues to operate the farm or closely held business, would not cause the qualified use of the property to cease. Subsequently, EGTRRA, Pub. L. No. 107-16, §581 (in a noncodified provision), specified that, for a one-year period after the date of EGTRRA's enactment, a taxpayer who paid the §2032A(c) recapture tax could bring a claim for any overpayment resulting from the application of §2032A(c)(7)(E), even if the claim was otherwise time-barred.
219. In *Schuneman v. United States*, 783 F.2d 694 (7th Cir. 1986), the court held that the qualified use requirement was satisfied where a rental adjustment clause, providing for a rent reduction if certain production and price levels were not met, made the rental substantially dependent on production. *See also Minter v. United States,* 19 F.3d 426 (8th Cir. 1994) (applying test of "substantial dependence upon production"). In contrast, in *Martin v. Commissioner,* 84 T.C. 620 (1985), *aff'd,* 783 F.2d 81 (7th Cir. 1986), the cash leasing of the decedent's farmland to an unrelated party was held to be the cessation of qualified use by a qualified heir even though some of the heirs materially participated in farming by assisting the tenant. The court reasoned that the cash lease shifted the economic risks to the lessee. *See also Estate of Gavin v. United States,* 113 F.3d 802 (8th Cir. 1997) (transferred real property of estate was entitled to continue to be valued as farmland even though land was rented for income because rent paid was dependent upon renter's proceeds from farming land).
220. §2032A(e)(4).
221. *Id.*
222. H.R. Rep. No. 94-1380, at 23 (1976). *Accord Estate of Heffley v. Commissioner,* 884 F.2d 279 (7th Cir. 1989) (cash lease of farmland is not qualified use under §2032A); *Williamson v. Commissioner,* 93 T.C. 242 (1989), *aff'd,* 974 F.2d 1525 (9th Cir. 1992).
223. §2032A(e)(5)(B), §2032A(e)(5)(C).
224. §2032A(e)(3); Reg. §20.2032A-3(b)(2).
225. Rev. Rul. 88-78, 1988-2 C.B. 330. *See also* TAM 9443003 (mineral rights were not includible as qualified real property under §2032A but associated buildings qualified for this purpose).
226. *See* Reg. §20.2032A-3(b)(2).
227. §2032A(b)(2)(B).

228. Section 2032A(g) authorizes the IRS to promulgate rules setting forth the application of the special valuation rules in this context. *See also* Reg. §20.2032A-3(b)(1), §20.2032A-3(f). Under §2032A(g), an interest in a closely held business is the same as defined for purposes of the deferred payment rules under §6166(b). *See Estate of Hoover v. Commissioner*, 69 F.3d 1044 (10th Cir. 1995), *acq.*, 1999-1 I.R.B. 5 (property ownership consisted of limited partnership interest). *See also Estate of Maddox v. Commissioner*, 93 T.C. 228 (1989).
229. §2032A(b)(1)(C)(ii).
230. Reg. §20.2032A-3(a). For example, in *Estate of Abell v. Commissioner*, 83 T.C. 696 (1984), the Tax Court held that the decedent's leasing of a ranch to an unrelated party constituted a passive rental of investment property rather than a qualified use of the property by the decedent for purposes of §2032A special use valuation. *See also Estate of Sherrod v. Commissioner*, 774 F.2d 1057 (11th Cir. 1985), *rev'g* 82 T.C. 523 (1984). However, in PLR 8939031, the lease of specially valued farm property to an unrelated farmer did not constitute cessation of the qualified use and, therefore, did not result in the imposition of the additional estate tax under §2032A(c)(1). This occurred because the property continued to be used as a farm and the qualified heir materially participated in its operation during the term of the lease. Material participation occurred because the qualified heir regularly advised and consulted with the lessee about farm management, regularly inspected production activities, furnished essential items of machinery, and lived on the premises.
231. §2032A(b)(1)(C), §2032A(c)(6)(B).
232. §2032A(b)(4). The material participation test need be satisfied only during periods aggregating five or more of the eight years ending with the earlier of the date of death, the date on which the decedent became disabled (if the condition lasted until the decedent's death), or the date on which the decedent began receiving Social Security retirement benefits (if that status continued until death).
233. §2032A(b)(5).
234. *Id.* To invoke the rule substituting "active management" for "material participation," the deceased spouse need not have elected special use valuation. Rather, that spouse must have held qualified real property. §2032A(b)(5)(B).
235. §2032A(e)(12).
236. §2032A(b)(1)(C)(ii), §2032A(b)(4)(A), §2032A(b)(5)(A). The surviving spouse must have been a surviving spouse at the time of active management in order for "active management" to substitute for "material participation." Therefore, active management of a farm operation by a spouse before becoming a "surviving spouse" may not count toward satisfying the material participation eligibility requirement. The "tacking" of material participation by a deceased spouse (even if there was a period of retirement or disability under §2032A(b)(4)) with the active management by the surviving spouse to qualify property for current use valuation is permitted. *See* §2032A(b)(5)(C).
237. §2032A(c)(7)(B). "Eligible qualified heir" means a qualified heir who is the surviving spouse of the decedent, has not attained age 21, is disabled, or is a student. §2032A(c)(7)(C).
238. *See* §2032A(e)(6), §1402(a)(1); Reg. §1.1402(a)-4. The IRS uses payment of self-employment tax as a test to determine whether material participation exists, but this tax payment is not conclusive. Reg. §20.2032A-3(e)(1).

239. Reg. §20.2032A-3(e)(2). Employment of the decedent or a family member on a full-time basis, or to any lesser extent necessary to allow full management of the farm or business, is considered material participation. Reg. §20.2032A-3(e)(1). Reg. §20.2032A-3(e)(2) states:

> At a minimum, the decedent and/or a family member must regularly advise or consult with the other managing party on the operation of the business. While they need not make all final management decisions alone, the decedent and/or family members must participate in making a substantial number of these decisions. Additionally, production activities on the land should be inspected regularly by the family participant, and funds should be advanced and financial responsibility assumed for a substantial portion of the expense involved in the operation of the farm or other business in which the real property is used. In the case of a farm, the furnishing by the owner or other family members of a substantial portion of the machinery, implements, and livestock used in the production activities is an important factor to consider in finding material participation.

240. Reg. §20.2032A-3(f)(1).
241. Reg. §20.2032A-3(f)(2). This regulation states:

> Where property is owned by a corporation, partnership or a trust, participation in the management and operation of the real property itself as a component of the business is the determinative factor. Nominally holding a position as a corporate officer or director and receiving a salary therefrom or merely being listed as a partner and sharing in profits and losses will not alone support a finding of material participation.

See also Reg. §20.2032A-3(g) *Exs. (5)* and *(6).*

242. Pub. L. No. 94-455.
243. *See* Staff of J. Comm. on Tax'n, 94th Cong., General Explanation of the Tax Reform Act of 1976, at 539 (J. Comm. Print 1976). *See also* former Reg. §20.2032A-3(b)(1).
244. §2032A(g), as amended by the Economic Recovery Tax Act of 1981 (ERTA), Pub. L. No. 97-34, §421. See 833 T.M., *Section 2032A—Special Use Valuation* (Bloomberg BNA), for a discussion of the ongoing controversy over whether §2032A contains a general present interest requirement. If successive interests are created by a decedent in otherwise qualified property, all of the interests must vest in qualified heirs and all of the interests must be specially valued if any part is valued under the special use valuation rules. Reg. §20.2032A-8(a)(2). Interests passing to nonfamily members will preclude special use valuation. However, in *Smoot v. United States*, 892 F.2d 597 (7th Cir. 1989), the court concluded that Reg. §20.2032A-8(a)(2), which requires that all successive interests created by a decedent be received by qualified heirs, is invalid. In that situation, the IRS sought to disqualify a transfer of farmland from special use valuation where only a very small and remote portion had the possibility of passing to nonqualified heirs. *Estate of Thompson v. Commissioner*, 864 F.2d 1128 (4th Cir. 1989), similarly specifies that property remains eligible even though the qualified heirs have the power to appoint their interest to nonqualified heirs. Leaving a remainder interest to a charitable organization does preclude special use valuation for the life interest left to eligible family members. Rev. Rul. 81-220, 1981-2 C.B. 175; PLR 9407015.
245. §1014(a)(3). *See, e.g., Van Alen v. Commissioner,* T.C. Memo 2013-235 (unequivocal language of §1014(a)(3) requires Trust's inherited basis in property interest to equal §2032A special-use valuation). The IRS and Tax Court may impose a duty of consistency on taxpayers who try to eschew §1014(a)(3) and assert a higher date-of-death value in order to avoid income tax on dispositions of property previously valued for estate tax purposes under §2032A. *Id.*

246. §1040(a).
247. §1040(c).
248. §2044(c). *See* Reg. §20.2044-1(b) (indicating that this rule applies for purposes of §1014).
249. §2032A(e)(7), §2032A(e)(8).
250. In Rev. Rul. 83-115, 1983-2 C.B. 155, the IRS allowed an executor to change the method of special use valuation of a decedent's qualified real property after the estate tax return had been filed and the election for special use valuation had been made. The IRS noted that, although an election for special use valuation is irrevocable, the selection of special use valuation methods under §2032A(e)(7) or §2032A(e)(8) depends upon information available to the executor. The executor was permitted to change the valuation method to reflect information not previously available to him to enable a more proper valuation.
251. §2032A(e)(7)(A). To insure the availability of the formula method in areas where "share" rather than cash rentals are used, "net share rentals" can be substituted for cash rentals if the executor cannot identify comparable farm tracts in the same locality that are rented for cash. §2032A(e)(7)(B). The amount of net share rental is equal to the gross value of the produce received by the lessor (or the agreed value of proceeds of sale thereof) of the comparable land during a calendar year, minus the applicable cash operating expenses. *Id.*
252. Actual cash rent figures from comparable land are required and only rentals from arm's-length transactions are eligible for consideration. Reg. §20.2032A-4(b)(1).
253. The rates are specified by the IRS according to Farm Credit System Bank Territory (formerly the Farm Credit Bank District). Rev. Rul. 81-70, 1981-1 C.B. 454, contains an illustrative computation of an average annual effective interest rate. The IRS publishes the rates annually. For the 2015 rates, see Rev. Rul. 2015-18, 2015-34 I.R.B. 209.
254. §2032A(e)(7)(A).
255. §2032A(e)(7)(C).
256. §2032A(e)(8). *See* Rev. Rul. 89-30, 1989-1 C.B. 274 (executor electing to value farm property under §2032A(e)(8) must apply all of factors stated in §2032A(e)(8) that are relevant in particular valuation). For extensive discussions of the application of this method, see *Estate of Wineman v. Commissioner,* T.C. Memo 2000-193, and *Estate of Rogers v. Commissioner,* T.C. Memo 2000-133.
257. See 833 T.M., *Section 2032A—Special Use Valuation* (Bloomberg BNA).
258. §2032A(e)(13). For a discussion of this provision, see *Estate of Rogers v. Commissioner,* T.C. Memo 2000-133.
259. *See* §2032A(e)(7).
260. *See* §2032A(e)(8).
261. *See* Rev. Rul. 89-22, 1989-1 C.B. 276 (noting that, if qualified heir disposes of specially valued property to transferee who is member of decedent's family, that is, a cousin, but who is not member of qualified heir's family, then family disposition exception to additional estate tax imposed by §2032A(c)(1) on the early disposition of specially valued property does not apply).
262. §2032A(c)(1). *See, e.g.,* Rev. Rul. 85-66, 1985-1 C.B. 324 (sale of five acres of farmland by three qualified heirs to another qualified heir and that heir's spouse and construction of house on those five acres did not constitute disposition or cessation of qualified use; purchasing qualified heir and that heir's spouse were required, however, to sign consent agreement for personal liability for additional estate tax); PLR 9519015 (no

taxable disposition occurred where qualified heir of specially valued property transferred property to revocable trust, retaining income interest for life; trustees and beneficiary were required to enter into agreement to be fully liable for any recapture tax).

263. Section 2032A(c)(2) specifies how the amount of additional tax is determined. Recapture does not occur on a tax-free transfer of qualified real property to a partnership or a corporation if: (1) the qualified heir retains the same equitable interest in the property, (2) the corporation or partnership would be considered a closely held business within the meaning of §6166, and (3) the corporation or partnership consents to personal liability for recapture tax. *See* H.R. Rep. No. 94-1380, at 25 (1976). Recapture does not occur if qualified real property is exchanged in a tax-free exchange for "qualified exchange property." §2032A(i); PLR 9604018. "Qualified exchange property" is real property used for the same qualified use as the property transferred. §2032A(i)(3). Recapture does not occur if qualified real property is involuntarily converted and "qualified replacement property" is acquired. §2032A(h). "Qualified replacement property" is real property used for the same qualified use as the property involuntarily converted. §2032A(h)(3).
264. §2032A(c)(2)(C).
265. §2032A(c)(2)(A).
266. §2032A(c)(2)(A). Form 706-A is used by individuals to compute and pay the additional estate taxes due under §2032A(c). The IRS uses the information to determine that the taxes have been properly computed. The form is also used for the tax basis election of §1016(c)(1). *See LeFever v. Commissioner,* 100 F.3d 778 (10th Cir. 1996) (after qualified use ceased, duty of consistency precluded taxpayer from denying validity of his original special use valuation election on inherited farmland where taxpayer attempted to change his position after running of statute of limitations).
267. §2032A(c)(6). *See Estate of Gibbs v. United States,* 161 F.3d 242 (3d Cir. 1998) (conveyance of development easement was disposition of interest in farm).
268. See PLR 201129018, where farmland passed from the decedent to his four children and to three trusts for grandchildren. The children and grandchildren were qualified heirs for purposes of §2032A. The children and the trusts transferred their undivided interests in the farm to LLCs in exchange for proportionate interests in the LLCs. Each trust and the children received an ownership interest in the LLC proportionate to the transferred interest in the farm. The interests in the farm were then owned indirectly through the LLCs. The IRS ruled that these transfers were not dispositions for purposes of triggering the additional tax.
269. §2032A(c)(6)(B)(ii). For this purpose, §2032A(c)(6)(B)(i) looks at the material participation by the decedent (or his or her family members) for periods in which the decedent held the property. The material participation requirement is considered satisfied through "active management" by the eligible qualified heir (or by a fiduciary if the qualified heir is under age 21 or disabled). §2032A(c)(7)(B). *See, e.g., Williamson v. Commissioner,* 93 T.C. 242 (1989), *aff'd,* 974 F.2d 1525 (9th Cir. 1992) (Tax Court determined that material participation by qualified heir had ceased).
270. §2032A(c)(7)(A).
271. §2032A(c)(3).
272. §2032A(c)(2)(B).
273. Rev. Rul. 89-22, 1989-1 C.B. 276.
274. §2032A(c)(1). Section 2032A(c)(7)(A)(ii) extends the 10-year period under §2032A(c)(1) if the qualified heir uses the two-year grace period.
275. Reg. §20.2032A-3(c).

276. *Id.* Apparently this rule would apply whether the interests are: (1) a legal life estate and a remainder or (2) an equitable life estate and a remainder interest under a trust arrangement.
277. §1016(c)(1). Section 1016(c)(5)(A) specifies that this election is irrevocable. Form 706-A (used by individuals to compute and pay additional estate taxes due under §2032A(c)) is also used for the basis election of §1016(c)(1).
278. §1016(c)(3).
279. §1016(c)(5)(B). Interest is computed at the rate(s) charged on tax deficiencies for the periods involved.
280. *See* §1016(c)(3) (referring to "any" basis increase).
281. §2032A(c)(5) (imposing such personal liability unless heir furnishes bond satisfying §2032A(e)(11) requirements).
282. §6324B(a).
283. §6324B(b).
284. §6324B(d). Reg. §20.6324B-1(c) specifies that upon the application of a qualified heir the IRS may issue a discharge of a lien after receiving an appropriate bond or other security.
285. §2032A(f).
286. §2032A(d)(1). When made, this election is irrevocable. *Id.*
287. §2032A(d)(1), as amended by ERTA, Pub. L. No. 97-34, §421 (deleting reference to return filed within time prescribed by §6075(a)). Where an estate does not qualify for special use valuation because the tests of §2032A(b)(1) are not satisfied, or where no estate tax is due at the time of the initial return, a protective election may be made to specially value qualified real property. This election is made by filing a notice of protective election with a timely estate tax return. The availability of special use valuation under this election is contingent upon values as finally determined satisfying the requirements of §2032A. Reg. §20.2032A-8(b).
288. §2032A(d)(2); Reg. §20.2032A-8(c)(1). *See* Rev. Proc. 81-14, 1981-1 C.B. 669 (which includes sample form of agreement). In *Estate of Pullin v. Commissioner,* 84 T.C. 789 (1985), *acq.,* 1988-2 C.B. 1, the Tax Court held that surviving tenants in common are not required to sign the agreement required by §2032A(d)(2) to enable the estate of a decedent/co-tenant to make a valid special use valuation election. The Tax Court concluded that Reg. §20.2032A-8(c)(2) is invalid to the extent that it includes surviving tenants in common as persons who must enter into this agreement. The IRS acquiesced in *Pullin* with respect to the decision that the estate could value farmland under §2032A without including the signatures of the surviving tenants in common on the recapture agreement.
289. §2032A(d)(3).
290. *Id.* A prior version of this provision specified that the executor had to be in "substantial compliance" with the regulations to modify a defective election. *See, e.g., Estate of Hudgins v. Commissioner,* 57 F.3d 1393 (5th Cir. 1995) (providing exhaustive analysis of §2032A, its legislative history, and cases dealing with substantial compliance issue and determining, in reversing Tax Court, that estate could not correct defective election where notice of election contained only nine of 14 items required by instructions and applicable regulations and notice and recapture agreement were signed by only three of five qualified heirs); *Prussner v. United States,* 896 F.2d 218 (7th Cir. 1990) (although taxpayer's failure to file recapture agreement with timely filed estate tax return precluded finding of substantial compliance, taxpayer entitled to relief under special provision in

§1421 of 1986 TRA, Pub. L. No. 99-514); *Estate of McAlpine v. Commissioner,* 96 T.C. 134 (1991); H.R. Rep. No. 98-861, at 1224 (1984); Staff of the J. Comm. on Tax'n, 98th Cong., General Explanation of the Revenue Provisions of the Deficit Reduction Act of 1984, at 1123-25 (J. Comm. Print 1984); Rev. Rul. 85-84, 1985-1 C.B. 326 (indicating that where notice of election of special use valuation failed to contain required legal description of qualifying real property, executor of estate could perfect election within required time period if original notice of election included reasonably clear description of property). The 1997 Act, Pub. L. No. 105-34, §1313(a), eliminated the substantial compliance requirement for estates of decedents dying after August 5, 1997.

291. For further discussion of the former family-owned business deduction, see 829 T.M., *The Family-Owned Business Deduction—Section 2057* (Bloomberg BNA).
292. Former §2057(j). EGTRRA, Pub. L. No. 107-16, §521, terminated former §2057 for estates of decedents dying after 2003 because Congress determined that the deduction was no longer necessary once the §2010(c) unified credit effective exemption amount exceeded $1.3 million in 2004.
293. Pub. L. No. 113-295, Div. A, §221(a)(97)(A). For convenience, this section continues to refer to former §2057 in the present tense, however readers should note that the section can no longer be found in the Code.
294. Pub. L. No. 105-34, §502(a).
295. *See* S. Rep. No. 105-174, at 155-158 (1998).
296. For example, it was unclear whether it provided an exclusion of value or an exclusion of property from the estate and, thus, it was unclear how former §2033A would interact with other Code provisions (e.g., §1014, §2032A, §2056, §2612, and §6166).
297. Pub. L. No. 105-206, §6007(a).
298. Like the provision it replaced, §2057 was effective for estates of decedents dying after December 31, 1997.
299. §2057(a).
300. As defined in §2032A(e)(6).
301. §2057(b)(1).
302. *See* §2057(b)(1)(c), §2057(b)(2), §2057(b)(3).
303. An interest in an entity does not include a debt interest (e.g., an unsecured loan) held and issued by that entity. *See Estate of Artall v. Commissioner,* 595 F.3d 605 (5th Cir. 2010); *Estate of Farnam v. Commissioner,* 583 F.3d 581 (8th Cir. 2009).
304. §2057(e)(1).
305. *Id.*
306. §2057(e)(3)(A)(i).
307. §2057(e)(3)(A)(ii).
308. §2057(e)(3)(B).
309. §2057(e)(3)(C).
310. §2057(e)(2) flush language.
311. §2057(e)(2)(C), §2057(e)(2)(D). *See* H.R. Rep. No. 105-599, at 93 (1998).
312. §2057(e)(2)(A).
313. §2057(e)(2)(B).
314. §2057(e)(2)(C). This income was as defined in §543(a) without regard to §543(a)(2)(B).
315. §2057(e)(2)(D).

316. Because this provision does not apply to estates of decedents dying after 2003, the potential 10-year recapture period will expire as of the end of the year 2013.
317. §2057(f)(1).
318. §2057(f)(3).
319. §2057(f)(2)(B).
320. §2057(f)(2)(A)(i), (C).
321. §2057(f)(2)(A)(ii).
322. §2057(i)(1).
323. §2057(g)(1).
324. §2057(g)(2).
325. §2057(j).

CHAPTER 11

Special Executive Compensation/Deferred Benefits Estate Planning

A. Executive Compensation Planning

1. Compensation Options

The estate planner often has the opportunity (and responsibility) to provide estate planning for a corporate executive or other highly compensated employee or professional. Many of these types of clients are commonly employees of a larger corporation that the client does not control as a shareholder. The client's wealth often consists significantly of: (1) stock in the employer company (often acquired through the exercise of employee stock options), (2) outstanding options to buy stock in that company, (3) nonqualified deferred compensation arrangements, (4) group term and split-dollar life insurance policy coverage, and (5) anticipated benefits under a qualified pension and profit-sharing plan.[1]

The situation may be complicated because the executive is a highly mobile individual and may previously have acquired these benefits (and other property interests) while domiciled in various jurisdictions, including community property states, in the United States.[2] If employed by a multinational corporation, that individual's situation may be even more complicated because he or she may have acquired property (including various employee compensation arrangements) in a foreign country while resident there. The property ownership rights concerning that compensation and related contractual arrangements would often be determined under the laws of that foreign country. Under applicable conflict of laws rules, however, that property may be subject (with respect to its testamentary disposition) to the laws of the jurisdiction of the individual's then current residence or domicile. This treatment will depend upon the specific type of property held at the time of death. Alternatively, the foreign based executive client may actually be resident abroad at the time of death. The disposition of property deemed located at the residence (e.g., compensation benefits and similar contractual rights) would then be governed by the laws of the foreign country.

The function of this section is (1) to identify the common issues that must be confronted in recommending estate planning options to clients having significant employment based benefits and (2) to identify those estate planning techniques that might best be implemented by such clients. If the employee is highly compensated and has current income subject to a high marginal federal income tax rate, the estate planner will also want to suggest that the client focus on possible techniques available to currently reduce potential income tax liabilities for that compensation income when received.

This discussion primarily addresses the federal income, estate, and gift taxation of these various benefits when accrued and when received upon distribution to the plan beneficiary or his or her successors. Probably the most important planning detail to address concerning these various benefits is to assure that the designation of the successor beneficiary is consistent with the client's intent. A designation in a last will that these benefits be distributed to an identified party will be ineffective, unless the plan benefits have been specified as being payable to the client's estate. Ordinarily, this designation must be accomplished through a plan benefits designation form filed with the administrator for the particular plan. Numerous situations have occurred (even when benefits were allocable away from a former spouse in a divorce settlement) where the plan administrator paid benefits consistent with the specific designation on file with that administrator.[3]

2. Deferred Compensation

a. Economic Components

The client might be advised to implement income deferral arrangements if: (1) the employer will facilitate a plan enabling income tax deferral for accruing compensation income, and (2) the interim risk of relying on the employer's continued creditworthiness is not significant.[4] This would be particularly valuable if the deferral arrangement permits the tax-free accumulation of additional value (i.e., the equivalent of interest income) to be credited on the deferred amount effectively as compensation from the employer for its continued use of the funds (to be accomplished through some type of phantom income account). The employee would not want to defer income, however, if a substantial risk exists that, at the time the subsequent deferred compensation payment is to be made, the employer may no longer have the financial capacity to actually satisfy that obligation to the employee. In some instances the employer may insist on a deferred compensation arrangement both (1) as an additional reward for service (i.e., part of the compensation package) and (2) as a means of retaining the employee's services (since the ultimate payment may be subject to certain contingencies).

This income deferral could permit realization of the income in a later year (1) when the employee's marginal income tax bracket has declined (e.g., after retirement), (2) when tax losses might be incurred (which could be used to offset that deferred income), or (3) when statutory income tax rates have been reduced by subsequent tax legislation. As with any income deferral arrangements, care must be exercised to avoid applicability of the constructive receipt rules that would cause the income to be treated as immediately received by the taxpayer for income tax purposes (even though not actually received).

b. Definition of Nonqualified Deferred Compensation

A deferred compensation arrangement is often the unsecured and (usually) unfunded obligation of the employer (often a corporation, sometimes a partnership) to its executives/employees to pay compensation at some date in the future, usually in several installments. Those payments will often begin upon the retirement from active employment or the earlier death of the executive. Deferred compensation can be available as the result of a comprehensive plan for many executives of the company, or can be provided under a specifically tailored arrangement between an individual employee and his or her company.

One important tax planning objective of this arrangement is to defer the receipt of additional compensation until the employee is in a lower income tax bracket (e.g., after retirement). A deferred compensation arrangement can be exceedingly flexible because it need not satisfy the detailed requirements for the qualification of a broad-based pension or profit-sharing plan, such as the funding, vesting, coverage, and anti-discrimination limitations, but must avoid potential constructive receipt treatment.

c. Facilitating Income Tax Deferral

The position of the IRS with respect to the income tax treatment of deferred compensation arrangements is enumerated in longstanding Rev. Rul. 60-31,[5] the fundamental IRS-prescribed authority in this setting.[6] Two examples from that revenue ruling are particularly pertinent in identifying income tax deferral opportunities and, also, limitations:

Example (1): Taxpayer and his employer corporation enter into a contract under which the taxpayer is to work for the corporation in an executive capacity for five years. Under the contract, the taxpayer is entitled to a stated annual salary and to additional compensation of 10x dollars each year. The additional compensation, being deferred, is credited to a bookkeeping reserve account on the books of the employer corporation and is to be paid in five annual installments upon: (1) termination of the taxpayer's employment by the corporation (e.g., by retirement or death); (2) the taxpayer's becoming a part-time employee of the corporation; or (3) the taxpayer's becoming partially or totally incapacitated.

Under the terms of this agreement, the corporation was merely under a contractual obligation to make the payments when due and the parties did not intend that the amounts treated as in reserve be held by the corporation in trust for the taxpayer. The agreement was entered into prior to the time the services were rendered.[7] Under such circumstances, the income tax liability is permitted to be deferred.[8]

Example (2): The corporation has a deferred compensation plan for certain officers and key employees. A percentage of the before-tax earnings of the corporation is earmarked for these employees in proportion to their salaries. The same type of crediting mechanism is used as in Example (1). Under such circumstances, the income tax liability for this compensation is deferred until the income is actually received.[9]

Under the principles of Rev. Rul. 60-31, deferral is not permitted for federal income tax purposes, however, if[10]:

- the employee has the right to draw on amounts that have been set apart (i.e., those amounts have thereby been constructively received by the employee);
- the obligation is evidenced by promissory notes that can be discounted (i.e., cash equivalency has been received); or
- an escrow account or trust with nonforfeitable rights for the employee is established (i.e., the obligation is funded).

In essence, to obtain deferral the employee must rely on the future creditworthiness of the corporate employer–obligor and not some third party.[11]

d. Variations on Cash Plans

Innovative executive compensation specialists have introduced variations on the basic cash scheme, so as both to induce greater executive incentive mechanisms and to counteract the impact of inflation on delayed cash transfers. This has been accomplished by:

- Phantom stock arrangements—by which the account of the employee is credited with the equivalent of shares of the employer corporation when earned, rather than being credited with cash. At the later time of the actual distribution, the employee will receive the benefit of the interim appreciation in the stock (and any accumulated dividends, perhaps treated as having been reinvested into the employer's stock as of the time of crediting).
- Investment by the employer in other listed securities (particularly where a closely held corporation might be involved) whereby, during the interim between the time (1) when the securities are deemed "earned" by the employee and (2) when they are actually distributed to the employee, that employee becomes entitled to the benefit of both (1) the appreciation in value of the acquired securities and (2) the cash dividends and accumulated interest income from the securities.[12]

e. "Rabbi" and Secular Trusts

The "rabbi trust" structure remains an important tool for segregating deferred compensation benefits for executive level employees.[13] Under this mechanism, the employer creates a grantor trust and funds that trust with assets eventually to be used to fund the deferred compensation obligations to the employees. Under such a trust arrangement, the trust assets remain subject to the claims of the employer company's creditors.[14] Participants hold only an unsecured right to the assets in the trust. For federal income tax purposes, amounts paid under the plan are includible in the participants' gross income only when actually received by the participants, unless rights earlier become vested.[15]

An alternative in this context is the use of the "secular trust" (as contrasted to the "rabbi trust"). A secular trust is an irrevocable trust in which the trust's funds are not subject to the claims of the employer's creditors.[16] A secular trust can provide a method to assure the availability of the employee's benefits against both a company's refusal to pay and its financial inability to pay. The employer's contribution to the nonqualified employee trust will be includible in the employee's gross income when made.[17]

An additional alternative in this context might be to create a rabbi trust (which enables gross income deferral for the employee) but include certain triggering devices that can automatically cause the trust to be transformed into an irrevocable trust upon certain events occurring.[18] For example, the trust might be converted into an irrevocable trust upon the corporation attaining certain levels of debt or going beyond certain debt to equity ratios. Although this shift in status would cause gross income to be recognized for federal income tax purposes, the employee would be assured of the availability of the funds, rather than being a general creditor seeking these funds in a bankruptcy proceeding (unless treated as receiving some preference in an insolvency proceeding).[19]

f. Estate Planning Considerations

The value of compensation that is deferred and unpaid at death is includible in the gross estate of the deceased employee for federal estate tax purposes.[20] Inclusion in the gross estate will also be required for the element of the compensation package that is payable after death as a death benefit.[21] If only a death benefit plan exists, the IRS has been unsuccessful in treating the death benefit payments as includible in the gross estate.[22] Similarly, except in closely held employer situations, the creation of these death benefits for survivors will not be treated as constituting donative transfers for gift tax purposes.[23]

When the estate receives this amount after the employee's death, it will be treated as "income in respect of a decedent" (IRD).[24] Further, a deduction is available against the amount of IRD included in gross income, limited to the portion of federal estate tax attributable to that included amount.[25] Because the deferred compensation is includible in gross income as IRD, a valuable income tax planning technique is to channel this post-death realized income to taxpayers having a low marginal rate for federal income tax purposes for the year of receipt. This can substantially reduce the overall tax cost for the receipt of this income within the family unit.[26] This would normally be accomplished through the exercise of a fiduciary's discretion in directing the distribution of the rights to this income. To accomplish this, the fiduciary must have the necessary authority, as enumerated in the powers clause of the applicable governing instrument.

The right to the receipt of the deferred income might be transferred by gift prior to death to another family member. For federal income tax purposes this income would still be taxed to the employee-donor (as an "anticipatory assignment of income"), however, when the income is received by the donee (assuming the donor to still be living).[27]

Ultimately, the decision to defer compensation normally depends on the relative income tax brackets for the year the compensation is earned and the year it will ultimately be paid. If the tax bracket differential between current and future gross income inclusion will be nonexistent or inconsequential, the better choice could be to receive the compensation presently, pay the applicable income tax liability, and invest the net proceeds. This position might change, however, if a significant "phantom income" deferral amount (i.e., the equivalent of interest) might be credited to this postponed income amount (the phantom income being credited to a pretax account). Other factors that might indicate the feasibility of taking the compensation currently include: (1) the risk before payment of the deferred compensation of the insolvency of the employer corporation, (2) the potential loss in the value of this account as a result of accelerating inflation, particularly if alternative investments could be made, and (3) possible legislation increasing the applicable federal income tax rate.[28]

3. Stock Options

a. Stock Option Alternatives

The corporate executive may hold options to acquire stock in the employer corporation. Assuming that (if not previously exercised) those options will have value at the time of death, estate planning considerations should certainly focus on: (1) how to transfer those options at death, and (2) how funds can be available to assure exercise of these stock options by the decedent's probate estate after death.[29]

Two basic types of stock options are ordinarily granted[30]:

- incentive stock options (ISOs)[31]; and
- nonqualified (or nonstatutory) stock options (NSOs).[32]

Either plan enables the employee to make a bargain purchase of the employer's stock. When an employee exercises an ISO, the employee realizes a bargain purchase and income recognition is deferred for federal income tax purposes until the acquired stock is ultimately sold, assuming the prescribed conditions are satisfied.[33] When an employee exercises an NSO (but not at the earlier time of the option grant), the entire bargain element must be immediately included in gross income.[34] In either situation, the payment of the exercise price may be in cash, a promissory note issued by the employee, or other shares of the employer already held by the employee.[35]

b. Incentive Stock Options

(1) Description and Tax Treatment

Under the ISO rules[36]: (1) no gross income inclusion is required when an ISO is granted or when the option is subsequently exercised,[37] (2) the employee is generally taxed at capital gain rates when the stock received on the exercise of the option is subsequently sold, and (3) no deduction for compensation paid is allowed to the employer with respect to the cost of an ISO.[38]

The employee, in order to receive this special income tax treatment, must not dispose of the stock within two years after the option is granted and must hold the stock itself for at least one year after the exercise of the option.[39] If all ISO requirements other than these holding period rules are satisfied, inclusion in gross income is deferred until the disposition of the option stock, but the gain (to the extent the value of the stock at the exercise of the option exceeds the exercise price) is treated as ordinary income, rather than as capital gain.[40] The employer is allowed an ordinary deduction at that time. Stock acquired on exercise of an ISO may be paid for with stock of the corporation granting the option.[41]

For an option to qualify as an ISO the following conditions must be satisfied[42]:

- The option must be granted under a plan specifying the aggregate number of shares of stock that may be issued and the employees or class of employees eligible to receive the options.[43] This plan must be approved by the stockholders of the granting corporation within 12 months before or after the plan is adopted.[44]
- The option is granted within 10 years from the earlier of the date the plan is adopted or the date the plan is approved by the stockholders.[45]
- The option must by its terms be exercisable only within 10 years of the date it is granted.[46]
- The option price must equal or exceed the fair market value of the stock at the time the option is granted.[47] This requirement will be deemed satisfied if a good faith attempt to value the stock accurately has been made, even if the option price is later determined to be less than the stock value.[48]
- The option by its terms must be nontransferable other than at death and must be exercisable during the employee's lifetime only by the employee.[49]
- The employee must not, at the time the option is granted, own stock representing more than 10% of the voting power of all classes of stock of the employer corporation or its parent or subsidiary.[50] This stock ownership limitation will not apply if the option price is at least 110% of the fair market value (at the time the option is granted) of the stock subject to the option and the option by its terms is not exercisable more than five years from the date it is granted.[51]
- The terms of the plan must limit the aggregate fair market value of the stock (determined at the time of the grant of the option) for which any employee may exercise ISOs in any calendar year to not more than \$100,000.[52] In applying this rule, ISOs are taken into account in the order in which they were granted.[53]

(2) Estate Planning Considerations

Since the ISO cannot be assigned during the lifetime of the holder, these options cannot be transferred by gift as part of a lifetime estate planning arrangement.[54] Additionally, if the long-term capital gains status is to be retained, the stock received upon exercise of the option cannot itself be transferred pursuant to a gift program within a one-year period after the exercise of the option or within a two-year period after the initial grant of the option.[55]

The unexercised stock option can be bequeathed to a named beneficiary (including the trustee of an inter vivos or testamentary trust).[56] Alternatively, the option could become a part of the decedent's residuary estate. In this situation, the executor should be vested with the necessary power to exercise the option and to allocate the shares acquired (upon the exercise of the option) among the various beneficiaries of the residuary estate. The holding period is waived for the stock acquired by the exercise of the option held by the decedent's successor after the optionee's death.[57] This holding period also will not apply to option shares held by the decedent at the time of death for less than the required period.[58]

The fiduciary certainly should have appropriate authority to exercise valuable options so that they do not expire unexercised (after their value has been included in the decedent's gross estate). This might be specifically identified in the "powers" clause of the client's will, although state law may be adequate for this purpose. The estate planner will need to focus on satisfying cash requirements if (1) the stock options become valuable (thereby constituting an asset in the gross estate) and, therefore, (2) they should be exercised by the executor after death. Particularly, this would necessitate assuring that the fiduciary has adequate authority to borrow funds (if necessary) to be used in exercising the options.

c. Nonqualified Stock Options

(1) Flexibility with Nonstatutory Options

Unlike an ISO, an NSO may be granted at any price the employer chooses, including a price below market value at the time of the grant.[59] No limit exists on the length of option period for NSOs. For tax purposes, the NSO plan does not require shareholder approval. NSOs may be granted to and exercised by individuals who are not employees, such as the outside members of a corporation's board of directors.

(2) Nonstatutory Options Without Readily Ascertainable Value

No income tax consequences result to the employee at the time of the grant of an NSO if the NSO then has no readily ascertainable value.[60] When the employee exercises the NSO, the entire bargain element (i.e., the difference between the fair market value of the stock at exercise, determined without regard to restrictions, and the option price) is included in taxable income as compensation, with a corresponding deduction to the employer for compensation paid.[61] If the stock acquired is nontransferable or is subject to a substantial risk of forfeiture, realization of income is postponed until the stock becomes transferable or the forfeiture risk expires.[62] Appreciation accruing subsequent to the income tax recognition of the bargain element of the NSO will be taxed as capital gain (short-term or long-term) when thereafter realized and required to be recognized.

(3) Nonstatutory Options Gross Income Inclusion Election

The corporate executive in a new and growing enterprise may prefer that his or her option be immediately treated as having a readily ascertainable value. On the transfer to the employee of an option, the employee may elect to immediately include in gross income the excess of the option's fair market value over the amount, if any, paid for the option.[63] The optionee, at the cost of electing to recognize ordinary income upon receipt of the option, can obtain deferral of additional income. Often the amount of this ordinary income will be small. The subsequent recognition of any additional income from the NSO transaction is postponed until the stock is sold and the appreciation in value of the stock will be taxed at capital gain rates.

(4) Estate Planning Implications

An assignment during lifetime by gift of the rights under an NSO grant (to the extent permitted) could shift the benefit of that stock investment to the donee. Subsequently the donor (not the donee) will be subject, however, to the inclusion of the income element in his or her gross income, when appropriate under the NSO rules. The gratuitous transfer of an NSO by the optionee becomes a completed gift for federal gift tax purposes at the later of: (1) the date or transfer or (2) when the right to exercise the option is no longer conditioned on the performance of services by the optionee.[64]

If upon death the NSO is transferred to the estate of the employee, that NSO will constitute an asset of the estate for federal estate tax purposes. No basis step up will be applicable at death and the income derived from the NSO will be IRD when the NSO is exercised by the recipient.[65] Similar to the ISO situation, the executor should be vested with sufficient authority to exercise the NSO and to borrow funds to enable the exercise of the NSO. Further, the parties should consider whether, under the client's last will, the NSO should be directed to a particular beneficiary or the executor should have the discretion to transfer the NSO (if not exercised during the probate administration phase).

d. Stock Appreciation Rights

Stock appreciation rights (SARs) can be granted to employees in tandem with ISOs or NSOs or other bonus arrangements. Alternatively, SARs can be provided to employees independent of any other compensation arrangements. A SAR is used to give the employee (often high-level executive) a stake in the growth of the company but without the capital outlay required for stock options or other stock purchase plans. The employee may be entitled to exercise both the stock option and the SAR or the exercise of one may cancel the other.

A SAR is a contract right stating that an employee may receive in cash the difference between: (1) the base value of the employer's stock (usually the fair market value at the date of the grant) and (2) the value of the stock on any date during a future time period. In some situations, the employee may receive employer stock equivalent to that value. The value of the SAR is includible in the employee's gross income when it is exercised.[66] That exercise will terminate the employee's right to receive any additional appreciation in the employer's stock with respect to that SAR. For income tax purposes, the amount paid by the employer is deductible as compensation.[67]

Estate planning considerations with respect to SARs will be similar to those for stock options. The income element will not be transferable to avoid gross income inclusion because of the applicability of the assignment of income doctrine. The SARs would become an asset of the estate. Under the will, the executor should be vested with adequate power to deal with the SARs.

B. Qualified Pension and Profit-Sharing Plans

1. Basic Tax Planning Structure

Various types of corporate employees will often be participants in a qualified pension or profit-sharing plan sponsored by the employer company.[68] This qualified plan will have the basic advantage of (1) deferring the receipt of gross income by cash basis employees on those amounts contributed by the employer for the employee under the plan even though (2) these contributed amounts have been segregated into a separate account for the employees. To enable qualified plan status, those amounts are to be contributed to an independent trust created to hold the contributions.

The income tax is deferred until these contributed amounts are distributed or otherwise made available to the employee. In the interim, the trust created to hold the employer's plan contributions is exempt from income tax, enabling the tax-free accumulation of investment income by the trust, pending actual distributions to the beneficiaries.[69] Unlike in the nonqualified executive compensation context, the income tax deferral for the employee is not dependent upon the continuing financial viability of the employer corporation. Rather, the deferred compensation under the qualified pension or profit-sharing plan is contributed to be held in a separate trust without causing gross income recognition to the employee-beneficiary (i.e., the contributed amount is not treated as constructively received by the employee-beneficiary).

Significant additional opportunities exist through the use of "cash or deferred" arrangements (or §401(k) plans) to accumulate further tax-deferred funds. A cash or deferred plan can be either a free-standing defined contribution plan or can be an arrangement that is part of a stock bonus or profit-sharing plan under which an employee can either elect to have the employer contribute to the plan for the employee a limited pretax amount or to pay that amount to the employee in cash. If the requirements for full vesting, nondiscrimination, and limited withdrawability are satisfied,[70] an employee's credited amounts will be excluded from his or her gross income[71] as employer contributions to a qualified plan.[72]

The estate planner will ordinarily be more concerned with assisting the individual estate planning client with anticipated plan distributions than with the rules concerning the structuring of qualified plans (and related trusts). The issues to be considered in the individual employee's context might include: (1) when distributions should be made; (2) how the distributions must and should be shared with a spouse; (3) the federal income tax effects on distributions received both during life and after the death of the primary beneficiary; and (4) the estate and gift tax effects of the transfer of benefits under a qualified plan.

2. Income Distribution Requirements

a. Joint and Survivorship Requirements

A joint and survivorship annuity and a pre-retirement survivor annuity are required in certain qualified deferred compensation plans when an employee-plan participant client has a spouse.[73] Joint and survivor requirements apply to: (1) any defined benefit plan and (2) any defined contribution plan that is subject to the specified funding standards, that is, a money purchase or target benefit plan, but not a profit-sharing or a stock bonus plan.[74] These requirements also apply to any other defined contribution plan unless the following three requirements are satisfied: (1) the defined contribution plan provides that the participant's vested benefit is payable in full, upon the death of the participant, to the participant's surviving spouse,[75] (2) the participant does not elect a payment of benefits in the form of a life annuity, and (3) with respect to the participant, the plan is not a direct or indirect transferee of a defined benefit plan or a defined contribution plan that is subject to funding standards.[76]

All vested benefits paid from a defined benefit plan or a defined contribution plan subject to a funding standard must be paid, therefore, in the form of a qualified joint and survivor annuity (with the survivor receiving at least 50% of the value).[77] Effectively, a forced heirship provision in favor of the surviving spouse is applicable to these distributions by application of the federal tax provisions. The qualified joint and survivor annuity requirement only needs to be applied if the participant and the participant's spouse have been married throughout the entire year before distributions commence.[78] A participant, with the consent of the spouse, may elect, however, to waive the qualified joint and survivor annuity.[79]

b. Death After Distributions Commence

The employee may die after distributions have commenced but before the entire interest under the qualified plan has been distributed. In this situation, the remaining portion of the employee's interest must be distributed to the designated successor to the plan benefits at least as rapidly as scheduled under the method of distribution in effect before the employee's death.[80] For the surviving spouse, the balance can be distributed using a single life divisor for the spouse's age each year, recalculated annually.[81] Other rules concerning the timing of the distributions apply where the participant's spouse is not the beneficiary or is not the sole beneficiary. If no beneficiary has been designated, the payment will ordinarily be made to the deceased participant's estate.[82]

c. Death Before Distributions Commence

If the employee dies before any distributions have commenced, the general rule is that the entire interest of the employee must be distributed within the five years following the employee's death.[83] Certain exceptions to this rule are permitted. For example, if the employee dies before any distributions have commenced, and if the employee has designated an "individual" as his or her beneficiary, the employee's interest may be distributed over the life of that designated beneficiary or over a period not extending beyond that beneficiary's life expectancy, provided that the distributions begin no later than one year after the date of the employee's death.[84] If the employee's designated beneficiary is a surviving spouse, distributions may be deferred until the time the employee would have reached age 70 1/2.[85]

3. Income Tax Treatment of Retirement Plan Distributions

a. Payment Options

The employee will often have the option at retirement of receiving a distribution of the proceeds in his or her qualified plan account either in: (1) periodic payments or (2) a lump sum distribution. Those payments will be included in gross income, as described below. A 10% additional tax will be applicable on early distributions from a qualified retirement plan, that is, distributions made before an individual reaches age 59 1/2.[86] Further, an additional income tax will be applicable to excessive distributions made to a participant who was a 5% or greater owner of the qualified trust sponsor.[87]

b. Periodic Payments

If the amounts are received periodically, the distributions received will be taxed under the general rules relating to the income tax treatment of annuity payments, subject to a simplified method for allocating tax basis to the payments anticipated to be received.[88] An individual is required to include in income some portion of every distribution made to him or her on or after his or her annuity starting date. An individual may exclude that portion attributable to his or her investment in the contract, as made on an after-tax basis.[89] In many instances in the employee annuity context, the employee will not have made any contributions on an after-tax basis.

An individual may not exclude from gross income more than the total amount of his or her after-tax employee contributions.[90] This situation could occur if the employee lives longer than the anticipated life expectancy on which the annuity payments were based. If the individual receiving the annuity dies after the annuity starting date, but before recovering the total amount of his or her after tax contributions, the unrecovered amount of those contributions may be:

- deducted on the annuitant's last income tax return; or
- deducted by the persons entitled to certain payments in the year in which they are received.[91]

c. Lump-Sum Distributions

The accumulated qualified plan balance may be paid in a lump-sum amount as of the client's retirement. The amount received will be included in gross income, subject to an offset for tax basis. For tax years beginning before 2000, certain taxpayers could elect to determine the tax on a lump sum distribution by reference to a five-year averaging mechanism, but that opportunity for income averaging was eliminated.[92]

d. Rollovers of Plan Distribution Amounts

Distributions of all or a portion of an employee's account under a qualified plan may be rolled over, tax-free, by the employee (or the surviving spouse of the employee) by causing that distribution to be transferred into an IRA or other eligible retirement plan.[93] A rollover of a partial distribution is not permitted if the distribution is one of a series of substantially equal payments that are required to be made.[94] In addition, hardship distributions are not eligible rollover distributions.[95]

4. Gift Tax Treatment at Retirement

A spouse may be entitled to plan benefits attributable to the work efforts of the other employee spouse. Before the death of the plan participant, the spouse can waive any survivor benefits or the rights to such benefits.[96] This waiver by the spouse is not treated as a transfer of property by gift for gift tax purposes from the nonemployee spouse to the employee spouse.[97]

5. Distributions After Death

a. Estate Tax Inclusion

Retirement benefits to be received by a survivor or estate after the death of the primary qualified plan beneficiary are fully includible in the gross estate of the deceased employee.[98] This is required whether the payments are periodic or lump sum.[99] For decedents dying before 1997, an additional 15% estate tax was imposed on "excess retirement accumulations," but this penalty provision was eliminated.[100]

b. Income Tax Considerations

The recipient of qualified plan benefits as a successor beneficiary to an employee participant must include the distributed amount in gross income (except to the extent of any allocable after-tax contributions).[101] These benefits would constitute IRD and, therefore, no income tax-basis step-up occurs as of the time of death.[102] Consequently, the successor recipient of these benefits would not have a fair market value basis established at death as an offset in determining the amount of gross income when these distributions are received. A deduction may be available for the estate tax allocable to this gross income. No estate tax will be incurred if this qualified plan amount is distributable to the surviving spouse (and is eligible for the marital deduction) and, therefore, this deduction provision would not be relevant.[103]

c. Community Property Considerations

A community property interest held by a nonparticipant spouse in the other spouse/employee's retirement account will be includible in the nonparticipant spouse's estate for estate tax purposes.[104] If this interest is transferred to the surviving spouse, it would ordinarily be eligible for the marital deduction.[105] Previously, controversy existed concerning whether: (1) the Employee Retirement Income Security Act of 1974 (ERISA)[106] or (2) state property law would determine the extent to which the nonparticipant spouse had an interest at death in the employee's account under a qualified retirement plan.[107] This could be a problem where the deceased nonemployee spouse transfers his or her interest (if any) under the plan to other beneficiaries (e.g., his or her children from a prior marriage) at the time of death. The Supreme Court resolved this issue as to ERISA plans by holding that state law community property rights in benefits provided under an ERISA plan are preempted by ERISA.[108] According to the Court's decision, a nonparticipant spouse does not have (by reason of community property rules) any property rights in the benefits available under an ERISA plan to the surviving employee spouse.

The qualified terminable interest property (QTIP) marital deduction is available for a nonparticipant spouse's interest in an annuity where he or she predeceases the participant spouse.[109] Thus, the nonparticipant spouse's interest in an annuity arising under state community property laws that passes to the surviving participant spouse may qualify as QTIP under §2056(b)(7).[110]

6. Estate Planning Considerations Summarized

a. Lump-Sum Distribution Election

Should the retiring employee elect to receive a lump sum distribution during life or should periodic payments be elected?[111] Relevant factors for making this determination include (1) the federal income tax impact, (2) investment considerations, and (3) whether the employee will consume the distributed amounts during his or her lifetime so that the value represented by that distribution (and any associated investment income) will not be subsequently includible in his or her gross estate for federal estate tax purposes.[112] If the distribution is delayed (except to the extent required to be made), the continued deferral will enable investment proceeds to be accumulated, including on the funds eventually to be used for income tax payments.

If the distribution is to be made pursuant to the satisfaction of a pecuniary bequest (whether into a credit shelter trust, marital deduction trust, or otherwise) the recipient will immediately recognize all the IRD associated with this transfer. In contrast, a specific bequest of that property interest will avoid this current income recognition, and the transfer of this property in kind, for example, under a fractional share bequest, will also postpone this IRD recognition until actual receipt of the periodic distributions.

b. Determining the Beneficiary at Death

(1) Decedent's Spouse

The decedent's spouse could be the beneficiary of the decedent's employee benefits. The surviving spouse could receive the proceeds in a lump sum.[113] Alternatively, the surviving spouse could make a special rollover of these funds into another qualifying plan.[114] The full amount of the employee benefit would be includible in the decedent employee's gross estate for federal estate tax purposes but would not be subject to tax if transferred to the surviving spouse and, therefore, protected by the unlimited estate tax marital deduction.

Disadvantages to this form of designation are that the funds received are exposed to the surviving spouse's creditors and, further, may be dissipated by the spouse as a result of improper management during his or her survival period. Upon the surviving spouse's death, these benefits would be included in the surviving spouse's gross estate, unless consumed during the spouse's lifetime. Since the distribution will be IRD when received by the surviving spouse, the surviving spouse will be required to pay income tax on that amount (at ordinary income tax rates), which will reduce the spouse's gross estate upon his or her subsequent death.

Rather than taking the proceeds outright in a lump sum, the transfer for the benefit of the spouse may be in an optional form qualifying for the unlimited marital deduction. This might include the acquisition of a single life annuity, with no refund feature, for the life of the surviving spouse. The distribution might be made into a testamentary marital deduction trust. Alternatively, the proceeds might be retained within the plan subject to disposition provisions that enable qualification for the marital deduction.[115]

(2) Credit Shelter Trust

The beneficiary of the qualified plan benefits may be the credit shelter or bypass trust, as established under the employee-decedent's will, assuming an appropriate waiver of the property rights by the surviving spouse to these benefits. The objective would be to deposit these payments into this type of trust for which the assets will subsequently not be includible in the gross estate of the surviving spouse (i.e., the exemption equivalent). No estate tax liability with respect to these benefits would be incurred upon the death of either spouse. In addition, this trust could offer professional management, a better potential for capital appreciation, limited generation-skipping possibilities, and protection of the assets for the children in the event of the remarriage of the surviving spouse.[116]

Because the distribution will constitute IRD, the distribution of these funds to the credit shelter trust will dilute the value of the exemption equivalent amount in this trust. For example, if the trust (or income beneficiary) were in a 39.6% income tax bracket[117] and the estate tax exemption equivalent were $2,045,800,[118] the exemption equivalent amount would be reduced by approximately $810,000, that is, the applicable federal income tax at the highest marginal rate on $2,045,800 of plan benefits. The amount remaining in the credit shelter trust after this income tax liability would total only $1,235,800.[119]

(3) Other Possible Beneficiaries

Individuals other than the surviving spouse may be beneficiaries of employee benefit plan distributions, assuming, if applicable, the necessary acquiescence of the surviving spouse. A lump sum distribution[120] may be an attractive option where the beneficiary of an employee benefit plan is other than the surviving spouse. That amount would be subject to inclusion in the recipient's gross income as IRD.

Alternatively, the qualified plan benefits distribution could be directly to a qualified charity. This would enable the avoidance of estate tax on the distributed amount, since an estate tax charitable deduction would be available for the amount to charity. Further, the payment to the charity of this IRD would not be diluted by federal income tax (on the IRD component) because of the charity's income tax-exempt position. The charitable recipients of this distribution could include a private charitable foundation established by the donor. For these reasons, charitable transfers funded with qualified retirement plan benefits are often very tax-effective arrangements for shifting no- or low-basis ordinary income assets since no dilution for tax liabilities occurs.

C. Self-Employed Individual

Representing an estate planning client who is self-employed, including a partner in a partnership, may present certain unique estate planning alternatives needing careful consideration when those individuals have accrued deferred compensation benefits. Most self-employed individuals are permitted to adopt qualified plans similar to those adopted by corporate employers for their employees. These self-employed individuals may organize their business activities in corporate form, including through the use of an S corporation, which permits income tax conduit treatment.[121] These individuals may also find other types of entities, such as partnerships, limited liability companies (LLCs) taxed as partnerships, or single-member LLCs disregarded for tax purposes, suitable for organizing their business activities, especially after the implementation of the check-the-box rules for determining entity classification for federal tax purposes.[122]

Certain employee benefit arrangements are available to employees when using the corporate form that are not available to self-employed individuals or partners. These include:

- group term life insurance up to $50,000 without the inclusion of the premium payments in the gross income of the employee[123];
- adoption of a sick pay plan[124];
- the possible tax sheltering of profits at a lower corporate tax rate level[125]; and
- the furnishing to the employee of meals and lodging for the convenience of the employer corporation without requiring the inclusion of the value of these items in the gross income of the employee.[126]

Particularly when several of these benefits are combined, the availability of these benefits when using the corporate form over an extended period can substantially enhance capital formation by the individual self-employed client. The use of the corporate form can facilitate additional intangible benefits, such as the transferability of the ownership interest and limited liability. The risk of malpractice liability is normally excepted from limitations in the statutes permitting professional practitioners to operate in incorporated form.[127] The two levels of corporate and shareholder taxation can be avoided if the S corporation tax option election is available and made.[128]

Acknowledging the availability of the corporate format for professionals and other self-employed individuals, the IRS has periodically questioned in individual situations (1) whether the professional corporation is actually functioning as a corporation or (2) whether the individual has merely assigned income to the corporation.[129] Accordingly, careful attention must be maintained to assure that the corporation is managed as a separate entity, including the continued observance of proper corporate form and the treatment of the corporation as an independent legal organization. Additionally, a tax-avoidance rule may be applicable where the personal service corporation is disregarded if availed of primarily to evade or avoid tax.[130]

D. Individual Retirement Account

1. Available Income Tax Deduction

With the enactment of qualified plans for self-employed persons, beneficiaries of qualified corporate plans and self-employed individuals were both able to take advantage of income tax incentives for retirement savings. Those individuals who were neither self-employed nor covered by a corporate qualified plan were unable, however, to take advantage of such incentives. Their retirement savings, if any, remained fully subject to tax and could only be accumulated on an after-tax basis. ERISA[131] enacted §408, which enabled employees who were not participants in qualified plans or governmental plans to deduct amounts contributed to a personal retirement account.[132]

The annual deduction limit for IRA contributions is the lesser of 100% of compensation or $5,000.[133] Since 2009, the $5,000 cap has been adjusted annually for inflation in $500 increments.[134] The 2015 (and 2016) limit is $5,500.[135] A higher limit (called a "catch-up contribution") applies to an individual who is at least 50 years old at the end of the tax year.[136]

Subject to a phase-out rule, an IRA deduction is not allowed when either the individual or his or her spouse is an active participant in a qualified retirement plan. The annual maximum dollar limit on the IRA deduction is phased out when either the taxpayer or the spouse is a participant in an employer plan and adjusted gross income exceeds a specified amount.[137] To the extent that the taxpayer is allowed a deduction that is less than the maximum allowed by §219(b), he or she can contribute the remaining portion without an income tax deduction (i.e., into a nondeductible traditional IRA or, in some cases, a Roth IRA). If the nondeductible contribution is to a traditional IRA, the contributed amount will earn income tax-free while in the account and the nondeductible contribution will be tax-free when subsequently distributed.[138] If the nondeductible contribution is to a Roth IRA, the earnings on the account (along with the after-tax investment) are generally tax-free when subsequently distributed.[139]

2. Treatment of Distributions from Traditional IRAs

The income and gain on amounts held under a traditional IRA (i.e., not a Roth IRA) are not included in gross income until distributed.[140] Except in the case of certain correcting distributions and nondeductible contributions, all traditional IRA distributions are includible in gross income. Distributions made before age 59 1/2 (other than those attributable to disability or death) are subject to an additional 10% income tax.[141] If an individual borrows from a traditional IRA or uses amounts in a traditional IRA as security for a loan, the transaction is treated as a distribution of the entire IRA amount and the usual tax rules for distributions apply.[142]

Distributions from a traditional IRA must commence no later than the taxable year in which the individual attains age 70 1/2 and special rules require distributions to be made within a prescribed time after the individual's death. In general, after death the entire amount must be distributed (1) no later than the "required beginning date," or (2) beginning no later than the "required beginning date" over the life of the IRA owner or of the owner and a designated beneficiary (or over the life expectancy of such individual).[143] The "required beginning date" is April 1 of the calendar year following the calendar year in which the owner attains age 70 1/2.[144]

Effective for taxable years beginning after 2005 and before 2015, §408(d)(8)[145] provided an exclusion from gross income for otherwise taxable IRA distributions from a traditional or a Roth IRA if the distributions are qualified charitable distributions.[146] The exclusion could not exceed $100,000 per taxpayer per taxable year. Distributions were eligible for the exclusion only if made on or after the date the IRA owner attained age 70 1/2.[147] Distributions excluded from gross income under §408(d)(8) were not taken into account in determining the §170 charitable income tax deduction.[148]

3. Estate Tax Treatment

IRA account accumulations are includible in the account owner's gross estate for estate tax purposes.[149] For some individuals, these proceeds could be significant amounts. These total proceeds might include: (1) amounts rolled over from qualified plans;

(2) amounts contributed during the period when no income or other qualified plan participation limitations for eligibility were imposed; and (3) amounts contributed to nondeductible IRAs.[150]

4. IRA Rollover Opportunities

Amounts previously held under a qualified retirement plan or an IRA may be rolled over to another IRA or other eligible retirement plan.[151] Consequently, a beneficiary of a qualified corporate plan may avoid the tax imposed on lump sum distributions by transferring the amount of any such distribution to an IRA. A rollover can also occur for the benefit of a spouse.

A tax-free rollover to an IRA is permitted for a total distribution and for certain partial distributions from a qualified plan.[152] The partial distribution, to be eligible for rollover treatment, must not be a distribution that is (1) one of a series of substantially equal periodic payments made for the life of the employee or the joint lives of the employee and the employee's designated beneficiary or (2) for a period of 10 years or more.[153] Tax-free rollover treatment is denied for hardship distributions made from a qualified plan after December 31, 2001.[154]

All IRA rollover account balances will be includible in the owner's gross estate for federal estate tax purposes.[155] If transferred to a surviving spouse, the unlimited marital deduction will be available, however, if the terminable interest rules are satisfied.[156]

5. Simplified Employee Pension

To provide employers with a simpler, although less flexible, alternative to the tax-qualified retirement plan, an increased deduction is available for contributions to an employee's individual retirement plan sponsored by his or her employer.[157] This alternative, a "simplified employee pension" (SEP) plan, involves the use of an IRA or individual retirement annuity. The maximum amount that can be contributed to an employee's IRA or individual retirement annuity under a SEP plan without the employee incurring current federal income tax is 25% of the employee's compensation or, if less, $40,000, as adjusted for inflation.[158] An employer that makes contributions to the SEP plans of its employees is essentially treated as if it were making contributions to a retirement plan subject to §404. Employee contributions can also be placed into a SEP plan.[159]

E. Business-Originated Life Insurance

1. Group Term Life Insurance

a. Benefits of Employee Insurance

The estate planner's client may receive life insurance benefits provided from an employment relationship. Usually, such insurance is either in the form of group term life insurance or "split-dollar" insurance.[160]

Many employers provide group term life insurance benefits to their employees. Providing this coverage is partially motivated by the favorable federal income tax treatment available to the employee.[161] An employer can provide insurance coverage under a group term life insurance policy to each employee to the extent of $50,000 of face value without the employee being required to include the value of that life insurance coverage in gross income.[162] Notwithstanding this exclusion from the employee's gross income, the employer can deduct the entire cost of this insurance as an ordinary and necessary business expense.[163]

b. Assignments of Group Term Insurance

The employee will have "incidents of ownership" in his or her interest under the group term policy and, therefore, the proceeds from this insurance coverage when received after death will be includible in the employee's gross estate for federal estate tax purposes.[164] These incidents of ownership might arise, for example, because the employee has the right to designate the beneficiary of the proceeds under this life insurance coverage.

To avoid estate tax inclusion, an employee might seek to assign all the incidents of ownership to another person or to an irrevocable trust. Controversy existed for a considerable period concerning whether group term insurance benefits could be effectively assigned to avoid federal estate tax, but this issue has been satisfactorily resolved in most situations.[165] The issues in this area are best presented by the examples posed in Rev. Rul. 69-54. In Situation 1, the insured employee made an irrevocable inter vivos assignment of his rights under a group term life policy. The employee had no right under either the master group policy or state law to convert the policy into individual insurance upon termination of his employment. Most state insurance laws require, however, that a conversion privilege must be included in group life contracts. The master policy provided that each employee's coverage ended upon termination of his employment. The IRS first ruled that the proceeds of a policy transferred under these circumstances were includible in the employee's gross estate since the employee's power to terminate his employment (and, thereby, cancel his insurance coverage) constituted a retained "incident of ownership." Rev. Rul. 69-54 noted that the assignee of the policy was powerless to prevent a termination of the employee's employment and the consequent loss of the assignee's interest under the policy. Modifying its position in Rev. Rul. 72-307, the IRS subsequently indicated, however, that the power to cancel rights under a group term life insurance policy solely by terminating employment is not an "incident of ownership." Rather, such a power was characterized as "a collateral consequence of the power that every employee has to terminate his employment."[166]

In Situation 2 of Rev. Rul. 69-54, the insured employee made an irrevocable assignment of the group term policy, but retained the conversion privilege required by state law. This privilege enabled the employee to convert the group coverage to an individual policy upon the occurrence of certain specified events. The master group policy provided that coverage under the group policy ceased on termination of employment. Both the master group plan and state law permitted assignment of group insurance, including the conversion privilege. The IRS concluded that the retained conversion privilege was an "incident of ownership," causing the proceeds to be includible in the employee's gross estate. The IRS also indicated that, if the master policy or state law prohibited an assignment of the conversion privilege, the insurance would be includible in the gross estate notwithstanding any attempted assignment. The IRS thereafter modified its position on this question, ruling that a conversion privilege exercisable only in the event of the termination of employment is not an incident of ownership.[167]

In Situation 3 of Rev. Rul. 69-54, the employee had made an irrevocable assignment of all rights under the group policy (including the conversion privilege). Both the master group policy and state law permitted the employee to assign all his incidents of ownership in the policy (including the conversion privilege). The master policy provided that an employee's group coverage ceased upon his termination of employment. The IRS ruled that the group insurance proceeds were not includible in the decedent's gross estate. The employee could not by his own action defeat the assignee's rights and had retained no "incidents of ownership." Even if the insured employee terminated his employment under these facts, the assignee could then exercise the conversion privilege to obtain an individual policy on the insured's life.

For estate tax planning purposes, the objective is to avoid the retention of any incidents of ownership concerning the individual coverage rights under a group term policy. Although most of the state law and federal estate tax law impediments to accomplishing this planning have been eliminated, this enumeration of the prior problem areas indicates that many mechanical hazards in this context must be carefully avoided.

Even though the employee's policy coverage has been transferred irrevocably by the insured employee, that coverage will continue to be provided when the insured employee's employment continues. If the coverage on the employee's life is greater than $50,000, the value of the excess coverage will constitute gross income to the employee (since not excluded from gross income under §79) on an annual basis. This amount will be gross income to the employee even though all the insurance benefits are to be paid at death for the benefit of the donee of the policy death benefits.[168]

c. Gift Tax Considerations

A transfer of an interest in a group term policy can be accomplished at minimal gift tax cost. Because a term policy has no cash or loan value, the value of a gift of group term insurance coverage benefits usually will not be significant.[169] After the employee irrevocably transfers his or her group term insurance coverage to another person or entity, the employee will be deemed to have also made an indirect gift to the donee of the policy interest each time the employer pays a renewal premium on that insurance coverage.[170] If the assignment of the interest in the policy is outright to an individual, payments of the subsequent premiums by the employer should qualify for the annual donee gift tax exclusion as to the employee/transferor.[171]

Where the interest under the insurance policy is assigned to an irrevocable trust, with the trust instrument specifying that the proceeds (when subsequently received) are to be invested and the net return paid to the donee-beneficiary during his or her lifetime, the transfer and the subsequent premium payments may represent gifts of future interests and no annual donee exclusion would be allowable.[172] If the trust is structured, however, so as to give the beneficiary a present interest in the form of a withdrawal power,[173] any transfer to the trust would appear to qualify for the annual donee exclusion for gift tax purposes. Where the trust corpus consists of group term insurance coverage, the demand right in the beneficiary seems illusory, however, because the insurance has no cash value and the premiums do not pass through the trust (but, rather, are paid by the employer directly to the insurance carrier). Nevertheless, the IRS has periodically issued favorable rulings with regard to the availability of the annual donee exclusion in this situation.

The requirement that the beneficiary of a demand trust have actual knowledge or notice of additions to the trust creates problems for all life insurance trusts and particularly for trusts holding group term life insurance rights. Notification of each addition to the trust is difficult in the case of employer-paid group term insurance since neither the insured nor the trustee is likely to know precisely when and how the premiums are paid by the employer. The trustee can often determine, however, the approximate times the premium payments are to be made and inform the beneficiary in writing in a single annual notice concerning the withdrawal right.

Where the trust is to be funded with an employee's group term insurance benefits and multiple beneficiaries hold a power of withdrawal from the trust, an issue can arise as to whether joint action would be required to exercise the withdrawal power and, if so, whether that action may jeopardize the availability of the annual donee exclusion.[174] This may necessitate a specific designation of a separate share for each beneficiary under this trust with a separate withdrawal power for each share.

d. Estate Tax Considerations

The objective for an employee in assigning away all of his incidents of ownership under a group term life insurance policy is to eliminate the policy proceeds from inclusion in the insured employee's gross estate.[175] The estate tax savings objective is defeated if the insured-transferor dies within three years of the transfer of the policy since, under §2035(a), the date of death value of the transferred property will be included in the transferor's gross estate.[176] An important planning issue in the §2035(a) context concerns whether the group term insurance policy is treated as a one-year contract that the employer repurchases and the employee transfers each year[177] or whether the coverage is of a continuing nature, automatically renewable each year, so that a new transfer (for §2035 purposes) does not occur each year.

Where the group term policy is renewable automatically upon the payment of the premium without further evidence of insurability, the rights and obligations of the parties continue from the policy's inception. The renewal does not create new rights or constitute a new purchase of insurance. Consequently, payment of the renewal premium is not a new "transfer" of an interest in the policy for §2035 purposes. Therefore, a renewable group term policy is not included in the decedent's gross estate under §2035 where the decedent transferred the interest under this policy more than three years before death, even though the decedent is considered to have continued to pay the premiums until death.[178]

A change in the employer's master insurance plan carrier may enable an IRS challenge that a new assignment of the employee's coverage necessitated by a change in insurance carriers starts another three-year period for §2035 purposes. Where the new assignment is necessitated by a change in the employer's master insurance plan carrier and the new policy is "identical in all relevant respects" to the previous arrangement, the value of the proceeds is not included, however, in the gross estate of the decedent under §2035. This assumes that at least three years have passed since the original assignment of the employee's insurance coverage rights.[179] Whenever an assignment of a group term policy is made, that assignment should be accompanied by an anticipatory assignment by the employee of all future insurance benefits provided by the employer. If a policy assignment has been made without an anticipatory assignment of future coverage and benefits, the employee should make an anticipatory assignment of all future benefits under the new policy promptly following any change of insurance carriers, so as to commence a new three-year period for §2035 purposes.

Another concern is whether an increase in the amount of face value insurance coverage under the same policy within the three-year period prior to death is a separate transfer of the increased coverage amount. The amount of coverage under many group insurance plans is linked to the specific level of compensation. In some compensation contexts, increases in coverage within the three-year period can be significant. The answer to any attempt to make such an increase a "transfer" for §2035 purposes is that the increased coverage is only an integral part of the original bundle of rights that was initially assigned. The initial transfer documents should be sufficiently inclusive to encompass all future increases in coverage under the terms of the plan as well as the amount of coverage at the time of the assignment.

The following matters should be specifically considered by an employee in assigning group term life insurance coverage:

- Both the insurance policy and local law must permit an absolute assignment of all incidents of ownership and both the statutory rules and the policy procedures should be carefully followed to assure the effective transfer of all policy rights.[180]
- The insured must make an absolute and irrevocable assignment of all rights under the policy, including any incidents of ownership enumerated in the policy[181] and any "nonpolicy" incidents.[182]
- The assignment of incidents of ownership should occur more than three years before death and should include an anticipatory assignment of all replacement coverage and any increases in coverage under the same or a different master policy.
- Steps must be taken to ensure that the policy does not return to the insured by the terms of the will of the donee or by intestate succession if the donee of the policy benefits dies first. Caution is also required if the policy may return to the insured in a capacity as (1) the executor of the estate of the donee or (2) the trustee of a trust created by the donee.

- The planner should consider how the policy proceeds can be made available to meet the liquidity needs of the insured's estate after the insured's death without having those proceeds included in the estate. This suggests the possible use of an irrevocable trust created by the insured to which these policy rights might be transferred.[183]

e. Retired Employees Coverage

An employer may provide group term insurance coverage to its retired employees, including through a pre-funding mechanism. A retired lives reserve (RLR) is a fund utilized by an employer as a method of prefunding the cost of continuing group term life insurance for retired employees or, at least, a select group of retired employees.[184] Accordingly, the RLR arrangement provides a mechanism through which the employer can allocate the cost of post-retirement insurance over the working lifetimes (or some segment thereof) of those employees. The most common method of funding such an arrangement is through a life insurance coverage reserve fund.

The continuation of insurance benefits on the life of an employee who has attained normal retirement age and whose employment has terminated does not result in gross income to the employee.[185] If, however, money or other property, including paid-up life insurance, is transferred or made available to the employee, that employee realizes gross income. In this and related contexts, RLR arrangements periodically have been subject to challenge by the IRS.[186]

2. Split-Dollar Insurance

a. Split-Dollar Concept

Split-dollar life insurance is an arrangement between two parties (usually an employer and employee)[187] to share the cost of life insurance premiums and to divide the proceeds between the employer and the employee's beneficiary.[188] Split-dollar insurance is not a special type of policy. Rather, split-dollar insurance, which generally involves permanent, cash-value life insurance, is simply an ownership and premium payment arrangement for a particular policy.[189]

The fundamental plan is that the employer pays that part of the annual premium cost equal to the current year's increase in cash surrender value of the policy, while the employee pays the balance (if any) of that premium cost.[190] Through this arrangement, the insured is enabled to acquire substantial life insurance not otherwise affordable by him or her. At death, the employer receives back its cost (its premium payments, usually the cash surrender value)[191] and a beneficiary designated by the employee receives the balance of the insurance proceeds.

b. Income Taxation

For income tax purposes, the employee must include in gross income the value of the economic benefit of the life insurance coverage accruing to him or her that exceeds the employee's insurance purchase cost.[192] Two different approaches to determining the compensation amount have been implemented under regulations,[193] that is, a compensation arrangement approach and a split-dollar loan approach.

Under the first approach, identified as the "economic benefit" arrangement, the owner of the split-dollar life insurance contract (e.g., the employer) is treated as providing economic benefits to the nonowner of the contract and those economic benefits must be accounted for by both the owner and the non-owner.[194] The tax consequences of the provision of economic benefits will depend on the relationship between the owner and the nonowner. The provision of the benefit may constitute a payment of compensation, a dividend distribution, a capital contribution, a gift, or a transfer having a different tax character. In a split-dollar life insurance arrangement in which an employer provides an employee with economic benefits, the employee would take into account those economic benefits by reporting them as compensation.[195] The employer reports the economic benefits on the appropriate employment tax and information returns. A transfer of the life insurance contract to the employee is taxed under §83.

Alternatively, under the second approach, the split-dollar life insurance arrangement may be a split-dollar loan.[196] Under this arrangement, the owner and the non-owner are treated as borrower or lender if: (1) the payment is made directly or indirectly by the non-owner to the owner; (2) the payment is a loan under general tax principles; and (3) the repayment is to be made from, or is secured by, either the policy's death benefit proceeds or its cash surrender value, or both.[197] Thus, if the employee is formally designated as the "owner" of the life insurance contract under a split-dollar arrangement, the premiums paid by the employer are treated as a series of loans by the employer to the employee if a reasonable person would expect the employee to repay the employer. If the employee is not obligated to repay the premiums paid by the employer, then such amounts are treated as compensation income to the employee at the time the premiums are paid by the employer. Except for specified arrangements, the loan regime applies to any split-dollar loan. This regime generally governs the taxation of collateral assignment arrangements.

Since to the employee the insurance cost will be a personal expense, no deduction of his or her premium payments is available.[198] Further, the employer will not be entitled to a business expense deduction for any portion of its premium payments since the employer is a beneficiary of the policy.[199]

When, after the death of the employee, the estate of the employee or his or her designated beneficiary receives the employee's portion of the split-dollar insurance proceeds, those proceeds will not be includible in the recipient's gross income for income tax purposes.[200] The receipt by the employer of its portion of the proceeds will constitute a recovery of its §1012 cost basis and, therefore, be without federal income tax effect. If the employer owns the policy this will be a recovery of the employer's tax basis in the policy. If the employee owns the policy, and is treated as borrowing funds from the employer, the employer will receive back its investment/tax basis in the promissory note.

c. Estate Tax Planning

The split-dollar proceeds will be includible in the employee's gross estate if payable to his or her estate.[201] The proceeds received by the employee's designated beneficiaries will be includible in the employee's gross estate for federal estate tax purposes if the employee at the time of his or her death had "incidents of ownership" in the policy.[202] Various techniques have evolved for removing the proceeds from the employee's gross estate for federal estate tax purposes.[203]

The employee can remove the risk portion of the insurance from his or her estate by making an irrevocable assignment of his or her rights under both the insurance policy and the accompanying split-dollar agreement.[204] An assignment by the employee is subject, however, to the usual rules with regard to assignment of life insurance policies, including §2035.[205] Alternatively, the prospective donee may enter into a split-dollar plan with the employer.[206] Whatever technique is used, the employer will want to be assured that it will be paid the cash surrender value when the employee dies.

Special planning problems arise in removing the proceeds of a split-dollar policy from the estate of an employee who is the controlling shareholder of the employer-corporation that is providing the funds equivalent to the annual increase in the cash surrender value. If the employee has majority voting control of a corporation, the incidents of ownership in the policy held by the corporation may flow through to the controlling shareholder.[207] The IRS originally took the position that, if the rights of a corporation in the policy were sufficiently limited to those of a secured creditor, no incident of ownership would be attributed to the controlling shareholder. This position was modified by the IRS to the extent that the right of a corporation to borrow against a portion of a policy is an incident of ownership attributable to the shareholder. This results in inclusion in the shareholder's estate of the entire proceeds of the policy that are not payable to the corporation.[208]

d. Gift Tax Planning

That value of the insurance protection annually provided by the employer that is included in the employee's gross income is a gift for gift tax purposes.[209] The employee's annual premium payment (if any) is also deemed to be a gift to the policy assignee.[210] If an irrevocable life insurance trust is the owner of the life insurance contract underlying the split-dollar life insurance arrangement and a reasonable person would expect that the donor, or the donor's estate, will recover an amount equal to the donor's premium payments, those premium payments are treated as loans made by the donor to the trust.[211] Payment of a premium by the donor is treated as a split-dollar loan to the trust in the amount of the premium payment. If the loan is repayable upon the death of the donor, the term of the loan is the donor's life expectancy.

If the donor is treated as the owner of the life insurance contract underlying the split-dollar life insurance arrangement, different rules apply.[212] Under these circumstances, the donor is treated as making a gift to the trust.[213] The value of the gift is the value of the economic benefits provided to the trust, less the amount of any premium paid by the trustee.[214]

The special gift tax valuation rules of Chapter 14 should not usually apply to split-dollar purchases of life insurance. Although the rules apply to joint purchases of property by family members,[215] no attribution applies in such cases to family members through controlled corporations or partnerships. Consequently, if a corporation controlled by one family member purchases split-dollar insurance with another family member employed by the corporation, Chapter 14 should not apply.

Notes

1. See, generally, Streng & Davis, *Retirement Planning: Tax and Financial Strategies* (2015).
2. See the discussion concerning community property in Chapter 9, B.
3. *See, e.g., Kennedy, Executrix, v. Plan Admin. for DuPont Sav. & Inv. Plan,* 555 U.S. 285 (2009). The plan benefits were paid to an ex-wife (even though she had waived benefits under the plan) because the decedent had not changed the beneficiary designation identifying her as the beneficiary of his benefits under this plan. Similarly, *see Egelhoff v. Egelhoff,* 532 U.S. 141 (2000). These questions are resolved under ERISA rules, as this federal law preempts state law (at least with respect to qualified plans). These federal rules do not apply to IRAs. Further, under federal common law the real intended beneficiary may be able to obtain the paid benefits from the named beneficiary. *See Kensinger v. URL Pharma, Inc.,* 674 F.3d 131 (3rd Cir. 2012). In some situations where ambiguity exists the plan administrator may interplead the benefits, necessitating a proceeding to determine the successor owner to these benefits. *See IBEW Pacific Coast Pension Fund v. Lee,* 52 EBC 2378 (6th Cir. 2012) (unpub. opin.).
4. See 358 T.M., *Cash or Deferred Arrangements* (Bloomberg BNA); 385 T.M., *Deferred Compensation Arrangements* (Bloomberg BNA).
5. 1960-1 C.B. 174.
6. For further limitations in this context, see §409A, as enacted by the American Jobs Creation Act of 2004 (AJCA), Pub. L. No. 108-357, §885(a), generally effective for amounts deferred after 2004. The IRS has issued an explanation of §409A in IRS Notice 2005-1, 2005-2 I.R.B. 274. This Notice indicates that, although §409A makes a number of fundamental changes, it does not alter or affect the application of any other provision of the Code or common law tax doctrine. Accordingly, deferred compensation not required to be included in income under §409A may nevertheless be required to be included in income under §451, the constructive receipt doctrine, the cash equivalency doctrine, §83, the economic benefit doctrine, the assignment of income doctrine, or any other applicable provision of the Code or common law tax doctrine. Q&A 4 in this Notice states:

   > A plan provides for the deferral of compensation only if, under the terms of the plan and the relevant facts and circumstances, the service provider has a legally binding right during a taxable year to compensation that has not been actually or constructively received and included in gross income, and that, pursuant to the terms of the plan, is payable to (or on behalf of) the service provider in a later year. A service provider does not have a legally binding right to compensation if that compensation may be unilaterally reduced or eliminated by the service recipient or other person after the services creating the right to the compensation have been performed. However, if the facts and circumstances indicate that the discretion to reduce or eliminate the compensation is available or exercisable only upon a condition that is unlikely to occur, or the discretion to reduce or eliminate the

compensation is unlikely to be exercised, a service provider will be considered to have a legally binding right to the compensation.

7. Sometimes an assertion is made by the IRS that tax deferral cannot occur after the services have been rendered but before an actual or constructive receipt of the compensation payment. *But see Oates v. Commissioner*, 18 T.C. 570 (1952), *aff'd*, 207 F.2d 711 (7th Cir. 1953), *acq.*, 1960-1 C.B. 5.
8. Rev. Rul. 60-31 (first example).
9. *Id.* (second example).
10. Other examples in Rev. Rul. 60-31 address certain of these issues. The fifth example in the ruling was modified in Rev. Rul. 70-435, 1970-2 C.B. 100. *See also* Rev. Proc. 71-19, 1971-1 C.B. 698 (listing conditions under which IRS will issue advance rulings concerning application of doctrine of constructive receipt to unfunded deferred compensation arrangements). Rev. Proc. 2015-3, 2015-1 I.R.B. 129, §3.01(60), indicates that no ruling will be issued as to the income tax consequences of a nonqualified unfunded deferred compensation arrangement with respect to a controlling shareholder eligible to participate in such an arrangement. Further, Rev. Proc. 92-65, 1992-2 C.B. 428, indicates that the IRS will not issue a favorable ruling on an unfunded deferred compensation contract unless the contract provides that the employee is a general, unsecured creditor and that the employee's rights to payments may not in any manner be anticipated, alienated, sold, transferred, assigned, pledged, encumbered, attached, or garnished by creditors of the employee or of the employee's beneficiary (e.g., a surviving spouse). *See also* Rev. Proc. 2015-3, §3.01(61).
11. PLR 200419006, for example, provides an extensive description of a plan enabling employee income deferral and extensively discusses Rev. Proc. 92-65. In PLR 200419006, an employer corporation established a plan to provide supplemental, nonqualified deferred compensation benefits to certain key employees. Under the plan, participants could elect to defer any portion of the salary, bonus, overtime pay, and commissions they earned during the plan year, which was the calendar year. To effect a deferral, participants had to submit an election form to the plan's administrator prior to the beginning of the plan year. Employees who became eligible to participate in the plan during the plan year could elect to participate and effect a deferral by submitting an election form to the plan's administrator within 30 days of becoming eligible to participate in the plan. Elections to defer amounts under the plan had to specify: (1) the amount that was to be deferred; (2) whether benefit payments were to commence on the plan's retirement date or on a fixed payment date; and (3) the manner in which benefits were to be paid. Elections under the plan were irrevocable, both as to the amount deferred and as to the time and manner of payment.
12. Presumably, the cash dividend and interest income will also have been reinvested as part of this phantom account for the executive. Of course, the employer may not actually acquire these shares, but an appropriate basket of listed shares could merely be used as the measuring vehicle to determine the eventual accrued and distributable amount.
13. This arrangement is so identified because it was first publicly used to secure benefits for a rabbi. PLR 8113107. *See* Rev. Proc. 92-64, 1992-2 C.B. 422 (model trust provisions for rabbi trusts so as to create safe harbor and to expedite advance ruling process). Notice 2000-56, 2000-2 I.R.B. 393, approves a modification to Rev. Proc. 92-46's model language and "provides guidance on which entity is treated as the grantor and owner of a grantor trust when a parent corporation contributes its stock to a rabbi trust for the benefit of the employees of a subsidiary." The model language was modified to provide

that parent corporation stock (or other assets) contributed by a parent corporation to a rabbi trust for the benefit of employees or service providers of a subsidiary is subject to the claims of the creditors of both the parent corporation and the subsidiary, and the remaining parent stock (or other assets) contributed by the parent corporation reverts to the parent corporation upon termination of the trust. *See* Rev. Proc. 2015-3, 2015-1 I.R.B. 129, §4.01(30) (ruling will ordinarily not be issued concerning tax consequences of nonqualified deferred compensation arrangement using grantor trust where trust fails to meet requirements of Rev. Proc. 92-64).

14. *See Bank of America, N.A. v. Moglia,* 330 F.3d 942 (7th Cir. 2003) (describing rabbi trust mechanism in creditors' rights dispute context).
15. For an extensive discussion in this context, see H.R. Conf. Rep. No. 108-755, at 706-724 (2004) (concerning enactment of §409A).
16. A secular trust is generally structured as a separate entity for tax purposes, and earnings are includible in the income of the trust.
17. *See* §83(a), §402(b)(1). In some cases, under the terms of the nonqualified deferred compensation arrangement, the employer pays the taxes attributable to the deferred compensation by grossing up the employees' current compensation by a corresponding amount.
18. See, however, the potential limitations in this context, as applicable under §409A, as enacted in the AJCA, Pub. L. No. 108-357.
19. Note that the legislative history for the enactment of §409A in the AJCA, Pub. L. No. 108-357, specifies that a transfer of property in connection with the performance of services (under §83) also occurs with respect to compensation deferred under a nonqualified deferred compensation plan if the plan provides that upon a change in the employer's financial health, assets will be restricted to the payment of nonqualified deferred compensation. An amount is treated as restricted even if the assets are available to satisfy the claims of general creditors. The transfer of property occurs as of the earlier of when the assets are so restricted or when the plan provides that assets will be restricted. See H.R. Conf. Rep. No. 108-755, at 706-724 (2004).
20. Under §2033 or §2039.
21. *See* Reg. §20.2039-1(b)(2) *Ex. (6)*; Rev. Rul. 76-304, 1976-2 C.B. 269. In Rev. Rul. 76-304, in consideration of performance of services, a corporation agreed to pay an employee a stated yearly salary and also agreed to pay a death benefit of a stated amount to the employee's designated beneficiary if the employee was employed by the corporation at the date of death. The decedent could change the beneficiary during the course of employment. The IRS ruled that the death benefit was includible in employee's gross estate under §2038(a)(1) since, at the date of death, the decedent possessed the power to alter the designated beneficiary of the death benefit.
22. *See Schelberg v. Commissioner,* 612 F.2d 25 (2d Cir. 1979) (declining to link several plans for purposes of requiring inclusion of survivor's benefits in decedent employee's gross estate). *Cf. Estate of Bahen v. United States,* 305 F.2d 827 (Ct. Cl. 1962) (gross estate inclusion resulted under §2039 because of coordination of several employee plans).
23. *See Estate of DiMarco v. Commissioner,* 87 T.C. 653 (1986), *acq. in result,* 1990-2 C.B. 1 (no gift transfer of survivor's income benefit occurs when that benefit was provided by publicly held corporation). *Cf. Estate of Levin v. Commissioner,* 90 T.C. 723 (1988) (benefit was provided by closely held corporation). In Rev. Rul. 92-68, 1992-2 C.B. 257, the IRS agreed with the result in the *DiMarco* decision that no transfer occurred for gift tax purposes at the time of death, revoking Rev. Rul. 81-31, 1981-1 C.B. 475, to the contrary.

24. IRD is subjected to gross income inclusion under §691 and as defined in the §691 regulations. See the discussion of IRD in Chapter 4, B.4.
25. §691(c). If deferred compensation is part of a marital deduction transfer, the deduction in respect of a decedent (under §691(c)) will not be relevant, since no federal estate tax will have been paid with respect to this item.
26. This could include deflection to children, assuming inapplicability of the "Kiddie Tax" rules which require certain unearned income of certain children under the age of 24 to be taxed at the marginal income tax rate of the child's parent. See §1(g). The Tax Increase Prevention and Reconciliation Act of 2005 (2005 TIPRA), Pub. L. No. 109-222, §510(a) and §510(d), increased the §1(g)(2)(A) age limit from 14 to 18, effective for taxable years beginning after 2005. Under §1(g)(2)(C), as added by 2005 TIPRA, Pub. L. No. 109-222, §510(c), the Kiddie Tax does not apply if the child files a joint return for the taxable year. The Small Business and Work Opportunity Tax Act of 2007, Pub. L. No. 110-28, §8241(a), and §8241(c), effective for taxable years beginning after May 25, 2007, amended §1(g)(2)(A) to expand the §1(g) tax to include certain children under the age of 24. For a complete discussion of the §1(g) tax, see 846 T.M., *Gifts to Minors* (Bloomberg BNA).
27. *Lucas v. Earl,* 281 U.S. 111 (1930). Often such rights are nonassignable during life.
28. Note, also, the possible limitation of deferral opportunities because of the provisions of §409A, as enacted in AJCA, Pub. L. No. 108-357.
29. See, generally, 381 T.M., *Statutory Stock Options* (Bloomberg BNA); 383 T.M., *Non-statutory Stock Options* (Bloomberg BNA); 384 T.M., *Restricted Property—Section 83* (Bloomberg BNA).
30. The tax treatment of stock options has been changed periodically in federal tax legislation: the Revenue Act of 1950, Pub. L. No. 81-814 (making provisions for "restricted stock options"); the Revenue Act of 1964, Pub. L. No. 88-272 (providing for "qualified stock options"); the Tax Reform Act of 1976 (1976 TRA), Pub. L. No. 94-455 (providing for repeal of qualified stock option treatment); and the Economic Recovery Tax Act of 1981 Pub. L. No. 97-34 (providing tax benefits for "incentive stock options").
31. §422.
32. §83; Reg. §1.83-7, §1.422-1, §1.422-2 (as added by T.D. 9144, 69 Fed. Reg. 46,401 [Aug. 3, 2004]).
33. The AJCA, Pub. L. No. 108-357, §251, added provisions in §421(b), §3121(a)(22), and §3306(b)(19), which provide specific exclusions from FICA and FUTA wages and income tax withholding for remuneration on account of the transfer of stock pursuant to the exercise of an ISO or under an employee stock purchase plan, or any disposition of such stock, effective for stock acquired pursuant to options exercised after October 22, 2004. Thus, FICA and FUTA taxes do not apply upon the exercise of a statutory stock option (i.e., an ISO described in §422(b)). The AJCA, Pub. L. No. 108-357, §251, also added §209(a)(19) to the Social Security Act providing that such remuneration is not taken into account for purposes of determining Social Security benefits. These changes are consistent with the earlier position of the IRS in Notice 2002-47, 2002-28 I.R.B. 97. *See also* Announcement 2005-55, 2005-55 I.R.B. 317.
34. *See Commissioner v. LoBue,* 351 U.S. 243 (1956). See also Notice 2004-28, 2004-16 I.R.B. 783 (identifying generally income tax treatment of options and noting that IRS is aware that certain promoters are advising taxpayers to take highly questionable and, in most cases, meritless, positions [described in this Notice] on current and amended

returns regarding income or alternative minimum tax due upon exercise of nonstatutory or statutory stock options).

35. Note that in Rev. Rul. 2004-37, 2004-1 C.B. 583, the IRS ruled that, when an employer and employee reduce the stated principal amount of a recourse note issued by an employee to the employer to acquire employer stock, the employee recognizes compensation income equal to the amount of the reduction.
36. See 381 T.M., *Statutory Stock Options* (Bloomberg BNA). In determining alternative minimum taxable income, §421 (specifying no income recognition upon transfer of stock acquired by exercise of ISO) does not apply, therefore requiring inclusion of this income in the alternative minimum tax base. §56(b)(3).
37. §421(a)(1).
38. §421(a)(2). These rules are similar to the tax treatment previously applied to restricted and qualified stock options. This treatment denying the compensation deduction to the employer mandates an analysis of whether the grant of an NSO might produce better overall after income tax effects when considering the tax situations of both the employer (a deduction against corporate income) and the employee (ordinary income treatment).
39. §422(a)(1). In addition, at all times from the grant of the option until three months before exercise, the individual must be an employee of the corporation, as specified by §422(a)(2) (subject to an extension to one year of the three-month period upon disability pursuant to §422(c)(6)).
40. §421(b). Where the amount realized on a premature disposition is less than the value at exercise, the amount includible in gross income and deductible by the employer will not exceed the excess, if any, of the amount realized on such sale over the adjusted basis. §422(c)(2). If capital gains and ordinary income are subject to tax at approximately the same rate, the employer may encourage a disqualifying disposition, so that the employer can obtain the deduction without significant additional income tax cost being incurred by the employee.
41. §422(c)(4)(A). See PLR 9736040.
42. These rules are also explained in the preamble to revised §421 and §422 regulations as published in T.D. 9144, 69 Fed. Reg. 46,401 (Aug. 3, 2004).
43. §422(b)(1). *See* PLR 9531031 (concerning specifying number of shares).
44. See *Moore v. Commissioner*, T.C. Memo 2007-123, where stock options were not ISOs because the options were not issued pursuant to a specific plan and the employer's shareholders had not approved the plan.
45. §422(b)(2).
46. §422(b)(3).
47. §422(b)(4). The fair market value of an ISO at the time the option is granted is to be determined without regard to any restriction except a restriction that by its terms will never lapse. §422(c)(7).
48. §422(c)(1).
49. §422(b)(5).
50. §422(b)(6).
51. §422(c)(5).
52. §422(d)(1).
53. §422(d)(2).
54. §422(b)(5).
55. §422(a)(1).

56. The unexercised option will be included in the gross estate of the decedent. Its value will be equal to the benefit of the bargain (i.e., the excess of the fair market value of the stock on the valuation date over the option price.)
57. See §421(c)(1)(A). This special rule will not affect the applicability of §1222 (relating to differentiating between short-term or long-term capital gain or loss). *See* Reg. §1.421-2(c)(1). For example, assume X's estate receives an ISO held by X at death. The executor exercises such option on June 1 and on June 30 disposes of the stock acquired under the option. Any gain or loss would be short-term (since held for a period shorter than the one-year long-term capital gains holding period). This could cause a material income tax difference when a substantial differential exists between long- and short-term capital gain tax rates.
58. §421(c)(1)(A).
59. See 383 T.M., *Nonstatutory Stock Options* (Bloomberg BNA); 808 T.M., *Estate Planning for the Corporate Executive* (Bloomberg BNA).
60. The rules of §83 are inapplicable to options without a readily ascertainable value. §83(e)(3). An NSO must have a "readily ascertainable" fair market value before its receipt (i.e., its grant) is taxable under §83. The tax status of such options is determined under the rules set forth in *Commissioner v. LoBue,* 351 U.S. 243 (1956). Few employee stock options are likely to be subject to §83 since most involve unlisted companies or, in the case of listed companies, may have a longer duration than traded options, cannot be freely transferred, and cover stock subject to restrictions on sale.
61. Reg. §1.83-7(a). In Notice 2004-28, 2004-16 I.R.B. 783, the IRS warned taxpayers against making frivolous claims on tax returns for avoiding income tax due upon the exercise of stock options. The IRS advised that NSOs rarely are subject to tax on the date of grant and taxation at grant typically occurs only if an option is actively traded on an established securities market on that date or, if not so traded, it has a readily ascertainable fair market value. The IRS added that a nonpublicly traded NSO is considered to have a readily ascertainable fair market value on the grant date only if, on that date, it satisfies four conditions: (1) the option is transferable; (2) the option is exercisable immediately in full by the optionee; (3) the option or the property subject to the option is not subject to any restriction or condition that has a significant effect upon the fair market value of the option; and (4) the fair market value of the option privilege is readily ascertainable.
62. §83.
63. §83(b).
64. Rev. Rul. 98-21, 1998-1 I.R.B. 975. Rev. Proc. 98-34, 1998-1 I.R.B. 983, describes how an unexercised compensatory stock option is valued for gift or estate tax purposes. The option pricing model provided takes into account factors similar to those established by the Financial Accounting Standards Board in Accounting for Stock-Based Compensation, Statement of Financial Accounting Standards No. 123 (1995) (FAS 123). The methodology in Rev. Proc. 98-34 applies only to the valuation of a nonpublicly traded stock option for stock that, on the valuation date, is publicly traded on an established securities market.
65. See §691(a). Under §691(c), however, a deduction in respect of a decedent may be available for the estate tax attributable to that IRD item.
66. Rev. Rul. 80-300, 1980-2 C.B. 165; Rev. Rul. 82-121, 1982-1 C.B. 79. If the employee elects to receive the appreciation in the form of employer stock, the stock received is taxable to the employee under §83(a) to the extent of the difference between its fair market value and the amount the employee paid for the stock. See also §409A, as enacted in AJCA, Pub. L. No. 108-357. The IRS has issued an explanation of §409A in Notice

2005-1, 2005-1 C.B. 274. This Notice indicates that §409A is applicable to SARs, although the Notice does identify various potential exceptions to that treatment. This Notice indicates that the Treasury Department and the IRS are concerned that a general exception for SARs may be exploited as a method to avoid application of §409A, particularly in regard to valuation of the underlying stock where the value is not established by and in an established securities market. The Notice states:

> In many respects, stock appreciation rights are similar to other forms of nonqualified deferred compensation, particularly where the recipient of a stock appreciation right may receive cash. In such cases, the taxation of stock appreciation rights generally is governed by §451 and the constructive receipt doctrine. See Rev. Rul. 80-300, 1982-2 C.B. 165.

Notice 2005-1, 2005-2 I.R.B. 274, was obsoleted in part by final regulations issued under §409A. See T.D. 9321, 72 Fed. Reg. 19,234 (Apr. 17, 2007) (effective for taxable years beginning on or after January 1, 2008). The final regulations reaffirm that stock appreciation rights (SARs) are treated similarly to stock options, and generally nondiscounted stock appreciation rights issued on service recipient stock that do not include any additional deferral feature are excluded from §409A. *Id. See* Reg. §1.409A-1(b)(5). For a complete discussion of deferred compensation, see 385 T.M., *Deferred Compensation Arrangements* (Bloomberg BNA).

67. An employer may claim a deduction for current compensation only after an amount of compensation has been "paid or accrued" within the meaning of §162(a)(1). Under §404(a)(5), the employer's deduction for a cash exercise of SARs arises when the cash is includible in the employee's income. If an employee exercises SARs for employer stock, because the taxation of the stock to the employee is governed by §83(a), the employer's deduction for the transfer of that stock is governed by §83(h).
68. Such plan will be "qualified" by satisfying the requirements specified in §401(a).
69. §401(a), §501(a).
70. *See* §401(k).
71. §402(e)(3).
72. The plan may be in the form of a salary reduction agreement. Section 401(k)(2) and §402(e)(3) make no reference to salary reduction plans (other than as to §403(b) plans in §402(e)(3)). Reg. §1.401(k)-1(a)(3) states that the plan may be in the form of a salary reduction agreement. Under such an agreement, an employee can elect to relinquish a portion of his or her current compensation and to have that amount contributed to a plan for his or her benefit. The employee receives less current cash and pays lower current income taxes. A salary reduction plan allows the employee to save for retirement with pre-tax dollars and to benefit from tax-free accumulation of income in the plan. Such a plan is similar in overall purpose to an individual retirement account (IRA) but may offer greater advantages. For a full discussion of §401(k) plans, see 358 T.M., *Cash or Deferred Arrangements* (Bloomberg BNA). Section 408, §219, and §401(k), as amended, inter alia, by the Small Business Job Protection Act of 1996 (SBJPA), Pub. L. No. 104-188, §1421, §1422, create a simplified retirement plan for small businesses known as a savings incentive match plan for employees (SIMPLE plan). A SIMPLE plan can be either an IRA for each employee or part of a qualified cash or deferred arrangement (§401(k) plan). The provisions relating to SIMPLE plans are effective for years beginning after December 31, 1996. In addition, §408(k)(6), as amended by SBJBA, Pub. L. No. 104-188, §1421(c), repealed salary reduction simplified employee pensions (SARSEPs).

73. *See* §401(a)(11), as enacted in the Retirement Equity Act of 1984 (1984 REA), Pub. L. No. 98-397. For further details, see 370 T.M., *Qualified Plans—Taxation of Distributions* (Bloomberg BNA).
74. See §401(a)(11)(B)(i), §401(a)(11)(B)(ii). These standards are specified in §412.
75. If no spouse survives or if the surviving spouse consents (in the manner prescribed in §417(a)(2)(A)), the payment may be made in full to a designated beneficiary other than the spouse.
76. §401(a)(11)(B)(iii).
77. *See* §401(a)(11)(B), §417(b).
78. Section 401(a)(11)(D) specifies a special rule where the participant and spouse are married less than one year and §417(d)(1) further specifies that the plan will not be treated as failing merely because the plan provides that a qualified joint and survivor annuity will not be provided unless the participant and spouse had been married throughout the one-year period ending on the earlier of: (1) the participant's annuity starting date or (2) the date of the participant's death.
79. §401(a)(11)(B)(iii)(I), §417(a)(1)(A), §417(a)(2). Generally effective for plan years beginning after 2007 (with special rules for collectively bargained plans), §417(a)(1)(A), §417(g), as added by the Pension Protection Act of 2006, Pub. L. No. 109-280, §1004(a), §1004(c), revises the minimum survivor annuity requirements to require that, at the election of the participant, benefits will be paid in the form of a "qualified optional survivor annuity" (QOSA), which is an annuity for the life of the participant with a survivor annuity for the life of the spouse equal to the applicable percentage of the amount of the annuity that is: (1) payable during the joint lives of the participant and the spouse; and (2) the actuarial equivalent of a single annuity for the life of the participant. If the survivor annuity provided by the plan's "qualified joint and survivor annuity" (QJSA) is less than 75% of the annuity payable during the joint lives of the participant and spouse, the applicable percentage is 75%. If the survivor annuity provided by the plan's QJSA is greater than or equal to 75% of the annuity payable during the joint lives of the participant and spouse, the applicable percentage is 50%. Thus, for example, if the survivor annuity provided by the QJSA under the plan is 50%, the survivor annuity provided under the QOSA must be 75%. For more information on the Pension Protection Act of 2006 amendments, see 814 T.M., *Estate and Gift Tax Issues for Employee Benefit Plans* (Bloomberg BNA).
80. §401(a)(9)(B)(i). For a general discussion of the required distribution rules for qualified plans, see 814 T.M., *Estate and Gift Tax Issues for Employee Benefit Plans* (Bloomberg BNA).
81. Reg. §1.401(a)(9)-5, §1.401(a)(9)-5(a)(1), §1.401(a)(9)-5(c)(2).
82. Reg. §1.401(a)(9)-8, A-11. Distribution from the estate must then satisfy the five year distribution rule.
83. §401(a)(9)(B)(ii).
84. §401(a)(9)(B)(iii).
85. §401(a)(9)(B)(iv). If a surviving spouse dies before distributions to that spouse commence, the distribution rules apply as if the surviving spouse were the participant. *Id.*
86. §72(t)(1), §72(t)(2)(A)(i). Certain exceptions to this penalty treatment apply, for example, (1) when the distribution is made to a beneficiary after the death or disability of the employee; (2) if the payment is part of a scheduled series of "substantially equal periodic payments" in the form of an annuity payable over the life of the participant (or several

participants); (3) the payment is made after separation from service after the employee has reached age 55; and (4) when the distributions are used to pay medical bills that are sufficiently large to be deductible under §213. §72(t)(2). For more information on these and other exceptions, see 814 T.M., *Estate and Gift Tax Issues for Employee Benefit Plans* (Bloomberg BNA).

87. §72(m)(5).
88. §72(b)(1), §72(d).
89. §72(d). Under a simplified method for taxing annuity payments, the portion of each annuity payment that represents a return of basis equals the employee's total basis as of the annuity starting date, divided by the number of anticipated payments under the table in §72(d)(1)(B) (see Chapter 9, D.2). Before its repeal by the Tax Reform Act of 1986 (1986 TRA), Pub. L. No. 99-514, former §72(d) contained a "three-year rule" allowing an individual to exclude from income the full amount of each distribution made after the annuity starting date until he or she recovered his or her total employee contributions to the plan, provided his or her "investment in the contract" was small enough to enable him or her to recover his or her entire investment within three years of the date that the distributions commenced. Subsequently, the Technical and Miscellaneous Revenue Act of 1988, Pub. L. No. 100-647, §1011A, revised §72(d). This section was further amended by the SBJPA, Pub. L. No. 104-188, §1403, effective with respect to annuity starting dates beginning 90 days after August 20, 1996, to provide that basis recovery on payments from qualified plans generally is determined under the method noted above for one annuitant. In the Taxpayer Relief Act of 1997 (1997 Act), Pub. L. No. 105-34, §1075(a), §72(d)(1)(A)(iv) was added to provide the table referenced above where the anticipated payments are to be made for more than one life.
90. §72(b)(2).
91. §72(b)(3), (4).
92. Former §402(d)(1), before its amendment by the SBJPA, Pub. L. No. 104-188, §1401. In repealing five-year averaging, the SBJPA also repealed the separate tax paid on a lump sum distribution and the deduction from gross income for taxpayers who elected to pay the separate tax on a lump sum distribution. Generally, only taxpayers over 59 1/2 could elect five-year averaging and then only once "with respect to any employee." Former §402(d)(4)(B). High wage earners often were not able to benefit from the five-year averaging because of the limited income tax brackets. The 1986 TRA, Pub. L. No. 99-514, which enacted the five-year averaging rules, repealed the prior 10-year forward averaging computation, effective for tax years beginning after 1986 (subject to a transitional rule in §1122(h) of the 1986 TRA permitting a plan participant who had attained age 50 before 1986 to elect 10-year averaging treatment under pre-1987 rates). Under the 10-year averaging rules, a participant receiving a lump sum distribution could elect: (1) to compute his or her tax on the distribution using a 10-year averaging computation, and (2) to treat the pre-1974 portion of the distribution as capital gains, subject to a maximum 20% tax.
93. §402(c)(1). Section 402(c)(8)(B) defines eligible retirement plans. Special rules apply if any portion of the distribution consists of the employee's after-tax (nondeductible) contributions to the qualified plan. *See* §402(c)(2). The rollover transfer into the eligible retirement plan must be made within 60 days of receipt but is ordinarily made directly from the qualified plan to the eligible retirement plan to avoid withholding tax at the source of the qualified plan trust distribution. The participant, but not the participant's spouse (while the participant lives) after a gift of those proceeds to the spouse, can make

a tax-free rollover from a qualified plan. *See Rodoni v. Commissioner,* 105 T.C. 29 (1995) (to constitute tax-free rollover to IRA, rollover must be to IRA established for benefit of employee who received lump sum distribution). A surviving spouse can elect rollover treatment, however, if not acquiring the proceeds from a third party.

94. §402(c)(4)(A).
95. §402(c)(4)(C), as amended by the Economic Growth and Tax Relief Reconciliation Act of 2001 (EGTRRA), Pub. L. No. 107-16, §636(b), effective for distributions made after December 31, 2001. Pursuant to the Pension Protection Act of 2006, Pub. L. No. 109-280, §811, the EGTRRA sunset (Pub. L. No. 107-16, §901) does not apply to the amendments made by EGTRRA, Pub. L. No. 107-16, §601-§666. For distributions after December 31, 1998 and before January 1, 2002, §402(c)(4)(C) provided that hardship distributions from a §401(k) plan could not be rolled over. Before the IRS Restructuring and Reform Act of 1998, Pub. L. No. 105-206, §6005(c)(2), added §402(c)(4)(C), effective for distributions after December 31, 1998, hardship distributions were generally eligible rollover distributions.
96. *See* §401(a)(11)(B)(iii)(I), §417(a)(2).
97. §2503(f). Even if so treated, a marital deduction would ordinarily be available. *See* §2523(f)(6). Further, this waiver does not constitute an assignment of income by the spouse in favor of the employee. §401(a)(13).
98. Section 2039 provides for inclusion in the gross estate of the value of annuity and similar benefits transferred to a survivor. Before the 1976 TRA, Pub. L. No. 94-455, former §2039(c) provided for the exclusion from the gross estate of an annuity (or other payment) received by a beneficiary other than the executor to the extent the payments were attributable to employer contributions to a qualified plan. In the 1976 TRA, this estate tax exclusion was eliminated for amounts payable in a single lump sum under a retirement plan. The exclusion was retained, however, for periodic payments. Under the Revenue Act of 1978, Pub. L. No. 95-600, the exclusion was made available for lump sum payments if the recipient elected not to take the 10-year averaging for income tax purposes formerly available and to take the taxable portion of the distribution into income as ordinary income. Under the Tax Equity and Fiscal Responsibility Act of 1982 (TEFRA), Pub. L. No. 97-248, the estate tax excludible amount was limited to $100,000. The Deficit Reduction Act of 1984 (DEFRA), Pub. L. No. 98-369, eliminated this $100,000 gross estate exclusion. Note, however, that this limitation is not applicable to the estate of a decedent who was a participant in a plan, who was in pay status on December 31, 1984, and irrevocably elected the form of benefit before July 18, 1984. *See* DEFRA, Pub. L. No. 98-369, §525(a). This could include proceeds from a rollover IRA where the election for the form of benefit was made before July 18, 1984. *See* Rev. Rul. 92-22, 1992-1 C.B. 313.
99. *Cf.* Rev. Rul. 76-380, 1976-2 C.B. 270, *obsoleted by*, Rev. Rul. 88-85, 1988-2 C.B. 333.
100. See former §4980A(d), before its repeal by the 1997 Act, Pub. L. No. 105-34, §1073. Similarly, if inter vivos annual distributions to a qualified plan participant were in excess of a specified amount, those excess distributions were subject to a 15% excise tax under former §4980A(a). This tax was also repealed, effective for excess distributions received after December 31, 1996.
101. Although §402(a) controls the timing for inclusion in gross income of qualified plan benefits, these benefits are, except as specifically provided in §402, taxable under §72 (relating to annuities). *See also* §61(a). A previously available $5,000 lump sum payment death benefit exclusion was repealed in 1996. *See* former §101(b)(1), §101(b)(2).

The $5,000 exclusion for employer-provided death benefits was repealed effective with respect to decedents dying after August 20, 1996. SBJPA, Pub. L. No. 104-188, §1402, (repealing former §101(b)).

102. See the discussion of IRD in Chapter 4, B.4.
103. *See* §691(c) (providing for deductions in respect of a decedent).
104. §2033. Prior to the 1986 TRA, Pub. L. No. 99-514, former §2039(c) provided that no portion of the employer's contributions would be includible in the gross estate of the employee's spouse if the spouse predeceased the employee and the couple had resided in a community property jurisdiction. Similarly, former §2517(c) provided that the value of the nonemployee's interest payable to other beneficiaries upon the employee's death was excluded from the taxable gifts of the surviving spouse to the extent the value arose solely by reason of the spouse's interest in the community income of the employee. No exclusion was available, however, for a property interest to the extent that it was attributable to the nondeductible contributions of the employee spouse. Former §2517(b). These provisions were repealed by the 1986 TRA, Pub. L. No. 99-514, §1852(e).
105. *See* TAM 8943006 (value of decedent's community property interest in her spouse's qualified pension plan account is includible in her gross estate under §2039(a) and qualifies for marital deduction under §2056(b)(7)(C)). The executor is treated as having made the QTIP election.
106. Pub. L. No. 93-406.
107. *See Allard v. Frech,* 754 S.W.2d 111 (Tex. 1988), *cert. denied,* 488 U.S. 1006 (1989) (under Texas law, nonparticipant spouse could transfer to other than surviving spouse her community property interest in surviving participant spouse's qualified plan account). *Cf. Ablamis v. Roper*, 937 F.2d 1450 (9th Cir. 1991) (California community property rules were superseded by federal law rules incorporated into ERISA, as amended by 1984 REA, Pub. L. No. 98-397; consequently, deceased spouse could not transfer her purported community property interest in surviving employee spouse's pension benefits).
108. *Boggs v. Boggs,* 520 U.S. 833 (1997), *rev'g* 82 F.3d 90 (5th Cir. 1996). The Fifth Circuit had rejected the Ninth Circuit's *Ablamis* analysis by holding that ERISA did not preempt Louisiana community property law and, thereby, a community property interest could be created in ERISA-qualified retirement benefit plans.
109. The 1997 Act, Pub. L. No. 105-34, §1311, clarified this marital deduction treatment of qualified plans for spouses who live in community property states, effective for estates of decedents dying after August 5, 1997. §2056(b)(7)(C).
110. The Conference Report for the 1997 Act stated that this provision was not intended to modify the result of the Supreme Court's decision in *Boggs.* H.R. Rep. No. 105-220, at 717–718 (1997).
111. This assumes the necessary spousal consent has been obtained, as required under the 1984 REA, Pub. L. No. 98-397. *See* §417(a)(2). For a note about the repeal of forward averaging for lump-sum distributions from qualified plans, see Chapter 11, B.3.c.
112. *See* 814 T.M., *Estate and Gift Tax Issues for Employee Benefit Plans* (Bloomberg BNA).
113. See Chapter 11, B.3.c., for a note about the repeal of forward averaging for lump sum distributions.
114. §402(c)(9).
115. *See* Rev. Rul. 2006-26, 2006-22 I.R.B. 939, identifying the circumstances under which delayed distributions from a qualified retirement plan into a QTIP trust do not preclude marital deduction eligibility.

116. If community property is involved, §2036 will result in the inclusion of the spouse's interest in this property in the spouse's gross estate upon death. The §2036 problem is avoided by a splitting of benefits between the surviving spouse and the trust.
117. The 39.6% rate is the highest individual income tax rate applicable in taxable years beginning after 2012. *See* §1(i), as amended by the American Taxpayer Relief Act of 2012 (ATRA), Pub. L. No. 112-240, §101(b). Prior to 2013, the maximum §1(i) income tax rate was 35%. See EGTRRA, Pub. L. No. 107-16, §101(a), amended by JGTRRA, Pub. L. No. 108-27, §104, and extended by the Tax Relief, Unemployment Insurance Reauthorization, and Job Creation Act of 2010 (2010 TRA), Pub. L. No. 111-312, §101(a), from December 31, 2010 to December 31, 2012.
118. As noted in Chapter 4, A.4.d., the amount exempted for estate tax purposes by the §2010(c) unified credit may vary depending on the year of the decedent's death. See Chapter 4, A.1., for a discussion of the changes made to §2010(c) by the 2010 TRA, Pub. L. No. 111-312, §301-§304, and ATRA, Pub. L. No. 112-240, §101(a).
119. *See* Rev. Rul. 83-121, 1983-2 C.B. 74 (special income tax treatment of lump-sum distributions to trust).
120. See Chapter 11, B.3.c., for a note about the repeal of the prior forward income averaging for lump sum distributions.
121. With an S corporation form, self-employed individuals may be able to reduce compensation payments, relying on dividend distributions, with the result that the employment taxes (particularly Social Security and the Medicare tax costs) are reduced.
122. See, generally, Staff of J. Comm. on Tax'n, 114th Cong., Choice of Business Entity: Present Law and Data Relating to C Corporations, Partnerships, and S Corporations (JCX-71-15) (Apr. 2015), available at www.jct.gov. Before the adoption of the check-the-box rules (found at Reg. §301.7701-1 through §301.7701-4, §301.7701-6, T.D. 8697, 61 Fed. Reg. 66,584 [Dec. 18, 1996], and generally effective as of January 1, 1997), an unincorporated business entity could be taxed as a partnership only if it lacked at least two of the following four characteristics of a corporation: (1) limited liability; (2) continuity of life; (3) free transferability of interests; and (4) centralization of management. The check-the-box rules make it far less difficult for owners to structure an unincorporated business entity that will satisfy both tax and nontax (i.e., limitation of liability) goals.
123. §79. Note that §79(d) provides nondiscrimination requirements with respect to making such insurance coverage available to employees. Notwithstanding this limited gross income exclusion these premiums will be deductible by the employer.
124. §105. Note that §105(g) specifies that a self-employed individual is not considered an employee for this purpose.
125. This assumes that, under §11(b), the applicable corporate tax rate is 15%, the rate available on the first $50,000 of taxable corporate income. Note, however, that §11(b)(2) provides that a 35% tax rate, rather than the lower graduated corporate tax rates, applies to certain personal service corporations. This situation can also exist where the highest marginal income tax rate for individuals (e.g., 39.6%) might be higher than the highest marginal income tax rate for a corporation (e.g., 35%).
126. §119. The cost for these meals would be deductible to the employer corporation pursuant to §162.
127. Under the check-the-box entity characterization regulations, noncorporate entities, such as LLCs, can have such "corporate" characteristics as free transferability and limited liability without the potential loss of partnership tax classification, to the extent these characteristics are available to the entity under the state governing statutes.

128. Depending on the shareholder ownership distribution, the profits could also be distributed as dividends, rather than as compensation, thereby avoiding the 2.9% Medicare tax that applies to compensation income without a dollar limitation. *See* §3101(b), §3111(b). The benefit of this approach is even greater for remuneration received and taxable years beginning after December 31, 2012, when changes introduced by the Patient Protection and Affordable Care Act, Pub. L. No. 111-148, §9015(a), §9015(b)(1), and §10906, and the Health Care and Education Reconciliation Act of 2010, Pub. L. No. 111-152, §1402(b), raised the Medicare tax on wages and self-employment income in excess of $200,000 ($250,000 for a joint return) by 0.9%, unindexed.
129. *See, e.g., Keller v. Commissioner*, 77 T.C. 1014 (1981); *Achiro v. Commissioner*, 77 T.C. 881 (1981); *Foglesong v. Commissioner*, 77 T.C. 1102 (1981). The *Keller* decision was effectively rejected by Congress when it enacted §269A.
130. Section 269A(a) specifies that if (1) substantially all of the services of a personal service corporation are performed for one other entity and (2) the principal purpose for forming, or availing of, such personal service corporation is the avoidance or evasion of federal income tax by reducing the income of, or securing the benefit of any expense, deduction, credit, exclusion, or other allowance for, any employee-owner that would not otherwise be available, the IRS may allocate all income, deductions, credits, exclusions, and other allowances between such personal service corporation and its employee-owners if such allocation is necessary to prevent avoidance or evasion of federal income tax or clearly to reflect the income of the personal service corporation or any of its employee-owners.
131. Pub. L. No. 93-406.
132. *See, generally*, §408, §219. Under §408, §219, and §401(k), as amended by the SBJPA, Pub. L. No. 104-188, §1421, §1422, a simplified retirement plan for small businesses, known as a SIMPLE plan, can be adopted by employers who employed no more than 100 employees with at least $5,000 in compensation for the preceding year and who do not maintain another employer-sponsored retirement plan. §408(p)(2). A SIMPLE plan can be either in the form of an IRA or as part of a qualified cash or deferred arrangement (§401(k) plan). §408(p)(1), §401(k)(11). The provisions relating to SIMPLE plans are effective for years beginning after December 31, 1996. For a full discussion of this legislative change and IRAs, see 367 T.M., *IRAs* (Bloomberg BNA), and 368 T.M., *SEPs and SIMPLEs* (Bloomberg BNA).
133. §219(a), §219(b)(1), §219(b)(5)(A).
134. §219(b)(5)(C), as redesignated by the Tax Increase Prevention Act of 2014, Pub. L. No. 113-295, Div. A, §221(a)(38)(C).
135. *See* Notice 2014-70, 2014-48 I.R.B. 905; IRS News Release IR-2015-118 (Oct. 21, 2015).
136. See §219(b)(5)(B), which increases the allowable deduction by $1,000 for qualifying individuals.
137. See §219(g)(1), §219(g)(2), §219(g)(3)(B), §219(g)(7)(a). The thresholds at which the phase-outs begin are adjusted annually for inflation. §219(g)(8). For 2015, the thresholds are: (1) $98,000 for joint filers and qualifying widow(er)s who are active participants; (2) $61,000 for all other taxpayers (except married taxpayers filing separately) who are active participants; and (3) $183,000 for a nonactive participant taxpayer whose spouse is an active participant. *See* Notice 2014-70. For 2016, the threshholds are: (1) $98,000 for joint filers and qualifying widow(er)s who are active participants; (2) $61,000 for all other taxpayers (except married taxpayers filing separately) who are active participants; and (3) $184,000 for a nonactive participant taxpayer whose spouse is an

active participant. *See* IRS News Release IR-2015-118 (Oct. 21, 2015). The threshold for married taxpayers filing separately is zero. §219(g)(3)(B)(iii).

138. §408(o).

139. Roth IRAs are governed by §408A. In general, a contribution to a Roth IRA will be preferable to a nondeductible contribution to a traditional IRA and, in some cases, a contribution to a Roth IRA may be preferable to a deductible contribution to a traditional IRA. Eligibility to contribute to a Roth IRA is subject to special modified adjusted gross income limits. §408A(c)(3). The age limits of §219(d)(1) and the active participation rules under §219(g) do not apply. §408A(c)(2)(A). As noted in Chapter 11, D.2., the §408(d)(8) (as added by the Pension Protection Act of 2006, Pub. L. No. 109-280, §1201(a), §1201(c)(1)) gross income exclusion for certain distributions from IRAs to charity available for taxable years beginning after 2005 and before 2015 applies to Roth IRAs as well as traditional IRAs. *See* §408(d)(8)(F). See 367 T.M., *IRAs* (Bloomberg BNA), for more information on Roth IRAs.

140. As noted in Chapter 11, D.1., the earnings on a Roth IRA generally are not taxed when distributed.

141. §72(q).

142. §408(e)(3).

143. §408(a)(6) (incorporating by reference the §401(a)(9) qualified plan rules for IRA distributions).

144. *See id.*

145. *See* Pension Protection Act of 2006, Pub. L. No. 109-280, §1201(a), §1201(c)(1); §408(d)(8)(F). The §408(d)(8) exclusion does not apply to distributions from employer-sponsored retirement plans, including SIMPLE IRAs and simplified employee pensions. *See* §408(d)(8)(B); Staff of J. Comm. on Tax'n, 109th Cong., Technical Explanation of H.R. 4, the 'Pension Protection Act of 2006,' at 266 (J. Comm. Print 2006).

146. Under §408(d)(8)(B), the IRA trustee must make the distribution from the IRA directly to a §170(b)(1)(A) charitable organization other than a §509(a)(3) supporting organization or a §4966(d)(2) (as added by the Pension Protection Act of 2006, Pub. L. No. 109-280, §1231(a)) donor advised fund. The §408(d)(8) exclusion only applies if a §170 charitable income tax deduction would otherwise have been allowable for the entire distribution (determined without regard to the §170(b) percentage limitations and §408(d)(8)). §408(d)(8)(C).

147. The legislative history indicates that qualified charitable distributions are taken into account for purposes of the minimum distribution rules applicable to traditional IRAs to the same extent the distributions would have been taken into account under such rules had the distributions not been directly distributed under the provision. Staff of J. Comm. on Tax'n, 109th Cong., Technical Explanation of H.R. 4, the 'Pension Protection Act of 2006,' at 266 (J. Comm. Print 2006).

148. §408(d)(8)(E). For more information on §408(d)(8), see 367 T.M., *IRAs* (Bloomberg BNA).

149. Before the 1976 TRA, Pub. L. No. 94-455, the estate tax exclusion under former §2039(c) for qualified plan benefits did not apply to an IRA. Subsequently, under the 1976 TRA, the value of an annuity receivable by a beneficiary under an IRA was excluded from a decedent's gross estate. Former §2039(e). TEFRA, Pub. L. No. 97-248, added former §2039(g), limiting this exclusion to $100,000. This exclusion was further limited when any payment to or for such an account was not allowable as a deduction for income tax

purposes. The estate tax exclusion for the value of an annuity receivable by a beneficiary under an IRA was eliminated by DEFRA, Pub. L. No. 98-369, §525.

150. Note §408(g) indicating that the IRA provision (§408) will be applied without regard to any community property laws. For a transaction in which a wife transmuted her interest in an IRA from community property to the separate property of her husband in return for the transmutation of his community property interest in other assets to her separate property, see PLR 8929046. This exchange transaction did not generate an income tax liability because §1041 is applied to all transfers of property between spouses, irrespective of differing state property laws. The transfers did not require the recognition of gain on the transferred assets but, instead, constituted an exchange of gifts. *See also* PLR 9439020 (effectively ruling that entering into partition agreement would not be taxable distribution).

151. §402(c), §408(d)(3), as amended by EGTRRA, Pub. L. No. 107-16, §641-§643, effective for distributions after December 31, 2000. Pursuant to the Pension Protection Act of 2006, Pub. L. No. 109-280, §811, the EGTRRA sunset (Pub. L. No. 107-16, §901) does not apply to the amendments made by EGTRRA, Pub. L. No. 107-16, §601–§666. Other eligible retirement plans are defined in §402(c)(8)(B). Rollovers from qualified plans are also discussed in Chapter 11, B.3.d. For a discussion of rollovers involving Roth IRAs, see 367 T.M., *IRAs* (Bloomberg BNA). An example of a rollover of a traditional IRA is described in TAM 9010007, where an individual's withdrawal of funds from an IRA for personal use was considered to be a qualifying roll over if redeposited into the same or another qualified IRA within 60 days of the original distribution. *See also Wood v. Commissioner*, 93 T.C. 114 (1989) (taxpayer attempting to roll over lump sum profit sharing distribution into IRA was not bound by brokerage house's failure to transfer cash to IRA within 60-day period required by former §402(a)(5)(C) where taxpayer transferred cash and stock to trustee and directed trustee to place amounts in IRA within required period).

152. §402(c)(1). Note that §3405(c) requires 20% tax withholding at source for an eligible rollover distribution unless the distribution is paid directly to another qualified plan.

153. *See* §402(c)(4)(A).

154. §402(c)(4)(C), as modified by EGTRRA, Pub. L. No. 107-16, §636. Pursuant to the Pension Protection Act of 2006, Pub. L. No. 109-280, §811, the EGTRRA sunset (Pub. L. No. 107-16, §901) does not apply to the amendments made by EGTRRA, Pub. L. No. 107-16, §601–§666.

155. Previously, the former §2039(c) estate tax exclusion (limited to $100,000 under TEFRA, Pub. L. No. 97-248) was available with respect to a rollover IRA contribution of a distribution from another qualified plan, even though no income tax deduction was allowable for the rollover contribution. This exclusion for rollover contributions of distributions from a qualified plan was repealed by DEFRA, Pub. L. No. 98-369, §525.

156. Rev. Rul. 2006-26, 2006-22 I.R.B. 939, *modifying and superseding* Rev. Rul. 2000-2, 2000-3 I.R.B. 305. Rev. Rul. 2006-26 provides guidelines for the funding of a QTIP trust with a decedent's IRA. The IRS requires a separate QTIP election for the trust and the IRA and relies on the spouse's power to compel the trustee of the trust to withdraw from the IRA an amount equal to all the income earned that year on the IRA assets, and then to pay that income to the spouse to meet the spousal income requirement. Among other things, Rev. Rul. 2006-26 added scenarios for QTIP treatment of an IRA or other qualified defined contribution retirement plan designating a QTIP trust as beneficiary

when income is determined under state law provisions defining income as a unitrust amount or allowing the trustee to make allocations between the income and remainder beneficiaries to fulfill the trustee's duty of impartiality. Rev. Rul. 2000-2 had clarified that the IRA distributions may be made under the normal distribution rules, rather than in equal amounts annually over the life of the surviving spouse, as implied by Rev. Rul. 89-89, 1989-2 C.B. 231, which Rev. Rul. 2000-2 obsoleted. Rev. Rul. 89-89 had ruled that an estate could elect QTIP treatment for an IRA if the IRA made annual distributions to a QTIP trust and the income on both the distributed and undistributed portion of the IRA was paid annually to the decedent's spouse for life. *See also* PLR 9544038, PLR 9537005. Note that special rules apply to trusts that are designated as the beneficiary of an IRA. See, generally, T.D. 9102, 69 Fed. Reg. 12 (Jan. 2, 2004) (amending regulations, including marital deduction regulations and Reg. §1.643(b)-1 definition of fiduciary accounting income, to take into account certain developments in state law, effective for taxable years ending after January 2, 2004).

157. *See* §408(j), §408(k), §415(c)(1). Section 408, §219, and §401(k), amended, inter alia, by the SBJPA, Pub. L. No. 104-188, §1421, §1422, created a simplified retirement plan for small businesses known as a SIMPLE plan. A SIMPLE plan can be either an IRA for each employee or part of a qualified cash or deferred arrangement (§401(k) plan). §408(p)(1), §401(k)(11). The provisions relating to SIMPLE plans were effective for years beginning after December 31, 1996.

158. *See* §402(h)(2), §415(c)(1)(A), §415(d). For both 2015 and 2016, the inflation-adjusted amount is $53,000. *See* Notice 2014-70, 2014-48 I.R.B. 905; IRS News Release IR-2015-118 (Oct. 21, 2015). For the amounts for other recent years, see the Worksheets in 371 T.M., *Employee Plans—Deductions, Contributions and Funding* (Bloomberg BNA).

159. The combined contributions of the employer and employee cannot exceed the overall limits discussed above and the employee's contributions cannot exceed the limits applicable to individual contributions to traditional IRAs, including the additional deduction for "catch-up" contributions by individuals over age 50 but subject to the deduction phase-out for active participants in qualified retirement plans. *See* §408(j), §408(k), §219, §415(c).

160. Insurance in the business context may also be acquired by other business owners, or the business itself, to fund obligations under a stock-retirement plan, a cross-purchase plan, or a combination plan, as discussed in Chapter 10, B.3. Further, insurance coverage can be provided under a qualified pension or profit-sharing plan.

161. *See* §79(a). Certain nondiscrimination requirements, as enumerated in §79(d), are applicable to group term policies. Benefits available to "key employees" must be available to all other participants, or the §79(a) gross income exclusion will not be available to the key employees.

162. §79(a). In T.D. 8821, 64 Fed. Reg. 29,788 (June 3, 1999), the IRS finalized regulations (effective July 1, 1999) that revise the uniform premium table used to calculate the cost of employer-provided group term life insurance coverage. Reg. §1.79-3(d)(2), §1.79-3(e). Reg. §1.79-3(d)(2) provides lower rates in the table to be applied for determining the value of the excess coverage. These rates were lowered based on improvements in mortality experience. The uniform premium table reflects a 50/50 blend of the male and female mortality rates. The resulting mortality projections have been adjusted to reflect a 10% load factor.

163. §162(a)(1).

164. *See* §2042(2).

165. The IRS attempted to resolve a major part of this controversy in Rev. Rul. 69-54, 1969-1 C.B. 221, published to clarify Rev. Rul. 68-334, 1968-1 C.B. 403 (which was retracted and superseded). Rev. Rul. 72-307, 1972-1 C.B. 307, subsequently modified Rev. Rul. 69-54. The questions presented concerned whether such an assignment was permitted both under (1) local law and (2) the master insurance policy. The local law problem has been solved in many instances by state legislation permitting transfers by employees of their interests under a group term policy. See 826 T.M., *Life Insurance* (Bloomberg BNA). Additionally, insurance companies often deleted a "no-assignment clause" from the master policy or developed a flexible attitude about waiving such a provision when the employee wanted to assign his or her rights under the policy.
166. *See Landorf v. United States,* 408 F.2d 461 (Ct. Cl. 1969) (rejecting proposition that right to terminate employment is "incident of ownership" in life insurance policy).
167. *See* Rev. Rul. 84-130, 1984-2 C.B. 194, acq'g *in Estate of Smead v. Commissioner,* 78 T.C. 43 (1982). In this instance, the decedent retained the right to convert a noncontributory group term life insurance policy in the event his employment was terminated. The IRS ruled that the power to cancel group policy coverage by termination of employment is an example of a power exercisable only as a result of a potentially costly related action and is, therefore, not an incident of ownership within the meaning of Reg. §20.2042-1(c)(2). The IRS noted that no distinction will be made between conversion rights exercisable upon voluntary termination of employment and any such rights exercisable upon involuntary termination. *See also* AOD 1984-056.
168. *See* Reg. §1.79-3(d).
169. Rev. Rul. 84-147, 1984-2 C.B. 201, indicates that an employee making an irrevocable assignment in trust of all his or her interest under an employer-provided group term life insurance policy can value the gift, for gift tax purposes, based upon Table I under Reg. §1.79-3(d)(2). Alternatively, the employee can value the gift by determining the actual cost of the life insurance coverage purchased by the employer. If the group term insurance plan is discriminatory, or the employee is a key employee, the value of the gift must be determined by reference to the actual cost of the employee's coverage.
170. Rev. Rul. 76-490, 1976-2 C.B. 300.
171. *See* Reg. §25.2503-3(a) (indicating that gift of interest in life insurance policy will not be deemed gift of future interest simply because obligations of insurance company "are to be discharged by payments in the future"). *See also* Reg. §25.2503-3(c) *Ex. (6).*
172. Rev. Rul. 79-47, 1979-1 C.B. 312; Reg. §25.2503-3(c) *Exs. (2), (3).*
173. *See Crummey v. Commissioner,* 397 F.2d 82 (9th Cir. 1968). The demand power is discussed in greater detail in Chapter 6, D.3.g.
174. *Skouras v. Commissioner,* 188 F.2d 831 (2d Cir. 1951).
175. *See, e.g.,* Rev. Rul. 83-148, 1983-2 C.B. 157 (proceeds of partnership group term life insurance policy were not includible in partner-decedent's gross estate because partner-decedent had assigned all right, title, and interest in policy more than three years before his death).
176. Any postassignment premiums paid by the insured or his or her employer should not be includible in the gross estate under §2042.
177. *See Bel v. United States,* 452 F.2d 683 (5th Cir. 1971), *cert. denied,* 406 U.S. 919 (1972) (holding that without automatic renewal privilege, annual premium payments constitute purchase of new policy).
178. Rev. Rul. 82-13, 1982-2 C.B. 132, noting that annual premium payments on renewable term life insurance was not a new transfer of insurance coverage.

179. The IRS ruled that when the employee-insured assigned all of his rights under the policy to his spouse, agreeing that the assignment would vest in her all rights under his group life coverage, and the corporation changed insurance carriers within three years of the employee-insured's death, the anticipatory assignment of future insurance benefits was not effective as a present transfer. Rev. Rul. 79-231, 1979-2 C.B. 323. Thereafter, the IRS changed its position on this issue. Rev. Rul. 80-289, 1980-2 C.B. 270. If the IRS insists on exact conformity of the policies, the benefits of its position may be illusory, however. Note that the IRS ruled in PLR 9436036 that an assignment of an interest in a group term policy was complete even though, after a merger and acquisition of the insurance company, the original insurance policies were replaced and thereafter the individual insured executed a confirmation of the assignment.
180. Assignment of group policies is permissible under the laws of all states and the District of Columbia, although some states limit the class of permissible assignees.
181. For example, these would include the power to change the beneficiary, to surrender and cancel the policy, to assign the policy, to convert the policy into other coverage, and to select an optional mode of settlement. *See* Reg. §20.2042-1(c).
182. For example, the possibility that the policy may return to the insured or his or her estate or otherwise become subject to his or her disposition pursuant to the terms of the assignment, the master policy, or an employment agreement. *See* Reg. §20.2042-1(c)(3). Attribution of incidents of ownership held by a corporation in a group term policy to its controlling shareholder may result. *See* Reg. §20.2042-1(c)(6). Incidents of ownership may be held in a fiduciary capacity or as a result of a divorce decree. *See* Reg. §20.2042-1(c)(4).
183. See the discussion of life insurance planning in Chapter 9, C.3.
184. The reserve has often been accumulated (without any guaranty as to sufficiency) for the benefit of employees as a group with: (1) an insurance company, (2) a §501(c)(9) trust, or (3) a nonexempt trust. The reserve is withdrawn as needed to pay premiums on individual term or group term policy coverage for retired employees.
185. *See* Reg. §1.79-2(b)(1). Section 79(e) specifies that the term "employee" includes a former employee, which extends the taxation and nondiscrimination provisions of §79 to any employee receiving coverage after termination of employment for any reason (including retirement) unless the employee is disabled. See, further, PLR 201136007.
186. In TAM 8342008, the IRS concluded that the post-retirement continuation of certain group term life insurance did not qualify for exclusion from gross income under §79. The IRS stated that the post-retirement fund was taxable to the individual under §83 at the time of retirement, noting that the post-retirement insurance was in effect "a permanent benefit" (as defined under Reg. §1.79-0).
187. Split-dollar insurance might also be used in a family context where a grandparent assists a parent in obtaining life insurance to protect grandchildren (i.e., children of the parent) in the event of the death of the parent.
188. *See* Reg. §1.61-22(b)(1) (identifying split-dollar life insurance arrangement as any arrangement between owner and nonowner of life insurance contract that satisfies specified criteria including that: (1) either party to arrangement pays, directly or indirectly, all or any portion of premiums on life insurance contract, including payment by means of loan to other party that is secured by life insurance contract, and (2) at least one of parties paying premiums is entitled to recover all or any portion of those premiums and such recovery is to be made from, or is secured by, proceeds of life insurance contract).

189. For a detailed discussion of the tax treatment of split-dollar arrangements, see 828 T.M., *Insurance-Related Compensation* (Bloomberg BNA).
190. Since the cash surrender value increases slowly during the early years of a policy, the employee bears a substantial portion of the premium cost during those years. After the first year, the employee's share of the premium decreases and, in some situations, that share becomes zero after the policy has been in force for several years. Life insurance companies have developed alternative programs for leveling these costs to the employee in the earlier years.
191. The two most commonly used methods to assure the recovery to the employer of its cost are: (1) the collateral assignment method and (2) the endorsement method. Under the collateral assignment method, the insured employee (or the employee's transferee) owns the policy and assigns the policy as collateral to the employer to secure the employer for the return of an amount equal to the employer's premium payments. Under the terms of the policy endorsement method, the employer owns the life insurance policy and the insured employee (or his or her transferee) has the right to name the beneficiary of the at-risk portion of the proceeds, i.e., the amount in excess of the cash value.
192. Rev. Rul. 64-328, 1964-2 C.B. 11, *amplified by*, Rev. Rul. 66-110, 1966-1 C.B. 12; Rev. Rul. 67-154, 1967-1 C.B. 11; Rev. Rul. 78-420, 1978-2 C.B. 67. In Notice 2002-8, 2002-4 I.R.B. 398, the IRS advised that Rev. Rul. 64-328 and Rev. Rul. 66-110, originally modified by now-revoked Notice 2001-10, 2001-5 I.R.B. 459, remain modified to the extent that they indicate that an employer's premium payments under a split-dollar arrangement should not be treated as loans where an employee is not expected to make repayment except out of the cash surrender value or proceeds of the life insurance contract. In REG-164754-01, 67 Fed. Reg. 45,414 (July 9, 2002), the IRS issued proposed regulations on the taxation of split-dollar life insurance arrangements that provided for two mutually exclusive regimes, based on either loans or economic benefit. The IRS stated that concurrent with the publication of the final regulations, the IRS would obsolete Rev. Rul. 64-328, Rev. Rul. 66-110, and Rev. Rul. 78-420 (with respect to income tax consequences). Taxpayers entering into split-dollar life insurance arrangements on or before the date of publication of the final regulations could continue to rely on these revenue rulings to the extent described in Notice 2002-8. The IRS stated that, under the proposed regulations, a split-dollar arrangement would be taxed as either: (1) the transfer of economic benefits from one party to the other; or (2) a series of loans to the benefited party. An arrangement would be taxed under the first regime if the employer was designated as the owner of the life insurance contract, and under the second regime if the employee was designated as the owner. These split-dollar regulations were finalized during 2003. T.D. 9092, 68 Fed. Reg. 54,336 (Sept. 17, 2003). The Preamble to the final regulations includes an extensive elaboration of these rules. In Rev. Rul. 2003-105, 2003-40 I.R.B. 696, the rulings identified above were listed as obsolete except as to certain limitations concerning transitional rules.
193. *See* Reg. §1.61-22, §1.7872-15, generally effective for split-dollar arrangements entered into or materially modified after September 17, 2003; T.D. 9092. For the applicable rules before the 2003 regulations, see Rev. Rul. 55-747, 1955-2 C.B. 228, *revoked by*, Notice 2002-8; PLR 9617042. In now-revoked Notice 2001-10, the IRS advised that the "P.S. 58" rates listed in Rev. Rul. 55-747 no longer bore an appropriate relationship to the fair market value of current life insurance protection. Thus, Notice 2001-10 revoked Rev. Rul. 55-747. Notice 2002-8, in turn, revoked Notice 2001-10. In Notice 2002-8, the

IRS indicated that Rev. Rul. 55-747 remains revoked. However, Notice 2002-8 provides that a taxpayer could continue to use the P.S. 58 rates set forth in Rev. Rul. 55-747 for a split-dollar life insurance arrangement entered into before January 28, 2002, in which a contractual arrangement between the employer and employee provided that the P.S. 58 rates will be used. For arrangements entered into before the effective date of final regulations, taxpayers may use the premium table (Table 2001) originally published in Notice 2001-10 and now set forth at the end of Notice 2002-8. For arrangements entered into before the effective date of final regulations, taxpayers can continue to use the insurer's lower rate instead of Table 2001 if certain conditions are satisfied. In addition, with the issuance of the proposed regulations in REG-164754-01, the IRS advised that taxpayers could rely on the proposed regulations for the treatment of any split-dollar life insurance arrangement entered into on or before the date final regulations were published in the Federal Register provided that all parties to the split-dollar life insurance arrangement treat the arrangement consistently.

194. Reg. §1.61-22 governs economic benefit arrangements.
195. *See* Reg. §1.61-22(d) (identifying valuation of economic benefits provided under such arrangements).
196. *See* Reg. §1.61-22(a)(1) (cross-referencing Reg. §1.7872-15).
197. Reg. §1.7872-15(a)(2).
198. §262.
199. §264(a)(1).
200. §101(a).
201. §2042(1).
202. §2042(2). *See* PLR 9026041 (proceeds of key man insurance policy bought under split-dollar agreement were includible in key man's estate under §2042 since he and company could cancel policy).
203. The Preamble to the 2003 regulations, discussed above, indicates that the inclusion of split-dollar policy proceeds in a decedent's gross estate continues to be governed by §2042, regardless of who is treated as the owner of the life insurance contract under the regulations. T.D. 9092. See PLR 200851013 for an example of the avoidance of estate tax inclusion when split dollar insurance proceeds were deflected to several trusts (the trust settlor/insured having no incidents of ownership in the policy).
204. Even though the employee is ultimately successful in having the proceeds removed from his or her gross estate for estate tax purposes, the employee must annually include in gross income for federal income tax purposes the value of the annual insurance protection exceeding the premiums paid by him or her (or his or her donee).
205. See 826 T.M., *Life Insurance* (Bloomberg BNA). An issue arises whether, when an employment relationship is necessary to the continuation of the policy, the right to terminate employment is an "incident of ownership." In Rev. Rul. 72-307, 1972-1 C.B. 307 (described above in the group term life insurance discussion), the right to terminate employment was determined to not be an incident of ownership in determining whether group term life insurance proceeds are includible in a decedent's gross estate.
206. Rev. Rul. 79-429, 1979-2 C.B. 321, recognized that a third party can arrange for a split-dollar policy on an employee's life. In the employment context, this will ordinarily require the consent of the employee. This will also ordinarily require that the donee have an insurable interest (as determined under applicable state insurance law) in the life of the employee.

207. *Estate of Levy v. Commissioner,* 70 T.C. 873 (1978); Reg. §20.2042-1(c)(6); Rev. Rul. 76-274, 1976-2 C.B. 278. *See also* Rev. Rul. 90-21, 1990-1 C.B. 172; PLR 9348009 (corporation's limited interest as irrevocably designated beneficiary of portion of policy was not incident of ownership that would be imputed to majority shareholder).
208. Rev. Rul. 76-274, 1976-2 C.B. 278, *modified by,* Rev. Rul. 82-145, 1982-2 C.B. 213. These rulings enumerate a number of specific restrictions on the corporation's rights in the policy that should be included in any split-dollar agreement where the employee is the controlling shareholder.
209. See PLR 200822003 providing that no gift transfer occurred (for federal gift tax purposes) where a trust owning the split dollar policy paid its share of the premiums and a husband and wife paid the remaining portion of premiums on a two-life policy.
210. Rev. Rul. 81-198, 1981-2 C.B. 188; Rev. Rul. 78-420, 1978-2 C.B. 67, *obsoleted by,* Rev. Rul. 2003-105, 2003-40 I.R.B. 696 (for split-dollar arrangements entered into on or before publication of final split-dollar regulations on September 17, 2003, taxpayers may continue to rely on Rev. Rul. 78-420 to extent described in Notice 2002-8, 2002-4 I.R.B. 398, but only if arrangement is not materially modified after September 17, 2003).
211. T.D. 9092 (preamble). Reg. §1.7872-15 would apply.
212. *See* Reg. §1.61-22(c).
213. *See* T.D. 9092 (preamble).
214. For example, assume that under the terms of the split-dollar life insurance arrangement, on termination of the arrangement or the donor's death, the donor or donor's estate is entitled to receive an amount equal to the greater of the aggregate premiums paid by the donor or the cash surrender value of the contract. In this case, the donor makes a gift to the trust equal to the cost of the current life insurance protection provided to the trust less any premium amount paid by the trustee. Thus, a payment by the donor will not constitute a gift if the trust pays the portion of the premium equal to the cost of the current life insurance protection and the donor pays the balance of the premium.
215. *See* §2702(c)(2).

CHAPTER 12

Post-Mortem Estate Planning

A. Planning Options

Possibilities for property transmission planning and related tax planning exist not only during the client's lifetime but, also, after death (i.e., during the process of administering the client's probate estate and funding any trusts created under either the will or any inter vivos trust agreements that became irrevocable at death). Important "post-mortem estate planning" matters to be considered by the advisor can include:

- Should the decedent's testamentary scheme (primarily in the last will) be altered through renunciations and disclaimers of property transfers as specified in the testamentary documents (or possibly by family settlements)?
- Should tax deductions be claimed for purposes of: (1) the federal estate tax or (2) the federal income tax when a choice is available (and a deduction for both purposes is not permitted)?
- What income tax planning positions should be implemented during the probate estate administration process, for example, concerning the timing of tax years, timing the activation of testamentary trusts, the timing of estate distributions to beneficiaries, and the disposition of "income in respect of a decedent" (IRD)?
- Should the executor's commissions be waived (not diluting the estate assets, thereby benefitting the estate beneficiaries)?
- Can and should the alternate estate tax valuation date option be used?

- Should the provisions to extend the time for making estate tax payments be used?
- Should a §303 corporate stock redemption be used?

These post-mortem tax savings opportunities relate to both federal income tax and estate tax planning.

B. Income Tax Planning Opportunities

1. Options

Various income tax elections and other federal income tax planning options can be used after the death of the client so as to produce an overall income tax savings for the decedent's family unit.[1] This planning can be done concerning (1) the decedent's final income tax return, (2) the fiduciary income tax return(s) for the probate estate, and (3) the potential income tax liabilities of the beneficiaries of the estate.[2]

2. Final Income Tax Return of the Decedent

a. Income Tax Planning Options

Several income tax planning opportunities with respect to the decedent's final federal income tax return can be implemented after the death of the decedent. This is the return filed for that part of the decedent's last year during which the decedent is alive. Obviously, this return for that "stub period" must be filed by the decedent's personal representative.

b. Medical Expenses

Expenses for the decedent's medical care paid out of his or her estate during the one-year period beginning at the date of his or her death can be treated as paid at the time actually incurred.[3] For this limited purpose, the cash basis taxpayer is transformed into an accrual basis taxpayer as to this item. This treatment would apply to medical deductions to be claimed on the decedent's last income tax return or, perhaps, to the last several income tax returns if the decedent dies shortly after the commencement of a tax year and before the time the federal income tax return for the prior year has been filed. This income tax deduction is not permitted, however, if the amount due for medical expenses is reported on the estate tax return as a claim against the estate.[4]

The decision as to whether the medical expense deduction should be taken on the last income tax return or as a claim against the estate for federal estate tax purposes will be based on the marginal tax rates applicable to the net income or net estate as reflected on each return. If the estate is in a taxable position for estate tax purposes, the deduction will ordinarily be more valuable when claimed on the estate tax return. If, however, the estate is protected from any estate tax liability (for example, because of the unified credit or the unlimited marital deduction, or both), an income tax deduction would be more valuable.

If the deduction for these medical expenses is taken on the decedent's last federal income tax return, the amount of the liability for any unpaid federal income tax will be reduced on the estate's estate tax return. Consequently, the federal estate tax liability would increase, since the income tax liability, which is a deductible debt of the estate, would have been reduced by the medical expense income tax deduction. This estate tax increase would be to the detriment of those estate beneficiaries entitled to the corpus, that is, the remainder beneficiaries.

If the deduction is taken on the estate tax return, the deduction will not be available for income tax purposes. Consequently, the income tax liability will increase. The estate tax liability would be reduced as a result of this deduction, thereby benefiting the remainder beneficiaries.

In some instances, the executor should examine whether the medical expense deduction should be divided between the decedent's last income tax return and the estate tax return so as to maximize overall federal tax savings. If the situation permits, however, the medical bills should be paid before death. If the last illness is lingering, and the decedent has implemented a durable power of attorney, payment before death might be completed by the attorney-in-fact, acting under this durable power of attorney. If this payment can be made, an income tax deduction would be available (subject to the §213(a) percentage limitation).[5] Further, the gross estate would be depleted by the amount of that actual payment.

c. Series E U.S. Savings Bonds

When investing in Series E U.S. savings bonds, individuals (assuming cash-basis taxpayers) are not required to report the current interest accrual, unlike other original issue discount debt obligations.[6] Therefore, these bondholders are required to recognize the entire amount of interest income when these obligations are redeemed or otherwise transferred in a taxable transaction. An election is available, however, to accelerate that income recognition, that is, to recognize currently the annual increase in the redemption value of Series E U.S. savings bonds (in addition to any previously accrued but unreported income).[7]

When a person dies holding these Series E bonds, the previously accrued but unreported interest income will not disappear from the income tax base. The §1014 date of death value tax basis rule will not be applicable. Rather, this accrued interest will be treated as an item of IRD.[8] A decedent may have died early in the income tax year and before he or she had realized much other income. In this situation, an election for the last individual short-period tax year (ending on the date of death) could be made to accrue for that year all previously realized but unrecognized income of the Series E bond. This would enable taking advantage of a low marginal tax rate, which might be applicable to that short-period tax year.[9]

The election, once made, will require annual income recognition thereafter as the interest accrues on the bonds to which the election is applicable.[10] If the tax attributable to this income is substantial and the bonds might be held for a considerable period, the value of the loss of the use of the tax funds should be considered if this election is made (unless it is subsequently revoked).

The increase in income tax liability resulting from the inclusion of this income in the decedent's final income tax return will increase the debt that is deductible on the estate tax return. This deduction will thereby reduce the estate tax liability. If the election is not made on the decedent's final return, the income would be reportable on the estate's fiduciary income tax return if either: (1) the bonds are disposed of by the fiduciary or (2) the fiduciary makes the election. Alternatively, the beneficiaries who receive these bonds in kind from the estate would realize this income when they subsequently dispose of the bonds or make the election to earlier accrue the income.[11] The income accrued up to the time of death would be IRD and, consequently, a deduction in respect of a decedent would be available for any allocable estate tax paid on the value of the income right included on the estate tax return.[12]

d. Joint Income Tax Return Status

For federal income tax purposes, the decedent's last tax year ends at the date of death. The final income tax return for the decedent can be filed on a joint return basis with the decedent's surviving spouse.[13] The income includible on that return would be (1) the decedent's income from the beginning of the tax year until the date of his or her death and (2) the surviving spouse's income for the entire tax year.

A joint return to which the surviving spouse acquiesces may reduce the total joint income tax liability. Likewise, advantages may accrue to the surviving spouse by having the executor consent to joint return filing status. In planning for this possibility, the estate planner should assure that the will actually authorizes the executor to participate in filing joint income tax returns (even where the surviving spouse's tax liability is reduced and the deceased taxpayer's tax liability is increased). Professional fiduciaries will want relief from liability for making this election, since the responsibility for the liability on the joint tax return is both joint and several.[14] Ordinarily, in this situation, the responsibility for the actual tax cost is divided proportionately between the two taxpayers (i.e., the estate and the surviving spouse).[15]

3. Fiduciary Returns

a. Fiduciary's First Return

The existence of a separate taxpayer will commence as of the date of death of a decedent with respect to: (1) his or her estate (ordinarily described as his or her "probate estate") and (2) any revocable inter vivos trusts created by the decedent (assuming those trusts continue after the decedent's death and become irrevocable as of death).[16] The existence of a testamentary trust for income tax purposes will commence when it is funded.[17]

As a new taxpayer, the estate can adopt a calendar or a fiscal tax year.[18] If a fiscal year is not elected, the taxable year will be the calendar year.[19] A return for a short period (i.e., less than 12 months) is permitted where the taxpayer is not in existence for what would otherwise be its entire tax year.[20] Under these circumstances, income is not required to be annualized.

These rules permit the estate to elect a fiscal year for the first year during which a small amount of income will be recognized. This will reduce the average income tax rate applicable to that income.[21] Additionally, the time at which the income tax liability accrues for later earned income will be deferred for a limited period.

Example: Decedent dies on March 15, 2015. A substantial income item is realized on April 15, 2015, as a result of a payment to the estate by the decedent's employer. The first tax year of the estate can be terminated as of April 30, 2015, thereby trapping only six weeks' income (from March 15 to April 30, 2015), as subject to income tax in that first, short tax year. If a lower income tax bracket is applicable to that period, income tax savings might accrue, even though the income tax liability is not deferred.

b. Deferral Through Staggered Fiscal Years

The use of varied fiscal years can permit the deferral of income tax liabilities. This is particularly pertinent where multiple taxpayers are involved.

Example: Death occurs March 15, 2015. The will provides that the residuary estate (which will receive the income of the probate estate) is to be paid to a testamentary trust required to distribute its income currently, such as a marital deduction trust. The testamentary trust is activated as a taxpayer on February 15, 2016, when the trust is funded. The estate adopts a February 28 fiscal year, with its first fiscal year starting on March 15, 2015, and ending on February 29, 2016 (the maximum period permitted). The trust must adopt a calendar year starting on February 15, 2016, and ending on December 31, 2016. The income realized by the estate from March 15, 2015, through February 29, 2016, will not be exposed to income tax until the individual beneficiary must report this income (treated as received through the trust) on April 15, 2017.[22] This result occurs because the trust is not deemed to have received and to have distributed the income distribution until as of the close of the estate's taxable year (i.e., February 29, 2016).[23]

c. Fiduciary Return Estimated Tax Payments

Estates must make estimated federal income tax payments only after the second complete tax year following the decedent's death.[24] Trusts are required from inception to make estimated tax payments, except that a pour-over trust, or a revocable living trust funded with a decedent's assets at the time of death, need not satisfy the estimated tax payment requirements for the two-year period after death.[25]

A trust may make an estimated tax payment but might thereafter make a distribution of all or most of its income. The estimated tax payments made by the trust could then be in excess of its income tax liability for that tax year. The trustee may elect to treat any portion of a payment of estimated tax made by that trust as a payment actually made by a beneficiary of the trust.[26] That amount is treated as paid or credited to the beneficiary on the January 15 following the trust's taxable year.[27]

d. Administration Expenses

Amounts allowable as deductions from the gross estate as administration expenses[28] or as losses[29] may, alternatively, be taken as a deduction on the federal income tax return of the estate.[30] For this purpose, administration expenses would include executor's commissions (if actually paid, but not if waived or if in the form of a bequest or devise to the executor in lieu of commissions), attorney's fees, and miscellaneous administration expenses (court costs, accountant's fees, and appraiser's fees).[31] The expense must be economically incurred by the estate (rather than by an associated trust) to qualify for this treatment.[32]

These administration expenses can include the costs of selling property (e.g., brokerage commissions for selling securities or real estate).[33] Items such as selling expenses may not be used to offset the sales price of property if they are deducted for estate tax purposes.[34] Under appropriate circumstances, these expenses might also include interest expense on continuing loans.[35]

The actual use of the deduction on the estate's income tax return (rather than on the estate tax return) will depend on the relative marginal tax rates on the estate tax return and the income tax return. Where these rates are the same (and other factors are neutral), the deduction may be split between the two tax returns.[36]

The estate planner should remember that, if the deduction is claimed on the income tax return, the estate tax will increase (to the detriment of the remainder beneficiaries). A decrease in the net income tax liability will benefit the income beneficiaries of the estate. To avoid conflict between income beneficiaries and remainder beneficiaries, the executor should be vested in the last will with appropriate discretion to claim the deduction on the income tax return or the estate tax return and without any obligation to reimburse a beneficiary who may be adversely affected by this decision.

e. Termination of the Probate Estate

(1) Timing

Continuing the existence of the probate estate as a separate taxpayer for an extended period can produce limited income tax savings. The existence of an additional taxable entity permits some spreading of income and diffusion of the income tax impact because of the reduced tax rates on lower tiers of taxable income. The maximum 39.6% income tax rate for an estate is reached when taxable income is $7,500, as adjusted for inflation, so the flexibility in this context is limited.[37] The accumulation trust rules (or "throwback" rules) do not apply to income taxed to the estate and subsequently distributed to the estate beneficiaries.[38]

The estate is permitted to remain in existence for a reasonable period for facilitating estate administration. This is the period actually required by the administrator or executor to perform the ordinary duties of administration (such as the collection of assets and the payment of debts, taxes, legacies, and bequests).[39] If sufficient assets are retained by the estate, thereby making legitimate its existence, income splitting can produce limited income tax savings during a reasonably extended period of probate administration.[40] This income tax savings consists only of the tax rate differential in the initial income tax rate brackets, however, and, as noted above, this is limited to taxable income below $7,500, as adjusted for inflation. The planning question to be addressed, therefore, is whether this tax savings is greater than the additional administration and tax compliance cost that might be incurred.

(2) Carryover of Excess Deductions

If, on termination of an estate (or trust), the estate (or trust) has for its last taxable year deductions in excess of gross income, that excess is allowed as a deduction to the beneficiaries succeeding to the property of the estate (or trust).[41] If a high-bracket beneficiary will be succeeding to the property of the estate, the estate before its termination might realize expenses that can constitute deductions to be carried out to the beneficiary.[42]

4. Distributing Items of Income in Respect of a Decedent

After death, the fiduciary should determine (if permitted) whether to allocate the items (or portions) of IRD to (1) the decedent's final income tax return (e.g., by making an election to recognize accrued interest income on Series E bonds), (2) the income tax returns of the estate, (3) any trust income tax returns, or (4) through distributions, the various individual beneficiaries who are part of the distributee family unit under the decedent's will and any trusts.[43] In making any such distributions, the fiduciary should be permitted to take into account the income tax impact upon the receipt of the IRD items by any beneficiary. To facilitate the exercise of this discretion, the fiduciary will need to be actually vested with the appropriate authority to implement these decisions. This authority should be included in the powers clauses and other provisions of the last will and any relevant trust instruments.

C. Renunciations and Disclaimers

1. Purposes of Renunciations

A renunciation or a disclaimer can be a valuable post-mortem estate planning device.[44] A renunciation can be used to shift property anticipated to be received by an older-generation member to a younger-generation member while avoiding a federal gift tax liability being imposed on the older-generation member.[45] This result is premised on the theory that the person making the renunciation never received the property being transferred and, therefore, that person could not be making a transfer by gift for federal gift tax purposes.[46]

A renunciation can also be used to save estate taxes that otherwise might later be imposed on an intermediate generation. For example, the daughter, who would otherwise receive property from her mother's estate, might renounce all or a part of a bequest. As a result, a per stirpes distribution might be made to the daughter's children (or a trust established for them) as contingent beneficiaries under the mother's last will.[47] The assets would thereby not be includible in the daughter's estate at her subsequent death.[48]

Similarly, a widow who would receive all the property from her deceased husband's estate might make a partial renunciation, thereby avoiding estate taxes at her later death with respect to the disclaimed property (then being held by younger-generation members), while enabling estate tax immunity for the renounced property in the husband's estate through the use of the unified credit amount (assuming available).[49] Alternatively, where a widow has not received a significant portion of the husband's estate, the other beneficiaries (e.g., a surviving son and daughter) might partially renounce their interests to enable their mother to receive more property and, thereby, their father's estate to have available a larger estate tax marital deduction.[50] A disclaimer may effectively prevent the income taxation to the person renouncing the property of the income from the disclaimed property[51] and, thereby, also serve to shift income within the family unit.

Various types of specific property interests can be the subject of renunciations or disclaimers. These could include[52]:

- testamentary bequests;
- intestate shares[53];
- income interests in trusts;
- remainder interests in trusts;
- nontestamentary property, such as (1) life insurance and (2) joint tenancies[54]; and
- powers held by a beneficiary or trustee.

A renunciation or a disclaimer can be a very useful post-mortem planning technique, but potential risks for challenge to the professional advisor can be significant.[55]

2. Definition of "Disclaimer"

A qualified disclaimer for federal gift tax purposes means an irrevocable and unqualified refusal to accept an interest in property when four conditions are satisfied[56]:

- The refusal is in writing.[57]
- The refusal is received by the transferor of the interest, his or her legal representative, or the holder of the legal title to the property not later than nine months after the day on which the transfer creating the interest was made[58]; however, the period for making the disclaimer is not to expire in any case until nine months after the day on which the person making the disclaimer has attained age 21.[59]
- The person must not have accepted the interest or any of its benefits before making the disclaimer.[60]
- As a result of the refusal, the interest passes either to[61] (1) the spouse of the decedent[62] or (2) a person other than the person making the disclaimer without any direction on the part of the person making the disclaimer.[63]

These disclaimer rules apply for purposes of the estate, gift, and GST taxes.[64]

If the requirements of §2518 are satisfied, a refusal to accept property is to be given effect for federal estate and gift tax purposes even if: (1) the applicable local law does not technically characterize the refusal as a "disclaimer" or (2) the person refusing the property was considered to have been the owner (under local law) of the legal title to the property before refusing acceptance of the property.[65] If a qualified disclaimer is made, the federal estate, gift, and generation-skipping transfer (GST) tax provisions apply to the property interest disclaimed as if the property interest had never been transferred to the person making the disclaimer.[66] The effect of the disclaimer is to treat the disclaimant as having predeceased the decedent. Accordingly, (1) the governing instrument, or (2) state intestacy laws, will determine who will be the recipient of the disclaimed property under these circumstances.[67]

3. Partial Disclaimers

A disclaimer of an undivided portion (but not all) of an interest in property is treated as a qualified disclaimer if it satisfies the requirements of §2518(b).[68] The undivided portion of the disclaimant's entire interest must consist of a fraction or percentage of each interest or right of the disclaimant in the property and must extend over the entire term of the disclaimant's interest in that property and any conversions thereof.[69] The IRS has taken a position in regulations against the "horizontal" disclaimer. Thus, a disclaimer of a remainder interest in a bequest of a fee interest, while retaining a life estate, is not treated as a qualified disclaimer.[70]

The surviving spouse can make a partial disclaimer with the disclaimed property then going into a non-marital or bypass trust.[71] Severable property (e.g., shares of stock) may be disclaimed,[72] and part of a specific pecuniary amount may be disclaimed.[73] With regard to transfers in trust, the disclaimer of the entire interest in the income, the corpus, or both, or an undivided portion of such interest, is required to enable a qualified disclaimer.[74] A disclaimer is not a qualified disclaimer if the beneficiary disclaims income derived from specific properties transferred in trust while continuing to accept income from the remaining properties in the same trust.[75] If separate taxable transfers to the same trust are made at different times or if transfers are made by different transferors, a qualified disclaimer can be made with respect to each transfer as though it were made to a separate trust.[76]

The question also arises as to whether a partial disclaimer may be used to reduce a general power of appointment to a limited power of appointment. The "without direction" requirement of §2518(b)(4) should preclude this result because the disclaimant would be retaining a continuing right to direct disposition of the property through the exercise of the special power.[77] Further, whether a partial disclaimer may be used to delete overly broad powers of distribution is uncertain. For example, where a beneficiary trustee has the power to invade corpus pursuant to a standard that is not "ascertainable," such as "support, health, and happiness," the beneficiary might disclaim the right to invade for "happiness." Any disclaimer of such a power would likely not be valid under §2518 because the beneficiary (who is not a surviving spouse) has retained the right to invade principal for support and maintenance and may have retained a right to direct the disposition of principal to remainder beneficiaries through his or her control over these invasions.[78]

4. Property Transfers as Qualifying Disclaimers

A written transfer of the transferor's entire interest in the property that otherwise satisfies the qualified disclaimer requirements, and that is to a person who would have received the property had the transferor made a qualified disclaimer, is to be treated as a qualified disclaimer.[79] This provision for a "putative disclaimer" introduced some uniformity for federal tax disclaimer purposes because shorter state disclaimer time limitation periods will no longer prevent a federal disclaimer if a qualifying "transfer" is made within the nine-month period. Although the transfer need not satisfy the requirements of the local law disclaimer statute, the writing effectuating the transfer must satisfy local property transfer laws. Further, the person to receive the transfer if a qualified disclaimer were made is to be determined under state law. Thus, uniformity problems do remain. Whether the term "entire interest" means only an "interest in property" as used elsewhere in §2518 or whether it imposes a requirement that all beneficial interests must be eliminated is uncertain. If the latter, the question arises as to whether the transfer-as-disclaimer can be used for a transfer by the surviving spouse into a bypass trust or for any type of partial disclaimer.

D. Waiver of Fee by Fiduciary

Post-mortem estate planning should include a consideration of whether a fiduciary should waive his or her fee for serving as executor. This contemplates a fiduciary who would be willing to decline such a fee, for example, a close relative of the decedent (rather than a professional corporate trustee). In the hands of the executor, the fee would constitute ordinary income for federal income tax purposes and this dilution of the fee might be avoided in appropriate circumstances.

If the executor is also the sole beneficiary of the estate (e.g., a spouse or child), a determination should be made as to whether enhanced net estate and income tax results would be produced by:

- the executor taking the fee as ordinary income and this fee being deductible for either estate tax or fiduciary income tax purposes; or
- the executor not accepting a fee, with (1) a larger amount being taxed in the estate (because no deduction is claimed) and estate income being greater (because no income tax deduction is claimed), but (2) the executor not realizing ordinary income reportable on his or her individual income tax return.

Additionally, if an older-generation person is the executor and is only one of several beneficiaries of the estate (e.g., the surviving spouse and a child being beneficiaries), economic value can be indirectly shifted from the older generation to the younger generation without gift tax cost when the executor waives his or her fee. This occurs because the estate is not reduced by any executor's fee and the younger generation member therefore shares in a larger distributable estate. The tax issues that might be raised by the IRS are (1) whether amounts to be received by the executor upon distribution of the estate are to be included in the executor's gross income, and (2) whether the waiver of the right to receive this executor's fee results in a gift transfer.[80] In essence, a waiver of this fee should be formalized promptly after the fiduciary's appointment, thereby clearly evidencing an intent by the fiduciary to render gratuitous services from the inception and for the duration of the estate administration. The income and gift tax results, therefore, will ultimately be determined by the timing, purpose, and effect of the waiver.[81]

E. Solving Estate Liquidity Problems

1. Corporate §303 Stock Redemptions

a. Purpose of Special Redemption Treatment

Under a stock redemption agreement effective as of death,[82] all the corporate shares held by the decedent would be redeemed and a complete termination would occur for purposes of enabling capital gains tax treatment of the sales proceeds received.[83] Since the tax basis for the redeemed shares will have been stepped up to fair market value at death, no gain would ordinarily be realized under these circumstances.[84] The decedent shareholder's heirs may wish, however, to retain the decedent's shares and, consequently, a stock purchase agreement would not have been implemented by the decedent.

In this situation, §303 could be a valuable post-mortem estate planning mechanism to permit a tax preferred corporate stock redemption of a sufficient number of shares to obtain adequate cash to satisfy tax liabilities of the estate and to pay funeral and administration expenses.[85] Section 303 was enacted to enable an estate to avoid ordinary dividend treatment otherwise applicable upon the redemption of only that stock necessary to amass these funds.[86]

The tax basis for the stock redeemed will be its estate tax basis as determined under §1014.[87] Therefore, notwithstanding that the redemption transaction is a sale for federal income tax purposes, if the stock is redeemed at its estate tax value, no actual gain or loss is realized for income tax purposes.[88]

b. Structure of §303

(1) Mathematical Tests

To be eligible for §303 capital gains redemption treatment, the value of the decedent's stock of the closely held corporation held at death must exceed 35% of the value of his or her adjusted gross estate.[89] For purposes of this eligibility rule, the stock of two or more corporations can be treated as the stock of a single corporation if 20% or more in value of the outstanding stock of each such corporation is included in determining the value of the decedent's gross estate.[90] For purposes of the 20% test, if the decedent and the surviving spouse hold stock as community property, the surviving spouse's interest in stock is treated as having been included in determining the value of the decedent's gross estate.[91] Only the value of stock of each redeeming corporation owned directly by the decedent at the date of his or her death and included in his or her gross estate can be considered (except for the community property exception) in determining whether the percentage requirements have been satisfied.[92]

(2) Limitation on Redemption Amount

Section 303 eligibility is available only to the extent of the total amount of (a) estate, inheritance, legacy, and succession taxes[93]; and (b) the funeral and administration expenses allowable as deductions to the estate.[94]

(3) Parties Eligible to Use §303

A redemption under §303 qualifies for sale or exchange treatment only to the extent that the interest of the shareholder is reduced either directly (or through a binding obligation to contribute) by any payment of an amount relating to death taxes or §2053 deductions.[95] Consequently, sale or exchange treatment is designed to be available under §303 only when the party whose shares are redeemed has an actual liability for death taxes or funeral or administration expenses in an amount at least equal to the amount of the stock redemption proceeds.[96] Consequently, stock used to satisfy the marital deduction bequest would ordinarily not be eligible for a §303 redemption since, if the tax allocation provision is properly constructed, the marital deduction gift should bear no responsibility for these taxes.[97] In the preparation of a will where the estate may want or need to use a §303 redemption after death to obtain funds, planners should give careful consideration to the potential allocation of taxes under state and federal law, as well as the tax clause under the will, so that §303 is actually available.

(4) Time Limitations

A stock redemption, to qualify under §303, must be made after the death of the decedent[98] and

- before the expiration of the three-year period of the statute of limitations for assessing an estate tax deficiency or within 90 days after the running of the three-year period of the statute of limitations[99];
- if a petition has been filed in the U.S. Tax Court, within 60 days after the decision of the Tax Court becomes final[100]; or
- before the due date of the last installment, where an election to defer payment has been made under §6166.[101]

The objective of this additional time provision is to more closely correlate the rules of §303 and the extended estate tax payment provisions.[102]

For any redemptions made more than four years after the decedent's death, sale or exchange treatment is available, however, only for a distribution in an amount which is the lesser of:

- the amount of the qualifying death taxes and funeral and administration expenses that are unpaid immediately before the distribution; or
- the aggregate of these amounts that are paid within one year after the distribution.[103]

c. Planning Opportunities

The estate planner will want to assure that a client's estate will satisfy the percentage requirements of §303 if a client holds a sizable block (or blocks) of stock in a corporation (or corporations).[104] The following planning possibilities should be examined in this context:

- Opportunities for §303 qualification can be improved by gifts of other property that will thereby produce an increase in the percentage of the total estate consisting of the closely held business stock.[105]
- Opportunities for qualification can be improved by the contribution of nonbusiness assets into the corporation.[106]
- Where a client holds the stock of several companies but does not satisfy the 20% control test with respect to one of the corporations, a personal holding company (holding the stock of those several corporations) might be created to enable satisfaction of the percentage tests.
- If the client's stock interest is only slightly more than a majority (e.g., 51%), and the client's children wish to retain control after the client's death, the corporation might recapitalize itself through the issuance of preferred stock. After death, the client's stock can be the subject of a §303 redemption without any loss of voting control occurring.[107]
- A slightly higher value for the closely held stock could be reported on the estate tax return than would otherwise normally be reported, so as to permit §303 qualification.[108]
- If the corporation does not have sufficient liquid assets within the time limitation to complete a §303 redemption and the estate has not made a §6166 election, the executor could exchange the stock in the redemption transaction for the corporation's promissory installment note.

2. Closely Held Business—Delayed Tax Payment

a. Purpose of Tax Deferral

As a matter of elective right, §6166 permits an extension of time for paying estate tax where the estate consists largely of an interest in a closely held business.[109] The basic tax policy purpose of §6166 is to enable the retention of a business enterprise where the death of one of the larger owners of a business results in the imposition of a significant estate tax attributable to that business.[110] Consequently, a "distress sale" of all or parts of a business is not necessary to generate sufficient funds to pay the federal estate tax liability. By extending the payment period, the estate tax can often be paid from post-death earnings of the business (e.g., dividends received by the estate). At a minimum, the heirs have more time during which to raise funds to pay the estate tax, thereby enabling retention of the business ownership within the family group.[111] The alert estate planner should recognize the possible availability of estate tax payment deferral[112] and should try to posture the client's assets to assure that the statutory criteria will be satisfied at the time of death.[113]

b. Elective Deferral

The executor of an estate that qualifies may elect to pay in up to 10 annual installments that estate tax liability attributable to an interest in a closely held business.[114] The first installment is payable no later than five years after the original due date of the estate tax return.[115] During the five years after the filing of the estate tax return, the executor's obligation with respect to the deferred estate tax is limited to the payment of interest in four annual installments of the interest amount on that deferred tax liability.[116] The interest rate is 2% for estates of decedents dying after 1997.[117] The 2% interest rate applies to that estate tax deferred that is attributable to the first $1 million (as adjusted for inflation) in taxable value of a closely held business (i.e., the first $1 million above the amount sheltered by the unified credit).[118] The deferred tax on holding companies and non-readily-tradable business interests, however, does not qualify for the 2% interest rate.[119] Interest on deferred taxes above the portion eligible for the 2% rate is payable at a rate equal to 45% of the §6621 underpayment rate.[120] Interest paid on the deferred estate tax, however, is not deductible for either estate or income tax purposes.[121]

The estate tax liability eligible to be deferred is that portion attributable to the business interest.[122] That specific portion of the total federal estate tax liability that may be deferred is determined by multiplying the total estate tax amount by a fraction, determined as follows[123]:

$$\frac{\text{value of closely held business}}{\text{value of adjusted gross estate}} \times \text{estate tax} = \text{estate tax amount payable in installments}$$

c. Percentage Threshold Test

Elective deferral is provided under §6166 only if the decedent owns an interest in a closely held business that exceeds 35% of the decedent's adjusted gross estate.[124] For this purpose, the "adjusted gross estate" means the decedent's gross estate less allowable §2053 and §2054 deductions.[125]

An aggregation rule allows the executor to amalgamate various closely held business interests owned by the decedent for purposes of satisfying this percentage qualification test. This opportunity is available whenever 20% or more of the total value of each business interest is included in the decedent's gross estate.[126] For purposes of satisfying the 20% requirement, a business interest of the decedent and the surviving spouse held as community property or in joint ownership is treated as having been included in determining the value of the decedent's gross estate.[127] This aggregation rule constitutes a recognition that even minority interests in multiple businesses can cause the decedent's estate to be illiquid.

d. Definition of "Interest in a Closely Held Business"

For §6166 purposes, the term "interest in a closely held business" includes:

- a sole proprietorship interest[128];
- a partnership interest, if (1) 20% or more of the total capital interest[129] in the partnership is included in the gross estate of the decedent, or (2) the partnership has 45 or fewer partners[130];
- stock in a corporation, if (1) 20% or more in value of the voting stock is included in the gross estate of the decedent,[131] or (2) the corporation has 45 or fewer shareholders.[132]

Several attribution rules apply automatically in the determination of whether the above numerical or percentage tests are satisfied.[133]

Stock or partnership interests held by a husband and wife as community property, joint tenants, tenants by the entirety, or tenants in common are treated as owned by one spouse.[134] Property owned, directly or indirectly, by a corporation, partnership, estate, or trust is considered owned proportionately by the stockholders, partners, or beneficiaries.[135] Further, all stock and all partnership interests held by the decedent or by any member of his or her family[136] are to be treated as owned by the decedent.[137]

The closely held business (whether proprietorship, partnership, or corporation) must be engaged in or be carrying on a trade or business at the time of the decedent's death.[138] The IRS interprets this requirement to mean an "active" as contrasted with a "passive" trade or business.[139] Thus, investment property does not constitute a trade or business.[140] Only where material, active management has been conducted by the decedent or his or her agent does the property qualify for this tax deferral.[141]

Where the business interest is a farm, that interest will include the residential buildings and related improvements on the farm if they are occupied on a regular basis by the owner or lessee for purposes of operating and maintaining the farm.[142] The value used for §6166 computations is the value determined for purposes of the estate tax.[143] Therefore, in the case of a farm where the executor has elected special use valuation under §2032A, that value is to be treated as the value for purposes of determining §6166 eligibility.

An executor may elect to treat stock of any holding company that represents direct ownership (or indirect ownership through one or more other holding companies) as stock in an active business in order to qualify for the §6166 estate tax installment payment provision.[144] Where this occurs, however, the five-year deferral will not be available[145] and the 2% interest rate on the deferred tax payment will not apply.[146] Further, to qualify for the election, none of the stock involved can be readily tradable.[147] For these tax deferral purposes, the value of a closely held business does not include the value of certain passive assets.[148]

A decedent's estate with an interest in a qualifying lending and financing business is eligible for installment payment of estate tax.[149] An estate with an interest in a qualifying lending and financing business that claims eligibility for installment payment of estate tax must make all installment payments (including principal and interest) without the 5-year deferral and over a 5-year (not 10-year) period.[150]

e. Termination of Installment Privilege

Under certain specified circumstances, a complete or partial termination of the §6166 installment payment privilege will result, with the payment of the remaining deferred taxes required to be accelerated in whole or part.[151] Such an acceleration will occur if:

- more than 50% of the value of the decedent's interest is withdrawn from the business[152];
- 50% or more of the decedent's interest in the closely held business has been distributed, sold,[153] exchanged, or otherwise disposed of[154];
- certain §303 redemption distributions occur[155];
- the estate has undistributed net income after the fourth taxable year[156]; or
- an installment payment of tax or interest is not made when due.[157]

A number of exceptions to the disposition and withdrawal rules apply. Redemptions under §303 do not count as dispositions or withdrawals provided the amount of property redeemed is applied against the federal estate tax on or before the date the next installment is due or, if earlier, on or before the day that is one year after the redemption date.[158] Withdrawals attributable to postdeath earnings of the business are excluded from the withdrawal rule.[159] Transfers of a closely held business interest under the decedent's will or inter vivos trust, or intestacy laws, will not constitute a disposition.[160] Certain exchanges of stock and corporate reorganizations[161] and changes in business form are also protected from this disposition/acceleration-of-payment rule.[162]

f. Election Procedure

The election under §6166 is to be made on a timely filed estate tax return.[163] This rule necessitates a "protective election" where qualification for the estate tax payment deferral is in doubt.[164] Section 6166(h)(1) permits an election to also be made during the tax return audit process if (1) the estate was originally eligible to make the deferred payment election but did not do so, or (2) the audit adjustments increase the valuation of the closely held business so that the estate then becomes eligible to make the election.[165] This delayed election permits tax payment deferral, however, of only the tax deficiency amount and not the entire unpaid tax amount then attributable to the closely held business.[166]

g. Interest Payable on Amounts Not Paid on Return Due Date

Interest is payable by a taxpayer if the entire tax is not paid on the due date of the return (disregarding extensions).[167] When the §6166 extension applies, the tax imposed on the sum of (a) $1 million (as adjusted for inflation), plus (b) the applicable exclusion amount in effect at the date of death, less (c) the applicable credit amount in effect at the date of death, is subject to a favorable 2% interest rate.[168] The $1 million amount is adjusted for cost-of-living adjustments determined under §1(f)(3) rounded to the next lowest multiple of $10,000.[169] All tax in excess of that amount subject to the 2% interest rate is subject to interest at 45% of the rate in effect from time to time under §6621.[170]

No deduction is allowed for estate tax purposes for any interest paid on the tax extended under §6166.[171] Each tax payment will be deemed to reduce a portion of the tax subject to the 2% interest rate and a portion subject to 45% of the normal §6621 rate. The reduction is in proportion to the amount of tax owed subject to each rate.[172]

h. Lien in Lieu of Executor's Personal Liability or Bond

The IRS may, if it deems necessary, require the executor to furnish a bond for the payment of the estate tax in an amount not more than double the amount of the tax for which an extension is granted.[173] In addition, the executor is personally liable for the payment of the tax unless discharged upon (1) payment of that tax due (excluding extended tax liability amounts) and (2) the furnishing of any bond or security that may be required for the tax not presently due because of an extension of time for payment.[174] Note that the executor can seek a discharge from personal liability and the IRS is to respond to such a request within nine months of the application.[175]

A special lien procedure is provided with respect to the payment of the deferred tax attributable to the closely held business where the executor has made an election under the extended payment provision rules.[176] This lien procedure is available for the tax deferred under §6166. This lien provision is elective. An executor and all parties who have an interest in the property that is to be subject to the lien must file an agreement consenting to the creation of the lien and designating a responsible person to be the agent for the beneficiaries of the estate and the persons who consented to the creation of the lien for purposes of dealing with the IRS.[177] This lien is to apply to real property and other designated assets that can be expected to survive the period for payment of tax under §6166.[178]

Where this lien procedure is followed and a party other than the executor is designated to make estate tax payments and to receive and transmit notices to and from the IRS, the executor would be discharged from personal liability. And, upon application, this other party would also be discharged from personal liability.[179] The IRS will have no authority to require a bond except to the extent of inadequate security for the unpaid principal amount of the tax liability, plus interest.[180] The value of property that the IRS may require under §6324A may not exceed the sum of the deferred principal amount of the taxes plus the aggregate amount of interest to be payable over the first four years of the deferral period.[181] The value of property to be subject to the lien is (1) to be determined as of the due date for the estate tax return and (2) to be reduced by taking into account other prior encumbrances, such as mortgages and liens under the provision relating to farm, etc., valuation recapture.[182]

As referenced above, if the property covered by the agreement or proposed to be covered by the agreement is insufficient, the IRS may accept a bond for the difference.[183] Also, additional lien property can be required by the IRS if the value is initially less or declines below the sum of the unpaid deferred amount of taxes and the "required interest amount." If additional property is not furnished as security within 90 days after notice and demand by the IRS, such failure will accelerate the tax payment.[184]

This special lien for deferred estate tax is in lieu of the regular tax lien under §6324.[185] The §6324A lien must be filed to be valid as against any purchaser, holder of a security interest, mechanic's lien, or judgment lien creditor.[186] Once filed, this lien need not be refiled every 10 years as is required, however, of tax liens generally. This lien arises when the executor is discharged from liability or, if earlier, when the notice is filed.[187] It continues until liability for the deferred amount of taxes is satisfied or becomes unenforceable by reason of the lapse of time.

The lien is inferior to certain "superpriorities."[188] These superpriorities are essentially the same as those relating to most other tax liens. Thus, even though a notice of the §6324A lien has been filed, the lien is not valid against (1) real property tax and special assessment liens (even those that come into existence after the date upon which the notice of lien is filed); (2) a mechanic's lien against real estate for repairs and improvements; or (3) a real property construction or improvement financing agreement, whether the security interest came into existence before or after the tax lien was filed. If the IRS files a notice that payment of the §6166 deferred amount has been accelerated, the §6324A tax lien will take priority over later mechanic's liens or real property construction or improvement financing agreements, but not over later real property tax or special assessment liens.[189]

3. Other Estate Tax Delayed Payment Opportunities

a. Section 6163—Reversions and Remainders

An extension of the time for the payment of estate tax attributable to the gross estate inclusion of the value of a reversionary or remainder interest in property is available.[190] The right to elect this tax payment extension is limited to reversionary and remainder interests.[191] It does not apply, for example, to any post-death installment payments of deferred compensation (although the same policy considerations would seem to be pertinent).[192]

At the election of the executor, the estate tax payment can be postponed until six months after the precedent interest in property is terminated. The postponement is limited to the estate tax attributable to the interest in the property.[193] A further deferral is permitted for no more than three years when the IRS finds "reasonable cause."[194]

b. Section 6161 — Commissioner's Discretion

The IRS can exercise discretion in permitting the deferral of payment of estate tax liabilities in circumstances that do not qualify for postponement under the elective provisions described above.[195] The IRS can extend the time for paying the tax for a "reasonable period" not to exceed 12 months.[196] The effect of a 12-month extension is to make the tax due 21 months after death. Upon the expiration of the extension period, the estate may apply for another extension. The IRS can grant an extension of the time to pay estate taxes for up to 10 years if "reasonable cause" exists.[197]

Reasonable cause might exist, for example, because estate assets cannot produce sufficient present cash to pay estate tax liabilities and a significant economic loss would be inflicted on the estate if these assets were required to be sold at distress prices.[198] The assets might be located in several different jurisdictions and not be otherwise immediately subject to the control of the executor. Alternatively, a claim to substantial assets might not be collectible without litigation, thereby postponing liquidity in the estate and the availability of cash for estate tax payments. The IRS will want to examine all the relevant facts and circumstances to verify that reasonable cause does exist for a payment extension.[199]

F. Alternate Valuation

The estate's representative may elect[200] under §2032 to determine the value of the gross estate by valuing all the property included in the gross estate as of an alternate valuation date.[201] This can enable estate tax savings where the total amount of estate assets depreciates during the period immediately after death.[202] The alternate valuation method may also be used in connection with the valuation for property subject to the GST tax in the case of a direct skip or a taxable termination that occurs as a result of death.[203] Specifically, in the situation of a direct skip occurring as a result of death, the property is valued for GST tax purposes the same as for estate tax purposes (including if the alternate valuation date election is made).[204] Where a taxable termination occurs as a result of an individual's death, the alternate valuation date may be used for GST tax purposes even if the estate does not elect its use for estate tax purposes.[205]

Under the alternate valuation approach, property held by the estate as of the date six months after death is valued as of that date.[206] If, however, property has been "distributed, sold, exchanged, or otherwise disposed of" within six months after the decedent's death, that property is to be valued as of the date of such distribution, sale, exchange, or other disposition.[207] Defining whether such a distribution, sale, or exchange has actually occurred may be subject to dispute.[208]

Notes

1. See 855 T.M., *Estate and Trust Administration—Tax Planning* (Bloomberg BNA).
2. Note that, until formal guidance is issued, the IRS will not rule on whether the assets in a grantor trust receive a §1014 basis adjustment for income tax purposes, at the death of the grantor when those assets are not includible in the grantor's gross estate. Rev. Proc. 2015-37, 2015-26 I.R.B. 1196, *amplifying* Rev. Proc. 2015-3, 2015-1 I.R.B. 129, §5.01.
3. *See* §213(c)(1).
4. §2053. *See* §213(c)(2); Reg. §1.213-1(d). The position of the IRS is that, where a medical expense is claimed as an income tax deduction, the amount below the §213(a) floor for this deduction is not deductible for either income or estate tax purposes. See Rev. Rul. 77-357, 1977-2 C.B. 328 (issued when 3% floor was applicable).
5. The Patient Protection and Affordable Care Act of 2010, Pub. L. No. 111-148, §9013, amended §213 to provide that, effective for taxable years beginning after December 31, 2012, only medical expenses exceeding 10% of adjusted gross income are deductible; under §213(f) if a taxpayer or the taxpayer's spouse is age 65 before the end of the taxable year, then the threshold remains at 7.5% for taxable years ending after December 31, 2012, and before January 1, 2017. For a discussion of the §213 percentage limitation, see 503 T.M., *Deductions: Overview and Conceptual Aspects* (Bloomberg BNA).
6. This discussion also applies to Series EE U.S. savings bonds and similar U.S. obligations received in exchange for Series E bonds, for example, Series H and HH bonds.
7. §454(a). Outside the estate planning context, this election might be made, for example, where the individual taxpayer has a loss (including a net-operating-loss carryforward) that can be used to offset the income, thereby avoiding an income tax liability on the previously accrued interest income.
8. *See* PLR 9024016 (under Reg. §1.691(a)-2(b), unreported increase in value of Series E bonds is income to joint owner when bonds are redeemed, disposed of, or mature, unless §454(a) is elected).
9. *See* Rev. Rul. 68-145, 1968-1 C.B. 203. This election can be made by the executor even though before death the decedent had transferred the bonds to a revocable trust. Rev. Rul. 79-409, 1979-2 C.B. 208.
10. Rev. Proc. 2015-14, 2015-5 I.R.B. 450, §16, identifies the procedure whereby a cash basis taxpayer may revoke an election under §454(a). This revocation is made using a cutoff method, requiring all postchange interest accrual to be included in income upon redemption. Previously, the IRS had a position precluding a revocation of this election. For example, in *West v. United States*, 701 F. Supp. 695 (W.D. Ark. 1988), the administrator elected under §454 to include in the decedent's final income tax return the increase in the Series E bonds' redemption value, believing that the bonds would pass to individuals who had a joint interest in a vault in which the bonds were located. Subsequent to that election, the Arkansas Supreme Court determined that the bonds passed to the state by escheat (*see Newton County v. West,* 293 Ark. 461 [1987]). The administrator attempted to revoke the election and claim a refund for income taxes paid on the interest. The district court held that the election could not be revoked in the absence of

a material mistake of fact and that an election under §454(a) may not be retroactively revoked even when made in good faith reliance on a material mistake of fact. The issue was seen as an attempt to retroactively change a method of accounting, something that generally cannot be done.

11. *See* PLR 9537011.
12. §691(c).
13. Reg. §1.6013-1(d). *See also* §6013(a)(2). See CCA 201049030, permitting this joint return filing even when the IRS has previously filed a substitute for a return for the taxpayer under §6020(b) (since this return does not constitute a "separate return" filed by the taxpayer).
14. The executor may derive some protection from the "innocent spouse" rule under §6015. This rule exempts a spouse from liability, including interest and penalties, for an "understatement of tax attributable to erroneous items" of the other spouse, provided the statutory conditions are satisfied. These conditions include: (1) establishing that the innocent spouse did not know or have reason to know that there was an understatement of tax; and (2) establishing that it would be "inequitable" to hold the innocent spouse liable. *See* §6015(b)(1).
15. Pursuant to Reg. §20.2053-6(f), for estate tax purposes, the executor can deduct the estate's share of the liability on the joint return that is equal to not more than the amount for which the estate would be liable under local law, as between the decedent and his or her spouse, after enforcement of any effective reimbursement or contribution right.
16. Before death, the revocable trust would be merely an agency for the decedent under the grantor trust income tax rules. Even if the revocable trust is to terminate at death, it does become irrevocable at death and may be a taxpayer during the short period when its activities are being concluded unless, under the trust agreement or applicable local law, the trust property is treated as immediately vested in the beneficiaries.
17. See, generally, 852 T.M., *Income Taxation of Trusts and Estates* (Bloomberg BNA).
18. §441(b)(1). Before the Tax Reform Act of 1986 (1986 TRA), Pub. L. No. 105-34, this option was also available to trusts. Section 644(a) (as enacted by the 1986 TRA, Pub. L. No. 105-34, §1403(a), and redesignated by the Taxpayer Relief Act of 1997 (1997 Act), Pub. L. No. 105-34, §507) provides that the taxable year of any trust must be the calendar year. Section 644(b) excepts trusts exempt from tax under §501(a) or described in §4947(a)(1).
19. §441(b), §441(g).
20. §443(a)(2).
21. This election can be made on a late filed return. *See* Rev. Rul. 68-125, 1968-1 C.B. 189 (fiduciary realized that return was delinquent for some months and elected short period first return, thereby minimizing delinquencies). Rev. Rul. 68-125 was obsoleted by T.D. 8996, 67 Fed. Reg. 35,009 (May 17, 2002).
22. The beneficiary's taxable year is calendar year 2016 (funds are distributed from trust to beneficiary during 2016 and income is treated as received by the beneficiary on December 31, 2016). However, he or she will need to examine the possible requirements for making earlier payments because of the estimated tax payment provisions.
23. *See, e.g.*, Reg. §1.662(c)-1.
24. §6654(l)(2)(A).
25. §6654(l)(2)(B).
26. §643(g)(1). *See* Form 1041-T (developed for this purpose and issued annually).

27. §643(g)(1). This election can only be made within 65 days of the close of the trust's year-end. §643(g)(2).
28. §2053.
29. §2054.
30. §642(g).
31. Reg. §20.2053-3.
32. *See Estate of Streeter v. Commissioner,* 491 F.2d 375 (3d Cir. 1974) (substantial expenses incurred by trust [rather than by decedent's estate] in disposing of American memorabilia collection were not deductible under §2053).
33. Reg. §20.2053-3(d)(2).
34. *See* §642(g), as amended by the Tax Reform Act of 1976 (1976 TRA), Pub. L. No. 94-455; H.R. Rep. No. 94-1380, at 71 (1976). These costs were previously deemed not to be an "expense," but rather an "offset" against the selling price in determining the amount of gain. *See Estate of Bray v. Commissioner,* 46 T.C. 577 (1966), *aff'd,* 396 F.2d 452 (6th Cir. 1968); Rev. Rul. 71-173, 1971-1 C.B. 204, *obsoleted by,* Rev. Rul. 89-75, 1989-1 C.B. 319. Consequently, these costs could be deducted on the estate tax return and, additionally, could be used to reduce capital gain as reported on the income tax return of the estate. Under the 1976 TRA, this differing tax treatment was eliminated for items considered "offsets" to the amount realized on the sale of property.
35. This might include interest on deferred estate tax payments. *See* PLR 9449011 (if interest on loan to pay estate taxes is not deductible for estate tax purposes, it is also not deductible for income tax purposes). Whether a loan is reasonably necessary to preserve the estate is a question of fact to be determined by the IRS. To preserve the right to a refund based on future interest expense deductions (after making a §642(g) election), the estate must file a tax refund protective claim on Form 843 before the expiration of the applicable statute of limitations. *See also* TAM 9604002 (including extensive discussion of this subject and concluding that interest paid pursuant to state law on delayed distribution of pecuniary bequest is not deductible administration expense under §2053). See *Estate of Stick v. Commissioner,* T.C. Memo 2010-192, where the Tax Court determined that the estate had sufficient liquidity and, therefore, borrowing (and an interest expense incurred) was not necessary.
36. *See* Reg. §1.642(g)-2. Further, under Rev. Rul. 70-361, 1970-2 C.B. 133, this election to take expenses on the income or estate tax return can be made on a year-by-year basis, as noted in *Estate of Street v. Commissioner,* T.C. Memo 1994-568.
37. *See* §1(e), §1(i), as amended by the American Taxpayer Relief Act of 2012 (ATRA), Pub. L. No. 112-240, §101(b). The 39.6% maximum rate applies to taxable years beginning after 2012. Prior to 2013, there was a maximum rate of 35%. *See* the Tax Relief, Unemployment Insurance Reauthorization, and Job Creation Act of 2010 (2010 TRA), Pub. L. No. 111-312, §101(a) (extending sunset provision in EGTRRA, Pub. L. No. 107-16, §901). Although the $7,500 amount is indexed for inflation under §1(f), this benefit is not significant.
38. Reg. §1.665(a)-0A(d). See the discussion of the throwback rules in Chapter 5, B.5.c.
39. Reg. §1.641(b)-3(a). The period of administration of an estate cannot be unduly prolonged. "If the administration of an estate is unreasonably prolonged, the estate is considered terminated for federal income tax purposes after the expiration of a reasonable period for the performance by the executor of all the duties of administration." *Id.* In Rev. Rul. 76-23, 1976-1 C.B. 264, the IRS ruled that, where the sole reason for

retaining stock of a subchapter S corporation in the estate of a deceased shareholder was to facilitate the deferred payment of the estate tax under §6166, the administration of the estate would not be considered unreasonably prolonged. *See also* PLR 200226031. *Cf. Brown v. United States*, 890 F.2d 1329 (5th Cir. 1989) (IRS properly exercised its authority under Reg. §1.641(b)-3(a) to terminate administration of estate after reasonable time). *See also Estate of Berger v. Commissioner*, T.C. Memo 1990-554.

40. The IRS will not rule whether the period of administration or settlement of an estate is reasonable or unduly prolonged. Rev. Proc. 2015-3, 2015-1 I.R.B. 129, §3.01(73).
41. §642(h)(2); Reg. §1.642(h)-2(a). Any net operating loss carryover (under §172) or capital loss carryover (under §1212) will also be allowed as a deduction to the beneficiary. §642(h)(1); Reg. §1.642(h)-1.
42. This deduction is allowable only in the tax year of the beneficiary in which the estate (or trust) terminates. If the deductions carried over from the estate exceed the beneficiary's gross income for the year of the estate's termination, no carryover of that excess to the beneficiary's next tax year is permitted. Reg. §1.642(h)-2(a). This deduction is also subject to the 2% floor applicable to miscellaneous deductions under §67. For a detailed discussion of the 2% floor on miscellaneous itemized deductions, see 852 T.M., *Income Taxation of Trusts and Estates* (Bloomberg BNA).
43. See the discussion in Chapter 4, B.4., concerning the identification of IRD items.
44. The "renunciation" or "disclaimer" should be distinguished from relinquishments, releases, compromises, and elections. See, generally, 848 T.M., *Disclaimers—Federal Estate, Gift and Generation-Skipping Tax Considerations* (Bloomberg BNA).
45. The transfer, even if treated as a generation-skipping transfer (GST), may not be taxable if within the exemption amount for GST tax.
46. A disclaimer may need to be executed by an attorney-in-fact under a durable power of attorney. *See* PLR 9015017 (permitting such result, premised upon assumption that disclaimer would be valid under state law recognizing that representative of incapacitated person has right to disclaim property).
47. This assumes that the last will provides for this asset disposition and will be so interpreted under local law.
48. Since these assets would go directly for the benefit of grandchildren, the applicability of the GST tax must be examined in this situation.
49. This can often be relevant where a decedent died with a will that used a specific, smaller unified credit exclusion equivalent amount, rather than a formula provision to use the particular credit amount available for the year of death under §2010(c).
50. This might happen, for example, where the husband dies intestate and the mother, son, and daughter would each receive a one-third interest under the applicable state laws of descent and distribution. To enable the marital deduction to be recognized, no restrictions should be imposed on this action, for example, that the surviving spouse commits to subsequently transfer these assets to the disclaimants.
51. *See* §678(d).
52. *See also Estate of Boyd v. Commissioner*, 819 F.2d 170 (7th Cir. 1987) (child was permitted to disclaim provisions of tax clause in his favor, thereby preserving marital bequest).
53. *See* Rev. Rul. 90-45, 1990-1 C.B. 175 (surviving spouse elected against decedent's will for statutory share and then made qualified disclaimer of undivided portion of that statutory share). *See also* PLR 200109041, PLR 200541038.

54. *See, e.g.,* PLR 200503024 (surviving spouse's disclaimer of her survivorship interest in joint brokerage account was qualified despite her withdrawals from account after death of other spouse; her withdrawals were attributable to her contributions into account).
55. See 848 T.M., *Disclaimers—Federal Estate, Gift and Generation-Skipping Tax Considerations* (Bloomberg BNA); 847 T.M., *Disclaimers—State Law Considerations* (Bloomberg BNA).
56. §2518(b). Before enactment of specific disclaimer rules in the 1976 TRA, Pub. L. No. 94-455, the basic federal gift tax requirements pertinent to making a renunciation immune from gift tax applicability were: (1) local law had to permit the renunciation; (2) the specific renunciation had to be effective under local law; (3) the renunciation had to occur within a reasonable time after learning of the existence of the transfer; and (4) the refusal had to be unequivocal. A renunciation in favor of the surviving spouse was explicitly permitted under the estate tax marital deduction provision. *See* former §2056(d)(2). A similar renunciation of a power of appointment was provided for in §2041. Problems arose because variations in local law could cause significantly different federal gift tax treatment. To achieve uniform treatment, definitive rules concerning disclaimers were provided in the 1976 TRA. Contrary to Congressional intent, the 1976 rules, as amended by the Revenue Act of 1978 (1978 RA), Pub. L. No. 95-600, did not provide uniform treatment of disclaimers under federal estate and gift tax law. Because local disclaimer laws differ, identical refusals to accept property were often being treated differently for federal estate and gift tax purposes, depending upon the applicable local statute. Accordingly, under the Economic Recovery Tax Act of 1981 (ERTA), Pub. L. No. 97-34, Congress authorized certain disclaimants to make the necessary transfers without regard to any requirements of a local law disclaimer provision. A transfer of the transferor's entire interest in property to the person(s) who would have otherwise received the property if an effective disclaimer under applicable local law had been made is treated as a valid disclaimer for purposes of the federal estate and gift taxes provided (1) the transfer is timely made and (2) the transferor has not accepted the interest or any of its benefits. *See* §2518(c)(3).
57. Section 2518 does not describe the specific requirements for a written disclaimer. Reg. §25.2518-2(b)(1) specifies that the instrument should identify the particular assets disclaimed and be signed by either the disclaimant or the disclaimant's legal representative. Also, although §2518(c)(3), as noted above, permits certain disclaimants to make qualified disclaimers without complying with local law provisions, compliance with local technical requirements (such as acknowledgements and recording) can still be important as local law may determine if an effective transfer has been made or if the disclaimant was authorized to make the disclaimer. *See, e.g.,* Rev. Rul. 90-110, 1990-2 C.B. 209.
58. An extension of time to file the estate tax return does not extend the time to make a qualified disclaimer. *Fitzgerald v. United States*, 94-1 USTC ¶60,152 (W.D. La. 1993). In accordance with the construction by the IRS of §2518 as requiring a disclaimer to be valid under state law as well as federal law, the nine-month period is a maximum time period but not a minimum period. If state law requires that the disclaimer be made within a shorter period, the shorter period is controlling (unless an effective transfer under §2518(c)(3) is made). The disclaimer period is determined with reference to the transfer creating the interest in the disclaimant. Reg. §25.2518-2(c)(3)(i). With respect to lifetime transfers, the transfer creating the interest occurs on the date a completed gift is made and, with respect to testamentary transfers or transfers that became irrevocable

at death, on the date of death. *Id.* With respect to a general power of appointment, the transfer relating to the holder occurs at creation of the power and, with respect to appointees or takers in default, occurs when the power is exercised or released or lapses. *Id.* The transfer with respect to a special power of appointment occurs when it is created. *Id.* Where the transfer is for the life of an income beneficiary with succeeding interests in other persons, both the life tenant and other takers must disclaim within nine months after the "original transfer creating the interest." *Id.* If the trust settlor retains the power to revoke or alter the trust, a contingent remainder beneficiary has nine months from the date of the trust settlor's death to disclaim the interest in the trust. PLR 8911028. In PLR 9001062, the IRS ruled that, where a transfer to an inter vivos trust is not a §2511 completed gift, the nine-month disclaimer period begins on the date of the transferor's death, not when the property was placed in the trust. *See also Estate of Fleming v. Commissioner,* T.C. Memo 1989-675 (disclaimer of bequest not qualified when filed nine months and three weeks after transferor's death). The IRS formerly took the position that the period within which a joint tenant must disclaim his or her interest in property received by surviving the other joint tenant begins on the date the joint tenancy was created, not on the date the other tenant died. *See Jewett v. Commissioner,* 455 U.S. 305 (1982); *Estate of O'Brien v. Commissioner,* T.C. Memo 1988-240. *But see Kennedy v. Commissioner,* 804 F.2d 1332 (7th Cir. 1986); *McDonald v. Commissioner,* 89 T.C. 293 (1987), *rev'd and rem'd,* 853 F.2d 1494 (8th Cir. 1988), *on remand,* T.C. Memo 1989-140; *Estate of Dancy v. Commissioner,* 89 T.C. 550 (1987), *rev'd and rem'd,* 872 F.2d 84 (4th Cir. 1989) (in case of revocable joint tenancies, transfer occurs for §2518 purposes upon death of joint tenant); PLR 8916070, PLR 8750023 (disclaimer made by surviving joint tenant of interest in joint brokerage account qualified because disclaimant never withdrew money from account and, thus, never accepted any benefits from account or income). In AOD 1990-06, the Chief Counsel's Office stated that it would no longer litigate the timeliness of a §2518 disclaimer of a survivorship interest where the joint tenant, under local law, has the right to sever the joint tenancy or to partition the property, thereby acquiescing in *McDonald. See also* PLR 9214022, PLR 9113011 (surviving spouse's timely disclaimer of fractional share of her survivorship interest in brokerage account held jointly with decedent qualifies); TAM 9140005 (surviving spouse's disclaimer of severable interest in joint bank account qualifies where disclaimant has not withdrawn funds from nor received benefits of portion disclaimed).

59. Reg. §25.2518-2(d)(3) indicates that any actions taken with regard to an interest in property by a beneficiary or a custodian before the beneficiary's 21st birthday will not be an acceptance by the beneficiary of the interest. *See* PLR 9436041 (receipt of income distributions before age 21 did not bar disclaimer of principal upon reaching age 21); PLR 201001007 (similar).
60. A prospective disclaimant should be careful not to take any proprietary action with regard to the property with respect to which he or she intends to disclaim (e.g., using the property, accepting income from the property or directing others to act as to the property) nor should he or she enter into any type of agreement whereby he or she receives consideration for his or her disclaimed interest. Reg. §25.2518-2(d)(1), §25.2518-2(d)(4) *Exs. (2)–(6).* In *Estate of Monroe v. Commissioner,* 104 T.C. 352 (1995), *rev'd in part,* 124 F.3d 699 (5th Cir. 1997), the Tax Court concluded that 29 legatees who requested to disclaim bequests under a will received consideration by receiving "gifts" shortly after their disclaimers. This suggests that the disclaimant should provide documentation that

he or she has not received and is not contemplating receiving any consideration for making the disclaimer. However, the Fifth Circuit reversed the Tax Court as to 23 of the 29 disclaimants, finding that an implied promise of a benefit in exchange for a disclaimer or the disclaimant's mere expectation of a benefit is not consideration that would invalidate the disclaimer. A joint tenant will not be considered to have accepted a survivorship interest in a personal residence even if he or she resides in the property before making the disclaimer. Reg. §25.2518-2(d)(1); PLR 9135043. In PLR 9210014, the IRS ruled that a trust beneficiary's disclaimer was qualified where she quickly withdrew a request for a distribution from the trust, noting that the withdrawn request did not constitute acceptance of the property or any benefits from the property. The exercise of a power of appointment to any extent by the donee of the power is an acceptance of its benefits. Reg. §25.2518-2(d)(1); Rev. Rul. 76-156, 1976-1 C.B. 292. Acts by a beneficiary who is also a fiduciary to preserve or maintain disclaimed property are not treated as acceptance. Reg. §25.2518-2(d)(2). A fiduciary who is also a disclaimant cannot retain discretionary power to direct the enjoyment of the disclaimed interest. Further, a disclaimer by a fiduciary will only be effective if the disclaimant has the fiduciary authority to make the disclaimer. Rev. Rul. 90-110, 1990-2 C.B. 209.

61. This "pass to" requirement injects the element of state law into the determination of whether there is a qualified disclaimer. For interests created in taxable transfers before 1982, the regulations state that a disclaimer that otherwise satisfies the requirements of §2518 and the regulations can be qualified even if the disclaimer is not effective to change the ownership of the property from the disclaimant to another person under local law. For this rule to apply, the disclaimed property must be transferred, under local law, as a result of the attempted disclaimer to another person without any direction on the disclaimant's part. Reg. §25.2518-1(c)(1)(i). A disclaimer that is void or that is voided by the disclaimant's creditors is not a qualified disclaimer. Reg. §25.2518-1(c)(2). However, a disclaimer is not disqualified under §2518 merely because it is voidable by the disclaimant's creditors. *Id.*
62. As originally enacted, §2518 required that the disclaimed interest pass only to a person other than the disclaimant. The 1978 RA, Pub. L. No. 95-60, amended §2518 to specify that a disclaimer by a surviving spouse can be effective where the disclaimed property passes to a trust in which the surviving spouse has an income interest. *See* Reg. §25.2518-2(e)(5) *Ex. (4).*
63. The "without direction" requirement can be a substantial impediment to post-mortem estate planning by surviving spouses. The retention by the surviving spouse in the non-marital trust of a special power to appoint among designated beneficiaries will result in an ineffective disclaimer. Reg. §25.2518-2(e)(5) *Ex. (5).* The retention of a power to direct enjoyment of the disclaimed property in a taxable transfer is not prohibited. Reg. §25.2518-2(e)(2). Thus, a retention by the spouse of a power to invade principal either under a five-and-five power, under an ascertainable standard, or through a trustee other than the surviving spouse should not constitute a prohibited power. Reg. §25.2518-2(e)(5) *Ex. (6).*
64. *See* §2518(a). *See, e.g.,* TAM 200437032 (potential estate beneficiary's taking of religious vow of poverty did not cause property in estate to be treated as going directly to charity, thereby enabling estate tax charitable contributions deduction).
65. H.R. Rep. No. 94-1380, at 67 (1976).
66. Reg. §25.2518-1(b).

67. For example, in TAM 8926001, the National Office indicated in an intestacy situation that, in a state having no statutory or decisional law specifically concerning the distribution of disclaimed property passing by intestacy, the state's highest court would follow the well-established rule that property subject to a disclaimer passes as if the disclaimant had predeceased the decedent. *See also* Uniform Disclaimer of Property Interests Act (2002) (part of Uniform Probate Code); PLR 200406038 (example of effective disclaimer made in intestacy context).
68. §2518(c)(1). *See, e.g.,* PLR 9437029 (amount of disclaimer was based on payment of specified amount of tax in decedent's estate), PLR 9435014 (partial disclaimer was based on zero-tax formula). In PLR 8514095, a formula-based disclaimer of an undivided portion of the interest left to the taxpayer by intestacy was treated as constituting a qualified disclaimer, provided the disclaimed amount was segregated from the remainder of the bequest.
69. Reg. §25.2518-3(b).
70. *Id.*; Reg. §25.2518-3(d) *Ex. (2).*
71. §2518(b)(4).
72. Reg. §25.2518-3(a)(1)(ii), §25.2518-3(d) *Exs. (1), (3).*
73. Reg. §25.2518-3(c).
74. Reg. §25.2518-3(a)(2). All interests in the corpus of a trust are ordinarily treated as a single interest and, if so treated, to have a qualified disclaimer, the disclaimant must disclaim all such interests or an undivided portion. Thus, if a disclaimant has a testamentary power of appointment over the trust corpus, coupled with an inter vivos power to invade or an interest as a discretionary appointee of corpus, both such interests must be disclaimed. *Id. See also* Reg. §25.2518-3(d) *Ex. (9). Walshire v. United States,* 288 F.3d 342 (8th Cir. 2002), held valid Reg. §25.2518-3(b), which prevents a disclaimer of a remainder interest, while retaining a life estate, from being considered a qualified disclaimer, but allows vertical divisions of an interest as opposed to horizontal divisions.
75. Reg. §25.2518-3(a)(2), §25.2518-3(d) *Exs. (5)-(7).*
76. See PLR 201515056, dealing with multiple issues in the disclaimer context: W had transferred stocks, bonds, and other securities to H's account during lifetime. H disclaimed specific securities within nine months of the transfers, including those added to a trust of which H was co-trustee and beneficiary. Under the trust agreement, the property disclaimed by H was to be placed into a separate trust where H would have no rights to income or principal, or hold any powers. The IRS ruled that, under the facts as specified, H did not accept any benefits from the disclaimed assets because the securities disclaimed were severable assets. Further, the IRS ruled that the provisions in the trust would prevent H from having the power to direct the enjoyment of the disclaimed assets, despite H's role as trustee and other administrative powers over the trust assets.
77. Reg. §25.2518-2(e)(5) *Ex. (5). See also Goudy v. United States,* 86-2 USTC ¶13,690 (D. Or. 1986), *rev'd in unpub. opin.*, 851 F.2d 360 (9th Cir. 1988) (Ninth Circuit holding that partial disclaimer of general power of appointment was not complete and qualified disclaimer since it was redirection of disclaimed property to persons other than those taking in default).
78. Reg. §25.2518-3(d) *Exs. (9)-(12).*
79. §2518(c)(3).
80. The applicable tax rules are prescribed in Rev. Rul. 64-225, 1964-2 C.B. 15, and Rev. Rul. 66-167, 1966-1 C.B. 20.

81. Claiming the fee paid as a tax deduction will obviously be inconsistent with an intent to serve on a gratuitous basis. *See Breidert v. Commissioner,* 50 T.C. 844 (1968), *acq.* 1969-2 C.B. 24; Rev. Rul. 66-167; PLR 200340015 (failure by trustees to pay themselves trustee fees authorized by trust was not to be treated as addition to trust for GST tax purposes).
82. See, generally, 809 T.M., *Estate Planning for Owners of Closely Held Business Interests* (Bloomberg BNA).
83. *See* §302(b)(3). Note that the applicability of all the "attribution of ownership" rules must be eliminated in this context. *See* §302(c)(2), §318.
84. This assumes that the redemption transaction is treated as a sale or exchange rather than as a dividend distribution.
85. No requirement exists that the estate must actually effectuate the redemption to pay estate taxes or that the redemption proceeds must be actually used for this purpose.
86. Proceeds of a redemption may be treated as a dividend under §301. The exceptions of §302(b) (which permit sale or exchange treatment) will not necessarily apply to this stock redemption. Consequently, §303 provides special relief in this context.
87. Previously this tax-basis step-up at death did not occur for shares held in a foreign personal holding company but, with the repeal of the foreign personal holding company rules in the American Jobs Creation Act of 2004 (AJCA), Pub. L. No. 108-357, §413(a), this limitation has been eliminated for decedents dying in 2005 and thereafter. *See* §1014(b)(5), as amended by AJCA, Pub. L. No. 108-357, §413(c)(18).
88. The corporation will realize gain if appreciated property is distributed to the shareholder in a §303 redemption. §311(b). Similarly, if the corporation distributes an asset subject to a liability or the redeeming shareholder assumes a corporate liability that exceeds the corporation's adjusted basis for the asset, the corporation realizes gain. *See* §311(b)(2). That gain when realized will increase the earnings and profits account of the distributing corporation.
89. §303(b)(2)(A).
90. §303(b)(2)(B).
91. *Id.*
92. *See Estate of Byrd v. Commissioner,* 388 F.2d 223 (5th Cir. 1967) (stock owned by decedent to be included in estate for purposes of satisfying percentage requirements). In Rev. Rul. 84-76, 1984-1 C.B. 91, a redemption of stock not actually owned by a decedent at death did not qualify for §303 redemption treatment even though such stock was included in the decedent's gross estate under §2035. The stock was includible in the decedent's gross estate, however, for the purpose of determining whether the percentage requirements for §303 eligibility were satisfied.
93. §303(a)(1).
94. §303(a)(2). If administration expenses are claimed on the fiduciary income tax return, a deduction would be foreclosed by §642(g) on the estate tax return. Such expenses would be "allowable" within the meaning of §303, however. Rev. Rul. 56-449, 1956-2 C.B. 180, Rev. Rul. 80-367, 1980-2 C.B. 386.
95. §303(b)(3).
96. This discussion also assumes that the other shareholders of the corporation will actually be agreeable to the redemption of the corporation's shares for this purpose. Some may decline to permit the redemption because of the impact on corporate cash availability. This dilemma could perhaps be solved through the issuance of an installment note in the redemption transaction. Other shareholders may prefer the redemption to occur because

the decedent's percentage ownership interest (otherwise received by the estate beneficiaries) will be diluted as a result of this redemption.

97. Section 303 is also not available to enable sale or exchange treatment to holders of stock acquired by purchase. The term "purchase" includes stock acquired from the estate in satisfaction of a specific monetary bequest. Reg. §1.303-2(f).
98. *See* §303(b)(1); Reg. §1.303-2(e).
99. §303(b)(1)(A). Note that this period is three years plus 90 days from the later of the due date of the return (not including extensions of time to file) or the date upon which the return was actually filed. Rev. Rul. 73-204, 1973-1 C.B. 170.
100. §303(b)(1)(B). This assumes that the litigation is not merely for purposes of extending the period during which a §303 redemption can be accomplished. *See* Reg. §1.303-2(e).
101. §303(b)(1)(C).
102. *See* H.R. Rep. No. 94-1380, at 35 (1976).
103. §303(b)(4).
104. After death, during the estate probate process, the executor may wish to assure that a proposed redemption transaction will be eligible for §303 treatment. The IRS will rule on §303 eligibility (although the taxpayer will need to make various factual representations to assure eligibility). *See, e.g.*, PLR 200327016.
105. If, however, the value of the stock is significantly appreciating while the other assets have limited appreciation potential, a dilemma exists concerning whether to risk incurring an increased estate tax cost on the high value stock.
106. Gain recognition on the transfer of appreciated property into the corporation can be avoided if the §351 nonrecognition rule applies. This transfer can either be for the receipt of additional shares or as a contribution to the capital of the corporation.
107. See the discussion of the use of recapitalization in estate planning in Chapter 10, B.2. A recapitalization might also be consummated after death to accomplish this objective. Any §306 taint resulting from a preferred stock bailout would be eliminated to the extent of the stock redeemed under a §303 redemption. *See* Reg. §1.303-2(d). An example of the application of a postdeath recapitalization is found in Rev. Rul. 87-132, 1987-2 C.B. 82. In this situation, an estate and an unrelated individual, Y, equally owned the 300 outstanding shares of voting common stock of X Corp. The estate satisfied the requirements for a §303 redemption. In order to maintain the 50–50 voting power equilibrium, X first issued 10 shares of a new class of nonvoting stock on each share of common stock outstanding. Immediately thereafter, X redeemed 1,000 shares of the nonvoting common stock from the estate for cash. The IRS applied §303(c), concluding that the new nonvoting stock, by reason of §305 and §307, had a basis determined by the basis of the old voting common stock. The IRS observed that, although the issuance of a new class of stock and redemption by the estate were part of the same plan, favorable treatment under §303 was nevertheless appropriate to carry out the Congressional intent in enacting §303 (i.e., §303(c) is a remedial provision expanding the application of §303 to the redemption of replacement stock that actually represents the same stock as that owned at death).
108. The higher value would result in a higher income tax basis (determined under §1014) and, therefore, would mitigate the effect of later capital gain realization. The risk must be avoided, however, of the possible application of an "accuracy-related penalty" due to an excessive valuation being claimed.
109. See, generally, 832 T.M., *Estate Tax Payments and Liabilities: Sections 6161 and 6166* (Bloomberg BNA). Note that provision is not limited to a decedent's interest as a shareholder in a corporation but includes others types of business interests.

110. Before the 1976 TRA, Pub. L. No. 94-455, under then-existing §6166, a 10-year extension for payment of estate tax was available where the value of the closely held business exceeded 35% of the value of the gross estate or 50% of the taxable estate. This provision was retained when the 1976 TRA was enacted, redesignating that version of §6166 as former §6166A. In addition, a revised §6166 was enacted whereby the estate tax attributable to the decedent's interest in a farm or other closely held business could be paid over a 15-year period, with all principal payments being deferred for 5 years and being thereafter payable in equal annual installments over the following 10 years. Thereafter, former §6166A was repealed by ERTA, Pub. L. No. 97-34, and §6166 was expanded.
111. Further, during any period of significant price inflation in the economy, this tax deferral permits the estate to pay the estate tax with "cheaper" dollars.
112. Rev. Rul. 86-38, 1986-1 C.B. 296, described the availability of a credit for state death taxes (previously allowable under former §2011) if the state death tax was paid in installments over a period of more than four years where the estate elected to pay the federal tax liability in 10 annual installments. Note that the state death credit was repealed for estates of decedents dying after 2004 and former §2011 was struck from the Code as deadwood by the Tax Increase Prevention Act of 2014, Pub. L. No. 113-295, Div. A, §221(a)(95)(B).
113. The objective is to either increase the numerator or decrease the denominator of the formula described below. For example, the predeath conversion of debt owing by the business to the owner into an equity interest in the business will increase the value of the closely held business interest held by the decedent at the time of death.
114. §6166. The Tax Court has jurisdiction to issue declaratory judgments as to an estate's initial and continuing eligibility for §6166 deferral. This remedy is available to estates of decedents dying after August 5, 1997. §7479, as added by the 1997 Act, Pub. L. No. 105-34, §505. Technical amendments to §7479(a) enacted by the IRS Restructuring and Reform Act of 1998 (1998 IRS Reform Act), Pub. L. No. 105-206, §6007(d), clarify that the Tax Court's jurisdiction extends to determining which businesses in an estate (whether or not part of the probate estate) are eligible for the deferral.
115. §6166(a)(1), §6166(a)(3).
116. §6166(f)(1). *See* Rev. Rul. 89-32, 1989-1 C.B. 307.
117. §6166(f) (cross-referencing §6601). For estates of decedents dying before 1998, the interest charged on the first $345,800 in estate tax (which is attributable to $1 million in value of an interest in a closely held business) was 4%. Pre-1997 Act §6601(j).
118. Section 6601(j), as amended by the 1997 Act, Pub. L. No. 105-34, §503. Under §6601(j)(3), the $1 million amount is indexed for inflation after 1998, rounded to the next lowest multiple of $10,000. In the years 2004 and 2005, the 2% interest rate applied to the tax on a closely held business interest valued (before this inflation adjustment) at between $1.5 million and $2.5 million; during 2006, 2007 and 2008, this range was between $2 million and $3 million, and in the year 2009, the rate applied on the closely held business valued between $3.5 million and $4.5 million. *See* §2010(c) (for amounts sheltered by unified credit each year). For the §6601(j) inflation-adjusted amount for recent years, see Worksheet 1.
119. §6166(b)(7)(A)(iii), §6166(b)(8)(A)(iii), as amended by the 1998 IRS Reform Act, Pub. L. No. 105-206, §6007(c).
120. *See* §6601(j)(1)(B), §6621.

121. §2053(c)(1)(D), §163(k), as enacted by the 1997 Act, Pub. L. No. 105-34, effective for estates of decedents dying after 1997. Estates of decedents dying before 1998 could elect to apply the 2% rate to installments due after 1997 that were previously subject to the 4% interest rate and forego the interest deduction. 1997 Act, Pub. L. No. 105-34, §503(d)(2). *See* Rev. Proc. 98-15, 1998-4 I.R.B. 25 (description of election, which was to be made before 1999).
122. *See, e.g.*, CCA 201226027 (property claimed for §6166 purposes as subject to this eligibility was not actually part of closely held business and, therefore, deferred tax amount was reduced).
123. §6166(a)(2).
124. §6166(a)(1).
125. §6166(b)(6).
126. §6166(c).
127. *Id.* This includes ownership both as tenants by the entirety and tenants in common.
128. §6166(b)(1)(A). Only assets actually used in the proprietorship business will qualify. Reg. §20.6166A-2(c)(2). The pre-ERTA (Pub. L. No. 97-34) regulations issued under former §6166A have not been redesignated to reflect ERTA's repeal of former §6166A or its enactment of the revised §6166. *See* Chapter 12, E.2.a. For the position of the IRS on the valuation of proprietorship assets, see Rev. Rul. 80-202, 1980-2 C.B. 363.
129. Note that this qualification is based on a partnership "capital interest" rather than a "profits interest" in a partnership.
130. §6166(b)(1)(B). In contrast to the requirement for the proprietorship, all assets of the partnership or corporation need not be utilized in the carrying on of a trade or business. Reg. §20.6166A-2(c)(2). This suggests the following planning opportunities: Where an individual has an active business in corporate or partnership form, investment assets can be contributed to the entity so as to gain deferral with regard to the estate tax attributable to these assets. Alternatively, such assets together with the active business could be contributed to a new corporation or partnership. An individual with a sole proprietorship holding investment assets may consider a change in business form to a partnership (which necessitates having a partner) or a corporation so as to qualify those assets for §6166. Effective for decedents dying after 2001, EGTRRA, Pub. L. No. 107-16, §571, increased the §6166(b)(1)(B)(ii) maximum number of partners in a partnership from 15 to 45. Under the 2010 TRA, Pub. L. No. 111-312, §101(a) (extending sunset provision in EGTRRA, Pub. L. No. 107-16, §901), EGTRRA's increase in the allowable partners applies to estates of decedents dying in 2010–2012. ATRA, Pub. L. No. 112-240, §101(a), made the increase from 15 to 45 partners permanent for estates of decedents dying after 2012.
131. Note that this test is based on fair market value, rather than on voting power, of voting stock. Presumably this does not include stock eligible to vote only on limited issues such as mergers and should not normally include nonvoting preferred stock.
132. §6166(b)(1)(C). Effective for decedents dying after 2001, EGTRRA, Pub. L. No. 107-16, §571, increased the §6166(b)(1)(C)(ii) maximum number of shareholders in a corporation from 15 to 45.
133. *See* §6166(b)(2). *See also* §2035(c)(2) (preserving three-year inclusion rule for purposes of §6166 qualification), §2035(c)(1)(C) (relating to special liens under subchapter C of chapter 64, which include §6324A liens for §6166 deferred estate taxes).

134. §6166(b)(2)(B).
135. §6166(b)(2)(C). Ownership attribution for trust beneficiaries is limited to those having present interests.
136. Members of the family for this purpose are as defined in §267(c)(4). *See* §6166(b)(2)(D).
137. §6166(b)(2)(D). Section 6166(b)(7) provides that, if the executor so elects, the ownership interest rules will be applied by reference to partnership interests and stock not readily tradable owned by the decedent and his or her family. If this election is made, the special §6601(j) 2% interest rate is not available. *See* §6166(b)(7)(A)(iii), as amended by the 1998 IRS Reform Act, Pub. L. No. 105-206, §6007(c) (clarifying that deferred payments of estate tax on holding companies and non-readily-tradable business interests do not qualify for 2% interest rate but instead are subject to interest rate equal to 45% of regular deficiency rate); PLR 9301014.
138. §6166(b)(1); Reg. §20.6166A-2(c)(1). The IRS will not rule on requests involving §6166 where there is no decedent. Rev. Proc. 2015-3, 2015-1 I.R.B. 129, §3.01(109).
139. *See* PLR 8514037 (when 95% of decedent's estate consisted of promissory notes secured by vendors' liens representing unpaid balance from sale of plots of land, ownership of those notes did not qualify as interest in closely held business). There is a special election available in this context, as described below.
140. *See* Rev. Rul. 2006-34, 2006-26 I.R.B. 1172, where the IRS provided a list of factors to use in determining whether a decedent's real estate interest qualifies as a closely held business for purposes of §6166. Rev. Rul. 75-365, 1975-2 C.B. 471 (rental properties and notes managed by decedent) was revoked. *See* PLR 200845023, PLR 200842012.
141. *See* Rev. Rul. 2006-34, 2006-26 I.R.B. 1172 (revoking Rev. Rul. 75-367's conclusion that rentals of single family homes were not active trade or business for §6166(b)(1) purposes). Various PLRs have been issued applying these rules, and the IRS might rule in response to an inquiry in this context. *See, e.g.,* PLR 200340012, PLR 200339043 (IRS responded to inquiries concerning qualifying status for §6166 purposes). *See also Estate of Heffley v. Commissioner,* 884 F.2d 279 (7th Cir. 1989) (estate did not qualify for installment payment eligibility because farm operation was not family business).
142. §6166(b)(3).
143. §6166(b)(4).
144. §6166(b)(8).
145. §6616(b)(8)(A)(ii).
146. *See* §6166(b)(8)(A)(iii), as amended by the 1998 IRS Reform Act, Pub. L. No. 105-206, §6007(c) (clarifying that deferred payments of estate tax on holding companies and non-readily-tradable business interests do not qualify for 2% interest rate but instead are subject to rate equal to 45% of regular deficiency rate).
147. §6166(b)(8)(B). Effective for decedents dying after 2001, EGTRRA, Pub. L. No. 107-16, §572, added to §6166(b)(8)(B) a provision clarifying that only the stock of the holding companies, not that of the operating subsidiaries, must be non-readily-tradable in order to qualify for installment payment of estate tax. *See* §6166(b)(8)(B)(ii). This provision specifies that an estate with a qualifying property interest held through holding companies must make all installment payments (including principal and interest) over 5 (rather than 10) years. *Id.* Under the 2010 TRA, Pub. L. No. 111-312, §101(a) (extending sunset provision in EGTRRA, Pub. L. No. 107-16, §901), EGTRRA's amendment to §6166(b)(8)(B) applies to estates of decedents dying in 2010–2012. ATRA, Pub. L.

No. 112-240, §101(a), made this provision permanent for estates of decedents dying after 2012.

148. §6166(b)(9)(A), §6166(b)(9)(B).
149. §6166(b)(10), as added by EGTRRA, Pub. L. No. 107-16, §572, effective for decedents dying after 2001. Under the 2010 TRA, Pub. L. No. 111-312, §101(a) (extending sunset provision in EGTRRA, Pub. L. No. 107-16, §901), §6166(b)(10) applies to estates of decedents dying in 2010-2012. ATRA, Pub. L. No. 112-240, §101(a), made this provision permanent for estates of decedents dying after 2012.
150. §6166(b)(10)(A)(ii), §6166(b)(10)(A)(iii).
151. §6166(g).
152. §6166(g)(1)(A)(ii). *See* Rev. Rul. 75-401, 1975-2 C.B. 473 (corporation's payment of ordinary cash dividend consisting of entire earnings and profits accumulated before and after death of corporation's sole shareholder was withdrawal of money or other property within meaning of §6166(g)(1)(A) to extent attributable to earnings and profits accumulated before decedent's death).
153. See Rev. Rul. 66-62, 1966-1 C.B. 272, specifying that a change in business form does not cause an acceleration of the tax; PLR 8922035 (indicating that liquidation or merger of subsidiaries into holding company solely owned by estate did not trigger acceleration of estate tax); PLR 201403012 (restructuring of business from general partnership to LLC would not trigger acceleration of §6166 estate tax installments).
154. §6166(g)(1)(A)(ii). In Rev. Rul. 89-4, 1989-1 C.B. 298, a decedent owned farm property consisting of two tracts, both encumbered by mortgages. The executor properly elected special use valuation under §2032A and deferral of tax under §6166. A few years later, when the farm had financial difficulties, one of the tracts was sold for $700,000, and the proceeds were used to pay the entire debt on both parcels ($700,000). The IRS concluded that there was no disposition for purposes of §6166 that would trigger acceleration of deferral of tax, explaining that the sale of property followed by a discharge in debt of an amount equal to the sales proceeds did not change the net value of the farm. The IRS added, however, that if the sales proceeds exceed the amount of debt that is discharged, the excess is treated as a withdrawal of funds from the business under §6166(g)(1)(A), that would be added to other dispositions to determine whether sales, exchanges or other dispositions exceed 50% of the value of the farm, an event which would trigger acceleration of estate tax. Further, a disposition did occur for recapture of the tax under §2032A(c). *See* PLR 200321006 (lease of certain farm properties did not constitute disposition for these purposes).
155. *See* §6166(g)(1)(B); Rev. Rul. 86-54, 1986-1 C.B. 356, *modifying* Rev. Rul. 72-188, 1972-1 C.B. 383 (permitting cumulative approach and redemption-by-redemption approach to be used interchangeably for determining application of this provision). For a complete discussion of these revenue rulings, see 832 T.M., *Estate Tax Payments and Liabilities: Sections 6161 and 6166* (Bloomberg BNA).
156. §6166(g)(2); Reg. §20.6166A-3(b). The undistributed net income rule does not operate to accelerate the entire unpaid portion of the deferred estate tax. This accumulation of income rule necessitates, however, the required payment of the accumulated income against the estate tax then owing.
157. §6166(g)(3)(A). If payment of principal and interest is made within six months of the due date, acceleration will not occur. Availability of the 2% interest rate (and the higher rate on tax above $1 million, as adjusted for inflation) is lost, however, and a 5%

per month penalty is incurred. §6166(g)(3)(B). *See* Rev. Rul. 85-43, 1985-1 C.B. 356 (for purposes of avoiding acceleration of federal estate tax installment payments under §6166(g)(1)(B), application of state death tax credit to reduce federal estate tax liability was not equivalent to amount of tax paid).

158. §6166(g)(1)(B).
159. Reg. §20.6166A-3(d)(1), §20.6166A-3(e)(1); Rev. Rul. 75-401, 1975-2 C.B. 473.
160. §6166(g)(1)(D). This exception further extends to transfers at death from the original transferee provided the subsequent transferee is a family member, without regard to the date of death of the original decedent. *Id.*
161. §6166(g)(1)(C).
162. Reg. §20.6166A-3(e)(2). *See* PLR 201403012, PLR 200129018 (citing Rev. Rul. 66-62, 1966-1 C.B. 272, which holds that where change in operation of business from corporate form to unincorporated form does not materially alter business or interest of estate in business, change does not cause termination of installment election under §6166 that was otherwise available to estate).
163. §6166(d). See *Estate of Woodbury v. Commissioner*, T.C. Memo 2014-66, where an estate's election was invalid because not made on a timely filed estate tax return and, further, the estate did not substantially comply with the election requirements concerning the providing of information. The requests for extensions did not include either the enumeration of the properties shown on the estate tax return that constituted the closely held business interests, or the statement of the facts that form the basis for the executor's conclusion that the estate did qualify for the payment of the estate tax in installments.
164. §6166(d); Reg. §20.6166-1(d). A timely filed election will automatically include any deficiency asserted on audit that is attributable to the closely held business interest.
165. This election is not available if the deficiency is due to negligence, to intentional disregard of rules and regulations, or to fraud with intent to evade tax.
166. §6166(h)(3). *See* CCA 201302037 (where no election is made when return is filed and, later, deficiency is determined, §6166(h) election for certain deficiencies only allows that portion of deficiency attributable to closely-held business to be paid in installments).
167. *See* §6601(a).
168. §6601(j)(2).
169. §6601(j)(3). See Chapter 12, E.2.b., for the inflation-adjusted amount.
170. §6601(j)(1).
171. §2053(c)(1)(D).
172. §6601(j)(4).
173. §6165. See Notice 2007-90, 2007-46 I.R.B. 1003, where the IRS specified that it will evaluate on a case-by-case basis whether security will be required. The factors which will be relevant in making this determination will include: (1) duration and stability of the business; (2) ability to pay the installments of tax and interest timely; and, (3) tax compliance history.
174. §2002, §2204(a). If the IRS and the estate's representative agree as to the amount of overassessment of an installment payment of tax, that amount will be abated. Future installments due will be recalculated and any overpayment of interest or tax will be applied to the next installment payment in accordance with §6403.
175. §2204(a).
176. §6324A.
177. §6324A(c).

178. §6324A(b).
179. §2204(b).
180. §6324A(b)(3), §6324A(d)(6).
181. §6324A(b)(2), §6324A(e)(2).
182. §6324A(b)(2). See §6324B concerning this special lien.
183. §6324A(b)(3).
184. §6324A(d)(5).
185. §6324A(d)(4).
186. §6324A(d)(1).
187. §6324A(d)(2).
188. §6324A(d)(3).
189. *Id.*
190. §6163.
191. Reg. §20.6163-1(a)(1) specifies that this provision does not extend to cases in which the decedent creates future interests by his or her own testamentary act.
192. Rev. Rul. 73-311, 1973-2 C.B. 405.
193. Reg. §20.6163-1(a)(1) indicates that "the part of the tax attributable" to the reversionary or remainder interest can be postponed. Reg. §20.6163-1(c) specifies that this amount is to be determined on a proportionate basis. An estate may prepay any portion of the outstanding tax liability postponed under §6163 without accelerating the remaining unpaid portion of the tax or accrued interest. Rev. Rul. 83-103, 1983-2 C.B. 238.
194. §6163(b); Reg. §20.6163-1(a)(2).
195. §6161.
196. §6161(a)(1).
197. §6161(a)(2).
198. *See* Reg. §20.6161-1(a)(1).
199. See, for example, *Estate of Mangiardi v. Commissioner,* T.C. Memo 2011-24, *aff'd.,* 2011 U.S. App. Lexis 20884 (11th Cir. 2011), for an example of such an examination.
200. A timely (irrevocable) election is to be made on the estate tax return. §2032(a). Under §2032(d)(2), the election can be made only if the return is filed within one year after the time prescribed for filing the estate tax return, including extensions. *Estate of Dixon v. Commissioner,* T.C. Memo 1990-17. *See also Estate of Eddy v. Commissioner,* 115 T.C. 135 (2000) (noting that estate's failure to make timely election precludes use of alternate valuation date even if reasonable cause existed for failure). See PLR 201431017 where an estate was granted a 120-day extension to elect the alternate valuation date when tax advisors had failed to alert the executors of the availability of this election when filing the return.
201. An alternate valuation date election may be made only if the election results in a decrease in both: (1) the value of the gross estate and (2) the amount of the federal estate and GST tax liability. §2032(c). This precludes the use of the alternate valuation date to increase the income tax basis of assets (thereby reducing subsequent income tax liabilities) when no estate tax liability exists (e.g., by reason of the unlimited marital deduction being utilized). *See* TAM 9001001.
202. §2032(a). In REG-112196-07, 76 Fed. Reg. 71,491 (Nov. 18, 2011), the IRS proposed regulations to clarify the types of factors that impact the fair market value of property and the effect of which will be recognized.
203. §2624(b), §2624(c)

204. §2624(b).
205. §2624(c).
206. §2032(a)(2). See *Estate of Holl v. Commissioner*, 54 F.3d 648 (10th Cir. 1995) (concerning dramatic change in value of oil and gas properties between date of death and alternate valuation date). Note in this context TAM 200343002, where the issue presented was whether amounts earned by a corporation during the alternate valuation period that were not distributed as a dividend to the shareholder and that remained in corporate solution as of the alternate valuation date constituted excluded property not included in the gross estate. The determinative question was whether these earnings represented a part of the property interest owned by the decedent at death or whether the earnings were, in effect, new property first owned by the estate. The IRS concluded that amounts earned by the corporation during the six-month period after the decedent's death, that were not distributed to the decedent's estate as the sole shareholder during that period, were not "excluded property" for purposes of Reg. §20.2032-1(d).
207. §2032(a)(1).
208. *See, e.g., Estate of Smith v. Commissioner*, 63 T.C. 722 (1975), *acq.*, 1976-2 C.B. 2; Rev. Rul. 77-221, 1977-1 C.B. 271 (concerning alternate valuation date where stock was exchanged for stock and warrants; exception to exchange treatment in this context is only applicable to transactions wholly tax free for income tax purposes).

CHAPTER 13

Estate Planner–Client Relationship

A. Professional's Responsibility

1. The Rules of Professional Conduct

a. The Attorney's Rules of Professional Conduct

Estate planning is an important component of the process of delivering legal services to individuals. To avoid professional sanctions (and possible malpractice claims[1]) the estate planner must comply with the standards of professional responsibility in performing these professional services.[2] The *Model Rules of Professional Conduct* mandate, among other responsibilities (as relevant in the estate tax planning context), an obligation to be competent[3] and to preserve confidences.[4] This duty of confidentiality continues after the death of a client and, consequently, a lawyer ordinarily should not disclose confidential information following a client's death.[5]

This professional obligation also requires the estate planner to avoid conflicts of interest.[6] This may necessitate advising an individual client's spouse that he or she should obtain independent counsel.[7] Some advisors take the position with respect to significant marital estates (particularly when involving second-marriage situations) that the conflict potential is so great that a waiver would really not be sufficient, and the other spouse should obtain independent legal counsel. At a minimum, the estate planner will want to send a cautionary letter to all participants apprising them of potential conflicts when multiple interests are being represented and obtaining their consent for this mutual representation.[8] Regarding confidentiality, these commentaries indicate that the same lawyer should be permitted to represent a husband and wife, or parent and child, whose dispositive plans are not entirely the same. When the lawyer is first consulted by the multiple potential clients, the lawyer should review with them the terms upon which the lawyer will undertake the representation, including the extent to which information will be shared among them.[9] The principal terms should, but need not, be reflected in writing, a copy of which is given to each client.[10] In some situations, the estate planner will specifically want to advise some parties that they should obtain their own independent counsel and that they should not rely on the estate planner for protecting their separate interests.[11]

The situations in which these conflicts can arise in the estate planning context can include[12]:

- identifying the ownership of specific assets by each spouse[13];
- suggesting varying asset disposition arrangements for spouses[14];
- disclosure of information between spouses, business partners, or parents and children[15];
- identifying the actual client, for example, when the child of an elderly person is seeking the implementation of asset disposition documents for the elder parent (who may be having mental capacity problems) or where a parent requests the estate planner to advise a minor child[16]; and
- for an attorney, responding to a suggestion (which may be inappropriate) made by an insurance agent or trust officer who has referred the client to the attorney.[17]

Where only one client is paying the estate planning fee for estate planning being done for several clients, this may create the possibility for compromised loyalties and the estate planner should obtain additional consents from the other clients concerning this precise situation.[18]

Other situations are clear, but sometimes bear repetition. The estate planner has an ethical responsibility not to self-deal with an estate or trust under that person's management. Further, the attorney preparing an instrument is prohibited from receiving from the client (or a related person) any substantial gift, including a testamentary gift, except where the client is related to the donee.[19] A lawyer can prepare a document that appoints the lawyer to a fiduciary office if (1) the client is properly informed, (2) the appointment does not violate the conflict-of-interest rules, and (3) the appointment is not the product of undue influence or improper solicitation by the lawyer.[20] If the attorney is asked to hold property of the client in connection with this representation, the client's property should be maintained separate from the lawyer's own property.[21]

This is often an area where multiple family members are seeking the advice of one attorney who is actually acting on behalf of a husband and wife, an elderly parent, or a decedent's estate. In these circumstances these other parties may not understand that they cannot also rely on the advice of the attorney, and the attorney should advise them to obtain their own legal representation in certain situations possibly producing conflict.[22]

b. Retaining Client's Estate Planning Documents After Completion

An important element of the document preparation process is the appropriate retention of the documents so that they are not lost or misplaced. The question then becomes whether the lawyer should seek to retain the executed original documents, partly with the view toward being employed in the future for the purpose of providing services to the fiduciaries. A lawyer who has prepared these documents may offer to the client to retain the executed originals subject to the client's instructions.[23] A lawyer who retains a client's documents for safekeeping should provide the client with a written document or letter noting that the documents are being held subject to the client's instructions.[24] Retention of these documents only in an electronic form is ordinarily not acceptable for eventually proving the existence and validity of these documents.

Notwithstanding that the original executed documents are retained, the advisor should consider sending a "termination" or "disengagement" letter to the client. One objective of this letter would be to reinforce the concept that this has been a positive experience for the client. Perhaps, more importantly, that letter could specify that (unless specifically requested) the advisor will be taking no further action on behalf of this client in the future. Consequently, if the transfer tax or other laws change significantly (which could adversely impact on the estate plan which has been implemented), the advisor would have no responsibility to track down this client and inform the client of the impact of these changes on the existing estate plan.

c. The Mentally Impaired Client

The lawyer may be certain of the identity of the client but the client's ability to make adequately considered decisions may be impaired, particularly because of mental disability. In this situation, the lawyer has a responsibility, as far as is reasonably possible, to maintain a normal client-lawyer relationship with the client.[25] The lawyer may seek the appointment of a guardian or take other protective action with respect to a client only when the lawyer reasonably believes that the client cannot adequately act in the client's own interest.[26] The lawyer should attempt, however, to earlier assist the client to avoid these problems through the implementation of such arrangements as (1) a durable power of attorney, (2) a health care power of attorney, (3) a designation of a potential guardian by the client, and (4) a funded revocable trust with an adequate mechanism for the appointment of a replacement trustee when the grantor (if acting as trustee) becomes incapacitated. The trust document could include having the determination of incapacity (which causes trustee replacement) made by an independent party, such as the trust grantor's personal physician or persons in similar status.[27]

The advisor also needs to be aware of the possible undue influence of one person (e.g., a child), who is seeking to encourage the client (and the advisor) in a particular direction. This situation would be accentuated if only one of several children is participating in this process on behalf of the older-generation member, and the participating child is receiving a disproportionately greater portion of the client's properties.

d. Applicable Professional Conduct Rules

Although the discussion above is based on the American Bar Association (ABA) *Model Rules of Professional Conduct*, these are only model rules as suggested to be adopted by each state jurisdiction. When adopted by various jurisdictions the rules may have been modified and amended and, therefore, their applicability is dependent upon local practice and customs. Attorneys are, however, also subject to the rules of conduct enunciated by the U.S. Department of the Treasury in "Circular 230" if practicing before the IRS. Further, the ABA *Model Rules of Professional Conduct* (rather than state law rules) may be applicable when practice is occurring before a national court, such as the U.S. Tax Court.[28]

2. Treasury Department Circular 230 Applicability

In addition to the professional conduct rules applicable to the estate planner under state law, and the applicability of the ABA rules of professional responsibility applicable to practice in special situations such as the U.S. Tax Court, the estate planner must also be aware of and carefully observe the mandates included in the U.S. Department of the Treasury's Circular 230.[29]

The portion of Circular 230 as modified in regulations finalized in 2002[30] is quite comprehensive in its application to individuals practicing before the IRS. For example, a practitioner who, having been retained by a client with respect to a matter administered by the IRS, knows that the client has not complied with the Code or has made an error in or omission from any return, document, affidavit, or other paper that the client submitted or executed under the Code, must advise the client promptly of the fact of such noncompliance, error, or omission.[31] The practitioner must advise the client of the consequences (as provided under the Code and regulations) of such noncompliance, error, or omission. A practitioner must exercise due diligence[32]: (1) in preparing or assisting in the preparation of, approving, and filing tax returns, documents, affidavits, and other papers relating to IRS matters; (2) in determining the correctness of oral or written representations made by the practitioner to the Treasury Department; and (3) in determining the correctness of oral or written representations made by the practitioner to clients with reference to any matter administered by the IRS. A practitioner will be presumed to have exercised due diligence if he or she relies on someone else's work product and "the practitioner used reasonable care in engaging, supervising, training, and evaluating the person, taking proper account of the nature of the relationship between the practitioner and the person."[33]

The portion of Circular 230 as modified in regulations finalized in 2004 and 2005 (the "tax shelter" segment of Circular 230)[34] specifies "best practices" for tax advisors.[35] Tax advisors are to "provide clients with the highest quality representation concerning Federal tax issues by adhering to best practices in providing advice and in preparing or assisting in the preparation of a submission to the Internal Revenue Service." In addition to compliance with the standards of practice provided elsewhere in Circular 230, best practices include[36]:

(1) Communicating clearly with the client regarding the terms of the engagement. For example, the advisor should determine the client's expected purpose for and use of the advice and should have a clear understanding with the client regarding the form and scope of the advice or assistance to be rendered.
(2) Establishing the facts, determining which facts are relevant, evaluating the reasonableness of any assumptions or representations, relating the applicable law (including potentially applicable judicial doctrines) to the relevant facts, and arriving at a conclusion supported by the law and the facts.
(3) Advising the client regarding the import of the conclusions reached, including, for example, whether a taxpayer may avoid accuracy-related penalties under the Internal Revenue Code if a taxpayer acts in reliance on the advice.
(4) Acting fairly and with integrity in practice before the Internal Revenue Service.

Thus, a "reasoned opinion" is to be provided in these situations.

The IRS has provided final Circular 230 regulations that eliminated the "covered opinion" rules for written tax advice rendered on or after June 12, 2014.[37] Instead, all written tax advice is now subject to one standard under the amended version of Circular 230 §10.37. The final regulations were intended to decrease the burden of compliance on practitioners, including the ability in many cases to eliminate the necessity of disclaimers attached to virtually all communications (even those not necessarily related to federal tax matters).

Circular 230 §10.37(a) provides that a practitioner may give written advice (including by means of electronic communication) concerning one or more Federal tax matters, but subject to the requirements in §10.37(a)(2). These requirements indicate that a practitioner must:

(1) base all written advice on reasonable factual and legal assumptions;
(2) exercise reasonable reliance and consider all relevant facts that he/she knows or reasonably should know;
(3) use reasonable efforts to identify and ascertain the facts relevant to written advice on a federal tax matter;
(4) not rely on representations, statements, findings, or agreements (including projections, financial forecasts, or appraisals) of the taxpayer or any other person if reliance on them would be unreasonable;
(5) relate applicable law and authorities to facts; and
(6) not, in evaluating a Federal tax matter, take into account the possibility that a tax return will not be audited or that a matter will not be raised on audit.

The final regulations do not specifically define "written advice," but do provide some clarification on the matter. For example, government submissions on matters of general policy (e.g., a law firm submitting comments on proposed regulations to the IRS on a client's behalf) are not considered written tax advice. Further, certain continuing education presentations are not considered written tax advice.

The final regulations do provide a definition of "federal tax matters." A federal tax matter is any matter concerning the application or interpretation of (1) a revenue provision as defined in §6110(i)(1)(B); (2) any provision of law impacting a person's obligations under the Code or regulations, including but not limited to the person's liability to pay tax or obligation to file returns; or (3) any other law or regulation administered by the IRS.[38]

Further, the final regulations modified the rules relating to a practitioner's reliance on other practitioners. The reliance provisions have been expanded to include other individuals not described as a practitioner in Circular 230 §10.2 and §10.3, including appraisers. However, reliance is prohibited when the practitioner knows or reasonably should know that the advice should not be relied on, the other person is not competent to provide the advice, or the other person has a conflict of interest.[39]

3. Professional Malpractice Risks

Exposure to ever increasing professional liability risk in the estate planning context mandates that the estate planning firm implement a quality control program to reduce that risk.[40] This includes pursuing the professional engagement with diligence and promptness, so as to avoid problems with the client.[41] Further, to avoid this risk the lawyer should keep the client reasonably informed about the status of the matter[42] and should explain a matter to the extent reasonably necessary to permit the client to make informed decisions regarding the representation.[43] Even though the estate planning attorney may be in violation of some rule of professional responsibility, a malpractice action will not necessarily succeed.[44] In some states, the concept of "privity" limits those seeking to pursue a claim for estate planning malpractice, particularly precluding some parties who have not had adequate "privity" with the professional advisor.

B. Determining the Amount of the Estate Planner's Fee

The estate planner is engaged in the practice of estate planning to (1) provide services to his or her clients, but also (2) to provide an adequate stream of income to that advisor. The inquiry then can concern how to estate planner should charge fair value for those services while maximizing the estate planning practice income.[45] That fee might be based on an hourly charge or on an agreed amount for the particular engagement. The estate planner's fee for the estate planning services provided is to be "reasonable."[46] The factors to be considered in determining the reasonableness of a fee include the following[47]:

(1) the time and labor required, the novelty and difficulty of the question involved, and the skill required to perform the legal service properly;
(2) the likelihood, if apparent to the client, that the acceptance of the particular employment by the estate planner will preclude other employment by the lawyer;
(3) the fee customarily charged in the locality for similar legal services;
(4) the amount involved and the results obtained;
(5) the time limitations imposed by the client or by the circumstances;

(6) the nature and length of the professional relationship with the client;
(7) the experience, reputation, and ability of the lawyer or lawyers performing the services; and,
(8) whether the fee is fixed or contingent.

The practice of basing a fee solely or primarily on the size of the fiduciary estate is inappropriate unless required or authorized by law. Courts in several states have prohibited or seriously limited the use of fees based upon a percentage of the estate.[48]

> "A fee may be contingent on the outcome of the matter for which the service is rendered except in a matter in which a contingent fee is prohibited."[49] A contingent fee agreement is to be in writing and must[50]: state the method by which the fee is to be determined, including the percentage or percentages that shall accrue to the lawyer in the event of settlement, trial or appeal; litigation and other expenses to be deducted from the recovery, and whether such expenses are to be deducted before or after the contingent fee is calculated. Upon conclusion of a contingent fee matter, the lawyer is to provide the client with a written statement stating the outcome of the matter and, if there is a recovery, showing the remittance to the client and the method of its determination.

Most states allow a lawyer who serves as (1) a fiduciary and (2) a lawyer for the trust or estate to be compensated for work being done in both capacities. The lawyer should not receive double compensation for the same work, however.

C. Income Tax Deduction of Estate Planning Fees

1. Availability of Deduction

The estate planning client should be appropriately advised as to the extent to which the legal and other fees incurred for estate planning can be deducted for current federal income tax purposes. Opportunities will be available to assist the client in reducing the net cost of the estate planning fees paid through the availability of an income tax deduction. This cost saving opportunity may be reduced, however, due to the 2% floor on miscellaneous itemized deductions.[51]

Under §68, an overall limitation on itemized deductions applies to certain individual taxpayers.[52] The §68 limitation applies only to individual taxpayers whose adjusted gross incomes exceed the applicable amount.[53] Generally, taxpayers whose adjusted gross incomes exceed the applicable amount must reduce the amount of otherwise allowable itemized deductions[54] by the lesser of 3% of the excess of adjusted gross income over the applicable amount,[55] or 80% of the amount of otherwise allowable itemized deductions.[56]

The applicable amounts for tax year 2016 are $311,300 for a joint return or a surviving spouse, $285,350 for a head of household, $259,400 for an unmarried individual who is not a surviving spouse or head of household, and $155,650 for a married individual filing a separate return.[57] The applicable amounts are adjusted for inflation for tax years beginning after 2013.[58] The applicable amounts for earlier taxable years are:

Calendar Year	Married Filing Joint Returns	Married Filing Separate Returns	Single (not HoH)	Head of Household
2015[59]	$309,900	$154,950	$258,250	$284,050
2014[60]	$305,050	$152,525	$254,200	$279,650
2013[61]	$300,000	$150,000	$250,000	$275,000
2010–2012[62]	No applicable amount	No applicable amount	No applicable amount	No applicable amount

The §68 limitation applies only to those individual taxpayers whose adjusted gross incomes exceed the applicable amount. The §68 limitation does not apply to any estate or trust.[63]

2. Allocation Among Related Taxpayers

Estate planning will often involve services rendered not only to the individual client but also to a related business entity. Some of these services may be for the direct benefit of that business entity and, accordingly, should be charged directly to that entity. These items might include preparing (1) buy-sell agreements, (2) family partnership agreements, (3) corporate restructuring documents, and (4) employee benefit plans (whether qualified pension and profit-sharing plans or executive compensation arrangements, such as incentive stock option and deferred compensation plans). These costs would be deductible by the business enterprise under §162 as ordinary and necessary business expenses.

In contrast, expenses may have been paid for by the employer that, however, are of direct and exclusive benefit to the employee (and only insignificantly benefit the employer). These items might include the cost of investment counseling for executives and legal services for the employee with respect to designating beneficiaries of pension and profit-sharing plans, deferred compensation arrangements, and key man and group term life insurance. These items should be appropriately billed to the individual employee, unless these amounts are to be paid by the employer, but treated as additional compensation to the employee.[64]

3. Individual Estate Planning Costs

a. Categories of Costs

The individual client may be permitted to deduct estate planning–related fees under §212 (subject to the 2% floor on certain deductions).[65] This section permits deductions for ordinary and necessary expenses paid or incurred during the taxable year:

- for the production or collection of income[66];
- for the management, conservation, or maintenance of property held for the production of income[67]; and
- in connection with the determination, collection, or refund of any tax.[68]

Court decisions with respect to the allowance of such deductions appear to allow limited deductions in the estate planning context,[69] but the rules are not very precisely defined. The preparation of simple estate planning documents such as a will, health care directive, and durable power of attorney is considered to be personal in nature and not deductible for federal income tax purposes.

b. Specific Professional Services

(1) Tax Advice

Subject to the 2% floor noted above, the client should be advised to deduct the portion of the estate planner's fee attributable to tax planning.[70] Expenses paid for tax "counsel" or paid in connection with any "proceedings" involved in determining the extent of tax liability are deductible.[71] Deductibility would be in accord with the position of the IRS.[72]

(2) Formulating the Last Will

The fee for drafting a will is normally considered to be not deductible for income tax purposes.[73] Various portions of the will often have substantial tax planning significance (e.g., a marital deduction formula clause, a tax apportionment clause, and provisions creating charitable remainder trusts). An allocation should be made for the time expended for these items and this amount should be included in the tax planning segment of the fee billing with an indication that it should be treated as deductible. Provisions dealing with most specific bequests and legacies would seem, however, to be personal and, therefore, nondeductible.

(3) Drafting Trust Documents

A deduction is available for expenses incurred "for the management, conservation, or maintenance of property."[74] Where a revocable trust is funded with income-producing property, the taxpayer could argue that (a) the trust is an arrangement for the management and conservation of property,[75] and (b) the property will be conserved and maintained by the avoidance of probate fees at the grantor's death (one of the primary factors motivating the creation of a revocable inter vivos trust). Where the trust corpus is property that produces tax-exempt income (e.g., state and local government bonds), a deduction would be completely foreclosed.[76]

Where the unfunded revocable trust or a testamentary trust is created, a deduction would ordinarily not be permitted. A taxpayer could reasonably argue, however, that the trust is a protective arrangement for the management and conservation of property and, therefore, the fees paid should be deductible.[77] Where an irrevocable trust is created and property is irrevocably transferred to the trust for the benefit of others, the origin of the transfer would seem to be personal and, therefore, nondeductible.[78]

(4) Other Property Adjustments

As part of estate planning, the attorney may prepare appropriate documents to sever joint tenancies, terminate trusts, and complete outright gifts. Legal fees for such items (except for the costs for related tax planning) would ordinarily not be deductible since the fees are personal expenses rather than tax planning related. In some situations, these costs could be added to the tax basis of the particular assets, to be recovered upon a subsequent disposition.

c. Preparing the Fee Statement

The estate planner should itemize his or her fee statement, with specific portions being attributed to[79]:

- tax counsel and planning[80];
- preparing documents and advice concerning property management, conservation, and maintenance[81]; and
- personal matters.[82]

The allocation should, of course, be reasonable.[83] The fee statement could be accompanied by a letter to the client emphasizing that the estate planning process is substantially devoted to reducing death transfer costs (both federal income and estate taxes and local court costs), as well as to implementing the client's basic scheme for lifetime and testamentary disposition of the client's properties.

Notes

1. Although the professional ethics rules do not establish an independent basis for civil liability, the rules (and violations of the rules) are usually admissible as evidence in malpractice actions.
2. This discussion analyzes the applicability of the American Bar Association (ABA) *Model Rules of Professional Conduct*, but the applicable rules will be the rules of professional conduct as adopted in the jurisdiction where the estate planner is rendering advice. See generally ACTEC (American College of Trust and Estate Counsel), Commentaries on the Model Rules of Professional Conduct (4th ed. 2006). A copy can be downloaded (in PDF format) at www.actec.org. This website location provides annotations to the ACTEC commentaries on the model rules of professional conduct. These annotations provide summaries of various ethics opinions relevant to the application of these rules in the estate planning context. See, further, American Bar Association, *Model Rules of Professional Conduct* (2011) (from the Center for Professional Responsibility); and *Annotated Model Rules of Professional Conduct*, Seventh Edition (2011). See, also, The American Law Institute's (ALI), Restatement (Third) of the Law Governing Lawyers, which deals comprehensively with the duties of lawyers and, accordingly, is relevant to the activities of estate planning attorneys. If estate planning services are being provided by a certified public accountant,

the professional conduct rules (prescribed by the American Institute of Certified Public Accountants) will be similar.

3. ABA Model Rules of Prof'l Conduct, R. 1.1 specifies that a lawyer is to provide competent representation to a client and that competent representation requires the legal knowledge, skill, thoroughness, and preparation reasonably necessary for the representation. The ACTEC Commentaries on the Model Rules of Professional Conduct (4th ed. 2006) indicate (in a segment entitled "Importance of Facts") that this rule means a lawyer who is engaged by a client in an estate planning matter should inform the client of the importance of giving the lawyer complete and accurate information regarding relevant matters such as the ownership and the value of assets and the state of beneficiary designations under life insurance policies and employee benefit plans. Having so cautioned a client, the lawyer is generally entitled to rely upon information supplied by the client unless the circumstances indicate that the information should be verified. The lawyer should verify the information provided by the client if the client appears to be uncertain about it or if other circumstances create doubts about its accuracy.
4. Model Rules of Prof'l Conduct R. 1.6(a) specifies that a lawyer should not reveal information relating to representation of a client unless the client consents after consultation, except for disclosures that are impliedly authorized in order to carry out the representation. This contemplates that the estate planner will ordinarily be permitted to share information with members of the lawyer's office staff to the extent reasonably necessary to the representation.
5. *See* Commentary to Model Rules of Prof'l Conduct R. 1.6(a).
6. Model Rules of Prof'l Conduct R. 1.7(a) provides that a lawyer is not to represent a client if (1) the representation of that client will be directly adverse to another client or (2) there is a significant risk that the lawyer's responsibilities to others or his or her personal interests will materially limit the representation. Model Rules of Prof'l Conduct R. 1.7(b) provides that, notwithstanding the existence of such a "concurrent conflict of interest," a lawyer may represent the client if (1) the lawyer reasonably believes that he or she will be able to provide competent and diligent representation to each affected client; (2) the representation is not prohibited by law; (3) the representation does not involve one client's assertion of a claim against another client represented by the lawyer in the same litigation or other tribunal proceeding; and (4) the affected clients all give informed consent, confirmed in writing.

   Model Rules of Prof'l Conduct R. 1.7 cmt. states:

   > It is often appropriate for a lawyer to represent more than one member of the same family in connection with their estate plans, more than one beneficiary with common interests in an estate or trust administration matter, co-fiduciaries of an estate or trust, or more than one of the investors in a closely held business. . . . In some instances, the clients may actually be better served by such a representation, which can result in more economical and better coordinated estate plans prepared by counsel who has a better overall understanding of all of the relevant family and property considerations. The fact that the estate planning goals of the clients are not entirely consistent does not necessarily preclude the lawyer from representing them: advising related clients who have somewhat differing goals may be consistent with their interests and the lawyer's traditional role as the lawyer for the "family." Multiple representation is also generally appropriate because the interests of the clients in cooperation, including obtaining cost effective representation and achieving common objectives, often clearly predominate over their limited inconsistent interests. Recognition should be given to the fact that estate planning is fundamentally nonadversarial in nature and estate administration is usually nonadversarial.

7. The ACTEC Commentaries of the Model Rules of Professional Conduct (4th ed. 2006) indicates that, under Model Rules of Prof'l Conduct R. 1.7 cmt.:

   before, or within a reasonable time after, commencing the representation, a lawyer who is consulted by multiple parties with related interests should discuss with them the implications of a joint representation (or a separate representation if the lawyer believes that mode of representation to be more appropriate and separate representation is permissible under the applicable local rules).... In particular, the prospective clients and the lawyer should discuss the extent to which material information imparted by either client would be shared with the other and the possibility that the lawyer would be required to withdraw if a conflict in their interests developed to the degree that the lawyer could not effectively represent each of them. The information may be best understood by the clients if it is discussed with them in person and also provided to them in written form, as in an engagement letter or brochure. Further, as noted in the ACTEC Commentary on MRPC 1.2 (Scope of Representation and Allocation of Authority Between Client and Lawyer), a lawyer may represent co-fiduciaries whose interests do not conflict to an impermissible degree. A lawyer who represents co-fiduciaries may also represent one or both of them as beneficiaries so long as no disabling conflict arises. . . . Before accepting a representation involving multiple parties a lawyer may wish to consider meeting with the prospective clients separately, which may allow each of them to be more candid and, perhaps, reveal conflicts of interest.

   If a confidence is revealed by one party after the joint representation has commenced the advisor (1) might take no action if determining that the confidence is not relevant to the representation, (2) may encourage the client to share that confidence with the other client, or permit the attorney to do so, or (3) might withdraw entirely from the representation if the confidence reflects serious adversity between the husband and wife clients. A concern in this context is that the spouses may subsequently divorce and one disgruntled ex-spouse might file some type of ethics complaint against the estate planning advisor who was perceived as being more supportive of the other ex-spouse.

8. The ACTEC Commentaries on the Model Rules of Professional Conduct (4th ed. 2006) indicates that, under Model Rules of Prof'l Conduct R. 1.7. "As indicated in the ACTEC Commentary on MRPC 1.6 (Confidentiality of Information), a lawyer usually represents multiple clients jointly. However, some experienced estate planners regularly represent husbands and wives as separate clients. They also undertake to represent other related clients separately with respect to related matters. Such representations should only be undertaken with the informed consent of each client, confirmed in writing." The Commentaries for R. 1.6 provide in this context:

   A lawyer may represent more than one client with related, but not necessarily identical, interests (e.g., several members of the same family, more than one investor in a business enterprise). The fact that the goals of the clients are not entirely consistent does not necessarily constitute a conflict of interest that precludes the same lawyer from representing them. *See* ACTEC Commentary on MRPC 1.7 (Conflict of Interest: General Rule). Thus, the same lawyer may represent a husband and wife, or parent and child, whose dispositive plans are not entirely the same. When the lawyer is first consulted by the multiple potential clients, the lawyer should review with them the terms upon which the lawyer will undertake the representation, including the extent to which information will be shared among them. In the absence of any agreement to the contrary (usually in writing), a lawyer is presumed to represent multiple clients with regard to related legal matters jointly with resulting full sharing of information between the clients. The better practice in all cases is to memorialize the clients' instructions in writing and give a copy of the writing to the client. Nothing in the foregoing should be construed as approving the representation by a lawyer of both parties in the creation of any inherently adversarial contract (e.g., a marital property agreement) which is not subject to rescission by one of the parties without the consent and joinder of the other. *See* ACTEC Commentary on MRPC 1.7 (Conflict of Interest: General Rule). The lawyer may wish to consider holding a separate interview with each prospective client, which may allow the clients to be more candid and, perhaps, reveal conflicts of interest that below would not otherwise be disclosed.

9. Having agreed to represent both spouses, conflict may later arise concerning disclosure of information from one spouse to another, and in this situation the estate planner may need to resign as to the representation of both spouses.
10. See the sample client engagement letter in the Worksheets. See also the ACTEC website (www.actec.org) for *ACTEC Engagement Letters: A Guide for Practitioners*, Second Edition 2007. This book does not deal with matters of post-death probate administration, but, it should be noted that, in the probate process, the advisor should similarly obtain a client engagement letter describing the activities to be undertaken by the attorney. These identified activities could include (1) filing necessary probate court notices of appointment and inventory, (2) completing reports to the Probate Court, (3) arranging for the filing of various tax returns (income and estate) and the payment of these taxes and the allocation of the responsibility for these taxes, and (4) providing counsel and advice concerning these various matters. In this situation the client would be the estate of the deceased and the executor of the estate (which may be conflicting interests).
11. If a representation is declined by the lawyer or a prospective client, the lawyer should consider sending a "nonengagement" letter to the prospective client so that no future misunderstandings on this matter can occur. Unfortunately, some potential clients in a family situation may still not take "no" for an answer to a request for legal representation and subsequently initiate a legal proceeding on the basis that their interests were not adequately protected.
12. For further discussion of these issues, see 801 T.M., *Conflicts, Confidentiality, and Other Ethical Considerations in Estate Planning* (Bloomberg BNA); 872 T.M., *Ethical Issues in International Estate Planning* (Bloomberg BNA).
13. This can be a complicated issue when the essential question is whether marital property has (1) a separate property or (2) a community property origin.
14. For example, one spouse may wish the transferred property for the benefit of the other spouse to be held in trust (such as a qualified terminable interest property trust), while the other spouse believes the transfers among them should be outright and unencumbered.
15. Particularly if the planning is to be done for unrelated business partners the concern might be that the advisor will tend to favor one party rather than another.
16. Model Rules of Prof'l Conduct R. 1.8(f) specifies that a lawyer is not to accept compensation for representing a client from someone else unless: (1) the client consents after consultation; (2) there is no interference with the lawyer's independence of professional judgment or with the client-lawyer relationship; and (3) information relating to representation of a client is protected as required by Model Rules of Prof'l Conduct R. 1.6. The ACTEC Commentaries on the Model Rules of Professional Conduct (4th ed. 2006) indicates that, under Model Rules of Prof'l Conduct R. 1.7, a lawyer should exercise

particular care if an existing client asks the lawyer to prepare for another person a will or trust that will benefit the client, particularly if the client will pay the cost of providing the estate planning services to the other person. Such a representation may be appropriate if the client and the other person are closely related, the other person is competent and adequately informed, and the terms of the will or trust do not unduly benefit the client. The lawyer should consider cautioning the client and the other party of the possibility that the client may be presumed to have exerted undue influence on the other person because the client was involved in the procurement of the document. *See also* ABA Comm. on Ethics and Prof'l Responsibility, Formal Op. 02-428 (2002) (Drafting Will on Recommendation of Potential Beneficiary Who Also Is Client). This opinion states that a lawyer who is recommended by a potential beneficiary to draft a will for a relative may represent the testator as long as the lawyer does not permit the person who recommends him or her to direct or regulate the lawyer's professional judgment pursuant to Model Rules of Prof'l Conduct R. 5.4(c). If the potential beneficiary agrees to pay or assure the lawyer's fee, the testator's informed consent to the arrangement must be obtained, and the other requirements of Model Rules of Prof'l Conduct R. 1.8(f) must be satisfied. If the person recommending the lawyer also is a client of the lawyer, the lawyer must obtain clear guidance from him or her as to the extent to which he or she may use or reveal that person's protected information in representing the testator. The lawyer should advise the testator that he or she also is concurrently performing estate planning services for the other person. Ordinarily, there is no significant risk that the lawyer's representation of either client will be materially limited by his or her representation of the other client; therefore, no conflict of interest arises under Model Rules of Prof'l Conduct R. 1.7.

17. This may also function in the opposite direction, for example, where the trust officer has concerns about the capability or integrity of an attorney who refers a client to the bank's trust department.
18. *See* Model Rules of Prof'l Conduct R. 1.8(f).
19. Model Rules of Prof'l Conduct R. 1.8(c). The ACTEC Commentaries on the Model Rules of Professional Conduct (4th ed. 2006) specify that, under Model Rules of Prof'l Conduct R. 1.8, the lawyer should exercise special care if a relative of either the lawyer or the lawyer's spouse proposes to make a gift that is disproportionately large in relation to gifts that the relative proposes to make to others who are equally related.
20. *See* ABA Comm. on Ethics and Prof'l Responsibility, Formal Op. 02-426 (2002) (Lawyer Serving as Fiduciary for an Estate or Trust). This opinion notes that a lawyer may accept appointment as fiduciary under a will or trust that the lawyer is preparing for a client, so long as the lawyer discusses with the client information reasonably necessary to enable the client to make an informed decision in selecting the fiduciary. If there is significant risk that the lawyer's interest in being named a fiduciary will materially limit his or her independent professional judgment in advising the client in his or her choice of a fiduciary, the lawyer also must obtain the client's informed consent, confirmed in writing. Although a lawyer serving as a fiduciary of an estate or trust may appoint himself, herself, or other lawyers in his or her law firm to represent him or her as fiduciary, his or her compensation received in both capacities must be considered in determining what is reasonable compensation for his or her services as lawyer. Finally, a lawyer who is serving as a fiduciary ordinarily must not represent a beneficiary or creditor of an estate or trust in a matter adverse to the estate or trust. When representing a beneficiary in a matter unrelated to the estate or trust, the lawyer must satisfy the requirements of Model Rules of Prof'l Conduct R. 1.7.

21. The comment to Model Rules of Prof'l Conduct R. 1.25(a) specifies that "[a] lawyer shall hold the funds and property of others using the care required of a professional fiduciary. . . . Separate trust accounts may be warranted or required when administering estate monies or acting in similar fiduciary capacities."
22. Model Rules of Prof'l Conduct R. 4.3 specifies that in dealing on behalf of a client with a person who is not represented by counsel, a lawyer shall not state or imply that the lawyer is disinterested. When the lawyer knows or reasonably should know that the unrepresented person misunderstands the lawyer's role in the matter, the lawyer shall make reasonable efforts to correct the misunderstanding. The lawyer shall not give legal advice to an unrepresented person other than the advice to secure counsel if the lawyer knows or reasonably should know that the interests of such person are or have a reasonable possibility of being in conflict with the interests of the client.
23. *See* ACTEC Commentaries on the Model Rules of Professional Conduct (4th ed. 2006) (concerning Model Rules of Prof'l Conduct R. 1.8).
24. The Commentary indicates that a lawyer who retains a client's documents for safekeeping should provide the client with a written receipt, which may be in the form of a letter, acknowledging that the documents are held subject to the client's order. The receipt may, but need not, also indicate that the fiduciary designated in the documents is not required to retain as counsel the lawyer with whom the documents were left for safekeeping. The documents should be held by the lawyer in a manner consistent with the requirements of MRPC 1.15 (Safekeeping Property) regarding the duties of a lawyer who receives and holds property on behalf of a client. In particular, the documents should be properly identified and appropriately safeguarded. Subject to otherwise applicable law, the lawyer should comply with the client's written directions regarding disposition of the documents. The retention of the client's original estate planning documents does not itself make the client an "active" client or impose any obligation on the lawyer to take steps to remain informed regarding the client's management of property and family status. Similarly, sending a client periodic letters encouraging the client to review the sufficiency of the client's estate plan or calling the client's attention to subsequent legal developments does not increase the lawyer's obligations to the client.
25. Model Rules of Prof'l Conduct R. 1.14(a).
26. Model Rules of Prof'l Conduct R. 1.14(b).
27. A similar determination could be provided for if the durable power of attorney is a "springing power"; that is, it is activated only when the principal becomes incapacitated.
28. The U.S. Tax Court has adopted the Model Rules of Prof'l Conduct. *See* U.S. Tax Ct. R. 201(a).
29. 31 C.F.R. Part 10, hereinafter Circular 230 (cited with appropriate identification of the specific section or sections to which reference is made). Circular 230 was issued by the Secretary of the Treasury pursuant to authority granted by 31 U.S.C. §330. Circular 230 (Rev. 6-2005, with amendments 2007), which applies to lawyers, accountants, enrolled agents, enrolled actuaries, and others practicing before the IRS, is generally effective July 26, 2002. Circular 230 §10.93. Circular 230 §10.91 contains a savings clause for a proceeding instituted under regulations in effect before July 26, 2002, if the proceeding was not final before that date. Violation of the rules prescribed in Circular 230 can lead to censure or suspension or disbarment from practice before the IRS. Circular 230 §§10.50, 10.52. Effective for actions taken after Oct. 22, 2004, the American Jobs Creation Act of 2004 (AJCA), Pub. L. No. 108-357, §822(a), amended 31 U.S.C. §330(b) to include

monetary penalties in the sanctions that may be imposed on practitioners under Circular 230. Although the 2004 and 2005 final Circular 230 regulations issued in T.D. 9165, 69 Fed. Reg. 75,839 (Dec. 20, 2004), and T.D. 9201, 70 Fed. Reg. 28,824 (May 19, 2005), do not reflect the amendments made by the AJCA, the preamble to T.D. 9165 indicates that Treasury and the IRS expect to propose additional regulations implementing the amendments. For subsequent regulations, *see* T.D. 9359, 72 Fed. Reg. 54,540 (Sept. 26, 2007). See 801 T.M., *Conflicts, Confidentiality, and Other Ethical Considerations in Estate Planning* (Bloomberg BNA), for more information on Circular 230.

30. T.D. 9011, 67 Fed. Reg. 48,760 (July 26, 2002).
31. Circular 230 §10.21 (entitled "Knowledge of client's omission").
32. Circular 230 §10.22 (entitled "Diligence as to accuracy").
33. *Id.*
34. T.D. 9165 and T.D. 9201, respectively, generally effective after June 20, 2005. News Release IR-2004-152 (Dec. 17, 2004), issued in conjunction with the 2004 regulations, stated that the revisions providing "standards of practice for written advice that reflect current best practices and are intended to restore and maintain public confidence in tax professionals. These revisions ensure that tax professionals do not provide inadequate advice, and increase transparency by requiring tax professionals to make disclosures if the advice is incomplete."
35. Circular 230 §10.33.
36. *Id.*
37. Preamble to T.D. 9668, 79 Fed. Reg. 33,685 (June 12, 2014).
38. Circular 230 §10.37(d), as amended by T.D. 9668.
39. Circular 230 §10.37(b)(1)-(3), as amended by T.D. 9668.
40. Note the prohibition in Model Rules of Prof'l Conduct R. 1.8(h) against agreeing with the client to a limitation of the attorney's liability to the client for malpractice, unless permitted by law and the client is independently represented when completing this agreement. Consequently, the client might incur tax penalties based on inadequate advice and then seek to be reimbursed by the professional advisor. *See United States v. Boyle,* 469 U.S. 241 (1985) (taxpayer's reliance upon counsel to timely file estate tax return does not constitute "reasonable cause" for late filing of return). In *Boyle,* the Court opined that Congress placed the burden of prompt filing on the executor, not his or her agent. In the Court's view, although retaining an attorney is an exercise of "ordinary business care and prudence" as required by Reg. §301.6651-1(c)(1), it does not relieve the taxpayer of his or her statutory duty. The Court distinguished the reliance in *Boyle* from reliance on erroneous advice of counsel concerning a question of law. For an application of this distinction, see, for example, *Estate of Buring v. Commissioner,* T.C. Memo 1985-610 (reliance upon accountant's advice that gift tax return did not have to be filed was reasonable cause). The "erroneous advice" exception was held not to apply, however, to excuse a professional executor from §6651 late filing penalties even though the executor was assured by the accountant that the return would be timely filed and also believed that no estate tax was due because of a charitable remainder bequest. *Estate of Cox v. United States,* 637 F. Supp. 1112 (S.D. Fla. 1986). In footnote 6 of its opinion, the Supreme Court in *Boyle* expressly left open the question of whether "reasonable cause" exists when a taxpayer relies on an attorney because the taxpayer is incapable (measured by objective standards) of meeting the criteria of "ordinary business care and prudence." Justice Brennan, with three Justices concurring, maintained that the "ordinary business care and prudence" standard applies

only to the ordinary person, that is, one who is capable of knowing, remembering, and complying with a filing deadline. The footnote 6 exception in *Boyle* was applied in *Brown v. United States,* 630 F. Supp. 57 (M.D. Tenn. 1985) (administrator who failed to timely file estate tax return due to old age, ill health, and inexperience was excused from §6651 late filing penalty).

41. Model Rules of Prof'l Conduct R. 1.3 provides that a lawyer should "act with reasonable diligence and promptness in representing a client." The ACTEC Commentaries on the Model Rules of Professional Conduct (4th ed. 2006) indicates that, under Model Rules of Prof'l Conduct R. 1.3 (concerning "diligence"), whether the representation relates to inter vivos estate planning or the administration of a fiduciary estate, it is usually desirable, early in the representation, for the lawyer and client to establish a timetable for completion of various tasks.
42. Model Rules of Prof'l Conduct R. 1.4(a).
43. Model Rules of Prof'l Conduct R. 1.4(b).
44. Note that a lawyer who is a specialist—or holds himself or herself out as having special skills—will be held to a higher standard of performance than a nonspecialist. *See* Restatement (Third) of the Law Governing Lawyers §74 cmt. (d).
45. This discussion does not concern such matters as to how one builds an estate planning practice (including through the use of a website), and the mechanics of this practice (such as computerization and going "paperless"), but these are all important matters to be decided upon by the practitioner, often with expert technical advice.
46. Model Rules of Prof'l Conduct R. 1.5. Circular 230 §10.28(a) specifies that "a practitioner may not charge an unconscionable fee for representing a client in a matter before the Internal Revenue Service."
47. Model Rules of Prof'l Conduct R. 1.5.
48. ACTEC Commentaries on the Model Rules of Professional Conduct (4th ed. 2006) (on Model Rules of Prof'l Conduct R. 1.5).
49. Model Rules of Prof'l Conduct R. 1.5(c).
50. *Id.*
51. Section 67(a) specifies that in the case of an individual, the miscellaneous itemized deductions for any taxable year are allowed only to the extent that the aggregate of such deductions exceeds 2% of adjusted gross income. *See also O'Neill Irrevocable Trust v. Commissioner,* 994 F.2d 302 (6th Cir. 1993) (payments by individual trustees for investment advisory services were deductible in full, and were not subject to 2% limitation); Rev. Rul. 89-68, 1989-2 C.B. 82. The *O'Neill* decision was not extended to individual taxpayers and other circuits have rejected its application to trust expenses. *See, e.g., Scott v. United States,* 328 F.3d 132 (4th Cir. 2003) (trust's deductions for outside investment advisory fees were subject to 2% floor for miscellaneous deductions); *Mellon Bank, N.A. v. United States,* 265 F.3d 1275 (Fed. Cir. 2001), *aff'g* 2001-1 USTC ¶50,153 (Fed. Cl. 2000) (investment advisory and management fees paid by trustee did not satisfy second prerequisite of §67(e)(1) exception to §67(a) 2% floor because such fees are commonly incurred outside trusts and individual investors not bound by fiduciary duties are likely to incur such costs when managing large sums); *Rudkin Testamentary Trust v. Commissioner,* 124 T.C. 304 (2005), *aff'd,* 467 F.3d 149 (2d Cir. 2006), *aff'd sub nom., Knight v. Commissioner,* 552 U.S. 181(2008) (§67(e)(1) excepts from 2% floor only those costs that it would be uncommon, unusual, or unlikely for hypothetical individual owning trust or estate property to incur; investment advisory fees are generally subject to 2% floor because

it would not be uncommon or unusual for individual owning trust or estate property and having same investment objectives as fiduciary to incur such expenses). On July 27, 2007, the IRS issued proposed regulations under §67 providing guidance on which costs incurred by estates and nongrantor trusts are subject to the 2% floor on the deduction of miscellaneous expenses. REG-128224-06, 72 Fed. Reg. 41,243 (July 27, 2007). This regulation was withdrawn on September 7, 2011, with newly proposed regulations. 76 Fed. Reg. 55,322 (Sept. 7, 2011). These proposed regulations provide that the portion of a bundled fee attributable to investment advice (including any related services that would be provided to any individual investor as part of the investment advisory fee) will be subject to the 2% floor. In addition, these proposed regulations provide that, except for the portion so allocated to investment advice, a fiduciary fee not computed on an hourly basis is fully deductible, with certain exceptions. The exceptions are payments made to third parties out of the bundled fee that would have been subject to the 2% floor if they had been paid directly by the nongrantor trust or estate, and any payments for expenses separately assessed (in addition to the usual or basic fiduciary fee or commission) by the fiduciary or other service provider that are commonly or customarily incurred by an individual owner of such property. These 2011 regulations were subsequently finalized essentially as re-proposed. T.D. 9664, 79 Fed. Reg. 26,616 (May 9, 2014).

52. §68(a).
53. *Id.*
54. *Id.*
55. §68(a)(1).
56. §68(a)(2). For taxable years beginning in 2006 and 2007, the reduction is two-thirds of what it otherwise would have been. Former §68(f)(2), repealed by the American Taxpayer Relief Act of 2012 (ATRA), Pub. L. No. 112-240, §101(b)(2)(A). For tax years beginning in 2010 through 2012, there is no reduction of itemized deductions under §68(a). However, the §68 reduction is reinstated for taxable years beginning in 2013 and thereafter. Former §68(g), repealed by ATRA, Pub. L. No. 112-240, §101(b)(2)(A).
57. §68(b)(1). Rev. Proc. 2015-53, 2015-44 I.R.B. 615, §3.15.
58. §68(b)(2).
59. Rev. Proc. 2014-61, 2014-47 I.R.B. 860, §3.15.
60. Rev. Proc. 2013-35, 2013-47 I.R.B. 537, §3.14.
61. §68(b)(1), as amended by ATRA, Pub. L. No. 112-240, §101(b)(2)(A); Rev. Proc. 2013-15, 2013-5 I.R.B. §3.08.
62. Former §68(g), repealed by ATRA, Pub. L. No. 112-240, §101(b)(2)(A).
63. §68(e).
64. ABA Comm. on Ethics and Prof'l Responsibility, Informal Op. 86-1517 (1986), stated that charging the fee to the corporation is permissible, provided that the basis of the fee is noted, specifically indicating the portion of the fee that was for personal work for the individual involved. The corporation can then determine whether to treat this benefit as income or as a dividend to the individual, whether to deduct any part of the fee paid from the individual's salary or dividends, and whether any part of the fee was a proper charge to the corporation or deduction from its income for tax purposes. Billing corporation for personal legal services for shareholder without identifying them as personal legal services and indicating amount applicable violates professional obligation to disclose.
65. Note that §262 disallows deductions for "personal, living, or family expenses" not otherwise allowed.

66. §212(1).
67. §212(2). *See Luman v. Commissioner,* 79 T.C. 846 (1982) (denying income tax deduction for costs of creation of family trust because no proof had been presented to allocate cost between income-producing and non-income-producing properties).
68. §212(3).
69. Of primary significance is *Merians v. Commissioner,* 60 T.C. 187 (1973), *acq.,* 1973-2 C.B. 2. In *Merians,* an individual retained a law firm to prepare an estate plan for him and his wife. He received a bill for $2,144 representing 42.8 hours of work by his attorney. The bill did not allocate between matters relating to tax advice and other services performed in the estate planning. The type of legal services provided included: (1) preparing a worksheet for the taxable estate, wills, and an irrevocable trust for the benefit of the wife; (2) transferring corporate stock to a trust; (3) dissolving a corporation; (4) creating a partnership to hold real estate belonging to the corporation; (5) creating an irrevocable life insurance trust for the benefit of the wife and transferring life insurance policies to the trust; and (6) preparing gift tax returns. The IRS agreed that some of the legal fee was for services deductible under §212(3), but asserted that the taxpayers failed to satisfy the burden of proof (because no specific allocation had been made) and, consequently, should be denied a deduction. The Tax Court (using the *Cohan v. Commissioner,* 39 F.2d 540 [2d Cir. 1930], rule permitting approximation) held that 20% of the total fee was paid for tax advice (although the court did not explain which specific tasks constituted deductible tax planning). Various concurring and dissenting opinions were filed to the effect that the *Merians* decision and Rev. Rul. 72-545, 1972-2 C.B. 179 (noted below), are erroneous. The Court of Claims had previously permitted deductions for tax services in conjunction with tax planning. *See, e.g., Carpenter v. United States,* 338 F.2d 366 (Ct. Cl. 1964). In Rev. Rul. 72-545, the IRS ruled that tax planning expenses incurred in conjunction with divorce proceedings are deductible under §212(3). This ruling noted that, if tax advice is rendered to a taxpayer by a law firm that limits its practice solely to matters of state and federal taxation, the entire fee is deductible. If tax matters are referred to a separate tax department within the law firm, the amount of the bill properly allocated to the tax department's fee is deductible. If an individual lawyer represents a client in all aspects of a divorce proceeding, the taxpayer can deduct that part of the fee properly allocable to tax advice. *See also Bagley v. Commissioner,* 8 T.C. 130 (1947), *acq.,* 1947-1 C.B. 1 (involving deductibility of estate planning fees); *Hesse v. Commissioner,* 60 T.C. 685 (1973), *acq.,* 1974-2 C.B. 3 (holding that legal expenses incurred in obtaining periodic payments in lieu of alimony were deductible as expense for production of income).
70. §212(3).
71. Reg. §1.212-1(l).
72. *See Merians v. Commissioner,* 60 T.C. 187 (1973), *acq.,* 1973-2 C.B. 2; Rev. Rul. 72-545, 1972-2 C.B. 179.
73. In *Estate of Pennell v. Commissioner,* 4 B.T.A. 1039 (1926), a legal fee for drafting a will was held not to be deductible. This decision was issued before the enactment of the predecessor provision of §212.
74. §212(2).
75. Compare the deductibility of investment counseling fees. Reg. §1.212-1(g) provides that fees for services of investment counsel paid by a taxpayer in connection with investments are deductible.

76. §265(a)(1), §265(a)(2). Query as to the availability of the income tax deduction where the trust is funded with non-income-producing property (e.g., life insurance or unimproved land).
77. *See* §212(2).
78. The deduction of such an expense was denied in *Mathews v. Commissioner,* 61 T.C. 12 (1973), *rev'd,* 520 F.2d 323 (5th Cir. 1975), *cert. denied,* 424 U.S. 967 (1976). To the extent that expenses are incurred for calculating gift tax exposure for these transfers that cost should be deductible under §212(3).
79. See, as another example suggesting why a specific billing allocation is important, *Wong v. Commissioner,* T.C. Memo 1989-683, where the Tax Court ruled that 20% of a nonitemized estate planning bill was deductible as tax advice, under §212(3), citing *Merians v. Commissioner,* 60 T.C. 187 (1973). The court noted that the taxpayers failed to establish that any portion of the legal expenses was deductible as ordinary and necessary expenses paid or incurred during the taxable year in carrying on any trade or business under §162 or, alternatively, was an ordinary and necessary expense paid or incurred during the taxable year for the production or collection of taxable income under §212(1). Further, the court found that the fees were not ordinary and necessary expenses paid or incurred during the taxable year for the management, conservation, or maintenance of property held for the production of income under §212(2).
80. *See* §212(3).
81. These costs are possibly deductible under §212(2), except to the extent attributable to property that produces tax-exempt income.
82. For a suggested format for a fee statement, see the Worksheets.
83. An identification of separate items ordinarily would have a better probability for assuring income tax deductions than the "all-or-nothing" approach used in the *Merians* case and which the Tax Court compromised with an application of the "Cohan rule" (enabling some estimate of the deductible expenses) as developed in *Cohan v. Commissioner,* 39 F.2d 540 (2d Cir. 1930).

Appendix: Worksheets

Table of Worksheets

Worksheet 1

Table of Selected Inflation-Adjusted Amounts

§1

The §1(e) $7,500 taxable income amount for determining when the highest §1(e) income tax rate applies to trusts and estates is indexed for inflation, in multiples of $50, for tax years beginning in calendar years after 1994 pursuant to §1(f).

Year	Amount	Source
2016	$12,400	Rev. Proc. 2015-53, 2015-44 I.R.B. 615, §3.01.
2015	$12,300	Rev. Proc. 2014-61, 2014-47 I.R.B. 860, §3.01.
2014	$12,150	Rev. Proc. 2013-35, 2013-47 I.R.B. 537, §3.01.
2013	$11,950	Rev. Proc. 2013-15, 2013-5 I.R.B. 444, §2.01.
2012	$11,650	Rev. Proc. 2011-52, 2011-45 I.R.B. 701, §3.01.
2011	$11,350	Rev. Proc. 2011-12, 2011-2 I.R.B. 297, §2.01.
2010	$11,200	Rev. Proc. 2009-50, 2009-45 I.R.B. 617, §3.01.
2009	$11,150	Rev. Proc. 2008-66, 2008-45 I.R.B. 1107, §3.01.

§68

The §68(b)(1) applicable amounts ($300,000 for taxpayers filing jointly and surviving spouses, $275,000 for heads of households, $250,000 for unmarried taxpayers who are not heads of households or surviving spouses, and 1/2 of the married-filing-jointly amount for married taxpayers filing separately) for determining the §68(a) limit on itemized deductions are indexed for inflation, in multiples of $50, for tax years after 2013 pursuant to §68(b)(2).

Year	Married Filing Jointly; Surviving Spouse	Married Filing Separately	Head of Household	Single	Source
2016	$311,300	$155,650	$285,350	$259,400	Rev. Proc. 2015-53, 2015-44 I.R.B. 615, §3.15.
2015	$309,900	$154,950	$284,050	$258,250	Rev. Proc. 2014-61, 2014-47 I.R.B. 860, §3.15.
2014	$305,050	$152,525	$279,650	$254,200	Rev. Proc. 2013-35, 2013-47 I.R.B. 537, §3.14.

§219

The §219(b)(5)(A) $5,000 amount for determining the maximum §219(a) qualified retirement contribution deduction is indexed for inflation, in multiples of $500, for tax years beginning in calendar years after 2008 pursuant to §219(b)(5)(C).

Year	Amount	Source
2016	$5,500	IRS News Release IR-2015-118 (Oct. 21, 2015).
2015	$5,500	Notice 2014-70, 2014-48 I.R.B. 905.
2014	$5,500	Notice 2013-73, 2013-49 I.R.B. 598.
2013	$5,500	Notice 2012-67, 2012-50 I.R.B. 671.
2012	$5,000	Notice 2011-90, 2011-47 I.R.B. 791.
2011	$5,000	Notice 2010-78, 2010-49 I.R.B. 808.
2010	$5,000	Notice 2009-94, 2009-50 I.R.B. 848.
2009	$5,000	Notice 2008-102, 2008-45 I.R.B. 1106.

§415

The §415(c)(1)(A) $40,000 amount for determining limits on contributions to certain retirement plans, including §408(k) simplified employee pensions via §408(j), is indexed for inflation, in multiples of $1,000, for calendar years after 2001 pursuant to §415(d).

Year	Amount	Source
2016	$53,000	IRS News Release IR-2015-118 (Oct. 21, 2015).
2015	$53,000	Notice 2014-70, 2014-48 I.R.B. 905.
2014	$52,000	Notice 2013-73, 2013-49 I.R.B. 598.
2013	$51,000	Notice 2012-67, 2012-50 I.R.B. 671.
2012	$50,000	Notice 2011-90, 2011-47 I.R.B. 791.
2011	$49,000	Notice 2010-78, 2010-49 I.R.B. 808.
2010	$49,000	Notice 2009-94, 2009-50 I.R.B. 848.
2009	$49,000	Notice 2008-102, 2008-45 I.R.B. 1106.

§§2010, 2505, 2631

The §2010(c)(3)(A) $5,000,000 estate tax basic exclusion amount is indexed for inflation, in multiples of $10,000, for decedents dying in calendar years after 2011 pursuant to §2010(c)(3)(B). The amount also serves as the §2505(a) gift tax basic exclusion amount by reference to §2010(c) in §2505(a)(1) and as the §2631 GST exemption amount by reference to §2010(c) in §2631(c).

Year	Exclusion Amount	Credit Amount	Source
2016	$5,450,000	$2,125,000	Rev. Proc. 2015-53, 2015-44 I.R.B. 615, §3.33.
2015	$5,430,000	$2,117,800	Rev. Proc. 2014-61, 2014-47 I.R.B. 860, §3.33.
2014	$5,340,000	$2,081,800	Rev. Proc. 2013-35, 2013-47 I.R.B. 537, §3.32.
2013	$5,250,000	$2,045,800	Rev. Proc. 2013-15, 2013-5 I.R.B. 444, §2.13.
2012	$5,120,000	$1,772,800	Rev. Proc. 2011-52, 2011-45 I.R.B. 701, §3.29.

§2032A

The §2032A(a)(2) $750,000 limit on the aggregate decrease in the value of qualified real property resulting from a special use valuation election is indexed for inflation, in multiples of $10,000, for decedents dying in calendar years after 1998 pursuant to §2032A(a)(3).

Year	Amount	Source
2016	$1,110,000	Rev. Proc. 2015-53, 2015-44 I.R.B. 615, §3.34.
2015	$1,100,000	Rev. Proc. 2014-61, 2014-47 I.R.B. 860, §3.34.
2014	$1,090,000	Rev. Proc. 2013-35, 2013-47 I.R.B. 537, §3.33.
2013	$1,070,000	Rev. Proc. 2012-41, 2012-45 I.R.B. 539, §3.18.
2012	$1,040,000	Rev. Proc. 2011-52, 2011-45 I.R.B. 701, §3.30.
2011	$1,020,000	Rev. Proc. 2010-40, 2010-46 I.R.B. 663, §3.20.
2010	$1,000,000	Rev. Proc. 2009-50, 2009-45 I.R.B. 617, §3.29.
2009	$1,000,000	Rev. Proc. 2008-66, 2008-45 I.R.B. 1107, §3.29.

§2503

The §2503(b)(1) $10,000 annual donee exclusion is indexed for inflation, in multiples of $1,000, for gifts made in calendar years after 1998 pursuant to §2503(b)(2).

Year	Amount	Source
2016	$14,000	Rev. Proc. 2015-53, 2015-44 I.R.B. 615, §3.35(1).
2015	$14,000	Rev. Proc. 2014-61, 2014-47 I.R.B. 860, §3.35(1).
2014	$14,000	Rev. Proc. 2013-35, 2013-47 I.R.B. 537, §3.34(1).
2013	$14,000	Rev. Proc. 2012-41, 2012-45 I.R.B. 539, §3.19(1).
2012	$13,000	Rev. Proc. 2011-52, 2011-45 I.R.B. 701, §3.31(1).

Year	Amount	Source
2011	$13,000	Rev. Proc. 2010-40, 2010-46 I.R.B. 663, §3.20.
2010	$13,000	Rev. Proc. 2009-50, 2009-45 I.R.B. 617, §3.21(1).
2009	$13,000	Rev. Proc. 2008-66, 2008-45 I.R.B. 1107, §3.30(1).

§2523

The §2523(i) $100,000 annual exclusion for gifts made to noncitizen spouses, which is provided via cross-reference to §2503(b), is indexed for inflation, in multiples of $1,000, for gifts made in calendar years after 1998 pursuant to §2503(b)(2).

Year	Amount	Source
2016	$148,000	Rev. Proc. 2015-53, 2015-44 I.R.B. 615, §3.35(2).
2015	$147,000	Rev. Proc. 2014-61, 2014-47 I.R.B. 860, §3.35(2).
2014	$145,000	Rev. Proc. 2013-35, 2013-47 I.R.B. 537, §3.34(2).
2013	$143,000	Rev. Proc. 2012-41, 2012-45 I.R.B. 539, §3.19(2).
2012	$139,000	Rev. Proc. 2011-52, 2011-45 I.R.B. 701, §3.31(2).
2011	$136,000	Rev. Proc. 2010-40, 2010-46 I.R.B. 663, §3.21(2).
2010	$134,000	Rev. Proc. 2009-50, 2009-45 I.R.B. 617, §3.30(2).
2009	$133,000	Rev. Proc. 2008-66, 2008-45 I.R.B. 1107, §3.30(2).

§6039F

The §6039F(a) $10,000 amount used to determine when a U.S. person must report a foreign gift to the IRS is indexed for inflation for tax years beginning after 1996 pursuant to §6039F(d).

Year	Amount	Source
2016	$15,671	Rev. Proc. 2015-53, 2015-44 I.R.B. 615, §3.39.
2015	$15,601	Rev. Proc. 2014-61, 2014-47 I.R.B. 860, §3.39.
2014	$15,358	Rev. Proc. 2013-35, 2013-47 I.R.B. 537, §3.38.
2013	$15,102	Rev. Proc. 2012-41, 2012-45 I.R.B. 539, §3.23.
2012	$14,723	Rev. Proc. 2011-52, 2011-45 I.R.B. 701, §3.35.
2011	$14,375	Rev. Proc. 2010-40, 2010-46 I.R.B. 663, §3.24.
2010	$14,165	Rev. Proc. 2009-50, 2009-45 I.R.B. 617, §3.33.
2009	$14,139	Rev. Proc. 2008-66, 2008-45 I.R.B. 1107, §3.34.

§6601

The §6601(j)(2)(A) $1,000,000 amount used to determine, when an estate makes a §6166 election, the portion of the deferred estate tax subject to the 2% interest rate is indexed for inflation, in multiples of $10,000, for decedents dying in calendar years after 1998 pursuant to §6601(j)(3).

Year	Amount	Source
2016	$1,480,000	Rev. Proc. 2015-53, 2015-44 I.R.B. 615, §3.42.
2015	$1,470,000	Rev. Proc. 2014-61, 2014-47 I.R.B. 860, §3.42.
2014	$1,450,000	Rev. Proc. 2013-35, 2013-47 I.R.B. 537, §3.41.
2013	$1,430,000	Rev. Proc. 2012-41, 2012-45 I.R.B. 539, §3.26.
2012	$1,390,000	Rev. Proc. 2011-52, 2011-45 I.R.B. 701, §3.38.
2011	$1,360,000	Rev. Proc. 2010-40, 2010-46 I.R.B. 663, §3.27.
2010	$1,340,000	Rev. Proc. 2009-50, 2009-45 I.R.B. 617, §3.36.
2009	$1,330,000	Rev. Proc. 2008-66, 2008-45 I.R.B. 1107, §3.37.

Worksheet 2

Estate and Gift Tax Rates for U.S. Citizens and Residents

2013 (and Thereafter) Decedents and Gifts

Taxable Amount Over	Taxable Amount Not Over	Tax on Amount in 1st Column	Tax Rate on Excess Over Amount in 1st Column
$0	$10,000	$0	18%
$10,000	$20,000	$1,800	20%
$20,000	$40,000	$3,800	22%
$40,000	$60,000	$8,200	24%
$60,000	$80,000	$13,000	26%
$80,000	$100,000	$18,200	28%
$100,000	$150,000	$23,800	30%
$150,000	$250,000	$38,800	32%
$250,000	$500,000	$70,800	34%
$500,000	$750,000	$155,800	37%
$750,000	$1,000,000	$248,300	39%
$1,000,000		$345,800	40%
2010–2012 Decedents and Gifts			
$0	$10,000	$0	18%
$10,000	$20,000	$1,800	20%
$20,000	$40,000	$3,800	22%
$40,000	$60,000	$8,200	24%
$60,000	$80,000	$13,000	26%
$80,000	$100,000	$18,200	28%
$100,000	$150,000	$23,800	30%
$150,000	$250,000	$38,800	32%
$250,000	$500,000	$70,800	34%
$500,000		$155,800	35%

2007–2009 Decedents and Gifts

Taxable Amount Over	Taxable Amount Not Over	Tax on Amount in 1st Column	Tax Rate on Excess Over Amount in 1st Column
$0	$10,000	$0	18%
$10,000	$20,000	$1,800	20%
$20,000	$40,000	$3,800	22%
$40,000	$60,000	$8,200	24%
$60,000	$80,000	$13,000	26%

2007–2009 Decedents and Gifts

Taxable Amount Over	Taxable Amount Not Over	Tax on Amount in 1st Column	Tax Rate on Excess Over Amount in 1st Column
$80,000	$100,000	$18,200	28%
$100,000	$150,000	$23,800	30%
$150,000	$250,000	$38,800	32%
$250,000	$500,000	$70,800	34%
$500,000	$750,000	$155,800	37%
$750,000	$1,000,000	$248,300	39%
$1,000,000	$1,250,000	$345,800	41%
$1,250,000	$1,500,000	$448,300	43%
$1,500,000		$555,800	45%

2006 Decedents and Gifts

Taxable Amount Over	Taxable Amount Not Over	Tax on Amount in 1st Column	Tax Rate on Excess Over Amount in 1st Column
$0	$10,000	$0	18%
$10,000	$20,000	$1,800	20%
$20,000	$40,000	$3,800	22%
$40,000	$60,000	$8,200	24%
$60,000	$80,000	$13,000	26%
$80,000	$100,000	$18,200	28%
$100,000	$150,000	$23,800	30%
$150,000	$250,000	$38,800	32%
$250,000	$500,000	$70,800	34%
$500,000	$750,000	$155,800	37%
$750,000	$1,000,000	$248,300	39%
$1,000,000	$1,250,000	$345,800	41%
$1,250,000	$1,500,000	$448,300	43%
$1,500,000	$2,000,000	$555,800	45%
$2,000,000		$780,800	46%

2005 Decedents and Gifts

Taxable Amount Over	Taxable Amount Not Over	Tax on Amount in 1st Column	Tax Rate on Excess Over Amount in 1st Column
$0	$10,000	$0	18%
$10,000	$20,000	$1,800	20%
$20,000	$40,000	$3,800	22%
$40,000	$60,000	$8,200	24%

2005 Decedents and Gifts

Taxable Amount Over	Taxable Amount Not Over	Tax on Amount in 1st Column	Tax Rate on Excess Over Amount in 1st Column
$60,000	$80,000	$13,000	26%
$80,000	$100,000	$18,200	28%
$100,000	$150,000	$23,800	30%
$150,000	$250,000	$38,800	32%
$250,000	$500,000	$70,800	34%
$500,000	$750,000	$155,800	37%
$750,000	$1,000,000	$248,300	39%
$1,000,000	$1,250,000	$345,800	41%
$1,250,000	$1,500,000	$448,300	43%
$1,500,000	$2,000,000	$555,800	45%
$2,000,000		$780,800	47%

Note that, for post-2005 decedents, estates are not actually subject to tax in the lower brackets because of the use of the "applicable exclusion amount," also known as the "unified credit." The same is true for post-2009 gifts with respect to the gift tax unified credit. For spouses dying after 2010, the applicable exclusion amount may also include the deceased spousal unused exclusion (DSUE) amount. The unified credit amounts for the estate and gift taxes are shown in a separate Worksheet.

Worksheet 3

Maximum Estate and Gift Tax Rates and Unified Credit Amounts

Federal Estate Tax—Maximum Tax Rates and Unified Credit Amounts

Year of Transfer	Maximum Tax Rate	Credit Amount	Maximum Value for Excluded Property
1997	55%	$192,800	$600,000
1998	55%	$202,050	$625,000
1999	55%	$211,300	$650,000
2000	55%	$220,550	$675,000
2001	55%	$220,550	$675,000
2002	50%	$345,800	$1,000,000
2003	49%	$345,800	$1,000,000
2004	48%	$555,800	$1,500,000
2005	47%	$555,800	$1,500,000
2006	46%	$780,800	$2,000,000
2007	45%	$780,800	$2,000,000
2008	45%	$780,800	$2,000,000
2009	45%	$1,455,800	$3,500,000
2010	35%	$1,730,800	$5,000,000
2011	35%	$1,730,800	$5,000,000
2012	35%	$1,772,800 (as indexed)	$5,120,000 (as indexed)[1]
2013	40%	$2,045,800 (as indexed)	$5,250,000 (as indexed)[2]
2014	40%	$2,081,800 (as indexed)	$5,340,000 (as indexed)[3]
2015	40%	$2,117,800 (as indexed)	$5,430,000 (as indexed)[4]
2016	40%	$2,125,000 (as indexed)	$5,450,000 (as indexed)[5]

Federal Gift Tax—Maximum Tax Rates and Unified Credit Amounts

Year of Transfer	Maximum Tax Rate	Credit Amount	Value of Excluded Property
1997	55%	$192,800	$600,000
1998	55%	$202,050	$625,000
1999	55%	$211,300	$650,000
2000	55%	$220,550	$675,000
2001	55%	$220,550	$675,000
2002	50%	$345,800	$1,000,000
2003	49%	$345,800	$1,000,000
2004	48%	$345,800	$1,000,000

Federal Estate Tax—Maximum Tax Rates and Unified Credit Amounts

Year of Transfer	Maximum Tax Rate	Credit Amount	Maximum Value for Excluded Property
2005	47%	$345,800	$1,000,000
2006	46%	$345,800	$1,000,000
2007	45%	$345,800	$1,000,000
2008	45%	$345,800	$1,000,000
2009	45%	$345,800	$1,000,000
2010	35%	$330,800	$1,000,000
2011	35%	$1,730,800	$5,000,000
2012	35%	$1,772,800 (as indexed)	$5,120,000 (as indexed)[6]
2013	40%	$2,045,800 (as indexed)	$5,250,000 (as indexed)[7]
2014	40%	$2,081,800 (as indexed)	$5,340,000 (as indexed)[8]
2015	40%	$2,117,800 (as indexed)	$5,430,000 (as indexed)[9]
2016	40%	$2,125,000 (as indexed)	$5,450,000 (as indexed)[10]

Worksheet 4

Estate Planning Checklist/Preliminary Questionnaire

This list identifies a variety of fundamental questions that the estate planner can use to initially determine whether the client/prospective client needs appropriate estate planning assistance. This listing could be reconfigured by the advisor to present to the client so that the client can consider these matters in detail either before or after an initial meeting with the estate planner.

A. Basic Asset Dispositions at Death

1. Does the client's current last will and testament reflect the client's basic objectives for transferring his/her property at death (a) in the amounts identified and (b) to the beneficiaries named?
2. Are any revisions to the client's basic estate plan essential because of changes in the client's family, including births, deaths, mental or physical incompetency, and divorces?
3. Are assets held by the client in an appropriate format that achieves property transfer efficiencies, maximizes estate tax savings, and avoids over funding or under funding of trusts at death?
4. If a marital gift (including a marital deduction trust) is included in the will, should the provisions for this gift be made more or less restrictive?
5. If a power of appointment to be held by another is included in the client's will, are the takers in default of the exercise of this power of appointment actually the desired recipients of the property subject to that power?
6. If the client holds a power of appointment under an instrument previously created by another, should that power be exercised, will that power be exercised consistent with current objectives, or should it not be exercised, with the takers-in-default provisions controlling the disposition of the assets subject to this power?

B. Nonprobate Asset Dispositions

1. Should a revocable/living trust be used to implement the estate plan with the assets thereby being placed beyond probate court jurisdiction, including, for example, to achieve privacy concerning the client's asset holdings?
2. If a living trust has been previously created, have all the desired assets been actually transferred into the trust so that the trustee (rather than the executor) has control over these assets (including a replacement trustee after the death of the grantor if the grantor is acting as current trustee)?
3. Should the dispositive provisions of this revocable trust agreement be amended to accommodate changed objectives or to recognize changes in the client's family situation, such as deaths, births, mental or physical incompetency, and divorces?

4. Are the ownership and beneficiary designations for other properties appropriate to assure consistency with the client's property transfer objectives, including:
   a) ownership of the personal residence and any secondary residences
   b) joint tenancy property
   c) payable on death (i.e., "POD") checking and savings accounts
   d) life insurance policy designations
   e) deferred compensation beneficiary designations, including for pension plans, profit sharing plans, 401(k) plans, IRAs, and similar accounts.

C. Related Property and Health Care Management and Asset Transfer Matters

1. Does the client have a durable power of attorney in effect and, if so, is the appropriate person designated as the "attorney-in-fact"; if so, is that person aware of this designation, willing to serve in that capacity, and in possession of an executed version of this document?
2. Does the client have in effect a power of attorney for health care (or a similar document as identified under local law)?
3. Does the client have a living will or advance medical directive? If the client has both a living will and a power of attorney for health care, are these documents consistent?
4. Does the client have in effect a designation for the guardian of the person of the client in the event of mental or physical incompetency?
5. If the client has minor children, has an appropriate identification been made of any successor guardian for both the person and the property of such children (particularly in the event the other parent is deceased)? If this designation has previously been made in a will, should this designation alternatively be stated in a separate document?
6. Are family members aware of funeral, organ donation, and related end-of-life instructions?
7. Does the client have effective adequate long-term care insurance and other insurance to manage the coverage of catastrophic financial costs during lifetime?

D. Possible Lifetime Gift Program

1. Does the client have sufficient financial flexibility to implement a gift program?
2. If so, but the client presently seems unwilling to make gifts, should the client be encouraged to make gifts; if so, what strategies are appropriate to surmounting this psychological barrier against making significant gifts?
3. Should the client make annual donee exclusion gifts to children and others?
4. Should separate trusts for educational purposes or §529 education funding plans be implemented for the benefit of grandchildren and others?

E. Additional Inquiries

1. Does the client have in effect adequate buy-sell agreements for joint investments and businesses and should those agreements be amended, including to properly reflect the current value of these properties?

2. Should an irrevocable life insurance trust be implemented and, if so, what should be the face value of the acquired life insurance? Who would be the trustee of that trust?
3. Should a family limited partnership be created and funded to (a) facilitate both the transfer of a family business and (b) achieve possible reductions in valuations for federal estate tax purposes?
4. Should charitable trusts and private charitable foundations be organized and, if so, who are the appropriate charitable beneficiaries and who are to be the individuals managing the private charitable foundation?
5. Should other estate planning alternatives be considered and possibly implemented, including:
   a) interest-free loans to family members (and trusts for family members),
   b) a grantor retained annuity trust (GRAT),
   c) a qualified personal residence trust (QPRT),
   d) self-canceling installment notes,
   e) joint- or split-property purchases, and
   f) similar arrangements?

Worksheet 5

Client Interview Materials—Factual Analysts and Inventory of Assets

As adapted to the estate planner's individual use, this prospective client inventory/questionnaire could be structured to facilitate the insertion of this information into a personal computer for use in conjunction with an estate tax projection software program. Some of this information may be available electronically from brokers, banks, mutual funds, and other financial institutions. Some estate planners ask clients to complete forms such as this, or ask assistants to work with clients to develop this information.

PART ONE

FAMILY DATA

1. Basic Information

Name:	**Date of Birth**	**Social Security Number**	**Status of Health**
Husband			
Wife			

2. Residence
   Permanent home address
   Business address
   Other temporary residences (Possibility of treatment of this residence as a "permanent residence" for any state tax purposes?)
   Period of residence in present state
   Prior residences (e.g., including any community property states?)

3. Citizenship Status

Husband:	U.S. ____________	Other ____________
Wife:	U.S. ____________	Other ____________

4. Children, Grandchildren, and Other Dependents

Name	**Address**	**Date of Birth**	**Status**

5. Marital History (each client)
   Date of marriage
   Prior marriages and divorces, including terms of any continuing obligations

6. Telephone Numbers and E-mail Addresses

PART TWO

INCOME DATA—PRESENT CASH FLOW—FUTURE REQUIREMENTS

I. Present Net Income/Cash Receipts Data	**Husband**	**Wife**	**Others**
A. Income/Cash Sources			
Salaries	______	______	______
Other Compensation	______	______	______
Dividends	______	______	______
Interest	______	______	______
Net Rents	______	______	______
Royalties	______	______	______
Business Profits	______	______	______
Trusts	______	______	______
Other	______	______	______
Total	______	______	______
B. Current Expenditures			
Living Expenses	______	______	______
Insurance Premiums	______	______	______
Tax Liabilities	______	______	______
Mortgage & Other Debt Payments	______	______	______
Other	______	______	______
Total	______	______	______
C. Amount Available for Savings			
(Income/Cash Sources Less Current Expenditures)	______	______	______

II. Future Annual Cash Requirements	**Husband**	**Wife**	**Others**
A. Future Cash Sources (after retirement)			
Dividends	______	______	______
Interest	______	______	______
Other Investment Income	______	______	______
Annuities & Insurance	______	______	______
Social Security	______	______	______
Employee Retirement Benefits	______	______	______
Other Employee Benefits (e.g., Deferred Compensation Arrangements)	______	______	______
Trusts	______	______	______
Other	______	______	______
Total	______	______	______

B. Future Cash Needs (after retirement)

Living Expenses	_______	_______	_______
Tax Liabilities	_______	_______	_______
Other Obligations	_______	_______	_______
Total	_______	_______	_______

C. Amount Available for Savings

(Future Cash Sources Less Future Cash Requirements)	_______	_______	_______

PART THREE

NET WORTH/SUMMARY OF ASSETS & LIABILITIES

	Husband (separate)	**Wife (separate)**	**Joint & Survivor & Community**
		(Identify Contributor)	
I. Assets			
A. Cash and Bank Accounts			
(see Attachment A)	_______	_______	_______
B. Notes, Accounts Receivable, Mortgages			
(see Attachment A)	_______	_______	_______
C. Bonds			
(see Attachment A)	_______	_______	_______
D. Stocks and Mutual Funds			
(see Attachment A)	_______	_______	_______
E. Closely Held Business Interests			
(see Attachment B)	_______	_______	_______
F. Real Estate			
(see Attachment C)	_______	_______	_______
G. Insurance			
(see Attachment D)	_______	_______	_______
H. Employee Benefits			
(see Attachment E)	_______	_______	_______
I. Miscellaneous (e.g., personal effects, collections, patents, trademarks, copyrights, etc.)			
(see Attachment F)	_______	_______	_______
Total	_______	_______	_______

II. Liabilities (see Attachment G)

A. Real Estate Mortgages	_______	_______	_______
B. Notes to Financial Institutions	_______	_______	_______
C. Loans on Insurance Policies	_______	_______	_______

D. Other Obligations	______	______	______
E. Charitable Pledges	______	______	______
F. Tax Liabilities	______	______	______
Total	______	______	______
III. Net Worth	______	______	______

PART FOUR

ESTATE PLANNING OBJECTIVES

A. Retirement Needs and Objectives
B. Provision for Spouse at Death
C. Provision for Children at Death
D. Gift Program for Spouse and Children
E. Gifts to Charities

PART FIVE

CHECKLIST OF ESTATE PLANNING DOCUMENTS & FAMILY ADVISORS

A. Safe Deposit Box

Location and Ownership ______________________

B. Present Documents (if any), and physical location

1) Will: dated ______________________

2) Revocable Trusts:

i) created by client ______________________

ii) created for client by others ______________________

3) Irrevocable Trusts:

i) created by client ______________________

ii) created for client by others ______________________

4) Gift Tax Returns—filed? location of copies? ______________________

5) Income Tax Returns—filed? location of copies? ______________________

6) Other Pertinent Documents (e.g., durable power of attorney, health care power of attorney, medical directive, life insurance policies, annuity contracts, real property deeds, etc.) ______________________

7) Location of computers passwords and similar electronic access information ______________________

C. Advisors (names, physical addresses, telephone numbers, and email addresses)

Other Attorneys ______________________

Accountant ______________________

Trust Officer ______________________

Commercial Banker (and bank account numbers) ______________________

Investment Advisor	______
Securities Broker (and account numbers)	______
Life Insurance Agent	______
Casualty Insurance Agent	______
Closest Relative(s)	______

Attachment "A"

LIQUID ASSETS

A. Cash and Bank Accounts **Amount**

	Bank	**Husband**	**Wife**	**Joint**
	(Identify whether husband, wife, or joint ownership)			
Cash	______	______	______	______
	______	______	______	______
Checking Account	______	______	______	______
	______	______	______	______
	______	______	______	______
Savings Account	______	______	______	______
	______	______	______	______

B. Accounts Receivable, Notes, & Mortgages

Debtor	**Nature of Debt**	**Security**	**Maturity**	**Face Amount**	**Present Value**
______	______	______	______	______	______
______	______	______	______	______	______
______	______	______	______	______	______

C. Bonds

Description of Bonds	**Ownership**	**Face Value**	**Cost**	**Current Value**	**Current Yield**
______	______	______	______	______	______
______	______	______	______	______	______
______	______	______	______	______	______
______	______	______	______	______	______

D. Stocks

	Description	**Ownership**	**Cost**	**Current Value**	**Current Yield**
	______	______	______	______	______
	______	______	______	______	______
	______	______	______	______	______

E. Mutual Fund (Regulated Investment Company) Shares & Exchange Traded Funds (ETFs)

Description	Ownership	Cost	Current Value	Current Yield
________	________	________	________	________
________	________	________	________	________
________	________	________	________	________

F. Limited Partnership Interests

Description	Ownership	Cost	Current Value	Current Yield
________	________	________	________	________
________	________	________	________	________
________	________	________	________	________

Attachment "B"

CLOSELY HELD BUSINESS INTERESTS *

A. Basic Information

1. Name of business ________________
2. Business address ________________
3. Type of business organization ________________

(e.g., regular corporation, S corporation, partnership, limited liability company, sole proprietorship)

4. Business advisors, accountants ________________

B. Capitalization (if corporation) (adapt to partnership use, if a partnership or limited liability company)

	Common	Preferred	Debentures
Outstanding	________	________	________
Authorized	________	________	________
Dividend Rate	________	________	________

C. Distribution of Entity Ownership

	Common	Preferred	Debentures
Client	________	________	________
Spouse	________	________	________
Children	________	________	________
Unrelated Parties	________	________	________

D. Buy-Sell Agreement

1. Does buy-sell agreement exist? ________________
2. If so, what type? (e.g., cross-purchase, stock redemption, combination) ________________
3. Is buy-sell obligation to be funded and, if so, how and amount? ________________

4. Method for determining value of business entity (e.g., book value, earnings multiple, appraisal, agreed value)	________________

E. Other Commitments of Business

1. Stock option agreements	________________
2. Deferred compensation agreements	________________
3. Other employee benefit plans	________________
4. Key-man insurance policies	________________

F. Anticipated Disposition of Stock (assuming no buy-sell agreement)

____

____

____

G. Anticipated Eligibility for Deferred Estate Tax Payments Attributable to Interest in Closely Held Business

____

____

____

* This form, as appropriately adapted, should be separately completed for each closely held business interest, whether in corporate, partnership, limited liability company, or sole proprietorship form and by each spouse (if this compilation is done for a marital unit). The total value can then be inserted into the Net Worth/Summary of Assets & Liabilities (Part Three in this Worksheet).

Attachment "C"

REAL ESTATE *
(including cooperative apartments and condominiums)

	Parcel One	Parcel Two
A. Basic Information		
1. Location	________	________
2. Type of property (e.g., residential, commercial, unimproved land)	________	________
3. Form of property ownership	________	________
4. If joint property, contribution amount by each joint tenant	________	________
5. Date property acquired	________	________
6. Income tax basis (and accumulated tax depreciation)	________	________
7. Present fair market value	________	________

B. Mortgage Obligations		
1. Original mortgage amount	______	______
2. Current principal amount of mortgage	______	______
3. Maturity and payment schedules	______	______
C. Cash Flow Analysis		
1. Annual gross income	______	______
2. Annual maintenance costs	______	______
3. Annual real estate taxes	______	______
4. Annual tax depreciation	______	______
5. Annual mortgage payments (principal and interest)	______	______
6. Net positive (or negative) cash flow	______	______
D. Farm		
1. Value of land	______	______
2. Farm machinery and equipment	______	______
3. Excess of value of land over value as operating farm	______	______

E. Estate Tax Special Use Valuation & Tax Payment Deferral Eligibility

1. Does real estate qualify for estate tax special use valuation? ______

2. Is eligibility anticipated for estate tax deferral for farming and other closely held business activities? ______

* This form, as appropriately adapted, should be separately completed for each spouse and for additional properties. The total value can then be inserted into the Net Worth/Summary of Assets & Liabilities (Part Three in this Worksheet).

Attachment "D"

LIFE INSURANCE *

	Face Value	Type of Policy	Annual Premium	Cash Surrender Value	Designated Beneficiary	Settlement Option
A. Policies Owned by Client on Own Life (Company & Policy Number)						
______	______	______	______	______	______	______
______	______	______	______	______	______	______
______	______	______	______	______	______	______

"Incidents of ownership" held by client in these policies?______

	Face Value	Type of Policy	Annual Premium	Cash Surrender Value	Designated Beneficiary	Settlement Option
B. Policies Owned by Others on Client's Life (Company & Policy Number)						
______	______	______	______	______	______	______
______	______	______	______	______	______	______
______	______	______	______	______	______	______

"Incidents of ownership" held by client in these policies?______________________

	Face Value	Type of Policy	Annual Premium	Cash Surrender Value	Designated Beneficiary	Settlement Option
C. Policies Owned by Client on Lives of Others (Company & Policy Number)						
______	______	______	______	______	______	______
______	______	______	______	______	______	______
______	______	______	______	______	______	______

* This form, as appropriately adapted, should be separately completed for each spouse. The total current value can then be inserted into the Net Worth/Summary of Assets & Liabilities (Part Three in this Worksheet). Adjustments will be required to reflect the differences between cash surrender values and the face values if the proceeds will be includible in the insured's gross estate for federal estate tax purposes.

Attachment "E"

EXECUTIVE COMPENSATION AND EMPLOYEE BENEFITS *

Employer's name and address ______________________________

A. Type of Plan	**Retirement Benefit**	**Amount Vested**	**Death Benefits**
1. Pension	______	______	______
2. Profit-sharing	______	______	______
3. Deferred compensation arrangement	______	______	______
4. Individual retirement account	______	______	______
5. Other	______	______	______

B. Stock Option Plan	Option Price	Current Value	Summary of Terms
1. Incentive stock plan	________	________	________
2. Nonqualified stock option plan	________	________	________
C. Other Benefits	**Company**	**Benefits**	**Beneficiary**
1. Group term life insurance	________	________	________
2. Disability income	________	________	________
3. Health and medical insurance	________	________	________
4. Other	________	________	________
TOTAL VALUES FOR NET WORTH INCLUSIONS	________	________	________

* This form, as appropriately adapted, should be separately completed for each spouse. The total value can then be inserted into the Net Worth/Summary of Assets & Liabilities (Part Three in this Worksheet).

Attachment "F"

MISCELLANEOUS ASSETS *
(at current fair market value)

	Client	Spouse	Joint
A. Personal Effects			
1. Clothing	________	________	________
2. Jewelry	________	________	________
3. Home furnishings	________	________	________
4. Other	________	________	________
B. Other Tangible Personal Property			
1. Collections (e.g., art, book, stamp, coin)	________	________	________
2. Automobiles	________	________	________
3. Other (e.g., boats, aircraft, office contents)	________	________	________
C. Patent, Trademark, Copyright Ownership & Royalty Arrangements	________	________	________
D. Mineral Interests			
1. Oil and gas	________	________	________
2. Coal	________	________	________
3. Other	________	________	________
E. Estates & Trusts			
1. Anticipated benefits under estates and trusts	________	________	________
2. Powers of appointment (general or limited?)	________	________	________

F. Social Club Memberships, Bonds, & Stock	________	________	________
G. Cemetery Plot	________	________	________
TOTAL VALUES	________	________	________

* This form, as appropriately adapted, should be completed for each spouse. The total value can then be inserted into the Net Worth/Summary of Assets & Liabilities (Part Three in this Worksheet).

Attachment "G"

PERSONAL LIABILITIES *

	Obligee	Amount	Interest Rate
A. Real Estate Mortgages	________	________	________
B. Promissory Notes Owing to Financial Institutions	________	________	________
C. Loans on Insurance Policies	________	________	________
D. Other Obligations	________	________	________
E. Charitable Pledges	________	________	________
F. Tax Liabilities	________	________	________
G. Contingent Liabilities	________	________	________
TOTAL LIABILITIES FOR INCLUSION IN NET-WORTH STATEMENT	________	________	________

* This form, as appropriately adapted, should be separately completed for each spouse. The total value can then be inserted into the Net Worth/Summary of Assets & Liabilities (Part Three in this Worksheet).

Worksheet 6

Client Engagement and Conflicts Letters

Client Joint Spousal Engagement and Spousal Conflicts Letter

NOTE: The objectives of this letter are to (i) specify the terms of the estate planning representation for both spouses in a marriage, (ii) identify the fee arrangement, and (iii) provide evidence that each client (spouse) agrees to a waiver of his or her privileges of confidentiality with respect to the other client.

Dear [Clients]:

You have asked our firm to provide certain estate planning services for both of you. As we have discussed, these services will include the preparation of (1) last wills, (2) trust agreements, and (3) tax projections showing the tax effects of various options that we have been discussing. These options include the preparation of documents reflecting the utilization of (a) the unlimited marital deduction, (b) the unified credit, and (c) generation-skipping transfers.

We will proceed with these matters and our firm will charge you a fee for such services in accordance with our usual hourly charges. At present our fees for our attorneys who will be working on your estate planning matters range from $___ to $___ per hour, and our fees for our legal assistants are $___ per hour. My personal billing rate is $___ per hour. Our customary practice is to prepare and send our fee statements on a monthly basis, covering services performed by us during the prior month. We expect those fee statements to be paid within thirty days after our invoice is sent, if the amount is in excess of the retainer previously paid. We would anticipate that we will complete this assignment promptly and, accordingly, the entire fee should be represented by only one billing.

Our firm's policy is to require a retainer to be paid before we provide services to new clients. For this matter we request a retainer amount of $___ to be received before we proceed with any legal work on your behalf. This retainer is not an estimate of our total fees to be incurred, but will constitute a prepayment of the fees to be incurred by you.

As I mentioned during our initial conference, we want to again inform you that, when estate planning is being implemented, a husband and wife may have conflicting interests that concern their various property interests. If, as you have both requested, we are to act as attorneys for both of you, we must try to balance all important factors concerning your properties and several interests. We cannot, therefore, be a proponent for either of you against the interests of the other spouse. Such a process could favor one of you to the detriment of the other spouse.

We must necessarily obtain confidential information from each of you. Because we will be representing both of you, we cannot, however, keep that information confidential from the other spouse.

We must make estate tax planning recommendations that affect the property interests of each of you after your deaths. A substantial conflict may exist in the determination of what constitutes community property and what is separate property and, therefore, who is assumed to be the owner of certain of your properties. That determination by us may be more beneficial for one of you than for the other. Although unlikely, the possibility of your divorce must also be recognized. Consequently, our present recommendations could affect the income, property, and support provisions either in any divorce or after the death of one or both of you.

We feel that, only after you have been informed by us as to the facts of these potential conflicts, can you decide whether you want us to represent both of you in the estate planning project you have requested. You are each, of course, welcome to have your own counsel for any part or all of the matters we are discussing.

We would be pleased to assist you with these matters. If you do wish us to proceed with estate planning assistance for both of you, please each sign the copy of this letter that is enclosed and return the copy to us. I want to assure you that our firm is committed to providing excellent estate planning services in an effective, timely, and cost efficient manner.

Very truly yours,
Estate Planning Law Firm

____

Consent to Joint Estate Planning Legal Representation

I have read the letter above and I understand that conflicts of interest exist between my [husband/wife] and me in the estate planning matters about which we are consulting you. If I wish to have separate counsel or desire that you not be involved in any aspect of estate planning on my behalf, I shall notify you. I do consent to have your firm represent both of us in our estate planning. I understand that, where you are representing both of us on the same matter, and between my [husband/wife], you, and me no confidential communications are possible.

Dated: ________________ ____________________
Spouse One

Dated: ________________ ____________________
Spouse Two

Client Family Business Client Engagement Letter

NOTE: The objective of this letter is to specify the terms of the representation of a family business enterprise and its owners in considering and implementing various arrangements to facilitate a business ownership succession plan, often in conjunction with estate planning for the individual owners (and their spouses).

[Date]
PERSONAL AND CONFIDENTIAL
Dear [Clients]:

You have asked our firm to provide certain services for you, as the owners of ABC Company, and also to assist ABC Company. These activities will concern the consideration of structures to implement a business succession plan for transferring ownership of the business enterprise to surviving owners and their successors. As we have discussed, these services may include the preparation of (1) buy-sell agreements, (2) other owner agreements, and (3) tax projections showing the tax effects of various options that we have discussed.

We will proceed with these matters and our firm will charge a fee for such services in accordance with our usual hourly charges. At present our fees for our attorneys who will be working on your estate planning matters range from $___ to $___ per hour, and our fees for our legal assistants are $___ per hour. My personal billing rate is $ ___ per hour. We anticipate that our fee statement will be issued to ABC Company to the extent that our services are provided in matters benefiting the company. However, we will not send a fee statement to the company for those services of direct and exclusive benefit to owners; rather, our fee for those services will be billed directly to the individual owner.

Our customary practice is to prepare and send our fee statements on a monthly basis, covering services performed by us during the prior month. We expect those fee statements to be paid within 30 days after our invoice is sent, if the amount is in excess of the retainer previously paid. We would anticipate that we will complete this assignment promptly and, accordingly, the entire fee should be represented by only one billing.

Our firm's policy is to require a retainer to be paid before we provide services to new clients. For this matter we request a retainer amount of $___ to be received before we proceed with any legal work on your behalf. This retainer is not an estimate of our total fees to be incurred, but will constitute a prepayment of the fees to be incurred by you.

As I mentioned during our initial conference, we want to again inform you that, when estate planning is being implemented in a situation involving a business and several owners, these various parties may have conflicting interests that concern their various interests. If, as you have requested, we are to act as attorneys for all of you (i.e., the owners and the business enterprise itself), we must try to balance all important factors concerning your properties and several interests. Therefore, for example, we cannot be a proponent for one owner against the interests of another owner. Such a process could favor one of you to the detriment of the other(s).

We must necessarily obtain confidential information from each of you. Because we will be representing all of you, we cannot, however, keep that information confidential from the other(s).

We believe that, only after you have been informed by us as to the facts of these potential conflicts, can you decide whether you want us to represent all of you in this business succession planning project you have requested. You are each, of course, welcome to have your own counsel for any part or all of the matters we are discussing.

We would be pleased to assist you with these matters. If you do wish us to proceed with this planning assistance, please sign the copy of this letter that is enclosed and return the copy to us. I want to assure you that our firm is committed to providing our business succession planning services in an effective, timely, and cost efficient manner.

Very truly yours,
Estate Planning Law Firm

____

CONSENT ISSUED TO LAW FIRM TO ITS JOINT REPRESENTATION FOR BUSINESS SUCCESSION PLANNING FOR ABC COMPANY

We are the owners of ABC Company. We have asked you to provide your services jointly to each of us in developing and implementing a business succession plan for ABC Company. We have previously discussed some of the options and want to go forward with this project.

We do realize that our several interests and objectives may differ, producing potential conflicts of interest between us in conjunction with matters involving implementing a business ownership succession plan (and related documentation) for our business. We realize that communications and information that you receive from any of us will be completely shared with the other owners.

After careful consideration we each request that your firm jointly represent ABC Company and its several owners individually in developing and implementing a comprehensive business succession plan for our business. We recognize that this may include buy-sell agreements (which will include valuation mechanisms and procedures) and other documentation relating to restructuring of the business ownership.

____

Signed: ABC Company

____

Signed: Owner One

____

Signed: Owner Two

Additional Resources: See the Sample Engagement Letter and the Sample Declination Letter in the Worksheets of 801 T.M., *Conflicts, Confidentiality, and Other Ethical Considerations in Estate Planning.*

Various other formats for engagement letters in the estate planning context may be found at the following website: http://www.actec.org/public/EngagementLettersPublic.asp. Included there are the following possible engagement letters: (1) joint spousal representation engagement letter and a concurrent separate spouse representation engagement letter (and a spousal representation checklist); (2) representation of multiple generations of the same family (and a representation of multiple generations of the same family checklist); (3) multiple-party representation in the business context (including a multiple-party representation in the business context checklist); (4) a letter accepting the nomination of a lawyer as fiduciary; (5) an estate administration engagement letter (and an estate administration representation checklist), and (6) an optional additional to a basic engagement letter when planning for disability (and a client under a disability checklist).

Worksheet 7

Fee Statement for Estate Planning Services

[Estate Planning Firm Letterhead]
Fee Statement for Estate Planning Services For professional services rendered in estate planning for Mr. and Ms. ______________ including:

(a) Drafting will—preparation of last wills and advice to clients with respect to the lifetime and testamentary disposition of personal property items: $__________
(b) Drafting trusts—preparation of trust documents and advice to clients to enable the management, conservation, and maintenance of their properties: $___________
(c) Tax advice—analysis of the potential estate, gift, and income tax impact on the present property situations of clients and the development of recommendations concerning wills and trusts to implement appropriate tax-saving arrangements when implementing property transfers to intended beneficiaries: $___________

TOTAL: $ ____________

Note: Under IRC §212, potential federal income tax deductions are available for the costs of (1) managing and conserving property and (2) tax assistance. These deductions, when coupled with various other deductions, may be subject to a floor of 2% of the taxpayer's adjusted gross income. IRC §67.

Worksheet 8

Estate Tax Projections

(Prepared Using Bloomberg BNA Estate and Gift Tax Planner)

Estate planners are often called upon to prepare client-specific federal estate tax projections to identify the probable federal estate tax costs and state death tax costs to be incurred upon the death of a client and, if married, on the death of the spouse. Various estate tax spreadsheet programs have been developed to make these projections with the use of a personal computer. The following pages include a sample of the calculations that can be made and the information that can be produced using the Estate and Gift Tax Planner published by Bloomberg BNA Software, a division of Bloomberg BNA.

These federal estate tax cost projections can be customized to enable inclusion of the name of the clients and information concerning the estate planner's firm in a form permitting attractive presentation to clients. The computer program contains numerous supporting schedules for items such as tax credits, previously paid gift taxes, prior transfers, state death taxes, state inheritance and estate taxes, generation-skipping transfer taxes, the estate tax due on the death of the testator's children (taking into account the projected appreciation of assets), and the resultant shares remaining for the grandchildren.

The use of the Bloomberg BNA Estate and Gift Tax Planner enables immediate estate tax (and related) projections based on a wide range of variables that are fully integrated into the calculations, including, for example: (1) marital deduction alternatives, including the minimum marital gift that will reduce the federal tax to zero or the lowest possible number; (2) assumptions concerning the future appreciation of asset values; (3) circular interrelated residue calculations; (4) charitable gift calculations, including charitable remainder and charitable lead trusts; (5) §303 analysis; (6) §6166 analysis and calculations; (7) generation-skipping transfer taxes (whether lifetime direct skip transfers or direct skip transfers on death), including projections of estate taxes on children's deaths for comparison with generation-skipping transfer taxes; (8) taxable gifts prior to death, including projections as to future gifts; (9) credits for estate tax on prior transfers and for foreign death taxes paid; (10) deductions for state death and inheritance taxes; (11) liquidity analyses; (12) the net family share remaining after all taxes on the estates of both parents; (13) gift taxes on grantor retained income trusts, grantor retained annuity trusts, and grantor unitrusts; and (14) valuation discounts.

The results can be displayed graphically for presentation to clients.

These projections can be made using a variety of assumptions, including: (1) the amount of the anticipated exclusion for estate tax purposes as of the time of death (this amount obviously being dependent upon estate tax law changes); (2) reversed order of deaths between spouses; (3) probable investment returns during the estate tax postponement period (when the maximum appropriate marital deduction amount has been claimed at the first death); and (4) subsequent investment returns.

The Bloomberg BNA Estate and Gift Tax Planner enables the simultaneous calculation and display of up to six cases for a single decedent or up to three family estate plans. For answers to questions about the Bloomberg BNA Estate and Gift Tax Planner, call toll-free: 1-800-424-2938.

Hypothetical Scenario

Paul and Margaret Client are married and have one daughter, Sally, and two adult grandchildren. The Clients are domiciled in Florida, a state that imposes no death taxes. Paul is age 80 and Margaret is age 79. It is anticipated that Paul will not survive Margaret. Paul owns approximately $10 million in separate property and Margaret's net worth is approximately $4 million. Their only joint property is the marital home, worth about $1 million. The Clients wish to use optimum marital deduction planning to take full advantage of each spouse's unified credit. Jointly owned property will pass outright to Margaret. Paul's estate will fund a $5.25 million credit shelter trust (premised on the year 2013 estate tax exclusion amount),[11] and the remaining portion will pass to a marital trust. The Clients anticipate that their assets will grow at a rate of 4% annually, which will create an estate exceeding $16 million (including the marital trust) at Margaret's death. An *assumed* estate tax exclusion amount of $5.65 million is used to illustrate the calculations at Margaret's death. The Clients also have charitable goals and wish to establish a charitable remainder annuity trust in the estate of the surviving spouse, funded with $3.5 million, with Sally as the noncharitable annuity beneficiary.

Case 1 illustrates the federal and state death consequences of these choices if Paul dies in 2013 and Margaret in 2016. No estate tax will be due in Paul's estate. The charitable deduction in Margaret's estate is based on Sally's age 62 in 2016, an *assumed* then-applicable §7520 rate of 5.6%, and an annuity amount of $230,000 paid annually. Case 1 also illustrates the estate tax due at Sally's death and the amount the grandchildren will receive on her death, assuming that the estate assets grow at 4% annually. Note that no tax would be saved by "balancing" Paul's and Margaret's estates because, after 2005, the estate tax is applied only at the highest rate. Although the Clients have fully used their unified credits in Case 1, they have not taken advantage of their generation-skipping transfer (GST) tax exemptions.

Case 2 illustrates the addition of GST tax planning. Rather than funding the credit shelter trust, Paul makes direct testamentary bequests of $5.25 million to trusts for the adult grandchildren, to which GST exemption is allocated. Margaret makes direct testamentary bequests to the grandchildren in the largest amount available to take advantage of the GST exemption, to which her executor will allocate GST exemption. Assuming the 4% growth rate, the GST tax planning will increase the grandchildren's share by approximately $6.9 million at Sally's death.

Case 3 illustrates the identical optimum marital deduction and GST tax planning, but eliminates the charitable remainder trust. This increases the grandchildren's share by approximately $6.76 million over Case 2.

Flowchart graphics generated by the Bloomberg BNA Estate and Gift Tax Planner illustrate the various scenarios in Cases 1, 2, and 3.

Estate and GST Tax Projection Prepared
Using BNA Estate & Gift Tax Planner

Paul and Margaret Client

Main Worksheet

	Case 1		Case 2		Case 3	
	Husband	Wife	Husband	Wife	Husband	Wife
Date of Death	1/1/2013	1/1/2016	1/1/2013	1/1/2016	1/1/2013	1/1/2016
Adjusted Gross Estate	10,500,000	10,967,424	10,500,000	10,967,424	10,500,000	10,967,424
Marital Deduction	5,250,000	0	5,250,000	0	5,250,000	0
Charitable Deduction	0	969,471	0	969,471	0	0
Taxable Estate	5,250,000	9,997,953	5,250,000	9,997,953	5,250,000	10,967,424
Federal Estate	5,250,000	9,997,953	5,250,000	9,997,953	5,250,000	10,967,424
Federal Tax per Schedule	2,045,800	3,944,981	2,045,800	3,944,981	2,045,800	4,332,770
Applicable Credit	2,045,800	2,205,800	2,045,800	2,205,800	2,045,800	2,205,800
Federal Tax + Max Credit	0	1,739,181	0	1,739,181	0	2,126,970
State Death Taxes - Max Credit	0	0	0	0	0	0
Federal Tax Before Special Credits	0	1,739,181	0	1,739,181	0	2,126,970
Federal Tax	0	1,739,181	0	1,739,181	0	2,126,970
Total Death Taxes	0	1,739,181	0	1,739,181	0	2,126,970
Family Share	5,905,536	8,258,772	5,905,536	8,258,772	5,905,536	8,840,454
Family Share Both Spouses	0	14,164,308	0	14,164,308	0	14,745,990
Grandchildren's Share Before Death	0	0	0	0	0	0
GC Shr Bef Death-Both Spouses	0	0	0	0	0	0
Grandchildren's Share on Death	0	0	12,442,074	0	12,442,074	11,849,594
Estate Tax on Children's Death	0	9,804,247	0	0	0	2,710,364
GST Tax on Children's Death	0	0	0	0	0	0
GC Shr on Chldrn Dth	0	14,706,371	0	0	0	4,065,545
Total GST Taxes	0	0	0	0	0	0
Total GC Sh After Chldrn Dth	0	14,706,371	0	0	0	28,357,213

Estate and GST Tax Projection Prepared
Using BNA Estate & Gift Tax Planner

Paul and Margaret Client
Adjusted Gross Estate

	Case 1		Case 2		Case 3	
	Husband	Wife	Husband	Wife	Husband	Wife
Separate Gross Estate	10,500,000	5,061,888	10,500,000	5,061,888	10,500,000	5,061,888
MD from Deceased Spouse	0	5,250,000	0	5,250,000	0	5,250,000
FVal Increase in MD & GE	0	655,536	0	655,536	0	655,536
Gross Estate	10,500,000	10,967,424	10,500,000	10,967,424	10,500,000	10,967,424
Funeral & Admin Exps in $	0	0	0	0	0	0
Total Funeral & Admin Exps						
State Death Tax Paid	0	0	0	0	0	0
Debts & Expenses	0	0	0	0	0	0
Adjusted Gross Estate	10,500,000	10,967,424	10,500,000	10,967,424	10,500,000	10,967,424
Fval %-Fam Shr Decedent 1	4	0	4	0	4	0
Fval $-Fam Shr Decedent 1	5,905,536	0	5,905,536	0	5,905,536	0
Fval %-Decedent 2 MD & GE	4	4	4	4	4	4
Fval $-Fam Shr Decedent 2	0	8,258,772	0	8,258,772	0	8,840,454
FVal Fam Share Bth Spouses	0	14,164,308	0	14,164,308	0	14,745,990
GST Fut Val at Chdrns Dth						
Est Yr Whn Chldrn are Dead	2035	2035	2035	2035	2035	2035
Fval % - Until Children's Deaths	4	0	4	0	4	0
Fval $-Fam Shr Decedent 1	12,442,074	0	12,442,074	0	12,442,074	0
Fval $-Fam Shr Decedent 2	0	17,399,987	0	17,399,987	0	18,625,503
FVal Fam Share Bth Spouses	0	29,842,061	0	29,842,061	0	31,067,577
Annual Inc % for Children's Life	4	4	4	4	4	4

Marital Deduction

	Case 1		Case 2		Case 3	
	Husband	Wife	Husband	Wife	Husband	Wife
Joint Property with Spouse	500,000	0	500,000	0	500,000	0
Plans/IRAs to Spouse	0	0	0	0	0	0
Zero Federal Tax Option	ZFT1	None	ZFT1	None	ZFT1	None
Phantom Assets	0	0	0	0	0	0
Interrelated Residue Calculation	None	None	None	None	None	None
Computed Marital Bequests	4,750,000	0	4,750,000	0	4,750,000	0
Toral Marital Bequests	5,250,000	0	5,250,000	0	5,250,000	0
Spousal Joint Property & Plan/IRA	500,000	0	500,000	0	500,000	0
QTIP Trust	4,750,000	0	4,750,000	0	4,750,000	0

Estate and GST Tax Projection Prepared
Using BNA Estate & Gift Tax Planner

Paul and Margaret Client

Charitable Deduction

	Case 1		Case 2		Case 3	
	Husband	Wife	Husband	Wife	Husband	Wife
Nonresiduary Trust Bequests	0	969,471	0	969,471	0	0
Residuary Interrelated Trusts	None	None	None	None	None	None
Interrelated Charitable Bequests	0	0	0	0	0	0
Total Charitable Bequests	0	969,471	0	969,471	0	0
Value of Fund after Taxes	0	0	0	0	0	0
Non-Interrelated Tr Calcs:						
Type of Fund	Annuity	Annuity	Annuity	Annuity	Annuity	Annuity
Fund Amt at Termination	0	0	0	0	0	0
Total Fund Payout for the Pd	0	0	0	0	0	0
CLA $5M Interest Factor	0	0	0	0	0	0
CLA Addition	0	0	0	0	0	0
CLA New Num Aft CLA Period	0	0	0	0	0	0
Exceed $5M Exemption Y/N	No	No	No	No	No	No
Exceed Available Prop Y/N	No	No	No	No	No	No

Nonresiduary Trust Bequests

	Case 1		Case 2		Case 3	
	Husband	Wife	Husband	Wife	Husband	Wife
Type of Fund 1	None	Rem Ann	None	Rem Ann	None	None
Nonresiduary Trust Amount 1	0	3,500,000	0	3,500,000	0	0

Nonresiduary Fund #1

	Case 1		Case 2		Case 3	
	Husband	Wife	Husband	Wife	Husband	Wife
First Age	0	62	0	62	0	0
Section 7520 Interest Rate	0	5.6	0	5.6	0	0
Dollar Payout	0	230,000	0	230,000	0	0
Payment Frequency	Annually	Annually	Annually	Annually	Annually	Annually
Pay @ Begin or End Period	End	End	End	End	End	End
Remainder Factor	0	0.38387	0	0.38387	0	0
Annuity Factor	0	11.00230	0	11.00230	0	0
Adjustment Factor	0	1.00000	0	1.00000	0	0
Adjusted Annuity Factor	0	11.00230	0	11.00230	0	0
Present Value of Annuity	0	2,530,529	0	2,530,529	0	0
Rem Annuity Deduction	0	969,471	0	969,471	0	0

Estate and GST Tax Projection Prepared
Using BNA Estate & Gift Tax Planner

Paul and Margaret Client

GST Taxes Payable on Death

	Case 1		Case 2		Case 3	
	Husband	Wife	Husband	Wife	Husband	Wife
$5M Exemption Used Bef Dth	0	0	0	0	0	0
$5M Alloc to DSTs by Exr	0	0	5,250,000	2,269,576	5,250,000	5,624,320
Direct Skip Transfers–DST	0	0	5,250,000	2,269,576	5,250,000	5,624,320
Reverse QTIP Election	No Election	No Election	No Election	No Election	No Election	No Election
GST Taxes Payable on Death	0	0	0	0	0	0
Family Shares at Death	5,250,000	8,258,772	5,250,000	8,258,772	5,250,000	8,840,454
Adjustments to Family Shares	0	−6,134,452	0	−6,134,452	0	−3,216,134
Adjusted Family Shares	5,250,000	2,124,320	5,250,000	2,124,320	5,250,000	5,624,320
DST Transfers & GST Taxes	0	0	5,250,000	2,269,576	5,250,000	5,624,320
Fam Shr Balance After GST	5,250,000	2,214,320	0	−145,256	0	0
Tentative QTIP Trust Amt	4,750,000	5,343,104	4,450,000	5,343,104	4,450,000	5,343,104
Adjustments to QTIP Trust	0	0	0	0	0	0
Balance is QTIP	0	5,343,104	0	5,343,104	0	5,343,104
Adjustments to QTIP Prop	0	−1,739,181	0	−1,739,181	0	−2,126,970
Adjusted QTIP Prop	0	3,603,923	0	3,603,923	0	3,216,134
DST QTIP Trfrs & GST Taxes	0	0	0	0	0	0
QTIP After GST Transfers	0	3,603,923	0	3,603,923	0	3,216,134
Total Fam Sh After GST Trfrs	5,250,000	5,728,243	0	3,458,667	0	3,216,134
Total $5M Exemption Used	0	0	5,250,000	2,269,576	5,250,000	5,624,320
Avail $5M GST Exemption	5,250,000	5,650,000	0	3,380,424	0	25,680
New Value of DSTs	0	0	0	0	0	0

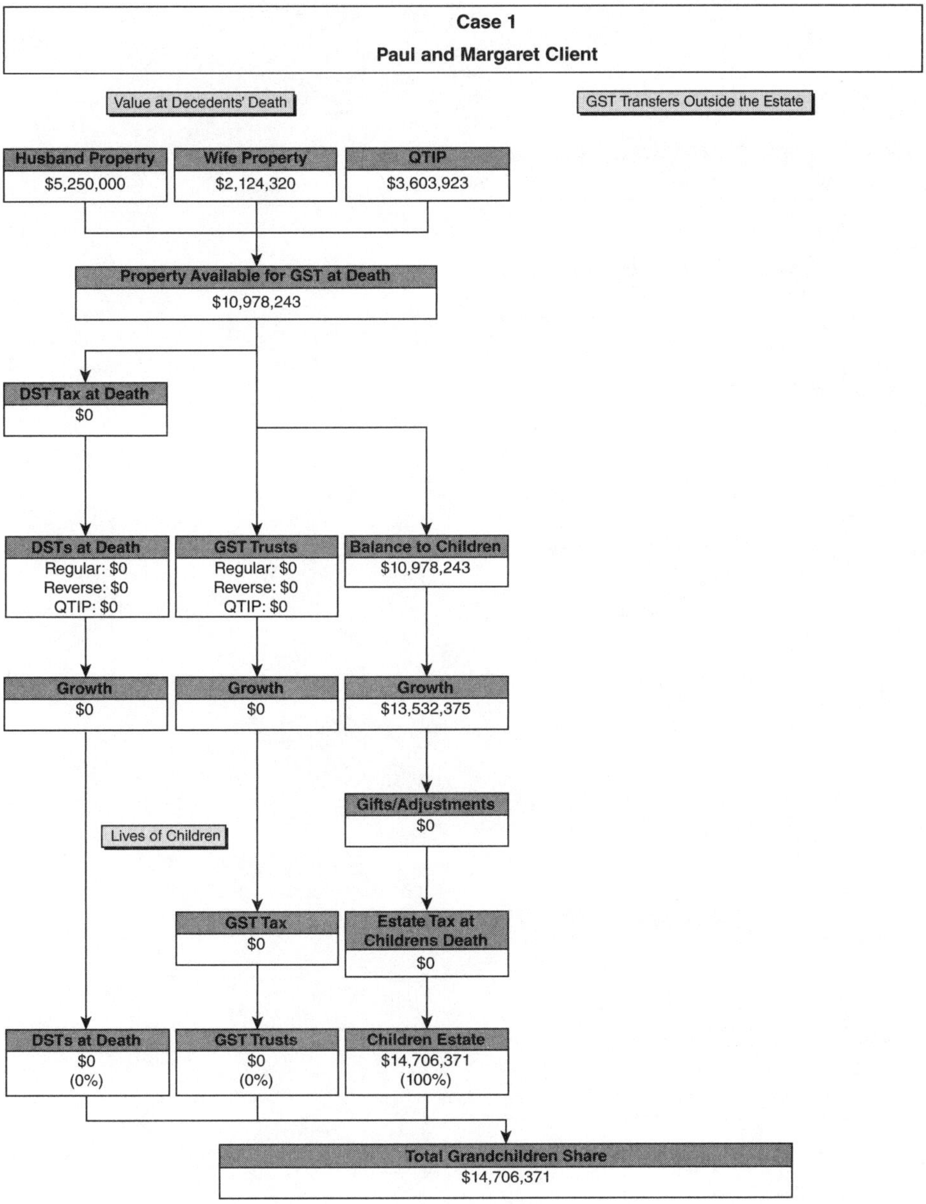
Case 1
Paul and Margaret Client
Value at Decedents' Death
GST Transfers Outside the Estate
Husband Property
$5,250,000
Wife Property
$2,124,320
QTIP
$3,603,923
Property Available for GST at Death
$10,978,243
DST Tax at Death
$0
DSTs at Death
Regular: $0
Reverse: $0
QTIP: $0
GST Trusts
Regular: $0
Reverse: $0
QTIP: $0
Balance to Children
$10,978,243
Growth
$0
Growth
$0
Growth
$13,532,375
Gifts/Adjustments
$0
Lives of Children
GST Tax
$0
Estate Tax at Childrens Death
$0
DSTs at Death
$0
(0%)
GST Trusts
$0
(0%)
Children Estate
$14,706,371
(100%)
Total Grandchildren Share
$14,706,371

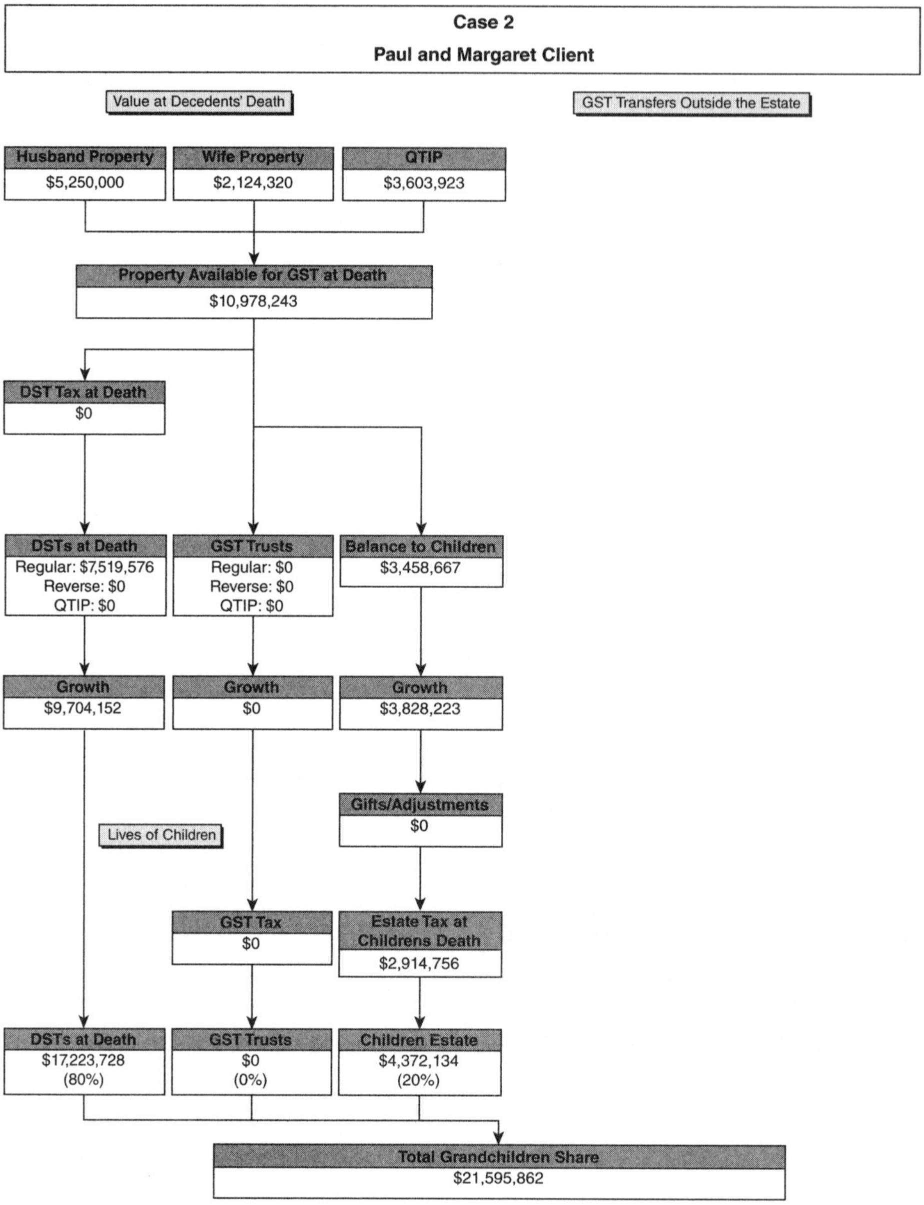
Case 2
Paul and Margaret Client
Value at Decedents' Death
GST Transfers Outside the Estate
Husband Property
$5,250,000
Wife Property
$2,124,320
QTIP
$3,603,923
Property Available for GST at Death
$10,978,243
DST Tax at Death
$0
DSTs at Death
Regular: $7,519,576
Reverse: $0
QTIP: $0
GST Trusts
Regular: $0
Reverse: $0
QTIP: $0
Balance to Children
$3,458,667
Growth
$9,704,152
Growth
$0
Growth
$3,828,223
Gifts/Adjustments
$0
Lives of Children
GST Tax
$0
Estate Tax at Childrens Death
$2,914,756
DSTs at Death
$17,223,728
(80%)
GST Trusts
$0
(0%)
Children Estate
$4,372,134
(20%)
Total Grandchildren Share
$21,595,862

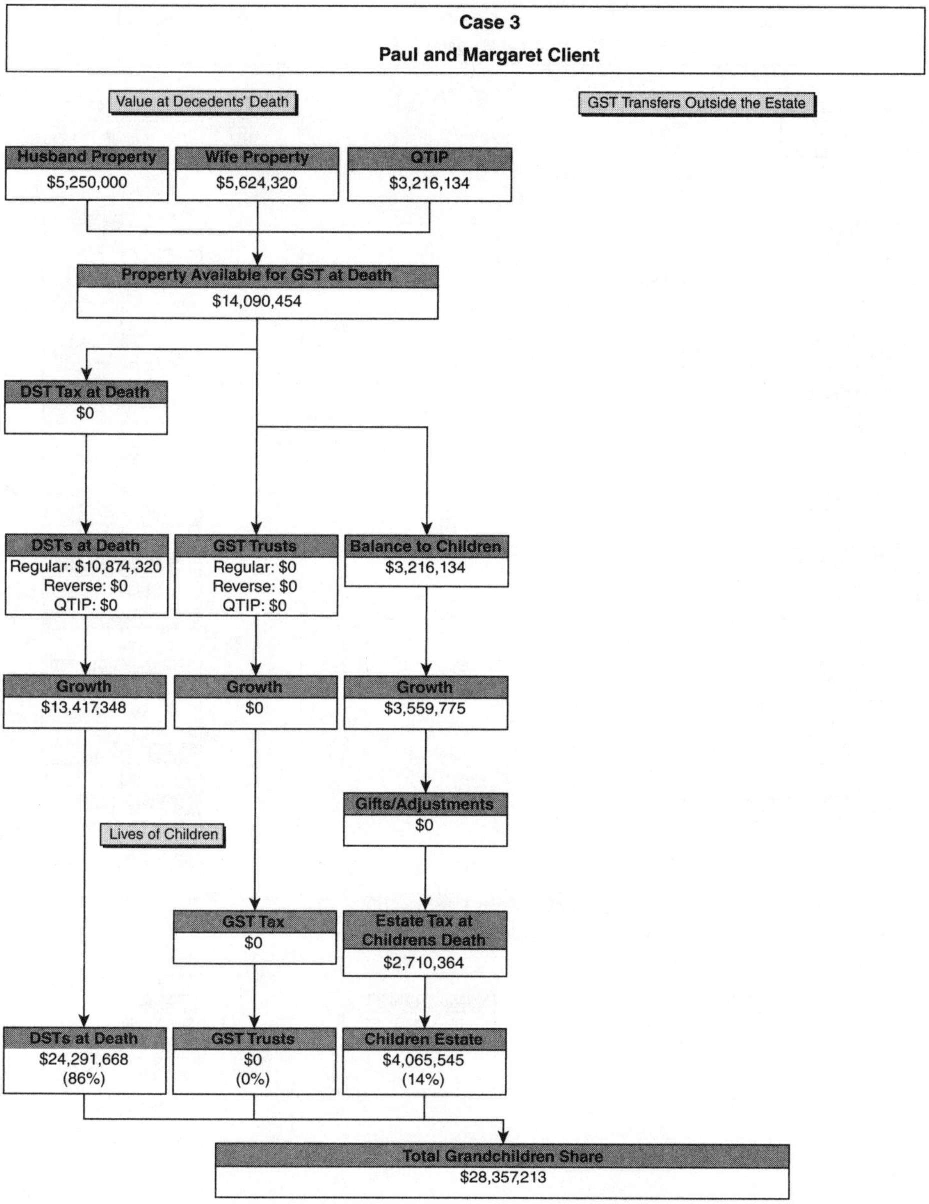
Case 3
Paul and Margaret Client
Value at Decedents' Death
GST Transfers Outside the Estate
Husband Property
$5,250,000
Wife Property
$5,624,320
QTIP
$3,216,134
Property Available for GST at Death
$14,090,454
DST Tax at Death
$0
DSTs at Death
Regular: $10,874,320
Reverse: $0
QTIP: $0
GST Trusts
Regular: $0
Reverse: $0
QTIP: $0
Balance to Children
$3,216,134
Growth
$13,417,348
Growth
$0
Growth
$3,559,775
Gifts/Adjustments
$0
Lives of Children
GST Tax
$0
Estate Tax at Childrens Death
$2,710,364
DSTs at Death
$24,291,668
(86%)
GST Trusts
$0
(0%)
Children Estate
$4,065,545
(14%)
Total Grandchildren Share
$28,357,213

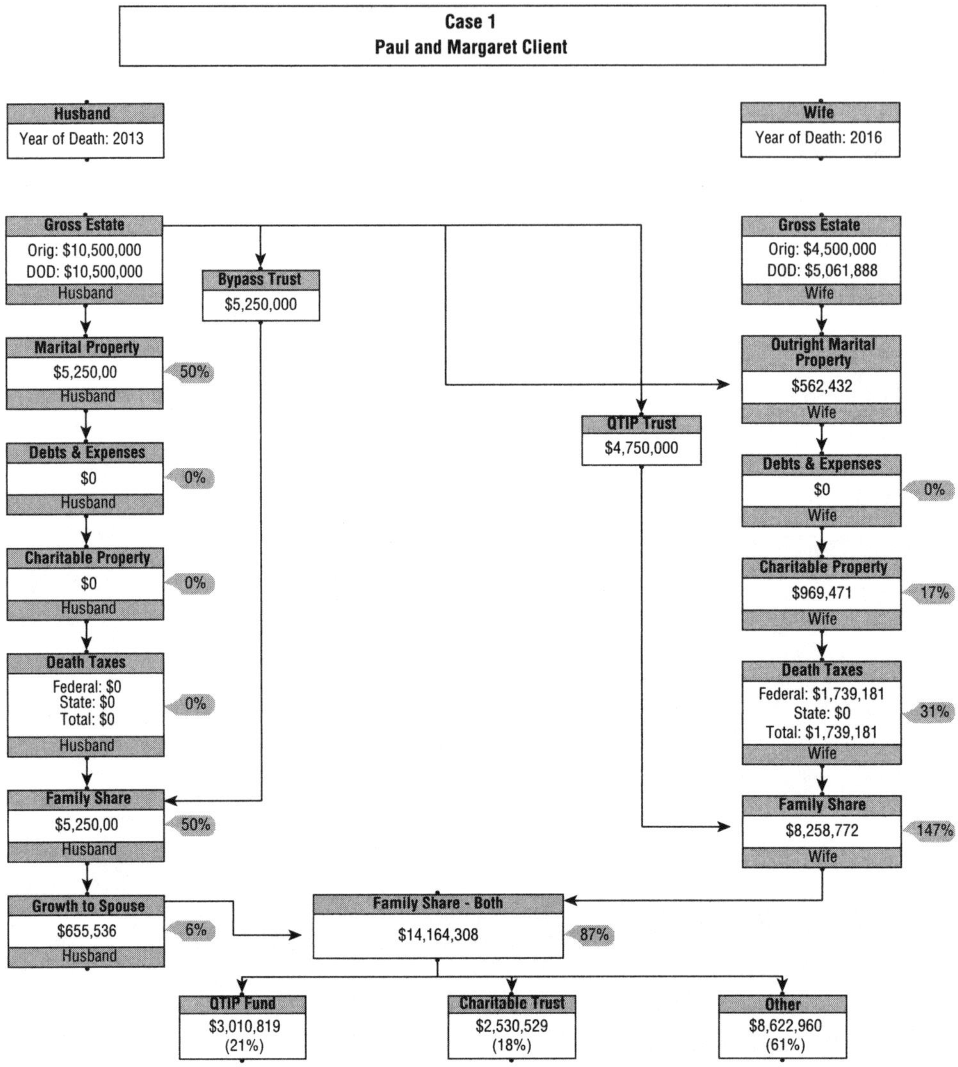
Case 1
Paul and Margaret Client
Husband
Year of Death: 2013
Wife
Year of Death: 2016
Gross Estate
Orig: $10,500,000
DOD: $10,500,000
Husband
Bypass Trust
$5,250,000
Gross Estate
Orig: $4,500,000
DOD: $5,061,888
Wife
Marital Property
$5,250,00
Husband
50%
Outright Marital Property
$562,432
Wife
QTIP Trust
$4,750,000
Debts & Expenses
$0
Husband
0%
Debts & Expenses
$0
Wife
0%
Charitable Property
$0
Husband
0%
Charitable Property
$969,471
Wife
17%
Death Taxes
Federal: $0
State: $0
Total: $0
Husband
0%
Death Taxes
Federal: $1,739,181
State: $0
Total: $1,739,181
Wife
31%
Family Share
$5,250,00
Husband
50%
Family Share
$8,258,772
Wife
147%
Growth to Spouse
$655,536
Husband
6%
Family Share - Both
$14,164,308
87%
QTIP Fund
$3,010,819
(21%)
Charitable Trust
$2,530,529
(18%)
Other
$8,622,960
(61%)

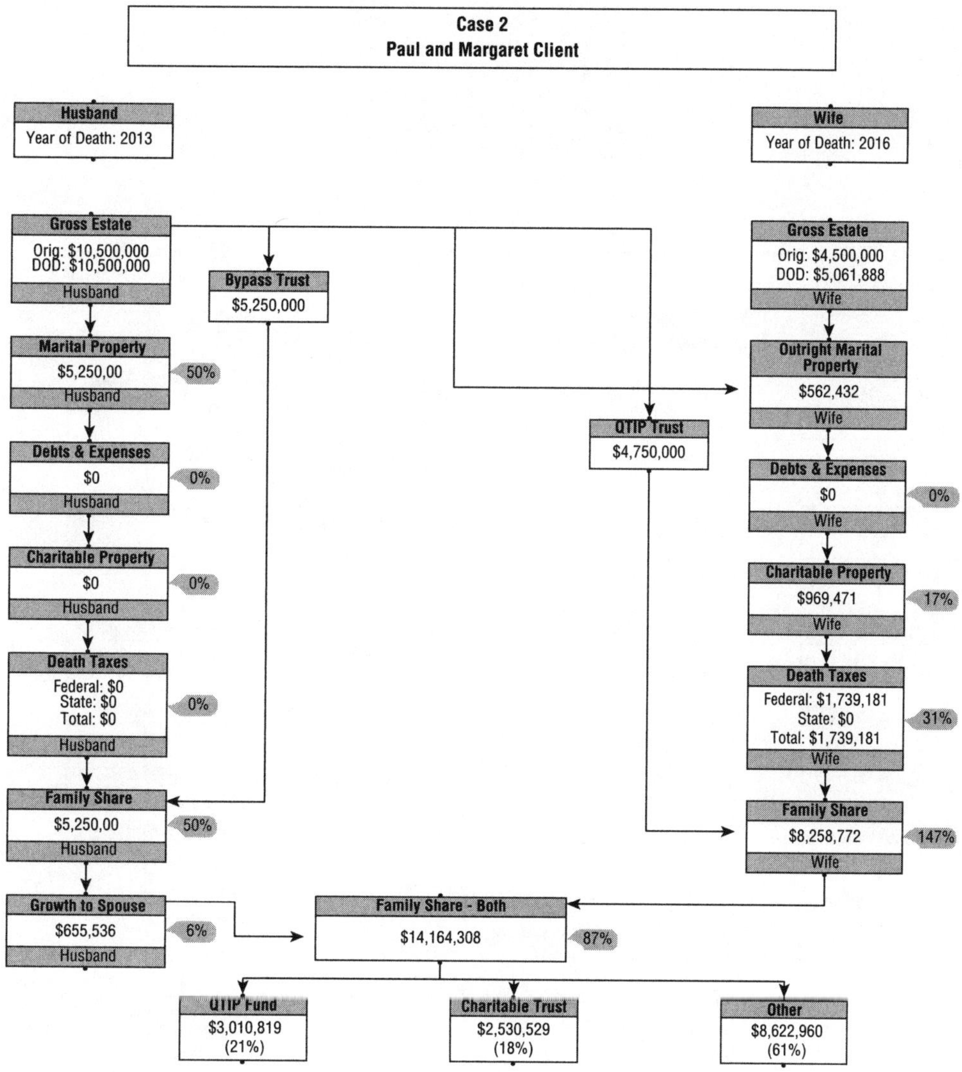
Case 2
Paul and Margaret Client
Husband
Year of Death: 2013
Wife
Year of Death: 2016
Gross Estate
Orig: $10,500,000
DOD: $10,500,000
Husband
Bypass Trust
$5,250,000
Gross Estate
Orig: $4,500,000
DOD: $5,061,888
Wife
Marital Property
$5,250,00
Husband
50%
Outright Marital Property
$562,432
Wife
QTIP Trust
$4,750,000
Debts & Expenses
$0
Husband
0%
Debts & Expenses
$0
Wife
0%
Charitable Property
$0
Husband
0%
Charitable Property
$969,471
Wife
17%
Death Taxes
Federal: $0
State: $0
Total: $0
Husband
0%
Death Taxes
Federal: $1,739,181
State: $0
Total: $1,739,181
Wife
31%
Family Share
$5,250,00
Husband
50%
Family Share
$8,258,772
Wife
147%
Growth to Spouse
$655,536
Husband
6%
Family Share - Both
$14,164,308
87%
QTIP Fund
$3,010,819
(21%)
Charitable Trust
$2,530,529
(18%)
Other
$8,622,960
(61%)

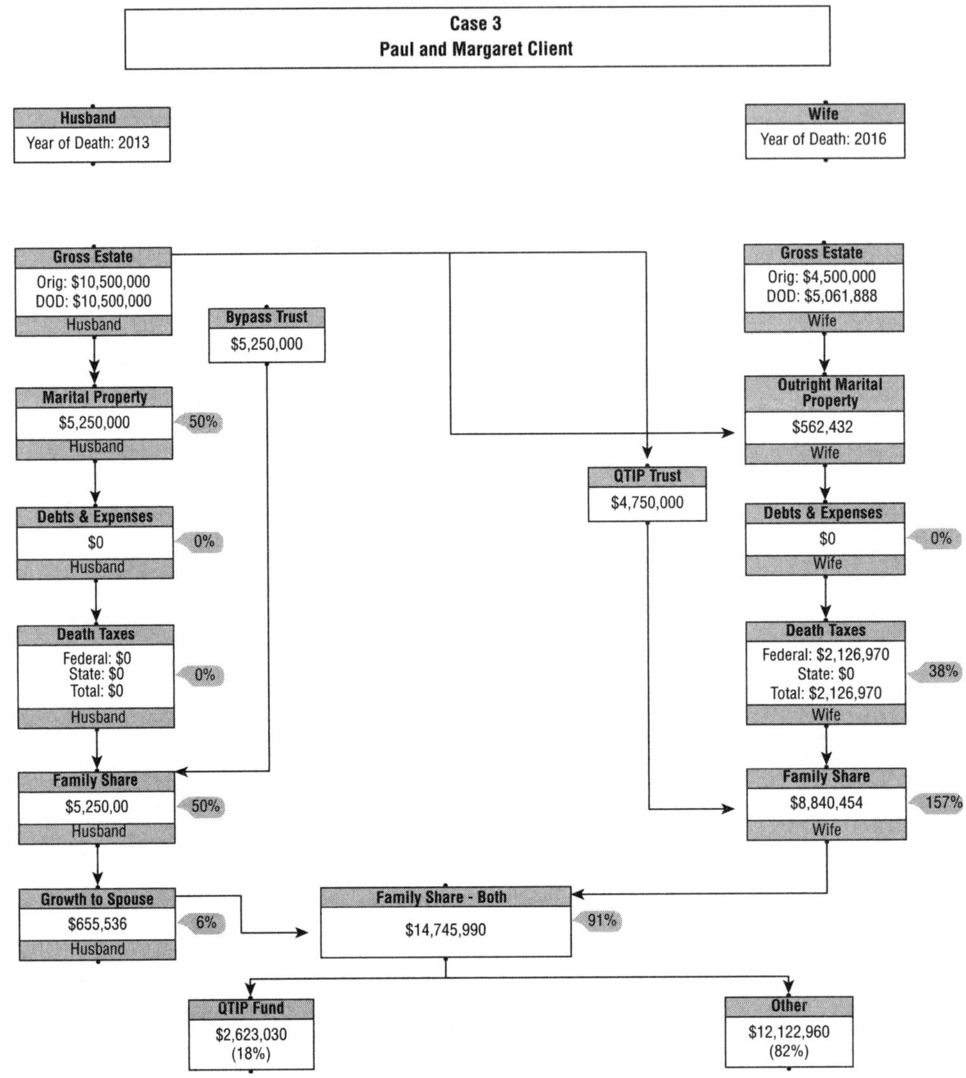
Case 3
Paul and Margaret Client
Husband
Year of Death: 2013
Wife
Year of Death: 2016
Gross Estate
Orig: $10,500,000
DOD: $10,500,000
Husband
Bypass Trust
$5,250,000
Gross Estate
Orig: $4,500,000
DOD: $5,061,888
Wife
Marital Property
$5,250,000
Husband
50%
Outright Marital Property
$562,432
Wife
QTIP Trust
$4,750,000
Debts & Expenses
$0
Husband
0%
Debts & Expenses
$0
Wife
0%
Death Taxes
Federal: $0
State: $0
Total: $0
Husband
0%
Death Taxes
Federal: $2,126,970
State: $0
Total: $2,126,970
Wife
38%
Family Share
$5,250,00
Husband
50%
Family Share
$8,840,454
Wife
157%
Growth to Spouse
$655,536
Husband
6%
Family Share - Both
$14,745,990
91%
QTIP Fund
$2,623,030
(18%)
Other
$12,122,960
(82%)

Worksheet 9

Checklist for Possible Estate Planning Client Documents

Client Representation Checklist: Options for Possible Basic Estate Planning Documents (Not Including Federal and State Tax Forms)

This checklist might be used by the estate planner to assure that the estate planner is fully aware of the numerous documents that either: (1) might previously have been implemented by the client and should be examined in reviewing the client's current estate planning situation, or (2) should be considered in a client situation because they could be usefully implemented for the client's arrangements for his/her transfer of wealth.

1. PRELIMINARY DOCUMENTS
   A) Client Engagement Letter
   B) Estate Planning Questionnaire (identifying various client assets [probate and nonprobate] and liabilities)
   C) Representation Letter (single or joint representation, including for any related business entities)
   D) Client Disengagement Letter (at termination of estate planning representation)
   E) List Identifying Client's Computer Passwords (or identifying location for their subsequent identification)
2. LAST WILL & TESTAMENT
   A) Basic Will with Outright Property Dispositions
   B) Will with Pour-Over Provisions
   C) Will with Basic Trust Provisions
   D) Will with Credit Shelter Trust and QTIP Provisions
   E) Will with Generation-Skipping Trust Provisions (including reverse QTIP provision)
   F) Separate Memorandum/Statement for Disposition of Personal Property (outside scope of will provisions)
   G) Codicil to Last Will
   H) Will with Disclaimer Provisions (enabling beneficiary to reject property, enabling deflection to others, including trusts)
   I) Revocation Documents for Prior Wills
   J) Any "Situs Wills" for Properties Located in Foreign Jurisdiction
3. TRUSTS
   A) Revocable Trust Agreement
   B) Revocable Trust—Subsequent Restatement and Amendment
   C) Irrevocable Trust Agreement
   D) Irrevocable Life Insurance Trust (ILIT) (with life insurance policy transfers to the trust)
   E) Annual Donee Exclusion Trust (with "*Crummey* power")

- F) Trust Exercising Power of Appointment (general or non-general)
- G) Spendthrift Trust Provisions
- H) Designation of Trust Protector
- I) Special Needs Trust

4. ALTERNATIVE CONTRACTUAL ARRANGEMENTS
   - A) Life Insurance Contracts Summary (including ownership, "incidents of ownership," and designated beneficiaries)
   - B) Memorandum Identifying Separate and Community Property Interests Among Spouses (including possible "partition agreement")
   - C) Grantor Retained Annuity Trust (GRAT)
   - D) Qualified Personal Residence Trust (QPRT)
   - E) Installment Sale Contract/Bargain Sales
   - F) Sales Contracts for Transfers to Intentionally Defective Grantor Trusts (IDGT)
   - G) Self-Canceling Installment Notes
   - H) Joint Purchase Arrangements
   - I) Private Annuity Contracts
   - J) Promissory Note for Below Market Loans to Family Members and Trusts for Family Members
5. COMPENSATION ARRANGEMENTS
   - A) Designation of Beneficiary Under Corporate-Owned/Provided Life Insurance
   - B) Designation of Successor to Deferred Compensation Arrangements
   - C) Designation of Beneficiary Under Pension, Profit-Sharing, 401(k), 403(b), and Other Qualified Deferred Compensation Arrangements
6. BUSINESS RESTRUCTURING/PLANNING
   - A) Memorandum Concerning Business Disposition/Restructuring Plan (including business valuation analysis)
   - B) Buy-Sell Agreement (entity redemption/purchase, cross-purchase, or combination, including installment sales provisions)
   - C) Limited Liability Company Organizational Documents
   - D) Family Limited Partnership Agreement
7. CHARITABLE GIFT PLANNING (LIFETIME/TESTAMENTARY)
   - A) Charitable Remainder Trust (CRAT or CRUT) (including "NIMCRUT" or "FLIPCRUT" provisions)
   - B) Charitable Lead Trust (CLUT or CLAT)
   - C) Charitable Private Foundation
   - D) Charitable Annuity
   - E) Charitable Bargain Sale Contract
   - F) Conservation Easements
   - G) Donor Advised Fund
8. NONTAX/DISABILITY & RELATED MATTERS
   - A) Durable Power of Attorney (including possible "springing power")
   - B) Health Care Power of Attorney

C) "Living Will" (i.e., medical directive)
D) Designation of Guardian of Person
E) Designation of Guardian for Minor Children
F) Instructions for Final Arrangements for Physical Remains
G) Organ Donation Documents
H) Long-Term Care Insurance and Similar Arrangements

Worksheet 10

Diagrams and Summaries of Estate Planning Document Structures

I. Options for Structures of Wills and Trusts

Although clients might profess to understand the complexities of the structures described to them for dividing their properties among various trusts for tax planning purposes, their comprehension process will often be significantly enhanced through the use of charts and diagrams. This Worksheet identifies the various fundamental approaches that might be used in structuring these arrangements. This planning can incorporate the use of some or all of three fundamental planning tools:

1) the unified credit against the estate tax (often utilized with a "family trust" or "bypass trust");
2) the unlimited marital deduction; and
3) the generation-skipping transfer exemption amount.

These various diagrams proceed from the less complicated to among the most complex of estate planning structures. These diagrams also assume that the clients do not desire to use less complicated arrangements and merely rely on the portability election to enable (1) the maximum marital deduction when the first spouse dies and (2) maximum estate tax protection upon the subsequent death of the surviving spouse through the use of an enhanced unified credit.

The diagrams in (i) Diagrams 10A through 10D and (ii) Diagrams 10E through 10L identify structures for various estate tax planning alternatives that can be implemented in the transfer of wealth, particularly in marital situations (i.e., transfers from a husband and wife to their descendants).

The essential elements of each of these diagrams, and the benefits available under each structure, are identified below. Each of these diagrams contemplates that the wealth being transferred has been accumulated within a marital unit. However, in many estate planning situations, the starting point is often not a marital unit. These various diagrams can certainly be adapted to those transfers where the marital deduction is not relevant to the wealth transfer planning arrangements.

In many instances, these planning arrangements may be implemented through the use of a funded revocable (or "living") trust, created under a trust agreement, rather than under a last will. In this situation, all or much of the marital wealth will have been previously incorporated into one (or several) trusts prior to the time of the death of the first spouse to die. Except for special items of tangible personal property, any properties directly held at death outside these trusts may often "pour over" into this revocable trust under the provisions of the last will. These diagrams can also be adapted to reflect the use of a trust (rather than the last will) as the vehicle for mandating the distribution of the assets includible in the estate of the deceased for federal estate tax purposes.

These diagrams are divided into two types:

(1) Diagrams 10A through 10D show the possible formats for disposition of assets at the death of the first spouse to die to the surviving spouse and/or children, and
(2) Diagrams 10E through 10L show the ultimate disposition of all marital assets from both spouses to younger generation members.

II. Detailed Structures Showing Disposition of Assets at Death of First Spouse to Die

Diagram 10A Direct Marital Gift; Residue to Family Trust

The structure in this diagram provides details concerning the transfer of assets as of the death of the first spouse to die (here assumed to be the husband). These provisions include:

1) Specific gifts are contemplated under the will, such as a gift of the residence, the employee benefit plan or IRA balances, and personal and household items.
2) The marital deduction gift is outright to the surviving spouse (i.e., not in trust), thereby avoiding applicability of the marital deduction limiting "terminable interest" rules. The amount transferred to the spouse is to be determined by a formula, i.e., the "minimum needed marital deduction amount" to eliminate any federal estate tax liability. This gift amount is determined as a "pecuniary amount" (rather than as a fractional share).
3) The residue is distributed to the "family trust." No federal estate tax is incurred because the amount transferred into this trust is equivalent to the exemption equivalent amount (as remaining after the transfer of the specific gift of the residence, etc. unless these transfers qualify for the unlimited marital deduction). Considerable flexibility can be provided concerning income and principal distributions from the family trust for various family members, including providing for the surviving spouse to have a special testamentary power of appointment.
4) At the death of the surviving spouse, the family trust assets are distributable to those beneficiaries having attained a specified age and, otherwise, the assets are held in contingent trusts for the particular beneficiary until reaching the specified age.

Diagram 10B Marital Trust; Residue to Family Trust

The structure in this diagram provides more extensive restrictions concerning the transfer of assets as of the death of the first spouse to die (here assumed to be the husband). These provisions include:

1) Specific gifts are contemplated under the will, such as a gift of the residence, the employee benefit plan or IRA balances, and personal and household items.
2) The marital deduction transfer is made into a marital deduction qualified terminable interest property (QTIP) trust for the benefit of the surviving

spouse. The amount transferred to this trust for the surviving spouse is determined by a formula, that is, the "minimum needed marital deduction amount" to eliminate any federal estate tax liability. This gift is identified as a pecuniary amount (rather than as a fractional share). To enable the marital deduction for the transfers into this trust (a) all net income must be payable at least annually to the surviving spouse and (b) the undistributed net income goes to the wife's estate. Additionally, in this format, principal can be distributed to the wife for health, education, support, and maintenance and the wife has a limited testamentary power of appointment. In default of the exercise of this power of appointment, at the death of the surviving spouse, this property is distributed to the husband's descendants, subject to the contingent trust provisions.

3) The residue is distributed to the family trust. No federal estate tax is incurred because the amount transferred into this trust is equivalent to the exemption equivalent amount (as remaining after the transfer of the specific gift of the residence, etc. unless these transfers qualify for the unlimited marital deduction). Considerable flexibility is provided concerning income and principal distributions from the family trust to various family members, including providing for the surviving spouse to have a special testamentary power of appointment.
4) At the death of the surviving spouse, the family trust assets are distributable to those beneficiaries having attained a specified age and, otherwise, the assets are held in trust for the particular beneficiary until reaching the specified age.

Diagram 10C Family Trust; Residue to Spouse Outright

The structure in this diagram provides for the funding of a family trust with the residue distributable outright to the surviving spouse (here assumed to be the wife). These provisions include:

1) Specific gifts are contemplated under the will, such as a gift of the residence, the employee benefit plan or IRA balances, and personal and household items.
2) The applicable exclusion amount is distributable to the family trust. No federal estate tax is incurred because the amount transferred into this trust is equivalent to the exemption equivalent amount (as remaining after the transfer of the specific gift of the residence, etc. unless these transfers qualify for the unlimited marital deduction). Considerable flexibility is provided concerning income and principal distributions from the family trust for various family members, including providing for the surviving spouse to have a special testamentary power of appointment.
3) The residue is distributed as a marital deduction gift outright to the surviving spouse (i.e., not in trust), thereby avoiding applicability of the marital deduction limiting terminable interest rules.
4) At the death of the surviving spouse, the family trust assets are distributable to those beneficiaries having attained a specified age and, otherwise, the assets are held in trust for the particular beneficiary until reaching the specified age.

Diagram 10D Family Trust; Residue to Marital Trust

The structure in this diagram provides for the funding a family trust with the residue distributable to a marital trust as of the death of the first spouse to die (here assumed to be the husband). These provisions include:

1) Specific gifts are contemplated under the will, such as a gift of the residence, the employee benefit plan or IRA balances, and personal and household items.
2) The applicable exclusion amount is distributable to the family trust. No federal estate tax is incurred because the amount transferred into this trust is equivalent to the exemption equivalent amount (as remaining after the transfer of the specific gift of the residence, etc. unless these transfers qualify for the unlimited marital deduction). Considerable flexibility is provided concerning income and principal distributions from the family trust for various family members, including providing for the surviving spouse to have a special testamentary power of appointment.
3) The residue is distributed as a marital deduction gift into a QTIP trust for the benefit of the surviving spouse. To enable the marital deduction for the transfers into this trust (a) all net income must be payable at least annually to the surviving spouse and (b) the undistributed net income goes to the wife's estate. Additionally, in this format, principal can be distributed to the wife for health, education, support, and maintenance and the wife has a limited testamentary power of appointment. In default of the exercise of this power of appointment, at the death of the surviving spouse, this property is distributed to the husband's descendants, subject to the contingent trust provisions.
4) At the death of the surviving spouse, the family trust assets are distributable (without estate tax impact) to those beneficiaries having attained a specified age and, otherwise, the assets are held in trust for the particular beneficiary until reaching the specified age. The descendants will also receive the assets of the QTIP trust (originally sourced from the first spouse to die). The estate tax liability (if any) arising on the subsequent death of the wife and attributable to the QTIP trust assets will be satisfied from the assets held in that trust.

II. Structures Showing Disposition of Assets After Deaths of Both Spouses to Younger Generation Members

Diagram 10E Direct Marital Gift; Residue to Family Trust

The structure in this diagram contemplates wills for a husband and wife where (assuming the husband dies first):

1) The amount held by the husband at death in excess of the applicable exclusion amount is transferred outright to the surviving spouse.
2) The residue (consisting of the applicable exclusion amount) is transferred to the family trust for the benefit of the surviving spouse and the descendants.
3) This results in (a) no federal estate tax liability at the earlier death of the husband and (b) the avoidance of any federal estate tax on the amount in the family trust at the death of both spouses, because the assets in this trust are also not subject to

federal estate tax inclusion when the surviving spouse subsequently dies. Federal estate tax liability will arise upon the death of the surviving spouse unless the total assets includible in her estate are less than the then available applicable exclusion amount for the estate of the surviving spouse (and after consideration of any available "deceased spousal unused exclusion amount").

4) The diagram shows that, at that subsequent death, the descendants will directly receive the after-tax assets from (a) the estate of the then deceased surviving spouse and (b) the family trust.

Diagram 10F Marital Trust; Residue to Family Trust

The structure in this diagram contemplates wills for a husband and wife where (assuming the husband dies first):

1) The amount held by the husband at death in excess of the applicable exclusion amount is transferred into a QTIP trust for the surviving spouse.
2) The residue (consisting of the applicable exclusion amount) is transferred to the family trust for the benefit of the surviving spouse and the descendants.
3) This results in (a) no federal estate tax liability at the earlier death of the husband and (b) the avoidance of federal estate tax on the amount in the family trust at the death of both spouses, because the assets in this trust are also not subject to federal estate tax inclusion when the surviving spouse subsequently dies. Federal estate tax liability will arise upon the death of the surviving spouse unless the total assets includible in her estate are less than the then available applicable exclusion amount for the estate of the surviving spouse (and after consideration of any available deceased spousal unused exclusion amount).
4) The diagram shows that, at that subsequent death, the descendants will receive (a) the after-tax assets from the estate of the then deceased surviving spouse, (b) the assets (not subject to estate tax) of the family trust, and (c) the assets of the QTIP trust. The federal estate tax liability (if any) arising on the subsequent death of the wife and attributable to the QTIP trust assets being includible in her estate will be satisfied from the assets held in that trust.

Diagram 10G Family Trust; Residue to Spouse Outright

The structure in this diagram contemplates wills for a husband and wife where (assuming the husband dies first):

1) The amount held by the husband at death equal to the applicable exclusion amount is transferred to the family trust for the benefit of the surviving spouse and the descendants.
2) The residue is transferred outright to the surviving spouse.
3) This results in (a) no federal estate tax liability at the earlier death of the husband and (b) avoidance of federal estate tax on the amount in the family trust after the death of both spouses, because the assets in this trust are also not subject to federal estate tax inclusion when the surviving spouse subsequently dies. Federal

estate tax liability will arise upon the death of the surviving spouse unless the total assets includible in her estate are less than the then available applicable exclusion amount for the estate of the surviving spouse (and after consideration of any available deceased spousal unused exclusion amount).

4) The diagram shows that, at that subsequent death, the descendants will directly receive the after-tax assets from (a) the estate of the then deceased surviving spouse and (b) the family trust.

Diagram 10H Family Trust; Residue to Marital Trust

The structure in this diagram contemplates wills for a husband and wife where (assuming the husband dies first):

1) The amount held by the husband at death in excess of the applicable exclusion amount is transferred to the family trust for the benefit of the surviving spouse and the descendants.
2) The residue (consisting of the applicable exclusion amount) is transferred into a QTIP trust for the surviving spouse.
3) This results in (a) no federal estate tax liability at the earlier death of the husband and (b) the avoidance of federal estate tax on the amount in the family trust at the death of both spouses, because the assets in this trust are also not subject to federal estate tax inclusion when the surviving spouse subsequently dies. Federal estate tax liability will arise upon the death of the surviving spouse unless the total assets includible in her estate are less than the then available applicable exclusion amount for the estate of the surviving spouse (and after consideration of any available deceased spousal unused exclusion amount).
4) The diagram shows that, at that subsequent death, the descendants will receive (a) the after-tax assets from the estate of the then deceased surviving spouse, (b) the assets (not subject to tax) of the family trust, and (c) the assets of the QTIP trust. The estate tax liability (if any) arising on the subsequent death of the wife and attributable to the QTIP trust assets will be satisfied from the assets held in that trust.

Diagram 10I Direct Marital Gift; Residue to Family Trust; Generation-Skipping Trusts

The structure in this diagram contemplates wills for a husband and wife where (assuming the husband dies first):

1) The amount held by the husband at death in excess of the applicable exclusion amount is transferred outright to the surviving spouse.
2) The residue (consisting of the applicable exclusion amount) is transferred to the family trust for the benefit of the surviving spouse and the descendants.
3) At the death of the surviving spouse, both the family trust assets and the assets held by the surviving spouse are transferred into various separate trusts for the descendants that are exempt and not exempt from the generation-skipping transfer tax.
4) This results in (a) no federal estate tax liability at the earlier death of the husband, (b) avoidance of federal estate tax on the amount in the family trust at the death

of both spouses (because the assets in this trust are also not subject to federal estate tax inclusion when the surviving spouse subsequently dies), and (c) avoidance of future generation-skipping transfer tax for those assets held in the exempt trusts. Federal estate tax liability will arise upon the death of the surviving spouse unless the total assets includible in her estate are less than the then available applicable exclusion amount for the estate of the surviving spouse (and after consideration of any available deceased spousal unused exclusion amount).

5) The diagram shows that, at that subsequent death, the after-tax assets from both (a) the estate of the then deceased surviving spouse and (b) the family trust will be transferred into several trusts for the descendants that are exempt or not exempt from the generation-skipping transfer tax.

Diagram 10J Marital Trust; Residue to Family Trust; Generation-Skipping Trusts

This structure in this diagram contemplates wills for a husband and wife where (assuming the husband dies first):

1) The amount held by the husband at death in excess of the applicable exclusion amount is transferred into a QTIP trust for the surviving spouse.
2) The residue (consisting of the applicable exclusion amount) is transferred to the family trust for the benefit of the surviving spouse and the descendants.
3) At the death of the surviving spouse, the family trust assets and the assets held by the QTIP trust and the surviving spouse are transferred into various separate trusts for the descendants that are exempt and not exempt from the generation-skipping transfer tax.
4) This results in (a) no federal estate tax liability at the earlier death of the husband, (b) avoidance of federal estate tax on the amount in the family trust at the death of both spouses (because the assets in this trust are also not subject to federal estate tax inclusion when the surviving spouse subsequently dies), and (c) avoidance of future generation-skipping transfer tax for those assets held in the exempt trusts. Federal estate tax liability will arise upon the death of the surviving spouse unless the total assets includible in her estate are less than the then available applicable exclusion amount for the estate of the surviving spouse (and after consideration of any available deceased spousal unused exclusion amount).
5) The diagram shows that, at that subsequent death, the after-tax assets from (a) the estate of the then deceased surviving spouse, (b) the family trust, and (c) the QTIP trust will be transferred into several trusts for the descendants that are exempt or not exempt from the generation-skipping transfer tax.

Diagram 10K Family Trust; Residue to Spouse Outright; Generation-Skipping Trusts

The structure in this diagram contemplates wills for a husband and wife where (assuming the husband dies first):

1) The amount held by the husband at death equal to the applicable exclusion amount is transferred to the family trust for the benefit of the surviving spouse and the descendants.

2) The residue is transferred outright to the surviving spouse.
3) At the death of the surviving spouse, both the family trust assets and the assets held by the surviving spouse are transferred into various separate trusts for the descendants that are exempt and not exempt from the generation-skipping transfer tax.
4) This results in (a) no federal estate tax liability at the earlier death of the husband, (b) avoidance of federal estate tax on the amount in the family trust at the death of both spouses, because the assets in this trust are also not subject to federal estate tax inclusion when the surviving spouse subsequently dies, and (c) avoidance of future generation-skipping transfer tax for those assets held in the exempt trusts. Federal estate tax liability will arise upon the death of the surviving spouse unless the total assets includible in her gross estate are less than the then available applicable exclusion amount for the estate of the surviving spouse (and after consideration of any available deceased spousal unused exclusion amount).
5) The diagram shows that, at that subsequent death, the after-tax assets from both (a) the estate of the then deceased surviving spouse and (b) the family trust will be transferred into several trusts for the descendants that are exempt or not exempt from the generation-skipping transfer tax.

Diagram 10L Family Trust; Residue to Marital Trust; Generation-Skipping Trusts

The structure in this diagram contemplates wills for a husband and wife where (assuming the husband dies first):

1) The amount held by the husband at death equal to the applicable exclusion amount is transferred to the family trust for the benefit of the surviving spouse and the descendants.
2) The residue (consisting of the applicable exclusion amount) is transferred into a QTIP trust for the surviving spouse.
3) At the death of the surviving spouse, the family trust assets and the assets held by the QTIP trust and the surviving spouse are transferred into various separate trusts for the descendants that are exempt and not exempt from the generation-skipping transfer tax.
4) This results in (a) no federal estate tax liability at the earlier death of the husband, (b) avoidance of federal estate tax on the amount in the family trust at the death of both spouses, because the assets in this trust are also not subject to federal estate tax inclusion when the surviving spouse subsequently dies, and (c) avoidance of future generation-skipping transfer tax for those assets held in the exempt trusts. Federal estate tax liability will arise upon the death of the surviving spouse unless the total assets includible in her gross estate are less than the then available applicable exclusion amount for the estate of the surviving spouse (and after consideration of any available deceased spousal unused exclusion amount).
5) The diagram shows that, at that subsequent death, the after-tax assets from (a) the estate of the then deceased surviving spouse, (b) the family trust, and (c) the

QTIP trust will be transferred into several trusts for the descendants that are exempt or not exempt from the generation-skipping transfer tax. The estate tax liability (if any) arising on the subsequent death of the wife and attributable to the QTIP trust assets will be satisfied from the assets held in that trust.

DIAGRAM 10A
LAST WILLS & TESTAMENTS OF HUSBAND
Direct Marital Gift; Residue to Family Trust

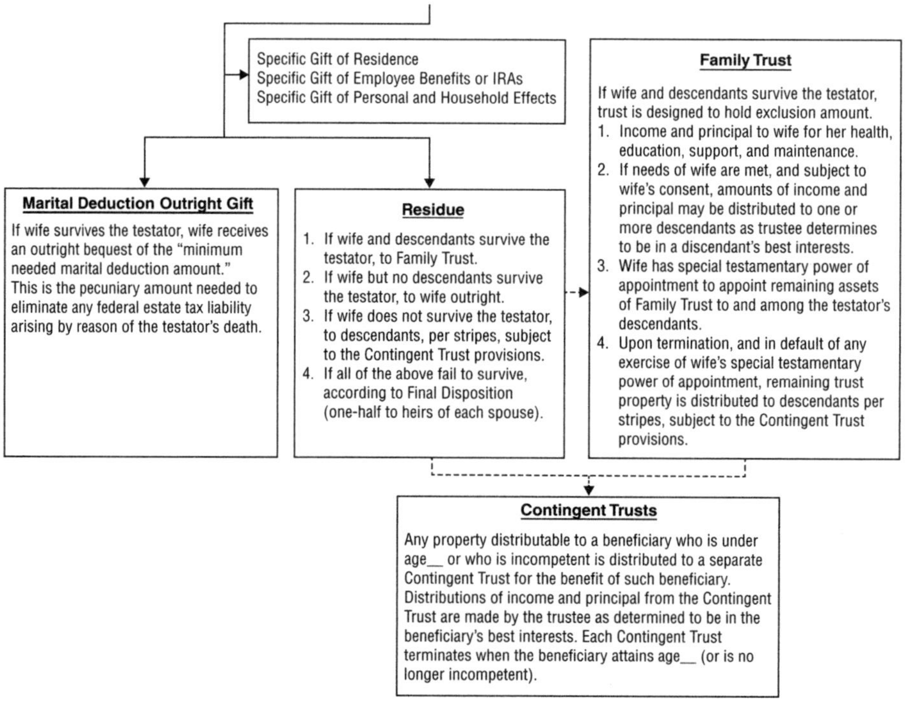

DIAGRAM 10B
LAST WILLS & TESTAMENTS OF HUSBAND

Marital Trust; Residue to Family Trust

Specific Gift of Residence
Specific Gift of Employee Benefits or IRAs
Specific Gift of Personal and Household Effects

Marital Trust

If wife survives the testator, Marital Trust receives a bequest of the "minimum needed marital deduction amount," which is the pecuniary amount needed to eliminate any federal estate tax liability arising by reason of the testator's death.

1. All net income to wife at least annually.
2. Principal to wife for health, education, support, and maintenance.
3. Upon termination, undistributed net income to wife's estate.
4. Wife has limited testamentary power of appointment to appoint remaining principal to and among descendants of the testator.
5. In default of any exercise of wife's limited power of appointment, remaining trust property is distributed to the testator's descendants, per stripes, subject to the Contingent Trust provisions.

Residue

1. If wife and descendants survive the testator, to Family Trust.
2. If wife but *no* descendants survive the testator, to wife outright.
3. If wife does not survive the testator, to descendants, per stripes, subject to the Contingent Trust provisions.
4. If all of the above fail to survive, according to Final Disposition (one-half to heirs of each spouse).

Family Trust

If wife and descentants survive the testator, trust is designed to hold exclusion amount.

1. Income and principal wife for her health, education, support, and maintenance
2. If needs of wife are met, and subject to wife's consent, amounts of income and principal may be distributed to one of more descendants as trustee determines to be in a discendant's best interest.
3. Wife has special testamentary power of appointment to appoint remaining assets of Family Trust to and among the testator's descendants.
4. Upon termination, and in default of any exercise of wife's special testamentary power of appointment, remaining trust property is distributed to descendants per stripes, subject to the Contingent Trust provisions.

Contingent Trusts

Any property distributable to a beneficiary who is under age__ or who is incompetent is distributed to a separate Contingent Trust for the benefit of such beneficiary. Distributions of income and principal from the Contingent Trust are made by the trustee as determined to be in the beneficiaty's best interests. Each Contingent Trust terminates when the beneficiary attains age__ (or is no longer incompetent).

DIAGRAM 10C
LAST WILLS & TESTAMENTS OF HUSBAND

Family Trust; Residue to Spouse Outright

Specific Gift of Residence
Specific Gift of Employee Benefits or IRAs
Specific Gift of Personal and Household Effects

Family Trust

If wife and one or more descendants survive the testator, trust is designed to hold the exclusion amount.

1. Income and principal to wife for her health, education, support, and maintenance.
2. If needs of wife are met, and subject to wife's consent, amounts of income and principal may be distributed to one or more descendants as trustee determines to be in a descendant's best interests.
3. Wife has special testamentary power of appointment to appoint remaining assets of Family Trust to and among children and other descendants.
4. Upon termination, and in default of any exercise of wife's special testamentary power of appointment, trust property distributed to discendants per stripes, subject to be the Contingent Trust provisions.

Residue

1. If wife survives, to wife outright.
2. If wife does not survive, to the testator's descendants, per stripes.
3. If all of the above fail to survive, one-half to the testator's heirs and one-half to wife's heirs.

Contingent Trusts

1. Any property distributable to a beneficiary (other than the testator's wife) who is under the age of __ or who is incompetent is distributed to a separate Contingent Trust for the benefit of such beneficiary.
2. Income and principal are distributable to the beneficiary in his or her best interests.
3. Terminates upon the beneficiary attaining the age of __ (provided the beneficiary is not incompetent) [or according to the following schedule:
   one-third upon attaining the age of__;
   one-half of the remaining trust property upon attaining the age of __; and all remaining trust property upon attaining the age of __ (provided the beneficiary is not incompetent).]
4. If terminated upon the beneficiary's earlier death,
   [A. Remainder Version–the beneficiary has a limited testamentary power of appointment (excluding the beneficiary, his or her creditors, his or her estate and the creditors of his or her estate), otherwise trust estate passes to the beneficiary's descendants, per stripes (or to the testator's descendants, per stripes, if the beneficiary has no descendants).]
   [B. Estate Trust Version–the trust property is distributed to the beneficiary's personal representative as part of his or her probate estate.]

DIAGRAM 10D
LAST WILLS & TESTAMENTS OF HUSBAND
Family Trust; Residue to Marital Trust

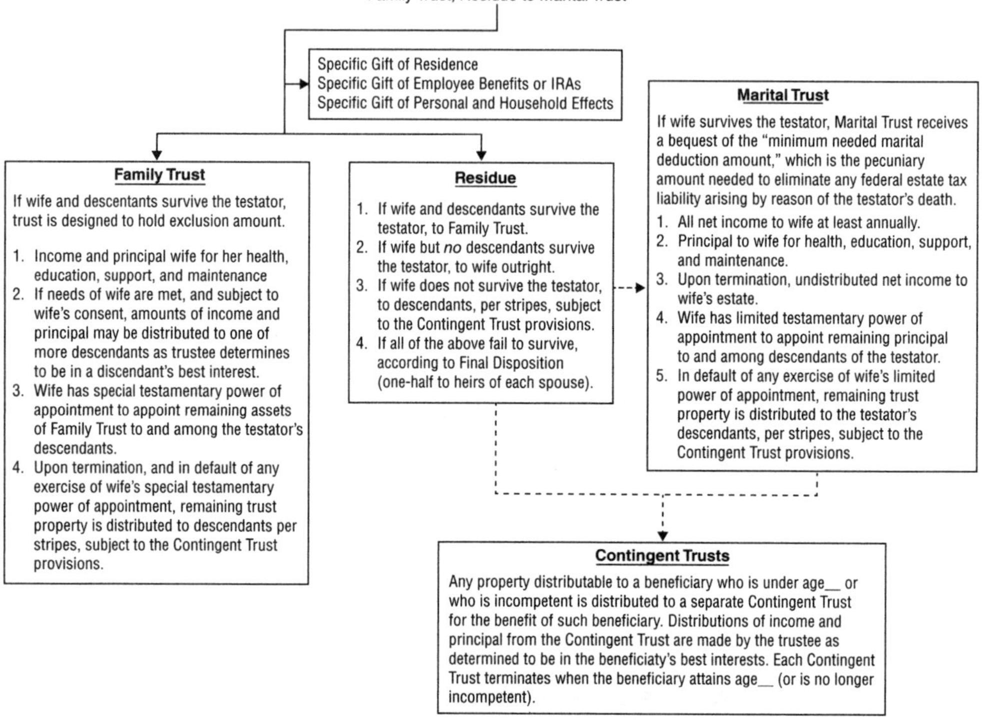

DIAGRAM 10E
LAST WILLS & TESTAMENTS FOR HUSBAND & WIFE
Direct Marital Gift; Residue to Family Trust

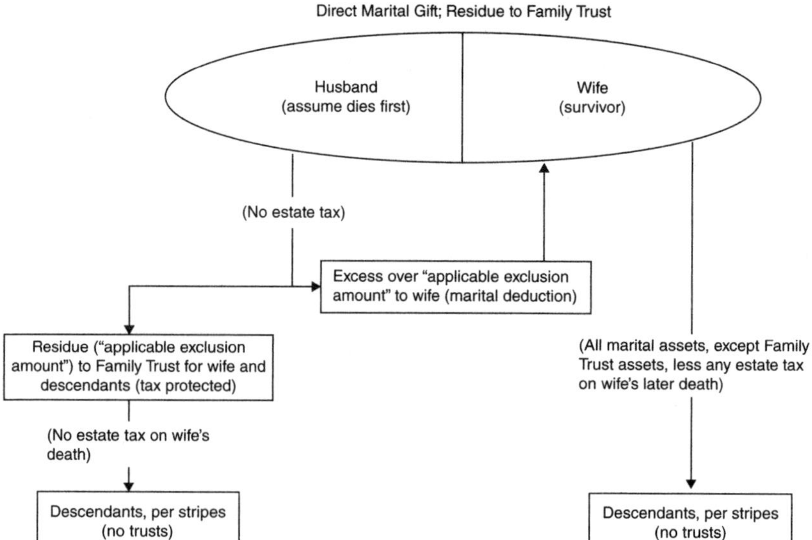

DIAGRAM 10F

LAST WILLS & TESTAMENTS FOR HUSBAND & WIFE

Family Trust; Residue to Family Trust

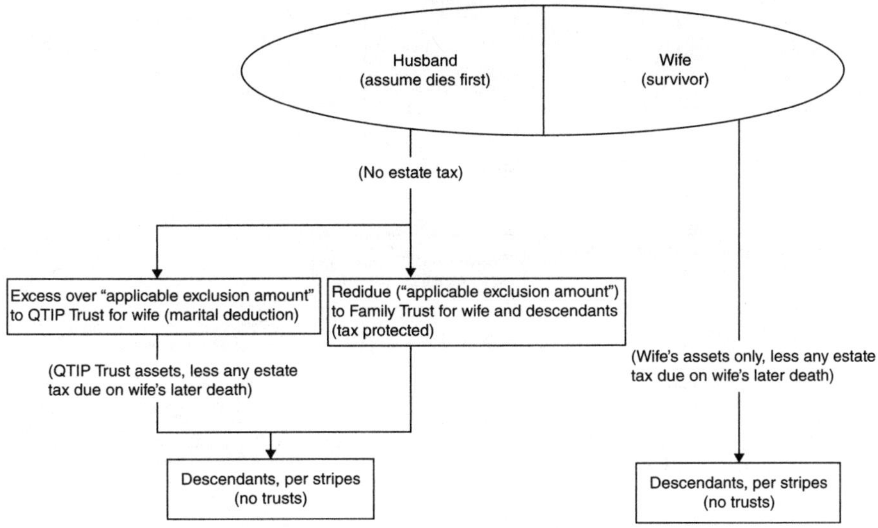

DIAGRAM 10G

LAST WILLS & TESTAMENTS FOR HUSBAND & WIFE

Family Trust; Residue to Spouse Outright

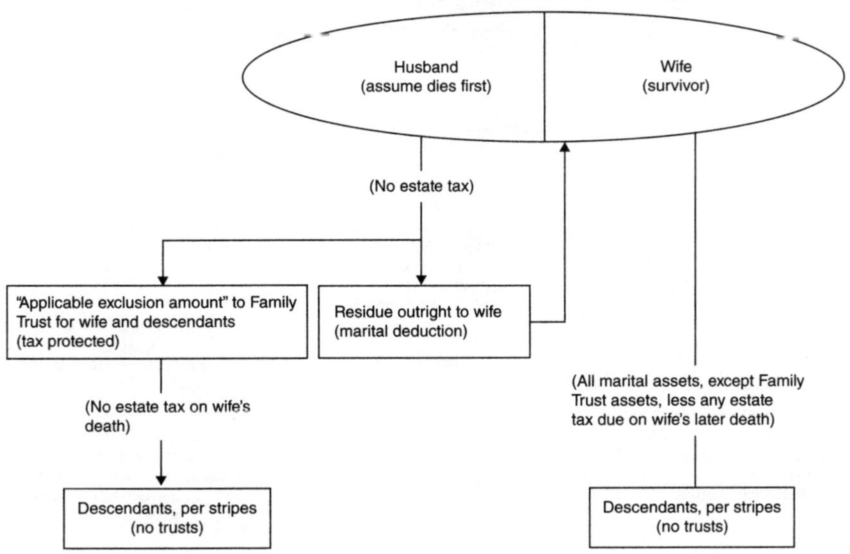

DIAGRAM 10H

LAST WILLS & TESTAMENTS FOR HUSBAND & WIFE

Marital Trust; Residue to Marital Trust

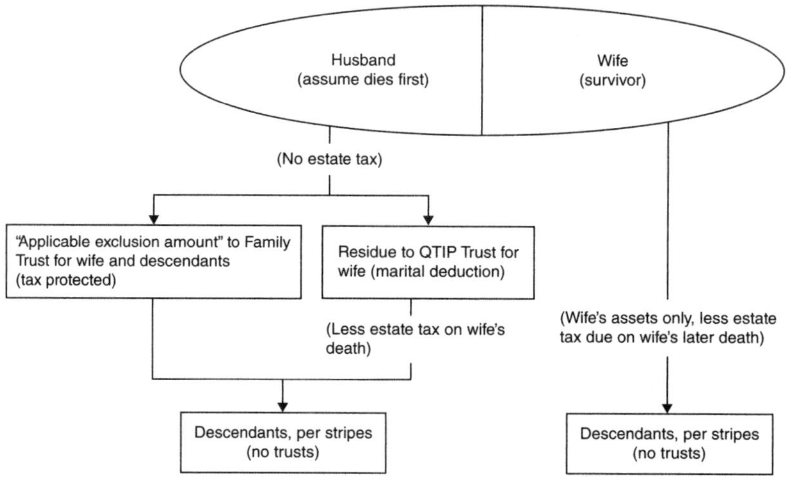

DIAGRAM 10I

LAST WILLS & TESTAMENTS FOR HUSBAND & WIFE

Direct Marital Gift; Residue to Family Trust; Generation-Skipping Trusts

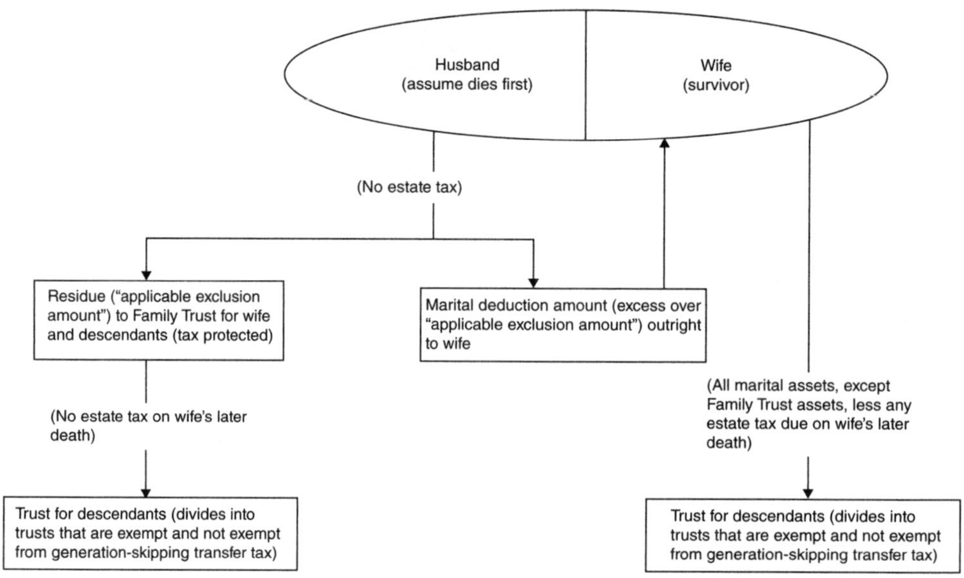

DIAGRAM 10J

LAST WILLS & TESTAMENTS FOR HUSBAND & WIFE

Marital Trust; Residue to Family Trust; Generation-Skipping Trusts

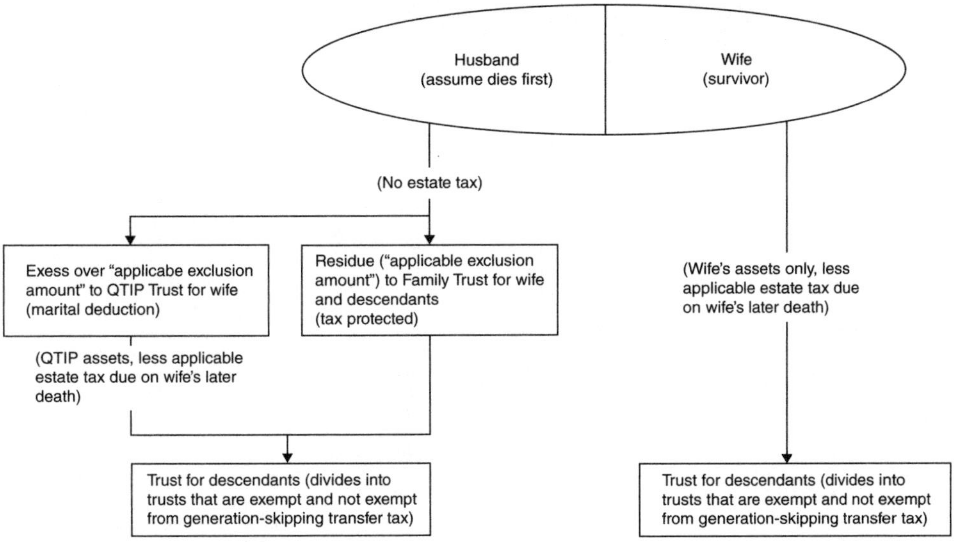

DIAGRAM 10K

LAST WILLS & TESTAMENTS FOR HUSBAND & WIFE

Family Trust; Residue to Spouse Outright; Generation-Skipping Trusts

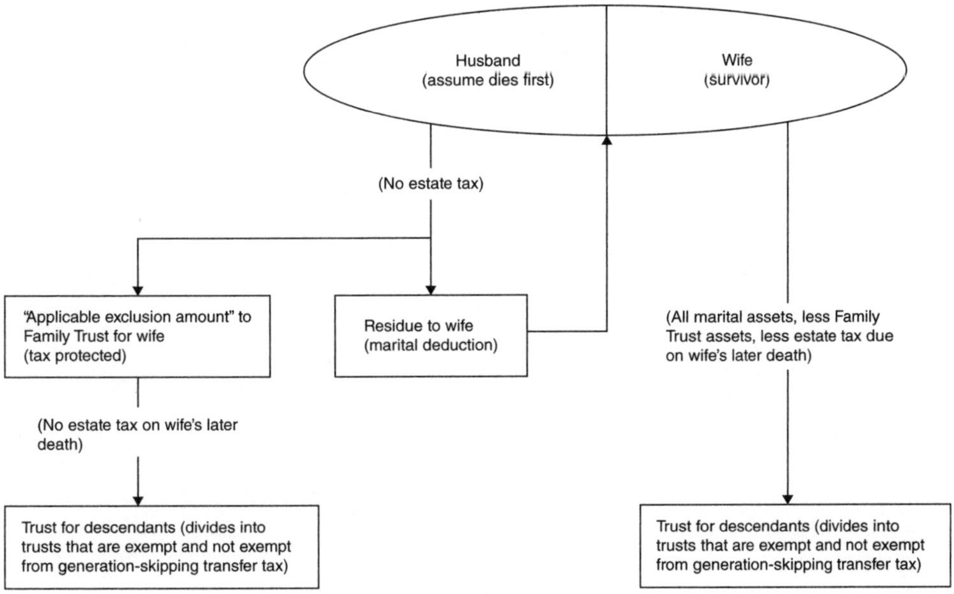

DIAGRAM 10L

LAST WILLS & TESTAMENTS FOR HUSBAND & WIFE

Family Trust; Residue to Marital Trust; Generation-Skipping Trusts

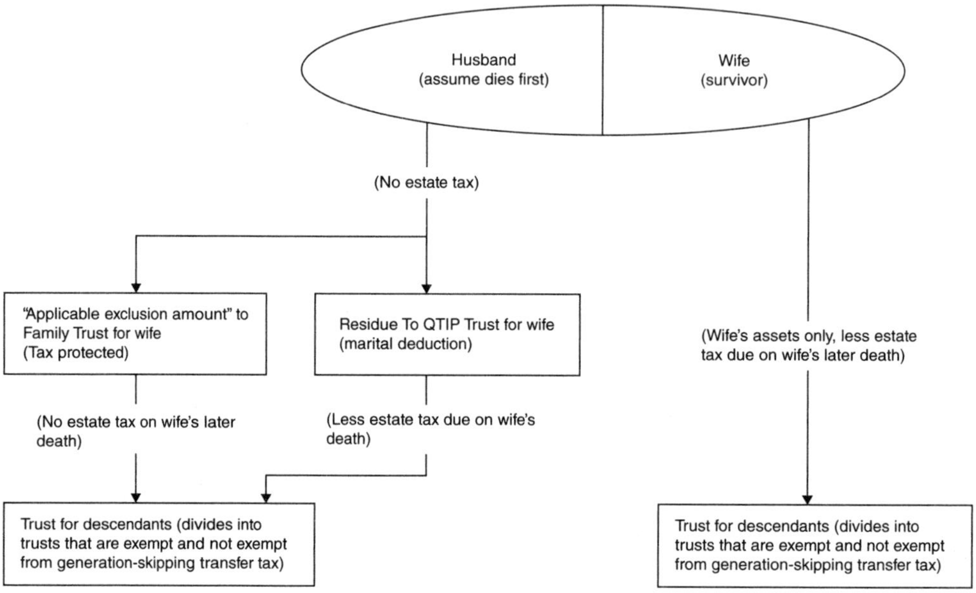

Worksheet 11
Client Letter Describing Uses and Purposes of Estate Planning Trusts

Law Firm Client

Re: Benefits Available from Using Trusts for Holding and Transferring Family Wealth

Dear Client:

In the process of examining your options for implementing a comprehensive plan for the eventual transfer of your wealth to your family beneficiaries, we have been discussing your possible establishment of one or more trusts. You indicated that you have limited experience and exposure to the use of trusts and would like some fundamental description of the trust mechanism and its possible uses. You noted that you will want to use this letter to discuss these matters with your family members. This letter is my response to your request.

1. What Is a "Trust"?

   A trust is a device to enable the holding of the legal title of property separate from its equitable ownership (i.e., the "beneficiaries" or the parties for whom the property is being held). Instructions can be provided to the "trustee," that is, the legal representative of the trust, concerning the investment, management, and distribution of the property held within the trust.
2. Uses and Types of Estate Planning Trusts

   Trusts are used in many different situations to enable the holding of the legal title of property separate from the equitable ownership. These situations are not limited to estate planning. We are discussing how you might use one or more trusts in the estate planning context to facilitate the transfer of your wealth to your intended beneficiaries. In some (but not all) instances, significant tax benefits might be achieved through the use of trusts that are "irrevocable," that is, cannot be changed.

The following are possible basic options for the use of a trust in your situation:

a) Revocable or "Living" Trust

During your lifetime, you can transfer some or many of your assets into a revocable trust. You can be the "trustee" of this trust during your lifetime (or until your earlier mental incapacity). You can designate who will be the successor trustee upon the occurrence of either of these events. This will enable the coordinated management of your various properties in the trust and can facilitate the transfer of the trust assets after your death without the impediment of probate court proceedings. Further, because you do not technically own that property for state property law purposes (it is held by another owner, the trust), any information about this property can be kept private at the time of death because it is not involved in the probate process.

The provisions of this trust agreement can specify the distribution of the trust property after your death, or the maintenance of the property in trust for management and subsequent periodic distributions to designated beneficiaries. This is a very useful device for easily transferring the ownership and management of property. It does not achieve any income tax, gift tax, or estate tax savings because the person funding the trust is the true "economic owner" of the trust assets. The "economic ownership," rather than the nominal, legal ownership, is the basis on which tax application occurs.

b) Testamentary Trusts

If you directly own your properties at the time of death (that is, they have not been transferred during lifetime into a revocable trust), in your Last Will and Testament you can specify the transfer of your properties into one or more trusts created under your Last Will and Testament. Many varieties of trust arrangements can be specified here, including for your spouse (enabling the postponement of any applicable estate taxes), a "family trust" or "credit shelter trust" to enable segregation of assets into a trust to benefit from the then available "unified credit," and other specialized trusts, for example, generation-skipping trusts for the eventual benefit of grandchildren.

c) Lifetime Irrevocable Trusts

During your lifetime, you can transfer certain of your assets irrevocably into one or more trusts for the benefit of others. In this situation, your objective will be to transfer these assets by gift (exposed to the federal gift tax) under circumstances where they subsequently will not be included in your estate for federal estate tax purposes. Consequently, the value of these assets held in the trust (including any post-transfer appreciation) will not be included in your gross estate for federal estate tax purposes. Further, the income from these assets will not be included in your gross income for federal income tax purposes. Careful planning is necessary to achieve these tax objectives.

Particularly, the transferor of the property may not retain rights to control the property or dictate its distribution.

d) Irrevocable Life Insurance Trust

An irrevocable trust can be created to hold one or more life insurance policies on the life of the creator of the trust. Although this is really only a variant of the lifetime irrevocable trust (noted immediately above), it is separately described here because of the extensive discussions that you may have encountered about life insurance trusts. The most important objective is to ensure that the life insurance policy proceeds received after death by the trust (as the designated beneficiary under the life insurance policy) are not includible in the insured's gross estate for federal estate tax purposes. This necessitates (1) acquisition of the life insurance policies directly by the trust and (2) no retention by the insured of "incidents of ownership" in these policies. Further, the policy proceeds when received after death may be in an amount significantly in excess of the "tax basis" for the policy, but that excess amount (even though "insurance gain") will not ordinarily be included in gross income for federal income tax purposes (whether of the trust or a trust beneficiary).

3. Options for Distributions of Income and Principal from Trusts

Many options exist for making distributions of both income and the principal from a trust to the beneficiaries:

a) Income and principal can be retained until a future date, including only for grandchildren or great-grandchildren at that future date.
b) Income can be distributed currently with principal held for future distribution.
c) Principal can be scheduled to be distributed periodically at specified dates.
d) Income and principal can be distributed to a specified beneficiary solely within the discretion of the trustee.
e) Income and principal can be distributed to one or more beneficiaries (to the possible exclusion other beneficiaries) within the discretion of the trustee.
f) Income and principal can be distributed to one or more beneficiaries pursuant to an "ascertainable standard," that is, for health, education, support, or maintenance.

These are representative of the types of alternatives that can be molded to the particular situation for disbursing income and principal from a trust.

4. Other Valuable Benefits from Trusts

Many other nontax benefits exist with the use of a trust, particularly for protecting property from certain creditors:

a) The trust may be structured as a "spendthrift" trust, meaning that a beneficiary is not able to obtain trust benefits until the due date for distributions (for example, the beneficiary can not sell the anticipated payments to be received in the future).
b) An ex-spouse of a beneficiary will not ordinarily be entitled to receive any of the beneficiary's trust benefits as a result of a property settlement in a divorce proceeding.
c) Children and grandchildren can act as advisors to the trustee or (if the trust provisions are appropriately constructed) as trustee or co-trustees, enabling them to participate in the active management of the family wealth. However, they would not have the capacity to waste the trust assets for their own benefit.

5. Summary

You can observe that the trust can be a quite useful arrangement in separating who controls property from who can receive the economic benefits from that property. That enables the beneficiaries to be protected from their own tendencies for wasting their assets and from importuning individuals seeking the beneficiaries' assets. The trustee can be either another individual (who must have integrity and an understanding of the responsibilities of a trustee) or a corporate trustee, such as a bank. In constructing the trust, I would encourage providing significant flexibility to the trustee for dealing with both the investments of the trust and the future distributions to the trust beneficiaries. In this manner, substantial flexibility for dealing with changed circumstances in the future will be possible.

We look forward to discussing these important matters further with you in the near future.

Sincerely,
Law Firm
By: ______________________________

Worksheet 12

Client Letter Identifying Gift Strategies and Value of Making Gifts

Law Firm Client

Subject: Implementing a Gift Program for Tax Planning Purposes

Dear Client:

When we met, I promised that I would provide a letter identifying how you can reduce the potential exposure of your assets to federal estate tax at the time of your death. We are aware of the fluidity in the federal estate and gift tax structure over the last several years and the potential for future changes. However, we must now assume that the federal estate tax will remain in existence, with the tax imposed at a significant rate. Further, based on our conversations, it seems quite likely that your net-worth situation will cause your assets to be exposed to a federal estate tax despite the relatively high unified credit exclusion equivalent amount.

Consequently, I have suggested that you implement a gift program to remove assets "off the top" that otherwise would be included in your gross estate and be subjected to federal estate tax. Further, with assets transferred into the ownership of younger generation members, the post-gift appreciation in the transferred assets would accrue in the hands of those transferees. That appreciation would then also be excluded from your gross estate.

Giving property to your children and grandchildren does not mean that they need to receive this property outright. The gifts could be made into trusts for the children or grandchildren, or could otherwise be transferred in arrangements (e.g., family limited partnerships) where the transferees would have only limited access to those properties (thereby limiting their possible wastage of these assets).

Many options exist for making tax-efficient gift transfers. We suggest that you consider some of these gift tax planning "guideposts":

1. Make gifts qualifying for the gift tax annual donee exclusion (the amount is subject to change each year because of an inflation-adjustment provision; please contact me to confirm the exclusion amount at the time of any gifts). This necessitates the transfer of a "present interest" gift but, if necessary, when funds are transferred into a trust, this can be facilitated through making available a temporary "withdrawal" power. However, this withdrawal power must be "real" or it could face a serious IRS challenge.
2. Double this annual donee exclusion benefit by having a spouse match these gifts, because the spouse can also make gifts eligible for the annual donee exclusion.
3. Make additional gifts by paying tuition bills directly to a school for the benefit of children and grandchildren. These are not treated as gifts for federal gift tax purposes, as long as they are paid directly to the educational institution. Similar treatment is available for the payment of health care costs.

4. Make gifts of highly appreciated capital gains property. The tax basis of the gifted property will transfer to the donee. This assumes that the donee can sell the property and that a lesser capital gains tax rate will be applicable.
5. Make larger gifts that will be tax protected through the unified credit exclusion equivalent amount (the amount is subject to change each year because of an inflation-adjustment provision; please contact me to confirm the exclusion amount at the time of any gifts).
6. Examine whether certain gifts can be valued with a discount (e.g., because of a minority interest), thereby permitting a larger gift that still fits within the annual donee exclusion and/or unified credit exclusion amount.
7. Pick as assets to be transferred those properties that might have the most significant opportunities for appreciation (that appreciation thereafter accruing outside the donor's estate for federal estate tax purposes).

These are some of the basic ideas relevant in considering a gift strategy that can (1) enable the transfer of assets out of the potentially taxable estate of the donor, (2) be without any gift tax cost to the donor, and (3) enable significant accumulation in the hands of the donees (or intermediaries, such as trusts).

If gifts are made of property that is difficult to value, we do encourage the filing of gift tax returns to report these gifts so that the statute of limitations can expire. This limits the chances of an IRS challenge of these transfers at some subsequent time.

We look forward to discussing these important matters further with you in the near future.

Sincerely,

Law Firm

By: ________________________________

Worksheet 13

Client Letter Explaining Benefits of Unified Credit Portability

Law Firm Client

Re: Portability of the Unused Estate Tax Exclusion Amount to Estate of Surviving Spouse

Dear Client:

For federal estate tax purposes, each individual's estate is entitled to a unified credit that enables (for deaths occurring in 2015) the equivalent of an exclusion in the amount of $5.43 million. In the situation of a married couple, this amount would be doubled, thereby facilitating the exclusion of $10.86 million in the transfer of assets by both spouses (for 2015 deaths). The amount for this exclusion equivalent may change in future years via an inflation-adjustment provision, but the numbers shown here demonstrate that the transfer of assets by spouses can be eligible for combined exclusions that are substantial in most estates.

In some situations, the spouse having fewer assets may die first without that deceased spouse's estate actually using the entire available unified credit exclusion amount. In pre-death planning, the spouse having greater assets could have transferred assets to the other spouse when anticipating the death of that spouse, but this property transfer process can be cumbersome and not always feasible when the poorer spouse is in extremis.

However, the U.S. Congress has decided that any unused exclusion amount of the deceased spouse should be transferred to the surviving spouse, to be available to be used at the subsequent death of that surviving spouse. Therefore, for example (using the 2015 numbers above), if, at the death of the first spouse to die, the exclusion amount is $5.43 million and only $1.0 million of that exclusion amount is used, then, at the death of the surviving spouse, an exclusion amount of $9.86 million (the deceased spouse's unused $4.43 million, plus the surviving spouse's $5.43 million) would be available to the surviving spouse's estate. Technically, this is known as the "deceased spousal unused exclusion amount" (sometimes "DSUEA" or "DSUE amount").

The use of the DSUE amount can be quite beneficial for eliminating estate tax in transferring the combined assets of two spouses. However, various limitations do apply to the potential use of this DSUE amount:

1) This exclusion amount is available only to the estate of a surviving spouse if an election is made on a timely filed estate tax return (including extensions) of the predeceased spouse on which the precise exclusion amount is computed. No election can be made on a late return. Once this election is made, it is irrevocable. This requirement applies regardless of whether the estate of the predeceased spouse is otherwise required to file a federal estate tax return. This means that, to have the DSUE amount available in the future, the estate of the first spouse to die is required to incur the cost of filing this federal estate tax return even though the subsequent usage of this exclusion amount appears to

be remote at that time. This will be a difficult decision in some situations. If you are an executor, you must be especially careful about making this election because you could be subsequently challenged for not doing so.

2) Notwithstanding the statute of limitations for assessing estate or gift tax with respect to the estate tax return of a predeceased spouse, the IRS may examine the estate tax return of the predeceased spouse for purposes of determining the DSUE amount to be available for use by the estate of the surviving spouse.
3) If a surviving spouse is predeceased by more than one spouse, the DSUE amount available for use by the estate of the surviving spouse is limited to the lesser of $5.43 million or the unused exclusion of the last deceased spouse. This suggests that the surviving spouse might not wish to remarry if he or she has significant wealth that would be absorbed by the exclusion from the first spouse to die.
4) The availability of the DSUE amount raises the possibility of not using the usual "credit shelter" or "bypass" trust upon the death of the first spouse to die. If these assets are instead held in the estate of the surviving spouse, the DSUE amount would be available to protect those assets from estate tax and the income tax basis for those assets would be stepped up to their fair market values when the surviving spouse dies. The counterarguments to this are that (1) creditor protection for those assets will not be available (such protection would be available if in a credit shelter trust), (2) the appreciation of the assets in that trust will be excluded from inclusion in the surviving spouse's estate (and, therefore, then non-eligible for a stepped-up income tax basis), and (3) the DSUE amount could be lost on remarriage of the surviving spouse.

Many planning opportunities exist to take advantage of the DSUE amount, such as using the DSUE amount to shelter significant lifetime gifts from gift tax. These techniques present some complications, but we can advise you about these if you wish to consider the possible refinement of your estate plan to accommodate this provision.

We look forward to discussing these important matters further with you in the near future.

Sincerely,

Law Firm

By: ______________________________

Worksheet 14

Client Letter on Effective Estate Planning with Family Limited Partnerships and Limited Liability Companies

Law Firm Client

Re: Using Family Limited Partnerships and Limited Liability Companies to Reduce Federal Transfer Tax Costs

Dear Client:

We have suggested to you that you consider the potential use of a family limited partnership (FLP) to hold your business and investment assets. Thereafter, you could give limited partnership interests to your children and grandchildren (or trusts for some or all of them). With careful planning, this would enable you to: (1) currently share your net wealth with younger generation members, (2) continue to control the management of the limited partnership without interference from younger generation members, (3) limit the amount of the gift transfers for federal gift taxes because of valuation discounts, and (4) limit the subsequent inclusion in your gross estate to only the interest in the partnership held by you at the time of death (and not including the interests previously transferred by you to other family members). A particular benefit of this mechanism is that, because of the restrictions imposed by the limited partnership arrangement on the properties held within the partnership, significant discounts can often be achieved in making transfers of the partnership interests. For example, if a discount of 30% can be achieved and the donor had a $4.9 million unified credit exclusion equivalent amount remaining after prior gifts, property having a value of approximating $7 million (before the discount) could be transferred without triggering gift tax exposure.

We note below some matters that you should consider if you wish to proceed with the implementation of a FLP plan:

1) A business entity will need to be organized under state business organization laws. Although this type of planning is often described as involving FLPs, we normally advise the use of a limited liability company (LLC) as organized under state law. This LLC can be organized so that it is treated as a partnership for federal tax purposes.
2) After organizing the LLC, you will need to transfer the desired business and investment assets into the LLC. These transfers will not have a federal tax effect because (at this juncture) you will merely be transferring assets "from your right pocket to your left pocket." You should not transfer all your assets so that, thereafter, you would need to rely on partnership distributions for current living expenses. This would appear as if you have retained (for federal estate tax purposes) a prohibited lifetime interest in all the properties that you have transferred into the LLC.
3) Thereafter, you can transfer LLC membership interests to your children and grandchildren (or trusts for them). These transfers will be transfers of LLC

interests for purposes of the federal gift tax. However, because these interests will be restricted, you can claim that the transferred LLC interests are valued at considerably less than the proportionate interests in the underlying value of the assets held by the LLC. This would result from asserting discounts based on the property interest transferred being a minority interest and having a lack of marketability. At this point (or earlier), we should arrange to have a competent, qualified appraisal firm conduct an analysis as to the (discounted) value of the interests transferred. The report of this appraiser will be useful for thereafter demonstrating the value of the transferred interests.

4) The LLC must continue to operate as a business/investment entity, rather than merely as a continuing part of the portfolio of assets owned by the older generation member. Many parties believe that the organization of the LLC is sufficient to achieve the ultimate estate tax exclusion objective, but this result cannot be ensured unless the operations of the LLC are regularly conducted in an orderly, business-like manner.

The LLC (or FLP) is very valuable in reducing the transfer tax cost in achieving the transfer of wealth to family members. Valid business and investment reasons supporting organization and funding of a FLP/LLC (as identified in various litigated cases) include: (1) protecting a large block of voting stock in a closely held corporation or other "legacy assets" of a family, (2) joint management of a single pool of assets for investment opportunities, (3) holding ownership of a closely held entity to enable later coordinated disposition, and (4) protecting depletion of family assets in the event of divorce, family disputes, etc.

However, we must emphasize that the IRS regularly challenges these arrangements based on a variety of arguments (e.g., the form of the gift transfers is of the underlying properties and not FLP/LLC interests). Further, legislative proposals are regularly made to limit the use of valuation discounts in this context. For this reason, if you decide to go forward, we encourage you to recognize at the outset that you will need to (1) carefully implement the various steps for organizing and transferring the LLC interests, and (2) continue obtaining regular legal and business advice, so as to assure the ultimate tax reduction objective.

We look forward to discussing these important matters further with you in the near future.

Sincerely,
Law Firm
By: ______________________________

Worksheet 15

Client Letter Outlining Advantages of Using Defined Value Clauses

Law Firm Client

Re: Effective Use of "Defined Value" Clauses to Avoid Federal Gift Tax

Dear Client:

Often those assets that have the greatest potential for appreciation and that have the greatest possibility for shifting wealth to younger generations through estate planning are the most difficult to value. Even when the transferor obtains an appraisal from a highly qualified appraiser, the significant possibility exists that the IRS will challenge the valuation of illiquid property gifted to younger generation members. For some time, taxpayers have sought to use some type of "savings clause" to provide that, if the IRS challenges and increases the claimed value of transferred property, the property representing the excess value will automatically be returned to the donor or excluded from the gift so that the gift tax will be inapplicable. The IRS has challenged these provisions for various reasons, including that they violated public policy. Although the IRS was successful initially, it has been losing litigated cases where the clauses have been carefully constructed to avoid the pitfalls of the earlier results.

1. What Is the Structure for Making These Gifts?

   A document to implement a gift when using a "savings clause" often provides for the conveyance of a specified portion of a property with the conditions that:

   (a) if the assumed value of the gifted property is successfully challenged by the IRS (with the result that gift tax liability would be triggered),

   (b) the gift will automatically be rescinded,

   (c) to the extent that it would be otherwise be subject to gift tax.

   When these conditions apply, the IRS would be frustrated because, as a result of its efforts, the transaction would be partially unwound with no tax being collected by IRS as a result of its audit activities.

2. The Case of *Commissioner v. Procter*

   Numerous years ago, the IRS was successful in the *Procter* case where a trust agreement included a savings clause providing that, if the IRS ultimately determined that any part of the property gifted to a trust was subject to gift tax, the portion of the property subject to the gift tax would automatically be excluded from the conveyance and would remain the donor's property. This was effectively an "adjustment" clause, which had the effect of changing the elements of the transaction if a subsequent tax challenge was made. The court of appeals denounced this savings clause as a tax-avoidance device that could be used to void a court's determination of whether gift tax was owed and that, as a matter of public policy, could not be given its intended effect. The court noted that the savings clause discouraged the collection of the tax because any attempt to collect the tax would actually defeat the gift. The court reasoned that the use of savings clauses would obstruct the administration of justice by requiring courts to decide moot cases and would reduce final judgments to being only declaratory in nature.

3. Subsequent Developments

   Much varied litigation has occurred in this context since the *Procter* case, but the net result is that tax planners have implemented a different approach than the "adjustment" clause approach. The alternative has been to use a "value definition" or "defined value" clause, defining the transfer itself in terms of the ultimate value (for tax purposes) intended to be transferred. The objective in using this type of clause is, simply, to give a fixed set of rights with uncertain value. The objective is not to vary the gift based on the results of a tax audit.

   Gradually, taxpayers are consistently winning cases that are based on a gift document that has no conditions that might defeat the contemplated transfer of property. We do note that many of these cases have involved situations in which the excess amount over the defined value passed to charity, thereby making the IRS challenge unproductive (because of the availability of a charitable contributions deduction). However, the IRS now seems to be on the losing side of this issue, including situations where charity would not take any value determined to be excessive.

   One requirement evolving from these cases is that the donor must ordinarily utilize the help of a qualified appraiser to assist in determining the value at which the gift will be converted from a dollar value into a percentage value of the transferred property. However, with careful planning, the risk of large gift tax exposure through the use of the defined value clause can be considerably moderated.

We hope this explanation is helpful to you in examining whether to go forward with your intended gift program for some of your family properties. We look forward to discussing these important matters further with you in the near future.

Sincerely,

Law Firm

By: ________________________________

Worksheet 16

Client Letter Concerning Use of Valuation Discounts for Estate and Gift Tax Purposes

Law Firm Client

Re: Exploiting Opportunities to Discount Property Values on Property Transfers Subject to Federal Gift or Federal Estate Tax

Dear Client:

You have asked us to identify for you those circumstances in which you can take advantage of recent developments in the federal tax laws so as to enable discounts in the valuation of properties for federal gift and estate tax purposes when property is transferred by gift or at death. This letter responds to that request.

Ordinarily, when property is transferred for federal gift or federal estate tax purposes, it must be valued at its fair market value at the time of the transfer. The "fair market value" is identified as the price at which the property would change hands between a willing buyer and a willing seller, neither being under any compulsion to buy or to sell and both having knowledge of the relevant facts. The fair market value of a particular item of property is not to be determined by a forced-sale price. Nor is the fair market value of an item to be determined by the sale price of the item in a market other than that in which such item is most commonly sold to the public, taking into account the location of the item wherever appropriate.

Notwithstanding these general rules, significant opportunities can exist to reduce the value of certain properties when transferred and potentially exposed to the federal gift tax or the federal estate tax. These opportunities arise in situations where various discount rules might apply. Those possible discount mechanisms are described here.

1) Minority Discounts

Probably the most common discount claimed is that for holding a minority position in a business or investment enterprise. The assumption is that this interest cannot be independently sold on a market or exchange. Therefore, the holder of the minority interest cannot influence the management decisions of the enterprise, including with respect to the distribution of profits to the owners.

The IRS has previously agreed (in its Revenue Ruling 93-12) that the interests of various family members who hold minority interests need not be amalgamated together to determine whether as a group they have a majority position. If such a rule were applicable, it would eliminate the opportunity to assert minority status (and eligibility for a minority discount). The IRS has indicated that each ownership position separately held must be independently evaluated (and, therefore, the minority status will be respected, even though much of the interests when combined are held by family members).

2) Blockage Discounts

In some situations, the holding in an enterprise may be so large that it cannot all be sold at one time without negatively impacting the market pricing. The excessive supply would cause disequilibrium in the market for that item and its price would deteriorate. For this reason, portions of the interest must be sold over an extended period to enable realizing adequate value (and not at a depressed price) for the properties. This is often described as a "blockage" problem. Under these circumstances, the value must be discounted to recognize that adequate value can be recognized only over a deferred period.

This analysis can be applied not only to shares of stock or other business interests but also to a variety of other assets. Depending on the circumstances, these can include multiple real estate parcels in a particular area and large collections, such as accumulations of the works of one artist.

3) Lack of Marketability Discount

Although the property may have significant value, it may not be listed on any regular sales exchange. As of result of the lack of liquidity or access to a ready market, the owner can assert that the market will severely discount the property interest because the owner/seller is limited as to potential purchasers. This "lack of marketability" discount can also enable a significant reduction in the assessed value for federal tax purposes.

Many opportunities exist for asserting eligibility for discounts, but careful planning is essential to ensure that both (1) the opportunity to use discounting is available and (2) the maximum percentage of discounting can be achieved. This latter item suggests that an integral part of this process is obtaining the assistance of valuation experts. Ultimately, if arranged appropriately, significant tax reduction may be possible on family asset transfers using discounting mechanisms.

We look forward to discussing these important matters further with you in the near future.

Sincerely,
Law Firm
By: _______________

Notes

1. Rev. Proc. 2011-52, 2011-45 I.R.B. 701, §3.29.
2. Rev. Proc. 2013-15, 2013-5 I.R.B. 444, §2.13.
3. Rev. Proc. 2013-35, 2013-47 I.R.B. 537, §3.32.
4. Rev. Proc. 2014-61, 2014-47 I.R.B. 860, §3.33.
5. Rev. Proc. 2015-53, 2015-44 I.R.B. 615, §3.29.
6. Rev. Proc. 2011-52, §3.29.
7. Rev. Proc. 2013-15, §2.13.
8. Rev. Proc. 2013-35, §3.32.
9. Rev. Proc. 2014-61, §3.33.
10. Rev. Proc. 2015-53, §3.33.
11. *See* §2010(c); Rev. Proc. 2013-15, §2.13.

Bibliography

Books and Treatises (Selected, Including Electronic Access)

ACTEC (American College of Trust and Estate Counsel), Commentaries on the Model Rules of Professional Conduct (4th ed. 2006).

American Bar Association, The ABA Practical Guide to Estate Planning, J. Soled, Editor, Senior Lawyer Division, 2011.

American Law Institute, Restatement (Third), of the Law Governing Lawyers (2000).

American Law Institute, Restatement of the Law of Trusts 3rd., Volumes 1 & 2 (2003) (trust creation and interpretation); Volume 3 (2007) (trust administration); Volume 4 (2012) (breaches of trust and legal remedies).

Checkpoint, Estate Planning Library, Estate Planning Analysis, Annotations & Explanations, available electronically.

Gazur & Phillips, *Estate Planning—Principles and Problems* (3rd ed., 2012), Wolters Kluwer.

Hume, The ABA Checklist for Family Heirs: A Guide to Family History, Financial Plans and Final Wishes, Senior Lawyer Division, American Bar Association (2011).

Madoff, Tenney, Hall, & Mingolla, *Practical Guide to Estate Planning* (2014 ed.), CCH (Wolters Kluwer).

McNulty & McCouch, Federal Estate and Gift Taxation in a Nutshell (7th ed.), West Group (Law), 2011.

Price & Donaldson, *Price on Contemporary Estate Planning* (2015 ed.), CCH (Wolters Kluwer).

Various estate planning treaties, available electronically on RIAG Checkpoint, including:

Streng & Davis, Retirement Planning: Tax & Financial Strategies.

Henkel, Estate Planning and Wealth Preservations—Strategies and Solutions.

Westfall & Mair, Estate Planning Law and Taxation.

Zaritsky, Tax Planning for Family Wealth Transfers: Analysis with Forms.

Government Reports and Materials

Congressional Research Service report entitled "A History of Federal Estate, Gift and Generation-Skipping Taxes," dated Jan. 24, 2011 (Order Code 95-444); see www.crs.gov.

Staff of Joint Committee on Taxation, Description and Analysis of Alternative Wealth Transfer Tax Systems (JCX-22-08), March 10, 2012; this document can be found at www.jct.gov.

Staff of Joint Committee on Taxation, History, Present Law, and Analysis of The Federal Wealth Transfer Tax System (JCX-52-15), March 16, 2015; this document can be found at www.jct.gov.

Staff of Joint Committee on Taxation, Present Law and Background Relating to the Tax Treatment of Retirement Savings (JCX-32-12), April 13, 2012; this document can be found at www.jct.gov.

Staff of Joint Committee on Taxation, Overview of the Federal Tax System as in Effect for 2015 (JCX-70-15), March 30, 2015; this document can be found at www.jct.gov.

Joulfaian, Office of Tax Analysis, U.S. Department of the Treasury, "The Federal Estate Tax: History, Law, and Economics," July 2010, available electronically at http://ssrn/com/abstract=1579829.

Estate Planning Course Materials (Selected)

American Law Institute – Continuing Legal Education:

"Advanced Estate Planning Techniques" (2015 and prior years).

"Charitable Planning Techniques" (2014 and prior years).

"Estate Planning in Depth" (2015 and prior years).

"Estate Planning for the Family Business Owner" (2015 and prior years).

"Sophisticated Estate Planning Techniques" (2011).

"Representing Estate and Trust Beneficiaries and Fiduciaries" (2015 and prior years).

"Heckerling Institute on Estate Planning," annual proceedings, University of Miami School of Law.

Estate Planning Periodicals (Selected)

American College of Trust and Estate Counsel, *ACTEC Law Journal.*

American Bar Association, Section of Real Property, Trust and Estate Law, *Real Property, Trust and Estate Law Journal*, online at www.abanet.org/rppt/journal.

American Bar Association, Section of Taxation, *Tax Lawyer.*

Tax Management, Inc., *Tax Mgmt. Est., Gifts and Tr. J.*

WG&L (Checkpoint), *Estate Planning Journal.*

Periodicals

2005

Kelley, *Practical Aspects of Intrafamily Loans*, 46 Tax Mgmt. Memo. 539 (Nov. 28).

2009

Akers, Blattmachr & Boyle, *Creating Intentional Grantor Trusts*, 44 Real Prop. Tr. and Est. Law J. 207 (Summer).

2010

Ausness, *The Role of Trust Protectors in American Trust Law*, 45 Real Prop. Tr. and Est. Law J. 319 (Summer).

Bekerman, *Is There Terror in In Terrorem Clauses*," 51 Tax Mgmt. Memo. 67 (Mar.).

Culp & Mellen, *Trust Decanting: An Overview and Introduction to Creative Planning Opportunities*, 45 Real Prop. Tr. and Est. Law J. 1 (Spring).

Law & Yokomoto, *Fiduciary and Reporting Challenges Created by the New Modified Carry-Over Basis and Reporting Rules Under §§1022 and 6018*, 51 Tax Mgmt. Memo. 179 (May 24).
Lee, Berry, & Hall, *Reeling, Rolling and Reining in "Shark-Fin CLATs,"* 51 Tax Mgmt. Memo. 435 (Dec. 6).
Tax Law Review, *Symposium on Wealth Transfer Taxation*, Vol. 63, No. 1.

2011

Bekerman, *Portability of Estate and Gift Tax Exemptions Under TRA 2010*, 52 Tax Mgmt. Memo. 315 (Aug.1).
Kiziah & Campbell, *Drafting to Effectuate Grantor's Retention Desires with Respect to Publicly Held Securities*, 46 Real Prop. Tr. and Est. Law J. 199 (Fall).
Medlin, Boyle, & Zaritsky, *2010: It Was a Very Good Year . . . to Die—Or Was It?* 45 Real Prop. Tr. and Est. Law J. 589 (Winter).
Ransome and Frances Schafer, *The GST Trust: Pulling Back the Layers to Find Its True Identity*, 2011 TNT 128-7 (Mar. 31).
Ruce, *The Trustee and the Remainderman: The Trustee's Duty to Inform*, 46 Real Prop. Tr. and Est. Law J. 173 (Spring).

2012

ABA Section of Taxation, *ABA Tax Section Suggests Options For Estate Tax Reform*, 2012 TNT 66-36 (Apr. 4).
Bekerman, *Back to the Future—Welcome to 2013*, 37 Tax Mgmt. Est., Gifts & Tr. J. 315 (Nov./Dec. 2012).
New York State Bar Association Tax Section & New York State Bar Association Trusts and Estate Law Section, Report on Notice 2011-101: Request for Comments Regarding the Income, Gift, Estate and Generations-Skipping Transfer Tax Consequences of Trust Decanting, Report No. 1265, April 26, 2012, available at www.nysba.org/taxsectionreports.
Horwood, *Family Ties: Leveraging Charitable Giving*, 53 Tax Mgmt. Memo. 211 (June 4).
New York State Bar Association Tax Section & New York State Bar Association Trusts and Estate Law Section, Report on "Portability" of Unused Estate Tax Exclusion, Report No. 1260, March 23, 2012, available at www.nysba.org/taxsectionreports.
Spica, *Future Perfect: How Tense and Mood Will Have Declawed the Claw-Back*, 46 Real Prop. Tr. and Est. Law J. 475 (Winter).
Zaluda, *Common Day to Day Ethical Issues When Serving as or Advising a Fiduciary*, 53 Tax Mgmt. Memo. 27 (Jan 16).

2013

Bekerman, *The 2012-2013 Trusts and Estates Stability Act*, 38 Tax. Mgmt. Est., Gifts & Tr. J. 279 (Sept./Oct.).
Blase, *The Case for the Continued Viability of Trusts in Estate Planning*, 38 Tax Mgmt. Est. Gifts & Tr. J. 255 (July/Aug.).

2014

Gassman & Blattmachr, *The Stepped-Up Basis Conversation*, 39 Tax Mgmt. Est., Gifts & Tr. J. 78 (Jan./Feb.).
Gerzog, *What's Wrong with a Federal Inheritance Tax?* 49 Real Prop., Tr. & Est. L.J. 163 (Spring).
Scroggin, *Income Tax Planning for Clients with Short Life Expectancies*, 41 Est. Plan. 32 (Nov.).

2015

Albright, *Looking Over the Past 30-Plus Years: Trends and Changes—Constantly Changing Landscape*, 40 Tax Mgmt. Est., Gifts & Tr. J. 3 (Jan./Feb.).

Beyer, *Web Meets the Will: Estate Planning for Digital Assets*, 42 Est. Plan. 28 (Mar.).

Bramwell & Socash, *Preserving Inherited Exclusion Amounts: The New Planning Frontier*, 50 Real Prop., Tr. & Est. L.J. 1 (Spring).

Glazier, Dixon, & Sweeney, *What Every Estate Planner Should Know About Undue Influence: Recognizing It, Insulating/Planning Against It. . .and Litigating It*, 40 Tax. Mgmt. Est., Gifts & Tr. J. 199 (July/Aug.).

LaPiana & Bekerman, *Estate Tax Planning in an Income Tax World*, 40 Tax Mgmt. Est., Gifts & Tr. J. 111 (Mar./Apr.).

Lee, *Run the Basis and Catch Maximum Tax Savings—Part I*, 42 Est. Plan. 3 (Jan.).

Nenno, *Getting a Stepped-Up Income-Tax Basis and More by Springing – or Not Springing – The Delaware Tax Trap the Old-Fashioned Way*, 40 Tax Mgmt. Est, Gifts & Tr. J. 215 (Sept./Oct.).

Pratt & Brown, *Estate Planning in 2015 and Beyond: No Longer a One-Size-Fits-All Approach*, 89 Fla. B.J. 24 (Feb. 2015).

Wilson, *The Chaos of Digital Assets Brings Opportunities for Planning Creativity*, 40 Tax Mgmt. Est., Gifts & Tr. J. 199 (July/Aug.).

Zaritsky, *The Year in Review: An Estate Planner's Perspective on Recent Tax Developments*, 40 Tax Mgmt. Est., Gifts & Tr. J. 19 (Jan./Feb.).